For Reference

Not to be taken from this room

Encyclopedia of the

NORTH AMERICAN COLONIES

Encyclopedia of the
NORTH AMERICAN COLONIES

EDITOR IN CHIEF
Jacob Ernest Cooke, *Lafayette College*

ASSOCIATE EDITORS
W. J. Eccles, *University of Toronto*
Ramón A. Gutiérrez, *University of California, San Diego*
Milton M. Klein, *University of Tennessee*
Gloria Lund Main, *University of Colorado*
Jackson Turner Main, *University of Colorado*
Alden Vaughan, *Columbia University*

SPECIAL CONSULTANTS
Mathé Allain, *University of Southwestern Louisiana*
Carl A. Brasseaux, *University of Southwestern Louisiana*
Charles T. Gehring, *New Netherland Project*
William C. Sturtevant, *Smithsonian Institution*

Volume III

CHARLES SCRIBNER'S SONS / NEW YORK
MAXWELL MACMILLAN CANADA / TORONTO
MAXWELL MACMILLAN INTERNATIONAL / NEW YORK   OXFORD   SINGAPORE   SYDNEY

Charles Scribner's Sons
Macmillan Publishing Company
866 Third Avenue
New York, NY 10022

Maxwell Macmillan Canada, Inc.
1200 Eglinton Avenue East
Suite 200
Don Mills, Ontario M3C 3N1

Library of Congress Cataloging-in-Publication Data

    Encyclopedia of the North American colonies/ editor in chief, Jacob Ernest Cooke; associate
editors, W. J. Eccles . . . [et al.]; special consultants, Mathé Allain . . . [et al].
      p cm.
    Includes bibliographical references and index.
    ISBN 0-684-19269-1 (set: alk. paper)
      1. Europe--Colonies--America--History--Encyclopedias. 2. North America--History--
Encyclopedias. I. Cooke, Jacob Ernest, 1924–
E45.E53   1993   93-7609
940′.03--dc20   CIP

ISBN 0-684-19269-1   Set
ISBN 0-684-19609-3   Volume 1
ISBN 0-684-19610-7   Volume 2
ISBN 0-684-19611-5   Volume 3

3 4 5 6 7 8 9 10

Printed in the United States of America

CONTENTS

Volume III

CONTENTS

CONTENTS

CONTENTS

LIST OF MAPS

Volume I

Volume II

Volume III

CONTENTS

VOLUME I

VOLUME II

Encyclopedia of the

NORTH AMERICAN COLONIES

XII

THE LIFE OF THE MIND

LITERACY

This essay construes *literacy* broadly to mean the speaking, reading, and writing practices that engaged the written word. During the seventeenth and eighteenth centuries, producing or understanding the written word often involved more than one person as well as a combination of linguistic skills. Friends and family often participated collectively in producing or interpreting written texts. Moreover, speaking, reading, and writing often worked together rather than separately to engage the written word. Since reading and writing were skills many did not possess, interactions with the written word often included oral production such as reading aloud before responding by writing or talking about the text.

It must be noted, however, that even though reading and writing were early concerns of those settling North America and words such as *reading* and *writing* were in use, the term *literacy* cannot be said to be widely used until the nineteenth century. This is probably due to the fact that early North Americans did not view these skills as constituting a coherent area of expertise. Reading and writing were often acquired quite independently of each other, either in different settings or through the tutelage of more than one individual. Writing was also learned after reading, and many individuals did not continue their formal or informal schooling long enough to learn to write. As a consequence, the two were not seen as inextricably tied together.

LITERACY AND THE LAW

Literacy was an early concern of British and Dutch colonists as well as among the Franciscans sent to convert and educate the inhabitants of New Spain. By the end of the seventeenth century, all of the colonies in New England, with the exception of Rhode Island, had passed laws requiring some form of education connected to literacy. This meant that children were to be educated in some way, not necessarily in a formal school setting. Through the seventeenth century, many of the colonies along the Atlantic coast passed local laws requiring that the young as well as apprentices receive some sort of education that would foster literacy. Often, early laws required that children be taught to read; instruction in writing was frequently included in later laws. In the absence of an educational system of even modest scope, such as could be offered by a minister, schoolmaster, or dame school, parents were responsible for seeing that their children learned to read. Legislation in New England provided fines for parents who failed to instruct their children and charges or to see that they were instructed. Repeated fines were progressively more severe, and children could be removed from their parents' care if all else failed.

Even though the role of widespread formal schooling in literacy instruction was not significant until the nineteenth century, as early as the seventeenth century communities demonstrated concern that children learn to read and write in institutions known as schools. Often, local mandates that instruction be offered were tied to an increase in population density. For example, in 1644 the Connecticut General Court ordered that "euery Towneshipp within this Jurissdiction, after the Lord hath increased them to the number of fifty houshoulders, shall then forthwith appoint one within theire Towne to teach all such children as shall resorte to him, to write and read."

The requirement for instruction based on population size grew out of the natural pressures keeping children out of school. Boys were needed to help with heavy agricultural work, and girls might be kept at home to help with domestic demands. As a result, schoolteachers would not have a sufficient number of scholars to teach in a geographic area with few inhabitants and many children kept at home to keep the family unit afloat. In addition, a minimum number of families was required to generate fees to pay a schoolmaster even a modest wage.

Four goals of literacy were frequently spelled out in early legislation. First, knowledge of the Scriptures was an intermediate goal of reading; the written Word was seen as the path to individual salvation. With Satan eager to keep men from knowing the Scriptures (the Protestant fear of Catholicism), colonial laws served to reinforce the need to foster reading competence. A 1647 law of Massachusetts Bay spelled out this peril: "It being one cheife piect of ye ould deluder, Satan, to keepe men from the knowledge of ye Scriptures." Religious motivations for requiring reading were found in early laws in colonies including Connecticut, Pennsylvania, Maryland, Virginia, and South Carolina.

The religious impetus toward literacy was not found everywhere in North America. The French Canadians did not demonstrate the same concern with literacy as the English and the Dutch colonists. Since they were Roman Catholics, the French Canadians were under no pressure to read the Bible. The priest explained everything and performed the requisite rites, officiating at baptisms, marriages, and burials. For the individual to take it upon himself or herself to interpret the holy writ was anathema. French Canadians were quite comfortable with this arrangement.

A second goal of literacy was to foster civic competence. In particular, laws specified that it was important for citizens to read the capital laws of the colonies. For example, in 1682 Pennsylvania required "that the Laws of this Province from time to time shall be publisht & Printed that Every Person may have the Knowlege thereof and they shall be one of the books taught in the Schooles of this Province and Territorys thereof." Despite the perceived importance of acquiring civic competence through literacy, illiteracy did not prevent participation in civic activities. Illiterate freemen elected town officials, served on juries, and offered testimony in cases ranging from witchcraft to murder.

The development of a cultured mind and proper behavior was a third goal of literacy. A 1696 Maryland Petitionary Act sought to establish a free school to promote "the Education of the Youth of this Province in good Letters and Manners." This particular framing is reminiscent of a contemporary definition of literacy as culturally shared knowledge.

The fourth goal of literacy was to maintain and regulate the legal rationality of the emerging bureaucratic state through written records. Numerous legal provisions required that many forms of social interaction be recorded. These ranged from marriage records to apprentice indentures, from wills to deeds recording the purchase or sale of land and slaves. These records were a part of the rhythms of life in places as distinct as Dedham, Massachusetts, and Santa Fe, New Mexico.

WHO WAS LITERATE?

Determining who was literate in the North American colonies is not a simple task. We are hampered in addressing this question because we are often without materials that record explicitly whether a person could read or write. In Sweden, for example, there are church examination registers as far back as the early seventeenth century that record to what degree, and what kinds of materials, a parishioner was able to read. In the United States, however, related information was not gathered systematically until the 1850 census. Exceptions to this situation can be found in New France and New Spain. In New France, all legal contracts included a declaration when a signatory was unable to write, or even sign his or her name: "ne scavoir escrire ny signer." Similar information is contained in military enlistment records in New Mexico, which concluded with an explicit statement as to whether the enlistee was able to sign his name. In the Spanish Borderlands more generally, all legal papers included a signature, an X in its place, or the signee's name written by someone else.

The most widely applied method of measuring literacy uses signatures on legal documents as an indication of some level of reading and writing skill. Because individuals generally learned to read before they learned to write, the ability to sign one's name, a very limited writing skill, probably meant that the signer could read at some level and knew something about writing. To obtain an estimate of literacy in a community, scholars sample a set of legal documents, counting the number of individuals who signed their names and those who marked with an X. The percentage who signed is taken to be a rough indication of the literacy of that population.

There has been a good deal of debate about the validity of signing as a measure of literacy. One concern centers on the representativeness of samples drawn from documents such as wills and military muster rolls. Many have pointed out that the number of women leaving wills was small because they were not property owners, and women did not enlist in the military. Thus, analyses employing wills examine a small, and hence unrepresentative, sample of women in a community. Other criticisms of signing center on the interpretation of marks. Some individuals marked because they were too infirm to sign their names. Others used initials rather than X, which may indicate that they could sign their full names but chose not to do so. In other cases, signatures may overestimate literacy skills. In New France, for example, wooden stencils were sometimes used to trace one's name when a signature was required. Hence, individuals able to stencil their names would be counted as literate despite their inability to read or to write beyond tracing their names. Despite these qualifications, however, signature rates offer a standard measure of a very limited exercise of writing ability that can be used to compare diverse populations over time.

Immigrants: Literacy in the Old World and the New

The literacy rate of immigrants to the North American colonies was higher than that of those who remained in England and Europe. In the seventeenth and early eighteenth centuries, the English in the British colonies, the Germans settling in Pennsylvania, and the Spanish in New Mexico had more literate individuals among their numbers than their continental counterparts when literacy is measured in terms of the ability to sign a document. A major reason for this pattern was that literacy and trade skills were valued in much of North America; premiums were sometimes paid for these skills. Thus in contrast to those without literacy skills, literates had incentives for migrating.

For example, in 1700, 30 percent of the males in England were literate, compared with 75 percent of the males in Elizabeth City, Virginia, and over 70 percent in Boston. This higher rate of literacy was found among women as well, although fewer women were literate in the new land as well as in the old. That the total colonial literacy rate was higher than England and Europe is due in part to the higher literacy rate of those immigrating.

A discussion of literacy among immigrants to New France must be qualified by the observation that the majority of those migrating eventually returned to France because they held time-limited contracts to work in the colony, return passage guaranteed. In the seventeenth century the rate of literacy among immigrants to New France was higher than that at home, with over 60 percent of the men able to sign their name. From 1672 on, migration was negligible because the Crown discontinued its policy of subsidizing emigration. As a consequence, literacy rates among French Canadians after that year are based on Canadian-born, Canadian-educated individuals. Throughout the seventeenth century, literacy was not a high priority due to the constant conflicts with the Iroquois confederacy. As a result, literacy rates fell substantially; by the end of the century, there were more French-born Canadians than native-born Canadians who could sign their names.

Patterns of Literacy

During the seventeenth and eighteenth centuries, the North American colonies, especially the British colonies, experienced considerable growth in the number of individuals with reading and writing skills. In the seventeenth century, women's literacy rates as determined by rates of signing were below that of men in most of North America. However, it is likely that such rates underestimate the number of women who could read but not write, since many features of colonial life worked against teaching women to write. Whereas local practice required that both males and females learn to read, writing instruction was offered primarily to males throughout the seventeenth century; females were taught to sew instead. Much didactic literature of the period depicts the pen as necessary for the young man eager for a life in commerce; the needle is portrayed as the woman's instrument of domestic organization, used to mark and decorate linen with lettering.

During the first half of the seventeenth century, roughly one-third of the women in New England were literate as defined by signing rates. This approached 50 percent by the end of the seventeenth century, increasing to 70 percent in the years around the Revolutionary War, with reports as high as 90 percent in some areas. By the end of the eighteenth century, women in New England seem to have been almost universally literate.

There are notable exceptions to the New England pattern, however. In New Netherland (New York), literacy was very high among women, with over 75 percent able to sign their names by the end of the seventeenth century. In other regions, rates were not as high. For example, in Perquimans County, North Carolina, only slightly more than one-third of the women were able to sign their names by the time of the Revolutionary War. In New France, after the Crown terminated its policy of subsidizing immigration to Acadia and Canada in 1672, a different pattern of male-female literacy began to emerge. In Canadian *habitants* (families holding title to a farm), it was the girls who went to school, where they learned to read, write, and keep accounts. Some visitors from France deplored the fact that *habitant* girls were too well educated and thus wanted to rise above their appointed station in life, marrying husbands of higher status and living in town.

By the end of the seventeenth century, literacy was quite high for men—nearly universal for those in New England and near 80 percent in the Middle Atlantic region. That many New England soldiers kept diaries during the Seven Years' War attests to the spread of literacy. By the revolution, from 80 percent to 100 percent of the men were literate everywhere except the Spanish Borderlands and New France, where rates were much lower. In New Mexico, for example, only roughly a third of men were able to sign their names by the end of the eighteenth century.

Despite regional differences, certain patterns of literacy were similar across the North American colonies. For one, place of residence, urban versus rural, affected literacy. From New England through New France to New Mexico, both male and female urban dwellers counted more literates among their numbers than did those in rural areas. This gap decreased over the seventeenth and eighteenth centuries in New England but still remained; in New France there were substantial urban-rural differences even through the middle of the eighteenth century. With more schools in town than in rural areas, there was greater access to resources promoting literacy. Even contracts for servants were less likely to include provisions for education in rural households as compared to urban. A child put out to serve a household in the country was less likely to receive the benefits of education than his or her urban counterpart. At the same time, however, there was a substantial increase in literacy among those in rural settings. For example, literacy among farmers in New England nearly doubled between the seventeenth and the mid eighteenth century.

Literacy varied among individuals along occupational lines. Occupations relying on the written word for conducting business demanded some measure of reading and writing skills. As a consequence, apprenticeships often provided individuals with the training and practice necessary to acquire some literacy skills.

Despite the overall increase in literacy, the trend toward universal literacy was not constant. In the first generation after immigration, the numbers of literate adults tended to decline. It has been suggested that the absence of formal education placed the burden of teaching children to read and write on the family. Since the challenges of establishing a life in a new land turned attention away from education to basic survival and placed lower value on literacy relative to other needs, literacy among the offspring of immigrants would have been lower. As population density grew, and with it financial resources, it is possible that access to schooling became both more affordable and easier, leading to a rise in literacy.

READING AND WRITING

The Intersection of Spoken and Written Words

Many features of life in seventeenth and eighteenth century North America contributed to bringing the spoken and written words together. For one, not all could read and fewer could write. Hence, settlers and their children often depended on those around them for help in participating in the world of literacy. Those who could not read well enough to assimilate written material were able to share in the world of the written word as others read aloud books and newspapers. A farmer who received a letter from relatives in England might ask a neighbor to read it to him. Letters might be written by one individual while others contributed orally or reviewed a draft before it was sent. Likewise, interactions with legal documents were often mediated by a friend or community member, or prepared entirely by another person. Members of a town who wanted to petition local government for road improvements, for example, might enlist the services of a scrivener to record their wishes. In rural areas, inhabitants might seek local individuals who could write to draft a petition. These individuals ranged from surveyors to soldiers.

This sharing occurred in both the private domain and the public. In New France, government edicts initially were read from the pulpit by the parish priest. In the early eighteenth century, this responsibility was transferred to parish militia captains, who read the decrees on the church steps after Mass. These public readings also took place in New Mexico, where a drum summoned inhabitants to plazas to hear notices read aloud, "published" in the medieval sense. Since New Mexico was a multilingual setting, public readings were in the language of the villagers, thus providing access to the written word regardless of native tongue.

Despite the intersection of speaking and writing, it would be misleading to cast colonial North America as "oral" in some of the senses in which that word is used. The simplest and least controversial meaning of oral is its application to cultures utterly outside the use of the written word, where communication is largely a face-to-face matter. Clearly seventeenth- and eighteenth-century North America does not fit here.

One sense in which oral does apply to colonial America can be found in New England. Here colonials perceived speech and writing as interwoven. Religious texts of all sorts repeatedly represented the word of God and the written word as interchangeable. The Word, God's word, was given orally, then written down only to be transmitted orally through sermons and oral discourse.

A second sense of oral found in the British and Dutch colonies comes from the educational emphasis on oral performance. Students were required to present aloud material they had read, to spell orally, and to show facility with grammar through an oral demonstration. These performances were offered in school as well as in special programs presented to parents and the community at large. In colleges, oral recitation of material learned was the norm. Graduates of Harvard College were expected to excel in such performance.

A third sense in which oral applies to colonial North America can be found in changes in the relative importance of writing. Although the written word was part of many interactions, much written information circulated by word of mouth because many were unable to read or write. The North American colonies made the transition from an oral to a literate culture by incorporating the written word into the lives of more people over the course of the seventeenth and eighteenth centuries. As increasing numbers acquired some level of literacy, the need for orally communicating what was written decreased; individuals became able to read and write on their own.

The shift from a culture more dependent on speech to communicate information to one more embedded in written communication was also evident in printed matter, most of which initially was produced in the British and Dutch colonies. While the production of printed materials is not an unambiguous measure of an increase in the rate of literacy, it does provide some evidence for it. The seventeenth century witnessed growth in the overall production of printed materials in what was to become the United States. In 1700 sixty-five imprints were produced. This approximately doubled in twenty-five years; by 1725 there were 124 items printed. Growth continued more slowly for the next twenty-five years—174 imprints in 1750—and then increased dramatically. In 1775, presses churned out 852 publications. Indeed, inexpensive chapbooks and almanacs were widely available through urban book dealers as well as rural shopkeepers and itinerant peddlers.

Newspapers are often used as an index of the literacy of a population. In 1690 there was a single issue of one newspaper in these colonies, published in Massachusetts. By 1740 twelve newspapers were printed in five colonies—Massachusetts, New York, Pennsylvania, South Carolina, and Virginia—and there were eighteen papers in nine colonies by 1760. The average number of weekly copies per paper was roughly six hundred in the mid eighteenth century, but readership was much larger because single copies were passed from reader to reader and were shared aloud as well. In addition, in 1778 the interest in news rose markedly, so much so that the *Connecticut Courant* (Hartford) claimed a circulation of eight thousand.

At the same time that many more of the colonies' inhabitants were able to participate directly in the world of the written word, their knowledge of it seems to have been closely tied to oral language. The many primers, readers, and self-help books of seventeenth- and certainly eighteenth-century America repeatedly tied the written word to the spoken. Early lessons cataloged discrepancies between the way words were heard or spoken and the way they were written. Students were taught that punctuation was a system for representing pauses of different duration in speaking: a comma was a pause of one interval,

a semicolon of two, a period of three. Today, in a culture more intimately embedded in the written word, the distribution of punctuation is typically described in syntactic terms. As a frame of reference, speech has shifted to the background for most types of punctuation.

Students also were taught that there were classes of words that began with one sound, such as *s*, but were spelled with another, such as *c* in "ceiling," "cinnamon," and "cypher." They were advised that many words had "extra" letters that were silent, not to be pronounced, such as the *g* in "sign," the *h* in "ghost," and the *c* in "science" or "sceptre." The connection between spelling and speaking can be readily found in the writing of common people during the period. Writers varied the spelling of the same word in a single text; they also cast the spelling of the word to more closely reflect their conception of the way it was spoken, such as "onist" for "honest."

Learning to Read and Write

Throughout North America in the seventeenth and eighteenth centuries, fewer people learned to write than read. There were many reasons for this. For one, reading was crucial to religious aims to a greater or lesser degree everywhere except among the Roman Catholics in New France; in contrast, the skill needed to draft original texts, religious or otherwise, was not a commonly shared goal or necessity. Second, writing was largely viewed as a technical skill needed by those pursuing occupations where writing was important. A third reason that fewer learned to write than read was the expense associated with writing instruction. Where the fees for reading and writing instruction were specified in local law, writing was costlier than reading. The charge per student might be four pence per week to learn "wrighting" and three pence for reading. Similarly, the books and materials used to teach penmanship were more expensive and more difficult to obtain than books used to teach reading.

The order in which reading and writing were taught contributed to more readers than writers. The expression "readin', ritin' and 'rithmetic" roughly describes the sequence in which these skills were taught and learned. Since writing was learned after reading, students were older when they were taught to write. Since older children were often needed to contribute to the family economy, they frequently did not remain in school long enough to master penmanship.

Although an increasing number of communities made efforts over the course of the seventeenth and eighteenth centuries to provide some sort of schooling outside the home, initial contacts with literacy often began with reading in the home, typically of religious texts. Children would become familiar with the Scriptures as they were read aloud by father and increasingly by mother. In New Mexico, this exposure to texts may have occurred in missions as well as in the homes of others in the community who were often paid to provide instruction in reading. There young children, known as *doctrinarios*, received religious indoctrination through reading. They were then able to provide a critical link to those who could not read by disseminating the Word.

The extensive use of reading aloud meant that the earliest encounters with texts entailed the word heard and the word spoken. Consequently, the implicit curriculum in early primers and schoolbooks was oriented toward reading aloud and being read to, both in the types of instructional material included in these books and in the tasks new readers were asked to perform. Initial instruction typically consisted of letters taught alongside words that began with the same sound and letter. *The New-England Primer,* the most widely used reader in the eighteenth century, opens with an oral alphabet set in verse:

> In Adam's Fall
> We Sinned all.
>
> Thy Life to Mend
> This Book Attend.

The correspondence between the sound of the letter and the initial sound of the word depended on those learning to read hearing the two spoken or read aloud. Likewise, the use of verse to present information drew on the assumption that individuals would hear these stretches of language read aloud and would repeat them, and that the rhyme would foster memorization, thereby facilitating their recitation to others. Similarly, primers frequently included passages specifically identified as for reading aloud.

The New-England Primer is emblematic of the type of content found in primers. For example, the 1727 edition includes an illustrated rhyming alphabet, a syllabarium (pairs of "easy syllables" such as *ab, eb, ib, ob, ub*), a longer alphabet with religious material, and longer religious passages including the Lord's Prayer, the Creed, the Ten Commandments, and a catechism. A shift away from religious material for reading instruction began to appear in the mid part of the eighteenth century, when such schoolbooks as Thomas Dilworth's *A New Guide to the English Tongue* (1747) and Noah Webster's *A Grammatical Institute* (1783) came out.

Although writing was second to reading both in the order in which it was learned and in the numbers of individuals who could employ it with any facility, access to writing instruction increased over the course of the seventeenth and eighteenth centuries. Its technology was certainly a limiting factor in its spread. Paper was expensive and scarce due to its composition and method of production. Through a tedious and labor-intensive process, rags, which were difficult to obtain, were turned into paper. And implements for writing were not readily available. Pencils were not widely available until the nineteenth century. One wrote instead with a goose quill, which had to be sliced and shaped until a fine point was achieved. Ink had to be prepared by mixing water with a special powder.

Unlike reading, writing was often regarded as an art. The goal of writing instruction was to develop a "faire" hand, that is, to produce beautiful penmanship. This was accomplished by having students proceed through a series of exercises aimed at developing the various flourishes and curves of cursive writing. George Bickham's *The Universal Penman* (1743), printed first in England, served as a model for many writing masters. It is likely that the numerous editions of George Fisher's *The (American) Instructor; or Young Man's Best Companion* (1748) served as an out-of-school model for improving penmanship throughout the eighteenth century. Toward the latter part of that period, books devoted solely to penmanship, such as John Jenkins's *The Art of Writing* (1791), began to be used for penmanship instruction.

In general, students began to learn penmanship by copying the basic components of letters, such as upward and downward curves, gradually moving to words, then phrases and sentences with moral content. The following, from Fisher's *Instructor,* illustrates the latter:

> Fair Words commonly dress foul Deeds,
> Fair Faces have sometimes foul Conditions.
> Few do good with what they have gotten ill.
> Future Events must be left to Providence. (p. 34)

Thus, while young scholars worked at perfecting a "faire" hand, they were exposed to maxims for living a righteous life.

The ultimate goal of penmanship instruction was to prepare individuals for commercial life. Copybooks for advanced students typically included, as part of the final lessons, samples of bills and pages from wastebooks or daybooks—the accounting records appropriate to anyone engaged in commerce. The fact that copying, rather than creating original compositions, was the major vehicle for learning manifested the belief that writing was not primarily for invention but to master the tools necessary to produce conventional kinds of material.

When writing instruction was provided at home, the prevailing view was that it was the domain of fathers rather than mothers. Some of the evidence for this comes from diary reports where fathers indicate they were involved in writing instruction; in other cases sons have recorded being taught to read by their mothers and to write by their fathers. That some women might have followed a different route in learning to produce letters is a possibility raised in recent work on women's literacy. Local ordinances sometimes specified that boys learn to read and write (and perhaps cipher) and that girls learn to read and do needlework. We know that women used letters to mark linen and that eighteenth century self-help books, such as *The American Instructor,* included alphabets for that purpose. This leaves open the possibility that boys learned to write on paper and that some girls, heretofore regarded as nonwriters, might instead be writers with the needle rather than the pen.

Those who learned to write outside the home were tutored by writing masters or in "wrighting" schools for several hours each day. It should be noted, however, that the teaching of reading and writing in different schools or by different persons was not quite so straightforward as it might seem. Certainly by the end of the eighteenth century, many persons taught both reading and writing, as well as other subjects. Undoubtedly, children still learned some reading before writing, but they were able to do so under the same roof.

Whether an individual was taught at home or in school, self-instruction or self-improvement undoubtedly boosted literacy. Diaries recount the stories of individuals who read in the evenings by candlelight or the fireside so they could improve their reading skills; others tell of taking a book to read while working in the field.

As the eighteenth century wore on, self-improvement books became widely available. A vade mecum aimed at improving one's literacy skills included such details as sound-grapheme correspondences, punctuation, capitalization, alphabets for copying, recipes for making ink, and model letters for personal as well as business correspondence, along with sample legal forms such as deeds.

MATERIAL LIMITS ON THE SPREAD OF LITERACY

The spread of literacy was limited by many material factors. Although printed matter had been imported from England since the seventeenth century, the presence of printing presses on American soil made it possible to produce reading matter more readily. Within roughly a decade after the mid eighteenth century, at least one printing press could be found in each of the thirteen colonies. But many of the tools of the printing trade were not readily obtained because of high cost or limited availability. In New France the picture was quite different from New England. There were neither printers nor book sellers until 1764, when the first newspaper was established. With the English conquest printing, bookselling, and libraries came to this region. In the Spanish Borderlands, the availability of the printing press was a nineteenth-century phenomenon. New Mexico and California did not have their first printing presses until the 1830s.

In the thirteen colonies, type was generally imported in the seventeenth and eighteenth centuries because skilled type makers were largely unknown in North America. At the same time, type was expensive, so few printers owned the number of fonts necessary to produce a steady stream of imprints. Printing ink, although not expensive, was messy to produce; recall also that paper was not widely available because of the scarcity of rags, the basis of colonial paper.

These scarcities were compounded by poor networks for distributing printed material. Books and other printed matter were typically sold near the city or within the colony where they were produced. General store owners from the country might come to the city two or three times a year to purchase books for a season; peddlers traveled around the countryside, hawking a limited number of publications. This meant that those outside of areas with heavy population density had very limited access to the range of materials imported from abroad or printed in North America.

Even where printed material was more widely available, the cost of books put them outside the reach of a goodly number of people. Evidence of book ownership from probate inventories indicates that few individuals owned more than a Bible and perhaps some miscellaneous small books. A Philadelphia laborer would have had to invest nearly two days' wages in *The Lady's Letter Writer* for his wife in 1767, and one and a half days' wages in a new copy of *The Young Man's Companion* for himself in 1768. To be sure, many books circulated as used copies. But still, faced with limited resources and the need to feed, clothe, and shelter a family, printed matter was not a major priority.

CONCLUSION

Over the course of the seventeenth and eighteenth centuries, colonial North America made an uneven journey toward more intimate interaction with the written word. Both men and women, city dwellers and those in the country, and individuals from a wide range of occupations were able to participate in the life of the written word. Even so, literacy was a set of contradictions. On the one hand, the absence of the term "literacy" in the vernacular language reflects the fact that many people were unable to read and to write because these skills were acquired separately. On the other hand, literacy was far more of a collective experience than it is today because people jointly encountered the written word. Acts of literacy were often the result of weaving together the strands of speaking, reading, and writing rather than experiencing them independently. Similarly, the linguistic skills entailed in literacy—speaking, reading, and writing—were taken to be more dependent on each other than we regard them today. Such a view sets in relief the present, where people generally possess the reading and writing skills reflected in our use of the term "literacy." At the same time, our conception of literacy is more highly differentiated, reflected in such terms as "information literacy," "math literacy," and "computer literacy."

BIBLIOGRAPHY

Auwers, Linda. "Reading the Marks of the Past: Exploring Female Literacy in Colonial Windsor, Connecticut." *Historical Methods* 13, no. 4 (Fall 1980):204–214.

Barth, Pius Joseph. "Franciscan Education and the Social Order in Spanish North America, 1501–1821." Ph.D. diss., University of Chicago, 1945.

Beales, Ross W., Jr., "Studying Literacy at the Community Level: A Research Note." *Journal of Interdisciplinary History* 9, no. 1 (Summer 1978):93–102.

Beckman, Gail McKnight, comp. *The Statutes at Large of Pennsylvania in the Time of William Penn.* Vol. 1. New York, 1976.

Cremin, Lawrence A. *American Education: The Colonial Experience, 1607–1683.* New York, 1970.

———. "Reading, Writing, and Literacy." *Review of Education* 1, no. 4 (1975):517–521.

Cressy, David. *Coming Over: Migration and Communication Between England and New England in the Seventeenth Century.* Cambridge, England, 1987.

———. *Literacy and the Social Order: Reading and Writing in Tudor and Stuart England.* Cambridge, England, 1980.

Curtis, Bruce. "Some Recent Work on the History of Literacy in Canada." *History of Education Quarterly* 30, no. 4 (1990):613–624.

Cushing, John D., ed. *The Laws of the Province of Maryland.* Wilmington, Del., 1978.

Fischer, David Hackett. *Albion's Seed: Four British Folkways in America.* New York, 1989.

Fisher, George. *The American Instructor; Or, Young Man's Best Companion*. Philadelphia, 1748.

Galarneau, Claude. "Livre et société à Québec (1976–1859)." In *L'imprimé au Québec: Aspects historiques (18ᵉ–20ᵉ siècles)*, edited by Yvan Lamonde. Quebec, 1983.

Galenson, David W. "Literacy and the Social Origins of Some Early Americans." *The Historical Journal* 22, no. 1 (1979):75–91.

Gallegos, Bernardo Phillip. "Literacy, Schooling, and Society in Colonial New Mexico: 1692–1821." Ph.D. diss., University of New Mexico, 1988.

Gallman, Robert E. "Changes in the Level of Literacy in a New Community of Early America." *Journal of Economic History* 48, no. 3 (1988):567–582.

———. "Two Problems in the Measurement of American Colonial Signature-Mark Literacy." *Historical Methods* 20, no. 4 (Fall 1987):137–141.

Greer, Alan. "L'alphabétisation et son histoire au Québec: État de la question." In *L'imprimé au Québec: Aspects historiques (18ᵉ–20ᵉ siècles)*, edited by Yvan Lamonde. Quebec, 1983.

Grubb, Farley W. "Colonial Immigrant Literacy: An Economic Analysis of Pennsylvania-German Evidence, 1727–1775." *Explorations in Economic History* 24, no. 1 (1987):63–76.

———. "Growth of Literacy in Colonial America: Longitudinal Patterns, Economic Models, and the Direction of Future Research." *Social Science History* 14, no. 4 (Winter 1990):451–482.

Hall, David D. "The Uses of Literacy in New England, 1600–1850." In *Printing and Society in Early America*, edited by William L. Joyce et al. Worcester, Mass., 1983.

———. *Worlds of Wonder, Days of Judgment: Popular Religious Belief in Early New England*. New York, 1989.

Kilpatrick, William H. *The Dutch Schools of New Netherland and Colonial New York*. Washington, D.C., 1912; repr. 1969.

Lockridge, Kenneth. *Literacy in Colonial New England*. New York, 1974.

Monaghan, E. Jennifer. "Literacy Instruction and Gender in Colonial New England." *American Quarterly* 40, no. 1 (1988):18–41.

Moogk, Peter N. "Reluctant Exiles: Emigrants from France in Canada Before 1760." *William and Mary Quarterly*, 3rd ser., 46, no. 3 (1989):463–505.

Mott, Frank. *American Journalism: A History of Newspapers in the United States Through 260 Years, 1690–1950*. New York, 1941; rev. ed. 1950.

The New-England Primer. Boston, 1727. Facs. repr. in *The New-England Primer*, edited by Paul Leicester Ford. New York, 1897; repr. 1962.

Perlmann, Joel, and Dennis Shirley. "When Did New England Women Acquire Literacy?" *William and Mary Quarterly*, 3rd ser., 48, no 1 (1991):50–67.

Raesly, Ellis L. *Portrait of New Netherland*. New York, 1945.

Shurtleff, Nathaniel B., comp. *Records of the Governor and Company of the Massachusetts Bay in New England*. Vol. 2. Boston, 1853.

Simmons, Marc. *Spanish Government in New Mexico*. Albuquerque, N.Mex., 1968; 2d ed., 1990.

Small, Walter H. "Girls in Colonial Schools." *Education* 22, no. 9 (1902):532–537.

Soltow, Lee, and Edward Stevens. *The Rise of Literacy and the Common School in the United States: A Socioeconomic Analysis to 1870*. Chicago, 1981.

Trumbull, J. Hammond, comp. *The Public Records of the Colony of Connecticut*. 15 vols. Hartford, Conn., 1850; repr. New York, 1968.

Tully, Alan. "Literacy Levels and Educational Development in Rural Pennsylvania, 1729–1775." *Pennsylvania History* 39, no. 3 (1972):301–312.

Warner, Michael. *The Letters of the Republic: Publication and the Public Sphere in Eighteenth-Century America*. Cambridge, Mass., 1990.

Wells, James M. "American Printing: The Search for Self-Sufficiency." *Proceedings of the American Antiquarian Society* 94, pt. 2 (1984):269–295.

*Deborah Keller-Cohen**

SEE ALSO **The Colonial Press; European Languages; Literature;** and **Protestant Pluralism;** and various essays in EDUCATION.

* I am indebted to W. J. Eccles for his comments as well as his generous help with the complexities of New France. David Hall, Anne Gene, Pamela Moss, and Becky Reed offered helpful feedback on earlier drafts. Keith Arbour provided crucial assistance with the research.

EUROPEAN LANGUAGES

COLONIAL ENGLISH

THE ENGLISH OF THE ENGLISH

SHAKESPEARE HAD ONLY recently completed *Macbeth* when the first English settlers brought their language to Jamestown, Virginia, in 1607. These early colonists had grown up in Elizabethan England and spoke the language of William Shakespeare, Sir Francis Bacon, and John Donne. It was a time of great change and new worlds, the beginning of the British Empire and of English as a world language.

English itself was undergoing major changes. The colonists as well as Londoners did not always pronounce such words as *meat, sea,* and *lean* with the same vowel. Sometimes they used the old pronunciation, making them sound like *mate, say,* and *lane;* and sometimes they used the pronunciation we use today. By about 1700 the old pronunciation was seldom heard. Similarly the vowels in words like *food, good,* and *flood* were in flux and the vowel in *cut* was a recent innovation. Words like *clerk* were sometimes rhymed with *jerk* and sometimes with *dark.*

Seventeenth-century English also preserved the double forms of the second person pronouns: the formal *you, ye,* and *your* used to address lords and ladies, and the informal *thou, thee,* and *thy*

reserved for everyone else. Despite the efforts of the Quakers of the Pennsylvania colony to use *thou* in all situations because it was supposed to be inherently egalitarian, by about 1750 the *thou* forms were largely dropped, and *you* and *your* were used without regard to status or social occasion.

Early colonial American writing now seems quaint with its Elizabethan features. When, for example, the governor and early historian of the Plymouth colony, William Bradford, describes a dramatic incident that took place in 1638, his language is essentially Elizabethan:

Amongst other *enormities* that fell out amongst them, this year 3. men were (after due triall) executed for robery & murder which they had committed . . . Arthur Peach . . . a *lustie* and a desperate yonge man . . . being now out of means, and *loath* to worke, and falling to idle *courses* & company, intended to goe to the Dutch plantation. . . . [Three others] *complotting* with him, rane away from their maisters in the night, and shaped such a course as they thought to avoyd the pursute of any. But falling into the way that *lyeth* betweene the Bay of Massachusetts and the Narrigansets, and being disposed to rest them selves, *struck fire,* and took tobaco, a litle out of the way, by the way side. At length ther came a Narigansett Indean by, who had been in the Bay *a trading,* and had both cloth & beads *aboute* him. . . . Peach tould the others he would kill him, and take what he had from him. But they were *some thing* afraid. . . . So they let him alone to doe as he would; and when he saw his time, he [Peach] tooke a rapier and rane him [the Indian] through the body once or twise, and tooke from him 5. *fathume* of *wampum,* and 3. coats of cloath, and wente their way, leaving him for dead. But he [the Indian] scrabbled away, when they were gone, and *made shift* to gett home (but dyed within a few days after,) by which means they were discovered; and by subtilty the Indeans tooke them. For they desiring a canow [canoe] to *sett them* over a water, (not thinking their *facte* had been known,) by the *sachems* comand they were carried to Aquidnett Iland, & ther accused of the murder. [Italics added]

Aside from the odd spellings, which were not yet uniformly established by printers, editors, or schools, one of the first things we notice about the passage is the number of words that are obsolete or archaic. *Amongst* for *'among,' loath* 'disinclined,' and *make shift* are little heard today. Bradford uses *enormity* in its old sense, 'a breach of law or morality,' whereas today, influenced by *enormous,* we reserve it for more monstrous crimes. *Courses* 'personal behavior,' *complotting* 'to plot or conspire,' and *fact* 'a crime' are all essentially obsolete, though we might still hear the last in *after the fact.* Bradford's *lustie* may mean 'healthy or vigorous,' which the *Oxford English Dictionary (OED)* labels "somewhat archaic," or he may be referring to Mr. Peach's arrogance and insolent self-confidence, in which case Bradford would be using it in an outright obsolete sense.

Fathom (a unit of length, about five feet) is still used, but exclusively in soundings or measuring water depths in navigation. Bradford uses it as a measurement of wampum strings. *Strike fire* is obsolete because fires today are rarely started by striking flint on steel. The awkward locution *make shift to get home* is marked "obsolete" by the *OED,* as is the equally ungainly expression, "a canow *to sett them over* a water." The preposition *a,* prefixed to a present participle in *a trading,* survives today only in folk speech and dialect, as does the adverbial use of *something* in *something afraid.*

Bradford's use of *lyeth* is also a sign that he is writing in essentially Elizabethan English, which had two inflectional endings for the third person singular, the earlier *-eth,* which was on its way out, and *-s,* the modern form.

Most of these Elizabethan features were defunct or obsolescent in America by the time of the Revolutionary War. Even so Bradford's lan-guage has elements of nascent American English, namely, the Indian loanwords *wampum* 'shell beads used as a medium of exchange' and *sachem* 'an Indian chief.'

ENGLISH BECOMES AMERICAN ENGLISH

American English, or as Samuel Johnson derisively called it, the "American dialect," was not generally recognized as distinct from British English until well into the eighteenth century. But the seeds of American English were planted before the first colonists set foot on New World soil. Even when immigrants, like those aboard the Mayflower, were relatively homogeneous—more or less from the same cultural region and speaking the same dialect in England—their experiences coming to America, such as contact with other languages, as well as sailor's jargon and pidgins, doubtless had an impact on their native speech patterns.

Most of the groups immigrating to the New World were more mixed than the Plymouth Rock pilgrims. The language they brought with them was not only subtly altered by the crossing but was a mixture of varieties of English, though the dominant speech was of southeastern England. American English was inchoate in this melting pot of English dialects and maritime varieties.

Borrowings from the Indians

The greatest changes in the process of distinguishing American from British English happened in the New World itself. The colonists encountered a strange landscape and unfamiliar forms of wildlife for which they had no English names. When, for example, they came upon a furry, cat-sized creature with a mask-like marking, they were at a loss for what to call it. They naturally adopted the Indian name, but it was difficult for Europeans to pronounce. Captain John Smith spelled it *rahaugcum* and *raugroughcum* in his 1608 account of the Virginia colony. He was trying to write the Algonquian word *ärä-'kun* from *ärä'kunem,* literally, 'he scratches with his hands,' which probably alludes to the racoon's habit of scrabbling for crabs and other tidbits on stream bottoms. The name was also used in the New England colonies and was spelled *rackoone* or *rockoon*. By 1672 the current spelling was established and the Native American word was fully assimilated into colonial English.

Some American Indian terms had already found their way into Elizabethan English, usually by way of Spanish and Portuguese borrowings from Nahuatl, the tongue of the Aztecs, and from various Native American dialects of the West Indies and Central and South America. Some of these words are *barbecue, cannibal, canoe, chocolate, cocoa, maize, potato, savannah,* and *tomato*.

About half of all the three hundred or so American Indian loanwords current today entered the language in the seventeenth century, including *caribou, hickory, hominy, moccasin, moose, possum, papoose, persimmon pone, powwow, skunk, squash, squaw, terrapin, tomahawk, totem, wigwam,* and *woodchuck*. Some, like William Bradford's *wampum* and *sachem*, dealt primarily with the Native American culture and today are not used much, even though *sachem* was extended to mean 'a political leader or government head.' Others, like *caucus, chipmunk, mackinaw, pecan, succotash,* and *toboggan*, were borrowed later and were not applied exclusively to Native American life.

A colonial Indian would probably not recognize any of these words because they were radically changed in the course of being adopted into American speech. Algonquian, the source of most of these borrowings, has many sounds and sound combinations that were completely foreign to English speakers and difficult for them to pronounce. Often the words were abbreviated or clipped (*hominy* from *rockahominy*, *squash* from *asquutasquash*, *hickory* from *pawcohiccora*). Sometimes the Indian word was changed by folk etymology, which was an attempt to make sense of a new and unusual sounding word by analyzing it (incorrectly) in terms of known words. For example, the Indian word *muskwessu* or *muscassus* became *muskrat*, a musky smelling rodent; and *otchek* or *odjik* became *woodchuck*.

The influence of the Native American culture was not negligible when we take into account the numerous combinations in which these loanwords occur (e.g., *skunk*-cabbage, *skunk* bear, *skunk* weed), not to mention the couple of hundred combinations with *Indian* (e.g., *Indian* pony, *Indian* mallow). In addition there are many expressions derived from features of Native American life: *on the warpath, peace pipe, to bury the hatchet, to hold a powwow, Indian summer, pale face, brave* (noun), *firewater, Indian file, Indian giver, happy hunting grounds, Great Spirit, medicine man, war paint, war dance, to scalp,* and *ticket scalper*.

American English also borrowed many words from non-English Europeans as well as from African slaves. These loanwords tend to be regionalized to wherever a given immigrant group settled—African in the South, French in Louisiana, Spanish in the Southwest, German in Pennsylvania, Dutch in New York—and assumed greater importance in the development of American regional dialects, which will be dealt with later.

Changes in English Words

The English spoken by the colonists almost immediately began drifting away from the mother tongue. Many words and pronunciations died out in England over two or three centuries but survived in America, such as *adze, andiron, baywindow, cesspool, clodhopper, copious, cross-purposes, din, flap-jack, foxfire, greenhorn, home-spun, jeans, loophole, molasses, offal, ragamuffin, stock* 'cattle,' *trash,* and *underpinning*. Sometimes it was one of the senses of a word that died out in England but survived in America, such as *cabin* 'a poor dwelling,' *fall* 'autumn,' *quit* 'to stop,' *raise* 'to breed, rear, grow,' *bug* 'insect,' and *baggage* 'luggage.'

Among the older English pronunciations surviving in America but not in England are the vowel sound in *fast, bath, aunt* and the postvocalic 'r' in *fire, course, board*. In England the vowel of the first group of words was originally enunciated like the vowel sound in *cat* but shifted to the vowel in *father* during the late sixteenth and the seventeenth centuries. The colonists of New England and Virginia, who looked to England for their standards of fashion in speech and culture, imitated the later British pronunciation. This articulation still survives in New England and parts of Virginia today, whereas the rest of the country uses the older (*cat*) pronunciation. The same thing happened during this period with the so-called postvocalic 'r,' which became the unstressed vowel 'uh' or was dropped altogether. In England, as well as in New England and the lower South, the words in the second group above are pronounced approximately 'fiuh,' 'ko-uhs,' and 'bo-uhd,' while in the rest of America the 'r' is pronounced.

Often English dialect terms became standard American words. This is the case for *cater-cornered, cordwood, deck, drool, pond, shoat, squirt, wilt,* and many others.

A word used in England with a particular sense frequently developed new meanings after being transplanted to America. This happened with *apartment, barn, cracker, creek, dry-goods, fraternity, lumber, pie, rock, shop, squat* 'to settle on land,' *store, tariff, team, to notify, to haul,* and many more. For example, *lumber* in eighteenth-century English meant 'disused goods,' the sense that survives in England today, as in *lumber room.* But the American colonists used it to designate cut timber. *To haul* in England meant and still means 'to move by force or violence.' In America since colonial times, it has meant 'to transport in a vehicle.'

THE UNIFORMITY OF COLONIAL AMERICAN ENGLISH

The differences in the varieties of British English that the colonists brought to America tended to be "leveled out" over a period of 150 years or so. Leveling is the obliteration of a linguistic distinction. For example the vowel in *kettle* was variously pronounced in colonial English with the short 'i,' *kittle,* and the short 'e,' *kettle.* Eventually the vowel was leveled to *kettle,* the variant *kittle* almost completely dying out except in folk speech.

The extent of leveling on a national basis is difficult to ascertain. There is evidence that at least for certain features, no leveling took place during the colonial period. The vowel sound in *keg,* for example, was sometimes pronounced with the same vowel as in *hat,* sometimes with the vowel as in *pain,* and sometimes with the vowel as in *shed. Devil* was sometimes *divil,* and *head* was often *haid.* These variations were used in urban as well as rural areas and by speakers of all social classes. A few centuries later they were restricted socially and regionally, but in the colonial period they were not yet leveled to a single pronunciation in general speech.

On the other hand there is evidence that colonial pronunciation, at least for certain other features, tended to level out in the direction of standard British English, the speech of eighteenth-century southeastern England, notably the language of Londoners. Colonial America, especially the coastal towns and seaports, maintained close ties with England. The leading colonial families, who spoke the prestige dialect, followed English fashions of speech and culture and were the model for the majority of uneducated settlers. When standard British English began dropping 'r' after vowels, for example, most colonial English speakers adopted this pronunciation, except in the middle colonies.

In general new British immigrants were under social pressure to assimilate their dialects into the general colonial vernacular, which most closely approximated the speech of the region around London. Whatever the degree of leveling, the main effect of this process was to unify American English during the colonial period in contrast to the more historically rooted regionalization of British English.

VARIETIES OF COLONIAL AMERICAN ENGLISH

Just as English in America began distinguishing itself from the English of Britain almost from the first day of colonial life, so the English spoken in each colonial region began differentiating itself from region to region.

Newcomers to the colonies speaking the dialects of the English homeland had an incentive to blend in, to assimilate and quickly adopt the speech patterns of the established colonists. But the speech patterns they heard and tried to conform to were the local or regional ones that were becoming more and more distinctive. Much of the linguistic leveling in the colonies really took place regionally rather than for the colonies as a whole.

Because language is one of the most important characteristics of a culture, the geography of language variation—or linguistic geography—is necessarily a branch of cultural geography. The guiding principle in this approach is that settlement patterns have shaped and defined the geography of American life and language. To understand the character of a given cultural region, its features and boundaries, we must begin by examining the cultures that the settlers brought to it.

On the broadest level, the British settlement on North America's Atlantic coast defined the boundaries within which American English established itself. The individual colonies along the coast then became the focal points, points of origin, or "hearths," out of which developed the various regional cultures and their dialects. There are five seminal hearths corresponding to the earliest colonies: New England, New York, the South (upper and lower), and African American influence.

Colonial New England

The first colonists established two dominant centers from which sprang New England's regional characteristics: the Massachusetts Bay area and the lower Connecticut River valley. The following words were current in colonial Massachusetts, Connecticut, or New Hampshire and today are still regionalisms confined primarily to New England or its northern settlement areas (the dates are of the earliest known printed occurrence of the word): *alewife* 'a fish of the herring family' (1633), *banker* 'fisherman or fishing vessel' (1704), *barvel* 'fisherman's apron' (1629), *basket-fish* 'a brittle star' (1670), *beaver meadow* 'an open grassy area' (1644), *black ash* 'an American ash' (1673), *bonnyclabber* 'solidified sour milk' (1731), *buttry* 'pantry' (1654), *caboose* 'cook's galley on a ship' (1747), *case* 'general health' (1634), *chamber* 'an upper room or floor' (1639), *clapboard* 'wooden siding' (1632), *creek stuff* (or *thatch*) 'cordgrass' (1669), *cusk* 'a saltwater fish' (1677), *deacon seat* 'front row seat in church' (1667), *dish kettle* 'a heavy pot for cooking' (1747), *drag* 'harrow' (1655), *dresser* 'sideboard,' 'cupboard' (1651), *ex* 'an axle' (1648), *fare* 'a catch of fish' (1707), *flake* 'a rack for drying fish' (1635), *flitch* 'salt pork' (1632), *general* 'bill of expenses' (1763), *green corn* 'sweet corn' (1645), and *hire* 'to borrow money' (1782).

To the seventeenth-century colonists, waterways were vital to trade and communication and were an integrative force for the region as a whole. Consequently the New England towns settled to about 1675 were all accessible by water, either along the coast or the rivers. It is not surprising, then, that many of the words and phrases that characterize the regional dialect to-

day are connected with the sea. Of the more or less random sample of colonial New England words cited above, note that almost half dealt with the sea: *alewife, banker, barvel, basket-fish, caboose, creek stuff, cusk, fare, flake,* and *general* 'bill of expenses incurred in a fishing expedition.'

Eastern New England speech is one of the most conservative of American regional dialects and is rooted in the colonial period. Many of its expressions date from before the revolution, such as *notch* 'mountain pass,' *hatchway* or *bulkhead* 'sloping cellar doors,' *buttry* 'pantry,' *swale* 'a marshy depression in level land,' *bannock* 'a thin corn cake' and *hasty pudding,* also known as *Indian pudding,* 'cornmeal mush with milk and molasses.' It borrowed words from the Indians, including *mummichog* 'a saltwater minnow or killifish,' *quahog* 'a thick-shelled edible clam,' and *pogy* and *scup* 'menhaden,' more reminders of this culture's close connection with the sea.

Like many conservative dialects, it tends to be euphemistic and avoids slang. Primarily in folk or rural speech *sire,* for example, is used instead of bull and *meadow* or *top dressing* instead of manure. *Gone by* is a euphemism for died, and a funeral wake is also known as *calling hours.* Two recent New Englandisms are *rotary* 'a traffic circle' and *parkway* 'a divided highway with extensive greenery.'

New York

The settlement of upstate New York primarily from western New England is evident in such vocabulary remnants as *a-yuh* 'yes,' *adder* 'snake,' *cow corn* 'field corn,' *go cross-lots* 'to take a short cut,' *hatchway (doors)* 'sloping cellar doors,' *matterate* 'suppurate,' *snap-the-whip* 'a game played on ice,' and *titman* 'the runt of a litter.'

The Dutch had been the first to colonize New York, though with little of the vigor that the English brought to the New World. Even so the Dutch culture and language persisted tenaciously well into the eighteenth century when Albany, for example, was still completely Dutch in character.

Inevitably the English spoken in the Hudson River valley became a regional variety marked by Dutch borrowings, including *hay barrack* 'a roofed structure for covering haystacks' (from *hooiberg*), *olicook* 'doughnut' (from *oliekoek* 'oil cake'), *rolliche* 'roulade' (from *rolletje* 'little roll'), *pot cheese* 'cottage cheese' (from potkaas), *suppawn* 'cornmeal mush' (borrowed by the Dutch from the Indians), *cruller* 'a doughnut or sweet cake,' and *teeter-totter* 'seesaw.' All of these are obsolete or rapidly dying out, except for the last two, which are also used in the northern and most of the western United States. One of the few Hudson River valley terms not borrowed from Dutch is *skimmilton* 'shivaree,' which derives from English dialect.

Many Dutch borrowings did not stay confined to the Hudson River valley or New York but are in general use in American English, including *boodle, boss, caboose, cole slaw, cookie, dingus, dope, dumb* 'stupid,' *logy, poppycock, Santa Claus, saw buck* 'saw horse,' *sleigh, snoop, spook, stoop* 'porch,' *waffle,* and probably *Yankee.*

The South
The following southern regionalisms were current in the Virginia or Carolina colonies: *ambeer* 'tobacco spit' (before 1763), *baldface* 'having a white face' (1709), *bamboo (briar)* 'a greenbrier' (1709), *bat* 'nighthawk' (1709), *black gum* 'a tupelo tree,' (1709), *blade* 'leaf of corn plant' (1688), *brake* 'a thicket' (1657), *branch* 'a stream' (1663), *case* 'a condition of tobacco leaves' (1640), *cat* 'catfish' (1705), *chicken snake* 'rat snake' (1709), *chinquapin* 'chestnut' (1612), *fanner* 'winnowing basket' (1797), *fever and ague* 'malaria' (1671), *Frenchman* 'spindly tobacco plant' (1688), *fresh* 'a stream' (1608), *gallbush* 'inkberry' (1728), *ground worm* 'cutworm' (1708), *ground pea* 'peanut' (1770), *groundnut* 'peanut' (1770), *(hog) crawl* 'enclosure of hogs' (1733), and *honey tree* 'honey locust' (1705).

Settlement of the upper South sprang essentially from the Virginia and Pennsylvania hearths. The early Virginia colonists and the tobacco economy they took into the upper South is hinted at in the regional vocabulary. Of the more or less random sample of colonial southern terms cited above, three have to do with tobacco: *ambeer, case,* and *Frenchman.*

In the 1730s the Germans from southeastern Pennsylvania moved into the Shenandoah valley, followed by the Scotch-Irish, who pressed into the Great Valley of Virginia and North Carolina and overflowed into the Carolina Piedmont. These two groups, especially the Scotch-Irish, left their mark on American English, giving it,

for example, the pronunciation of postvocalic 'r,' as well as many words and phrases. A partial list would include: *poor* 'scrawny,' 'weak,' *nicker* 'the sound that a horse makes,' *blate* 'the sound of a sheep,' *hippin* 'a baby's diaper,' *back* 'to address an envelope,' and *to pet a child to death* 'to overindulge or spoil a child,' all of which are used in the South as a whole. Representative Scotch-Irish words confined primarily to the upper South include *brickle* 'brittle,' *fornent* or *ferninst* 'near to,' 'opposite,' *scoot* 'to move or slide something,' and *muley* 'a hornless cow.'

The language of the upper South region, which harbors many old-fashioned and relic expressions, reflects its isolation and conservatism. Some scholars have even claimed that Ozark and southern Appalachian speech is a form of Elizabethan English, a claim that is probably more poetic than true. The old-fashioned, folk flavor of the upper South is heard in expressions like *hidy* 'hello,' *smothering spell* 'a momentary feeling of weakness,' *cuss fight* 'an argument,' *carrion crow* 'vulture,' and *cur dog* 'a mongrel.'

The lower South is the historical extension of Charleston and to a lesser extent tidewater Virginia. In this region one can hear such expressions as *cracker* 'a poor white person,' *frog skin* 'dollar bill,' *lightwood* 'dried pine used for kindling,' and *ground peas* 'peanuts.' The Atlantic South also shares a number of expressions with eastern New England, which like the loss of postvocalic 'r,' are fossil evidence of a shared and relatively unified colonial lexicon. These include *piazza* 'porch,' 'veranda,' *bush hook* 'a hand tool for cutting underbrush,' *belly girt* 'harness band,' *adder* 'snake,' and *hog's head cheese,* these last two also occurring in the lower South, the settlement region of the Atlantic South. This pattern of words distributed in New England and the Atlantic South is fading. Many expressions that were formerly shared, such as *haslet* 'edible organs of a hog,' *whicker* 'neigh,' and *lulling down* 'a subsiding of the wind,' are viable today only in the Atlantic South, which tends to be more linguistically conservative than New England.

Influence of African American English
Though the picture has changed considerably since World War II with the migration of southern blacks to the urban North, the early African-American subculture, the product of social isola-

tion and the remnants of African culture, has left a lasting influence on the religious, artistic, and linguistic aspects of lower southern culture. Many expressions unique to its lexicon are African in origin, such as: *cooter* 'turtle,' *goober* 'peanut,' *gumbo* 'dish made with okra,' *juke* 'immoral,' 'disorderly,' *juju* 'amulet,' 'fetish,' *okra* 'edible pods of a tall annual plant,' *pinder* 'peanut,' *poor joe* 'great blue heron,' and *tote* 'carry.' Many of the African words brought to the South by the slaves have spread through the United States, including *banjo, bogus, boogie-woogie, chigger, hep* or *hip, jazz, jitter, jive, mumbo-jumbo, phoney, voodoo, yam,* and *zombie.* Black speech has had a creative influence on American English, but today, instead of being confined to the South, it is national and primarily urban.

CONCLUSION

The development of American English began the moment the English colonists set sail for a new world that would demand their language have the same vigorous, democratic, and self-confident qualities that they themselves would need to flourish in the wilderness. This first involved a gradual but clear break from the mother language, the Elizabethan tongue of Shakespeare. After one or two generations, the direction of American English was set and all subsequent settlers had to assimilate to it.

But as American English became distinctive, so did its regional dialects, so much so that one is hard pressed to find any such entity as American English. Except perhaps in writing, there is no national or standard form of American speech. Southerners speak just as pure a version of American English as their Yankee cousins. The history of colonial American English, then, is also the story of its regional settlements and the emergence of its varied cultures and dialects.

BIBLIOGRAPHY

Babcock, C. Merton, ed. *The Ordeal of American English.* Boston, Mass., 1961.

Bradford, William. *Bradford's History "Of Plimoth Plantation."* Boston, Mass., 1901.

Carver, Craig M. *American Regional Dialects: A Word Geography.* Ann Arbor, Mich., 1987.

Forgue, Guy Jean. "American English at the Time of the Revolution." In *Dialect and Language Variation,* edited by Harold B. Allen and Michael Linn. Orlando, Fla., 1986.

Krapp, George Philip. *The English Language in America.* 2 vols. New York, 1925.

Kurath, Hans. "British Sources of Selected Features of American Pronunciation: Problems and Methods." In *Readings in American Dialectology,* edited by Harold B. Allen and Gary Underwood. New York, 1971.

———. *A Word Geography of the Eastern United States.* Ann Arbor, Mich., 1949.

Marckwardt, Albert H. *American English.* New York, 1958.

Mathews, Mitford McLeod, ed. *The Beginnings of American English.* 1931. Chicago, Ill., 1963.

Mencken, H. L. *The American Language: An Inquiry into the Development of English in the United States.* 4th ed. 2 supplements. New York, 1947.

Read, Allen Walker. "The Assimilation of the Speech of British Immigrants in Colonial America." *Journal of English and Germanic Philology* 37, no. 1 (1983):70–79.

———. "British Recognition of American Speech in the Eighteenth Century." *Dialect Notes* 6, part 6 (1933):313–334.

Sen. Ann Louise Frisinger. "Dialect Variation in Early American English." *Journal of English Linguistics* 8 (1974):41–47.

Craig M. Carver

SEE ALSO **Literacy** and **Literature**.

COLONIAL DUTCH

IN 1643 WILLIAM KIEFT, director-general of New Netherland, informed a visiting Jesuit missionary that eighteen languages could be heard spoken on and about the island of Manhattan. This reference to linguistic and ethnic diversity in the Dutch colony remains a characteristic of this international city today.

Although approximately one-half of the colonists sent over by the West India Company were not native-born Netherlanders, they were quickly assimilated into the Dutch colonial society of New Netherland. Whether it was Norwegians brought over for lumbering, German refugees from the Thirty Years' War, or Croatians, Poles, or Bohemians, they were required to adhere to the laws and ordinances of the West India Company in New Netherland. As with most immigrants in a new land, the first necessity was to learn the dominant language, which would provide access to the law, the economy, and society.

ASSIMILATION AFTER 1674

After England permanently expelled Dutch authority in 1674, assimilation of the colonists who had arrived in the New Netherland era was a slow and uneven process. In New York City by the mid 1700s, it was reported that while the elderly continued to speak Dutch, the younger generation almost always spoke English and were insulted if taken for Dutch. However, certain areas of New Jersey and especially the upper Hudson region of New York, with its center at Albany, became strongholds of the Dutch language. Because of their isolation during the New Netherland period, the Dutch in the Albany area and in Bergen County, New Jersey, maintained their native language and distinct ethnic characteristics the longest.

Most visitors to Albany in the eighteenth century made note of the Dutch character of the town and the use of the Dutch language by the inhabitants. In 1749 a Swedish botanist observed that "the inhabitants of Albany and its environs are almost all Dutchmen. They speak Dutch, have Dutch preachers and the divine service is performed in that language. Their manners are likewise quite Dutch." By 1755, however, the Dutch society in and around Albany experienced its first serious cultural invasion. Plans for a British expedition against Quebec brought thousands of English-speaking troops into the area; many of these soldiers were billeted with families in town. For three years the troops poured in until Quebec fell to General Wolfe. In 1760 the British soldiers left Albany to garrison Quebec. The exposure of the younger generation to foreign manners and ways accelerated the process of assimilation that had been slowly proceeding since the English conquest.

However, Dutch social tradition and the Dutch language in which it was articulated survived in remote areas well into the nineteenth century. During the revolution an officer of Dutch descent stationed in New Jersey wrote to his wife back in Albany: "The inhabitants are all Dutch people from whom I can git every think [sic] by speaking Dutch to them." As late as 1793 a group of French refugees traveling up the Mohawk River observed that most of the inhabitants west of Schenectady were of Holland origin and carefully pointed out that they were Dutch and not English. The following year an English traveler to Albany noted that

the people are of a mixed race, but chiefly Dutch, which language, as they call it, they generally speak, but it is so corrupted, and so replete with new words, which a new country, new subjects, and new circumstances would unavoidably require, that a minister some time since arrived from Amsterdam, could neither understand his congregation, nor could they understand him to their satisfaction, and it has been necessary for him to study to lower his language to theirs. (William Strickland. "Journal of a Tour," p. 160)

EVOLUTION OF *LAEG-DUITS*

After almost 130 years of separation from the Netherlands, the Dutch language in North America, or *Laeg-Duits* (Low Dutch)—called *de taal* (pronounced and later written *tawl*), "the language," by its speakers—had diverged considerably from the tongue of the fatherland. The so-called *corrupted* language, as it was referred to in the quote above, was actually characterized by new or divergent forms of phonology, morphology, and syntax, that resulted from the long separation and isolation during which dialectal variations were allowed to spread. The development of these forms was possible because of the lack of reinforcement from standardizing developments occurring in the Netherlands. The absence of a socially prestigious standard to emulate, especially among the younger generation, caused the dialectal variations to flourish and seek their own level of communal acceptability. This is evident from a nineteenth-century observation of *Laeg-Duits* speakers that "no Laag Dauitser ever corrects any speaker no matter how gross his mistake. The reason seems to be that none of them, even the most fluent, is ever quite certain that *he* has the right of it."

It should be remembered that the majority of the speakers came from the farming and tradesmen class in the Netherlands. Their social level of speech became predominant in New York as the educated class found it increasingly necessary to communicate in English in order to participate in colonial politics and the commerce of New York. This left the burden of language preservation on a socially stratified class of speakers, composed of farmers and tradesmen, more accustomed to speaking their local dialects than the cultured speech of a more educated class. The extensive vocabulary borrowed from English by *de tawl* was a result of the ever-increasing isolation of the Dutch-speaking communities from one another along with the lack of steady contact with the Netherlands. Both interdialectal contact and injection of new blood and ideas from the home country are necessary reinforcements for vocabulary growth. As the older generation of Dutch speakers gave way to the bilingual generation, English was relied upon increasingly for vocabulary expansion. When a new system is adopted by a people, whether by choice or by force, many semantic elements of the language associated with the new system are also embraced. A typical example of borrowings from English by *Laeg-Duits* speakers in matters associated with the legal system appeared in a certificate issued in 1716 stating that the undersigned had been present in the court at Albany when a case was tried: *"Deese sertiefieseeren dat wy . . . geweest syn int coert huis der stat Albany sijnde in open coert waer een actic getryt wiert. . . ."* In addition to the English loans for "certify," "court," and "courthouse," the verb "to try" has also been restructured as the Dutch past participle *getryt*.

The most divergent feature of *de tawl* that made it difficult for visitors from the Netherlands to understand or to be understood, was the intonation pattern. A speaker of *de tawl* in the nineteenth century described it as a rising and falling inflection having a peculiar singing intonation. Contemporary speakers claimed that people could not be understood if they did not use it.

Some older speakers thought that it may have come from the imitation of the mannerism and tone used by the domines (Dutch Reformed ministers); some thought that it imitated the speech of old Holland. All agreed that every speaker used it and that it was necessary in order to be understood. There is some evidence that the former explanation may be closer to the truth. In the mid 1800s, a prominent Albany attorney made an official visit to the Netherlands. When he delivered a public speech in the Dutch he had learned as a boy, he found to his dismay that it was unintelligible to all of his audience except for an old man who stated that when he was a boy, his church had a very old pastor who had spoken in a similar way during the service. It is possible that the descendants of New Netherland imitated this feature of the domines' delivery during the service because the Reformed church had become one of the most important institutions for the preservation of their ethnic identity.

A visitor to New York City in the 1740s remarked:

There have been a great number of Dutch here, tho now their language and customs begin pritty much to wear out and would very soon die were it not for a parcell of Dutch domines here who, in the education of their children, endeavour to preserve the Dutch customs as much as possible. (Alexander Hamilton. *Gentleman's Progress*, p. 89)

It is not surprising that the domines, who had become the only representatives of a socially prestigious standard of the language worthy of emulation, would have influenced the shape of the speech patterns of *de tawl*.

In the late 1700s, English-speaking pastors began to replace the Dutch domines, so that by the mid 1800s Dutch was rarely heard in the Reformed churches. Some of the bilingual speakers had eventually transferred to English churches because they could no longer understand the Holland Dutch of the Reformed domines. A speaker of *Laeg-Duits* in the nineteenth century remembered that when he was a boy in the 1830s, there had now and then been Sunday services in which the domines used Low Dutch, i.e., Holland Dutch, rather than the spoken vernacular called *Laeg-Duits*. He recalled that when the domine preached all the children, and some of the parents, too, sat idly staring. As Dutch gradually became relegated to use in the home and on the farm, contact with the outside world became increasingly associated with English, the common language of the people who were shaping the future of the country. A nineteenth-century *Laeg-Duits* speaker in the Mohawk valley observed that if a stranger attempted to speak *de tawl* and was not as fluent as his listeners, they would switch at once to English.

REMNANTS OF THE DUTCH LANGUAGE

Today the only remnants of the language survive in a handful of words and phrases used mostly by speakers of American English in the Hudson and Mohawk valleys and in Bergen County, New Jersey. These are words such as "winkelhawk," a right-angle tear in a garment, from Dutch *winkelhaak,* a carpenter's square, in addition to the more commonly identified borrowings: cookie, cruller, and pit (instead of stone, as in a peach). Also fondly remembered by descendants of New Netherland's settlers is the nursery rhyme "Trippa, Troppa, Trontje," which President Theodore Roosevelt recited at a dinner party to the delight of his Afrikaans-speaking guest from South Africa, a general in the insurgent Boer army. Unlike the South African Boers, who maintained their linguistic and social identity in reaction to British imperial pressure, after the revolution the descendants of New Netherland became just one more component of the new American nation. They were no longer an ethnic minority guarding against foreign encroachment, but a participant in the development of a new national identity.

BIBLIOGRAPHY

Bachman, Van Cleef. "What Is Low Dutch?" *De Halve Maen* 57, no. 3 (1983):14–17, 23–24.

Cohen, David Steven. "How Dutch Were the Dutch of New Netherland?" *New York History* 62, no. 1 (1981):43–60.

Gehring, Charles T. "The Dutch Language in Colonial New York: An Investigation of a Language in Decline and Its Relationship to Social Change." Ph.D. diss., Indiana University, 1973.

Goodfriend, Joyce D. *Before the Melting Pot: Society and Culture in Colonial New York City, 1664–1730.* Princeton, N.J., 1992.

Hamilton, Alexander. *Gentleman's Progress: The Itinerarium of Dr. Alexander Hamilton, 1744.* Edited by Carl Bridenbaugh. Chapel Hill, N.C., 1948; repr. 1973.

Jameson, J. Franklin, ed. *Narratives of New Netherland 1609–1664.* New York, 1909.

Kalm, Peter. *The America of 1750: Peter Kalm's Travels in North America.* Edited by Adolph B. Benson. 2 vols. New York, 1937.

Kenney, Alice P. *Stubborn for Liberty: The Dutch in New York.* Syracuse, N.Y., 1975.

Rink, Oliver A. "The People of New Netherland: Notes on Non-English Immigration to New York in the Seventeenth Century." *New York History* 62, no. 1 (1981):5–42.

Strickland, William. "Journal of a Tour in the United States of America, 1794–1795," *New York Historical Society Collections* 83 (1971):160–161.

Charles T. Gehring

See also **Dutch and Swedish Settlements; Literacy;** and **Literature.**

COLONIAL FRENCH

We have only a sketchy knowledge of the dialects spoken in France during the colonial period. We do know that until the early nineteenth century at least, the French provinces spoke assorted patois. Standard French, originally the dialect of the Paris region, had become the prestige language abroad and in the French cities, but we cannot estimate how much it was understood by the masses. A widely held opinion is that standard French was not spoken in the provinces. From this, one concludes that the New France colonists spoke mainly patois, which they gradually abandoned in favor of standard French that alone could function as a lingua franca.

It is certain that few New France colonists claimed standard French as their mother tongue.

Yet scholars increasingly agree that seventeenth-century France spoke a variety of French that formed the matrix of North American French dialects. Interestingly, studies of American and Creole dialects have enabled specialists to evaluate the extent to which standard French might have been spoken in contemporary metropolitan provinces.

LINGUISTIC VARIATIONS AMONG SETTLEMENTS

In the seventeenth century, New France encompassed an immense territory stretching from the Hudson Bay to the Gulf of Mexico and beyond Lake Superior. Today, the North American French communities form an archipelago in which Quebec, Acadia, and Louisiana, the points where French civilization was strongly anchored in America, stand out. Quebec (or rather Canada, as it was called then) and Acadia were developed by colonists who settled during the early seventeenth century, while Louisiana, thus named by the explorer René-Robert Cavalier de La Salle in 1682 in honor of Louis XIV, did not really come into existence until the early eighteenth century. These three colonies received immigrants from the same regions of France, but in different proportions and at different times, facts that influenced their language. Moreover, the settlement of Louisiana was less homogeneous than was that of the other regions, so that a great linguistic diversity still exists there.

Acadia was founded by Samuel de Champlain in 1605 at Port Royal (today Annapolis Royal, Nova Scotia), three years before Quebec, which became the first permanent colony. Acadia was really settled after 1635, however, with the arrival of families, the bulk of which came from the Loudun region in what is today the department of Vienne. Two-thirds of the early Acadian settlers came from regions south of the Loire, a provenance that endowed this colony with its linguistic identity. Conversely, the colony along the Saint Lawrence River (first Quebec, then Trois-Rivières in 1634, and Montreal in 1642) was populated mainly by settlers from regions north of the Loire, though nearly one-third came from the western regions of Poitou and Saintonge. Acadian French and Quebec French have

many traits in common, but they are distinguished from one another by usages that reflect the linguistic division between northern and southern France. Thus, the tree that grows in damp terrain is called *aune* in Quebec, as in the regions north of the Loire, while the Acadians use *verne,* the word of the southern French regions.

The settlement of Louisiana was more complex. In the early eighteenth century, the colony consisted of a few Canadians and immigrants who came directly from France, especially from the Paris region. Those pioneers were joined by other groups, notably a rather large German community and a smaller number of black slaves. After 1763 the colony received Acadian immigrants seeking a home after their deportation by the English. Their arrival had a major impact on Louisiana, for there developed west of New Orleans, in the region of Bayou La Fourche, a French community distinct from the others, whose linguistic influence eventually proved crucial.

The history of the settlement thus explains the coexistence in Louisiana of two varieties of French as well as a distinct Creole dialect: a colonial French influenced by the speech of the Paris region; an Acadian French; and a French-based Creole that evolved in the black slave community. In the Acadian settlement areas, Acadian French became the most common means of oral communication among francophones and between whites and blacks. It also played an important role in the assimilation of German immigrants. Refugees from Saint Domingue (Haiti), having learned a French-based Creole dialect from black slaves in the islands, taught it to their own slaves in Louisiana, where it flourished.

Creole dialects arise when a language has to be developed for communication between two groups, one dominant, one dominated, both speaking different tongues. A simplified version of the dominant language develops, called "pidgin," as long as both groups continue using their own language except for communicating with each other. When the "pidgin" becomes the sole language of one group, or of both, it becomes a Creole. There are Dutch-based and English-based Creoles as well as the French-based variety encountered in Louisiana, the Antilles, and the islands of the Indian Ocean.

STUDYING THE ORIGINS THROUGH COMPARISON

A brief comparison of the American French dialects shows that they evolved from a variety of French that must have been widely spoken in colonial times. Quebecois, Acadian, and Louisiana French present many common traits that distinguish them from the French spoken in France—in pronunciation, in lexicon, and in morphology. A frequently mentioned example is that of the nautical terms which in all three are applied to terrestrial realities: for instance, *amarrer,* originally "to tie a boat with cables," is used for "to tie up"; *se greyer,* from *gréer,* "to outfit a boat with sails," means "to dress." Pursuing the comparison further, and taking into account the history of each of these French-speaking communities, one reaches illuminating conclusions about the French spoken in America in the seventeenth century.

The Acadian speech is exemplary. The Acadian community was formed by families originating far from Paris. It evolved in a *vase-clos* because of its separation from France. (Acadia was invaded by the English several times in the seventeenth century and was ceded to them in 1713). Until the 1960s it had little contact with Quebec or Paris. This isolated population, which always lived in a rural environment, obviously did not learn French by itself after the seventeenth century, hence the early immigrants must have spoken it rather than a patois. Since the nucleus of immigrants that gave Acadia its characteristics came from Poitou, one can hypothesize that French was spoken in that region, distant though it was from Paris, in the seventeenth century.

Acadian French is the one that has evolved least since colonial times. In Acadia, for example, one still uses *bailler* (rather than *donner*) for "to give" and *point* for *pas* in negative constructions. The historical study of pronunciation shows that an evolution took place in Quebec, though the Laurentian colony was quite conservative. There, one notes, for example, that seventeenth-century pronunciations such as "tchoeur" for *coeur* (heart) and "djeule" for *gueule* (mouth) have disappeared, while they have persisted in Acadian French.

One should remember that the Paris region sent an appreciable number of immigrants to Quebec (some 20 percent), especially in the region of Quebec City, and that Quebec administrators came from France. In Ville Marie (Montreal), on the other hand, two-thirds of the settlers came from a limited region of western France, between the Garonne and the Loire, and 65 percent of them were rural. One can expect the linguistic influence of Paris to be less in Montreal, as is confirmed by the retention of an older pronunciation of "r," which is still pronounced there with the tip of the tongue (the apical "r"), while the "r" in the Quebec City area now resembles that of Paris.

The evolution undergone by the North American French settlers since the seventeenth century shows up most clearly in the vocabulary, through semantic innovations and borrowing from English. Pronunciation gradually aligned itself with that of Paris, especially in Quebec City, or developed tendencies already present during the colonial period. An example of the latter is the case of the pronunciation of "t" and "d." In Quebec they are followed by a slight "s" or "z" (affrication) when they precede "i" or "u": thus the pronoun *tu* is pronounced "tˢu" and the verb *dire* is "dᶻire." This characteristic is found in some Creole dialects, but not in Acadian nor in Louisianian. Here again the comparison is interesting, especially in communities founded by the three earlier colonies. The region of Baie Saint Paul, near Quebec, which was settled in the 1680s by Quebecois, remained isolated into the twentieth century and was unaffected by the affrication phenomenon. But in the Missouri village of Old Mines, which was founded by Quebec settlers in the 1720s and still preserves some vestiges of French, the "t" and "d" are affricated. One can conclude that, on the other hand, the phenomenon occurred sporadically in France before the immigrants left, since it is found not only in Quebec but also in some Creole dialects, but that, on the other hand, it did not become widespread in Quebec until the early eighteenth century.

The influence of Amerindian languages on the French spoken in North America is limited to loanwords borrowed in the distant past. These loanwords are used for plants, animals, or objects—physical realities—such as *babiche* meaning "strips of leather," or *ouaouaron* for a large frog, both in general use. Another example is *bayou* for a slow-flowing, shallow stream, a term used generally in Louisiana but spread by explorers through the Mississippi Valley. The Amerindian influence was important in toponomy: Canada, Quebec, Saguenay, Baton Rouge (the last means "red stick" and is a French translation of an Indian place name). In Louisiana, French and Creole long coexisted and influenced one another; each retained essentially its morphology and syntax, but they have a common French lexical base.

FRENCH IN THE COLONIAL PERIOD

The comparison of the French dialects spoken in America leads one to conclude that the early immigrants shared a common variety of French even if for most of them the mother tongue was a patois. This conclusion is confirmed by the accounts of missionaries and travelers, the earliest of which is that of Simon Denys in 1651. Later, Claude-Charles Bacqueville de La Potherie (1700), Pierre François Xavier de Charlevoix (1720), and Jean-Baptiste d'Aleyrac (1755) expressed favorable opinions of the French spoken in Canada. "Nowhere else is our language better spoken," says Charlevoix. These statements must be understood within the linguistic context of a France where standard French was not the spoken dialect of the provinces; nonetheless, one may conclude that there existed in France a variety of French that served as lingua franca among patois speakers.

This variety must have been strongly marked with regional and dialectic characteristics, since a number of those found their way into North American French. Some linguists think that this French developed in the Atlantic harbors, especially La Rochelle and Nantes, from which it would have spread. Others think that it was a variety of vernacular spoken in much of the French territory. Whatever the case in France, one must acknowledge that the colonial immigrants had more chances than their compatriots back home to improve their knowledge of standard French. They had a particular linguistic experience when they came into contact, in the harbors and during the crossing, with groups who spoke a dialect more or less distant from their own though these dialects had already colored the common variety.

BIBLIOGRAPHY

Hull, Alexander. "Evidence for the Original Unity of North American French Dialects." *Louisiana Review* 3, no. 1 (1974):59–70.
Juneau, Marcel. *Contribution à l'histoire de la prononciation française au Québec.* Quebec, 1972.
Massignon, Geneviève. *Les parlers français d'Acadie.* 2 vols. Paris, 1962.
Poirier, Claude, et al., eds. *Dictionnaire du français québécois: Volume de présentation.* Sainte-Foy, Quebec, 1985.
Valdman, Albert, ed. *Le français hors de France.* Paris, 1979.

Claude Poirier

SEE ALSO **The Conquest of Acadia; French Settlements; Literacy;** and **Literature.**

COLONIAL SPANISH

THE SPANISH COLONIAL period extends from 1492 to the beginning of the nineteenth century, with the specific termination date dependent upon one's source. Some consider it to be 1810, the year of the *grito de Dolores* (the battle cry of the Mexican Revolution), others claim 1825, the year of American victories and publication of the commemorative poem "La victoria de Junín. Canto a Bolívar" by Ecuadorian poet José Joaquín de Olmedo. Although official documents of a commercial or political nature abound in several archives in both the Old and New World—for example, the Archivo General de Indias in Seville or the Biblioteca del Obispo Palafox y Mendoza in Puebla, Mexico—an equally important source for our knowledge of colonial Spanish language is the literature of the period. When attempting to discuss language of any period exclusively on the basis of written records, the perennial chasm between written and spoken language must always be borne in mind, a caveat which certainly holds true in this discussion. Although New World Spanish toward the end of the colonial period differed substantially from the Spanish brought in 1492, in its initial phase it was essentially fifteenth-century Peninsular Spanish.

LINGUISTIC FLUX AND STANDARDIZATION

The year 1492 marks not only the encounter between two worlds but also the unification of Spain nationally, religiously, and linguistically. Shortly after Ferdinand and Isabella became joint rulers of Castile and Aragón in 1479, on 2 January 1492 the last Moorish stronghold, Granada, surrendered to them. Spain was now one politically. On 30 March 1492 the Catholic monarchs signed an edict ordering the expulsion of all who professed Judaism and were unwilling to convert to Christianity. Spain was now one religiously. Linguistic unity, if not in fact achieved, was at least advanced in August 1492 with the publication of Elio Antonio de Nebrija's *Gramática sobre la lengua castellana,* in which, following Latin models, he strove to give a standard account of Spanish phonetics, orthography, and syntax. In addition to Nebrija's grammar, the move toward linguistic standardization was enhanced considerably by nearly three hundred years of university instruction, which had promoted greater literacy among the populace, and by the recent advent of the printing press.

Examples of the state of flux reside in the syntax—that is, the word order—which was considerably less rigid than today. The sampling below is taken from one text, Bartolomé de las Casas's *Brevísima relación* (Briefest Account). It is intended to be representative and not exhaustive of language in the early colonial period. Las Casas's work was written in 1552, so some of the more archaic characteristics of the language—using objects of small value to reinforce negation ("Quanto dexo no lo precio un figo" [All that I leave behind I value less than a fig], in *Poema de mio Cid*) or using two negatives before the verb ("Nadie no me quiere" [No one loves me], in *Celestina,* IX)—are not easily found.

Other early characteristics, however, readily appear. The superlative suffix *-issimus* (possibly reinforced in the fifteenth century) abounds— "brevissima," "felicissima," "obedientissima," and "fidelissima" (most brief, most happy, most obedient, most faithful)—occur on the first page of the text. Contraction of the preposition *de* plus the pronoun is common (*deste, dellos, destos* [of this, of them, of these]). Vestiges of a synthetic pluperfect can be found—"delibere por no ser reo callando de las perdiciones . . . que los tales perpetaran [=habían perpetrado]" (I deliberated lest I be guilty of hushing the iniquities . . . that the aforesaid had perpetrated).

Las Casas's work shows the use of *haber* in expressions of time—"Pocos dias ha" (It has been a few days)—and the postponement of subject or verb to end of the sense group "Antes que acabase de morir, lo baptizo un frayle" (Before he had died, a friar baptized him). It also has the variable placement of atonic object pronouns—"Y por mas los apretar mando que no les metiessen alguna comida" (And to press them even more, he ordered that they not be given any food) or "Arremetio la madre por se la quitar" (He attacked the mother to take her away from her). The narrative's syntax does not begin a breath group with an atonic pronoun—"Descubrierouse las yndias" (The Indies were discovered) or "Hase de considerar" (It is considered). There is regular use of the future subjunctive— "persuadir a su magestad que deniegue a quien las pidiere" (to convince your majesty to deny whomever may request them). Other linguistic features common to the Peninsula during this early period remain common in colonial Spanish as well.

EVOLUTION OF AMERICAN SPANISH

With the passage of time several factors combined to cause American Spanish to diverge somewhat from that of the motherland, distance—that is, isolation—not being the least of them. An analogy at the personal level will clarify this: persons who have left their homeland for as short a period as five years upon their return realize that although they have retained the essence of their language, they are deficient when it comes to the latest clichés. In short, their language is slightly outmoded. On a larger scale, the same happened to the Spanish spoken in America. Not only could it not evolve with all the nuances and neologisms of Peninsular Spanish, primarily because of its physical separation in an age when technology capable of dissolving the distance did not exist, but also because the realities encountered in the new land demanded new language. What better source for neologisms than indigenous languages, which had words for what must have been novelties to the Europeans?

Thus another major factor having an impact on American Spanish was the substratum (sometimes the adstratum). We know for example that *canoa* (canoe) and *cazabe* (mandioc bread) are recorded in Peninsular writings of 1492. Other loanwords quickly followed—so quickly that scholars debate whether certain words were used in more than one language group or were in fact spread to various groups by the Spaniards themselves.

At any rate, from Caribbean languages including Arawak, Taína, and Carib the following words reinforced Spanish: *bohío* (hut), *cacique* (chief), *hamaca* (hammock), *huracán* (hurricane), *iguana*, *maíz* (corn), *(en)aguas* (slip), *sabana* (savannah), *carey* (sea turtle), *niqua* (chigger), *guacamayo* (macaw), *manatí* (manatee), *piragua* (canoe), *caimán* (cayman), *caníbal* (cannibal), *loro* (parrot), *butaca* (farm chair).

Nahauatl offered, and Spanish gratefully accepted, *aguacate* (avocado), *cacahuete* (peanut), *chocolate*, *tomate*, *cacao*, *hule* (rubber), *petate* (sleeping mat), *nopal* (prickly pear), *petaca* (hump), *jícara* (calabosh cup), *tiza* (chalk), *guajolote* (turkey), *tecolote* (owl), *zopilote* (vulture), *sinsote* (mocking bird).

Quechua enhanced Spanish with *coca*, *quina* (cinchona bark), *papa* (potato), *alpaca* (alpaca), *vicuña*, *guano*, *cóndor*, *mate* (calabash tea), *puma* (mountain lion), *llano* (pampa plain), and *puna* (high plateau).

Tupi-Guaraní added *ananas* (pineapple), *jaguar*, *maracá* (musical gourd rattle), *tapioca*, *mandioca* (cassava), *ombú* (tree of the Phyto-laccaceae family), *capibara* (capybara, a South American rodent that does not have a tail), *ñandú* (ostrich), *urubú* (vulture), and *tiburón* (shark).

Later, when Africans were imported as slaves, ironically, in exchange for the inhumanity, they bettered American Spanish with *malanga* (malanga, a root vegetable), *banana*, *guarapo* (cane liquor), *funche* (corn flour porridge), *bongó*, *conga*, *samba*, *mambo*, *macuto* (basket), *bembe* (thick lip), *burundanga* (jumble), *matungo* (skinny), and *ñangotarse* (to squat). The exact manner in which these words were incorporated, and the question of their original geographic extension, offer scholars of colonial Spanish substantial grist for their mills.

By the beginning of the nineteenth century, the end of the colonial Spanish period, the major differences between Peninsular and American Spanish lay in the slightly more archaic lexical flavor of the latter, as well as a greater abundance of loanwords from the Native substratum and resolution of the sibilant confusion of the fifteenth and sixteenth centuries in much the same way that had been done in Andalusia. The final major difference occurs in the Spanish American pronunciation of a voiced palatal lateral as a voiced palatal fricative /y/, which today is the dominant pronunciation in the Peninsula as well.

BIBLIOGRAPHY

Casas, Bartolomé de las. *Brevísima relación de la destrucción de las Indias*. Edited by Olga Camps. 3rd ed. Barcelona, Spain, 1981.

Entwistle, William J. "The Extension of Spanish to Spanish America." In his *The Spanish Language, Together with Portuguese, Catalan, and Basque*. London, 1936; 2nd ed. 1962.

Lapesa, Rafael. "El español de América." In his *Historia de la lengua española*, 9th ed. Madrid, Spain, 1981.

Spaulding, Robert K. *How Spanish Grew*. Berkeley, Calif., 1971.

Anthony J. Cárdenas

SEE ALSO **Literacy**; **Literature**; **Mission Communities**; and **Settlements in the Spanish Borderlands**.

INDIAN LANGUAGES

INTRODUCTION

WHEN EUROPEANS FIRST ARRIVED in the New World, they encountered extraordinary linguistic diversity, a diversity far beyond their imagination. Several hundred distinct, mutually unintelligible languages were spoken. These languages differed substantially among themselves, a fact that is not surprising given the vast territory over which they were spoken. Over fifty genetic groups or language families were represented.

GENETIC RELATIONSHIP

Languages are said to be genetically related if they are descended from the same ancestral language. English and German, for example, have a common source in a language called Proto-Germanic and are relatively closely related. Similarly, French and Spanish, both descended from Latin, are closely related. The two parent languages, Proto-Germanic and Latin, along with Slavic, Celtic, Greek, Armenian, Albanian, Persian, Sanskrit, and other languages, are ultimately descended from a common parent as well, termed Proto-Indo-European. English and Spanish are thus distantly related to each other. All of the languages descended from a common parent language are said to constitute a **language family.** English is a member of the Indo-European language family.

Identifying genetic relationships among languages involves the painstaking discovery of words and structures that the modern languages have inherited from their common parent. All languages change over time, in their sounds, their grammars, and their vocabularies. When two languages have been apart for only a short time, they retain so much of their common inheritance that a relationship is easy to spot. The close relationship between French and Spanish, languages that separated perhaps two thousand years ago, can be discerned immediately. As time goes by, however, and each language discards some old structures and transforms others, relationships become more difficult to perceive, such as the more distant relationship between English and Armenian, languages that separated five or six thousand years ago.

Identifying common inheritances among languages involves much more than recognizing superficial resemblances. Languages may show similarities for a variety of reasons. One is chance. Central Pomo spoken in the California region contains a verb *čʰuw,* pronounced like English *chew.* It means 'eat,' specifically 'gulp down.' The similarity between the Central Pomo and English verbs is sheer coincidence. The human vocal tract is capable of a relatively small set of sounds, and both languages happened to have settled on the same sequence for these two verbs.

A second reason for resemblances among languages is borrowing. The English word *dentist* resembles the French *dentiste* because English speakers borrowed the word from French, not because both languages inherited the word from Proto-Indo-European. Central Pomo contains the word *sánṭi·ya* for 'watermelon,' strikingly similar to the Spanish term for the same thing: *sandía*. Of course Central Pomo and Spanish are not genetically related. Central Pomo speakers adopted the Spanish term when they adopted the fruit.

Only the third reason for similarity, common inheritance, constitutes evidence of a genetic relationship. Distinguishing common inheritances requires special techniques, among them the Comparative Method. This procedure is based on the search for regular sound correspondences over many sets of words. English *tooth* and French *dent*, for example, are not superficially alike, but regular sound correspondences demonstrate that they are in fact both retentions from their common parent, or **cognates.** In cognates, English *t* regularly corresponds to French *d* (*two:deux, ten:dix*). English *th* regularly corresponds to French *t* (*three:trois, thunder:tonnerre*). During the development of English, speakers shifted their pronunciation of original Indo-European *t* to *th* and of *d* to *t*, while French speakers retained the original pronunciation.

Genetic relationships among the languages of North America, just as among those in Europe, have been identified primarily on the basis of regular sound correspondences. The Mohawk *onò:tsa'* and Tuscarora *utúʔθæh* both mean 'tooth,' but certainly sound different. The two words are cognates, however, descended from the same word in their common parent, Proto-Northern-Iroquoian. Regular recurring sound correspondences, in large numbers of words, confirm their status. Mohawk *o* systematically corresponds to Tuscarora *u* in cognates (*ohsóhkwa':uhθúhkwæh* 'color'), Mohawk *n* to Tuscarora *t* (*onéhwa':utǽhwæh* 'skin'), etc. Reconstructions of forms in the parent language are indicated by an asterisk (*). The Proto-Northern-Iroquoian noun root for 'color,' for example, is reconstructed as *-hθohkw-*, and that for 'skin' as *-nehw-*. The asterisk indicates that the form is hypothesized

on the basis of the modern daughter languages, but no actual record of it exists. The longer languages have been separated, developing independently, the fewer cognates will remain, and the more dissimilar those cognates will appear. Particularly in such cases of distant relationship, a thorough knowledge of the languages compared is crucial if the remaining correspondences are to be perceived.

Genetic relationships in North America have been reconstructed dating back at least as far as those of Indo-European. Some North American families are quite large, with as many as thirty or forty related languages, such as Algonquian, Uto-Aztecan, and Athabaskan. Others are much smaller, such as Iroquoian, Muskogean, Caddoan, and Eskimo-Aleut. For some languages, such as Beothuk in the Northeast and Zuni in the Southwest, no relatives have ever been found. Such languages are known as **language isolates.**

It can never be proven that two languages are not genetically related; it can be determined only that no evidence of a relationship can be found. Over fifty families have been established in North America with certainty. Several more distant relationships between families have been investigated. Some of these hypotheses have ultimately been shown to be true, others unfounded. Some will probably never be resolved, because the languages are scantily documented and no longer spoken, and the proposed relationships are so remote that it is difficult to distinguish true cognates from similarities due to ancient borrowing or to chance. Among the more intriguing proposals are the hypothesized Gulf stock of the Southeast, the Siouan-Caddoan-Iroquoian stock of the Plains and the East, and the Aztec-Tanoan, Hokan, Penutian, and Mosan stocks of the West. In all cases, substantial additional evidence would be necessary before the relationships were considered established.

In 1929, Edward Sapir hypothesized that the languages of North America might ultimately be reducible to six 'superstocks.' One aspect of the hypothesis, a link between the Algonquian family and two California languages, Wiyot and Yurok, has been validated with further research. Other aspects have been shown to be untenable as more data have become available. Still others remain open issues. Unfortunately, what Sapir had proposed as a preliminary proposal for research, "suggestive but far from demonstrable," was sometimes taken as an established classification by scholars in other fields.

In 1987 a proposal was made by Joseph Greenberg, a specialist in Indo-European and African languages, that all of the languages indigenous to North, Central, and South America fall into just three genetic groups. Although it offers a tantalizing prospect, and was therefore discussed in the popular press at the time, that work is not generally accepted by specialists in the field, due to the method used of superficial inspection for similarities among words, a lack of understanding of the grammars of the languages, and serious problems with the data on which it is based.

STRUCTURES OF THE LANGUAGES

North American languages exhibit a rich variety of structures in both their sounds and their grammars.

Sounds
Some of the languages contain surprisingly small inventories of consonants. Plains Cree, an Algonquian language spoken across western Canada, contains only eleven:

p, t, č, k, s, š, h, m, n, w, and *y.*

Mohawk, an Iroquoian language of Quebec, Ontario, and New York State, contains only nine:

t, k, s, n, r, w, y, h, and *'.*

Others, particularly in California and the Northwest, show large numbers. Central Pomo, of northern California, contains thirty:

b, d; p, ṭ, t, č, k, q; pʰ, ṭʰ, tʰ, čʰ, kʰ, qʰ, h; ṗ, ṭ̣, ṭ, č̣, k̇, q̇, ʔ; s, š, ṭs, m, n, l, w, and *y.*

Nootka, a language of the Wakashan family spoken on Vancouver Island in British Columbia, contains thirty-five:

p, t, c, č, λ, k, kʷ, q, qʷ; ṗ, ṭ, ċ, č̣, ƛ̇, k̇, k̇ʷ ʔ; ʕ, s, š, ł, x, xʷ, x̣, ḥ, ḥʷ, h; m, n, ṁ, ṅ, y, w, ẏ, ẇ.

Obviously the English spelling system is inadequate for representing the sounds of these languages. Some of the languages have been written in non-Roman-based orthographies developed for the use of speakers, such as the syllabaries for Cherokee, Cree, and Eskimo. Especially where there is no such tradition, linguists now generally transcribe the languages with the International Phonetic Alphabet (IPA) or a similar Americanist system developed earlier in this century. In many communities, practical spelling systems have been devised for the use of speakers based on the IPA or Americanist systems, with more familiar symbols, found on most typewriters, substituted for certain technical ones.

Sounds in all languages are easily classified according to the way they are produced in the mouth. **Stops,** such as *p, t,* and *k,* are made by completely closing off the flow of air somewhere in the mouth. **Fricatives** involve a near closure that results in a hissing or buzzing, such as *s* or *z.* **Affricates** consist of a stop plus fricative, like *č* (English *ch*). **Nasals** result when the flow of air passes through the nose, such as *m* or *n.* **Laterals** involve a contact between the tongue and one or both sides of the roof of the mouth, as for *l.* **Glides** consist of a tongue movement without closure, *w, y.*

The **plain stops,** written *p, t,* etc., are pronounced much as in French, Spanish, or Italian. Of course many North American languages contain considerably more stops than the Romance languages. Some California languages distinguish a dental stop *ṭ,* made with the tongue tip touching the teeth, from a back *t,* in which the tongue touches the ridge behind the teeth. Many languages distinguish the velar stop *k* (as in English *skip*) from a uvular stop *q,* made even further back in the mouth. Substituting *ṭ* for *t* or *k* for *q* can completely change the meaning of a word in these languages, just like substituting *t* for *p* in English (*skit, skip*). Many languages contain labialized stops like *kʷ,* pronounced like *k* with rounded lips. The glottal stop, written *ʔ* or *',* is common across the continent. It is the sound between the vowels in English *ohoh* 'woops' (*ʔóʔo*).

Some languages contain **aspirated stops,** written *pʰ, tʰ, kʰ,* etc. These sounds, which include a puff of air, are pronounced like the first sounds of English *pot, top,* and *cop.*

A striking feature of a large number of North American languages are **ejectives,** written *ṗ, ṫ, k̇, q̇,* etc. English contains no ejectives, but they can be approximated. If English *upon* is pronounced as a single word, the aspirated stop *pʰ* is normally used. If its parts are pronounced forcefully as two separate words, *up ón,* something near ejective *ṗ* may result: *p* with a pop. Ejective *ṫ* can be approximated with forceful pronunciation of *at áll* as two distinct words, *k̇* with *pack úp.*

Other common symbols used for consonants in North American languages are the following. *š* ('esh') is a palatal fricative like the *sh* of English ***ship.*** *c* is an affricate like the *ts* of *cats.* *č* is a palatal affricate like the *ch* of ***chair.*** *n* ('eng') is a velar nasal like the *ng* of *sing.* *x* is a velar fricative like the *ch* of German *Bach.* *x̣* ('x-dot') is a uvular fricative, further back in the mouth. Lateral fricatives are represented by *ɬ* or λ, sometimes spelled *hl,* pronounced as a hissed *l,* with air rushing through a side of the mouth. *ƛ* is a lateral affricate, a combination of *t* plus hissed *l,* or *tλ.* *ʕ* and *h* are pharyngeals, also found in Hebrew and Arabic, pronounced with tightened pharynx.

In contrast with the consonants, vowel systems in North American languages are generally simple. Symbols *i, e, a, o, u* are pronounced as in Spanish or Italian. The symbol *ə* ('schwa') is pronounced like the first vowel in English ***about*** or the last in *sofa.* A number of languages have nasalized vowels, similar to those in French ***un bon vin blanc.*** Nasalized vowels are written with a hook under the vowel (*ǫ*), or a tilde (*õ*). Some languages have whispered vowels, indicated with a circle beneath the vowel (*o̥*). Vowel length may be indicated by a raised dot or colon after the vowel (*o·* or *o:*) or double vowels (*oo*). Long vowels simply last longer than short ones.

There are a number of tone languages in North America, some in the Algonquian family, such as Cheyenne, the Iroquoian family (Cherokee), the Muskogean family (Koasati), the Caddoan family (Caddo), the Tanoan family (Kiowa), Athabaskan family (Navajo), and many others. In these languages, the relative pitch of a syllable affects the meaning of the word just like a change of consonant or vowel. In Kiowa, for example, *gú·* (high tone) means 'clever,' but *gû·* (falling tone) means 'hit'; *pʰą́y* is 'dust,' but *pʰą̂y* is 'tie.'

Grammatical Structures

Like their sound systems, the grammatical structures of North American languages show tremendous diversity. One feature of many languages that is particularly striking to speakers of Indo-European languages is **polysynthesis,** the propensity for long, complex words. Not all North American languages are polysynthetic, but a large proportion of them are, among them those of the Algonquian, Iroquoian, Muskogean, Caddoan, Athabaskan, and Eskimo-Aleut families.

An example of polysynthesis can be seen in Susan Rose's study of Kyuquot Nootka. The first line shows how the word is pronounced, the second line its meaningful parts, called **morphemes,** the third the meaning of each morpheme, and the fourth the definition of the word as a whole.

> *hu·ʼni ʕi-ƛ ʔa·qƛcu·wa·ʕš*
> *hu·ʼniq- ʔiƛ- ʔa·qƛ-c-u·w-a·ʕš*
> whale-go to take-FUTURE-INFERENTIAL-you
> all-evidently
> 'You're all going to get some whale!'

This word corresponds in meaning to a whole sentence in English, and indeed could stand alone as a full sentence in Nootka. It is clearly a single word in Nootka, however, and is recognized as such by speakers. If any of its parts were uttered alone, they would be meaningless.

Morphemes are of several kinds. The root carries the principal meaning of the word, like *read* of English *re-read* or *friend* of *friend-ly.* Affixes modify the meanings of roots. Those that appear before the root are **prefixes,** as in *re-read;* those that follow are **suffixes,** as in *friend-ly.* Some languages, such as those of the Athabaskan family, are primarily prefixing; words often contain large numbers of prefixes but few if any suffixes. Others, like those of the Eskimo-Aleut and Wakashan families, are primarily suffixing. Many more languages, including those of the Algonquian and Iroquoian families, contain large numbers of both prefixes and suffixes.

In the Nootka example above, the root for 'whale' is the first morpheme in the word. All of the other morphemes in the word are suffixes, even the one translated 'go to take.' The inferential and evidential suffixes specify the source of the information conveyed, deduction from some kind of visual or aural evidence. Even the subject 'you all' is expressed with a suffix.

Certain semantic distinctions are systematically expressed in these polysynthetic languages that are less commonly noted in Indo-European languages. In many languages, for example, speakers routinely express the source of information, as above, specifying whether a statement is based on direct observation, hearsay, deduction, or general knowledge. While a difference between masculine and feminine gender ('he' versus 'she') is not routinely specified in many languages, that between animate and inanimate entities may be. Past and present tense may not be distinguished, but single events ('strike once'), repetitive events ('beat a drum'), and ongoing states ('be seated') may be differentiated. Additional examples of the kinds of distinctions encoded by grammars can be seen in the articles in this volume on individual language families.

The distinctions encoded in morphological structure vary considerably from one language to the next, but they are far from arbitrary. They can provide us with a view of what speakers have said the most often during the thousands of years over which the languages have evolved. A morpheme like the evidential suffix -a·šɕ of Nootka above probably began life as a full phrase, perhaps with a meaning something like 'it is evident that.' The more often it was used, the more speakers shortened the form, perhaps first to a word meaning something like 'evidently,' and ultimately to a single syllable, only part of another word.

THE LINGUISTIC LEGACY OF COLONIALIZATION

The arrival of European colonists has had a devastating impact on the languages indigenous to North America. Of the several hundred languages spoken here three hundred years ago, no more than a dozen will survive very far into the next century. Nearly all are endangered, no

longer being learned by children as mother tongues.

These languages have left relatively little mark on the European languages that are replacing them. Loanwords into English are limited principally to names for indigenous objects, such as *moose* and *moccasin* from Algonquian nouns for 'moose' and 'shoe' or *tipi* from the Siouan word for 'house,' and to place-names, such as *Canada* and *Schenectady* from Iroquoian terms meaning 'settlement' and 'beyond the pines' respectively.

The limited borrowing is related to the fact that comparatively few Europeans learned indigenous languages themselves. For the most part, they used their own languages with Native translators, or rudimentary communication systems such as the pidgin Massachusett of New England; the Delaware Jargon of the Eastern seaboard; the Mobilian Jargon of the Southeast; Trader Navajo; the Chinook Jargon of the Northwest from the northern California border up into Alaska and inland to Montana; or the Eskimo Jargon of Alaska, the Yukon, and the Northwest Territories. Such systems, rarely spoken as mother tongues by anyone, are often composed of elements from several different languages. They typically show simple but highly variable sound systems and grammars, with few if any affixes. Most served as lingua francas for speakers of many languages. Chinook Jargon was probably used by speakers of over a hundred indigenous languages in addition to speakers of English, French, Russian, Chinese, Japanese, and Hawaiian. A few words have been borrowed from the pidgins into European languages, such as the pejorative *siwash* 'Indian,' from Chinook Jargon, originally from French *sauvage*.

Another linguistic option was the use of the Plains Indian sign language, first documented in the southern Plains. Over the past two and a half centuries variants of the system have spread up through the northern Plains and the Northern Plateau, providing a valuable tool in areas with considerable linguistic diversity.

It might be argued that the disappearance of the languages indigenous to North America is a good thing, reducing barriers to international communication. In fact it represents a tremendous cultural and intellectual loss, both to the descendants of the speakers and to the rest of mankind. With the death of each language we lose the essence of a culture, a particular perspective on life, an alternative way of categorizing and relating elements of the human experience that has evolved over thousands of years, as grammatical structures have been honed by use to meet the needs of their speakers.

The study of these languages offers both extraordinary intellectual discoveries and glimpses of irretrievably lost opportunities.

Marianne Mithun

BIBLIOGRAPHY

Current Trends in Linguistics, edited by Thomas A. Sebeok. Vol. 10, *Linguistics in North America.* The Hague, 1973. Largely reprinted in *Native Languages of the Americas,* edited by Thomas A. Sebeok. New York, 1976.
Handbook of North American Indians, edited by William C. Sturtevant. Washington, D.C., 1978–.
The Languages of Native America: Historical and Comparative Assessment, edited by Lyle Campbell and Marianne Mithun. Austin, Tex., 1979.
Rose, Susan Maria. "Kyuquot Grammar." Ph.D. diss., University of Victoria, 1981.
Sapir, Edward. "Central and North American Languages." *Encyclopaedia Britannica.* 14th edition. London and New York, 1929.

SEE ALSO **The First Americans** and **Literature, Native Americans;** the maps accompanying **The First Americans.**

ALGONQUIAN

ALGONQUIAN IS A FAMILY OF twenty-five or more languages spoken during the colonial period in northeastern and central North America. These languages are similar enough in structure and basic vocabulary for their relationship to have been evident from the time of first acquaintance.

SUBGROUPS AND LOCATIONS

The Algonquian languages of the Maritimes, New England, and the East Coast as far south as North Carolina constitute Eastern Algonquian. These languages included Micmac (in Nova Scotia, eastern New Brunswick, and Prince Edward Island); Malecite-Passamaquoddy (western New Brunswick and eastern Maine); Eastern Abenaki (most of Maine); Western Abenaki (New Hampshire and Vermont); Massachusett (southeastern Massachusetts); Narragansett (Rhode Island); Nipmuck (central Massachusetts); Mohegan-Pequot-Montauk (eastern Connecticut and eastern Long Island); Quiripi-Unquachog (western Connecticut and central Long Island); Mahican (upper Hudson and Housatonic rivers in New York and western Massachusetts); Munsee (lower Hudson valley and western Long Island in New York and northern New Jersey); Unami (eastern Pennsylvania, central and southern New Jersey, and northern Delaware); Nanticoke (Eastern Shore of Maryland); Piscataway or Conoy (central Maryland), Virginia Algonquian or Powhatan (tidewater Virginia); and Carolina Algonquian (northeastern North Carolina).

The languages listed are those for which there is some direct documentation. The precise aboriginal geographical demarcations between these languages are often uncertain, and in the linguistically undocumented interstitial areas there may have been, and in some cases certainly were, additional distinct languages. The most important of these undocumented gaps are the area from the North Shore of Massachusetts Bay to the Kennebec River and the adjacent interior, parts of Connecticut and interior Massachusetts, and parts of the coastal plain south of Delaware Bay.

The languages north of the Gulf of Saint Lawrence and the Saint Lawrence River and around the Upper Great Lakes are grouped as Central Algonquian. These included Cree-Montagnais, a dialect continuum probably to be counted as several languages (in Quebec and Ontario, from the Lower North Shore at least as far west as northwestern Ontario); Ojibwa-Ottawa-Algonquin, also a dialect continuum (from the Ottawa River valley to Lake Superior); Menominee (northeastern Wisconsin); Potawa tomi (Green Bay of Wisconsin); Fox-Sauk-Kickapoo (southern Wisconsin), Shawnee (Ohio); and Miami-Illinois (Illinois and northwestern Indiana).

The westernmost languages are classed as Plains Algonquian. These were Blackfoot (on the Canadian Plains); Arapaho-Atsina (South Saskatchewan River and areas to the south); and Cheyenne, in western Minnesota and eastern North Dakota.

Although there are some undocumented or poorly documented major dialects among the Central and Plains languages, there do not appear to be major gaps of the kind found among the Eastern languages.

European knowledge of the linguistic divisions of the Algonquian family was often imprecise in the colonial period, and the contemporary political labels often do not correspond to the linguistic divisions and labels recognized by later linguists. For example, all the Algonquian of northern New England were called Abenaki, and the term Algonquin, originally used for those first encountered by the French in the Ottawa River valley, was extended to other dialects and ultimately to the entire family.

RELOCATIONS

The speakers of a number of languages were relocated during the colonial period, affecting the geographical distribution of the languages outlined above. Micmac was extended to southern Newfoundland. Eastern Abenaki speakers were drawn off into French missions in the Saint Lawrence valley, later to be joined by Western Abenaki and Nipmuck speakers. Unami was carried westward to the Susquehanna River valley and later the Allegheny-Ohio valley. Some Munsee and Mahican speakers were associated with these Unami speakers, and Unami and Munsee came to be referred to, often without differentiation, as Delaware. Most Munsee-speakers ended up in Upper Canada (western Ontario). Some Nanticoke and Conoy joined the Six Nations Iroquois in New York, as did some Christian Indians from southern New England and Long Island.

Cree and Ojibwa were spread westward, and by the end of the colonial period in Canada, Plains Cree extended as far as the Rocky Mountains. Ojibwa dialects spread north of Lake Superior and south and west of the upper Great Lakes, bringing the Saulteaux dialect to Lake Winnipeg, Southwestern Ojibwa (Chippewa) to northern Minnesota, Wisconsin, and Michigan, and the Ottawa dialect to the Lower Peninsula of Michigan and Sault Sainte Marie, in addition to its earlier location on Manitoulin Island. Potawatomi spread around the southern end of Lake Michigan. Fox, Sauk, and Kickapoo moved into eastern Iowa, northern Illinois, and western Indiana. Before direct European contact, Shawnee speakers were dispersed from Ohio to scattered locations in the east, southeast, and midwest, whence they eventually coalesced again in the Ohio country in the first half of the eighteenth century.

The Plains Algonquian languages, little contacted during the colonial period, all moved west on the Plains.

CONTACT LANGUAGES

Communication between Europeans and Algonquian speakers was carried out through a variety of contact languages. In some cases specific languages or dialects emerged as the common means of communication over extended areas, both between the races and among Indians of different languages. This was the case with Eastern Abenaki in the French missions to the northern New England populations (which included Western Abenaki speakers and others), Northern Unami in the Moravian missions, and Ottawa in the Upper Great Lakes (used also by speakers of Ojibwa proper, Potawatomi, and Menominee).

In some areas pidgins emerged. The earliest of these known was a Basque-Algonquian pidgin used on the North Atlantic coast in the sixteenth century. There were also Algonquian-based pidgins in southern New England and Virginia, and a Unami-based Pidgin Delaware that was widely used by Dutch, British, and Swedish colonists on the Middle Atlantic Coast.

The widespread knowledge of Algonquian languages or at least Pidgin Algonquian among

European colonists is reflected in the large numbers of Algonquian loanwords that were adopted in colonial North American English and French, and apparently also (to judge from available evidence) Dutch and Swedish.

LITERACY

Missionary efforts to translate Christian religious materials for the use of Indian converts led to Native literacy in some cases, the most successful being among the Massachusett-speakers of Massachusetts. There is also some evidence of Native literacy in Eastern Abenaki and Unami. The development of the Cree Syllabary in the 1830s by the Reverend James Evans established Cree literacy in Canada, and literacy in alphabetic Ojibwa also seems to have emerged in the Canadian missions.

STRUCTURE AND STUDY

The Algonquian languages have generally simple phonologies that made it possible for Europeans to transcribe them adequately for practical use. Their complex inflectional and derivational morphology received extensive study from French, English, and German missionary linguists.

The dialect of Algonquin first studied by French scholars in the seventeenth century had the consonants *p, t, č, k, s, š, ʔ* (lax, short, perhaps optionally voiced); *pp, tt, čč, kk, ss, šš* (tense, long); and *r, m, n, w, y* (voiced), and the vowels *a, i, o* (short), and *a·, e·, i·, o·* (long). In the French recordings the tense and lax series were not consistently kept apart and the long vowels were marked only where potential ambiguity was noted, but the transcriptions proved generally adequate for practical use. The segment that was *r* in this early dialect shifted to *l* and had become *n* by the nineteenth century in all varieties of Ojibwa-Ottawa-Algonquin.

To write the sounds *w* and long *o·* (and in some cases short *o*), which would have been represented by *ou* in French spelling, the French adopted the omicron-upsilon digraph used in Classical Greek manuscripts and early printing. This character resembles a figure *8* open at the top and has often been printed as an *8* when special type was unavailable; alternatively it has been transliterated as *ou* or (incorrectly) *ŏ* and *w*.

In some languages the series corresponding to the Algonquin tense consonants is preaspirated (*hp, ht,* etc.). With varying consistency English transcriptions of these in Massachusett use *h* (e.g., *ohke* for *áhkəy* 'earth'), and French transcriptions of Eastern Abenaki use the Greek rough breathing mark ʻ (for example, *temaʻk8é* for *təmahkwe* 'beaver').

Algonquin words consist of stems, often composed of several meaningful elements, and inflections, which mark numerous categories including all the pronominal subjects and objects of verbs. For example, Munsee *mpaxkšə́mən* 'I cut it (e.g. a string)' and *ntəmšə́mən* 'I cut it (e.g. meat from bone)' share the inflectional affixes *n-* (or assimilated *m-*) and *-əmən*, which together specify a first person singular pronoun ('I') acting on a definite inanimate object in the general indicative mode (referring to present or past time). The two stems are bipartite; they share an element *-š,* used for action on an inanimate object by a cutting instrument, but their initial elements indicate different configurations resulting from the action of cutting: *paxk-* 'string-like entity medially severed' and *təm-* 'lopped, bobbed' or, from the other perspective, 'cut off, severed and removed.'

The derivation of stems from other stems produces many types of secondary derivatives, which John Eliot illustrated for Massachusett *koowadchansh* 'I keep thee' (stem *wadchan-*): *noowadchanittimun* 'we keep each other' (with reciprocal suffix *-itti-*); *koowadchanumoush* 'I keep it for thee' (with ditransitive *-umou-*); *kooweeche-wadchanumwomsh* 'I keep it with thee' (with comitative preverb *weeche* and suffixes *-umwo-m-*); and *koowadchanumwanshun* (with benefactive *-umwa-nsh-*).

Ives Goddard

BIBLIOGRAPHY

Bakker, Peter. " 'The Language of the Coast Tribes Is Half Basque': A Basque–American Indian Pidgin in Use Between Europeans and Native Americans in North America, ca. 1540–ca. 1640." *Anthropological Linguistics* 31 (1989):117–147.

Eliot, John. *The Indian Grammar Begun*. Cambridge, Mass., 1666. Reprinted as *A Grammar of the Massachusetts Indian Language*, edited by Peter S. Duponceau, in *Massachusetts Historical Society Collections*, series 2, vol. 9 (1822):i–liv, 223–312.

Goddard, Ives. "Eastern Algonquian Languages." In *Handbook of North American Indians*, edited by William C. Sturtevant, Vol. 15, *Northeast*, edited by Bruce G. Trigger (1978) (abbreviated below as HNAI).

Goddard, Ives, and Kathleen J. Bragdon. *Native Writings in Massachusett*. 2 vols. Philadelphia, 1988. An edition of all known documents written by Native speakers of Massachusett.

Hanzeli, Victor E. *Missionary Linguistics in New France: A Study of Seventeenth- and Eighteenth-Century Descriptions of American Indian Languages*. The Hague, 1969.

Pentland, David H., and H. Christoph Wolfart. *Bibliography of Algonquian Linguistics*. Winnipeg, Manitoba, 1982.

Pilling, James C. *Bibliography of the Algonquian Languages*. Washington, D.C., 1891.

Rhodes, Richard A., and Evelyn M. Todd. "Subarctic Algonquian Languages." In *HNAI*, vol. 6, *Subarctic*, edited by June Helm (1981).

SEE ALSO **The First Americans** and **Literature, Native American**; the maps accompanying **The First Americans.**

IROQUOIAN

THE IROQUOIAN LANGUAGE family is centered in northeastern North America. The Southern branch of the family is represented by a single language, Cherokee. At contact, the Cherokee occupied an area ranging over what is now Tennessee, North Carolina, Virginia, South Carolina, Georgia, and Alabama. The language is now spoken by over a thousand people in North Carolina and by about ten thousand in Oklahoma.

The Northern branch is composed of several subbranches. First to separate from the main branch were the Tuscarora and Nottoway, originally encountered by Europeans in North Carolina and Virginia, respectively. Most Tuscarora moved northward in the early eighteenth century. The language is now spoken by a few individuals in New York State near Niagara Falls and in southern Ontario at Six Nations. Nottoway was last spoken in Virginia in the mid nineteenth century.

A second Northern subbranch is Huron. At contact the Huron occupied a large area in what is now southern Ontario, but in 1649, decimated by disease and war, they scattered. Some moved to Lorette near Quebec City, where the Huron language was spoken into this century. Some settled among other Iroquois groups and the Ottawa. Some joined other defeated Iroquoian groups, the Petun, Erie, Wenro, and Neutral, and moved westward ultimately into Oklahoma. The language of this community, termed Wyandot, was last spoken in the mid twentieth century.

The other principal Northern subbranch is Iroquois proper, consisting essentially of Seneca, Cayuga, Onondaga, Oneida, and Mohawk. At contact, these groups, who constituted the Iroquois confederacy, inhabited what is now New York State. The Seneca, traditionally the Keepers of the Western Door, occupy the westernmost portion of the territory. Their language is now spoken by several hundred people primarily in three communities there: Allegany, Cattaraugus, and Tonawanda. To the east of the Seneca were the Cayuga. After the American Revolution, the Cayuga moved to Six Nations, Ontario, and to Oklahoma. Their language is spoken today by over three hundred people in Ontario and by one or two individuals in Oklahoma. Occupying central New York State are the Onondaga. Their language is now spoken by fewer than fifty in New York and at Six Nations, Ontario. To the east of the Onondaga were the Oneida. A few Oneida remain in New York, but most now live near London, Ontario, and Green Bay, Wisconsin. There are perhaps two hundred Oneida-speakers in Ontario and fewer than fifty in Wisconsin. Finally, to the east of the Oneida were the Mohawk, the Keepers of the Eastern Door. Mohawk is spoken by several thousand people in a number of communities: Kahnawà:ke (Caughnawaga) and Kanehsatà:ke (Oka), Quebec, near Montreal; Ahkwesáhsne (Saint Regis) straddling the Quebec–New York–Ontario borders; and Deseronto, Six Nations, and Gibson, in Ontario.

Several Northern Iroquoian languages are little known because documentation is sparse. Among these are Meherrin from what is now North Carolina; Petun (Tobacco Nation or Tionontati), Neutral, Wenro, and Erie (Kahkwah) from around Lake Erie; Susquehannock from what is now Pennsylvania; and Laurentian, actually a group of languages from communities along the Saint Lawrence preserved in word lists appended to accounts of Cartier's voyages of 1534 and 1535. When Champlain returned to the region in 1603, the Laurentian had vanished.

The sound systems of the Iroquoian languages are relatively simple, generally containing around 9–11 consonants and 5–7 vowels. Oklahoma Cherokee, Oneida, and Mohawk have developed distinctive tone.

The grammatical structures of the Iroquoian languages differ strikingly from those of more familiar European languages. Words, especially verbs, can be quite long, composed of many meaningful parts. Because of their elaborate structure, verbs can and often do serve as complete sentences in themselves.

All verbs contain minimally a pronominal prefix and a root. The Mohawk verb *shehró:ri* 'tell them!,' for example, consists of a pronoun *she-* 'you/them' plus the verb root *-hrori* 'tell.' (Mohawk forms are given in the community orthography.) The pronominal categories differ from those in most European languages. Instead of subjects and objects, Iroquoian pronouns distinguish agents (those who instigate and control events) from patients (those to whom things happen). The Mohawk verb *ktákhe'* 'I'm running,' for example, contains the agent pronoun *k-* 'I,' but the verb *wakya'tishónhkhwa'* 'I'm trembling' contains the patient pronoun *wak-* 'I.' Singular, dual, and plural number are distinguished, and inclusive (including the hearer) and exclusive first person. There are thus many equivalents of English 'we': *teni-* 'you and I (agent),' *tewa-* 'you all and I (agent),' *iaken-* 'he/she and I (agent),' *iakwa-* 'they and I (agent),' *ionkeni-* 'we two (patient),' and *ionkwa-* 'we all (patient).' Masculine, feminine/indefinite, and neuter/zoic (animal) gender are distinguished, but some female persons are referred to with feminine/indefinite

forms, others with neuter/zoic forms. In all, there are over fifty different pronominal prefixes.

Other verbal prefixes can indicate negation, surprise, simultaneity, direction, repetition, tense, reflexive actions, reciprocity, and middle voice. Suffixes can reverse an action ('*untie*'), indicate the coming into being of a state ('*get* rich'), causation ('*cause* to break'), use of an instrument ('write *with*'), action for someone else's benefit ('cook *for*'), action distributed over a time, place, or participants ('go visiting *here and there*'), and habitual, punctual, or stative aspect. Noun roots may be incorporated into verbs. Words, especially verbs, can thus be quite long. The verb *ionsahatihwistaniión:ten* 'they hung the bell back up there,' for example, contains the following parts: *i-* 'there,' *on-* past tense, *sa-* 'back,' *ha-* masculine agent, *-ti-* plural, *-hwist-* noun root 'metal' ('bell'), and *niionten* verb root 'hang.'

Perhaps because of their rich structure, verbs serve more functions in Iroquoian languages than in most European languages. The full Mohawk term for 'bell' is actually a verb, *iehwista'ékstha':* *ie-* 'one,' *-hwist-* 'metal,' *-'ek* 'strike,' *-st* instrumental, *-ha* habitual; literally, 'one strikes metal with it.' Verbs have provided an important resource for creating names for introduced items, so that it has seldom been necessary to borrow foreign words. Some names of this type are *akohsá:tens* 'it carries one on the back' = 'horse,' *iontenonhsohare'táhkhwa'* 'one cleans one's house with it' = 'mop,' *teietharáhkhwa'* 'one talks with it' = 'telephone,' and *teiohnekatsikhè:tare'* 'liquid has sugar in it' = 'soft drink.'

Iroquoian sentence structure also differs substantially from that of most European languages. The order of words in sentences does not depend on their roles as subjects or predicates, but on their importance to the discussion. More newsworthy information appears early in sentences, followed by less significant material. Both the following sentences are grammatical:

1. *Wahonnesákha'ne iehwista'ékstha'.*
2. *Iehwista'ékstha' wahonnesákha'.*
   'They went to look for the/a bell.'

The verb *wahonnesákha'* 'they went to look for' can either precede or follow *iehwista'ékstha'* 'bell.' It would precede if the audience were already aware of a lost bell and the search was the most important point of the sentence. It would follow if the bell represented a new idea. Speakers use word order as a stylistic device in every sentence, foregrounding significant information and backgrounding incidental material.

Elaborate word structure and word order are only a sample of the rich repertoires of stylistic devices available to speakers. Such devices are used with great skill among the Iroquois, who have traditionally cultivated and appreciated language and have long been recognized for their eloquence.

Marianne Mithun

BIBLIOGRAPHY

Chafe, Wallace. *The Caddoan, Iroquoian, and Siouan Languages.* The Hague, 1976 (revised from *Current Trends in Linguistics,* edited by Thomas A. Sebeok. Vol. 10, *Linguistics in North America,* The Hague, 1973).

Mithun, Marianne. "Iroquoian." In *The Languages of Native America: Historical and Comparative Assessment,* edited by Lyle Campbell and Marianne Mithun, Austin, Tex., 1979.

SEE ALSO **The First Americans** and **Literature, Native American;** the maps accompanying **The First Americans.**

MUSKOGEAN AND OTHER SOUTHEASTERN FAMILIES

INTRODUCTION

THE MUSKOGEAN LANGUAGE FAMILY is the only North American linguistic family limited to the southeastern United States. Languages of the Algonquian, Siouan, and Caddoan families are found bordering the Muskogean languages, or with a few isolated enclaves in the area. The southeast was an area of great linguistic diversity: besides the Muskogean family, six language isolates or small families survived to be recorded;

many other languages are known only by names in the historical record, and their affiliations are unknown. Among these are the Coree in North Carolina; the Cusabo and Santee in South Carolina; the Guale in Georgia; the Calusa, Tequesta, and Ais in Florida; the Chatot in Alabama; the Koroa and Yazoo in Mississippi; the Washa, Chawasha, and Avoyel in Louisiana; and the Tamahitan in Tennessee.

Although place names all over the Southeast have been borrowed from the Native languages, from Tallahassee in Florida (Creek *talaha·si·* 'abandoned town') to Calcasieu in Louisiana (Atakapa *katka siw* 'crying eagle'), other borrowings are relatively uncommon. Two plant names borrowed from Creek into English are the catalpa (*kataɬpa*) and the wahoo (*aha·hwa*). Borrowings into the colonial Spanish of Florida include *mico* 'chief' (Creek *mi·kko*) and *chicasa* 'abandoned town' (Apalachee *čikasa*). Borrowings from Choctaw (or Mobilian) are more common in Cajun French, due to the persistence of Native Americans in Louisiana. Such items include *chaoi* 'raccoon' (Choctaw *šawi*), *patasa* 'perch' (Choctaw *nani patassa*), and *sac-a-lait* 'white crappie' (Choctaw *sakli* 'trout').

Loans from European languages of the colonial period come primarily from Spanish: *chivato* 'goat,' Creek *čowa·ta,* Seminole *čawa·ta,* Mikasuki *čowa:ti,* Koasati *čowa:ta, capitán* 'captain,' Creek *kapitani,* Mikasuki *kapitani,* Koasati *kapitani,* Chickasaw *kapittani?, naranja* 'orange,' Creek *yala·ha,* Mikasuki *yala:hi,* Koasati *yilaha.* A few borrowings came from Colonial French: *escalin* 'twelve and a half cents,' Koasati *skali,* Alabama *iskali,* Choctaw *iskali* 'money'; *picaillon* 'half an escalin,' Koasati *pikayo,* Alabama *pikayo,* and Choctaw *pikayo* 'nickel.' Only one word clearly was borrowed from English of the colonial period. That is the place-name *Virginia,* which is interpreted as referring to Englishmen, the 'English language,' and later to Americans: Shawnee *yewacena·ki* 'Americans,' Yuchi *wajine* 'white people,' Koasati *wacina* 'English language' or 'Englishman,' Alabama *wa:cina* 'speak English,' Creek *wacina* 'United States' or 'American.'

MUSKOGEAN LANGUAGES

The Muskogean family consists of eight languages: Alabama, Apalachee, Chickasaw, Choctaw, Creek, Hitchiti, Koasati, and Mikasuki. Chickasaw is very closely related to Choctaw, and Mikasuki is to Hitchiti. Alabama and Koasati are more similar to each other than to any other of the languages but are still mutually unintelligible. At the beginning of the historical period, Creek was spoken in northern Georgia and north-central Alabama, Hitchiti and Mikasuki in southern Georgia, Apalachee in northwestern Florida, Koasati in eastern Tennessee, Alabama in northern Alabama, Chickasaw in northern Mississippi, and Choctaw in central and southern Mississippi and the Florida parishes of Louisiana. In addition, there was a trading jargon called Mobilian, probably developed in the pre-contact period and spoken widely in Louisiana in the nineteenth century, whose vocabulary came from Alabama, Chickasaw, and Choctaw.

The Muskogean languages are related to each other at a time depth comparable to that of the Romance languages; Choctaw and Creek are about as different from each other as French and Romanian are.

Muskogean languages are typified by a relatively simple phonology and syllable type, consonant-vowel-consonant-vowel (CVCV). All the languages possess the stops *p, t, č,* and *k;* the fricatives *f, ł,* s, and *h;* and the resonants *m, n, l, w,* and *y.* All the languages but Creek have just one voiced stop, *b;* in Creek, cognates have *k* or *p* depending on conditioning factors; these sounds descend from Proto-Muskogean $*k^w$. Creek has an additional consonant ŋ, of limited distribution, historically derived from one of the other nasal consonants. All the languages have a three-vowel system, *i, a, o,* both long and short. Creek has a fourth vowel, *e,* historically derived from the sequence *ay.* All the Muskogean languages have pitch accent—that is, one or more syllables of a word can bear a musical pitch that serves to distinguish words. The details of this system vary greatly from language to language.

Noun morphology is less complex than verb morphology. All the languages mark at least two marked nominal cases, nominative and accusative; most indicate plural only for nouns referring to human beings. Choctaw, Chickasaw, Koasati, and Alabama have developed nominal suffixes, often called "articles," which encode discourse information such as focus and topic. Koasati article suffixes go even further, and indicate

that a noun has a particular location in time, as well as prior mention in a discourse. There are two classes of noun possession: inalienable possession, which includes all body parts and most kin terms, and alienable possession, which includes all other items. These two classes are indicated by two different sets of possessive pronoun prefixes.

Verb morphology is extremely complex. All the languages divide verbs into two categories, active and stative, depending on the degree of control the agent has over the performance of the action; if the degree of control is high, the verb is active, if it is low, the verb is stative. In all the languages, subjects of stative verbs are marked by verbal prefixes that mark direct or indirect objects of active verbs. Subject cross-reference markers have distinct affirmative and negative forms. In Choctaw and Chickasaw, subject cross-reference markers are prefixed to the verb root, in Creek, Hitchiti, Mikasuki, and Apalachee they are suffixed, and in Alabama and Koasati, the cross-reference markers can be prefixed (1), suffixed (2), or infixed (3) (examples from Koasati):

1. *ak-hí:c-q̣*
   I(negative)-SEE-negative:complement
   'I do not see'
2. *holás-tákkq̣*
   LIE-I(negative)
   'I do not lie'
3. *ho,ká,hc-ó-hč*
   DIG,I(negative),-negative:complement-
   can
   'I can't dig'

Infixation is found in other languages only as fossilized derivational morphology. A notable category of verbs has roots that indicate that the subject or the object of the verb is singular or plural. A number of motion verbs also indicate a dual subject; in Creek, Hitchiti, and Mikasuki, the indication of dual in verbs is quite widespread.

Tense is weakly developed in the Muskogean languages, actions generally being divided into completed, ongoing, and potential aspects, rather than past, present, and future tenses. Verbal aspect is highly developed, using both verbal suffixes and infixed elements. Evidentials are also present; these can indicate the fact that an action has occurred has been deduced, overheard, or reported by another.

A major feature of the syntax of Muskogean languages is the use of reference-indexing, also known as "anticipatory switch-reference." This feature marks each clause or sentence as to whether it has the same subject as, or a different subject from, the following clause or sentence. A result of switch-reference is that there is little need for relative clauses, and they are completely absent from languages such as Alabama and Koasati.

The normal word order in a sentence is subject, object, verb, locative. Adjectives, which are nominalized verbs, follow the nouns they modify, while adverbs, also derived from verbs, precede the verbs they modify. When a special locative case is not found, locatives are marked either by the accusative or by postpositions. When a postposition occurs with a pronoun, it appears as an inalienably possessed noun rather than with the pronoun.

OTHER SOUTHEASTERN LANGUAGES

The non-Muskogean languages of the Southeast about which something is known are six in number: Atakapa, Chitimacha, Natchez, Timucua, Tunica, and Yuchi. Atakapa was spoken in south-central and southwestern Louisiana and adjoining parts of Texas, Chitimacha in southeastern Louisiana, Natchez in southwestern Mississippi, Timucua in northern and central Florida, Tunica in west-central Mississippi, and Yuchi in the Appalachian foothills of Tennessee and Georgia.

Atakapa

Atakapa forms a small, closely related language family, with three known members, Eastern Atakapa, Western Atakapa, and Akokisa. Atakapa has a simple consonantal phonology and five vowels; its syllable type is CVC. It has very little noun morphology, aside from a few discourse suffixes; its verb morphology is agglutinative and simple. Verbs are divided into active and stative. Word order is subject, object, verb, and switch-reference is not present.

Chitimacha

Chitimacha phonology distinguishes glottalized and unglottalized stops, with some of the latter arising from clusters of a stop and the glottal stop. It has five vowels with length distinctions, stress, and CVC syllables. It has minimal nominal morphology; most notable are the nonsystematic noun plurals. Verb morphology for person distinguishes only between first and non-first person; however, pronouns are not obligatory in sentences. Verbs have a form which is used when a following verb has the same subject, but this operates only within a sentence, not between sentences.

Natchez

Natchez has a five-vowel system, and in addition to the stops p, t, $č$, and k, a labiovelar k^w and the glottal stop $ʔ$. The most notable feature of Natchez phonology is the voiceless sonorants $m̥$, $n̥$, $l̥$, $w̥$, and $y̥$; Mary R. Haas has shown that most of the voiceless sonorants have come from sonorant-stop clusters. There are five nominal affixes with case functions and an articular suffix. Case relations are not nominative-accusative, but rather ergative-absolutive. Verbal morphology is highly complex. Verbs are divided into inflected verbs and verbs requiring an auxiliary; there are over thirty auxiliary verbs. Most verbs are inflected for singular, dual, and plural subject; all transitive verbs have four roots which encode the singularity and plurality of both object and subject. There are also two classes of impersonal (stative) verbs. Suffixes are used to coordinate verbs; the basic word order is subject, object, verb, although variant orders occur.

Timucua

It is possible that the Timucua language of Florida is distantly related to the Macro-Chibchan languages of South America. Long extinct, it is only known through missionary works of the seventeenth century. Timucua phonology is simple, five vowels and fourteen consonants. Words are made up of strings of V or CV syllables. Verbs have a complex affixal morphology, with apparently active processes of vowel harmony.

Tunica

Tunica has seven vowels, but its consonantal system is simple, like those of other southeastern languages. The language has fixed stress; pitch is a feature of the sentence, not the word. The Tunica nominal system is unusual for the Southeast, as it marks masculine and feminine gender in all nouns. In addition gender of a third person subject is marked on verbs. There are three classes of verbs, auxiliary, active, and static (stative); verb morphology is complex. The basic word order is subject, object, verb, and there is no switch-reference marking.

Yuchi

Yuchi has the richest phonological inventory of any southeastern language with a series of unaspirated, aspirated, voiced, and glottalized stops, with the addition of glottalized fricatives, resonants, and glides—a total of thirty-eight consonantal segments. There are also fourteen phonetic vowels, seven oral and seven nasal, though their phonemic status is not certain. The basic syllable type is (C)CV and (C)CV(C)CV. Noun morphology is simple, and verb morphology is complex. Basic word order seems to be subject, object, and verb, and there is no switch-reference marking.

Geoffrey D. Kimball

BIBLIOGRAPHY

Booker, Karen M. *Languages of the Aboriginal Southeast: An Annotated Bibliography.* Metuchen, N.J., 1991. This is the most recent and the most extensive bibliography of material pertaining to all the languages of the Southeast.

Crawford, James M. "Southeastern Indian Languages." In *Studies in Southeastern Indian Languages,* edited by James M. Crawford. Athens, Ga., 1975. Provides good, succinct historical sketches of Southeastern languages and linguistic work done on them up to that time.

Haas, Mary R. *The Prehistory of Languages.* The Hague, 1969. Contains a concise and succinct overview of comparative Muskogean phonology and morphology.

———. "The Southeast." In *Current Trends in Linguistics,* edited by Thomas A. Sebeok. Vol. 10, *Linguistics in North America.* The Hague, 1993.

SEE ALSO **The First Americans** and **Literature, Native American**; the maps accompanying **The First Americans**.

SIOUAN-CADDOAN

AT THE TIME OF FIRST EUROPEAN contact, most of the languages that lay directly west of the Algonquian, Iroquoian, and Muskogean languages of the East were members of the far-flung Siouan and Caddoan language families. Extending from the Eastern Woodlands across the plains, these were the languages of the Sioux and Pawnee, the Mandan and the Wichita, and many other tribes. There is some evidence that the Siouan and Caddoan languages, along with those of the Iroquoian family, sprang from a single common ancestor, sometimes referred to as Macro-Siouan. That ancestor language must have been spoken well over five thousand years ago, perhaps somewhere in the Southeast.

The Siouan languages were spoken by the following tribes. In the Northwest were the Crow, settled on and near the Yellowstone River in Montana. The Hidatsa or Gros Ventres lived along the Missouri River in North Dakota, as did the related Mandan. The Dakota or Sioux, speaking various dialects such as Teton (Lakota), Santee, Assiniboine, Stoney, and Yankton, were first encountered in what is now western Wisconsin and Minnesota. Another group of dialects called Chiwere, consisting of Iowa, Oto, and Missouri, were located in the area of present Iowa and Missouri. The closely related Winnebago lived to the northeast in present-day Wisconsin. A third dialect group, called Dhegiha, consisting of Omaha, Ponca, Kansa, Osage, and Quapaw, was distributed over much of the central plains from Nebraska south through Kansas and Missouri to Arkansas. The Ofo lived on the Yazoo River in Mississippi, and the Biloxi on the lower Pascagoula River in the same state. The Tutelo were in western Virginia. Two other languages of the Southeast, Catawba in northern South Carolina and Woccon in eastern North Carolina, were evidently more distantly related to these Siouan languages. More distantly related still were the Yuchi in the mountains of eastern Tennessee and northwest Georgia.

There were not as many Caddoan languages, but they too covered a large area. The

Caddo, speaking a variety of dialects, were spread from eastern Texas (the Hasinai dialects) across northern Louisiana into Arkansas (the Kadohadacho dialects). Not far from the Texas Caddo were the Kitsai. The Wichita were first encountered in central Kansas, and the Pawnee, with two major dialects, in Nebraska. The Arikara or Ree were a northern offshoot of the Pawnee.

Most of these languages are still spoken, though many by only a few old people. Thus, the following remarks on the sound systems and grammatical properties that are typical of these languages are given in the present tense.

The Siouan languages generally have a fairly large number of consonants, conspicuous among which to European ears were the glottalized or ejective stops, a full range of stops and fricatives in the velar tongue position, and a distinction between unaspirated and aspirated stops. The vowel systems tend to consist of the five vowels familiar in many languages (such as Spanish), along with three nasalized vowels. The Caddoan languages lack the considerable variety of the Siouan consonants, although Caddo has two ejective stops. Caddo developed several affricate consonants which are not present in the other languages. The earliest Caddoan vowel system seems to have consisted of only three vowels, but Kitsai, Pawnee, and Arikara have added one or two others.

In both the Siouan and Caddoan languages the most complex words are verbs, within which a variety of inflectional and derivational elements may be incorporated. In both families, the first and second person participants in events and states are indicated with pronominal prefixes, as with the prefix *wa* 'I' in Lakota *walówā* 'sang,' or the prefix *tsi* 'I' in Caddo *tsínáy'áwnah* with the same meaning. These prefixes come in pairs resembling English *I* and *me,* but the distinction is made differently. Whereas English distinguishes *I* and *me* as the subject and object of a verb respectively, in Siouan and Caddoan languages one of the prefixes indicates a person who does something, the other a person to whom something happens. Thus, the Caddo prefix *tsi* means 'I' as the one who did the singing in the word cited above, but a different prefix, *ku,* is translated 'I' in *kutnáwkáwtakah* 'I got sick,' because it was something that happened to me, not something I did.

Noteworthy in Siouan languages is a set of so-called instrumental prefixes that indicate the instrument or manner with which an action is performed. Thus, the Lakota verb *bleca* 'break' can be supplemented with a variety of prefixes as in *yabléca* 'break with the teeth,' *yubléca* 'break with the hands,' *nabléca* 'break by stepping on,' *pabléca* 'break by pressing on,' *kabléca* 'break by striking,' and *wobléca* 'break by jabbing or shooting.'

Caddoan languages have verbs that can be more complex than those of Siouan languages. Many contain incorporated noun roots indicating the thing affected by an event. For example, Caddo *bashúkah* 'it dried up' can be prefixed with *kam* 'water' to form *kambashúkah* 'the water dried up.' Many other kinds of elements can be added. As an example, a not unusual word in Caddo is *kánʔuʔintáywáyúhʔaʔ* 'I hear they are going to tell us.' The initial prefix *kán-* indicates that the fact that they are going to tell us is something I heard from another party, not something I learned directly. The next syllable -*ʔu*- indicates that it is *us* who are to be told, and furthermore an *us* that includes the person I am now talking to, a distinction not made in English. The beginning of the next syllable, -*ʔi*-, pronounced with a falling pitch, indicates that there are exactly two of us (you and I). The -*nt*- that follows marks us as the beneficiaries of this potential event. There follows a discontinuous verb root -*áy-yúh*- 'tell.' Inserted within this root is a syllable -*wá*-, which indicates that the tellers are plural. Finally, the word ends with the syllable -*ʔaʔ*, indicating that the event will take place in the future. This example suggests why the few early colonists and missionaries who observed these languages with care decided that their speakers could say in one word what for Europeans would require an entire sentence.

Wallace Chafe

BIBLIOGRAPHY

Chafe, Wallace. "Caddoan." In *The Languages of Native America: Historical and Comparative Assessment,* edited by Lyle Campbell and Marianne Mithum, Austin, Tex., 1979 (abbreviated before as LNA).

———. *The Caddoan, Iroquoian, and Siouan Languages.* The Hague, 1976 (revised from *Current Trends in Linguistics*, edited by Thomas A. Sebeok. Vol. 10, *Linguistics in North America,* The Hague, 1973. Reviews the history of scholarship on these languages and includes a grammatical sketch of Caddo.

Rood, David. "Siouan." In *LNA.*

SEE ALSO **The First Americans** and **Literature, Native American;** the maps accompanying **The First Americans.**

UTO-AZTECAN

LANGUAGES OF THE UTO-AZTECAN family, named by Daniel Brinton in 1891, are spoken from Southern Idaho (Shoshone) to El Salvador (Pipil), and from the California coast (Luiseño) to the Texas plains (Comanche). While Uto-Aztecan unity was first recognized (and attributed to diffusion) by J. K. E. Buschmann in 1859, a 1913 publication by Edward Sapir is the first scientific demonstration that all branches of the family must descend from a single protolanguage. The ancestral speech community occupied mixed woodland-grassland zones from eastern California to northwest Mexico, probably about five thousand years ago. An early expansion to the Pacific Coast was followed by migration south into the Sonoran Desert and the Mexican tropics; Aztecans reached Central America by the tenth century. Numic peoples entered the Great Basin as recently as a thousand years ago. Numic groups like the Wind River Shoshone and Comanche expanded into the Plains in the historic period. Most recently, Yaqui refugees fleeing Mexican repression entered Arizona from about 1900 to 1925. At the peak of the Uto-Aztecan expansion, speech communities ranged from small, highly mobile groups of hunters and collectors in the Great Basin to the great city-states of Central Mexico.

Links between the approximately thirty known languages suggest that within the two major subgroups, Northern and Southern Uto-Aztecan, language differentiation was gradual in a complex chain or mesh of regional variants. The Table illustrates one subgrouping hypothesis, with languages spoken in the United States listed within their subgroups. Languages within the family are as diverse as those of Indo-European. Thus the difference between Luiseño in California and Tohono O'odham in Arizona is comparable to the level of differentiation between Russian and Italian, while within the Takic subgroup Cupan, the difference between Cupeño and Cahuilla might be compared to that between Spanish and Portuguese.

Table 1. Uto-Aztecan Subgroups

Northern Uto-Aztecan

Numic:
Western—Mono, Monachi, Paviotso, Northern Paiute
Central—Shoshone-Comanche
Southern—Chemehuevi-Southern Paiute-Ute, Kawaiisu
Tubatulabal:
Tubatulabal
Takic:
Serranan—Serrano-Kitanemuk, Gabrielinan, Gabrielño-Ferdanño
Cupan—Luiseño, Cahuilla, Cupeño
Hopi:
Hopi

Southern Uto-Aztecan

Sonoran:
Tepiman—Tohono O'odham (Papago)-Akimel O'odham (Pima)
Taracahitian—Yaqui (spoken in Arizona and Sonora, Mexico)
Tubar—(Extinct)
Corachol
Aztecan:
Aztecan

Uto-Aztecan peoples have often been in close contact with speakers of other languages; multilingual individuals like Doña Marina (Nahuatl [Aztecan]), interpreter for Hernán Cortés, and Sacagawea (Shoshone), interpreter for part of the Lewis and Clark expedition, were probably never rare. Multilingualism yielded convergence of Aztecan languages with other language groups of Mesoamerica, and borrowing is attested as well between all the northern groups and their non–Uto-Aztecan neighbors. Ancient

44

Tohono O'odham contact with Puebloans yielded *ki:he* 'brother-in-law' from Zuni *kiha* 'ceremonial brother,' and *siwañ*, the name of a wicked leader in several myths, from Zuni *shiwani* 'rain priest' (probably in turn a loan word from a Keresan language). Tohono O'odham *su:dagĭ* 'water,' incorporates River Yuman *wasú* 'blue, green' with *-dagĭ*, an abstract-noun formative; cognates of this word are found throughout Tepiman and replace Proto-Uto-Aztecan **pa* 'water.'

The encounter with Europeans stimulated a new episode of multilingualism and convergence. Contact with Nahuatl speakers who accompanied the first missionaries yielded Tohono O'odham words like *ciopĭ* 'church' from Nahuatl *teopan* and *cikpan* 'working' from Nahuatl *tequipanoa*. Hopi *tota'tsi* 'dictator, extremely demanding person' from Nahuatl *totahtzin* 'our father, priest' attests eloquently to Hopi attitudes toward early missionaries. All the Mexican languages and the Yaqui spoken in Arizona exhibit hundreds of Spanish loans, many of which replace indigenous words. However, languages farther north have Spanish loans only for a hundred or so European animals, plants, household goods, and the vocabulary of the Catholic religion and the regime of the missions. Thus Tohono O'odham includes *siwol* 'onion' from Spanish *cebolla*, *kawĭyu* 'horse' from Spanish *caballo*, and *kownal* 'village headman' from Spanish *gobernador*. In the Takic languages of California we find Cupeño *tevxaa'* 'to work' from Spanish *trabajar*, Cahuilla *káama'* 'bed' from Spanish *cama*, and Luiseño *múisi-* 'to attend mass.' Hopi has only about fifty Spanish loans, attesting to Hopi resistance to Spanish influence after the Pueblo Rebellion of 1680, and Spanish loanwords are virtually absent from the Numic languages.

In spite of near-universal bilingualism in English among their speakers, there are relatively few well-established English loanwords in most Uto-Aztecan languages in the United States. This suggests relatively greater social distance from English speakers in the years after 1848 than was the case with Spanish-speaking colonists. For instance, Cupeño has only *kri:tu* 'streetcar.' Tohono O'odham has only *kili* 'kitty.' Big Smokey Valley Shoshone has a few dozen English loans, including *posyh* 'boss,' *pĭini* 'penny,' *appon* 'apple,' and *cikkinah* 'chicken.' Some registers of Hopi are apparently quite open to English loans, and include loan blends like *tónatsmo'a* 'sweet talker', from English 'doughnuts' and Hopi *mo'a* 'mouth,' and *tsolaaylawu* 'be celebrating the Fourth of July,' from English 'July' and Hopi *-lawu* (a continuative suffix).

Among Uto-Aztecan loanwords in English, the best known come from Nahuatl by way of Spanish, as with 'chocolate' and 'tomato' from Nahuatl *chocolatl* and *tomatl* respectively. Otherwise, loans are almost exclusively restricted to place names like Azusa (California), from Gabrielino *'asuksavit*, of unknown meaning; Tucson (Arizona), from old Tohono O'odham *tuk son* 'black base (of a mountain),' or Kanab (Utah), from Southern Paiute *kanavɨ* 'willow sp.' The few additional Uto-Aztecan loans into English include 'kiva' from Hopi *kiva* 'underground ceremonial chamber,' and 'chuckwalla,' a kind of lizard, from Cahuilla *cakwal*.

Descriptive studies of Uto-Aztecan languages began in the sixteenth century with works by missionary grammarians on Nahuatl, the language of the Aztecs. Pablo Tac's grammatical sketch and brief dictionary of Luiseño, written in the late 1830s, is the first grammar of an indigenous American language composed by a North American Indian. Juan Dolores published on Tohono O'odham early in this century. Today several Native speakers contribute to Uto-Aztecan linguistics.

Among the interesting typological features of Uto-Aztecan syntax is a rare pattern of marking case (subject or object) on both nouns and verbs. This can be reconstructed for the proto-language. In sentence 1, Cupeño shows both a pronominal object prefix on the verb and an object case suffix on the noun. (Read abbreviations in examples as follows: 1, 2, 3 for first, second, third person; SG, PL: singular, plural).

1. Muku'ut 'aya *hunwe-t-i p-i-čakpen*
   BEAR-ABSOLUTIVE-OBJECT
   3SG-OBJECT-CAUGHT
   'And then he caught a bear, it is said.'

AUX, an independent grammatical category marked for modality, subject person and number, and tense, is reconstructed for the second position in the protolanguage syntax, and has reflexes in all modern languages, as in Tohono O'odham:

2. 'Id *'a-p-t* o hu: ha'icu bahidag
   AUX-2SG-PERFECTIVE
   'You will eat this fruit.'

In some of the languages simultaneous marking for the same argument values on noun, verb, AUX, and other elements gives a startling impression of "redundancy," as in the Luiseño sentence below.

3. čam-taax ča čam-yaax 'ari-wun
   1PL-REFLEXIVE AUX:1PL 1PL-TRY KICK-PRE-SENT.PL
   'We are trying to kick ourselves.'

In addition to object-case suffixes, a series of "absolutive" suffixes on nouns, with diverse functions in the daughter languages, can be reconstructed for the protolanguage. The well-known *-tl* suffix of Nahuatl is an absolutive; for example, *conē-tl* (child-ABS). Absolutive nouns contrast with nouns marked with possessive prefixes and suffixes; for example, Nahuatl *no-conē-uh* (my-child-POSS).

Other phenomena of linguistic interest include free word order and discontinuous constituency (the latter seen in *'Id . . . ha'icu bahidag* [this . . . something ripeness (this fruit) in sentence 2]), the semantics of locatives in the Sonoran languages, and spatio-temporal reference in Hopi.

In comparison to many other languages of North America, the sound systems of Uto-Aztecan are relatively straightforward. Thus, in contrast to the multiple series of stops in languages in California, the Northwest, and in the Pueblo area, Uto-Aztecan languages typically manifest but a single series /p, t, č, k/, although in the Tepiman languages the Uto-Aztecan sonorants have become constricted-glottis stops /b,d/ j,g/ from /*w, *y, *kʷ/ respectively. Syllable structures are usually simple, with onsets restricted to single consonants and coda consonant clusters also not permitted in most of the languages. Most of the languages have four or five vowels. While stress systems are diverse and intricate, only Hopi exhibits tone.

All the languages exhibit internal diversity. "Shoshone" is a continuum of many dialects, and Tohono O'odham includes at least four closely related regional varieties. Gender differentiation is little developed (although some registers are restricted to, or preferred by, males or females). In the aboriginal speech communities a continuum of registers distinguished everyday colloquial speech from esoteric high languages of political and religious specialists. Piman speakers recognize at least three genres of oral literature; ranked in order of sacredness, these are song, oratory, and narrative. Each has several subgenres, mastered by community leaders, ritual and curing specialists, and laypersons who become "dreamers of songs." Yaqui deer songs share many metaphors with Aztec poetry; they are composed to accompany deer dancers in performances that reveal to the community the "flower world." Celebration of the beauty of this spirit world in sung poetry, seen also in Hopi kachina songs and the "round dance" songs of Numic peoples, is distinctive of Uto-Aztecan oral literature.

Several Sonoran and Takic languages became extinct by the early years of the twentieth century. In the United States, the surviving Takic languages and Tubatulabal have only a few very elderly speakers. In contrast, speakers of Yaqui and Hopi preserve vigorous creative power in ritual and "public" registers, and Hopi and Tohono O'odham in Arizona and Ute in Colorado have thousands of speakers who use the language in everyday contexts. Thus, while many Uto-Aztecan languages have become extinct and others are threatened, increasing cultural pride among Uto-Aztecan–speaking people makes survival and development of the languages, especially through increased literacy and formal education in the languages through bilingual education programs, possible in many communities.

Jane H. Hill

BIBLIOGRAPHY

Evers, Larry, and Felipe S. Molina. *Yaqui Ocer Songs/ Maso Bwikam.* Tucson, Ariz., 1987. Includes many bilingual texts. Molina is a deer singer.
Langacker, Ronald W. *An Overview of Uto-Aztecan Grammar.* Studies in Uto-Aztecan Grammar, vol.

1. Arlington, Tex., 1977. The introductory volume to a series of grammatical sketches of modern Uto-Aztecan languages.

Malotki, Ekkehart. *Hopi Time.* Berlin, 1983. Attacks a cornerstone of the "Whorf Hypothesis" on linguistic relativity with massive evidence against Whorf's claim that Hopi is a "timeless" language.

Miller, Wick R. "Uto-Aztecan Languages." In *HNAI,* vol. 10, *Southwest,* edited by Alfonso Ortiz (1983). Includes a language map and several lists of cognates.

Steele, Susan. "Uto-Aztecan: An Assessment for Historical and Comparative Linguistics." In *The Languages of Native America: Historical and Comparative Assessment,* edited by Lyle Campbell and Marianne Mithun. Austin, Tex., 1979.

Underhill, Ruth. *Singing for Power.* 1938; Repr. Berkeley, Calif., 1976. A sensitive, much admired study of Tohono O'odham sung poetry; all texts in English.

Zepeda, Ofelia. *A Papago Grammar.* Tucson, Ariz., 1983. An easy-to-understand pedagogical grammar authored by a Native-speaker linguist.

SEE ALSO **The First Americans** and **Literature, Native American;** the maps accompanying **The First Americans.**

WESTERN

DISTRIBUTION OF FAMILIES

THE LARGE NUMBER OF LANGUAGE families in North America north of Mexico have an uneven geographical distribution. Taking a conservative inventory of families, that is, groups of languages whose relationship by virtue of descent from a single language of the past is not in serious doubt, there appear to be some fifty-five of them in this area. Two regions of extreme diversity stand out, both of them coastal. One is along the coast of the Gulf of Mexico, west of the Muskogean family, from the lower Mississippi to the lower Rio Grande, which contains at least eleven localized families; the other is the long Pacific strip west of the Coast Mountains–Cascade Range–Sierra Nevada, which contains fully half the fami-

lies. The larger area between the Rocky Mountains and the Pacific, moreover, includes over two-thirds of the total number. This survey is organized by these three geographical areas.

Coastal Texas

Besides the small families treated in the essay on southeastern languages herein, it is likely that there were at least seven additional families, mostly poorly attested, between the Mississippi and the lower Rio Grande, and there may well have been yet other languages for which direct attestation is lacking. West of Atakapa along about half the Texas coast was Karankawa, and inland (around Austin) was Tonkawa. South and west of these there were five less easily localizable families that have inappropriately been grouped together under the label Coahuiltecan: Coahuilteco, Comecrudan (a family consisting of Comecrudo, Garza, and Mamulique), Cotoname, Solano, and Aranama-Tamique.

Intermontane West

The Intermontane area is largely taken up by five families: Uto-Aztecan and Athabaskan (see the essays directly preceding and following this one), plus Salish, Sahaptian, and Yuman, in addition to which there are seven localized families or language isolates (single languages comprising a family by themselves). South of Athabaskan in British Columbia, northern Washington and Idaho, and western Montana is the Interior branch of the deeply diversified Salish family, which also extends to the coast. Interior Salish comprises some seven languages: northern Lillooet, Thompson, and Shuswap, and southern Columbian (including Wenatchi), Okanagan (including Sanpoil, Colville, and Spokane), Kalispel (including Flathead and Pend d'Oreille), and Coeur d'Alene. Between Thompson and Okanagan is located Nicola, an offshoot of more northerly Athabaskan. At the eastern edge of this northern Plateau region, in southeastern British Columbia and nearby Idaho and Montana, is the isolate Kutenai.

South of Salish in southern Washington and Idaho and northern Oregon is the Sahaptian family, comprising two languages, Nez Perce to the east and Sahaptin (including dialects such as Yakima, Klikitat, and Umatilla) to the west. Sahaptian is distantly related to Klamath-Modoc, a single language, in northeasternmost California and nearby Oregon. Poorly attested Cayuse is located between the two branches of Sahaptian.

South of Klamath-Modoc in northeastern California (in the gap between the Cascades and the Sierras) is the Palaihnihan family, with two sharply divergent branches: Achumawi (or Pit River) and Atsugewi (or Hat Creek). Most of the Great Basin is occupied by the Numic branch of the Uto-Aztecan family, but at its western edge, in an area centering on Lake Tahoe, is found the Washo isolate.

The Southwest area is largely occupied in its eastern half by languages of the Apachean branch of Athabaskan. In its western half, in addition to Uto-Aztecan groups, Hopi and Pima-Papago (O'odham), is found the Yuman family, also extending to the coast, in western Arizona, southern California, and nearby Mexico. In the Upland region of northwestern Arizona is Walapai-Havasupai-Yavapai (a single language), which is most closely related to Paipai (or Akwa'ala) of Baja California. In the Colorado River drainage are Mohave, Quechan (or Yuma), and Maricopa (plus now-extinct dialects Halchidhoma and Kavelchadom). The Yuman family as a whole is related to Cochimí, which adjoins it to the south in Baja California. And finally, within the eastern half, in pueblos of New Mexico surrounded by Apachean, are three additional groups: the isolates Zuni and Keres, and the Tanoan family consisting of three branches, Tiwa (three languages, including Taos and Picuris), Tewa, and Towa (or Jemez). Tanoan is related to Kiowa of the southern Plains, to make up the Kiowa-Tanoan family.

Pacific Strip

As mentioned, the Pacific Strip—two hundred miles (320 kilometers) or less in width—is an area of great diversity. Some twenty-nine families (including numerous language isolates) are found here, only six of which have either members or external relations extending to the east.

Moving south along the coast from Eskimo, we first encounter Eyak in the Copper River delta, which is related to the Athabaskan family as a whole. South of this is Tlingit, covering a lengthy stretch of the panhandle of Alaska. Tlingit is distantly related to Athabaskan-Eyak, forming a narrow version of the Na-Dene family.

On the Queen Charlotte Islands and adjacent mainland of British Columbia is Haida, with two rather divergent dialects. This has often been considered to be related to Tlingit and Athabaskan-Eyak to form a broader version of Na-Dene, but the evidence for this now seems insufficient.

Next to the south is Tsimshian, with two languages, Coast Tsimshian and Nass-Gitksan. South of this we reach Wakashan, a family consisting of two distantly related branches. The Northern or Kwakiutlan branch contains Haisla, Heiltsuk-Oowekyala (including Bella Bella and Oowekeeno), and Kwakiutl, this last spoken on the northeastern portion of Vancouver Island and the opposite mainland. Inland from Heiltsuk is Bella Coola, a separated and linguistically distant offshoot of Salish. The Southern or Nootkan branch of Wakashan consists of Nootka and Nitinat on the west coast of Vancouver Island, and Makah on the northwestern tip of the Olympic Peninsula (Washington State).

A stretch of ten additional Salish languages runs south from Kwakiutl on both sides of the Strait of Georgia and Puget Sound, making up the Central group. These are Comox, Pentlatch, Sechelt, Squamish, Halkomelem (including Chiliwack, Musqueam, and Cowichan), Nooksack, Northern Straits (including Saanich, Sooke, Songhees, Samish, Lummi, and Semiahmoo), Clallam, Lushootseed, and Twana. The Tsamosan group of Salish, in southwestern Washington, contains Quinault, Lower Chehalis, Upper Chehalis, and Cowlitz. The Chimakuan family of the northern Olympic Peninsula consists of Quileute on the Pacific coast (between Makah and Quinault) and Chemakum on the northeast tip.

Along both sides of the Columbia River is Chinook, subsuming two languages, Lower and Upper Chinook (including Cathlamet, Multnomah, and Kiksht). On either side of this near the coast are two dialects of an Athabaskan language, Kwalhiokwa and Clatskanie. Next to the south on the Oregon coast is the Tillamook outlier of Salish (including Siletz). Then come three small groups: the Yakonan family, consisting of Alsea and Yaquina, Siuslaw (including Lower Umpqua), and the Coos family, made up of Hanis and Miluk. Then Pacific Athabaskan groups run on down the coast into northern

California. Inland in the Willamette Valley is Kalapuya, a family of three languages, which is quite distantly related to Takelma to its south (separated by Athabaskan Upper Umpqua) in the Rogue River drainage. Along the Cascade foothills east of Kalapuya is the isolate Molala.

South of Athabaskan on the northwest California coast are two languages, Yurok and Wiyot, which are rather distantly related to each other to make up a family that has been termed Ritwan; they in turn are related to the widespread Algonquian family east of the Rockies (see the separate article) to make up Algonquian-Ritwan (or Algic). East of Yurok is isolate Karok, and to its east Shasta, a family of four languages: Shasta, New River Shasta, Okwanuchu, and Konomihu. Another Athabaskan-speaking area is found starting inland from Wiyot and running south of it on the coast. Just east of this and south of New River Shasta is the isolate Chimariko. Most of the area near the coast south of Athabaskan and north of San Francisco Bay is occupied by Pomo, a family of seven languages. Some Pomo languages separate the two divergent branches of Yukian, Yuki (including Coast Yuki and Huchnom) and Wappo. Spread along the Sacramento Valley is the Wintun family, with three languages, Wintu, Nomlaki, and Huchnom. To the east in the Sierra foothills are Yana, with two languages (including Yahi), and Maiduan, with three languages: Maidu, Konkow, and Nisenan.

The Miwok family, with some seven languages, runs across central California from the coast into the Sierras south of Pomo, Wintun, and Maiduan. This is distantly related to Costanoan, running south from the Bay, with some eight languages, these together constituting the Utian family. Then extending south along the coast are the isolates Esselen and Salinan, and the Chumash family, incorporating at least six languages.

Inland in the San Joaquin Valley and Sierra foothills is the Yokuts family, with perhaps six languages, divided into numerous intergrading dialects. East of this in the Sierras are Uto-Aztecan representatives: Western Mono of the Numic branch and Tubatulabal; the Takic branch of Uto-Aztecan cuts a wide swath across southern California to the coast east and south of Chumash. Finally, running across southernmost California and extending somewhat south

of the border is the Yuman language Diegueño (including Ipai, Tipai, and Kamia).

DEEPER GENETIC RELATIONSHIPS

Indications have long been noted of possible relationships among some of these families, leading to groupings into certain deeper, more comprehensive families. Four of these are most commonly mentioned, the restricted Aztec-Tanoan and Mosan, and the more inclusive Hokan and Penutian. Aztec-Tanoan combines two families that center on the Southwest, Uto-Aztecan and Kiowa-Tanoan, while Mosan brings together three families of the Northwest: Salish, Wakashan, and Chimakuan. Hokan unites eleven families scattered around the edge of California, with at least two more families south of the border. Penutian combines eight families of Oregon and southern Washington and four families covering a broad area in central and northern California, with the northern outlier Tsimshian and two or more additional families of southern Mexico. These postulations remain controversial; probably some subset of them, or yet other combinations, are valid, but it should be emphasized that the relationship between any two of these families must be very distant at best, seemingly greater, for instance, than that obtaining between two languages of different branches of Indo-European, such as English and Russian. Drastic reductions, such as those of Edward Sapir in 1929, although often cited, must at present be regarded merely as hypotheses. Sapir put all languages north of Mexico into six groups, now often referred to as "superstocks," all of them represented in the Pacific Strip. Joseph Greenberg finds only three groups for all of the Americas, with the great majority of the languages belonging to a widespread "Amerind" family; the other two are Eskimo-Aleut and Na-Dene, and all three are well represented in the West.

WIDESPREAD STRUCTURAL CHARACTERISTICS

This group of over forty language families, not surprisingly, exhibits a large diversity of language structures. But certain characteristics not typical of European languages are present in many of them, and in certain areas shared features cut across the boundaries of different languages and families. The most salient such linguistic area is one combining the Northwest Coast (stretching from the panhandle of Alaska into northwestern California) and the inland Plateau, in which there are as many as seventeen different families.

Phonology

Widespread shared traits of the Northwest-Plateau area include a series of glottalized stops or ejectives (*p' t' k'*, etc.) made with a simultaneous closure of the vocal cords, a distinction between velar and postvelar consonants (*k/q, k'/q', x/x̲*, etc.), plain versus labialized dorsal consonants (*k/kʷ, q/qʷ, x/xʷ*, etc.), and a series of laterals (*l ɬ ƛ'*, etc.). Many of these languages also allow clusters of several successive consonants. The glottalized stops also extend to the south through central California, in most languages of the Pacific Strip bordered on the east by Uto-Aztecan, and in southwestern Pueblo languages; a subset of these languages also have glottalized resonants (*m' n' l' w' y'*, etc.); postvelar consonants (mostly *q*) also occur more sporadically in California, the Great Basin, and the western Southwest; and labialized velars (mostly *kʷ*) are found widely in the Great Basin and the Southwest. In central California several families share a distinction between plain and apico-alveolar stops (*t/ṭ*). In an area including the Great Basin and nearby eastern California occur both the velar nasal (ŋ) and a high central vowel (*ɨ*). Many other phonological characteristics must perforce be omitted here, because they are either more localized or less exotic.

Grammar

In the area of morphology, the occurrence of one or more patterns of reduplication is extremely widespread, expressing meanings such as plurality and distributive, and sometimes the diminutive. Patterns of alternation of consonants to express diminutive or augmentative variants, so-called consonantal symbolism, occur in some languages of the Northwest-Plateau and the more southerly Pacific Strip.

Many of these languages exhibit the trait of polysynthesis, meaning that words—especially verbs—can be relatively long on the average, combining several meaningful parts. Several grammatical factors contribute to this. One is what has been called pronoun incorporation: the inclusion in verbs of markers not only of their subjects, but also of their objects. Nouns also often take prefixes or suffixes expressing their possessor. Verbs additionally may contain affixes or compounded stems with relatively concrete meanings—so-called instrumental prefixes or (suffixal) locative-directional markers or (especially in the Northwest) lexical suffixes or (especially in the Southwest) noun incorporation.

The Northwestern languages grouped as Mosan show an unusually weak differentiation between nouns and verbs, in that most stems can serve as predicates. Several Northwest-Plateau languages have numeral classifiers—suffixes on numerals classifying the objects counted into categories, predominantly of shape. And several languages have some verbs that are specialized for either the number or the shape of their subject or object.

In pronouns, a dual number category is attested sporadically, especially in Penutian groups and in the Great Basin and Pueblo Southwest. A distinction between inclusive and exclusive plural (and sometimes dual) first persons (i.e., including or not the person[s] spoken to) occurs primarily in the Great Basin and central and northern California. A device for keeping track of pronominal reference called switch-reference is encountered in the Great Basin, central California, and the western Southwest; this is manifested by suffixes on the verb or on sentence-introducing particles that indicate whether the subject of the following clause will be the same as or different from that of the preceding.

Various Western languages exhibit categories of evidentials, which indicate the source of information that the speaker cannot vouch for by direct personal experience, such as by hearsay or by indirect auditory or visual evidence. An example of a geographically constrained category is grammatical sex gender, which, while not typical of Western languages, does occur in the Northwest in an area comprised of Coast Salish, Chimakuan, and Chinook.

William H. Jacobsen, Jr.

BIBLIOGRAPHY

Bright, William. *Bibliography of the Languages of Native California, Including Closely Related Languages of Adjacent Areas.* Metuchen, N.J., 1982.

Davis, Irvine. "The Kiowa-Tanoan, Keresan, and Zuni Languages." In *The Languages of Native America: Historical and Comparative Assessment,* edited by Lyle Campbell and Marianne Mithun. Austin, Tex., 1979 (abbreviated below as *LNA*).

Goddard, Ives. "The Languages of South Texas and the Lower Rio Grande." In *LNA*.

Hale, Kenneth, and David Harris. "Historical Linguistics and Archeology." In *Handbook of North American Indians,* edited by William C. Sturtevant. Vol. 9, *Southwest,* edited by Alfonso Ortiz (1979) (abbreviated below as *HNAI*).

Jacobsen, William H., Jr. "Chimakuan Comparative Studies." In *LNA*.

———. "Hokan Inter-Branch Comparisons." In *LNA*.

———. "Wakashan Comparative Studies." In *LNA*.

———. "Washoe Language." In *HNAI*, vol. 11, *Great Basin,* edited by Warren L. d'Azevedo (1986).

Kendall, Martha B. "Yuman Languages." In *HNAI*, vol. 10, *Southwest,* edited by Alfonso Ortiz (1983).

Sherzer, Joel F. "Areal Linguistics in North America." In *Current Trends in Linguistics,* edited by Thomas A. Sebeok. Vol. 10, *Linguistics in North America.* The Hague, 1973 (abbreviated below as CTL).

Shipley, William F. "California." In *CTL*.

———. "Native Languages of California." In *HNAI*, vol. 8, *California,* edited by Robert F. Heizer (1978).

Silverstein, Michael. "Penutian: An Assessment." In *LNA*.

Thompson, Laurence C. "The Northwest." In *CTL*.

———. "Salishan and the Northwest." In *LNA*.

Thompson, Laurence C., and M. Dale Kinkade. "Languages." In *HNAI*, vol. 7, *Northwest Coast,* edited by Wayne Suttles (1990).

Voegelin, C. F., and F. M. Voegelin. "The Southwest and Great Basin." In *CTL*.

SEE ALSO **The First Americans** and **Literature, Native American**; the maps accompanying **The First Americans**.

ATHABASKAN

THE ATHABASKAN LANGUAGE family is a group of thirty-some languages descended from a common ancestor that was spoken over two thousand years ago. It has differentiated and spread, probably from a homeland in the interior of Alaska and the Yukon, through northwest Canada east as far as Hudson's Bay and south to southern British Columbia; from there to Oregon and California as well, perhaps a thousand years ago; and in a separate movement, somewhat later, from the North through the Plains to the Southwest, where they are now known as Navajo and Apache, having arrived not long before the Spanish.

The first European–Athabaskan contact was between Hudson's Bay Company men and individuals of the "Northern Indians" (Chipewyan) at York Factory, in 1686, and especially at Churchill, beginning in 1714. More widespread direct, steady trade contact did not begin until the late eighteenth or early nineteenth century in the North; in northern British Columbia, the Yukon, and interior Alaska it did not begin until after 1867, the end of the colonial period. Anglican and Catholic (Oblate) missionary contact had reached the Chipewyan-Beaver-Dogrib-Slavey area by the 1850s but did not pervade the Athabaskan North until after 1867, and no literacy developed in any of these languages during the period.

So too for Oregon-California Athabaskan and Apache-Navajo: contact did not begin until the first half of the nineteenth century, and literacy not until the twentieth. Nevertheless, so distinctive and similar are the Athabaskan languages that as early as 1826 Albert Gallatin accurately defined the extent of the northern Athabaskan languages, naming them, arbitrarily, after Lake Athabasca; then in 1841 Horatio Hale recognized that the Oregon(-California) group was also Athabaskan; and W. W. Turner in 1852 finished defining the remarkable extent of this family by recognizing that Navajo and Apache are Athabaskan as well.

The Athabaskan languages differ among themselves about as much as the Romance or Germanic languages do, hence the estimate that they began to diverge from a common ancestor (called Proto-Athabaskan) something on the order of two thousand years ago. Aside from the large geographical gaps, within their continuous territories they formed a sort of continuum of dialects (adjacent communities could understand each other's speech, while those that were farther apart had to exert some effort to do so). Even where the differences were more abrupt, Athabaskans routinely learned the neighboring dialects or languages, to communicate and remain a coherent people throughout the great breadth of their territory.

By comparing its modern-day descendants, linguists are able to reconstruct a fairly clear picture of the Proto-Athabaskan sound system, grammar, and vocabulary, and to explain how each of the modern languages has changed in its own way from that prototype. The sound system consisted of the (full) vowels *i e a u* and (their reduced counterparts) *a ʊ* and (from *i* and *e*) *ə* ; the sonorants *m n ŋ w y;* and the following rich pattern of obstruent consonants:

plain stops:

d	*dl*	*dz*	*j*	*j^w*	*g*	*G*		*ʔ*

aspirated stops:

	t	*tl*	*ts*	*č*	*č^w*	*k*	*q*	

glottalized stops:

	t'	*tl'*	*ts'*	*č'*	*č^w*	*k'*	*q'*	

voiceless fricatives:

		ł	*s*	*š*	*š^w*	*x*	*x̣*	*h*

voiced fricatives:

		l	*z*	*ž*	*ž^w*	*ɣ*	*ʀ*	

where the *G–q* column represents a series pronounced far back in the mouth. Note that there are no labial obstruents, (*b p f*), made by closure of the lips; this lack is an unusual trait, held in common with the only languages that have been proven to be genetically related to Proto-Athabaskan, the coastal Eyak and Tlingit.

No modern Athabaskan language has retained this system unchanged; the Tanana language, spoken at Minto and Nenana, near Fairbanks, Alaska, has kept the vowels (except *a,* changed to *ʊ*), has changed *m* and *ŋ* to *n,* *w* to *b,* and has changed most of the obstruents but kept them all distinct, as follows, corresponding item for item to the table above:

d	*dl*	*dð*	*dz*	*j*	*dr*	*g*	*ʔ*
t	*tl*	*tθ*	*ts*	*č*	*tr*	*k*	
t'	*tl'*	*tθ'*	*ts'*	*č'*	*tr'*	*k'*	
	ł	*θ*	*s*	*š*	*sr*	*x*	*h*
	l	*ð*	*z*	*y*	*zr*	*ɣ*	

There was, in addition, a constricted voice quality marking certain vowels in Proto-Athabaskan, which has given rise to high tone (distinctive pitch) in some of the modern Athabaskan languages (e.g., Chipewyan) and low in others (e.g., Navajo), but in Tanana this is preserved, as low tone, only in certain verb prefixes. The main grammatical categories are nominal and verbal. Nouns are relatively simple, without number or case, but can have possessive prefixes (kin and anatomical terms must have them), as in Tanana *sətaʔ* 'my father,' *nətaʔ* 'your father' (the stem *-taʔ* cannot occur alone); *łət* 'smoke,' *sələdeʔ* 'my smoke,' *nələdeʔ* 'your smoke' (with a suffix, originally *-əʔ*); and they can be compounded: *sra* 'sun,' *tətθ-zraʔ* 'moon' ('night-sun'). Verbs, on the other hand, are extremely complex. They include long strings of prefixes preceding the stem, which is a monosyllable that itself varies somewhat in shape, and a small number of suffixes that may follow it. The core of Athabaskan grammar is this "polysynthetic" complexity of the verb, a combination of the "verb theme," often composed of a stem and prefixes with highly abstract meaning, plus several more derivational and inflectional prefixes, all interlocking and closely fused in a rigid order. To take a simple example from the Tanana language:

1. *nnət łʔen* 'I see you'
   from *nə-nə-s- łʔen*

is composed of the stem *-ʔen,* the "thematic" (second) prefix *-nə-* (perhaps originally meaning 'face'), and the "classifier" *- ł-* (partly connected with the idea of transitive-active), to form the theme *-ne- ł-ʔen* 'see'; this is combined with the second person singular object prefix 'you' *n(ə)-,* at the beginning of the word, and the first person singular subject prefix 'I' *-s-,* which becomes *-ł-* before the *- ł-.* The future of that,

2. *ntənəɣət łʔi ł* 'I'll see you (someday)'
   from *nə-tə-nə-ɣə-s- ł-ʔen- ł*

has added a discontinuous sequence *-tə-ɣə-* on either side of "thematic" *-nə-,* and a suffix *- ł* to the stem, which as a result changes from *-ʔən* to *-ʔi-.* The next form,

3. *nantənəɣəjaʔi ł* 'I'll see you again'
   from *na-nə-tə-nə-ɣə-s-lə-ʔen- ł,*

has added to (2) the prefix *na-* 'again' and has (somewhat irregularly for a transitive verb) changed the *-ł-* classifier to *-lə-,* which combines with the *-s-* subject prefix to form *-jə-,* a peculiar but old trait. The following example,

4. *nastənəðəʁilʔilé* 'You won't see me again' from *na-sə-tə-nə-ðə-ʁə-i-lə-ʔen- ł-é,*

has two suffixes and eight prefixes, still not the maximum possible: the object *s(ə)-* 'me' replaces *n(ə)-* 'you'; the 'you' *n(ə)-* (now in subject position) changes to *i-* before the *l(ə)-* classifier, which now appears as such; and negation is represented by the prefix *ðə-* and the suffix *-é* (with high tone and nasality), the addition of which has changed the future suffix *-ł* to *-l*. The components are largely discontinuous: *-nə-* . . . *-lə-ʔen-* 'see,' future *-tə-* . . . *-ʁə-* . . . *ł,* 'again' *na-* . . . plus change of *-ł-* to *-lə-,* negative *-ðə-* . . . *-é,* and *-s(ə)-* 'me' (object) plus *-n(ə)-* or *-i-* 'you' (subject), all combined interlockingly in a definite order.

Another characteristic of Athabaskan is verb themes or stems which refer to physical classes of objects, as in

5. *ja ðə-ʔan* 'it (roundish object) lies here'
6. *ja ðə-tan* 'it (sticklike object) lies here'

Moreover, where European languages have prepositions, Athabaskan has postpositions, noun-like stems which follow their object, such as *sə-ts'ənʔ* 'me-to,' as in the sentence

7. *čile dəčən səts'ənʔ dèðtan* boy stick to-me he-moved-it (sticklike) 'the boy moved the stick toward me'

where the verb now has a classificatory prefix *də-* referring to wooden objects (among other things) which when directly combining with the prefix *-ð (ə)-* "perfective" (completion of action) forms the sequence *dèð-* with low tone. To say that the boy moved (plural) sticks toward me, the noun *dəčən* 'stick(s)' would not change, but the verb stem *-tan* would change to *-dla* 'handle plural objects,' at the very end of the sentence, thus

8. *čile dəčən səts'ənʔ dèðdla* 'the boy moved sticks toward me'

Finally, from (7) and (8) it can also be seen that the basic order of words in a sentence is first subject (*čile* 'boy'), then direct object (*dəčən* 'stick(s)'), then postpositional phrase (closely connected to and sometimes fused with the verb, *səts'ənʔ* 'to me'), and last the verb (*dèðtan* 'he moved it [sticklike]' or *dèðdla* 'he moved them'). The structure of Athabaskan languages clearly has its own genius, its own very distinctive understanding of the universe of human experience.

Michael Edward Krauss

BIBLIOGRAPHY

Krauss, Michael. "Na-Dene." In *Current Trends in Linguistics,* edited by Thomas A. Sebeok. Vol. 10, *Linguistics in North America.* The Hague, 1973.

———. "Na-Dene and Eskimo-Aleut." In *The Languages of North America: Historical and Comparative Assessment,* edited by Lyle Campbell and Marianne Mithun. Austin, Tex., 1979.

Krauss, Michael, and Victor Golla. "Northern Athapascan Languages." In *Handbook of North American Indians,* edited by William C. Sturtevant. Washington, D.C., 1978. Vol. 6, *Subarctic,* edited by June Helm (1981).

SEE ALSO **The First Americans** and **Literatures, Native American;** maps accompanying **The First Americans.**

ESKIMO-ALEUT FAMILY

ESKIMO-ALEUT IS A NORTHERN family of languages, sharply divided into two main branches, Aleut and Eskimo. Aleut in 1741 occupied the Aleutian Islands and the tip of the Alaska Peninsula, and in the 1820s also was settled on the Pribilof and Commander Islands. It is a single language, with relatively minor dialect differences. Eskimo, on the other hand, is itself a family of five to eight languages (counting as separate languages, forms of speech that are not mutually intelligible). The ancient home of Eskimo-Aleut was the Bering Sea area, and maximum linguistic diversity is found where a language family has been settled longest; therefore nearly all the different languages of the family are at the Alaskan end of its range. The language of Canadian and Greenlandic Eskimos—now the majority—is only part of one branch of Eskimo, the Inuit.

The Inuit branch of Eskimo (*inuit* 'people,' plural of *inuk* 'person') forms an unbroken dialect chain which, over the past thousand years, has spread from the Bering Strait across northern Alaska and Canada to Greenland. It could be considered a single language, though the extremes could not understand each other well without some weeks' or months' accommodation.

The other branch of Eskimo, Yupik, is a series of four languages comprising a broken chain of dialects: 1. Pacific Yupik or Alutiiq (also called "Aleut" in local English) of Prince William Sound and the tip of the Kenai Peninsula, Kodiak Island, and the Alaska Peninsula; 2. Central (Alaskan) Yupik, from Bristol Bay through southwestern Alaska to Unalakleet and the pocket of Elim and Golovin on the Seward Peninsula (a Yupik continuum reaching to Siberia was interrupted during the last few hundred years by the nearly complete Inuit occupation of the Seward Peninsula); 3. Naukanski Yupik of East Cape, Siberia—their village, Naukan, was evacuated by Soviet authorities in 1957—was the link to 4. (Central) Siberian Yupik of the southeast tip of Chukotka, Russia, and the adjacent Saint Lawrence Island (since the American purchase of Alaska in 1867 it has been an international language). Sirenikski, either a very divergent fifth Yupik language or a third branch of Eskimo, was spoken beyond (Central) Siberian Yupik on the southern coast of Chukotka, and in the early 1990s was a relic remembered only by two old women at the village of Sireniki.

Several words of Eskimo origin are widely known in English: *kayak, igloo, mukluk, umiak, anorak;* over a dozen more are to be found in one or more of the general major dictionaries of English: *angakok, kamik, kashim, komatik, koole-tah/kuletuk, kuspuk, muktuk, nunatak, piblokto, pingo, qiviut, tupik, ugrug, ulu* (spellings may vary). Some dozens more can be found in dictionaries of regional English for Alaska and Canada, and there are many Eskimo place-names and ethnic group names; for example, *Nunamiut, Malemute, Kabloona, Inuit* (singular *Inuk*), *Inupiat* (singular *Inupiaq*), *Yupik,* also more or less widely used in English.

HISTORY

Russian colonization of Alaska began in 1745 after Vitus Bering's discovery of the Aleutians in 1741. For forty years, steady Russian fur-trading contact was confined to the Aleutians, bringing mainly death to the Aleut population, which was reduced from perhaps sixteen thousand to twenty-five hundred. With the need to find less depleted sea-otter grounds and to counter British, American, Spanish, and French movement into the area that started in the 1770s, the Russians established a company with headquarters on Kodiak Island in 1784 (moving farther to Sitka in 1799). During the second forty-year period, the Alutiiq and southern Central Yupik (as well as Tlingit and some Athabaskan-speakers) were also affected. The first long-term missionary and educational efforts began during this period, including writing in Alutiiq at Kodiak, but they were sporadic and short-lived, 1794–1807. The third period began in 1824, with the arrival of Ioann Veniaminov (canonized as Saint Innocent) as priest to the Aleutians. Among the many important humanistic accomplishments of this man was the establishment, with the help of the Aleut Ivan Pan'kov, of a remarkably good adaptation of the Cyrillic alphabet for writing Aleut. This had special signs for the uvular (guttural) *k, g,* and *ch* sounds which are characteristic of all Eskimo-Aleut languages. The first printed Alaskan languages were Aleut (Primer, Catechism, Gospel of Matthew, 1834, 1840), then Alutiiq (1847–1848). Manuscript religious literature also began in Central Yupik, but none was printed until the 1890s. In Aleut, especially, there was very widespread literacy by the time of the Alaska Purchase in 1867.

After a twenty-year period of "neglect," American educators began, and in the case of Aleut and Alutiiq, eventually succeeded in, a campaign to eradicate these languages and literatures. Central Yupik and Siberian Yupik on Saint Lawrence Island remained unaffected for the most part because of their isolation, and, unlike

Aleut and Alutiiq, are still being naturally passed on to and spoken by children.

The influence of Russian on these languages can clearly be seen and assessed via the quantity of Russian loanwords found in them: over 800 in Aleut, about 600 in Alutiiq, but only 190 in Central Yupik. Alaskan Eskimo languages farther north were barely affected, with perhaps a dozen loans in Inuit (which in Alaska is called Inupiaq) and still fewer in Siberian Yupik on Saint Lawrence Island.

For Canadian Inuit, the first European contacts were with the French and English during the second half of the sixteenth century, along the Labrador coast and Baffin Island. The first Eskimo vocabulary ever printed (in Richard Hakluyt's *Principal Navigations, Voyages, and Discoveries of the English Nation* of 1589) contained seventeen words written down in 1576 by a member of Martin Frobisher's expedition in the bay that bears his name. Though there were intermittent or seasonal contacts between Inuit and European explorers, traders, and fishermen during the seventeenth and eighteenth centuries in the Canadian East, the earliest colonization was by the Moravians (United Brethren), at first from Greenland (which Denmark had colonized in 1721), in Labrador, then a part of Newfoundland, with the establishment of a mission at Nain in 1771 and a school there in 1791. By 1809 printing of religious literature in Labrador Inuit (Inuttut) had begun, in a roman alphabet derived from that used for Greenlandic. The Moravian educational system for Labrador developed in the language, and literacy in it there became widespread. The German-speaking Moravians brought a large number of loanwords to Labrador Inuttut, such as *kaattuupalak* 'potato' and *mitivuuk* 'Wednesday,' from German *Kartoffel* and *Mittwoch*. When Newfoundland joined the Canadian Confederation in 1949, strictly English-language education took over, and Labrador Inuttut, alone of the Inuit dialects of Eastern Canada, is now in serious decline.

Inuit dialects of the rest of Canada were little or not at all affected during the colonial period (taken to end with the Canadian Confederation in 1867, the same year as the sale of Alaska). The western Inuit groups had barely been contacted, and there was no steady colonial presence in northern Quebec beyond Labrador except at the very end of the period. Most importantly at that point for the Canadian Inuit language (Inuktitut), a syllabic form of writing devised for Cree in the 1830s was adapted for Inuktitut in the 1860s. It was spread by the Anglican Edmund Peck among the Inuit starting in the 1870s in Quebec, and in this century it spread also to Baffin Island and the central Canadian Arctic, where the language remains strong and literacy flourishes as a part of Inuit culture.

GRAMMAR

The consonant system of Eskimo languages typically includes the following sounds:

p	*t*	*c*	*k*	*q*
v	*l*	*y*	*ɤ*	*r*
m	*n*		*ŋ*	

where *p t k* are unaspirated as in French, or as in English *spy*, *sty*, *sky*; *c* is *ch* or *s*; *ɤ* (spelled *g*) is as in Spanish *haga* or German *sagen*, and *ŋ* is as in English *singer*. The *q* is pronounced farther back in the mouth than *k*, like Arabic *q*, and the *r* farther back than *g*, like Parisian *r*. These two uvular sounds are essential to all languages of this family.

The vowels are the simple triangle *i a u* (with a fourth vowel, schwa, written *e*, in Yupik). Any two vowels (except *e*) can combine to form diphthongs *ia*, *iu*, *ai*, *au*, *ui*, *ua*, and also *ii*, *aa*, *uu* (long, that is double, vowels). In addition, Inuit can also have double consonants, so that, as for example in Finnish, long and short vowel and consonant sequences, such as *ata*, *aata*, *atta*, and *aatta*, are all importantly different. Yupik also has prosodic lengthenings and shortenings, whereby for instance the name *Alutiiq* is pronounced *alútĭq*, with secondarily accented and lengthened *u*, primarily accented but secondarily shortened *ii*, so that the "single" vowel actually sounds longer than the "double" one—which is impossible in Inuit. To pronounce any Eskimo language well, in addition to *q* and *r*, mastery of vowel and consonant length is essential.

Eskimo, like Latin or Russian, has inflectional endings, including cases for nouns, in dual as well as singular and plural number (all examples here are Central Alaskan Yupik):

1. *arnaq qavartuq*
   '(a) woman is sleeping'
2. *arnak qavartuk*
   '(two) women are sleeping'
3. *arnat qavartut*
   '(three or more) women are sleeping'

Case endings are crucial: with *nukalpiaq* 'young man,' *nanuaq* 'polar bear,' and the transitive verb *tuqutaa* 'A killed B,' the actor is marked by replacing the absolutive singular case ending *-q* with the relative singular *-m,* and the patient remains in the absolutive. The three words *nukalpiam nanuaq tuqutaa, nanuaq tuqutaa nukalpiam,* etc., in any order (as in Latin or Russian) mean 'man killed bear,' whereas *nukalpiaq nanuam tuqutaa,* in any order, mean 'bear killed man.' But the use of the cases is not only unlike English, but also unlike Latin or Russian, where the same ending is used for the subject of a transitive or an intransitive verb, while in Eskimo it is the object of the transitive verb that has the same ending as the subject of the intransitive:

4. *nanuaq qavartuq*
   'the polar bear is sleeping'
5. *nanuaq tuqutaa*
   '(he) killed the bear'

This trait puts Eskimo in the typological category of "ergative" languages.

What puts Eskimo-Aleut at a typological extreme, however, is that it can build very long words with suffixes (not compounding or prefixes), derivational as well as inflectional, added to a single base:

6. *qayarpaliyugciqarpetegkut*
   qayaq-pak-li-yug-ciq-ar-peteg-kut
   ' you (two) will want to make a big kayak for us (three or more)'

from the base *qayaq* 'kayak' with the derivational suffixes *-pak* 'big,' *-li* 'to make for', *-yug* 'to want,' *-ciq* 'will,' *-ar* 'transitive,' and inflectional endings *-peteg* 'you (dual) subject' with *-kut* 'us (plural) object,' would be a perfectly ordinary Yupik word, and such examples could be multiplied indefinitely in any Eskimo-Aleut language.

Michael Edward Krauss

BIBIOGRAPHY

Arctic Languages: An Awakening, Paris, 1990. Includes Lawrence D. Kaplan, "The Language of the Alaskan Inuit"; Edna Ahgeak MacLean, "Culture and Change for Inupiat and Yupiks of Alaska"; Knut Bergsland, "The Aleut Language of Alaska"; and Louis-Jacques Dorais, "The Canadian Inuit and Their Language," the last a particularly excellent survey.

Bergsland, Knut. "Comparative Eskimo-Aleut Phonology and Lexicon." *Journal de la Société Finno-ougrienne* 80 (1986):63–167. Basic on Eskimo-Aleut relationship.

Damas, David, ed., *Arctic* vol. 5 of *Handbook of North American Indians,* edited by William C. Sturtevant. Washington, D.C., 1984. The most important single book available on Eskimo-Aleut, with articles on each major group, and one on languages by Anthony Woodbury. Includes most basic references for further reading, to 1983.

Dorais, Louis-Jacques. *Inuit Uqausiqatigiit: Inuit Languages and Dialects.* Iqaluit, Ala., 1990. Survey of Eskimo and Aleut languages for the general reader, including bibliography.

Krauss, Michael. *Alaska Native Languages: Past, Present, and Future.* Fairbanks, Ala., 1980.

———. "Eskimo-Aleut." In *Current Trends in Linguistics,* edited by Thomas A. Sebeok. Vol. 10, *Linguistics in North America.* The Hague, 1973. Includes comprehensive bibliography especially for 1945–1972.

———., ed. *Yupik Eskimo Prosodic Systems: Descriptive and Comparative Studies.* Fairbanks, Ala., 1985. Includes articles by M. Krauss, J. Leer, S. Jacobson, O. Miyaoka, and L. Kaplan on Eskimo language relationships.

SEE ALSO **The First Americans** and **Literature, Native American**; the maps accompanying **The First Americans**.

LITERATURE

THE BRITISH COLONIES

THE LITERATURE OF the British colonial empire was written over a vast geographic area, from India and Malaysia to Australia and New Zealand. English North American colonial literature ranges from the literature of exploration, which dates from the late sixteenth century and includes accounts like Thomas Harriot's *A Brief and True Report . . . of Virginia* (1590) and Richard Hakluyt's collection of *Principal Navigations* (1598–1600), to the true "colonial" literature which emerged in the century and a half before the American Revolution. All literature composed in English in America during this period was heavily indebted to English models and authorial influences, but colonial writers developed themes and forms or genres unique to the American experience while remaining technically British colonial subjects. It is the purpose of this essay to review and to develop a strategy for understanding the literature of the original thirteen British colonies during the years from 1600 to 1783.

AN OVERVIEW OF COLONIAL LITERATURE

The colonies were all on the eastern seaboard of North America and were grouped into three regions. The most prominent was New England, which included Massachusetts Bay, Rhode Island, Connecticut, New Hampshire, and what is now Vermont and Maine. The Middle Atlantic colonies of New Jersey, Pennsylvania, and Delaware developed some indigenous regional characteristics, while New England's major rival for regional dominance in the colonial period was the South, those colonies from Maryland to Georgia. The New England and southern colonies dominated the literature produced from 1600 to 1783. Each of the three geographic regions developed qualities in its literature that are distinctive and identifiable as both colonial and regional; however, the voice of America during the colonial period was most clearly that of New England Puritanism.

The colonial and revolutionary poet Philip Freneau, who graduated from the College of New Jersey (now Princeton University), and his classmate Hugh Henry Brackenridge, author of *Modern Chivalry* (1792–1815), were both early American authors of the Middle Atlantic colonies who developed a literature unique to their region. Brackenridge and Freneau jointly authored a long epic poem, called "The Rising Glory of America," which they read at the graduation exercise in 1771. In it, the economic and political promise of the revolting colonies was celebrated in the language of biblical millennialism. The "language of Canaan" employed in this way clearly reflects the influence of New England Puritan theology and of the Calvinist teachings of Princeton; however, like Benjamin Franklin's *Autobiography* (1771–1789), "Rising Glory" offers only an echo of the doctrinally didactic literature of Puritanism, and it celebrates with prophetic enthusiasm mainly the secular promise of the yet unrealized new nation. Freneau's epic celebrates America's future without significant political teaching; rather, the poet suggests that the colonies are a recapitulation of the Garden of Eden or of a neoclassical paradise in which peace and harmony will characterize the life of all citizens.

Paradise anew
Shall flourish, by no second Adam lost,
No dangerous tree with deadly fruit shall grow,
No tempting serpent to allure the soul
From native innocence. . . . The lion and the lamb
In mutual friendship linked, shall browse the shrub,
And timorous deer with softened tigers stray
O'er mead, or lofty hill, or grassy plain

This obvious allusion to the Book of Isaiah and its prophecy of the Peaceable Kingdom is a good place to commence our excursion into colonial American writing, for although it comes at the end, rather than the beginning, of the colonial period, it was composed by an essentially secular, neoclassical, Middle Atlantic writer whose language reflected both the pastoral vision of his neighbors to the South and the biblical prophetic phrasing of the New England Puritans to the North. Thus, "The Rising Glory of America" is a synthetic work, like the later epic poems of Joel Barlow, one of the Connecticut Wits. In 1787 Barlow published the first of his poems, "The Vision of Columbus," an epic that appropriates the themes if not the language of Philip Freneau.

If the regional characteristics of colonial literature may be roughly summarized as southern, Middle Atlantic, and New England, it is also important to approach the material from the perspective of genre, because writers employ those genres most appropriate to the literary and cultural needs of their historical period. For example, the colonial period in America witnessed the production of hundreds of travel diaries, long letters mailed to those who had not crossed the Atlantic, and more formal documents, such as promotional literature, histories, and writings on discovery, exploration, and settlement. In New England, the histories took the form of extensions of biblical history, such as Cotton Mather's *Magnalia Christi Americana* (1702), or The Great Works of Christ in America. Genres peculiar to a particular region and time also developed. These include the Indian captivity narratives, accounts written by captives of the Native Americans.

Political literature was another genre that characterized this period, as English colonists in all three regions debated the merits of remaining British subjects or forming a new nation. In New England especially, sermon literature developed as a significant genre, and many of the most prominent theses and ideas of English settlement are carried in the religious histories of New England and in the sermons preached during the seventeenth and eighteenth centuries. The sermons of New England were numerous, and they were generally published more regularly than those delivered in the southern colonies. In Massachusetts Bay colony, for example, the Mather dynasty of ministers controlled the printing of literature in Boston (though dissident authors were often published elsewhere).

Once again, regional qualities become important in assessing these divisions. The denominations of southern churches varied by colony, from predominantly Anglican in Virginia to early Methodist and Baptist in the Carolinas and Georgia. In contrast, New England was settled by Puritans, a dissident group who sought to purify the Anglican liturgy; the hegemonic voice of the New England writers from the 1600s to 1750 can largely be ascribed to the powerful influence of Puritanism. The genres of New England writing—histories, diaries, journals, autobiographies, poetry, inspirational and instructional writing, biography, and captivity narratives—all reflect a unity of voice and theme that gives this literature a much more prominent place in our reconstruction of the literary past than is given to the voices of the Middle Atlantic colonies or the South.

All regions produced promotional writing, literature designed to attract converts to the settlement cause and to lure additional people from the Old World to the New. The need was often urgent. In Plymouth colony, the subject of William Bradford's *Of Plimouth Plantation* (1630–

1651), the Separatists who crossed on the *Mayflower* numbered only 103; by April 1621, after the colonists had spent the first desperate winter on board the ship in Plymouth harbor, there were only about sixty souls remaining.

All colonies produced historical accounts, not only to promote settlement but also to justify their enterprise in the larger context of God's divine plan for the New World. Early historical writings thus have the quality of myth about them, and they are often unreliable as history because the authors deliberately intervene in the texts to universalize their moment in history, to give their experience a larger, more significant context. The very titles of some of these historical accounts suggest this tendency, such as *The Wonder-Working Providence of Sion's Saviour in New England. Wonder-Working Providence* (1654) is a blatant example, but many of the early colonial accounts carried the providential emphasis, especially in New England. A partial list of titles includes *Leah and Rachel* (1656) by Joseph Hammond; *A Character of the Province of Maryland* (1666) by George Alsop; *New England's Rarities* (1672) by John Joselyn; *A Further Account of the Province of Pennsylvania* (1685) by William Penn; *A New Voyage to Carolina* (1709) by John Lawson; and the historical writings of Captain John Smith. Smith is the most prominent Virginia writer of the colonial period, though he is rivaled by Robert Beverley, whose *The History and Present State of Virginia* (1705) provides a retrospective account of the Virginia colony just as Cotton Mather had traced the history of New England in his *Magnalia Christi Americana*. William Byrd II's *A History of the Dividing Line Betwixt Virginia and North Carolina, Run in the Year of Our Lord 1728* (1728) gives much information about the early settlement of North Carolina and Virginia, while Patrick Tailfer delivered a satirical attack on James Oglethorpe, the founding settler of Georgia, in his *A True and Historical Narrative of the Colony of Georgia* (1741).

This type of historical writing continued throughout the eighteenth century, though the emphasis was less on settlement, discovery, and exploration and more on the character of the community that had developed under the guidance of God. Thomas Prince published *A Chronological History of New England in the Form of Annuals*, commencing in 1726, to counter the heavily religious emphasis of such histories as Bradford's *Of Plimouth Plantation*, Johnson's *Wonder-Working Providence,* and Mather's *Magnalia*. Some specialized historical works were attempted, such as Cadwallader Colden's *History of the Five Indian Nations* (1727). Clearly, the colonial British settlers were engaged in an exhaustive process of self-definition.

REGIONAL CHARACTERISTICS IN LITERATURE

It is important to realize that the culture of the New World was regional and that the settlements that developed along the east coast of America reflected differing responses to the New World experience. The "melting pot" ideal was most fully realized in the so-called middle colonies— New York, New Jersey, Pennsylvania, and Delaware. Pennsylvania was originally established under the leadership of the Quaker William Penn, who authored *Letter to the Free Society of Traders* (1683), which became a propaganda piece for his new colony. This treatise was a first edition, so to speak, of a much longer document, *An Historical and Geographical Account . . . Of Pensilvania and of West New-Jersey* (1698), which was written by a Quaker named Gabriel Thomas. These long "reports" were actually a blend of history and anthropology and served as promotional brochures for those in England who anticipated emigration. Thomas Hutchinson's *History of the Colony of Massachusetts Bay* (1764–1828) provided a lengthy documentary history of that colony, and John Woolman, a New Jersey Quaker, was a voice in the middle colonies that sounded very close to the spiritual autobiographers of the New England settlements.

The middle colonies turned early to science, partly because Benjamin Franklin, the most prominent writer to emerge from this region, was so fervently interested in science and had founded not only the College of Philadelphia but also the American Philosophical Society in Philadelphia, an organization modeled on the Royal Society of London. Thus, writers like Lewis Evans, who was originally a Philadelphia cartographer, wrote an encyclopedic work called *Geographical, Historical, Philosophical, and Mechanical Essays* (1755–1756), something of a comprehensive treatment of the learning of the time. But the middle colonies were themselves an encyclopedia of culture. "Few areas of the earth embraced such a conglomerate population," Frederick B. Tolles observes in "Writers of the Middle Colonies."

There were Dutch patroons on the Hudson; Anglican, Jewish, Huguenot, and Dutch Calvinist merchants in New York; English Quakers and transplanted New England Puritans on Long Island and in New Jersey; English and Welsh Quaker merchants and farmers in Philadelphia and the surrounding counties; industrious German sectarians farming the fertile hinterland of Philadelphia; hardy Scots-Irish Presbyterians on the frontiers; descendants of Swedish and Finnish traders along Delaware Bay; Negro servants and slaves; Iroquois, Delaware, and Susquehanna Indians. This mixed people, restless and inquiring, was always on the move; by the middle of the eighteenth century it could no longer be contained by the region drained by the Hudson and the Delaware and had begun to spill over into the watershed of the Susquehanna, where it entered the arena of Anglo-French imperial conflict. Here were the people from whom, as [Hector St. Jean de] Crèvecoeur was to write, "that race now called Americans have arisen." (Robert Spiller, et al., eds. *The Literary History of the United States,* pp. 83–84)

This melting pot phenomenon was also partially realized in the southern colonies, perhaps the most distinctive literary and cultural region in America. Southerners have always been self-conscious writers, and from the very beginning they have articulated a vision of their region that has been endowed with mythic, neoclassical qualities and an abundance of local color. The South has been viewed as a type of paradise, not only in metaphorical terms, which was often the view advanced in the New England histories, but as a real arena of fulfillment and pleasure. Alexander Whitaker wrote *Good News from Virginia* (1613) as a promotional document long before John Smith developed his *The Generall Historie of Virginia, New-England, and the Summer Isles* (1624), which included a history of New England. In 1656 John Hammond wrote a promotional tract entitled *Leah and Rachel, or, the Two Fruitful Sisters, Virginia and Maryland: Their Present Condition, Impartially Stated and Related.* This pamphlet is typical of the many promotional tracts produced by southerners during the

seventeenth and eighteenth centuries, in which the Chesapeake region is described as a land of milk and honey. Hammond praised the region as "plentiful, pleasant and profitable . . . pleasant in the brightness of the weather, pleasant in their building, pleasant in observing their stocks and flocks of cattle, hogs, and poultry, grazing, whisking, and skipping in their sights, pleasant in having all things of their own, growing or breeding without drawing the penny to send for this and that, without which, in England, they cannot be supplied." This utopian paradise, this pastoral Eden, quickly became a metaphor for the entire colonial enterprise, but the southern writers were responsible for these early images of an Edenic paradise on the "American Strand."

The most prominent example of this type of writing was Robert Beverley's *History and Present State of Virginia . . . by a Native of the Place* (1705). Unlike Hammond, Beverley engaged in political debate and attacked the system of royal governors that ruled the colonies. William Byrd's *History of the Dividing Line* is a social history of the region, containing some unflattering portraits of southern characters. Another unflattering picture of southern living was rendered in verse by Ebenezer Cook in *The Sot-Weed Factor* (1728). Based upon Cook's experience as a visitor to Maryland, this amusing narrative satirized American manners and customs, presented the South in very modern terms, and created the antithesis of the image New England was fostering of itself: "May wrath divine then lay those regions waste / Where no man's faithful nor a woman chaste."

The colony of Georgia was first settled by James Oglethorpe. A group of his dissatisfied followers—Patrick Tailfer, Hugh Anderson, David Dougles, and others—wrote a scathing and skillful satire called *A True and Historical Narrative of the Colony of Georgia* (1741), which satirized the settlement and the entire colonial enterprise. Because Tailfer, Anderson, Dougles, and their accomplices were also politically motivated, their satire was more scathing than that in Ebenezer Cook's poem; they attacked Oglethorpe for his denunciations of slavery and of the rum trade.

These authors were perhaps the earliest in a long tradition of southern letters to establish hyperbolic anecdote as an "historical" methodology. The "tall tale" is a peculiarly southern phenomenon, a regional characteristic that spread widely throughout the colonies but is originally associated with the southern tradition of oral storytelling. The important quality that emerges from southern writing during the colonial period is a strong, well-defined sense of region. This sense of place was later crystallized not only in the cultural and economic isolation the South suffered during the Civil War but in the self-consciousness its authors have always shared about their "peculiar" region of the United States.

Regionalism is exceptionally strong in the South because it is the one part of colonial America where the melting pot ideology of Crèvecoeur did not easily obtain. In a region that was "Cavalier" rather than "Yankee" by cultural orientation, the southern system of plantation agriculture, with its incessant and eternal demands for inexpensive labor sources, gave wealthy planters an enviable life-style from a material perspective; however, it also led the South to become the center of the one burning issue against which the rest of the nation rose in opposition in the first half-century after independence: the importation and subjugation of African slaves. The South was not the only region engaged in slavery. New England was more industrial and less agricultural than the agrarian South, which needed slave labor to harvest the tobacco and rice crops that had become a staple of the plantation economy. However, wealthy merchants in New England also held slaves for domestic purposes; the Reverend Jonathan Edwards of Northampton, the leading minister of the Great Awakening, had a household servant who was a purchased slave. And Phyllis Wheatley of Boston, a domestic slave who was tutored and educated by her owners, became one of the leading poets of the colonial period.

The literature of the New England region dominated the seventeenth and eighteenth centuries, not only because of the quantity of writings produced but also because the Puritan vision of the New World extended biblical mandates for God's "New English Israel," an "errand into the wilderness" that was a divinely sanctioned human achievement. Thus the writers of New England during the colonial period reflected a worldview that was at once hegemonic and diverse, encouraging a tradition of dissent from the established authorities of church and state that ran from Roger Williams's *A Key into the Language of America* (1643), a work that engages the Narragansett Indian culture fully, to revolutionary-era documents like the Declaration of Independence. Despite its seeming monolithic voice, raised always in the service of God, the colonial writings of New England contain many dissenting opinions. The founding of Connecticut by Thomas Hooker in 1639 was the direct result of a dispute between Hooker and the Massachusetts Bay colony authorities. Roger Williams in 1636 and Anne Hutchinson and others implicated in the Antinomian Controversy of 1636–1638 make clear that the hegemonic authority of the New England colonies was often checked by radical dissenters (which the Puritan settlers themselves had been when they revolted against the Church of England and fled to Holland or the New World for asylum).

The English vision of the New World is represented in the various literary genres the colonial writers left behind: histories, political tracts, almanacs, magazines, poetry, naturalistic accounts of New World discovery, travel narratives, promotional documents, diaries and journals, popular literature, such as Ben Franklin's *Poor Richard's Almanack,* and the flourishing newspapers, like the *Pennsylvania Gazette* or Isaiah Thomas's *Massachusetts Spy.*

Writers in New England were particularly fond of historical and biographical accounts, which helped them to define their mission in the New World and to understand their experience in the larger context of God's providential plan for the redemption of the world, in which they saw themselves as having a specific role. Just as historical writings gave meaning to a community, the biographies and autobiographies produced in New England gave meaning to the lives of individual saints. One particular variant of the historical narrative and spiritual autobiography peculiar to New England was the Puritan captivity narrative, inappropriately named the Indian captivity narrative. The narratives were a kind of autobiographical spiritual literature in which the subject described the experience of being held captive by the Indians in a narrative that always took the form of a journey away from the community of Christian saints, through a type of "dark night of the soul" in the tortuous migration to Canada or into the Indian wilderness, from which the subject would be "redeemed" by God's providential agency.

EARLY AMERICAN HISTORIES

Even though the earliest English settlement was the Jamestown colony (1607), the historical literature of Virginia was overshadowed by the writings produced by the Puritans of New England. Captain John Smith's *Generall Historie* written in 1624 furnishes an example of historical literature in Virginia, and it treated the historical events of the early settlements in episodic fashion, covering not only the New England region but also the southern colonies, especially Virginia.

The story of the Puritans' emigration from Leiden, Holland, in 1619, journey through Southampton and Plymouth, England, and settlement in what is now Provincetown on Cape Cod in December 1620 was told by the colony's governor, William Bradford. Bradford's chronological narrative *Of Plimouth Plantation* was begun in 1630 and added onto until 1650, with the narrative strategy shifting in later years to "annals," or accounts of events told by each year. Occasionally, Bradford shifts the focus to the lives of eminent leaders, such as the Elder William Brewster, whose life story occupies "Annal 1643." Thus the Bradford history, like many histories that would follow, obeys the doctrine of Emerson that "there is properly no history, only biography." (Bradford's history remained in manuscript and was stored in a chest in the Old South Church in Boston. The British carried the chest with them on their removal from Boston in 1777, depositing it in London, where the manuscript remained until the late nineteenth century, when the British returned it to America in a grand ceremony at the Parker House Hotel in Boston. Thereafter, the manuscript was edited several times for publication; the most authoritative edition was edited by Samuel Eliot Morison of Harvard and published in 1962.)

It is important to understand that for the Puritan settlers, recording history was a way of emphasizing God's divine providential intervention in human affairs, just as writing biography and autobiography was seen as a way of reinforcing their belief that God was guiding individual human experience. Indeed, the conflation of these genres is a feature of many early historical accounts, and the modern reader must keep in mind the Puritan writer's view of personal experience as divine drama.

Cotton Mather's conviction that history should be the biography of saints derived from a commonly shared belief that scriptural history itself worked in this manner and that the Bible was a compilation of achievements among God's chosen people, so that their story was best told through biographical and autobiographical narratives. The *Magnalia Christi Americana,* his long ecclesiatical history of New England, contains the history of Harvard College and the biographies of more than sixty men who led the settlers in New England from the time colonization began. For Mather, the models of Scripture and of classical literature sufficiently justified the method of composing contemporary biography and history. In the pagan writers of Greece and Rome, he found analogies to the providentially guided writers of biblical history.

In the *Magnalia* itself, Mather clearly stated the relationship between classical and Christian models, particularly in *Pietas in Patriam, The Life of His Excellency Sir William Phips* (1697), first published separately but reprinted in the *Magnalia.* Mather wrote: "So *obscure* was the *original* of that memorable person, whose *actions* I am going to relate, that I must, in a way of writing, like that of *Plutarch,* prepare my reader for the intended relation, by first searching the *archives* of antiquity for a *parallel.*" Those archives of antiquity included the Old Testament, Greek and Roman mythology, and ancient and classical history. Mather's work was extensive; he wrote more than 444 printed volumes. But he spoke for all Puritan writers when he showed how the genres were inextricably bound to each other through the shared Christian doctrines they expressed. All narratives, poetry or prose, were a means of understanding the Divine will acted out in human time, and historical writing was thus filled with various literary genres, exemplary accounts of eminent lives which would thus become sources for comprehending God's teleological plan for New England.

Not only did the Puritan writers regard the history of New England to be evidence of God's continuing Providence as leader of His New English Chosen; they also attempted to use parallels to the Scriptures metaphorically to establish specific correspondences between Old Israel and New England. It was the calling or duty of the Puritan saint to establish a life and a society of lives that could advance the eternal struggle between the good and evil forces that governed the universe; if parallels between contemporary events and ancient and biblical narratives could be identified, it could also be asserted that New England was moving toward the Second Coming and the Millennium. In this context, the settlement of the New World, and New England in particular, was perceived as an historical episode within the larger framework of the "History of the Work of Redemption" as Jonathan Edwards would title his 1774 masterpiece. The Puritan writer's foremost objective was to show that New England was under the continuous guidance of Providence, and the purpose of the parallels with pagan figures or the analogies between contemporary leaders and Old Testament leaders (both William Bradford and John Winthrop were called Moses in their life-accounts in Mather's *Magnalia*) was primarily illustrative. Cotton Mather, for example, did not believe Greek or Roman history to be guided by Providence, from which both Old Israel and New England had received direction. Mather's adaptation of Plutarch's reading of history to rely on biographical accounts of the lives of eminent individuals and special events was, moreover, not unique, but a sense of biographical composition as being important to historical redemption gave the life-writers of seventeenth-century New England a specific role in shaping the inspired accounts of God's revealed historical purpose.

THE INDIAN CAPTIVITY NARRATIVES

The sermon literature of New England may have been the most widely disseminated and quantifiable documents produced, but the Indian captivity narratives were the most popular form of writing and many of the stories they tell were circulated well into the nineteenth century. The presence of Native Americans on the continent of North America was a continuing problem for the English settlers, and the highly romanticized tableau of the Plymouth pilgrims sitting down with their Indian neighbors at the first Thanksgiving in 1621 does not adequately represent the relationship between English and Native American contestants for dominance in the New World. Hostility and brutality were present on both sides. The captivity narratives contain numerous accounts of torture and slaughter by Indians; on the other hand, Captain John Mason led a band of Puritans on a mission against the Pequot tribe at Mystic, Connecticut, in 1636 that resulted in the slaughter of the entire tribe.

The most valuable collection of captivity narratives has been assembled by Alden T. Vaughan and Edward W. Clark in their volume, *Puritans Among the Indians: Accounts of Captivity and Redemption, 1676–1724*. This edition contains *A Narrative of the Captivity, Sufferings, and Removes of Mrs. Mary Rowlandson* (1682) and the story of the Deerfield Massacre, in which the entire town of Deerfield, Massachusetts, was killed or captured by Indians in the winter of 1704 and the surviving population transported to Canada, where they were imperiled by the assaults of the "savages" who had conquered them and also indoctrinated by the French Catholics. *The Redeemed Captive Returning Unto Zion*, an account of this massacre and captivity published in 1707, tells the dramatic story of John Williams, minister at Deerfield, and his family history. Williams's narrative does not, however, contain the full story of Eunice Williams, his daughter, who was eight years old at the time of the captivity and who became fully assimilated into the Indian tribe, eventually marrying an Indian and refusing to return to Deerfield. Eunice Williams was not fully understood until the twentieth century, when modern social historians and anthropologists reconstructed her story.

The demonic "other" in the Indian captivity narratives is the barbarous Indian group, those descendants of Satan who bore the mark of Cain or made the journey to the New World across the polar ice cap as descendants of the ten lost tribes of Israel. Mythmaking intended to define and isolate the Indians from Christian culture was common among the captivity narrators and among early New England historians, as the example of Increase Mather clearly shows. The task of these writers was to make sense of their suffering in the New World by arguing that the experience was part of a larger, divine drama, teleological and even eschatological, out of which would emerge a Brave New World of Christian redemption precisely because these beleaguered captives had held firm to the cause of God in the face of immense physical and psychological adversity. The emphasis on Puritan tribalism, noted by scholars like Alden Vaughan and Cecelia Tichi, is enhanced by the separation of the "other," particularly a "demonic other," a distinct group differentiated by culture, race, ethnicity, religion, and origin. In the late eighteenth through the antebellum nineteenth century, the assigning of "otherness" to the Indians was bolstered by arguments over the monogenetic and polygenetic theories of human evolution. These arguments were indiscriminately applied to African Americans and Indians in attempts to justify slavery and to preserve white ethnic hegemony.

Mary Rowlandson, in her account of her captivity following an Indian massacre in Deerfield, Massachusetts, in 1704, associates blackness and darkness with images of hell and night, all connected with Indian behavior. The narrative is rendered even more poignant because it describes in the first person a mother losing her family, especially her children, to the cruelty of barbarians who thwart the divine design of the Christian God.

Oh, the doleful sight that now was to behold this house. Of thirty-seven persons who were in this one house, none escaped either present death or a bitter captivity save only one. . . . There were twelve killed, some shot, some stabbed with their spears, some knocked down with their hatchets. . . . There was one child who was chopped into the head with a hatchet and stripped naked, and yet was crawling up and down. It is a solemn sight to see so many Christians lying in their blood, some here and some there, like a company of sheep torn by wolves, all of them stripped naked by a company of hell hounds, roaring, singing, ranting, and insulting, as if they would have torn our very hearts out. . . . Oh, the roaring and singing and dancing and yelling of *those black creatures in the night, which made the place a lively resemblance of hell.* Yet the Lord by his almighty power preserved a number of us from death, for there were twenty-four of us taken alive and carried captive. (Quoted in George Perkins, ed., *The American Tradition in Literature* [New York, 1985], p. 63)

Like the Holocaust narrators of the twentieth century, Rowlandson adds the purposeful intent of her chronologically arranged story: "And that I may the better *declare* what happened to me during that grievous captivity, I shall particularly *speak* of the several removes we had up and down the wilderness." It is interesting to note that the slave narratives of the nineteenth century will reverse and invert the association of demonic otherness found in the Indian captivity narratives, portraying hypocritical Christian masters as the demons.

The original thirteen colonies were not, of course, the first settlements in the New World; Spain had sent explorers to the Southwest, and French explorers would advance into Canada and into the western and southern territories and would rival the English claims to sovereignty over these Native American lands. But the original thirteen English colonies, all established along the east coast of North America, were populated by settlers who brought with them a cultural legacy in language and literature that became dominant in the settled land. "Native Americans," of course, were "Christianized or exterminated," as Roy Harvey Pearce has pointed out. Leading colonial thinkers debated how best to control the Native populations— through force or religion. These alternatives are reflected in such documents as Increase Mather's *A Relation of the Troubles Which Have Hapn'd in New England, by Reason of the Indians There* (1677). The title gives away the author's bias. John Eliot, the "apostle to the Indians," translated the entire Old and New Testaments into an Algonquian language and acted as a missionary to the Indians, but he was unusual in a culture that sought conquest rather than assimilation. More typical was Increase Mather's *A Briefe History of the Warr With the Indians in New England,* published in Boston in 1676, which includes the story of the loyal Uncas; it also contains a full account of the Pequot Massacre at Mystic in 1636, where the tribe for whom Melville would later name his doomed whaling ship were trapped inside their fort by a small army of English settlers:

The Indians some were slain, some fled, others crept under their beds, where they slept their last; the Captain going out of the Wigwams met with many of them and put them to the sword; in which time of flight several English were wounded. Captain [John] Mason perceiving his Men wounded, and the Enemy

64

not yet routed, saw Cause himself to go into a Wigwam, and fetch out a Firebrand, and putting it in one of the Mats with which the Wigwams were covered; commanded one of his Souldiers to throw some powder upon it, which set the Mat on fire, which the Wind taking, it was quickly thoroughly kindled, which made the Indians run as Men most dreadfully amazed. And indeed such a dreadful Terror did the Almighty let fall upon their spirits, that they would fly from the Sword, and cast themselves into the very Flames, where many of them perished. . . . And here we may take notice of God's Judgment upon this bloody Generation, in sending the Night before the Assault an hundred and fifty Men from their [the Pequot's] other fort to join with this Fort, who were designing, as some of themselves have related, to go forth against the English at that very instant when this Stroke came upon them, where the most of them perished with their fellows, so that the Mischief they intended against us came upon themselves; they were taken in their own snare and we through the Mercy of God escaped. . . . Thus was God seen in the Mount, crushing his proud Enemies, and the Enemies of his People, so that they who were ere while a Terror to all that were round about them, who resolved to destroy all the English and root their very Name out of this Country, were by weak Meanes thus vanquished and destroyed, and the Mischief they plotted, and the Violence they offered, and brought on their own Heads in a Moment; for the Lord burnt them up in the Fire of His Wrath, and dunged the Ground with their Flesh, it was the Lords doing, and it was marvelous in our Eyes. (*A Briefe History,* pp. 136–143)

It is hardly any wonder that the literature or culture of the North American Indians was rarely assimilated by the English colonists.

BIOGRAPHY AND AUTOBIOGRAPHY

The Puritan sense of divine purpose permeates all genres of New England colonial literature. History, biography, captivity narratives, and personal narratives are all controlled by the dominant ideology, and all reflect its powerful, didactic intent. The rhetorical strategies of each genre are governed by the author's sense of belonging to a much larger, more universally significant cause, rather than reflecting the mere recording of personal experience. This cultural emphasis is nowhere more prominently seen than in the composition of biography and autobiography, the process of "life-writing" that allowed the New England writers to link their personal narratives to the history of the community and region.

The genres of biography and autobiography during the colonial period were less concerned with fidelity to factual truth and accuracy of detail than with establishing an account in the biblical, spiritual tradition. Although some life-writing was produced in the southern colonies, and while the *Secret Diary of William Byrd of Westover, 1709–1712,* written by a prominent Virginia planter, is representative of autobiography in early America, the overwhelming literary output of New Englanders in this genre, as in others, during the seventeenth and eighteenth centuries must form the core of any discussion of literary production during this period. Some European travelers, such as William Bartram, wrote accounts of their experiences in North America. But for the Puritans, particularly the life-writers, the experiences of eminent figures became the most prominent means of articulating New England's place in providential history.

This didactic approach to the recording of a life quickly found a place in Puritan New England, so that life-writing became the examination of a saint's life. Formulaically, these accounts tended to emphasize the process of conversion at an early age. The earliest examples of this process, as we know from Patricia Caldwell's study, are the autobiographical confessions of faith given by Massachusetts colonists during the settlement's first decades as a qualification for church membership and transcribed by such pastors as Thomas Shepard and Michael Wigglesworth. The sanctified life and good works described in the later portions of confessional narratives had a clear foundation in the spiritual experience of conversion and personal transformation. These formulas govern Increase Mather's biography of his father, *The Life and Death of That Reverend Man of God, Mr. Richard Mather* (1670), honoring the man who was the founder of the Mather dynasty and a patriarch of the Massachusetts Bay colony.

The habit of mind that led Increase Mather to compose his own *Autobiography* (first published in 1966) is represented in a statement of purpose articulated by Cotton Mather, a doctrinal statement that speaks volumes about the intention of each colonial life-writer: "I know not how the *Pen* of an *Historian* can better be Employ'd than in *Reporting* the *Vertuous* tempers and Actions of Men that have therein *shown forth the Vertues of our Blessed Redeemer,* and been the *Epis-*

tles of Christ unto the Rest of Mankind" (*Parentator*, 1724). As I have shown earlier in this essay, this basic principle of the "saint's life" as an imitation of the life of Christ governed the uniformly crafted sixty-odd biographies that appear in Cotton Mather's *Magnalia Christi Americana*. However, the *Apologia* of the merchant Robert Keayne (1653), who was arraigned before the General Court for charging excessive interest rates, is a secular version of a spiritual confession that does not conform to the divine paradigm.

This spiritual and cultural unity was the result of Puritan tribalism, as reflected in the works of the "Lord's Remembrancers," those historians and biographers who saw in the lives of New England's spiritual leaders parallels to biblical leaders. Similarly, the colonial historians paralleled early New England biographers by comparing the experiences of the colonists to those of Christian wayfarers journeying from the earthly city of Babylon to the eternal and holy city upon a hill, Jerusalem. This metaphor was used extensively, but never more effectively than in the "Model of Christian Charity," a sermon preached on board the flagship *Arbella* by Governor John Winthrop of the Massachusetts Bay colony as the group awaited departure from England:

For we must consider that we shall be as a city upon a hill. The eyes of all people are upon us, so that if we shall deal falsely with our God in this work we have undertaken, and so cause Him to withdraw His present help from us, we shall be made a story and a by-word through the world. We shall open the mouths of enemies to speak evil of the ways of God, and all professors for God's sake. (Quoted in Miller, *The American Puritans*, p. 83)

Winthrop's vision is derived from the concept of the biblical covenant by which God will reward his faithful servants with success as long as fidelity to the principles of God's eternal law is maintained. Conversely, punishment awaits those sinners who digress from the straight and narrow path to heaven, as the linear model of Puritan history was represented: "We shall shame the faces of many of God's worthy servants, and cause their prayers to be turned into curses upon us 'til we be consumed out of the good land whither we are agoing." The fate of those sinners who are found wanting at the time

of the Last Judgment is described in Michael Wigglesworth's "The Day of Doom" (1662), a long, narrative poem in doggerel verses of eight lines per stanza. This was so pervasive and popular a concept in seventeenth-century New England that no extant copies of the first edition of Wigglesworth's poem survived: they were all read to death and even used as sermons from the pulpit on occasion.

In colonial New England, history and biography are best represented by Cotton Mather's *Magnalia*. The autobiography is well represented by Benjamin Franklin in his *Autobiography*, composed in sections in France and in America between 1771 and 1790 but not published until 1791, when it was first printed in French. Though Franklin's work is one of the best-known autobiographical studies produced by an American, it is incomplete; the narrative concludes in 1759, even though Franklin lived until 1790. Franklin, whose image and life were popularized by the wide circulation of his *Autobiography*, came to represent the American economic dream realized and actualized. Cotton Mather immortalized the "saints' lives" of seventeenth-century Puritan leaders; Franklin explored the question posed by Crèvecoeur's "What is the American, this new man?" in graphic detail, showing how the secular version of the American Dream would eventually replace the religious motivation for the "errand into the wilderness." As autobiographical writers, Franklin and revivalist Jonathan Edwards, author of *Personal Narrative of Conversion* (ca. 1740), represent two diametrically opposed "theologies" for colonial America, the one rationalist and secular and the other pietistic. Franklin was able to rise from rags to riches in the New World during his lifetime. Not only was he wealthy at a relatively early age, but he became one of the most significant figures in the era of the American Revolution—a signer of the Declaration of Independence, a framer of the Constitution, and a negotiator of the Treaty of Paris (by which the Revolutionary War was officially ended in 1783).

Franklin was a skilled writer as well. The *Autobiography* is his most significant contribution to the development of American literature and is one of the most widely circulated American works ever printed. The reader of the *Autobiography* must, however, distinguish between the real events of Franklin's life and the image of Franklin that appears in that text. The *Autobiography* carries the reader only to Franklin at the age of fifty-three, though he lived to be eighty-four. Yet the image of Franklin as perpetuated by the *Autobiography* is immortal. In a scant fifty-odd years, the *Autobiography*'s subject moves from youthful apprenticeship to great wealth and prominence in public life. The image developed in the narrative creates a formula for earthly success, a plan by which a person may realize the secular American Dream and enjoy its benefits while still on this earth. This image is as important as Franklin's life itself, for the *Autobiography* was translated from the French and English originals into many languages during the nineteenth century. The account gave the entire world some idea of the type of new nation that was evolving under a highly experimental government, referred to as "Democracy in America" (1835) by Alexis de Tocqueville, a Frenchman who visited the United States in its infancy. As commissioner to France for the new nation, Franklin established himself as a representative American and was known as being shrewd, politically tough, and extremely clever.

Franklin's own life story and satirical style, as exemplified by "The Speech of Polly Baker" and "The Way to Wealth" were ideal materials for Parson Mason Locke Weems's mythologizing of the American hero. Together, both accounts of Franklin give the world a vision that wonderfully represents his own approach to the writing of literature; speaking through an invented persona to an audience that is receptive to the process of image making more than it is concerned about fidelity to truth and accuracy of portraiture. For example, in "The Way to Wealth," the narrator, Richard Saunders, comes upon a group gathered in a public marketplace where an elderly man, Father Abraham, is "preaching" a sermon that develops a strategy for monetary success. The quoted maxims that make up the text for the sermon are taken primarily from Franklin's most successful journalism, *Poor Richard's Almanack*, which became the source of his fortune as a publisher and a writer.

Franklin's *Autobiography* consists of four parts. Part 1 commences, like many Puritan autobiographies, with "Dear Son," an address to posterity, as though Franklin were writing to a young man who, in moving from adolescence to adulthood, could benefit from the wisdom of his parent. These words were addressed to William Franklin, Franklin's illegitimate son, then forty-two years old and the governor of New Jersey. Part 1 moves forward in a conventional, autobiographical style that idealizes the subject and that was borrowed from the Puritan autobiographers, Franklin's literary antecedents. It discusses generations past, with fathers instructing sons concerning their ancestors and with each succeeding generation enjoying a more successful life than the preceding one.

In part 2, Franklin shifts away from the persona of a parent instructing a child and expands his audience to include all his followers who wish to learn how to become virtuous, industrious, and successful. He lists thirteen "virtues" and includes a chart by which he measures his personal habits, a programmed approach to personal living that has been adapted by self-improvement advisers. This section of the narrative is the best known and the most often quoted.

Parts 3 and 4, written just before his death, describe how the author's moral behavior led not only to worldly success but also to a role as a public figure. Franklin's significant public achievements of the late eighteenth century, such as his important role in the Continental Congress and his ambassadorship in Paris, are not recorded in the *Autobiography*. However, that Franklin turned his own personal success into a contribution to the public good is clear. The persona of the adult Benjamin Franklin is less judgmental and self-righteous than that of the youthful figure who during his lunch breaks drank only water and read by himself while his peers indulged themselves with stronger refreshment and lengthy, trifling conversation.

Significantly, many of Franklin's themes were inherited from the Puritans who preceded and surrounded him. His *Autobiography* was written in a form developed by Puritan authors of spiritual autobiographies. Franklin adapted the form to a secular purpose and used as his "text" the wisdom of the ancients and the practical wisdom of his own *Poor Richard's Almanack*, which is often cited in the *Autobiography*. The work ethic Franklin developed so fully in his *Autobiography* was an extension of the earlier Protestant/Puritan work ethic of European and English origins, which held that the most visible sign of sanctification and of being chosen by God is worldly success. (A sad corollary of this ethic placed the impoverished in league with the Devil.) Even his "Dogood Papers" (1722) were echoes of Cotton Mather's *Bonifacius: An Essay upon the Good* (1710). If Franklin's rhetorical style commonly resembles that of the English essayists Joseph Addison and Richard Steele and the satirist Jonathan Swift, his content is typically the legacy of English and American Puritanism. All the essential elements of spiritual autobiography are there: the first-person account of a deliverance from earthly peril by divine Providence; the journey motif, suggesting a linear migration governed by God, who moves the action forward toward a predetermined end, and the essential, innate depravity of humanity, except for those saintly few who, like Franklin and his contemporary Jonathan Edwards, are especially designated to carry forward the course of divine history.

Jonathan Edwards's *Personal Narrative* (ca. 1740–1745) is a superb example of colonial life-writing, as are the Indian captivity narratives of Mary Rowlandson and John Williams. Another variation of the autobiographical formula is found in the Puritan conversion narratives, such as the *Diary* of Cotton Mather and the *Autobiography* of Increase Mather. Quaker narratives were also prominent in colonial America. The *Journal of John Woolman* (1774) traces the author's struggle with his conscience over the matter of writing an indenture for the sale of a Negro slave, while his *Some Considerations on the Keeping of Negroes* (1754) is an early example of the type of discourse over slavery that would later characterize the slavery debates of the nineteenth century.

Another Quaker narrative is that of Elizabeth Ashbridge, entitled *Some Account of the Fore-Part of the Life of Elizabeth Ashbridge* (1774). Elizabeth Ashbridge's voice is that of an abused wife, and her conditions are quite specific and very modern, because she wrote as one lost in the turmoil of the political debates that followed the military events of 1776–1783. Ashbridge provides an illuminating portrait of a remarkable woman whose spiritual and marital struggles reflect the religious imperatives and gender roles of colonial American culture. Born in England,

she eloped at fourteen and was soon widowed, then immigrated to America as an indentured servant. She eventually purchased her freedom and married a man named Sullivan who, she claims, "fell in love with me for my dancing." But it was her conversion to Quakerism that led to the severe marital conflict that occupies most of her narrative: "Before he reached me, he heard I was turned Quaker; at which he stamped, and said, 'I had rather have heard she was dead, well as I love her, for, if it be so, all my comfort is gone.' He then came to me; it was after an absence of four months; . . . he flew into a great rage, exclaiming, 'The devil thee, thee, thee, don't *thee* me!'" Ashbridge was assaulted and beaten regularly by her demonic husband, for whom she continues to express a dutiful obedience, except in matters of religious conscience:

Finding that all the means he had yet used could not alter my resolutions, he several times struck me with severe blows. I endeavored to bear all with patience, believing that time would come when he would see I was in the right. . . . Once, he came up to me, took out his penknife, and said, 'if you offer to go to meeting tomorrow, with this knife I'll cripple you, for you shall not be a Quaker.' I made him no answer. In the morning, I set out as usual; he did not attempt to harm me.

But Elizabeth Ashbridge did suffer horribly in this marital captivity narrative; she often walked to Quaker meeting barefoot, as her husband refused to allow her to have shoes as long as she persisted in resisting his authority over her. The distance she covered was several miles, through snow and ice in the winter.

Ashbridge's triumph through suffering, even at the hands of her husband, is typical of the Puritan spiritual autobiographies on which her account is based. It is also very characteristic of much Puritan literature of the seventeenth century, when many of the doctrinal positions of the early American colonists were taken from earlier Protestant positions of Luther and Calvin in Europe. Listen, for example, to Governor John Winthrop of Massachusetts Bay colony in his Address to the General Court, "On Liberty," in 1645:

There are two kinds of liberty, the one is natural. . . . The other kind of liberty is civil or federal, it may also be termed moral, in reference to the covenant between God and man, in the moral law, and the politic covenants and constitutions amongst men themselves. This liberty is the proper end and object of authority, and cannot subsist without it. . . . This liberty is exercised and maintained in a way of subjection to authority, and it is the same kind of Liberty wherewith Christ has made us free.

The Woman's choice makes such a man her husband—yet, being so chosen, he is her Lord, and she is to be subject to him, yet in a way of liberty, not of bondage. And a *true wife* accounts her subjection her honor and freedom, and would not think her condition safe and free but in her subjection to her husband's authority. . . . whether her Lord smiles upon her, embraceth her in his arms, or whether he frowns or rebukes or smites her, she apprehends the sweetness of his life in all, and is refreshed, supported, and instructed by every such dispensation of his authority over her. (Quoted in Nina Baym, ed., *The Norton Anthology of American Literature* [New York, 1989], p. 63)

Elizabeth Ashbridge, like Anne Bradstreet before her, was a colonial New England woman writer who resisted the patriarchal authority of the system in which she was placed, and her mid-century protest against marital abuse of authority foreshadowed the more militant reform movements that would characterize women's personal accounts in the following century.

Life-writers, whether biographers or autobiographers, captivity-narrators, or diarists and keepers of spiritual and meditative life-accounts, all shared the common vision of a life governed by Providence and played out within the tension of individual free will constrained by God's omnipotent guidance. These life-writings constitute some of the most interesting and fascinating of all colonial literature, and the juxtaposition of Benjamin Franklin and Jonathan Edwards provides a unique view of the secular and spiritual cultures that were rapidly developing in prerevolutionary America.

POETRY

In the poetry of Anne Bradstreet, we find reflections of the Pauline/Augustinian doctrine of male authority. Bradstreet asserts her right to compose verse in a world dominated by male writers (see the Prologue to "The Tenth Muse Lately Sprung Up in America" [1650]) with words like

Men can do best, and women know it well
Preeminence in all and each is yours;
Yet grant some small acknowledgement of ours.

Yet her verses addressed to her husband—such as "To My Dear and Loving Husband"—are loud testaments to the Puritan view of marital authority.

If ever two were one, then surely we
If ever man were loved by wife, then thee
If ever wife was happy in a man, Compare
with me, ye women, if you can.

("To My Dear and Loving Husband")

"A Letter to Her Husband, Absent Upon Public Employment," begins "My head, my heart, mine eyes, my life, nay more / My job, my magazine of earthly store . . ." and goes on to compare her husband to Christ, through a succession of sun/son analogies, in a poem that reflects the early Pauline/Augustinian doctrine of marriage authority on more personal terms than the Winthrop court statement; however, both represent the Puritan/scriptural hierarchical system of governance that was based on Bible, where kings ruled entire nations *dei gratia*, by divine right, and women were represented either in support of the patriarchal system or as evil miscreants who subvert the divine cause. Either way, the social order is male-dominated, and the English Puritan poet John Milton devoted twelve thousand lines of verse to examining "the ways of God to men," concluding, in Book 9 of *Paradise Lost* that "fully and clearly warned," Adam's reason had given way to his passion, represented by Eve, the subordinate partner in the creation process.

These complex beliefs influenced all genres of literature in New England during the colonial period. The *Meditations* (1682–1725) of Edward Taylor also reflect the pattern of belief by which the mortal sinner seeks assurance that divine grace had been sufficiently imparted to make salvation possible. In his well-known sustained analogy, "Huswifery," Taylor pleads,

Make me, O, Lord, Thy spinning wheel complete
Thy Holy Word my distaff make for me. . . .
Then clothe therewith mine understanding, will
Affections, judgment, conscience, memory,
My words and actions, that their shine may fill

My ways with glory and Thee glorify.
Then mine apparel shall display before Ye
That I am clothed in holy robes for glory.

(Quoted in George Perkins, ed.,
*The American Tradition in Liter-
ature* [New York, 1985], p. 102)

Taylor praises God's saving power in his poetry
and in the fifty known sermons that accompany
the *Meditations*. (There are some 212 meditations
but fewer known sermons.) He poetically renders
man's insignificance in comparison with God's
glory:

I am this crumb of dust which is designed
To make my pen unto Thy praise alone,
And my dull fancy I would gladly grind
Unto an edge on Zion's precious stone.

(Quoted in Baym, ed.,
*The Norton Anthology of
American Literature*, p. 103)

DIARIES AND JOURNALS

Colonial poets and historians, biographers and
autobiographers wrote with the intention of discovering patterns in the events of one's life that
would provide some indication that one had been
elected for salvation. Moreover, in writing a
chronicle of one's life or in narrating events in
the history of a group, authors sought some clues
as to the final outcome of the subject's earthly
trial. Diaries and journals were kept by many
colonial New Englanders, and all human activity
was considered to be directed by God through
Providence, according to the Calvinist idea of
predestination and election. Puritans shared the
common view that some were fortunate members
of God's elect or chosen, but they were always
uncertain of their actual roles in this grand design. However, it was also believed that God
would provide signs along the way to indicate
those whom he had elected to save and those
who were not filled with grace. These signs were
usually manifested in everyday life, and "special
Providences" or particular examples of God's unusual concern for the individual needs of His
saints were considered to be excellent indications
of the subject's election for salvation.

This early and functional system of diary
composition gradually underwent some sophistication and refinement, so that by the mid seventeenth century diaries and journals were part
of the larger literature of self-examination, as
Daniel Shea has shown in *Spiritual Autobiography
in Early America*. The result was a literary and
theological art form among New England Puritans that complemented the formal histories and
biographies. Despite the fragmentary nature of
some diaries like Michael Wigglesworth's, which
covers only the years 1653 to 1657, or Edward
Taylor's, which is even briefer, the diaries suggest
forcibly the writer's experience of Puritan doctrine, as when Wigglesworth complains "my
goodness (if any there be) is like the morning
dew that is dried up." This is no less true of
Edward Taylor's "Spiritual Relation" or Anne
Bradstreet's "To My Dear Children," two important personal testimonies by the two major colonial American poets, who invert the process of
creating diaries and autobiographies by com-
pressing their spiritual experiences into utterances of a single moment.

Probably the most prominent examples of
personal diaries are the Puritan diaries of Cotton
Mather and Samuel Sewall, the *Personal Narrative*
of Jonathan Edwards, and the *Journal* of the
Quaker John Woolman, and the journal-like autobiography of the Quaker Elizabeth Ashbridge.
Southern writers are well represented by the *Diary* (1709–1712) of William Byrd of Westover
plantation in Virginia. In each of these accounts,
the reader is provided unique insights into the
personality of the author. Unlike the truncated
accounts by Anne Bradstreet, Michael Wigglesworth, and Edward Taylor, these longer diaries
are expansive and comprehensive for the years
they purport to cover, and they are sufficiently
full of examples to allow the modern reader an
opportunity to assess each author as a richly, if
not fully developed, personality.

In more public journals like John Winthrop's account of his years in the Massachusetts
Bay colony, or in more deliberately didactic historical narratives like Bradford's *Of Plimouth
Plantation*, the focus is less on the individual than
it is on the "community of gathered saints" whose
special purpose overshadows the entire narrative. Samuel Sewall was able to make his diary
a compelling reflection of both his secular and
sacred experience, and his narrative voice is endowed with the unique qualities of his anguished
personality. Sewall had been a judge at the Salem

witchcraft trials of 1692, a role which he later regretted and an event of whose cruel actions he repented publicly. His *Diary* (1673–1729) carries an account of this transformation, including his courageous act in asking his pastor to read a public apology for his participation in the Salem witch trials. The Sewall and Mather documents are both seventeenth-century accounts that reflect the formulaic expression of an individual's personal encounter with God, and each is an exhaustive record, kept over a long period of time in a chronological fashion, indicating God's interactions with the personal life of His elected saint, as each diarist hoped to become.

Because of this pious focus, the diary accounts of Sewall, Mather, and Thomas Shepard differ greatly from the record kept by William Byrd II, the son of a wealthy Virginia planter and a very well-bred young man who was given an English education in London schools, where he was essentially trained in the ways of the world rather than instructed in the pathways to Heaven. His *Diary* clearly reflects the differences between the Cavalier and the Yankee, between the southern aristocrat and the bourgeois New England Puritan. Byrd traveled in sophisticated, urban social circles, and he attended the latest London drama, whereas New England Puritans banished theater altogether. Thus his account is more a record of daily experience than it is a document designed to exemplify the sanctified or providentially guided life of a saint. We are told repeatedly of his daily habits and how "I did my dance," a form of physical, not spiritual, exercise, possibly ablutions. Though he occasionally used the metaphorical structures of New England's journey into the wilderness and once wrote that "we are very happy in our Canaans if we could but forget the onions and fleshpots of Egypt," Byrd was a southern Anglican, essentially concerned with commercial trade with Britain, and his "new Canaan," unlike its New England equivalent, was a neoclassical earthly paradise, a pastoral plantation that in no way resembled the Garden of Eden sought by the Puritans. His conceptual framework for the *Diary* was a long way from the "howling wilderness" in which the New England Puritans found themselves abandoned by all except God.

Diary writing and the keeping of journals gradually were shaped into the self-conscious patterns of the life-narrative in which writers selected and edited the events of their lives in order to tell a story from a particular, and often biased, point of view. During the later colonial period, life-writing in America as well as in England was much more an expression of human personality, even in its relations to God, than it was a recording of divine intervention in human affairs. For example, Thomas Shepard's *Autobiography* presents a human personality that comes through the pervasive concern with the spiritual frame of reference in which that personality develops. Shepard's account is a narrative rather than a chronicle, and because of the shift toward life-reckoning rather than life-chronicling it provides an excellent example of the shaped life narrative with a theocentric focus. And yet, the Shepard *Autobiography* is also a fine example of personality development, even though it is primarily a record of providential guidance of an early New England community in its encounter with Indian antagonists, a record in which the personality is often subordinated to the spiritual doctrine. Cotton Mather's *Diary* and his autobiographical *Paterna* also reflect this tension between the human personality and the divine presence.

SERMON LITERATURE

Like colonial diaries, the sermon literature of the period, particularly in New England's Puritan churches, reflects the determination of the settlers to expand God's "errand into the wilderness" into a conquest not only of the Native American inhabitants but also of the landscape and the environment itself. Samuel Danforth preached "A Brief Recognition of New England's Errand Into the Wilderness" (1671), along with a number of millennial and judgmental sermons that expressed the vision of the colonial enterprise while lamenting the loss of the spiritual and psychological power of the first-generation settlers. Increase Mather preached and published "Ichabod, or, the Glory has Departed" in 1702, in which he spoke like the ancient prophet Jeremiah, who denounced the Israel of old when the Chosen People departed from the preordained path; this sermon form became known as the Jeremiad. Sacvan Bercovitch has examined this type of sermon writing in his study

The American Jeremiad and has found that its most popular expression in colonial America was in Jonathan Edwards's sermon "Sinners in the Hands of an Angry God" (1741), which Edwards preached during the Great Awakening, a revivalist movement that he, along with the Reverend George Whitefield, led in New England in the 1730s and 1740s.

"Sinners" follows the conventional Puritan sermon form in which the speaker selects a biblical text to give his sermon divine authority, then expounds on a doctrine derived from that text, and finally applies that doctrine to the congregation seated before him. Edwards wrote with "affection," utilizing images well known to his parishioners, such as fire and floods (his Northampton, Massachusetts, congregation lived on the shore of the Connecticut River, which annually floods near his church site). He paved the way for the language of nature found in Ralph Waldo Emerson's essays with imagery like

The God that holds you over the pit of hell, much as one holds a spider or some loathsome insect over the fire, abhors you, and is dreadfully provoked; His wrath towards you burns like fire; He looks upon you as worthy of nothing else but to be cast into the fire; He is of purer eyes than to bear to have you in His sight; you are ten thousand times more abominable in His eyes than the most hateful, venomous serpent is in ours. . . . O sinner! Consider the fearful danger you are in; it is a great furnace of wrath, a wide and bottomless pit, full of the fire of wrath, that you are held over in the hand of that God, whose wrath is provoked and incensed as much against you, as against many of the damned in hell. You hang by a slender thread, with the flames of divine wrath flashing about it, and ready every moment to singe it, and burn it asunder, and you have no interest in any Mediator, and nothing to lay hold of to save yourself, nothing to keep off the flames of wrath, nothing of your own, nothing that you ever have done, nothing that you can do, to induce God to spare you one moment. (Quoted in George Perkins, ed., *The American Tradition in Literature* [New York, 1985], p. 171)

Edwards was writing and preaching one hundred years after the first generation of Puritan settlers preached in New England, but his Calvinist message of judgment and salvation was essentially the same. The three most prolific ministers during the colonies' first century were: Thomas She-

pard ("The Sound Believer" [1645]; "The Sincere Convert" [1646]), John Cotton ("The Way of Life" [1641]; "God's Promise to His Plantations" [1646]), and Thomas Hooker, founder of Connecticut, who preached "The Soule's Preparation" (1632), "The Soule's Humiliation" (1637), "The Soule's Vocation" (1637), "The Soule's Implantation" (1637), and "The Soule's Exaltation" (1638), a series that Hooker later revised and published under the title *The Application of Redemption* (1656). These preachers, and many others like them, filled the century with the voice of God who spoke to His New English Israel through the Scripture texts and through the many interpretations that ministers gave twice each week.

Thus, sermons, like histories and biographies, reflected the New England settlers' sense of self and their bold assertions about providential guidance and divine sanction for their holy mission. But New Englanders, like the inhabitants of the Middle Atlantic colonies and the southern colonies, were rapidly confronting a new question by the third quarter of the eighteenth century; political events were rapidly unfolding so that their colonial status was threatened by the possibility of becoming a new nation, independent of Britain and perhaps independent of British cultural influences. The colonies had all developed genres of literature that expressed the uniqueness of their New World experience. However, the writers were British subjects writing literature in the English language and expressing their feelings in forms derived from English models. Thus "colonial" America ended abruptly in the period 1776–1783, but this was a political and social fact more than a literary and cultural one. English writers continued to influence Americans well into the nineteenth century, and it is clear from cargo manifests of books imported to the colonies and from studies like Lawrence Wroth's *American Bookshelf: 1755* (Philadelphia, 1934) that the North American colonies consumed vast quantities of imported English literature.

It is therefore poignant that in 1782, at the close of the colonial period, the French visitor Hector St. Jean de Crèvecoeur would observe that an American was one "who, leaving behind him all his ancient prejudices and manners, receives new ones from the new mode of life he has embraced, the new government he obeys, and the new rank he holds. He becomes an American by being received into the broad lap of our great Alma Mater." In America, "individuals of all nations are melted into a new race of men, whose labours and posterity will one day cause great changes in the world." Crèvecoeur concluded that "the American is a new man. He "acts upon new principles; he must therefore entertain new ideas and form new opinions. From involuntary idleness, servile dependence, penury, and useless labor, he has passed to toils of a very different nature, rewarded by ample subsistence. This is an American."

BIBLIOGRAPHY

Elliot, Emory, ed. *American Literature: A Prentice Hall Anthology.* Vol. 1. Englewood Cliffs, N.J., 1991.

Gottesman, Ronald, ed. *The Norton Anthology of American Literature.* Vol. 1. New York, 1989.

Lauter, Paul, ed. *The Heath Anthology of American Literature.* Vol. 1. Lexington, Ky., 1990.

Miller, Perry, ed. *The American Puritans: Their Prose and Poetry.* New York, 1956.

Vaughan, Alden T., and Edward W. Clark. *Puritans Among the Indians: Accounts of Captivity and Redemption, 1676–1714.* Cambridge, Mass., 1981.

Literary Histories

Elliott, Emory, ed. *The Columbia Literary History of the United States.* New York, 1988.

Spiller, Robert, ed. *The Literary History of the United States.* New York, 1957.

Critical and Historical Studies

Andrews, William. *To Tell a Free Story: The First Century of Afro-American Autobiography, 1760–1865.* Urbana and Chicago, Ill., 1986.

Bercovitch, Sacvan. *The Puritan Origins of the American Self.* New Haven, Conn., 1975.

Caldwell, Patricia. *The Puritan Conversion Narrative.* Cambridge, Mass., 1983.

Emerson, Everett, ed. *Major Writers of Early American Literature.* Madison, Wis., 1972.

Grabo, Norman. *Edward Taylor.* New York, 1961.

Heimert. Alan. *Religion and the American Mind.* Cambridge, Mass., 1966.

Howard, Alan B. "Art and History in Bradford's *Of Plimouth Plantation.*" *William and Mary Quarterly,* 3rd ser., 28 (1971):237–266.

Keller, Karl. *The Example of Edward Taylor.* Amherst, Mass., 1975.

Leary, Lewis. *That Rascal Freneau: A Study in Literary Failure.* New Brunswick, N.J., 1941; repr. New York, 1964, 1971.

Lowance, Mason I. *The Language of Canaan: Metaphor and Symbol in New England From the Puritans to the Transcendentalists.* Cambridge, Mass., 1980.

Marambaud, Pierre. *William Byrd of Westover, 1674–1744.* Charlottesville, Va., 1971.

Middlekauff, Robert. *The Mathers: Three Generations of Puritan Intellectuals, 1596–1728.* New York, 1971.

Miller, Perry. *Errand Into the Wilderness.* Cambridge, Mass., 1956.

———. *Jonathan Edwards.* New York, 1949.

———. *The New England Mind: From Colony to Province.* Cambridge, Mass., 1953.

———. *The New England Mind: The Seventeenth Century.* Cambridge, Mass., 1954.

Murdock, Kenneth B. *Literature and Theology in Colonial New England.* Cambridge, Mass., 1949; repr. New York, 1963.

Pearce, Roy Harvey. *Savagism and Civilization: A Study of the Indian and the American Mind.* Baltimore, Md., 1967.

Piercy, Josephine K. *Anne Bradstreet.* New Haven, Conn., 1965.

Shea, Daniel. *Spiritual Autobiography in Early America.* Princeton, N.J., 1968.

Silverman, Kenneth. *The Life and Times of Cotton Mather.* New York, 1985.

Vaughan, Alden T. *New England Frontier, Puritans and Indians, 1620–1675.* Boston, 1965; rev. ed., New York, 1979.

Winslow, Ola E. *Jonathan Edwards, 1703–1758: A Biography.* New York, 1940.

Mason I. Lowance, Jr.

SEE ALSO **Colonial Political Thought; The Colonial Press; Drama; Libraries and Learned Societies; and Schools and Schooling.**

THE DUTCH COLONY

THE EXISTENCE OF LITERATURE in New Netherland is rarely acknowledged; it has received virtually no critical attention. Pragmatic rather than literary purposes underlie its prose, and, to some extent, its poetry. Netherlanders who involved themselves with the colony and those who lived there wrote to inform, to explain, or to persuade, be their utterances public, private, or both. Yet their books, periodicals, pamphlets, journals, and letters rarely hide the personality of the author; his attitude toward the native inhabitants, flora, and fauna; or the nature of his audience. These writings often portray colorful characters in a minutely detailed description of the natural scene and present a vivid picture of the colony's social life and customs. They also reveal their author's sense of structure and, in many cases, his conscious literary effort.

EARLY LITERATURE ON NEW NETHERLAND

The "Provincial Regulations" for New Netherland, adopted by the Assembly of Nineteen of the West India Company in 1624, enumerate the colonists' duties and privileges. They are valuable for their tone and emphasis, as are the two sets of instructions for director Willem Verhulst (Van Laer, *Documents*).

Early-seventeenth-century Dutch histories and geographies already included New Netherland. Johan de Laet's *New World* (1625) relies on the written accounts of early explorers, including Henry Hudson's now-lost journal, and emphasizes the colony's plant life and apparent fruitfulness (Jameson, *Narratives*).

Similarly, several periodicals informed the public at home. Nicolaes van Wassenaer's *Historical Account,* a semi-annual (1624–1630), frequently directs its information at potential emigrants. Although the disadvantages of life in New Netherland are not disguised, the tone remains optimistic. Biblical and classical analogies demonstrate a literary bent (Jameson, *Narratives*).

Promotional and polemical books and pamphlets appeared in which financially or politically motivated authors argued for or against the colony. Such writings often included descriptions of New Netherland, and frequently resorted to the dialogue form, employed allegory or classical analogy, or contained poetry. For example, in *Kort en Klaer Ontwerp,* published in 1662, Peter

C. Plockhoy successfully encouraged settlement in New Netherland by presenting a "short and clear plan" for a community in the Delaware region. It includes Karel Verloove's poem on the project and Steendam's promotional spurring verses.

The lawyer Adriaen van der Donck, a Leyden University graduate and a New Netherland landowner, composed the highly polemical *Representation of New Netherland* or *Remonstrance* in 1649 for an audience in the Netherlands. Hence this work, which is both complaint and promotion literature, repeatedly explains the unfamiliar through comparisons with the fatherland. His style is literate but simple; the work, tightly structured. The even, factual tone in the descriptive section yields to one of urgency and indignation at foreign usurpation and mismanagement by the West India Company. A promotional section indicates the colony's promise, followed by reasons this promise remains unfulfilled. Alternately emotional and ironic, this section uses many familiar sayings to support the argument. In a more submissive tone, the closing offers suggestions for the colony's improvement (Jameson, *Narratives*).

Van der Donck also wrote *A Description of the New Netherlands* in 1655. The first book about New York, it was penned and published well before William Bradford composed his *Of Plymouth Plantation*. It expands upon the descriptive aspects of the *Remonstrance* and omits the latter's elements of complaint and acrimony. Beginning with the publisher's dedications, one of which is in verse, the work encourages settlement. Tightly organized, rich in practical detail and illustrative incidents, the *Description* demonstrates the author's delight in the colony's natural beauty. His literary inclination is evident in references to the arts and the classics. A concluding dialogue acknowledges the West India Company's mismanagement but remains optimistic about the colony's future.

NEW NETHERLAND JOURNALS

Extant New Netherland journals—simple chronological accounts with entries varying in length—were clearly composed either to impart information to a private audience who would read the manuscript or to be published. Harmen van den Bogaert, barber-surgeon at Fort Orange, led a small expedition among the Iroquois to investigate the decline of the fur trade and to renegotiate fur prices. Marked by an even tone, his journal of this expedition provides vivid details of hardship, danger, and Indian life.

David de Vries, seaman and patroonship partner, composed his journal using his own contemporary notes and some borrowed material, then reworked it for publication in 1655. The journal often moves abruptly from a relation of events to a description of the scene. He regularly uses comparisons with their homeland to acquaint his readers with New Netherland and relates a wealth of practical information for sailors and settlers. His tone is self-assured; his characterizations and descriptions of events are compelling and often humorous. At times poetic, the journal also demonstrates genuine religious feeling (Jameson, *Narratives,* and Myers, *Early Pennsylvania*).

The search of Jasper Danckaerts, a Labadist missionary and intelligent observer, for a suitable place to found a community took him through the entire New Netherland area and beyond. Danckaerts's journal provides lively characterizations, often with background detail, that are occasionally colored by a self-satisfied tone and religious cant. Landscape descriptions alternate with deftly inserted explanatory material where needed. Realistically rendered dialogue imparts a sense of immediacy to his journal.

CORRESPONDENCE AS LITERATURE

Letters from administrators, clergymen, and patroons document the variety of personalities at the top of New Netherland's society. While Van den Bogaert's is an impersonal account, Isaack de Rasieres's reveals his adventurousness, humor, sensitivity, and frustration. The reports written by the New Amsterdam town council and Director General Peter Stuyvesant upon the colony's surrender to England are marked by sadness.

The clergy's letters are naturally preoccupied with the condition of the Church in New Netherland, yet they differ markedly among themselves in tone and content. Henricus Se-

lyns's letters are unique for their spirit of tolerance. The letters between Jeremias and Maria van Rensselaer and their correspondents, often devoted to business concerns, nevertheless reveal the personalities of both writers and recipients. Jeremias's writings are particularly notable for his use of Dutch maxims.

THE NEW NETHERLAND POETS

To date, three important New Netherland poets have come to light. Jacob Steendam, a trader, was already known as a poet before his arrival in New Netherland. In his "The Complaint of New Amsterdam," the city is personified as the thriving daughter of a neglectful mother, Amsterdam; its envious neighbor, New England, is depicted as swine. "The Praise of New Netherland," also by Steendam, is epic in its introduction of the four elements, its immense catalog of species, and its insistence on the nobility of its subject, the new colony. The poem is Christian in its biblical and religious allusions, its prayer for peace, and its exhortation to gratitude. Steendam's "spurring" verses stress the colony's abundance and minimize the dangers of Indian attacks.

Henricus Selyns was minister of the Dutch Reformed church in New Netherland from 1660 to 1664 and from 1682 to his death in 1701. His "Nuptial Song" celebrates the marriage of another minister at Christmastime while "Bridal Torch" contrasts the joy of these occasions with the recent Indian war and direful natural phenomena. Many of Selyns's other occasional poems are secular. He wrote epitaphs for prominent New Netherlanders, including one for Stuyvesant, that rely on wordplay for humor. Similarly, in miscellaneous punning verses, he aims his good-natured satire at a variety of human foibles. Selyns also composed in Latin; one such poem is prefixed to Mather's *Magnalia*.

Nicasius de Sille served Director General Stuyvesant as councillor and held other administrative posts. His most important poem, "The Earth Speaks to Its Cultivators," is especially noteworthy for its main character of "new Adam" who clears the land and names the place [New] Utrecht (Murphy, *Anthology of New Netherland*).

IMPORTED WORKS

Most New Netherlanders were simple folk. Those who could read and had means imported books from the Netherlands. Such works included religious treatises, biographies, histories, and works by contemporary authors such as Pieter Cornelisz, P. C. Hooft, Constantyn Huygens, and Joost van den Vondel, the greatest poet of the Dutch Golden Age. No author was as popular, however, as Jacob Cats.

Affectionately known as Father Cats, he swiftly became and remained an indispensable guide for everyday living well into the nineteenth century. His *Spiegel* (Mirror), first published in 1632, served as a counterpart to the family Bible. Some of the New Netherland writers quoted Cats, and historian Alice Kenney cites evidence that his verses survived in oral form into the early-twentieth-century Hudson valley.

CONCLUSION

The literature of New Netherland did not end when the colony became definitively English in 1674 by a treaty legitimizing the end of New Netherland as a Dutch colony. Dutch prose and poetry were produced as long as the language remained in use. And even after Dutch was eclipsed by English, New Netherland's oral tradition of legends and tales survived in the works of Washington Irving, James K. Paulding, and James Fenimore Cooper.

BIBLIOGRAPHY

Asher, G. M. *A Bibliographical and Historical Essay on the Dutch Books and Pamphlets relating to New-Netherland and to the Dutch West-India Company and to its Possessions, 1854–1867.* Amsterdam, The Netherlands, 1960.

Cats, Jacob. "Spiegel van den ouden en nieuwen tyt." In *Alle de Wercken van den Heere Jacob Cats.* 2 vols. 1712. Repr., Utrecht, The Netherlands, 1976. Readers should refer to volume 1, pages 477–666 for Cats's work.

James, Bartlett B., and J. Franklin Jameson, eds. *Journal of Jasper Danckaerts, 1679–1680.* New York, 1913.

Jameson, J. Franklin, ed. *Narratives of New Netherland, 1609–1664.* New York, 1959.

A Journey into Mohawk and Oneida Country, 1634–1635: The Journal of Harmen Meyndertsz van den Bogaert. Translated and edited by Charles T. Gehring and William A. Starna. Syracuse, N.Y., 1988.

Kenney, Alice P. "'Het Poelmeisie': An Introduction to the Hudson Valley Dutch Dialect." *New York History* 61, no. 2 (April 1980): 161–167

Murphy, Henry C. *Anthology of New Netherland or Translations from the Early Dutch Poets of New York with Memoirs of Their Lives.* Amsterdam, The Netherlands, 1966. Steendam's, Selyns's, and De Sille's poetry in Dutch texts with English translations. Murphy's transcription of the Dutch texts may contain errors; his translation is occasionally flawed.

Myers, Albert C. *Narratives of Early Pennsylvania, West New Jersey, and Delaware, 1630–1707.* New York, 1912.

Van Boheemen, Christine. "Dutch-American Poets of the Seventeenth Century." In *The Dutch in North-America: Their Immigration and Cultural Continuity.* European Contributions to American Studies 20. Amsterdam, The Netherlands, 1991.

Van der Donck, Adriaen. *A Description of the New Netherlands.* Edited by Thomas F. O'Donnell. Syracuse, N.Y., 1968. This text is flawed; a new translation is being prepared for publication in 1992.

Van Laer, A. J. F., ed. and trans. *Correspondence of Jeremias van Rensselaer, 1651–1674.* Albany, N.Y., 1932.

———. *Corresponderance of Maria van Rensselaer, 1669–1689.* Albany, N.Y., 1935.

———. *Documents Relating to New Netherland 1624–1626 in the Henry E. Huntington Library.* San Marino, Calif., 1924.

Elisabeth Paling Funk

See also **Literacy** and **Schools and Schooling**.

THE FRENCH COLONIES

Canada

A CONSIDERABLE BODY OF writing originating in the colonies was published in France, as well as some in England and Holland, and many other manuscripts have been published in our own times. These works bear witness to their colonial roots, even though, there being no printing press in any of the French colonies in North America before 1764, they could not develop as an autonomous literary institution. Yet although there is no clear boundary between colonial and French literature or between "literature" and other writing, we can identify a coherent main corpus of works with a specific character. The most important genre in the French colonies is the narration of travel and discovery, varying from the semifabulous to the bureaucratic. Other kinds are geographical descriptions, sermons, satirical and occasional verse, memoirs, letters, and chronicles. Something like a hundred writers might be considered, in periods ranging from the sixteenth to the late eighteenth century, so comments will have to be restricted to the best-known works or those of the most striking interest.

NARRATIVES OF TRAVEL
AND DISCOVERY

Jacques Cartier and Jean de Léry traveled, respectively, to Canada and Brazil as part of the first French colonial tentatives, and both left pithy accounts of their encounters with the strange continent and its inhabitants. Cartier's *Brief récit* (1545 is the first date in a complicated publication history) is rich in anecdote, while Léry's *Histoire d'un voyage fait en la terre de Brésil* (1578) attempts a more comprehensive view of the so-called savages. Both of these texts influenced the Frenchmen who later resumed attempts to found a colony, such as Marc Lescarbot, author of *Histoire de la Nouvelle-France* (1609–1618).

Lescarbot wrote to promote French colonialism, despite its very unpromising start on the Atlantic seaboard, and he created a cheerful picture of the New World, influenced by the classical myth of Arcadia. He had a sense of the reading public, which was still captivated by the great voyages of discovery; according to some witnesses of the time, travel literature was the most popular form of reading. The work of this cultivated Renaissance man includes original poetry and a masque, generally recognized as the first theatrical performance in North America. The bulk of his *Histoire*, besides the story of his own voyages and his impressions of Port Royal (later Annapolis Royal), consists of copies of the travel stories of his predecessors. The chief of these

is Samuel de Champlain, who published several versions of his own voyages (1603–1632). A strong, distinct personality is evident in each of these writers, despite frequent borrowings from other authors and passages probably inserted by their editors.

The year 1632, one of rival publicity, saw three important publications: Gabriel Sagard's *Le grand voyage du pays des Hurons*, Champlain's major volume, and the first of the annual *Jesuit Relations* (1632–1673), launched by Paul Le Jeune. Another Jesuit, Pierre Biard, had already published a *Relation de la Nouvelle France* (1616), a long and systematic study of Port Royal. Sagard's *Grand voyage* is generally found to be the most spontaneous of these travel stories (though written, presumably from field notes, eight years later), and it is certainly the first full-length account of the journey inland into Canada and of life shared with the natives. His later *Histoire du Canada* (1636), though much more discursive and polemical, is a more complete account of early contact. All of these writers were motivated by the desire to tell their adventurous story, as well as by political and fund-raising aims. They all appear to have been convincing: Champlain and the Jesuits were authorized to continue colonizing, and while Sagard's brethren lost their cause, his work had won them the support of Rome.

A new development in promotional writing came with Pierre Boucher's *Histoire véritable et naturelle . . . [du] Canada* (1664). Boucher, having lived in Canada since the age of thirteen, wrote from the point of view of the colonist, answering questions about Canada that had been put to him in the French court. The result is a mixture of local history, natural history, geographical description, and economic argument. Like most of the other writers of this time, he borrowed considerably from the *Jesuit Relations*.

Boucher's life was a colonial success story at a time when failure seemed imminent (because of the Iroquois wars, in which he played a vigorous part). From being an interpreter among the Indians, he had become an important landowner and leader of a thriving settlement. When he was sent to France to boost interest in the colony and attract more settlers, Jean-Baptiste Colbert, minister of finance to Louis XIV, encouraged him to write about the country. While borrowing from his predecessors, and probably accepting a certain amount of editorial assistance, he wrote, on his return to Trois-Rivières, in the simple manner of a practical man.

Marie de l'Incarnation is the name in religion of Mme Guyart-Martin, who died in Quebec in 1672, after living there for thirty years with her religious order. Her letters (collected and published in 1681) are outstanding among the several interesting writings of colonial nuns. They contain a striking mixture of mystical lyricism and shrewd observations on life in and around her convent hospital.

Nicolas Perrot was an outstanding man of action whose memoirs (not published until 1864) are rich in knowledge of the Indians and their relations with the French. His frontier life fitted him to write sober ethnographic descriptions, strongly influenced by the Jesuits, for whom he had also worked as interpreter. He later held various commands for the colonial government, and, without indulging in heroics, he leaves a gripping picture of his action in the westward spread.

The rich and varied content of the *Jesuit Relations* includes some very daring episodes, especially those relating the violent deaths of certain missionaries, including Jean de Brébeuf and Gabriel Lalemant, who were later canonized (1930). The heroic strain was continued with great effect, especially by the Sulpician priest François Dollier de Casson, whose history of Montreal from 1640 to 1672 gave an epic tone to the henceforth legendary exploits of Dollard Des Ormeaux, Lambert Closse, and other fighters against the Iroquois.

SATIRE AND THE BURLESQUE

The mock-heroic genre known as burlesque, made popular in France by Paul Scarron in 1648, was applied by René-Louis Chartier de la Lotbinière to Rémy de Courcelle's 1666 expedition against the Mohawk. His verse narrative turns hardships into soldierly tales and a miserable failure into victory. The bantering tone of the poem seems quite satirical, but Chartier de la Lotbinière's precise intentions are not known. Nor do we know whether the manuscript, which is well corrected and annotated, was intended for publication; this comic picture of colonial military life could have circulated in salons and officers' messes in Canada and France. This was the custom in France, and the few surviving pieces suggest that it flourished in the colonies.

Chartier de la Lotbinière's main literary devices are a jarring mix of litotes and hyperbole, of noble allusion and low-life detail. The octosyllabic verse is deliberately close to doggerel, and the entire narrative is in the second person, addressed to Courcelle. The following lines (my translation) are a sample of how he described the extreme privations of the expeditionary force:

> Hunting, with the foe so near,
> you bagged no bear nor moose nor deer,
> your sleep was not upset the least
> by the excesses of a feast.

Increasingly frequent criticism of the authorities, especially by disgruntled army officers, is best known through Louis-Armand de Lom d'Arce de Lahontan. His *Nouveaux voyages* and *Dialogues* (1703) are the most profoundly satirical works to emerge from the French colonies. The first parts are a fairly straightforward narration of the author's extensive travels, while the last part, supposedly dialogues between Lahontan and a Huron named Adario, creates the rhetorical figure of the "savage" as a falsely ingenuous critic of French society. Adario may be based to some extent on a real Huron, but the conversations the narrator has with him are a provocative mix of reality and obvious fiction. By setting them in the framework of his authentic travels, Lahontan gives authority to the opinions he expresses through Adario.

All the travel writers do this to some degree, while the scope of satire varies enormously. Dière de Diéreville's *Relation du voyage du Port Royal de l'Acadie* (1708) is a more lighthearted use of the same strategy. His verse narrative mingles geographical description with humorous comments on life in that region, in the manner of a salon wit.

Claude Lebeau continues this tradition with the most gripping personal adventure story, richly illustrated with observations on the Indians and other aspects of the country. Although it is obvious that *Avantures du s. C. Le Beau* (1738) does not tell the whole truth, this book abounds in circumstantial detail. Sent to the colonies by his irate father, Lebeau worked for a year in Quebec and then set off on his adventures in the forest, hunting beaver with Huron partners, living in Iroquoian villages, falling prisoner to another band, escaping with his Abenaki mistress, and much more. Lebeau adopts a dignified narrative manner not far removed from Abbé Antoine François Prévost's *Histoire de Chevalier des Grieux et de Manon Lescaut,* while the content of his story is equivalent to that of a thriller, set in a mysterious and dangerous world.

DESCRIPTION OF THE NATIVE PEOPLES

The "savage" in this literature goes well beyond the satirical device of Lahontan. From the earliest contact, travelers give violently contrasting pictures of the Native peoples encountered. The stereotypes and rhetorical figures persist and continue to color even the most circumstantial stories. Yet there also emerges an increasingly scientific ethnology. Joseph-François Lafitau, after serving in the Jesuit mission in Canada, wrote his *Moeurs des sauvages amériquains . . .* (1724), comparing Amerindian culture with that of the earliest Greeks. His primitivist hypothesis (true human nature could be found by going back to uncontaminated man) was common in eighteenth-century Europe, but it derived new substance from the missionary experience, which thus contributed to the development in France of the highly complex myth of the noble savage (*le bon sauvage*).

LETTERS

Epistolary art, with all the elegance of its age, was well known in the colonies through the new generation of French officers arriving in the eighteenth century. A striking case is that of Élisabeth Bégon (née Marie-Élisabeth Rocbert de la Morandière, 1696–1755), whose letters give highly individual expression to a curious love story. Mme Bégon, Canadian-born widow of the governor of Trois-Rivières, was hopelessly in love with her son-in-law, and her letters use every

pretext to engage his attention. At the same time, they give a shrewd and sometimes bitter portrait of life in the colonial elite. Frustrated and embittered at home, Mme Bégon finally descended on her cousins in France, where her letters express a new disappointment. Though not written for the public eye, this series (eventually published in 1934) seems like life imitating art, as known in the epistolary novels of the time.

ORAL TRADITION

Canada inherited a rich tradition of oral stories and songs, which were not much recorded until the nineteenth-century folklorists began to conserve them. Most of this material goes back to medieval French sources, and we know little about its diffusion and development in New France under the old regime. Among the surviving manuscript fragments, the following lines (of uncertain origin) show the innuendo typical of the genre:

> Je veux faire un grand voyage
> a ceste St Nicolas . . .
> Mon mary vous este vieux
> Reposez vous
> Votre valet my menera bien mieux que vous

> (I want to go on a long trip this Christmas holiday / . . . Husband you are old / Take a rest / Your servant will take me there much better than you)

LATER WORKS

Alongside these diversified new kinds of writing, the histories and descriptions and the voyages of discovery continued to be the most important genre. The great Jesuit historian Pierre-François-Xavier de Charlevoix imposed his sweeping views on Japan (1715), Santo Domingo (1730–1731), New France (1744), and Paraguay (1756). *Histoire de l'Amérique septentrionale* (1722) by Claude-Charles Le Roy de La Potherie, *dit* Bacqueville de La Potherie, born in Guadeloupe, is another example of increased cultural contact between the different colonies. Louis Hennepin and Henri de Tonty wrote different accounts of the expedition of René-Robert Cavelier de

La Salle from Quebec to Louisiana; they show the endless tendency to inject personal bias into otherwise factual accounts. Mathieu Sagean, who claimed to have met with lions and leopards on his way from Montreal to his version of El Dorado, is an extreme and belated case of the tendency to create travelers' tales. In general, the fabulous content declined after the mid seventeenth century, giving way to more factual-sounding narratives, as westward exploration proceeded in an increasingly rational age. Finally, the voyage of Saint-Luc de la Corne Saint-Luc (published in 1778) reverses the whole process. Though real, his story seems like a symbol of the end of the French colonies, for he relates the shipwreck and hardships of a group of Canadian seigneurs leaving for France after the capitulation to the English.

A COLONIAL LEGACY

It is evident that discovery of the New World by travelers from Europe was a major fascination throughout the colonial period. Writing by people born or chiefly resident in the colonies grew in importance toward the end of the old regime, but did not achieve a dominant position. However, the high level of intertextual reference within the corpus, especially the discovery literature, argues the existence of a specifically colonial literature, despite the strictures mentioned above. The literary figure of the savage, arising from the contact of ancient myth with real Amerindians, is only one of its most significant developments. As in most countries in this period, folklore and popular writing continued in their own way, without having much impact on published literature. Nor is there much Amerindian influence, although some pastiches of Indian oratory are scattered among the discovery writings.

The corpus as a whole is colonial, in the precise sense that its creation is conditioned both by the genius loci and by its relations with metropolitan antecedents, publishers, and readership. It is literary, in that it goes far beyond the immediate practical aims that prompted most of the writings. Its specific characteristics leave a double legacy: a certain impact on French literature and a solid testimony to a living culture, which is being increasingly recuperated by the heirs to the French colonial regime.

BIBLIOGRAPHY

Primary Works

An important new series now appearing in the collection Bibliothèque du Nouveau Monde (Montreal) may be expected to supply more works in modern critical editions. Various reprint houses are reproducing older editions. The following is a collection of manuscript items transcribed in modern times:

Margry, Pierre. *Découvertes et établissements des Français dans l'ouest et dans le sud de l'Amérique septentrionale (1614–1754)*. 6 vols. Paris, 1879–1888.

Others have continued to appear in *Bulletin des recherches historiques*.

The following choice of editions is suggested for the works mentioned in this article:

Bégon, Élisabeth. *Lettres au cher fils*. Edited by Nicole Deschamps. Montreal, 1972.

Boucher, Pierre. *Histoire véritable et naturelle des moeurs et productions du pays de la Nouvelle-France, vulgairement dite le Canada*. Boucherville, Quebec, 1964.

Cartier, Jacques. *Relations*. Edited by Michel Bideaux. Montreal, 1986.

———. *The Voyages of Jacques Cartier*. Edited by H. P. Biggar. Ottawa, 1924.

Champlain, Samuel de. *Works*. Edited by H. P. Biggar. 6 vols. Toronto, Ontario, 1922–1936.

Charlevoix, Pierre-François-Xavier de. *History and General Description of New France*. Edited by John Gilmary Shea. 6 vols. New York, 1866–1872; repr. Chicago, 1962.

Chartier de la Lotbinière, Louis-Théandre. "Sur le voyage de Monsieur de Courcelles Gouverneur et Lieutenant General pour le Roy en la Nouvelle france en l'année 1666." *Bulletin des recherches historiques*, 1927.

Dièreville, Dière de. *Relation of the Voyage to Port-Royal*. Edited by J. C. Webster. Toronto, Ontario, 1933.

Dollier de Casson, François. *Histoire de Montréal, 1640–1672*. Quebec, 1871. Ralph Flenley edited an edition that was published in London in 1928.

Hennepin, Louis. *A New Discovery of a Vast Country in America*. London, 1698; repr. Toronto, Ontario, 1974.

———. *Nouveau voyage d'un païs plus grand que l'Europe*. 2nd ed., Boston, 1903.

Lafitau, Joseph-François. *Customs of the American Indians Compared with the Customs of Primitive Times.* 2 vols. Edited by William N. Fenton and Elizabeth L. Moore. Toronto, Ontario, 1974, 1977.

———. *Moeurs des sauvages amériquains, comparées aux moeurs des premiers temps.* 4 vols. Paris, 1724.

Lahontan, Louis-Armand de Lom d'Arce, baron de. *Lahontan's Voyages.* Edited by Stephen Leacock. Ottawa, 1932.

———. *Oeuvres complètes.* Edited by Réal Ouellet. 2 vols. Montreal, 1990.

Le Beau, Claude. *Avantures du sr. C. Le Beau, avocat en parlement; ou, Voyage curieux et nouveau parmi les sauvages de l'Amérique septentrionale.* 2 vols. Amsterdam, 1738.

Le Roy de la Potherie, Claude-Charles, dit Bacqueville de la Potherie. *Histoire de l'Amérique septentrionale.* 4 vols. Rouen, France, 1722.

Léry, Jean de. *Histoire d'un voyage fait en la terre de Brésil, autrement dite Amérique.* Edited by Sophie Delpech. Paris, 1980.

Lescarbot, Marc. *The History of New France.* Edited by W. F. Ganong. 3 vols. Toronto, Ontario, 1907–1914.

Marie de l'Incarnation (Guyart-Martin). *Écrits spirituels et historiques.* Edited by Albert Jamet. 4 vols. Paris, 1929–1939.

———. *Word from New France: The Selected Letters of Marie de l'Incarnation.* Translated by Joyce Marshall. Toronto, Ontario, 1967.

Perrot, Nicolas. *Mémoire sur les moeurs coustumes et religion des sauvages de l'Amérique septentrionale.* Edited by Jules Tailhan. Paris, 1864; repr. Montreal, 1973.

Sagard, le F. Gabriel. *The Long Journey to the Country of the Hurons.* Edited by George McKinnon Wrong. Toronto, Ontario, 1939.

Sagean, Mathieu. *Extrait de la relation des avantures et voyage de Mathieu Sagean.* Edited by M. Shea. New York, 1863.

Saint-Luc de la Corne. *Journal du voyage de m. Saint-Luc de la Corne . . . dans le navire "l'Auguste," en l'an 1761.* Quebec, 1863.

Tonty, Henri de (attributed to). *Dernières découvertes dans l'Amérique septentrionales de M. de la Salle.* Paris, 1697.

Thwaites, Reuben Gold, ed. and trans. *The Jesuit Relations and Allied Documents: Travels and Exploration of the Jesuit Missionaries in New France, 1610–1791; The Original French, Latin, and Italian Texts, with English Translations and Notes.* 73 vols. Cleveland, Ohio, 1896–1901; repr. New York, 1959.

Studies and Reference

Atkinson, Geoffroy. *The Extraordinary Voyage in French Literature Before 1700.* New York, 1920.

———. *The Extraordinary Voyage in French Literature from 1700 to 1720.* New York, 1969.

Berthiaume, Pierre. *L'Aventure américaine au XVIIIe siècle: Du voyage à l'écriture.* Ottawa, 1990.

Dictionary of Canadian Biography. Vols. 1 and 2. Edited by George W. Brown and David M. Hayne. Toronto, Ontario, 1966, 1969.

Lemire, Maurice, ed. *Dictionnaire des oeuvres littéraires du Québec.* Vol. 1. Montreal, 1978.

Toye, William, ed. *Oxford Companion to Canadian Literature.* Toronto, Ontario, 1983.

Warwick, Jack. "Récits de voyages en Nouvelle-France au XVIIe siècle: Bibliographie d'introduction." In *Voyages, récits et imaginaire.* Biblio 17. Paris, 1984. Also published in *Scritti sulla Nouvelle-France nel seicento.* Quaderni del seicento francese, vol. 6. Bari, Italy, 1984.

Jack Warwick

SEE ALSO **Colonial Political Thought; The Colonial Press; Drama; Higher Education; Libraries and Learned Societies; Literacy;** and **Schools and Schooling.**

Louisiana

THE EARLIEST EXTANT texts written with a literary intent date from the Spanish period. As with other emergent literature, that of colonial Louisiana began with poetry and drama. In the Louisiana colony, as in Canada, the chief literary genres were travel relations, geographical descriptions, and historical accounts. Only a few personal letters have survived from the colonial period.

TRAVEL AND HISTORICAL ACCOUNTS

The earliest accounts are, naturally, those of the explorer René-Robert Cavalier de La Salle and his companions, especially Henri de Tonty and Henri Joutel. The *Jesuit Relations* included interesting accounts of Louisiana by Jacques Gravier (vols. 65 and 66), Nicolas de Beaubois (vol. 67), and Paul du Poisson (vol. 67). Father du Poisson, in particular, provides a rather jaundiced, totally unromantic view of the Louisiana landscape (as well as a spirited description of the ferocity of the Louisiana mosquito) that can serve as a useful corrective to Vicomte François René de Chateaubriand's fustian prose.

While the official correspondence, including innumerable memoirs describing the potential wealth of the colony and suggesting means of exploiting it, is voluminous, personal letters are few. Two sets do stand out: the letters written by an Ursuline nun to her father and those of a colonist. Sister Marie-Madeleine Hachard, who arrived in the colony in 1727 with a group of other Ursulines, sent home lively descriptions of life in colonial New Orleans intended above all to reassure her father back in Rouen about conditions in the New World. The Chevalier de Pradel's correspondence provides an excellent description of daily life outside of New Orleans during the early years of French colonization.

Histories of the colony were of course produced by settlers, missionaries, and officers. The Jesuit Pierre François Xavier de Charlevoix included Louisiana in his monumental 1744 *History and General Description of New France with the Historical Journal of a Voyage Made in North America*. The Louisiana chapters retrace the history of La Salle's explorations and assassination and the establishment of the colony up to the Natchez rebellion in 1729. The *Journal* contains descriptions of the countryside and of the Natchez Indians. Antoine Simon Le Page du Pratz, a colonist, published in 1758 an *Histoire de la Louisiane* that is actually a memoir of his stay in the colony from 1718 to 1734. Le Page du Pratz is especially valuable as a source for the Natchez Indians, among whom he lived for eight years. Jean-Bernard Bossu, a naval officer detached to Louisiana from 1751 to 1763, recorded his observations and the stories he had heard in a two-volume work published in 1768 and favorably reviewed in Friedrich Melchior von Grimm's *Correspondance littéraire*.

Literary production as such, however, had to wait until the Spanish period. In the 1740s, Dumont de Montigny penned "Poème en vers," relating the founding of the colony and its history from 1716 to 1746, but the work was first published in the *Journal des Américanistes de Paris* in 1931. The first documented works of literature published in the Louisiana province are poems replete with allusions to Greek mythology produced by a planter, Julien Poydras, to praise the Spanish governor. *La prise du Morne de Baton Rouge* (1779) celebrates the capture of the British-held fort at Baton Rouge by Bernardo de Gálvez, Louisiana's sole foray into the American War of Independence. An earlier poem (1777), "Le Dieu et les nayades du Fleuve St. Louis" (the God and the water nymphs of the Mississippi), rejoiced in fulsome fashion at Gálvez's recovery from illness. Though it seems that Paul Louis LeBlanc de Villeneufve was already writing during the colonial period, his only play, Louisiana's first, was not published and performed until after the Louisiana Purchase. This work, a classical tragedy entitled *The Festival of the Young Corn; or, The Heroism of Poucha-Houmma*, celebrated the virtue and nobility of the Louisiana Indians as they were during the heroic period of early colonization, before they were corrupted by contact with the white man. With its nostalgic notes, it can be considered a fitting conclusion to the literature of colonial Louisiana.

BIBLIOGRAPHY

Baillarde, A., and A. Prioult. *Le chevalier de Pradel: Vie d'un colon français en Louisiane au XVIIIe siècle.* Paris, 1928.

Bossu, Jean-Bernard. *Nouveaux voyages en Louisiane, 1751–1768.* Paris, 1980.

———. *Travels in the Interior of North America, 1751–1762.* Edited and translated by Seymour Feiler. Norman, Okla., 1962.

Carpenter, John R. *Histoire de la littérature française sur la Louisiane 1673 jusqu'à 1766.* Paris, 1966.

Charlevoix, Pierre François Xavier de. *Charlevoix's Louisiana: Selections from the "History" and the "Journal."* Edited by Charles Edward O'Neill. Baton Rouge, La., 1977.

Hachard, Marie-Madeleine. *Relation du voyage des dames religieuses ursulines de Rouen à la Nouvelle-Orléans.* Paris, 1872.

LeBlanc de Villeneufve, Paul Louis. *The Festival of the Young Corn; or, The Heroism of Poucha-Houmma.* Edited and translated by Mathé Allain. Lafayette, La., 1964.

Le Page du Pratz, Antoine Simon. *Histoire de la Louisiane . . .* Paris, 1758.

———. *The History of Louisiana.* Edited by Joseph G. Tregle. Baton Rouge, La., 1975.

Thwaites, Reuben Gold, ed. *The Jesuit Relations and Allied Documents: Travels and Explorations of the Jesuit Missionaries in New France, 1610–1791.* 73 vols. New York, 1959.

Tinker, Edward Larocque. *Louisiana's Earliest Poet: Julien Poydras and the Paeans to Gálvez.* New York, 1933.

Mathé Allain
Carl Brasseaux

See also **Drama; Literacy;** and **Schools and Schooling.**

THE SPANISH BORDERLANDS

DURING A PERIOD OF three hundred years, between roughly 1521 and 1821, the Spanish explored and mapped the North American interior from Florida to the Mississippi River, the deserts of Arizona and New Mexico to the plains of Texas and Kansas, and the Pacific Coast to the Sierra Nevada mountain range in northern California. Spanish soldiers; tradesmen; Franciscan friars; and common men, women, and children also established settlements in New Mexico as early as 1598, parts of Texas and Arizona during the seventeenth and eighteenth centuries were settled, and in California a line of missions, *presidios,* and towns was established between present-day San Diego and San Francisco. Over these three centuries, the people who explored and settled the Spanish Borderlands produced a vast body of writing that chronicled their long journey to the New World and that gave voice to their colonial experience in exploration narratives, diaries, and histories, as well as epic poetry, liturgical and secular drama, and verse. This essay will present an overview of the various forms and rich expression of Spain's colonial period.

Hernán Cortés initiated the Spanish conquest of the Americas with his destruction of the marvelous city of Tenochtitlan in the Valley of Mexico. Cortés himself led numerous explorations westward and northward from the Valley of Mexico—now Mexico City—but other Spaniards joined him in exploring and exploiting the new land. Among these was Pánfilo de Narváez, who at the head of some three hundred men, was authorized to take possession of Florida in 1527. While most of the party was exploring the interior, a series of brutal storms destroyed the three Spanish vessels on the western coast of Florida, leaving the men stranded. This contingency led to an astonishing journey overland by Alvar Nuñez Cabeza de Vaca and his three companions—Alfonso del Castillo Maldonado; Andrés Dorantes de Carranza; and Estevanico, "a black Arab, native of Azamjor."

CABEZA DE VACA

It was also the first narrative cartography of land entirely unknown to Europeans. Between 1528 and 1535, Cabeza de Vaca and his three companions made their way overland from Florida to the western coast of Mexico, some six thousand miles (9,600 kilometers). The narrative of the journey provides a detailed ethnographic description of scores of Native tribes, including their daily material and cultural practices; languages; familial and tribal practices and ceremonies; and modes of food gathering, processing, and consumption. It also reflects Cabeza de Vaca's gradual understanding of Native cosmologies and the acculturation of the Spaniards into tribal life over the period of their eight-year journey westward from Florida through Texas, southern New Mexico, and Arizona and down the Mexican central plateau and western coast to Culiacan and Mazatlan.

It is surmised that when he returned to Spain in 1537, he revised and considerably extended the thirty-page report he, Castillo, and Dorantes delivered to the authorities. His *La Relación* was published in Spain in 1542, with a second, interpolated edition appearing in 1555 (under the title *Naufragios*). The first section describes Pánfilo de Narváez's expedition of five ships and six hundred men to explore the coast and interior of Florida. The ill-fated expedition began to encounter trouble while ported in Santo Domingo and Cuba, where storms constantly threatened and finally forced them, before they were fully provisioned, toward Florida in April 1528. From April through November, the explorers wandered in the Florida interior, lost most of the time and stranded in marshes. They encountered Native groups, interacting with them sometimes peacefully but just as often trying to destroy them. Straggling to the coast, the men constructed three rafts and floated for days off the Gulf coast before being tossed ashore on Malhado (Galveston Island) on 6 November during another storm. Cabeza de Vaca described their miserable condition: "We were left naked, as we were born. . . . We were in the bitter cold of November, so emaciated our bones could be counted; we were the figure of death."

Like the English Pilgrims, those other wretched Europeans of a century later, Cabeza de Vaca and his men were pitied and cared for by Native people who shared their food and shelter. The perspective of Cabeza de Vaca's narrative of the Native habitat soon began to shift from fear to admiration for the Native people: "These people love their children more than any other, treating them in the best fashion. When someone's child dies, the parents and relatives and all the villagers cry, and the lament lasts a year, during which every day just before sun rise the weeping begins."

Like Mary Rowlandson's *Captivity Narrative* (1682), which opens with a fearful scene of assault and captivity by the Algonquian and initially presents Native life and culture as an abomination, Cabeza de Vaca's narrative begins with straggling Europeans alone and afraid on territory they do understand, held captive by people whose language, dress, and daily life they can not comprehend. In both narratives, however, fear gradually turns to cultural adaptation, and finally, in the case of Cabeza de Vaca, to admiration for the resilience and integrity of scores of Native groups spread over the continent. A full century before Rowlandson bartered her skill at sewing for food, clothing, and favorable treatment, Cabeza de Vaca became a successful merchant, trading "pieces of sea snails, their hearts, conches" in exchange for "skins, red ocher with which they dye their faces and hair . . . flints for arrowheads, paste, hard cane to make arrows." When he appeared to heal a dead man ("I found the Indian's eyes rolled up; he had no pulse all the signs of death"), he was elevated from slave to shaman. Over the course of his journey, he was held in increasing respect and awe by numerous tribes that had heard about

him and traveled long distances to beg him to heal their sick. In return for his medicine, they offered him everything they owned and then escorted him en masse to the next tribe.

Cabeza de Vaca's narrative provides the first ethnographic information on marriage and sexual practices. For example, he noted that in many tribes, there were no sexual relations for two years after a woman became pregnant and that "the children suckle until the age of 12, which is when they are old enough to find their food." His account provides an inventory of tribal names—Cauoque, Han, Charruco, Deguene, Mendica, Atayo, Yeguaze, Quitole, Chavavare, Cultalchulche, Susola, Camole—"all of whom had diverse habits, villages, and languages," and it presents the first detailed description of the grasslands, birds, plants, and animals (among which the buffalo are remembered as ranging from the "seacoast of Florida . . . over a tract of more than 400 leagues" [1,200 miles, 1,920 kilometers], weather patterns, and geological formations.

After years of living among various groups while the Europeans traveled west, they were at first joyous when they heard that other Christians were nearby but were then disillusioned when they found that Spanish soldiers were enslaving and decimating Indian people: "We grieved seeing their fertile and beautiful land with abundant waters and rivers being depopulated and burned and its skinny and sick people fleeing and hiding all the time. . . . They were so malnourished they looked like they were about to die." Ironically the Indians regarded them as protectors from the Spanish. Indeed after their long journey they looked more Indian than Spanish, as their first encounter with other Europeans indicates: "I reached four Christian horsemen who were dumbfounded upon seeing me so strangely undressed and in company of Indians. Stunned, they stared a long time neither speaking to me nor asking anything." Even after they presumably had been culturally restored, they were never able to convince the Indians that they were Christians: "they replied that the Christians lied: We had come from the sunrise, they from the sunset; we healed the sick, they killed the sound; we came naked and barefoot, they clothed, horsed, and lanced." De Vaca adds, "we coveted nothing but gave whatever we were given, while they robbed whomever they found and bestowed nothing on anyone."

The transformation Cabeza de Vaca and his companions underwent during the course of their physical and spiritual journey in the New World was, as William Pilkington suggests, what gives *La Relación* its "peculiarly American" narrative configuration. Pilkington might well have said that Cabeza de Vaca's story of his encounter with the New World actually established the narrative prototype of transformation for later European encounters with the people and geography of the new world.

THE DE SOTO EXPEDITION

Even before Cabeza de Vaca's narrative was published, people in Mexico had heard him say that there were large cities in the interior; as the whisper flamed into fabulous tales, these became the Seven Cities of Cíbola. As early as 1537, the year Cabeza de Vaca sailed to Spain, Hernando de Soto was appointed governor of Cuba with authority to conduct all exploration and settlement of the area from Florida to the central interior to the Gulf Coast of Mexico. In fact, de Soto met Cabeza de Vaca in Spain and asked him to return to Florida as his second in command, a request Cabeza de Vaca refused because, given his journey of some eight years, he thought he should command the expedition himself. In 1539 de Soto sailed to Florida with 600 soldiers, 213 horses, supplies for two years, and several monks and priests. Between August 1539 and January 1543, de Soto's expedition covered a huge expanse of terrain, from the west coast of Florida, through central Georgia, portions of the Carolinas, much of Alabama, the northern half of Mississippi, central Arkansas, and as far west as Texas. The expedition members were the first Europeans to sail the Mississippi, using four barges they built in April 1541. A year later, after wandering through swamps, forests, and up and down the Mississippi, de Soto died on 21 May 1542 of fever in Arkansas, and although initially buried, he was quickly disinterred and lowered into the Mississippi because it was feared he would be dug up by the Indians and mutilated in retaliation for the cruelties he had perpetrated upon them. The expedition continued under the leadership of Luis de Moscoso, but when after six months of pointless marching, the expedition failed to find the treasures Cabeza de Vaca had hinted at in his *Relación*, the straggling group of three hundred men made its way down the Mississippi, along the Gulf coast, and back to Mexico by September 1543.

The most famous story of de Soto's exploits was a contemporary account that reads like a chivalaric romance. *La Florida del Inca: O historia de Adelantado Hernando de Soto* (1605) was composed in the 1590s by Inca Garcilaso de la Vega, who relied on two first-hand expeditionary accounts, Roderigo Rangel's *Relación de la expedición de Hernando de Soto* and Luis H. de Biedma's *Relato de la expedición,* for his historical information. *La Florida del Inca* generally exaggerates de Soto's exploits, turning the usually uneventful actual journey into an extravagant series of epic encounters with dangerous Indians and harrowing natural obstacles. As narrative, it exploits the tradition of the medieval romance in a manner that is far more colorful than the relatively stark narrative of Cabeza de Vaca. Just as the latter provided the impetus for de Soto's expedition of 1539, so *La Florida de Inca,* coupled with the narrative of Fray Marcos de Niza (see below), would drive the even bigger expedition of Francisco Vasquez de Coronado in 1540.

THE CORONADO JOURNEY

Soon after Cabeza de Vaca returned to Mexico, Fray Marcos de Niza, with Estevanico as his guide, made his way toward Cíbola. Although it is now believed that he never advanced into the pueblos of New Mexico, where Cíbola supposedly existed, his report, *Descubrimiento de las siete ciudades de Cíbola* (1539), fueled the Spanish imagination by claiming that Cíbola (Hawikuh, a Zuni pueblo in southwestern New Mexico) was "larger than the city of Mexico" and that the entire surrounding land was the "greatest and best of all that have been discovered." It was de Niza's report that inspired the preparation of the most ambitious expedition into the interior ever made by the Spanish; Francisco Vasquez de Coronado's journey of 1540–1542. Although there were numerous letters and journals of the expedition, Pedro de Casteñeda's retrospective

Relación de la jornada de Cíbola de 1540 provided the most detailed, vivid, and narratively stylized chronicle of the journey.

One of Coronado's common soldiers, Casteñeda wrote about the failed expedition some twenty years after the event, because having heard the fabulous stories that had accrued over time, he felt that someone should write a sober and reliable version of events. Casteñeda's self-effacing narrative—"Although not in a polished style, I write that which happened, that which I heard, experienced, saw, and did"—normalizes the geography and presents a fair-minded description of the many different tribes encountered by the Europeans, even criticizing the Spanish for their arrogant, unsympathetic, casually cruel treatment of the Pueblo Indians.

But what gives the narrative its imaginative quality is its nostalgia for the expedition, the land, and people encountered. It is as though twenty years after riding through a vast stretch of terrain that was unappreciated during the exploration itself, he and many of his comrades came to realize the potential for settling a land they had before only been interested in plundering for its riches. The prefatory sigh of lost opportunity gives nuance to the entire narrative:

Granted that they did not find the riches of which they had been told, they found a place in which to search for them and the beginning of a good country to settle in. . . . Since they came back from the country which they had conquered and abandoned, time has given them a chance to understand the direction and locality in which they were, and the borders of the good country they had in their hands, and their hearts weep for having lost so favorable an opportunity." (George Parker Winship. *The Coronado Expedition,* p. 3)

Casteñeda's desire to narratively restore the past seems an almost anguished attempt to regain what he has lost, at least through literary imagination. Like the others who went along and who years later spun one story and tale after another as a means of filling the emptiness, all Casteñeda had was memories of a journey he "experienced, saw, and did." But it is precisely the power of Casteñeda's sense of wonder for the past that gives the narrative a literary rather than just a historical or documentary value.

Like Cabeza de Vaca, Casteñeda provides an outsider's view of Indian society that, on one hand, is culturally biased and judgmental but, on the other, sympathetic and critical of European brutality. In his attention to the cruelty visited upon the Indians, as well as his interest in their customs and habits, Casteñeda, perhaps unwittingly, calls into question the very colonial enterprise of which he was a part. A typical conquistador might well have erased certain events, but he refused to gloss over Coronado's savage order, during the siege of a Tiguex village, to burn two hundred men at the stake "as an example so that the other natives would fear the Spaniards." His subsequent description of the orderly life of these same Tiguex only deepens our sense of the tragic effects of Spanish cruelty:

In general, these villages all have the same habits and customs. . . . They are governed by the opinions of the elders. They all work together to build the villages, the women being engaged in making the mixture and the walls, while the men bring the wood and put it in place. . . . The men spin and weave. The women bring up the children and prepare the food. The country is so fertile that they do not have to break up the ground the year round, but only have to sow the seed. . . . In one year they gather enough for seven." (George Parker Winship. *The Coronado Expedition,* pp. 53–54)

As was usually the case with Europeans' myopic encounter with New World peoples, Coronado and most of his party failed to see the richness of the cultural and social structures before their very eyes. Rather, they pushed on as far as Kansas looking for the fabled cities of gold until, exhausted and disillusioned, they returned to Mexico City, the expedition a failure and Coronado ruined. Casteñeda gave a sense of the scope of that failure when he noted that the land erased all trace of their huge train: "Who could believe that 1,000 horses and 500 of our cows and more than 5,000 rams and ewes and more than 1,500 friendly Indians and servants, in traveling over those plains, would leave no more trace where they had passed than if nothing had been there—nothing." Yet though the expedition was a failure in its singular quest to find cities paved with gold, Casteñeda counted as heroic the men who made the difficult and dangerous journey of some two thousand miles (3,200 kilometers). In a stunning passage anticipating

Miguel de Cervantes by forty years, he referred to books of chivalry as but fables filled with heroes possessed of "deadly strength" and "resplendent arms," while in the real world the "small stature of the men of our time" made the more "remarkable" those "things which our people have undertaken and accomplished," feats to be "more wondered at today than those of which the ancients write."

GALLEGOS AND ESPEJO NARRATIVES

For forty years after 1542, the northern frontier was virtually closed to further exploration. In 1581 the Rodriguez-Chamuscado expedition of some thirty men traveled as far as Taos, New Mexico. Hernán Gallegos's account, *Relación y concudío de el viage* (1582), is modeled after Cabeza de Vaca's and Casteñeda's already-famous narratives. Like Casteñeda, Gallegos described Native customs and traditions (for example, the Hopi snake dance and a wedding ceremony), Native dress and social structures, and, of course, the buffalo. The narrative provides useful cartographic and especially ethnographic information on the region, but it has little of the imaginative quality found in Casteñeda. Gallegos, however, did report how two friars staged a drama in which they saved a group of Indians just before they were to be executed as a demonstration of their sympathy and good will toward the people with whom they expected to stay. The two friars did, in fact, remain to Christianize the Indians.

The next year another small group, led by Antonio de Espejo, went in search of the two, who had been given only a few days to proselytize before they were sent to their heaven (or hell) by irate Indians. Espejo, as it turned out, was much more interested in the material than the spiritual potential of the area, which he renamed Nueva Andalucía in remembrance of his Spanish homeland. In fact Espejo's *Relación* of 1583 prefigures Captain John Smith's promotional narratives, *A True Relation of Virginia* (1608) and *A Description of New England* (1616), in its focus upon the vast material potential of the new land. However, rather than holding out the ever-elusive promise of gold and silver, Espejo noted that Nueva Andalucía was a land ripe for perma-

nent settlement. Espejo wrote that there was "much game to be hunted on the ground and in the air, rabbits and hares, deer and the cattle [buffalo] of that country, and ducks and geese, and cranes and pheasants and other birds; good mountains with all types of woods, salt pits, and rivers with a wide diversity of fish." He added that "in the greater part of these lands wagons and carts can be used; there are very good pastures for the cattle, and lands from which to make farms, large gardens, and fields for both dry farming and irrigations, many rich veins, from which I brought ore to be assessed for its fineness." It was precisely such promise that opened the way fifteen years later for Juan de Oñate to lead over five hundred people into New Mexico, where they would establish the first permanent European settlement in what is now the United States, a project to be discussed below.

THE CALIFORNIA COAST

Between 1521, the year Mexico was conquered by Hernán Cortés, and the 1540s, numerous exploratory parties inched their way along the Pacific coast. Cortés himself led a group up the California Peninsula in 1535, but the effort to colonize the area was quickly abandoned. However, the first major voyage along the California coast was carried out by Juan Rodriguez Cabrillo between 1542 and 1543, the same period during which Coronado's expedition was mapping the interior. The "Relación, o Diário," kept by Juan Paez, charts its progress during the stormy winter months along what is now San Diego Bay, Santa Barbara, Monterey, the Golden Gate, and beyond Drake's Bay. The diary proved to be generally accurate, identifying some seventy coastal points that would be useful for later exploration and providing the first detailed information on Native people encountered during the two-year voyage. An entry written along the coast of Santa Barbara reads:

All this coast which they have passed is very thickly settled. The Indians brought for them many sardines, fresh and very good. . . . They were dressed in skins, and wore their hair very long and tied up with long strings interwoven with the hair, there being attached to the strings many gewgaws of flint, bond, and wood. The country appears to be very fine. (Herbert E. Bolton, ed., *Spanish Exploration*, p. 27)

Juan Cabrillo himself sustained an injury during the first leg of the trip and died on the return voyage in January 1543, on the island of Ciquimuymu, renamed for him but now called San Miguel Island.

At the same time that Cabrillo's expedition was taking place, a route to the Philippines was charted and a vigorous galleon trade established that brought goods to Mexico. Because the best return was across the Pacific to the Cape Mendocino latitude, and because the English and the French were pirating Spanish galleons along the California coast, interest in securing a port of call led to renewed exploration and coastal charting. At the same time that Juan de Oñate was settling New Mexico, Sebastian Vizcaino, a merchant seaman familiar with the Philippine trade, was contracted to explore and to secure a settlement in California. His voyage of 1602–1603 was described in the obligatory diary, which was not published until 1882, as well as in a journal, or navigational description of the route, and thirty-three charts mapping the coast. Like Cabrillo's voyage some forty years earlier, Vizcaino's expedition was carried out largely during the winter months. Storms halted progress and repeatedly separated the three ships; and cold and rain created such severe conditions that most of the men were sick, many of them dying aboard ship. Of their condition in January 1603, after reaching the northernmost point of Cape Mendocino and sailing back into Monterey Bay, Vizcaino wrote in his *Diário:*

The state of our health was so bad and the sick clamoring, although there was neither assistance nor medicines nor food to give them except rotten jerked beef, gruel, biscuits and bean and chick-peas spoiled by weevils. The mouths of all were sore, and their gums were swollen larger than their teeth, so that they could hardly drink water, and the ship seemed more like a hospital than a ship of an armada. (Herbert E. Bolton, ed. *Spanish Exploration*, p. 97)

KINO IN PIMERÍA ALTA

In Pimería Alta, the name then applied to southern Arizona and northern Sonora, exploration and mission settlement was carried out in the late seventeenth and early eighteenth centuries under the direction of Padre Eusebio Francisco Kino. Between 1687 and 1711, Kino made some fifty journeys of from one hundred to about one thousand miles (from 160 to 1,600 kilometers) on foot and on horseback inland from the Tucson mission. Kino's magisterial *Favores celestiales* provides an astonishing general history of the founding of Pimería Alta and Kino's fearless travels into the interior. Historians have long known and had access to a diary, three *relaciones,* two or three letters, and a famous 1705 map of Kino's missionary work. However, not until Herbert E. Bolton discovered the Kino text of *Favores celestiales* in the Archivo General y Público in Mexico City in the early 1900s has Kino's history been offered widely in text and translation. The original contains 433 small folio pages of text in five parts. Part I consists of an account of the "spiritual affairs, the explorations, the Indian troubles, and other temporal interests in Pimería Alta from March 1687 to November 1699, with a discussion of the spiritual and temporal advantages which might be derived from further conquests in this most extensive northern portion of this North America" (Bolton, *Kino's Historical Memoir*, p. 71). Parts II, III, and IV cover in a similar way the period from 1700 to 1707, with particular emphasis upon Kino's own exploring expeditions in Pimería Alta along the Gila and Colorado rivers and along the Gulf coast. According to Bolton, Kino wrote from and referred to some "two hundred sources, giving some in their entirety and citing others," mostly letters, from his superiors and "seven diaries of exploring expeditions."

SETTLEMENT OF TEXAS AND CALIFORNIA

During the seventeenth and eighteenth centuries, the Spanish turned to the development of settlements in present-day California and Texas that would consolidate Spain's possession of the northern provinces and western seacoast. In Texas, exploration during the late seventeenth century produced a few cartographic and missionary narratives. Supposedly at the behest of Indians from Coahuil in present-day Texas, Fray Juan Larios traveled to the frontier alone to establish a mission. Between 1673 and 1675, he and Fernando del Bosque journeyed hundreds of leagues through the plains of Texas and along the Rio Grande and Pecos, reporting their findings in the *Autos de la conquista de la Provincia de Coahuila* (1688). Some twelve years later, Alonso de León led a series of five expeditions through much of the same territory with a view to founding a permanent settlement. In 1690 two missions were built near the Nueces River but were abandoned in 1693, and it was more than twenty years before Texas was resettled. The de León expeditions produced a series of letters, journals, and narratives that, published as a group in *Historia de Nuevo León . . . por el Capitán Alonso de León* (1909), may be useful in recharting this early period in Texas history.

In California, diaries, journals, and narratives describing exploration of both the California and upper northwest coast and routes into the eastern interior provide a thorough inventory of personal and collective reflections on the California tribes, coastal bays, forest and grasslands, and so on. Bolton's *Spanish Exploration,* a collection of original materials in translation on the exploration and settlement of the Spanish Borderlands, remains one of the standards for those interested in reading about the founding of New Mexico, California, Texas, and Arizona.

THE LATER NARRATIVES

During the eighteenth century, exploration was rather limited, and that which did take place assumed a scientific aspect, with the Spanish Crown sponsoring expeditions that were expected to provide useful cartographic, botanical, navigational, and ethnological information. By the end of the eighteenth century, present-day California, New Mexico, and Texas had been sufficiently mapped so that the elaborate narratives, chronicles, and journals of earlier years fell into decline. The reasons may best be understood in light of a cartographic metaphor. The cartographic narrative served what William Boelhower, referring to European mapmaking of New World territory, called a "military apparatus, a means of monitoring possessions, a tool of power, an operational scheme."

The Spanish colonial charting of what David Weber referred to as "New Spain's far northern frontier" had by the end of the eighteenth century been mostly completed. The last great wave

of narratives consisted of those composed during the establishment of settlements in northern California during the last quarter of the eighteenth century. Among them are the narratives of Juan Bautista Anza's two expeditions, one into the interior to chart the terrain between Sonora and California and the other to settle San Francisco in 1776. For the two expeditions, a total of thirteen diaries were kept, including: Anza's own official *Diário de la rutta y operaciones* (1775–1776); Fray Pedro Fónt's brief *Diário* (1775–1776) and its expanded four-hundred-page version, *Diário completa* (1777); Fray Francisco Gárces's *Diário y derrotero* (1775–1776); Joaquin de Moraga's *Carta de la ocupación de San Francisco* (1776); and Fray Francisco Palóu's *Noticias de Nueva California* (1776), a narrative describing Fray Junipero Serra's missionary work in California. There is also the narrative of the Dominguez-Escalante expedition that set out from Santa Fe in 1776 to find a new route to California to replace the difficult and often dangerous sea voyage from Mexico to Monterey, California. Although a more satisfactory route was not found, the expedition did chart new terrain through what is now Utah and Nevada.

The cartographic function of such narrative practice whereby information about new possessions was recorded was largely complete by the beginning of the nineteenth century. There were a handful of other *relaciones* and diaries produced during this period, but the forementioned are really the final examples of an imperial discourse charting Spain's possessions in the northern provinces. Once the map was complete at the end of the eighteenth century—complete in the sense that the Spanish colonial project had calcified, had marked its boundaries, and would be satisfied with building its home upon terra cognita—further mapping was deemphasized. Cartographic narrative had renamed the rivers, bays, valleys, mountains, and Native people encountered by the Spanish; such toponymic transformation, along with a line of *presidios,* missions, and towns, signaled the finality of Spanish colonial domination of what had long been indigenous terrain.

Domination and settlement of areas along the Rio Grande Valley in New Mexico, parts of Texas, and the California coast mission system meant that numerous official reports were produced to detail social and economic conditions in colonial settlements. Once again these narratives provided information on intercultural relations with various Indian groups as well as botanical, geographic, church, and military issues; and information on natural resources, trade, and commerce. Most importantly they served as advocates on behalf of the colonists for material supplies, military support, political recognition, and economic backing in the far northern settlements. Among these narratives are Miguel de Costanso's *Report of 1791* on the California *presidios;* Governor Juan Bautista de Elguezábal's *A Description of Texas in 1803* and Manuel de Salcedo's *A Governor's Report on Texas in 1809;* and Governor Fernando de Chacón's *Economic Report of 1803* for New Mexico, Pedro Bautista Pino's *Exposición sucinta y sencilla de la Provincia del Nuevo México* (1812), and Antonio Barreiro's *Ojeada sobre Nuevo Mexico que da una idea de sus producciones naturales* (1832). While they are occasionally interesting for the information they impart, these narratives have little of the imagination or passion of the early narratives, which are filled with awe and wonder at seeing another world for the first time.

In 1821, the year Mexico won its independence from Spain, Luis Antonio Argüello was sent on the very last expedition into California. Ironically for Spain he was dispatched, with seventy men and a cannon, to have a look for the Crown following rumors that Americans had established a colony in northern California that might pose a threat to Spanish interests. His brief *Diário* (1821) shows that, during their month-long reconnoiter, they found no Americans. His report was the last narrative composed during Spanish rule in the borderlands. The new republic of Mexico would continue to commission official narratives until 1846, when the Americans would indeed pose a threat and in the Mexican War (1846–1848) complete their conquest of the vast area explored and settled by the Spanish and Mexican governments over a period of three centuries.

GASPAR PÉREZ DE VILLAGRÁ'S EPIC

As indicated, although Spanish explorers wrote scores of narratives, journals, and diaries about their journeys into the North American conti-nent after Hernan Cortés conquered Mexico in 1521, the literature—the aesthetic enterprise—of the Spanish Borderlands began most properly in 1610 with the publication of Gaspar Pérez de Villagrá's monumental *Historia de la Nuevo-Mexico,* the epic account of the first Spanish settlement of the province of New Mexico by Juan de Oñate and some six hundred colonists in 1598. Published fourteen years before Captain John Smith's celebrated *General History of Virginia* (1624), Villagrá's work is both the first history and the first epic of the country's early colonial period.

Villagrá, born in New Spain (around 1555), had joined Oñate's expedition in 1596 as a captain and legal officer, and he remained with the colony until 1600, when Oñate sent him back to Mexico for more colonists. When the viceroy not only denied Oñate's request but ordered him brought up on charges of misconduct, Villagrá disappeared and never returned to New Mexico. It is possible that he wrote the poem while in Mexico, perhaps already having drafted sections while in New Mexico. At any rate he was in Spain by 1609, living in Alcalá de Henares, where his epic was published in 1610. During a prolonged trial from 1612 to 1614, Villagrá himself was charged with misconduct for his part in the campaign against the Acoma tribe, the exploits of which are celebrated in his *Historia.* In 1614 he was banned from the province of New Mexico for six years. It was not until 1620 that he restored himself before the king and was granted permission to return to the New World in a position of authority. Ironically, Villagrá died in a shipwreck while returning to New Spain to serve as *alcade mayor* (mayor) of Zapoltitlán in Guatemala.

Opening with a direct allusion to Virgil's epic invocation in the *Aeneid,* Villagrá salutes Juan de Oñate, and with him the entire Spanish colonial enterprise in the New World:

> Las armas y el varón heroico canto,
> El ser, valor, prudencia y alto esfuerzo
> De aquel cuya paciencia no rendida,
> Por un mar de disgustos arrojada
> A pesar de la envidia ponzoñosa
> El ser, valor, prudencia y alto esfuerzo
> De aquellos españoles valerosos
> Que en la Occidental India remontados.

> (Villagrá, Canto I, ll. 1–8)

LITERATURE: SPANISH

(I sing of arms and of that heroic man, / Of him whose courage, care and high emprise / Of him whose unconquered patience / Though cast upon a sea of cares, / Who spite of envy slanderous, / Is raising to new heights the feats, / The deeds of those valorous Spaniards / Who go forth in the Western Indies.)

Published in 287 folios of text, the poem is written in thirty-four cantos of blank hendeca-syllabics, an eleven-syllable line common in Greek and Latin poetry. This form departed from the royal octave practiced by most Renaissance epic poets, but allowed Villagrá more prose-like freedom of expression in narrating the heroism of the Oñate expedition. Like other writers of New World epics, Villagrá participated in the events he narrated; therefore the poem is imbued with autobiographical authority and passion for exploring terrain largely unknown and mysterious. The first two cantos describe the migration to the Valley of Mexico of the legendary Aztecs from the northern regions of a mythical land thought to be somewhere in New Mexico. These two cantos are filled with marvelous events and characters, not the least interesting of which is the devil in the guise of a witch with face *"descarnado macilento"* (fleshless and emaciated):

> Desmesuradoes pechos, largas tetas,
> Hambrientas, flacas, secas y fruncidas,

(Misshapen breasts and dangling teats, / Starved, flaccid, dry and wrinkled,)

> Disforme boca desde oreja a oreja,
> Por cuyos labios secos desmedidos,
> Cuatro solos colmillos hacia afuera,
> De un largo palmo corvos se mostraban;

(A mouth malformed, from ear to ear, / Through whose dry and distorted lips / Of fangs just four protruded / And, curving, showed themselves a good palm's length;)

(Villagrá, Canto II, ll. 16–23)

Cantos III through V recount the famous journeys and expeditionary narratives of Cabeza de Vaca, whose *Relación* (1542) fueled Spanish desire for a city of gold in the north that would match the grandeur of Tenochtitlán; Fray Marco de Niza's report, *Descubimiento de las siete ciudades de Cíbola* (1539), of his expedition to the north

in which he greatly amplified the story of the cities of gold; Pedro de Casteñeda's narrative of the Francisco Vasquez de Coronado expedition of 1540–1542 in search of the seven cities of gold; and Antonio de Espejo's exploration of New Mexico in 1582, *Relación del viage* (1583). Cantos VI through XVII provide a detailed chronicle of the long trip from interior Mexico to the upper Rio Grande above present-day Santa Fe. The expedition involved some four hundred colonists, many of them in families, carrying supplies for building a permanent settlement—cloth and domestic furnishings and thousands of sheep, cattle, pigs, mules, and horses. The epic ends with the tragic and brutal destruction in 1599 of Acoma, a Pueblo village famed as an inaccessible fortress high on a desert butte. Villagrá's description of the strangeness and great numbers of buffalo echoes that of Pedro de Casteñeda's *Relación* some seventy years earlier:

> Lanudos por extremo, corcobados,
> De regalada carne y negros cuernos,
> Lindísima manteca, y rico sebo,
> Y como los chivatos tienen barbas,
> Y son de una mano tan ligeros,
> Que corren mucho más que los venados,
> Y andan en atajos tanta suma,
> Que viente y treinta mil cabezas juntas,
> Se hallan ordinarias muchas veces.

(They are extremely wooly, hump-backed, / Black-horned, and have splendid flesh, / Wonderfully fat and rich in tallow. They / Have beards like billy-goats, / Yet are so fleet of foot / That they run much faster than deer, / And gather in herds of such great numbers, / That twenty or thirty thousand head / Are commonly and often found)

(Villagrá, Canto XVII, ll. 93–101)

Villagrá's representation of Native people is generally like that offered in other New World epics; they are barbarous and yet intriguing, at once placid and fearful, a people to be brought into the new Christian nation, and yet a people steadfast in their idolatry. The account of the conquest of Acoma is indeed of epic, if imperially self-serving, proportions. Villagrá's graphic description of the death and destruction on both sides is fashioned in the classical mold of Virgil's *Aeneid* as well as in the contemporary style of other New World epics describing the often-bloody encounters between the Spanish and Native people. Yet the poem is historically sound on many aspects of the Oñate expedition. The closing cantos, in fact, were used as evidence against Oñate, Villagrá, and other Spaniards for their mistreatment of Indian captives after the siege, including Villagrá's own execution of two deserters and his alleged transporting of Acoman women and children to Mexico to be distributed among convents.

However faithfully Villagrá chronicled the settling of New Mexico, his epic poem has, unfortunately, been used primarily as a historical document instead of being read as one of the major literary texts of the New World. Hubert H. Bancroft, for example, relied upon the epic extensively for his *History of Arizona and New Mexico* (1889), and in *Don Juan de Oñate and the Colonization of New Mexico, 1595–1628* (1953), George Hammond and Agapito Rey often worked as directly from Villagrá's epic as from official documents and Oñate's own letters. As the editors of the 1992 and only verse translation suggest, the *Historia* is "a literary recreation that not only holds strictly to the historical events and their chronology, but that introduces a very bare minimum of fictional material." Yet although Villagrá wrote from the actual historical events surrounding the exploration and settlement of New Mexico, the poem is of course an imaginative reconstruction, displaying all of the free play we commonly associate with epic structure. Although Villagrá was a direct witness of the events narrated in the poem, there are numerous scenes that must be regarded as purely imagined. Restoring the poem to its rightful place at the fountainhead of American literature requires a revision of our national literary history, a revision that recognizes the Spanish literary production in the borderlands alongside that of British colonial literatures of the eastern seaboard.

MOROS Y CRISTIANOS

Villagrá's *Historia* notes that the first European play performed in New Mexico was *Moros y Cristianos* (The Moors and the Christians). Oñate and his group of colonists arrived in July at Okhe, a Tewa village on the convergence of the Rio Chama and the Rio Grande. The Spanish took possession of the village, renaming it San Juan de los Caballeros. After constructing a church in little over three weeks, Mass was offered in late August, followed by a week of festivities intended to encourage the settlers, many of whom were already disillusioned with the land they saw and the riches they did not see, and, more subtly, to remind them of their covenant with Oñate and the Mexican viceroy:

> . . . se ordenaron
> Unas solemnas fiestas que duraron
> Una semana entera, donde ubo
> luego de canas, toros, y sortija,
> Y una alegre comedia bien compuesta,
> Regozijos de moros y Cristianos,
> Con mucha artilleria, cuio estruendo,
> Causo notable espanto y maravilla,
> A muchos bravos barbaros que avian
> Venido por espias a espiarnos . . .

(. . . they organized / Solemn festivities lasting / An entire week, during which there were / Jousting matches and bull-fights, / A wonderful, well-written comedy, / And the Moors and Christians play, / Acted with such thunderous artillery / That it created great fear and awe / Among the barbarous warriors who / Had come to spy upon us.)

(Villagrá, Canto XXII, ll. 88–97)

Moros y Cristianos and the comedies were the first colonial dramatic productions performed in what is now the United States. Although we have no idea which *comedias* were performed, the play *Moros y Cristianos* is traceable to medieval Spain, where it was staged as part of the Christian reconquest against the Moors, who were finally expelled from Spain in 1492. Staged at the moment the colonialists established their first settlement in 1598, the play appears to have served dual ideological functions. At the behest of the priests, the colonists were being reminded that their mission in the new province was not gaining wealth but rather gaining souls for Christianity. At the same time, the Pueblo Indians were witnessing a show of Spanish military force. For Indians and Spaniards both, *Moros y Cristianos* was a form of conquest drama that signaled the role both groups would play in the colonial enterprise. It appears that versions of the medieval play remained in the cultural repertoire of the Spanish-Mexican population through the contemporary period in New Mexico, where it is occasionally performed in towns and villages even in the late twentieth century.

LITERARY CULTURE

During the colonial period, settlers in the Spanish Borderlands both sustained and adapted literary forms carried with them from Spain. As indicated above, the Spanish medieval play *Moros y Cristianos* was produced in New Mexico as early as 1598 and continues in performance today along with various other dramatic, poetic, and narrative traditions introduced and developed in the Hispanic Southwest.

Ecclesiastical drama, or *autos,* were used extensively by the Franciscans to proselytize Native American groups from Texas to California as well as to provide religious instruction for the colonists. Most of this religious drama was imported from Spanish allegorical drama that had its origin in medieval Europe, or it was composed in Mexico. *Los pastores, Los tres reyes magos, Adan y eva, Los cuatro apariciones de la Virgen de Guadalupe,* and *La primera persecución de Jesus* all functioned to establish the church's authority within colonial society, but the regular performance of the plays also established an aesthetic habitat within different communities through which folk dramatists, poets, singers, and storytellers developed strong traditions of their own.

Many of the songs and poems contained in the religious plays provided material and verse forms for more original compositions by *trobadores.* These roving musicians sang traditional poems and engaged in verbal dueling contests with other folk poets in which they extemporaneously composed *trovos,* or verses, to the applause or disdain of community audiences. Popular folk poets also sustained and modified other verse forms like the *décima,* an elaborate verse form containing an opening quatrain and four ten-verse stanzas. In its more traditional form, the *décima* was offered as a religious or philosophical meditation, but there were also secular and localized *décimas* celebrating local events or eulogizing individuals. The *alabado,* formal and somber meditative hymns, are an offshoot of the *décima.* They were common in New Mexico during the colonial period and are still widely chanted during Lent in villages and towns today.

Another very popular verse form in the Spanish Borderlands was the *romance,* an octosyllabic narrative ballad related to the *corrido;* both are forms that have their origins in Spain. In addition to their value as entertainment, the *romances* functioned to inculcate community and familial responsibilities. Such *romances* as "Delgadina," "La esposa infiel," and "La amiga de Bernal" reminded men and women of their marital obligations as well as the consequences of infidelity. There were also scores of social burlesque *romances,* pastoral *romances,* and religious *romances. Inditas* were a poetic form that evolved from the *romance.* These narrative poems were accompanied by drumbeat and dance, the most famous of which described the various encounters with Native Americans. In the more recent period, the traditional *romance* has given way to the *corrido* as the dominant narrative ballad.

Perhaps the most popular and pervasive narrative tradition circulating in the Spanish Borderlands was the practice of relating *cuentos.* In his pioneering *Cuentos Españoles de Colorado y de Nuevo México,* Juan B. Rael points out that the majority of the five hundred tales he collected between 1930 to 1940 "represent a part of the cultural heritage that the first settlers of this former Spanish frontier brought with them, a heritage which their descendants have faithfully preserved through more than three centuries." The *cuentos* gathered by Rael and his predecessor, Aurelio M. Espinosa, represent a huge repository of orally transmitted narratives that are old-world in type-origin but were modified by the Spanish colonial society in which they circulated. There were scores of tales of picaresque rogues, tales of enchantment filled with witches, ghosts, devils, spellbound young men and women, and animals with the gift of speech and wisdom who reminded adults of their familial and social responsibilities. *Cuentos morales* like "Los tres hermanos" and "Los tres consejos" were highly moralistic, functioning to instill a complex religious, social, and familial sensibility in young listeners. In "La comadre Sebastiana," death is personified, actually given full status as a character: a familial figure, *una comadre,* or friend, who maintains filial ties with an individual over a lifetime. Along with *dichos* (proverbs), *adivinanzas* (riddles), plays, and the improvisational compositions of folk poets, the *cuentos* provided rich entertainment embedded with moral guidance, social mores, and historical and cultural knowledge. They were the cornerstone of a powerful and pervasive oral literature sustained throughout the Southwest from the seventeenth century to the present.

Although drama, poetry, and folktale traditions were part of a complex oral culture, they nevertheless emerged from a Spanish literary culture through books people took with them into the borderland provinces. Although the most prominent textual influence was religious rather than secular, both played a significant part in the formation of a literary culture in the Spanish Borderlands. The Franciscans, who either led or accompanied the many expeditions into the Spanish colonies, brought missals, breviaries, books about the lives of the saints, and other books of a religious nature. The inventory of the Oñate expedition indicates that Captain Alonso de Quesada carried a small batch of religious and nonreligious books, while another colonist, Juan del Caso Baraona, took medical books along with him to New Mexico. If, as it has been conjectured, Gaspar de Villagrá drafted some of his epic *Historia* while in New Mexico, it is quite possible that he carried the *Aeneid,* works by Ovid, a chivalric romance or two, and the Bible. Moreover, one of the major influences on Villagrá was Alonso de Ercilla's *La Araucana,* the epic description of the Spanish conquest of the Araucanian people of Chile in the mid sixteenth century. And, of course, one of the first books to return to the New World during the seventeenth century was Villagrá's own *Historia de la Nueva Mexico.* Governor Diego de Peñalosa had a copy of the *Historia* in his possession in 1661, but it is likely that the epic poem had made its way to the province soon after its publication. Yet, it was rare enough that it disappeared from public circulation almost entirely during the eighteenth century and was not rediscovered until the 1890s by Adolph Bandelier in Mexico's National Museum.

Of course, most of the books brought to the northern provinces belonged to the Franciscans. In 1776 Fray Francisco Domínguez, after the failed expedition to discover a route to California, conducted a lengthy review of a number of missions in New Mexico that, among other matters, provided an inventory of books in the province. Domínguez's inventory now gives us a good idea of the kinds of books that made their way from Spain and Mexico all the way to the far northern reaches of New Mexico's towns and missions. Although there were books scattered throughout the missions, the largest single library was kept in the convent at Santo Domingo pueblo. Domínguez catalogued some 256 titles, many of which apparently had been taken out by various friars and never returned. As one might suppose, most of these books were religious: sermons, missals, lives of the saints, theological treatises, works of the Spanish mystics, catechisms, meditations, and books on canon law. There were a few classics, Virgil and Ovid especially. Yet, among the more interesting and useful to the friars were a group of books on the grammar and vocabulary of Native languages published in Mexico, which provided not only linguistic information but strategies for teaching the Indians in their own languages. *Camino del cielo en lengua mexicana* and *Advertencias para los confesores de indios* (1599) are two such examples.

While the Franciscans' books were generally religious or instructional, those owned by civil officials were usually histories, scientific and medical treatises, the classics, and popular romances and epics of the day. As part of the contest for authority between clerics and public officials, the friars often accused lay officials and their families of reading scandalous books. One such incident during the governorship of Bernardo López de Mendizábal (1659–1661) led to a trial of Mendizábal and his wife, Doña Teresa de Aguilera, by the Holy Office of the Inquisition. The records of the trial, in addition to providing a fascinating narrative of colonial life in the province, detail the governor's effects, including all of his books.

These Inquisition records indicate that the library of the governor's palace in Santa Fe had copies of Roman histories; Aristotle's *Topics;* works by Plato, Boccaccio, and Saint Augustine; Ovid's *Metamorphoses;* Saint Thomas Aquinas's *Summa Theologiae;* as well as a number of secular books including a volume of *comedias* (secular drama), *Don Quixote,* and Ariosto's *Orlando Furioso.* Ariosto's epic poem was enormously popular in Europe but not so with the Inquisition. When it was discovered that the governor's wife, Doña

Teresa, had a copy in the original Italian, she was accused of heresy (it should be added that she and the governor were accused of being Jews as well). Both were sent off to Mexico to stand trial before the Inquisition; the governor died in jail while awaiting trial, but Doña Teresa persevered, defending her behavior as well as her reading habits, which she argued were rather more religious in scope than the charges indicated. She was vindicated but never returned to Santa Fe.

At the end of the seventeenth century, when Don Diego de Vargas reconquered the province of New Mexico after the Pueblo rose against the Spanish in 1680, he brought along with him a batch of books, the titles of which were listed in his will. De Vargas's collection of thirty-three books are for the most part histories and biographies about the Spanish nobility and the affairs of the Spanish Crown in European politics. There is another group of books that deals specifically with the New World, especially about military and religious strategies toward Native people. Among these are *Varones ilustres del Nuevo Mundo, descubridores, conquistadores, y pacificadores* (1639), *Política indiana* (1648), and *Teatro eclesiástico de la primitiva iglesia de las Indias* (1649–1655). He also had a copy of María Jesús de Agreda's famous *Mística Ciudad de Dios* (1670) and a cookbook, *Arte de Cocina* (1611).

The literature of the Spanish Borderlands may, therefore, be said to have emerged from the rich literary culture—both textual and oral—of medieval and Renaissance Europe. Spanish colonial drama had its sources in seasonal religious allegories acted out before church altars or in popular street theater. Poetry, in its various forms, emerged from epics like Spain's famous *El Cid* and the scandalous *Orlando Furioso,* from Franciscan prayer books and hymns, and from popular songs. *Cuentos* were part of the rich storytelling tradition that can be found in Boccaccio and Ovid, as well as in the stories of the *Arabian Nights* that circulated in Spain, a gift of the Moors who had inhabited the country for hundreds of years. In the New World, this European literary culture was used to dramatize military and religious control over both Native people and Spanish colonists, but it was modified by geography, social and cultural change, and by political transformations. Even after 1821, the literary

culture of the Spanish Borderlands occupies a central place in the imagination of a people who still reenact the *pastorelas*, who compose new *corridos*, and who have incorporated the *cuento* tradition into their short stories and novels.

BIBLIOGRAPHY

Anza, Juan Bautista. *Anza's California Expeditions.* Edited by Herbert E. Bolton. 5 vols. Berkley, Calif., 1930.

Argüello, Luis Antonio. *The Diary of Captain Luis Antonio Argüello, 1821.* Edited and translated by Vivian Fisher. Berkeley, Calif., 1992.

Boelhower, William Q. *Through a Glass Darkly: Ethnic Semiosis in American Literature.* New York, 1987.

Bolton, Herbert E. *Spanish Exploration in the Southwest, 1542–1706.* New York, 1916. Includes the *Diary of Fernando del Bosque.*

Bourne, Edward G. *Narratives of the Career of Hernando de Soto in the Conquest of Florida.* 2 vols. New York, 1904.

Cabeza de Vaca, Alvar Nuñez. *La Relación,* 1542, 1555 (titled *Naufragios*). For an English translation, see Cyclone Covey's *Adventures in the Unknown Interior of America,* Albuquerque, N. Mex., 1960.

Coues, Elliot, ed. *On the Trail of a Spanish Pioneer: The Diary and Itinerary of Francisco Garcés in His Travels Through Sonora, Arizona, and California, 1775–1776.* 2 vols. New York, 1900.

Cutter, Donald C., ed. *The California Coast: A Bilingual Edition of Documents from the Sutro Collection.* Norman, Okla., 1969.

Geiger, Maynard, ed. and trans. *As the Padres Saw Them: California Indian Life and Customs as Reported by the Franciscan Missionaries, 1813–1815.* Santa Barbara, Calif., 1976.

Gonzales-Berry, Erlinda, ed. *Paso por Aqui: Critical Essays on the New Mexico Literary Tradition, 1542–1988.* Albuquerque, N.Mex., 1989.

Hammond, George P., and Agapito Rey, trans. *Expedition into New Mexico Made by Antonio de Espejo, 1582–1583, as Revealed in the Journal of Diego Pérez de Luxan, a Member of the Party.* Los Angeles, 1929.

———. *The Gallegos Relation of the Rodriguez Expedition to New Mexico.* Santa Fe, N.Mex., 1927.

———. *Narratives of the Coronado Expedition, 1540–1542.* Albuquerque, N.Mex., 1940. Includes the "Report of Fray Marcos de Niza."

———. *The Rediscovery of New Mexico, 1580–1594: The Explorations of Chamuscado, Espejo, Castaño de Sosa, Morlete, and Leyna de Bonilla and Humaña.* Albuquerque, N.Mex., 1966.

Hodge, Frederick W., and Theodore H. Lewis. *Spanish Explorers in the Southern United States, 1528–1543.* New York, 1907.

Kino, Eusebio. *Kino's Historical Memoir of Pimería Alta.* Edited and translated by Herbert E. Bolton. 2 vols. Cleveland, Ohio, 1919.

de León, Alonso. *Historia de Nuevo León con noticias sobre Coahuila, Tejas, y Nuevo Mexico.* Mexico City, 1909.

McCarty, Kieran, comp. *Desert Documentary: The Spanish Years, 1767–1821.* Arizona Historical Society, Historical Monograph no. 4. Tucson, Ariz., 1976.

Moziño, José Mariano. *Noticias de Nutka: An Account of Nootka Sound in 1792.* Edited and translated by Iris Higbie Wilson. Seattle, Wash., 1972.

Palóu, Francisco. *Historical Memoirs of New California.* Edited by Herbert E. Bolton. 4 vols. Berkeley, Calif., 1926.

Smith, Buckingham, ed. *Colección de varios documentos para la historia de la Florida y tierras adyacentes.* London, 1857.

de la Vega, Inca Garcilaso. *The Florida of the Inca: A History of the Adelantado, Hernando de Soto.* Edited and translated by John Grier Varner and Jeannett Johnson Varner. Austin, Tex., 1951.

Velez de Escalante, Silvestre. *The Domínguez-Escalante Journal: Their Expedition Through Colorado, Utah, Arizona, and New Mexico in 1776.* Edited by Ted J. Warner. Translated by Angelico Chavez. Provo, Utah, 1976.

Villagrá, Gaspar Perez de. *Gaspar de Villagrá's Historia de Nuevo Mexico, 1610: A Critical and Annotated Edition.* Edited and translated by Miguel Encinias, Alfredo Rodriguez, and Joseph P. Sanchez. Albuquerque, N.Mex., 1992.

Wagner, Henry R. *From the Spanish Southwest, 1542–1794: An Annotated Bibliography.* Albuquerque, N.Mex., 1937.

———. *Spanish Voyages to the Northwest Coast of America in the Sixteenth Century.* San Francisco, Calif., 1929.

Warman, Arturo. *La danca de moros y cristianos.* Mexico City, 1972.

Winship, George Parker. *The Coronado Expedition, 1540–1542.* Washington, D.C., 1896; repr. Garden City, N.J., 1990.

Genaro Padilla

SEE ALSO **Colonial Political Thought; The Colonial Press; Drama; Libraries and Learned Societies; Literacy; and Schools and Schooling.**

AFRICAN AMERICAN

THE PROBLEM OF COLONIAL African-American literature is one of recognition and definition. Black African slaves were imported to the Virginia colony as early as 1619. During the first two centuries of colonial conquest in North America, the African immigrants' efforts to achieve social and political recognition were impeded because most blacks were enslaved and denied all forms of participation in the American achievement, while educational opportunities for all blacks, slave and free, were severely limited before the nineteenth century. As slaves, blacks were denied basic skills such as reading and writing, either by regional custom or by local practice. However, communication in the slave communities was strong from the very beginning; slaves desperately attempted to preserve some vestiges of their African heritage through stories and folktales brought across the Atlantic. Their traditions were dominated by oral forms of communication, and one prominent theme in the early slave narrative literature of colonial America is the slaveowner's attempt to prevent oral communication and political expression.

At the end of the colonial era, according to the 1790 census, there were some 700,000 black slaves in the United States, contrasted with 55,000 free blacks, living mostly in the northern states. The census takers estimated that in 1776, the year of the Declaration of Independence, some 20 percent of the population of the colonies was enslaved, in both the North and the South. In 1808 congressional legislation prohibiting the importation of slaves went into effect. However, by 1820, there were over 1,000,000 slaves of African heritage, and by 1860, on the eve of the Civil War, there were over 4,000,000 slaves, living primarily in the South, whereas the free black population had grown to only 250,000. Defining one's self under the conditions of chattel slavery was extremely difficult, and many white leaders, northern and southern, suppressed the emergence of an African-American colonial literature because they believed in the superiority of English literature over colonial

American writing, white or black, and assumed a natural inferiority of African-American literary abilities. Published black writers were few.

Paradoxically, the distressing situation of blacks during the colonial period is probably responsible for the strong tradition of black literature in America today, for those untutored, often illiterate early slaves were not assimilated into the dominant white culture but were instead thrown back on their own imported resources for the development of a subculture within the colonies. This subculture included the maintenance of a folk tradition through African oral narratives, folktales, and myths that were transformed into anglicized versions. Those versions, in turn, appeared as early American folk narratives. Negro spirituals owe much to this powerful cultural identity; they speak of suffering and trial in the New World while suggesting a better life in the world to come.

The Bible offered justifications for both the abolition of, and perpetuation of, slavery (both sides arguing from scriptural texts). But for black writers it also provided a mythic narrative analogous to their experience as slaves, one with which white readers could understand and identify but which still preserved the integrity of the African-American experience. For example, the African slave in colonial America was confronted with such complex questions of cultural identity that assimilation was virtually impossible. Slave owners were neither European nor British but were themselves colonial "subjects," whose primary culture was appropriated from England and Europe and whose allegiances were often more Old World than New. Slaves, meanwhile, were not permitted access to the literate culture of the colonies and were forced to develop alternative resources or to learn "American" culture secretly. Thus, like the Puritan settlers of New England, many of the colonial slave narrators developed analogies between their own personal sagas and the sufferings of ancient Israel, and they appealed for emancipation from slavery just as the colonists were appealing to England for fairer treatment under English rule. For half a century after the Constitutional Convention of 1787, American literature suffered neglect because Americans were uncertain of their cultural roots, so that in 1782 a visitor, Hector St. Jean de Crève-

coeur, would ask, "What is this American, this new man?" We are still responding to this question.

Moreover, the white perception of the Negro slave during the colonial period, and the frequent debates about Christianizing the African that emanated from colonial pulpits and from eighteenth-century printers, circulated an image of African Americans that was not their own but that reflected how they were perceived by the dominant white culture. For example, one of the judges at the Salem witch trials of 1692, Samuel Sewall, penned *The Selling of Joseph,* one of the earliest antislavery tracts and the first by an American Puritan. Printed in Boston on 12 June 1700, it was promptly answered by John Saffin, another colonial judge and writer of the first proslavery document printed in colonial America. Racial stereotyping abounds in these tracts; the Saffin piece is venomous and contains attacks on African Americans that represent one side of a debate about "the Negroes' Character" and intellect. Soon after, in 1721, Cotton Mather entered the debate with his *The Negro Christianized,* a softened proslavery treatise, in which he argued that "Your servants will be Better Servants, for being Christian Servants."

ROOTS OF
BLACK LITERARY TRADITION

It would take the powerful voice of Phillis Wheatley to offset these sentiments in prerevolutionary America. Wheatley was not only an accomplished poet; she was also one of the early voices for the abolition of slavery. In a letter to the Reverend Samson Occom, dated 11 February 1774, she argues that "in every human breast God has implanted a principle, which we call love of freedom; it is impatient of oppression, and pants for deliverance . . . that same principle lives in us." Wheatley adds, "God grant deliverance in his own way and time, and get him honour upon all those whose avarice impels them to countenance and help forward the calamities of their fellow creatures. This I desire . . . to convince them of the strange absurdity of their conduct." But Wheatley cried out against such writers as William Byrd II (*A History of the Divid-*

ing Line, 1728) and Thomas Jefferson (particularly his *Notes on the State of Virginia,* 1784–1785). These highly inflammatory pieces were answered by writers like Anthony Benezet, a French Huguenot who became a prominent propogandist against the slave trade with his *A Caution and Warning to Great Britain and Her Colonies, in a Short Representation of the Calamitous State of the Enslaved Negroes in the British Dominions* (1766), and the Quaker John Woolman, whose *Some Considerations on the Keeping of Negroes* (1754) became one of the most eloquent treatises in opposition to the cruelty of slavery.

Colonial African-American literature has its roots in some isolated poetry, like that of Phillis Wheatley, and in the slave narratives. Slave narratives had their beginnings in a little-known form called the "petition," a brief statement to the owner requesting a release from bondage, usually delivered to the master in person. Many of these petitions argued for manumission, and often the slave offered to pay for his freedom. Most important, the petitions contained articulations of selfhood, statements that the slave was an individual, not a nameless appendage to the master's inventory of property. As one scholar has shown, these petitions were enlarged into longer narratives and letters in which slaves began to write of their experiences in order to bear witness to the horrors of the "peculiar institution." Through these narratives, the white reader was provided evidence of the inhumanity of slavery and clear testimony about the eloquence of the slave. By the end of the eighteenth century, the writing of slave narratives was well established, as William Andrews has shown, and it was often supported by a growing abolitionist movement.

As in all literature, African-American writing during the colonial period sought a voice, a way of expressing the self so that the overwhelming force of slaveholding would not wholly subordinate African culture to European culture. This was not an easy task, as Bernard Bell notes, because "the struggle of blacks for freedom during the War for Independence . . . was always in tension with the economic, political, and psychological compulsion of whites to transform them into docile Christians and subhumans." Cotton Mather, the most prominent rep-

resentative of the powerful Mather dynasty of Boston, provided ample evidence of this habit of mind in his *Rules for the Societies of Negroes* (1693) and later in *The Negro Christianized.* And the Puritans were not the only colonists who oppressed the African Americans; the framers of the Declaration of Independence and the Constitution deleted all references to slavery, thus creating a democratic charter even while slavery was still part of the new nation's heritage; both Jonathan Edwards and Thomas Jefferson owned slaves.

In this context, the achievement of two figures, Wheatley and the slave writer Gustavas Vassa (Oladuah Equiano) assumes enormous importance. These gifted writers were struggling against almost insurmountable odds in their efforts to gain recognition. As Thomas Jefferson wrote of Wheatley's poetry in his *Notes on the State of Virginia,* "Misery is often the parent of the most affecting touches in poetry. Among the blacks is misery enough, God knows, but no poetry. Love is the peculiar oestrum of the poet. Their love is ardent, but it kindles the senses only, not the imagination." He added, "Religion, indeed, has produced a Phillis Wheatley; but it could not produce a poet. The compositions published under her name are below the dignity of criticism." This highly biased dismissal was countered by Wheatley's own eloquent voice.

Born in Africa, Wheatley was kidnapped into slavery when she was very young and sold to the Wheatley family of Boston, which raised her in a family as one of its members. She was manumitted in 1773, but was only nominally a slave before that. Her Christian piety obscures the fine quality of some of her heroic verses; she was tutored in the home (as were all women in colonial times) and absorbed the literature of England, modeling her style on the regular couplet of heroic verse and her themes on both classical and biblical subjects. She wrote many elegiac verses, one on the death of evangelist George Whitefield, and several addresses to "To His Excellency George Washington" and even one to Harvard, "To the University in Cambridge in New England." But she is best known for "Liberty and Peace" (1784) and for "On Being Brought from Africa to America" (1773), which contains a warning, similar to that Harriet

Beecher Stowe would deliver in 1852—"Remember; *Christians, Negros,* black as *Cain,* / May be refin'd, and join th' angelic train."

The sophistication and quality of Wheatley's poetry contrast markedly with the brutal accounts written by some of her contemporaries, who were slaves in the South and who wrote to bring an end to the sufferings of their brothers and sisters. Paradoxically, slave narrators wrote bitter accounts of their personal experiences just at the moment of their emancipation, when they might have been expected to wish to forget the past. But they were energized by their visions of a better world in which the institution of slavery would be abolished. The conflation of biblical Christianity as a religious foundation with the actual experience of African Americans laid the groundwork for a rich literature in colonial America, resulting in extraordinary works such as Jupiter Hammon's "Evening Thought: Salvation by Christ, With Penetential Cries" (1760), his "Address to the Negroes in the State of New York" (1787), and the finest slave narrative of the eighteenth century, Equiano's *The Interesting Narrative of the Life of Olaudah Equiano, or Gustavas Vassa, the African, Written by Himself* (1789).

The "written by himself" is exceedingly important, as part of the title, for it clearly shows the emphasis Equiano placed on his literacy and his power to articulate his own story as a means of identifying the autobiographical self. The models for his narrative were the conversion narratives and the spiritual autobiographies of earlier settlers, but his vision and experience were his own, and he affirmed himself by the act of articulating his own experience. The "petition" thus evolved into a very sophisticated, extremely powerful, literary form. Equiano's language is erudite and polished, obviously the work of a learned writer, though self-taught. Like many of the Puritan narratives it resembles, his commences with an apology that contains many apostrophes to God but that, in this instance, reveals much about the personality of the author. Very self-conscious about thrusting his life story onto a reading public, Equiano says that "it is not a little hazardous in a private and obscure individual . . . thus to solicit the indulgent attention of the public." This modesty pervades the narrative, but Equiano, like Phillis Wheatley in her poetry, ascribes the good fortune of his life to the operations of divine providence. "I might say that my sufferings were great; but when I compare my lot with that of most of my countrymen, I regard myself, as a particular favorite of heaven, and acknowledge the mercies of providence in every occurrence of my life." Like Wheatley, Equiano affirms rather than censures Christianity, even though Christian doctrine was often used to support proslavery arguments in colonial America.

The best-known of the colonial slave narratives were that of Equiano, *A Narrative of the Uncommon Sufferings, and Surprizing Deliverance of Briton Hammon, a Negro Man* (1760); John Marrant's *A Narrative of the Lord's Wonderful Dealings with John Marrant, a Black, Now Going to Preach the Gospel in Nova Scotia, Born in New York, in North America* (1785); and Venture Smith's *A Narrative of the Life and Adventures of Venture, a Native of Africa* (1798). These early slave narratives, like the Indian captivity narratives, contain formulaic accounts of brutality and deliverance. The pervasive metaphor of all life-writing of this type is the teleological journey, that purposeful trek from birth to death that is punctuated by episodes and digressions and observations about the world external to the autobiographical self. Like many slave narratives written in the nineteenth century, such as Frederick Douglass's *The Slave's Narrative* (1845) and *My Bondage and My Freedom* (1855) or Harriet Jacobs's *Incidents in the Life of a Slave Girl Written by Herself* (1861), these early accounts reveal that the deepest impulse of colonial African-American writings was the achievement of personal freedom and the fulfillment of a life that was ultimately governed by divine providence. It is these voices, rather than those of the white owners and masters, that modern readers should consult when seeking to know the truth about the colonial African-American experience.

BIBLIOGRAPHY

Andrews, William. *To Tell a Free Story: The First Century of Afro-American Autobiography, 1760–1865.* Urbana and Chicago, 1986.

Bell, Bernard. *The Afro-American Novel and Its Tradition.* Amherst, Mass., 1987.

Davis, Charles, and H. L. Gates. *The Slave's Narrative.* New York, 1985.

Eakin, John Paul, ed. *American Autobiography: Retrospect and Prospect.* Madison, Wis., 1991.

Olney, James, ed. *Autobiography: Essays Theoretical and Critical.* Princeton, N.J., 1980.

Pearce, Roy Harvey. *Savagism and Civilization.* Baltimore, Md., 1965.

Ruchames, Louis, ed. *Racial Thought in America from the Puritans to Abraham Lincoln.* Amherst, Mass., 1969.

Shea, Daniel B. *Spiritual Autobiography in Early America.* Princeton, N.J., 1968.

Tise, Larry E. *Proslavery: A History of the Defense of Slavery in America, 1701–1840.* Athens, Ga., 1987.

Mason I. Lowance, Jr.

SEE ALSO **African-American Culture; Free Blacks;** and **Slavery.**

NATIVE AMERICAN

SEBASTIEN RASLES, A JESUIT missionary among the Illinois in the late seventeenth century, found much to praise in the oratory of one of the Native leaders. "I confess to you that I admired his flow of language," he noted in a letter to his brother written in 1723. Also impressed by "the justness and force of the arguments that he presented, the eloquent turn he gave to them, and the choice and nicety of the expressions with which he adorned his speech," Rasles believed that the oration bore comparison to what "the most able Europeans . . . after much thought and study," could compose. The missionary to the Illinois was not the only Jesuit in New France to be impressed with the eloquence of Native Americans. The *Jesuit Relations,* the yearly reports of these missionaries to their superiors in France, contain many descriptions of speechmaking by Huron, Iroquois, and other Native orators, occasional accounts of how they narrated their "fables," and a number of speech, lyric poem (that is, song without the music), and story texts rendered from oral performance and usually translated into French.

If missionaries and colonizers in other parts of North America had provided records of Native American verbal art as useful as those of the Jesuits in New France, our understanding of that art would not be as sketchy as it now is. Sadly, though, the Jesuits were virtually alone in taking what the *sauvages* said seriously enough to document it. The Puritans in New England recorded few evidences of verbal art from people whom they considered—in the words of the editor of the account of Mary Rowlandson's captivity—"atheisticall, proud, wild, cruel, bruitish (in one word) diabolicall creatures," beings who had fallen as far as it was possible to fall into the snares of evil. It was better, the Puritans undoubtedly thought, to preserve no record of anything that these minions of Satan might say.

The middle and southern English colonists provided somewhat better data, and accounts of oratorical performances along with translated texts of speeches from eighteenth-century sources offer some information about this important genre of Native American oral literature. But even they shared the generally held notion that Native American languages were too "primitive" for the sort of discourse that merited translation except for practical reasons. Consequently, the earliest song text from the middle and southern colonies, a Cherokee "war song" recorded by Henry Timberlake, dates only from the 1760s. Story texts are equally scarce. Dutch and Swedish colonizers, as well as those from other nations who settled along the eastern seaboard of North America, preserved nothing of significance about Native American verbal art. Nor did the Spanish explorers and colonizers in Florida and the Southwest, though they became a significant presence among the Pueblo by the early seventeenth century.

That Europeans in the New World failed to recognize the literary artistry in the oral traditions of Native Americans should not be surprising. Not only were the natives of North America considered, at best, representatives of untamed natural humanity (the *sauvages* of the French Jesuits), whose languages were inherently too simple and childlike to produce anything resembling literature, but also the possibility of an "oral" literature had not received consideration. In fact, centuries would pass before descendants of the European colonizers began to realize that Native groups had traditional aesthetic systems that generated literary expressions as rich as any known in Europe.

THE NATURE OF ORAL LITERATURE

The verbal artistry of Native North Americans in the colonial period emerged from what Walter Ong has called "primary oral culture," a social situation in which oral communication provides virtually the only means of preserving and circulating knowledge. Our scant records of the specifics of that artistry as it existed immediately following the Columbian "discovery" of the New World prevent us from offering categorical assessments. Nonetheless, we can assume that the speeches, stories, songs, prayers, ritual texts, and other verbal art forms from the sixteenth through the eighteenth centuries shared some traits with oral literatures encountered among their descendants and throughout the world.

In contrast to its written counterpart, for which the text is basic, performance is the fundamental entity for oral literature. Thus, the words of a creation myth, for example, do not exist until a storyteller utters them. The performance actually includes much more than the words, which may become a "text" if someone records and transcribes them for print. As a communicative event, performance involves not only what a storyteller, orator, or other verbal artist says, but also how he or she says it, to whom it is said, and the physical, cultural, and psychological contexts of the saying. Since variation in any of these components may transform the others, each performance of the creation myth may be unique. The storyteller creates anew the story— the potential "text" of the myth—in response to a perception of the audience and the surroundings and under the distinctive cultural and psychological influences of the moment. Such creation, however, occurs within the context of a tradition, of many repeated performances of the same myth, which may extend back through several generations.

Some genres of oral literature evince more resistance to textual variation than others. The words of a prayer or ritual text, for example, will vary much less from performance to performance than those of a personal-experience narrative or historical legend. But without a fixed, written text, variation will occur no matter how intent the performer is on verbatim repetition. Conversely, even the most loosely structured genre of oral literature exhibits a degree of constancy. For as verbal artists perform what they conceive to be the most innovative material, they employ verbal formulas and structural patterns that have been used over and over again.

A tension exists in oral literature, then, between the tendency for material that has no permanently preserved versions to vary and the performer's use of conventional modes of presentation. On the one hand, oral literature is in a constant state of fluctuation, but on the other, even myths, legends, songs, or orations that have never been heard before seem very familiar. For example, consider the story of Sedna, frequently collected since the late nineteenth century among various Inuit groups in northern Canada and Alaska and undoubtedly performed by storytellers during the colonial period. Performers generally relate how a young girl refuses all human suitors to marry a bird or dog, who promises her marital bliss. When he fails to deliver on his promise and she becomes miserable, Sedna's father kills the bird or dog husband and escapes with his daughter by boat. A storm arises, perhaps caused by kin of the murdered husband, and the father throws Sedna overboard to save himself. As she clings to the side of their boat, he cuts off her fingers, which are transformed into various kinds of fish, thus accounting for the origin of sea life. Sedna's animal children destroy the father, and she becomes queen of the lower world.

The unadorned structure of this plot may remain relatively constant, so that no matter who tells it or when, it remains recognizably the story of Sedna. But variations may occur in simple wording; in secondary plot elements, such as the specifics of the bird or dog husband's prenuptial promises; or even in primary plot elements, such as the disposition of the father after he tries to get rid of Sedna. How the narrative is articulated depends upon the specific tradition with which each storyteller is familiar, the nature of the audience (children or adults, for instance), and even such prosaic factors as the physical situation of the performance (the relative comfort or discomfort of performer and audience). The essential plot pattern, however, identifies the story as that of Sedna. Moreover, even an Inuit who had never heard the story might deem it familiar because of certain elements (marriage to a bird or animal husband, for example) heard in other stories.

Characterizations of an oral culture's literature, then, involve two descriptive levels: the general patterns, such as plot outlines and recurrent episodes; and recurrent stylistic devices, such as figurative language and conventionalized imagery. One should also note how performers use the general patterns in distinctive ways to create unique instances of verbal art.

In most cases, even into the twentieth century, commentators have tended to emphasize the more general aspects of oral literature, writing in broad terms of Iroquois mythology, Huron oratory, or Cherokee lyric poetry. The role of the individual creator-performer has usually been ignored or minimized. But the general approach, though representing only a portion of verbal art, allows comparative surveys of the oral literary genres found in different cultures. For example, by drawing upon the scanty contemporary records from the colonial period and by making inferences based on later findings, we can determine some of the features of the stories, lyric poetry, oratory, prayers, and other ritual utterances encountered by the colonizers.

STORIES

The memoirs (1736) of John Gyles, who commanded a garrison on the Saint George River in Massachusetts Bay colony, contain summaries of two Native American oral narratives, included to show readers how "deluded or under the influence of Satan" the storytellers were. One tale tells of a boy, eight or ten years old, carried off by a giant bird that intends him for a meal for her young. When they refuse to eat him, the bird returns the boy to where she found him. Gyles reported that his Native informants were able to point out the site of the bird's nest. The other story tells of a maiden so beautiful and accomplished that her parents can find no suit-

able husband for her. One day they discover her missing but locate her in the company of a remarkably handsome youth, a supernatural being whom the parents look upon as their son-in-law. As is customary, he provides for their needs for the rest of their lives.

Such retellings of traditional narratives are found in the writings of other colonial officials, missionaries, and explorers. Usually labeled "a very odd story," a "fond and idle" fancy, or otherwise dismissively, the texts seldom attempt to reproduce how the storytellers told them but are usually presented to illustrate the benighted nature of the savage mentality and spirit. Even in the writings of the most sympathetic observers, traditional narratives are seldom identified as evidence of serious art or thought.

Colonial observers were most intrigued by Native American mythologies, not only because North American accounts of Creation, gods, and other themes confirmed belief in the Natives' savagery, but also because myths could sometimes be used to support pet theories about Native American origins, especially the belief that the natives of North America were descendants of the ten lost tribes of Israel. For example, Louis Hennepin, whose account of his North American explorations appeared in 1698, found in the Creation mythology of an unnamed Native group living apparently "at the Mouth of the River of St. Laurence and Mississippi" clear parallels with the Hebrew myth: the sleep of a primordial human resembling that of Adam when Eve was created from his rib, two quarreling brothers like Cain and Abel, and events similar to the death of Abel and the subsequent curse upon Cain.

The Creation mythologies of North America actually represent considerable diversity, and a survey of three hundred Creation-myth texts has yielded several distinct types. One of the most widely known, reported from throughout North America with the exception of the desert Southwest, assigns creative power to a being known as Earth-Diver, who plunges to the bottom of the primordial ocean to bring up a few fragments of soil. These particles of dirt, cast upon the waters, expand to form the earth. Many southwestern native groups have traced the world's origins to a series of emergences from the earth's interior. Three or four previous worlds had been inhabited by the ancestors of modern humanity before their emergence into the present world. Some southwesterners also attribute Creation, at least in part, to a spider deity, usually female, who after the emergence was responsible for ordering the present cosmos.

Other theories of Creation posit the existence of world parents, the personified sky and earth, whose union ignites the creation process; the development of the cosmos from the body of a dead giant; competition between rival deities as the source of the creative energy that results in the cosmos; or Prometheus-like theft of fire or light as the generator of Creation. Some Native American myths treat the origins of specific natural and cultural phenomena rather than dealing with the creation of the world in general, as in the reference to the origin of sea life in the Inuit story of Sedna.

In addition to Creation, Native American mythologies have also dealt with culture heroes. Some may be involved with aspects of the Creation process; others seem to serve as embodiments of central values and attitudes. Among the most interesting figures is the trickster, manifested variously as deity, primordial human, prototypical animal, or sometimes amorphous entity. Frequently an amoral marplot who in some way spoils the perfection of Creation by introducing a negative force such as disease or want, the trickster is often depicted as gluttonous, sexually promiscuous, unable to settle in one spot, and perpetually at odds with his environment. In such manifestations as Glooskap among New England groups, Manibozho among Algonquian-speakers in the Great Lakes area, or Coyote in the West and Southwest, the trickster may be regarded positively or negatively, as the villainous source of such evils as death or as the comic personification of license and misrule. Stories of his actions may have been part of cycles or may have existed as independent episodes. The most extensive collection of trickster myths comes from the Winnebago, who have lived in the upper Midwest west of the Great Lakes. The forty-nine episodes in the Winnebago trickster cycle trace his wanderings, his sexual and scatological escapades, and his ultimate transfiguration into a deity in charge of a world parallel to ours.

In addition to such mythological narratives, Native American stories recount the post-Creation history of their peoples, often preserving knowledge of what archaeological investigation has proved to be historical fact. Typically such historical narratives may trace the group's wanderings before it settled in its present homeland, attempt to account for the relics left by previous inhabitants of the homeland, and characterize the interaction between the group and its neighbors. By the time Europeans began to record such stories, they often found accounts of the natives' initial contact with the invaders in the repertoires of storytellers. Other stories, such as those summarized by John Gyles, validate beliefs about the natural and supernatural worlds by giving specific examples of how these worlds operate. Tales of personal experiences also have figured in the narrative repertoires of many Native American performers, who may relate them in formal situations such as councils or religious rituals or as part of their casual interchanges. Remarkable experiences when hunting or fishing, supernatural encounters—including dreams—and military heroics may be favored themes.

The telling of certain kinds of stories has often required particular contexts, times, or seasons, and telling a tale out of season may result in negative consequences for both the teller and the group. The valued storyteller must know when and where to tell stories and can dramatize the material while recalling it with richly detailed accuracy. In his relation for 1645–1646, the Jesuit Paul Ragueneau provided a good description of the context and functions of storytelling among the Huron when their "elders" assembled "for the election of a very celebrated Captain." Their custom was to use such occasions to recount the stories "which they have learned regarding their ancestors, even those most remote." The purpose was to "transmit to posterity the history and the annals of the country" and consequently "to supply the lack of . . . books." Myths and historical narratives also served to explain how and why the present world had come to be, thus justifying the procedures that particular groups had developed to deal with it.

LYRIC POETRY

Some modern commentators have argued that all oral literature should be viewed as poetry. Prose, they assert, is a product of the printed page and represents something entirely foreign in primary oral cultures. For example, oral narratives—which careful analysis reveals to be more like dramatic poetry than the prose fiction of European literary tradition—often rely on such devices usually associated with poetry as parallelism, rhythm, and patterned repetition. The oral narratives from the Zuni of the Southwest, the Tonkawa of the southern Plains, and the Clackamas Chinook of the Northwest have been presented effectively in print as poetic pieces, measured into lines, verses, and stanzas. Similar treatment has been given to oratory. A distinct category of poetry, then, may seem unnecessary. Moreover, what Europeans have designated as Native American "poetry" has almost always been the words of songs, whose impact when removed from the performance context is even more adulterated than that of other forms of oral literature.

A survey of Native American literature during the colonial period nonetheless needs to account for those forms of verbal art which resemble what Europeans knew as lyric poetry. Poem texts are extremely rare in colonial sources; even the Jesuits, who devoted considerable attention to Native American singing, included only a few in their *Relations*. Apparently the earliest is that which Paul Le Jeune recorded (without translation) in 1634 in the Algonquian language of the Montagnais. Hence, we are especially reliant upon the later findings for ideas about this genre.

Even the material available from later observers is often of especially questionable worth. Native American poems, like most lyric poetry, resist translation. Those who have tried to convert them into a European language have often obscured their nature by imposing their own poetic aesthetic upon the material. Thus, we encounter rhyme, regularized meter, and other conventions of European poetic expression not used in the original performances. When Henry Timberlake translated a Cherokee war song for his 1765 memoirs, for example, he rendered it in heroic couplets, the rhymed lines of iambic pentameter that dominated English and American poetic composition of his time. Furthermore, while adding European features to their treatments of Native American lyric poetry, European translators have omitted some of the devices used by Native singers, especially vocables,

often dismissed as "meaningless nonsense syllables."

With these reservations in mind, we can note that the poetry of Native American song has generally evinced several qualities across cultural boundaries. Among the most important are brevity and terseness, qualities that have tempted some translators to render the material in the manner of the imagist poetry of the early twentieth century. Native American singers have often employed extreme economy of expression, saying a great deal in a few words and images. What Maria Chona, a woman of the Tohono O'odham (formerly Papago), told anthropologist Ruth Underhill holds true for lyric poetry in many Native American literary traditions: "The song is very short because we understand so much." Texts are brief because the performers and their audiences are able to make a multitude of evocative associations from their cultural background.

Lyric poetry also places a high value upon the musical quality of language, the ways in which the sounds reflect meaning. This explains the frequent use of those vocables which translators have so often ignored. Such sounds, while not words or even morphemes, are frequently rich in meaning because of their onomatopoeic associations, their recurrence in a variety of poetic texts, and their resonance with actual words in the poet's language. The emphasis on sound also explains the repetitions of single words or phrases throughout a lyric poem, as well as the tendency to play upon the sounds of words by lengthening them or reiterating a single syllable. Sound may also play a part in the retention of archaic language, even after the precise meanings of some terms have been lost to common usage, though this trait may often stem just as much from the ritual functions of much poetry.

Attitudes toward lyric poetry vary among Native groups. In most cases, some distinction may be drawn between sacred and secular poetry, but strict application of those categories often involves the imposition of European modes of classification. Singing, the performance of lyric poetry, may be group or solo, public or private. Poems may derive strictly from tradition, be the creation of the individual, be the gift of a spirit perhaps in a dream, or combine these factors. In his relation for 1637, Paul Le Jeune recorded the Algonquian-language text of a Montagnais song used for hunting magic. The singer claimed that its efficacy derived from his having learned it in a dream. Songs figure in most religious rituals. Jacques Marquette's relation describing his first voyage, in 1673, includes the words of a song used among the Illinois in the Calumet Dance. One of the earliest attempts to translate Native American lyric poetry into a European language, which appears in Jesuit Jean de Quens's relation for 1655–1656, involves French renderings of six "chants" performed by Christian Iroquois in appreciation for favors granted them by the missionaries. At the same time, singing occurred in situations such as social dancing that would be considered entirely secular from the European perspective.

Perhaps the most important generalization about lyric poetry—and the only one that holds up under cross-cultural scrutiny—is that it is the genre of Native American oral literature most dependent upon the performance situation. The conversion of a song into a verbal text has almost invariably resulted in a lessening of meaning and impact, sometimes almost to the vanishing point. This factor, along with the utter foreignness of the musical settings, may explain why lyric poetry fared so poorly when colonizers tried to document Native American traditions.

ORATORY

Colonial resources provide more information on oratory than on any other genre, principally because many more Europeans witnessed oratorical performances than heard storytelling or singing. Moreover, Native excellence in oratory confirmed presuppositions about the "savages." The "natural eloquence" on which observers repeatedly commented actually lent credence to belief in the "poverty" of Native languages, which allegedly were incapable of abstraction. Consequently, Native American speakers had to rely on concrete imagery, figures of speech that referred to natural phenomena often within sight of the orators as they made their speeches. At the same time, oratorical performances reinforced the image of the native as the particular adversary of Christian civilization, since in many cases orators articulated their avid resistance to the colonizers' various causes.

The Jesuits, who reproduced the texts of a number of Huron and Iroquois oratorical performances in their *Relations*, were almost all avid admirers of the speech-making skills of the *sauvages*. Though Pierre Biard may have taken an extreme position by claiming that the natives were "the greatest speech-makers in the world," most French and Italian missionaries commented on how effective their speeches, often called "harangues," might be. Focusing especially on the richness of their figures of speech, which proved both their innate mental ability as well as the undeveloped condition of their languages, the Jesuits left relatively detailed descriptions of not only what the orators said but how they said it.

Though their records are not as rich and their attitudes toward the Native Americans less positive than those of the Jesuits, even the New England Puritans found Native oratorical skills praiseworthy, especially if they could be rechanneled for Christian ends. Hence, in 1685 John Eliot, who pioneered the study of Native American languages realizing that knowledge of Massachusett would contribute to his missionizing efforts, offered *The Dying Speeches of Several Indians* to demonstrate the advances of the Gospel in North America. Speeches and sermons by Native converts appeared in other publications of the period.

The most famous speech by an Indian during the colonial period, that of the Cayuga sachem Tahgahjute (James Logan), was delivered in 1774. A response to the murder of some of his people by European colonizers, Tahgahjute gave his speech to his brother-in-law John Gibson, who wrote it down and conveyed it to John Murray, earl of Dunmore, governor of Virginia. Thomas Jefferson recorded it in his memorandum book for 1774, and a text was first published in the *Virginia Gazette* in February 1775. Jefferson's acclaim for the speech in *Notes on the State of Virginia* enshrined it as one of the most important events in Native American oratorical history.

The traditional contexts for oratory in Native American cultures have been the assembly and council, but any public or semipublic event might provide the occasion for oratory. Although the claims of some observers that skill in oratory was the only Native American measure of a man probably are inaccurate, speech-making must have been an important factor in the acquisition and maintenance of political power. Though specific tribal traditions varied, admired oratory might involve both content and manner of presentation. A speaker might assume a traditional oratorical stance, which could involve holding a cane or some other object that signified his right to speak. He would then apply images from a body of traditional figures as well as original metaphors and symbols to the matter at hand, using both voice and body to enhance his performance. Changes in vocal pitch, dynamics, tempo, and timbre as well as apt gestures complemented what he had to say. Audience response, which should be accounted as part of the performance, depended upon group convention and could range from stony silence to vociferous endorsement of or opposition to the speaker's points. The skills honed by orators for generations in the contexts of tribal political maneuvering endured in their encounters with the colonizers, even though some of the performance components suffered from the necessity to pause frequently for translation and from the inability of the audience to appreciate their implications fully.

Not only is oratory the most richly described oral literary genre in colonial sources, it is the only kind of Native verbal art in which room for individual genius seems to have been recognized. This is evident in the careful preservation of the names of orators, including widely known figures such as the Cayuga James Logan, Onondaga speechmakers Garangula and Sadekanatie, and Kognethagecton of the Delaware, as well as lesser figures such as Thanayieson, a Seneca whose speech to a delegation from the Commonwealth of Pennsylvania was recorded and commented upon by the delegation's leader, Conrad Weiser, in 1748. Though no colonial observer seems to have been sensitive enough to the niceties of the relevant Native language to show how individual rather than cultural genius found specific expression in oratory, the identification of speakers by name suggests some awareness of individual creativity.

PRAYERS AND OTHER RITUAL UTTERANCES

Although other genres of oral literature, especially lyric poetry and orations, occurred in ritual contexts, some groups utilized forms intended exclusively for ritual. These included short prayers and other formulas offered directly to supernatural beings and forces, as well as longer material that sometimes functioned almost liturgically. The function of most ritual texts among Native Americans has been to return ceremonial participants to the sacred time of myth. By transporting them into the realm of Creation and culture heroes, these texts allow people to communicate intimately and, perhaps, to identify with some of the forces that set the cosmos in motion. As such, ritual texts may be reconstitutive and revitalizing. They can also be sources of power. As participants enter into the time frame of the fundamental creative forces, they may be able to draw upon them. Hence, sacred formulas such as those which some Cherokee preserved in their syllabary during the nineteenth century, and that had undoubtedly been circulating orally during the colonial period, might move an individual into the realm of the mythic, allowing him or her to draw upon sources of potency that in European terms would be deemed "supernatural." Power thus acquired was used for such purposes as winning affection or avenging oneself on an enemy.

Ritual texts longer than prayers also figured into many literary traditions. Though largely unrecorded during the colonial period, a ritual text that must have been known to some European observers in lower Canada and western New England was the Iroquois condolence ceremony performed upon the death of a leader. For the five nations that constituted the League of the Iroquois during the colonial era, the death of someone in political authority could precipitate serious catastrophe. Though disturbed by anyone's death, the Iroquois regarded a leader's demise as especially calamitous and took immediate steps to avert negative repercussions. Soon after a chief died, a condolence council was convened to cleanse of their grief those whom the deceased leader had represented and, more important, to install his successor. The greetings, prayers, and exchanges of condolence emphasized the importance of renewed life; and when the new leader was introduced, the ceremony included formulaic instructions for his conduct in fulfilling his responsibilities. The event ended with general festivity directed toward maintaining and renewing the vitality of the individual and the group. The functions of various parts of the ceremony found literary expression in a lengthy series of formulas used each time the need arose.

Another important kind of ritual text, not recorded by Spanish colonizers in the Southwest but certainly known by Navajo inhabitants of the region during colonial times, was the verbal component of the healing ceremony called a "sing" or a "chant." Navajo disease theory has held that sickness arises from an individual's loss of balance with the cosmos. Someone who is ailing first consults a diagnostician, who ascertains exactly how the person has become out of harmony—perhaps by violating a taboo. Then the sick person seeks out a singer, who knows how to perform the ritual needed to restore balance. The singer then schedules a healing ritual, which may take up to nine days to perform, designed to return the sick person to the time when the cosmos was coming into being. The ritual, which enables the afflicted to return to a state of harmony, consists of songs, prayers, and poetic recitations of mythology, illustrated by large dry-paintings in such media as sand and pollen on which the sick person sits or reclines.

THE BEGINNINGS OF
A WRITTEN LITERATURE

Although literatures during the colonial period were principally oral, some groups had developed traditional methods for recording oral literary texts in "written" form. Among the Ojibwa who lived on the western shores of the Great Lakes, for example, some songs might be accompanied by birchbark drawings, consisting of ideograms that represented the images of the songs and from which they might be sung. These probably served as aids to memory but may have also embodied some of the same power as the songs in performance. Most such songs accompanied by birchbark drawings come from the Mide Society, the basic organization in Ojibwa traditional religion. Traditional rock art, both pictographs (painted on rocks) and petroglyphs (incised into stones), may have had similar relations with literature. Some contemporary Zuni, descendents of those who have resided in a southwestern pueblo since long before the first *entradas* by the Spanish colonizers to the south, have inter-

preted the rock art inscribed by their ancestors as depictions of the same mythic events about which oral narratives are still told.

Nonetheless, a written literature in the European sense was only beginning during the colonial period. The first important Native American writer was Samson Occom (1723–1792), a Mohegan who converted to Christianity at the age of sixteen. He spent four years under the tutelage of Eleazar Wheelock, founder of the Indian Charity School (predecessor to Dartmouth College), and became an ordained minister in 1759. He delivered some three hundred sermons while on a tour of England during 1764 and 1765 to raise money for Wheelock's school. Occom's principal publication was *A Sermon at the Execution of Moses Paul: An Indian, Who Had Been Guilty of Murder,* which went through nineteen editions after its publication in 1772. He also coauthored a collection of hymns that appeared in 1774, and his history of the Montauk nation, to whom he ministered, was posthumously published in 1809. Today he is known mainly for his autobiography, "A Short Narrative of My Life," written in 1768 but unpublished during his lifetime. One of Occom's students, the Mohegan Joseph Johnson (1752–1777), published several letters on topics of Christian spirituality in local newspapers.

CONCLUSION

Native American literatures offer a rich trove of often-misunderstood treasures. The temptation by European commentators has often been to appreciate Native literary traditions in terms that diminish them, usually as the primitive effusions of a race that either had fallen into savagery since the Creation or had not yet evolved culturally beyond the most basic stage of development. Even when these literatures have been regarded more highly, they have often been forced into European generic categories and analyzed from the perspective of European literary criticism.

Only in the latter part of the twentieth century have extensive attempts been made to appreciate Native American literatures ethnopoetically—that is, from the perspectives of the indigenous artistic systems. As anthropologists, linguists, poets, folklorists, and literary critics come to understand Native American literatures on their own terms, as products of Native aesthetics and of oral performances, they have recognized both the strengths and weaknesses of the colonial records. The weaknesses are obvious. Without the methodology or technology for accurately recording what they heard, and with a mind-set that usually regarded anything said by "savages" dismissively at best, colonizers included very few texts of oral performances that represent with any accuracy what storytellers, singers, and orators said. While there are exceptions, especially among the Jesuits in New France, one can safely claim that the records preserve very little of value.

On the other hand, in these accounts, we do find the earliest documentation of oral literature in performance. These descriptions may be less scrupulous than those recorded by later observers, but they at least tell us how and on what occasions some of the literary material was performed in cultural contexts that are as close to the pre-Columbian as possible. In that light they contribute to our appreciation of Native American traditional literatures specifically and of oral literature in general.

BIBLIOGRAPHY

Primary Sources

Erdoes, Richard, and Alfonso Ortiz, eds. *American Indian Myths and Legends.* New York, 1984. This intercultural anthology includes material recently collected by the editors and their revisions of story texts published earlier.

Gyles, John. *Memoirs of Odd Adventures, Strange Deliverances, Etc., in the Captivity of John Gyles, Esq., Commander of the Garrison on Saint George River.* Boston, 1736; repr. Cincinnati, Ohio, 1869.

Hennepin, Louis. *A New Discovery of a Vast Country in America.* 2 vols. 1698; repr. Chicago, 1903; Toronto, Ontario, 1974.

The Memoirs of Lieut. Henry Timberlake, (Who Accompanied the Three Cherokee Indians to England in the Year 1762) Containing Whatever he observed Remarkable, or worthy of public Notice. . . . London, 1765.

Peyer, Bernd, ed. *The Elders Wrote: An Anthology of Early Prose by North American Indians, 1768–1931.* Berlin, 1982. Includes material by Samson Occom and Joseph Johnson.

Radin, Paul. *The Trickster: A Study in American Indian Mythology.* New York, 1956; repr. 1972. Presents the Winnebago cycle of trickster myths.

Rothenberg Jerome, ed. *Shaking the Pumpkin: Traditional Poetry of the Indian North Americas.* Rev. ed. Albuquerque, N.Mex., 1991. Though Rothenberg's own method for translating "lyric poetry" remains controversial, this volume is one of the best samplings of this genre of Native American oral literature.

Thwaites, Reuben Gold, ed. *The Jesuit Relations and Allied Documents: Travels and Explorations of the Jesuit Missionaries in New France 1610–1791.* 79 vols. 1896–1901; repr. New York, 1959.

Underhill, Ruth Murray, ed. *The Autobiography of a Papago Woman.* Memoirs of the American Anthropological Association, no. 46 (1936); repr. Millwood, N.Y., 1974.

Vanderwerth, W. C. *Indian Oratory: Famous Speeches by Noted Indian Chieftains.* Norman, Okla., 1971. Includes texts of several orations from the colonial period.

Secondary Sources

Bauman, Richard. *Verbal Art As Performance.* Rowley, Mass., 1977; repr. Prospect Heights, Ill., 1984. Articulates the idea that oral literature must be understood as a performance event that includes much more than what is said (the text): that is, such elements as the composition of the audience, the particulars of the context, and the cultural influences upon the performer.

Clements, William M., and Frances M. Malpezzi. *Native American Folklore, 1879–1979: An Annotated Bibliography.* Athens, Ohio, 1984. Contains some fifty-five hundred entries on works dealing with oral literatures, arranged by culture area and tribal group.

Finnegan, Ruth. *Oral Poetry: Its Nature, Significance and Social Context.* Cambridge, England, 1977. The best cross-cultural survey of the nature of oral literature.

Hymes, Dell. *"In Vain I Tried to Tell You": Essays in Native American Ethnopoetics.* Philadelphia, 1981. Hymes shows that both oral stories and orations should be viewed as poetic. He also emphasizes the importance of performance in the nature of oral literature.

Murray, David, ed. *Forked Tongues: Speech, Writing, and Representation in North American Indian Texts.* Bloomington, Ind., 1991. Shows how the interpretation of Native American oral and written literatures, including some examples from the colonial period, has reflected ideological concerns of the interpreters.

Ong, Walter J. *Orality and Literacy: The Technologizing of the Word.* London, 1982. This theoretical treatment of the nature of orality and of primary oral cultures summarizes the work of one of the most influential students of oral literatures.

Pearce, Roy Harvey. *Savagism and Civilization: A Study of the Indian and the American Mind.* Berkeley, Calif., 1988. Originally published as *The Savages of America* in 1953, this is one of the most important treatments of European-American attitudes toward Native Americans. Part 1, which deals with the colonial period, explicates some of the ideas that shaped how the colonizers viewed Native American oral literatures.

Rooth, Anna Birgitta. "The Creation Myths of the North American Indians." *Anthropos* 52 (1957): 497–508. Based on a survey of three hundred myth texts, Rooth identifies eight major types of Native American creation myths.

Swann, Brian, ed. *Smoothing the Ground: Essays on Native American Oral Literature.* Berkeley, Calif., 1983. An important collection of pieces that reflect contemporary thinking about Native American oral literatures.

Swann, Brian, and Arnold Krupat, eds. *Recovering the Word: Essays on Native American Literature.* Berkeley, Calif., 1987. As important as Swann's earlier collection of essays.

Tedlock, Dennis. *The Spoken Word and the Work of Interpretation.* Philadelphia, 1983. Based primarily upon work with Zuni storytellers, Tedlock has developed a method for rendering Native American oral literature ethnopoetically—that is, taking into account the Native aesthetic systems.

Zumthor, Paul. *Oral Poetry: An Introduction.* Minneapolis, Minn., 1990. Though not grounded as firmly in actual experience with the performance of oral literature as Finnegan's survey, this volume applies some theories and methodologies of postmodern literary criticism to oral-literature study.

William M. Clements

SEE ALSO **The First Americans** and **Indian Languages.**

THE COLONIAL PRESS

Printing began in British North America in 1639, one hundred years after Spanish missionaries established a press in Mexico City. Neither the Dutch nor the French colonies had printers or printing presses until after they were conquered by the English. The earliest documents printed by the Spanish-American press and Anglo-American press were quite similar in their fundamentally religious and governmental character. Once in operation, however, the press of English America was soon diversifying its output to a greater extent than that of New Spain. The former came to play a more complex, more varied, and undoubtedly more central cultural role than its Latin counterpart. Moreover while books and reading took their place as conspicuous components of the mission and official life of the Spanish Borderlands, the actual production of Spanish-American printed materials occurred only south of the Rio Grande. This essay, therefore, concerns primarily the press of British North America.

The first purpose of printing in the British colonies, as in Mexico, was to serve the needs of church and state. The first press, located in Cambridge, Massachusetts, also operated in a close relationship with Harvard College. When printing presses were established in successive colonies after Massachusetts, beginning with Maryland and Pennsylvania in 1685, the main impetus came from each colonial government's need to print laws and other official documents.

By the early eighteenth century, however, the American press had assumed a considerably larger cultural purpose as well.

In addition to contracting for official work with governments, colonial printers produced religious books and pamphlets, a wide variety of broadsides for information and entertainment, primers and other instructional books for the education of children, copies of English works of fiction and political writings, almanacs, newspapers, and magazines. Other press work included business and legal forms, handbills, and other types of miscellaneous job printing plus innumerable bits of ephemera. The printed word in colonial America thus served as a vehicle for government and commerce, a spiritual resource and indispensable aid to organized religion, a means of education, a medium of public information and entertainment, and a significant factor in the formation of public opinion. More broadly the press in its various manifestations helped create a community of shared ideas, perceptions, and values.

THE PRINTING TRADE IN BRITISH AMERICA

The central figure in the production of printed materials in colonial America was the printer himself. He was a tradesman who had learned his craft through apprenticeship and owned or had the use of one or more wooden printing presses, an assortment of metal type, and the other necessary equipment and furnishings of a small printing office. Unlike the great printing houses found in London, Oxford, and Cambridge, the typical American printing office resembled most of the printing establishments of eighteenth-century provincial England. It contained but one or two—or occasionally three—presses and was operated by from two to perhaps eight or ten persons. The master printer, or a partnership of two such printers, usually owned the business. Depending upon the size and complexity of the operation, others in the office might include one or more journeymen who worked for wages and one or more bound apprentices who lived in the master's household for a specified term of years while learning the craft. Several American printers in the North and South were assisted by skilled black slaves, and others were helped by their wives and by their children of both sexes.

As in all the trades, the overwhelming majority of American printers in the colonial era were male. Occasionally a widow or a daughter succeeded to her husband's or father's business, and sometimes a woman achieved sole or partial control of a printing establishment by other means. Anne Timothy, Cornelia Bradford, Anne Franklin, Sarah Goddard, and Mary Katherine Goddard were among the notable women printers of the mid and later eighteenth century.

Stephen Day (or Daye) is usually credited with being the first printer in the British colonies (though it may actually have been his son Matthew who did most or all of the printing). He fell into the management of a press by accident. He came to America in 1638 with Jose (or perhaps Joseph) Glover, a Puritan clergyman who had hired him to set up an iron works. Glover, who had brought along a printing press, died during the voyage. Upon settling in Cambridge, Massachusetts, Glover's widow entrusted Day with setting up the press. In 1649 Harvard president Henry Dunster, having married the Widow Glover, transferred control of the press to Samuel Green. Green was no more trained in printing than Day, but he served for many years as official printer both to Harvard College and to the Massachusetts General Court. More important, he began a family printing dynasty that

was to dominate New England publishing for well over a century. In 1675 one of his two shops then in Cambridge moved to Boston, which in the eighteenth century became by far the leading center of printing in America.

Printing came to the middle colonies with the arrival of London-trained printer William Bradford in Philadelphia in 1685. There was no permanent printing establishment in the Chesapeake region until William Parks came to Annapolis in 1726. In 1682 there had been a brief venture in printing, immediately suppressed, in Jamestown, Virginia, followed by several marginally more successful but short-lived attempts to establish printing enterprises in Maryland near the end of the seventeenth century.

The number of printers at work in the Anglo-American colonies grew from six in 1700 to eleven in 1720, twenty-eight in 1740, sixty in 1760, and well over one hundred in 1776. The greatest concentrations of printers were in the principal seaport towns of Boston, New York, and Philadelphia, Boston boasting the highest concentration. By 1750, however, printing was also being carried on in New London, Newport, Annapolis, Williamsburg, and Charleston, and there were German language presses in Germantown and Ephrata, Pennsylvania. Several of the British West Indian islands already had printers by mid century, one having been set up in Jamaica as early as 1720. In the 1750s printing spread to Woodbridge, New Jersey; New Bern, North Carolina; Portsmouth, New Hampshire; New Haven; and Halifax, Nova Scotia. By 1770 none of the colonies that would comprise the thirteen United States lacked a printing establishment, and by then a bilingual press had also been established in British-occupied Quebec. In 1776 there was at least one printer in each of twenty-nine separate locations on the continent and on six of the British islands in the Caribbean.

Few Anglo-American printers worked in isolation from their fellow printers. Family and professional contacts resulted in patterns of association, sponsorship, and mutual help. The most dramatic familial printing network was that of the Green-Kneeland-Draper clan in New England, composed of several generations of descendants and descendants-in-law of the same Green who had taken over the Cambridge press in 1649. For a comparable network that stressed professional rather than family ties, one turns to the far-flung band of former apprentices and beneficiaries of Benjamin Franklin, who was the second most prolific printer in the American colonies, exceeded only by Bartholomew Green of Boston. Franklin was certainly the most famous printer and by almost any measure the most successful. Franklin ran his printing business in Philadelphia from 1729 until he formed a partnership in 1748 with David Hall, after which he remained a silent partner in the business until 1766. His encouragement and sponsorship of former apprentices and employees resulted in the establishment of new printing houses in Charleston, Annapolis, Wilmington, New York, New Haven, and Antigua.

Many American printers also served as postmasters in their respective communities, especially after 1753 when Franklin became deputy postmaster general for the colonies. A book- and job-printing business combined with the colonial government printing contract, the publication of a newspaper, and the local postmastership with its franking privilege proved a characteristic key to success for the most fortunate. The combination, repeated in a string of colonial capitals along the seaboard, was also instrumental in the easy exchange of news and opinion and thus in the forging of a common Anglo-American culture. Most printers, whether or not they enjoyed this privileged combination, conducted some kind of retail shop along with their printing business.

Printers, while central to any act of publishing, did not operate alone. Most printing jobs were undertaken not at the printer's own financial risk but under contract with a sponsor or publisher. The sponsor might have been a branch of the provincial government in the case of a book of laws, a clergyman or his congregation in the case of a printed sermon, a college, an author, a bookseller, a club of anonymous politicians, or almost anyone else who wanted to get something into print and had the means to pay for it. The most systematic and professional publishing operations, however, were carried on by booksellers operating according to the mode long established in London.

The surviving records of one especially prolific and influential bookseller and publisher, Daniel Henchman of Boston, disclose a developing business relationship between publisher and author as well as between publisher and printer. During a half-century career that ended shortly before the beginning of the revolutionary crisis, Henchman published more than three hundred titles, mostly religious works, by at least 116 authors.

In the beginning the separation of printer and publisher applied to newspapers as well as to most other printed materials, but the conventions of newspaper publishing gradually changed, and by about 1740 all but one newspaper in America was being published by its printer on his or her own account. By then almanacs were also generally printers' productions.

Booksellers were essential to the publication process not only as publishers in many cases but also as distributors of printed materials. Since books usually came from the printer in sheets, some American booksellers added a bindery to their operations, though binders could also work independently or, less frequently, under the sponsorship of a printer. In America more than in England, it was possible to find printers who were also booksellers. American booksellers almost invariably imported and sold books printed in England as well as the domestic publications they sponsored.

THE PRODUCTS OF THE PRESS

The Seventeenth Century

The products of seventeenth-century American printing presses leaned heavily toward government and religious documents. The reputed first piece of printing off the Cambridge press of Stephen Day, though there is no extant copy to prove it, was the "Oath of a Free-Man," by which a subscriber swore loyalty to the Massachusetts Bay Colony and promised to obey its laws. The next, also with no surviving copy, was an almanac. The third, the celebrated *Whole Booke of Psalmes Faithfully Translated into English Metre* or "Bay Psalm Book," was printed in 1640 and was the first book printed in English America. The Days, their successor, Samuel Green, and Marmaduke Johnson, who started a second printing establishment in Cambridge in 1660, together turned out close to five hundred pieces of printing in Cambridge before 1700. Many of these were broadsides such as the periodic Harvard commencement program listing the "quaestiones" to be upheld or refuted by the graduates, various oaths, of which the famous Freeman's Oath of 1639 was the first, government proclamations setting fast and thanksgiving days, and printed orders to town constables and selectmen to collect taxes for the colony. The Cambridge printers also produced many works that were more substantial, such as catechisms, books of psalms and hymns, various editions of the Massachusetts laws and orders of the General Court, many printed sermons, and even the first British-American edition of the Bible. Issued in 1663, the Bible was printed in the language of the Algonquians.

The Cambridge press provides evidence that beginning in 1667 New England reading tastes went beyond the official and religious productions that dominated the Cambridge press. Green and Johnson each printed an edition of a book describing the recent plague and Great Fire of London. The same two printers jointly published an account of the eruption of Mount Etna. Johnson printed a semihumorous collection of maxims called *Old Mr. Dod's Sayings* and even a mildly erotic piece of fiction entitled *The Isle of Pines,* for which he was fined by the authorities.

John Foster's introduction of printing to Boston in 1675 was significant both for the development of printing in America and for the rapid pace of change in that town toward the end of the seventeenth century. In 1685 an American press was harnessed for the first time for the publication of an immediate piece of news when Samuel Green, Jr., then in Boston, reprinted the *London Gazette* that reported the death of English king Charles II and the accession of James II. From then to the end of the century, occasional news broadsides took their place among the productions of the Boston press.

From 1689 to 1691 Boston was caught up in the tumultuous events surrounding the Glorious Revolution, the local revolt against Sir Edmund Andros and the Dominion of New England, the outbreak of the War of the League of Augsburg, and the establishment of a restored Massachusetts government under a new charter. The printing press did not merely record these events; it was itself a central actor. In April 1689 a proclamation urging Andros to surrender the government to a caretaker committee was not only read to a Boston crowd but printed by Green for distribution throughout the province. Late in the same year, a newspaper-like broadside entitled *The Present State of the New-English Affairs* informed its Massachusetts readership of the progress of Increase Mather's mission to England. The mission had begun as a complaint against the Andros regime but as a consequence of the Glorious Revolution had been transformed into what would become a successful quest for a new charter.

On 25 September 1690 the exiled English journalist and propagandist Benjamin Harris carried the logic of *The Present State* a step further by publishing what was intended to be the first number of a periodical newspaper, *Publick Occurrences Both Forreign and Domestick,* but which the temporary government of the province immediately suppressed. Before returning to England in 1695, however, Harris made a much more lasting contribution to American publishing by commissioning and possibly compiling the first of many editions of *The New England Primer,* which became a staple of elementary education in the region over the century to come.

The role of the press as vital actor in the political transformation of New England at the end of the century had its counterpart first in Philadelphia and then in New York with the activities of William Bradford. Bringing his press and his London training to Pennsylvania with the specific endorsement of William Penn, Bradford began in 1685 to fill his intended role as official printer to the colony and to the Society of Friends. Pennsylvania's Quakers, however, were factionalized, and by 1690 Bradford was in trouble with the authorities for printing the tracts of the minority faction. After several episodes of repression, a period in jail, and an inconclusive trial for seditious libel, he moved to New York in 1693 at the invitation of Governor Benjamin Fletcher, who was prompted in part by his desire to see his own military exploits recorded in print. At the age of thirty, Bradford began a fifty-nine-year career in New York as the leading printer of the city, a newspaper publisher, and a prominent citizen and churchman. His son, Andrew Bradford, once having been trained in his father's New York shop, returned to Philadelphia to reestablish a branch of the Bradford press in that city in 1712.

The Eighteenth Century

The increase in the number and variety of American imprints during the last decade and a half of the seventeenth century proved to be only a foreshadowing of the growth and role of the press once the eighteenth century got under way. The best estimate of numbers of imprints, based on standard bibliographies but weighted to account for known patterns of error, produces a total of 1,264 for the first sixty-four years of printing from the "Freeman's Oath" in 1639 through 1703, the year before the establishment of the first successful American newspaper. During the next twenty years, from 1704 through 1723, American printers turned out 1,582 imprints. The corresponding figures for successive twenty-year periods are 2,997 for 1724–1743; 4,965 for 1744–1763; and 11,098 for 1764–1783, the years of the revolutionary crisis and the War for American Independence. This adds up to 21,905 imprints from 1639 to 1783. (These figures do not include the weekly numbers of the several dozen newspapers appearing entirely in the eighteenth century.)

Fewer than 6 percent of these were printed before 1704, while over half were printed after 1763. Except for 1764 Massachusetts led all the colonies in the number of imprints from 1638 until 1775, when Pennsylvania printers took the lead in production for the rest of the century.

Books and Almanacs

Before the revolution American printers did not produce many books of substantial size. Books of this nature required a relatively heavy investment, a larger supply of type and equipment than most American printers had, and an assured market. Thus the steady sellers and other larger-sized books that circulated in the British colonies tended for the most part to be imported from the mother country.

American printers did, however, turn out pamphlet-sized books in great variety. The printed sermon constituted the most characteristic publication of this sort, especially in New England. Political pamphlets, instruction books and guidebooks, law books, brief works of fiction,

primers, and descriptions and discussions of topical matters were also produced in this format. Theological and other religious writings, including portions of the Bible, remained the leading subject category of imprints throughout the colonial period. As the revolution approached, however, the proportion of such works declined in relation to works on politics, history, current events, and law.

The pamphlet format, often simply eight octavo leaves yielding sixteen pages, was also widely employed for almanacs. If we are to believe John Winthrop, an almanac was the second piece of printing off Stephen Day's Cambridge press in 1639, and from that year on, at least one almanac was published annually by nearly every printer in British America. Aside from the Bible, there was no more ubiquitous genre to be found in homes throughout the colonies. At first consisting of little more than a calendar page for each month with astronomical data, weather predictions, and farming tips, the almanac increased in size, complexity, and literary scope throughout the eighteenth century. An almanac could take on a distinctly partisan flavor, depending upon the religious or political inclinations of its author. But the twelve calendar pages, later usually doubled to create a two-page spread for each month, always remained the one essential ingredient. It was on those pages, or on leaves stitched between them, that countless farmers and householders kept their diaries. The "man of signs," a woodcut of a human figure showing the influence of the twelve signs of the zodiac over various parts of the anatomy, often preceded the calendar pages.

Throughout the colonial period, the number of separate almanacs published exceeded that of all other books combined, and many of them were printed in extremely large quantities. Benjamin Franklin's *Poor Richard's Almanack,* to cite the most famous and most spectacular example, sold 141,257 copies during the years 1752–1765, an average of some ten thousand per year.

Newspapers

The colonial newspaper got off to a much slower start than did the almanac, but its cultural importance was no less great and its political importance ultimately very much greater. The first attempt at an American news periodical, Benjamin Harris's *Publick Occurrences* of 1690, was decidedly premature. At the time of its publication, the only other newspapers in the English-speaking world were the official *London Gazette* and the *News-Letter* of Dublin. An act for the regulation of printing, one practical consequence of which was to prevent the legal publication of private newspapers in competition with the *Gazette,* would remain in effect in England until 1694. Although the applicability of the printing act in the colonies was open to question, *Publick Occurrences* was immediately suppressed on other grounds by the very tenuous revolutionary government that temporarily held power in Massachusetts.

The first successful newspaper in America, the *Boston News-Letter,* was begun in 1704 by the Boston postmaster John Campbell. Under Campbell's ownership, which lasted nineteen years, the *News-Letter* was insufferably dull and unimaginative and by Campbell's own account began with a circulation of only 250 copies. In the context of British publishing, however, it was hardly less precocious than Harris's abortive attempt fourteen years earlier. The end of the English licensing act had allowed the flourishing of private newspapers in London during the second half of the 1690s, but newspapers did not come to the outlying cities of England until either 1700 or 1701.

Considered as an extension of English provincial newspaper publishing, Campbell's *News-Letter* was either the third or the fourth such newspaper to be established. This does not take account of the small newspaper that continued to serve the alien English population of Dublin or the start-up of a new *Edinburgh Gazette* in 1699. But even considering these additional British publications, the *Boston News-Letter* was a very early entry in the field of English provincial journalism. It remained the only newspaper in America until December 1719, when a competing *Boston Gazette* appeared one day before Andrew Bradford's *American Weekly Mercury,* Philadelphia's first newspaper.

By 1740 there were twelve American newspapers (in addition to one each in Jamaica and Barbados). In 1750 there were nineteen and in 1765, twenty-five. These papers included one in Halifax, Nova Scotia, begun in 1752, and a short-lived bilingual newspaper in Quebec, be-

gun in 1765, a few years after the British conquest, but cut short the same year by the Stamp Act. A more enduring version of that experiment commenced in 1774. Beginning as early as 1739, American newspapers consistently included at least one German-language newspaper in Pennsylvania. Of the thirteen colonies that declared independence in 1776, only Delaware lacked at least one newspaper. In that year thirty-nine newspapers were being published in twenty-three different places in the new United States. The number had risen to fifty-eight in twenty-six places by the end of the war in 1783.

Practically without exception prerevolutionary American newspapers came out weekly, their publication day usually keyed to the arrival or departure of the post. In the early part of the eighteenth century, a typical newspaper had only two small pages, occasionally expanded to four. By the middle of the century, four-page papers were more common. Only one newspaper ever exceeded four pages and that was the *Pennsylvania Gazette,* to which Benjamin Franklin and David Hall occasionally had to add extra pages beyond the normal four to accommodate the need for extra advertising space. The size of the typical page, which in the earliest *Boston News-Letter* and *Boston Gazette* was not much different from today's standard piece of typing paper, gradually increased through the century.

Circulation, most often effected by delivery to subscribers rather than by street sales, was startlingly small both by nineteenth and twentieth century standards and in comparison to contemporary figures from London. The average newspaper publisher before the revolution probably sold about six hundred copies weekly, though of course the number of readers of those copies was certainly much larger.

The main content of colonial newspapers was the news of Europe, copied from London newspapers that arrived in American ports from six weeks to three months after publication, depending on the season. This preponderance of European news did not end until the revolutionary crisis. This does not mean that the nature of newspaper content remained static until 1763. As the number of American newspapers slowly increased during the 1720s and 1730s, colonial printers took to copying each other as well as the "prints" of London. This practice, eventually encouraged and stimulated by an improved postal system, motivated newspaper publishers to take their part in what was becoming a rudimentary provincial information exchange by collecting and printing area news and locally produced letters and essays. In this way, a Boston printer could provide his counterpart in Philadelphia or Charleston with news and comment from New England, while he in turn shared material copied from other colonial newspapers with his own readers.

A significant turning point came in 1739. At that time a new war with Spain and the first American tour of the evangelist George Whitefield provoked American publishers into giving new prominence to substantial accounts and letters of opinion regarding events and issues that were close to home. This tendency continued for the remainder of the colonial era, though never to the eclipsing of foreign news, which continued to be the major staple of the colonial newspaper.

Newspapers also contained advertisements, though the few surviving printers' accounts of the period suggest that advertising revenues were less important in newspaper publishing than subscribers' fees. The few advertisements in the earliest Boston newspapers leaned heavily toward book announcements. The same was true of the earliest newspaper advertising in Philadelphia, but in that city advertising eventually proliferated more than in any other during the colonial era. From 1748 to 1765 advertisements, averaging about sixty a week, occupied more than half the space of the *Pennsylvania Gazette.* Goods at retail, an increasing proportion of goods at wholesale, slaves and indentures for sale, runaways, animals and animal services for sale, real estate, and ship departures, among many other things, were advertised. Nowhere as much as in Philadelphia did advertisers and publishers collaborate in a way that discloses quite such a sophisticated awareness of how a newspaper could function in an increasingly complex economy. Nevertheless, the tendency was at work to some degree everywhere an American newspaper was published.

In Boston, where a relatively large number of printers produced a correspondingly disproportionate number of colonial newspaper titles,

a distinctive genre of literary newspaper flourished in the 1720s and 1730s. Beginning with James Franklin's *New England Courant,* founded as America's first opposition newspaper in 1721, this genre combined features of the essay journals of Augustan England with those of the standard English newspaper. The same literary emphasis was continued in the *New-England Weekly Journal,* a thoroughly "establishment" paper begun in 1727 soon after the *Courant* died, and in the *Weekly Rehearsal,* owned by an aspiring writer from its founding in 1731 until it was acquired by its printer, who transformed it into a standard newspaper and changed its name to the *Boston Evening-Post* in 1735. Although none of the literary journals lasted very long, they did help newspaper readers develop a taste for speculative and imaginative writing. This in turn established a strong precedent for the inclusion of this kind of material, along with occasional verse, as part of the varied content of the provincial newspaper as it continued to mature.

Except for a time in Boston, where the first newspaper publishers were postmasters who were not printers, where one writer was briefly a publisher, and where literary "clubs" were sponsors of printer-owned newspapers, the owners and publishers of newspapers were always their printers. That was technically true even in the case of John Peter Zenger's *New-York Weekly Journal.* The *Journal* was begun in 1733 specifically as a vehicle for the province's opposition political faction and thus, while the controversy endured, was sponsored and largely edited by the members of that faction.

Even though the circulation of most individual American newspapers was comparatively small—the main exception was probably the *Pennsylvania Gazette,* which may have circulated as many as two thousand copies weekly—the total production of newspapers was sufficient to reach much of the literate population. One can estimate roughly that from mid century to the eve of the revolution, one copy of an American newspaper was being printed each week for every 100 to 120 inhabitants of the English colonies. Multiple readership in households and in taverns and coffeehouses assured that each copy influenced several, perhaps even many, persons. The practice of mutual copying and the essential unanimity of publishers on fundamental social, cultural, and political values—though not always on specific issues—assured quite a broad distribution and confirmation of shared values and beliefs as well as what the publishers agreed was "news." Perhaps more effectively than any other print medium, therefore, the newspapers served as both creators and vehicles of what was becoming in the pre-revolutionary decades a coherent provincial culture.

Magazines

Just as one inventive and influential newspaper, the *London Gazette,* served as the ultimate model for its English and American imitators, two London-based monthly magazines became the joint prototype of that genre. The difference was that no American magazine before the revolution survived nearly as long or rewarded its publisher remotely as well as even the more modestly successful newspapers.

Gentleman's Magazine, founded in 1731, and its competitor, the *London Magazine,* begun in 1732, became exceptionally popular in England in the late 1730s and 1740s. Their success stemmed in part from their substantial literary content but also from their reports of the proceedings of Parliament—often under the thin guise of various fictional devices. The contemporary success of these two famous journals inspired Benjamin Franklin and Andrew Bradford, rival printers and newspaper publishers in Philadelphia, to issue competing magazines almost simultaneously in February 1741. The appearance of Bradford's *American Magazine* and Franklin's *General Magazine* three days later climaxed a bitter exchange between the two printers in which Franklin accused his rival of stealing the idea of a magazine from him. The *American Magazine,* heavy on reports of the proceedings of colonial legislatures and little else, lasted three months. The *General Magazine,* running from seventy to seventy-six duodecimo pages, was more varied in content than its rival. It also extended in a new format the newspaper debates over George Whitefield and the burning contemporary question of paper currency. Yet it lasted only six months.

Clearly there was not yet an American reading market sufficient to absorb a diet consisting of both weekly newspapers and monthly magazines. From the failure of the *General Magazine* to the outbreak of the War for Independence, there were eighteen more attempts to start magazines in Boston, New York, Philadelphia, and in one case, Woodbridge, New Jersey. Ten lasted a year or less. The most successful, measured at least in terms of longevity, was the very next effort after Bradford's and Franklin's failed attempts. This was the *American Magazine and Historical Chronicle,* published by the Boston printing firm of Rogers and Fowle and edited by the same Jeremiah Gridley who had earlier founded the *Weekly Rehearsal* and would go on to become a distinguished jurist.

During its existence from September 1743 to December 1746, the *American Magazine and Historical Chronicle* closely followed the *London Magazine* both in content and format. Its fifty octavo pages each month were devoted largely to Parliamentary debates, proceedings of colonial legislatures, and reports from both the European and American theaters of the War of the Austrian Succession. The longevity of this magazine compared to the others may have been partly due to its publishers' desperate quest for a niche in Boston's crowded periodical market. The partnership of Rogers and Fowle was at the time one of the only two of the town's six printing firms that did not publish newspapers and the only firm not printing one.

This observation merely heightens the conclusion that although there was clearly a colonial appetite for periodical literature and a desire to be kept current on public affairs, the vast majority of printers found that the most practical and profitable way to meet it was with a weekly newspaper and an annual almanac.

FREEDOM OF THE PRESS IN COLONIAL AMERICA

Since 1960, no aspect of colonial American publishing has attracted as much scholarly attention as the question of press freedom. To printers of the pre-revolutionary period, the term meant the accessibility of a fundamentally neutral press to expressions of various opinions. In the twentieth century, the term usually refers to the degree to which the press is free to operate without interference from government. It is that meaning of "press freedom" that has interested most modern scholars.

The question as usually framed focuses on the colonial background and original intent of the "freedom of the press" clause of the First Amendment. Did the founders, based on colonial and revolutionary experience, intend "freedom of the press" to mean simply freedom from censorship and prior restraint, or did they also intend to abolish the common law principle of "seditious libel"? English courts, operating under the assumption that the safety of government depends upon the "good opinion" of the people, had long found it their duty to punish seditious libel. Defined as statements tending to beget "an ill opinion of the government," in the words of a noted decision of 1704, seditious libel charges existed whether or not any legislative provisions for actual censorship were actually in effect.

In 1960 Leonard W. Levy appalled various well-known libertarian legal historians and jurists by arguing, in *Legacy of Suppression,* that contrary to the prevailing assumption, the First Amendment was not intended to abolish the law of seditious libel in the United States. A broader theoretical understanding of freedom of expression than that held by the framers, Levy suggested, had to await subsequent political and legal developments. In 1985 Levy modified his findings in *Emergence of a Free Press* in which he softened but did not abandon his main argument and enlarged his consideration of the colonial experience beyond the strictly theoretical to the actual practices of printers in their criticisms of government. The emergence of a full-fledged libertarian theory, he continued to insist, lagged well behind actual behavior—as well as behind the enactment of the First Amendment.

The debate between Levy and his many critics constituted one of the liveliest chapters in early American historiography during the quarter century between *Legacy of Suppression* and its 1985 revision. In 1988 Jeffery A. Smith sought to demonstrate, in *Printers and Press Freedom,* the development during the colonial era of an explicit ideology of press freedom that was linked to republican theory and thus constituted a self-conscious departure from English legal and political assumptions. It is upon this ideology, he

asserted in opposition to Levy's findings, that the freedom of speech and press clause of the First Amendment is based. There is no reason to suppose that this rich scholarly debate will end there.

The numerous instances in which American colonial printers brushed against authority demonstrate, among other things, a gradual shift from control by "prior restraint," a legislative function, to control by prosecution for illegal utterances, a judicial function. A third stage might be described as control by public opinion.

In the seventeenth century control of the press by prior restraint was the general though not the invariable rule. Colonial authorities simply took for granted their duty to "supervise" the press. Official suppression of a printing operation in Virginia in 1682 demonstrated this control as did the order of the Massachusetts General Court in 1664, which prohibited the establishment of any press outside Cambridge and provided for the prior licensing of any piece of printing. The Massachusetts government's order suppressing *Publick Occurrences* in 1690 does not make clear on what grounds the suppression was based. Was it the Massachusetts act of 1664 or one like it, the Parliamentary licensing act that would remain in effect in England until 1694, or did the paper's contents provoke the governor's and the council's "high Resentment"? The same order forbade any future printing without government license. In Pennsylvania, on the other hand, the Quaker-dominated government's prosecution of William Bradford in 1692 and his long imprisonment awaiting a trial that was never completed resulted from a charge of seditious libel. Prior licensing of the offending pamphlets, or the lack thereof, was never at issue.

The legislative abandonment of prior licensing in England in 1694 did not automatically signal the colonial governments that such licensing was either unconstitutional or outmoded. When John Campbell started up the *Boston News-Letter* in 1704, he took care to secure the governor's or the province secretary's "approbation" of each week's proposed contents ahead of time. It is not clear, however, that there was any law in force under the new charter that required this. The Massachusetts General Court tried to impose prior licensing for the last time in January

1723. In its dealings with the obstreperous *New England Courant* the previous June, the General Court had jailed James Franklin for contempt during the remainder of the legislative session. This time, after fresh assaults in the *Courant* upon the dignity and authority of religion and government, the General Court passed an order forbidding Franklin to publish the *Courant* "or any Pamphlet or Paper of the like Nature" except under the supervision of the province secretary, and compelling him to post a bond to prevent "the like offense for the future." Franklin quite easily got around the order by turning over the paper in name to his apprentice, brother Benjamin Franklin. When the General Court tried to prosecute him for violating the order, the grand jury refused to hand down the indictment. This was the de facto end of prior licensing in America, since no government ever tried it again.

The most celebrated confrontation between press and government in the colonial period was the one-day trial of John Peter Zenger on 4 August 1735. Zenger's *New-York Weekly Journal*, like the *New England Courant* in the previous decade, was conspicuous in its community as an opposition paper. Unlike Franklin and his "Couranteer" colleagues, however, Zenger was only a hired tool of the political faction surrounding the dismissed Chief Justice Lewis Morris. This faction essentially rented the *Weekly Journal* in order to carry on its regular printed harangues against Governor William Cosby.

For several of these attacks on the governor, Zenger was jailed for eight months before being tried for seditious libel. His defense attorney, Andrew Hamilton of Philadelphia, argued contrary to the received law of libel at the time that the truth of an utterance should be admitted as a defense against libel and moreover that the jury had the right to determine questions of law as well as the facts of the case. The jury, easily swayed by Hamilton's libertarian rhetoric and acting really, as Hamilton knew, as a court of public opinion rather than as an agent of the law, quickly found Zenger innocent, and the city celebrated.

Though the Zenger decision did not change any law or create any legal precedent, the publicity that it gained through the wide distribution of the case's printed record discouraged further common-law prosecutions for seditious libel.

The chief source of actions against the press thereafter came to be the popular assemblies, which, in pursuit of their Whiggish claims to be champions of the liberties of the people, could easily and occasionally did take action against printers for contempt or for breach of legislative privilege. Thus all a printer needed to do to stay out of trouble was not to offend majority opinion. The same principle applied during the mounting revolutionary crisis, when neither legislatures nor patriotic mobs seemed quite able to grasp the illogic of attacking, in the name of liberty, the publication of unpopular opinions.

THE PRESS AND THE AMERICAN REVOLUTION

The role of American printers in forwarding the revolt against Britain has long been asserted and celebrated. The founder of this historiographical tradition no doubt was Isaiah Thomas, himself a printer and newspaper publisher during the years of turbulence, whose 1810 publication, *The History of Printing in America*, laid the essential groundwork for all subsequent histories of books and printing in colonial and revolutionary America. The broadest treatment of the theme in the twentieth century has been Arthur M. Schlesinger's 1958 monograph, the title of which speaks for itself: *Prelude to Independence: The Newspaper War on Britain, 1764–1776*. Later scholars who have examined more limited aspects of the topic have shown less interest in how the press helped bring about independence, if it did, than in the response of printers to revolutionary circumstances and how the nature of the press was changed as a result.

For one thing, the revolutionary crisis and the ensuing war vastly increased the productions of the press. More than half of the nonnewspaper imprints that came off North American presses in the 144 years between the "Freeman's Oath" and the end of the War for Independence were concentrated in the twenty years after 1763.

Especially significant, both in numbers and in their substantive importance as the principal vehicle by which the crucial constitutional ideas of the era were developed and argued both in America and in England, was the political pamphlet. Exact numbers of such publications are difficult to determine. But one careful study, Thomas R. Adams's *American Independence: The Growth of an Idea* (1965), identifies 195 pamphlets on the question of independence first published in America between 1764 and 4 July 1776 and another 190 American reprints of such pamphlets first printed either in America or abroad. Thomas Paine's *Common Sense* alone, by far the most reprinted pamphlet of the era, went through twenty-five American editions and another five abroad. The most influential analysis of the arguments that are developed in this extensive pamphlet literature is in Bernard Bailyn's *Ideological Origins of the American Revolution,* published in 1967 as an enlarged version of the introduction to his important collection of 1965, *Pamphlets of the American Revolution, 1750–1776.*

The revolutionary crisis also affected newspapers, catalyzing a permanent change in their character. The Stamp Act of 1765 confronted printers, especially the great majority who published newspapers, with a challenge not only to continued economic viability but also to the traditional stance of political neutrality to which most of them had adhered. Although virtually all printers opposed the legislation out of obvious self-interest, only a few at first issued strong public statements or engaged in printed demonstrations of protest. Printers as a whole soon discovered to their surprise and discomfiture that the Stamp Act was being used throughout the colonies as a rallying cause for radical protest against tyranny.

Reluctantly and in some cases ambiguously, printers were forced by public opinion to take sides, thus abandoning a principle of press freedom—a neutral press accessible to varying opinions—that most had accepted until then as their guide. A few ceased publishing newspapers altogether. Subsequent episodes during the ensuing revolutionary crisis further heightened patriot passions and drove ever-deepening wedges between the committed and the uncommitted as well as between Loyalist, however moderate, and burgeoning revolutionary. Most printers eventually adjusted to this unfamiliar atmosphere of polarization, some taking the Loyalist side but the majority the Patriot side. As the printers of Patriot newspapers took on the unaccustomed role of leaders of opinion, their stature rose in the eyes of the revolutionary and post-revolutionary generation from the status of "mechanic" to that of significant public figure whose press was a safeguard against tyranny. From then until the early nineteenth century, a vigorously partisan press, each paper and journal commanded by a zealous and fearless guardian of some version of the public good, became the norm and the expectation.

BIBLIOGRAPHY

Adams, Thomas R. *American Independence: The Growth of an Idea.* Providence, R.I., 1965.

Alexander, James. *A Brief Narrative of the Case and Trial of John Peter Zenger.* Edited by Stanley Nider Katz. Cambridge, Mass., 1963. This edited edition of Alexander's chronicle, with interpretive commentary, may be the single best available source on the Zenger case.

Bailyn, Bernard. *Ideological Origins of the American Revolution.* Cambridge, Mass., 1967.

———. *Pamphlets of the American Revolution, 1750–1776,* Vol. 1. Cambridge, Mass., 1965.

Bailyn, Bernard, and John B. Hench, eds. *The Press and the American Revolution.* Worcester, Mass., 1980. A superb collection of papers derived from a conference at the American Antiquarian Society. All nine essays are useful, but those by Stephen Botein, Richard Buel, and G. Thomas Tanselle are particularly relevant to the themes discussed above.

Botein, Stephen. " 'Meer Mechanics' and an Open Press: The Business and Political Strategies of Colonial American Printers." *Perspectives in American History* 9 (1975):127–225. A strong statement of the thesis that pre-revolutionary American printers conducted an impartial, or "free" press as a matter of economic self-interest.

Brigham, Clarence S. *History and Bibliography of American Newspapers, 1690–1820.* 2 vols. Worcester, Mass., 1947; repr., 1975.

Brown, Richard D. *Knowledge Is Power: The Diffusion of Information in Early America, 1700–1865.* New York, 1989. Restricted neither to the colonial period nor to the medium of print, this work furnishes a provocative treatment of the significance of the changing methods and scale of the transmission of information.

Clark, Charles E. "The Newspapers of Provincial America." *American Antiquarian Society Proceedings* 100 (1990), 367–89. Reprinted in *Three Hundred Years of the American Newspaper,* edited by John B. Hench. Worcester, Mass., 1991.

Franklin, Benjamin V., ed. *Boston Printers, Publishers, and Booksellers: 1640–1800*. Boston, 1980. A most engaging reference book.

Hall, David D. "The World of Print and Collective Mentality in Seventeenth-Century New England." In *New Directions in American Intellectual History*, edited by John Higham and Paul K. Conkin. Baltimore, Md., 1979.

Joyce, William L., David D. Hall, Richard D. Brown, and John B. Hench, eds. *Printing and Society in Early America*. Worcester, Mass., 1983. Another fine collection of American Antiquarian Society conference papers. The introductory essay by David Hall is especially stimulating.

Levy, Leonard W. *Emergence of a Free Press*. New York, 1985. See text above for significance of this book and its relationship to Levy's earlier version, *Legacy of Suppression: Freedom of Speech and Press in Early American History*. Cambridge, Mass., 1960.

Mott, Frank Luther. *A History of American Magazines, 1741–1850*. New York, 1930.

Schlesinger, Arthur M. *Prelude to Independence: The Newspaper War on Britain, 1764–1776*. New York, 1958.

Smith, Jeffery A. *Printers and Press Freedom: The Ideology of Early American Journalism*. New York, 1988.

Steele, Ian K. *The English Atlantic, 1675–1740: An Exploration of Communication and Community*. New York, 1986. Good on communications within and between England and America, with some special attention to newspapers on both sides of the Atlantic.

Thomas, Isaiah. *The History of Printing in America*. Edited by Marcus A. McCorison. 2nd ed. Barre, Mass., 1874; repr. 1970. The starting point for any study of the colonial press. Thomas's first edition appeared in 1810.

Wetherell, Charles. "Brokers of the Word: An Essay in the Social History of the Early American Press, 1639–1783." Ph.D. diss., University of New Hampshire, 1980. A sophisticated analysis of the early American printing trade and the relationships within it.

Wroth, Lawrence C. *The Colonial Printer*. 2nd ed. Charlottesville, Va., 1964.

Charles E. Clark

SEE ALSO **Artisans; Colonial Political Culture; Colonial Political Thought; Libraries and Learned Societies;** and **Literature.**

LIBRARIES AND LEARNED SOCIETIES

BOOKS WERE AMONG THE MOST important provisions early colonists brought to North America. Navigation books helped them cross the Atlantic. Promotional tracts provided encouraging descriptions of the continent. Religious treatises, belletristic works, and histories let them transplant Old World culture to the New. Regardless of their content, books held symbolic value as hallmarks of civilization and bulwarks against the wilderness. The earliest American libraries were personal collections, but as the colonies developed during the seventeenth century, church and college libraries were established. In the eighteenth century, subscription libraries, and eventually learned societies, were founded to meet the intellectual needs of colonial Americans.

INDIVIDUAL LIBRARIES

Spanish explorers and merchantmen had prodigious quantities of histories and romantic fiction shipped to the New World. Conquistadors favored *Amadís de Gaul* (1508), the *Palmerín* cycle that began in 1511, Mateo Alemán's *Guzmán de Alfarache* (1599), Miguel de Cervantes's *Don Quixote* (1605), and Garci-Rodríguez Montalvo's *Sergas de Esplandián* (1510). In these romantic adventures, the Spanish explorers found analogues

of their New World experience. In *The True History of the Conquest of New Spain*, Bernal Diaz del Castillo compared Mexico City to the "enchantments they tell of in the legend of Amadis." Once the conquistadors had come and gone, New World interest in romantic fiction, with the notable exception of *Don Quixote*, waned until the mid eighteenth century. Other sixteenth-century Spanish works such as Pedro Mexía's *Historia imperial y cesárea* (1547) and Antonio de Guevara's didactic historical novel, *Libro áureo de Marco Aurelio* (1529), remained popular (in translation) among English colonists.

Spanish book collections surviving in North America beyond the sixteenth century were generally mission libraries. Though liturgical books such as missals and breviaries predominated, these collections also included philosophical works, biblical commentaries, church-law books, ecclesiastical histories, and Latin classics. Our Father Santo Domingo mission library southwest of Santa Fe, for example, had such diverse works as Diego de Baeza's *Commentaria moralia in Evangelicam Historiarum* (1624); Antonio de Solìs y Rivadeneyra's *Historia de la conquista de México* (1684); Fray Domingo de Soto's *In dialecticam Aristolelis commetarii* (1554); Philipp Clüver's *Introductio in universam geographiam* (1624); works by Virgil, Ovid, and Horace; and several Mexico City imprints.

French colonists brought books with them to the early settlements. Canada's first man of letters, Marc Lescarbot, had a library at Acadia (Nova Scotia) in 1606 and generously shared his books with other Port Royal settlers. Since Lescarbot's library was destroyed, scholars can only surmise that the collection probably would have included belletristic works, histories, law books, and medical treatises. When the Port Royal settlement was disbanded the following year he returned to France, but later French settlers shared his penchant for books. Individuals had their own libraries: judges had the usual legal tomes, the *Coutume de Paris* and the various learned commentaries on it; merchants had accounting books, especially Jacques Savary's *Le parfait negociant* (1675) and Jacques Savary des Bruslons's *Dictionnaire universel de commerce* (1723). Attorney-general Louis-Guillaume Verrier accumulated a notable legal collection, and he generously shared it with his law students. Among them was François-Joseph Cugnet, the French secretary to Quebec's governor and council, who assembled one of the first libraries in the colony.

Michel de Montaigne's *Essais* (1571–1580 and 1588) and Fénelon's *Les Aventures de Télémaque* (1699) were among the most well-read works in New France. Plays by Pierre Corneille, Molière, and Jean Racine were popular, and in the later eighteenth century, Voltaire and Jean-Jacques Rousseau were widely read. Baron Lahontan's statement in his *Nouveau Voyages* that the "clergy prohibit and burn all the Books that treat of any subject but Devotion" was fanciful hyperbole. Books reached the colonial French settlements throughout North America. At his death in 1778, Saint Louis's first citizen, Pierre de Laclède Liguest, had over two hundred volumes including works by René Descartes, Fénelon, and Charles Rollin; French translations of Bacon and Locke; and Benjamin Franklin's *Experiences et observations sur l'electricité* (1752).

Many schools in New France developed fine book collections—the Jesuit College at Quebec, the Sulpicians' Seminary in Montreal, and the Quebec Ursulines. The Jesuit College, established in 1635, owned the single greatest library in New France. By the mid eighteenth century, the collection had grown to five thousand volumes. The library was pillaged by the British during the 1759 occupation, but surviving evidence indicates that it included a wide variety of theological treatises, ecclesiastical histories, saints' lives, devotional works, classical histories, and medical books.

Although New France lacked learned societies, undiscovered flora and fauna gave colonists abundant opportunity to contribute to L'Académie Royale des Sciences de Paris. Michel Sarrazin, the surgeon-major of the colonial regular troops, frequently sent descriptions and botanical samples to the Académie. The French colonial impulse for scientific discovery continued well into the eighteenth century. Traveler Peter Kalm reported in 1750 that the French Canadians had a great taste for "natural history and other learning."

New Netherlanders read for piety and practicality. Jonas Bronck's library, inventoried in 1643, appears to have been quite old, even then. He owned a fifteenth-century Dutch translation of the eschatological work *Cordiale quattuor novissimorum* and many manuscript books possibly even older. His other volumes helped guide body and soul. He owned navigational works such as Willem Janszoon Blaeu's *Seespiegel* (1623) and religious works including Abraham Scultetus's book of homilies, *Idea concionum dominicalium* (1607). New Netherland merchant Gysbert van Imborch often provided customers with Bibles and school books, but he occasionally sold histories and medical books.

Individual libraries had been part of English colonial life since the sixteenth century. John White brought books with him to the 1585 Roanoke settlement. The original Jamestown colonists, most notably the Reverend Robert Hunt, brought their libraries to Virginia. Jamestown settler John Pory remarked in 1619: "I am resolved to have some good book always in store, being in solitude the best and choicest company. Besides among these crystal rivers, and odoriferous woods I do escape much expense, envy, contempt, vanity, and vexation of mind." Precise details concerning colonial American libraries frequently do not survive, however. White's books are known only because he wrote that he later found them "torne from the covers." The Reverend Hunt's library is known because Captain John Smith recorded that it burned. In New England, the Bradstreet family's eight-hundred-plus-volume library suffered the same fate later in the century. References in Anne Bradstreet's poetry only hint at the library's breadth. Wills and estate inventories provide the most complete information, but many are frustratingly brief listing only a "parcel" of books. William Fitzhugh's library, possibly the largest in seventeenth-century Virginia, was listed in his will as a "study of books."

Based on surviving inventories, seventeenth-century reading preferences from Jamestown to Plymouth can be subdivided into three basic categories: practical works, divinity, and the classics. Books were bought to be used, and pragmatism guided many colonial book acquisitions. The British colonists read works similar to their French and Dutch neighbors. Many provided basic, practical information. Medical works helped them cope with illness. Legal treatises and books on trade helped establish the colonies and situate them within the world community. The most popular religious books were also practical works. Lewis Bayly's *The Practice of Piety* (1611) could be found throughout the colonies: there were English editions in New England and Virginia, the Dutch *De practijcke of te oeffeninge der Godtsaligheyt* (1676) in New York, and John Eliot's Algonquian translation *Manitowompae pomantamoonk* (1665) in New England.

All learned colonials read Greek and Latin histories. Other ancient classics more belletristic in nature—tragedies, comedies, poems—were also read widely. Most seventeenth-century colonists frowned on reading chiefly for pleasure, but they did not object to getting pleasure from reading—as long as it served a practical purpose. The comedies of the Roman dramatist Plautus, for example, were immensely popular with colonial Americans. Such bawdy plays could be justifiably read, and coincidentally enjoyed, because they served a useful purpose, teaching language. Contemporary English belletristic literature could seldom be justified similarly. The most popular English poets in the colonies were John Milton and George Herbert, men whose pleasing works taught piety. Horace's dictum, "to delight and instruct," guided book purchases throughout America.

The first New England colonists brought their libraries with them. William Bradford had books on geography, history, and divinity. Miles Standish owned a fifty-volume library that included Sir Walter Raleigh's *History of the World* (1614), many contemporary historical works, and, of course, John Calvin's 1536 work *Institutes of the Christian Religion*. William Brewster and John Harvard owned substantial libraries. At his death in 1644, Brewster left nearly four hundred volumes. His collection included Captain John Smith's *A Description of New England* (1616), a work that encouraged and directed many early settlers. Sir Francis Bacon's *Advancement of Learning* (1605) helped direct colonial intellectual development; both Harvard and Brewster owned the work.

John Winthrop II, the first governor of Connecticut, owned seventeenth-century New England's most extraordinary library. Winthrop brought his books when he came to the New World in 1631, and he soon contacted English friends to obtain additional volumes necessary for his scientific research. According to his father's *Journal*, the library had grown to one thousand volumes by 1640. What makes the collection remarkable is not its size, but its contents. Winthrop gathered an alchemical, mathematical, and astronomical library that rivaled Old World collections. Many volumes had a distinguished provenance; several were formerly in the possession of John Dee and contain his marginal notes.

In 1661, Winthrop traveled to England, renewed contacts with London scientists, and became an original member of the Royal Society of London. While there, he remained active with the society, serving on committees and presenting papers; he was the first of several prominent colonials who could proudly place the initials "F.R.S." after his name. Returning to New England as governor of Connecticut, Winthrop maintained contact with the society, providing it with a variety of reports and specimens. He continued to develop his library and generously loaned books to neighbors. At his death in 1676, his collection was probably the largest and most erudite in New England.

In 1686 Samuel Lee left England to become pastor at Bristol, Rhode Island, bringing his thirteen-hundred-volume library with him. Returning to England in 1691, Lee was seized by a French privateer and died a prisoner. His library remained in New England and was sold in 1693. He owned medical, mathematical, and astronomy books; works on divinity; legal treatises; classical histories, local English histories; and many classical works including Plutarch's *Parallel Lives* and Martial's *Epigrams*. John Winthrop's son, Wait Still Winthrop, and Increase Mather were fortunate enough to acquire volumes from Lee's library.

Virginian Ralph Wormeley II of Rosegill accumulated nearly four hundred titles by his death in 1701. Though smaller than the libraries of John Winthrop or Samuel Lee, Wormeley's collection displays wide-ranging intellectual interests. He owned sermons from Lancelot Andrewes and Jeremy Taylor; a basic law-book collection that included Michael Dalton's popular *Country Justice* (1618); medical books; and many belletristic works including Ben Jonson's *Every Man in His Humour* (1598), Francis Beaumont's and John Fletcher's *Fifty Comedies and Tragedies* (1647), Robert Burton's *The Anatomy of Melancholy* (1621), and Samuel Butler's *Hudibras* (1663–1678). Wormeley's interest in geography reveals his eagerness to understand Virginia's place in the world. He owned John Speed's *A Prospect of ye Most Famous Parts of the World* (1611), Peter Heylyn's *Cosmographie* (1642), Richard Blome's *A Geographical Description of the Four Parts of the World* (1670), and John Ogilby's *America* (1671).

Anglican minister Thomas Teackle gathered a comparably sized library at his Accomack home, but the collection's makeup greatly differed. Teackle owned biblical commentaries, Puritan works, and occult books; English prose works by Thomas Browne and Francis Bacon; Latin verse; and many medical books. Teackle's book inventory is especially important because it designates which books went to his children. The books Elizabeth and Catharine Teackle received provide clues to the reading tastes of colonial American women of their class. Elizabeth got many theological works; a Greek and Latin dictionary; and Latin works by Lucian, Cicero, Horace, and Sallust. Catharine, equally accomplished in languages and divinity, inherited many Latin works and several biblical commentaries. She apparently had a greater interest in the sciences than her sister and received books on astronomy and geography.

During the first half of the eighteenth century, several great individual libraries were formed in Boston, Philadelphia, and Virginia; each collection reflected its owner's personality. Massachusetts scholar and historian Thomas Prince's collection shows the profound importance he attached to New England's colonization. Virginia gentleman William Byrd's diverse library reflects the various roles he undertook throughout his life and writings: man of letters, healer, historian, lawyer, natural philosopher, religious thinker. Prominent New England divine Cotton Mather's library confirms his profound theological interests as well as his scientific and medical interests. Philadelphia statesman and chief justice James Logan's erudite library reveals his scientific curiosity as well as his elite, and sometimes cantankerous, scholarly attitude. He never hesitated to fill the margins of his books with challenges to authors' theories or to express scorn for an author's ignorance. Isaac Norris, Logan's son-in-law, shared his erudition, and he too gathered many Hebrew, Greek, Latin, and French works. The greatest interest among Byrd, Logan, and Norris was their concern with classical scholarship. Titles common to their libraries include many Latin and Greek works with variorum annotations.

When Thomas Prince entered Harvard in 1703, he established the New England Library, a collection designed to chronicle the establishment and growth of New England. Prince eventually assembled the greatest collection of Americana during the colonial period. His primary purpose was to gather source material for his *A Chronological History of New England* (1736). Both the *History* and the library reflect Prince's belief that he and his fellow colonists were enacting God's great historical design by carving a New Canaan from the American wilderness. The collection included histories, travels, promotion literature, and works written by New Englanders.

Cotton Mather, of course, owned a great theological collection, but his library shows that he was also well read in travel literature, history, the ancients, medicine, and natural philosophy. Like Thomas Prince, Mather believed that the establishment of Puritan New England was a significant event in the unfolding of providential history. His view of history was much the same as Sir Walter Raleigh's in the *History of the World*, the most popular historical work in colonial America. Herbert's *The Temple* (1633) was one of the few volumes of poetry Mather owned.

William Byrd's library was unsurpassed in colonial America for its depth and variety. Like most colonial Americans, he gathered books to use them and regularly read poetry by Geoffrey Chaucer, John Dryden, Alexander Pope, and Edmund Spenser among others. His excellent drama and belletristic prose collection included the writings of Thomas Browne, Daniel Defoe, Joseph Addison, and Jonathan Swift. Indeed, his books on art, architecture, medicine, history, and travel formed a unique library. His diaries show that nearly every morning he read the Hebrew Bible and some Greek. In the afternoons and evenings, Byrd read Latin, Dutch, English, French, or Italian. He generously shared his collection with neighbors and visitors. William Stith applauded Byrd in the *History of the First Discovery and Settlement of Virginia* (1747) for letting him use whatever books he needed.

James Logan's linguistic and scholarly abilities surpassed even Byrd's accomplishments. Besides being an expert in languages from Arabic to Syriac, Logan also mastered differential calculus, optics, astronomy, and botany. He was, as Benjamin Franklin described him in his *Proposals Relating to the Education of Youth in Pensilvania,* "a Gentleman distinguished for his universal knowledge, no less than for his judgment in Books." He often exasperated London correspondents, sparing no effort to obtain the best edited, scholarly, authoritative editions at the lowest prices. Though Logan owned some extremely rare books, he was not a rare-book collector per se. Like Byrd, he acquired books to use them, and he rated a volume not by how well it was printed but by what he could learn from the text. One detail he did appreciate, however, was a good margin. His intricate understanding of classical scholarship often surpassed the editor's, and he did not hesitate to point out blunders in his extensive marginal notes.

Logan steadily expanded his personal collection until the early 1740s when he decided to endow a public library in Philadelphia. He then stepped up his book-buying pace. He once sent Benjamin Franklin a description of the collection, which Franklin adapted for a footnote in his *Proposals Relating to the Education of Youth in Pensilvania* (1749). The collection contained "the best Authors in the best Editions," including the polyglot Bible, nearly all the classical Greek authors in diverse editions, the Byzantine historians, Ptolemy's *Almagest,* all of the Roman classics without exception, and an excellent collection of mathematical works.

Isaac Norris, Logan's son-in-law, shared his bookish inclinations. Once Logan decided to donate his collection to the Philadelphia public library, he chose Norris to catalog it. Norris's manuscript catalog of Logan's library is noteworthy because it is the earliest American book that contains such bibliographic details as full titles and places and dates. Norris's own library suggests similar meticulousness. He often annotated his books, filling up blank leaves with biographical and bibliographical information. Norris owned books on French religious history, sorcery and alchemy, medical works, and bookseller's catalogs. Like Byrd, he owned many French books, but unlike Byrd, Norris took reading French seriously. Whereas Byrd described his French books as "chiefly entertainment," Norris owned French legal works, political tracts, and Catholic treatises. Both Norris and Logan, like John Winthrop of Connecticut, owned books with distinguished provenances. Some of Norris's books were once owned by Ben Jonson, George Sandys, and Oliver Cromwell. John Dickinson eventually inherited Norris's collection and donated many volumes to the college that bears his name.

Though no known private collections in other early eighteenth-century English colonies equaled these collections in size, there were many other very good libraries. New York governor John Montgomerie owned more than thirteen hundred volumes at his death in 1731. The Maryland minister Thomas Bacon, as well as other members of the Tuesday Club, owned good libraries. Club member Robert Morris, characterized by Dr. Alexander Hamilton as "Merry Makefun," owned books reflecting his nickname: besides an excellent collection of English essayists, he owned works on poetry, music, painting, brewing beer, and fencing. Edward Moseley of North Carolina owned more than four hundred volumes at his death in 1749, probably the largest private library in that colony at the time. Estimating the total number of books in the colonies is impossible, but it is not unreasonable to think that for every library inventory that survives, there are at least four that do not. The readership for any given book is likewise difficult to estimate, since so many readers shared their collection with family members, friends, and neighbors that every book listed in each inventory may have been read many times over. Furthermore, reading aloud was a favorite entertainment among many colonial families.

Benjamin Franklin and Thomas Jefferson gathered the two most remarkable collections during the second half of the eighteenth century. "From a Child I was fond of Reading," Franklin wrote in his *Autobiography,* "and all the little Money that came into my Hands was ever laid out in Books." At his death in 1790, his library contained more than four thousand volumes. Early in life, Franklin read Plutarch's *Parallel Lives,* Antoine Arnauld's *Logic; or, the Art of Thinking* (1662), John Bunyan's *Pilgrim's Progress* (1678), John Locke's *An Essay Concerning Human Understanding* (1690), Defoe's *Essay on Projects* (1698), and Cotton Mather's *Essays To Do Good* (1710). Surviving volumes Franklin owned include works on printing; histories and political works, many with a Whiggish bent such as Algernon Sidney's *Discourses Concerning Government* (1698); a fine collection of medical books including some applying electricity to physical ailments; and European scientific works including presentation copies from the greatest contemporary scientists. Besides being an excellent private collector, Franklin was the single most important figure in colonial American library development.

Thomas Jefferson's library became the foundation for the Library of Congress. As a youth, Jefferson bought law and architecture books to advance his studies. In 1770 fire destroyed his library of nearly four hundred volumes but Jefferson rebuilt his holdings to more than twenty-six hundred books by 1783. He classified his books according to the hierarchy of knowledge set forth by Francis Bacon in the *Advancement of Learning* (1605); the three general categories—history, philosophy, and fine arts—corresponded to the faculties of the mind—memory, reason, and imagination. Assembling a library that encompassed the complete range of human knowledge, Jefferson acquired volumes from many great colonial American bookmen: William Byrd, Peyton Randolph, Richard Bland, and Benjamin Franklin among others. After the

British burned the congressional library in 1814, Jefferson sold his private collection to his country.

COLLEGE LIBRARIES

The first American college library opened in 1638 when John Harvard included his personal library with the donation that resulted in the college being named in his honor. Besides theology, Harvard's library included such works as Roger Ascham's *Epistolae* (1590), Erasmus's *Colloquia* (1519), Sir Thomas North's translation of Plutarch, and poetry by George Wither and Francis Quarles. Gifts from generous patrons helped the library grow throughout the seventeenth century. In 1723 the first Harvard library catalog listed nearly twenty-nine hundred volumes. Although theology predominated, the collection also included works on jurisprudence, civil history, natural history and philosophy, mathematics, philology, and medicine. After fire ravaged Harvard's growing collection of nearly five thousand volumes in 1764, the college quickly rebuilt Harvard Hall and by 1790 the library housed nearly ten thousand books.

The William and Mary library was the second college library established in the English colonies. After the school's establishment in 1693, James Blair, its first president, secured donations from English divines and men of letters and from Virginia citizens. The largest early donation came from Governor Francis Nicholson. The library, including its acquisition records, burned in 1705; only one volume, Paolo Sarpi's history of the Council of Trent, remains from the original collection. Nicholson's donation inventory survives; it lists theological works, travels, histories, poetry, gardening books, works on trade, and English essays, but these works more accurately reflect Nicholson's tastes than the library's overall makeup.

The Yale College library developed quickly during the early eighteenth century through donations from such English men of letters and science such as Richard Steele, Isaac Newton, and Edmund Halley. In 1718, Elihu Yale donated over four hundred books along with other goods substantial enough to give the college his name. The collection was predominantly theological, but it included works with widely varying viewpoints. The non-theological works included history, travel, biography, trade, and natural history: Charles Davenant's *Essay upon . . . the Ballance of Trade* (1699), John Ray's *Methodus plantarum* (1682), and Antoine Varillas's *Reflexions on Dr. Gilbert Burnet's Travels* (1688), to name a few. The Yale library's greatest early benefactor was George Berkeley, who donated eight cases of books to the college in 1733. The cases contained many Latin classics in the Dauphin editions but also English literature including works by Milton, Spenser, Ben Jonson, and William Shakespeare.

When Samuel Davies became president of the College of New Jersey (Princeton) in 1759, one of his first undertakings was to catalog the library. Theology and the classics were the two largest categories, but English literature was well-represented by Dryden, Shakespeare, Defoe, and Abraham Cowley. Works by Fénelon and Montaigne attest to their continuing popularity. The collection also included several contemporary essayistic journals including the *Tatler*, the *Spectator*, the *Guardian*, and the *Freeholder*.

PAROCHIAL AND PROVINCIAL LIBRARIES

The efforts of Thomas Bray brought about the establishment of parochial and provincial libraries throughout the English colonies in the late seventeenth and early eighteenth centuries. These mostly theological collections were assembled for the clergy's benefit, but Bray believed that understanding God's works required understanding a broad range of knowledge, and the libraries included European and English histories, books on gardening, and the Latin classics in the well-respected Dauphin editions. Bray also recognized the book needs of isolated communities visited infrequently by clergymen, and he established many laymen's libraries composed mainly of devotional works. With more than one thousand volumes, the Annapolitan Library was Bray's greatest colonial library. The Annapolitan served as a model for similar, though smaller, libraries in Boston, New York, Philadelphia, and Charleston. These collections were divided into twelve subject categories, eleven theological and one "historical and geographical," which in-

cluded subcategories for books on trade, medicine, poetry, and rhetoric. With the advent of subscription libraries in the eighteenth century, Bray's impressive efforts to establish public collections were somewhat neglected by later colonial readers.

SUBSCRIPTION LIBRARIES

The "Mother of all the North American Subscription Libraries," as Benjamin Franklin called it in his *Autobiography*, was the Library Company of Philadelphia. After forming his intellectual club, the Junto, in the late 1720s, Franklin suggested to the others that they pool their individual book collections to make a common library for everyone's benefit. The Junto library did not work as well as he had hoped, but convinced that a communal library made good economic and educational sense, Franklin founded the Library Company of Philadelphia in 1731. Unlike contemporary college libraries, the Library Company contained primarily nonreligious works in English. There were more histories than anything else, but the collection included practical works on architecture, gardening, medicine; many English essay collections; and political works reflecting the colonial American's burgeoning awareness of self-government. In the "Short Account of the Library" that ended the 1741 catalog, Franklin wrote,

It is now Ten Years since the Company was first established; and we have the Pleasure of observing, That tho' 'tis compos'd of so many Persons of different Sects, Parties and Ways of Thinking, yet no Differences relating to the Affairs of the Library, have arisen among us; but every Thing has been conducted with great Harmony, and to general Satisfaction.

By 1770 the library contained more than two thousand titles. When the first Continental Congress convened in Philadelphia, its members took advantage of the collection; in 1776, ten signers of the Declaration of Independence held shares in the Library Company.

The Library Company of Philadelphia provided a pattern for later subscription libraries. Merchants, tradesmen, and artisans, none of whom could individually afford a library comparable to William Byrd's or James Logan's, had the opportunity to form a collective library. Each subscriber would purchase a share in the company that would give them the privilege of borrowing books as well as the opportunity to determine library acquisitions. Franklin explained in the *Autobiography* that these libraries "improv'd the general Conversation of the Americans, made the common Tradesman and Farmers as intelligent as most Gentlemen from other Countries, and perhaps have contributed in some degree to the Stand so generally made throughout the Colonies in Defence of their Privileges."

The Redwood Library in Newport, Rhode Island, was chartered in 1747 when Abraham Redwood, inspired by a visit to the Philadelphia Library Company, donated five hundred pounds for books. His gift stipulated that additional funds be raised for the building. Architect Peter Harrison designed a stately Palladian structure, which was completed by 1750. A catalog printed in 1764 lists nearly nine hundred titles in more than fifteen hundred volumes. The collection's composition is similar to the Library Company's—primarily secular, English works. The Redwood's higher concentration of art and architecture books may have reflected Harrison's input.

The Charleston Library Society was also patterned after the Library Company. Founded in 1748 by a diverse group that included Scots, French Huguenots, and British colonists, it was incorporated in 1754. Designed to be neither theological nor commercial, the collection included plays by William Congreve, John Gay, and Shakespeare; historical works, including an impressive collection of Americana; and many Whiggish works including *Cato's Letters* and Robert Molesworth's *An Account of Denmark* (1694). The 1772 catalog supplement suggests fiction's growing popularity; it included Laurence Sterne's *Tristam Shandy* (1760), Tobias Smollett's *The Expedition of Humphrey Clinker* (1770), and Henry Mackenzie's *The Man of Feeling* (1771).

The New York Society library was founded in 1754. Earlier attempts to start public libraries in New York had been well-intended, but misdirected. Both the seventeenth-century Dr. Thomas Bray library and the Reverend John Sharpe's 1713 donation to New York (eventually transferred to the Corporation Library in 1730) contained few works that interested mid-

eighteenth-century merchants and lawyers. Sharpe's strongly theological collection contained biblical commentaries and erudite works by church fathers and schoolmen. The new society collection was similar in content to the other subscription libraries. It contained many English histories, voyages from various parts of the world, biographies, and works by Shakespeare, Defoe, and Pope.

LEARNED SOCIETIES

Learned societies and colonial libraries shared close ties. The most prominent colonial fellows of the Royal Society of London—John Winthrop II, Cotton Mather, William Byrd, Benjamin Franklin—were among the greatest colonial bookmen. Furthermore, the colonies' subscription libraries frequently took on similar responsibilities to learned societies. When the Library Company received an air pump from proprietor John Penn in 1738, it suddenly became a center for research and a place to display scientific curiosities. Atmospherical, astronomical, zoological, and electrical experiments were soon performed under its auspices. When the American Philosophical Society was established in 1743, several original members had been part of Benjamin Franklin's Junto; all were members of the Library Company of Philadelphia.

In 1743 Franklin printed "A Proposal for Promoting Useful Knowledge Among the British Plantations in America," in which he proposed the American Philosophical Society. The original members included Franklin, the botanist John Bartram, and the physician Thomas Bond, among others. By the mid 1740s, the society had stopped meeting. In 1750 another Philadelphia scientific society was established. The new organization went through several name changes but became known as the American Society by the mid 1760s. Its popularity led Bond to revive the Philosophical Society in 1767. The two groups clashed because each was dominated by a different political faction: the American Society by the liberal Quakers, the American Philosophical Society by the Proprietary party. Scientific curiosity won out over political differences, and in 1768 the two societies set aside differences to concentrate on the forthcoming transit of Venus. At the end of that year, they united as the American Philosophical Society.

In January 1769 the newly formed group met for the first time, electing Benjamin Franklin president and Thomas Bond vice-president. Since Franklin was in England, Bond took the reins of leadership and assuaged any remaining antagonism. In June 1769, the society's methodical observations of the transit of Venus were successful. In 1771, the society entered the world scientific community when it published the first volume of its *Transactions*. Franklin capitalized on the publication of the *Transactions* by arranging to have all European learned societies receive a copy. The European societies reciprocated by sending their own *Transactions* to the American Philosophical Society. The exchange improved the society's stature as well as its library's holdings.

Other learned societies were started elsewhere in the colonies. New Yorkers formed the Society for the Promotion of Arts, Agriculture, and Oeconomy in 1764, but its members were more interested in fostering the linen industry than encouraging pure scientific research. In 1772 the Virginian Society for the Promotion of Usefull Knowledge, ostensibly patterned after the Royal Society, also emphasized science's practical applications. Neither the New York nor the Virginia Society survived beyond the Revolutionary War. The American Philosophical Society, however, had gained such an international reputation by the late 1770s that John Adams heard its praises sung in Paris and subsequently helped the leaders of Boston's scientific community to form their own learned society, the American Academy of Arts and Sciences, chartered in 1780. Americans had achieved their intellectual independence.

BIBLIOGRAPHY

Davis, Richard Beale. *Intellectual Life in the Colonial South, 1585–1763.* 3 vols. Knoxville, Tenn., 1978. Davis's thoroughly documented work is the first place to look for additional information on southern colonial libraries.

Drolet, Antonio. *Les Bibliothèques Canadiennes, 1604–1960.* Ottawa, 1965. A thorough overview of early libraries in New France. For more specific information on the Jesuit College library at Quebec, see Drolet, "La Bibliothèque du Collège des Jésuites," *Revue d'Histoire de L'Amérique Française* 14 (1961):487–544.

Hayes, Kevin J. "William Byrd's Library." Ph.D. diss., University of Delaware, 1991. A reconstruction of Byrd's library based on the manuscript catalog made by John Stretch in the early 1750s.

Korey, Marie Elena. *The Books of Isaac Norris (1701–1766) at Dickinson College.* Carlisle, Pa., 1976. A bibliography of the books that John Dickinson inherited from Norris and donated to the college. Edwin Wolf II, in an excellent introduction, suspects that the collection presented to the college reflected the obscure, erudite Norris books Dickinson did not want.

Korty, Margaret Barton. "Benjamin Franklin and Eighteenth-Century American Libraries." Philadelphia, 1965. In *Transactions of the American Philosophical Society,* n.s. 55, pt. 9. Korty's study shows the tremendous influence Franklin had on libraries throughout the English colonies.

Leonard, Irving A. *Books of the Brave: Being an Account of Books and of Men in the Spanish Conquest and Settlement of the Sixteenth-Century New World.* Cambridge, Mass., 1949. Leonard describes the reading tastes of the sixteenth-century Spanish conquistadors.

McCorison, Marcus A. *The 1764 Catalogue of the Redwood Library Company at Newport, Rhode Island.* New Haven, Conn., 1965. A reconstruction of the Redwood Library, based on the 1764 catalog. For a letter from James Logan to Abraham Redwood, see Edwin Wolf II's review in *William and Mary Quarterly,* 3rd ser., 23 (1966):327–328.

Raesly, Ellis Lawrence. *Portrait of New Netherland.* New York, 1945. Raesly devotes one chapter to the reading tastes of the New Netherlanders. For Jonas Bronck's inventory, see *New York Historical Manuscripts: Dutch.* Baltimore, Md., 1974, 2:121–122.

Sowerby, E. Millicent. *Catalogue of the Library of Thomas Jefferson.* 5 vols. Charlottesville, Va., 1952–1959. A catalog and reconstruction of Jefferson's library based on the books Jefferson sold to the Library of Congress in 1815. More recent work by James Gilreath and Douglas L. Wilson provides additional insights into Jefferson's library and his system of organization. See their retrospective reviews in *PBSA* 78 (1984):219–232 and *WMQ,* 3rd ser., 41 (1984):615–628; also see their edition of the 1783 catalog, which was unavailable to Sowerby, *Thomas Jefferson's Library: A Catalog with the Entries in His Own Order,* Washington, D.C., 1989. Wilson provides a well-balanced analysis in "Jefferson's Library," in *Thomas Jefferson: A Reference Biography,* edited by Merrill D. Peterson, New York, 1986.

Tuttle, Julius Herbert. "The Libraries of the Mathers." *Proceedings of the American Antiquarian Society* 20 (1910):269–356. Tuttle's work remains the most thorough treatment of the Mather library.

Winans, Robert B. *A Descriptive Checklist of Book Catalogues Separately Printed in America 1693–1800.* Worcester, Mass., 1981. The first place to look for any separately printed colonial American library catalogs. Winans provides a short description of each collection including its size and organization. The libraries mentioned here which Winans lists are Lee, Logan, Harvard, Yale, Princeton, the Library Company, the Charleston Library Society, the New York Library Society, and the Redwood Library.

Wolf, Edwin II. "Great American Book Collectors to 1800." *Gazette of the Grolier Club,* n.s., no. 16 (June 1971):3–70. Wolf's exhibition catalog provides fascinating tidbits of bibliographic lore about the libraries of the Winthrop family, the Mathers, William Byrd, James Logan, Thomas Prince, Isaac Norris, Benjamin Franklin, John Adams, and Thomas Jefferson, among others.

————. *The Library of James Logan of Philadelphia, 1674–1751.* Philadelphia, 1974. This catalog of Logan's library includes extensive annotations from Logan's correspondence and marginalia.

————. "The Reconstruction of Benjamin Franklin's Library: An Unorthodox Jigsaw Puzzle." *PBSA* 56 (1962):1–16. Wolf tells the story of his discovery and identification of Benjamin Franklin shelfmark. For other information on Franklin's library see Wolf, "Report of the Librarian," *The Annual Report of the Library Company of Philadelphia for the Year 1956*; Wolf, "Frustration and Benjamin Franklin's Medical Books," in *Science and Society in Early America: Essays in Honor of Whitfield J. Bell, Jr.,* edited by Randolph Shipley Klein, Philadelphia, 1986; and James Green, *Poor Richard's Books,* Philadelphia, 1990.

Kevin J. Hayes

SEE ALSO **Higher Education; Literature; Philosophy;** and **Scientific Inquiry.**

PHILOSOPHY

PRACTICE OF PHILOSOPHY IN ANGLO-AMERICA

ALL THOUGHT PROGRESSES by way of dialogue. Stimulating conversation with peers, oral and written intellectual exchange, and similar kinds of supportive conditions are prerequisites of advanced intellectual life. Where men and women who have the drive to think deeply about fundamental matters are isolated from prevailing currents of thought, philosophy cannot prosper. If there are to be progress and development, the reflections of others must be made available, either at firsthand or through books and magazines.

Looking at the Americas during the colonial period in the broadest context, the only territory in the Western Hemisphere where a European intellectual environment was replicated to any degree was that controlled by the Spanish. In Mexico and Peru there were full-fledged universities and humanistic "colleges" by the sixteenth century, with hundreds of learned priests in the cities and missions and thousands of well-educated laymen. Such cultural growth, which was made possible above all by mining wealth, did not extend to the barren and underpopulated area north of the Rio Grande, where no Spanish universities were founded.

In contrast to Mexico and Peru, in the economically and socially underdeveloped English colonies in North America, the layers of literary and philosophical culture were necessarily thin. The variety of social institutions that undergirded technical philosophical speculation in the European tradition—monastic schools and missionary orders, aristocratic and church patronage, great private and public libraries, salons, coffeehouses, learned periodicals, a leisured class, royal and ecclesiastical courts, colleges and universities, bourgeois ambition, postal communications—all were either totally absent in the English colonies or in a relatively primitive state.

It hardly needs saying that in the Dutch and the French colonies in North America—which also lacked large, rich cities such as could be found south of the Rio Grande—the social conditions for the growth of philosophical culture were even more lacking than in the English colonies, although learned individuals might be present from time to time. In such institutions as the Collège de Québec, founded by the Jesuits in 1635, a classical education, including philosophy, was offered to youth, but the emphasis was necessarily on rote learning rather than on philosophical examination or speculation.

Conditions of deprivation in Anglo-America not only took their toll directly, making it difficult for "philosophers" to function as such, they also had an indirect psychic consequence, imposing a debilitating sense of inferiority on intellectuals. For among other requirements, first-rate philosophical achievement depends upon confidence, and it was difficult to be self-consciously a provincial and at the same time feel intellectually confident. Colonists of sensitivity and learning—including those who were emigrants from Britain or native Americans who had visited Europe, as well as colonial intellectuals who had never crossed the ocean—were, and tended to feel like, provincials or "hicks," out of touch with the most recent intellectual trends and unread in the works of the latest fashionable luminaries.

It was a characteristic of the philosophical activity that did exist in early English America, and symptomatic of its nature, that it had little significant internal history of ideas; that is, the passing of influence from one colonial philosopher to another. (Of course, actual inter-American intellectual connections, at least until the late eighteenth century, when a kind of pan-American colonial or "Creole" self-consciousness arose in political affairs, were virtually nonexistent.) Although some of the best philosophical minds within the English colonies were in touch with one another to some degree, we generally must deal with culturally isolated figures who looked abroad for philosophical leadership and inspiration rather than to their compatriots. It was not until the second half of the eighteenth century, after the Massachusetts minister Jonathan Edwards began to publish extensively, that a true indigenous "school" of thinkers emerged in the British colonies, the so-called Edwardsian philosophical theologians of varying stripes.

Some twentieth-century commentators on the history of colonial Anglo-American philosophy, notably Isaac Woodbridge Riley, the author of the pioneering work *American Philosophy: The Early Schools* (1907), and others influenced by him, have engaged in rather fervid and tendentious talk about the "contributions" or "advancements" of the colonial American "schools" of philosophy—the idealist school, the materialist school, and so on—as though the New World bordering on the Atlantic Ocean circa 1750 bore some resemblance to the Old World bordering on the Aegean two millennia earlier. The more exact truth, however, was stated in a 1959 *William and Mary Quarterly* journal article by Vincent Buranelli: "The study of colonial philosophy has one virtue almost peculiar to itself. It is a cure for chauvinism." Most colonial American intellectuals correctly saw themselves in a satellite role, tinkering with received ideas from overseas and looking forward to the day when various institutions—social, economic, educational—would exist at home in sufficient strength to sustain independent work.

These truths aside, it is revealing that for all this isolation, the progress of thought throughout North America in the seventeenth and eighteenth centuries more or less kept pace with the broad lines of the development of thought all over the Western world in this period, with a time lag of perhaps twenty years or so. In English America one sees, for example, the gradual weakening among certain key intellectuals of some of the major tenets of Protestant religious orthodoxy, such as the doctrines of original sin and reprobation, and the acceptance of more optimistic and humanitarian views, as well as the gradual rejection of the theory of final causes and teleological explanations in favor of a more mechanistic and naturalistic world view. That the intellectual class in the English colonies remained, despite the cultural lag, somewhat up to date is attributable in good part to the relative freedom of publication that prevailed in Britain and its colonies and to the free flow of printed works. In the Spanish colonies in the New World, which, as we have noted, had a far more developed intellectual life in the seventeenth century, with Dominicans and Jesuits and the learned of other international religious orders serving as teachers and philosophical guides, there was often concerted government and ecclesiastical opposition to the importation of new ideas, including outright censorship and the banning of certain books. Nevertheless, as Max Savelle has commented in *Empires to Nations: Expansion in America, 1713–1824*, "The private libraries of learned men in Latin America, as well as in Canada, contained copies of the great *Encyclopédie* of Denis Diderot and his associates, not to mention the books of such writers as Montesquieu, d'Alembert, and Voltaire, and, above all, the work of Rousseau."

Vast sea changes in mental outlook such as occurred in the seventeenth and eighteenth centuries in both Europe and America are always difficult to "explain" or even to trace in detail. Given the dependence of America on European thought, the principal challenge presented to historians and philosophers studying the colonial period is that of reconstructing the international context within which American philosophical activity occurred and of studying the specific ramifications in the colonies of the fundamental developments in the Western mind that took place between 1500 and 1800. These developments included the demise of Latinate culture and of Scholasticism, particularly the academic dependence on Aristotle; the effects of secularization upon ethics and metaphysics; the fascination with the problems of epistemology, although that word was not used at the time; the consequences of the rise of the new mathematical science; and the variety of ways in which the concept of "nature" became a force in moral and political thought.

In no area of investigation did European and American philosophers work more collaboratively than in the study of natural history—namely, the effort to describe and categorize the flora and fauna of the New World—an enterprise that in the seventeenth and eighteenth centuries was still considered part of philosophy.

Although the cultural lag was real and the dependence on Europe was inescapable, historians have generally underestimated how up-to-date American intellectuals could be, an underestimation, that is, of the efficiency of the circulation of thought from Europe to America. British colonials read European books and journals. They also benefited from selective European immigration, although not to the degree that the Catholic empires in the Americas benefited from the immigration of university-trained missionaries from all over Europe. Charles Morton, for example, came at the end of the seventeenth century from an English dissenting academy to teach at Harvard at nearly sixty years of age and had an important effect, and John Witherspoon arrived from Scotland in 1768, when he was forty-five, to be president of the College of New Jersey (later Princeton).

Americans who left to study overseas also had a significant influence, even if they never returned to the colonies. Jeremiah Dummer of Massachusetts studied at Utrecht and settled in London, from where he donated to Yale a superb collection of books, including many in philosophy.

Others who went to Europe returned with much-increased intellectual sophistication. One such traveler was William Byrd II, the Virginia aristocrat who gained considerable intellectual culture from his years in London. It was, nevertheless, extremely hard for American writers to get a real hearing in Europe, although almost anyone with any pretensions sought that goal as soon as the last "i" was dotted on his manuscript, and to remain truly au courant took persistent effort.

Cadwallader Colden, who held important political positions in the colony of New York, experienced terrible frustration in trying to get a serious reading in Europe of his works on the metaphysics of gravity, *First Causes of Action in Matter and of the Cause of Gravitation* (1746) and *The Principles of Action in Matter* (1751), even though he was Scottish-born and held a bachelor's degree from the University of Edinburgh. His experience paralleled almost exactly the efforts of James Logan, the learned Philadelphia Quaker and agent of William Penn, who had been born in Ireland. Logan composed a treatise on moral philosophy that contained a theory on the anatomical foundations of the passions. He sought sound criticism of his ideas by writing to medical authorities in Europe. In the case of both Colden and Logan, the criticism from overseas, when it came—Logan had to wait two years to get a reply from an eminent British neurologist—was severe, but that is beside the point. If, in the first place, there had been a continual interchange of ideas with qualified European thinkers, neither man would have found himself in such an exposed and embarrassing position.

Taking all of these facts together, then, it is not surprising that the practice of philosophy in colonial British America, with only a few major exceptions to be discussed later in this essay, tended to be elementary, often slightly outdated, and nearly always derivative. The present-day historian or student of philosophy who turns to this region in search of great original works will generally experience only disillusionment. If one is seeking a comprehensive picture or a typical picture, the proper approach to early American philosophy cannot be, for the most part, the search for great representative works and their elucidation. It is more fruitful, instead, to concentrate simply on the philosophical *activity* of the time as it was, whether homegrown American or not. It is necessary to distinguish, in other words, between philosophy *in* America and genuine "American" philosophy and not to make the mistake of scanting the former or artificially inflating the latter.

To fully comprehend our subject, moreover, we must make a basic distinction between academic and independent philosophy. Academic philosophy refers to the intellectual training that had been incorporated into the curricula of colleges and universities since the founding of such institutions in the Middle Ages, training that in most respects was conservative and deferrent and generally not conducive to original thought. Independent philosophy, on the other hand, comprise the work of would-be thinkers outside the academy, such as Colden and Logan, who had the ambition, at least, of making an original contribution to philosophy, however flawed and insufficient that contribution might be.

The teaching of academic philosophy continued virtually uninterruptedly throughout the colonial period, beginning in the English colonies with the founding of Harvard in 1636. Reasonably good records of philosophical or quasi-philosophical activity have survived from Harvard, Yale (founded 1701), College of New Jersey (Princeton, founded 1746), and King's College (Columbia, founded 1754), for example, as well as from other institutions. Generally speaking, the books and authors that were studied in the seventeenth century were part of a broad European Latinate inheritance. Based on educational traditions originating in the Middle Ages and the Renaissance, it was nearly universal and easily crossed the usual lines of division between Protestants and Catholics.

The entirely transnational university tradition provides what links there may be between English colonies in North America and the French and Spanish colonies. Although the conditions for advanced intellectual life south of the Rio Grande were far superior to those in the English colonies and began a century earlier, the university student in Mexico or Lima would have found the curriculum at Harvard in the seventeenth century quite intelligible, and vice versa. The same would apply to the Jesuit Collège de Québec in New France, where the teaching of the classics in accordance with the Ratio Studiorum was operating by the 1660s. The Latinate republic of letters knew no national boundaries.

In the frail Harvard College of the seventeenth century, for example, questions concerning the nature of the will and the basis of human freedom probably engendered more debate than any other topic in moral philosophy. The Roman Catholic authorities and adversaries on this subject were read as much in this Protestant institution as were Protestant writers. Despite the deep political divide between Catholics and Protestants, serious philosophical disputes crossed over these lines all the time.

In the eighteenth century, this universality began to be lost. The use of vernacular languages rather than Latin created new barriers to international debate, and philosophical education in Catholic institutions, with the exception of education in the natural sciences, had to contend with the prevailing anticlericalism that grew out of the French Enlightenment. Philosophical thought in all of the American colonies in the eighteenth century came under the influence of the new science and of the revolution in philosophy that began with René Descartes, but in the English colonies, in addition, the Scottish Enlightenment was a major source of fresh thinking.

The writing of philosophy outside the academy was necessarily sporadic, yet most of the figures who are thought of as "philosophers" in eighteenth-century British America happened to be nonacademics. These writers have tended to get the most attention, although the great preponderance of philosophical activity per se, however routine, was always within the academy. The "philosophy" that was taught in early American colleges as an ongoing and traditional part of the curriculum has never received the attention it deserves from historians, but it can be reconstructed from what we know of textbooks that were in use, from surviving student notebooks and précis, from the printed commencement broadsides that listed topics for disputation (the so-called *quaestiones* and *theses*), and from the topics chosen for orations.

The training in disputation that flourished in universities bred combativeness and ingenuity in argument, although this posture was almost always within the context of deference to traditional textual authorities. Such deference to past texts is the essence of the Scholasticism that dominated European thought, both Catholic and Protestant, for so many centuries and prevailed throughout American thought, too, into the eighteenth century.

Yet there was a long-standing dissatisfaction with Scholasticism, a dissatisfaction that emerged fully in the colonial period and was made evident by the warm welcome with which Cartesian innovations were received in the last quarter of the seventeenth century. Scholasticism was vulnerable to attack from two different camps in particular, apodictic rationalism (exemplified above all by Descartes's method for attaining truth) and empiricism (exemplified by the inductive method advocated by Francis Bacon). Neither of these approaches—free-standing a priori logic on the one side, based on self-evident principles, and close attention to the evidence from observation of natural events on the other—depended upon the authority of earlier texts. Within both, originality and innovation could find an outlet.

The very use, in this essay, of such phrases as "prevailing currents of thought," "training" in philosophy, and "original contribution" implies that there was a received tradition, an accepted body of thought, that in the colonial period constituted the discipline, or the specific literature, of philosophy. Indeed, the rudiments of such a tradition existed, although, as was the case also in all the other academic disciplines, the meaning of what constituted academic philosophy was continuously in evolution and, in this case, always somewhat indistinguishable around its edges from theology and natural science.

Much philosophy was buried in theology; logic and rhetoric, standard in the curriculum, also included an array of philosophical subjects under their unrevealing headings. In particular, "logic" included what we would now call "epistemology," the examination of the question of how we can truly know anything, which was at the center of the most important seventeenth-century philosophical debates. Logic also included the study of the methods by which truth is best attained, out of which our concept of the "scientific method" arose. The social sciences as such had not yet become established as separate disciplines, and areas of observation and speculation that we now denominate anthropology, psychology, sociology, and economics were more or less subsumed under "moral philosophy." In other words, to find philosophy in colo-

nial America one must make a determined effort, because it was often not labeled as such, and some of what was labeled "philosophy" would not be called such today.

At the beginning of the period under discussion, philosophy meant, in essence, the body of thought and commentary derived from Plato and Aristotle, especially the latter. In 1800, at the end of the period, philosophy consisted also of the anti-Aristotelian work of, and the responses to, Descartes in the seventeenth century and ultimately of the whole range of European philosophical writing in the late seventeenth and eighteenth centuries by major original thinkers such as Nicolas Malebranche, Gottfried Wilhelm Leibniz, John Locke, Samuel Clarke, Anthony Ashley Cooper—the third earl of Shaftesbury—Francis Hutcheson, Bishop George Berkeley, Adam Smith, Thomas Reid, and David Hume, one of the greatest philosophical minds of the eighteenth century. It also included the work of dozens of lesser known or altogether forgotten figures. The teaching of philosophy became eclectic and came to include also a self-consciousness about its own history, that is, about the development of thought from the time of the ancient world.

FOUR DISTINGUISHED AMERICAN CONTRIBUTIONS

Before scanning the interesting, if unspectacular, provincial intellectual enterprise that typified philosophy in colonial North America, it is necessary to isolate the great exceptions, the instances where colonial Anglo-Americans transcended the limitations of their time and place and produced work that may be called genuinely American, true indigenous products. Only four candidates come to mind as instances of true "American" philosophy, as opposed to "philosophy in America," and the eligibility of even these four may be questioned. However that may be, these four are the glories of early American philosophy in this writer's view, but they must not be thought of as representative or typical. Moreover, the reader must once again be reminded that the splendors of Hispanic-American culture are excluded by the geographical limitations of this essay.

Puritan Thought

The seventeenth-century English Puritan movement, as a result of a highly unusual migration, was located partly in America. Significant and well-educated writers with acute minds, alert to all the developments of international Calvinism and of humanistic learning—writers such as John Cotton, Thomas Shepard, Roger Williams, Charles Chauncy, and Thomas Hooker—moved to New England and brought with them the intellectual energy characteristic of their sect. Thus, a living branch of English Puritanism momentarily flourished on American shores; as such, it would be inaccurate to call it merely derivative from overseas. It was a projection, not a derivation (analogous in some respects to the migration of learned Jesuits to Peru), and the challenges of the heady new environment of the Western Hemisphere seemed to stimulate fresh thinking.

New England Puritanism was for a time as influential in old England as ideas from old England were in New England. For a brief moment there was equality and reciprocity in the intellectual exchange. Hence, students of Reformed Protestantism will always have to take seriously the religious mind of New England in the seventeenth century no less than that in Great Britain, since American Puritanism was a source of independent philosophical energy.

On the other hand, it would be misleading to suggest that the New England Puritans made some kind of original technical contribution to the central tradition of Western philosophy as it descends from the Greeks. Their place was analogous, roughly, to that of Saint Augustine in relation to the classical intellectual giants. Puritanism fostered a point of view, one that was profoundly pessimistic about the human condition and at the same time hopeful about humanity because of God's unimpeded freedom to intervene to rescue men and women from themselves. Because of their concern for the individual's relationship to God, the Puritans formulated a philosophical anthropology that emphasized the inescapable human propensity to evil and the necessity for redemption from outside the individual will, by grace alone.

Because of their anxiety about the condition of their souls in the eyes of God, the Puritans were inveterately introspective, and a number of Puritan authors thought deeply and perceptively about the dynamics of human psychology, anticipating in the process insights we associate with, for example, twentieth-century Freudianism. (They were, in this respect, similar to their fellow Augustinian Calvinists in France, the Jansenists). On the rational side, they saw the individual as a dependent creature but endowed with intellect that could apprehend dimly the divine pattern according to which the universe was created. The advancement of knowledge, therefore, insofar as it revealed the laws of creation and of the Creator, was considered a religious act. Puritans engaged diligently in the quest for truth, and this quest was backed by a philosophical theology and by a theory of knowledge that made the quest meaningful.

Although colonial American Puritanism was essentially a religious movement within the Calvinist tradition, rather than a secular philosophy, every religion has a metaphysics of some sort, although it may not be rigorous or ever become explicit. Many Puritan intellectuals in British America subscribed to a version of Neoplatonist metaphysics based on a theory of types—archetype in the Creator, entypal object in nature representing the archetype, and ectypal innate idea in the human mind—that helped to make sense of the natural world and of the relationship of the human intellect to that world. According to this metaphysic, the natural material world has hidden in it the great eternal system of ideas, although this system appears to humankind in a fragmented form. The task of *scientia*, or systematic knowledge, is to reconstruct the world mentally in accordance with the archetypes. When the task is complete, if ever it can be, the human mind thus informed will correspond to the divine mind in detail, as it does potentially at any time. The mind of each person, now a shattered mirror reflecting the archetypes fragmentarily and chaotically, will one day be truly an image of God.

The Puritans' deep attachment to, and reliance upon, Scripture led them to reject in name (but not entirely in practice) the tradition of classical metaphysics and ethics descended from Aristotle, for Scripture was dogmatically presented as an adequate guide to both thought and morals. Classical metaphysics, unconnected to a theory of conduct, was rejected as being arid, vain, and unredeeming, while at the same time the pagan tradition in ethics was dismissed as being without divine authority, capable of leading humanity to terrible sins, and also inadequate for redemption.

To fill the philosophical void, the Puritans adhered to a kind of Platonic idealism, as has been noted, but one that deliberately linked idea and action, God as the creator of good in both nature and conduct, and humankind as God's dependents in this enterprise. The theory found classic expression within Puritanism in certain publications of the English minister William Ames, who never came to America but who was closely associated with the English ministers who did. They were all influenced by the anti-Aristotelian, sixteenth-century writings of Peter Ramus, the French Protestant logician and Christian humanist, who among other things wished to emphasize the importance of an actively righteous life over a merely blessed life and who attempted to reorganize the system of the disciplines. Theology in particular was redefined to encompass and supplant Aristotelian ethics and metaphysics, in principle eliminating these studies from the curriculum.

The basic idea, as expressed by William Ames and his predecessors and successors, was that of "living to God" as the essential definition of theology. Theology must not be simply belief separated from action; it must be practical. Yet at the same time, truly righteous action requires theological grounding.

Because Puritanism was a philosophy of action, of life, of pious *doing*, it was adverse to "mere" contemplation. A Puritan metaphysic had to be a metaphysic of action, and such was the case. Right thinking ought to lead necessarily to right action. God, as the Creator and Judge, was an actor, and each individual must emulate God in this.

American Puritanism thus may be said to have had an underlying "philosophy" or philosophical theology, and it is commonplace for histories of British American colonial philosophy (such as Elizabeth Flower and Murray G. Murphey's *A History of Philosophy in America*) to treat Puritanism as one of the foundation stones of American thought. But it is an approach that tends to create a misimpression. Historians of American philosophy are tempted to begin with Puritanism because it was big, important, and genuinely American. Yet by treating an essentially religious movement as the initial stage of American philosophy, one runs the danger of building in a discontinuity with subsequent developments. Such a beginning tempts us to look at the seventeenth century in the history of British America as the essentially "religious" century, typified by Puritan piety, which was supposedly followed by a great falling away, a declension, to the secular philosophy of the Enlightenment in the eighteenth century. This schema creates a greatly exaggerated gap between the two centuries. Such a contrast is artificial and simplistic.

The fact is, of course, that both in the academy and outside it, the seventeenth century sustained a tradition of enlightened and naturalistic academic thought that ran parallel to Puritanism, and the eighteenth century had its own religious philosophy (consider, for example, Joseph Butler in England and Jonathan Edwards in America). The umbrella term "Puritanism," which belongs properly to the history of religion, can obscure the signs of the strictly *philosophical* (as opposed to theological) enterprise in seventeenth-century New England that fed directly into the development of American thought in the eighteenth century and that has generally been understudied.

As Perry Miller, the influential twentieth-century historian of American Puritanism, has enduringly described, the transplantation of English Puritans from their native soil caused root damage that ultimately took its toll. There was a decline in the quality and originality of religious thought in America after the passing away of the immigrant generation for the very reason that the great immigrant generation of Puritans, trained in Europe, were not a truly indigenous American group in the first place.

Whereas in England, after the restoration of the Stuart monarchy in 1661, Puritans metamorphosed into nonconformists, Dissenters, latitudinarians, Cambridge Platonists, and other such schools and groups, all of which had considerable vitality and influence, in America the situation was quite different. The dying away of the founding generation inevitably left a void because there was no context in America to sustain a first-rate intellectual movement. After the Restoration, if one is to look for philosophical activity within the Puritan movement, it is necessary to turn to the dissenting academies in England, where philosophical studies flourished, rather than to Massachusetts.

In fact, however, it is pointless to confine one's investigations to the Dissenters alone if one is searching for the main influences on the development of American thought in the period from, let us say, 1670 to 1730. Anglican writers—such as Isaac Barrow (who was a Newtonian), Bishop John Tillotson, the great preacher, and Samuel Clarke, who did annotations for Jacques Rohault's Cartesian *Physica* (London, 1697), adapting it to Newtonianism—not Dissenters, were as influential, or more influential, in both England and America, than any descendant of the Puritans. In this same period, too, the Cambridge Platonists in England, a number of whom had explicitly rejected Calvinist severity, attracted a following in both England and America. Works by Henry More, who had a profound influence upon both natural and moral philosophy as a transitional figure, began to be used as the basis of lectures at Harvard as early as the 1690s.

In the colonies, a third-generation American Puritan, Cotton Mather, proves the rule. In his quasi-philosophical work—most importantly his treatise on natural philosophy, *The Christian Philosopher* (1721)—he performed the typical provincial function of importing and interpreting the newest ideas for local consumption, rather than being himself a generator of original insights.

One final point, however, must be made concerning the relationship between Puritanism and the development of philosophy in the colonial period. Insofar as Puritanism embraced Protestant (and even Catholic) Scholasticism, Renaissance humanism, and the new seventeenth-century methodologies for acquiring knowledge, beginning with those propounded by Bacon and Descartes, it was ipso facto hospitable to secular philosophy. This religious group founded Harvard College in 1636, which from the start was something more than a parochial seminary. Harvard attempted to offer an education in the European philosophical tradition, even in areas where that tradition had the potential to subvert orthodox doctrine and practice. To summarize, the temporary intellectual efflorescence of the Puritan movement in New England in the seventeenth century does not seriously undermine the argument that early American philosophical thought was derivative, gaining what strength it had from importation.

The Writings of Benjamin Franklin

The first exception to the prevailing derivative character of American philosophical culture, Puritanism, is ambiguous in its implications. The second exception is, perhaps, stronger, namely the writings of Benjamin Franklin. Franklin is completely American; he is original in much of what he says; to this day, he makes good reading. In sum, he is a classic. There is no European contemporary or group of contemporaries to whom one can turn and find everything said better than it was said by Franklin himself. Franklin deserves a small place in histories of American philosophy—in histories of natural philosophy or physical science, it goes without saying, but also in histories of moral philosophy.

Yet here, too, there are manifest reservations. Franklin was a *philosophe*, not a philosopher. He had no college education—which certainly did not impair his mind; indeed, it may have preserved its originality from destruction—but this deprivation kept him separate from the academic tradition in philosophy and probably engendered in him, from his youthful resentment at being too poor to go to college, a hostility or at least an ambivalence toward formal philosophy. Franklin is worth reading because he is a charming stylist, a delightful wit, and a perceptive reasoner. But his virtues are literary rather than strictly philosophical, and he made no lasting contributions to the history of formal philosophy.

As we have noted, philosophy, indeed nearly all academic learning, was heavily polemical in Franklin's day, or perhaps disputatious would be the more appropriate word. Franklin is quoted as once having stated, "Of all things, I hate altercation," which if true would have made him unsuited for the philosophical battleground. His one youthful venture into formal philosophy, the *Dissertation on Liberty and Necessity, Pleasure and Pain*, a remarkably nihilistic and cynical work written in London in 1725 when he was only nineteen years old, he later repudiated as a futile exercise in metaphysics. The rules for the discussion group Franklin organized in Philadelphia, the Junto, specified that debates were to be conducted "without Fondness for Dispute, or Desire of Victory," and "Direct Contradiction" was prohibited.

On the other hand, it is noteworthy that Franklin significantly facilitated the development of American philosophy. He undertook, for example, to publish Samuel Johnson's *Elementa Philosophica* (Philadelphia, 1752), which he probably realized was a bad business decision, and befriended men with philosophical interests, such as James Logan. These facts may appear to contradict the argument that Franklin was hostile to formal philosophy, but they may be explained by the recognition that Franklin was also a booster of nascent American culture, and this urge overcame his distaste for philosophical controversy and its abstractions.

In any case, Franklin's principal aversion was to metaphysics, which, in concurrence with the Massachusetts Puritans among whom he grew up, he considered unhelpful for the improvement of conduct. He himself ventured into moral philosophy and for thirty years tinkered with an essentially neopagan book on ethics, specifically on the practical means by which one could attain virtue or acquire individual virtues. Franklin's "Art of Virtue" was never published, but the core of the idea that informed the book appears in his famous *Autobiography,* in which he describes his method of slow incremental modification of external behavior for the purpose of achieving temperance, silence, order, frugality, cleanliness, and so on.

Franklin was a friend of the Scottish jurist and philosopher Henry Home, Lord Kames, and of the great Scottish intellect David Hume. When one reads some of the letters between Hume and Franklin, one feels the two men are equals in sophistication. There were very few other Americans in this period of whom that can be said, but still it may be fairly maintained that Franklin was no philosopher, except in the special sense that he was one of those extremely rare individuals who somehow lend themselves to discussion as the very embodiment of certain ambient ideas, the spirit of the new age in the Hegelian sense. It is worth nothing in this regard that Herbert Schneider, perhaps the premier contributor in the mid twentieth century to the historiography of early American philosophy, published an article in which he argued, paradoxically, that Franklin was significant as an American philosopher precisely because, in typical American pragmatic fashion, he did *not* espouse a formal, rigorous, fixed philosophy.

For an intellectual living in America before the mid eighteenth century, Franklin was unusual, too, in the ease and rapidity with which he shed much of the baggage of orthodox Christianity. Creating for himself a kind of customized, personal theism, Franklin was able to pick and choose from among the tenets of institutional religion those elements that suited his needs and seemed to him to make sense judged in terms of general beneficence. Thomas Jefferson would later do more or less the same thing. Most philosophical activity in America, it must be emphasized, was directed to the protection of inherited religious tenets. Franklin seemed to have no such religious commitments to protect.

The Work of Jonathan Edwards

The third instance of what might be called genuinely indigenous American philosophy, rather than simply European philosophy that was taught or discussed or restated in America, is the work of Jonathan Edwards. Although it is true that more of Edwards's thinking was borrowed or imitative than has been assumed, there can be no doubt that he was capable of unique insights and of advances in thought that are not entirely reducible to any background or borrowing. The Yale University Press's multivolume edition of Edwards's writings makes clear that Edwards was less of an isolated, wholly original giant than has been hitherto believed, that his thought took place in a preexisting intellectual context, as all thought must. But these volumes also demonstrate that Edwards was, nonetheless, the only early American philosopher (now using the term "philosopher" in a strict sense) who had the capacity to transform almost everything he touched into a personal expression of his style and system of thought. Edwards's true genius is widely recognized and does not require belaboring. The student of the history of Western philosophy—not just of American philosophy—can gain fresh understanding from reading Edwards that is not to be found anywhere else.

Edwards wrote with great originality and penetration on dozens of philosophical subjects, most notably, perhaps, on moral psychology, analyzing such questions as to what degree self-love may legitimately play a role in virtuous acts and whether punishment for crime can be justified under a deterministic theory of motivation. He wrote brilliantly also on the theory of causation, basing his thinking on the conviction that the universe is sustained from instant to instant only by divine will. Like a Malebranchian occasionalist, Edwards maintained that mechanical, secondary causation between objects is an illusion. God chooses to be orderly and regular in his continuous sustenance of the world and its seemingly fixed relations, but he may also be arbitrary. The Creation itself was the Lord's greatest arbitrary act, and in general God's arbitrariness appears in his supreme originality, not in whimsy or capriciousness. God's total freedom to act is revealed in what is new, unique, unprecedented, and particular in the world, qualities that are most evident in human affairs, not in "nature," so-called, where God chooses to observe undeviating order.

The creation of the human mind totally transcended the natural order, Edwards argued, one consequence of which is that there can never be a complete behavioral or social "science." Human nature and human affairs in their entirety are not reducible to fixed laws, not even in theory. The human mind is the closest thing on earth to a perpetual miracle, with the exception of the extraordinary operations of the Holy Spirit.

There is a continuum in effect from the arbitrary to the fixed in the universe, or from grace to nature. What appears to the observer to be unique or arbitrary is no more miraculous, in itself, than what is seemingly fixed, since even those phenomena that are most uniform are part of the Creation, are the product of divine will.

Looked at in relation to the entire span of time, God was most arbitrary at the beginning, when He created the universe ex nihilo. He will be arbitrary again at the end of time, when he will "arrest" the laws of nature everywhere, in all parts of the visible universe, and "by an entire new disposition" change "all things at once." "In the execution of the sentence on both the righteous and the wicked," Edwards wrote, "the glorious powers of God will be wonderfully and most extraordinarily manifested, in many respects, above all that ever was before in the arbitrary exertions of it."

Looked at vertically or spatially, so to speak, the higher we go in the chain of being, the more the conduct of things is "arbitrary." God's dealings with the angels are "quite above those rules which we call the laws of nature," whereas the lowest rank of material things, the worms and the stones, are governed completely by the most general positive laws of matter and motion.

It is a central key to Edwards's thought to understand that, according to his thinking, spiritual relations are rare and refined occurrences and, in that sense, arbitrary, since God's will in these matters is largely unknowable on earth. But Edwards pointedly rejected the notion that spiritual relations are therefore amorphous and fuzzy. Their precision is not below that of mathematical physics but above it, hence unmeasurable with humankind's rough calibrators.

Despite Edwards's association in the popular mind with a deterministic philosophy, his theory of causation espouses an open and creative universe, pregnant always with the possibility of new beginnings and unique events. Ultimately, both God and humankind are free, not in the sense that their choices are likely to be gratuitous or beyond the grasp of reason but in the sense that they can never be reduced to fixed laws, or that which may be consistently predicted.

Edwards is most famous in philosophical circles, perhaps, for having brilliantly derived, independently of both Bishop George Berkeley and Nicolas Malebranche (although in all probability not without some suggestions from the writings of the latter, directly or indirectly received), an immaterialist metaphysics. He arrived at his immaterialism from at least two, or possibly three, different directions, one of them, along a path similar to that followed by Bishop Berkeley, from an analysis of the sensationalist epistemology of John Locke—all that we can know is through our senses, from which we gain only mental impressions—and one of them from an analysis of the concept of solidity, or matter, as consisting essentially of resistance, or impenetrability, which is a power with which God imbues certain parts of space. Matter, reducible to resistance, thus becomes a form of divine energy.

Neither Edwards's nor Berkeley's nor Malebranche's metaphysical idealism was subjectivist or skeptical, that is, conducive to doubt about the reality and reliability of our knowledge of the world. Our knowledge of the world is necessarily mediated through ideas, or mental phenomena, but because the world itself is ideal, matter itself being the great illusion, this conclusion does not weaken our grasp of the truth. All three of these thinkers had in common a profound religious faith, and each took up metaphysics not as a means of undermining theological truths but of reinforcing them.

Like his Puritan predecessors, Edwards believed that the human quest for understanding of the universe through thought, speculation, and reflection and by offering praise was a holy exercise, indeed, the most fundamental purpose of human existence. Edwards's conviction that God created humankind so that the universe would be conscious of itself was simply a metaphysical extension of the basic confessional tenet that the purpose of the Creation is the manifestation of the glory of God, with the creation of humankind and angels supremely important in this scheme.

"Tis certain that God did not create the world for nothing," Edwards wrote in one of his earliest philosophical notes.

Tis most certain that, if there were no intelligent beings in the world, all the world would be without any good at all; for senseless matter, in whatever excellent order it is placed, would be useless if there were no intelligent beings at all, neither God nor others.

"Men, or intelligent beings, are the consciousness of the creation, whereby the universe is conscious of its own being, . . ." he continued. "Now except the world had such consciousness of itself, it would be altogether vain that it was. If the world is not conscious of its being, it had as good as not be as be."

Most of this metaphysical work by Edwards was not published in his lifetime and hence had no contemporary influence. What has survived is now incorporated in the Yale edition of his works.

Edwards was widely conversant with British and continental thought, but from an early age he judged everything he read in terms of its conformity to his brand of Calvinist orthodoxy. He was a superb analyst of the fallacies and weaknesses of much eighteenth-century moral and religious thought and was gifted at transmuting the tenets of Christianity (which he understood as deeply as anyone ever has) into philosophical principles that could hold their own in the marketplace of free ideas. He was not only the third Anglo-American thinker to achieve a degree of international stature before the revolutionary period—Cotton Mather and Benjamin Franklin antedated him in this—but one of the most profound philosophical thinkers in the whole span of American history.

American Political Philosophy, 1760–1790

The final exception to the generalization that for the colonial period we can discuss only "philosophy in America," rather than "American philosophy" per se, is only slightly less indisputable than the case of Jonathan Edwards. Between 1760 and 1790 there was a unique flowering of political philosophy in America, which was in good part indigenous and original and which for a time reversed the normal order of things, making all of Europe a pupil to the American teacher. The remarkable creativity of Americans in this area was not perfectly understood until recently, but it is the one fact that makes the American Revolution itself an event of world-historical importance. Before Hegel and the advent of the French Revolution, a number of European observers saw correctly that in British America reason and history had for the first time joined hands.

But one may ask here, too, as we did with reference to Puritanism, whether the best political thought of the era of the American Revolution—works by Thomas Jefferson, John Adams, James Wilson, and James Madison—was a true species of philosophy. If one believes that Aristotle's *Politics* is philosophy, then the answer must be yes. Political thought of the highest order, political thought that has lasting significance and universal application, such as is found in the *Federalist* papers, is often tied to actual political crises. "The Americans of the Revolutionary generation had constructed not simply new forms of government," the historian Gordon Wood has written, "but an entirely new conception of politics." The great German historian Leopold von Ranke observed in 1854 that the North Americans, "by abandoning English constitutionalism and creating a new republic based on the rights of the individual . . . introduced a new force into the world. For ideas spread most rapidly when they have found adequate concrete expression."

During the founding years, numerous ideas that had been floating about for decades or even centuries, and some that were hardly conceived of before, were brought together into a coherent whole, and these ideas in combination, formed in the vortex of political crisis and war, were original creations. The claim, for example, that all political power inheres ultimately in the people and that government must be derived from the will of the people was not new in itself, nor was the doctrine of inalienable individual rights. But these two notions locked together in dynamic tension, with the constitutional establishment of individual rights checking the possible tyranny of the majority, had never before been instituted. The concern for individual rights previously had focused on the rights of the "people" versus the will of their rulers. But when the people are their own rulers, how may they be protected from themselves?

Similarly the combination of overlapping local, state, and national government broke with all prior assumptions about the necessary structure of government. "The proposed Constitution," Madison wrote in *Federalist* 39, ". . . is in strictness, neither a national nor a federal Constitution, but a composition of both." It had been assumed hitherto that sovereignty could not be practically divided, that national sovereignty demanded undivided centralized power if a people were to have a real state. But the federal principle allows for concurrent political powers.

The concept of the constituent assembly—a body elected by the people for the sole purpose of drawing up a fundamental constitution, a structure of government, after which it disbands—was also a new combination. It brought together the notion of a kind of representative assembly that is situated outside of ordinary legislative activity and the notion of the autarchic individual lawgiver who has Solonic power and creates a set of fundamental laws that no ordinary political action or legislation may tamper with. The American Constitution, Tom Paine wrote, was "not the act of a government, but of a people constituting a government."

Most remarkably, in the new American government the internal structure was created without reference either to social classes and orders—aristocracy, monarchy, and populace—or to the alleged inherent virtue of any group. The invention of the Senate, for example, was one of the means of dividing power in government, thereby creating checks and balances, without using class relations as the basis of its formation. The traditional belief that a republic relied particularly upon the rectitude of the people was abandoned in favor of a structure of government designed to prevent or at least to limit abuses that, given the assumed inherent propensities of human nature, were inevitable. The retention of sovereignty by the entire voting population, which meted out power to various divisions of government for the sole purpose of accomplishing ends that served the voting population, was a means of forcing those temporarily in power—and all power in government is temporary—to serve the interests of the majority.

In the new invention of representative democracy, all power flows from and periodically returns to the people. The divisions of government differ only in their functions, not in the source or nature of their authority, for all authority springs equally from the people, whether the function be executive, legislative, or judicial or whether the power be exercised by federal, state, or local government. Government speaks and acts in the name of the people and is in fact part of the people. Those in government come from the people and will return to the people because of rotation in office and the elective power of the people.

The Founding Fathers solved the problem (at least as far as it could be solved) of how to create republican governments with sufficient power to act effectively and yet with that power diffused to such an extent that it can never be concentrated to the degree that it can be a threat to the people or to liberty. The separation of powers, with power checking and balancing other power, does not destroy power but limits it in particular cases.

The process for amending the Constitution and the concept of the Supreme Court as the interpreter of fundamental law were other original creations that ensured the possibility of continuous revisions in government, thereby overcoming the rigidity and ossification that doomed the empires of the past. The philosophical basis of some of these ideas was brilliantly delineated some years ago by Arthur O. Lovejoy in *Reflections on Human Nature*, and American political and constitutional thought is also looked at from the point of view of philosophical foundations by Hannah Arendt in *On Revolution*. Both these books give examples of how the European inheritance of philosophical ideas was incorporated and applied by the Founders. The problem, as Lovejoy remarks, was how "to construct an ideal political society out of bad human materials—to frame a rational scheme of government." A rational scheme would be one in which "the general good [is] realized, without presupposing that the individuals who exercise ultimate political power will be severally actuated in their use by rational motives, or primarily solicitous about the general good."

Once more to follow Gordon Wood,

So piecemeal was the American's formulation of this [new political] system, so diverse and scattered in authorship, and so much a simple response to the pressures of democratic politics, . . . that the originality and the theoretical consistency and completeness of their constitutional thinking have been obscured. It was a political theory that was diffusive and open-ended; it was not delineated in a single book; it was peculiarly the product of a democratic society, without precise beginning or ending. It was not political theory in the grand manner, but it was political theory worthy of a prominent place in the history of Western thought. (*The Creation of the American Republic, 1776–1787*, p. 615)

THE CHARACTER OF PHILOSOPHICAL ACTIVITY

With these special four cases out of the way, we can turn to our second purpose, which is (without chauvinism) to note some aspects of the character of philosophical activity in colonial Anglo-America. We have already stressed the relative isolation of colonial intellectuals and consequently the feeble nature of the philosophical enterprise in the colonies, thought of in social or group terms. English America lacked the clubs and coffeehouses, the wealthy educational and religious institutions, and the general economic surplus to support a leisure class that could nourish or patronize philosophical discussion and criticism.

For the seventeenth century in Anglo-America, outside of the special case of the Puritans and Harvard College, the historian must be content to record whatever small evidence exists merely of philosophical *reading*. It is a delight to find, for example, that one Richard Lee of Westmoreland County in Virginia, who died in 1715 at age 68, had in his library a logic text by the Dutch academic philosopher Franco Burgersdyck, whose works were pervasive in Protestant circles at the time. Lee also owned a commentary on Aristotle's ethics and some works by Descartes, all in Latin, and, in English, Antoine LeGrand's *Entire Body of Philosophy According to . . . Descartes, Written Originally in Latin* (London, 1694) and no less than two works by Thomas Hobbes, something called his "Elements," which could be any of three different Hobbes titles, and his *Philosophical Rudiments Concerning Government and Society* (1651).

The library of Captain Arthur Spicer, who died in Richmond County, Virginia, in 1699, also had a copy of Burgersdyck's work on logic, which is enough to suggest that Burgersdyck was as important an educational tool in Virginia as in New England. Such a conclusion is not very impressive, but there is not much more one can do with philosophy in seventeenth-century Virginia, or in any of the British colonies other than Massachusetts, than investigate libraries and education.

The study of library inventories and of documented references to what actually was read in the colonies does not provide the ingredients for the construction of a fleshed-out, synthetic picture of philosophical activity, but it may be helpful in breaking down a particular kind of myth concerning the transmission of thought to America. These are myths that rely on the impressions of a single individual or on the actions of a single individual as the determinants of our knowing what actually happened in the history of thought.

There are two classic instances of such myths concerning the history of early Anglo-American philosophy, one involving Samuel Johnson, the Connecticut descendant of Puritans, who after graduating from Yale became an Anglican, and the other, John Witherspoon, the president of the College of New Jersey.

In an autobiographical memoir written by Johnson around 1770, about seven years after his retirement from the presidency of King's College, he reflected back on his education at Yale some fifty years before and how he was "changed to the New Learning." He wrote, referring to himself in the third person, "They heard indeed in 1714 when he took his Bachelor's Degree of a new philosophy that of late was all in vogue and of such names as *Descartes, Boyle, Locke,* and *Newton.*" However, "they were cautioned against thinking anything of them because the new philosophy it was said would soon bring in a new divinity and corrupt the pure religion of the country." There were no books of learning to be had, Johnson continued, under 100 or 150 years old, "such as the first settlers of the country brought with them seventy or eighty years before," but he was fortunate to have accidently discovered a copy of "Lord Bacon's *Instauratio Magna,* or *Advancement of Learning* (perhaps the only copy in the country and nobody knew its value)," whereupon "he found himself like one at once emerging out of the glimmer of twilight into the full sunshine of open day."

Autobiographies referring to events decades earlier are notoriously unreliable, and Johnson had a motive for deprecating the state of learning in the colonies in his youth—among other things, it helped to justify his conversion to the Anglican church and his lifelong Anglophilia—but it would be particularly absurd to take seriously his belief that he was alone in reading Francis Bacon in 1714. Suffice it to say that William Ames, one of the Massachusetts Bay colony's spiritual fathers had, decades earlier, quoted Bacon with approval and that a copy of *The Advancement of Learning* (of which there were editions in English in 1605, 1629, and 1633, to mention the earliest) was in Elder William Brewster's library when he died in Plymouth Colony in 1644. A copy was also in John Harvard's library, bequeathed to Harvard College in 1638. Thus, knowing where books were can offset biased or ill-remembered personal testimony.

It is important to remember, too, that, typically, new books and new ideas seep into a culture and into consciousness in many different ways and at many different levels. Some of the "New Learning" that Johnson discovered in 1714 was already much under discussion at Harvard at least twenty years earlier.

Similarly, it has long been premised in simplified accounts of American philosophy that John Witherspoon "introduced" the Scottish philosophy to America, like some sort of Moses descending with the tablets of the law. Thus, James McCosh, in *The Scottish Philosophy, . . . From Hutcheson to Hamilton* (New York, 1875), referred to Witherspoon as the "energetic man who actually introduced Scottish thought into the new world." Witherspoon was certainly conversant with philosophical trends in Scotland, but Americans were studying, and were already influenced by, a half-dozen Scottish thinkers many years before Witherspoon's arrival at the College of New Jersey. There was no single conduit by which the influence of Scottish philosophers reached eighteenth-century America; there were many, and the influence of the Scots was pervasive in social, economic, and political thought, as well as in logic, rhetoric, and metaphysics.

The celebrated burgeoning of original philosophical thought in Scotland in the eighteenth century began to be felt in America by the 1720s when Francis Hutcheson's *Inquiry Into the Original of Our Ideas of Beauty and Virtue* (1725) was first taught at Harvard, and thereafter there is continuous influence in logic, rhetoric, metaphysics, and epistemology as well as in moral philosophy. The Calvinist heritage of Scotland ensured that there would be a natural affinity between many American intellectuals and the great minds of the northern British state, as distinguished, let us say, from French thought in the mid eighteenth century, which in opposition to Roman Catholic domination harbored views far too skeptical, materialistic, anticlerical, or even nihilistic for the taste of most Americans. Hume was, of course, the big exception among the Scots, but much of the most influential Scottish thought was written in opposition to the intellectual challenge presented by Hume's skepticism.

Misinformation about the spread of new ideas, similar to that purveyed by Samuel Johnson of Connecticut or James McCosh, is also prevalent in commentary about the Spanish colonies. As noted by John Tate Lanning, a historian writing in the 1840s could still claim, ridiculously, that "the names of Locke, Bacon, Galileo, Descartes, Newton, and Leibnitz, were never heard in the schools of America until the nineteenth century was far advanced." Drawing on manuscript and printed theses composed at universities in Mexico, Guatemala, Caracas, Chile, and Córdoba, among other sources, Lanning has shown the utter falsity of that conclusion.

If the history of early American philosophy must be in good part a detailed study of the dispersion and discussion of European ideas, it is necessary to examine the means of transmission and communication. For example, as has already been noted, from time to time, European visitors made a significant difference, bringing in books, ideas, money, and the affirmation of the importance of ideas. One small area that has received only minimal exploration is that of the contributions of the royal governors to American cultural growth. Despite the political opposition these men regularly generated, they were sometimes patrons or even students of thought and often brought with them good libraries, as well as the aura of the metropolis. Colonial intellectuals, hungry for mental nourishment from "home"—that is, London—flocked to the governors if they showed any semblance of philosophical intellect. The nucleus of the College of William and Mary's library was supplied in 1698 by Governor Francis Nicholson, who was the executive of Virginia between that year and 1705. Nicholson was basically a soldier, but he was elected to the Royal Society in 1706 and because of his interest in higher education was the kind of person who could serve as a catalyst.

William Burnet, the son of the famous bishop and historian Gilbert Burnet, is a clearer case. Royal governor of New York in the 1720s, and briefly of Massachusetts, owner of a massive library and a person of definite cultivation, he had the good judgment to befriend Benjamin Franklin when the latter was just a youth and corresponded with James Logan, the learned Philadelphia Quaker; with Samuel Johnson in Connecticut, the closest thing in colonial British America to a true philosopher; with Cadwallader Colden in New York, who was interested in natural philosophy; and with Henry Flynt, the Harvard tutor who reigned in Cambridge, Massachu-

setts, for more than fifty years, from 1699 to 1754.

Another example is that of Governor Francis Fauquier, who was in Virginia between 1758 and 1768 and who formed an intellectual circle to which Thomas Jefferson belonged for a time and that Jefferson remembered all of his life with gratitude. The group included the Scottish professor of mathematics and natural philosophy at the College of William and Mary, William Small, whom Jefferson credited as an important influence on his intellectual development. Fauquier, like Nicholson, was a fellow of the Royal Society.

By far the most spectacularly important philosophical visitor to America in the colonial period was the great Anglo-Irish luminary George Berkeley, who lived in Rhode Island from 1728 to 1731. Berkeley, noted for his metaphysical idealism, was at the time of the visit a dean in the English church and not yet a bishop. He had come with the whiggish intention of rescuing Britain and the empire from corruption and decay by establishing in the New World a seminary of religion and virtue, specifically an Anglican college from which would pour forth men of good morals and learning. He was also possessed of the dream, already a century or two old, of using such an institution to train Indian converts who would themselves become missionaries to their kindred.

The entire plan came to nought because Berkeley never received the financial backing from Parliament that he had been expecting, but his sojourn in America had a pronounced effect on philosophical speculation in the colonies. One of his most important works, *Alciphron, or the Minute Philosopher,* was written while he was living in Rhode Island, and he carried on an earnest and revealing correspondence with the Reverend Samuel Johnson on the most difficult metaphysical questions. Berkeley also endowed the first graduate fellowships in America (at Yale) and gave unparalleled gifts of books to both Harvard and the young Yale College, including many that were exemplary of recent philosophical speculation from Britain and the Continent. These books overnight made it possible for those living in proximity to Yale to have access to works that were not otherwise readily available in America.

Colleges, of course, acted as centers of intellectual activity. They provided refuge for instructors who spent some part of their time in study; they supported learned libraries; they offered the stimulus of students; and they often attracted a coterie of educated men who were interested in ideas. Moreover, it is impossible to do research on the curriculum of the colonial colleges between 1650 and 1800 without coming upon the study of philosophy every step of the way. The major portions of the curriculum were sometimes called the "three philosophies"—natural, moral, and rational—for good reason. The state of learning was prescientific, in the sense that the physical sciences had not yet become the prevailing models of rigor and progress in learning. The procedure in all studies was philosophical in essence, which is to say that it was textual, disputatious and dialectical, speculative, and syllogistic.

In this period, too, the curriculum itself—its divisions, its organization, its methods, and its ends—was a subject of intensive and constant philosophical study, as though an error in the order of learning were itself a matter of vast substantive consequence. This concern was expressed in the discipline of "technologia," the art of organizing knowledge, so to speak, wherein the method and the ordering of the sciences in order to achieve truth and to link the divine with the earthly was the object of study. Concern with the role and place of each of the disciplines, inherited from the Middle Ages, was a continuous theme in American thought from Peter Ramus to John Witherspoon. Francis Bacon, John Locke, and Gottfried Wilhelm Leibniz, among many other distinguished European thinkers, likewise were interested in this subject.

The earliest work we have from the hand of Samuel Johnson, who was preoccupied throughout his life with the problem of the organization of knowledge, is illustrative of this concern. It is a manuscript dating from 1714, Johnson's last year in college, and entitled "Technologia Sive Technometria or Ars Encyclopaidia, Manualis Ceu Philisphia." Designed to be a synopsis of all of the arts of learning, and containing 1,271 numbered and ordered propositions, the work is highly revealing of what was taught at Yale in the early eighteenth century and of what had been taught at Harvard prior

to about 1680, when the Harvard curriculum was reformed.

The first philosophical article written by an Anglo-American to be published in Europe was Johnson's "Introduction to the Study of Philosophy, Exhibiting a General View of All the Arts and Sciences," which appeared in the London journal the *Present State of the Republic of Letters* in May 1731. This piece was intended to be "a general View of the whole System of Learning . . . in Miniature," wherein may be beheld "not only the Objects, Boundaries, Ends and uses of each of the Sciences, but at the same time the natural Order wherein they stand, . . . both with respect one to another, and to the great general End, *viz.* our Happiness, which is pursued thro' them all."

Mention of the influence of the seventeenth-century English philosopher John Locke has for many years figured prominently in even the briefest discussions of colonial philosophy. This influence is often presented in vague terms, with Locke serving as a kind of magical icon of modernity and progress. One problem with this focus on Locke is that he was the author of a number of works in different areas, each of which reached different audiences and had a different impact, not always the obvious one.

Debate still rages, for example, about the importance of Locke's *Two Treatises of Government* (1690) for the political thought of the Founding Fathers of the United States. This is an entirely different question from that of the influence of Locke's *Essay Concerning Human Understanding* (1689), regarded at the time as a logic treatise, on Samuel Johnson or Jonathan Edwards, or the influence of Locke's *Thoughts Concerning Education* (1695) on American pedagogy, or the influence of his *Reasonableness of Christianity* (1695) on American clergy. When admiration for Locke was expressed in America in the eighteenth century, it was rarely indicated which work of Locke's was being admired, with the result that his name can be inserted into almost any context. Moreover, it is always important to know what strands of Locke's thought are under consideration at any given time.

Samuel Johnson's first comments on Locke had to do not with Locke's epistemology or his critique of syllogistic logic in favor of empiricism, but with the section in the *Essay Concerning Hu-*

man Understanding on the "Division of the Sciences," which was Johnson's great preoccupation. It was recognized early that the implications of some of Locke's thought, in the *Essay* in particular, ran counter to Calvinist orthodoxy, and most Americans in the eighteenth century were, with Jonathan Edwards, looking for philosophical ideas that reinforced and protected their religious tradition, not ideas that threatened to subvert it.

SECULARIZATION

The history of philosophy, like the history of literature, cannot be told in terms of alleged linear progress. Human understanding has broadened and deepened in the course of two and a half millennia of Western philosophy—the height of psychological penetration achieved in Adam Smith's influential *Theory of Moral Sentiments* (1759), for example, was the direct result of the preceding two centuries of close investigation and could not have been written in, let us say, 1500. But there has been no evident progress in the sheer ability of human minds to reason deeply, acutely, and imaginatively about essential questions, many of which can have no definitive answers.

Historians of eighteenth-century American philosophy have tended to single out as *the* course of development the rise of Unitarianism, which eventuates in such great figures as Ralph Waldo Emerson. Yet at the same time, in colleges and seminaries, serious and subtle philosophical debates continued among orthodox Trinitarian theologians. To neglect this losing side in the battle for cultural dominance is to leave out half of the story.

It is generally true that the trend in the course of the colonial period was toward secularization, meaning, as the twentieth-century sociologist Talcott Parsons once defined the term, that traditional Christian orthodoxy was in control of less and less of the full span of human activity—politics, economics, education, social conduct, and so on. Secularization does not mean that religious belief itself became diluted or that fewer and fewer people had any religious beliefs at all. The traditional Christian worldview was confined to a smaller space, but in eighteenth-century North America, it certainly did not lose intensity.

BIBLIOGRAPHY

Arendt, Hannah. *On Revolution.* New York, 1963.

Blau, Joseph L. *American Philosophic Addresses, 1700–1900.* New York, 1946.

Bushman, Richard. "On the Uses of Psychology: Conflict and Conciliation in Benjamin Franklin." *History and Theory* 5 (1966):225–240.

Curti, Merle. *The Growth of American Thought.* 2nd ed. New York, 1951.

Edwards, Jonathan. *Ethical Writings,* edited by Paul Ramsey. New Haven, Conn., 1989.

———. *Scientific and Philosophical Writings.* Edited by Wallace E. Anderson. New Haven, Conn., 1980.

Ellis, Joseph J. *The New England Mind in Transition: Samuel Johnson of Connecticut, 1696–1772.* New Haven, Conn., 1973.

Fiering, Norman. "Benjamin Franklin and the Way to Virtue." *American Quarterly* 30 (Summer 1978): 199–223.

———. *Jonathan Edwards's Moral Thought and Its British Context.* Chapel Hill, N.C., 1981.

———. *Moral Philosophy at Seventeenth-Century Harvard: A Discipline in Transition.* Chapel Hill, N.C., 1981.

———. "President Samuel Johnson and the Circle of Knowledge." *William and Mary Quarterly,* 3rd ser., 28 (April 1971):199–236.

———. "The Rationalist Foundations of Jonathan Edwards's Metaphysics." In *Jonathan Edwards and the American Experience,* edited by Nathan O. Hatch and Harry S. Stout. New York, 1988.

Flower, Elizabeth, and Murray G. Murphey. *A History of Philosophy in America.* Vol. 1. New York, 1977.

Gibbs, Lee Wayland. "The Technometry of William Ames." Th.D. diss., Harvard Divinity School, 1967.

Hindle, Brooke. *The Pursuit of Science in Revolutionary America, 1735–1789.* Chapel Hill, N.C., 1956.

Johnson, Samuel. *Samuel Johnson: His Career and Writings.* Edited by Herbert and Carol Schneider. 4 vols. New York, 1929.

Kennedy, Rick. "The Alliance Between Puritanism and Cartesian Logic at Harvard, 1687–1735." *Journal of the History of Ideas* 51 (October–December 1990):549–572.

Kuklick, Bruce. *Churchmen and Philosophers: From Jonathan Edwards to John Dewey.* New Haven, Conn., 1985.

Lanning, John T. *Academic Culture in the Spanish Colonies.* New York, 1960.

PHILOSOPHY

Lovejoy, Arthur O. *Reflections on Human Nature.* Baltimore, Md., 1961.

May, Henry F. *The Enlightenment in America.* New York, 1976.

Miller, Perry. *The New England Mind: The Seventeenth Century.* New York, 1939.

Savelle, Max. *Empires to Nations: Expansion in America, 1713–1824.* Minneapolis, Minn., 1974.

Schneider, Herbert W. *A History of American Philosophy.* 2nd ed. New York, 1963.

———. "The Significance of Benjamin Franklin's Moral Philosophy." In his *Studies in the History of Ideas,* Vol. 2. New York, 1922.

Witherspoon, John. *Lectures on Moral Philosophy: An Annotated Edition.* Edited by Jack Scott. Newark, Del., 1982.

Wood, Gordon S. *The Creation of the American Republic, 1776–1787.* Chapel Hill, N.C., 1969.

Norman Fiering

SEE ALSO **Colonial Political Thought; The Enlightenment; Higher Education; Libraries and Learned Societies; and Scientific Inquiry.**

THE ENLIGHTENMENT

EUROPEAN ORIGINS

FOLLOWING THE SENTIMENTS of the French philosopher and Anglophile Voltaire, Thomas Jefferson regarded Francis Bacon, Isaac Newton, and John Locke as his "trinity of immortals." These were the brilliant and learned Englishmen whose thought and understanding of the world made them, to Jefferson, more praiseworthy than the mighty monarchs, valiant warriors, or even saintly mystics generally held up as the greatest human beings. Although greatly influenced by the writings of such figures as Descartes, Galileo, a notable group of Dutch scientists, and others, this trinity's rationale—empirical, reasonable, scientific, and mundane—transformed the European intellectual universe in the seventeenth century. Their views laid the foundation both, as Voltaire foresaw, for English prosperity and power and for the world of ideas known as the Enlightenment.

Spreading across the Atlantic Ocean to a North America peopled by European colonists, this worldview had particular impact on the British continental colonies where it was basic to the founding documents and political thought of the new United States. When Anne-Robert-Jacques Turgot, the baron de l'Aulne, said of Benjamin Franklin in 1778 that he had "snatched the lightning from the sky, and the sceptre from the tyrants," the Frenchman captured something of the spirit of the Enlightenment and of its special relevance to the European colonies in North America.

The essence of the Enlightenment was an attitude toward humankind and the world it inhabited, past, present, and future. As the French mathematician and philosopher the Marquis de Condorcet, writing in 1794, expressed it,

Scholarship, which seemed doomed by its respect for the past and its deference towards authority always to lend its support to harmful superstitions, has nevertheless contributed to their eradication, for it was able to borrow the torch of a sounder criticism from philosophy and the sciences. It already knew how to weigh up authorities and compare them; it now learned how to bring every authority before the bar of Reason. It had already discounted prodigies, fantastic anecdotes, facts contrary to all probability; but after attacking the evidence on which such absurdities relied, it now learned that all extraordinary facts must always be rejected, however impressive the evidence in their favour, unless this can truly turn the scale against the weight of their physical or moral probability.

Thus all the intellectual activities of man, however different they may be in their aims, their methods, or the qualities of mind they exact, have combined to further the progress of human reason. Indeed the whole system of human labour is like a well-made machine, whose several parts have been systematically distinguished but none the less, being intimately bound together, form a single whole, and work towards a single end. . . .

The sole foundation for belief in the natural sciences is . . . that the general laws directing the phe-

151

nomena of the universe, known or unknown, are necessary and constant. Why should this principle be any less true for the development of the intellectual and moral faculties of man than for the other operations of nature? . . .

Our hopes for the future condition of the human race can be subsumed under three important heads: the abolition of inequality between nations, the progress of equality within each nation, and the true perfection of mankind. Will all nations one day attain that state of civilization which the most enlightened, the freest and the least burdened by prejudices, such as the French and the Anglo-Americans, have attained already? Will the vast gulf that separates these peoples from the slavery of nations under the rule of monarchs, from the barbarism of African tribes, from the ignorance of savages, little by little disappear?

Is there on the face of the earth a nation whose inhabitants have been debarred by nature herself from the enjoyment of freedom and the exercise of reason? . . .

Will men approach a condition in which everyone will have the knowledge necessary to conduct himself in the ordinary affairs of life according to the light of his own reason, to preserve his mind free from prejudice, to understand his rights and to exercise them in accordance with his conscience and his creed; in which everyone will become able, through the development of his faculties, to find the means of providing for his needs; and in which at last misery and folly will be the exception, and no longer the habitual lot of a section of society? (Marquis Antoine-Nicolas Condorcet. *Progress of the Human Mind,* pp. 168, 173–174)

ENLIGHTENMENT PRINCIPLES

Though this was the general spirit of the Enlightenment, and properly captures its essential meaning among its American devotees in the eighteenth century, the Enlightenment was by no means clear and simple either in its timing in history or in its philosophic content. In general, the Enlightenment drew its strength from the repudiation of what it regarded as the millennium of superstition, other-worldliness, mysticism, and dogma known as the "Middle," or "Dark," Ages, when Christianity reigned in Europe, as doctrine, as institution, and as ritual. Before the Middle, or Dark, Ages, there had been the vibrant, mundane, and intellectually critical classical world of Greece and Rome, and after it the Renaissance ("rebirth") of learning

and the growth of knowledge and science in the era of Galileo, Christiaan Huygens, and William Harvey. The Enlightenment, then, sought to overcome the superstitious Dark Ages by flooding it, reasonably and systematically, with the "light" of the classical writers and of modern science.

Though the Enlightenment, like the Renaissance, exalted an individualism and a universalism that owed much to Christianity, its more direct attention was "ancient," that is, turned toward the culture of Greece and Rome. Virtually all the great thinkers of the Enlightenment were learned in the ancient languages (some even continued to write in Latin) and adopted some of the worldview of their classic texts. Although simple exposure to non-Christian thought and culture produced a substantial enlargement of perspective, the critical and probing nature of many of the rediscovered ancient texts also provoked burst after burst of intellectual energy. This provided impetus to more human understanding in the creative new directions heralded by Condorcet, but it stirred as well a deep reverence for the whole of classical civilization. As the Renaissance stimulated "progress," then, it also restored to Europeans the heritage of Greece and Rome. When colonists in North America sought to sustain enlightened civilization in the New World, they attended to both of these sources or means of intellectual and cultural enlargement.

In England, as the seventeenth-century thought of Bacon, René Descartes, and others propelled the scientific revolution of the seventeenth century and led to the founding of the Royal Society and other scholarly institutions, the "ancient" wisdom of Greece and Rome was reevoked so powerfully that English letters entered a neoclassical age. As Alexander Pope made immensely popular translations of Homer and Virgil and imitated Horace and Seneca, and Jonathan Swift satirized the presumption of science and made the "ancients" the clear winner in the "Battle of the Books," English society found itself enthralled by the culture of Greece and Rome. In aesthetics, rhetoric, morality, and politics especially, ancient wisdom and classical models became the vogue. Ciceronian rhetoric, stoic moderation and self-control, Epicurean love of life, Plutarchian moral leadership, Homeric patriotism, Aristotelian emphasis on political obligation, and Socratic love of public discourse all became the models for students and for a wide variety of aspiring writers and leaders. Since this classical emphasis came early in life as students learned Greek and Latin, and was regarded as well as a means of broadening and enlightening Christianity itself, it existed as a foundation undergirding the novel and exciting ideas of modernity. Jefferson, that is, came to his reverence for Bacon, Newton, and Locke only after he had been stirred by Cicero's republican patriotism, enriched by Epicurean morality, and impressed with Aristotle's sense of the importance of the political in human life. The Enlightenment thus was, at least in its earlier phases, profoundly neoclassical. This "ancient" orientation, though, being part of the Enlightenment critique of the fanaticism and irrationalism of the Christian Dark Ages, was also a repudiation of a more recent past.

The more innovative aspects of the Enlightenment, however, flowed from its enthusiasm for science. Following the new inductive approach (the scientific method) explained by Bacon and Descartes, scientists in the seventeenth century paid careful attention to the collection of facts about everything in the natural universe, sought to "induce" from them hypotheses and "laws" to explain all phenomena, tested these hypotheses in careful experiments, and presumed they could thus understand and explain the entire physical universe. "The true and lawful goal of the sciences," Bacon wrote in *Novum Organum* (1605), "is none other than this: that human life be endowed with new discoveries and powers." Descartes made the same confident, forward-looking point in his *Discourse on Method* (1637) when he scorned "the syllogisms . . . of the Schools" as capable only of "explaining to others things that are [already] known," while the inductive method was effective in "learning what is new." This method, he declared, was a "more powerful instrument of knowledge than any other that has been bequeathed to us by human agency," and would, if properly applied, enable men to "render [themselves] the masters and possessors of nature."

Thus the Enlightenment meant not only a revival of ancient learning and wisdom, but, perhaps more significantly, a resolute search for new facts and new principles that would propel the rational progress of humankind to previously unknown heights. Henry Oldenburg, the first secretary of the Royal Society of London (chartered in 1662), stated that its members were "followers of nature itself, and of truth, and moreover they judge that the world has not grown so old, nor our age so feeble, that nothing memorable can again be brought forth." In beginning publication of the Society's to-be-famous *Philosophical Transactions* in 1665, Oldenburg declared its purpose to be that scientific observations and experiments of people might be "clearly and truly communicated, desires after solid and usefull knowledge may be further entertained, ingenious endeavours and Undertakings cherished . . . and invited and encouraged to search, try, and find out new things." Oldenburg added that the Society members might "impart their knowledge to one another, and contribute what they can to the Grand design of improving Natural knowledge, and perfecting all Philosophical Arts, and Sciences. All for the Glory of God, the Honour and Advantage of these Kingdoms, and the Universal Good of Mankind." This was in effect the manifesto of the European Enlightenment.

European settlers in North America not only took this outlook with them to the New World (indeed such an outlook furnished an important part of the impetus and confidence to seek and settle what were to them new worlds), but once there they found an environment unsuited to rigid orthodoxies but rather welcoming to the new, the untried, and the unformed. In Quebec and New Amsterdam (New York), Saint Augustine and Santa Fe, as well as in Boston, Philadelphia and Williamsburg, the Enlightenment impulse to pursue and exploit the new and the unknown was an integral part of European settlement in North America.

SCIENCE

The most obvious and direct way for North Americans to take part in the Enlightenment zeal for science was to report "the facts" of their new environment to European colleagues. With the end of the War of the Spanish Succession in 1713 and the death of Louis XIV in 1715, the Regent, the duc d'Orleans, and the Conseil de Marine were eager to have the mystery of the continent west of the Great Lakes and the Mississippi River unravelled. Thus it was that the explorations of the La Vérendryes and Legardeur de Saint-Pierre were undertaken under Crown auspices and the Mallet brothers reached the barrier of the Cordilleras before the English colonists had struggled across the Appalachians.

Within New France proper, in Canada at least, scientists were at work. The Jesuits at the Collège de Québec kept meticulous twice-daily records of the temperature. The Intendant Jacques Raudot was an ardent entomologist and collector of moths and butterflies. A successor, the Intendant Claude-Thomas Dupuy, posted to Canada in 1726, took with him a library of over a thousand books, a well equipped physics laboratory, and numerous instruments for the study of astronomy.

During the first third of the century Dr. Michel Sarrazin, in addition to his medical practice and work as Royal Surgeon Major and as a member of the Conseil Superieur, was also a brilliant botanist, biologist, zoologist, and mineralogist with an international reputation as a scientist. His publications were many and well received by his peers in France and England. Year after year he shipped botanical specimens to the Royal Jardin des Plantes—some still survive at Oxford—along with learned papers on plants previously unknown in Europe and on the strange animals that he had dissected. These papers went to the Académie des Sciences, of which he was a corresponding member. After his death in 1734 his work was carried on by professors at the Collège de Québec and by his contemporary, Jean-François Gaultier, a fellow corresponding member of the Académie. Similarly, in Louisiana during those years, the Sieur Duprat, doctor of medicine and botanist, was in receipt of a stipend of 2,000 livres a year from the Crown to support his scientific investigations.

Given this intellectual climate in New France it is not surprising that the Swedish scientist Pehr Kalm, during his sojourn in Canada in 1749, was much impressed and wrote in his journal, "Great efforts are made here for the advancement of Natural History, and there are few places in the world where such good regulations are made for this purpose." Kalm was greatly taken

by the departing Governor General, the marquis de La Galissonière, a scientist in his own right, who had ordered seeds, roots, minerals, and strange animals gathered at the western posts for shipment to France along with information on the plants used by the Indians for medicinal purposes. Most of these discoveries and reportings, however, were made by Frenchmen only temporarily in New France, and hence had only limited impact in establishing an Enlightenment milieu in Quebec or other cities.

The same pattern was evident in the Spanish Borderlands to the south and west of what eventually became the United States. From the first voyages of Columbus, Spanish explorers sent back geographic, ethnographic, and biological information about North America. In the eighteenth century, first under the impetus of Philip V, who ruled from 1700 to 1746, and then especially of the "Enlightened" monarch Charles III, king from 1759 to 1788, Spanish military leaders and governors of Mexico sponsored scientific expeditions to the Pacific coast and to the Colorado and Rio Grande valleys. Again, since the emphasis was on gathering data for Spanish military and scientific purposes, and expeditions were conducted often by only temporary residents of the colonies, the impact in the New World was limited. A continuing insistence on religious orthodoxy in the colonies, and a suspicion that scientific initiatives abetted an officially unwelcome "liberalism," further curtailed the growth of a broadly enlightened culture in the Spanish domains.

In the British colonies, colonists took part enthusiastically in the European fascination with the New World environment. Beginning with John Winthrop, Jr., in 1662, more than thirty colonials became fellows of the Royal Society. John Clayton and John Mitchell in Virginia, Alexander Garden in South Carolina, and especially John Bartram in Pennsylvania sent accounts to Linnaeus and others of hundreds of plants unknown in Europe. Cadwallader Colden of New York made notable contributions in botany and the study of North American natives, though his treatise on gravitation proved to be utterly misguided.

The most remarkable flowering of Enlightenment science, however, took place in Philadelphia in the circle of Benjamin Franklin. Proposals in 1743 for what became a year later the American Philosophical Society; the conduct by Franklin and his friends of increasingly sophisticated electrical experiments (also in the 1740s); the careful reporting of these experiments to English correspondents; and Franklin's retirement from active business in 1748: together they amounted to a fulfillment of the Enlightenment ideal. The collection and communication of facts about the natural world, the building of rational, practical organizations to facilitate progress, and the turn of energies from private affairs to the public good (in this case, "to promote useful knowledge") were cardinal tenets of that ideal. As was also true in the Spanish and French colonies, there was growing confidence in the propositions that scientific knowledge could be applied to the improvement of human life, that societies organized for that purpose should be encouraged, and that this was especially the case in the unformed New World. Franklin summarized the essential perspective in a letter about electricity:

Electrical fluid [produced by static electricity devices] agrees with lightning in these particulars: 1. Giving light. 2. Colour of the light. 3. Crooked direction. 4. Swift motion. 5. Being conducted by metals. 6. Crack or noise in exploding. 7. Subsisting in water or ice. 8. Rending bodies it passes through. 9. Destroying animals. 10. Melting metals. 11. Firing inflammable substances. 12. Sulphereous smell. The electrical fluid is attracted by points. We do not know whether this is a property of lightning. But since they agree in all the particulars wherein we can already compare them, is it not probable they agree likewise in this? Let the experiment be made. (L.W. Labaree, ed. *The Papers of Benjamin Franklin.* Vol. 5, pp. 523–524)

In the revolutionary and early national eras, others besides Franklin made notable scientific and technological discoveries. The physician Benjamin Rush, the physicist and mathematician David Rittenhouse, the naturalist Thomas Nuttall, the chemist Benjamin Silliman, the paleontologist Thomas Jefferson, the black mathematician Benjamin Banneker, the inventors Robert Fulton, John Fitch, and Eli Whitney, and others made important contributions. Philip Freneau had explained poetically in "The Rising Glory of America" (1771) the special link many Enlightenment thinkers saw between science and the public sphere:

This is the land of every joyous sound,
Of liberty and life, sweet liberty!
Without whose aid the noblest genius
fails,
And science irretrievably must die.

(H. H. Clark, ed. *Major American Poets,*
New York, 1936, p. 7).

In science as in many other fields it seemed that the open environment and the growth of political independence in the New World would be especially congenial to fulfillment of Enlightenment ideals.

RELIGION

Though the Enlightenment, especially in its critical, materialistic, and scientific features, seemed hostile to religion, in fact it stimulated whole new understandings of and approaches to religion. In 1717 the Puritan clergyman John Wise of Ipswich, Massachusetts, already influenced by such Enlightenment intellectuals as Samuel von Pufendorf and John Locke, sought to rest both ecclesiastical and secular government on reason alone. When Wise endorsed Plutarch's dictum that "to follow God and obey Reason is the same thing," he expressed the essence of the Enlightenment impact on religion. Following "Arminian" (free will) theologians in the Netherlands and other continental rationalists, but harking especially to liberal English clerics such as Archbishop John Tillotson and the Arian Samuel Clarke, American preachers and writers responded vigorously to the religious implications of the emphasis on reason. When the great Locke himself wrote *The Reasonableness of Christianity* (1695), he stated the keynote of the impact of the Enlightenment on religion in the American colonies.

Within all religious denominations, but especially notable in the large Anglican and Calvinist (including both Congregationalists and Presbyterians) persuasions, the religion of reason made its mark. For Anglicans the impact came slowly and unevenly as individual clergymen and laymen responded to the ideas of "latitudinarian" clerics such as Tillotson and Clarke. Thus some churches and intellectual circles made reason more and more the test of doctrine, religious practice, and even understanding of the Scripture. Controversy and tension over the "Religion of Reason" affected Anglican congregations throughout the British colonies. In the French and Spanish colonies, where authorities much more rigidly controlled religious affairs and were generally orthodox, the impact of Enlightenment thought was much less evident.

In New England, the congregational organization of the churches allowed Enlightenment ideas of religion to enter the churches both easily and unevenly throughout the eighteenth century. As individual clergymen such as John Wise, Elisha Williams, and Ezra Stiles absorbed the "Age of Reason" approach, that worldview gained more or less currency in the region. The new thinking exercised, in particular, such a strong influence at Harvard College that it provoked hostile outbursts from the more orthodox. Through the leadership of two Boston clergymen, Jonathan Mayhew and Charles Chauncy, the religion of Reason had spread broadly through Congregationalism by mid century.

The Enlightenment's impact, however, was most significant in its pervading, by degrees, many segments of religious life. Most extremely, it led, in the fashion of the so-called radical Enlightenment of Holbach and Helvétius, to an aggressive anti-Christianity and even militant materialism. Although such intellectuals as Franklin, Adams, Jefferson, and Paine knew of this radicalism, it had little influence or following in North America. Even the non-Christian natural religion usually called deism, which accepted a so-called watch maker God who created an orderly world that ever after ran in accord with Newtonian and other natural laws, had little publicly avowed or organizational impact in North America. Many sophisticated and learned individuals (including Paine, Franklin, and Jefferson), though, could probably best have been characterized as deists.

Far more influential were Christian "latitudinarians" or "Arminians" who believed that Christianity itself, properly understood, was reasonable and in accord with the laws of nature. These "Arminians," as their orthodox foes termed them, believed that God had created a rational universe, that human beings had "freedom of the will" to determine the course of their lives, that they were endowed with reason to discern right from wrong, that Jesus of Nazareth was a great moral teacher, that humans were obliged to live in accord with right reason in this world, and that their lives would be judged by that standard. This outlook gained wide currency across a wide spectrum of religious denominations. It had its most important institutional outgrowth in the gradual transition, during the late eighteenth and early nineteenth centuries, of Congregational churches into Unitarian Societies. By 1825 there were 125 Unitarian Societies in the United States, mostly in New England. So congenial was this transition to Jefferson, a devotee of rational religion, that he hoped and expected "Unitarianism [would] become the general religion of the United States."

Even where more orthodox Anglican or Calvinist theologies were upheld, the ideas of the Enlightenment had a considerable influence. Moderates of all Protestant denominations—Anglicans, Presbyterians, Congregationalists, Lutherans, Quakers, and even the new, surging Baptists and Methodists—affected in some degree by the Enlightenment, sought a middle ground between deism and even atheism on the one hand, and rigid, dogmatic creeds on the other. They sought to remain good Christians, believing in a just and loving God, in the general if not literal authority of the Bible, and in the moral teachings of Jesus, which they saw as compatible with the rational ideals of the Enlightenment.

These "moderates" even made some reconciliation with the often irrational fervor of the Great Awakening that swept over the British colonies, reaching its height in the 1740s. Though the revivalistic extremes of some preachers were anathema, the ecumenical optimism of the Methodists and others, the egalitarianism of spiritual experience, and the emphasis on the free choice of individuals to seek their salvation, all echoed Enlightenment themes. Jonathan Edwards himself, the intellectual and at times even the pastoral leader of the Great Awakening, was thoroughly conversant with the "new philosophy" of John Locke and the Scottish "common sense" thinkers. In some fashion Edwards adjusted Calvinist theology to current modes of thought. Finally, though, Edwards, and especially his followers whose "New Divinity" was influential into the nineteenth century, became the most resolute defenders of Calvinist orthodoxy against the Arminian, free will, Unitarian tendencies of the Enlightenment. They revealed in North America a version of the antagonism between reason and religion expressed more pungently in Europe by Voltaire, Edward Gibbon, and other Enlightened intellectuals.

The growth of rational religion, and the understanding that freedom of religion was a natural right, led throughout the British colonies to challenges to religious orthodoxies and to the tradition of established churches. This insistence on the right of "liberty of conscience," as the Virginia Declaration of Rights of 1776 put it, plus the difficulty of sustaining orthodoxy or establishment amidst the "multiplicity of sects" (Madison's phrase) in the colonies, led to the firm guarantees of religious freedom in the constitutions of many states as well as in the federal Bill of Rights of 1791. Madison wrote Jefferson in 1786, after the passage of the Virginia Bill for Establishing Religious Freedom, that he believed the state had "extinguished forever the ambitious hope of making laws for the human mind"—a cardinal tenet of the Enlightenment.

GOVERNMENT

The most important and lasting impact of the Enlightenment in North America, however, came through its influence on the political thinking and government of the thirteen British colonies that in 1776 became the United States of America. The appeal in the Declaration of Independence to "the Law of Nature and of Nature's God," and the assertion in the preamble of the Constitution that Justice, domestic tranquility, the common defense, the general welfare, and the Blessings of Liberty were the proper purposes of government all reveal devotion to the Enlightenment creed of reason. The preference in *The Federalist Papers* for "reflection and choice" over "accident and force" as the foundation of political society reflects this fidelity as well. Though these ideas drew on classical and Judeo-Christian patterns of thought and were thus much older than the Enlightenment, that era so heightened such thinking that it gave systematic and lasting expression to a theory of government resting on reason.

Documents such as the Mayflower Compact (1620) and William Penn's Frame of Government for Pennsylvania (1682) show that ideas of government resting in some degree on reason and consent had long been part of North American experience. Yet, it was the move toward reaffirmed autonomy after the victorious conclusion of the Seven Years' War (1763), culminating in the American Revolution and independence, that most stimulated the application of Enlightenment thought to political questions. John Wise argued in 1717 that like church organization, the foundations of civil government could be "the Produce of Man's Reason, of Humane and Rational Combinations," rather than dependent on divine right, immemorial custom, or even Scriptural authority. That is, one could *reason* toward the proper and just principles that should guide human government. Wise called these principles natural law, which, of course, he thought were entirely consistent with God's law.

In 1744 another Puritan clergyman, Elisha Williams, declared that "all are born . . . naturally equal" and everyone "is a *reasonable . . . moral* and *accountable* Being: and therefore . . . must reason, judge, and determine for himself," thus laying important groundwork, in reason, for freedom of belief and expression. Then, in 1776, yet another Puritan clergyman, Samuel Hopkins, extended what he thought were the obvious (reasonable) implications of the Enlightenment for the institution of slavery. African Americans brought as slaves to North America, had "never forfeited their liberty or given anyone the right to enslave and sell them," Hopkins asserted in *A Dialogue Concerning the Slavery of Africans,* and then pointed to "the shocking, the intolerable inconsistence," of American proclamations of liberty while slavery existed in the new nation. Reason abhorred the circumstance, he said. Though, as the case of slavery demonstrates especially, the projection of the principles of reason did not always achieve either intellectual agreement or quick practical results. It was nevertheless clear that those principles were fraught with significance for politics.

As early as 1750, a leading exponent of rational religion, Jonathan Mayhew, had made an important linkage of Enlightenment and Christian thought to bring each to bear on the subject of political obedience. Noting that both Scripture and reason insisted that the conduct of rulers be judged according to a "higher law," Mayhew justified the execution a century earlier of the "perfectly wild and arbitrary tyrant" Charles I. The act was "a most righteous and glorious stand, made in defence of the natural and legal rights of the people, against the unnatural and illegal encroachments of arbitrary power. . . . Resistance was absolutely necessary in order to preserve the nation from slavery, misery, and ruin."

Fourteen years later James Otis of Boston declared that every Briton in North America "is by the law of God and nature, by the common law, and by act of parliament . . . entitled to all the natural, essential, inherent and inseparable rights of our fellow subjects in Great Britain." Otis thus conflates divine, natural, and constitutional rights into what to him was an entirely consistent amalgam. The rule of reason in government was that certain propositions should be absolute and universal simply because they accorded with human reason as follows: the power of legislation should be exercised as the people prescribed; the means or ends of legislation could not be altered arbitrarily; the people must be governed by stated laws; and those laws should have no ultimate end but the good of the people. These propositions, Otis held, were "natural and essential" in that in reason one could not deny their justice and applicability in human affairs. Furthermore, once these fundamental propositions about *how* government was to be conducted were in place, the protection of individual rights would also be assured. Was it reasonable to suppose, Otis and others asked, that government resting on the will of the people would violate or abridge their rights? The Enlightenment believed that in government as elsewhere reason provided necessary, proper, and universal guidelines.

Though Mayhew, Otis, and other Enlightenment thinkers had foreshadowed many of the arguments of the American Revolution, a considerable development of thought was still necessary before independence would be justified. The critical problem, at least for the Enlightened mind, was the one Otis passed over so lightly in equating God's law, natural law, and English law. The joining of divine and natural law had been proceeding apace for nearly a century by clergymen influenced by the early phases of the

Enlightenment. What seemed reasonable in matters of religion—the basing of belief on individual conscience and conviction, and the government of churches by congregations rather than by kings or bishops, for example—when applied to public affairs called for freedom of religion and expression as well as a form of government resting on the consent of the governed. At the same time the validation through reason of certain scriptural injunctions (such as the Ten Commandments and the Sermon on the Mount) strengthened the ideas of human rights and universal principles so essential to the Enlightenment. Thus the articulation of a "higher law," both conforming to reason and coming from God, became a crucial part of the coming of the American Revolution.

As Otis implied, the British Constitution itself, as "settled" in the Glorious Revolution of 1688 and defended by Locke, was held to be in conformity to right reason. Its limitation on the power of the monarch, its declaration of the rights of the people, and its establishment of parliamentary supremacy (with particular power over taxation given to the House of Commons) were regarded by Voltaire and Montesquieu, as well as a host of British thinkers, as the embodiment of Enlightened government. Following this near orthodoxy of political thought in the first half of the eighteenth century, transatlantic Britons saw appeals to natural rights and to "the rights of Englishmen" as two sides of the same coin. Since the rights of Englishmen were more immediately relevant in courts of law, the first appeals were made ordinarily to them. Hence, as particular disputes over taxation, legal rights, control of trade, colonial legislative power, quartering of troops, and so on became more intense after the victory in the war against France (concluded in the Treaty of Paris in 1763), colonists appealed initially to English rights. But their spokesmen, often in the same breath, appealed as well to God's law and to natural right—since all conformed to reason.

When the alleged rights of Englishmen seemed more and more subject to restriction at the hands of the British court and officials, however, colonists, adhering to Enlightenment ideology, asserted the primacy of natural law and natural right, and of course God's law. These tenets were held *above* the laws and constitution of the British Empire. After the passage in 1765 by Parliament of the Stamp Act, many colonial protests against it appealed beyond English rights. At a mass meeting that year in New London, Connecticut, colonists declared that if application of English principles in North America required payment of a tax not levied by colonial legislatures, it was time for the colony to "resume their natural rights and the authority the laws of nature and of God have vested them with." After Parliament passed the Declaratory Act in 1766, which asserted its right—despite the absence of colonial representation there—to legislate for the colonies "in all cases whatsoever," William Hicks of Pennsylvania asked "how can the colonists be said to possess the *Natural rights of mankind* or the *peculiar privileges of Englishmen?*" In repudiating the Declaratory Act, defended as authorized under the British constitution, Hicks underscored both the limitation of English rights and the priority of natural rights—as Enlightenment thought required.

As the struggle between the mother country and her colonies intensified in the 1770s, the issue increasingly became whether the very idea of *colonies*—one part of the world ruled by another—was not itself a violation of the law of nature, and, therefore, of reason. In reason and nature, could an island rule a continent? Could a legislature (or, eventually, a king) in London be expected to rule provinces thirty-five hundred miles (5,600 kilometers) away with an understanding of their common good? In 1772 Samuel Adams once again proclaimed colonial protests of British acts were justified by "the Rights of the Colonists as Subjects" of the British Crown and by "the Rights of the Colonists as Christians." Preeminently, though, he claimed justification under the "Natural Rights of the Colonists as Men, [including] . . . First, a Right to *Life*; Secondly to *Liberty*; [and] Thirdly, to *Property*." Continuing his paraphrase of John Locke, Adams insisted that "all positive and civil laws, should conform as far as possible, to the Law of natural reason and equity." In a categorical statement of Enlightenment faith, Adams concluded that "the natural liberty of man is to be free of any superior power on earth, and not to be under the will or legislative authority of man; but only to have the law of nature for his rule." John Adams, Alexander Hamilton, James Wilson, Thomas Jefferson, and other spokesmen for American rights wrote pamphlets making largely similar arguments based on the Enlightenment worldview.

The culminating expression of this worldview and its most telling projection to the issue of Independence was, of course, Tom Paine's *Common Sense*, first published in January 1776. Paine declared that he wrote under "the influence of reason and principle," in circumstances that were "not local, but universal," and that made "the cause of America . . . in a great measure the cause of all mankind." So great was Paine's faith in man's goodness and reason that he thought "Government even in its best state is but a necessary evil." It was, however, "rendered necessary by the inability of moral virtue to govern the world." This did not authorize government to go beyond its only legitimate end, the "freedom and security" of the governed. "The simple voice of nature and of reason," Paine declared, affirmed this basic proposition. Drawing his idea of government "from a principle in nature . . . that the more simple any thing is, the less liable it is to be disordered, and the easier repaired when disordered," Paine condemned the "exceedingly complex . . . constitution of England." Worst of all was the Crown itself that had its "paltry rascally origin . . . [when] a French Bastard landed with an armed Banditti and established himself King of England against the consent of the natives." Since this conquest, the English Crown had helped lay "the World in blood and ashes," and had proved itself adept at little more than to "make war and give away places." "TIS TIME TO PART," he concluded, so that the colonies would suffer no more from the wholly unjust and unnatural deeds of "the Royal Brute of Great Britain." In a famous peroration Paine foreshadowed Condorcet's Enlightenment creed of the global march of freedom:

O ye that love mankind! Ye that dare oppose not only the tyranny but the tyrant, stand forth! Every spot of the old world is overrun with oppression. Freedom hath been hunted round the Globe. Asia and Africa have long expelled her. Europe regards her like a stranger, and England hath given her warning to depart. O! receive the fugitive, and prepare in time an asylum for mankind. (Thomas Paine. *Writings*. Vol. 1, pp. 100–101)

The spirit of *Common Sense* was throughout that of the Enlightenment. Indeed, the phrase itself was a fitting expression of faith in the existence of conscience, good judgment, and reason in people. This was present potentially, and consistent with underlying Enlightenment belief in a benign and universal human nature, in *all* people of whatever race or gender. (Though Enlightenment stalwarts, including Jefferson and other Americans, did not generally hold late-twentieth-century views on race and gender equality, any serious effort to project Enlightenment thought in that direction encountered at once the obvious contradictions of existing slavery, racism, and gender disqualification.) Paine later stated succinctly his Enlightened idea of government:

Establish the Rights of Man, enthrone Equality . . . let there be no privileges, no distinctions of birth . . . make safe the liberty of industry and of trade, the equal distribution of [family] inheritance, publicity of administration, freedom of press; these things all established, you will be assured of good laws. (Thomas Paine. *Writings.* Vol. 3, pp. 107–108)

REALIZATION OF ENLIGHTENMENT IDEALS

The American Revolution and its ideology of natural law in fact became the symbol throughout the world for a freer and better life. A French historian, M. J. Chénier, wrote poetically in 1789 of North America that "this vast continent that the seas surround will soon change Europe and the world. There arise for us, in the fields of America, new interests and a new system of politics." A Russian poet earned the ire of Catherine the Great and exile in Siberia for writing about America, "to you my inflamed soul aspires, to you, renowned land, . . . Your example has revealed the goal." A British vessel, stopping at the Comoro Islands in the Mozambique Channel in 1784, even found natives in revolt against their Arab masters saying "America is free. Could we not be?"

These extravagant, even romantic statements, along with Paine's own rhetoric, suggest a closeness with what has been termed a late-eighteenth-century revolutionary or radical Enlightenment centering on the European continent. This contrasted with an earlier, British, "moderate" Enlightenment. Yet, in North America at least, the movement was more general and

more seamless. Men of ideas, whether scientists, preachers, or politicians, had responded since the mid and late seventeenth century to the new ways of thinking that were to characterize the Enlightenment. As time went by, of course, Enlightenment thought broadened, deepened, and strengthened as it pushed its implications into more and more areas. Some thinkers welcomed these projections while others condemned them. (John Adams, for example, called the ideas of government in *Common Sense* a "Star of Disaster" because they ignored what he thought were necessary checks and balances.) But the tension between "moderates" and "revolutionaries" was an ongoing one that, at least in the colonial era, achieved no clear drawing of lines or taking of sides. Much more significant was the steady, exciting impact of Enlightenment ideas, both those crossing the Atlantic and those being generated in North America, on all aspects of American thought and culture.

The Declaration of Independence, for example, is best understood as a document responding generally to the Enlightenment, rather than to any particular "phases" or thinkers. In it Jefferson said he depended on no "particular and previous writing" but rather sought to "harmonize sentiments of the day." He did so by setting forth "the common sense" on the subject of government that would be "an expression of the American mind." The basis of this "common sense," so pervasively accepted that explicit citation or quotation was entirely unnecessary, was Locke's thought, especially the *Second Treatise on Civil Government* (1690). In 1790 Jefferson termed this treatise "perfect as far as it goes." By that he meant that it needed supplement by such "practical" works as *The Federalist Papers* (1788), James Burgh's *Political Disquisitions* (1774–1775), and David Hume's *Essays, Moral, Political and Literary* (1741). Jefferson also recommended Montesquieu's *Spirit of Laws* (1741), Adam Smith's *Wealth of Nations* (1776), and the works of Turgot and the French physiocrats as basic books.

It is clear from such listings that in addition to Locke himself, Enlightenment intellectuals in North America read the Scottish thinkers, English radical Whigs, and continental theorists. Also admired were the great Augustan stylists Joseph Addison, Pope, and Swift. Jefferson once even called the Tory publicist Bolingbroke an "advocate for liberty" comparable to Paine. North Americans were also reading and beginning to respond to Rousseau, Claude-Adrien Helvétius, Beccaria, Condorcet, Diderot, Richard Price, Mary Wollstonecraft Godwin, William Godwin, and other later European Enlightenment figures, but their influence was relatively small, especially in the colonial period.

Scholarly efforts to show how Americans misunderstood the fine points of Locke, to assert the primary influence of the Scottish thinkers above that of Locke, or to be precise about the "liberal" or "civic republican" character of the American Revolution, all miss the more basic point. Colonials absorbed something from many streams of thought. They were far more impressed with the general, Enlightened quality of it *all*, than with the contradictions or philosophic niceties that later critics might have combed out of the flood of texts. When John Adams observed that of all ages "the Eighteenth Century . . . had been . . . the most honorable to human nature," he meant that "knowledge and Virtues were increased and diffused, Arts, Sciences useful to Men, ameliorated their condition, were improved, more than in any former equal period." Jefferson agreed in these "eulogies." This was the broad meaning of the Enlightenment in America.

The greatest influence, though, of the Enlightenment ideals implanted in the Declaration of Independence came in their projection into the government of the new United States. Alexander Hamilton expressed the basic hope in the first of the *Federalist Papers*, when he wrote that it fell to the new country to decide "whether societies of men are really capable or not of establishing good government from reflection and choice, or whether they are forever destined to depend for their political constitutions on accident and force." The Declaration of 1776, defended in the Revolutionary War, would achieve its fulfillment, Hamilton hoped, in a political system reasoned about and agreed to by the people. This system would embody the Enlightenment ideals of rule by consent and of natural rights, and would altogether result, finally in human history, in good government.

Hamilton and other American revolutionists understood, too, the importance of Enlightened thinking in those who took part, leaders and citizens, in this government. Following Diderot's definition of a *philosophe*, the need was "to act out of a feeling for Order and Reason, . . . suffused with concern for the good of civil society." Such good government, moreover, was understood to be essential to the spread of science, the growth of rational religion, and other Enlightenment hallmarks.

The American Revolution and the formation of government under the Constitution, then, were in a way a climax of the Enlightenment. They seemed to prove to the rest of the world that in that most fateful arrangement of human society, government itself, ideals of freedom and choice could be put in practice. They showed that popular sovereignty, a social contract, responsible citizenship, religious liberty, freedom of expression, balance of powers, human rights, and other rational ideals could be written into constitutions. These ideals could, as Robert R. Palmer has observed in *The Age of Democratic Revolution*, "be made the actual fabric of public life among real people, in this world, now," as Condorcet had hoped in 1794. George Washington, writing in 1783 as he turned his attention from war to statecraft, expressed the Enlightened mood of the new nation:

The foundation of our Empire was not laid in the gloomy age of Ignorance and Superstition, but at an Epocha when the rights of mankind were better understood and more clearly defined, than at any former period; the researches of the human mind, after social happiness, have been carried to a great extent, the Treasures of knowledge, acquired . . . by the labours of Philosophers, Sages, and Legislators are laid open for our use, and the collected wisdom may be happily applied in the Establishment of our forms of Government. (W.B. Allen, ed. *George Washington: A Collection*, Indianapolis, Ind., 1988, pp. 240–241)

Though in government, as in other areas, the ideals remained far from fulfillment. They were themselves subject to serious challenge for their superficiality, naiveté, and insufficiency. Nonetheless a powerful and beckoning aspiration, "the heavenly city of the eighteenth-century philosophers" in historian Carl Becker's apt phrase, had been articulated and set before humankind. As is implicit in the very word itself, then, the Enlightenment, especially in North America (where—compared with the Old World—life was less formed by dogma and custom), was fundamentally a way of thinking about humankind and the world it inhabited more open to choice, new knowledge, progress, and, especially, reason, than most other eras of intellectual history.

BIBLIOGRAPHY

The basic sources, of course, for the ideas of the Enlightenment in colonial North America are the writings of the major figures—such as Benjamin Franklin, John Adams, Thomas Jefferson, and Benjamin Rush—now published in many complete *Papers* editions and more convenient selected editions. Of the hundreds of fine books on the Enlightenment generally, on various aspects of it, and on major and minor figures in it, the following are among the most helpful and most authoritative:

Bannon, John. *The Spanish Borderlands Frontier, 1513–1821.* New York, 1970.

Becker, Carl L. *The Declaration of Independence.* New York, 1922.

Cohen, I. Bernard. *Franklin and Newton, an Inquiry into Speculative Newtonian Experimental Science and Franklin's Work in Electricity as an Example Thereof.* Philadelphia, 1956.

Commager, Henry Steele. *The Empire of Reason: How Europe Imagined and America Realized the Enlightenment.* Garden City, N.Y., 1977.

Condorcet, Marquis Antoine-Nicolas. *Sketch for a Historical Picture of the Progress of the Human Mind.* Paris, 1794. Translated by June Barraclough. London, 1955.

Cunningham, Noble E. *In Pursuit of Reason: The Life of Thomas Jefferson.* Baton Rouge, La., 1987.

Eccles, William J. *France in America.* New York, 1972; rev. ed. Markham, Ontario, 1990.

Gay, Peter. *The Enlightenment: An Interpretation.* 2 vols. New York, 1966–1969.

Hindle, Brooke. *The Pursuit of Science in Revolutionary America, 1735–1789.* Chapel Hill, N.C., 1956.

Ketcham, Ralph. *Benjamin Franklin.* New York, 1965.
———. *From Colony to Country: The Revolution in American Thought, 1750–1820.* New York, 1974.

Malone, Dumas. *Jefferson and His Time.* 6 vols. Boston, 1948–1981.

May, Henry F. *The Enlightenment in America.* New York, 1976.

Mousnier, Roland, and Labrousse Ernest. *Le XVIIIe Siècle. Révolution intellectuelle, technique at politique (1715–1815).* Paris, 1955.

Paine, Thomas. *The Writings of Thomas Paine.* Edited by Moncure Daniel Conway. 4 vols. New York, 1894–1896.

Palmer, Robert R. *The Age of the Democratic Revolution; a Political History of Europe and America.* 2 vols. Princeton, N.J., 1959–1964.

White, Morton. *The Philosophy of the American Revolution.* New York, 1978.

Whitehead, Alfred North. *Science and the Modern World.* New York, 1925.

Wills, Garry. *Inventing America: Jefferson's Declaration of Independence.* Garden City, N.Y., 1978.

Wright, Esmond. *Franklin of Philadelphia.* Cambridge, Mass., 1986.

Ralph Ketcham

SEE ALSO **Colonial Political Culture; Colonial Political Thought; Philosophy; The Reorganization of Empires;** and **Revivalism and the Great Awakening.**

XIII

SCIENCE AND TECHNOLOGY

SCIENTIFIC INQUIRY
MEDICAL PRACTICE
TECHNOLOGY

SCIENTIFIC INQUIRY

THE BRITISH COLONIES

ONE MUST ABANDON any strictly modern notion of "science" and of "inquiry" fully to grasp the character of the intellectual activity that is the subject of this essay. The form of the encyclopedia (a term first employed in the modern sense in the mid seventeenth century) itself represented an unprecedented arrangement of facts, a magisterial ordering of knowledge that at once identified and defined the practice of science in the seventeenth and eighteenth centuries, for the age of discovery was so in two senses. Even as adventurers sought to appropriate and exploit the physical space and natural resources of North America, intellectuals undertook to systematize knowledge of the New World. In the near century before Isaac Newton offered up his *Opticks* (1704), upon which the "experimental philosophy" as it was practiced in the colonies rests, the exigencies of the marketplace and the emerging English state combined to establish the margins of knowledge. This close correlation between ideology and inquiry persists throughout the duration of English settlement.

The notion of an encyclopedia would have perplexed the first naturalists and philosophers to contemplate the problem of describing the nature of the world, new or old. Though one might broadly mark the division between natural philosophy and natural history, where the former concerned itself with the study of optics, mathematics, astronomy, magnetism, and physics, and the latter with botany, zoology, geology, and mineralogy, few early practitioners of science recognized any disciplinary boundaries. Though trained as a surgeon, John Gerard nevertheless composed the first great English botanical text, *The Herball; or, General Historie of Plantes* (1597). The Elizabethan mathematician John Dee moved effortlessly between astrology, which he viewed as a natural extension of his interest in numerology, and alchemy. Newton, also, found no incongruity between the study of optics and the pursuit of the philosophers' stone.

Colonial governor John Winthrop, Jr., of Connecticut, then, is no mere provincial type. Born in England, educated at Trinity College in Dublin and at the Inner Temple in London, drawn to medicine and alchemy, well-traveled and cosmopolitan, Winthrop numbered Samuel Hartlib, who first proposed the cultivation of silk in Virginia, and Moravian bishop Jan Amos Komensky (Comenius), the philosopher of education, among his acquaintances. During his long tenure in North America (1636–1676), Winthrop pursued the study of alchemy and astronomy with equal gusto, maintained a colonywide medical practice, imported the first telescope to New England, and became a charter member of the Royal Society and its "chief Correspondent . . . in the West."

That Winthrop should have served on two committees within the society—"Mechanical. To consider and improve all mechanical conventions," and "For Histories of Trade"—perfectly illustrates the convergence of the practice of science, which his life otherwise exemplifies, and the emergent ideology of English mercantilism, which came to full fruition during his term as governor. Winthrop's interests and activities and those of other North American naturalists and philosophers were shaped most immediately by historical processes and social and cultural imperatives of which they were at once unwitting and deliberate agents.

THE SOCIAL CONSTRUCTION OF SCIENCE

An almost giddy sense of movement and transformation characterized the intellectual life of the sixteenth and early seventeenth centuries, in which the presence—and the unknown promise—of the New World figured dramatically. While the number of Englishmen who actually viewed with their own eyes the coasts of Virginia or Maine remained small, their reports circulated widely, a part of the expanding print culture of literature, science, and medicine. Sometimes fabulous, sometimes accurate, these reports fed the imagination, and long before the settlement of the Chesapeake and the Puritan migrations of the 1620s and 1630s created a generation of actual inhabitants, America had already established in the English mind a set of images and associations.

"Plantations are amongst ancient, primitive, and heroical works," wrote Francis Bacon, in the thirty-third of his *Essays* (1612). By "plantation," he meant colony, and the fact that he chose to include this subject among other philosophical matters reveals the extent to which the idea of "colonizing" had become resonant in his time. More than a mere guideline, however, the essay exhibits several assumptions about the English mission in the New World and reveals the attitudes to which English science would conform. He goes on: "When the world was young, it begat more children; but now it is old, it begets fewer; for I may justly account new plantations to be the children of former kingdoms." A long intellectual tradition, derived from the ancients, rec-

ognized that the vitality of nature was in a steady decline. Bacon plays here both on the notion of age and infertility and on the reality of the geopolitical circumstance of his time. This metaphor of planting and its concomitant preoccupation with fertility and vitality—or infertility and vitiation—conveys the sense of urgency and necessity that surrounded the settlement and exploitation of North America and with it the drive for mastery and domination (ever present in Bacon's work) that, in turn, sustained England's commercial and political ambitions in the seventeenth century.

The most famous promoter of English colonialism and mercantilism was Richard Hakluyt, who published his *Principall Navigations, Voiages, and Discoveries of the English Nation* in 1589. Hakluyt never voyaged to the New World; his own volumes are compilations of the reports of others. Dozens of these reports filtered back, and Hakluyt dutifully transcribed and printed them, with copious annotations of his own. Additional narratives appeared in separate volumes, so that by the beginning of the seventeenth century, this literature amounted almost to a distinct genre, with its own conventions of structure and language, comprising the first natural histories of British North America.

Two of Sir Walter Raleigh's captains visited the coast of North Carolina in 1584; in *The Elizabethan's America*, Louis B. Wright collects their descriptions of a small island that they called "A New Land Like unto That of the Golden Age" (a report to Raleigh, published by Hakluyt):

This island had many goodly woods full of dear, conies, hares, and fowl, even in the midst of summer, in incredible abundance. The woods are not such as you find in Bohemia, Muscovia, or Hyrcania, barren and fruitless, but the highest and reddest cedars of the world, far bettering the cedars of the Azores, of the Indies, or of Libanus, pines, cypress, sassafras, the lentisk, or the tree that beareth the mastic, the tree that beareth the rind of black cinnamon of which Master Winter brought from the Straits of Magellan, and many other of excellent smell and quality (p. 105)

Another of Raleigh's associates was the well-educated Thomas Harriot, who wrote *A Briefe and True Report of the New Found Land of Virginia* (1588), illustrated with drawings by John White, which are the earliest firsthand images of North America. Harriot, who had some training as a naturalist, drew up his own list of the "merchantable commodities" he found in Virginia. Each specimen he identified accurately, but, more important, he described precisely the value and potential market for each item.

Captain John Smith wholly captures the sensibility of the first English explorers in his *Generall Historie of Virginia, New-England, and the Summer Isles* (1624). Smith interlards his hardheaded observations on the natural history of the Chesapeake with accounts of his encounters with the Native inhabitants, in which he reveals much about his own engagement with science. Presenting the natives with a magnetic compass, Smith reveals how central such instruments had become to the European sense of place and perspective. Smith notes that the "globe-like jewel" enabled him to demonstrate not only the "roundness of the earth and skies, the sphere of the sun, moon, and stars, and how the sun did chase the night round about the world continually," but also "the greatness of the land and sea, the diversity of nations, varieties of complexions, and how we were to them antipodes, and many other such-like matters," to a crowd of amazed natives. Yet even Smith framed his history with an eye toward English investors, who were more easily pleased by catalogs of market goods than by the curious manner of the aborigines. Powhatan and the Algonquian genuinely fascinated Smith, but his narratives went to their own purpose. The Chesapeake afforded few easily enumerated resources—at least to English eyes—and he had necessarily to produce a compelling account. What better than the story of Pocahontas's dramatic rescue of "mine host"? Native Americans became in this way a variety of commodity, exotica, something to pique the intellectual palate of his European audience.

New England promised equal rewards to those intrepid enough to attempt colonization there. After visiting Cape Cod, Nantucket, and Martha's Vineyard, and after a short stay on Cuttyhunk Island in Buzzard's Bay, John Brereton published *A Briefe and True Relation on the Discouerie of the North Part of Virginia* (1602), which carried on the tradition of the southern narratives and confined itself largely to descriptions of things palatable, potable, and portable.

This reflex unifies the literature of early American exploration and settlement, which is neither scientific nor belletristic, but rather falls somewhere between. Authors invoke with poetic intensity the great fecundity of America, the incredible diversity of its flora and fauna, the richness of its produce, but typically categorize their perceptions according to use or market value. Empiricism and the demands of commerce dictated a style of scientific inquiry that approached nature much as one enters the grocery: shopping list in hand. Early naturalists simultaneously described and appraised their subjects, and little separated Jacob Bobart the elder's *Catalogus Plantarum Horti Medici Oxoniensis* (1648) from any response John Winthrop, Jr., might have offered to the Royal Society's request for "a history of trade" in the New World.

NATURAL HISTORY AND NATURAL PHILOSOPHY

Some early observers departed notably from this convention as coastal exploration gave way to the interior settlement of British North America in the seventeenth and eighteenth centuries. The act of imagining America surrendered to the fact of being there. John Lawson, of North Carolina, and Virginians John Mitchell and the elder and younger John Claytons assembled catalogs of southern flora, corresponded indefatigably with English collectors, and in a more general fashion sustained and promoted interest among the colonial gentry in matters relating to science. The elder Clayton much praised planter William Byrd I of Westover in Virginia for his close study of Native Americans, and Byrd acted as a patron to the naturalist John Banister. His son, William Byrd II, took his election to fellow of the Royal Society seriously enough to circulate his manuscripts among English readers; but, perhaps more significantly, he stood as a patron to Mark Catesby, whose *Natural History of Carolina, Florida, and the Bahama Islands* (1731) remains a monument to North American natural history as it was practiced in the age before Linnaeus.

The Swedish botanist Carolus Linnaeus so influenced the practice of natural history in the eighteenth century that the "Linnaean system" and "proper" science became virtually synonymous terms. Confronting the vexing problem of classification—that is, how might a description of a specimen be constructed in such a way as to describe clearly and systematically its identifying traits—Linnaeus proposed two comparatively radical solutions. The first, that plants tended to group themselves according to sexual characteristics, helped to establish the utility of imposing *artificial* categories upon natural phenomena. The second, that the nomenclature of natural history might itself benefit from a similar reorganization, ultimately established the binomial system (genus/species) of classification as the basis for all descriptive taxonomy.

Catesby came of intellectual age in a world in which Cotton Mather's *Christian Philosopher* (1721) could claim respectability as a treatise on natural history, but even by midcentury such a passage as this, from "Of the Vegetables" (quoted by Kenneth Murdock in *Selections from Cotton Mather,* p. 337), would seem quaintly antique:

Indeed *all* the *Plants* in the whole *Vegetable Kingdom* are every one of them so *useful,* as to *rise up* for thy Condemnation, *O Man, who dost little Good in the World.* But sometimes the *Uses* of one *single Plant* are so many, so various, that a wise Man can scarce behold it without some *Emulation* as well as *Admiration,* or without some wishing, that if a *Metamorphosis* were to befal him, it might be into one of these. *Plutarch* reports, that the *Babylonians* out of the *Palm-tree* fetch'd more than three hundred several sorts of Commodities.

Mather's fascination with utility, his emphasis on purposefulness of nature, was amplified by his staunch Puritanism, but not overly exaggerated by it. In contrast, John Mitchell's divigations on the problem of classification in his "Dissertatio brevis de principiis botanicorum et zoologicorum" (1738) seem a world apart. Writing of plants, Mitchell followed Linnaeus and emphasized structure over application: "In determining new genera, when nature seemed to allow it, I noted the differences, closely taking into account the whole plant, as well as any more outstanding part." In adopting this systematic approach to classification, Mitchell effectively abandoned the market-driven empiricism of the early naturalists.

American intellectuals like Mitchell took a part, though often a limited one, in the European Enlightenment. Though exceptional, the career

of Benjamin Franklin conveniently symbolizes the transformation of the practice of science in provincial and pre-revolutionary America. Franklin seized quickly upon the value of the mails in creating and maintaining a far-flung network of correspondents, both domestic and foreign, and thus perfected communication among successive generations of naturalists. His own considerable fame as a natural philosopher depended largely on his ability to put his work before a European audience. Through his correspondent Peter Collinson, he submitted reports to English savants on "the properties and Effects of Electrical Matter." Collinson transmitted these papers to the Royal Society and to the English editor Edward Cave, who published them in London in 1751 and at once established Franklin as a leading theorist of the phenomenon of electricity. Franklin's contribution of the terms "plus" and "minus," "positive" and "negative," "charge" and "battery" took hold immediately, and on the strength of his science alone, Franklin gained a vast popular following in Europe. He achieved international celebrity not only for his work in experimental physics, but also for his published inquiries into diverse topics, including population growth, which Thomas Malthus found informative a half century after its publication. Others contributed less spectacularly—or not at all.

As Linnaeus's *Systema Naturae* (1737) supplanted John Ray's *Historia Generalis Plantarum* (3 vols., 1686, 1688, 1704), Newton's *Principia* (1687) and his *Opticks* replaced Charles Morton's *Compendium Physicae* (circulated in manuscript form ca. 1687–1728) in the lecture rooms of colonial colleges. Like many of their European counterparts, colleges in North America afforded only limited formal exposure to the extraordinary range of Enlightenment science—usually a single course of lectures on "natural philosophy," including, perhaps, astronomy and optics. Laboratory work, as such, commonly confined itself to demonstrations of basic physical processes: the laws of motion, the refraction of light, the generation of electricity, the creation of a vacuum, and so on. The apparatus of science in America, then, though far from primitive, was not abundant and did not support research on the scale established by the best private laboratories in Europe. Eighteenth-century Harvard

College boasted at different times several sorts of telescopes (a particular interest of the Winthrop clan in the eighteenth as well as the seventeenth centuries), an orrery, various sextants and surveying instruments, clocks, a water pump, and miscellaneous other equipment, and it was probably as well supplied as any American school. Philadelphian David Rittenhouse achieved provincial renown for his design and construction of orreries, notably one destined for Princeton University. Based on clockwork mechanism, these elegant instruments faithfully represented the motion of the planets and moons of the solar system. Extraordinarily complex and delicate, the Rittenhouse orreries stand as the highest achievement of colonial scientific technology. That they seldom functioned properly and were of comparatively small value in the classroom—proportionate to their great expense—points to one difficulty of advancing scientific education in a colonial setting, where all but the most basic apparatus was scarce, expensive, and of necessity imported. Still, goaded by convention, colleges struggled to secure the high-status instruments commonly associated with European institutions.

Colleges were not the locus of scientific practice in colonial North America; instead, gentlemen amateurs imitated their English correspondents and undertook privately to experiment and observe. One could buy contemporary works of European science in the bookshops of Boston, New York, and Philadelphia, and ships returned to Europe with certain productions native to North America—as they had John Banister's catalogs of the shrubs, seeds, and plants of Virginia, for instance (which appeared in John Ray's magnificent *Historia Generalis Plantarum*), or William Byrd's manuscript *History of the Dividing Line*, which he had circulated among his friends in the Royal Society. Science—or, rather, the disciplines of natural history and natural philosophy as they were known in the eighteenth century—enjoyed great popularity in the colonies as it did in Europe. Jonathan Edwards, author of the terrifying "Sinners in the Hands of an Angry God" (1741), wrote a treatise on "flying spiders" in his youth. His opponent in theology, the Congregationalist president of Yale College, Thomas Clap, urged a version of Arminianism from the pulpit—against Edwards, James Davenport, and

their supporters in the Awakening—and simultaneously begged his English friends to help him to publish an essay on "terrestrial comets."

These titles sound merely eccentric now, but they capture the flavor of eighteenth-century science, in which the American Englishmen acted a crucial though supporting role. American naturalists and collectors were, with few exceptions, the only observers of the vast panorama of nondescript New World flora and fauna, and they contributed impressively to the travel and scientific literature of an age obsessed with such things. Mark Catesby, for instance, had traveled widely through Virginia in the early eighteenth century. Through the influence of William Byrd II, he secured a meeting with Governor Alexander Spotswood, who, in turn, provided additional introductions; these elite connections eventually shaped the conduits through which Catesby's seeds and specimens reached English collectors and naturalists. The *History of the Dividing Line*, for all its curious humor, intended to impress and inform English aristocrats, who were themselves often, like Byrd, patrons of science.

In the north, Cadwallader Colden served in a similar capacity to promote and encourage scientific activity among gentlemen. Surveyor general of the Province of New York, for nearly forty years a member of the council, lieutenant governor, and at times acting governor, Colden was well situated to play out the life of the amateur naturalist. He maintained a broad correspondence with prominent researchers: Linnaeus, the Dutch botanist Johann Friedrich Gronovius, and Peter Collinson in Europe; Benjamin Franklin, John Mitchell, and John Bartram in America, to name but a few. Colden gave slight original research to natural history, but he tirelessly copied and transmitted information by post and encouraged a rising generation of naturalists, including his daughter, Jane Colden. He lived long enough to witness the maturation of Enlightenment science, and even if he did not fully grasp the consequences of that revolution in method, he nevertheless contributed significantly to the education of those who did.

Science, then, seemed a sort of neutral ground, where Puritan, Quaker, or Cavalier gentlemen of opposing philosophical, political, and theological views deported themselves *as* gentlemen. In the realm of learning, so reasoned the intellectuals of the Enlightenment, resided truly a "republic of letters," the ultimate realization of classical republicanism. That scientific prestige was inevitably a matter of national pride was not entirely obvious during the first century of English expansion, but as the modern state emerged from the eighteenth century, the pursuit of science reflected the changing character of nationalism. In response to this and other pressures, scientific societies first appeared in the colonies as part of a general movement to establish autonomous regional and professional identities. Amateurs, joined in common cause, attempted to regularize the informal exchange that had distinguished colonial scientific activity since first settlement and to establish a center apart from that of the Royal Society in London.

While the practice of medicine was not in any modern sense a scientific undertaking during the colonial period, it, too, was subject to the institutionalizing impulse of the 1760s. Though a great number of colonial naturalists received some training in medicine, few evinced significant research interest in medical matters. Cotton Mather's *The Angel of Bethesda,* composed in the 1720s, is perhaps the only systematic work on medicine attempted during the colonial period, but it failed to draw subscribers enough to publish and remained in manuscript until the twentieth century. Significantly under-educated by European standards, colonial practitioners rarely acquired the academic degrees of European physicians. Indeed, no American college of the colonial period offered a degree in medicine. Instead, colonial doctors combined skills that in England demarcated particular branches of medicine: apothecary, surgeon, and physician; though relatively few of the latter actually found their way to North America. More often than not, aspiring doctors apprenticed themselves to local practitioners, where they learned to cup, bleed, and purge, to amputate limbs and set bones, and to administer materia medica and dispense whatever folk remedies enjoyed local currency. A college education was not a prerequisite. Prominent physicians of the late colonial period—John Morgan and Benjamin Rush to name but two—were invariably educated abroad. Morgan's bold attempt to set American medical education on a European footing by establishing a medical school and hospital as part of Franklin's College

of Philadelphia did not altogether succeed; but his *Discourse upon the Institution of Medical Schools in America* (1765), like the incorporation of Franklin's American Philosophical Society, imparted additional momentum to the swing toward consolidation during the mid 1760s.

THE TRANSIT OF VENUS

Colonial society had not yet developed the habits of association and degree of expectation that sustained truly professional medical practice and education in Europe, which, in any event, more commonly found its provenance in the city than in the country or province. In many ways this indifference or backwardness translated to the practice of science, which found few occasions to engage the attention of the general public. In the years following the close of the Seven Years' War and Pontiac's rebellion, the British government set in motion policies that would culminate in the Stamp Act crises and, eventually, revolution. The greatest scientific event of the colonial period—at least as it touched upon the North American shore—took place against this backdrop of shifting social, economic, and political circumstances, at a time when the American English had necessarily to confront sharply the distinction implicit in that double label. In 1788 some wealthy patrons of science in Boston attempted to raise by subscription the purchase price of an orrery constructed by a watchmaker named Joseph Pope. They implored reluctant subscribers to admit "the desire of a great number of persons to retain within this state the valuable piece of mechanism, which does so much honour to the artist, and to the country to which he belongs." Twenty-five years earlier, few would have dared so directly to proclaim the desirability of a purely American science, but the episode of the transit of Venus reveals how quickly science and the prestige attending invention or discovery could be put to political service or ideological use.

A matter of pressing concern to astronomers and natural philosophers of the eighteenth century was that they obtain some accurate notion of the size of the solar system. Astronomy conceived of the spatial relation of the sun and planets in relative terms; that is, whether they were closer or farther away than the earth. In 1716 Edmund Halley devised a method to compute the solar parallax by observing the transit of Venus across the sun's disk from points widely separated on earth, but such transits were rare and occurred only twice during the eighteenth century, in 1761 and 1769. Despite heroic efforts (England sent expeditions to the Cape of Good Hope and Saint Helena in the southern Atlantic; France sent a team of observers to the East Indies; and the Russians mounted an expedition that covered nearly four thousand miles (6,400 kilometers) to set up a telescope in Tobolsk, Siberia) observations of the 1761 spectacle failed to produce the required data, and only one chance remained. Clearly international cooperation was the absolute key to the solution of the problem, but the scale of the task and the importance of the result naturally created a climate in which nations vied for prestige. Whoever best solved the problem was, by this logic, the most advanced in science. Oxford astronomer Thomas Hornsby clearly understood this reasoning, declaring "We may be assured that the several Powers of Europe will again contend which of them shall be most instrumental in contributing to the solution of this grand problem."

Colonists were aware of, but not entirely alive to, the opportunity the transit offered to them as *American* Englishmen. Franklin was skeptical from the start that any worthwhile observations should take place in North America. No single province, he wrote to the Astronomer Royal of England (Nevil Maskelyne), was "likely to have a spirit for such an undertaking, unless it be Massachusetts," and there was the additional problem of securing the appropriate instruments, for only Professor John Winthrop of Harvard (descended from the Massachusetts governor) possessed telescopes of the optical quality needed for precise measurement. Franklin also may have been discouraged by the prospect of mounting an expedition to Lake Superior, the only location in North America where both the ingress and egress of Venus would be visible. Nevertheless he contacted his close friend, Winthrop, who expressed himself as quite willing to undertake the venture. The problem of finding support for so expensive a project still loomed. The Massachusetts Assembly had funded Winthrop's observation of the 1761 tran-

sit, but the assembly had been disbanded in retaliation for its Circular Letter urging opposition to the Townshend Acts. From the start, then, the Winthrop expedition lay bound in a tangled skein of ideological controversy and political defiance.

Meanwhile, several Philadelphians had reached the conclusion that they might mount their own expedition and wrote to General Thomas Gage requesting support from his military command. Gage reasonably suggested that the Philadelphians, who had the money, combine their resources with Harvard, which had the telescope and, in the person of Winthrop, a competent observer. Neither the Cantabrigians nor the Philadelphians wanted very much to work with each other. Time and distance operated here, of course, but this does not entirely account for the reluctance. Both parties identified with local interests, and in this enacted in miniature the competition among European nations. The transit itself, and the data it would produce, was secondary to the higher purpose—as the Philadelphians saw it—of creating the first permanent observatory in North America, which carried with it considerable regional prestige—in contrast, say, to less well-endowed facilities in Massachusetts—but also promised in the long term to attract European attention.

Other provincial centers, in the outlying provinces of England, Scotland, and Ireland—towns like Manchester or Glasgow—would soon begin to form their own societies and to create their own scientific institutions on the model of the Royal Society and other London-based organizations. Likewise, Philadelphians sought to establish new institutions in response to the demands of cultural elites who were growing increasingly to resemble their counterparts at the heart of the empire. Philadelphians saw themselves simultaneously as separated from the cultural world of Boston but joined to London and other English metropolitan centers. The transit of Venus episode reveals American science in its formative state: Philadelphia intellectuals, even those opposed ideologically to English rule, nevertheless aspired to cultural forms emanating from the mother country, a reflex that exactly captures the spirit of scientific inquiry in the British colonies during the eighteenth century. Even amid the growing violence of the patriot movement, the mass actions, economic instability, and increasing threat of conflict with Great Britain, American Europeans persisted in viewing themselves as part of a greater English culture whose center was in London. In science, at least, few thought of themselves as Americans—as "new" men, in J. Hector St. John de Crèvecoeur's sense. Rather than abandon the manners of the English savants, many Americans wished to adopt them as their own.

AMERICAN VALUES AND THE "MIRROR" OF NATURE

American intellectuals could draw upon distinct customs of thought that, while not strictly related to the practice of science, did affect the ways in which they viewed nature; such customs of thought must take their place along the continuum of observation that began with Raleigh and his captains. Fed equally by the new divinity of Jonathan Edwards and the coalescing values of radical Whig ideology, the Great Awakening had given a special force to theories of environmentalism derived from the French philosophes and John Locke alike. Just as the first English naturalists translated nature into a list of commodities, eighteenth-century Americans extracted their own meaning from the landscape, and this, in turn, ordered the practice of their science. For even as the landscape shaped the mind of Thomas Jefferson (by his own admission), Jefferson and John Bartram and others like them in turn projected something of their own character into the environment, which became at once something more majestic, more sublime, more grand and wild than anyplace else in the world: a physical environment as exceptional, they imagined, as the nation that inhabited it. Although this development is not properly in the venue of colonial science, it does in an essential way represent the culmination of it.

Europeans may have been the first to take notice of the unusual style of William Bartram's natural histories of the middle Atlantic and southern regions of North America. For example, *Travels Through North and South Carolina, Georgia, East and West Florida,* published first in Philadelphia in 1791, was quickly reprinted in

London, where it found a wide circulation among English readers, notably among a young generation of English writers: Samuel Taylor Coleridge, William Wordsworth, Thomas Carlyle, and the other founders of the romantic movement in English literature. "Do you know Bartram's 'Travels'?" Thomas Carlyle wrote to Ralph Waldo Emerson after the two had met. "Treats of Florida chiefly, has a wonderful kind of floundering eloquence in it; and has grown immeasurably old. All American libraries ought to provide themselves with that kind of book; and keep them as a future *biblical* article." It is hard to know exactly what Carlyle meant by his reference to the "immeasurable" age of the book. Bartram undertook his journey to the Carolinas, Georgia, Florida, and the southwest in the early 1770s. The manuscript circulated privately, like William Byrd's diary, for almost twenty years. But Carlyle did not refer to this delay in publication. Instead, he looked back from a vantage of some fifty years on a peculiar form of enthusiasm that grasped American writers and naturalists of the revolutionary era.

Carlyle responds, we imagine, to the language of the *Travels,* which for the most part tends to the vividly descriptive—scientific in its own way—but that frequently gives way to this intriguing "floundering eloquence." He gives no examples, but one ventures to guess at what struck the Englishman most forcibly. Having returned from one jaunt, Bartram prepares for another, this time to the trading post on the Gulf of Mexico. He writes that the various scenes of nature have imprinted in his mind a "flattering contemplation" that gives "strength and agility to my steps, anxiously to press forward to the delightful fields and groves of Apalatche." This sentence rings with a wonderful resonance, and would have caught Carlyle's eye, because it invests an almost perfect romantic sensibility in the person of the narrator. The sentence follows a rigorously logical sequence from cause to effect, a fluid transit from perception to action. A "deeply graven impression" provokes an act of "contemplation" (an association of stimulus and idea within the mind). This "contemplation" generates sentiment and agile action and an anxiety to press on. The whole cycle of romantic psychology is embedded in these lines.

It is a special sort of nature that Bartram encounters in his travels, one that is surprisingly sensual and, as it were, talkative. Riding through a pine barrens, the "most dreary, solitary, desert waste" he had ever seen, he nevertheless finds a remarkable expression of harmonious life, "the symphony of the western breeze, through the bristly pine leaves, or solitary crickets screech, or at best the more social converse of the frogs, in solemn charus [sic] with the swift breezes, brought from distant fens and forests." Everywhere he turns, Bartram finds community and coherence, an ordered nature that in its forms of cooperation provides a model for human, even national interaction. After being served a good dinner of crane soup (which he does not scruple to eat), he regrets the killing of the bird, which has a higher use:

We had this fowl dressed for supper, and it made excellent soup; nevertheless, as long as I can get any other necessary food, I shall prefer their seraphic music in the ethereal skies, and my eyes and understanding gratified in observing their economy and social communities, in the expansive green savannas of Florida. (*Travels,* p. 189)

At a far remove from the Elizabethan explorers, Bartram is far closer to Jonathan Edwards—or even Charles Darwin—in a passage like this. Edwards records in his *Personal Narrative* (1808) similar moments of contentment and delight as he viewed his God "in the sun, in the moon and stars; in the clouds, and blue sky; in the grass, flowers, trees; in the water and all nature."

The evangelical Edwards sought types and antitypes in nature that would sustain his millennial aspirations: to "gather" Christians into a commonwealth of saints, to purify society, and to build upon the unspoiled plains of the Connecticut River valley a community of regenerate souls. Edwards here merely ushers in a way of viewing nature, for he could never see it as anything more than an "image and shadow" of divine things, as the irradiated expression of divine presence in the world. Bartram's vision is at once more secular—even the terms "economy" and "social community" derive from the political rhetoric of the 1760s and 1770s—and more material, for he sees in nature not a simulacrum of divinity, but a version of regulated government connected by degree to similar, human organizations. The *Travels* asserts in effect that the natural environment of America foreordains the shape of the civic order of the revolutionary republic. Thomas Jefferson, too, created a revolutionary text in *Notes on the State of Virginia,* which, like his "Declaration of Independence," attempted to set America apart from Europe; in this case he was keen first to establish at least parity—against assertions that the New World was home to creatures inferior in size and variety to the old. Jefferson quite persuasively demonstrates that the opposite is true, but the deeper question is to ask why it mattered at all.

Jefferson was himself something of a reservoir of the intellectual currents of his age; he was motivated by his own clarifying sense of patriotism to advance the cause of the exceptionality of the American environment, and this motive at times shaped his science. Jefferson had resided in France and had suffered at firsthand the patronizing bite of European intellectuals—whose chauvinism must simply have stunned him. His response in the *Notes,* then, arose from a variety of sentiments: patriotism, a loyalty to his own state of Virginia, and, one that we must not underestimate, his own desire to assert himself as an American mind engaged in the act of interpreting American natural history—an almost unprecedented role. For along with the catalog of resources and animal and vegetable productions that the *Notes* afforded the curious European reader (similar, it is worth noting, to those first accounts of the Chesapeake and New England in the seventeenth century), Jefferson included sharp and wonderfully wrought glimpses into a landscape that few Europeans could imagine: the famous description of the natural bridge, for instance, or the carefully contrived description of the passage of the Potomac River through the Blue Ridge Mountains. It is, wrote Jefferson, "one of the most stupendous scenes in nature":

You stand on a very high point of land. On your right comes up the Shenandoah, having ranged along the foot of the mountain an hundred miles to seek a vent. On your left approaches the Patowmac, in quest of a passage also. In the moment of their junction they rush together against the mountain, rend it asunder, and pass off to the sea. The first glance of this scene hurries our senses into the opinion, that this earth has been created in time, that the mountains were formed first, that the rivers began to flow afterwards, that in this place, particularly, they have been damned up by the Blue Ridge of mountains, and have formed an ocean which filled the whole valley; that continuing to rise they have at length broken over this spot, and have torn the mountain down from its summit to its base. . . . But the distant finishing which nature has given to the picture, is of a very different character. It is a true contrast to the foreground. It is as placid and delightful, as that is wild and tremendous. For the mountain being cloven asunder, she presents to your eye, through the cleft, a small catch of smooth blue horizon, at an infinite distance in the plain country, inviting you, as it were, from the riot and tumult roaring around, to pass through the breach and participate of the calm below. (*Notes*, p. 19)

The circumstances both of the writing of this passage and of its publication are noteworthy. Invited in 1781 to respond to a series of enquiries regarding the state of Virginia, Jefferson published the *Notes* privately in 1784 and 1785. An authorized edition appeared in *London* in 1787—this intended for general circulation. These facts shape the strategy of his presentation; and in this selection of what does, in fact, signify the meaning of American natural history, Jefferson sets the agenda for the first generation of post-revolutionary naturalists. Like Bartram, and, in a curious way, like Mather and the earliest naturalists, Jefferson avoids the synthetic taxonomy of Linnaeus—toward which he was at times hostile. Instead he searches out correspondences, that is, the way in which natural processes anticipate the historical moment of which he was part, even as they validate the progress of republican civilization in the New World. The passage above is central to the science of the *Notes* and thus to American science at the close of the eighteenth century. Jefferson invokes the now-commonplace association of physical nature with a state of mind, but moves from there to a truly grand theory of geology—not original, but current with common practice. The earth is old and was not created of a piece. Rivers and other natural forces are transforming it, and the evidence of this transformation contributes to a natural history of progressive development. This change is not steady, but a progress punctuated by cataclysmic events. In contrast to the sublime ruggedness and disarray of the foreground—the physi-

cal record of great natural forces in ancient conflict—is the placid background, the "smooth blue horizon" and the "plain country." This "inviting" prospect attracts the eye, just as the flow of the river draws one irresistibly to the sea.

Jefferson advances in this seemingly neutral description of a geological phenomena a theory of history, one that is revolutionary and progressive. As natural history serves Bartram, geology becomes here for Jefferson a medium through which to examine a more fundamental plane of existence. Forces analogous to those that rend mountains unseat empires; neither granite nor proclamations check the natural course of history. An expanding population exerts pressure in its own right, and will, finally, find free passage. Jefferson emphasizes how natural is this event, how inevitable, and how fully dictated by natural law. The natural outcome of such expansion is a transformed landscape, one characterized by domesticity and productivity: "placid and delightful." In this short passage, one of many in the *Notes*, Jefferson encapsulates a whole universe of ideological commitment, to his own historical mission, to that of his nation, and to the prosperous future that he believed was its certain destiny—despite his expressing elsewhere a variety of cautious doubts. His enthusiasm rings out in his concluding utterance that "this scene is worth a voyage across the Atlantic."

We see in the example of Jefferson and Bartram, and in the generations of naturalists that preceded them, that science never constituted an activity separate from society and the values that sustain it. The first explorers were compelled to see one sort of America; the last colonial naturalists were equally obliged to construct quite another. Throughout the colonial period, the North American environment mirrored the peculiar character of American intellectuals, even as it influenced the shape of their science. Desperate at the end of the eighteenth century to validate the principles for which a revolution was waged, uncertain (in some respects) whether these endured outside the short-lived expression of rhetoric, Americans deployed science to discover in nature a permanent corollary to their values. This urge to discover, and ultimately to create or invent, such reassuring messages of transcendental approval, born in colony and in province, would preoccupy the naturalists of the early republic, who felt perhaps more urgently the need to recover the lessons, so obvious to Bartram or Jefferson, whispered from the "expansive green savannas of Florida."

BIBLIOGRAPHY

Bartram, William. *The Travels of William Bartram.* Edited by Mark Van Doren. New York, 1955.

Bedini, Silvio. *Thinkers and Tinkers: Early American Men of Science.* New York, 1975.

Bell, Whitfield. *Early American Science: Needs and Opportunities for Study.* Chapel Hill, N.C., 1955.

Cohen, I. Bernard. *Franklin and Newton: An Inquiry into Speculative Newtonian Experimental Science and Franklin's Work in Electricity as an Example Thereof.* Philadelphia, 1956.

———. *The Newtonian Revolution: With Illustrations of the Transformation of Scientific Ideas.* New York, 1980.

Crosland, Maurice P., ed. *The Emergence of Science in Western Europe.* New York, 1976.

Greene, John C. *American Science in the Age of Jefferson.* Ames, Iowa, 1984.

Hall, Marie Boas. *Promoting Experimental Learning: Experiment and the Royal Society, 1660–1727.* New York, 1991.

Hindle, Brooke. *David Rittenhouse.* Princeton, N.J., 1964.

———. *The Pursuit of Science in Revolutionary America, 1735–1789.* Chapel Hill, N.C., 1956.

Inkster, Ian, and Jack Morrell, eds. *Metropolis and Province: Science in British Culture, 1780–1850.* Philadelphia, 1983.

Jefferson, Thomas. *Notes on the State of Virginia.* Edited by William Peden. Chapel Hill, N.C., 1955.

Mather, Cotton. *Selections from Cotton Mather.* Edited by Kenneth B. Murdock. New York, 1926.

Miller, Perry, and Thomas H. Johnson, eds. *The Puritans.* Rev. ed. 2 vols. New York, 1963.

Oleson, Alexandra, and Sanborn C. Brown. *The Pursuit of Knowledge in the Early American Republic: American Scientific and Learned Societies from Colonial Times to the Civil War.* Baltimore, Md., 1976.

Porter, Roy. *The Making of Geology: Earth Science in Britain, 1660–1815.* New York, 1977.

Stearns, Raymond Phineas. *Science in the British Colonies of America.* Urbana, Ill., 1970.

Thackray, Arnold, and Jack Morrell. *Gentlemen of Science: Early Years of the British Association for the Advancement of Science.* New York, 1981.

Wright, Louis B., ed. *The Elizabethan's America: A Collection of Early Reports by Englishmen on the New World.* Cambridge, Mass., 1965.

Chandos Michael Brown

SEE ALSO **Colonial Political Thought; The Enlightenment; Higher Education; Libraries and Learned Societies; Medical Practice, Colonial Medicine; Philosophy; and Technology.**

THE DUTCH COLONY

SCIENTIFIC INQUIRY IN NEW Netherland consisted chiefly of mapping and charting the land and its waters and describing its flora and fauna and the Native Americans who inhabited it.

The Low Countries were in the forefront of European cartography in the sixteenth and seventeenth centuries. The sixteenth-century Flemish cartographer Gerardus Mercator (1512–1594) was the most notable geographer of his time. His Mercator map, a straight-line projection on a chart of the curved lines of longitude and latitude on a globe, was especially useful to mariners, who needed to chart a straight course. Later, rival cartographic firms founded by Judocus Hondius (1563–1612) and Willem Janszoon Blaeu (1571–1638), both located in Amsterdam, published globes, maps, and *paskaarten* (sea charts). Their maps were based on the observations and charts of European explorers, including those who explored the coast of New Netherland.

Henry Hudson (*c.* 1565–1611), the English navigator, came to America in 1609 on his third voyage to discover a northern passage to the Orient for the Dutch East India Company. Because of a feared mutiny among his crew, on the return trip Hudson stopped at Dartmouth, England, rather than going directly to the Netherlands. He sent a brief summary of his voyage to the directors of the company; however, the English did not allow him to report fully any of his discoveries, since he had not obtained permission from the king of England for his foreign service.

MAPS AND CHARTS

The earliest maps and charts of New Netherland came from the observations of the fur traders and explorers sent by Dutch merchants between Hudson's voyage in 1609 and the founding of the Dutch West India Company in 1621. One of them was Captain Adriaen Block, who made several trips to New Netherland during this period. The Figurative Map, presented to the States-General by thirteen merchants of Amsterdam and Hoorn, was based on information Block had gathered on his trip along the coast of North America in the spring of 1614. It was the first map to use the name New Netherland. Another of these early traders and explorers was Cornelis Hendricksen, who spent three years in America. The map he is thought to have drawn was submitted by his patrons in 1616 as part of their petition to the States-General for a trading privilege. Hendricksen obtained information about the tribes living along the Susquehanna River from several Dutch traders he ransomed from the Indians.

NATURE AND INDIAN CULTURE

Information provided by Block and Hendricksen was used by promotional writers such as Johan de Laet (1582–1649). De Laet was a director of the West India Company and a shareholder in the patroonships of Swanendael and Rensselaerswyck, but he never visited New Netherland in person. In 1625 he published *New World, or Descriptions of the West Indies*. The book is especially important because in it de Laet quoted extracts from the lost journal of Henry Hudson. It also contains descriptions of the geography of New Netherland, the customs and manners of the Indians, maps and charts, and in later editions, plates of American animals and plants. De Laet was a botanist of some note; Carolus Linnaeus named a botanical species after him. Plant specimens sent from New Netherland at his request were planted in the medical garden at the University of Leyden. He also wrote two small books

in which he attempted to refute Hugo Grotius's theory that the American Indians were descended from Europeans.

While de Laet wrote about America from afar, another writer, Adriaen van der Donck (1620?–1655), lived in New Netherland. Because he assisted Director General Willem Kieft in making peace with the Mohawk Indians, van der Donck was rewarded in 1646 with a land patent that included present-day Yonkers. The modern place-name is derived from van der Donck's title *Jonkheer*, a common title for a gentleman farmer. Van der Donck served on the colony's Board of Nine Men and was probably the author of a protest written in 1649 and titled the *Remonstrance of New Netherland*, which not only listed the charges against Director General Peter Stuyvesant but also described the colony. It became a preliminary sketch for his later work, *A Description of New Netherland*. In 1649 van der Donck led a delegation that traveled to the Hague to take its protest against Stuyvesant and the West India Company before the States-General. He remained in the Netherlands until 1653, during which time he wrote his *Description of New Netherland*. It was not published until 1655, the year van der Donck died at about the age of thirty-five.

It has been noted that van der Donck took some of the information in his *Description* from published sources without attribution. While this might be considered plagiarism today, it was common practice during the seventeenth century. At any rate much of the book came from his own experiences in America. Although van der Donck was not trained as a scientist and his purpose in writing was to encourage settlers to come to the colony, the book does contain observations on the land, climate, flora and fauna, and culture of the Indians. Some of it is folklore:

I have also been frequently told by the Mohawk Indians, that far in the interior parts of the country, there were animals which were seldom seen, of the size and form of horses, with cloven hoofs, having one horn in the forehead, from a foot and a half to two feet in length, and that because of their fleetness and strength they were seldom caught or ensnared. I have never seen any certain token or sign of such animals, but that such creatures exist in the country, is supported by the concurrent declarations of the Indian hunters. (van der Donck. *Description*, p. 46)

In 1628 Isaak de Rasieres, who was the chief commercial agent and secretary of the colony of New Netherland, repeated similar Indian legends about unicorn-like creatures.

The book also contains a detailed section on the North American beaver, which was central to the fur trade. Van der Donck mentions his own experiments to determine whether castor, a brownish substance secreted by glands in the groin of the beaver and prized for its medicinal properties, came from the male or female beaver.

It happened at this time that beavers were found not far from my residence, and several were brought to me by the Indian hunters, unopened and fresh; these I opened and examined with great care for the real castor cods, but to no purpose. . . . At last, a discreet Indian hunter, who had assisted me in my experimental dissections, . . . advised the opening of a female beaver. (van der Donck, *Description*, p. 119)

Van der Donck took this advice and found the glands he was looking for. He showed them to Doctor Johannes la Montagne, the resident physician in New Netherland, for verification. "Afterwards I have opened more beavers with the like result," he wrote, concluding that "therefore, without prejudice to the feelings of any person, I am decidedly of opinion, that the real *castorium* is found in the females and not in the males."

Seventeenth-century science must be defined by different criteria than the science of today. Many of the above-mentioned activities combined observation with folklore, politics, and art. Yet it all contributed to expanding European knowledge of the natural world in America and the culture of Native Americans.

BIBLIOGRAPHY

Deak, Gloria Gilda. *Picturing America, 1497–1899: Prints, Maps, and Drawings Bearing on the New World Discoveries and on the Development of the Territory that Is Now the United States.* 2 vols. Princeton, N.J., 1988. Contains early prints, maps, and drawings from the print and photograph collections of the New York Public Library, including maps by Block, Hendricksen, Hondius, and Blaeu.

de Laet, Johan. "From the 'New World' by Johan de Laet, 1625, 1630, 1633, 1640." In *Narratives of New Netherland, 1609–1664,* edited by J. Franklin Jameson. New York, 1909. Contains selections pertaining to New Netherland from the four editions of de Laet's promotional book, *New World, or Descriptions of the West Indies.* Includes extracts from the lost journal of Henry Hudson.

Donck, Adriaen van der. *A Description of the New Netherlands.* Edited by Thomas F. O'Donnell. Syracuse, N.Y., 1968. A reprint of the most detailed eyewitness description of New Netherland by the first lawyer in the colony, originally published in 1655.

Stokes, I. N. Phelps. *The Iconography of Manhattan Island, 1498–1909.* Vol. 1. New York, 1916. Contains early maps and prints of New Netherland and extended essays on the Dutch cartography of America.

David Steven Cohen

SEE ALSO **Technology**

THE FRENCH COLONIES

IN 1749 PETER KALM, a Swedish professor of natural history sent to North America in search of hardy seeds and plants, was astonished at the apparent breadth and organization of scientific inquiry in New France. "Great efforts are made here for the advancement of natural history," he wrote; and so great was his surprise that he quite forgot the men whom he had earlier met in British America. In New France, he claimed, "people of distinction had . . . in general a much greater taste for natural history and other learning than in the English colonies."

What struck Kalm so forcefully was that scientific inquiry in New France was not a private matter but appeared to be inspired and supported by the state. Commanders at remote fur trading posts received written instructions concerning the collection of minerals, roots, and seed specimens and the cultivation of plants for shipment to Paris. They were advised how to observe and collect animals and enjoined to inquire into the uses that Indians made of medicinal plants. Officers were even instructed to identify for promotion or later reward private soldiers who displayed zeal and diligence in furthering the aims of these instructions. But though the

French state supported scientific inquiry in the colonies, the beneficial effect of such encouragement was not all that Kalm imagined.

Scientific inquiry in New France centered on questions concerning the earth's measurement (geodesy) and natural history (biology). These fields of study included astronomy, cartography, and hydrography in the first instance, and meteorology and ethnography in the second. Though curiosity stimulated these inquiries, utility also motivated French scientific research. It also reflected the reformulation of notions that came to characterize the Scientific Revolution in the seventeenth century and the appearance of science as organized social activity inspired and supported by the state.

THE FIRST ATTEMPTS

The earliest observations of nature in the New World occurred in the sixteenth century and accompanied the Scientific Revolution itself. They were made within prevailing categories of thought about nature, which included a strong sense of the occult and of the presence of mysterious forces in nature. Astrology was more important than astronomy, though accurate measurement was essential to both. The facts of nature were just as likely to include an amphibious horselike fish reported by Jacques Cartier at the mouth of the Moisie River, inexplicable deflections of the compass, or a new species of whale. Moreover, astrology continued to assert a strong influence long afterward. Upon recording the passage of a comet across the winter skies of Quebec from January to March 1661, Father Jérôme Lalemant noted that to many colonists it portended an Iroquois invasion, an idea repeated twenty-one years later by Father Jean de Lamberville after a similar sighting.

Although the early explorers of Canada were professional navigators, they often saw only what they sought: gold, silver, rubies, cloves, nutmeg, and cinnamon. The only observations of that age that might be termed scientific concerned navigators' attempts to locate themselves in the New World relative to the Old.

Observations using sea astrolabes and crossstaffs in conjunction with an agreed system of latitude and longitude (such as provided by Ptolemy's world system) enabled explorers to locate their positions once they reached land. In the absence of reliable timekeepers, they relied on dead reckoning. Navigators, probably including Christopher Columbus, also depended upon eclipses of the moon, observing the local time of the beginning or end of an event and comparing it to previously predicted times of occurrence at a European location. Knowing that one hour was equivalent to fifteen degrees of longitude enabled any navigator to determine his new meridian. The accuracy of his conclusion, however, depended on variables from which errors could not be removed: the determination of local time (a function of the precision of the instrument and the skill of the observer), and the reliability of the predictive tables. The second variable could be removed by replacing the tables with simultaneous observations of a lunar eclipse from two different points on the earth's surface.

The work of Samuel de Champlain marked the culmination of Renaissance geography. No other contemporary even approached the quality and extent of his mapping of North America. He traced over one thousand miles (sixteen hundred kilometers) of Atlantic coastline, and his general map of 1612 was the first to delineate the shores of northeastern North America with any degree of accuracy. In 1608 Champlain founded Quebec, and during the next two decades he penetrated deep into the interior of the continent, being credited with discovering Lake Huron and the entrance to Lake Superior. Champlain's maps became the bases of all maps of New France until long after his death.

THE JESUITS

After 1632 missionaries of the Society of Jesus became the primary geographers of New France. Others also contributed, but chiefly Jesuit missionaries, often in conjunction with Canadian fur traders, unrolled the map of North America to nearly ninety-five degrees west longitude. During the seventeenth century Jesuit missionaries in New France also observed no less than ten lunar and seven solar eclipses and several comets. In all, it was a magnificent achievement unmatched by any other group of explorers in American history.

While Jesuit missionaries were recruited from among the best-educated men in Europe, their geographical and cartographic work nonetheless involved less speculative thought than careful measurement. This was just as well, for their theoretical notions remained firmly tied to the Aristotelian corpus of natural philosophy until the early eighteenth century, when they shifted to Cartesian texts. The Jesuit "Relation" for 1664–1665 contains an entire chapter, "On Comets and Extraordinary Signs Which Have Appeared at Quebec and Environs." While noting the passage of two comets and recording their daily positions in degrees, minutes, and sometimes seconds of arc, with respect to several stars, the account also records the comets' astrological significance. Here is captured the profound conflict between astrology and astronomy during the seventeenth century that reminds us not to overemphasize the impact of scientific method on contemporary thought.

A course in astronomy taught at the Collège des Jésuites at Quebec in 1677 rejected the Copernican heliocentric theory of planetary rotation as contrary to Holy Scripture. More than three-quarters of a century later, in 1754, the situation had changed only to the extent of allowing the Copernican system to be taught as a hypothesis. Students learned the proposition that the Earth orbited about the sun even if, in not conforming to the Bible, the statement was considered false.

Even though the work of Jesuit missionaries was often of high quality, it was only a means to another end: the conversion of natives. They studied Indians carefully, but their aim in geographical observation was to locate Indian tribes as much as to describe a continent.

As well-educated men, however, the Jesuits did contribute during the middle decades of the seventeenth century to the development of surveying and the training of ships' pilots in New France. Both activities required skilled practitioners of accurate measurement. The strong utilitarian aspect of the work appealed to Jesuit desires to assist in the formation of community.

In 1634 Jean Bourdon arrived in New France and established the first standard units of measurement, the *perche* and the arpent of Paris of 5.85 and 58.5 meters (roughly 6.5 and 64.5 yards), respectively. During the early years, when New France numbered about three hundred souls, Bourdon surveyed properties with a compass and a wheel for direction and distance, but on New Year's Day 1646, the Jesuit fathers gave him a Galilean telescope on which a compass had been mounted. Designated the governor's engineer, Bourdon advanced from laying out streets in Quebec to constructing the first cadastral map of the colony and directing construction of the governor's official residence and other forts.

As the population grew, disputes increased along with the number of land grants. Surveying needed to be controlled and instruments inspected. Following Bourdon's death in 1668, colonial authorities appointed a lay brother with the Jesuits, Martin Boutet de Saint-Martin, to license aspiring surveyors and regulate their instruments. He had begun to teach mathematics in the Collège des Jésuites, where he also taught navigation to a few select pupils destined to become masters and pilots in the colony. During the 1660s, however, special events in France rapidly transformed the colony, and gave a major stimulus to scientific inquiry.

PARIS ACADEMY OF SCIENCES

In 1661 Louis XIV announced that henceforth he would rule as well as reign. New France soon ceased to be a proprietary colony and in 1663 became a royal province under the direct authority of the king and his minister Jean-Baptiste Colbert. Two years later, the Royal Academy of Sciences, called by some historians the Paris Academy, was officially established under the agency of the same Colbert, who was also busily engaged in creating a permanent French navy. One man became responsible for colonies, science, and the navy, and the direction of all three was forever altered.

The first evidence of the change appeared in New France during the 1670s when Boutet was transformed from a simple teacher of mathematics into an instructor of hydrography and examiner and licenser of the colony's surveyors and their instruments. During the same decade, Canadian and French explorers such as Louis Jolliet, Father Jacques Marquette, and René-Robert Cavalier de La Salle rapidly penetrated the interior of North America as far west as the Mississippi River and north to Hudson Bay, discovering new Indians, flora, and fauna.

The Royal Academy of Sciences was organized to undertake research into basic scientific questions according to an agenda established by the state. Prominent among them was the determination of longitude at sea. The Academy was a government-sponsored brain trust whose elite membership was not confined to Frenchmen. It was not an educational or propagandizing agency. Owing to generous financial support, the members of the Academy were able to undertake large projects. As a result, excellent astronomical, cartographical, and hydrographical work was carried out in New France and long remained unsurpassed in the New World.

As time went on, however, the Academy gradually became transformed into a regulatory body, deciding what might, or might not, be a legitimate subject of investigation, authorizing (and thereby delaying, limiting, and even retarding) scientific publication, and diverting members from science to the investigation of technical inventions at best and trivia at worst. Encouraging others, developing broad channels of communication, spreading news of experiments, and stimulating debate never composed part of the Academy's mandate. The well-financed, increasingly influential, but rigidly structured Royal Academy did not answer all the needs of seventeenth-century science, which, in the words of historian Richard Westfall, was still largely informal and frequently chaotic. Subsequent developments in nautical science in New France well illustrate the evolution of French cartography from dominance at the end of the seventeenth century to decline and even stagnation by the middle of the next.

Further reward came to Martin Boutet ten years after his first appointment. In 1678 he was appointed royal engineer in the colony. But he was succeeded in that capacity by Jean-Baptiste-Louis Franquelin, who had been constructing maps of New France for Governor General Louis de Buade de Frontenac since 1674. The new absolute government needed information on which to base its policies. In 1687, four years after Boutet's death, Franquelin also succeeded to Boutet's post as professor of hydrography, but it is not clear that he ever taught mathe-matics at the Collège des Jésuites or trained masters and pilots in navigation. Franquelin was little more than a draftsman. He never traveled west of Montreal himself, and his famous maps of the interior of North America, of which twenty-four have survived, are remarkable for their beauty rather than scientific accuracy. Moreover, during the years 1689–1691, his duties as engineer, working on the fortifications of Quebec and preparing maps for a proposed invasion of New England, occupied most of his time. Franquelin left New France in 1692, but state-supported scientific inquiry had declined during his periods in office.

He was succeeded three years later as royal hydrographer by Louis Jolliet, one of Canada's foremost explorers, but the post had lost much of its importance. The Paris Academy had imposed a highly centralized organization on scientific inquiry that reached to the colonies and reduced the influence of other potentially useful positions. The appointment of colonists as harbormasters at Quebec and Louisbourg, for example, did little to improve hydrographic knowledge or increase chart production, for surveys by such men were not carried out under the aegis of the Academy and most remained in colonial and naval archives.

The Academy's ventures were not all bad. Indeed, it sponsored a voyage to Acadia (modern Nova Scotia and New Brunswick) in 1670 that may well be called the first modern scientific expedition to North America. But the expedition of Jean Richer, one of the Academy's "élève astronomes," did not meet with success. Its first mission, to test one of Christiaan Huyghens's marine clocks, failed when the experimental clock stopped soon after leaving France. The expedition was also to test a method for finding longitude based on lunar distances, but no trace of that experiment has ever been found. Richer's sole achievement was to fix the latitude of two points on the coast of present-day Maine and New Brunswick and report his observations in seconds of arc, a radically new departure, reflecting his use of telescopically mounted instruments equipped with filar micrometers, such as those devised a few years earlier by Abbé Jean Picard.

Despite its modest results, the expedition illustrates how the Academy drew America into its program to measure the earth. But the program itself illustrates another important point about French scientific inquiry. Although the measurement of the earth had great commercial, political, or military significance, it was conceived of as a purely scientific problem. The question of determining longitude at sea, however, was a practical problem of immense difficulty and enormous significance. Yet French science had not been organized to solve a single question but to adjudicate among many in need of support.

Fifteen years later, another scientist, Jean Deshayes, arrived in New France to carry out a hydrographic survey, construct a nautical chart of the Saint Lawrence River, and establish a meridian at Quebec. Already associated with the Paris Academy as a corresponding member and a veteran of overseas expeditions, Deshayes met with considerable success in the colony. He reached New France in August 1685 armed with a commission as royal hydrographer. In the late summer he accompanied the new governor on a rapid journey some 350 miles (560 kilometers) up the Saint Lawrence River from Quebec to Lake Ontario. Deshayes traced the course of the river, marked the inhabited locations, and frequently halted to observe latitudes. He was unable to establish stations for angles and obtained latitudes by sighting on the polestar with a quadrant, reporting them only to the nearest five minutes of arc. He met with better fortune on 11 December when he observed a lunar eclipse at Quebec and established a meridian of longitude. As a result the colonial capital appeared as the only astronomically determined position north of Mexico City in the Western Hemisphere in Giovanni Domenico Cassini's great world planisphere published in 1696.

A mathematician and surveyor, Deshayes was completely at home with up-to-date instruments. During the next spring and summer, he carried out a major hydrographic survey of the Saint Lawrence River, employing a plane table equipped with fixed and movable telescopes. Through the use of such optically advanced instruments, the French came to dominate topographical surveying and cartography during the late seventeenth century. But the fate of his work reveals the other side of scientific inquiry in the

colonies. A chart appeared fourteen years later about 1700, only after receiving the Academy's official approval. A second edition accompanied by new sailing directions was issued in 1715, but the excellence of the survey was overshadowed by the long delay before initial publication and its limited availability to seafarers, for the chart was published in Paris rather than in a seaport.

The location of France's map-publishing industry in Paris, close to scientists and far from the practical concerns of merchants and seafarers, failed to stimulate a commercial chart-printing industry, despite the excellent quality of French topographical and hydrographic surveying. Cheaply produced, outdated Dutch sea charts continued to dominate the French market to such an extent that it was not until about 1750 that the French navy began to publish its own charts. The organization of French geographic inquiry under the aegis of the Academy encouraged speculative cartography which accounts for the growing interest in a Mer de l'Ouest (Western Sea) that was thought to exist in western North America between forty and sixty degrees north latitudes. Even though Father Charlevoix was sent to America in 1720 to find out everything he could about the Mer de l'Ouest and concluded that it might exist, the French government was no longer interested. Perhaps this was why French mapmakers continued to publish maps of America showing the nonexistent sea long afterwards.

In 1702 Deshayes returned to New France where he ended his few remaining years as professor of hydrography. But the state's demands for surveying, mapmaking, and teaching clashed, leading to a decline in the field of scientific inquiry. Following his death in 1706, the teaching of hydrography was confined to the Jesuits, while mapping and surveying fell increasingly to naval officers and colonial harbormasters who, though proficient, were far from the men and prestige associated with the Paris Academy. In 1737 the professor of hydrography at the Collège des Jésuites was reported to be so occupied with his obligations as principal and a missionary that he taught only the barest essentials. Indeed, nautical science, astronomy, and cartography in New France all suffered from constraints imposed by the French organization of scientific inquiry during the eighteenth century.

The appearance of Father Joseph-Pierre de Bonnécamps and Roland-Michel Barrin, marquis de La Galissonière, during the 1740s introduced a brief revival. Father de Bonnécamps was appointed professor of hydrography at the Collège des Jésuites in 1744. He sought to provide up-to-date instruction for his future pupils by obtaining advanced instruments for them. Four years later he was still requesting the same instruments: a seconds pendulum, an observing telescope, a quadrant with a three-foot radius equipped with a telescope rather than sighting vanes, and a new lodestone. The following year, when Peter Kalm was in New France, Bonnécamps was unable to take any accurate astronomical observations during his exploration of the Ohio Valley, because he still lacked his instruments and could not rely even on the accuracy of his watch.

The encouragement of science attested to by Kalm was chiefly due to one man, the marquis de La Galissonière, commander-in-chief and interim governor of the colony from 1747 to 1750. La Galissonière had a surprising knowledge of all branches of science, especially natural history, and was its greatest promoter in the colony. Following his departure in 1749 the old constraints reappeared.

On the other hand, La Galissonière was subsequently appointed director of the French navy's hydrographic office and nominated to the Anglo-French commission established to settle the boundary claims between Acadia and Nova Scotia. The work of these institutions quickly led to the first accurate surveys of the coast of Nova Scotia based on astronomical observations. The work was carried out in 1750–1751 by Joseph-Bernard de Chabert de Cogolin, a naval ensign who later went on to become perhaps the most distinguished French hydrographer of the ancien régime.

The chief significance of the survey of the Nova Scotian coast was threefold. First, it illustrated that scientific inquiry in New France continued to be initiated in France. Second, by the middle of the eighteenth century the organization of science under the Royal Academy had become so constraining that the French navy was moving to develop its own ability to initiate and undertake scientific inquiry. Finally, the work of men like La Galissonière mattered more than rules and regulations of institutions.

THE STUDY OF NATURE

An examination of the development of natural history in New France, on the other hand, suggests that while institutions might be constraining, only they could provide any general plan of action, direction, or long-term support. The ever-increasing number of plants and animals continually being discovered in the New World profoundly affected the way Europeans thought about nature. Natural historians in the French colonies played small but significant roles in the collective enterprise that contributed to the most significant speculative thought concerning the theory of generation. During the eighteenth century most of this was carried out in institutions established under royal auspices.

Seventeenth- and eighteenth-century natural philosophers were chiefly concerned with taxonomy, or the classification of animals, plants, and minerals. They expended their greatest efforts to find similarities among specimens, and though most agreed that minerals belonged to their study, they disagreed on how life ought to be classified.

In France, the strong influence of René Descartes dominated speculation concerning nature. There the great naturalists of the age led a strong reaction against artificial taxonomies, such as those of Carl Linnaeus (von Linné). They were influenced, in part, by the major expansion of plant and animal specimens sent from America that challenged attempts to impose hierarchical concepts on nature, which they conceived of both as uniform and individual.

The great naturalists of the age—Joseph Pitton de Tournefort, and Georges Louis Leclerc de Buffon, keepers of the royal gardens at Paris; Antoine and Bernard de Jussieu, of the royal gardens at Trianon; and their nephew, Antoine-Laurent de Jussieu—corresponded with men in Canada and elsewhere in America while they advanced a "natural" system of classification based on the belief that there existed "real" features in nature independent of observers. Slowly they developed the modern sciences of plant pathology and comparative anatomy.

Natural history was closely tied to medicine, owing to the deep interest in herbal plants and the organization of medical education where botany was taught. Around 1660 Parisian medical theory asserted that God put in every area of the world plants to cure the diseases incident therein. This promoted botanizing among physicians. The few natural historians in the French colonies were physicians who sought out new specimens for description and dispatch to France. They participated in scientific inquiry from a distance. Their position was modest, and their science was chaotic. Nonetheless their contribution was important. For it was from the far reaches of the world that man confirmed the critical notion of the uniformity of species.

Interest in natural history went back to the earliest days of French exploration during the early sixteenth century, when the human beings inhabiting the New World led to endless speculation. Jacques Cartier reported learning of pygmies, of people possessing no anus, and others having only one leg. Human specimens were among the first to be brought to Europe initiating a never-ending fascination with America's indigenous inhabitants.

Long before the establishment of the first permanent French settlement, Canadian plant specimens found a home in the herbal garden of the medical faculty of the University of Paris. Curiosity extended to everything imaginable. But interest remained episodic, unfocused, and unplanned, swinging from a rage for the exotic to inquiries into utility. The King's Garden at Paris owed its origin to the creation of the Royal Garden of Medicinal Plants in 1626 and it was here that almost all American specimens were sent. The first book on North America flora, *Canadensium Plantarum Aliarumque Nondum Editarum Historia,* published by a Parisian doctor, Jacques Philippe Cornuti, appeared in 1635 and described some one hundred plants.

A generation later a Jesuit missionary, Louis Nicolas, who labored in Canada between 1664 and 1675, left descriptions of nearly two hundred plants accompanied by a collection of illustrations. The depictions often included notes on the use made of the plants by Indians, which reflects well on Nicolas, for most missionaries saw Indian shamans as obstacles to conversion and linked their use of medicinal plants to sorcery and witchcraft. Such preconceived notions did not affect Louis-Armand de Lom d'Arce (active in the 1680s), who observed that there was no wound or dislocation that Indians could not cure with their simples and plants.

Without organization, natural history inquiry in French America would never have done more than satisfy curiosity. Just as the Royal Academy of Sciences transformed the organization of the physical sciences, it led to significant changes in the pursuit of the natural sciences. During the 1670s the Royal Garden at Paris became an experimental laboratory for academicians, and the public lectures on anatomy and botany given there transformed the garden into one of the strongholds of modern critical inquiry. The impetus that the new direction of the gardens and its close connection to the teaching of medicine gave to natural history can be seen in the careers of two doctors who worked in New France during the late seventeenth and early eighteenth centuries.

Michel Sarrazin, a naval surgeon, came to Canada in 1685 but returned to France nine years later in order to complete his studies in medicine. While in Paris he met Tournefort, who taught at the Royal Garden at Paris between 1683 and 1708 and was transforming the garden from a regulating body established to control the trade and distribution of herbal medicines to a center for the collection and study of botanical specimens. Tournefort had just published his major work, *Éléments de botanique* (1694), in which he broke with the older "artificial" system and outlined a new taxonomy that aimed to describe the natural order of nature. Tournefort befriended Sarrazin, asking him to write once he returned to Canada as royal physician in 1697. Thanks to the same influence, two years later Sarrazin became an official corresponding member of the Paris Academy charged with collecting natural history specimens.

During the next thirty-five years Sarrazin served the interests of science. But although it appeared to be his first love, the work was neither appreciated by colonial officials nor sufficiently rewarded in Sarrazin's own eyes. Authorities criticized his interest in natural history, fearing that any recognition or rewards might draw him back to France and leave the colony in the hands of barber surgeons without the ministrations of a physician. Sarrazin, on the other hand, thought his post as royal physician insufficiently rewarding and made several bad business decisions hoping to increase his wealth and prestige. During the last years of his life, he constantly appealed for recognition, requesting membership in the Paris Academy. But in spite of his difficulties and disappointments over lack of personal reward, Sarrazin never stopped working.

His contribution to the knowledge of American flora and fauna remains impressive, but it was his association with the Academy that made it significant. Taxonomy requires access to enormous amounts of data, which was then held only in the greatest collections in Europe. Without such a connection no one in America could have made a significant contribution to a science still in the process of becoming. Sarrazin's botanical work first appeared in Tournefort's addenda to his *Éléments,* published in 1700. His work on the natural and anatomical history of the beaver appeared in the *Mémoires* (or annual reports) of the Academy for 1704. Reports of his descriptions and dissections of the wolverine, porcupine, muskrat, seal, marmot, and skunk appeared in later editions.

Shortly after 1700 Tournefort turned his correspondence with Sarrazin over to Sébastien Vaillant, a demonstrator of plants at the Royal Garden whose major contribution established plant sexuality in France. In 1708, in an important advance in colonial botany, Sarrazin and Vaillant jointly authored a catalog or history of plants of Canada that identified, classified, and named over two hundred plants. Sarrazin also corresponded with Antoine de Jussieu and, following Tournefort's and later Vaillant's death, with René-Antoine Ferchault de Réaumur.

Sarrazin and others annually loaded their carefully gathered and prepared specimens together with descriptive notes and reports on board ships for dispatch to Paris. In the French capital the recipients classified them by genus and species, elaborating where possible. They gratefully acknowledged their correspondents by naming new species after them and arranging to publish their work in reports of the Academy. Thus, Tournefort named the most original botanical specimen to arrive from Sarrazin, a family of insect-eating plants, Sarraceniaceae. The best-known, *Sarracenia purpurea,* is the common pitcher plant, found in sphagnum bogs and wet peaty woods from northern Labrador to Maryland, and west to Minnesota and Iowa. *Diervilla lonicera,* or bush honeysuckle, remains Tournefort's acknowledgement of his correspondent from Acadia. Sieur Dière de Dièreville, a surgeon, visited Port Royal (later Annapolis Royal) between 1699 and 1700 and returned with specimens that he sent to the King's Garden at Paris. Some of Sarrazin's work found its way into Europe's premier scientific publication, the *Journal des sçavans.*

The highly centralized organization of science under the auspices of the Royal Academy gave significance to the work of men otherwise isolated in the field. But it left control of the agenda in the hands of a few academicians at Paris. The names of other colonial botanists are known to historians, but their obscurity affirms the importance of organization to scientific inquiry.

Eight years passed subsequent to Michel Sarrazin's death in 1734 before the Paris Academy found a new correspondent to replace him. But Jean-François Gaultier, who arrived in Canada in 1742 as the colony's new royal physician, was more than adequate. He was already acquainted with Bernard de Jussieu of the Royal Garden at the Trianon who had entrusted him with Sarrazin's great manuscript work, the *Histoire des plantes de Canada,* which he carried back to Canada. In 1745 the Academy named Gaultier official correspondent of the distinguished academician Henri-Louis Duhamel du Monceau. Réaumur and the mineralogist Jean-Étienne Guettard also corresponded with him.

At Duhamel du Monceau's request, soon after arriving in the colony, Gaultier established its first meteorological station, and like his patron he took a keen interest in agriculture. For fourteen years Gaultier kept daily records of temperature—the first in Canada. Like Duhamel du Monceau, he was more interested in the utility of his observations than in the more speculative work of Sarrazin's patrons. Gaultier also recorded dates of plowing, sowing, ripening, and harvesting. His scientific instruments, however, were not the best. The extremes of Canadian winters gave him some difficulties measuring temperatures at Quebec using a thermometer of Philippe de La Hire's invention. Finally, in 1754 Réaumur sent him a thermometer of his own design. But at Montreal, Abbé Jean-Marie Castagnac de Pontarion had possessed one since 1749 and had been compiling similar meteorological data.

Gaultier's mineral samples were sent to Jean-Étienne Guettard, whose theory of the geological distribution of minerals and the structure of continents appeared in 1746. Six years later, relying on Gaultier's descriptive notes and specimens, he published the first mineralogical map of Canada accompanied by the designs of several fossils. Gaultier's greatest work, however, never saw the light of day. A four-hundred-page manuscript on plant species not investigated by his predecessor, it was to be part of a planned six-volume work on North American flora promoted and planned by Jussieu and Duhamel du Monceau. It was abandoned for reasons unknown.

Works that did see print reflected the growing utilitarian interest of the state. They dealt with maple sugar, pine pitch, resin, and wintergreen tea. *Gaultheria procumbens*, checkerberry, also called spicy wintergreen, remains a reminder of Gaultier's work on this last species. Gaultier served as Peter Kalm's guide when the latter visited New France in 1749 and may have contributed to the marquis de La Galissonière's publication on the preparation, care, and transportation of botanical specimens by sea, which earned him admission to the Royal Academy as an associate member on his return from Canada in 1750.

EARLY ETHNOGRAPHY

Ethnographic observations began with Europeans' first view of America's indigenous inhabitants, but serious studies awaited the appearance of missionaries whose observations on society and language continue to receive serious consideration from today's anthropologists and ethnohistorians. With a single exception, however, none of the earlier religious attempted to speculate concerning the origins of man in America. The odd man out was Father Joseph-François Lafitau. After spending nearly six years (1712–1717) at the mission of Sault Sainte Louis (Caughnawaga) among the Iroquois, where he made all of the observations that would go into his work, he returned to France to write his treatise in order, so he claimed, to contribute to "a science of manners and customs of peoples." In 1724 he published his *Moeurs des sauvages amériquains comparées aux moeurs des premiers temps* in Paris.

Lafitau was an acute social observer. He is credited with being the first European to have understood the importance of the council of elders in Iroquois political organization and to have linked the longhouse to social structure. He was also the first to describe the complex rules of Iroquois kinship. Though farfetched, his speculations concerning the origins of man in America were just as significant as his observations. He affirmed that customs are shaped by nature, an early argument in favor of environmentalism, and argued that some, such as marriage and incest taboo, are universal. More significant still, Lafitau developed the most complete theory up to that time of the Asian origins of Americans. Whether the discovery of Canadian ginseng, following predictions emanating from China, sparked his thought or not, Lafitau developed his idea, tracing the migration of men from ancient Greece across Asia to America via the Bering Strait. His comparison of the Iroquois and ancient Greeks based on language and custom has led his work to be viewed as having more in common with modern anthropology and comparative ethnology than many works of his own times.

His comments on the writings of his predecessors in the *Jesuit Relations* reflect his enormous intellectual advance. He decried their mistaken emphasis on lack of religion and ignorance of laws and forms of government among the Indians. Lafitau was far ahead of his time and though his work was quickly translated into German and Dutch an English edition appeared only 250 years later.

COLONIAL LEGACY

Scientific inquiry in the French colonies in America in all its categories is astonishing. In the mid eighteenth century, French American colonial populations were small (fewer than 100,000), and settlements widely dispersed from Nova Scotia through the Saint Lawrence Valley to the Illinois and lower Mississippi. Social structures based on a combination of agricultural subsistence and single commodity exports were simple, and demands limited. Yet, precisely because this simplicity allowed direct intervention of the state, with its highly centralizing political powers and organizing skills, scientific inquiry in the colonies contributed more than might have been expected. In so doing it tied America to the European world of empirical observation and speculative thought more profoundly than the small numbers suggest.

The metropolitan intellectual milieu and the available social political institutions profoundly shaped scientific inquiry in New France, more than the New World environment. As a consequence, although Frenchmen were often the first to investigate phenomena in North America, they obtained few lasting benefits. Their researches had little impact. Their greatest legacy lies in the vast body of maps, the fruits of more than a century and a half of endeavor that unrolled the contours of North America from Hudson Bay to the Gulf of Mexico and the Atlantic coast westward beyond the Mississippi toward the Rocky Mountains. Nearly all of the investigation and resulting maps, however, were the product of Frenchmen, not colonists.

Despite the broad spectrum of scientific inquiry that was encouraged and undertaken, it had little impact on the colony's development or the cultural evolution of its inhabitants. No traditional scientific outlook appeared to persist in the educational institutions of French Canada. Indeed, much that occurred still remains to be discovered by today's historians.

BIBLIOGRAPHY

Broughton, Peter. "Astronomy in Seventeenth-Century Canada." *Journal of the Royal Astronomical Society of Canada* 75, no. 4 (1981):175–208.

————. "Canadian Comet Discoveries." *Journal of the Royal Astronomical Society of Canada* 70, no. 6 (1976):311–319.

Chartrand, Luc, Raymond Duchesne, and Ynes Gingras. *Histoire des sciences au Québec.* Montreal, 1987.

Dictionary of Canadian Biography. Vols. 1–5. Toronto, Ontario, 1966–1983.

Dictionary of Scientific Biography. 16 vols. New York, 1970–1980.

Evans, Brian L. "Ginseng: Root of Chinese-Canadian Relations." *Canadian Historical Review* 66, no. 1 (March 1985):1–26.

Hahn, Roger. *The Anatomy of a Scientific Institution: The Paris Academy of Sciences, 1666–1803.* Berkeley, Calif., 1971.

Heidenreich, C. E., *Explorations and Mapping of Samuel de Champlain, 1603–1632.* Cartographica, Monograph No. 17. Toronto, Ontario, 1976.

Jarrell, Richard A. *The Cold Light of Dawn: A History of Canadian Astronomy.* Toronto, Ontario, 1988.

Kalm, Peter. *Peter Kalm's Travels in North America.* Revised and edited by Adolph B. Benson. 2 vols. New York, 1937; repr. 1966.

Lafitau, Joseph-François. *Customs of the American Indians Compared with the Customs of Primitive Times.* Edited by William N. Fenton and Elizabeth L. Moore. 2 vols. Toronto, Ontario, 1974–1979.

Levere, Trevor H., and Richard A. Jarrell, eds. *A Curious Field Book: Science and Society in Canadian History.* Toronto, Ontario, 1974.

Olmstead, J. W. "The Voyage of Jean Richer to Acadia in 1670: A Study in the Relations of Science and Navigation under Colbert." *Proceedings of the American Philosophical Society* 104, sec. 6 (1960):612–634.

Pritchard, James S. "French Charting of the East Coast of Canada." In *Five Hundred Years of Nautical Science, 1400–1900,* edited by Derek House. Greenwich, England, 1981.

————. "The Problem of North America in French Nautical Science During the Seventeenth and Eighteenth Centuries." In *Les marines de guerre européennes XVII–XVIIIe siècles,* edited by Martine Acerra, José Merino, and Jean Meyer. Paris, 1985.

Roger, Jacques. *Les sciences de la vie dans la pensée française du XVIIIe siècle.* 2nd ed. Paris, 1971.

Westfall, Richard S. *The Construction of Modern Science: Mechanisms and Mechanics.* New York, 1971; Cambridge, England, 1977.

James S. Pritchard

SEE ALSO **The Enlightenment; Philosophy;** and **Technology.**

THE SPANISH BORDERLANDS

THAT EXPLORATION AND EMPIRE have been so closely associated with Spanish colonial history might have led to widespread public awareness of a logical by-product: scientific inquiry. That the reverse may well be true—an almost complete popular ignorance of Spanish participation in scientific pursuit—is related both to a general (and often negative) misconception of Spanish and Spanish colonial accomplishments and to those political circumstances at the end of the colonial period that prevented publication of the results of much sophisticated scientific investigation in the Spanish Borderlands.

There, during the Spanish period and in the same area when it became United States territory, science, along with exploration, was the servant of empire. From the earliest *entradas* into the borderlands, scientific material was collected and applied to various purposes of empire. Invariably this included general geographical information. Sometimes more specific topographical observations were noted; and ethnographic, biological, and geological material was often collected. Such data would later be collected more systematically and would be arranged according to prevailing rules of classification by discipline. Those procedures were instituted in the eighteenth century by persons specially trained in the new scientific methodologies. The Spanish manifestation of the new science and its significance in the borderlands during the period of that region's most intensive exploration and settlement did not receive great scholarly attention until about three decades ago.

EXPLORATION AS SCIENTIFIC PURSUIT

Purposeful exploration was a hallmark of Spanish colonial activities from Columbus's first voyage practically to the last moment of the American empire. Always linked to Crown-driven, Crown-supported, and Crown-directed exploration were admirable and prolific efforts to record the results of exploration, most regularly by means of cartography. As a record of what had been seen—sometimes for the first time—and as a navigational aid for return trips, maps were the first and most constant type of scientific documentation. Besides describing the limits and contents of any territory, they were political statements to delineate empire, illustrations of geographical theory, and designs for future as well as existing towns and settlements.

Maritime or hydrographic maps take on a significance not readily recognized by those who think of the borderlands principally as interior, continental space. Throughout the colonial period, the easiest and safest means of transportation was by sea. Opportune long-distance travel was conceived in maritime terms, and adherence to what now seems like a foolish belief in imaginary geography was associated with sea travel. Locating and laying sovereign claim to the Strait of Anián or Northwest Passage, for example, contributed to an extraordinary amount of exploration, cartographical effort, and political finagling.

Maritime cartography, as well as mathematics, astronomy, and hydrography, were pursued at the naval academies established in Spain in the eighteenth century, and cadets preparing for the Royal Navy were intensively trained in the newest technologies. Superlatively skilled naval officers were attached to the Department of San Blas, established in 1767 in what is now Nayarit and founded as the naval headquarters and depot for the Spanish North Pacific. Among its other functions, it served as a center for shipbuilding, as home base for all ships plying the coast northward for exploration, settlement, and subsequent supply of Alta California and Nootka Sound, and as a launching point for scientific investigations.

While exploration may have been the oldest scientific pursuit applied to the borderlands, by the eighteenth century other enterprises were under way. The Enlightenment brought context to scientific inquiry in the New World, and without the Old World background provided by knowledge of this intellectual revolution, events in the borderlands ring distant, isolated, and disconnected.

INSTRUMENT OF INQUIRY: THE ROYAL CORPS OF ENGINEERS

Enlightenment-oriented expertise in the borderlands initially appeared in the first quarter of the eighteenth century. Francisco Álvarez Barreiro, a member of the elite Royal Corps of Engineers, accompanied the Martín de Alarcón expedition in 1718–1719 to reinforce the fragile Texas settlements and, as a consequence, to found San Antonio. Again from 1724 to 1728, the same engineer tramped the borderlands, this time with Brigadier Pedro de Rivera on his eight-thousand-mile (28,800 kilometer) review and inspection of frontier military garrisons, including El Paso and Santa Fe. Material included in Rivera's diary, such as demographic and ethnographic data as well as coordinates for thirty settlements, was probably Álvarez Barreiro's work, as were four detailed maps. Although these are the only surviving documents from his reconnaissance, his early presence in the northern region is emblematic of the Crown's concern for establishing the Royal Corps and indicative of its later activity in the borderlands.

Founded in 1711 by Philip V, the Royal Corps of Engineers was based on Flemish and Prussian models. The Corps was elite; that is, it consisted only of officers and never comprised more than two hundred men trained in military, civil, and hydraulic engineering, mathematics, architecture, and in other subjects now considered distinct and mutually exclusive specialties. Like other scientists of their time, engineers received training in and then practiced various specialties.

In cartography, reconnaissance, observation, and general expertise on technical and scientific matters, the Royal Corps of Engineers had no peer. It was the only elite military unit in New Spain; and corpsmen were assigned to the borderlands as well as to projects in Veracruz, Acapulco, Mexico City, and other sites in central Mexico, thus indicating the significance placed by the Crown and by viceroys on that region.

After the Seven Years' War (1756–1763), borderland concerns played an integral role in colonial policy making and implementation. Since scientific inquiry was a much broader concept in the eighteenth century and individuals' efforts were more broadly directed, corpsmen participated in an advisory and practical role in many considerations related to geopolitical dynamics. Francisco Fersén, for example, assisted in ascertaining the nature of the northwestern frontier in preparation for a reorganization of political, religious, and military affairs ordered by Charles III (1716–1788) and effected by Visitor General José de Gálvez. Engineer Nicolás de Lafora accompanied the marquis of Rubí on a military reconnaissance of the borderlands and joined him in proposals for a new military organization for the Apache-troubled area. Miguel Costansó, probably the best-known engineer, was a member of the Sacred Expedition to settle Alta California in 1769, wrote a widely published account of that venture, and then continued his engineering service in New Spain for another forty-five years. Alberto de Córdoba was the second engineer to work in Alta California, where he attempted to improve defenses against foreign invasion and laid out the Villa de Branciforte, near Santa Cruz. Four other engineers—Gerónimo de la Rocha, Manuel Mascaró, Juan Pagazaurtundúa, and José Cortés—worked under the commandant general of the Interior Provinces.

In addition to defense surveys and recommendations, which was a principal part of their work, corpsmen completed many commissions of civil and church architecture as well as more strictly engineering projects such as the construction of dams, roads, and bridges. Descriptions of their surveys include geological observations, ethnographic notes, language vocabularies, hydrographic analyses, biotic surveys, and navigational computations for establishing land routes. These works constitute primary field reports and include data, details, and systematic descriptions that make them valuable both as historical and scientific documents. The engineers' maps remain the best examples of cartographical knowledge of the Spanish Borderlands in the colonial period.

THE SCIENTIFIC SPIRIT

One way in which Charles III opened Spain to the Enlightenment was by fostering expeditions designed to survey subjects in the natural sciences. In New Spain and the borderlands, the atmosphere of scientific inquiry thus initiated lasted beyond his reign (1759–1788) until almost the end of the century, sustained in large part by the count of Revilla Gigedo while he was viceroy. The patronage provided by other key figures made possible the flowering of Spanish science from the 1760s on. The withdrawal of support and encouragement by later kings, ministers, and viceroys doomed to near-oblivion the accomplishments of Spanish scientists until very recent times.

Even before Charles III's reign, news of scientific developments in other nations had reached Spain. For example Pehr Loefling, a student of the famous Swedish botanist and taxonomist, Carolus Linnaeus (1707–1778), had visited Spain in 1751. Buffon's encyclopedic *Natural History of Animals* was known and was translated into Spanish in the 1780s. A spirit of internationalism and cooperation was developing on the Iberian peninsula and elsewhere as one of the earmarks of modern science.

Scientists also exchanged research observations and results, published their work, often in multiple and foreign editions, and participated in field trips at home and studies abroad. Above all scientists made investigations and observations based on the assumption that the whole universe of mind and matter was guided and controlled by natural law.

The questioning spirit of the times filled the tropical, mountain, and coastal airs of Spanish America, and the Crown's major scientific expeditions concentrated on biological taxonomy, ethnology, and geology. Botany was given considerable emphasis, as in eighteenth-century British and French field investigations. Individual scientists were supported or commissioned by those with an interest in the fruits of their research. Beneficiaries of the discovery of new species and the demystification of the natural world included all people affected by commerce, medicine, political sovereignty, and power—in short everyone. In Madrid new institutions such as the Royal Academy of Medicine, the Museum of Natural Science, and the Royal Botanical Garden trained scientists and served as repositories for specimens collected and for notes, reports, and illustrations generated in the field.

MAJOR EXPEDITIONS TO NORTH AMERICA'S WESTERN COAST

Two formal scientific expeditions to New Spain engaged the borderlands in crucial and extraordinary ways. Before they began in the 1780s the borderlands, at the edge of colonial settlement, had benefited from less systematic efforts carried on by two centuries of missionary-ethnographers and explorer-naturalists. Whether these protoscientists were missionizing or extending military or civilian settlement, their observations provided often-utilized background. Members of the later scientific expeditions, army and navy officers, and others frequently refer in their reports to the memorials and other documents from the 1540s by previous observers like Father Eusebio Francisco Kino, Father Silvestre Vélez de Escalante, and Father Francisco Atanasio Domínguez. Because eighteenth-century Spanish scientists reviewed the literature before and while undertaking research, they were aware of the earlier work—or of its absence.

The Royal Scientific Expedition

In 1787 the Royal Scientific Expedition to New Spain, also called the Royal Botanical Expedition, was dispatched from Madrid. Covering territory from Guatemala to Vancouver Island, it would serve as the focal point for all scientific endeavors in New Spain until the end of the century. That the leader was a physician, Martín de Sessé, was no coincidence. Much of the expedition's work related to botany, which was then of particular importance for physicians, surgeons, and pharmacists. The therapeutic properties of plants constituted the practical attraction to botany, while thousands of unclassified American species must have served as a powerful lure to the botanical explorer and field-worker.

Among the tasks included in the expedition's initial six-year funding was the introduction of the new scientific methods to the University of Mexico. A further purpose was hard scientific inquiry for both pure and applied knowledge in the augmentation of commerce, the promotion of medicine, and textile dyeing. Certain activities of the expedition were extended and did not terminate until 1802.

In 1792 one member of the expedition, José Longinos Martínez, traveled overland from Mexico City to San Blas. From there he crossed the Gulf of California to Loreto, and from this old capital of Baja California he went south before traversing the whole peninsula from Cabo San Lucas northward. Longinos crossed into Alta California near San Diego and visited the mission there as well as San Juan Capistrano and San Gabriel. After a stop at Rancho La Brea, within today's Los Angeles, where he collected fossils from the now famous tar pits, he continued northward to Santa Barbara and then Monterey. By the time he returned to Mexico by sail, he had sent ahead some thirty boxes of specimens. The journal he wrote after returning to Mexico includes his observations on mineralogy, geology, paleontology, entomology, ornithology, botany, and ethnology. Longinos's field collection and journal constitute the first detailed record of broad-based scientific observation in Baja California.

Naturalist and ethnographer José Mariano Moziño was one of the most extensive contributors to borderlands scientific inquiry. Born and educated in Mexico, he became professor of philosophy at Oaxaca. He gave up this post to study medicine at the University of Mexico and had also studied mathematics there under Engineer Miguel Costansó by the time he joined the Royal Scientific Expedition in 1790. Field studies in areas northwest of Mexico City led to his assignment to join the 1792 Expedition of Limits led by Juan Francisco de la Bodega y Quadra, commandant at the Naval Department of San Blas.

During the several months Moziño spent at Nootka Sound, on the west coast of Vancouver Island, he conducted a detailed survey of the biota and an ethnographic study of the inhabitants. He observed the politicoreligious organization of the Indians and provided detail so descriptive that his observations are still useful to ethnologists. He also added subjective judgments no longer considered appropriate: Nootkans, he said, would benefit from the introduction of Christianity and European agriculture. Not only is this ethnocentrism to be expected as part of the sociopolitical mentality of the time, but it is well within the bounds of science in the service of political aims, which was always at least an implicit item on exploration agendas. The naturalist further observed that the "noble savage" at Nootka was not tainted by the "vices" of private property and acquisitiveness until European trade goods had been introduced there.

Moziño's lengthy report concerning Nootka provided a wealth of systematically collected detail on the Indians' historical chronology, rituals, music, government, and economy as well as a dictionary of the Nootka language and a classification of some two hundred species of biota. On the way back to Mexico, he spent about two months in California, classifying flora and fauna, particularly in the Monterey area.

In Mexico, Moziño continued work with the Royal Scientific Expedition. He climbed the erupting volcano at Tuxtla in 1793 and studied leprosy, smallpox, drinking-water supplies, and indigo herbal cures and published a Spanish edition of John Brown's *Elements of Medicine*. With the recall of the expedition, he traveled to Spain, where he worked for the government, mainly in medicine. Moziño flourished under French occupation as director of the Royal Museum of Natural History, but when Spanish sovereignty was restored, he was treated as a traitor. His political misfortunes and trials were manifold: pushing a handcart filled with his biological illustrations and notes to the French border and beyond, experiencing an unhappy exile, making fruitless attempts to return to Spain, and having no success in publishing his precious scientific illustrations.

As with most other Spanish scientists and explorers of the era, most of Moziño's work was not published in his lifetime because of political circumstances around 1800. For all the support to scientific inquiry of Charles III, subsequent years saw dissipation and dispersal of the royal will. Charles IV had little if any interest in science; and his pretentious prime minister and chief of state, Manuel de Godoy, had none. The Napoleonic wars brought the French occupation, followed by restoration and a liberal government. But for Moziño, as well as for Alejandro Malaspina, leader of the other major expedition to the Spanish Borderlands, it was too late; their scientific achievements went unpublished for nearly two hundred years.

The Malaspina Expedition

Malaspina was the dominant coleader of the grandest and most ambitious eighteenth-century Spanish expedition: the around-the-world scientific and political expedition from July 1789 to September 1794. Together with José de Bustamante, his co-captain, the Italian-born Alejandro Malaspina had first circumnavigated the globe on the *Astrea* in 1786–1788. Their proposal for a new expedition was based on a desire to extend knowledge of navigation, geography, and natural history and to ascertain conclusively whether or not a Northwest Passage existed. Comprising experts in cartography, astronomy, botany, zoology, scientific illustration, and general artistic production, the expedition embarked in two specially built and extravagantly outfitted corvettes. After visiting sites in South America, it anchored in Acapulco early in 1791. Some members were left behind for scientific surveys of the coast and inland, while the main body proceeded to the Northwest Coast for exploration and natural history surveys.

Among the active participants was Felipe Bauzá, the chief of charts and maps, who later became director of the Depósito Hidrográfico in Madrid, predecessor of the archives at the Naval Museum. Bauzá was driven into exile in 1822 by the return of Ferdinand VII. Laden with hundreds of documents and drawings from the Malaspina Expedition as well as other borderland reports, he fled to England.

Publication of Bauzá's extensive writings had not materialized upon his return to Spain in 1794 because the commander had become embroiled in court intrigues with Queen María Luisa that led to his imprisonment and exile. Tens of thousands of pages of documentation were confiscated and relegated to an uncertain, but certainly unpublished, future. They included diaries, reports, letters, charts, coastal profiles, maps, and illustrations, many of them beautiful watercolors, as well as artifacts and specimens concerning his Northwest Coast visit and other stops in the Americas, Australia, New Zealand, and Pacific islands.

While the Malaspina party was in the Pacific Northwest, it made a nine-day stop at Mulgrave Sound (Yakutat Bay), where expedition members collected ethnological material, compiled a vocabulary, and tried to learn the language of the Tlingit Indians. Some of the men tried to climb the glacier later named for Malaspina, while others calculated the height of Mount Saint Elias. Still others described the biota, compiling a catalog of the wood immediately available and the zoological assemblage, such as local fauna and animals.

Certain specific cartographic and geographic investigations had been added to the Malaspina Expedition's priority list in consideration of the Nootka Sound Controversy, which involved conflicting territorial claims of Spain and England. While the expedition was at Nootka for two weeks in 1791, a temporary observatory recorded astronomical data of value for navigation, maps of the coastal regions were developed, and the labyrinthine canals around the sound were charted.

While the main body proceeded to Monterey for further observations and then sailed west across the Pacific, in 1792 a subexpedition made a detailed reconnaissance of the Strait of Juan de Fuca and the complicated waterways within. Under command of Dionisio Alcalá Galiano and Cayetano Valdés, the crews aboard the *Sutil* and *Mexicana* explored, charted, and described the sounds, bays, inlets, and passages between Vancouver Island and the mainland. The Spaniards met and joined the Englishman George Vancouver and his expedition, which was involved in the same kind of work. Demonstrating astonishing scientific cooperation despite their political mistrust, the specialists of two rival European powers for the first time circumnavigated the largest island on the west coast of North America, shortly to be named Qjadra and Vancouver Island in honor of the Englishman and his Spanish counterpart.

Unlike the great mass of Malaspina's work and that of many other Spanish scientists, the results of the *Sutil* and *Mexicana* expedition were published in 1802, eight years after the event, and included the text of Moziño's "Noticias de Nootka." But still more of the scientific data collected on the Northwest Coast were left unanalyzed and unused until recent times. For example, José Maldonado with Jacinto Caamaño traveled to points north of the Queen Charlotte Islands and to the Alaska coast. In three months, they collected a wealth of animal and plant specimens and made detailed lists of other natural resources.

SCIENCE ACROSS BORDERS

There are other examples of international scientific cooperation in the late eighteenth century. The count of La Pérouse sailed to California, Hawaii, and the South Pacific in 1785–1786 on behalf of France and sent back comments, drawings, and botanical specimens. La Pérouse was treated cordially in California and was provided with fresh food that greatly restored his ailing crew. Furthermore the French commander had determined that attempting to establish a French claim on the Northwest Coast in order to take part in the fur trade was not worth the risk of incurring the enmity of the Spanish Crown.

Venus Crosses the Sun:
Cooperation in Astronomy

International cooperation was amply demonstrated with the observation of the transit of Venus across the face of the sun in 1769. At that time Spaniards assisted French astronomers, under the leadership of the Abbé Jean-Baptiste Chappe d'Auteroche of the Royal Academy of Sciences in Paris, in establishing an observatory in Baja California to record this rare celestial occurrence. The observations were used to calculate the solar parallax, the mean distance between earth and the sun.

The premier eighteenth-century astronomical event for Western astronomers, the transit of Venus, would not recur until 1874 (and then in 1882) and not at all in the twentieth century. Transit observations in 1761 had been made by 120 people at sixty-two stations throughout the world from south of the Arctic Circle to Peking and Siberia, where l'Abbé Chappe d'Auteroche recorded them. As part of the international effort in 1769, British scientists were sent to observe the transit from Tahiti with James Cook, who was on his first Pacific voyage.

In Baja California the self-taught astronomer Joaquín Velázquez Cárdenas de León, who was the mining district administrator at Real de Santa Ana, generated his own data on the transit, which agreed extraordinarily well with the observations made by Chappe d'Auteroche and Spanish scientists Vicente de Doz and Salvador de Medina, who were part of the Frenchmen's party. Visitor General José de Gálvez had done his best to outfit Mission San José del Cabo so that the French academicians would be comfortable and would not think the place a wilderness. The original plans had called for British scientists to be hosted by Jesuit missionaries, but the Spanish expulsion of the Society of Jesus in 1767 and the growing tension between Spain and Britain had forced a change. That a terrible plague killed Chappe d'Auteroche and most of the other members of the party in Baja California was the sad ending to this joint venture; that their data survived and were used, along with those of the other 151 observers at seventy-seven stations worldwide, was the happy scientific ending.

THE ENLIGHTENMENT AND
SCIENTIFIC INQUIRY

Mixed results also summarize the accomplishments of Spanish scientific inquiry in the borderlands and all of Spanish America. While remarkable advances were made, and international cooperation and investigation had resulted in the collection and analysis of magnificent data, the course of Spanish history made it difficult for scientists to build on this achievement. For as the Enlightenment had engendered a spirit of scientific inquiry, so it generated liberal ideas in support of individual rights and in opposition to tyrannical government that ultimately left Spanish scientific efforts in disarray. The complicated political results were the French occupation followed by a restoration government without the authority to salvage an empire in disintegration—partially from the dissemination of those same liberal ideas. In sum the Enlightenment that sparked scientific forays into the borderlands also helped to create political conditions that impeded such efforts.

BIBLIOGRAPHY

Calatayud Arinero, María de los Angeles. *Catálogo de los Expediciones y Viajes Científicos Españoles: Siglos XVIII y XIX*. Madrid, 1984.

Cutter, Donald C. *California in 1792: Report of a Spanish Naval Visit.* Norman, Okla., 1990. The visit of the *Sutil* and *Mexicana*.

———. *Malaspina and Galiano: Spanish Voyages to the Northwest Coast, 1791 and 1792.* Seattle, Wash., 1991. Includes cartographic advances, ethnographic observations, and helpful maps and illustrations.

———. *Malaspina in California.* San Francisco, 1960.

[Engstrand] Wilson, Iris Higbie, ed. and trans. *Noticias de Nutka: An Account of Nootka Sound in 1792.* Seattle, Wash., 1970; repr. 1988; paper repr. 1991. Contains José Mariano Moziño's journal, plus an excellent introduction and illustrations.

Engstrand, Iris H. W. *Spanish Scientists in the New World: The Eighteenth-Century Expeditions.* Seattle, Wash., 1981. Contains the best information and analysis of the Royal Scientific Expedition and of scientific efforts associated with the Malaspina Expedition on the northwest coast.

Espinoso y Tello, José. *Relacion del viaje hecho por las goletas "Sutil" y "Mexicana" en el año 1792.* Madrid, 1802; repr. 1958, 1991. The 1991 version is an important facsimile reprint, using the original title with the addition of the words *para reconocer el estrecho de Juan de Fuca,* complete with tipped-in astronomical charts, maps, and illustrations. It also contains an informative introduction by the editors María Dolores Higueras Rodriguez and María Luisa Martín-Merás. John Kendrick has translated, provided an introduction, and added valuable material to this important work. It appears as *The Voyage of Sutil and Mexicana, 1792: The Last Exploration of the Northwest Coast of America.* Spokane, Wash., 1991.

Fireman, Janet R. *The Spanish Royal Corps of Engineers in the Western Borderlands: Instrument of Bourbon Reform, 1764–1815.* Glendale, Calif., 1977.

González Claverán, Virginia. *La Expedicón Científica de Malaspina en Nueva Expaña: 1789–1794.* Mexico City, Mexico, 1988.

John, Elizabeth A. H., ed. *Views from the Apache Frontier: Report on the Northern Provinces of New Spain by José Cortés, Lieutenant in the Royal Corps of Engineers, 1799.* Norman, Okla., 1989.

Novo y Colson, Pedro de., ed. *Viaje político-científico alrededor del mundo por las Corbetas "Descubierta" y "Atrevida" al mando de los Capitanes de Navío D. Alejandro Malaspina y D. José de Bustamante y Guerra, desde 1789 á 1794.* Madrid, 1885; repr., 1984.

Nunis, Doyce B., Jr., ed. *The 1769 Transit of Venus: The Baja California Observations of Jean-Baptiste Chappe d'Auteroche, Vincente de Doz, and Joaquín Velázquez Cárdenas de León.* Los Angeles, 1982.

Puerto Sarmiento, Francisco Javier. *La ilusión quebrada: Botánica, sanidad y política científica en la España ilustrada.* Barcelona, Spain, 1988. A fine example of new Spanish scholarship on the important role of science, and especially botany, in the Spanish and Spanish colonial Enlightenment and the integral part it played in scientific inquiry, particularly with application to hygiene and medicine.

Simpson, Lesley Bird, ed. and trans. *Journal of José Longinos Martinez, Notes and Observations of the Naturalist of the Botanical Expedition in Old and New California and the South Coast.* San Francisco, 1961.

Thurman, Michael E. *The Naval Department of San Blas: New Spain's Bastion for Alta California and Nootka, 1767 to 1798.* Glendale, Calif., 1967.

Janet R. Fireman

SEE ALSO **The Enlightenment; Philosophy;** and **Technology.**

MEDICAL PRACTICE

HEALTH AND DISEASE

HEALTH IS INFLUENCED by many factors. It is dependent on birth—the genetic traits of individuals and groups—and may be modified by any peculiar developments such as birthing complications. It is also shaped by diet. Levels of physical well-being and exposure to disease-causing agents are affected to varying degrees by the physical environment: geography, climate, population distribution, clothing, sanitation, and shelter. As a corollary, the ways in which food is obtained, especially agricultural and fishing techniques, will be influential. Given the fact that many of these elements must be acquired by individuals, the issue of access to essential resources enters into the picture—the economic structure of the society, particularly the distribution of wealth. In broader terms, health is also affected by the social environment: conditions in the family and community, levels of violence in the society. Finally, ethnicity or cultural factors may be influential: attitudes to a range of things associated with life and illness. In the North American colonies, this combination of elements produced a great variation in the health of inhabitants—Amerindians, Europeans, and Africans.

Discussing and documenting the state of health and levels of disease in the colonies is beset by several problems. Reports of physical condition and diseases encountered are often vague, generally not systematic, and rarely quantitative—few observers (doctors, government officials, colonists, visitors) had the resources or the inclination to take meticulous notes. There are only a few series of detailed records from the hospitals in Spanish, French, and later, English colonies. It is difficult to say precisely which modern disease entity corresponds with some of the old medical descriptions. Often the cause of illness or death was only dimly recognized, and the way perceptions were recorded makes the picture obscure to researchers. Church records of births, marriages, and deaths are valuable sources but they vary between parish and type of church, and many are simply missing. People in cities did better at identifying diseases than those in rural regions.

In general, what information we have is skewed: as in any age, people were most impressed by spectacular problems—catastrophic epidemics, anomalies, and freak accidents. There are far fewer comments about common maladies from which people recovered or mysterious troubles that ended individual lives. Moreover, the actual cause of death or illness might be obscured by identification of another ailment that flared up at the same time or by a symptom, such as

195

fever or convulsions, that could be attributed to several causes. It is therefore seldom possible to embark on the kind of detailed discussion favored by present-day epidemiologists.

LIFE EXPECTANCY

Observers at time of contact marveled at the physique of Native Americans. Many found them tall, well-built, with good muscles and white teeth. Deformities were rare. Later contact with tribes in less hospitable lands produced varied reports. Twentieth-century anthropologists, archaeologists, and historians have generally confirmed the impression that Amerindians were predominantly well-developed and suffered from few diseases for which evidence can be recovered. This is probably due in part to relatively low populations spread over large territories with access to plentiful and varied food.

Contact, however, proved disastrous for Native Americans. Although the figures are varied and still disputed, the population of most Amerindian tribes was reduced by at least half and some by as much as 90 percent by smallpox, diphtheria, measles, yellow fever, typhoid, and malaria. The explanation for this ecological catastrophe appears to rest in the isolation of the Americas. Archaeologists believe that early inhabitants trickling across the Bering Strait encountered a "cold screen" that severely reduced both pathogens and vectors. "Crowd diseases" such as smallpox and measles that require large numbers of susceptible subjects to maintain their viability would also be eliminated if they had been present.

Calculating mortality and life expectancy is difficult given the fragmentary nature of most records, and historical demographers have produced a range of figures. There were at times very high death rates in the English and French colonies, particularly in the earliest days of settlement. In Plymouth, for example, almost half the population died in the winter of 1620–1621. Thereafter conditions steadily improved. Life expectancy of infants born in New England between 1620 and 1650 has been calculated at 42.5 years for males and 41.8 years for females. By the eighteenth century, life expectancy at birth

in the northern colonies of Britain and France was between 35 and 38 years. If these figures are correct, people in North America were faring just a little better than Western Europeans. Of course most colonists should not have begun to count their days after their thirty-fifth birthday. Premature death was a frequent misfortune. Much of this occurred in the first months and years of life, so the low figures reflect high infant and child mortality. People who lived to marriageable age (in their mid twenties) had a much greater likelihood of living into their fifties or sixties, and some lived well beyond that.

Many people soon discovered the dangers to life in the southern English colonies, including the Chesapeake region. French colonists likewise found the Mississippi Delta region of Louisiana unattractive. This was part of the reason that these colonies resorted to the use of slave labor. Rich plantation owners often avoided the colonies, others who were better-off could distance themselves from trouble in the time of an outbreak of disease. Poorer whites and indentured servants fared much less well. Africans who were brought to the continent to serve as slaves, chiefly in the southern colonies of Britain and France, often fared badly.

PHYSICAL ENVIRONMENT

The quality of life depended to an important extent on the land that was settled. There were significant differences between colonies and across the territories of each colony, between rich soils and more limited soils that were quickly depleted. For example, the sandy soils of coastal Virginia were quickly exhausted by tobacco cultivation. Marshy lands around the Mississippi Delta in Louisiana, in Florida, and along the southeastern coast of the continent also affected both agriculture and disease patterns. The rocky rugged terrain and poorer soils of Newfoundland, Cape Breton Island, and parts of present-day Maine and New Brunswick would limit settlements in those regions, although people there were largely committed to fishing, which would produce a different settlement pattern.

Predictably, conditions were not nearly as good in the frontier agricultural regions of any colony, with their volatile social conditions and erratic economies disrupted by frequent war. On the other hand, the people who lived a nomadic existence in the west (*coureurs de bois,* or woods runners, for example) were often said to be in remarkably good health; and given the prodigious distances they paddled in their canoes, they were undoubtedly more fit than just about anyone but their Indian confreres.

The climate would also affect health and patterns of illness. From the Gulf of Mexico to the Saint Lawrence and along large parts of eastern North America, long hot humid summers fostered growth of organisms and vectors like mosquitoes. People spent much time outdoors, and this increased exposure to certain organisms proliferating on objects and animals and in the soil and water. In more northerly colonies, particularly in New France, short growing seasons and long winters reduced access to certain foods and therefore to certain essential nutrients. Winter kept people cooped up indoors, increasing exposure to organisms that infected the respiratory system.

Population distribution affected the spread of some diseases. Urban centers might suffer rapid spread of infections but small villages isolated and reliant on their own resources could on occasion suffer more severely. Isolation in the course of time could reduce the collective immunity of some small settlements and farming regions, leading to particularly severe outbreaks of some infections. Finally, patterns of trade brought many port cities in North America into contact with vessels sailing from tropical locations that carried more exotic parasites in their holds.

Shelter was often less than adequate to assure good health. As the Swedish botanist Peter Kalm noted in 1749–1750, sanitation in the cities of the northern English colonies and in Canada was not that impressive. Ships and carts dumped offal and other refuse into the rivers. Wells were shallow. Streets were mostly unpaved. Little care was taken with the disposal of garbage from houses. Many colonists' houses were small, poorly ventilated, and overcrowded. In the early days of each colony or region, many people slept in the same small room. Such conditions persisted among the poorer people throughout the

seventeenth and eighteenth centuries. Fears of "bad air" and cold, damp night air discouraged many from ventilating houses. Spitting onto the floor or street was a common practice in all colonies.

Conditions in the countryside often were not better. In early stages, and often even later, farmers slept with the animals, particularly in the winter, to conserve heat. If an animal died, it was left to rot. Latrines often were not constructed. Water was taken directly from rivers and streams or from shallow wells, all contaminated on occasion, especially after storms and during the spring runoff. Even when improvements were made in the later stages of development, living conditions among the poorer settlers and black slaves, particularly those in "quarters" on southern plantations, remained crude.

Conditions in Amerindian villages varied considerably by tribe, from the elaborate long-houses of Iroquoian peoples to the tepees of northern nomads. Natives were often fastidious about disposal of waste, and since most were nomadic or seminomadic they could avoid living for long periods in badly contaminated environments.

Colonists generally had few changes of clothing, and washing was limited, though it occurred more frequently than legend sometimes suggests. Clothing could be inhabited by mites and lice as well as people, and with these could come disease. Inadequacies of clothing could at times affect health, particularly in the winter. This was especially a problem for the poor and for those in military service. In 1700 the governor of New York wrote that the soldiers on garrison at Albany were in a "shameful and miserable condition for want of cloaths that the like was never seen, in so much that those parts of 'em which modesty forbids me to name, are expos'd to view, the women forced to lay their hands on their eyes as often as they pass by 'em."

DIET AND NUTRITION

Diet varied considerably between regions and between classes or ethnic groups. Research has revealed that many Amerindians, particularly the Iroquoian peoples with their mixed hunter-gatherer and farming economies, had remarkably balanced diets. The staples of the French Canadian diet were wheat, white beans, peas, and pork; in the northern English colonies beef and pork, corn, beans, squash, and later wheat. These were supplemented in all colonies by smaller quantities of other meat either from domestic or wild animals, birds, and fish, and by vegetables as they became available in season. A surprising amount of fruit was available in many places during the summer and autumn. The diet was more limited in the southern colonies. The basic diet of slaves there consisted of corn and meat, usually ham, supplemented by some vegetables, fruit, fish, and lesser amounts of other items.

Analyzing these diets with data provided by modern nutrition science, historians have concluded that all people generally received adequate quantities of protein and carbohydrate, though generally more than enough fat. They were also able to meet their energy requirements in terms of calories required for work performed. Preliminary analysis of data for the height of people in the British colonies confirms the impression that conditions were actually good. Diet plays a central role in the final height and it appears that by the time of the American Revolution, native-born white males aged twenty-four to thirty-five were on average 68.1-inches (170-centimeters) tall, which was above the average for many European populations. Contrary to the popular impression that there has been an almost continuous improvement in nutrition and height since the seventeenth century, it now looks as though there were good and bad periods as well as good and bad places.

There were, however, a number of problems. The most significant was a low intake of vitamin C. In the north, a shortage of fruit and vegetables, long winters, and short growing seasons could lead to subclinical or frank cases of scurvy by late winter or early spring. This problem was even more obvious among slaves. Rickets, a bone disorder resulting from vitamin D deficiency, was not common in the way it became in nineteenth-century industrial cities. Goiter, resulting from iodine deficiency, was also evidently uncommon, probably due to consumption of fish. Parasites were common. Beef and pork tapeworms were a frequent problem for all races in all colonies. In Canada, government officials correctly noted that little worms (i.e., pork tapeworm) could cause a form of seizure resembling epilepsy. Slaves could also be short of essential amino acids, vitamin B, and essential minerals, notably calcium and iron. There were some more exotic disorders. For example, in some colonies, notably Pennsylvania, "milk sickness"—also known as "the trembles," "the slows," "the tires," and "the puking fever"—was widespread. It resulted from cattle eating white snakeroot, which contains the poison tremetol, while in pasture. Colonists who drank milk or ate meat from these animals came down with the classic symptoms. Survivors might be left in a weakened state for months, and many never completely recovered.

Dietetic diseases rarely killed, but they paved the way for other illnesses. Much of colonial agriculture in the northern colonies of England and France operated near the subsistence level. Poor farming techniques could lead to soil exhaustion that reduced crop yields. Lack of care with breeding might reduce the quality of animals. This would present problems for farmers in times of dearth, and even greater troubles for urban and military populations which depended on that surplus (although some food was imported). Although food shortage was less of a possibility in North America than in Europe, it did occur and shortage due to repeated poor harvests could lead to malnutrition, which then opened up possibilities for infectious disease to ravage the population.

Malnutrition was a frequent problem for military expeditions, especially those venturing far from the agricultural base of their colonies. Expeditions would have to rely increasingly on stores brought with them—hordes of men ruin hunting and quickly exhaust whatever fruit and vegetables they may come upon in a forest. This was a problem from the days of early explorers such as Jacques Cartier in the Saint Lawrence in 1535 and Hernando de Soto in the borderlands between 1539 and 1543. It was a problem for William Phips at the siege of Quebec in 1690, and it crippled Paul Marin's expedition to the Ohio in 1753. During the American Revolution, the constant shortage of supplies undermined the condition of men in the Continental Army.

DEFORMITIES AND DISORDERS

Eye disorders are quite frequently encountered today, and they would not have been that much less common in the seventeenth and eighteenth centuries. In older people, opacified lenses (cataracts) were a fairly common problem. Errors of refraction are well-known: nearsightedness and farsightedness are prevalent in people of all ages. Presbyopia, a form of farsightedness, affects many people from middle age onward. All such cases require corrective lenses. These were being produced in the eighteenth century; everyone remembers them in portraits of Benjamin Franklin. If they were not on the noses of many men, they would not have been very good shots—an important consideration for hunting and even more so during the frequent wars. Mention of spectacles is made in probate inventories from eighteenth century New England. There are only the briefest indications, however, for the southern colonies or for Canada. For example, in 1755 François Clement Boucher de La Perrière, a captain in the Canadian regulars, wrote to a friend that "I am old [he was 48] and no longer see clearly even though I have glasses on my nose." We do not know where most glasses were made, nor how many people could afford them. La Perrière, an aristocrat, was a member of the elite. He died at the Battle of the Plains of Abraham in 1759; one wonders what he saw.

Hernias, bladder stones, and kidney problems are mentioned from time to time. Ulcers were also noted but without sufficient detail for us to say now what they were. Many people also suffered from tooth decay. In some Amerindian and Inuit societies, wear and tear on teeth was especially common among individuals, particularly women, who used their teeth in preparing hides to make clothing.

DISEASES OF DEGENERATION

Colonial records have many unhelpful entries such as "atrophy," "decay of nature," and "old age." In a few instances, death can clearly be attributed to cardiovascular disease but often a diagnosis cannot now be made. Many ailments were not recognized as cardiovascular. This included some quite common troubles: "dropsy" (edema, an accumulation of excessive fluid in tissues or cavities, which can be the result of congestive heart failure), "palsy," and "apoplexy" (the effects of strokes). It is even more difficult to say anything concrete about Amerindians and Africans, although some contemporaries, and historians following them, maintained that heart and vascular diseases were rare among pre-contact Indians.

The word "cancer" appears from time to time but like many colonial terms, it was imprecise and included a variety of surface disorders and growths. Given the major limitations of what we would now call pathology, only external cancers were identified at the time. Again, it is difficult to say anything with confidence about Amerindians and slaves, however cancer and skin diseases were apparently rare among pre-Columbian Indians.

"Arthritis" is noted with considerable frequency as one of the most common ailments of older people. "Rheumatism" and "gout" are also easy to recognize in colonial documents, though some cases were probably degenerative arthritis. Many observers reported that arthritis and rheumatism were widespread among natives, most likely the consequence of heavy exertion and constant exposure. Some cases in all groups may have been rheumatoid or infectious arthritis. This would have been the case particularly with joint disease among people in their twenties and thirties. To some extent it resulted from inadequate clothing and shelter. Not surprisingly, there was a relatively high incidence of "rheumatism" in the Continental Army during the revolution.

INFECTIOUS DISEASES

There were many opportunities for the spread of infectious diseases but none as rich as the transatlantic crossing. Cramped quarters, poor sanitation, and reliance on barreled water quickly caused problems. Food consisted of dried and salted meat and biscuit. Not only was the nutritional content limited but it was also further reduced by the manner of preparation, particularly heavy salting. Spanish, French, and English officials all recorded many deaths at sea. Sometimes the tragedy reached epic proportions. In 1738, fifteen ships arrived at Philadelphia after suffering losses totaling sixteen hundred. In 1749, the year of heaviest immigration to Philadelphia, two thousand Germans died. Much the same conditions prevailed on slave ships. Herbert Klein found that while mortality was at times very high, it was not consistently higher for Africans, and could run lower than for Europeans making the crossing at the same time. This is not surprising: slaves were a valuable cargo and had to be delivered "sound in wind and limb."

Repeated outbreaks of fevers and other infections often follow the arrival of ships. This reveals a classic pattern of disease in colonial North America: major infections were regularly "imported." High morbidity and mortality rates were expected among new arrivals. Colonials referred to this as "seasoning."

Diseases were spread by European explorers, missionaries, and traders along major transportation routes from Europe, Africa, and the Caribbean to North America, then along rivers into the interior. The process was accelerated by Indians who came to trade or to fight alongside Europeans. Farmers who led expansion along the frontiers also contributed to the spread of some diseases. Military operations were frequent and helped spread a great variety of diseases among natives, Europeans, and Africans alike. These infections affected not only the individual, they also disrupted trade, reduced production, and touched off tensions between regions and between racial and ethnic groups.

Maternal and Infant Illnesses

Historical demographers have found that 1 percent to 2 percent of French women who gave birth in Canada would die, and 2 percent to 3 percent of women died in the northern English colonies, though the actual figure may have been higher. This was the effect of either complications of the birth process or attendant infections. Puerperal fever, resulting from infection at the time of childbirth, was a persistent worry for women in the colonies. It was a frequent enough occurrence, though less often a cause of maternal death than was once assumed. Large families were common in all colonies and women's risk of dying increased with the number of children they bore and the frequency of pregnancies.

Newborns and infants were particularly vulnerable to disease and since little was known about the infections, little could be done. Many succumbed—between 11 percent and 14 per-

cent—within the first year of life. This is nonetheless marginally better than figures for England (12–15 percent) and appreciably better than those for France (17–27 percent). Intestinal disorders were a common occurrence, notably "summer diarrhea" (also referred to as "cholera infantum" although not related to cholera, which did not appear in North America until 1832). While the details of neonatal health among slaves are not well documented, historians have noted a high incidence of tetanus in the antebellum south. This resulted from the practice among African Americans of applying mud to the umbilical stump.

Diphtheria and Scarlet Fever

Two throat diseases troubled the lives of many colonial children: diphtheria and scarlet fever. They were not well-distinguished by contemporaries who referred to them both by a variety of names including "throat distemper," "bladders," and "quincy." Both had appeared in the seventeenth century in relatively mild forms. In 1735 an especially virulent strain of diphtheria swept through New England. It was followed or accompanied by a severe form of scarlet fever called *scarlatina anginosa*. It was especially prevalent in rural regions. Over one thousand died in New Hampshire alone, mostly children—a major loss in a population of twenty thousand. After the initial devastation, the diseases returned each year until 1740 although they never struck again in quite such a deadly fashion. It is estimated that between 1735 and 1740, five thousand died in New England, again a significant loss in a population of two hundred thousand. Though New England suffered the heaviest losses, the disease spread to most parts of the English colonies and into French and Spanish territory. Amerindians, who had not been exposed to the diseases before contact, rapidly succumbed to the infection. This became another of the diseases that sharply reduced the Native population.

Measles

Although it is now considered a relatively minor ailment of childhood, measles was much more serious in early colonial times and struck all age groups. It was particularly severe among Native Americans and Africans who had not been exposed before and so had not built up an immune response. In Canada a severe outbreak in 1687–1688 left five hundred dead—three and a half times the annual rate. It returned to New France in 1710–1711, 1714, and 1730. Measles was first reported in Boston in 1657, and the most destructive outbreak in the English colonies occurred in 1713 when over one hundred died. There were scattered outbreaks thereafter, notably in 1739–1741, 1747–1748, and 1758–1759 but none as severe. By the end of the century it was primarily a disease of childhood.

Respiratory Diseases

Native, European, and African inhabitants of all the northern colonies—from Newfoundland to Canada, New England, and the middle colonies—often suffered from respiratory problems. People at the time were not that good about distinguishing pulmonary diseases. Often there was a general attribution, just as people today say "I have the flu" when in fact they have the common cold. Colds were predictably ubiquitous in many parts of the continent, particularly to the north and east, and were noted by doctors and by travelers like Peter Kalm. Pneumonia was widespread and while not often fatal on its own, it could be the final blow for an individual crippled by other infections, malnutrition, or old age. There were a number of epidemics that appear to be influenza. One struck Virginia in 1688, another New England in 1697–1699 and New France in 1700–1701. During the eighteenth century there are frequent instances of "violent cold" in many colonies from South Carolina to Canada, but there is no way of establishing just what these illnesses were. We do know, however, that the great influenza pandemic of 1729 reached North America and lingered there until 1733. Pleurisy, inflamations of the lungs, and bronchitis are mentioned often enough among all races.

Evidence, though fragmentary and vague, gives the impression that tuberculosis, often referred to as "consumption," was widespread. Though levels of infection are disputed, tuberculosis may have been responsible for as many as one quarter of all deaths. It is common to associate tuberculosis with a cold damp climate; however, medical historians now recognize that important factors in the pattern of this disease include diet, shelter, clothing, and the proximity of infected individuals to a larger population. Tuberculosis was a widespread and ferocious disease among African slaves. "Galloping consumption"—rapid deterioration of lung tissue—was also given the name "Negro consumption" or *struma africana*. It seems most likely that the reason for this pattern is that while Europeans had been exposed to the disease for centuries, Africans had not and therefore they had not developed an elevated immune response to tuberculosis. The same applies to Amerindians and Inuit (Eskimo), though it is not clear whether tuberculosis was at all present in pre-Columbian America.

Gastrointestinal Ailments

Diarrhea was a major problem, usually in the summer and autumn, among natives, Europeans, and Africans in almost all North American colonies. It could be serious and sometimes fatal. Many of these cases are usually attributed to dysentery, called "the flux" or "bloody flux." The signs of dysentery (bloody stools and severe abdominal pain) were not always noted so one cannot be absolutely sure. Diarrhea has several causes, all plausible in the context. A classic disease of military campaigns in Europe, dysentery, or diarrhea, troubled many military operations in North America, including General Edward Braddock's ill-fated expedition into the Ohio Valley in 1755. Diarrhea and dysentery were serious problems during the American Revolution, for example during the siege of Boston in 1775 and at Ticonderoga in 1776. The incidence of diarrhea was usually highest at the outset of hostilities because armies had not implemented adequate sanitation measures, nor had the troops developed sufficient discipline to adhere to regulations. The New England troops gathered around Boston in the early years of the revolutionary war were notorious for urinating and defecating in areas around their camps without building adequate facilities. American forces also suffered from the fact that many men served short terms and never learned the intricacies of surviving military service.

Smallpox

Probably the most dreaded disease of colonial times was smallpox. It was shocking to observe:

pustules gradually formed on the skin which then broke down and a hard crust would form over large areas. Smallpox was extremely infectious and often appallingly disfiguring. Complications and extensive degeneration of tissue led to death in 15 percent to 25 percent of all cases among Europeans. An outbreak could account for 8 percent to 10 percent of all deaths in a city during that year. In Boston during the famous outbreak of 1721–1722, there were nearly six thousand cases in a population of 10,670, of which 844 died. Smallpox struck port cities in particular. Often ships brought the disease to the colonies from Europe or the West Indies. Occasionally trade between two North American colonies (for example, between Albany, New York, and Montreal, Canada) reintroduced it to an area. It might also oscillate between Amerindian nations and individual colonies as a consequence of trade or war. There was a very widespread epidemic throughout eastern North America between 1688 and 1691 aided, no doubt, by military operations in several theaters.

Smallpox first appeared in English and French colonies in the 1630s. The first general outbreak in New England only occurred in 1648, and others followed in 1666, 1677, 1689, 1702, 1721, 1730–1731, 1751–1752, and 1764. A similar pattern of punctuated devastation appears in other colonies or regions from Florida to Canada usually a year either way of these dates. New York, Pennsylvania, and Canada all suffered repeated outbreaks during the 1730s. Smallpox was a serious problem throughout the American Revolution. The most memorable outbreak occurred in 1775 when General Richard Montgomery's invasion of Canada was crippled by the disease.

Smallpox was responsible above all other diseases for reducing the Amerindian populations. Never before exposed to the disease, they had developed no resistance and often died of the infection. Although smallpox may have appeared earlier in Spanish territories, the first severe outbreaks appear to have occurred at the end of the 1630s among the Huron and other Indians around the Great Lakes. The large numbers and the horrific consequences must have profoundly shaken not just the economic, military, and political strength of individual nations but also the morale of those who survived.

Fevers

Many different infections produce elevated temperatures but the descriptions of the time are vague. There were general categories—"slow," "nervous," "malignant"—but these were wide enough to include several different diseases. Records from every colony in North America often make reference to fevers, but since many were penned by people who could not distinguish them it is difficult now to be very precise. Louse-borne typhus (ship or jail fever) probably accounts for fevers on more than a few vessels that crossed the Atlantic and perhaps in military camps. In general, however, epidemiologists have concluded that it was not widespread in North America. Typhoid, a water-borne disease causing a long, continued, slow fever, appeared early in the colonial period and increased in incidence as the population grew. "Camp fever," which reappeared in many locations during the American Revolution, was probably one or both of these.

Yellow Fever

The awful symptoms of "bilious plague" were soon recognized and feared. First a flushed face, scarlet lips and tongue, fever and chills; then after a few days the skin turned yellow, and in severe cases partially digested blood from hemorrhaging in the stomach would produce the dreaded "black vomit." Mortality could be very high, generally between 10 percent and 25 percent of all cases though it could sometimes be much higher.

Epidemics of yellow fever varied markedly in extent and intensity. The disease would strike then disappear. To contemporaries it was a mystery. It first appeared in ports trading with the West Indies: Boston in 1693, Charleston and Philadelphia in 1699, New York in 1702, Quebec and Montreal in 1710–1711. It appeared intermittently in the eighteenth century, generally affecting port cities, and was less common in colonies with few large seacoast towns. It struck New York in 1732, 1743, and 1745; Philadelphia in 1741, 1747, and 1762. After that, yellow fever disappeared until the 1790s when it returned to devastate Philadelphia in 1793.

A tropical disease not native to North America, yellow fever was introduced from Africa through the West Indies. Both the virus and the vector, the *aëdes aegypti* mosquito, found a new ecological niche in the subtropical setting of the southern colonies. The coming of frost would bring an end to outbreaks in more northerly locations. Southern winters, however, were mild enough that a few mosquitoes and eggs could survive and activity then resume the following spring. As a result, recurring outbreaks troubled Florida, Louisiana, and the Spanish Borderlands to the southwest, as well as parts of the southern British colonies. Because of its climate and its trade with the West Indies, Charleston, South Carolina, bore the brunt of the disease. Yellow fever struck in 1706, 1711, 1718, 1728, 1732, 1739, 1745, 1748, 1753, 1755, and 1761. Observers noted that it affected Europeans much more than Africans, and again the explanation lies in the fact that one population had not previously been exposed to the disease; indeed some Africans had built up resistance to yellow fever before they were taken to the Americas.

Malaria

Colonists referred to malaria as "remitting" or "intermittent" fever and distinguished three types according to the frequency with which the debilitating paroxysms of chill (ague) and fever recurred: twenty-four, forty-eight, or seventy-two hours. This more or less corresponds to present-day understanding. Malaria takes three major forms: *vivax* produces an episode lasting one to eight hours every forty-eight hours, *malariae* every seventy-two. *Falciparum,* which some called "hemorrhagic" or "pernicious" fever, produces an episode lasting twenty to thirty-six hours, recurring at irregular intervals of thirty-six to seventy-two hours. This was a far more severe illness and could quickly prove fatal. In addition, someone weakened by chronic malaria could fall prey to other infections including typhoid and various gastrointestinal diseases that could complicate the pattern of fevers.

Malaria is caused by protozoa carried by the anopheles mosquito that breeds in still, freshwater pools, swamps, lakes, and river bottoms. Evidently not native to North America, malaria was probably introduced by Europeans and Africans from tropical locations in the mid seventeenth century. Perhaps the earliest reference was penned by a Dutch official in 1659. Malaria spread through the seaboard regions of English, French, and Spanish colonies. The combination of geography and climate helped to make malaria endemic in the southern colonies by the end of the century. In towns and plantations that were often located in low-lying and marshy areas, many colonists suffered from chronic vivax malaria. It gradually spread up the Mississippi. By 1700 it had reached the Illinois territory, the Ohio Valley, and parts of the Great Lakes.

Most adults, white and black, gradually built up a measure of resistance to the two milder forms. Around 90 percent of blacks coming from West Africa, the principal source of slaves, had an immunity to vivax, while 10–20 percent carried the sickle-cell trait that produced elevated resistance to *falciparum.* With their imperfect understanding of the disease, European settlers were puzzled by the fact that their slaves clearly had higher resistance but then periodically suffered outbreaks of malaria. For those who did not build up resistance, malaria could be incapacitating. Troops on both sides suffered during the revolution. Predictably, northern troops sent south were particularly susceptible. The incidence was especially high among French and New England troops at the siege of Yorktown in 1781.

Sexually Transmitted Disease

Although there are actually several different sexually transmitted diseases, their separate identities were not established until the nineteenth century. The most notorious in colonial times was syphilis. Many in the sixteenth century considered it a new disease and some attributed it to the Americas. Historians such as Alfred Crosby suggest that syphilis may be what America gave to Europe in return for all the diseases brought to its shores. But syphilis was not as prevalent in North America as one might therefore expect. There is only limited evidence of infections, and these relate chiefly to soldiers and sailors—English, French, and Spanish. The disease was first noted among the English in 1646 and made periodic appearances thereafter, especially in the mid eighteenth century with the influx of British and European troops. The same thing occurred in New France. In 1775 a mysterious illness broke out in Canada and came to be known as the "mal de la Baie St. Paul."

Contemporary accounts give it a certain resemblance to a form of syphilis, but its actual nature remains unclear. The infection spread gradually until almost all regions of the colony were involved, and it was especially prevalent in rural populations. The disease lingered through the 1780s then disappeared as mysteriously as it arrived.

ALCOHOL

Colonial authorities in the Spanish, French, and English colonies frequently penned accounts of drunken misbehavior, and alcohol figures prominently in court records. There is little doubt that a significant minority of colonists consumed prodigious amounts and that would surely produce cases of alcoholism. Problems with alcohol were particularly severe among Africans and even more so among Amerindians, both of whom had low toleration of alcohol either because of differences in their metabolism, or because these people had little or no exposure to fermented drinks before contact with whites. Contemporary observers were unanimous in recording the devastations caused by alcohol in Native communities, and indeed, members of the Iroquois confederacy acknowledged the severity of its effect after the establishment of Forts Niagara and Oswego on their territory in the 1720s.

PHYSICAL INJURY

Accidents
Although most of the information we have is anecdotal, it appears that there were many accidents in the colonies, and injuries were often enough fatal. There were few safety precautions and virtually no traffic or safety regulations. People fell from buildings and precipices. They suffered dislocations and broken bones, including compound fractures. Limbs might be crushed by an object. Workers and farmers might be cut by axes, saws, and scythe blades. People fell victim to the hazards of travel in a time when there were few roads, and those available were often in poor condition. They were hit by carriages and carts. On the road and in farms they might

have misadventures with animals: a riding accident or a sharp blow from a hoof could kill outright or cause serious internal injury that colonial doctors and surgeons could do nothing about. Few people knew how to swim, and swimming techniques were limited in the colonial period. Reports appeared regularly of people drowning in rivers, in lakes, and in the sea. This was not simply the hazard of fishing or sea voyages; much transportation in all the colonies, particularly New France, relied on rivers. There were also a fair number of hunting mishaps. In colonies with harsh winters, individuals suffered from exposure and frostbite, and from time to time someone was found frozen to death. In the small multi-use rooms of many colonial homes, family members got burned or scalded. In the countryside, people might also run into trouble with snakes, bears, and other predators, and on occasion there is a reference to "hydrophobia" (rabies). Another complication of wounds was "lockjaw" (tetanus). Almost always fatal, it sometimes accompanied only minor injuries, and at the time no one could establish the cause.

Physical Abuse
Slaves faced the danger of injury from the various punishments that were meted out, particularly with the whip. Whips, of course, caused indescribable pain. Multiple lacerations of the skin opened a route for organisms. Bleeding and injury to muscle and internal organs could further weaken an individual. More difficult to document, except for extraordinary cases, are instances of wife and child abuse among European colonists.

Murder
Killing a man in a fight was a common enough occurrence, and court records for most colonies regularly note trials for murder. Deaths from dueling did occur, even though dueling was made illegal in many colonies.

Wounds of War
In colonies where warfare with both Europeans and Amerindians was frequent, wounds would be common. Civilians and soldiers would suffer blows to the head, cuts, puncture wounds, and arrowheads and bullets lodged in limbs and in-

side the body cavity. Bombardment in a siege could lead to the severing or shredding of limbs. Accidental explosions killed some and mangled others. It is worth underlining, however, the fact that battle casualties were nowhere as numerous as in the age of mechanized warfare that began in the nineteenth century. The range and accuracy of muskets was distinctly limited, which was one reason for the elaborate formations in regular European warfare and the close range of most battles up to the Napoleonic era. Nearly every observer agreed that the ratio of sick to battle casualties in eighteenth-century wars was very high. In 1776 the Continental Army numbered some forty-seven thousand, the militia twenty-seven thousand. That year, one thousand were killed in action, twelve hundred wounded, and ten thousand died of disease. Historians have confirmed contemporary estimates that ten thousand Americans died each year between 1775 and 1781 with nine deaths from disease for every death in action.

Postoperative Infections

Given the limitations of surgical technique and the absence of any awareness of microorganisms, postoperative infections were common. Many patients had to endure severe infections before recovering—or succumbing. Reporting was limited so it is difficult to say how well or poorly surgeons fared but their popular reputation was generally low.

PSYCHOLOGICAL CONDITIONS

In the realm of mental illness and madness, the usual problems with documentation are compounded by the fact that perceptions differed significantly from those of the present, and norms in any society are loaded with cultural values. Moreover, different groups—Native American, European, African—perceived mental processes differently. Many things that we might see as mental disorders were not identified as such, and disorders of the day might not be considered such now.

Psychological factors figured prominently in the perceptions of health and illness in many Amerindian tribes. Isolating these is not exactly possible, given the very different conceptualiza-

tion of disease. Still, the importance of psychology is evident in the attention paid to dreams, to bizarre behavior attributed to the working of spirits and sorcery. This intricate worldview was greatly complicated by the arrival of Europeans and Africans, after which Native Americans faced the stress of epidemic disease, alcohol, and military defeat, as well as the challenges of adjusting to radically different cultures.

Beyond individual troubles and constitutional conditions that might bring about mental illness, Europeans faced the initial trauma of pulling up roots and venturing to strange and often violent lands. Periodically, there are indications of mental illness, including insanity (the most easily identified) and depression. On rare occasions there is mention of a suicide. Hallucinations and paranoia may be read into some accounts of strange behavior. Psychological historians have tried to analyze the extraordinary behavior associated with some individuals in religious revivals or witch-hunts as symptoms of certain mental states. There are also references to "convulsions," "seizures," and other symptoms indicating troubles we can only guess about.

For blacks, especially those actually seized in Africa, the possibilities of mental illness were increased by the experience of being deprived of freedom and subjected to hard manual labor, severe punishments, crude living conditions, and the breakup of families. Precious little is said in the records about the Africans' state of mind, which only testifies to the capacity of humans to overlook suffering in others.

BIBLIOGRAPHY

Archer, Richard. "New England Mosaic: A Demographic Analysis for the Seventeenth Century." *William and Mary Quarterly*, 3rd ser., 47, no. 4 (1990):477–502.

Benson, Adolph B., trans. and ed. *The America of 1750: Peter Kalm's Travels in North America.* New York, 1927; repr. 1966.

Blake, John B. *Public Health in the Town of Boston, 1630–1822.* Cambridge, Mass., 1959.

Blanton, Wyndham B. *Medicine in Virginia in the Eighteenth Century.* Richmond, Va., 1931.

———. *Medicine in Virginia in the Seventeenth Century.* Richmond, Va., 1930.

Burkhart, Larry L. *The Good Fight: Medicine in Colonial Pennsylvania.* New York and London, 1989.

Cassedy, James H. *Demography in Early America: Beginnings of the Statistical Mind,* 1600–1800. Cambridge, Mass., 1969.

Caulfield, Ernest. *A True History of the Terrible Epidemic Vulgarly Called The Throat Distemper. . . .* New Haven, Conn., 1939.

Cook, Sherburne, and Woodrow Borah, eds. *Essays in Population History: Mexico and the Caribbean.* 3 vols. Berkeley, Calif., 1971–1979.

Cowan, David L. *Medicine and Health in New Jersey: A History.* Princeton and New York, 1964.

Crosby, Alfred W., Jr. *The Columbian Exchange: Biological and Cultural Consequences of 1492.* Westport, Conn., 1972.

Duffy, John. *Epidemics in Colonial America.* Baton Rouge, La., 1953.

———. *A History of Public Health in New York City, 1625–1866.* New York, 1968.

Fogel, Robert W., Stanley L. Engerman, and James Trussell. "Exploring the Uses of Data on Height." *Social Science History* 6, no. 4 (1982):401–421.

Heagerty, John J. *Four Centuries of Medical History in Canada.* 2 vols. Toronto, Ontario, 1928.

Kiple, Kenneth F., and Virginia H. King. *Another Dimension to the Black Diaspora: Diet, Disease, and Racism.* Cambridge and New York, 1984.

Klein, Herbert S. *The Middle Passage: Comparative Studies in the Atlantic Slave Trade.* Princeton, N.J., 1978.

Lessard, Renald. *Se soigner au Canada aux XVIIe et XVIIIe siècles.* Hull, Quebec, 1990.

Numbers, Ronald L. *Medicine in the New World: New Spain, New France, and New England.* Knoxville, Tenn., 1987.

O'Callaghan, E. B., ed. *Documents Relating to the Colonial History of New York.* 13 vols. Albany, N.Y., 1856–1883.

Patterson, K. David. *Pandemic Influenza, 1700–1900: A Study in Historical Epidemiology.* Totowa, N.J., 1986.

Salisbury, Neil. *Manitou and Providence: Indians, Europeans, and the Making of New England, 1500–1643.* New York, 1982.

Savitt, Todd, and James Harvey Young, eds. *Disease and Distinctiveness in the American South.* Knoxville, Tenn., 1988.

Shammas, Carole. *The Pre-industrial Consumer in England and America.* Oxford, 1990.

Shryock, Richard H. *Medicine and Society in America, 1660–1860.* Ithaca, N.Y., 1962.

Sturtevant, William C., gen. ed. *Handbook of North American Indians.* Vols. 5–15. Washington, D.C., 1978–1988.

Tate, T. W., and Ammerman, D. L., eds. *The Chesapeake in the Seventeenth Century: Essays on Anglo-American Society.* Chapel Hill, N.C., 1979.

Wallace, Anthony F. C. *The Death and Rebirth of the Seneca.* New York, 1972.

Waring, Joseph I. *A History of Medicine in South Carolina, 1670–1825.* Charleston, S.C., 1964.

Jay Cassel

SEE ALSO **Ecological Consequences of Economic Development; Old Age and Death;** and the essays under COLONIAL SETTINGS.

COLONIAL MEDICINE

THE EUROPEANS WHO SETTLED North America, and their descendants, held ideas of health and disease that were shared, for the most part, by English-, French-, Spanish-, Dutch-, and German-speaking peoples on both sides of the Atlantic. The inhabitants of some colonies might differ from others in their views of death and in the structure of their medical institutions, but their common medical culture mimicked that of Europe as a whole during the colonial period. That is, all colonial European Americans recognized the fifth-century B.C. Greek physician Hippocrates as the father of medicine, especially as perpetuated by his major interpreter, Galen, a prolific Greco-Roman physician of the second century A.D. As a result, later developments in the healing arts were regarded simply as improvements on the Hippocratic-Galenic tradition.

EXPLANATIONS OF DISEASE

The colonists' concepts of disease and its causation were largely speculative. It could not have been otherwise before either the emergence of modern pathology in the nineteenth century or the invention of diagnostic tools such as microscopes and bacterial cultures, which made it possible to identify the specific causes of specific illnesses. Thus, until about 1850 or even later, disease was explained by a two-tiered set of causes.

External Causes

The first tier of hypothetical causes comprised the "external" or "proximate" causes, which triggered the "internal" changes that produced the patient's symptoms. The most common triggers were "miasmas" or "effluvia," invisible particles released into the air from putrefying animal or vegetable matter, or from noxious or poisonous objects, thus inducing disease from a distance. When threatened by illnesses transmitted in this way, colonists protected themselves by fumigating their homes, shops, or ships; by cleaning their privies; by taking hygienic steps ordered by municipal authorities; or by fleeing the epidemic, as smallpox sometimes forced colonial legislatures to do.

Contagion, the spread of illness by direct contact with sick animals or patients or with tainted objects, was a second major external cause of disease. Common sense dictated that it could be prevented by isolating affected or potential victims, by quarantine, or by flight.

A third putative cause of disease was the weather, especially changes in temperature or humidity. Physicians used thermometers to measure body temperature far less often than to measure air temperature, because it, along with estimates of rain- and snowfall, helped doctors predict the onset or disappearance of epidemics. This was especially true for mosquito-borne epidemic diseases such as malaria and yellow fever until the mosquito's role in their transmission was demonstrated at the very end of the nineteenth century. Individuals could protect themselves from meteorologically induced illness in their homes, it was believed, by controlling drafts.

Several contemporary observers of the colonial scene rejoiced that they found greater health and longevity in America than in Europe, although it was sometimes suggested that immigrants to the southern colonies should plan to arrive in the autumn, to permit "seasoning" of their bodies and diets before their first experience of the hottest months. Americans' relative healthiness—if the observation was indeed valid—was usually ascribed to their cleaner air, although it was more likely related to both their better diet and the lesser likelihood of transmitting infectious diseases among the relatively thinly scattered North American populations.

Closely related to meteorological theories of illness was the notion that it could be caused—even at great distances—by natural disasters such as earthquakes, volcanic eruptions, floods, and droughts, or by astronomical events such as comets. Little could be done to avoid this fourth external cause of disease, although it was thought that conventional precautions such as rest, appropriate diet, and cleanliness might help render the body fit to counterbalance the adverse effects of such unpredictable occurrences.

Finally, illness could be inflicted by a vengeful deity, a concept that was especially strong among both Calvinists and Counter-Reformation Catholics. Because sin was the obvious stimulus of pathogenic divine wrath, it could be avoided by obeying biblical injunctions or mitigated by prayer and penance.

Internal Causes

Although one or more external factors might trigger illness, specific symptoms were explained separately, as the results of internal derangements of a normal physiology that were unique to the patient alone, associated with his own lifestyle and environment. Colonial physicians used this second tier of disease causation to explain how the body was healthy when its parts were in harmonious equilibrium, and how illness indicated weakness or dominance in one or more of the patient's organs, an imbalance reflected in his special cluster of symptoms. Physicians trained in the ancient Hippocratic-Galenic tradition believed that the body was healthy when its four fluid humors—blood, phlegm, yellow bile, and black bile—remained in their appropriate balance, and that an excess or deficit of one or more humors, whatever the cause, resulted in disease. This concept survives in our words "sanguine," "phlegmatic," "bilious" or "choleric" (*chole* was Greek for bile), and "melancholic" (*melan* was Greek for black), and we still describe people as in a good or foul "humor" in both English and French.

Humoral imbalances were detected clinically by assessing four correlative qualities: heat, cold, moisture, and dryness. An excess or deficit of any one of these represented a disequilibrium between two humors associated with it. For instance, if a patient's nose was overflowing with phlegm but the skin was not warm to the touch, the diagnosis would be a "cold," whereas if the patient coughed up copious phlegm and felt warm, the illness was a "fever."

Although doctors relied on humoral explanations of disease until well into the nineteenth century, they did adopt new theories that offered improved explanations of specific symptoms, even if the new ideas did not completely replace older ones. Thus, late-eighteenth-century physicians had absorbed an eclectic group of theories that they continually molded to their own clinical observations. For instance, the sixteenth-century mystical Swiss-German physician Paracelsus had taught that disease was related to chemical disturbances (among other factors). In the seventeenth century many physicians adopted this "iatrochemical" approach to medicine, which led them to prescribe a number of inorganic chemical remedies in tandem with classical botanical drugs. The emergence of recognizably modern chemistry in the 1780s led doctors to use Paracelsus's explicitly antihumoral theory to explain the heat generated in the feverish body in terms of unbalanced amounts of mercury, sulfur, and salt in the blood.

The most important new pathophysiological concept was promoted in 1695 by Friedrich Hoffmann of Halle, and then by Hermann Boerhaave of Leiden. Because several of the medical faculty at Edinburgh had studied at Leiden and in turn taught many leading physicians in British North America, by the 1750s Hoffmann's ideas were taking firm root on both sides of the Atlantic (although they had had close parallels in ancient Greece). His theory, now called solidism to distinguish it from humoralism, postulated that disease was caused by imbalances in the tone, or innate strength, of the fibers assumed to comprise the basic structure of conducting tubes such as blood vessels and nerves (the latter were thought to convey nerve "fluids" through the body).

Thus, for instance, physicians blamed convulsions on hyperactive nerves, and paralytic strokes on weak nerves. Similarly, they thought that fever was caused by hyperactive and constricted arteries because heat was always associated with hyperactivity (as in boiling water), and because the fast pulse usually associated with elevated body temperature was assumed to generate heat through friction within the arteries. Jaundice was interpreted as an excess of bilious humor caused by obstruction of the passages through which the liver secreted bile into the intestinal lumen. Dropsy (now known as congestive heart failure) was seen in humoral terms as an accumulation of fluid in the chest (hydrothorax) and abdomen (ascites), and in solidist terms as a weakness of the vascular fibers that normally resorbed excess fluid from body tissues. Thus, humoralism and solidism were not mutually exclusive; each complemented and extended the other.

Several physicians were tempted by the urge to classify that permeated the Enlightenment. In accord with solidist tenets, John Brown of Edinburgh proposed in the early 1780s that all disease could be classified as "sthenic" or "asthenic"; that is, as due to increased or decreased "excitability." Although his theory was as logical as any other, it was ridiculed by his colleagues as an unwarranted oversimplification. His major book was not published in America until after the revolution, but his teaching had already been imported by his pupil Benjamin Rush of Philadelphia, who earned his M.D. at Edinburgh in 1768. He later carried Brown's teaching even further by reducing all disease to a generalized "debility," a notion just as controversial as Brown's "asthenia."

DIAGNOSIS AND TREATMENT

Diagnosis

Physicians relied chiefly on the patient's history to assess humors and tones. Physical examination was rudimentary. Most disorders were diagnosed by typical symptoms and physical signs such as superficial sores, rashes, jaundice, pallor, edema (tissue fluid), ascites, urethral discharge, or blindness due to opacified lenses (that is, cataracts).

Pulse and respiratory rate were assessed in fever patients, because both were thought to be proportional to body temperature. Doctors also palpated wounds, deep or superficial swellings, and the birth canal of women in labor. Urine and sputum were sometimes examined for evidence of inflammation.

Doctors seldom changed their diagnoses, although they did recognize new symptoms as complications of a patient's primary illness. Sometimes they sought permission for postmortem examination of the body when they were unsure of the cause of death or to learn more about a patient's disease. Birth defects and, rarely, medicolegal queries were other reasons for autopsies.

We have little information about the actual disease burden in the North American colonies beyond what can be inferred from sporadic diaries, bills of mortality, and accounts of devastating epidemics. That is, we know little about the majority of patients who were afflicted by, but survived, the ordinary illnesses of everyday life. Still, a few generalizations are possible.

The leading cause of death was consumption (most cases were tuberculosis), which caused 20 to 25 percent of deaths in communities of all sizes throughout North America (and Europe). Other pulmonary afflictions, such as pneumonia and influenza, accounted for another 5 percent of deaths and for a large but unknown number of nonfatal respiratory illnesses. Other common serious or fatal diseases included diarrhea and dysentery (diarrhea accompanied by bloody stools and severe abdominal pain); yellow fever (especially in the southernmost colonies); and a group of fevers called, in increasing order of severity, slow, nervous, petechial (characterized by skin hemorrhages), typhus (or ship or jail), and malignant, although such terms cannot now be equated with specific causative microorganisms with any certainty. Bilious fever and colic were accompanied by jaundice. All these fevers were termed "continued fevers," in contrast with "intermittent fevers," fits of fever and shaking chills that recurred every forty-eight or seventy-two hours (they are now called malarias, which means "bad air," because of their presumed miasmatic origin).

Smallpox was an ever-present threat, especially in port towns throughout North America, where 15 percent to 25 percent of those afflicted died of it. In 1721 Dr. Zabdiel Boylston and Rev. Cotton Mather of Boston introduced the practice of protecting uninfected people by inoculating them with pus from smallpox patients. Boylston and Mather had learned about inoculation, later called variolation (*variola* is the Latin for smallpox), from reports of its use in Constantinople and West Africa. After coming down with a mild case that was usually fatal in fewer than 1 percent, inoculated persons would not be struck down in future epidemics of smallpox. British doctors introduced the technique to New France about 1765. George Washington, who had had smallpox when he was nineteen, had his entire army inoculated during the winter of 1777–1778.

Children succumbed to intestinal disorders such as cholera infantum (a "summer diarrhea" unrelated to true cholera), as well as to measles, chicken pox, scarlet fever, diphtheria, croup, whooping cough, erysipelas, and worms. A particularly devastating combination of scarlet fever and diphtheria swept through New England in 1735–1740. Called the "throat distemper," it killed large numbers of infants in many rural towns but mysteriously spared both neighboring communities and seaports.

Many bacterial or viral causes of death are camouflaged by the diseases named in bills of mortality, such as the childhood deaths attributed to convulsions but undoubtedly caused by febrile illnesses. A few deaths were clearly related to cardiovascular disease, but most such conditions were not recognized as such. For instance, dropsy was not yet associated with heart failure, nor was palsy or apoplexy associated with strokes. In addition, many cardiovascular and cancer deaths are masked by diagnoses such as "atrophy," "bedridden," "decay of nature," "lethargy," "marasmus" (now used for protein and calorie malnutrition), "old age," and "suddenly." Still, since the average life expectancy at birth was only about thirty-eight (largely because of the high mortality rates during childhood), and less in the larger towns, heart disease and cancer were not as prevalent in colonial America as they are in the late twentieth century.

Bladder stones, syphilis, and kidney infections are easier to recognize in colonial documents, as are "rheumatism" and "gout," even if most of the latter two were probably caused by degenerative arthritis. Stillbirths and congenital malformations of the spine, face, and heart occurred about as often in the North American colonies as now, but puerperal (childbed) fever was less often a cause of maternal death than is now usually assumed. On the other hand, accidental deaths and trauma were about as frequent among colonists as they are today. Infants were burned, scalded, smothered, or overdosed with opium (given to calm them); and adults fell from roofs, froze, committed suicide, were run over by carriages, and—especially in port towns— drowned.

Medical Treatment

Colonists throughout North America relied on about 225 different drugs, compounded from about 100 presumed active ingredients, although each doctor had his own favorites. Because the body was thought to be in a state of healthy balance when blood or nerve fluids could circulate freely, or when feces, urine, sweat, phlegm, or menstrual flow could be expelled easily, drugs were judged effective when they stimulated the release of secretions and excretions that contained or represented foul humors. Thus, once a physician had determined whether his patient's symptoms were associated with hypoactivity or hyperactivity of the blood vessels or nerves, and had concluded which humors were most seriously affected, he chose those remedies which he thought best suited for the illness at hand: stimulating drugs for patients with weak systems, or sedative drugs for illnesses characterized by overactive systems.

However, the first colonists, who arrived in Plymouth, Jamestown, and Quebec, well before solidist ideas had permeated European practice, relied chiefly on ancient humoral concepts and on Dioscorides, the first-century Greek physician whose work was the progenitor of the herbals that the colonists brought with them. Thus, the first European-American physicians usually chose drugs that they thought would correct humoral imbalances. They also chose drugs recommended by Paracelsus, both his inorganic chemical remedies and those which he said were indicated by the "doctrine of signatures" (or "similars"). Like humoralism, that idea had first surfaced in the ancient world. It supposed that illness was appropriately treated by materials that physically resembled the patient's symptoms or the affected organs. For instance, yellow flowers were suitable for jaundice, walnut meats for afflictions of the brain, bloodstone for hemorrhage, and toad skins for illnesses characterized by wartlike eruptions.

The colonists imported most of their drugs from Europe or the West Indies but, when possible, planted species that they could cultivate themselves, whether in their home gardens or in those which supplied the hospitals of New France. In 1672 John Josselyn described for the first time, in his *New-Englands Rarities Discovered*, a few medicinal plants used by Indians in New England. The descriptions of drug plants found in the early eighteenth century by Dr. Michel Sarrazin, who was also known as a botanist, were widely disseminated in his native France.

Several physicians sought useful remedies among the new plant species that they encountered in the New World chiefly because a corollary of the doctrine of similars dictated that appropriate remedies would be found growing near places where disease occurred. However, surprisingly few of the plant remedies used by Indians anywhere on the continent were adopted by Anglo-American practitioners. Not only did they find most indigenous remedies to be no more effective than those which they brought with them, they could not relate the Indians' usage to their time-honored Galenic and Paracelsian notions of drug action. Among the newly introduced Native American plant drugs were sassafras, ginseng, Virginia snakeroot, and jimsonweed, but none of them surpassed in medical popularity any European import used for the same therapeutic purposes. By the 1750s most European-American physicians had lost interest in seeking indigenous or Indian remedies and in the doctrine of similars. By then their therapeutic choices were almost entirely among those dictated by the conjunction of humoral and solidist concepts.

The most frequently prescribed drugs had laxative or cathartic properties, especially medicinal rhubarb, castor oil, jalap, niter, licorice, senna, aloes, cream of tartar (potassium bitartrate), calomel (mercurous chloride), Glauber's salt (sodium sulfate), and soapy saline enemas. Not only did these drugs flush out unbalanced humors via the intestines, but they were also thought to relax the abnormal tensions that could inhibit normal evacuations. Constipation alone was seldom an indication for prescribing cathartics. Indeed, they were often prescribed for patients with diarrhea when the physician associated it with hyperactive fiber tones that could be reduced by drugs which simultaneously stimulated bowel movements. All the cathartics used in colonial America could indeed move the bowels, although the resulting evacuation did not contribute much to the restoration of health.

The next most popular remedies were the "tonics" used to increase the tone of weakened blood vessels and nerve fibers. The drug most often prescribed for this purpose was Peruvian bark (or cinchona), which we now know contains quinine. After its introduction to Europe from South America in the 1630s as a highly effective remedy for "intermittent fevers" (that is, malaria), doctors went on to reason that it should be equally effective against other fevers. The bark's astringent bitterness supported the notion that it could strengthen a body that had been weakened by any fever, whether intermittent or continued. Other common tonics included acids such as vitriol (sulfuric acid), probably because they could denature animal tissue, thus making it appear more solid.

Colonial physicians also gave their febrile patients emetics, drugs that caused vomiting, to strengthen what they took to be weak ("dyspeptic") stomachs. Drugs such as tartar emetic (antimony potassium tartrate) and ipecac were thought to give new tone to organs that had been weakened by disease, via the nerves that connected the stomach to the rest of the body. Thus, the act of vomiting was not merely evidence that foul humors had been evacuated. It also showed that the drug had acted as it was supposed to do, as a generalized tonic that first strengthened the stomach.

Diaphoretics, drugs that made patients sweat, were thought to strengthen the blood vessels that carried fluid to the sweat glands in the skin. Not only did such drugs remove excess fluids, they were also tonics that made fever patients "sweat out" their disease. Most were salts of antimony, but Dover's powder, a mixture of opium and ipecac, was sometimes prescribed for the same purpose. Similarly, "absorbent" drugs,

such as magnesia alba (magnesium carbonate) and kaolin (a fine clay), were thought to absorb pathogenic materials out of the blood and into the intestines, so that they could be flushed out with the stools.

Diuretics formed a final category of humor-depleting drugs, and according to solidist reasoning, it was their tonic effect on renal arteries that enhanced the production of urine. Although squill and several inorganic salts were used for the same purpose, none was thought to be dependable. Digitalis, the first drug that could be relied on to induce diuresis in patients who were bloated by dropsy, was not introduced until 1785.

Narcotics—opium preparations like laudanum (an alcohol solution of 6 percent to 10 percent opium)—were important multipurpose drugs. About fifteen opium-based remedies were used in the eighteenth century. Often prescribed as analgesics (painkillers), they were also given to induce sleep (especially to quiet crying infants) and to control diarrhea (the weak camphorated laudanum formula called paregoric, which means "soothing," is still used for that purpose).

Drugs made with mercury and its salts were used as cathartics, diaphoretics, diuretics, and even as emetics. These properties, as well as the salivation invariably induced by mercury, convinced physicians that it was tonic to all organs. As a result, mercurials were prescribed for many fevers, notably syphilis, on the assumption that they could help the body to eliminate the offending noxious factors.

Physicians reserved two treatments for their patients with the worst fevers or injuries. One was blistering the skin with an "epispastic," an alcohol solution of pulverized cantharides beetles (also called Spanish flies). Employed in ancient Greece to draw pathogenic humors from the body, by the 1750s the blister was also regarded as an artificial inflammation that neutralized the naturally occurring inflammation which had caused the febrile patient's symptoms in the first place, by the process called counterirritation.

The other drastic treatment was bleeding, on the humoral grounds that it removed chemically or otherwise unbalanced blood, and on the solidist grounds that reducing the blood volume relaxed tension on the hyperactive fibers of the fevered cardiovascular system. Patients were bled only if they had rapid pulses, indicating that their circulatory system was overexcited and needed to be calmed, or sedated, by draining off excess blood. Doctors bled up to 20 percent of their adult fever patients, removing an average of twelve ounces at a time, although they sometimes bled a patient repeatedly, even on the same day. The usual technique was to cut the vein in the front of the elbow ("venesection" or phlebotomy) and let blood drain from it into a bowl. However, until the late eighteenth century children were sometimes bled through a cut on the underside of the tongue, on the gums, or on the top of the foot. Leeches, each of which removed about half an ounce of blood, were far more popular in the Middle Atlantic and southern British colonies than in New England, New France, or Louisiana.

Because the most prevalent illnesses throughout colonial North America, as everywhere, were fevers, physicians relied on a general approach to their cure, the "antiphlogistic regimen," which emerged in Germany about 1700. The Greek word *phlogiston* referred to a combustible substance that gave off heat (that is, fever) when burned; although its existence was disproved in the late 1780s, the concept survived in medical therapeutics well into the nineteenth century. Also called "depletive" treatment, antiphlogistic therapy required that the patient minimize the physiological irritations which increased body heat, chiefly by avoiding external heat (for example, fires), exercise, and excessive food and mental activity; putrefaction of humors in the stomach, by taking emetics or acids; fecal retention, by taking cathartics; and abnormal tissue fluids, by taking diaphoretics or diuretics. Blisters and bleeding, too, were depletive, but they were prescribed only for the sickest patients.

A "low," or meatless, diet was a standard component of the antiphlogistic regimen, since red meat was considered a tonic because it contained iron. A stronger diet, one with meat, was prescribed for patients convalescing from debilitating fevers or from nonfebrile illnesses characterized by weakness. Hence our dictum to "feed a cold, starve a fever."

One last therapeutic option was to prescribe no remedy at all, to rely on what colonial physicians called the *vis medicatrix naturae,* the healing power of nature. The notion that the body could heal of its own accord had been known in the ancient world, and doctors trained in the European medical tradition knew that it could be relied upon from time to time. On the other hand, excessive reliance on nature would have been professionally unsatisfying to most healers and, perhaps, most patients. Not until after 1835 did the concept of self-limited disease begin to gain explicit acceptance throughout North America.

Surgical Treatment

Although English custom and law distinguished carefully among surgeons, physicians, and apothecaries, English colonists in the Americas did not. Most colonial physicians had few special surgical skills other than those required for basic emergency care: they could dress wounds, reduce dislocations and simple fractures, excise wens, open and drain abscesses, and remove fluid from the abdomen through a large, hollow needle. Doctors called themselves surgeons only if they could also perform complex operations, such as amputating limbs injured in accidents or in battle, especially involving compound fractures, as well as those which had been frozen or were gangrenous because of arterial occlusion. Only a few performed the operations that made headlines in colonial newspapers, such as removing bladder stones ("lithotomy") and cataracts ("couching"). The latter involved depressing the opacified lens into the back of the eye, a procedure first described in Rome about A.D. 35, or total removal of the lens, introduced in France in 1747. Hall Jackson of Portsmouth, New Hampshire, was among the small number of highly imaginative eighteenth-century surgeons who devised essentially *ad hoc* lifesaving operations for patients with extensive wounds, but the chest and the abdomen remained beyond surgical treatment until well after the advent of general anesthesia (in 1846) and antiseptic techniques (from the 1870s).

Surviving documents do not verify the regular use of alcohol to provide anesthesia during surgery in the North American colonies, although opiates were sometimes used to minimize postoperative pain. Nor is it known why the amputations performed by some surgeons, such as Jackson, seldom became fatally infected; perhaps they were intuitively more attentive to cleanliness than others, even if they did not recognize its true importance. Many doctors, unwilling to subject patients to the pain and putrefaction ("sepsis") that often accompanied operations, limited their practices to what is now called internal medicine and minor surgery.

However, most physicians did provide two quasi-surgical services. Tooth extraction was among their standard procedures until just after the revolution, when it began to be performed largely by the specialists who were then emerging in cities like Boston. Specific prenatal care was virtually unknown during the colonial centuries, but doctors did deliver some babies and care for postpartum illnesses. However, most infants were delivered by midwives or other women, although they were beginning to be replaced by physicians in large towns like Boston and Portsmouth at the time of the revolution.

In retrospect, it is clear that physicians of the colonial era had few drugs that could have contributed to their patients' recoveries. Nevertheless, about 95 percent of adult patients did recover, as far as they or their doctors could tell, at least when not afflicted by a serious epidemic disease such as smallpox. Their "cures" really testify to the body's ability to heal itself through normal physiological mechanisms such as the immune and inflammatory responses. On the other hand, it can be concluded that those who survived the rigors of surgery did benefit directly from their physicians' professional skills.

HEALTH CARE PROVIDERS

Colonial Americans relied on two tiers of health care providers. Most first-line healing occurred in the home, occasionally with the help of a part-time practitioner. Trained physicians were consulted chiefly when home-based medical care failed to restore health.

Healing in the Home

The most important healers in the homes of North American colonists were women, who took care not only of their families but also of their servants and farm laborers. Women also occasionally took into their homes, at town expense, indigent town residents unable to care for themselves (after about 1700 this function was taken over by almshouses in New England). In addition, southern plantation owners often took care

of their slaves or delegated that responsibility to their farm overseers, much as shipowners delegated it to their captains.

Although colonial women may have learned about the care of the sick primarily from their mothers or other women, they could also rely on books such as George Hartman's *The Family Physitian or a Collection of Choice . . . Remedies for the Cure of Almost All Diseases Incident to Humane Bodies* (London, 1696). Popular British home medical texts that were exported to North America and reprinted in the colonies included Nicholas Culpeper's *The English Physitian* (London, 1652) and John Wesley's *Primitive Physick* (London, 1747). Many women grew their own medicinal herbs, guided by local oral tradition or by herbals in the Hippocratic tradition of Dioscorides. Of these, the most important was probably Thomas Johnson's 1633 revision of John Gerard's *The Herball or Generall Historie of Plantes*, originally published in 1597. However, because few households had such books, some women kept journals in which they wrote home remedies gleaned from their own reading or from their friends. Similarly, shipmasters could rely on John Woodall's *The Surgions Mate* (London, 1617, 1639, 1653, 1655) and its successors, written partly to fill the need created as the number of transatlantic voyages increased.

Women made home remedies with the same ingredients that physicians prescribed for their patients. In addition, proprietary or patented medicines imported from England after 1700 were made with similar drug materials, also in the humoral tradition. Cheaper alternatives to the remedies prescribed by doctors, such over-the-counter remedies as Turlington's Balsam, Daffy's Elixir, Stoughton's Drops, and Juniper's Essence of Peppermint, were integral to early American do-it-yourself medicine. However, they were sold largely in taverns and other shops, not in apothecary shops. Many of the latter were owned by physicians, who publicly decried such remedies as unscientific while privately fearing them as potential competition for patients' shillings.

Some well-to-do colonial homes had a medicine chest stocked with the most frequently used cathartics, emetics, diaphoretics, and diuretics. The chests usually included scales and other equipment for compounding drugs for the sick-room, and lancet-shaped blades for bleeding. Apothecaries stocked similar but proportionately larger chests for militia commanders, sea captains, and the hospitals of New France.

Reverend Cotton Mather's 1724 manuscript "The Angel of Bethesda" (eventually published in 1972) illuminates the healing role of Calvinist preachers in early New England. While interpreting sickness to their congregations in terms of a wrathful deity, many ministers absorbed medical information that they used to heal individual parishioners. The preachers' wide reading, combined with their less than generous cash income, made it easier for them to assume the role of fee-for-service healers, especially when theocracy and its perquisites waned. Several ministers who lost pulpits in the Great Awakening began to practice medicine full time. In general, medical ministers performed nearly the whole range of services provided by regular physicians, except for major surgery. Similarly, as early as the 1620s Jesuit missionaries in New France provided medical care for Indians, as well as for French settlers, at least partly to help win converts.

Two groups of women practitioners—midwives and ministers' wives—provided fee-for-service medical care outside their own homes on a regular basis, as integral parts of the network of mutual assistance that sustained colonial communities. They were self-taught or instructed by other women, but some ministers' wives also knew or consulted their husbands' medical books. Although both kinds of female practitioners assisted at childbirth, they also cared for patients of both sexes with many kinds of illness, just as male physicians or ministers cared for women at term as well as for their gynecological complaints. That is, gender appears not to have been a major issue at the time of sickness or delivery, and the remedies prescribed by women healers were the same as those prescribed by regularly trained male physicians.

Overt quacks, mountebanks in the European tradition, were rare in colonial America. As early as 1649 the Massachusetts legislature found it necessary to restrain the practice of healers who were not trained in traditional Hippocratic-Galenic medicine, but the law was unenforceable. In 1736 the Virginia House of Burgesses tried to limit rising medical costs by setting maximum fees that regular physicians could charge; by inference, irregular practitioners were not allowed to practice at all.

After 1720 a small number of itinerant healers began to advertise in newspapers. Most promoted themselves, chiefly to the poor, as specialists in treating venereal complaints, tumors, and diseases of the eyes or ears; as bonesetters; or, the most numerous, as surgeon-dentists. Among the last to appear, surgeon-dentists were more reputable than the other advertisers and helped pave the way for modern dentistry. The others may have been entrepreneurs, but their medical concepts were consistent with those of regular physicians.

Regular Physicians

It has been estimated that at the outbreak of the American Revolution, about thirty-five hundred physicians trained in the ancient traditions were practicing medicine in the thirteen British colonies. Fewer than 10 percent are thought to have had a professional degree, and no more than 6 percent to 7 percent were immigrants trained before coming to America. The only two medical schools in British North America were still new in 1776: that at the College of Philadelphia (now the University of Pennsylvania) was founded in 1765, and that at King's College (now Columbia University) in New York two years later. Consequently, most Americans who wished to study medicine at a university had to go abroad, but the cost was too great for most aspiring doctors. A few went to Padua and Leiden on the Continent, or to Oxford or Cambridge; but most went to Edinburgh (popular among students from Philadelphia, New York, and the southern British colonies), or to hospitals in London (favored by New Englanders, perhaps because of the greater emphasis there on practical than on theoretical medicine). Some colonial physicians attended college, but the majority did not. In any event, the college curriculum would have contributed little to a doctor's preprofessional education.

It has been nearly impossible to identify the substantial proportion of colonial doctors, especially in the decades just before the revolution, who were self-taught—much less to assess their professional skills. Most of those whose training can be documented earned their credentials as apprentices to other physicians (often relatives) even if they also went to college or medical school, or they took a postgraduate course in London or elsewhere. The quality and extent of on-the-job medical training varied considerably, since it had no standardized curriculum. The term of apprenticeship in the colonies was generally one to two years, far shorter than under the more restrictive conditions common in England, but it was occasionally as long as five years. Moreover, apothecaries were not clearly differentiated from physicians, and training in one trade could lead to a career in the other.

The earliest English settlements sometimes found it difficult to recruit physicians. Few who had been trained in Britain would willingly abandon financial safety there for the uncertainty of earning a living in the American wilderness. The ratio of physicians to population remained about 1 to 1,000 between 1620 and 1700 in Massachusetts; it was local men who increased the ratio to 1 to 420–800 in towns of all sizes by 1780.

New England physicians treated four to ten patients daily, about half of them on house calls. Their fees averaged about two shillings per patient visit in rural areas, and three to six shillings in Boston and New York. The latter charges were larger partly because they included fees for services, such as deliveries of babies and major surgery, seldom provided in less populous areas. Another coveted source of professional income was the award of municipal contracts for almshouse physicians or those attached to military units even during times of peace.

Unlike the salaried physicians and surgeons of New France and New Spain, healers in British America were paid almost entirely on a fee-for-service basis. However, they seldom had enough patients to provide them with substantial or dependable professional incomes. As a rule, accounts were settled once or twice a year, and when cash was scarce, payment was likely to be in labor or goods. Thus, many physicians had to supplement their incomes as farmers, lawyers, judges, landlords, or merchants, especially of drugs, which they imported wholesale and sold at retail. Only after the revolution did most Anglo-European physicians abandon drug sales to apothecaries, although important towns such as Boston and Williamsburg supported retail drug-

gists soon after their founding. Still, even if doctors did not become wealthy by practicing medicine, they were esteemed in their communities, chiefly because of their time-honored role as members of a learned, care-giving profession.

Beginning in 1721 doctors in and near Boston organized at least twelve short-lived local medical societies. Their goals included professional self-improvement, the prevention of competition, the adoption of minimum-fee schedules, and regulation through licensing. However, these societies soon degenerated into social organizations. The first long-lived colony (or state) medical societies were established in New Jersey (1766) and Massachusetts (1781), to set fees and regulate licensing. Thus, medicine did not begin to become fully professionalized in British America until after the revolution, when medical schools and journals, as well as societies, began to proliferate.

New France had fewer doctors with medical degrees. The majority, called *chirurgiens*, resembled today's general practitioners; the elite minority, the *médecins*, resembled modern specialists. Both earned their medical credentials in France or elsewhere in Europe, often by apprenticeship. The distinguished Michel Sarrazin, for example, emigrated as a *chirurgien* but went back, to Rheims, to qualify for appointment as a *médecin* when he returned to New France in 1697. The military nature of the French colonization necessitated an abundance (about six per one thousand population) of *chirurgiens*, who were supervised by a royal navy appointee at Quebec. Charged to examine the qualifications of prospective *chirurgiens*, he had to accept many who were poorly trained because the French were so thinly spread throughout their provinces.

A similar official at Mexico City, called the *protomedicato*, examined physicians and surgeons for service in New Spain. In addition to assessing their professional competence, he had to certify that they were not of Moorish or Jewish descent. The Royal and Pontifical University of Mexico (founded in 1551) began teaching medicine in 1572, and in 1646 it became illegal to practice medicine in New Spain without a university degree. However, those physicians in Mexico City who already had degrees tried to obstruct the influx of trained physicians from Spain, and of students into the new degree program, in order to preserve their lucrative monopoly. As a result, much medical care in New Spain was provided by illegal folk healers who practiced a blend of Hippocratic-Galenic and indigenous Aztec medicine, especially in rural areas such as the Spanish Borderlands.

Beginning in the 1630s, barber-surgeons accompanied colonists to both New Sweden and New Netherlands, where they were called *balbieren*. Although some did not remain for any length of time, those who did stay performed common medical and surgical procedures that they had learned at home. Thus, like the *chirurgiens* of New France, the *balbieren* were general practitioners, but they also gave shaves.

Hospitals

If colonial medical practice was less hierarchical than that of the French and Spanish colonies, so was the British colonial *ad hoc* hospital system. Its roots were in the infirmaries of municipal almshouses, which usually contracted with a local physician for his services when they were needed. Boston had an almshouse in 1662, Portsmouth, New Hampshire, in 1711, and most other major towns by 1750.

The almshouse (*armenhuis,* "poor house") established in 1652 at Beverswyck (Albany) may have been the first in North America. However, unlike its British counterparts, it seems to have provided medical services to indigents who were not inmates. It remained in operation until after the American Revolution.

Many towns established temporary pesthouses at the advent of serious epidemics, while ports, which were at the greatest risk of imported epidemics, maintained them on a permanent basis. Between the introduction of smallpox inoculation at Boston in 1721 and its replacement by vaccination with cowpox at the end of the century, town governments at Boston and elsewhere authorized the establishment of temporary inoculation hospitals, where people could undergo the three-week preventive treatment when smallpox threatened their communities. Beginning in Boston in 1764, town-funded inoculation hospitals sometimes inoculated indigent residents without charge, as did several private for-profit operations.

The one single-purpose permanent hospital established in British America before the revolution was the hospital for the insane at Williamsburg, Virginia, opened in 1773. Built and supported by the province, it permitted removing the pauper insane from jails to roomier cells, although still in chains, in a more easily controllable environment.

Moreover, only one general hospital opened in British America before 1776. The Pennsylvania Hospital in Philadelphia (1751) admitted its first patients to a recently acquired house in 1752 and to a new permanent building in 1756. Modeled in part on the Royal Infirmary in Edinburgh, which was well known to the founders of the new hospital, it had British America's first medical library (1762). However, the nursing care that it provided was more custodial than remedial, since modern nursing techniques would not evolve for another century. The New York Hospital, designed along similar lines, was chartered in 1771 but did not accept patients until 1791.

The Continental Army relied on an ill-governed hospital system during the revolution. It was often mired in disputes over lines of authority between the frontline hospitals of the provincial regiments, staffed by surgeons familiar to their wounded patients, and rearline general hospitals, staffed by physicians appointed by the Continental Congress. Regimental hospitals, which were more temporary than the general hospitals, were designed to give immediate care to the wounded; general hospitals served those convalescing from wounds and major surgery or from contagious diseases. Many military hospitals were established in large private homes, especially those confiscated from fleeing Tories, or in suitable public buildings, such as the College of Rhode Island (Brown University) at Providence, or the Governor's Palace and the College of William and Mary at Williamsburg. None of the few military hospital structures built for that purpose has survived, although archaeologists are excavating one at the site of Fort Independence in Vermont.

The owners of the largest southern plantations called the infirmaries that they built for their slaves "hospitals." In addition to custodial services, they had the additional special charge of providing adequate pre- and postnatal care for pregnant slaves and their children, because of their value to their owners. Much medical care was rendered by the slave owners themselves or their overseers, by midwives, or by local physicians on an annual retainer; but black "doctors" and "doctoresses" were also employed. However, in 1746 the Virginia legislature made it a capital offense for blacks to administer medicines, apparently because the slave-owning lawmakers feared being poisoned by them.

By contrast, French and Spanish colonists, as citizens of more highly centralized states whose hospitals were usually staffed by religious orders, re-created similar institutions, and many of them are still operating. The cornerstones of the health care system in New France were the general hospitals (*Hôtels-Dieu*) for medical and surgical patients in Quebec (1639), Montreal (1642), and Trois-Rivières (1694); and the hospitals for the elderly, infirm, and insane (*hôpitaux-généraux*) in Quebec and Montreal (both, 1692). The *Hôtel-Dieu* in Quebec, modeled on the famous *Hôtel-Dieu* in Paris, is the oldest hospital in North America. The oldest hospital in the present United States is the Charité in New Orleans, established in 1736 for the sick poor under the will of a sailor boatbuilder named Jean Louis. However, that city's first two hospitals had appeared in 1722–1725 and 1732–1734, and a *Hôtel-Dieu* was begun at Biloxi in the 1710s. Established by the church, the royal government, or wealthy benefactors, whose purses bore the medical costs of the needy poor, the well-endowed French colonial hospitals were administered along the progressive lines typical of the Enlightenment. A *chirurgien* and a *médecin* were attached to each, and nursing orders were responsible for everyday operations. Military *chirurgiens* cared for troops at major forts, although soldiers were also treated in civilian hospitals. A field hospital was established for the Lake Champlain army during the Seven Years' War.

Beginning in 1521 New Spain developed an equally well-organized hospital system, centered on Mexico City. Run by the Crown, the Spanish hospitals were staffed by religious orders, although they were financed by tribute exacted from the Indian communities that they served, especially in areas furthest removed from the colonial capital. A few institutions were devoted to specific diseases, such as leprosy and rabies. By 1700 the hospitals of New Spain had become important tools for acculturating the Indians.

SUMMARY

The European doctors who came to North America brought with them not only their ancient Hippocratic-Galenic notions of health and sickness but also newly emerging modifications of those theories that offered what they thought were better explanations of their patients' symptoms. Although the doctors adopted a few new plant remedies that they found on this side of the Atlantic, they did not adopt indigenous medical ideas. Many of the illnesses that affected the colonists were familiar to their compatriots at home, and death rates from each illness on both sides of the Atlantic were probably comparable over the long run. However, sporadic epidemics of highly fatal diseases that were endemic in Europe, such as smallpox, were far more threatening to the stability of colonies maintained for the economic benefit of their home countries. Because of the professional heritage common to doctors throughout North America, their treatments and results of those treatments resembled those of their professional colleagues throughout Europe.

So did the institutions and individuals who provided medical care in New France, New Spain, and the English colonies. Women or clergy met the most frequent therapeutic needs, while regular physicians were consulted chiefly when such frontline healers were unable to restore health. Few university-trained physicians settled in any North American province; most colonial doctors began their careers as apprentices. On the other hand, the French and Spanish brought to the New World the highly structured and well-supported hospital systems that they knew at home. The English did not even begin to build hospitals (for which they had to raise public subscriptions, as was often customary at home), until late in the colonial era. Still, it is nearly impossible to make meaningful comparisons of the quality of medical care given to the colonists, either among the various colonies or with that given in their homelands. Most non-surgical adult patients recovered regardless of the treatment they received, thanks to the body's remarkable ability to heal itself.

BIBLIOGRAPHY

Benes, Peter, ed. *Annual Proceedings of the Dublin Seminar for New England Folklife.* Vol. 15, *Medicine and Healing.* Boston, 1992.

Blanton, Wyndham B. *Medicine in Virginia in the Eighteenth Century.* Richmond, Va., 1931.

Cash, Philip. *Medical Men at the Siege of Boston, April 1775–April 1776.* Philadelphia, 1973.

Cash, Philip, Eric H. Christiansen, and J. Worth Estes, eds. *Medicine in Colonial Massachusetts, 1620–1820.* Boston, 1980.

Estes, J. Worth. *Dictionary of Protopharmacology: Therapeutic Practices, 1700–1850.* Canton, Mass., 1990.

———. *Hall Jackson and the Purple Foxglove: Medical Practice and Research in Revolutionary America, 1760–1820.* Hanover, N.H., 1979.

———. "Patterns of Drug Use in Colonial America." *New York State Journal of Medicine* 87 (January 1987):37–45.

———. "The Practice of Medicine in 18th-Century Massachusetts: A Bicentennial Perspective." *New England Journal of Medicine* 305, no. 19 (1981): 1040–1047.

———. "Quantitative Observations of Fever and Its Treatment Before the Advent of Short Clinical Thermometers." *Medical History* 35, no. 2 (1991): 189–216.

Estes, J. Worth, and David M. Goodman. *The Changing Humors of Portsmouth: The Medical Biography of an American Town, 1623–1983.* Boston, 1986.

Hein, Wolfgang-Hagen, ed. *Botanical Drugs of the Americas in the Old and New Worlds.* Stuttgart, Germany, 1984.

King, Lester S. *The Medical World of the Eighteenth Century.* Chicago, 1958.

Lessard, Renald. *Se Soigner au Canada aux XVIIe et XVIIIe siècles.* Hull, Quebec, 1990.

Numbers, Ronald L., ed. *Medicine in the New World: New Spain, New France, and New England.* Knoxville, Tenn., 1987.

Ortiz de Montellano, Bernard R. *Aztec Medicine, Health, and Nutrition.* New Brunswick, N.J., 1990.

Radbill, Samuel X. "The Barber Surgeons Among the Early Dutch and Swedes Along the Delaware." *Bulletin of the Institute of the History of Medicine* 4, no. 4 (1936):718–744.

Risse, Guenter B. *Hospital Life in Enlightenment Scotland.* New York, 1986.

Ulrich, Laurel Thatcher. *A Midwife's Tale: The Life of Martha Ballard, Based on Her Diary, 1785–1812.* New York, 1990.

Wangensteen, Owen H., and Sarah D. Wangensteen. *The Rise of Surgery, from Empiric Craft to Scientific Discipline.* Minneapolis, Minn., 1978.

Watson, Patricia A. *The Angelical Conjunction: The Preacher-Physicians of Colonial New England.* Knoxville, Tenn., 1991.

J. Worth Estes, M.D.*

SEE ALSO **Gender Relations** and **Scientific Inquiry.**

NATIVE AMERICAN MEDICINE

IN THE EARLY NINETEENTH CENTURY, a leader of a Kutchin Indian band languished at a Hudson's Bay Company post in the western sub-Arctic. He accused the local trader of sorcery—of "throwing bad medicine" on him—and, hoping for a cure, hired a "juggler" who blew on and said a spell over him. Barbue, as the traders called him, was also given a phlebotomy from which he bled profusely, then was placed in a shallow pit around which four fires were lit. The European traders offered Barbue some "salts" and a "physic," which he accepted. But to no avail; Barbue died from debilitating disease like many other natives of North America who succumbed to European-introduced epidemic diseases.

The story of Barbue's demise contains basic elements of North American Indian disease theory and curing practice, as well as a historical scene repeated often in the last five hundred years. When they became sick, the Kutchin and other western sub-Arctic Indians often suspected sorcery. They accounted for disease in other ways too, sometimes blaming themselves for violating taboos or the spirits of animals. For cures, they unhesitatingly hired people with special knowl-

---

* I am indebted to Dr. Jay Cassel of York University for much of the material on New France, including the results of some of his own unpublished work.

edge who diagnosed the cause of their sickness and sought, through ritual, their recovery. Their knowledge of the medicinal properties of plants was extensive. When Europeans arrived, they brought new diseases against which shamans and old cures were ineffective. In time, Native people contemplated and accepted alternative European theories and techniques but also adhered to partly eroded traditional belief systems and techniques. Even today, an amalgam of new and old remains for many.

TRADITIONAL DISEASE THEORY

Native American disease theory was richly varied. But despite the cultural specificity among belief systems, two broad statements can be made: American Indians tended to ascribe illness and death to several major sources including sorcery, transgression of taboos, spirits of various types (including ghosts), desires and loss of the soul, and dreams, as well as to "natural" causes; and of these, sorcery, spiritual aggression, and taboo transgression were indicated most often. Of course, not all these categories were equally important (or present) throughout Native America. Moreover, diagnosis was rarely a straightforward matter; although specific causes were considered likely for particular ailments, specialists were required to identify sources of sickness and prescribe cures. Sometimes, two or more causes "worked" together to cause illness: souls were lost because they wandered in dreams, for example, or a spirit's wrath was incited because of the transgression of a taboo.

The illustrations that follow are drawn from societies in which particular beliefs were fairly marked. It is worth keeping in mind that basic categories like religion and the supernatural may have been meaningful to Europeans, but not to Native Americans who did not have, or may not have had, words for them, nor did they draw lines between natural and supernatural, or animate and inanimate, in the same way or at all.

Sorcery

One of the commonest explanations of illness and disease throughout Native America was some form of sorcery, which involved an agent who was human or who belonged to a special

category of human and some form of supernatural aggression. In this essay, sorcery embraces several culturally constructed forms of supernatural aggression through human or special-human agency, variously called, in addition to sorcery itself, witchcraft, wizardry, and conjury. Distinctions between witchcraft as innate and inherent in a special class of humans, on the one hand, and sorcery as willfully acquired by any humans, on the other, are often drawn but are invalid in many cultures; the use of these labels requires great caution.

The fear of sorcery was especially marked among Navajo, Apache, and Puebloan peoples in the Southwest. For the Western Apache, certain types of illness were the result of sorcery. As Keith Basso shows in *Western Apache Witchcraft* the Western Apache distinguished two types of people with power: the medicine man, who diagnosed and cured illness, and the sorcerer-witch, who caused sickness. There were two types of sorcerer-witch: the love witch, who could make a person uncontrollably sexually obsessed with another; and the sorcerer—usually male, nocturnal, and highly dangerous—who made his victims sick by using poison made from powdered corpse skin and menstrual fluid, by spells, or by the magical injection of objects. The Western Apache believed that an incapacitating illness was caused by intense cold, bad food, or ghosts, or by a power; that one type of power was the sorcerer's; and that sudden paralysis or hurt, or dizziness or fainting were symptoms of sorcery.

Clyde Kluckhohn described four categories employed by the Navajo to distinguish principal techniques and agents of sorcery (which he termed witchcraft): witchery, the technique of witches; sorcery, or sorcerers; wizardry, or wizards; and frenzy witchcraft, whose practitioners were quite different from the other three. Witchery involved the nocturnal use, by men or women who had learned their craft, of corpse poison to injure or kill a victim. Some dramatic symptom such as lockjaw or fainting, or a gradual wasting away, were signs of having been bewitched. In sorcery, a spell was used together with an image of the victim or a bit of the victim's personal belongings to cause injury—or to kill, for victims were said to die four days after the spell was uttered. Wizardry involved the injection of ashes—or fragments of bone, charcoal, or other material—into the victim, who became emaciated. In frenzy, the Navajo used the power that they believed was contained in datura and other plants to gain success in trading, gambling, and hunting. That power could also be used malevolently against the rich.

Outbreaks of accusations of sorcery in societies experiencing stress, or engaged in disputes over power, have been abundantly described in Native America; this reminds us that no explanation of disease theory is adequate in the absence of historical contextualization. Different scholars have argued that one function of the belief in sorcery is as a form of social control.

Spirits

Many Native Americans believed that spirits or forces conceptualized in various ways and perhaps drawing on a diffuse, neutral power in the universe could be found inhering in specific objects or classes of objects, in great beings or lesser beings, or in human and other-than-human persons. When angered, these spirits through their constituting entities could make people sick. For some American Indians, great beings—"gods" in English—might be held responsible for certain types of illness. In the Northeast, the Huron attributed sickness in epidemic form to Aataentsic, an important supernatural being who was conceptualized as female and the moon. For many others, spirits of various sorts caused disease and death: the Shasta, in California, believed that spirits which inhered in meteorological phenomena, geophysical features and astral bodies, animals, and other objects—some of which were manufactured (including mortars)—caused disease and death by shooting "pains" into people.

Many Native Americans held that angered animal spirits might cause specific ailments—although if the spirit was angered by breach of taboo, one might argue that the person who transgressed was responsible. For groups like the Creek, Cherokee, and other Indians of the Southeast, animal spirits were an important cause of disease. If animals, especially deer, were treated or killed disrespectfully—by breaking one of several important hunting taboos—then vengeful spirits might cause illness. The Creek believed that specific animals (and even specific

parts of specific animals) brought specific illnesses: eye problems were caused by the eye of the deer, rheumatoid pains by deer spirits angered by their improper treatment, high fever with thirst and diarrhea by bear, inflamed gums by squirrels, vomiting and severe bowel pains by dog, liver complaint by beaver, otter, or muskrat, chronic cough by turtle and hoarse cough by millipede, and so on. Diseases were also caused by other spirits like rainbow, fire, sun, and thunder, who were angered by taboo transgression, as well as by the spirits inherent to ghosts and sorcerers.

Most Native Americans believed in the existence of ghosts, who were not neutral toward the living. For some, like the Navajo, ghosts were believed to be inherently malignant and dangerous and were deeply feared; most people who died returned, the Navajo believed, to harass the living. Ghosts assumed different forms, appeared usually at night, made certain sounds, and both presaged and caused illness and death.

Transgressions of Taboos

For many Native Americans, extensive and elaborate taboos governed personal actions, especially with respect to hunting activities, rites of passage, and bodily functions. Breaking a taboo—including, for the Plains-dwelling Arapahoe and others, a taboo on speaking about one's health—was followed by ill health. The Netsilik Eskimo were just one example of people who connected countless observances to such activities as hunting, the treatment of living and dead animals, women's work, childbirth, menstruation, and death. Transgressions of prohibitions were almost unavoidable and had negative consequences including sickness.

Causation in such instances must be made explicit. If, as Indians in the Southeast believed, a man became ill because a menstruating woman came into contact with him, who was responsible for his sickness? In some instances, taboo transgression incurred the wrath of a spirit who caused illness. But human agency was also involved, and if intent could be established then the transgressor was at fault. For many, including the Lake Winnipeg Saulteaux, this personalized theory of causation was very important. Taboo transgression, which might be followed by sickness of oneself or another, could be one's own fault; even if a sorcerer made a person sick, it may have been because that person offended the sorcerer.

The Soul: Desires and Loss

The Iroquois and Huron were like other Native Americans in having not one but several possible causes of illness. For both groups, natural injuries, sorcery, and the desires of the souls of the living (and the recently dead) all caused illness. Despite having many causes, sickness and death were persistently explained by the Iroquois and Huron by the desires of the soul and sorcery. Often hidden, the soul's secret desires were nevertheless contained in dreams, although a specialist in interpretation may have been required to reveal what was not manifest. Sickness resulted when a person did not get what his or her soul desired, or when a supernatural being who was revealed in a dream to want something was frustrated in not obtaining it.

For other Native Americans, soul loss was a potential danger. The Kwakiutl of the Northwest Coast believed they became ill because spirits could cause a soul to jump out of the body and be taken away, because their souls were lost, or because some shaman had thrown sickness into their bodies. Shamans could attract and catch the lost soul and blow it back into the patient's body. There were other circumstances of soul loss (and consequent illness) in Native America. One's soul might have been induced to follow a recently dead person's soul, or may have left the sleeping body, refusing to return from dreams. The soul could be wandering because a taboo was broken or it could have been stolen by a shaman or sorcerer.

Dreams

For many Native Americans, including the Iroquois and Huron, dreams were rigorously interpreted for hidden insights into the desires of the soul. For a few, like the Mojave in the Southwest, dreams and their interpretation were absolutely fundamental for theories of disease causation. The Mojave believed that certain agents like ghosts or sorcerers might trigger disease, but the cause of mental illness could be found in the struggle in a patient's psyche between various forces. Through dreams, one could foretell the future or receive the power to cure. Bad

dreaming could make one sick. Good dreaming could make one well.

Natural Causes

Most Native Americans attributed some of their sickness or infirmities to natural causes including such things as accident, warfare, and intense cold. Of course, it is impossible to predict that a particular "accident" had a "natural" cause in any single society. Unusual accidents often elicited explanations of sorcery. Like other categories, what is "natural" is everywhere culturally constructed, and even a "natural" accident does not account for the particularities of misfortune: why a particular person, in a particular place and time, was affected.

CURING PRACTICES

When Native Americans became sick, or when they died, they often could point to more than one possible cause. The first problem, then, was diagnosis, which usually required seeking out and hiring a specialist: one who possessed authority because of special knowledge or special techniques and/or power from a tutelary or masterful relationship with one or more spirits. People with such knowledge or power have been given different names: medicine man (or woman), herbalist, curer, shaman, practitioner, conjuror, priest. For convenience, they are collectively termed shamans. Substantial variation existed among tribes in the shaman's permissible gender, in the relative importance of apprenticeship and personal quest in acquiring a relationship with and power over spirits, in the shaman's specialty (or general practice), and in the specificity of shamanic roles. In their cures, shamans diagnosed or divined cause, then resorted to a variety of techniques including sucking, singing, physical therapy, use of plants, and surgery, in ritual behavior ranging from perfunctory to elaborate. Rarely was only one of these techniques used; often, as the cure progressed through various stages, different techniques came to the fore. The settings in which cures took place varied substantially, from the small private rite devoted exclusively to a cure, to community-wide public rituals of which curing was just one aspect. The shaman functioned as physician, psychiatrist, and psychotherapist but was often regarded with ambivalence because the same powers that granted the ability to cure could also be used for malevolent ends.

Plants and Pharmacopeia

In their cures, most Native Americans used plants in various ways: applied like a poultice, mixed with grease and rubbed on the body, inhaled in steam, chewed, boiled and drunk, and so forth. Each plant often had quite specific applications, even though particular symptoms—like those associated with rheumatism or stomachaches—might be relieved by several alternative plants. American Indian knowledge of plants was prodigious. The Southwestern Chippewa of the Great Lakes used almost 150 different types of plants for medicinal purposes alone, about half of which were long ago regarded by pharmacologists or in medicine as being of "therapeutic" value—psychosomatic considerations aside. On the Plains, the Cheyenne distinguished over fifty plants to cure a variety of highly specific ailments, including a tight cough, abdominal cramps, carbuncles, bowel pains, excessive menstrual bleeding, headache, rheumatism, fever, insufficient milk, diarrhea, numbness, paralysis, vomiting, insomnia, bloody stools, sore gums, and rattlesnake venom. Creek Indians derived herbal medicines from more than one hundred plants, including "red root" from willow as a purgative for fever and nausea, malaria, and other illnesses; "button snakeroot" as an expectorant and emetic for snakebite, kidney ailments, and rheumatism; "white medicine," or ginseng root, to induce sweat in a fever, to staunch the flow of blood, or to assuage croup and shortness of breath; angelica root for stomachache, worms, back pain, and hysteria; wormseed for worms and fever; red cedar for aches and as a tonic; spicewood to induce perspiration or vomiting; horsemint to reduce leg swelling and induce perspiration; red sumac or post oak for dysentery. Many options existed for general purgatives, emetics, and the like. In all, about 170 drugs at one time or still in official pharmacopeias were used by American Indians.

Sucking, Blowing, Singing, and Chanting

Blowing and, especially, sucking on the body were among the commonest shamanic techniques, no doubt because of the widespread belief that illness resulted from the intrusion of objects in the body. Shamans rubbed and sucked on the body, especially on its fleshier parts, and might make small incisions; then, by concealing objects and by sleight of hand, they produced things they said had been magically injected.

For many American Indians—like the Blackfoot of the Plains and the Hupa in California—words themselves, in formulaic phrases, chants, prayers, and songs, possessed crucial curative power, although various other techniques and herbal-based medicines were also used to cure. Chants constituted valuable property whose use was restricted in various ways; in some societies chants were inherited by the next generation, and in others they could not be sold. For their cures, Navajo shamans relied heavily on chants (they also sucked out intruded objects, obtained confessions of taboo violations, and made sandpaintings whose images in combination with chants contained curative power), which were greatly elaborated and owed much to Puebloan influence. Elaborate and lasting up to nine nights, two dozen Navajo ceremonials (called "chantways" from the prominence of chanting) were intended to cure illness and restore health by attracting good beings or spirits, exorcising ghosts, or combating sorcery.

Divination

Many Native Americans engaged in divination to discover the cause of illness. The Cherokee, for example, manipulated a stick in a river and then "read" the water around it for actions or conditions that would indicate one or another cause of illness. Divination with crystals or beads gave favorable or unfavorable prognosis for ill people. Techniques of divination were extremely varied.

Confession

Confession, both in cases of taboo transgression and sorcery, was often necessary to a successful cure. The Lake Winnipeg Saulteaux were like many other American Indians in believing that one must confess "bad conduct" (taboo violation) in order to get well. And for many Native Americans, one of the most important ways for a victim of sorcery to recover was for the sorcerer to confess—willingly or under duress—his or her culpability. The Navajo believed that if the victim was not too close to death, confession would be followed by improvement.

Granting the Soul Its Desires

For people like the Huron and Iroquois, for whom the soul's desires caused sickness, granting the desires was required for a cure. Desires were revealed in dreams and could range from property to feasts or dances, from what should be done to what should not. Announcement of the desires was public and they or agreeable substitutes were granted.

Vows and Sacrifice

For some Native Americans, a vow during illness was followed by action after recovery, like joining a medicine association in some Puebloan societies. Many American Indians who lived on the Plains believed that one could make a personal sacrifice in the hope of achieving restored health. The sacrifice was either made on the spot—like cutting off one's finger or fasting—or at the next annual Sun Dance, which was the major pan-tribal religious ceremony of the Plains when vows made to (dis)embodied sacredness (the "Great Spirit") were fulfilled.

Sweat Baths

Sweating in a sudatory to keep in good health or purify the self, or as a preventive measure against disease, was common among Native Americans. Some American Indians also employed the sweat bath in order to cure illness. The Kwakiutl, for example, took sweat baths when their ailments were generalized and vague. Covered with blankets, they lay down on kelp-covered fire-heated stones on which seawater had been poured, and were rubbed with cedar bark that, they believed, would soak up diseases.

Surgical Procedures

Many American Indians resorted to a variety of surgical measures to effect cures. Surgery was used to remove arrowheads lodged in the body, set broken bones, and perform amputations and other operations. Some American Indians used sinew sutures to close wounds. They bandaged hernias, splinted or bound fractures, drained ab-

scesses with incisions, amputated fingers (commonly in mortuary and other rituals, and occasionally when frozen), pulled teeth, and even practiced trephination for various reasons. For Native Americans, scarification and phlebotomy, both bloodletting techniques, were common (phlebotomy less so); for a long time bloodletting was also commonly resorted to by Europeans.

Formal Organizations

Sodalities devoted to curing were important for many Native Americans, especially in the Puebloan Southwest where medicine societies (usually four major ones) recruited members from people recovered from sickness. Members were responsible for curing individuals, cleansing the entire village of evil, and purging witches. Twelve Zuni societies were concerned with curing, but to eradicate sorcerers responsible for drought, sickness, or epidemics, a priesthood—the Bow Priesthood—took responsibility for forcing witches to confess. Elsewhere in Native America, formal organizations in which curing might figure prominently were fairly widespread and included the Iroquois Society of Faces (one of a number of medicine societies), members of which cured ailing individuals and periodically purged communities of illness; and the Midewiwin, which provided instruction for Chippewa members to both prevent and combat disease in subsequent individual cures.

PREVENTIVE AND PROTECTIVE MEASURES

American Indians undertook a variety of prophylactic measures to ensure protection and health, ranging from keeping amulets to protect the individual from supernaturally caused illness, taking care not to break taboos, eating foods intended to make one strong, and using plants and sweat baths, to ceremonials for the individual, group, or entire society intended to prevent malevolence and illness. The Western Apache, for example, believed that one could acquire protective power from an inexhaustible supply of power in the universe, but if offended the power would withdraw, exposing the person to sickness. Many Native Americans performed elaborate ceremonies intended to keep balance in the universe or pestilence at bay, or to achieve health and well-being, as in many Puebloan ceremonials, the Hupa jumping dance, California Kuksu cult, Chippewa Midewiwin, and others.

DISEASE THEORY AND CURING: PERSISTENCE AND EUROPEAN ALTERNATIVES

Like Barbue, the Kutchin leader whose demise was charted at the outset, most Native Americans after contact with Europeans combined their own and European disease theories and curing practices. For some Native people, theories about sickness and well-being have persisted tenaciously in the face of technological, social, and political change. Many Western Apache, for example, today believe in and carry protection against sorcery, and many Navajo continue to have fear of ghosts and sorcerers. Not all do, however; some are openly skeptical about these traditional beliefs.

But nowhere were aboriginal systems uninfluenced by European contact. While chantways are used today by the Navajo to restore health, most have withered and disappeared. Everywhere, Native disease theory and curing practices altered. The onslaught of epidemic diseases, from which many fell sick and died, both strengthened and weakened native theories, in that many Native people concurrently considered Europeans as powerful sorcerers and lost faith in the efficacy of their own shamans. In time, missionaries, who rigorously attacked Native American religions (and thus attacked curing rituals), eroded Native systems of belief and rituals. Themselves sometimes regarded as sorcerers, and their rituals (like baptism) and paraphernalia as powerful medicine, missionaries achieved results in ways they never intended or sanctioned. During the early centuries of contact, one must question whether European diagnosis and cures represented an advancement on Native American practices. Nevertheless, Native people tried new practices especially when their own specialists seemed unable to cure new and epidemic diseases. In instances, Christianity and Native religions as well as European and Native techniques, were reconciled in disease theory and cure. For many Native people, a distinction has evolved between long-present Indian diseases whose symptoms often include ennui and sadness or which are slow-developing, and white-man diseases, which are new and have other symptoms. In some instances, "Indian disease" embraces ailments which might be better responded to by white-man medicines. For many, each type of disease demands a different physician, Indian- or white-trained. The Indian Health Service has finally hired Native healers selectively, at last recognizing their psychotherapeutic value, and given formal recognition to what is well known: when they become sick, many Native Americans continue to draw upon a reservoir of traditional knowledge about etiology and cure, about sickness and health.

BIBLIOGRAPHY

Ackerknecht, Erwin H. "Primitive Surgery." *American Anthropologist* 49, no. 1 (1947):25–45.

Adair, John. "Physicians, Medicine Men, and Their Navajo Patients." In *Man's Image in Medicine and Anthropology,* edited by Iago Galdston. New York, 1963.

Balikci, Asen. *The Netsilik Eskimo.* Garden City, New York, 1970.

Basso, Keith H. *Western Apache Witchcraft.* University of Arizona Papers in Anthropology, no. 15. Tucson, Ariz., 1969.

Boas, Franz. *Kwakiutl Ethnography,* edited by Helen Codere. Chicago, 1966.

Bunzel, Ruth L. "Introduction to Zuni Ceremonialism." *Forty-seventh Annual Report of the Bureau of Ethnology.* Washington, D.C., 1932.

Densmore, Frances. "Use of Plants by the Chippewa Indians." *Forty-fourth Annual Report of the Bureau of Ethnology.* Washington, D.C., 1928.

Devereux, George. *Mohave Ethnopsychiatry: The Psychic Disturbances of an Indian Tribe.* Smithsonian Institution. Bureau of American Ethnology, Bulletin 175. Washington, D.C., 1969.

Fogelson, Raymond D. "Change, Persistence, and Accommodation in Cherokee Medico-Magical Beliefs." In *Symposium on Cherokee and Iroquois Culture,* edited by W. N. Fenton and J. Gulick. Smithsonian Institution, Bureau of American Ethnology, Bulletin 180. Washington, D.C., 1961.

Grinnell, George Bird. *The Cheyenne Indians: Their History and Ways of Life*. Vols. 1 and 2. Lincoln, Nebr., 1972.

Hallowell, A. Irving. "Ojibwa World View and Disease." In *Contributions to Anthropology: Selected Papers of A. Irving Hallowell*. Chicago, 1976.

———. "The Social Function of Anxiety in a Primitive Society." In *Culture and Experience*. Philadelphia, 1955.

Hudson, Charles. *The Southeastern Indians*. Knoxville, Tenn., 1976.

———. "Why the Southeastern Indians Slaughtered Deer." In *Indians, Animals, and the Fur Trade: A Critique of "Keepers of the Game*," edited by Shepard Krech III. Athens, Ga., 1981.

Kluckhohn, Clyde. *Navajo Witchcraft*. Boston, 1967.

Kluckhohn, Clyde, and Dorothea Leighton. *The Navaho*. Rev. ed. Cambridge, Mass., 1974.

Krech, Shepard III. "The Death of Barbue, a Kutchin Trading Chief." *Arctic* 35, no. 3 (1982):429–437.

———. " 'Throwing Bad Medicine': Sorcery, Disease, and the Fur Trade Among the Kutchin and Other Northern Athapaskans." In *Indians, Animals, and the Fur Trade: A Critique of "Keepers of the Game*," edited by Shepard Krech III. Athens, Ga., 1981.

Kroeber, Alfred. *Handbook of the Indians of California*. Bureau of American Ethnology, Smithsonian Institution, Bulletin 78. Washington, D.C., 1925.

Powers, William K. "Alternatives to Western Psychotherapy: The Modern-day Medicine Man." Chapter in *Beyond the Vision: Essays on American Indian Culture*. Norman, Okla., 1987.

Spencer, Robert F. *The North Alaskan Eskimo: A Study in Ecology and Society*. Washington, D.C., 1969.

Sturtevant, William C., ed. *Handbook of North American Indians*. 20 vols. (projected). Washington, D.C., 1978—.

Swanton, John R. "Religious Beliefs and Medical Practices of the Creek Indians." *Forty-second Annual Report of the Bureau of Ethnology*. Washington, D.C., 1928.

Tooker, Elisabeth. *An Ethnography of the Huron Indians, 1615–1649*. Syracuse, N.Y., 1991.

Vogel, Virgil J. *American Indian Medicine*. Norman, Okla., 1970.

Wallace, Anthony F. C. *The Death and Rebirth of the Seneca*. New York, 1970.

Walker, Deward E., Jr., ed. *Witchcraft and Sorcery of the American Native Peoples*. Moscow, Idaho, 1989.

Wyman, Leland C. "Navajo Ceremonial System." In *Handbook of North American Indians*, edited by William C. Sturtevant. Vol. 10, *Southwest*, edited by Alfonso Ortiz. Washington, D.C., 1983.

Shepard Krech III

SEE ALSO **Ecological Consequences of Economic Development; The First Americans; Magic and Witchcraft;** and **Native American Religions.**

AFRICAN-AMERICAN MEDICINE

SLAVES IN THE AMERICAS had a substantially different experience with disease than did their white masters. Understandably, most of these differences became apparent in the face of the so-called "African" diseases, which reached the Western Hemisphere along with the slaves. Africans possessed a genetic resistance to both vivax and falciparum malaria that their white owners lacked, and, for reasons not yet understood, they were resistant to yellow fever and hookworm disease as well.

Yet a long history of exposure to certain pathogens in Africa did not always confer protection against them, and slaves suffered much more than whites in the West Indies from tropical ailments, such as yaws (as evidenced by open sores on the body) and filariasis (when it appeared as elephantiasis). In addition, they seem to have been more susceptible to smallpox throughout the hemisphere and to swellings designated as "scrofula" and "dropsy." In many cases these latter symptoms (rather than illnesses) were doubtless the result of nutritional deficiency diseases such as pellagra and beriberi. In others, however, they were probably evidence of tuberculosis and hypertension—two major black-related diseases that were not really recognized as such until the late nineteenth and twentieth centuries, respectively.

Unfortunately, we do not know a great deal about how the slaves viewed their differential experiences with disease or how they went about combating those illnesses that tormented them. Part of the reason for this lack of knowledge is that until the latter part of the nineteenth century, "white" or European medicine was frequently of the "heroic" nature, with remedies seemingly more fearsome than the diseases they were intended to cure.

AFRICAN-AMERICAN HEALERS

Many slaves wisely hid their illnesses from their owners and overseers and slipped behind owners' backs to consult their own black healers for help. But part of the reason is that these healers were often "conjure doctors," their medical practice based to a large extent on magico-religious rites that were in themselves secret. These individuals were frequently viewed by slaves not only as men and women who could cure illnesses that white medicine was helpless against, but also as instigators of disease through the "spells" that they were able to cast. These conjure doctors, not to be confused with the Obeah men and voodoo priests of the West Indies, gradually declined in importance when the slave trade to North America ended, and thus cultural connections with Africa came to an end. But there is little reason to doubt their influence and importance during the colonial period.

More respectable, at least in the eyes of the masters, were the "root" and "herb" doctors among the slaves. Whites as well as slaves frequently consulted them, although whites, who were always concerned about poisons the slaves were reputedly expert in concocting, did so with some wariness. Sustained by the conviction that there was a root or herb for every illness, these practitioners could be found in almost every neighborhood. Often they were plantation nurses whose intimate knowledge of illnesses helped them in matching roots and herbs with diseases. To be sure, when they succeeded in effecting a cure, it was as likely to be the result of their ability as psychologists and of the faith of the patient as it was the efficacy of their pharmacology. Today's pharmaceutical industry, however, rests on yesterday's pharmocognosy, and doubtless important knowledge of many herbs and roots with healing qualities has been lost in the transition. Among those frequently relied upon by African-American practitioners are comfrey, sage, garlic, catnip, peach tree leaves, pine needles, raspberry leaves, polk root, mustard weed, sweet william roots, "lion's tongue" (wintergreen tea), "life everlasting" (rab-

bit tobacco), elephant tongue, Jerusalem oak, red oak bark, wild cherry bark, chinaberry tea, dogwood, Peter's root, may apple, tansey leaves, and snakeroot.

These and other roots and herbs were generally dispensed with many flourishes and charms intended to enlist the supernatural in buttressing the remedy, as were other far less palatable concoctions, often consisting of such unpleasantries as boiled cockroaches, fried "young mice," and sheep's dung tea. But even these were less painful and harmful than the leeching, cupping, lancing, and mercuralizing done by the white physicians.

In addition, of course, slaves also treated themselves and their families without recourse to conjurers, root doctors, or white medicine. However, their remedies might embrace all three approaches, combining extracts of the local plants esteemed for their medicinal and magical properties with one or another of the purgatives or some other mainstay of the master's medicine chest.

Needless to say, much of black medical self-help was viewed dimly by self-interested professional physicians, who vehemently denounced it as quackery. On the other hand, in most cases the day-to-day health problems of plantation and farm were resolved without the assistance of physicians, but with blacks playing a significant role in the administering of European medicine as dispensers of purgatives, nurses, tooth-pullers, and blood-letters.

One significant area of health care that was almost invariably left in the hands of the slaves was prenatal and obstetrical care. In fact, in addition to delivering the infants of slave mothers, black midwives regularly oversaw the births of white infants. In the nineteenth century, black midwives were blamed by regular physicians for the high rate of infant mortality. Certainly the practice of applying mud to the umbilical stump contributed to many cases of neonatal tetanus during the antebellum period; there is reason to believe that this practice also prevailed in colonial America. To some unmeasurable extent, the relatively high incidence of uterine disease among black women can also be attributed to those midwives who were in the habit of forcing their patients to stand erect immediately after delivery and shaking them until the placenta was delivered. But in an age when it seems remarkable that anyone survived medical care, these practices were no more wrongheaded than many of those of regular medicine.

The medical practices of Africans on their mother continent had included techniques for inoculation against yaws (borrowing the yaws) and smallpox. Yet certainly the latter was the single most important killer of both blacks and whites on the North American continent during the days of Cotton Mather, a minister in the Massachusetts Bay colony, who in 1706 learned from his African slave Onesimus that the man had undergone a procedure in Africa to protect him from smallpox forever. Shortly after this, Mather and others launched an inoculation campaign using Onesimus's remedy that signaled the beginning of preventive medicine in the Western Hemisphere and marked the beginning of the end of smallpox's reign of terror in North America.

BIBLIOGRAPHY

Breeden, James O., ed. *Advice Among Masters: The Ideal in Slave Management in the Old South.* Westport, Conn., 1980.

Genovese, Eugene D. *Roll, Jordan, Roll: The World the Slaves Made.* New York, 1974.

Kiple, Kenneth F., and Virginia H. King. *Another Dimension to the Black Diaspora: Diet, Disease and Racism.* Cambridge, England, and New York, 1984.

Postell, William D. *The Health of Slaves on Southern Plantations.* Baton Rouge, La., 1951.

Savitt, Todd L. *Medicine and Slavery: The Diseases and Health Care of Blacks in Antebellum Virginia.* Urbana, Ill., 1978.

Kenneth F. Kiple

SEE ALSO **African-American Culture; Slavery;** and **The Slave Trade.**

TECHNOLOGY

THE BRITISH COLONIES

EUROPEANS CONQUERED the New World during what Lewis Mumford called the "dawn" of the modern age. With that dawn came a growing appreciation for the power of technology, a realization that better machines and improved techniques could bring about fundamental change. Therefore, to say that Europe throughout the colonial era was largely preindustrial does not in any sense mean that it was also pretechnological. Humans had established themselves as the planet's most successful toolmakers and tool users long before Europeans came to the Americas. And some of those transplanted Europeans knew that what we now refer to as technology underlay their economic and political power, their ability to compete against rivals in the New World—rivals who included other Europeans as well as Native Americans.

Even so, technology did not mean as much to colonial Americans as it does to Americans of the present generation. If many Americans today are aware of the power bestowed by advanced technologies, their forebears had only glimmers of what is now taken for granted. Indeed, the word "technology," despite its Greek roots, was almost never used before the nineteenth century. Samuel Johnson did not include it in his *Dictionary of the English Language* (1755).

In 1828 it finally appeared in the first edition of Noah Webster's Americanized version of Johnson's tome. Technology, as defined by Webster, was synonymous with what people of Johnson's generation called the "useful" or "mechanical" arts. Webster, significantly, did not link technology to science. For many of his (as well as Johnson's) contemporaries, science and technology occupied separate realms that only occasionally overlapped.

At the same time, elements of what we now consider essential for rapid technological change were brought together more often in Webster's lifetime than they had been in Johnson's, a shift traceable in the altered meaning of some old words. For example, in Johnson's dictionary an invention was defined as a "fiction" or a "forgery," as an "excogitation" or "discovery." Webster had similar definitions, but he also described an invention as a "skill or ingenuity which is or may be employed in contriving any thing new." Webster linked invention to what we commonly think of as technology; Johnson had not. Johnson and Webster also gave somewhat different meanings for "manufacture." Johnson's befitted a preindustrial frame of reference, an older understanding of the word that reflected the original Latin—*manus* (hand) and *facio* (make). Webster added made "by machinery" to his definition.

Something had happened during the intervening years. Water- and steam-driven machines had begun to take the place of hand work, and they did so under the roof of a "factory." Johnson in 1755 had defined a factory as a trading establishment. In 1828 Webster listed that definition but noted that "factory" was a shortened form of "manufactory, a building or collection of buildings, appropriated to the manufacture of goods." For Webster, who lived in an industrializing nation, "factory" and "manufacture" had taken on new meanings. Johnson drew from literary sources such as Shakespeare, Dryden, and Pope to illustrate his definitions. Webster turned more to his surroundings, to the machine-equipped enterprises transforming the landscape of New England. Words like "factory," "manufacture," "invention," and "technology" did not change their denotation and connotation just for the Americans of Webster's generation. The meaning altered in Britain, too, as that nation industrialized during the closing years of Johnson's life.

The colonies rose to maturity at a time when the meanings had not changed, and yet the new technologies behind Webster's new lexicon were soon to appear. It would be well to remember that political or economic turning points in the colonial experience do not necessarily mirror watersheds in the history of technology. The rise of an industrial Britain does not perfectly correspond to the emergence of British North America. That said, it is also evident that by the end of the colonial period, some sought to make more purposeful what were once seemingly accidental or incidental connections between technology and society, especially those Americans seeking greater autonomy within the British Empire and, by July 1776, total independence. Although they still called technology "the mechanical arts," and they did not always see how invention could be tied to technological innovation, much less to science, their quest for political and economic freedom helped them to make that connection. Their level of technological awareness increased along with the rate of technological change. The Americans whom Horace Mann called a "mechanical people" in 1845 were the lineal descendants of colonists who groped more haltingly toward technological change.

IMITATION AND INNOVATION

As John W. Oliver put it, the beginnings of colonial American technology came with "the efforts of the first settlers to provide the necessities of life for themselves and their families." Such efforts were simultaneously imitative and innovative: imitative in that the colonists imported or copied many of their tools and techniques; innovative in that, whatever the original source, they had to adapt to a different environment and a new set of demands. The familiar adage "necessity is the mother of invention" often held true.

Those first settlers, despite their feelings of cultural superiority, depended to some extent on Native Americans for their survival. From them the colonists learned planting and fertilizing skills; Native Americans also introduced them to domesticated crops like maize, potatoes, and tobacco. If they already knew how to fish, they nonetheless studied how the natives used nets, weirs, and tackle. They may have been able to build superior seagoing vessels, but they learned from the natives how to make canoes for inland waterways. Although Native American techniques were quickly absorbed within the larger social system of the European colonists, in the early days of settlement, at least, technological transfer flowed both ways. Colonial American technology was in part an amalgam, drawing from continental European and British sources and from the African as well as the Native American experience. These varied sources notwithstanding, the major technologies that emerged, and the attitudes that underlay them, were essentially Western European.

Some innovative changes came quite rapidly. The felling ax brought to the colonies from Europe was transformed into a more dynamic tool—not because of an innate genius distinguishing those who left Europe for the New World but because what was adequate in one clime proved inadequate in another. Given the importance of wood to the colonial economy, both as a source of fuel and as a basic building material, and given the colonists' perception of the forest as an obstacle to progress, the need for an improved felling ax quickly became apparent. Ax handles were lengthened to maximize the force and impact of the swing; the ax head was redesigned to produce a broader, sharper, and thinner blade combined with a flat poll of roughly the same weight as the blade for better balance. No single model was used by all, and certainly there was no standardized machine production of heads or handles; nevertheless, there was an underlying logic that pushed design changes in the same direction. As with so many of the technological improvements developed during the colonial era, change was incremental and gradual, initiated by nameless men and women whose individual efforts are lost to the historical record.

On a larger scale, water-driven sawmills supplemented pit and treadle saws early on. Virginia and New York (when it was New Netherlands) had sawmills within the first two decades of European settlement. Massachusetts had a sawmill by the end of the 1630s, and more soon followed. Each generation saw some refinement, some improvement in the sawmills that spread along the Atlantic seaboard—such as cogwheel-driven carriages for pushing a log toward the saw blade that replaced hand spikes once used for the task. And sawmills were not the only enterprises to make use of water-driven and geared machinery. Gristmills and flour mills dotted riverbanks by 1700, and if, like sawmills, they were essentially extensions to the New World of devices and techniques known in the Old, their existence was proof that colonial Americans could be just as interested in machinery as their cousins back in Europe. In some cases that interest was even more pronounced: English sawyers resisted innovations that threatened their long-established hand-tool trade; colonial sawyers were part of an economy that suffered from a chronic shortage of skilled workers, so they readily adapted to the more mechanized mill. Thus, what was spurned and consequently delayed on one side of the Atlantic was more eagerly embraced on the other.

What would someday be celebrated as "Yankee ingenuity" was undeniably part of the colonial American experience. This does not mean, however, that all of the colonists had embarked on a conscious quest to improve their technologies, that they were determined to improve them any way they could. Even some of their axes and adzes changed little over time, and they relied on claw hammers whose basic design had been familiar to Romans sixteen centuries before. As often as not, they were content to follow tradition or to combine old and new as it suited their purposes. In the early 1620s George Sandys, treasurer of the Virginia colony, pressed the settlers in and around Jamestown to diversify. He wanted to steer them away from their obsession with tobacco growing, which was lucrative but inherently risky because it could lead to a one-crop economy. Sandys recruited skilled workers from Britain and the Continent to introduce new enterprises: an ironworks, a shipyard, glassblowing, cotton for cloth, indigo for dye, corn for subsistence, vine cuttings for wine, and even mulberry trees for silkworms. Tobacco continued to flourish; most of the alternatives to it failed, and Sandys's attempts at diversification came to naught.

What happened to Sandys illustrates a general rule of thumb that is as valid now as it was then: successful technological change depends on a complex combination of factors, on what has been characterized as a technological "infrastructure" or "hierarchy." These factors include the available natural resources, a sufficient market demand, the level of craft skills, the prevailing system of labor, and the types of machines already in use. The availability or lack of risk-taking entrepreneurs, secure financing, government support, and popular enthusiasm also played a part. Change can be accelerated or slowed, depending on the absence or presence of any of these factors. In assessing why one technology caught on and another did not, why change and Yankee ingenuity seemed to mark one enterprise but not another, the arrangement of these factors must be kept in mind. At the northern end of the Chesapeake there might be farmers who innovatively employed improved plows to dig deeper furrows and cradle scythes to reap their wheat. At the other end of the bay there might be tobacco farmers who scratched at the ground with hoes and mattocks, who preferred to girdle trees rather than clear the land, and who exhausted the soil rather than rotate crops or fertilize their fields. Before we generalize about all of this, we have to be aware of the variables—of how particular circumstances affected technological choices. Not everyone, not even the ingenious Yankees of New England lore, automatically adopted the latest device or newest invention; for some, to have done so would have made little sense.

PROMOTING INVENTION

And yet invention proceeded apace, sometimes because of the constraints imposed by labor scarcity, sometimes despite them. Just how important were those inventions? "The history of the United States is fundamentally a history of invention," argued Roger Burlingame in his 1938 work, *March of the Iron Men*. This book's subtitle— *A Social History of Union Through Invention*— hinted at Burlingame's thesis: that inventors laid the foundation for an independent nation by making new devices which, as technological innovations, revolutionized ways of life and styles of thought as well as modes of production. Burlingame started his story with the printing press. Invented in the fifteenth century, the press carried word of Columbus's discovery and hastened European migration to the New World. The press likewise helped to spread the Protestant Reformation from the Continent to England, and it was dissident English Puritans who would later play a prominent role in founding the American colonies. Eventually, Burlingame contended, the press stimulated a distinct sense of identity among the colonists; not coincidentally, it was a colonial printer, Benjamin Franklin, who deserved credit as the "inventor of American civilization."

Burlingame confessed that he might have oversimplified. His exaggerations aside, however, he showed why the history of technology is no mere appendage to the history of science or economic development. He argued for a reformulation of how we think about the national experience. In the years since *March of the Iron Men* appeared, other writers, especially those who concentrate on the history of technology, have shared Burlingame's view about the importance of technological change. They stress that technology is not just machines and techniques; in a cultural context it reflects—and in turn shapes—ideas and values. People who put a premium on invention tend to be those who are trying to harness nature. And indeed, in the long run, perhaps it is the inventor rather than the politician who has had the greatest impact on society. At the same time, inventors are to some extent products of their environment, and in societies like that of colonial America, they often labored in obscurity and fought in vain to attract public notice.

Recognition of the Value of Inventions

Colonial society did not routinely promote inventions that required immediate, large-scale change because there was little precedent for direct backing, it could have been prohibitively expensive, and invention did not seem to be important for short-term economic prosperity. Support of invention was haphazard at best, a haphazardness seen in colonial patent-granting practices. Patents are not the primary source of the inventive impulse or even the most important stimulus to technological innovation. Nevertheless, they do reflect a certain awareness of the importance of invention, whether or not they hurt individual inventors while helping others, because they signify the social worth attached to the process of invention as well as to the utility of new devices. Governments instituting patent codes make invention part of the public domain even as they protect the property of individuals. By recognizing and elevating invention as a form of intellectual property, patents give inventors a special legal status.

Patent law has medieval origins. In England, the Statute of Monopolies passed by Parliament in 1623 marked the full emergence of the patented invention, which theretofore had been mixed in with grants of royal favor for manufacturing privileges or import monopolies. Under this act the rights to "the sole working and making of any manner of new manufactures" were reserved to the "true first inventor and inventors" for fourteen years. By the end of the seventeenth century, patenting inventions had become common in England; and by the middle of the next century, the patent system had matured enough to play a part, however small, in promoting Britain's industrial revolution.

Patents or "monopolies" in the colonies were much rarer, with some colonies making provision for them and others not. The Massachusetts general laws of 1641 had a patent clause stating that "there shall be no *Monopolies* graunted or allowed amongst us, but of such new inventions that are Profitable to the Country, and that for a short time." Five years later Joseph Jenkes received the first patent in the colonies for a mechanical device when Massachusetts gave him a monopoly on water-powered mills in that province. Jenkes went on to design a scythe, which he patented in 1655, and to build a fire engine and sawmill. Connecticut followed Massachusetts in 1672 with a similarly worded statute. By 1691 South Carolina had a patent clause "for the better encouragement of engines for the propagating of the staples of the Province," or new farm tools. In all three colonies, the legislatures set their own terms for patent granting; there was no uniform length, nor was there any statutory standard that aspiring inventors had to satisfy. They were treated on an ad hoc basis. Even if they secured a patent, inventors had no assurance that their rights would be honored within their own colony, much less neighboring provinces, and they still had to generate interest in their ideas if they hoped to make a profit.

Accordingly, instead of seeking patents, many inventors applied for "awards" or "premiums" offered by towns, counties, and provinces. These usually took the form of a small cash prize. Furthermore, colonial legislatures periodically passed acts to stimulate manufactures or agriculture, and inventors endeavored to have their genius recognized by demonstrating the immediate practicality and financial promise of their designs. A few managed to garner commissions for special projects. Notably, Hans Christiansen of Bethlehem, Pennsylvania, fulfilled a contract in 1754–1755 to erect a municipal waterworks by making wood pipes and self-acting pumps to carry water from a holding tank in the town square. On a more ambitious scale, Christopher Colles modified New York City's water supply system twenty years later. He used a Newcomen-type steam engine to pump water from a pond to a hillside reservoir; from there the water flowed through fourteen miles of hollowed-out pine pipes buried beneath city streets.

Opportunities of this type were few and far between, so most inventors had to be content with less. Virginian John Hobday designed a thresher capable of processing 120 bushels a day. Rather than keep the details of his invention a secret, he and his brother toured several tidewater counties in 1772, giving instructions on how to make the device. Two years later the House of Burgesses bestowed £100 on him, and the Virginia Society for the Advancement of Useful Knowledge added a medal and a small bonus for his "very ingenious and useful Machine." In Philadelphia, Arthur Donaldson invented a horse-powered clamshell dredge. The Pennsylvania General Assembly honored Donaldson with £100, and his dredge drew a favorable re-

view from the American Philosophical Society, the leading organization of its kind in British North America.

Benjamin Franklin and the American Philosophical Society

Promoting invention was a pet project of Benjamin Franklin, the American Philosophical Society's founder. Himself an inventor—of the lightning rod, a blown-glass musical instrument (the armonica), and a stove that he christened the "Pennsylvania fireplace"—Franklin had long wanted to form a group that would study "New Mechanical Inventions for saving Labour" and all improvements that "tend to increase the Power of Man over Matter, and multiply the Conveniences or Pleasures of Life." The society that finally emerged in January 1769 had six standing committees, two of which dealt directly with invention: the committee on mechanics and architecture, and the committee on husbandry and American improvements. Society members threw themselves into a variety of projects, from canal-building plans to a silk-producing experiment. They also tried, without avail, to keep a faltering Philadelphia paper factory from closing.

Perhaps most important, the American Philosophical Society helped bring invention to public notice, and its self-proclaimed raison d'être showed that there were men like Franklin, inventors and scientists, who understood that invention was connected to improved technology, and technology ultimately to science. Society members corresponded with the Society for the Encouragement of Arts, Manufactures and Commerce, founded in London by like-minded individuals in 1754. But neither society accelerated the rate of technological change in its land. The American Philosophical Society's promise to promote the work of "ingenious artists, who might otherwise remain in obscurity" paved the way for a national commitment to invention, but that was still decades away.

Fascination with invention was restricted to a comparatively small group of scientifically minded men. Colonial Americans were just beginning to tie technological change to their visions of social progress. Science probably struck most as being a gentleman's hobby. The innovations of isolated mechanics and millers, farmers and gunsmiths, which undoubtedly occurred constantly, were too subtle, too anonymous to have a sudden impact or strike the public fancy. A frustrated Benjamin Franklin complained that inventors were treated shabbily because there were people "who being totally destitute of inventive faculty themselves, do not readily conceive that others may possess it." Unfortunately, lamented Franklin, such people "think of inventions as miracles," and inventors, alas, endured cruel misfortune.

Thus through Envy, Jealousy, and the Vanity of competitors for Fame, the origin of many of the most extraordinary inventions, though produced within but a few centuries past, is involved in doubt and uncertainty. We scarce know to whom we are indebted for the *compass,* and for *spectacles,* nor have even *paper* and *printing,* that record every thing else, been able to preserve with certainty the name and reputation of their inventors. One would not, therefore, of all faculties, or qualities of the mind, wish, for a friend, or a child, that he should have that of invention. For his attempts to benefit mankind in that way, however well imagined, if they do not succeed, expose him, though very unjustly, to general ridicule and contempt; and, if they do succeed, to envy, robbery, and abuse. (Leonard Labaree, ed. *Papers of Benjamin Franklin.* Vol. 5, pp. 526–527)

Franklin enjoyed fame and fortune, though not because of his inventions. He sought neither patents nor profits from his ideas. His reputation rested on his public service and scientific discoveries. Christopher Colles's experience was much more representative of the ambitious inventor in colonial America: a taste of success accompanied by a larger dose of frustration. New York's water supply system fell into disrepair during the War for Independence, and Colles spent fruitless years trying to interest investors in other projects. Inventors like Colles had not yet become important to the public because they had not proved themselves to enough people. Colonial living stimulated the genius of innumerable tinkerers who modified old tools and brought forth new ones; colonial society, for reasons associated with gaps in the technological "hierarchy," did not always nourish that genius or adopt those tools. Although the men who belonged to the American Philosophical Society had a better feel for the latent power of invention, even they did not see invention the way they would after the

War for Independence, when yet another technological transfer from Britain brought the beginnings of industrialization.

THE QUEST FOR INDEPENDENCE

American desires to further mechanize, even industrialize, can be considered one cause of the push for independence. The carrot-and-stick approach that Britain took in developing its mercantilist empire had technological as well as economic and political implications. By the mid 1760s, conspiracy theories were proliferating among future revolutionaries, and many of them believed that British plots against American liberty included restrictions on technology. Not surprisingly, the further that some Americans drifted from the mother country politically, the greater became their desire for technological autonomy.

Constraints on Colonial Industry

One Pennsylvanian complained in the *Pennsylvania Gazette* in 1771 that "the mechanic Arts and Manufactures cannot be encouraged by our Legislature with the same Propriety that they promote the liberal Arts and Sciences." For this he blamed Britain and the imperial tie choking his colony. No doubt the Iron Act passed by Parliament seemed proof of his charge. Under that 1750 law, colonial ironmasters were encouraged to produce pig and bar iron; they were also instructed not to make finished products for export. If they generally ignored clauses that forbade the erection of new steel or slitting and plating mills, ironmasters still resented the restrictions as they existed on paper. By 1775 the iron industry had become a bone of contention. The colonies produced a substantial amount of iron and did so with the blessing of mercantilists in London; colonial agitators demanded more. They hoped to expand their facilities and move into new types of production; they wanted to make iron and steel tools, not just iron bars and pigs. Their ambitions ran at cross-purposes with those of imperial authorities, who wanted the iron industry to prosper—within the limits they had set.

Parliamentary restrictions also extended to textiles. Beginning in 1718, British textile workers were barred from immigrating to the colonies; in 1774 textile machinery was added to the list of proscribed exports. Britain had begun to industrialize, and politicians there understood that allowing ideas, individuals, and machines to spread abroad could redound to the advantage of potential competitors, manufacturers in the American colonies included.

Encouraging American Manufactures

Tightened restrictions contributed to a home manufactures craze that swept the colonies. In response to a succession of new laws—the Stamp Act in 1765, the Townshend duties two years later, and the much-resented "Coercive Acts" in 1774—Americans were urged by protesters and pamphleteers to buy more homespun cloth and other local products. "Let the Manufactures of *America* be the Symbol of Dignity, the badge of Virtue," wrote Daniel Dulany in his influential critique of the Stamp Act, "and it will soon break the Fetters of Distress." Colonial legislatures and, by the end of 1774, newly formed provincial conventions and committees of safety became involved by awarding premiums; merchants pooled their resources to begin new enterprises; consumers were asked to buy wares at special market days intended to promote American goods. The Association called for by the Continental Congress in October 1774 imposed a boycott of British imports and called for support of the "agriculture, arts and manufactures of this country." Congress, then, showed a willingness to wage economic warfare before resorting to the use of military force, and its members realized that only improved technologies would make that economic warfare possible.

In the midst of this politicized drive for improved technologies, a group of Pennsylvanians initiated the most ambitious textile manufacturing scheme to be seen in the colonies before independence when, in February 1775, they founded the United Company of Philadelphia for Promoting American Manufactures. Dr. Benjamin Rush, driving force behind the company and its first president, had been a home manufactures advocate for some years. "There is but one expedient left whereby we can save our sinking country," he had proclaimed in 1768, "and that is by encouraging American manufactures." He repeated that theme seven years later when ad-

dressing subscribers who had invested in the United Company. "Manufactures, next to agriculture, are the basis of the riches of every country," he told his listeners and fellow enthusiasts. A combination of home spinning and weaving and factory finishing work would, he predicted, employ the poor, invigorate the economy, bring about self-sufficiency, and show Britain the error of its mercantilist ways.

Shares in the United Company sold quickly, at £10 apiece. Half of the money went to erecting a factory; half went to paying a dozen managers to run it. The managers recruited spinners and weavers, and soon boasted a labor force of four hundred—some of whom worked in the factory, others of whom worked as part of a putting-out system. Local women were asked to bring in their yarn for weaving, finishing, and sale as cloth. The company purchased what was reportedly the first cotton and wool spinning machine made in the colonies, a device constructed by Christopher Tully that had been built along the lines of a Hargreaves spinning jenny. The Pennsylvania General Assembly awarded Tully and John Hague, a Derbyshire weaver who eluded authorities and made his way to the colonies, £15 apiece for their spinning machines. The company paid dividends and survived until 1777, collapsing only with the British occupation of Philadelphia.

Even though it survived for two years, after the first blush of success the United Company had not prospered. Despite the initial enthusiasm, it was crippled by a shortage of capital, experienced workers, good machines, and consistent demand for what it produced. Other factory experiments begun on the eve of war met similar fates. Widespread support for home manufactures had been difficult to sustain, fluctuating with the ebb and flow of imperial crisis. Pledges that relied solely on moral suasion were easily and often broken. Production rose and fell, and hope often turned to dismay, because political agitation took manufactures beyond the point where they could compete profitably. American patriots had tried to condense a major movement into a brief decade, expanding their technological horizons as they increased their political demands. As a result they jumped ahead of their expertise and the flexibility of limited markets. And yet they did not, probably could not, know this at the time. Only after the political tie with Britain had been severed and they were on their own would they discover the complexities of large-scale technological retooling.

The grand visions of manufacturing enthusiasts before the War for Independence remained visions—technological expressions of wishful thinking. American society would have to change a good deal before the enthusiasts would see their dreams become reality. They needed more capital, more advanced machines, more artisans and mechanics, more talented entrepreneurs, a political system intended to promote rather than discourage manufacturing experiments, and a general public more interested in and committed to technological change.

By expanding their political aspirations, the technological enthusiasts had put more pressure on the economy. The greater the pressure they exerted on the economy to sustain their political ambitions, the more pronounced became the need for significant technological change. After the war Americans would continue searching for ways to achieve economic independence, and in the process they would learn just how technologically limited they were, given their ambitions. What is more, after the war they came to see inventors and inventions as crucial to technological change, just as some saw technological change in manufacturing as the answer to their most basic economic woes. Those who were caught up in the vision of future technological greatness charted the course for the new nation, a course that Americans are still trying to follow.

CONCLUSION

Looking back over the colonial period, historian Thomas Cochran observed that "compared to later periods, technology in America from 1607 to 1783 was static." The key word here is "compared." Cochran did not mean that there was no change at all, but that there were no radical departures from, no grand additions to, the technologies that colonists had available to them from the beginning. For the most part they were able to feed, clothe, and house themselves with tools that had originated in Europe and had been but slightly altered in the colonies. On the level of prime motive forces, we could go even further and say that the colonists had not really advanced beyond the ancients. They relied on humans, animals, wind, and water to drive their machines, all of which had been known in the Old World for thousands of years.

The fifth great driving force—steam—was not effectively brought into play until an industrial revolution that had barely taken hold in Britain by the outbreak of the War for Independence. A few steam engines had been imported into the colonies before 1775, but they were all Newcomen atmospheric models, suitable for pumping and little else. Americans broke free from the empire at the same moment that James Watt designed a vastly improved steam engine. Watt had applied direct steam power when he added a separate condenser in 1765. He obtained his first patent in 1769, teamed with Matthew Boulton in 1773, saw a successful commercial application of his improvements three years later, and advanced to his double-acting model in 1782. Watt's pioneering work stretched over almost two decades; it took that long for his ideas to mature and his reputation to be made.

Inventions, noted S. C. Gilfillan, tend to be cumulative, the result of a "multitudinous accretion of little details." He believed that they evolve in an almost biological process. If simultaneity and spontaneity cannot be ruled out in some cases, a progression of sorts can be traced in others. Watt built on the work of Thomas Newcomen, as Newcomen had on the experiments of Thomas Savery, just as Savery had on the earlier efforts of Denis Papin. And the first recorded attempts to harness steam power date back to the first century of the Christian era and the experiments of Hero of Alexandria. Naturally those who came after Watt picked up where he left off in a process that will not end until steam power is abandoned.

The colonists produced no great engines of change; they did design and use countless gadgets and innovative devices. The improved felling ax, the cradle scythe, the Conestoga wagon, and the Pennsylvania rifle often—and rightly—turn up on lists compiled to show the extent of Yankee ingenuity. Proud of what Americans had accomplished even before they won their independence, Thomas Jefferson defended the genius of his countrymen in *Notes on the State of Virginia* (1785). George Washington's memory, he prophesied, "will be adored while liberty shall have votaries"; as for Benjamin Franklin, "no one of the present age has made more important discoveries"; and David Rittenhouse, because of his orrery, "has exhibited as great a proof of mechanical genius as the world has ever produced."

Jefferson's choice of heroes—one general and two inventors—is instructive. In later years Jefferson personified the complicated, even contradictory, technological impulses of Americans once they began to experience large-scale change. He was ambivalent about industrialization and feared the consequences of reducing independent yeoman farmers to an urban proletariat of factory workers. But he was a champion of inventors and an inveterate tinkerer, as a tour of his beloved Monticello attests. If the Jeffersonian inventive curiosity had already manifested itself in the colonial era, so had the Hamiltonian desire to promote technological change through governmental intervention. Hamilton's famous reports, including his recommendations on manufactures (1791), had antecedents in policies pursued by colonial legislatures. Hamilton wanted to promote manufactures as a means to a political end; so had those legislatures. However halfhearted and marginal their efforts, the technological interventionism of colonial governments reminds us that we have no pure laissez-faire past to which we can return.

Colonial antecedents do not end there. If modern Americans are often guilty of seeing the environment as matter to be manipulated for human needs, it is an attitude that has its colonial—and ancient—parallels. So, too, with the tendency to use a technological yardstick for making cultural judgments, as colonists did when they encountered "primitive" peoples who had no books and no firearms, no spinning wheels or plows. Moreover, Americans of the present day, frustrated by the loss of technological leadership, might recall that the "ingenious Yankees" never had a monopoly on ingenuity. The colonists borrowed shamelessly from others as they sought to become more technologically proficient. No people, no nation, has for very long been able to monopolize technological leadership, and most leaders begin as followers.

The attachment to technology that had always been an implicit part of the colonial experience had by the early national period become more explicit; the unconscious choice became more conscious. It could be argued that this attitudinal change, more than any single mechanical improvement, was the most important technological development to occur before 1800. Technology was increasingly on the public mind—as both a policy concern and a source of national pride.

With successful industrialization in the nineteenth century, the United States took its place among the great powers. To that extent, changed circumstances stand out. In another sense, that change was the result of continuity, of retaining values that had floated beneath the surface in the West long before the founding of Jamestown. It has often been stated that colonial American technology was essentially medieval in character because the colonists depended on tools that had been common in Europe perhaps five hundred years earlier. But to concede this does not make the colonists fundamentally different from us. To Lewis Mumford the most important invention marking the emergence of a modern mentality was the mechanical clock, not the steam engine, and the mechanical clock dates back to the Middle Ages.

It might also be argued that modern technology is simply the most tangible expression of a human desire that goes back further still. There had been a utopian strain in Western thought centuries before the Age of Discovery, and it had a technological side to it, a hope that better machines could bring a better life. When writing about the mythical isle of Atlantis, Plato described a people who had risen to power through their genius. They had superior crops, excellent livestock, and impressive ships; their craft skills enabled them to cut canals and adorn their cities with beautiful temples. On Atlantis could be seen the interaction of ingenious humans with a naturally fertile environment. Francis Bacon's updated version of this utopian tale two thousand years later was even more explicitly tied to science and technology. As Bacon imagined it, the "New Atlantis" (1624) had been contemporaneous with Plato's original but outlived it. Its centerpiece, its creative heart, was "Solomon's House," otherwise known as the "College of the Six Days' Work." The men of Solomon's House believed that "the end of our foundation is the knowledge of causes, and secret motions of things; and the enlarging of the bounds of human empire, to the effecting of all things possible." They experimented constantly on new machines and "upon every invention of value we erect a statue to the inventor, and give him a liberal and honorable reward"—the very fame and fortune, based on subsidized research and development, that real inventors in the colonies found so elusive.

Jonathan Swift would someday lampoon the assumptions that underlay Bacon's imaginary world. Plato's Atlantis sank and disappeared, its civilization crushed after its people fell into moral decay and a more virtuous Athens rose to take its place. If the Greek notion of hubris was at the core of Plato's allegory, modern-day critics of technological excess echo that warning when they advise against conflating a higher standard of living with a better quality of life. Busy carving their new civilization from the wilderness, the colonists did not stop to ponder such matters.

BIBLIOGRAPHY

Bishop, James L. *A History of American Manufactures from 1608 to 1860.* 2 vols. Philadelphia, 1864; 3rd ed., revised and enlarged 3 vols., 1966. Contains details missing in later surveys.

Bridenbaugh, Carl. *The Colonial Craftsman.* New York, 1950.

Burke, James. *Connections.* Boston, 1978. Introduces readers—as it did viewers of the BBC television production from which it was taken—to the importance of technology in society.

———. *The Day the Universe Changed.* Boston, 1985.

Burlingame, Roger. *Engines of Democracy.* New York, 1940.

———. *March of the Iron Men: A Social History of Union Through Invention.* New York, 1938.

Cipolla, Carlo M. *Guns, Sails and Empire: Technological Innovation and the Early Phases of European Expansion, 1400–1700.* New York, 1965. Sketches the role of superior technology in European overseas empire building.

Cochran, Thomas C. *Frontiers of Change: Early Industrialism in America.* Oxford, 1981.

Cronon, William. *Changes in the Land: Indians, Colonists, and the Ecology of New England.* New York, 1983.

Crosby, Alfred W. *Ecological Imperialism: The Biological Expansion of Europe.* Cambridge, England, 1986.

Daniels, George H. "The Big Questions in the History of American Technology." *Technology and Culture* 11, no. 1 (1970):1–21.

Derry, Thomas K., and Trevor I. Williams. *A Short History of Technology from Earliest Times to 1900.* New York, 1960. An attempt to condense Charles Singer et al., eds., *A History of Technology* (see below).

Gilfillan, S. Colum. *The Sociology of Invention: An Essay in the Social Causes, Ways, and Effects of Technic Invention.* Cambridge, Mass., 1935. Lays out general principles for the process of invention and the emergence of technological innovations.

Goldenberg, Joseph A. *Shipbuilding in Colonial America.* Charlottesville, Va., 1976.

Heald, Morrell, ed. *America's Wooden Age: Aspects of Its Early Technology.* Tarrytown, N.Y., 1975.

———. *The Pursuit of Science in Revolutionary America, 1735–1789.* Chapel Hill, N.C., 1956. Contains much that bears on technology as well as science.

———. "Technology in American Culture." *Stetson University Bulletin* 62 (1962):1–18.

———. *Technology in Early America: Needs and Opportunities for Study.* Chapel Hill, N.C., 1966. Assesses what has been done and what needs to be done in the history of early American technology. A good starting point.

Hindle, Brooke, and Steven Lubar. *Engines of Change: The American Industrial Revolution.* Washington, D.C., 1986.

Hounshell, David A. *From the American System to Mass Production.* Baltimore, Md., 1984. Explains how technological transformation—especially the substitution of machine action for human skills—was a gradual, piecemeal process.

Kasson, John F. *Civilizing the Machine: Technology and Republican Values in America.* New York, 1976. Traces how Americans linked technology with progress and republicanism.

Labaree, Leonard, Claude Lopez, Barbara B. Oberg, and William B. Willcox, eds. *The Papers of Benjamin Franklin,* 28 vols. New Haven, Conn., 1959–.

Marcus, Alan I., and Howard P. Segal. *Technology in America.* San Diego, Calif., 1989. The most notable recent survey of invention and technological change in America.

Merchant, Carolyn. *Ecological Revolutions: Nature, Gender, and Science in New England.* Chapel Hill, N.C., 1989.

Mumford, Lewis. *The Myth of the Machine.* 2 vols. New York, 1967–1970. Less optimistic than the earlier work.

———. *Technics and Civilization.* New York, 1934. Guardedly optimistic about technology and the human future.

Oliver, John W. *History of American Technology*. New York, 1956.

Parry, John H. *The Age of Reconnaissance*. London, 1963.

Shumway, George. *Rifles of Colonial America*. York, Pa., 1980.

Singer, Charles J., E. J. Holmyard, A. R. Hall, and Trevor I. Williams, eds. *A History of Technology*. 8 vols. Oxford, 1954–1984. A massive compendium.

Sloane, Eric. *Museum of Early American Tools*. New York, 1964.

———. *A Reverence for Wood*. New York, 1965.

White, Lynn, Jr. "Cultural Climates and Technological Advance in the Middle Ages." *Viator* 2 (1971):171–201.

———. "The Historic Roots of Our Ecologic Crisis." *Science* 155, no. 3767 (1967):1203–1207.

———. *Medieval Technology and Social Change*. Oxford, 1962.

York, Neil L. *Mechanical Metamorphosis: Technological Change in Revolutionary America*. Westport, Conn., 1985.

Neil L. York

SEE ALSO **Libraries and Learned Societies; Manufacturing and Extractive Industries; and Scientific Inquiry.**

THE DUTCH COLONY

THE DUTCH BROUGHT a whole array of European technology with them to New Netherland. The desire of Native Americans to acquire some of the products of this technology, including textiles, iron tools and implements, firearms, and alcohol, was a major underpinning of trade.

FORTIFICATIONS

It is significant that among the earliest settlers sent to New Netherland by the Dutch West India Company was an engineer and surveyor named Cryn Fredericksz. In April 1625 the company sent him specific instructions, including exact measurements, for laying out the fort and streets of New Amsterdam (New York City). His plan was never fully realized. By 1627 the fort had been staked out, but it was still under construction in 1628. In 1646 Father Isaac Jogues, a Jesuit priest who had been a captive of the Indians, described Fort Amsterdam as having four bastions mounted with pieces of artillery, although these bastions were nothing more than "mounds, most of which had crumbled away."

When Peter Stuyvesant became director general of New Netherland in 1647, he found the fort "more a molehill than a fortress, without gates, the walls and bastions trodden under foot by men and cattle." Stuyvesant tried to repair the fort, but his efforts were resisted by the inhabitants, who did not want to pay for the work. He was successful, however, in building a wall to set off the town from the rest of Manhattan Island. Work on the wall was begun in 1653 and completed in 1660. It ran along what is today Wall Street.

Fort Orange (in present-day Albany) was built in 1624 on the west bank of the Hudson River to replace an earlier fort named Fort Nassau, which had been built in 1614 about a mile to the south but later abandoned. Fort Orange originally was constructed of wood, had four bastions, and was surrounded by a moat. In the winter of 1647–1648, it was almost entirely washed away by flood waters, and Stuyvesant ordered that it be rebuilt with stone. The fort, which contained several houses and a brewery, was primarily a trading center. By the time of the English conquest in 1664, Fort Orange was in bad condition, and the English abandoned it in 1676 when they built a new fort on a hill overlooking Albany.

DIKES

Besides building fortifications the Dutch constructed ditches and dikes, for which they had become famous. Since around A.D. 1000, the Dutch had been building dikes to reclaim land from the sea. By the end of the Middle Ages, they had constructed an elaborate network of dikes and a system of drainage boards to maintain the dikes and control the water.

The Dutch brought this land-shaping technology to America. Jasper Danckaerts, who traveled through the middle colonies in 1679–1680, noted that at the early Dutch settlement on Burlington Island in the Delaware River, the Dutch governor "dyked and cultivated a large piece of meadow or marsh, from which he gathered more grain than from any land which had been made from woodland into tillable land."

On Manhattan Island work was begun in 1638 to reclaim the marsh known as Blommaert's Vly. Between 1657 and 1659 the ditch was widened and deepened into a canal, known as the Heere Gracht, which literally means the "gentlemen's canal." (This was a reference to its being a public thoroughfare like a canal of the same name in Amsterdam.) Its sides were sheathed with wooden planks and there were two bridges across it and a lock where it met the East River.

The diking of marshes continued after the English conquest, although much of the work was done by Dutch settlers who were experienced in land reclamation. In 1675 Governor Edmund Andros ordered that three Dutch men be placed in charge of the construction of a dike on marshland north of New Castle, Delaware, because "there are few here who have the knowledge of such work, especially among those living in New Castle." Dikes remained a distinctive feature of the built landscape along the Delaware into the mid eighteenth century. At that time the Swedish naturalist Peter Kalm noted that

dykes were made along all rivers here to confine their water; therefore when the tide was highest, the water in the rivers was much higher than the meadows; in the dykes were gates through which the water can be drawn from, or led into the meadows; they were sometimes placed on the outward side of the wall, so that the water in the meadows forced it open, but the river water shut it. (*The America of 1750.* Vol. 1, p. 175)

MILLS

Several types of mills are known to have been constructed in New Netherland. The earliest was evidently a mill powered by horses. In 1626 Fran-çois Molemaecker (literally, the millwright) was "building a horse-mill, over which shall be constructed a spacious room sufficient to accommodate a large congregation." Horse-mills were used in the Netherlands for a number of processes from grinding bark for tanning pits to churning butter. The mill just cited, which doubled as a church, was probably a gristmill. Horse-mills are known to have been built in Rensselaerswyck as early as 1646 and in New Amstel (New Castle) prior to 1659. Because of their power source, they had the advantage of being portable. A horse-mill constructed on Manhattan Island in 1656 was moved to New Utrecht (today part of Brooklyn) in 1660. They continued to be used in New York through the 1740s, when, as Peter Kalm noted, "Some people made use of a wheel made of thick oak planks, which turned upon a wooden axis, by means of a horse drawing it."

In 1628 the Dutch Reformed minister Jonas Michaëlius wrote: "They are making a windmill to saw the wood. . . ." This mill was probably located on Nutten Island (Governor's Island). A survey done in 1639 shows two additional windmills located near Fort Amsterdam. While most people associate windmills exclusively with the Netherlands, both horse-mills and windmills were known to have existed in England as early as the twelfth century. In America windmills were built by the English in Massachusetts; Rhode Island; Nantucket, Mass.; Long Island, N.Y.; Virginia; and Maryland.

The Dutch also built water-powered mills. The instructions sent to Director-General Willem Verhulst in 1625 ordered him to "see that a note be made of all the falls or affluent streams whereby sawmills or other mills might be operated." In 1656 there were at least three water-powered mills in Rensselaerswyck, two sawmills and a combination sawmill and gristmill. In 1658 a water-powered mill was constructed on Manhattan Island at a place known as the Fresh Water (near present-day James and Cherry streets). It was probably powered by the force of the tides.

With the possible exception of the diking of fields, little of the technology brought by the Dutch to New Netherland was uniquely Dutch. It was part of a general western European technology.

BIBLIOGRAPHY

Holt, Richard. *The Mills of Medieval England.* Oxford, 1988. Makes the point that both horse-mills and windmills were built in England as early as the twelfth century.

Innes, J. H. *New Amsterdam and Its People. 2 vols.* 1902; repr., Port Washington, N.Y., 1969. A detailed description of the layout of many of the streets, fortifications, ditches, and walls in Dutch New Amsterdam

Kalm, Peter. *The America of 1870: Peter Kalm's Travels in North America—The English Version of 1770.* 2 vols. Edited by Adolph B. Benson, New York, 1937. Contains first hand descriptions of Dutch dikes on the Delaware River and horse-mills in New York.

Lambert, Audrey M. *The Making of the Dutch Landscape: An Historical Geography of the Netherlands.* New York, 1971. Contains information on Dutch land reclamation projects in the Middle Ages.

David Steven Cohen

SEE ALSO **Scientific Inquiry.**

THE FRENCH COLONIES

TECHNOLOGY CROSSED national and cultural lines in colonial North America. Colonists adapted European techniques to particular North American environments, and Native American techniques to particular European-American settings. Some adaptations varied from one nationality to another; others were virtually identical. Contrary to long-accepted North American myths pervading English-language historical works, the French colonies were not a technological backwater.

French military engineers designed and built some of the most elaborate and attractive civil and military architecture on the North American continent. French surveyors laid out well-planned townsites and a distinctive agricul-

tural landholding pattern. A thriving shipbuilding industry emerged. Native food and drink, such as Indian corn, various squashes, and spruce beer, were developed along with the European staples such as beer, dairy products, fruits, vegetables, meats, and, notably, baked goods (which involved grain growing and milling as well as baking). Spinning and weaving, practiced chiefly for economic self-sufficiency, were highly developed, generating goods of exceptional quality. French colonial artisans practiced virtually every manual craft, and utilized an impressive array of tools. French-colonial metalworkers mined and smelted iron, copper, and lead, while stonecutters and miners extracted building stone, limestone, slate, tar, and potash. Finally, entrepreneurs produced bricks and tiles. Soap and lamp-oil were extracted from seals and beluga whales, and tallow was made for candles.

Several French-colonial adaptations of European and American Indian food technology, land reclamation, wind and water power, transportation, and mining and metallurgy merit examination.

FOOD TECHNOLOGY

The Fisheries

Colonial fisheries were by-products of the French metropolitan cod fishery. In and around the Gulf of Saint Lawrence, some of the practitioners of the "dry" fishery, whereby cod was cleaned, laid out to dry in the sun and wind, and lightly salted, settled in Canada and Île Royale instead of returning to Europe with the catch and, joined by other settlers, developed a resident fishery. Canada provided a market, not only for cod but also for other fish, and France an important market for much sought-after Canadian eels.

Maple Sugar

French colonists borrowed the Native American technique of producing sugar and syrup from sugar-maple tree sap. Europeans introduced metal vessels (which American Indians themselves were happy to adopt) for the boiling process, replacing the wood, bark, and earthenware vessels used before contact. Colonists gathered and boiled the sap and poured the resulting syrup into a mold to solidify when producing maple sugar. Syrup and sugar producers first notched trees with a brace-and-bit or axe; a spout, small trough, or knife blade was inserted to drain the sap from the tree into an earthenware jar or pot, or perhaps a bark vessel. Collecting the sap into wooden buckets, colonists carried the liquid to one of the several sugar bush sheds in the forest sheltering great kettles and caldrons. Placing these cast-iron pots on a stove, French Canadians boiled the sap down to syrup. (Colonists less frequently used a large tin dripping pan for this purpose.) The product was tested by pouring the sap along a spatula with a small hole in one end; the sap had boiled enough when the syrup reached the hole instead of running over the sides of the utensil. Small wooden sugar molds carved with a traditional design, such as that of a heart, beaver, fish, or cross, eventually became a Canadian folk-art form.

The Canadian maple sugar industry had so developed by 1706 that thirty thousand pounds were produced that year in the districts of Montreal and Trois-Rivières alone.

LAND RECLAMATION

The Acadian Dikes
Acadian colonists from western France, who were evidently familiar with Dutch methods of lowland reclamation, developed techniques for the agricultural development of tidal marshlands. The phenomenal high-to-low range of the Bay of Fundy tides varied from 23 feet (about 7 meters) at the Saint John River, 29.5 (8.8 meters) at Port Royal, 42.6 (12.7 meters) at Grand-Pré on the Minas Basin and Beaubassin at the top of Chignecto Bay, to 49 feet (14.7 meters) at the top of the Minas Basin. Acadian farmers undertook to prevent inundation of their fields by seawater and, with annual precipitation hovering at about 50 inches (12.5 centimeters), to drain from them the large quantities of surplus fresh water.

The dikes required for these purposes had to be protected while they were under construction. Acadians erected a barrier, at least five feet high (1.5 meters, and 4.5 to 6 meters or 15 to 20 feet at Minas) with a base at least twice the height, of deep sods held together by the matted roots of salt-marsh grasses cut in rectangular shapes like peat. In order to withstand the force of the tides, the colonists built the dikes eleven to twelve feet (3.3 to 3.6 meters) thick at the bottom and gradually sloped them until they became about eighteen inches (54 centimeters) thick at the top. The mixture of dry sod and marsh grass (which acted as mortar) quickly rendered them compact. Soon covered with grass, the firm and durable barriers supported footpaths on the summit.

Acadian dikes had been limited to enclosing areas adjacent to rivers, until the colonists realized that there must be egress for water drained from marshlands for cultivation and pasture. Acadians consequently built dams as close to the sea as possible, across creeks which drained both uplands behind the marshes and, at low tide, the marshes themselves. Composed of sprucebrush and sods reinforced by logs or branches, these dams featured large sluices with gates or valves both to stop the sea water and to draw off the fresh water. The closer to the sea they were constructed, the higher the dikes and the stronger the sluices became in order to withstand the tide.

WIND AND WATER POWER

Mills: Grist and Saw
To encourage the planting and harvesting of grain as well as flour production, the French Crown granted every seigneur in Canada a monopoly on milling facilities on the seigneurie. Seigneurs provided mills for their *censitaires*, who were required to use them at least for making flour for their own needs. Widespread if not universal conformity to this law made the mill an important institution throughout New France. Since there were also local requirements for lumber, seigneurs equipped some of the first water mills with saws and millstones running off the same waterwheel; however, most mills specialized as either gristmills or sawmills. In Acadia few, if any, mills appear to have exploited the great potential of tidal power. Windmills did function in the maritime colony, however. In Canada, particularly in the Montreal district,

some farms were so dependent on windmills that a week without wind left them bereft of bread.

At Kaskaskia, Illinois, in 1732, 11 mills served a population of 388; two years later, in Canada, 118 mills provided flour and lumber for a population of 37,700. The Kaskaskia mills derived their power from either wind, horses, or water. Regardless of their power source, the mills were sufficiently productive to permit the Illinois region to supply all of Louisiana with flour (for wheat could not be grown in the lower Mississippi Valley) and to feed it entirely during times of distress when semitropical produce was lacking.

Most mills were small, about the size of a small farmhouse, although the largest in French North America, at Terrebonne, was one hundred twenty feet (36 meters) long, forty feet (12 meters) wide, and three stories high, and had granaries on the top floor and four pairs of water-powered millstones. A Montreal mill, of stone construction, boasted three waterwheels and three pairs of millstones. The mill's builders used white oak for the wheels and axles and hardwood, chiefly the sugar maple, for the cogs in the wheel and other parts. The millstones, from France, consisted of "a conglomerate and quartz grains, both of the size of hazelnuts and ordinary sand, all bound together by white limestone," according to Peter Kalm. A masonry dike normally contained the millpond's waters.

Windmills, usually round stone towers, generally stood about twenty feet (6 meters) high and twelve to fifteen feet (3.6 to 4.5 meters) in diameter. The board roof, attached to the massive arms, or wings, of the windmill, sometimes rotated with the blades, as did one near Fort Chambly. The wings often consisted of thin boards, sometimes of linen sails that were removed from their frames after each flour-milling operation.

TRANSPORTATION

The French adapted European watercraft of various sizes and types to their North American needs, whether sailing on the Great Lakes or the navigable portion of the Saint Lawrence River. French Canadians employed the American Indian birchbark canoe to navigate the rivers and lakes of the interior, while for winter travel they used the native toboggan and snowshoe (*raquette*). Horses and horse-drawn vehicles were used locally on cleared land, over winter roads and trails, on frozen rivers and lakes, in towns, and eventually on limited summer-road systems. Spring and fall afforded the most difficult travel conditions, because snow was inadequate and ice too soft for winter modes of transportation, while the water and land routes were either impassable or too dangerous for summer modes. In the towns during the eighteenth century, the affluent could protect their clothes and persons from water and mud by being carried about in sedan chairs.

Travelers circumvented waterfalls and rapids by carrying canoes to the waterway's next navigable section (the *portage*) or, where it was feasible, by "running the rapids." A canal around the Lachine rapids on the Saint Lawrence above Montreal was begun in 1700 but not completed because of the contractor's inaccurate cost projections.

Shipbuilding

During the century 1663 to 1763 some 230 vessels of several sizes and types were built in the dockyards of Quebec. At Louisbourg and other ports on Île Royale during the periods 1733–1739 and 1750–1753, about 75 ships ranging in size from 12 to 160 tons were constructed, in addition to a large number purchased from New England traders. In the interior, four vessels were built on Lake Ontario in 1677 to 1678, one a single-decked barque of ten tons; and the famous *Griffon* was constructed on the Niagara River in 1679 for service on Lake Erie. During the period 1732–1745, six ships were built for Lake Ontario and one for Lake Superior. Four ships, one of fourteen and one of twelve guns, were built for the French navy on Lake Ontario in 1755–1756.

The colonial shipwright was a highly skilled, versatile craftsman who coped with every stage in shipbuilding from cutting the right sizes of timber to finishing and launching the vessel. His seven basic tools were the crosscut saw, felling axe, adze, plane, pod auger, pick, and mallet, although the use of various others could lighten his task. When the great French minister, Colbert, in 1663 initiated shipbuilding at Quebec to facilitate internal communications and trade and diversify the colonial economy, colonial ship-wrights were lacking. Prefabricated craft had to be sent out from France and assembled at Quebec until French master-craftsmen had brought journeymen and apprentices to an appropriate level of training.

In the seventeenth century the Quebec yards produced lifeboats, flat-bottomed boats for transporting troops and supplies in the war against the Iroquois, shallops with one or two sails for hunting and fishing on the Saint Lawrence and smaller ones for the tributaries, and two to three-masted, twenty-five- to thirty-ton barques for internal trade and the transshipment of cargo to and from ocean-going vessels. In the eighteenth century a more ambitious program comprised twenty- to seventy-ton schooners and the larger brigantines (to just under one hundred tons) for use as coasters and on the Saint Lawrence River and Gulf, corvettes of twenty to thirty guns for the navy, one-hundred-fifty- to three-hundred-ton frigates (reaching four hundred tons in wartime with twenty to thirty guns) for trade and privateering, the all-purpose oceangoing Marine Department vessel known as the *flûte*, and even the third-rate man-of-war of sixty guns or more.

The Birchbark Canoe

In the hands of strong, skillful paddlers the birchbark canoe was fast and maneuverable. Its light construction made the canoe portable, though vulnerable to damage from rocks or, when a sail was used, from a mast blown down in a storm. French Canadians nevertheless employed canoes as the primary means of transporting trade goods, food, furs, traders and troops, and for general purposes. Though colonists continued to make small craft, Canadian boatbuilders constructed progressively longer canoes for the routes between Montreal and the interior in response to the greater quantities of trade goods and furs transported over those routes and to regulations favoring larger craft. By 1752 a workshop at Trois-Rivières was producing each year about twenty eight-man canoes of a model almost thirty-six English feet (10.8 meters) in length, five and a half feet (1.7 meters) wide and three feet (about 1 meter) deep.

The exterior skin of this large model ordinarily consisted of six pieces of birchbark, the inner side of which always became the outer side of the boat. Boatbuilders used white cedar—sometimes fir—for the ribs and the strips. The space between the ribs was two and a half English inches (65 to 90 millimeters), but the strips were so close together that the birchbark could not be seen between them. Seams, usually held together by spruce roots, resembled a tailor's cross-stitch with the bark folded double. Waterproof melted resin (fir or spruce gum) sealed the seams and stopped small holes. Other repairs required varying degrees of partial reconstruction.

Sleighs and Carriages

Of the land vehicles used in the French colonies, the *carriole* and the *calèche* deserve special mention.

The **Carriole.** The Canadian sleigh, the *carriole,* was so efficiently designed and constructed that it could glide over eighty miles (120 kilometers) of deep snow in one day with the same horse. Some *carrioles* were covered, while others were open with a front panel or splash-board. French Canadians usually equipped their sleighs with a front seat for the driver and a rear seat for the passengers. Town sleighs required one horse. *Carrioles* used for longer trips sometimes had two, one in front of the other; the rear animal was driven and it, in turn, guided the lead horse.

The vehicle's body rested on a frame comprising three or four wooden crossbars and a pair of low wooden runners curved at the front and girded underneath by an iron strip. Shafts for the horse or horses were connected by two crossbars, the one nearest to the sleigh being attached to it by a piece of chain and a catch located at the driver's feet. The front ends of the shafts were attached to the backstrap of the horse's harness.

The **Calèche.** The *calèche*, a light, one-horse, sometimes two-horse, exceptionally well-sprung carriage that could be made to reach remarkable speeds, served as the *carriole's* summer counterpart. Quite unlike the heavier, cumbersome four-wheeled European vehicle of the same name, the *calèche* resembled the European post chaise, its body being suspended by large straps or springs between two shafts and mounted on two wheels. The passengers' seat, which could accommodate two occupants, rested on the wooden or leather springs. The vehicle swayed so much at high speeds that inexperienced riders often suffered motion sickness. The narrow driver's seat, located immediately behind the splashboard, permitted the driver to position his feet on the shafts. Until a few years before the end of the French regime *calèches,* some with a hood over the passengers' seat for protection against rain and sun, were something of a luxury vehicle.

MINING AND METALLURGY

The Saint Maurice Ironworks

Located about twelve miles (19 kilometers) from Trois-Rivières, on the tributary of the Saint Lawrence called the Saint Maurice River, two large-scale forges and two smaller ones, all under the same roof, collectively produced high-quality iron and iron products from bog ore mined nearby. Having opened in 1738, the ironworks failed as a private enterprise for various reasons, among them insufficient capital, poor management, inadequate marketing of products, and failure to recruit enough specialized workers. In 1743 the ironworks became an agency of the French Crown. Employing more than one hundred twenty workers, this facility smelted ore and produced pig iron for export, as well as chimney plates, stoves, pots, nails, gun and mortar barrels, and shot, for domestic, commercial, and military purposes.

At various sites three to nine miles (5 to 14 kilometers) from the forges, the very rich, soft ore lay in lumps six inches (150 millimeters) to a foot below the surface, within veins six to eighteen inches (150 to 450 millimeters) deep. After extracting the ore with relative ease, workers transported it to the ironworks in winter on sledges. The ore was then smelted with locally quarried gray limestone and a local clay marl, in furnaces fueled by locally produced charcoal.

Workers manufactured the charcoal used in the forges from local fir, which, in 1749 when Peter Kalm visited the works, was extremely

plentiful. Craftsmen fashioned bellows of wood. The iron manufactured at the forges was soft, but pliable and tough. Observers claimed that it was less susceptible to rust than iron produced elsewhere, which (if the assertion was true) would have made Saint Maurice iron especially valuable in hardware used in shipbuilding. French iron producers long resisted the introduction of high-quality Saint Maurice products into France, until they were made to realize that any iron it was likely to replace on the French market would not be their inferior French products, but rather the high-quality Spanish, German, and Swedish goods. Master craftsmen, however, were unsuccessful in applying known techniques to manufacture steel from Canadian iron; nor were they able to devise new ones. European manufacturers could conceivably have utilized it for that purpose if the iron was indeed suitable for steel, had France continued to own the works after 1763.

Water power drove the forges' great hammers (*martinets*), used to fashion pieces of iron. One rapidly flowing stream descending steeply from the forest above the site of the ironworks (for the Precambrian Shield almost reaches the valley of the Saint Lawrence throughout much of its course) was dammed at three places before its confluence with the Saint Maurice, thereby creating three waterfalls. The water behind the first dam was released for the use of a forge on the stream's left bank, just below; it then passed to the second dam, where it was released to operate a hammer; and finally it passed to the third dam, where it operated a second hammer. Hammers were also built on the left bank; in 1753 forge employees informed a visitor that three more hammers could have been on the right bank of the same stream, two opposite the existing ones and the third between the lower dam and the Saint Maurice. The informer also noted that surplus water could be released during the flood periods for use by the forges.

To cast an ingot fifteen feet (4.5 meters) long and six inches (150 millimeters) thick, workers plugged a channel of that size, formed between two small banks of sand. This crude channel constituted the mold into which the molten iron was poured. In casting one part of a stove, craftsmen carefully turned upside down a ladleful of molten iron and poured its contents into the hollow of the mold, up to the top of the sides, so that the underside of the section would be in relief. The dimensions of each individual part of a stove were so precise that when they were all put together they fitted perfectly. Workers produced chimney plates in a similar fashion, their molds being fixed to an accurately level table two to three feet (about 1 meter) off the floor to facilitate the worker's task.

A special nook contained molds for pots, kettles, and other round objects. These molds were box-shaped wooden cubes, held at the angles by iron angle-plates and revetted with masonry the thickness of a brick. Workmen could cast more than one object at the same time in these, provided the ladle had enough capacity for the molten iron required to form each object.

TECHNOLOGICAL ADAPTATION

Of the foregoing examples, most represent noteworthy adaptations of European technology to particular North American circumstances, while some represent borrowings from Native American technology. Some of these techniques demonstrate a particular technical flair in French colonists that distinguishes them from their fellows in other colonial empires.

BIBLIOGRAPHY

Belting, Natalia Maree. *Kaskaskia Under the French Regime.* Urbana, Ill., 1948. Contains some incidental information on mills.

Boissonnault, Réal. *Les Forges du Saint-Maurice, 1729–1883.* Trois-Rivières, Quebec, 1983. A short business history of the ironworks written chiefly for visitors to the Forges national historic site.

Brisson, Réal. *La charpenterie navale à Québec sous le régime français.* Quebec, 1983. Contains, among other things, detail on the art of ship's carpentry and the tools of the craft.

Clark, Andrew Hill. *Acadia: The Geography of Early Nova Scotia to 1760.* Madison, Wis., 1968. This work has not been superseded. Includes information on dikes, mills, and shipbuilding.

Fauteux, Joseph-Noël. *Essai sur l'industrie au Canada sous le régime français.* 2 vols. Quebec, 1927. An introduction to the subject for the largest of the French colonies.

Franquet, Louis. *Voyages et mémoires sur le Canada en 1752–1753.* Montreal, 1974. Astute observations on colonial society in the 1750s by an eminent military engineer. Useful for the ironworks, canoes, *carrioles, calèches,* and mills.

Harris, R. C. *The Seigneurial System in Early Canada.* Madison, Wis., 1966. Useful information about mills on Canadian seigneuries.

Harris, R. C., ed., and G. J. Matthews, cartographer/designer. *Historical Atlas of Canada.* Vol. 1. *From the Beginning to 1800.* Toronto, Ontario, 1987. Includes a diagram of an Acadian dike and extensive maps of canoe routes. See especially Plate 29.

Kalm, Peter. *Peter Kalm's Travels in North America: The English Version of 1770,* edited by Adolph B. Benson. New York, 1966. Observations on North American colonial society in the late 1740s by a Finnish botanist (a Swedish subject), a former student of Linnaeus. Useful for the ironworks, canoes, *carrioles, calèches,* and mills.

Lunn, Alice Jean E. *Développement économique de la Nouvelle-France (1713–1760).* Montreal, 1986. An outstanding, much-cited McGill University doctoral thesis now published in translation from the original English.

McLennan, J. S. *Louisbourg from its Foundation to its Fall, 1713–1758.* London, 1918. Only this first edition contains the appendices, such as Appendix V on shipping and trade, including ships built in certain years.

Mathieu, Jacques. *La construction navale royale à Québec, 1739–1759.* Quebec, 1971. Important first study on shipbuilding, beginning with the initiatives of the Intendant Gilles Hocquart and carrying the story to the end of the French period.

Pendergast, James F. *The Origin of Maple Sugar.* Ottawa, 1982. The National Museum of Natural Sciences, "Syllogeus" no. 36, 1982. The author offers strong evidence that maple sugarmaking originated with American Indians and puts to rest for good the notion that it was introduced to America by Europeans.

Séguin, Robert-Lionel. *La Civilisation traditionnelle de l'"habitant" aux 17e et 18e siècles.* Montreal, 1967. A reference work based chiefly on estate inventories and other documents. Valuable for information on vehicles, maple sugar, and farm equipment, for example.

Trottier, Louise. *Les Forges. Historiographie des Forges du Saint-Maurice.* Montreal, 1980.

Frederick J. Thorpe

SEE ALSO **Scientific Inquiry.**

THE SPANISH BORDERLANDS

COMPARED WITH MORE developed areas of Spanish colonial control, technology in the Spanish Borderlands was at a low level. There were obvious limits to the possibilities of technological advance in the borderlands. Except for missionaries (usually Franciscans) and a few military officers, the level of education was low. Outside contacts, restricted by distance, were few, and the latest innovations were costly. So most developments in frontier technology became a matter of applying to local resources some knowledge of practical alien influences. California, the last frontier, was an exception. Almost from its beginning in 1769 artisans and craftsmen, mostly recruited from San Blas and Guadalajara, were contracted in substantial numbers for service in the missions and *presidios*.

Technology, defined here as the application of scientific and engineering knowledge to everyday life through the industrial arts, played an unnoticed role. Three hundred years of history over a wide expanse of territory invite sweeping generalizations, but specific knowledge is necessary to establish a general framework in which to fit specific technological experience. Almost all technological developments were Hispanic-based, with minimal utilization of Native American technology, except as noted below. The fact that the Indians were not advanced technologically limited the amount of cultural borrowing from them. Two exceptions come to mind: the curing of meat, frequently buffalo beef, by means of a sun and wind drying process referred to as jerkeying, by which protein could be long preserved and transported great distances, was of importance for borderland survival and for the quality of life; and the long-established Native American skill in artistic and utilitarian basket making, though not copied by borderland Spaniards to any great extent, was utilized and encouraged through the purchase of Indian handicrafts. There are, of course, other examples, but an examination of their aggregate significance leads to the conclusion that only a very limited amount of cultural borrowing or adaptation from Native Americans can be classed as technological.

ASCERTAINING LATITUDE AND LONGITUDE

Few borderlanders knew even the rudiments of astronomy and therefore had an imperfect knowledge of the exact location of places within their own world. In the case of latitude, their elementary knowledge of the North Star, Polaris, gave a knowledge of their distance from the equator that was imprecise but useful in practice. Comparison provided the relative position of other places north and south. There is no evidence of any notion of compensation for elevation or declination. It was not until the late colonial period that an even elementary sextant was available to make more accurate measurements, and even then there was no consideration of magnetic north or of the elevation of the point of observation. Errors in latitude were considerably less when made along the coasts by mariners, who had better equipment and more experience in determining their coordinates. While latitude was inaccurate by modern standards even late in the colonial period, at least it had a fairly standard error.

Longitude was impossible to measure precisely, since the instruments and skill needed for precise measurement of longitude were far beyond local possibilities. Measurement was strictly a matter of dead reckoning. Assuming that the point of origin was known, which was doubtful, a person calculated any subsequent position based on his or her estimate of time and direction traveled, which can be in dispute even among members of the same traveling group. It was not until the latter part of the eighteenth century, a mere three decades before the end of the colonial period, that longitudes were calculated in most areas, specifically remote regions, with any astronomical certainty. In fact so far off were most estimates that rather than start with the great suspected error, cartographers, mariners, and travelers began their dead reckoning by establishing a new prime meridian. The naval station established in 1767 at San Blas in Nayarit was utilized for that purpose. Until then various conventions were used in efforts to determine the location of a specific place, none of which were fully satisfactory.

MILITARY EQUIPMENT AND FIREARMS

Technological advance occurred in warfare and its accoutrements. Although from first contact the Spanish were technologically superior to the Indians in arms and ammunition, the borderland experience altered Spanish military orientation to some extent, as technological improvements based on and conditioned by frontier existence became important to survival. Experience and sometimes sheer necessity dictated a change from the steel and chain mail armor of the early conquistadores to innovative armor based on the scarcity of traditional equipment and the utility of the substitute gear.

The *cuera,* a short, heavy buckskin jacket of five-to-seven-ply thickness of hide laminated together with animal glue, replaced metal armor. From this piece of equipment emerged the name *soldados de cuera* for many of the borderland soldiers, whose unique armor was nearly impervious to anything but a direct hit by a well-propelled arrow. The buckskin armor gave the frontier soldier great confidence, sometimes to the point of foolhardiness. He also bore an even more impervious piece of equipment: the *adarga,* a shield made of the same material as the *cuera* that, having the advantage of lightness and of maneuverability, replaced the metal shield.

The frontier weapons of the borderlands were second rate compared with those available to soldiers nearer the important centers of New Spain's population and industry. There was also a scarcity of competent gunsmiths on the frontier. Furthermore, considerable time was necessary for reloading, a lapse sufficient for a native adversary to discharge multiple arrows. The obvious tactical answer to that drawback was to fire by the numbers, with perhaps as few as one-third of the arms firing in one round, with others being held in reserve for discharge when battle conditions required. With all drawbacks considered, Spanish arms at the borderlands were far superior to the weapons of Native Americans.

TRANSPORTATION VEHICLES

In all borderland areas, there was a shortage of wheeled vehicles, particularly of four-wheeled wagons. Such paucity of transportation facilities was in large measure made up for by use of mule trains (*recuas*). For heavier and more cumbersome freight, carts were the normal means of locomotion. Legend says the first wagons in New Mexico were those of the Santa Fe traders in 1822, but close reading of early New Mexico documentation indicates that in 1598 Juan de Oñate and his party had with them a considerable number of wagons. It can be hypothesized that as those vehicles became unserviceable, the use of such four-wheeled conveyances was no longer possible in the absence of the necessary expertise and the component parts for making wheels. A lack of wheelwrights necessitated the use of a much more rudimentary wheel, one made of solid rounds of wood and attached to a simple axle.

The conveyance using this type of wheel was a *carreta,* the motive power for which was often a yoke of oxen. In California, founded later than New Mexico, the solid wheels were of giant oaks of suitable size and roundness. Lubrication of such wheels was essential, and beef tallow was the most available form of grease; it may have been far short of ideal, however, since the *carretas* could be heard from a great distance because of the squeaking, grating sound of the massive wheels against the wooden axle. All parts of the *carreta* were made of wood; with a flatbed of pine and upright stakes of small poles of even size laced together with thongs, the vehicle was sturdy enough to prevent freight from slipping. The *carretas* made lengthy trips and were the major vehicle in all parts of the borderlands.

DOMESTIC CRAFTS

Though the Indians, particularly in New Mexico, were skilled in weaving prior to the arrival of the first Spaniards, their skills and materials were suited to the manufacture of light cotton blankets, such as the four thousand blankets given to explorer Antonio Espejo in 1581 as a gift from the Hopi. This capacity for weaving was transferred at a later date to the manufacture of woolen blankets after the Spaniards had introduced sheep and, more importantly, had instructed the local Indians in the more complicated techniques of floor looms for weaving of woolens. Indian adoption of these techniques permanently changed their craft for weaving blankets, cloth, and rugs. It is hard now to imagine the Navajo and Pueblo without their looms for weaving woolens, but these were introduced by the Spaniards, and this is an example of the enrichment of Indian life by contact with an alien culture. New techniques of dyeing fabrics combined vegetable and earth dyes.

In the area of silversmithing, it is uncertain what skills, if any, were possessed by the pre-contact Indians. However, after long contact the art and capacity of the Indians grew to the point where many designs introduced by the Spaniards were thought to be indigenous, such as the squash blossom (really the pomegranate), the concho belt, and other adornments of silver that are so prized today. The use of turquoise was reasonably well developed in the pre-contact period. The Spaniards became borrowers from the Indians of this important semiprecious stone. Spaniards and southwestern Indians created an artistic style that depended on the technical skill of both groups and that continues to be of importance.

Other technology applied by Spaniards to the domestic scene included the making of candles and the construction of beehive-shaped ovens for outdoor baking, a long tradition of Moorish origin.

THE ERECTION OF BUILDINGS

Architecture, or perhaps more accurately, building, depended greatly upon native resources. Within that obvious conditioning influence, the Spaniards had more highly developed skills. Stone was available in considerable quantity but was not extensively used, except for some foundations, owing to a frontier scarcity of stonemasons. An early example of use of stone is the missions established for the Tompiro Indians in the Estancia Valley, consisting of the missions of Tajique, Abó, Chililí, and Quarai in New Mexico. (These buildings, abandoned even before the Pueblo Revolt of 1680, and their remains

are today at the Salinas Pueblo Missions National Monument.)

Though building methods were pragmatic, they were as technologically advanced as frontier circumstances permitted. Occasionally master craftsmen were sent to the frontier to assist in major building projects. Setting aside those notable exceptions, Spaniards early introduced adobe and the construction methods associated with these sun-dried bricks, made of earth with a suitable binder. As a building material, adobe was available in abundance, with a sandy loam soil being considered best, and was bound with straw, grass, pine needles, weeds, or even manure. Adobe had long been used in Spain; it was a Moorish import deriving its name from the Arabic word atob. In the borderlands it was adapted to local usage, at least in the case of the Pueblo Indians of New Mexico, who had worked with a less manageable but similar material in constructing their buildings.

The advantages of adobe construction were the availability of the component parts, its cheapness, its insulative properties, its immunity from infestation, and its fireproof and soundproof characteristics. With these advantages came some disadvantages. If there was too much sand, the adobe bricks crumbled, whereas if they had too much clay, they were subject to shrinkage and cracking. Other disadvantages were their extreme susceptibility to earthquake damage, water and wind erosion, and the great downward pressure exerted by such heavy building materials, which could cause the structure to collapse. The melting factor was somewhat reduced by the installation of moistureproof roofs and frequent plastering.

In making adobes, a thorough mixing of the materials was required. Then the mixture was placed in open, four-sided molds (frames without tops or bottoms). The dimensions of the bricks were characteristically convenient fractions of the Spanish yard (the vara, equaling thirty-three inches [82.5 centimeters]). Individual bricks, weighing from forty to sixty pounds (18 to 27 kilograms), were left to dry long enough to become cured, the amount of time depending on weather conditions and climate.

At least some of the early buildings had foundations. This necessitated rough quarrying of stones, which were placed in a suitable open trench in an effort to create a more solid footing upon which to build. Lack of technological skill in matching plans to actual construction has led to considerable problems in excavating and subsequently reconstructing edifices dating from the colonial period. Skill in surveying was almost nonexistent, and building methods were not sufficiently precise to permit following any plans that might have been drawn up in advance. Borderland builders had no trouble establishing a straight line, but they did not always build up to that line. Pragmatic solutions were reached that would permit the continuation of construction. Upon the foundation, if there was any, adobes were laid so that no vertical joint would continue from one course to the next, but rather, so that there would be overlapping. Mortar between adobes was made of the same materials as the adobe except for the binder; thus adobe mud was used with varying success depending upon whether greater binding quality was needed for the mortar's hold. Horizontal joints were always quite satisfactory, since the extreme weight from above was conducive to such seams becoming almost invisible and imperceptible. Vertical joints were not as easily made, and there was some separation. Most of these mortared joints had the advantage of regular coats of stucco made of quicklime and sand. With repeated application, a strong exterior coat was in time provided for most buildings.

Since building methods required many wooden structural pieces, the cutting and moving of timbers took much time. Unless forests were near at hand, which was rare, the transporting of timbers took some knowledge of terrain, much patience, and a great deal of manpower. Floodwater-assisted or gravity-aided transport of timbers was highly preferred, with most structural pieces shaped at the point of cutting to reduce the weight of the material being transported. Smaller structural members were either dragged or transported by *carreta* or mule back.

Roofing was much more complicated as far as construction methods were concerned. Tiles were made of clay and formed to the proper shape for laying over heavy beams. Other areas not supported by the heavy beams made use of wattles, long a method in regular use in parts of Spain and still utilized in rural areas. Wattle construction required many long, strong, and easily obtained rods of wood over which thatch could be laid.

The type of tools and equipment available reflected the level of technological development in the building arts. Squares and spirit levels were in use, and inventories of the 1770s in California indicate the existence of axes, adzes, augers, hoes, nails and tacks, machetes, bucksaws, hammers, pincers, soldering irons, compasses, crowbars, forges, planes, joiners, jack planes, plumb bobs, scales, trowels, drills, and chisels. In earlier years there would have been a considerably smaller assortment, and inland areas would have had less access to such technology as forges, since only when supply by ship to California began could such heavier items be transported to the borderlands.

WORKING WITH METAL AND RAWHIDE

Iron, and later steel, was at times imported from the outside. Metal locks, hinges, and crossbars, the latter for use in doors and windows, were listed in some inventories. The major use of iron was in agricultural equipment, especially in the late eighteenth century, when concerted efforts were made to modernize frontier methods of agriculture. Steel was always in short supply, if available at all.

Demonstrating the adaptability of the borderlanders, rawhide was often used as a substitute material for many structural pieces. For example, it took the place of nails and hinges. Thongs were used in place of nails and spikes to fasten together major structural members such as *vigas* (beams) and rafters. When tightly wound and tied, the rawhide shrank on drying, making a rigid joint. Scraped very thin and made translucent by application of oil, it became the substitute glass for windowpanes.

In California, where the sale of hides and tallow was a principal industry, tanning was a three- to six-month process of soaking the hides in a solution containing oak bark, in which the tannic acid changed the hide into leather, with some assistance from oil, grease, or tallow. Everywhere in the borderlands rawhide was the universal plaster, or glue, for repairing broken implements and meeting household requirements.

SURVEYING

The same lack of skill evident in rudimentary building plans was of more lasting significance when it came to surveying property and preparing plats and maps. The lack of precision in measurement of land was frequently indicated by the expression that the area contained, for example, three leagues, *poco más o menos* (more or less). Such lack of precision was of only minimal importance when much land was available and its value was insignificant. Later, after much of the better lands had been preempted by the earliest settlers, precise measurement became more important. It was not until the period of United States control that there was great attention paid to a new system of measurement, that of metes and bounds. By U.S. standards, holding land in the large parcels of the Spanish colonial period seemed immoral, even illegal under U.S. laws limiting the size of holdings from the public domain. At the very least, it seemed unwise. The people who suffered most under these circumstances were those who could not prove beyond a reasonable doubt that they not only had a valid deed of conveyance but also were in actual possession of the land in question.

Surveys from early days, based frequently on unstable descriptive boundaries, were attacked as invalid or became less expansive. By claiming a lesser area, claimants had less challenge and more promptness in validation. Such boundary descriptions as "the lone tree atop the second range of mountains, and from there to where the old highway crosses the arroyo coming down from the far sierra," seemed especially vague. The impact of imprecision was later compounded when it became evident that there were overlapping boundaries among various grants, resulting in dual claims, both with the authority of title. The lack of technological skill to construct detailed maps of real property was the major culprit.

TRANSPORTING WATER

Conduction of water was a concern not only for agriculture but for other purposes as well, although there was never any attempt to distinguish between domestic and farm use of water.

In recent years there has been a great deal of litigation over water, and attempts have been made to consider water as a transferable property right vested in an individual or individuals, but such was not the case in colonial times. Water, like air, was available to all, so long as its use was not to the detriment of others. Practical frontier considerations of water utilization led to the construction of diversion and storage works. Furthermore, the semi-arid characteristics of the Southwest made people particularly cognizant of the need for conservation. Town residents, living in a communal arrangement, were required to spend specific amounts of time working on a dam or on diversion ditches so that a year-round supply would be available.

In New Mexico's mountain villages, an ingenious system of transporting water was developed. Trunks of trees were hollowed out and laid end to end; through these *canoas* ran a copious supply of water. The hollow tree trunks, an inexpensive substitute for more complicated gravity flow systems, were propped up by trestles to conduct water over canyons and gorges. Because of the need for upkeep and maintenance, the use of such log flumes was restricted to mountainous areas where both trees of appropriate size and untapped water supplies were available. Other water channels were diverted to power small, rudimentary grinding mills. More sophisticated devices presented problems. In California, for example, when French visitor Jean François Galaup de Lapérouse presented a grinding stone in 1786, it was never used for lack of technological expertise to set it in motion.

CONCLUSION

In summary, technology was relatively undeveloped in the borderlands. Technological expertise made non-Hispanics, even those with only moderate claim to any such skills, welcome in an area that otherwise might have considered entry of such immigrants totally unacceptable. Such lack of skills became an important opening wedge for penetration by the neighboring United States into what had long been Hispanic territory.

BIBLIOGRAPHY

Brinckerhoff, Sidney B., and Odie B. Faulk. *Lancers for the King: A Study of the Frontier Military System of Northern New Spain.* Phoenix, Ariz., 1965.

Jordan, Louann, and St. George Cooke. *El Rancho de Las Golondrinas: Spanish Colonial Life in New Mexico.* Santa Fe, N.Mex., 1977.

Webb, Edith Buckland. *Indian Life at the Old Missions.* Los Angeles, Calif., 1952.

Wroth, William, ed. *Hispanic Crafts of the Southwest.* Colorado Springs, Colo., 1977.

Donald C. Cutter

NATIVE AMERICAN

TECHNOLOGICAL DEVELOPMENTS USING NATIVE MATERIALS

Stoneworking

UNTIL THE ARRIVAL of Europeans, stone was the basic tool material over the entire North American continent. Igneous, sedimentary, or metamorphic stone was used, depending on an object's intended use. All stones might be shaped by abrading, grinding, or pecking away superfluous material. These methods were usually chosen when making large tools such as hammers and woodworking celts. With the denser stones, it was possible to make well-shaped and highly polished tools by these processes. Igneous and metamorphic rocks were also shaped by pressure flaking—that is, spalling away long slices that were then refined into sharp tools such as knife blades and arrowheads.

Leatherworking

Throughout the New World, all tanning was done with animal products, usually the brain and sometimes the liver of the same animals from which the hides were obtained. If the aim was to tan furs, only the flesh sides of the raw skins were scraped clean; then, after being allowed to dry, the partially cooked, mashed tanning material was rubbed in. Finally the hides were softened by rubbing them briskly with a blunt tool. The Old World method of tanning with vegetable compounds was unknown. Leather without fur was made in the same way, but both sides were scraped and treated with the tanning compound.

Most North American natives used their leather for some form of clothing, ranging from simple robes and kilts wrapped around the body to elaborately cut garments suitable for the Arctic. However, true tailoring by European definition was not achieved. An especially ingenious leather construction was the tipi, the portable tent of the Plains and Prairie Indians. It was precisely designed to withstand strong winds and provide a warm shelter in subzero conditions. Leather objects were decorated with self fringes (those cut from the edge of the actual garment), painting, and embroidery.

Rawhide—cleaned but untanned skin—was also produced and used extensively. Strips or pieces of rawhide were softened in water and then applied as lashing or as a binding cover to objects such as saddle frames and Eskimo kayaks. It was effective because animal skins shrink considerably as they dry, thus consolidating whatever they enclosed. Sheets of rawhide were also cut into various storage containers. Here the material's rigidity protected the contents. The rawhide, semi-translucent when cleaned, was usually made opaque prior to decoration by abrading the whole surface with a stone hammer. Rawhide objects were decorated with painting and at times by incising and pyrography.

Weaving

True weaving was well established in the southwestern and southeastern regions of the continent, using both native animal and vegetable fibers as well as cotton introduced about A.D. 1000 from present-day Mexico and Guatemala. In the Southwest native weavers knew all the basic techniques including brocade, velvet, tapestry, and some unusual ones such as eccentric warping. They also practiced such nonloom processes as braiding and frame plaiting. There was evidently a similarly high level of expertise in the Southeast, but only a few fragments have survived to verify this belief. Elsewhere there was widespread use of proto-weaving techniques, especially twining. This is a basketry technique that could be modified to make two-dimensional robes and containers. Cloth, both woven and twined, was generally used for clothing and bedding. In addition to self-patterns, those made with the basic warps and wefts of a fabric, cloth was decorated with embroidery of many kinds and sometimes painted.

Embroidery

Objects made of leather, cloth, and birchbark were often decorated with various kinds of superstructural embroidery. Over most of the continent, quills from the porcupine were a favorite medium. The quills—modified hairs with sharp, barbed ends—are hollow and take dye readily. The barbs were cut off and the quills were flattened and applied in various ways. Other animal materials used for embroidery included deer hair, marine shells, teeth, claws, and bits of feather. Besides being sewn to a surface, quills, feathers, and deer hair were also woven with fiber warps and wefts into simple decorative bands. Embroidery in all the materials listed above was applied extensively to almost any suitable object, and some of the methods used appear to have been unique to North America.

Ceramics

Pottery was made in most areas south of the Great Lakes and, to a limited degree, in eastern Canada and the western Arctic. The potter's wheel was unknown throughout the entire New World, and the principal building methods were coiling, direct shaping, and patching. Although firing was generally done at low temperatures, some true reduction wares (involving a sealed kiln and often very high temperatures) were produced in the Southwest and Southeast. Before firing, pottery was often burnished to a glossy luster with smooth pebbles, giving it the appearance of a deeply glazed finish. But, with one short-lived exception, true vitreous glazes were unknown in the Western Hemisphere before European arrival.

There were two underlying North American pottery traditions: northern and southern. The northern, or woodland, was found north of the Ohio River, from the Saint Lawrence Valley west onto the Great Plains. Pottery in this tradition was made by direct shaping or patching, tended toward round-bottom forms, and decorated by incising, modeling, or appliqué. Northern pottery was seldom painted. Southern pottery was found through the Southeast and Southwest and in the California peninsula. It tended more toward flat-bottomed shapes and was made principally by coiling. In the West most pottery was painted. In the Southeast incising before firing or engraving afterward was more common than painting. In some of its elements, such as tripod feet and effigy vessels, southeastern pottery also showed Mexican and Central American influence. Besides the undecorated wares made for cooking, mixing, or storing dried foods, there were decorated ceramics for carrying water, serving food and drink, and using as containers for especially valued personal objects. In the Southeast ceramic effigy heads were made as mortuary gifts.

Basketry

Basketry was made practically everywhere in North America, and some of it (for example, that from the Aleutian Islands and north of San Francisco Bay) was technically and aesthetically unrivaled anywhere in the world. There were three principal construction methods—coiling, twining, and plaiting—with many variations of each. Coiling was actually a sewing process. A foundation of thin rods or a bundle of grass was wrapped for a very short distance with a fine fiber sewing element. This was bent into a tight circle and the sewing fiber was then used both to continue wrapping the foundation and to sew it to the preceding coil. By changing the placement of the new coil upon the old, the worker could change the shape from a flat disk to a three-dimensional bowl. Decoration of coiled basketry was usually done by simply changing the color of the sewing element as needed to create a pattern. In the Columbia River plateau, coiled baskets were also decorated by the imbrication method, in which a flat strand of decorative fiber was folded and inserted in turn under each individual stitch, creating a surface resembling many small tesserae. Coiled basketry predominated in the Southwest, in the Great Plains, in most places west of the Rockies, and in the Arctic.

Twined basketry was made with separate warps and wefts. Basically, each warp was enclosed in turn between a pair of wefts, which then made a half-turn around one another before engaging the next warp. Since these turns were always made in the same direction, the result looked like a fine textile of many small stitches angled downwards to the right or left. Twined basketry was usually decorated by adding elements during basic construction. There were numerous methods for doing this. On the northern Pacific Coast, the finished baskets were also painted with the heraldic designs peculiar to the area. Twined basketry was once common in the Northeast and Southwest and still is in the Great Lakes region. It predominated along the Pacific Coast from around San Francisco Bay north to the Aleutians.

Plaited basketry was made of flat fiber strips interlaced in a repeated pattern. It resembled a coarse, simply woven fabric. When the elements were round in cross section, plaiting became wicker. The variations in plaiting were limited only by the maker's imagination, and ranged from the simple "over-one-under-one" of utilitarian winnowing baskets to the fanciful double-layered treasure boxes made by the Chitimacha tribe of the Mississippi River delta. Decoration of plaited baskets usually consisted of self-pattern, plain or in several colors. Plaited basketry was found over most of eastern North America and, to a lesser degree, in the Southwest and in the region around Vancouver Island. The finest plaiting came from the Southeast.

Metals

Although smelting and casting of metals were known in Mexico and Central and South America, this knowledge had not diffused into North America upon European arrival. Over much of the continent east of the Mississippi, native copper was hammered cold into sheets and simple forms. Because of its softness, it was used principally for ornaments and less often for tools. In the Southeast metal smiths decorated thin plates with repoussé figures, but more often copper ornaments were decorated only with simple incising. Native copper is readily available on the northern Pacific Coast, and one distinctive northwestern form was tubular beads made by rolling thin rectangles into cylinders. Another was the larger, thicker plaque variously called "Copper Shield" or simply "Copper" in the literature but actually serving only as a wealth symbol.

TECHNOLOGICAL DEVELOPMENTS WITH EUROPEAN MATERIALS

Beginning soon after their initial appearance in the New World, Europeans introduced many new materials to North American Native people, who in most cases found their own applications for these goods.

Beads

Glass beads from Murano, and later from other parts of Europe, had been used for centuries in the Old World as components of necklaces and as light edge trimming for garments, hangings, and the like. But in North America, there was a tendency to cover large areas of leather and cloth with these beads. The glass beads were esteemed for the contrast in texture and color that they offered. Blue in particular was often very popular, since in many areas there had been no readily obtainable native blue coloring. Apart from one or two unsuccessful attempts in the nineteenth century, Indians themselves never made glass products.

Cloth

Europeans brought fine woolen flannel and broadcloth as well as colored calico. All these were very popular and used extensively. One favorite trade cloth was strouding from Gloucestershire. This woolen fabric was woven first and then dyed, leaving white selvages that the Indians exploited by using as sleeve ends, dress bottoms, and so forth. Another favorite fabric was plain canvas, which soon became the favorite material for tipis because of its lighter weight compared with leather and because of its translucency. European-printed cotton cloth was used to some extent, being most popular in the Ohio River valley area.

Ribbons

Europeans used silk ribbons as ornaments or adjuncts to clothing. But tribes in the Great Lakes area and the midwestern United States developed a unique kind of appliqué embroidery with overlapping layers of ribbon. Called ribbonwork, this craft is still widely practiced today.

Yarn

Wool yarns were meant for knitting or possibly weaving, but northeastern tribes substituted them for native fiber cordage in making braided bands. They also developed a method of exchanging warp and weft strands to produce flamelike figures. This technique was later borrowed by the colonists in New France for their distinctive Assomption sashes, named for the parish of Saint Jacques de l'Assomption where most of them were produced.

Metal

In the late seventeenth century, European colonists along the Atlantic Coast began making silver ornaments for Indian trade. Soon the natives themselves learned the basic techniques and were producing their own. They were, however, always dependent upon the traders for a supply of silver sheets. Their technology included only stamping, incising, cold hammering, and simple soldering. These eastern Indian smiths drew upon both Native ornament forms previously made in copper or seashell and European ones like the Scots Luckenbooth brooch. In the Southwest, Indians learned to work metals from Spanish blacksmiths in the nineteenth century. Besides the basic technology, the southwesterners also did extensive casting and eventually began setting stones into their work.

CONCLUSION

The cultures of the New World developed in isolation from those of Europe and Asia, which may explain why basic inventions like the wheel and iron smelting were unknown or rudimentary. On the other hand, if European arrival had happened a century or two later, others like gold working might have diffused from Mexico and Central America north. Despite their isolation North American Native peoples did manage to use their natural resources in imaginative ways. In doing so they hit upon some basic inventions that have been adopted into North American European culture. These include bark and dugout canoes, snowshoes, the toboggan, Arctic winter clothing, and moccasins. These contributions enabled European colonists to cope more effectively with the unfamiliar North American environment.

BIBLIOGRAPHY

Adovasio, J. M. *Basketry Technology: A Guide to Identification and Analysis.* Chicago, 1977.
Bourret, Françoise, and Lucie Lavigne. *La Fléché.* Montreal, 1973.
Conn, Richard. *Robes of White Shell and Sunrise: Personal Decorative Arts of the Native American.* Denver, Colo., 1974.
Horse Capture, George, ed. *Native American Ribbonwork: A Rainbow Tradition.* Cody, Wyo., 1980.
Kent, Kate Peck. *The Cultivation and Weaving of Cotton in the Prehistoric Southwestern United States.* Transactions of the American Philosophical Society, vol. 47, pt. 3. Philadelphia, 1957.
Morrow, Mable. *Indian Rawhide: An American Folk Art.* Norman, Okla., 1975.
Orchard, William C. "Beads and Beadwork of the American Indians." *Contributions from the Museum of the American Indian* 11 (1929):3–140.
———. "The Technique of Porcupine-Quill Decoration Among the North American Indians." *Contributions from the Museum of the American Indian* 4, no. 1 (1916):1–53.
Shepard, Anna O. *Ceramics for the Archaeologist.* Carnegie Institution of Washington, Publication 609. Washington, D.C., 1956.

Richard C. Conn

SEE ALSO **The First Americans** and **Native American Economies.**

XIV

THE ARTS

ARCHITECTURE
PAINTING AND SCULPTURE
CRAFTS
MUSIC AND DANCE
DRAMA
NATIVE AMERICAN AESTHETICS

ARCHITECTURE

THE BRITISH COLONIES

FISKE KIMBALL'S PIONEERING INTERPRETATION of early American domestic architecture, *Domestic Architecture of the American Colonies and of the Early Republic,* first published in 1922, gave the story of British colonial architecture its familiar shape. Following a period of pioneer improvisation, seventeenth-century British North American colonists closely reproduced the medieval models of English folk architecture. Around 1700 a new generation of American builders, informed by the architectural treatises and handbooks that flowed from English presses beginning in the late seventeenth century and spurred on by the cultural aspirations of an American elite, began to imitate the classical mansions of Georgian England. In the eighteenth century British-American architecture grew in ambition and sophistication. After a hiatus in building during the revolution, novel neoclassical architectural ideas appeared in America simultaneously with the first professional architects, who brought to a close the colonial Georgian tradition in the early years of the republic.

Both Kimball's developmental interpretation, in which traditional architecture constituted an initial phase of American architectural history that was later replaced by classical design, and the emulative, transfer-of-culture model stood unchallenged for nearly seventy years. While scholars recognize the continuing value of Kimball's work—it remains the best survey of colonial British architecture—new assumptions, new interests, and new research have undermined its interpretive structure and corrected some of its details. No new synthesis comparable in breadth to Kimball's has yet been attempted, but interest has shifted from the transfer of culture to the formation of culture, from chronicles of North American imitations of European buildings to the investigation of a much more complex indigenous social and material landscape.

Vernacular practice and academic architectural ideas, rather than constituting successive phases, were entwined throughout the colonial era. Various regions each had a distinctive architectural idiom shaped by the histories peculiar to North America: by local but also by international patterns of social structure, technological knowledge, and economic development; by British tradition and European high culture but also by North American interethnic and cross-cultural contact; by memories of home but also by the expectations and the unforeseeable surprises of the imperial enterprise. British North American architecture was very much a colonial, or facing-both-ways, phenomenon, but principally it faced inward. In recognition of this, the traditional themes of colonial architectural history are being rethought and their emphases reordered.

ENCOUNTERING NORTH AMERICA

English colonists brought a complex ideology of domination articulated in the language of civility and given specific form by imperial experience in Europe. Civil people lived according to Christian imperatives, under the rule of law. They practiced agriculture within settled, hierarchical, authoritarian communities. In short, they visibly occupied the land. The English concluded that orderly towns and buildings were both indices and generators of civility. Thus they came armed with strong, specific ideas about the kind of landscape they should create, and they carefully and simultaneously scrutinized both indigenous building practices and their own performance. It is important to understand British expectations and perceptions of North America to understand what they initially built.

Although Native cultures varied in many significant ways, the Eastern Woodland Indians who occupied most of what became British North America shared an architectural technology among themselves that Europeans could readily understand. Their domestic structures varied from small domed houses ten to fifteen feet (3 to 4.5 meters) in diameter, up to multifamily structures one hundred or more feet (30 or more meters) long, yet nearly all were constructed of saplings lashed together into a frame and covered with reeds, grasses, or woven mats. Many were surrounded by palisaded defenses, constructed by inserting sharpened poles into the ground at close intervals.

In contrast to neolithic societies, the British possessed metal implements and manufactured building materials, such as nails, glass, plaster, and baked brick, with which some built enormous mansions and others large and comfortable farmhouses. However these amenities were expensive and narrowly distributed in early modern Europe. Many British peasants lived considerably more roughly, in small houses lacking glass, plaster, floors, ceilings, or chimneys, houses that were little different in comfort or technological sophistication from those of Native

Americans. Some specific Indian practices, such as palisading and the construction of buildings lacking foundations, with their wooden frames set directly in the ground, directly paralleled the British tradition.

Consequently, the Native landscape lay within the comprehension of the British in North America and the possibility of interpreting it sympathetically as a familiar and acceptable one lay open. The choice to do so was conditioned by individual predisposition, inflected by European values. From the time John White made his late-sixteenth-century drawings in (present) North Carolina, English observers reported agricultural villages containing houses similar in size, construction, and comfort to their own. Other early artists and commentators were interested in the architecture of kingship. They reported unconvincingly complex, labyrinthine regal spaces within rulers' houses, and depicted Indian leaders sitting on thronelike constructions, surrounded by their followers arrayed as a court.

Yet even friendly descriptions were informed by assumptions about civility. White's images conspicuously featured pagan religious rituals at the center of his ordered agricultural villages. The more numerous hostile descriptions gave no benefit of the doubt. Indian houses were described as crude, uncomfortable, impermanent, feeble substitutes for civilized architecture. From this point of view the land was not truly occupied and was available for the taking.

The numerous projects to cajole or force Indians into civil settings revealed British assumptions about landscape and civility even more clearly. New England praying towns such as Natick, Massachusetts, where Native Americans were gathered to learn Christianity, are the most famous of the efforts mounted in several colonies to civilize the Indians through architecture. For example, Opechancanough, who later led the Powhatan uprising in Virginia, was asked to select Indian families to be placed among the English in English-style houses, and he was given one himself. It was believed that these efforts would settle the Indians, who would grow attached to European goods and abandon their way of life to obtain them. Underlying all such schemes was the seductive materialist belief in the civilizing power of the landscape.

The early colonial landscape had two aspects: instilling civility and repelling savagery. Both were applied equally to the Native population and to the colonists. English officials ordered their subjects to build substantial houses of frame and even of brick and they reported the success of their building programs to audiences at home as a sign of the triumph of civility. Documentary and archaeological evidence, however, paint a far different picture. Ralph Hamor's famous 1615 description of Henrico town in Virginia, with its rows of two-story houses and the foundation of a hundred-foot brick church has been a key document for histories of early American architecture, yet the House of Burgesses, with Hamor sitting as a member, confessed in 1624 that it had fabricated the account. The colony was a shambles, its housing poor, its towns and public buildings non-existent.

In fact, far from being models of European civility, the initial English settlements incorporated strong doses of the Indian landscape. Indian trade routes shaped European settlement patterns, while Native fields and village sites were commandeered for English building. Close correspondence between English and Native American building practices encouraged syntheses of the two. In Virginia bark was often used in place of tiles for English houses, and the colonists bought or stole woven reed mats to decorate the interiors of their houses. In New England, some of the initial English houses were described as wigwams, an Algonquian word.

It is unlikely that many were literal copies of Indian houses. Rather, the initial dwellings of every colony ran the gamut of bottom-of-the-scale European building reinforced and modified by analogous Indian practices. The free-standing wigwams, supported on posts driven into the ground and unframed, covered with roughly split boards or with bark and mats in the Indian fashion, were similar in quality to the houses of English peasants but superior to the caves and subterranean dugouts, sometimes crudely roofed over, that early colonists occupied in Virginia, Pennsylvania, New Netherland, and New England. Nevertheless, English officials thought these practices veered dangerously close to Indian ways and Indian savagery and attempted to eradicate them by decree.

EUROPEAN VERNACULAR TRADITION AND AMERICAN REGIONALISM

Despite grandiose official building schemes and flirtations with Indian architecture, seventeenth-century Anglo-American building was shaped predominantly by the British vernacular tradition in planning and aesthetic principles, building technology, and craft practice. On the one hand, the British vernacular was highly regionalized, with building traditions changing significantly over short distances. In this sense, seventeenth-century English colonists in North America had to come to terms with each other (and occasionally with other Europeans) as well as with the Native American population. On the other hand, local variations were encompassed within overarching continuities that made them comprehensible to other British builders, and more broadly to other Europeans, and promoted new architectural syntheses in North America.

One of the continuities was the use of the house as a farmhouse, sheltering servants (farm laborers) as well as the immediate family, and accommodating agricultural as well as domestic tasks. Another was a spatial division that centered the house around a large main living, working, and often sleeping room commonly called the hall. At one end—the "upper" end—of the hall the head of the household customarily sat; at the other, "lower," end was a passage into which doors opened from the road and from the farmyard, or simply front and rear doors opening directly into the hall. The hall was the core of all houses, but larger ones might also have a parlor, or main sleeping and storage room, and one or more service rooms, such as a buttery and pantry for wet and dry food storage or a kitchen. In many regions, the three spaces were arranged along a horizontal "up-down" axis, with the parlor at the upper end and the service rooms at the lower end beyond the passage. The resulting building was one story or a story and a half high, asymmetrical, since the door was off center, and lacked a formal facade, since the house faced both the road and its farmyard.

As the British came to North America, British vernacular houses were changing. In southern England, economic prosperity and stabilization lead to the improvement of many farmers' houses beginning in the late sixteenth century. Where halls had been open to the roof to allow the smoke from their open hearths to escape, they now included chimneys and as a result second floors could be inserted in the roof space above the hall. Glazed windows were more common, resulting in a tighter, warmer house. At the same time, farm laborers and farm processes began to be confined to lower ends of the house and segregated upper stories or excluded from the house altogether. Free access to the house through the passage was replaced in larger houses by restricted access, often through a vestibule (or lobby or porch) placed between two of the ground-floor rooms in front of the chimney. Upper floors began to be used more extensively for sleeping, and service spaces were moved to newly created cellars or around to the rear of the house. The result was a house that presented a roughly symmetrical, two-room long, often multi-story facade to the road, and that might have additional space in a rear ell or lean-to. It was a house less permeable to the comings and goings of agricultural life, one reserved more narrowly for the use of the immediate family.

This is a composite picture of changes occurring at differing paces, in varying combinations, in many parts of England and Wales. Indeed, the vernacular house at the time of the English colonization of North America was a house in flux. The common characterization of seventeenth-century American building as medieval architecture is wrong. With few exceptions the kinds of houses that the first English colonists built in North America did not exist a century earlier.

As well-built houses ("fair houses") succeeded the caves, dugouts, and wigwams of the first years, the emerging domestic architecture of all the British colonies was bewilderingly heterogeneous. The physical and documentary record reveals a wide variety of house sizes and types in the early seventeenth century, reflecting the changing British tradition and the scattered regional origins of the population.

One-room houses dominated the British colonies throughout the colonial period; they form the constant background against which all the succeeding remarks must be understood. Among builders of larger houses, a variety of other plans could be found in every colony, including the newer two-room houses and older three-room-long ones. None of the latter survive in any American colony, but examples have been excavated in Massachusetts, Maryland, and Virginia, and others are documented in those colonies and in Newfoundland. The largest houses north and south incorporated both through passages and lobby entries.

Historians such as Bernard Bailyn and Edmund Morgan have interpreted the third quarter of the seventeenth century as a period of formation of native elites in the American colonies. It may be that this stabilization of a local social structure accounts for a similar pattern of localization in domestic architecture, for variation within regions was replaced by variation among regions at that time. The house types now popularly associated with New England and the South came to dominate their regions during the years 1650–1700.

Builders in Massachusetts and Connecticut selected the most up-to-date English house type, the two-room, central-chimney, lobby-entry house. Following the lead of Norman M. Isham and Albert F. Brown, historians such as Kimball and J. Frederick Kelly assumed an evolutionary development of this New England plan from one-room pioneer houses to two-room houses, to houses with lean-tos, and finally to houses with a full rear file of rooms on both first and second floors. This interpretation is still occasionally offered, although since the publication in 1951 of Anthony N. B. Garvan's *Architecture and Town Planning in Colonial Connecticut,* we have understood that all variants except the last were present from the beginning, and that the selection had more to do with a person's ability to pay and with evolving patterns of house use than with evolutionary development. But if house form did not evolve, the uses of the principal rooms did. As lean-tos became common and their functions concretized, the hall or kitchen and the parlor were redefined. The Fairbanks house (ca. 1637) at Dedham, Massachusetts, for instance, had a lean-to added early in its history. This unspecialized, unfinished work and storage space was divided into two roughly equal parts, and can usefully be contrasted with the lean-to at the late-seventeenth-century Boardman house, Saugus, Massachusetts.

Its two-room, hall-and-kitchen plan was augmented with a lean-to within a decade of its construction. Now, the lean-to was carefully finished and fitted with a large, central kitchen, flanked by smaller sleeping chambers and service rooms. The kitchen at the front of the house became a kind of second-best parlor. This five-room pattern of spatial organization, with two public front rooms and a large central rear kitchen flanked by small sleeping and storage rooms, could be found through most of New England by the early eighteenth century and continued to be used until the middle of the nineteenth century.

Within this larger regional pattern, subregional differences developed as well. In prosperous areas such as the North Shore of Massachusetts Bay and the Connecticut River valley, the familiar two-story version of the five-room-plan dominated. In less prosperous southeastern Massachusetts (old Plymouth Colony) one-story variants of the five-room plan were so numerous that they came to be known as Cape Cod houses by the end of the eighteenth century. However, Cape Cod houses were not the only dwellings built in southeastern Massachusetts, nor were they confined there. They could be found throughout New England and were conspicuous in other economically marginal regions such as Maine, the hills of New Hampshire, and inland Connecticut.

Northern Rhode Island was an exception to the general New England pattern. In the third quarter of the seventeenth century, it emerged from heterogeneity and moved in a different direction. Rhode Island's large houses were organized according to the common British spatial principles and as in the rest of New England demonstrated the new importance of the vertical and front-back axes, but the results were different. Rhode Islanders tended to build second main rooms behind the hall or away from the chimney, rather than bracketing the chimney. These resulting stone-end houses were apparently based on a small-house model from the English-Welsh border, a region with a pastoral economy like early Rhode Island's. Rhode Island's integration into the broader New England society and economy by 1750 may account for the abandonment of the stone-ender in the second quarter of the eighteenth century and its replacement by the standard five-room plan.

The earliest surviving houses in the middle colonies also have two-room-long (hall-parlor or

hall-chamber) plans, but with end chimneys. The entrance led directly into the larger of the two unequal-sized rooms, which was generally the kitchen. This plan is often attributed to the western regions of Britain, an attribution strengthened by the presence of minor details and peculiarities of plan that can more certainly be called western English or Welsh characteristics.

Vernacular architecture with a west-of-England accent in the middle colonies was juxtaposed with other European traditions. Both the pockets of Dutch colonists in the Hudson valley and northern New Jersey and Germanic immigrants to New York and Pennsylvania built Continental variants of the two-room plan house, which was a widespread phenomenon in Europe in the early modern period. Germans built two- to four-room versions of an asymmetrical house sometimes called a *Flurküchenhaus*. The basic house consisted of a narrow kitchen, into which the front door opened, containing a large cooking hearth and the stairs to the upper floor. Opposite the chimney was a square *Stube*, or best room, usually heated from a ceramic or iron stove built into the wall and fed from the kitchen. Behind the *Stube* might be a small, narrow chamber, and a fourth small room was sometimes built behind the kitchen. Most houses had partial cellars that were often insulated or barrel-vaulted to aid in the preservation of the food stored in them.

If the northern houses represented local choices from common British vernacular patterns, the situation in the Chesapeake was more complex. On the one hand, even more than in the northern and middle colonies, small, poorly built, usually one-room houses sheltered most white and black southerners. On the other hand, well-to-do Chesapeakers, like New Englanders, chose a preferred house plan in the late seventeenth century. As labor-intensive tobacco cultivation led southerners to import more servants to the region, prosperous planters tended to enlarge their houses to accommodate them, adding wings and new rooms as needed.

The solidification of social power after the mid seventeenth century and a great increase in the numbers of servants who were imported prompted a change in this pattern. Instead of enlarging their houses, planters reduced their size, opting for two-room, end-chimney houses like those described in Pennsylvania and New

Jersey, but most commonly a story and a half high. Kitchens and other spaces that had housed servants and domestic tasks and that in New England had been accommodated in lean-tos and cellars, were pushed out of the house altogether into freestanding outbuildings and servants' quarters, scattering the house into several small buildings and creating a complex that visitors repeatedly likened to a village.

The transformation, which should be seen as a greatly accelerated version of a process begun in Britain in the late sixteenth century but not completed until the nineteenth, is attested in the aggregate by probate inventories and documents, and in detail by sites such as the Clifts plantation, a fortified house built in the 1670s in Westmoreland County, Virginia. It had a through passage and an entrance vestibule, interior workrooms, and an ell that probably housed workers, as well as a small, poorly built servants' house. By the time the Clifts burned in the early eighteenth century, the service spaces were exiled to small outbuildings at a distance from the house, the passage that gave access to them had been closed off, and the servants themselves were moved to a much enlarged and rebuilt quarter.

By the end of the seventeenth century, then, southerners had developed the pattern of a relatively small main house and associated domestic outbuildings and slave quarters that would characterize it until the Civil War. In this sense, the architectural envelope of slavery was created before black slave labor dominated Chesapeake agriculture and developed from changing relations between planters and their white laborers.

THE GEORGIANIZATION OF DOMESTIC ARCHITECTURE

In the eighteenth century, North American buildings in every region, of every type and ethnic derivation were transformed by a process that folklorists and anthropologists have called Georgianization. It introduced several changes to houses. A central passage isolated every room from every other room and changed the ways the house could be used, introducing the potential for greater specialization and for privacy as that concept developed. Houses were more commonly built a full two rooms deep. And a more controlled symmetry, a greater regularity of appearance, met the eye. Art historians such as Kimball and William H. Pierson have lumped these changes together and attributed them to the influence of new Renaissance house forms popular in mid-seventeenth-century England. It seems more useful to consider these innovations as independent variables introduced for disparate reasons, combined in various ways, and derived from diverse, often multiple, sources.

The central passage, introduced in the late seventeenth century, continued the closing-off of the house begun with the introduction of entrance lobbies in England and New England and with the construction of a projecting porch tower on large southern hall-parlor houses. With the passage, all rooms were now separately accessible; each had in effect its own lobby. Although the central passage has been attributed by historians to the influence of high-style Dutch ideas on mid seventeenth-century English country-house builders, the passage had multiple roots that made it familiar and acceptable. Off-center, if less formal, more utilitarian through passages in the older type of British vernacular house were still well known, and circulation passages separating upper-floor chambers in hall-parlor houses were also familiar in vernacular practice. Thus the central passage was a social concept, available for use in any kind of house. After the mid eighteenth century, one-room houses, end-chimney hall-parlor houses, Dutch two-room houses, and German *Flürkuchenhauser* were all commonly built or remodeled with passages. Even five-room-plan New England houses were sometimes built with a stair passage splitting or displacing the chimney mass.

Similarly, two-room-deep (double-pile) massing had already appeared in the lean-to service rooms of British vernacular houses, in the large country houses of the aristocratic political opponents of the Crown, and in small-size houses of the gentry that had complex, two-room-deep plans, even before Dutch classical models reached Britain. Thus the two-room-deep form was familiar to British American builders, who, about 1700, began to add a room called the dining room. This room might be more accurately described as a general-purpose second-best public room buffering the transition from the hall or parlor to the ground-floor chambers. For convenience of circulation, this often led to the creation of double-pile plans, with or without passages.

When the central passage and double-pile massing were combined, a house form resulted that scholars have named the Georgian plan. Among the earliest known are the Tufts house (ca. 1678) in Medford, Massachusetts, and Boston's Sergeant, or Province, house (1679; demolished). Georgian-plan houses were rare before 1700, however. Even in the eighteenth century only very large colonial houses were built this way. Nevertheless, they constitute a major, enduring eighteenth-century contribution to the American vernacular building repertoire.

In addition to their circulation advantages, the new planning devices helped to organize a proliferation of domestic public spaces, as a core of elite Americans in all the colonies adopted new modes of genteel living that demanded one or more dining rooms and, increasingly, refined parlors. The central passage itself might be transformed, as the wealthiest builders promoted it from a simple reception or circulation space to something grander that took on great ceremonial importance, challenging or usurping the functions of the major formal rooms. In the late colonial period, the passage might be replaced by a revived and redefined hall, or by an entry-saloon suite, a scaled-down version of a common English country-house pattern.

Ultimately, gentility chafed at the bounds of the Georgian plan, and elite houses were rethought as systems of spaces rather than as collections of independent rooms. Both George Washington and Thomas Jefferson were pushed by their fame to remodel their houses. Like many large English houses, Mount Vernon and Monticello were quasi-public attractions, besieged by invited and uninvited visitors. As Washington first knew it, Mount Vernon was a one-story Georgian-plan house, with a hall, dining room, chamber, and fourth room (which commonly lacked a specific name in eighteenth-century Virginia) flanking a central passage. In the 1770s and 1780s, Washington added a grand dining room at one end of the building and a library at the other. The resulting double circulation pattern is the key to understanding the house, as Mark Girouard has shown for comparable English houses in *Life in the English Country House*

(1978). Entering the land-side door, a visitor could turn left and pass through what were then called the great parlor, the banquet hall, and the little parlor, and then return to the passage. A more intimate acquaintance might turn right into the smaller dining room, the library (which Girouard has shown was an informal family sitting room in the late eighteenth century), and back through a chamber to the passage. An outside door to the banquet hall provided access for slaves serving that room, while secondary entries and stairways into the library end allowed the Washington family and their slaves direct access, bypassing the main entry. Jefferson's Monticello was remodeled from 1793 to 1809 along similar lines, with a central entrance hall-saloon suite separating a public circuit through guest rooms and dining room to one side and a more private suite of rooms reserved to Jefferson on the other.

The important point to note is that these changes to the North American house arose from social conventions and demanded no specific formal manifestation. Many small houses and some large ones incorporated the new spaces in unique ways, demonstrating that their builders were experimenting with social, rather than formal, ideas. Nevertheless, the desire to conform to visual fashion was an important aspect of gentility and some of the largest eighteenth-century American houses did so. This aesthetic aspect of Georgianization will be discussed in a subsequent section.

Urban Houses

Colonial urban housing has been less thoroughly studied than rural houses and mansions. Throughout the period, the wealthiest residents of all cities built freestanding houses that could easily have stood in the country. The first specifically urban houses known in North America were the three contiguous houses designated Structure 17, the so-called First Statehouse at Jamestown. The surviving cellar plans of these ruined structures reveal houses one room wide and two rooms deep, with a chimney between the rooms. Stairs probably rose beside the chimney of each house, and there may have been a narrow passage leading from the front door back to the stairs. This is a house plan that appeared in London after the 1666 fire and it seems probable that the Virginia examples were the products of government efforts to enforce urbanization in the 1660s and 1670s.

In addition to the ubiquitous single-room houses, late-seventeenth-century urban builders in Philadelphia, Boston, and the former Dutch towns of New York all adopted the narrow-end-to-the-street, two-room-deep plan, usually with circulation space between the rooms. By the second quarter of the eighteenth century, large urban houses acquired side passages the full depth of the house, that were the social and spatial equivalents of the Georgian central passage. Often, trailing ells or back buildings accommodated service rooms. Yet small passageless houses continued to be built into the nineteenth century. It may be that the famous single-houses of Charleston, South Carolina, are examples of the earlier kind of urban house plan as well, although they have been even less well studied than other colonial urban housing.

Public Buildings

Houses were the most numerous, the most significant, and the most varied buildings of colonial America. Nevertheless, public buildings were increasingly visible in the landscape, particularly in cities, over the course of the colonial era.

The most common public buildings served religious congregations. Characteristically these were rectangular and usually entered on the long side. Their seats faced a speaker situated near the center of the long wall. A gallery, or balcony, around three sides might increase the house's capacity. Historians have named this the meetinghouse type, to distinguish it from a church, a building with its entrance in one end and an altar at the far end. Although the term meetinghouse was used primarily by New England Puritans and by Quakers, meetinghouses were built by members of every mainstream European Protestant denomination.

The origin of the meetinghouse is uncertain, since North American examples seem to antedate European ones. One theory is that the New England variety of the meetinghouse derives from secular halls above markets in English villages. Another is that meetinghouses are radical revisions of medieval parish churches, which consisted of two separate parts, the chancel, or sacred area containing the altar, and the nave, or area where the people stood or sat. The nave

and chancel were separated by a screen and often were structurally independent and separately financed by clergy and laity, respectively. Most parish churches were entered along one long side, near the end farthest from the chancel.

The Protestant emphasis on the word, anticipated by the introduction of preaching in the late middle ages, led to the divorce among dissenters of the nave from its chancel. Like the late medieval nave, the new Protestant church was an auditorium, filled with seating often arranged according to social standing. Some congregations separated men and women as well. Even the explicit desacralization of Quaker and Calvinist meetinghouses (and the failure of many Anglican congregations to consecrate their churches) is congruent with the lay-owned medieval nave, which often served as a community hall.

In the meetinghouse, the status of the chancel or altar varied by denomination. Quakers eliminated both chancel and pulpit in favor of benches that faced the majority of the congregation. Here sat an unofficial spiritual elite. This arrangement introduced a hierarchical element to this most egalitarian of religious groups. Congregationalists and Presbyterians substituted a communion table—sometimes simply a hinged board—at the front of the pulpit for the chancel. Anglicans and Lutherans, who retained a formal liturgy, also retained a chancel. In low church style, it was reduced to a railed-off table at the east end of an east-west oriented building. The pews still faced toward a pulpit near the center of the building.

Church-plan buildings were built by Anglicans in late seventeenth century New York and Boston, and after the 1720s they were standard in cities. All eighteenth-century examples were influenced by the London churches of Christopher Wren. In planning for the reconstruction of many of London's churches after the 1666 fire Wren, like other English Protestants, was faced with the task of combining an axial ritual building with a centralized auditorium. He chose a basilican plan, one with a central nave flanked by aisles, to emphasize the axis from entry to chancel. Next, he placed galleries around three sides as in a meetinghouse, making a kind of stadium focusing on a pulpit in the middle of the floor. Wren also confronted the problem of making his churches visible on cramped sites, and created the now-familiar classical steeple tower. The tower could stand anywhere on Wren's building sites. Both the basilican auditorium church and the classical spire were first brought to America at Christ (Old North) Church, Boston (1723–1745), and introduced independently into most American cities in the second quarter of the eighteenth century.

Aside from churches, the commonest (if not as widely preserved) public buildings were markets and administrative buildings. The two are appropriately mentioned together, since they were often the same structures in seventeenth- and early-eighteenth-century cities. Boston's first town house, a bequest of Robert Keayne in 1656, consisted of court and meeting rooms above an open arcaded shed that sheltered the farmers' market, as did Philadelphia's Court House of 1709. The practice of building public halls above markets lasted in small cities well into the nineteenth century. In large cities, however, the two were separated early in the eighteenth century. When Boston's town house burned in 1711, it was succeeded by two buildings: the State House of 1711 occupied the site of the destroyed building while Faneuil Hall (1742; enlarged 1805), another hall-over-arcades structure, eventually replaced the market.

The new State House, a building with a prominent lantern and pedimented gable end flanked by the royal lion and unicorn and provided with a balcony facing out over Long Wharf, took as its typological model the European urban administrative palace. It was an attractive model in eighteenth-century America, where it commonly took the form of a building approximately the size and appearance of a large house, dignified with a central spire or lantern, and often with a prominent pediment and second-floor balcony for public appearances. Newport's Colony House, built by the local carpenter Richard Munday in 1739–1741, is a modest example. Pennsylvania's state house (1733–1748; 1753), now known as Independence Hall, was a mansion with a tower added and Maryland's 1772 Capitol was also a mansion with a dome. Williamsburg's first Capitol (1701–1705) resembled an urban merchants' exchange. Two separate wings were connected by a meeting room above an open arcade, and surmounted by a tall lantern. The name Capitol, reputedly the first modern use of the word, was chosen as a specific reference to ancient Rome, as were the apses in the meeting rooms of the two houses of the legislature, that imitated those occupied by judges and imperial statues in Roman basilicas. Yet when the Capitol was rebuilt between 1751 to 1753 after a fire in 1747, most of these distinctive features were removed, and the reworked building was made to look more like a house.

The conception of a government building as a grandiose domestic structure outlasted the colonial period. Although Thomas Jefferson's Virginia state Capitol (1785–1789) took a different approach, William Thornton's winning design for the United States Capitol was an overblown country house that was modified but not reconceived as built.

Two points are worth noting about the public buildings, particularly the urban public buildings, of eighteenth-century British America. First, the early eighteenth century marks a significant turning point in ambition. Like Boston's first town house, most seventeenth-century public buildings were wooden, many were built flimsily and had to be replaced frequently, and few made any pretensions to grandeur. In the early eighteenth century, British North America had higher aspirations and constructed more substantial buildings than before. Construction in brick attested to a new urban economic stability. Wren church forms and urban palaces embodied public values as much as the later works of Jefferson or the builders of Washington, D.C.

Second, while a new solvency was sufficient to undertake the buildings that urban maturity demanded, it was not always adequate to carry them off. Late colonial America abounds with large public buildings that were never finished or were finished only after the revolution. Boston's King's Chapel (1749–1754) had no portico until 1785–1787 and still lacks a spire. A tower and portico were added to New York's Saint Paul's chapel (1764–1766) only in the 1790s. In Annapolis, the new governor's house (1742) stood as a hollow shell until it was reclaimed by Saint John's college after the revolution. Even Williamsburg's modest courthouse of 1770 never had columns installed in its portico.

THE BUILDING PROCESS

The discussion so far has treated the development and proliferation of building types in colonial British America as a product of social change and economic development. Intentionally, little has been said about the structure or appearance of the buildings. To understand these requires consideration of the craft organization of early American architecture.

Two themes characterize the analysis of colonial builders. One is the search for architects. Such eighteenth-century figures as William Buckland of Annapolis or Peter Harrison of Newport, sometimes called the first American architect, served in this capacity. As currently used, architect refers to someone willing to and capable of directing every aspect of construction and someone, moreover, who strives in some sense to create a unified, personal work of art as a result. However, the concept of the creative personality, although invented in the Renaissance, made little impression on colonial American architecture. In addition, the organization of building around a single aesthetic-administrative head is a nineteenth-century phenomenon, arising out of the peculiar circumstances of the architect in a commercializing society.

Another theme is that of the struggle between the clever but stubborn and uneducated master builders and the gentleman amateur architects who did their best to bring new ideas and architectural sophistication to America over the objections of their workmen. In the late twentieth century it has been argued by Dell Upton in *Holy Things and Profane* and by Catherine Bishir and her coauthors in *Architects and Builders in North Carolina* that builders cannot be so easily categorized. They worked at many levels of sophistication and ambition. Moreover, those who built the most elaborate buildings were often gentlemen themselves. The pure architectural dilettante was rare. Thus it seems more fruitful to examine colonial architecture in terms of building process rather than builders' status, examining changes resulting from the imperatives of craft practice and from a desire to cater to consumerist impulses in the eighteenth century.

Trained craftsmen always controlled British colonial building. None but the flimsiest and least important buildings, and certainly nothing that has survived until the present, was owner built. American builders in the colonial era were trained through formal or informal apprenticeship. They differed from their European counterparts in compartmentalizing their work less rigidly. Housewrights, responsible for the frame, and joiners, responsible for the trim, might be the same people. Similarly, makers of buildings might also be makers of furniture. Samuel McIntire identified on his tombstone erected in 1811 as "architect and carver of Salem," Massachusetts, is an example of a man renowned in both fields.

In the South, some craftsmen were African-Americans, either slaves bound to an owner who employed them personally or rented them out, or free men of color. As was true of white builders, free and enslaved blacks were employed at all levels of the building industry; many underwent regular apprenticeships alongside whites. Large-scale plantations, such as Landon Carter's Sabine Hall in Virginia, had skilled craftsmen among their slave crews, enabling them to bid on small public construction jobs. Full-time builders, as well, might use black as easily as white craftsmen, and large construction crews often contained both.

While small plantation buildings in the South might be erected by the resident slave craftsmen, most colonial building was carried out by undertakers, or contractors, who most commonly agreed to erect a building for a fixed price. Building contracts specified the measurable data of the building—dimensions, number of stories or rooms, material—and sometimes called for the inclusion of particular decorative features, such as a pediment or a wall of paneling. Floor plans and simple elevation (facade) drawings were sometimes made for large buildings, but detail drawings were rare. The finish and precise appearance of a building were left to be worked out on the site by the workmen in consultation with the client, guided by shared aesthetic standards, the builder's skills, and often by contract clauses that identified extant buildings as models. Since details and even some major elements of buildings were determined in the course of construction, supplemental payments were common on large projects.

Colonial building was a highly organized business. Builders received an initial payment, one or more others at specified stages in the course of construction, and a final reckoning when all parties agreed that the building was satisfactorily completed. It was not the slow pace of the work that stretched major projects over several years, but the time that clients, and even governments, needed to raise the money. Hence payment and construction were both distributed over three or four years, and the builder worked on several projects during that time. Until the client could pay, a building stood unfinished.

At the same time, undertakers gave a bond, usually double the amount of the contract, for satisfactory completion of the work. For a large project, the undertaker needed to be personally wealthy or well-connected with elite patrons or partners able to afford the bond. For this reason, the building industry was highly stratified; some builders' practices were confined to small repairs and farm structures they could erect themselves, others worked mostly on houses, and a few were able to construct public buildings and large houses using sizable crews. They were entrepreneurs who were effectively the social and economic peers of their clients.

Although guilds in the European sense were never established in North America, building workers in Boston, Providence, and other northern cities had formed trade organizations by the 1770s. The best-known, the Carpenters' Company of the City and County of Philadelphia, founded in the 1720s, was one of several such building-craft groups in that pre-revolutionary city. Where medieval guilds had guarded the mysteries of their trades and maintained the distinctions among sub-crafts jealously, the colonial craft companies were designed primarily to regulate competition among themselves through controlling prices or, more accurately, the methods of determining prices. Their published price books were secret documents recalled on a members' death or expulsion. In practice, these figures were relative, not absolute. Building contracts regularly called for payment at some percent above the book price. One unintended effect of price books was to limit the kinds of work carpenters were willing to do to those encompassed by the book. The growing gulf between consumer demand and the price book's categories forced the Philadelphia Carpenters' Company to revise its prices in 1786.

BUILDING TECHNOLOGIES

Apprenticeship was a means of transmitting knowledge. Properly trained craftsmen knew how to use their tools and knew the properties of materials, but more importantly they knew how to organize familiar tasks: to lay out a rafter pattern or a floor plan, to find the angle of a joint. This meant that building practices tended to be operationally conservative: those elements of the building that affected the ways the builder accomplished his task, but not its appearance or other features of concern to the client, changed slowly.

Theoretical understanding of statics and methods for calculating structural loads were developed in the eighteenth century and disseminated to carpenters through popular publications in the early nineteenth century. Historians sometimes characterize the builder's approach to structure before the nineteenth century as trial and error, but the opposite is true. Builders operated by rules of thumb, designed to reduce labor and to eliminate error by eliminating trial. Apprentices learned standard ratios for the thickness of brick walls to their heights, formulas to determine the lengths of rafters, ways to lay out stairs, and means for joining one timber to another that did not require calculations. The transmission of these formulas through apprenticeship created regional and ethnic patterns of building technology analogous to those in building planning, but longer lasting.

While brick and stone buildings are conspicuous among the surviving buildings of the middle and southern colonies, timber framing was by far the dominant structural system in every part of colonial European America. Here the labor-conservative ethos of timber framing is most conspicuous and most radical in its unforeseen consequences.

The New England framing tradition remained very close to that of eastern England. The frame distinguished major framing members (posts, sills, girts, summer beams, principal rafters) that supported the house from minor members (studs, joists, common rafters) that filled the intervals. The size of the parts was adjusted according to their importance, and the structural bay (the space between major members) was likewise varied to match room sizes. Labor conservation altered even this most traditional of systems.

Seventeenth-century English builders confronted an increasing scarcity of timber and invested relatively large amounts of labor to make do with inferior materials. Seventeenth-century

Americans were confronted with the opposite problem: an abundance of materials and a relative scarcity of labor. As a result, the New England frame was simplified by reducing joinery and the number of parts. For example, southeastern New Englanders developed a system called plank framing, where the infilling studs, which required labor to cut them to size and labor to make joints at top and bottom, were replaced with wide, thick, mill-sawn planks simply nailed or pegged to the outside of the frame. Exterior cladding and interior plaster or whitewash were applied directly to the planks.

The most thoroughgoing labor-based transformation of the traditional system occurred in the Chesapeake. Among the quick and dirty building techniques of the first English colonists was the ancient practice of setting the vertical parts of the frame directly into the earth, eliminating the costs of joinery at the bottom and of preparing a foundation. While these earthfast, or post, structures are documented in all the British and French colonies, Chesapeake builders constructed them over a longer time period. Earthfast construction was used in most houses and many public buildings into the early eighteenth century and small earthfast houses and outbuildings were put up long after the revolution.

The uncertainty of life in the Chesapeake, the hope of returning to England, and most of all the desire to devote all available hands to the labor-intensive cultivation of tobacco all contributed to the seventeenth-century dominance of earthfast construction. By the end of the century, techniques developed by post builders to conserve labor and to adapt timber framing to the necessary imprecision of earthfast building had crept into inherited British timber building methods as well. A non-earthfast southern framing system was created that eliminated the complex joinery, the hierarchical gradation of part sizes, the multidimensional bracing, and the relation of bay size to plan that characterized the traditional braced frame in England and New England in favor of a rationalized, all-purpose system with simplified joints, two standard timber sizes, and uniform bays. The carpenter's conservative quest to minimize and routinize labor had generated an unexpected abandonment of tradition.

AESTHETIC CHANGE AND THE DESIGN PROCESS

Just as vernacular planning and building technology structured British-American architecture throughout the colonial period, so high-style—meaning classical—architectural ideas, far from being eighteenth-century innovations, were present from the seventeenth century in three ways.

First, the underlying language of architecture, even of vernacular architecture, was classical. Visitors to surviving seventeenth-century houses will note sheathing (paneling), exposed framing, window trim, fireplace lintels, all finished with classical moldings. Over the course of the seventeenth century, novel classical details were introduced to America by publications, imported decorative objects, and most important the constant stream of emigrating craftsmen who counteracted some of the ingrowth of apprentice training. Shaped Anglo-Netherlandish gables, attached pediments, baroque gadroons, and similar classical devices entered the builder's and joiner's visual repertoire.

Second, what might be called a classical eye appeared in American architecture in the seventeenth century. It was not an issue of introducing aesthetics to a utilitarian tradition. Vernacular buildings were governed by specific and recognizable aesthetic criteria. The Connecticut minister Thomas Hooker compared the beauty of orderly social hierarchy to that derived from viewing an exposed frame whose parts were carefully differentiated. In addition, seventeenth-century vernacular builders liked to emphasize mass and volume by overhanging second stories beyond first stories, exposing and decorating framing, and treating chimneys as sculptural objects.

By the mid seventeenth century, the new eye had already shaped the appearance of a few buildings. It imposed a strict symmetry as well as regularity over variety and differentiation, and it preferred surface over mass, increasingly hiding structural details behind a smooth plastered surface. This is the third aspect of the Georgianization process discussed above. Bacon's Castle, the Arthur Allen house (1665) in Surry County, Virginia, is the earliest extant example of the new aesthetic. Socially, it represents the reorganized ultramodern house discussed earlier: its service rooms are placed in a basement, leaving a two-room, hall-parlor core, while major chambers occupy the second floor, and a porch tower projects from the front, with a corresponding stair tower at the back. It has classical exterior details as well, such as shaped gables and molded window frames, a horizontal belt course (now covered with concrete) between the floors, and a pediment (now removed) over the entrance. These all attest to the wealth of Arthur Allen in a colony of earthfast houses, but none is surprising in a seventeenth-century context. What is surprising is the regularity of the facade, with its pairs of evenly spaced windows flanking the central entry, creating a building symmetrical in appearance though not in plan, regular on the outside, while still exposing and decorating its structure inside.

In the seventeenth century, only a few exceptional houses employed such careful symmetry. In the eighteenth century, it reorganized the appearance of most surviving buildings of every ethnicity in the British colonies, even those with no other connection to the high-style aesthetic. This preference for regularity cannot be ascribed to a particular style or design source, but should be seen more generally, though more accurately, as part of an impulse toward modular order that suffused European-American culture. Dutch-American builders often placed central-entry, five-bay facades on the fronts of their houses while retaining traditional plans and four-bay, two-door rear facades. English and German vernacular builders, as well, made their houses symmetrical while clinging to traditional plans, structure, and often decoration.

A third, and more familiar, way to use classicism in British colonial building was not merely to incorporate the odd classical detail or an eye for order and symmetry, but to attempt to participate in the main currents of European architectural fashion. Here Fiske Kimball's pioneering work has retained its largest audience. Kimball's method was to search colonial American architecture for elements that could be compared to images published in the architectural treatises and handbooks that flowed from British presses after 1680. For Kimball, the eighteenth century marked a significant change in American architecture, as it became book educated.

Scholars have tended to accept Kimball's interpretation, enlarging the scope of possible sources to Dutch and other Continental publications, or claiming, as Thomas T. Waterman did in *The Dwellings of Colonial America* (1950), specific British mansions as the sources of certain American houses. However, the newest work, while recognizing that books were an important element in British-American architecture, has explored avenues of aesthetic change that challenge the Kimball school's preoccupation with classicism as an eighteenth-century book-based phenomenon.

Research by Jonathan L. Fairbanks and Robert F. Trent finds mannerism, a variant of Renaissance classicism, in early seventeenth-century New England. Introduced through imported decorative arts and Continental publications, mannerism is evident mainly in American decorative arts but affected architecture as well. From this perspective, our image of a drab Puritan landscape must be considerably enriched and the novelty of eighteenth-century classicism downplayed.

Moreover, the continuing influx of new craftworkers from Europe was at least as important as books in importing new ideas. Abbott Lowell Cummings, the noted architectural historian, has ascribed to immigrants a new, late-seventeenth-century Boston provincial Renaissance that brought full-height pilasters and other urban domestic classicism to the city. Eighteenth-century American newspapers were full of advertisements from craftsmen who announced that they had just arrived with the latest fashionable ideas under their caps. A famous example is William Buckland, a London-trained joiner who imigrated to Virginia to work on the Mason family's Gunston Hall in the 1750s and stayed to have a brief, productive career in Virginia and Maryland. He was responsible, among other works, for the elaborate decoration in the Chase-Lloyd (1769–1773) and Hammond-Harwood (1773–1774) houses in Annapolis.

Finally, just as the study of plans has moved from origins to development, the study of architectural books now seems more fruitfully directed toward reasons for using books and the ways they were used than toward identifying sources of specific American details. The bookish classical aesthetic should be considered in its wider connotations for its users, rather than simply for its faithfulness to published images.

On one level, the language of classicism was the language of dignity. To place a pediment above the entry of a house or church was to make an ancient, nearly reflexive, gesture of respect. On another level, classicism was increasingly the visual language of the new genteel social values. Although passages and double-pile plans, dining rooms and parlors might be arranged in numerous ways, many builders chose to cloak them in the classical architecture of genteel Europe.

Handbooks taught Americans something about these forms. Among the most popular works were James Gibbs's self-promoting *A Book of Architecture* (1728), Abraham Swan's *The British Architect* (1745; republished in Philadelphia in 1775 and Boston in 1794), and the many handbooks of Batty Langley and William and John Halfpenny. Occasionally, weightier works such as Colin Campbell's *Vitruvius Britannicus* (1715–1725), a folio of representative designs by England's most powerful early-eighteenth-century architects, appeared in American libraries. Harvard even owned the Italian Renaissance architect Andrea Palladio's *Four Books of Architecture* (1570), but the more practical books were most popular. Architectural books initiated the native-born builder to classicism, refreshed the memory of the immigrant worker, and whetted the imagination of the client, creating a demand for the new forms. With these books in hand, most of the renowned gentleman architects of colonial America could work like shoppers with catalogs. The merchant Joseph Brown, for example, marked a steeple design in his copy of Gibbs's book to direct carpenter James Sumner in constructing Providence's First Baptist Church (1774–1775).

Books, then, taught American builders and clients the rudiments of architectural gentility, but they did not teach them what to build, for book ideas were relentlessly reworked in America. The use of Gibbs's work is a case in point. His book contained many examples of houses with central pedimented projections, or pavilions. It was a common English formula that Gibbs helped to popularize in America, and vaguely Gibbsian facades were built on large houses of all sorts in the mid eighteenth century. The Hammond-Harwood house, Mount Pleasant (1761–1762), Philadelphia, and the Lady Pepperrell house (ca. 1760), Kittery, Maine, all differ significantly in plan, material, and detail, but all use the facade formula. Gibbs's church designs, particularly for Saint Martin-in-the-Fields (1723–1726), London, were even more popular. The general form of a Wren-type basilican church, with a shallow chancel, a portico, and a gable-end tower (over the portico, in Gibbs's case) provided a readymade solution for urban churches, and towers adapted from Gibbs's multiple designs rose over most American cities. Versions' of Saint Martin's east end were also common. The fenestration of Gibbs's churches, with tall, round-arched windows above shorter, round- or segmental-headed ones, also proved popular. Nearly every major eighteenth-century American urban church owes something to Gibbs, but none imitates him.

The use of English books can mislead us about the significance of classicism in American colonial building. It had less to do with imitation of Europe for its own sake than with drawing on metropolitan references to make points in local discourse. The career of the Wren-type church in New England is an example. Once introduced by the Anglicans at Old North Church in 1723, it inspired a spate of new churches and meetinghouses. Soon after it was built, Bostonians adapted it to Puritan usage in the Third (Old South) meetinghouse (1729) retaining the traditional long-side entry and pulpit, but placing a steepled bell tower on the gable end. Eighteenth-century views of Boston, with their forest of spires, suggest that architecture had become a weapon in the complex struggle for power among locals and imperials, Puritans and Anglicans. Old North's image inspired Newport's Anglicans as well. Richard Munday's Trinity Church (1725–1726; spire 1741, rebuilt 1768) was a wooden version of the Boston church.

In the countryside, both Old North and Old South, as Bostonian buildings, offered appealing architectural models. Wethersfield, Connecticut, for example, built a new meetinghouse between 1761 and 1764 with a spire modeled on Old North's. The use of a forty-year-old Anglican model by a Puritan congregation suggests that being up to date by European standards or partisan by Bostonian ones was not the issue. The rural churches made invidious reference to Boston, as Bostonians did to London, for the benefit of neighbors. This is evident at Brooklyn, Connecticut, where the town's new Congregational (now Unitarian) meetinghouse (1770–1771) copied Old South's tower. In response, the rusticated Newport merchant Godfrey Malbone financed Trinity Anglican Church (1770–1771), which borrowed its name from Munday's church and its facade from Gibbs by way of Peter Harrison's King's Chapel in Boston.

In the late eighteenth century, English manufacturers like Josiah Wedgwood promoted fashionable consumption—the precise imitation of current visual modes—as a means of marketing ever-changing, mass-produced goods. Since books (and immigrant craftsmen) traveled the same channels as other consumer goods, it is not surprising that architecture should be affected by the new consumerist ethos with its emphasis on fashionable competition. Consequently, late colonial elite clients began to demand more precise copies from books and other buildings, as the Providence example suggests.

One of the most assiduous copyists was Peter Harrison. In two documented spates of building, around 1750 and around 1760, Harrison designed buildings for his wealthy friends in Newport, as well as churches for their peers in Boston and Cambridge. But "designed" makes Harrison seem too much an architect in the current sense. Instead, he clothed familiar building types in imagery closely though skillfully cribbed from his library. His Brick Market (1762), for example, drapes a standard hall-over-arcade market hall in the borrowed grandeur of Inigo Jones's seventeenth-century New Gallery at Somerset House, London, itself indebted to Palladio. The Redwood Library (1748–1750), essentially a single-room building, adopts a pediment-on-pediment image from a published English garden pavilion, whose designer had also borrowed from Palladio. To make the facade work, Harrison had to append a small closet to each side of the building to carry one of the pediments.

For historians, Palladian-derived buildings such as Harrison's have been among the most interesting aspects of American colonial architecture. In the mid eighteenth century, particularly in the South, several large houses were constructed with features such as porticoes, modular, symmetrical plans, and multi-part massing that descended from Palladian villas by way of English publications. Cued by the study of the ideological Anglo-Palladianism of the vocal early-eighteenth-century Burlington circle, scholars have associated these houses with that tradition.

The argument for an American Palladianism has been questioned on several grounds. First, the Palladians' contemporary audience was limited. Most builders and clients on both sides of the Atlantic approached Palladianism in the same spirit as Gibbs, who published some Palladian designs: as aesthetic consumers picking and choosing among images from a variety of sources, rather than allying with a school of thought. For colonial builders, whose contact with architectural thought was almost exclusively visual and who did not know Palladio's book first hand, the eclecticism was even less theoretical. It is unlikely that many clients or builders before Thomas Jefferson conceived of their work in terms of adherence to an intellectual movement, or of books as a key to membership in it. Once again, it may be more important to situate these exceptional houses in their American contexts, among the more numerous non-Palladian houses, and seek local meanings for the imagery.

The contrast in interpretations can be illustrated by the most famous of the Palladian houses, the Tayloe family's Mount Airy (1758–1762), Richmond County, Virginia. Mount Airy's plan and elevation derived from plates in Gibbs's book and the Tuscan pilasters of the entrance front and the rustication of the garden front evoke standards of rural decorum common in classical architectural practice. The house can thus be seen as a monument to late colonial architectural sophistication. At the same time, however, even this most imitative of houses is not an exact copy of the book. The plan departs from it, the hyphens connecting the house to the dependencies were not originally present, and every facade is different. The Palladian formula of an architecturally coordinated house and flanking, often matched, dependencies, or architecturally coordinated domestic outbuildings, readily accommodates the late-seventeenth-century southern domestic pattern of a planter's house with domestic outbuildings, and the classical decoration articulates and dignifies this pattern. Public, garden, family, and slave entrances were carefully distinguished architecturally, highlighting subtle distinctions in the way the house was used and in the process asserting the ordered social hierarchy southern planters sought. Mount Airy told a Virginia story in a European accent.

As a house that was superficially English in appearance but deeply Virginian in ethos, Mount Airy brings the story of colonial British architecture to a fitting stop, if not to a close. Many of the patterns of colonial British architecture continued into the early national period. The organization of the building industry, building typologies and technologies, and specific social uses of architectural form informed much North American architecture well into the nineteenth century. It was not until the second quarter of the nineteenth century that the reorganization of building prompted by the commercialization of architectural imagery, the introduction of new technologies, and the establishment of the architectural profession closed the book on British colonial architectural history.

BIBLIOGRAPHY

American Philosophical Society. "Historic Philadelphia, From the Founding Until the Early Nineteenth Century. Papers Dealing with its People and Buildings, with an Illustrated Map." *Transactions of the American Philosophical Society* 43, pt. 1 (1953). Studies of the principal buildings and building types in the largest colonial American city.

Bailyn, Bernard. "Politics and Social Structure in Virginia." In *Seventeenth-Century America: Essays in Colonial History,* edited by James Morton Smith. Chapel Hill, N.C., 1959.

Bishir, Catherine W. "Black Builders in Antebellum North Carolina." *North Carolina Historical Review* 61 (1984):423–461. Important overview of the many roles of African-American craftsmen in early southern architecture.

Bishir, Catherine W., Charlotte V. Brown, Carl R. Lounsbury, and Ernest Wood. *Architects and Builders in North Carolina: A History of the Practice of Building.* Chapel Hill, N.C., 1990. The best source for understanding the colonial building process.

Carson, Cary, Norman F. Barka, William M. Kelso, Garry Wheeler Stone, and Dell Upton. "Impermanent Architecture in the Southern American Colonies." *Winterthur Portfolio* 16 (1981):135–196. Radical revision of the traditional picture of seventeenth-century southern architecture, based on extensive new architectural, archaeological, and archival study.

Cummings, Abbott Lowell. "The Beginnings of Provincial Renaissance Architecture in Boston, 1690–1725: Current Observations and Suggestions for Further Study." *Journal of the Society of Architectural Historians* 42 (1983):43–53.

———. *The Framed Houses of Massachusetts Bay, 1625–1725.* Cambridge, Mass., 1979. Synthesizes and revises a century of scholarship about seventeenth-century New England.

Fairbanks, Jonathan L., and Robert F. Trent, eds. *New England Begins: the Seventeenth Century.* 3 vols. Boston, 1982. Argument about mannerism challenges the traditional view of plain Puritan New England.

Garvan, Anthony N. B. *Architecture and Town Planning in Colonial Connecticut.* New Haven, Conn., 1951.

Girouard, Mark. *Life in the English Country House: A Social and Architectural History.* New Haven, Conn., 1978. One of the great recent works of architectural history, important for understanding the social patterns of colonial American elite houses.

Glassie, Henry. *Pattern in the Material Folk Culture of the Eastern United States.* Philadelphia, 1969. An old but still essential overview of folk housing.

Gowans, Alan. *Building Canada: An Architectural History of Canadian Life.* Toronto, Ontario, 1966.

Isham, Norman M., and Albert F. Brown. *Early Connecticut Houses: An Historical and Architectural Study.* Providence, R.I., 1900; repr. New York, 1965.

———. *Early Rhode Island Houses: An Historical and Architectural Study.* Providence, R.I., 1895. The first scholarly study of British colonial architecture, and still useful.

Kelly, J. Frederick. *Early Domestic Architecture of Connecticut.* New Haven, Conn., 1924; repr. New York, 1963.

Kimball, Fiske. *Domestic Architecture of the American Colonies and of the Early Republic.* New York, 1922; repr. 1966. The founding survey of colonial architecture, superior to all its successors.

Mercer, Eric. *English Vernacular Houses: A Study of Tra-*

ditional Farmhouses and Cottages. London, 1975. The best overview of the vernacular tradition from which seventeenth-century American houses derived.

Morgan, Edmund S. American Slavery, American Freedom: The Ordeal of Colonial Virginia. New York, 1975.

Nabokov, Peter, and Robert Easton. Native American Architecture. New York, 1988. Important summary of scattered historical and ethnographic data.

Neiman, Fraser D. "Domestic Architecture at the Clifts Plantation: The Social Context of Early Virginia Building." In Common Places: Reading in American Vernacular Architecture, edited by Dell Upton and John Michael Vlach. Athens, Ga., 1986.

Pierson, William H. American Buildings and Their Architects, 1: The Colonial and Neoclassical Styles. Garden City, N.Y., 1971.

Roos, Frank J. Bibliography of Early American Architecture; Writings on Architecture Constructed Before 1860 in Eastern and Central United States. Rev. ed. Urbana, Ill., 1968. Old and inadequate, but has not been superseded.

St. George, Robert Blair, ed. Material Life in America, 1600–1860. Boston, 1988. Collects many important recent articles on colonial architecture, together with major social-history essays.

Tatum, George B. Philadelphia Georgian: The City House of Samuel Powel and Some of its Eighteenth-Century Neighbors. Middletown, Conn., 1976. The best of the few studies of urban architecture.

Upton, Dell. Holy Things and Profane: Anglican Parish Churches in Colonial Virginia. New York, 1986.

————. "Traditional Timber Framing." In Material Culture of the Wooden Age, edited by Brooke Hindle. Tarrytown, N.Y., 1981. Succinct overview of British, German, and Dutch timber-building technologies.

Upton, Dell, and John Michael Vlach, eds. Common Places: Readings in American Vernacular Architecture. Athens, Ga., 1986. Together with St. George (1988), collects most of the basic articles in early American vernacular architecture.

Waterman, Thomas T. The Dwellings of Colonial America. Chapel Hill, N.C., 1950. After Kimball's, the best survey; more attention to the South and to houses below the mansion level.

Whiffen, Marcus. The Eighteenth-Century Houses of Williamsburg: A Study of Architecture and Building in the Colonial Capital of Virginia. Rev. ed. Williamsburg, Va., 1984. The collective wisdom of Colonial Williamsburg's architectural staff; a good primer of colonial building construction.

Dell Upton

SEE ALSO **Artisans; Crafts; Home and Hearth; Rural Life; The Structure of Society;** and **Urban Life.**

THE DUTCH COLONY

FROM THE FIRST settlement in New Netherland in the 1620s to the last Dutch-style structures over two centuries later, Dutch architecture spread throughout the colony in a series of waves. Dugout huts, which served as temporary shelters for the first inhabitants, were followed by rudimentary one-story structures. Next came one- or two-room, one-and-a-half-story houses in Dutch medieval style. By the 1650s newly affluent colonists were building commodious houses of some stylistic pretension that closely resembled middle-class houses in the Netherlands.

After the English gained control of the colony in 1664, their architectural traditions began to influence houses built by people of Dutch descent, a process that continued for a century and a half. Change emanated slowly from New York City, in some cases reaching remote areas only decades later. Architecture proved to be the most conservative expression of Dutch material culture in both New York and New Jersey. As late as the 1830s, fully fifty years after most characteristically Dutch furnishings were no longer being made, some Dutch features were still being incorporated in rural houses and barns.

URBAN DUTCH ARCHITECTURE

Netherland Origins of Dutch Houses
To understand Dutch architecture in America, it is useful first to understand its medieval beginnings in the Netherlands. Examination of the oldest surviving structures, parts of which date back eight hundred years, as well as the archaeological record of earlier structures, shows that urban houses developed from rural houses when

cities began to form about the year 1200. Single-room, one-story thatched houses with a central fireplace but no chimney began to evolve slowly in the towns into larger structures with specialized rooms.

Through centuries of development, one can trace the continued interaction of environmental conditions with human needs for shelter from the cold; fire to see by, to cook over and get warm by; and windows and doors to supply light and air. A house also supplied security for family and possessions, a place to preserve the family and enrich the culture of living. By meeting these needs, Netherland houses were like houses anywhere in Europe. It was the peculiar character of the land and climate that gave Dutch homes their distinctive character.

Half of the Netherlands was land reclaimed (poldered) from the sea. These poldered areas were soft peat bogs on which not even an outhouse could be built without driving tree-trunk pilings down about twenty-five feet (8 meters), where a layer of glacial sand provided support. All the houses on this land, including all those in the major cities, had dozens of pilings beneath them. Because of this condition, houses had to be built of light construction. In cities, for example, a common or party wall of brick was only eight inches (200 millimeters) thick, even if the adjacent houses were five stories high. A wood frame of posts and joists carried the weight of the house; while the brick side walls were used as a firebreak, and the brick-and-stone front wall, with its large windows, presented an impressive facade. Although heavier than wood, brick became the principal building because wood (as well as stone) was scarce and had to be imported, while brick was made from clay, which was abundant. Stone, too heavy as well as scarce, was used only for ornaments on facades.

Other features of Dutch houses reflected climatic conditions. The angle of the roof was steep so that wind-driven rain would be less likely to penetrate beneath loosely set earthenware roof pantiles. In the towns and cities, use of pantiles was specified by law to retard the spread of fire. Thatched roofs were and still are common in the countryside, where the threat of fire was not as great. Wood shingles, common in the New World, were almost never used because of expense.

Since land was at a premium in Netherland walled cities and towns, maximum use had to be made of the narrow eighteen- to twenty-foot-wide (8 meter-wide) plots; houses expanded vertically. However the use of upper floors depended on controlling fireplace smoke, necessitating the development of the fireplace chimney. Access to those floors required stairways, built steeply to make the most of limited space. Because they were too steep for carrying large or heavy objects, a rope and pulley attached to a post beam in the front gable was used to hoist material to gable-end windows or doors. Inside, ceilings were increased in height so that large expanses of glass on the facade could provide more generous illumination. In some houses the back wall of the front room was also of glass, letting light into the next room and thus allowing the construction of houses three rooms deep. A short stairway and small porch in front of the door—the "stoop"—gave access to the main floor, which was elevated well above the sodden ground. In cities the stoop also gave shelter to a lower entryway, much as with Victorian town houses in America.

By the seventeenth century—the Netherlands's golden age—houses and warehouses in the major cities had as many as seven floors. Yet they retained their essentially medieval structure, which was partly hidden under Renaissance-inspired decoration. Not surprisingly, this long-standing tradition became the basis for structures built in the New World.

New World Urban Houses

Of necessity, the first houses built at Manhattan, and probably elsewhere, had more in common with the ancient one-room hovels than with the Netherland town houses. Accounts of Manhattan in the 1620s describe its first shelters as square cellars or pits, with bark or sod roofs, used as shelter while the urgent necessity of clearing and cultivating the land was pursued. Within a decade substantial Dutch-type houses of wood were being built, and by 1646 similar dwellings were being constructed upriver in Beverswyck (later Albany). Father Isaac Jogues, a Jesuit missionary among the Iroquois, wrote, "Their houses are solely of boards and thatched, with no mason work but the chimneys."

At the same time, larger houses were being constructed within the walls of adjacent Fort Orange. Recently excavated cellars show such pretensions to Old World elegance as leaded glass windows and green-glazed clay floor tiles. However, cellar walls made of timber and boards instead of stone indicate the temporary nature of even these houses.

As English control was secured, in 1664, some of the finest examples of urban Dutch architecture were beginning to be built. The design of Dutch houses built in Albany and New York during the late seventeenth and early eighteenth centuries followed closely those of urban houses in the main cities of the Netherlands until the early seventeenth century and as late as a century later in towns. In the New World, almost all such houses built with brick facades and parapet gables had either a step- or spout-shaped front gable.

Our knowledge of these houses comes from contracts and engraved and painted images. The clearest images are of houses in Albany, which was as Dutch-looking as a Netherland town from at least the 1660s until the last urban Dutch houses were constructed a century later. The fortifications and walls of the frontier town, combined with the cultural divisions within its Dutch majority, made its building less susceptible to fashion and innovation and accounts for the persistence of Dutch ways in architecture and other respects long after they were superseded in New York City. To English travelers, Albany was an anachronistic, medieval holdover from an alien land and ancient culture. Even during the first decade of the nineteenth century, Gorham Worth found it little changed:

All the old buildings in the city—and they constituted a large majority—were but one story high, with sharp peaked roofs, surmounted by a rooster, vulgarly called a weathercock. Every house, having any pretensions to dignity, was placed with its gable end to the street, and was ornamented with huge iron numericals, announcing the date of its erection; while from its eaves long wooden gutters, or spouts, projected in front from six or seven feet, when it rained, directly over the center of the sidewalk. This was probably contrived for the benefit of those who were compelled to be out in wet weather, as it furnished them with an extra shower both free of expense. (*Random Recollections of Albany*. Vol. 10, pp. 194–195)

That aggravating adherence to old ways characterized the attitude of many Dutch toward the English. But it slowly dissipated as a result of increased contact with English government, society, and culture, as historian William Smith observed in the early 1760s:

The manner of the people differ as well as their language. . . . In the city of New York, through our intercourse with the Europeans, we follow the London fashions; though by the time we adopt them, they [have] become disused in England. Our affluence during the late war [probably King George's War in the 1740s] introduced a degree of luxury in tables, dress, and furniture, with which we were before unacquainted. But still we are not so gay a people as our neighbors in Boston, and several of the southern colonies. The Dutch counties, in some measure follow the example of New-York [City], but still retain many modes peculiar to the Hollanders. (*The History of the Late Province of New-York*. Vol. 1, p. 277)

The architectural development experienced in New York City and Albany also occurred on a smaller scale in Schenectady, where at least four urban Dutch houses survive in various states of alteration. The naturalist Peter Kalm mentioned that New Brunswick, New Jersey, also had this type of house. In New Castle, Delaware—settled by the Dutch from 1655, when it was taken from New Sweden—one especially handsome brick house with a stepped gable, built about 1687, survived to be drawn by Benjamin Henry Latrobe in 1804–1805 and photographed before being demolished in 1884.

The plan of the two-room, side-hall Yates House (1732) in Schenectady is typical of urban Dutch houses. The front room (*voorhuis*) was often used as a shop; the rear room was a kitchen and general living and sleeping quarters. In most urban houses there was only one fireplace, most often located on a side wall in the kitchen. The Yates house, however, had a central chimney and originally had one or possibly two fireplaces (back-to-back in two rooms). The entryway was separate from both rooms for privacy and to suppress outside drafts, which could cause the large open fireplace to smoke. The traditional Dutch fireplace (which had no smoke shelf or side jambs in the English manner) did not handle heat and smoke efficiently. This was well known even to the Dutch. Their continued use of this outmoded fireplace can best be accounted for by the Dutch penchant for stubbornly maintaining symbols of their identity with their old country.

The cleanliness of Dutch houses was remarked on with some astonishment by visitors, including Peter Kalm.

> The floors of the houses were kept quite clean by the women who sometimes scrubbed them several times a week, and Saturday was the day especially set aside for that task. In many houses in the town they had partitioned off the part of the room where the beds stood by placing large doors before them [like cupboards], and thus completely concealing the beds from view. (*Peter Kalm's Travels in North America*, p. 613)

The structure and procedure for building Dutch houses, whether urban or rural, had changed little in centuries. Kalm described them:

> The houses hereabouts are generally built of beams and of unburnt bricks dried by the sun and the air. The beams are first erected, and upon them a gable with two walls, and the spars. The wall on the gable is made of nothing but boards. The roof is covered with shingles of fir. They make the walls of unburnt bricks, between the beams, to keep the rooms warmer; and that they might not easily be destroyed by rain and air they are covered with boards on the outside. There is generally a cellar beneath the house. The fireplaces among the Dutch were always built in, so that nothing projected out, and it looked as though they made a fire against the wall itself. (p. 356)

Dutch Reformed Churches

Worship by Dutch immigrants commenced from the day of debarkation, though it was some years before any church structures were built, and their architecture varied widely. The church in the New Amsterdam (later New York City) fort (begun in 1642 but completed after 1647) was built of stone, seventy-two by fifty-two feet (22 by 16 meters), with a belfry straddling a curious twin roof line. The 1656 church at Albany was described as the "blockhouse" church, apparently serving a double purpose at this frontier enclave. Its 1715 successor was a conventional Netherlands-type church, built on a square plan with a steeply pitched roof on which a high open belfry was erected. Similar examples can be seen in the Dutch province of Zeeland.

On Long Island and in New Jersey, several small churches followed the small octagonal form—with a high pointed roof and belfry—of the earliest Protestant churches in the Netherlands (the first being at Willemstad in 1595). These included churches at New Utrecht (Brooklyn) in 1700, Bushwick (Brooklyn) around 1708–1711, and Bergen (Jersey City) in 1680. The Midwout (Brooklyn) church of 1654–1655 was cruciform in plan, sixty-five by eighty-five feet (19 by 25 meters), the *domine* dwelling in the rear. By 1717 New York City had three additional churches, each a rectangular plan with a bell tower on the gable end. The English church was built in the current English style, while the Dutch and French churches were closely related to the Dutch style.

Following Calvinist reaction to Catholicism, churches were devoid of ornate decoration, especially graven images (Scripture paintings were for the home). With a new emphasis on preaching rather than the mass, the pulpit replaced the altar as the focal point of the interior.

Warehouses

A third type of urban structure common to Dutch towns was the warehouse, the structural embodiment of prosperity among this mercantile people. In New York the relationship between houses and warehouses was close, and most houses were actually residences with a shop or office in the front room and commercial storage in the upper floors. Those which served this dual purpose tended to be larger and to have exterior gable doors in the upper levels while retaining the structural system of a house (a single aisle, multiple bays, and from three to five levels, including garrets).

RURAL DUTCH ARCHITECTURE

Netherland Prototypes

Unlike Netherland and New York City town houses, which are often quite similar in response to the same urban constraints, farmhouses in the two countries were dissimilar, with the Dutch having primarily house-barns, with living quarters attached to animal quarters. In New Netherland such structures—like the large farmhouse with thatched roof contracted for in 1643 by Arent Van Cuyler, the Rensselaerswyck patroon's agent—are known only from early descriptions. It was 28 feet (8 meters) wide and 120 feet (36 meters) long—40 feet (12 meters) for dwelling and 80 (24 meters) for the quarters of farm laborers, cattle, and horses. This combination house and barn, so popular in the Netherlands, was quickly forgotten in New Netherland, where only separate structures were built after the 1680s.

This discontinuity is explained by the fact that New World farms were primarily crop farms, specializing in wheat, and not dairy farms, where a man's entire livelihood depended on the close care of his stock. While much of the Netherlands has long been dependent on dairy farming, in the province of Zeeland, where crop farming is dominant, barns and houses are separated in the New World manner.

New World Rural Houses

While the Hudson River valley, Long Island, and New Jersey are thought of as the settlement areas of the Dutch, in fact they were more widely disbursed. During the eighteenth century, both Dutch and Germans settled former Indian lands in the Mohawk and Schoharie valleys to the west of Albany. There are vestigial remnants of Dutch structures in western Massachusetts, New Castle, and even North Carolina, to which a few families went in the late seventeenth century.

The oldest surviving rural Dutch houses date from the 1660s; one of them, the Pieter Bronck House, is believed to date as early as 1663. It was built by the first settlers of an area near the Upper Hudson River. Its steep roof, masonry walls, and casement windows combine traditional medieval-style Dutch architecture with the indigenous stone of New Netherland.

From the 1660s (and into the nineteenth century in remoter areas), people of Dutch descent built houses that adhered to the medieval plan, though with regional variations in materials and style. Most houses had two rooms, each measuring about twenty feet square (2 square meters), and with an exterior door or with a hall with front and back doors between the two. One room was used for a kitchen and eating area; the other, similar in structure, was more formal— a *groot kamer*, or "best room," for sleeping and social occasions. The garret was open and was used only for work and storage. The cellars, too, were for storage, although in some houses a fireplace was built for cooking. Many houses had an additional wing with one or more rooms.

Farmhouses along the Upper Hudson and Mohawk rivers in Schenectady, Albany, Rensse-laer, Columbia, and Greene counties were constructed primarily of brick or wood; others were built of stone. Clay for bricks and large pitch-pine trees for structural members were abundant along these rivers. Surviving brick houses are especially reminiscent of construction in the Netherlands, where clay was the most readily available building material. Where once there were hundreds of houses of this material, fewer than a dozen built before 1750 remain intact, of which the 1737 Luykas Van Alen House is one of the finest examples. Its Dutch bond brick-work encasing a wood structure, parapet gables with chimneys, casement windows, and divided doors are features of seventeenth-century Netherlands houses.

Formerly much more numerous than brick houses, wood houses of the period are also rare, most of them victims of neglect that their vulnerable material could not withstand. Such a clapboard house as Kalm described was built for the farmer Cornelis Schermerhorn at Kinderhook ("children's corner"), about twenty miles (32 kilometers) south of Albany, about 1713 (with additions later that century). Anne Grant observed that houses constructed like this one required only the generally known skills of a self-sufficient rural population:

It is to be observed that the people in the interior of New York were so exceedingly skillful in the use not only of the axe, but all ordinary tools used in planing and joining timber, that with the aid of a regular carpenter or two to carry on the nicer parts of the work, a man could build an ordinary house, if it were a wooden one, with very little more than his own domestics. (*Memoirs of an American Lady.* Vol. 2, p. 49–50)

This, the essence of the so-called vernacular tradition, helps account for the persistence of that type of house for generations after all direct knowledge of its Netherlands prototypes had faded.

Farther from the Hudson River, stratified limestone outcroppings provided the principal building material, especially on the west side of the Hudson from Albany County southward into New Jersey, where isolated but fertile valleys attracted scattered Dutch settlement. In Ulster County, populated after the 1650s by Dutch and Huguenot settlers, houses were laid up with stone from the surface of newly cleared land or from adjacent quarries. These pitched-roof dwellings were one-and-a-half stories high and contained two rooms, sometimes separated by a hall. This type of rough stone house was built well into the nineteenth century, in a remarkably durable tradition reflecting the isolation of the settlers in this mountainous country.

Dutchess and Westchester county architectural styles were akin to those in other Hudson River valley counties, except that more houses were covered with weatherboards or shingles. A high proportion of tenant farmhouses probably accounts for the lack of more substantial structures.

On the west end of Long Island, across the East River from Manhattan, Dutch farmers commonly built houses of wood, the most plentiful material available there. They differed from Hudson River houses in a number of ways. The eaves of the roof frequently curved outward and overhung the side walls. The houses had lower-pitched gable roofs, allowing for a deeper house with twice as many rooms on the ground floor. The Minnie Schenck House, built at Manhasset (now at Old Bethpage Village) in 1730 is a typical example.

The wide overhanging eaves of the Schenck house are found on other rural houses of Long Island and northern New Jersey, often with the "bell cast," or curved sweep, seen here. This feature is also seen on French houses in rural Quebec; and its origins are traced to Normandy, where brick houses similar in appearance to the Dutch parapet gable houses of the Netherlands and New York indicate that this early form of medieval architecture had wide acceptance.

The same deep roof overhang, curved at the eaves, is found in Bergen County, New Jersey, and in adjacent Rockland County, New York, where quarried red sandstone was a common building material. In both counties the double-slanted (gambrel) roof prevailed. Deeper houses with gambrel roofs resulted not only in more rooms but also more adequate headroom on the second floor, something that the pitched roof did not allow. Although often associated with Dutch construction, the gambrel roof was actually borrowed from New England.

Other areas of Dutch settlement in New Jersey with similar houses include eastern Passaic County and adjacent areas of Morris and Essex counties. Farther south, the Dutch settled most of Somerset County and parts of eastern Hunterdon and western Middlesex counties. Monmouth County, the southernmost Dutch area in New Jersey, was inhabited by a Dutch enclave from Long Island. Their Long Island origin is reflected there in an occasional asymmetrical roofline.

English Influence

The process of incorporating English features into Dutch houses was remarkably slow. The English influence was first seen in late seventeenth-century structures around New York City, on Long Island, and in New Jersey. Not until the 1750s did the English style reach Albany. Houses became larger, with center halls and balanced window openings. They were more symmetrical than Dutch houses and more differentiated in room function, including separate eating, socializing, working, and sleeping areas. Concurrently, decorative moldings and paneling gave the interiors a formal appearance. With these changes the tradition of vernacular medieval Dutch architecture slowly succumbed to the new classical English style.

The motivation for adopting these changes was not simply fashion but a complex cultural "argument" over the owner's conservatism, their ambition, their relative wealth, and the availability of certain building materials and skills. The shift was first seen in public buildings, especially town halls funded by the English government. It then became apparent in taverns and other semipublic structures and in urban houses, more slowly in churches and rural houses, and hardly at all until well into the nineteenth century in rural utilitarian structures like barns, farm outbuildings, and mills. In the Mohawk valley, Dutch barns were still being built in the mid nineteenth century, and in New Jersey hay barracks were erected into the twentieth.

The Dutch Farm

A painting of the Marten Van Bergen family and farm completed in 1733 conveys more information about Dutch life in America than any other surviving object of the period. It is the only contemporary representation of a Dutch farm and among the earliest representations of the inhabited landscape. Depicting Van Bergen's farm near the village of Leeds, about thirty miles (48 kilometers) south of Albany, it shows Marten Van Bergen and his wife, their seven children, Indians, black slaves, and whites, the last probably hired hands or indentured servants. In addition to the stone farmhouse there is a Dutch barn, two Dutch hay barracks, and a blacksmith shop. Most Dutch farms were primarily devoted to such cash crops as wheat and peas and to the farm animals seen here—horses, cows, sheep, and chickens, which supplied the needs only of the family and servants.

In most respects Van Bergen's house is a Dutch farmhouse of superior quality. There were rooms with fireplaces at the gable ends, a cellar below and a garret above, and probably an upper garret as well. A 1729 date stone was matched by dated iron wall anchors once reported over the front door. The addition on the north side, perhaps built shortly after the house, was probably intended to provide quarters for farm workers and an expanding family.

The house was constructed of the stratified limestone found in abundance on the west bank of the Hudson River, but the red earthenware color of the parapet gable ends suggests that brick was used above eave level. As an elegant flourish Van Bergen used pantiles for roofing and finished off the two dormers with roll-gable pediments, unusual features in rural houses. The roll gable, a late-seventeenth-century feature in Netherlands architecture, reached New York just before English architecture eclipsed the Dutch style. It is the only visible Renaissance feature in an otherwise medieval house.

Unusual in New York is the single shutter seen at each two-light casement window. In the Netherlands this type of window, with leaded-glass casement sash in one half and a hinged shutter in the other, is called a *bolkozyn*. The glazed casement sash admitted light, and the shutter was for controlling ventilation. The bright red, white, and brown of the shutters constitute another example of Dutch tradition transferred to the New World. The only known representation of an original rural Dutch stoop in front of the main door is also visible.

The hay barrack is an easily built Dutch farm structure for storing hay. As the amount of hay changed, the roof could be raised or lowered by a jack on poles as high as fifty feet. Most American Dutch barracks were made of four posts about twenty-four feet (7 meters) high and set about sixteen feet (5 meters) apart. The two barracks on the Van Bergen farm are unusual for the number of poles and overall size. A raised floor on one allowed for sheltering stock underneath. Barracks were useful and inexpensive structures that continued to be built into the early twentieth century in the Dutch-settled regions of America, and a few survive today, primarily in northern New Jersey. They are still made and used extensively in the Netherlands.

The barn conforms to the Dutch style, with a large double doorway in the center of each gable, through which vehicles could enter, and a smaller door at each corner of each gable, by which animals entered pens and stalls in the side aisles. The wide center aisle was designed for grain threshing; opening the doors at the gable ends admitted a breeze that could aid in separating wheat from chaff. Thus this Netherlands barn type was well adapted to the wheat farming of the Upper Hudson River valley, a region renowned as the breadbasket of the colonies.

The structural system of a Dutch barn is chiefly characterized by a prominent series of "bents" or posts and crossbeams (now known as anchor beams) set parallel to each other over a central aisle. On these rested long poles or "sleepers" on which lay a prodigious amount of wheat or other crops. Long rafters extended the roof beyond the bents to form an additional aisle on each side. Barns, like that of Johannes Decker in Ulster County, New York (about 1750), were built with four, five, or six bays (the spaces between adjacent sets of bents), creating a square or nearly square floor plan of from forty-five to fifty feet (13.5 to 15 meters) on a side. A pentice (hood) over the main doors provided protection from rain. Small openings in the upper gable, called "martin holes" for the then-common denizens of these upper reaches, were made to permit the circulation of air to crops stored on the "sleepers."

This type of barn originated in the Netherlands and elsewhere in northern Europe, where its lineage can be traced back for at least a millennium, and its close affinity to the three-aisle Gothic church is evident. Several hundred of these barns survive in America, the greatest concentration being in the Mohawk valley, where Dutch farming practice continued well into the nineteenth century.

Mills

In the background of Abraham Wendell's 1737 portrait appears his father's mill, the only known contemporary picture of a colonial-era Dutch water mill in New York or New Jersey. Located on the Beaver Kill (now within the city of Albany), it was one of many such mills throughout the Hudson River valley from the early years of the New Netherland colony until the late nineteenth century. Many, like this one, were gristmills, for grinding grain into flour.

The structure is of wood, one aisle deep and two stories high—much the same proportion, construction, and size of a two-room Dutch farmhouse. Its apparent height, a full two stories, is unusual and allows for a second-floor exterior door as well as a garret door above it, both for access to stored bags of grain and for grinding. In the pediment over the doors are three holes. In Netherland barns similar holes allowed owls to enter and nest, reducing the population of mice and rats that fed on stored grain.

Two doors at ground level give access to the mill proper and to what is either the miller's residence or possibly a bakery. There are curtains in the window, and the back end of a brick bake oven protrudes from the gable end. At the end of the mill building is an overshot waterwheel that powered the grinding stones within.

BIBLIOGRAPHY

Bailey, Rosalie Fellows. *Pre-Revolutionary Dutch Houses and Families in Northern New Jersey and Southern New York*. New York, 1968.

Blackburn, Roderic H., and Ruth Piwonka. *Remembrance of Patria: Dutch Arts and Culture in Colonial America, 1609–1776*. Albany, N.Y., 1988.

Fitchen, John. *The New World Dutch Barn: A Study of Its Characteristics, Its Structural System, and Its Probable Erectional Procedures*. Syracuse, N.Y., 1968.

Grant, Anne. *Memoirs of an American Lady: With Sketches of Manners and Scenery in America, As They Existed Previous to the Revolution*. London, 1808; repr. 1901. Anne McVicar (1755–1838) (later the wife of the Reverend James Grant) of Scotland lived with her parents mostly at Albany from 1757 to about 1763 (the period of her *Memoirs*) and then in Vermont until about 1770.

Kalm, Peter. *Peter Kalm's Travels in North America*. 2 vols. Edited by Adolph B. Benson. New York, 1937; repr. 1964. Peter [Pehr] Kalm (1716–1779), a Swedish naturalist, collected scientific data in North America for Linnaeus between 1748 and 1751.

Reynolds, Helen Wilkinson. *Dutch Houses in the Hudson Valley Before 1776*. New York, 1929.

Smith, William. *The History of the Late Province of New-York*. 2 vols. New York, 1829. William Smith (1728–1793) spent most of his life in New York province. His *History* comprises the period from New York's discovery to the appointment of Governor Colden in 1762.

Stayton, Kevin L. *Dutch by Design: Tradition and Chance in Two Historic Brooklyn Houses*. New York, 1990.

Worth, Gorham A. *Random Recollections of Albany, from 1800 to 1808*. Albany, N.Y., 1849. Gorham A. Worth (1783–1856), writing under the pseudonym Ignatius Jones, first published his *Recollections* of 1800–1808 in 1848.

Roderic Hall Blackburn

SEE ALSO **Artisans; Crafts; Home and Hearth; Rural Life;** and **Urban Life.**

THE FRENCH COLONIES

ARCHITECTURE IS DETERMINED by available materials, climate, and social needs and by cultural traditions. French North America's institutional architecture was always dominated by the parent state's fashions, and public buildings were a statement of metropolitan values. In such projects adaptation to the new environment was slight. It was domestic architecture that responded fully to the new setting and reflected the geographic diversity of France's empire on the North American mainland.

DOMESTIC ARCHITECTURE

Seventeenth-century immigrants from France brought the architectural language of their provinces to North America. The building traditions of northwestern France were most influential. Half-timbered construction, in which the walls of a pegged wooden frame were filled in with other materials, provided the common vernacular from Acadia to Louisiana. Improvised dwellings were of post-in-ground construction, but such palisade walls rotted quickly and collapsed unless externally braced. They had a life expectancy of twelve to fifteen years in Canada and three to five years in Louisiana. Fishermen's shelters on the Atlantic coast were erected in this fashion, which required no carpentry skills. Turf was sometimes added to the exterior for insulation. Post-in-ground barns and outbuildings were still visible in the Saint Lawrence Valley in the mid 1700s and the technique persisted in the Illinois country for homes.

Colombage or *charpente* (heavy wooden framing) was the starting point for more durable homes. In New France cedar and oak timbers were preferred for their resistance to decay, just as cypress wood was favored by house framers in Louisiana. Masonry construction was too expensive for most colonists, but the fact that surviving seventeenth-century buildings are built of stone misleads one into thinking that such structures are representative of their generation. Rubble fill or vertical wooden posts (*piquets*) completed the walls in Louisbourg houses, just as bricks or a moss-and-clay mixture called *bousillage* over wattles filled framed walls in eighteenth-century Louisiana. Whitewashed roughcasting was laid over the exterior to harmonize the different constituents and to protect the fragile infill from the weather. Such dwellings could be expected to last for forty to fifty years or even longer.

Colonists from France brought an aesthetic with them that favored verticality. Half the height of a house or barn was encompassed by the roof, usually covered with wood shingles or battened boards. Tree bark was used as roofing in the fishing settlements. Inland, early rural houses had clay and log chimneys and thatched roofs. In the 1700s thatch was relegated to farm outbuildings.

The steep roofs were often hipped and the eaves terminated in a projecting, bell-cast curve that had as many disadvantages as benefits for the occupant. The curved eaves provided shade in summer but retained ice, snow, and moisture, thereby accelerating wood decay. These eaves were extended and supported by posts, emerging as the raised verandas (*galeries*) that are characteristic of late-eighteenth-century French colonial homes from Canada to Louisiana. In the Saint Lawrence Valley gable walls were eventually raised to the roof crest, leaving only two roof planes in tent fashion; thus the veranda only covered the front and back of the house. Their southern cousins had covered walkways around the entire house. The pitch of eighteenth-century roofs was lower—another example of taste overcoming practicality, since the gentler slope did not shed rain or snow as effectively as the steep one.

Another French legacy was a preference for the casement window over sliding sash. Ground-floor windows were given the additional protection of shutters. Glass was costly, and oiled parchment was used as a substitute by countryfolk. Doors were usually paneled, and construction contracts describe the ornamented yet functional wrought-iron hinges, drawbolts, and latches used to secure windows, shutters, and doors. Doorknobs and knockers are not mentioned. House construction drew on the talents of blacksmiths as well as those of stonemasons, carpenters, roofers, and joiners. Openings were not located with the same concern for symmetry apparent in the Georgian buildings built by the British colonists in North America. French builders had a relaxed, additive approach that placed extensions or windows where they were needed. Access to cheap and heavy timber allowed carpenters to simplify the structure of colonial roof trusses.

French half-timbering had developed in response to a dwindling supply of good building wood. In New France there was no shortage of forests, and wood fill superseded stone and mortar. Wood gave better insulation against the cold, and it expanded and contracted in harmony with the wooden frame. At first the timber infill was installed vertically and was roughly hewn on two faces. Full squaring provided a tighter fit. Upright timber fill alternating with panels of stone and mortar remained common in Cahokia and elsewhere in the Illinois country. There and on the Atlantic coast this variant of French half-timbering may have been forced on the colonists by the rarity of large trees.

In the Saint Lawrence Valley the squared timbers were later laid horizontally with end tenons slotted into a vertical groove in the frame uprights (*poteaux en coulisse*). This technique was usually called building *en-pièces-sur-pièces*. As aging wood shrank, the horizontal pieces settled and the wall remained snug, whereas vertical posts left widening gaps that had to be chinked with moss and mortar. Later builders sometimes dispensed with corner posts and dovetailed the horizontal members together. The fact that contracts specifically add *à queue d'aronde* (dovetailed) to the description *en-pièces-sur-pièces* indicates that interlocking corners were an exception to the general pattern of construction. Clients' specifications are often vague, citing another house as a model for certain features, and it would require supernatural powers to state exactly what percentage of dwellings were erected in one way or another.

Domestic houses underwent a progressive increase in height and size. In the Montreal region during the late seventeenth century houses were from nineteen to twenty-eight feet long (some 5.5 to 8.5 meters), with a depth four-fifths of the length. They were usually one or one-and-a-half stories high. At Louisbourg legislators tried in vain to limit building height, so as not to block the ocean breezes needed to dry cod fillets. Intendant Claude-Thomas Dupuy's 1727 comprehensive building ordinance insisted that houses in Quebec and Montreal have a cellar and more than one story, to make the best use of city lots.

Taxation encouraged Spanish Louisiana's residents to place the staircases leading to the upper story or attic *garçonnière* (bachelor's quarters) on the exterior. Canadians, being concerned with winter comfort, preferred interior staircases and provided themselves with additional protection by double-boarded tongue-and-groove roofs under shingles, by installing insulated floors and doorway vestibules called *tambours*. The Louisianian preoccupation with dissipating heat resulted in detached kitchens and large windows opening onto a *galerie* that permitted cross-breezes to blow through the house on sultry and rainy days. Rooms were divided laterally, so that they had windows on both side walls. Because of the Mississippi Delta's high water table, brick piers and foundations supported the wooden frame to protect it from damp rot and termites. In grander homes the entire ground floor might

be of brick and mortar construction. The rarity of freestone led to a greater use of brick than was seen in the Saint Lawrence Valley, where its use was confined to ovens and hearths.

Private dwellings in the French colonies rarely had hallways; rooms opened onto other rooms. The functional division of a Canadian farmhouse was one large open area for eating and family gatherings and an enclosed sleeping area divided by pine-board partitions. The partitions were movable and could be adjusted to the family's changing makeup; an overflow of children and the occasional servant would be accommodated in the attic. Both ground-floor areas were warmed by hearths on either side of a central chimney; end-wall chimneys wasted heat. The iron stove was welcomed in New France (except for Louisiana) during the 1700s as an even more efficient heater. Townhouses had a more complex layout, with rooms for a shop or office at the front and a kitchen and dining room near the rear.

Urban housing could not express the builder's fancy because it was subject to fire-prevention regulations that favored stone construction and outlawed cedar shingle roofs—except in the Atlantic settlements, where shingles were considered an improvement over bark roofing. Building laws were inconsistently enforced, and wood shingle roofs were still seen in towns during the 1750s. Mansard roofs, which had been fashionable in the seventeenth century, were forbidden in the 1720s because of the mass of combustible framing involved.

Since 1673 Quebec's houses were required to have stone fire gables that extended above the roof line, to prevent the spread of any conflagration. This requirement and specifications for chimneys to facilitate sweeping and to prevent sparks from landing on adjacent roofs spread to Montreal. In towns of the Saint Lawrence Valley, building facades had to follow street alignments, and this produced a continuous wall of house fronts on either side of a street, broken only by dressed stone corbels that terminated the projecting parapet wall of the gable. Urban fireplaces and flues were built into the stone gables, and massive paired chimneys formed the apex of the gable. Because of the high cost of dressed stone, trimmed masonry merely outlined openings; the balance of the front wall was rubblestone, generously mortared and smoothed over with a sand plaster. Behind the urban facades were courtyards, stables, and small gardens that gave town life a rural aspect.

INSTITUTIONAL ARCHITECTURE

French North America's architects were usually master builders who had risen from the ranks of stonecutters and masons. Without academic instruction they learned how to draft scaled plans, prepare detailed estimates, and use the classical orders of decoration. Quebec builders Claude Baillif and Jean-Baptiste Maillou owned copies of the architectural works of Vitruvius, Giacomo Barozzi da Vignola, Louis Savot, and Emile-François de Pagan. The library of Quebec's Collège des Jésuites held additional architectural books by Philibert de l'Orme, Mathurin Jousse, Antoine DeVille, and Bernardo da Gimignano. Skill and knowledge of fashionable styles recommended these builders to clients of the upper ranks, and good social connections helped win government contracts. Masonry builders appreciated by the administration received the honorific title *architecte du roi,* which involved no regular duties.

Private contractors learned more architectural theory from government projects, which were designed by men with professional training in draftsmanship and architecture. Military engineers sent out to the colonies not only prepared plans for fortifications, using Sébastien Le Prestre de Vauban's manual as their principal guide; they also designed public buildings. Army engineer Gaspard-Joseph Chaussegros de Léry planned new facades for Quebec's cathedral and Montreal's parish church, while New Orleans's second Ursuline Convent followed plans by Ignace-François Broutin, the chief king's engineer in Louisiana. Simplified baroque facades were preferred for churches, and touches of French neoclassicism lent dignity to secular structures, such as a barracks or an administrator's residence. A central two-story core with an imposing entrance might be flanked by wings, whose decoration gave a faint echo of the main body. Public buildings were a formal statement of the regime's attachment to order, discipline, and stability. These styles were sometimes applied to an older fabric, without altering the basic structure.

Because the first bishop of Quebec refused to consecrate wooden chapels, in order to reduce the number of individuals who could claim patronage rights, most places of worship were built of fieldstone. (An act of 1679 decreed that a seigneur who had a stone church built in his parish would be granted the advowson.) The typical eighteenth-century rural church in Canada had a simple nave, without transepts, ending in a half-round apse. Large half-round windows lined the nave walls. An attenuated spire superimposed over double lanterns was placed above the doorway, which had neoclassical decoration in low relief. A circular window over the main door was another popular feature. Because of the risk of frost damage to masonry and stone statuary, church facades were simple and sober. They gave no clue to the splendor within.

Inside, worshipers were dazzled by gilded wood carving that became more elaborate as one approached the high altar and tabernacle. Thanks to ecclesiastical support, wood sculpture flourished in the French colonies. The altar was framed by pilasters or columns supporting an arch; a baroque oil painting of the parish's namesake was placed over the tabernacle. One could not doubt that this was indeed the house of God; the interior decor in provincial rococo was a celebration of the divinity and gave a pictorial account of his messengers' lives. The churchwardens and seigneur of the parish sat close to the high altar in special pews; the benches behind were rented to local notables. The rest of the congregation stood or kneeled on the bare floor. Equality before God did not erase earthly distinctions in the highly stratified society of the colonies.

Because the colonial elite of administrators, military officers, and merchants adhered to the mother country's fashions and prided itself on fidelity to European ways, institutional architecture made few compromises with the North American environment. The mass of French colonials, who were guided more by pragmatism than by building manuals, responded freely to the resources and climate of their new homeland. It was in humble domestic buildings, particularly those of the countryside, that the originality of French North America expressed itself.

BIBLIOGRAPHY

Ekberg, Carl J. *Colonial Ste. Genevieve.* Gerald, Mo., 1985.

Farnsworth, Jean M., and Ann M. Masson, eds. *The Architecture of Colonial Louisiana: Collected Essays of Samuel Wilson, Jr.* Lafayette, La., 1987.

Gowans, Alan. *Church Architecture in New France.* Toronto, Ontario, 1955.

Heck, Robert W. "Building Traditions in the Acadian Parishes." In *The Cajuns: Essays on Their History and Culture,* edited by Glenn R. Conrad. Lafayette, La., 1978.

Moogk, Peter N. *Building a House in New France.* Toronto, Ontario, 1977.

Richardson, A. J. H., Geneviève Bastien, Doris Dubé, and Marthe Lacombe. *Quebec City: Architects, Artisans, and Builders.* Ottawa, 1984.

Ritchie, Thomas. *Canada Builds, 1867–1967.* Toronto, Ontario, 1967.

Peter N. Moogk

SEE ALSO **Artisans; Crafts; Home and Hearth; Rural Life;** and **Urban Life.**

THE SPANISH BORDERLANDS

THE SPANIARDS BROUGHT with them to New Spain a rich architectural heritage derived from Roman-Byzantine and Arabic sources. Although buildings on the northern frontier are, for the most part, pale reflections of richer structures of the more southerly provinces, there are a few truly noteworthy mission churches and regional differences of vernacular buildings to be admired.

Since the late 1960s Spanish colonial sites in the United States have received growing attention from archaeologists and historians. Their intensive studies have added significant data to our knowledge of Spanish architectural practices and the artisans involved that are slowly stripping away the romantic twaddle surrounding most of the more visible monuments. Building upon their studies, this essay will survey all types of architecture built by the Spaniards—structures associated with towns, ranches, *presidios,* and missions—the materials used, and the builders.

MATERIALS AND BUILDING TECHNOLOGY

It goes without saying that in a preindustrial society without a system of rapid and cheap transportation, people are restricted to building with the materials at hand. Therefore, our starting point is the materials and how they were used.

The simplest and quickest buildings to erect were thatched *jacales* (huts) made of upright poles set in a trench. There were two variations: a *palisado* (palisade), in which the vertical members were close-spaced, and a more open structure of the wattle-and-daub type. Walls were sealed with mud. *Jacales* generally had gabled roofs made from four heavier uprights with forked branches set at the four corners to support horizontal wall plates and two taller ones centered in the end walls to take a ridgepole. To these were affixed rafters and small perpendicular members to which thatch of palm, tules, or grass could be tied. Another type of temporary structure, usually referred to as a *horcón,* utilized the forked-pole framework of the jacal, but the walls were built of adobes set between the supporting vertical members. Yet another was a framework to which vertical boards were nailed. These structures were finished with thatched gable roofs or flat *terrado* or *azotea* roofs built up of large *vigas* (beams), ceiled with reeds, then layered with tules or grass and compacted earth, and topped with plaster. Such simple buildings as the *jacal* and *horcón* were still prominent in the borderlands in the nineteenth century, and isolated samples can yet be found.

Buildings made of more durable materials replaced the temporary ones as circumstances allowed. Adobe bricks, long used in Mexico, were introduced where suitable clay (with the addition of straw, potsherds, or small stones to help counteract cracking) was available and a relatively dry climate permitted. They were used in New Mexico and Sonora (Arizona) at the beginning of, and later in, the seventeenth century, respectively, and in California starting in 1773. The climate and the abundance of timber in Florida perhaps militated against their use there. Adobes, formed in wooden molds and air-dried, were set up with mud or lime mortar. The thick wall mass retained heat in winter and kept the interior cool in summer. Adobe walls were sometimes built on the ground without foundations, but more often were built on stone or *tipichil* foundations to protect their bases from water erosion. The latter material was a concrete made by adding small gravel aggregate to lime mortar. It was used as a roof sealer as well. Walls were sometimes protected by lime plaster and whitewash, and occasionally painted to look like ashlars. Roofs on adobe buildings were either gabled and covered with thatch or fired tiles, or were *terrado*. Flat roofs were actually slightly pitched to allow drainage through *canales,* waterspouts made of wood, fired clay, or stone. In Florida the Spaniards used tabby for walls, roofs, and floors. Tabby was made by adding sand, pebbles, and shells to lime mortar that could be poured into wood forms, like rammed earth, for raising walls.

In areas where building stone and artisans knowledgeable in masonry and stonecutting were available, more solid structures could be erected. Two techniques were employed: cut stone ashlars set in mortar or *mampostería* (rubble stone) set in lime mortar or mud. In the case of the latter, corners, and sometimes openings, were reinforced with dressed quoins, jambs, and lintels. *Mampostería* walls were cheaper to build and could be disguised by plastering, whitewashing, or being painted to resemble cut stone. Either flat or pitched roofs were used on these buildings. Another type of durable housing was of log construction, although it is less well known because of its limited distribution, mostly in mountain communities in New Mexico, where the raw material was close at hand. (It will be described more fully under regional adaptations.)

The manufacture of fired brick was standardized in Mexico City with the recognition of two better and two inferior grades. Both first- and second-quality bricks (*ladrillos de marca* and *ladrillos común*) measured 11 inches (27.5 centimeters) long, 4.5 inches (11.25 centimeters) wide, and 1.5 inches (3.75 centimeters) thick; the former were better fired. *Ladrillos* were used as flooring in houses and paving in laundry areas, and were found in other contexts as well. As a ceiling material they were laid straight or in a herringbone pattern across close-set *vigas.* They were thus used in a priest's cell at San Francisco de la Espada, Texas, in 1772 and in the church at San Gabriel, California, in 1808. Chimneys in the California missions often had handsome caps of brick. San Francisco de la Espada had a henhouse and a baking oven made of brick in 1772. A brick lantern was over the crossing of the stone church at San Juan de Capistrano, California (1797–1806), and San Luis Obispo, California, had a dovecote made of brick in 1812. Brick was used to finish the *espadaña* (bell parapet) at San Francisco de la Espada. The only large structure that appears to have been constructed entirely of fired brick was the church of San Buenaventura, California (ca. 1793–1809), although San Antonio de Padua, California, added a brick narthex with a barrel-vaulted roof to the church in 1821, and the adobe tower at San Luis Rey de Francia, California, was faced with brick.

When the California missions began protecting their exposed adobe walls with the addition of porticoes, the pillars were made of fired brick and the roofs of clay tiles. Fired brick was brought to Sonora by the Franciscans in 1768, when they took over that mission field following the Jesuit expulsion. Brick was only rarely used in New Mexico. Another use of brick was to form architectural details of moldings, scrolls, columns, and the like. These were made by breaking standard bricks to the needed sizes, stacking and counterlevering them to conform to the pattern, and finishing the element with thick coats of plaster. Bricks molded to desired architectural shapes, evident at missions San José de Tumacácori and San Xavier del Bac, Arizona, and at La Purísima, California, suggest their wider use, although the evidence is disguised under coats of plaster.

In central Mexico building stones, even for rubble construction, were graded according to their hardness. And stones dressed for use as window lintels or pilasters came in prescribed dimensions.

Door and window openings were framed with wood lintels, sills, and jambs. Doors (solid plank, plain or carved panel, and those set with *rejas* or grills) were made with mortise and tenon. They were hung on wrought-iron hinges or, where metal was scarce, pintles made by carving pegs or extensions at the top and bottom of one stile that fit into sockets made in the threshold and lintel. Hinges were either butterfly-shaped or consisted of two linked eye rings with split shanks that were hammered through the wood and the ends flattened to secure the shank. Exterior doors were provided with iron locks that were usually shipped to the frontier from Mexico.

Windows were frequently provided with wood or wrought-iron *rejas* for protection from unwanted entry and were shuttered on the inside. Door and window openings in thick-walled adobe and stone buildings were in some cases splayed to both the outside and inside for further light enhancement. Glass was a precious commodity. Although the manufacture of glass had been started in Puebla, Mexico, in the sixteenth century, the production never kept pace with the demand; only three furnaces were operating between 1721 and 1800. Into the early nineteenth century most glass used in New Spain was manufactured in Catalonia and Naples. It is therefore not surprising that glass was limited to church windows. The exception to its non-use in vernacular architecture was in Saint Augustine, Florida, where the British introduced glazed sash windows after their capture of the town in 1763. Some substitutes for glass were found, however. Translucent panes of selenite and *rejas* equipped with sheets of mica or talc were used in New Mexico, and oiled parchment in San Antonio, Texas.

Floors of tamped earth were found all across the borderlands. In Texas and New Mexico these were sometimes sealed by applying a coat of animal blood (sometimes mixed with ashes). Compacted earth floors with a coating of burnished lime mortar were archaeologically identified at San Juan Capistrano, Texas, and were used in the church at San Antonio de Padua, California. Adobe bricks were used as paving in the church at Santa Clara, California (1781–1784). Fired brick was being produced at San Francisco de la Espada, Texas, by 1772, and it was used as flooring at San José and Concepción as well. Brick floors were used extensively in California

mission and presidial buildings. The stone church at San Juan de Capistrano, California (1797–1806), sported a floor of diamond-shaped bricks across its transepts and into the sanctuary.

It is likely, too, that flagstone flooring was widely used. It is known from San Buenaventura and Santa Barbara, California (1793), and San Juan de Capistrano and San Francisco de la Espada, Texas, earlier in the century. The church at Santa Barbara (1815–1820) boasted an unusual floor made from oil and lime that took a polish.

Lime was usually produced by burning alternating layers of calcium carbonate and wood in kilns. In coastal settlements of California and Florida, seashells provided the lime. Fossilized oysters were used in the lower Rio Grande settlements of Texas-Coahuila-Nuevo León. Exposed limestone strata provided the raw material elsewhere, except in New Mexico, where gypsum (calcium sulfate) and micaceous clay were substituted. Lime was used for making mortar, plaster, and whitewash. There were various grades of mortar: *la real,* one basket of lime to one of sand; *mescla segunda,* one basket of lime to two of sand; and *mescla fina,* one part lime to one of sifted sand. Mortar for plastering was one basket of sand to one of lime, mixed together and then sifted. *Mescla terciada,* primarily used for foundations, was composed of three boxes of lime, six of sand, and twelve of earth.

Mortar was used to consolidate foundations; lay up brick, adobe, and stone walls; weatherproof walls and roofs; and as a floor finish. In California the adhesive and water-repellant qualities of mortar were said to be enhanced by using water in which chopped opuntia (prickly pear) cactus had been steeped for several days. Lime mortar was not used in New Mexico until the late nineteenth century.

Whitewash provided a finish coat for both exterior and interior walls of even *jacales* and provided a smooth surface for painted decoration. Goat's milk mixed with a little salt improved the surface even more for dry frescoing, according to California sources. Interior rooms often were painted with a brick-red dado, while more elaborate rooms might have a dado of tile patterns in perspective. Standard decorative motifs were architectural elements, lambrequin friezes, floral and acanthus borders, money chains, cherubs, vases of flowers, marbleized pilasters and cornices, and, in the case of mission buildings, the coats of arms of the Franciscan orders.

Exterior walls, too, were embellished with dry fresco work. Floral designs around principal doors and architectural motifs of pilasters with capitals and entablatures decorated structures in the lower Rio Grande Valley of Texas. The entire front facades of San José and Concepción, Texas, were originally painted with tile designs in imitation of the glazed tile used so extensively in Puebla, Mexico. The plain front facade of the adobe church at Santa Clara, California (1821–1825), was elaborately decorated in 1835 by Augustín Dávila with paired columns and entablatures bracketing niches. (This charming church was destroyed by fire in 1926.)

Some interior walls were completely painted with brocade designs, as is documented by several rooms in California missions. Mission San José, California, in 1835 commissioned Augustín Dávila to paint a landscape on its sacristy wall. The spectacularly painted interior of San Xavier del Bac, Arizona, has survived with minimum damage. It includes not only architectural detailing but also "framed pictures" and a false door. The palette was generally limited to yellow and red ochers derived from limonite and hematite, black from charcoal or manganese, and blue from indigo imported from central Mexico. Whitewashing and decorating rooms fell within the province of masons and stonecutters in central Mexico, but others, including "Sunday painters," executed the work in the borderlands.

Fired roof tiles, long used in Mexico, were first employed in Florida on the first completed stone structure—a powder magazine built at Saint Augustine in 1675. However, they appear not to have been used to any extent in Florida. The first tile roofs in California were at San Antonio de Padua in 1776. The clay was tempered with sand and straw. Tiles were formed in molds, turned out to dry in the sun, and finally kiln-fired. Only in California did their use become widespread.

TOWNS AND VERNACULAR ARCHITECTURE

From the earliest period of conquest the Crown took an active enough interest in the quality of the environment for its colonizers that building codes were written into the Ordinances of Discovery by Philip II (1573). Town sites were to be carefully selected according to considerations of defense, the availability of building materials, the climate, and adequate water for the construction of irrigation systems. Spanish settlements were to be laid out following prescribed proportional systems and with the health and safety of the people in mind. For example, plazas were to be "not less than 200 feet [60 meters] wide and 300 feet [90 meters] long, nor larger than 800 feet [240 meters] long and 532 feet [160 meters] wide," a proportion judged "best for fiestas in which horses are used and for any other fiestas that shall be held." Streets were to be wide in cold places and narrow in hot climes, so that the street would be warmed by the sun in the former and shaded in the latter.

Edifices were to have their openings placed to "enjoy the air of the south and north as these are the best." Businesses such as slaughterhouses or fish markets were to be sited to prevent pollution to the town. Settlers were given a town lot upon which to build their house, plus a piece of land on which to cultivate sufficient grain to maintain themselves. Settlers were generally provided with a small stipend for several years, seed for their first crop, the needed agricultural tools, and livestock (cattle, horses, sheep, goats) to build herds.

The Floridas

The oldest Spanish city in the United States is Saint Augustine, Florida, which was founded as a military base in 1565. It had a dramatic history: burned by Sir Francis Drake in 1586, sacked by freebooters in 1668, burned by South Carolinians in 1702, bombarded by the British in 1740, and, beginning in 1763, occupied by the latter for some twenty years before reverting to Spain. When Drake raided Saint Augustine, he found a "village without walls, built of wooden houses." The small, rectangular houses with pitched roofs were laid out in blocks near the bay, south of the original wooden fort. From historical sources and archaeological evidence uncovered at Santa Elena (Port Royal, South Carolina) and Saint Catherines Island, Georgia (founded in 1575), these houses are known to have been *jacales*, either of the wattle-and-daub type utilized by some of the indigenous populations prior to contact, or with vertical cypress board siding and palm thatch roofs. Wall studs were set in clay-filled postholes, wall trenches filled with clay, prepared clay foundations, or thin shell footings. Floors were clay.

From such humble structures evolved a distinctive style of architecture now known as the "Saint Augustine plan," probably basically Spanish with West Indies adaptations, that prevailed until 1763. Made of shellstone, wood, tabby (which became common by 1740), or a combination of these, the houses were one, one and a half, or two stories (two rooms to each floor), their long axis perpendicular to the street and entrance through a loggia facing the side yard. Privacy was afforded by a high fence that was part of the street facade; entry, through a gate into the yard. Roofs were either flat and sealed with tabby, drained with ceramic *canales*, or gabled and covered with thatch or shingles.

The houses were oriented so that the loggias admitted the winter sun and excluded the cold winds, and in summer admitted cooling breezes but kept the sun off the wall. North walls were doubled, providing a six-to-eight-foot (1.8- to 2.4- meter) space for cellars and pantries, and devoid of windows for further warmth. West windows were small, but east windows projected sixteen to eighteen inches (40 to 45 centimeters). Front windows were large and equipped with *rejas* and inside shutters. Street balconies were common. Loggias had built-in benches, and a staircase at the end gave access to the upper floor. Both masonry and wood houses were finished with whitewash. Heating was generally accomplished with braziers, there being few chimneys. The simple *jacal* still served the poorer folk, but even these had windows with *rejas;* a smokehole in the roof aired the interior.

Saint Augustine had its first hospital (a palm-thatched building), a public market, and a town plaza by the end of the sixteenth century. Around 1675 a two-story wooden house on a stone foundation and houses for the treasurer and accountant were built within the confines of the Castillo de San Marcos that was under construction. All had shingle roofs that were "customary in this *presidio*." A new governor's house was being built in stone in 1696. At the turn of the century, it and the mission of Nombre de Dios, north of

the city, were the only stone structures that had been built, aside from the *presidio*. After 1702 better constructed, more substantial structures resulted from an improved economy and security, and the presence of able craftsmen engaged on the construction of the stone fort.

After the British takeover in 1763 chimneys became common, glazed sash windows and outside shutters were introduced, and houses were built or modified with street entries. When the Spaniards regained the city in 1784, the Florida *crillos* and Canary Islanders constituted a minority; the architecture increasingly mirrored the cosmopolitan population of Minorcans, Italians, and Greeks who had come as indentured plantation workers even before the arrival of the British. Tabby went out of favor, and stone houses became more numerous. Common house forms were a single room, a single room with attic and dormer, and two-stories with several rooms. Thatched or shingled roofs might be gable, hip, pyramid, or parapet gable. The royal engineer, Mariano de la Roque, remodeled older houses into customshouses and countinghouses, and designed a magazine and a parish church.

The plan of Roque's 1788 stone church (now the cathedral), which survives in the East Florida Papers in the Library of Congress, shows the edifice prior to its later alterations. It was a hall church with a single tower, a curved parapet facade pierced for a bell, engaged columns bracketing the portal, and a choir window. It is the only borderland church designed by a royal engineer.

New Mexico

The seat of government in New Mexico was moved to Santa Fe, the second oldest Spanish city in the United States, in 1609. The Spanish settlement quickly took on the look of a modified Native pueblo. Late precontact pueblos had consisted of terraced blocks of apartments facing or surrounding open plazas where ceremonies were held and where subterranean or semisubterranean kivas were located. They were built of adobe of rammed earth construction, adobe bricks, or stone in areas where there were outcroppings of ledge stone. Roofs were flat, built up of layers of wood poles, vegetable matter, and mud over large *vigas* (beams). Rooms were as narrow as seven feet (2 meters); available timbers that could span the space from wall to wall determined the limits. For protection there were no openings at ground level, access being via ladders. For warmth, door openings were small with raised thresholds. Dark interiors were sometimes lightened by setting panes of translucent gypsum into the walls.

It has long been held that the Spaniards, accustomed to adobe construction, introduced the manufacture of adobe bricks. However, finds of adobe bricks dating from the Pueblo III period (latter half of the thirteenth century) at Homolovi, Arizona, indicate their use prior to European contact. The Spaniards did put up individual family dwellings, increased the dimensions of doors, built window openings protected by *rejas* and shutters, plastered and whitewashed their walls, and added bell-shaped corner fireplaces, outdoor beehive-shaped bread ovens, and porticoes, thus modifying the indigenous architecture. Larger rooms could be built because metal tools could fell larger trees, and carts and draft animals could haul timbers from greater distances. Thus the size of an Indian room in a pueblo might easily be doubled in a Spaniard's house.

Houses were generally a single room deep. Flat roofs were embellished. *Vigas* were sometimes adzed and carved or painted. Gracefully sawn *zapatas* (corbel brackets) helped distribute the weight of the heavy earthen roof across the *vigas*. Ceilings were made by placing *tablas* (boards), *latias* (small peeled poles), or reeds across the *vigas*. *Tablas* and *latias* were sometimes painted, and the latter might be laid in a herringbone pattern. *Latias* were sometimes called by the wood used—*sabinos* (juniper) or *cedros* (cedar)—and might be split.

In settlements remote from the protection of the presidial garrison at Santa Fe, there was the threat of Indian attack. Small villages were constructed with contiguous houses around a large plaza into which the livestock could be driven. With their windowless exterior walls, these were truly defensive structures. The only example left is the village of Chimayó. Another defensive building was the *torreón,* a round tower, generally two stories high, that served as a lookout and a refuge for besieged settlers.

Haciendas, too, were vulnerable and were constructed with defense in mind. They were built as single or double squares. In the latter, family quarters surrounded the first patio; barns and storerooms surrounded the second; and the two were connected by a passageway. Entry into the first patio was through a *zaguán,* large double doors that could admit a horse-drawn cart. Livestock were protected in the patio. Windowless, flat-topped, contiguous rooms having a defensive parapet pierced with loopholes doubled as ramparts.

Colonists who moved into the mountainous areas above seven thousand feet (2,100 meters) between Santa Fe and Taos adopted an altogether different type of architecture, based largely on log construction. Such construction can be traced southward through the Sierra Madres in the states of Chihuahua and Durango, where the techniques were introduced to Tarahumara and Tepehuan Indians. Just when log construction was introduced is unknown, but the earliest documented example is a gristmill referred to in 1756. The horizontal logs were usually peeled to reduce decay and damage by woodboring insects. They were often trimmed and squared with adz or broadax, and were fitted together with U-shaped saddle notches. Not only were homes thus constructed but barns, storehouses for food and utensils, cribs for small livestock, stables, corrals, and flat-topped corn sheds whose roofs were used for drying. Some examples of log construction are plastered over with adobe and therefore not clearly identifiable.

Texas

Although a mission (San Antonio de Valero) and *presidio* (San Antonio de Bexar) had been established on the San Antonio River in 1718, it did not become a *villa,* a town with its own *cabildo* (government), until 1731, when a group of Canary Islanders arrived to augment the local population. A plan for the town was drawn up by the Mexican geographer Joseph Villaseñor in accordance with the Laws of the Indies: church dominating the square at one short end of a large rectangular plaza, *casas reales* (government buildings) at the other, two blocks on each side of the long axis, and a grid of additional blocks surrounding the core. Despite the good intentions that San Fernando be an orderly town, the Franciscan chronicler Father Juan Augustín Morfi reported in 1777–1778 that its poorly built fifty-nine houses of stone and mud and seventy-nine of wood were situated along muddy, tortuous streets lacking a preconceived plan. The spacious parish church boasted a vaulted roof but was poorly built.

The church had been started in 1738, with the local populace serving as workmen (under penalty of a fine and jail sentence in 1745); there were no trained artisans on the project until 1748, when the master builder-stonemason Gerónimo Ibarra and the stonecutter Felipe de Santiago were hired in San Luis Potosí to finish the structure. The church was dedicated in 1755.

Judging from San Antonio houses depicted by European artists in the early nineteenth century, Morfi's "wood" houses were *jacales* of the wattle-and-daub type with thatched roofs. They were a constant fire hazard, so attempts were made to prohibit using tule or straw as thatching. In 1810 the governor complained that the citizens were still building with wood and thatch, "not only for kitchens, but living quarters as well." An ordinance dated 1831 again prohibited the use of tule or straw for roofing on *jacales* under penalty of up to fifty pesos, or up to fifteen days' arrest, or labor on public works if unable to pay.

From 1790 through 1793 the entire populace appears to have been engaged in the construction of new *casas reales*. Although the master masons Juan Mendes and Antonio Aguilar and the carpenters Pedro Huizar and Antonio Conar were paid wages for overseeing the work, most citizens put in from four to twelve days of labor as peons. More prominent citizens transported up to thirty-six cartloads of construction materials, some donated. The blacksmith José Francisco Pobedano donated the locks, hinges, and nails.

More substantial houses were built as more trained artisans were drawn to Texas. Some of the finer examples survived in the lower Rio Grande Valley until most were inundated by waters of the Falcón Reservoir in 1953. Many were handsome structures with gabled and thatched roofs (later shingled)—some with parapeted end walls, and massive stone fireplaces with chimneys and fireboxes protruding from an end wall. The geometrically commensurable proportions of floor plans and door openings, and the craftsmanship of both masonry and carpentry, reveal the presence of skilled artisans.

Vigas were sometimes squared and used with *zapatas* and *tablas* or *latias*. Interiors might have banquettes and shelves set on wood or stone brackets, or niches set into the walls. Another distinctive feature was bollasters, semicircular reinforcements on the corners of houses which may have protected the quoins from gouging by axle hubs of carts. Lime kilns, built into arroyo banks, produced the raw materials for mortar and plaster. One-room dwellings were expanded by adding a room on the long axis or a lean-to of stone, wood planks, or wattle and daub.

The houses described, typical of town and ranch alike, had flammable roofs that hostile Apache easily set ablaze. Although a few haciendas had outer defensive walls, most were composed of randomly placed buildings with no connecting walls for protection. There is mention in 1813 of a circular stone *torreón* like those reported in New Mexico, but the more typical local solution was a fortified, windowless stone structure with a flat roof and defensive parapet, often placed on high ground to serve as a lookout. The roof was made fire-resistant with a coating of *tipichil*, lime concrete with small gravel aggregate. The parapet and loopholes set into the walls provided protected defense positions for the besieged.

Nothing is known of the eighteenth-century ranch buildings other than the living quarters. However, a few *horcón* shelters with grass-thatched rooms, some enclosed or semienclosed with *palisado* or adobe walls, observed by the author on back roads of the northern Mexican states stretching from Nuevo León-Tamaulipas through Sonora, provide a clue to the probable type.

California

Settlements in California were all missions and *presidios* until the establishment of the *villas* of San Jose in 1777, Los Angeles in 1781, and Branciforte in 1797. Colonists for each were recruited in central Mexico by offering the usual inducements of land, seed, livestock, tools, and stipend. Once established, they were expected to reimburse the treasury through delivered grain. The settlers were responsible for the construction of their own houses (originally *palisados*) and community buildings. Citizens were not always willing to donate their time to the public good, and some in San Jose were imprisoned and put in irons for refusing to work on the town council house. When the residents of that town began construction of their own church in 1802, the cost was borne by the townsmen, who pledged half a *fanega* (1 *fanega* equals approximately 1.5 bushels) of grain apiece.

By the end of 1790 the Angeleños had replaced their temporary *palisados* with adobe houses, erected public buildings, and enclosed the town. In 1814 the master builder José Antonio Ramírez was engaged to build a church for the town, but lack of funds delayed its completion until 1822. Because of the poverty of the Angeleños, the southern missions contributed heavily by donating barrels of wine and brandy; cattle to be sold in Los Angeles to pay for materials and Indian carpenters; and masons, sawyers, and peons, who earned one real and board per day.

When it came time to found Branciforte, the Plan of Pitic had been in force throughout the Provincias Internas since 1789. According to the plan, no new pueblo was to be established within five leagues of any other settlement. A new community was to encompass a tract of four square leagues in the form of a square or rectangle (to the extent the topography would allow), and its boundaries were to be fixed and marked. The town plat was to be arranged symmetrically on a grid, with commons and communal pasturage and irrigated fields surrounding the core. The administration would be handled by a *comisionado,* the governor's representative, until the population reached thirty heads of households, at which point an *ayuntamiento,* or *cabildo,* would take over.

It was the wish of Viceroy Miguel de la Grúa Talamanca y Braciforte that the new *villa* named for him be a "proper town" with permanent buildings, not another "squalid community like Los Angeles or San José." Therefore he entrusted the military engineer Alberto de Córdoba, sent to bolster California's coastal defenses in 1797, with the task of laying out the new town. Córdoba was to draw plats and plans for fields, irrigation works, and buildings; gather building materials; construct temporary houses; assure a water supply; construct a bridge between the town and mission Santa Cruz; and build a water mill and lime kilns. But instead of the exemplary colonists expected, who were to include all categories of craftsmen, those who arrived were mostly impoverished, unskilled,

syphilitic outcasts and petty criminals. Branciforte never lived up to its glorious expectations.

MILLS

Apart from presses for crushing grapes or extracting olive oil found only in California, the most visible evidence of industrial architecture was mills. The Hispanic water-powered gristmill was of the Norse type, with a horizontal wheel with straight paddles. The type was used from Texas to California, and probably in Florida as well. Two Norse mills were built in San Antonio, Texas: mission San Jose built one in 1730–1731; the *villa* of San Fernando, in 1733. The housing of both was constructed of stone and mortar. The earliest reference to a water-powered gristmill in New Mexico was to one owned by Vicar Roybal in 1756. Santa Fe had three mills operating in 1776; others were located in Chimayó, Pojoaque, and Ojo Caliente. All were in log housing. The first to be built in California were constructed by the master carpenter and millwright Cayetano López, who in 1792 signed a four-year contract to teach his trade. He built mills at Santa Clara and San Luis Obispo, and perhaps at other localities. All California mills were housed in stone and mortar buildings.

The vertical New England type of mill, with both overshot and undershot wheels, was introduced into California by the Bostonian shipwright José Juan Chapman. He constructed a fulling mill at Santa Inés in 1821, flour and saw mills at San Gabriel from 1823 to 1825, and perhaps at Santa Barbara and La Purísima as well. All were housed in stone buildings. From 1822 to 1823 workers at La Purísima began constructing the only windmill in Hispanic California. The mission had a contract with Ferencio Ruíz to undertake its construction. Ruíz may have been the mason who put up the four stone pillars to support the elevated housing, while it was the intention to have Chapman build the mill itself. The structure, possibly never completed, was to operate as a fulling mill.

PRESIDIOS

Presidios changed very little over the course of time across the Hispanic United States. They were square or rectangular, with bastions on one, two (capable of covering two curtains anyway), or four corners. Within the enclosure were guard room and jail, usually adjacent to the entrance; chapel and priest's house; officers' quarters; barracks for the troop; kitchen and storerooms; carpenter's shop and smithy. When located at the seat of government, such as Monterey, Santa Fe, San Antonio, and Saint Augustine, the governor's house and official offices were incorporated. *Presidios* in coastal areas were reinforced with batteries, sentry boxes, and casemates to protect bay entrances. Building materials were usually adobes and *palisados* that required constant repairs and rebuilding. Within a few years of construction most were in ruinous condition.

The only permanent *presidio* within the United States was built at Saint Augustine to replace the earlier wooden fort. Construction of the stone Castillo de San Marcos became possible when coquina quarries were opened on Anastasia Island, and kilns were built on the mainland to produce the lime needed for mortar. The military engineer Ignacio Daza, masons, and lime burners were brought from Havana in late 1671, and the first stone was laid 9 November 1672. During the twenty-three years of its construction, it relied heavily upon local paid Indian laborers, some of whom were trained stonecutters and carpenters. Spanish peons and convict labor (either local or from Caribbean ports), and English prisoners, trained as masons and carpenters, also worked on the fort. Daza died within seven months of his arrival and was replaced by Lorenzo Lajones as master of construction. Spanish masons, stonecutters, and carpenters oversaw the work within their specialties. A new engineer, Juan de Céscara, was brought from Havana in 1681, and the fort was finished in 1695.

The activity of English settlers in Georgia prompted some improvements to be designed by the engineer Antonio de Arredondo; the engineer Pedro Ruiz de Olano from Venezuela and a new crew of artisans began work in 1738. The master of construction Blas de Ortega from Havana replaced a man named Castillo. A masonry tower and battery were added in 1742 at Matanzas Inlet, to guard the "back door" of the fort.

MISSIONS

Missions were established in Indian settlements or, in the case of nomadic tribes, in locations central to numerous bands. Invariably the first structures to be erected were a chapel and a house for the priest, followed by kitchen, storerooms, and barracks for the military escort, all enclosed within the protective walls of a stockade. As mission populations grew, so did the complexes that ministered to their spiritual and physical needs, and taught them skills needed to make the transition to a white-dominated society. The simple house for the priest expanded into a friary (*convento*)—generally a square surrounding a private patio containing rooms for the priests, kitchen, refectory, offices, storerooms, and sometimes guest rooms and/or hospital. Within an adjacent quadrangle might be weaving and carpentry shops; the smithy, tannery vats, and mills were isolated.

Houses for hired *criollo* servants and families of the military escort were usually set apart. Provisions were made for livestock: corrals, henhouses, dovecotes, and lambing pens. Kilns for making lime or firing brick and tile were built outside mission walls as well. Irrigation ditches, and sometimes dams and aqueducts, were built to bring water to the missions as well as to water fields under cultivation. Vineyards and gardens were protected by walled enclosures.

The Floridas

Although no Spanish mission structures survived the onslaught of periodic fires, hurricanes, and British destruction of the entire mission system in 1704, the typical plan of those founded in Las Floridas is depicted on a surviving 1691 plan of Santa Catalina on the island of Santa María (Amelia Island, Florida). It appears to be almost identical to the archaeologically excavated one of Santa Catalina de Guale (Saint Catherines Island, Georgia) that dates to the previous century. A nine-foot-high (3-meter) rectangular stockade with loopholes and bastions on four corners was protected by a moat. Within the compound were the church on one side, separate priests' house and kitchen opposite, with a plaza between, and a house for the garrison behind the church. Indian houses were outside the compound. The buildings were of wattle and daub, a framework with vertical board siding, or a combination of both. Excavations at other mission sites reveal the same construction techniques that were described under vernacular architecture. The churches had single naves with the sanctuaries elevated and reduced in width. The first mission church erected of stone was that of Nombre de Dios, north of Saint Augustine, built in the 1790s.

New Mexico

Missions in New Mexico were established within existing, densely populated towns, the inhabitants of which were known as Pueblo, or town dwellers. The churches and friaries were simply added to the settlements. Churches built prior to the 1680 rebellion of the Pueblo were similar to the fortress type typical of central Mexico, but with some important differences. The massive high walls were built of fieldstone or adobe set in adobe mortar that tapered toward the top. Foundations were nonexistent or primitive, consisting of adobe, stone slabs, or fieldstone set in trenches no wider than the walls. With the exception of Abó, which dates from about 1646, walls were unbuttressed, the mass of the walls alone counteracting the thrust and weight of the built-up flat roofs. Only Pecos incorporated a true arch, and there were no domes. Taking the place of a dome, however, was a transverse clerestory of selenite placed perpendicular to the long axis between the nave and sanctuary; this was made possible by raising the height of the latter above that of the former.

The churches were single-naved, with or without transepts, and with narrowed and elevated sanctuaries that might be rectangular, trapezoidal, or, more unusually, apsidal. Available roofing timbers dictated the width, which rarely exceeded thirty-three or thirty-four feet (10 meters). Windows were few and small, and except for the front choir window, were generally high on one lateral wall. Window openings were splayed to the outside, inside, or both. Except for the stone churches in the Salinas district, where flagstone pavers were used, floors were compacted earth or adobe clay. Access to the choir, typically over the main entrance, was more often by a straight exterior staircase, less frequently by a *caracol* (circular stair set in a tower). Since New Mexico's early churches were built within existing pueblos, they were not necessarily centrally located among the building units but might sit peripherally or be contiguous to a preexisting block.

Post-rebellion churches were all adobe, with the exception of the now-destroyed eighteenth century church of Nuestra Señora de la Luz (Cas-

trense) in Santa Fe. Facades took several forms: a plain end wall with a simple door and choir loft window; flanking towers or truncated buttresses; an ornamental parapet, often terraced, with bell arches; or a balcony set between projecting towers. It has been suggested that the balconied facades served the same function as the open chapel in central Mexico: a place from which the missionary could preach to a multitude too large to be accommodated within.

Texas

Early mission construction in Texas was typified by *jacales,* sometimes protected by stockades. By the mid eighteenth century a modicum of stability had been achieved, and it was time to replace temporary buildings with permanent ones. For the construction of stone churches trained artificers were needed, and the priests contracted with masters of masonry and stonecutting, carpenters, and smiths available in older provinces of Mexico. All five of the missions in San Antonio had stone churches. One was started at San Antonio de Valero in 1744, but for various reasons, construction was delayed from time to time. It was still incomplete in 1785. Over the years a procession of artisans worked on it for varying periods of time: master mason Antonio de Tello from Zacatecas (1741–1744); master mason Gerónimo Ybarra from San Luis Potosí (1755); master of the church project and master mason Estevan del Oio (or Losoya) from Aguascalientes (1766–1767); and master of the works Domingo González (1767).

Laborers at Nuestra Señora de la Purísima Concepción started construction on a stone church about 1740 and dedicated it in 1755. It is said to be the oldest unrestored church in the Southwest and the oldest stone church in the United States. The *maestro* who planned this masterpiece of geometric design is unknown, but two artisans who worked on it were Nicolás, a Tilpacopal neophyte who was recognized as a *maestro* in the 1760s and master stonecutter Felipe de Santiago of San Luis Potosí in 1755. In plan the missions of San Antonio and Concepción are similar: cruciform, twin towers (planned for the former), barrel-vaulted ceilings, domed crossings, and friary attached to one side. The facades are dissimilar, but both exhibit skillful carving in bas-relief.

The cornerstone of San José y San Miguel de Aguayo was laid 19 May 1768, and the church was nearing completion in 1777. The master mason Antonio Salazar from Zacatecas appears to have been the architect; Pedro Huizar, who had moved to San Antonio from Aguascalientes in the 1770s, was probably the carpenter. This beautiful baroque temple with its elegantly carved frontispiece has several unusual features. It is a hall church but has a dome. The roof is barrel-vaulted with lunettes set into the bays preceding and succeeding the one with the dome. The attached sacristy has a roof of three domical vaults. And the attached friary shares a common axis with the church rather than being to one side.

The churches of San Juan de Capistrano and San Francisco de la Espada were not intended as the permanent churches planned during the zenith of mission development. At the former, a stone church with a hexagonal sacristy and a single bell tower sits as an unfinished reminder of a dream never realized. Another building was enlarged and embellished with an *espadaña* (bell-wall) to serve as the late colonial church. Work on the grand church planned at San Francisco ceased in 1762 for lack of good building stone. A portal of faceted stone that had been cut for the new church was finally incorporated into a smaller structure that served as the church. The entry is the only Mudéjar horseshoe-shaped arch found in the northern borderlands.

The San Antonio missions were all built with defensive walls, and permanent Indian houses were incorporated within, forming portions of the ramparts. At San Antonio de Valero the church stood outside the enclosure but was attached to the *convento*, which in turn was connected to a second courtyard surrounded by the craftsmen's shops. The Indian dwellings were built into the walls of a long quadrangle that abutted the two courtyards. The churches at Concepción and San Jose were more or less centrally located within their compounds. The back sanctuary wall of San Francisco formed part of the rampart. In other words, the nave was perpendicular to the rampart. San Juan's long axis actually formed part of the defensive wall rather than being perpendicular to it, and its entry was placed on that axis. This arrangement is known

for only one other mission of the northern borderlands: Tubutama in Sonora.

California

The colonization of California was not undertaken until 1769, some fifty years after the first mission was planted on the San Antonio River in Texas and more than two hundred after Saint Augustine's founding. The rich natural resources of land and sea sustained a large Native population of hunters and gatherers who, like the nomadic peoples of Texas, lived in scattered settlements called *rancherías*. To effect their conversion to Christianity and the European way of life, Indians were relocated into mission complexes known as *congregaciones* or *reducciones*. In comparison with the missions of Texas, those of California were enormous. Furthermore, settlement of the province was in response to suspected Russian and English attempts to establish outposts on the Pacific Coast, to which Spain laid claim. The Spanish met the threat by establishing the Naval Department of San Blas in the state of Nayarit, not only as a shipyard to build the vessels with which to supply the new colonies but also to protect Spain's claims to the Pacific Coast and to safeguard the Manila trade route.

In fifty-four years four *presidios*, twenty-one missions, and three towns were founded. The missions not only produced the grain and cattle to feed the Spanish populace but also developed industries far beyond what had been attempted in other mission fields. This was possible through the sizable Indian labor force and the government's active recruitment of master artisans—carpenters, masons and stonecutters, blacksmiths, tailors, saddlemakers, tanners and cobblers, millwrights, weavers, potters and tilemakers, and even a lacemaker—who signed contracts, generally for two to four years to teach their trades to neophytes. The missions, therefore, reflected these and other activities, such as the making of wine and brandy, soap, and candles, through buildings erected for those specialties. They also developed sophisticated water systems that irrigated the fields, ran grist and fulling mills, brought water into the missions themselves, and fed fountains and brick-lined laundry areas.

The careers of over two hundred fifty trained artisans associated with the building trades in California prior to the beginning of the Anglo period in 1848 have been traced, making it possible to determine the professionals involved in many building phases of missions, *presidios*, and towns. Of special interest are those who were responsible for the mission churches. Today we think in terms of a "California mission style" of architecture: whitewashed adobe buildings with rather plain facades, red tile roofs, and parapet walls pierced with bell arches. Actually there was considerable diversity, and today's impression of a "typical" California style derives from "improvements" made after 1848 and churches rebuilt of whole cloth in the twentieth century. Part of the diversity of the originals emanated from the remarkable craftsmanship of the men involved.

Because stonecutters and masons were few in the province, only a handful of stone churches were constructed: San Carlos Borromeo, the presidial chapel at Monterey, San Gabriel, San Juan de Capistrano, and Santa Barbara. And these are all quite different. The baroque church of San Carlos (1793–1797) is unique with its asymmetrical yet geometrically commensurable facade, its star window over the portal, and its soaring plank-vaulted ceiling over stone parabolic arches. It was designed, and the work was directed, by the master stonecutter and mason Manuel Estevan Ruíz of Guadalajara with the help of his journeymen Joaquín Rivera and, later, Pedro Alcántara Ruíz. The carpentry work was under the supervision of master José Antonio Ramírez, a native of Zapotlán el Grande, Jalisco.

Master Ruíz also designed (with some modifications of the upper registers by Antonio González Velásquez, director of architecture at the Academy of San Carlos, Mexico City) and began work on the presidial chapel at Monterey (1791–1794). Its facade was based upon more classical lines of paired columns bracketing niches. In 1792 the day-to-day work was taken over by the master mason and stonecutter Santiago Ruíz and his journeyman, Manuel Doroteo Ruíz. Master carpenters who were engaged on its construction were probably Manuel Rodríguez and Leocadio Martínez. Master smith José Santos Ulloa is known to have been making, repairing, and sharpening tools for the workmen engaged on the chapel in 1791. Master Gregorio Segura was

at Monterey during the period of construction and surely was involved in it.

San Gabriel's church, under construction from 1794 to 1801, hearkened back to the fortress churches of sixteenth-century Mexico with its high walls emphasized with capped buttresses, long narrow windows, and vaulted roof. The original portal, at the end of the long axis, and the *espadaña* to the side of it, were severely damaged in the earthquake of 1812. Fifteen years later the *espadaña* was rebuilt at the other end of the church's axis and in alignment with it, elongating the building considerably. Several artisans can be linked to the initial church construction. The architect was probably Miguel Blanco, an Indian master mason from Baja, California. The journeyman mason and stonecutter Toribio Ruíz arrived to help during the first year. The master carpenter Salvador Carabantes probably framed and outfitted the doors and windows. Master Santiago Moreno was the blacksmith on the job.

The missionaries at San Juan de Capistrano aspired to build "the most important and pretentious" church in the province in 1797. Plans for the edifice were sent from Mexico, and a mason from Culiacán, Sinaloa, master Isidro Aguilar, was contracted to build it. The stone church was cruciform in plan with a domical-vaulted ceiling supported by elegant arches, a baptistery and single bell tower, a fired-brick lantern over the crossing, and diamond-shaped brick flooring. Aguilar died in 1803, and the masonry work may have been taken over by Basilio Rosas, an original Indian colonist and mason of Los Angeles. The carpenter on the job was the master José Antonio Ramírez. The church, finished in 1806, was destroyed by the great 1812 earthquake; forty neophytes attending Mass were buried under tons of stone and mortar.

José Antonio Ramírez was the architect of two missions built later: San Luis Rey de Francia (1811–1815) and Santa Barbara (1815–1820). Santa Barbara is unique in being the only church on the northern frontier built in the neoclassic style that had been espoused for some time in central Mexico. The design is clearly derived from a Greek prostyle-tetrastyle temple depicted in a 1787 Spanish edition of Vitruvius's *Ten Books of Architecture* found in the mission library. Ramírez altered the Greek temple by geometrically widening the pagan temple to accommodate twin towers (the second was not built until 1831), geometrically reducing the temple to form the frontispiece and adding two more columns. The statues of Faith, Hope, and Charity atop the acroteria and that of Santa Barbara set in a niche in the pediment were the work of a Ventureño Chumash Indian named Paciano. The Portuguese carpenter Antonio José Rocha doubtless had a hand in the construction during his stay there.

Before leaving California churches, one other example will illustrate the involvement of ship's carpenters from the arsenal at San Blas. Santa Cruz's first permanent adobe church, built in 1792–1794 and completely destroyed in the nineteenth century, was constructed entirely under the direction of ten men from the arsenal. First and second carpenters and first and second caulkers (also carpenters) from at least two ships were involved at different periods. San Blas had also sent the master mason and stonecutter José María López to lay the foundations, direct the work, and carve the stone portal for the facade. López was one of a team of masons and stonecutters brought from Guadalajara to San Blas to erect the stone church and various buildings of the town and arsenal in the 1780s. When the dedication of the Santa Cruz temple was entered into the Book of Baptisms, among the signatories were López; the carpenter Ignacio Chumacero, who had been there the year before; and the *maestro mayor de carpinteros* at the shipyard, Francisco Gómez. Ships' personnel had commonly been involved in construction efforts in missions and presidios in California, but the example of Santa Cruz stands out because of the sheer numbers of highly skilled artisans employed on a single building.

Arizona

During the period when many of California's permanent mission churches were being erected, friars at the missions of the province of Sonora, which included Arizona, were busily improving their churches. One of the borderlands' finest examples is that of San Xavier del Bac, started in the late 1770s to early 1780s and finished in 1797. The baroque exterior has a handsome frontispiece with three registers, the lower ones featuring engaged *estipite* columns bracketing

niches, a choir window-door with balcony, and heavy stepped towers (one missing its cupola and lantern). It is constructed of double fired-brick walls set with lime mortar and filled with rubble. The cruciform interior is topped with domical vaults and an octagonal dome. The frescoed interior and numerous images can best be described as "exuberant baroque" or rococo with a definite folk quality. The church was the inspiration of master mason Ygnacio Gaona, who went on to build a near-twin of it at Caborca, Sonora, from about 1805 to 1809.

The only other extant mission church in Arizona, albeit an unfinished one, is the adobe edifice of San José de Tumacácori that was being rebuilt in the early nineteenth century. A strange structure with a bell tower as wide as the frontispiece, it boasts the use of formed, fired bricks on cornices, cap courses, and other finishing details.

MISSION CHURCHES AND VERNACULAR STRUCTURES: A FINAL STATEMENT

Limitations on the length of this essay have prevented reporting on every Spanish church in the United States. Such an inventory would not add substantially to our knowledge. I have selected examples that show the range in style and building materials or that illustrate the origins of their builders. An important point to keep in mind is that all extant structures were built by the Franciscans, even though Jesuits founded the missions of northern Sonora and some of those in the Floridas. Obviously there is no "Franciscan style." The form a permanent church assumed depended upon its architect—either a master mason or a master carpenter, depending upon the basic material used, his particular level of skill and imagination, and ideas of style derived from the preferences of the priests or from Renaissance pattern books which were part of the tool kit of every artisan and were often found in mission libraries. The baroque style into which most border examples would fall (New Mexico excepted) lagged behind contemporary structures in more central areas of Mexico, where the trend was to neoclassicism.

Although there are very rare instances of builder-priests (excepting temporary structures, I know of only two who designed permanent churches), design and construction were almost exclusively in the hands of masters trained in their respective guilds through years of apprenticeship and licensed by the *cabildos* of their home towns. Some artisans, including hundreds of Indians, received their training on the frontier, and San Fernando de Béxar (San Antonio, Texas) had a recognized guild structure as late as 1809. It may have been unique, although elsewhere there is evidence of at least an extralegal system of apprentice-journeyman-master hierarchy.

Only the province of New Mexico evolved a regional style of church architecture based upon adobe structures with massive walls and flat roofs. Other border regions also built adobe churches with flat roofs, but went beyond that phase to build more individual structures while New Mexico became locked into a standard formula. We must assume that the relative isolation of the territory, the innate conservatism of its Hispanic population, and the similar structural properties of puebloan Indian architecture were deciding factors.

The vernacular architecture reflects more regionalism than does the ecclesiastical. The Caribbean and English influences on Florida styles produced house forms far different from those built in the lower Rio Grande Valley of Texas, which were probably derived from prototypes found in interior provinces from which colonists were drawn. New Mexican houses were smaller adaptations of monumental buildings and have survived as the "Santa Fe style." New Mexican colonists also introduced unique log construction in their mountain communities. California houses evolved into the whitewashed adobes with red tile roofs and porticoes adapted from mission buildings to become the popular "California mission style" so widely copied across the United States.

BIBLIOGRAPHY

Arana, Luis Rafael, and Albert Manucy. *The Building of Castillo de San Marcos.* Saint Augustine, Fla., 1977.

Benavides, Adán, Jr. "Building a Church in 18th Century Texas: Notes on the San Fernando Parish Church." Unpublished MS, 1991.

Bunting, Bainbridge. *Early Architecture in New Mexico.* Albuquerque, N.Mex., 1976.

———. *Taos Adobes: Spanish Colonial and Territorial Architecture of the Taos Valley.* Santa Fe, N.Mex., 1964; repr. Albuquerque, N.Mex., 1992.

George, Eugene. *Historic Architecture of Texas: The Falcón Reservoir.* Austin, Tex., 1975.

Gerald, Rex E. *Spanish Presidios of the Late Eighteenth Century in Northern New Spain.* Santa Fe, N.Mex., 1968.

Gritzner, Charles F. "Hispanic Log Construction of New Mexico." *El Palacio* 85 (Winter 1979–1980):20–29.

———. "Hispano Gristmills in New Mexico." *Annals of the Association of American Geographers* 64 (December 1974):514–524.

Kubler, George. *The Religious Architecture of New Mexico in the Colonial Period and Since the American Occupation.* Colorado Springs, Colo., 1940; 4th ed. titled *The Religious Architecture of New Mexico.* Albuquerque, N.Mex., 1972.

Manucy, Albert C. *The Houses of St. Augustine: Notes on the Architecture from 1565 to 1821.* Saint Augustine, Fla., 1962.

Neuerburg, Norman. *The Decoration of the California Missions.* Santa Barbara, Calif., 1987.

Romero de Terreros y Vinent, Manuel. *Las artes industriales en la Nueva España.* Mexico City, 1923.

Saunders, Rebecca. "Ideal and Innovation: Spanish Mission Architecture in the Southeast." In *Columbian Consequences,* edited by David Hurst Thomas. Washington, D.C., 1991.

Schuetz, Mardith K. *Architectural Practice in Mexico City: A Manual for Journeymen Architects of the Eighteenth Century.* Tucson, Ariz., 1987.

———. "Professional Artisans in the Hispanic Southwest." *The Americas* 40, no. 1 (July 1983):17–71.

Thomas, David Hurst. *The Archaeology of Mission Santa Catalina de Guale. 1. Search and Discovery.* Anthropological Papers of the American Museum of Natural History 63, pt. 2. New York, 1987.

Toussaint, Manuel. *Colonial Art in Mexico.* Translated and edited by Elizabeth Wilder Weismann. Austin, Tex., 1967.

Webb, Edith Buckland. *Indian Life at the Old Missions.* Los Angeles, 1952; repr. Lincoln, Nebr., 1983.

Mardith K. Schuetz-Miller

SEE ALSO **Artisans; Crafts; Home and Hearth; Rural Life;** and **Urban Life.**

PAINTING AND SCULPTURE

THE BRITISH COLONIES

ART AND EXPLORATION

WESTERN ART FORMS came to North America with the earliest explorers, intent upon charting in maps, drawings, and watercolors the inhabitants, flora, and fauna of the new land. Some of the European exploring parties included trained artists. In the sixteenth-century Jacques le Moyne des Morgues accompanied a Huguenot settlement to Florida, and his drawings, engraved and published by the Flemish engraver Theodore de Bry, provided a major source of information about the New World. John White came to Roanoke, Virginia, in 1585 with Walter Raleigh's first colony and returned as governor in 1587 and again in 1590. White's album of sixty-five watercolor drawings, engraved by de Bry and published in White's *True Report of Voyages* (1590), depicts aspects of Native life such as Indian dwellings and ceremonial dances, together with portraits of natives and studies of New World flowers, birds, fish, and animals.

Throughout the eighteenth century other artist-explorers followed. One of the more prominent was the naturalist Mark Catesby who arrived in Virginia in 1712 and, attracted by the region's exotic plants, animals, and birds, re-turned ten years later to illustrate these in his 1731 publication *The Natural History of Carolina, Florida, and the Bahama Islands*.

THE SEVENTEENTH CENTURY

Professional artists did not come to the New World until the latter half of the seventeenth century, after societies had been established, towns formed, and practical necessities met. The most popular kind of art was the portrait print; the first formal paintings were also portraits, while carved gravestones expressed three-dimensionally or in relief the fears and hopes of the new Americans.

Because it represented the kind of art with which most well-placed Englishmen were acquainted, the portrait became the major art form in the New World. From medieval times to the Puritan Rebellion and the civil war in 1641, English religious reformers had waged an iconoclastic campaign resulting in almost total destruction of all religious images and paintings. The portrait survived this anti-art fever primarily because it was an inexpensive and small-scale form that met political, familial, and social needs. It was believed that portraits of public figures enhanced national prestige, demonstrated the authority of leaders, and provided examples of virtue, thus contributing to public morality. In 1595 Sir Philip Sidney defined the portrait's public function in his *A Defence of Poetry:* "For as the Image of each Action stirreth and instructeth the minde, so the loftie image of such woorthies must enflameth the minde with desire to bee worthie." Such portraits also served as a *memento mori;* with the introduction of a death's head, they were expected to counter undue pride in achievement and remind viewers of the transitory nature of possessions and power. Private portraits that expressed family pride and social status suggest how important family connections were for middle- and upper-class Englishmen.

The first artists who came to the British colonies were Englishmen, who brought with them English styles and tastes. Although anonymous for the most part, these early limners were not untrained "naive" painters but artists who had received some studio training and who arrived in America skilled in the "mysteries" of their craft. Of the British colonies visited, New England was the most popular region, although, occasionally, the arrival of painters or painting supplies was noted in Virginia. In 1679, for example, a Thomas Powell received five hundred pounds of tobacco for "draweing the Cherubim" for a church at Poplar Springs. Southern gentlemen who enjoyed close commercial ties with England usually had their portraits painted in London, and generally pictures that hung in southern homes during the seventeenth century were of English origin.

It is perhaps ironic that New England, the colony that entertained the most severe strictures against the frivolous or ornamental, became the most hospitable to the arts during the colonial period. Middle class for the most part, with a strong interest in history and a religious concern for the family, mid-seventeenth-century New England settlers enjoyed a prosperity and stability that encouraged portraitists, print makers, and decorative painters. Economic expansion invited new immigrants, especially after the Restoration in 1660, when Protestant dissenters fled to America to escape the exactions of Catholic Charles II's court. It is from this time onward that documents note the presence of artists in the New World.

Prints

Middle-class English colonists were well acquainted with prints, especially portrait prints. Sold by street peddlers in English towns and ports and inserted in books as frontispieces or illustrations, such inexpensive prints featured "heads," maps, and topographical views. In 1622, advising readers of his *The Compleat Gentleman* how to judge character, Henry Peacham suggested that they be guided by portrait prints "cut to the life": "Their pieces will best instruct you in the countenance, for the naturall shadowes thereof, the cast and forme of the eye, the touch of the mouth, the true fall, turning and curling of the hair, for ruffes, Armor, &c." By the early seventeenth century, Englishmen—and by extension, those transplanted to America—could choose from many portrait prints, mostly of famous individuals and occasionally by such prominent artists as Raphael, Rubens, or Van Dyke. Issued singly, the prints were framed and hung in parlors, hallways, and along staircases. Seventeenth-century inventories list, along with linens, kitchen equipment, and clothing, "pictures"—occasionally in such numbers that it must be surmised that they were small engravings or mezzotints rather than larger oil paintings.

One of these may have been a woodcut of the Reverend Richard Mather done around 1670 by John Foster, Boston engraver and book publisher, who made an almost exact transcription of an oil portrait of Mather (by either Foster himself or Augustine Clement). Foster's woodcut is the earliest known and the only extant portrait print executed in America. Its ministerial subject, simplicity, and absence of ornament or elaborate background suggests the didactic function accorded to portrait prints that were intended to memorialize individuals of character and achievement and remind the community of their place in its history.

Painting

As far as we know, artists who came to the colonies during the seventeenth century were British. Joseph Allen, for instance, an ironmonger's apprentice, arrived in Boston around 1684 bearing a letter of recommendation to Increase Mather from Increase's brother Nathaniel in Dublin. A brooding portrait of Increase Mather has been attributed to him. Some painters who did decorative or funerary work were also present in the colonies, such as the self-styled "painter-stainer"

Tom Child, about whose death in 1706 Samuel Sewall wrote:

Tom Child had often painted Death,
But never to the Life, before:
Doing it now, he's out of Breath;
He paints it once, and paints no more.

(*Diary*, vol. 1, p. 554)

A few artists stand out for the quality of their work. Augustine Clement came to Boston in June 1635 from the important provincial artistic center of Reading, England, and remained there for the rest of his life. Attributed to him are portraits of the revered minister Richard Mather; of Dr. John Clark, the first physician in America to perform the operation of trepanning the skull; and of the uncompromising Puritan John Endicott, first governor of the Massachusetts Bay colony. Since these portraits memorialized civilian heroes, the artist gave prominence to the head and to such iconographical details as book, skull, surgical instruments, and gloves—emblems of occupation and status.

Seven portraits of children and their parents by an unknown artist or artists, painted between 1670 and 1674, express the New England Puritan's pride in family and the desire to retain likenesses of family members in the face of the uncertainty of life in the seventeenth-century wilderness. *John Freake* and *Mrs. Freake with Baby Mary*, are probably the most well known of the paintings surviving from the seventeenth century, and certainly the best manifestations of the Elizabethan painting tradition in New England art. Characterized by flat lighting and linear ornamentation emphasizing pattern, elaborate dress, and inscrutability of features, the Elizabethan style at its best was nonrepresentational and purely decorative. According to Jonathan Fairbanks in *New England Begins*, the style evolved from sixteenth-century Italian mannerism as defined in the writings of Giovanni Paolo Lomazzo and adapted by such English aestheticians as Richard Haydocke and John Bate and the artist Nicholas Hilliard. In his use of full frontal pose in bright light, the careful articulation of details of costume, concentration on design, conformity to the mannerist perspective system, and skillful use of strong color, the Freake artist clearly demonstrates his studio training in the English provinces, where rules for painting as well as scientific ideas about light and color were available.

Similar in design and style are the portraits of the Gibbs and Mason children, probably from the same hand as the Freake paintings. Descended from English gentry, the Gibbs children were the offspring of a successful New England merchant. In their portraits, Robert, Henry, and Margaret Gibbs wear expensive clothing appropriate for members of their class and carry symbols of their gender, age, and position. Henry holds a bird, a soul image found in many Elizabethan portraits of young children; Margaret's fan marks her as an upper-class lady; while Robert's gloves and hand-on-hip pose indicate his status as a gentleman and heir to a fortune. Like the Freake portraits, the paintings of the Gibbs children reflect the interest of Elizabethan artists in color, decorative pattern, and minimal shadowing; the red ground that shines through the canvas's surface imparts a liveliness to the figures, while the patterned black-and-white tiled floor provides a rhythm and movement to an otherwise static composition.

The Mason Children and *Alice Mason* are also painted on a red ground; a rhythmic pattern is achieved in the group portrait by the descending height of the children, the succession of objects each holds—the cane of the gentleman, the fan of the lady, and the rose of innocent childhood—the repetitive sleeve shapes and inserts, and the kerchiefs tied neatly under the girls' chins. Not concerned with three-dimensionality, the artist provided just enough resemblance to satisfy the parents' wish to preserve images of their children. Given the Neoplatonic nature of Protestant thought in the seventeenth century that tended to regard material reality as emblematic or symbolic, an objective reproduction of a three-dimensional likeness was not necessary. A diagrammatic, or simplified, representation of appearance sufficed to recall to mind the person or thing depicted.

The style of the portraits of Elizabeth Paddy Wensley and her husband, John Wensley, also dating from the decade 1670 to 1680, clearly indicates that a second artist worked in Boston who was more concerned with presenting figures in space and was knowledgeable about the symbolic meaning of portrait elements. Thinly painted on red ground, the matching three-quarter-length portraits are full of iconographic detail: flowers in Elizabeth Wensley's portrait probably denote her five children, born between 1664 and 1675; two roses fallen on the table perhaps refer to two who died, while two tulips among the flowers in the vase promise their resurrection. Tree and vines in the matching landscape cutouts represent the marriage state, a motif repeated in Elizabeth Wensley's dress; her fan establishes her status as a lady, while John Wensley's books mark him as a learned gentleman as well as mariner.

Thomas Smith was a mariner who may have learned his art in either England or Holland and practiced it in New England as an avocation. His signed *Self-Portrait,* painted sometime between 1670 and 1691, exemplifies the *memento mori* theme. In the convention of emblematic portraits such as those in the Norwich Castle Museum in Norfolk, England—of civic leaders in the full panoply of office, with a death's head lurking in the background and explained by a literary comment—Smith painted himself holding fast to a skull that rests upon a poem that rejects the world and asserts faith in eternal life after death.

In the cutout window a scene of a naval conflict, which may actually represent one of Smith's encounters as a ship's captain, symbolizes the world's battle. The skull, with its heart-shaped nose, resembles a "headstone" or "afterlife" spirit such as appeared on gravestone carvings of the time as a symbol of eternal life and rejection of worldly ambitions. Smith's *Self-Portrait* is the artistic expression of a religious conception that lay at the center of the Puritan effort in the New World.

Smith is also associated with a group of important public portraits of seventeenth-century military and civic leaders painted in a style similar to the *Self-Portrait: Major Thomas Savage, Captain George Corwin,* and *"An Unknown Gentleman," Probably Elisha Hutchinson, Also Identified As Sir George Downing* (1675–1690). Despite efforts to achieve three-dimensionality, Smith's figures remain linear and flat against the drapery. Costumes are painted with an eye to pattern, but they are also probably quite true to their actual appearance and appropriate to the high positions held by their wearers. The cutout landscapes and attempts to suggest projection through light and shadow distinguish these portraits from those created by the Freake-Gibbs-Mason limner and indicate that Smith was acquainted with the new continental or baroque style being introduced at the time into England by Anglo-Dutch painters, particularly Anton Van Dyck. These large three-quarter figures in all their fine regalia of uniform, baldric, and sword reveal clearly that portraits were considered the prerogative of individuals of rank and achievement, models of virtue worthy of emulation. The sitters are representative of the class of New Englanders who had their portraits painted in the seventeenth century, a ruling elite—magistrates, ministers, military leaders, naval captains, and merchants—who came from comfortable English backgrounds and assumed leadership in the colony at least up to the American Revolution. Capable of importing or commissioning such luxuries as engravings, alabaster images, fine silver, wood carvings, and decorative objects, these individuals soon rejected Puritan austerity and introduced into the community an artistic culture of great importance in the following century.

Sculpture: Gravestone Carvings

Even while they were enjoying a more sophisticated culture, seventeenth-century Englishmen continued to participate in the magical or sacred tradition that encouraged more primitive groups' practice of the visual arts. We see this tendency in the gravestone carving replicated in Smith's *Self-Portrait,* which, apart from the wood carvings of Bible boxes, ships' figureheads, furniture, shop signs, and architectural ornaments of the period, represents the major sculptural effort of New Englanders from about 1688 to 1815. A vernacular art, the carved gravestones convey the transplanted Englishman's effort to overcome his terror of death by symbolizing it as transformation to a new life. With such formalized and traditional images as, for instance, a cinerary urn out of which flowers grow, a soul effigy emerging from the mouth of a death's head or skull, a soul flying heavenward on the belly of an eagle, trees of life, palms of victory, peacocks, flowers, sun, moon, and stars, and an-

304

gels, the Puritan stone carvings fulfill a fundamental need to assert the triumph of the soul over the death of the body, or of "sweet grace" over "grim death."

Like the limner's portraits, the tombstone carvings emphasize line rather than three-dimensional volume, a style that resulted in an abstraction from, rather than an imitation of, naturalistic reality. The carvings emerged just when the first known portraits were being painted, when New England society was becoming more stable, more prosperous. The carvers, however, like the limners, remained itinerant and anonymous, perhaps because they were considered craftsmen rather than artists. By the beginning of the eighteenth century, however, carvers became more professional and began to sign their work. "N. L." left his initials on an "effigy portrait" of the Reverend Jonathan Pierpont of Wakefield, Massachusetts, while Henry Emmes carved his marker on similar gravestone portraits in Boston, Virginia, and Charleston, South Carolina, during the 1740s.

THE EIGHTEENTH CENTURY

By 1700 there was no question that the strongest influence in the New World would continue to be English—at least in the Northern Hemisphere. Great Britain was now the chief market from which the colonies drew everything of significance, including art. British painting, as experienced through mezzotints and engravings and a few originals, continued to provide the influences and models most important for American art of this century.

In the eighteenth century, under the influence of English collectors of Italian Renaissance art and the discovery of the classical, British writers began to justify art as the source of a great national culture. Those writers emphasized art's importance not only because of its capacity to endow status, power, or wealth, but because of its civilizing influence as an expression of sublimity and pure emotions. Regarded as fulfilling an important social role, artists were elevated to positions of prominence. By the middle of the century, the English artist had moved beyond the craft status of the seventeenth century into

a professionalism that was to leave its mark upon the world of American art as well.

The artist's status in the colonies also underwent change as a result of the introduction of the academic system of English eighteenth-century art through the importation of numerous engravings, mezzotints, and books about art. These sources introduced Americans to artistic formulas that expressed the English aristocratic world of the eighteenth century, with its aspirations toward graceful living and the increased consumerism resulting from importation of rich textiles, expensive furniture, and ornamental hangings. British mezzotints taught Americans how to render silks and satins, design fabric folds, formalize costumes and poses, paint landscape or marine backgrounds, place figures attractively in space, and master the tricks of chiaroscuro and use of shadow and light. Lacking academies in which new styles and painting methods could be formally taught and studios where they might serve apprenticeships, colonial artists did not hesitate to copy whatever came to hand to fulfill their purposes. In doing so, they produced works that combined cosmopolitan influences and models with a particularly provincial way of seeing: awkwardly constructed, dully painted at times, simplified in drawing and detail, and yet, frequently, penetratingly naturalistic.

Mezzotints and Engravings

As in the seventeenth century, prints constituted the principal source of artistic experience for Americans during the eighteenth century, especially with the expansion of book publishing to include broadsides, pamphlets, and almanacs. Although most prints available were imported from England and occasionally from the Continent, prints produced in America were primarily portraits. Portraits were used as frontispieces for books and illustrations in almanacs. Like other early American art forms, printmaking followed the British example, especially the metal engraving and the mezzotint. In 1728 Thomas Emmes made a copperplate engraving of a portrait of the Reverend Increase Mather that, copied from an English engraving of the minister, became the prototype for future ministerial portraits used as frontispieces in books. A simple bust image in an oval frame within a rectangle, the engraving emphasized the head as representative of the subject's calling.

James Franklin made particular use of such frontispieces, as in his portrait of Hugh Peter, which appeared in *A Dying Father's Last Legacy to an Only Child; or, Mr. Hugh Peter's Advice to His Daughter* (1717). Apprenticed to a publisher in London, Franklin returned to Boston with training in white-line engraving in relief. Since trained engravers were not to be found in the city, he probably made his own relief cuts for the books and almanacs he published. Other publishers turned to such images for republication in works by various authors, many anonymous. Actual identification of author with portrait was not necessary; any illustration would do. As the relief cut passed through the republication process, it gradually lost clarity, especially when it was used for illustrating almanac articles. Later in the century, greater effort was expended to obtain an accurate likeness, and the engraving process was refined and improved.

By the time of the revolution, engravers appeared who were able to combine portraiture with scenes illustrating events, satirizing social and political movements, reproducing topographical views or landscapes, or recording history. Among the more important metal engravers working in the major colonial cities was Thomas Johnston, who in 1755 produced the line engraving *A Prospective Plan of the Battle Fought near Lake George on the 8th of September 1755,* possibly the country's first historical print. During the revolutionary crisis, Paul Revere, Henry Pelham, and Nathaniel Hurd in Boston, John Norman, Henry Dawkins, and James Claypoole in Philadelphia, and Amos Doolittle in Connecticut published more elaborate engravings of views and battles.

Mezzotints were executed in the colonies as early as 1710, when John Simon published four full-length portraits of Iroquois chieftains from portraits painted by John Verelst for the queen. The first American portrait mezzotint appeared in 1728, the work of the recently arrived Peter Pelham. Based on Pelham's oil portrait of Cotton Mather, the mezzotint was issued upon subscription, because the talent, time, and effort invested in mezzotint production were so much greater than for other types of engraving. Mezzotint engraving required good original paintings, assistants to help prepare the plates, imported supplies, and publishers willing to risk the investment. Prints resulting from this process usually provided better likenesses; greatly valued, they were framed and hung. Until his death in 1751, Pelham continued to produce mezzotint portraits of eminent New Englanders, usually utilizing images from the portraits of John Smibert after his arrival in Boston in 1729. Pelham's bust portraits of ministers were drawn skillfully and with an eye to the dramatic, while his three-quarter prints of the heroes of Louisbourg—Sir William Pepperrell and Governor William Shirley—published in 1747 and based on Smibert's portraits, were masterpieces of the art.

William Burgis, who worked in America between 1716 and 1731, published topographical views such as *View of Fort George* (1729–1731) and *The Boston Lighthouse* (1729). Pelham taught his art to painters John Greenwood, his stepson John Singleton Copley, and Richard Kennys. In the 1770s the English mezzotint artist Samuel Oakey came to Newport, Rhode Island, where he worked for a time; his plates were reprinted many times, particularly one of Sam Adams taken from a copy of Copley's famous portrait.

After the revolution, Charles Willson Peale and Edward Savage began to produce elaborate and excellent mezzotints, but by this time, stipple engraving, which was faster and less expensive, became a more popular medium.

Painting

The early years of the eighteenth century witnessed many more artists migrating to the New World for temporary visits or permanent settlement. By mid century, a large number of painters were working in the American colonies, particularly in Boston, New York, and Philadelphia, with occasional visits to the southern plantations. As early as 1712, Gustavus Hesselius arrived from Sweden and maintained a residence in Philadelphia until 1720 and then again from 1734 until his death. Hesselius's output in the colonies was not large—about twenty portraits have been attributed to him, along with three religious compositions and one or two mythological works—and his influence on American painting was not strong. He did teach his art to his son John, who in turn gave a few lessons to Charles Willson Peale. Hesselius introduced a professionalism into the middle colonies that had a long-range effect on the young Benjamin West, and he was the first artist in America to be commissioned to adorn a public building. His *Last Supper* was painted for the vestry of Saint Barnabas's Church in Queen Anne's Parish in Maryland between 1721 and 1722.

Despite his cosmopolitan training and considerable technical ability, in temperament and capacity Hesselius fitted into the colonial craft environment; advertising himself as a "Face-Painter," he was willing to undertake "Coats of Arms drawn on Coaches . . . or any other kind of Ornaments, Landskips, Signs, Shewboards, Ship and House Painting, Gilding of all Sorts, Writing in Gold or Colour." He also made spinet pianos and built pipe organs. His portraits are direct representations of people he knew well or whose character he carefully realized—not outstanding works of art, but excellent memorials of a time passed and of people who once lived. Two portraits of Indian chiefs—*Tishcohan* and *Lapowinsa*—are sensitive interpretations of character. His *Self-Portrait* and his portrait of his wife, *Lydia Hesselius*, are unpretentious and forthright, marked by lively color, rich texture, and sense of form.

Charles Bridges arrived in Virginia in 1735 already advanced in years and training. His portraits possess the sophisticated elegance that marked the tradition of Sir Godfrey Kneller in England. The German-born Justus Engelhardt Kuhn worked in Maryland, Henrietta Dering Johnston, Jeremiah Theus, and William Burgis painted miniatures and portraits for plantation and town houses in Charleston, South Carolina, while in Albany, Schenectady, and the upper Hudson River region Nehemiah Partridge and Pieter Vanderlyn among other—anonymous—artists filled homes with delicate portrait images. In New York City, a group of portraitists painted some distinctive, and in many instances, pleasing portraits of the DePeysters, Beekmans, van Cortlandts, Livingstons, Gansevoorts, Bleeckers, Schuylers, and other Dutch patroons and their families between 1715 and 1740; most important among these were John Watson and Gerardus Duyckinck. During the following decades, in the 1750s and 1760s, Gerardus Duyckinck II, John Mare, John Wollaston, Abraham Delanoy, Jr., Lawrence Kilburn, Thomas McIlworth, Cosmo

Alexander, and John Durand experienced uncertain careers in the city, frequently remaining there for only short periods of time.

Of all the colonial settlements at this time, however, Boston remained at the hub of the New World's artistic life—at least until the onset of the revolutionary movement, after which Philadelphia and then New York surged ahead. Because of Boston's preeminence in trade and merchandising, its increasing aristocratic class ready to provide an appreciative patronage, its tradition of craftsmanship and diversity of occupational structure, its urban organization, and a pride in its own history that encouraged the collection of family portraits and records, the city invited emigrating Old World artists and aspiring native painters.

In 1729 Boston basked in an aura of artistic glory largely as a result of the arrival of John Smibert. Born in Edinburgh and trained in Thornhill's London Academy, Smibert had traveled in Italy studying and copying Renaissance masterpieces. He arrived in Newport, Rhode Island, in January 1729, as a member of the entourage accompanying Bishop George Berkeley to Bermuda to found a college for European and Indian children. Even before this utopian project collapsed for lack of funds, in April of that year Smibert left Newport for the more promising Boston.

Smibert's *Bishop Berkeley and His Family* (*The Bermuda Group*), although not the first group portrait executed in the colonies, became the prototype for many group portraits to follow. A commemorative portrait, it is at once allegorical as it is historical: Berkeley, an eminent philosopher, is dictating his visionary pronouncements to a scribe identified as the patron who had commissioned the picture, John Wainwright. Berkeley is surrounded by his entourage, whose positions in the painting are established by their social status. Neither a member of the family, nor a donor to Berkeley's project as are the three men in the center of the canvas, Smibert portrayed himself modestly at the left, on the outskirts of the group and not quite a part of it. In the men's images and in the rhythmic yet easy organization of the figures we see Smibert's vigorous style modified by a sophisticated cosmopolitanism. *Judge Samuel Sewell* and *Nathaniel Byfield*, among other portraits by him, are characterized by a strong grasp of fact and mastery of expression. Although his compositions follow those created by fashionable London portraitists, Smibert's subjects are rendered naturalistically, with every double chin, sunken mouth, or unrefined feature carefully presented, a straightforwardness that marks him as a provincial painter.

Smibert's shop for the sale of artists' materials and pictures was the first specifically established for this purpose in the New World. His copies of Old World paintings—retained in his studio for many years after his death—served as a school for young artists. Perhaps the first American student to learn from Smibert and the first to surpass him as an artist was Robert Feke.

Little is known about Feke. He was born probably into an Oyster Bay, New York, family and perhaps met Smibert while he was working on his group portrait of the Berkeley entourage. Feke's *Isaac Royal Family* of 1741 is modeled after *The Bermuda Group,* as is his early *Self-Portrait,* which closely resembles Smibert's self-portrait in that picture. Despite some awkwardness in the twist of the body, the flat, thin character of the painting, absence of hands and, indeed, of any attempt at composition, Feke's *Self-Portrait* is not a novice's work. In the commanding presence of the head and the expressiveness of the features, Feke revealed how capable he was of wielding an artist's brush.

Feke may have attempted painting before coming to Newport. His work shows the influence of the New York artists whose paintings in the Dutch tradition have a gaiety and charm not present in Smibert's more sober portraits. Such a feeling appears in a modified way in Feke's portraits of women, shown with graceful hands, colorful satin dresses, and flower bouquets. Feke's subjects represented the prospering elements of eighteenth-century colonial society—worldly men and women who sought to appear elegant, wealthy, and aristocratic. In his rendering of rich textures and fashionable clothing—as in the brown velvet coat of *James Bowdoin II* or the blue satin of his wife's gown—Feke met these desires. In these portraits and those of *Mr. and Mrs. William Bowdoin*—all owned by the Walker Art Gallery at Bowdoin College—Feke introduced aristocratic accessories such as gold braid, lapdog, bouquet, book, jewelry, and

curls, and provided an English-style background borrowed from British mezzotints: a pillar or draped curtain or landscape of clouds, hills, woods, and sky.

Despite his British mannerisms, Feke was concerned with the essential human being under the trappings of silks and satins. Especially in his portraits of men, such as the haughty *Rev. Thomas Hiscox* or the keenly appraising merchant *Charles Apthorp* (both works of the 1740s), Feke achieved a characterization both in dress and features that indicates quite clearly who these men were and what they did.

Feke's paintings reveal their mezzotint source. His landscapes are flat, as viewed secondhand from a print, rather than spatially conceived, reminiscent to some extent of the linear vision of the seventeenth-century limner, and his figures are not thoroughly integrated with their background. Much of his charm as a painter lies in his emphasis on drawing, his use of color, and his strong sense of design.

Feke's influence fell on a group of minor painters who followed him and attempted to apply the same formula to their own work, with, however, less success. Joseph Badger of Boston remained always a primitive, despite attempts at elegance. His paintings do not achieve Feke's fresh colors, sense of design, or pearliness of surface; rather, the colors are dull, lines blurred, forms awkwardly drawn and paint thin.

The English artist John Wollston, who practiced in the larger American cities and towns, was influenced by the provincial Feke's more skillful work, and despite its lighter rococo manner, his portrait of *Mrs. William Walton,* painted around 1749 to 1751, bears close resemblance to some of Feke's female portraits. John Greenwood, who painted in Boston between 1747 and 1752, attempted to copy the details of Feke's portraits without, however, achieving Feke's charm and lightness of touch.

Only Copley surpassed Feke. Copley was influenced by him either through his actual presence in Boston or through the works he left behind. Perhaps it is not unexpected that John Singleton Copley should have emerged from eighteenth-century Boston society, for the willingness of Boston's wealthy merchants and officials to pay for large portraits provided scope for more complex and eventually more successful work. The possibilities of incorporating landscape, marine scenes, animals, still life, and other figures into the portrait allowed him to experiment beyond the narrow limits of the likeness.

Like Feke, Copley's style shows the assimilation of the English rococo as practiced by the academically oriented English painter Joseph Blackburn, with his own provincial art education derived from prints and emphasizing line, design, bright colors, and strong contrasts. In *Ann Tyng* Blackburn's influence appears in the excessively pink landscape, the diagonal of the shepherdess's crook, the lamb munching a leaf from Ann's awkwardly placed left hand, the profusion of ribbons and laces, and Ann's simpering turned-up mouth. Yet, despite the artificialities derived from his English model, Copley's emphasis on visual fact and "likeness" emerges. This emphasis had characterized his earlier, plainer—almost angular—portrait of Mrs. Joseph Mann and continued to characterize his work, even as he successfully assimilated British traditions.

In his portrait of Mrs. Jerathmael Bowers we see Copley's mature colonial style: the surfaces are more highly polished, the modeling of the figure fuller, and the pose more relaxed. Mary Bowers sits on a garden bench and in a landscape similar to those in Sir Joshua Reynolds' *Duchess of Marlborough*. She wears the same clothing from the rose in her bosom and the shawl draped around her shoulders to the full satin skirt, in which the same little spaniel dog nestles. Despite this borrowing, she is beautifully rendered, and her quiet dignity and charm mark the individual rather than the type.

Copley's realization of character appears most successfully in a group of portraits of men dressed and posed familiarly that he painted between 1765 and 1770. In *Nathaniel Hurd, Paul Revere,* and *Samuel Adams,* Copley avoided formulas while concentrating on the texture and shape of objects and on the personalities of his sitters.

Under the influence of books about art and artists emanating from England during the middle half of the eighteenth century, Copley consciously worked at his paintings to make them conform to theory as well as to his own conception of the art. As these studies expanded his views of the artist's profession, he grew restless and began looking to London for expanded artistic opportunities. In 1765 he painted *Boy with a Squirrel*, which he submitted to the exhibition of the Society of Artists in London. The portrait not only earned for Copley election in 1766 to the society, but elicited from Sir Joshua Reynolds both praise as "a wonderful performance" and advice that he should come to Europe for study "before [his] Manner and Taste were corrupted or fixed by working in [his] little way at Boston."

Encouraged by the Philadelphia artist Benjamin West, Copley left for London in 1774, at the height of the revolutionary fervor. Before he took ship, he painted two double portraits—*Mr. and Mrs. Isaac Winslow* and *Governor and Mrs. Thomas Mifflin*—pictures that sum up his colonial achievements and capture the bourgeois world of men and women that characterized urban America on the eve of the American Revolution, a world in which men and women moved toward aristocratic pretensions within a growing republicanism of political sentiment. In these double portraits, we see that mercantile world, with its polished mahogany, fine yet conservative clothing, ease of expression and posture, and generally benign social attitude. In his portraits of men especially, Copley revealed the world of business activity that marked the last decades of America's colonial experience—in the impressive *Jacob Fowle*, the monumental *Eppes Sargent,* the short, stout, and pompous *Jeremiah Lee,* and the shrewd *Isaac Smith*.

When Copley arrived in London, he encountered a developing artistic interest in contemporary history. Popularized by West in 1769 in his *Death of General Wolfe*, these kinds of paintings permitted Copley to combine portraiture with history imaginatively, as in *The Death of Chatham, Watson and the Shark, The Death of Major Peirson,* and *The Siege of Gibraltar*. With his concern for details of costuming, textures and materials, interest in lighting, and factualism, Copley gave to his historical paintings elements of pictorial journalism that constituted their popular appeal. The English works fulfilled his colonial promise.

Like Copley, Benjamin West of Philadelphia absorbed an ideal of the professional artist from books on artistic theory and from the example of visiting foreign artists. West's youth was spent in rural Pennsylvania, where he displayed a genius for drawing at age seven. In Philadelphia, he received some instruction or encouragement from the English scene painter William Williams. The generous patronage of Philadelphia art collectors made possible a trip to Italy in 1758, where he met many of Rome's most influential "dilettanti," including Cardinal Albani, the city's most famous art connoisseur. He quickly absorbed Rome's neoclassical aesthetics, popularized by Johann Joachim Winckelmann and Anton-Raphael Mengs, which influenced changes in artistic styles and introduced a new system of values that further enhanced the Renaissance idea of the artist as moral and religious educator.

To achieve "classic grandeur" became the eighteenth-century artist's aim. Art's function, writers on aesthetics emphasized, was not to amuse or represent, but to elevate the mind with what was broadly representative and universal. The themes most conducive to such elevation were religious, mythical, or historical. Since it was believed that the work of the classical sculptors and Renaissance masters had come closer to achieving universal truth than any other artists before or after their time, it seemed reasonable that modern artists should draw upon them as the occasion demanded—a head, arm, or leg position, landscapes, groupings, furnishings. Thus, West's history paintings were highly eclectic, revealing "borrowings" or quotations from earlier masters' works. Yet, despite their lack of originality and mechanical groupings, West's paintings captured the American imagination, from the picturing of the death of the military hero in his *Death of Wolfe* to the dignified *Penn's Treaty with the Indians* of 1771.

West's influence on American art was immeasurable. The first American artist to venture into the stronghold of art at Rome and emerge triumphant, he became the subject of legend early in his career. Even more important an influence was the fact that his extensive oeuvre paralleled the course of Western aesthetic movements from classicism to romanticism. Americans who watched the canvasses emerge from his easel responded to the changes in taste his paintings introduced. They found his pictorial rhetoric satisfying. His accurate rendering of subject matter, particularly his attempt to convey moral lessons through realistic detail of costume and accessories, provided an immediacy missing from classical painting up to that time. Equally exciting

was his revolutionary interest in contemporary subjects, his melodramatic presentation of national themes, and his capacity to create a sense of awe—as in such later works as *Death on a Pale Horse*.

Hospitable to numerous young Americans who traveled to London to study art, West communicated neoclassical and then early romantic aesthetic ideas to Americans through such men as Matthew Pratt, Charles Willson Peale, Ralph Earl, John Trumbull, Robert Fulton, Washington Allston, and Samuel F. B. Morse, among others.

Charles Willson Peale was one of West's earliest pupils. Born on the Eastern Shore of Maryland, Peale's colonial career is associated with the cosmopolitan capitals Annapolis and Williamsburg. The first son of an exiled English schoolteacher, Peale was apprenticed at age thirteen to a saddlemaker and was trained in the mechanical arts. His interest in painting developed from examining portraits in a mansion in Norfolk, Virginia. From books, he learned how to prepare a canvas and mix pigments; later, on a trip to Boston he watched Copley at work and arranged for a lesson from John Hesselius in exchange for a saddle. His quick talent soon brought him to the attention of a group of Maryland landowners, who provided the funds for study in London. Upon his return to Annapolis two and a half years later, Peale produced accomplished portraits in the best English style, such as *Margaret Harwood*, charming conversation pieces, such as *The John Cadwalader Family*, paintings of mothers and children, such as *Mrs. John Dickinson and Her Daughter Sally*, and such grand portraits as *Nancy Hallam As Fidèle in Cymbeline*.

An ardent republican, Peale responded to prevailing political sentiments with such revolutionary propaganda as *William Pitt*, which he also published as a mezzotint, *John Beale Bordley*, and *William Paca*, among others. His sophisticated and pleasant portraits proved him to be one of the most versatile and popular colonial artists—especially after Copley left for England, abandoning the field almost entirely to Peale. On the eve of the revolution, in 1776, Peale moved his family to Philadelphia, where he spent the rest and most significant part of his career as a portraitist and museum keeper.

PAINTING AND SCULPTURE: BRITISH

Peale continued in the Middle Atlantic region the idea of the professional artist that Hesselius had introduced and that Smibert and Copley had nurtured in Boston. His portraits conveyed and strengthened the Anglo-American portrait tradition that was to exercise considerable influence in the post-revolutionary United States.

ROLE OF ART BY 1776

By 1776 the fine art of painting as it had developed in western Europe up to this time had been introduced into the American colonies through books and prints, European visitors and immigrants, and traveling Americans who brought back copies (and a few originals) of old master paintings and acquaintance with European art institutions.

Americans' acquaintance with sculpture also expanded by 1776. Elaborate marble tombstones imported from England as early as the 1740s for wealthy merchants and government officials introduced stonecarvers to classical imagery and abstract design such as marked European aristocratic sculpture. With prosperity came an interest in more finely carved furniture and decorative pieces, a demand met by such carvers as Simeon Skillins, Sr., of Boston, who trained three of his ten children to carve ships' figureheads, architectural ornaments, and furnishings. Just before the revolution, in 1775, William Rush, one of the last of the woodcarvers, opened his shop in Philadelphia; his post-revolutionary career connects the earlier native woodcarving tradition to the era of the imported stonecarver who would continue to provide the country with its sculptured art into the second decade of the nineteenth century.

By the outbreak of the revolution, the status of the artist underwent change. In the mid eighteenth century, painters had been willing to assume such artisan-related tasks as varnishing, gilding, teaching, keeping shops, and painting wheel carriages, houses, and signs. The terminology by which artists were described suggest their status: limner was usually applied to the anonymous portrait painter up to the 1760s; painter characterized anyone who could paint a flat surface. By the second half of the century,

artists who were trained in England or educated in the classics rejected the status of laborer and thought of themselves as artists and gentlemen. Usually urban portraitists, they were aware that in Europe artists were, as William Dunlap quoted West, "the companions of kings and emperors." Copley, West, and Peale married women from prosperous and upper-middle-class families and experienced no difficulty in consorting with affluent patrons. Although subject to economic downturns, before the revolution all three enjoyed sufficient patronage to allow them to maintain a self-image as professional artist, an image indicated by their custom of signing their paintings, frequently adding "pinxit" to underline their professional status. A few art collectors—James Bowdoin III of Boston, William Byrd of Virginia, and the Allens and Hamiltons of Philadelphia—introduced European art traditions to those Americans privileged to visit their galleries, especially aspiring artists, and established in their respective communities the idea of the value of art and the need for institutions devoted to its encouragement.

Although American taste favored portraits, it also accepted as appropriate artistic subjects landscapes, topographical views, historical works, and political engravings. With independence, a sufficient number of artists and artistic examples were available to serve nationalistic purposes. The achievements of the colonial artists, particularly Copley, West, and Peale, lent credence to the American boast that the new nation was capable of encouraging genius and that political liberty was congenial to the development of taste—a necessary step before art could assume an important role in the new republic.

BIBLIOGRAPHY

Works cited are listed in the following reference books:

General Works

American Art, 1750–1800: Towards Independence. Published for the Yale University Art Gallery (New Haven, Conn.) and the Victoria and Albert Museum (London). Boston, 1976.

Arts of the Anglo-American Community in the Seventeenth Century. Winterthur Conference Report, 1974. Charlottesville, Va., 1975.

Craven, Wayne. *Colonial American Portraiture: The Economic, Religious, Social, Cultural, Philosophical, Scientific, and Aesthetic Foundations.* Cambridge, England, and New York, 1986. Heavily one-sided in its emphasis on American materialism and the influence of the work ethic, this volume is perhaps the most complete history of colonial painting in print; useful for its information and bibliography, controversial in its interpretation.

Dresser, Louisa. "The Background of Colonial American Portraiture: Some Pages from a European Notebook." *Proceedings of the American Antiquarian Society* 76 (April 1966):19–58.

———. "Portraits in Boston, 1630–1720." *Journal of the Archives of American Art* 6 (July–October 1966):1–34.

———. *Sculpture in America.* New York, 1968.

———. *Seventeenth-Century Painting in New England.* Worcester, Mass., 1935. Dresser's three publications are classics in the field and began the process of identifying the several artists and their English backgrounds.

Fairbanks, Jonathan L., and Robert F. Trent. *New England Begins: The Seventeenth Century.* 3 vols. Boston, 1982. Offers extensive original essays by leading colonial scholars and informed entries of objects displayed in the exhibition of the Museum of Fine Arts, Boston, in 1982, celebrating the three-hundredth year of the founding of the New England colonies. Volume 3, "Style," is particularly important for the arts.

Flexner, James Thomas. *First Flowers of Our Wilderness: American Painting.* Boston, 1947.

Green, Samuel. "English Origins of Seventeenth-Century Painting in New England." In *American Painting to 1776: A Reappraisal.* Winterthur Conference Report, 1971. Charlottesville, Va., 1971.

Miller, Lillian B. "The Puritan Portrait: Its Function in Old and New England." In *Seventeenth-Century New England,* edited by David D. Hall and David Grayson Allen. Boston, 1984.

Mooz, R. Peter, et al. *Philadelphia Painting and Printing to 1776.* Philadelphia, 1971.

Peacham, Henry. *The Compleat Gentleman.* London, 1622.

Poesch, Jessie. *The Art of the Old South: Painting, Sculpture, Architecture, and the Products of Craftsmen, 1560–1860.* New York, 1983.

Reutlinger, Dagmar E. *The Colonial Epoch in America.* Worcester, Mass., 1975.

Saunders, Richard H., and Ellen G. Miles. *American Colonial Portraits, 1700–1776.* Washington, D.C., 1987. A scholarly and informed catalog of an exhibition held in 1987 at the National Portrait Gallery, Smithsonian Institution.

Sewall, Samuel, *The Diary of Samuel Sewall, 1674–1729.* 2 vols. Edited by M. Halsey Thomas. New York, 1973.

Sidney, Sir Philip. *A Defence of Poetry.* Rev. ed. London, 1966.

Prints and Engravings

Colonial Society of Massachusetts. *Boston Prints and Printmakers, 1670–1775.* Boston, 1973.

Dolmetsch, Joan D., ed. *Eighteenth-Century Prints in Colonial America: To Educate and Decorate.* Williamsburg, Va., 1979.

Morse, John D., ed. *Prints in and of America to 1850.* Charlottesville, Va., 1970.

Reaves, Wendy Wick. "Effigies Curiously Engraven: Eighteenth-Century American Portrait Prints." In *Prints of New England,* edited by Georgia B. Barnhill. Worcester, Mass., 1991.

Reilly, Elizabeth. *A Dictionary of Colonial American Printers Ornaments and Illustrations.* Worcester, Mass., 1975.

Sculpture: Gravestone Carvings

Benes, Peter. *The Masks of Orthodoxy: Folk Gravestone Carving in Plymouth County, Massachusetts, 1689–1805.* Amherst, Mass., 1977.

Forbes, Harriette Merrifield. *Gravestones of Early New England.* Boston, 1927.

Ludwig, Allan I. *Graven Images: New England Stonecarving and Its Symbols, 1650–1815.* Middletown, Conn., 1966.

Artists

Abrams, Ann Uhry. *The Valiant Hero: Benjamin West and Grand-Style History Painting.* Washington, D.C., 1985.

Allard, Joseph. "The Painted Sermon: The Self-Portrait of Thomas Smith." *Journal of American Studies* 10 (December 1976):341–348.

Evans, Dorinda. *Benjamin West and His American Students.* Washington, D.C., 1980. Catalog of an exhibition at the National Portrait Gallery in 1980.

Fairbrother, Trevor J. "John Singleton Copley's Use of British Mezzotints for His American Portraits: A Reappraisal Prompted by New Discoveries." *Arts Magazine* 55 (March 1981):122–130.

Fleischer, Roland E. "Gustavus Hesselius." Ph.D. diss., The Johns Hopkins University, 1964.

———. "Gustavus Hesselius: A Study of His Style." In *American Painting to 1776: A Reappraisal.* Winterthur Conference Report, 1971. Charlottesville, Va., 1971.

Foote, Henry Wilder. *John Smibert, Painter.* Cambridge, Mass., 1950.

———. *Robert Feke, Colonial Portrait Painter.* Cambridge, Mass., 1930.

Goodrich, Lloyd. *Robert Feke.* New York, 1946.

Massachusetts Historical Society. *Letters and Papers of John Singleton Copley and Henry Pelham, 1739–1776.* 1914. Reprint. New York, 1970.

Miller, Lillian B., ed. *The Collected Papers of Charles Willson Peale and His Family.* Millwood, N.Y., 1980. Microfiche edition.

Miller, Lillian B., Sidney Hart, and David C. Ward, eds. *The Selected Papers of Charles Willson Peale and His Family.* Vol. 1: *The Artist in the Revolution, 1735–1791.* New Haven, Conn., and London, 1983. Selected from the *Collected Papers* (above) and annotated.

Miller, Lillian B., and David Ward, eds. *New Perspectives on Charles Willson Peale.* Pittsburgh, Pa., 1991.

Mooz, R. Peter. "The Art of Robert Feke." Ph.D. diss., University of Pennsylvania, 1970.

———. "Robert Feke: The Philadelphia Story." In *American Painting to 1776: A Reappraisal.* Winterthur Conference Report, 1971. Charlottesville, Va., 1971.

———. "Smibert's Bermuda Group—A Reevaluation," *Art Quarterly* 33, no. 2 (1970):147–157.

Prown, Jules David. *John Singleton Copley.* 2 vols. Cambridge, Mass., 1966. The most authoritative account of the artist's work in America and England.

Richardson, Edgar P., Brooke Hindle, and Lillian B. Miller. *Charles Willson Peale and His World.* New York, 1983. Essays relating to Peale's art, natural history, his museum, and efforts in technology; also a catalog of major exhibition devoted to Peale's art at the National Portrait Gallery and Metropolitan Museum of Art in 1983.

Saunders, Richard H., III. "John Smibert (1688–1751): Anglo-American Portrait Painter." 2 vols. Ph.D. diss., Yale University, 1979.

Sellers, Charles Coleman. *Charles Willson Peale: A Biography.* New York, 1969. The first important biographical study of the artist written by a descendant.

Stein, Roger B. "Thomas Smith's Self-Portrait: Image/Text As Artifact." *Art Journal* 44 (Winter 1984):316–327.

Von Erffa, Helmut, and Allen Staley. *The Paintings of Benjamin West.* New Haven, Conn., and London, 1986.

Lillian B. Miller

SEE ALSO **Crafts; Home and Hearth; Libraries and Learned Societies;** and **The Structure of Society.**

THE DUTCH COLONY

ANNE GRANT WRITES in her *Memoirs of an American Lady* that in the Schuyler home near Albany "the best bedroom was hung with family portraits, some of which were admirably executed; and in the eating room . . . were some fine scripture paintings . . . one of Esau coming to demand the anticipated blessing." Visiting the home around 1760, Anne Grant's memory coincided with the close of an era of Dutch art in America. For a century families of mostly Dutch descent had kept alive an art tradition derived from Europe but interpreted by New York and New Jersey "limners" (from the Latin *luminare*, to illuminate, to depict by drawing). Shortly thereafter this tradition of sometimes self-taught and itinerant portraitists and sketch artists was to go out of fashion, as English culture inexorably overshadowed the colony's Dutch legacy. Yet despite the loss and misidentification of countless paintings during the intervening centuries, more paintings (over five hundred) survive than from any other province. Information about the artists and their trade, however, has been very difficult to uncover. And as for sculpture (if any was made) not a trace other than gravestones has survived. But of the latter, there are many in sandstone and slate. They often depict winged faces varying from cherubs to skulls.

ART IN THE DUTCH TRADITION

The immigrant Dutch brought with them a knowledge of a sophisticated Netherlands art tradition, and they even imported paintings and prints, to judge by their cryptic mention in estate inventories from the last half of the seventeenth century and by the comments of an antiquarian a century later. While visiting New York in 1768, the Swiss artist, naturalist, and art collector Pierre Eugène du Simitière was shown a large landscape with two figures, of Samuel and Anna Marika (Stuyvesant) Bayard. He was told that she, a widow, had come to the colony in 1647 with this painting, accompanied by her brother Petrus Stuyvesant, the newly appointed director general. In 1779 du Simitière offered for sale a number of "pictures, chiefly painted in oils, on boards . . . of those kinds the Dutch settlers brought a great many with their furniture." He had found them in New York garrets, where they had been "confined as unfashionable when that city was modernized." This brief comment provides a clue to the near disappearance of early New York's Netherlandish art, though the process was no doubt hastened by several large city fires.

Of the paintings produced here in the Dutch tradition, we can with assurance point to only three, all attributed to the Huguenot Henri Coutourier (1592–1672) and done about 1661–1666. His strong characterization of Governor Peter Stuyvesant surpasses in sophistication all subsequent paintings made in New York and New Jersey. Afterward there is a tantalizing void of nearly fifty more years in which hardly any paintings can be identified with assurance.

Inventories only suggest how much has been lost. In New York City, Doctor Jacob deLange owned, according to a 1685 inventory, sixty-one paintings, many large, consisting of still lifes, landscapes, and genre and Scripture paintings, as well as deLange's coat of arms and portrait. The range of subjects more closely reflects Netherland paintings of the time than contemporaneous English paintings, and his collection was probably imported from the Netherlands. Cornelis Steenwyck, the third mayor of New York City, had a portrait done by Coutourier and owned twenty-nine others of unknown subjects. Margarita Van Varick owned paintings of subjects much like those of Doctor deLange. Far more frequently mentioned in many inventories were maps and prints, all of them undoubtedly imported.

Besides Coutourier, other limners, painters (house and decorative painters), and glaziers (glassmakers and decorators) have been identified from public and private records. The earliest was Evert Duyckinck (1621 to ca. 1703), a glazier who came to New Amsterdam before 1640 and left us some coats of arms enameled on the windows of the Dutch Reformed church at Beverswyck (Albany) in 1656. While he is recorded late in life as a limner, a logical extension of the glazier's craft, no identifiable easel works by him are known.

Ordinarily a man who had proper training for an occupation—generally by apprenticeship for seven years—could register as a freeman, thereby obtaining certain rights, including the freedom of the city to pursue his work. Evert Duyckinck's youngest son Gerrit (1660 to ca. 1712) likely followed this procedure, as he registered as a limner in 1699 at the age of thirty-nine. Upwards of ten portraits are tentatively attributed to him. Gerrit's son Gerardus (1695 to ca. 1746), most likely instructed by his father, produced an early scripture painting, *The Birth of the Virgin*. He signed and dated the painting in 1713, making it the only known early New York painting bearing a limner's name. Over the next thirty years he painted many portraits and Scripture paintings while carrying on an active art-supply business. He was followed by his eldest son, also named Gerardus, though no known paintings by him can confirm his work as a limner.

There was one more limner in this Duyckinck dynasty, Evert III (1677 to ca. 1725), a son of Evert II, a mariner. Registering as a freeman in 1698, this Evert's New York City portraits share much in color and line with those of his cousin Gerardus.

While the Duyckincks were prominent for a century, other limners came to New York during its greatest period of colonial prosperity, 1714–1744. These years were also the only extended period of peace amid a series of four French wars.

Pieter Vanderlyn came to New York from the Netherlands via Curaçao around 1718, but his known portraits date from 1730 to 1745 and were of prominent Kingston and Albany families. Nehemiah Partridge came from Boston and also painted many leading families in Albany and later in other colonies. John Watson arrived from Scotland before 1715 and through the 1730s painted some of the prominent citizens in New Jersey, New York City, and Albany. The last clearly identifiable limner in the early New York tradition was John Heaten, who arrived in Albany by 1730, married a Dutch woman, and for fifteen years painted merchants and farmers in the Upper Hudson valley. His works include unique landscape and genre painting of Marten Van Bergen's farm (ca. 1733).

A SHIFT IN ARTISTIC TASTE

Heaten and Vanderlyn tended to paint their subjects as they found them; their contemporaries, however, favored poses and costumes copied from prints based on English court portraits. Many of these limners' patrons were, ironically, Dutch, but they were also persons who had succeeded and become wealthy under English rule and were thus more disposed to accept English culture than were their less affluent and more conservative relatives.

Indeed, a decided shift in subject matter as well as national style had taken place. Seventeenth-century paintings in New York appear from inventories to have been largely imports of an impressive range of Netherlandish art produced for art's sake.

But by the eighteenth century, painting had narrowed to portrait, scriptural, and genre subjects and had also become more provincial in origin, originality, and quality. Paintings were locally produced but stiffly and unimaginatively derived from European prints.

Furthermore, this shift suggests a loss of cultural self-confidence replaced, as the collective memory of the homeland faded, with a self-conscious need for art as a manifestation of identity, reassuring the Dutch that they were not just a remnant in the wilderness. Therefore portraits as symbols of personal identity needed only to be recognized, not evoke character; scripture paintings as symbols of cultural identity needed only to convey the message not the aesthetic inspiration. Young Anne Grant unwittingly appreciated this as she roamed the Schuyler house near Albany in the mid eighteenth century: "The family pictures, and scripture paintings, were to me particularly awful [awe-inspiring] and impressive. I compared them to the models which had before existed in my imagination, and was delighted or mortified, as I found they did or did not resemble them." Art had become folk art, the fallen culture of the upper class.

By the mid eighteenth century, another change was at hand. With the spread of King George's War to America in 1744, the greatest flowering of colonial art was over. Limners in New York and New Jersey appear to have left, died, or retired almost en masse. It would be several years before "artists," Englishmen with a new style, found the confidence to seek patronage in New York.

BIBLIOGRAPHY

Belknap, Waldron Phoenix, Jr. *American Colonial Painting: Materials for a History.* Cambridge, Mass., 1959.

Black, Mary. "Contributions Toward a History of Early Eighteenth-Century New York Portraiture: The Identification of the Aetatis Suae and Wendell Limners." *American Art Journal* 12, no. 4 (1980):4–31.

————. "Tracking Down John Watson." *American Arts and Antiques* 2, no. 6 (1979):78–85.

Blackburn, Roderic H., and Ruth Piwonka. *Remembrance of Patria: Dutch Arts and Culture in Colonial America, 1609–1776.* Albany, N.Y., 1988.

Grant, Anne. *Memoirs of an American Lady: With Sketches of Manners and Scenery in America, As They Existed Previous to the Revolution.* London, 1808; repr. 1901.

Piwonka, Ruth, and Roderic H. Blackburn. *A Remnant in the Wilderness.* Albany, N.Y., 1980.

Roderic H. Blackburn

SEE ALSO **Crafts; Home and Hearth;** and **Libraries and Learned Societies.**

THE FRENCH COLONIES

Canada

No sooner had French colonists begun the settlement of New France than a need for art was felt. The missionaries required religious paintings or engravings to aid them in instructing the Indians in the rudiments of the Christian religion. Bishop François Xavier de Laval-Montmorency wanted paintings and statues to decorate the parish churches that had been built during the first half of the seventeenth century. And the secular power could not do without a portrait of the queen or a bust of the king.

SCULPTURE

The intendant Jean Bochart de Champigny, when posted to Quebec in 1686, took with him a copy of Giovanni Lorenzo Bernini's bronze head of Louis XIV to show the Canadians what their monarch looked like. He had it mounted on a pedestal in the marketplace of Lower Town, Quebec. It was perhaps the only piece of sculpture imported from France during the colonial era. The art of sculpture had to develop in the colony for a simple reason. One could not carry sculpture as easily as one could carry paintings, which could be rolled on a stick and stretched later. Altarpieces or life-size statues were too bulky and heavy to import. The only sculptures that ships could carry were the figures that adorned their prows—sculptures that they took back with them! This situation accounts for the extraordinary and early development of sculpture in New France.

Bishop Laval was said to have created around 1700 a school in Saint-Joachim near Quebec where sculpture and painting were taught, but this is no longer maintained by modern scholars. The method by which sculpture was taught and learned in Canada was rather the system of apprenticeship, in which a master sculptor, himself usually trained in France, taught his skill to young apprentices. The archives of the province of Quebec have saved many apprenticeship contracts, which can be moving to read. The master promises to take good care of the young apprentice—to feed him, to clothe him, and to keep him on the right track—but in return expects much work from the poor boy.

By no means have all the sculptures made in the colony been saved. Carved in wood, sometimes painted, sometimes gilded or polychromed (decorated in several colors), many of the sculptures have been destroyed by fire or otherwise. But we do have some instances of somewhat miraculous conservation. The elaborate retable (altar screen) made by Pierre-Noël Levasseur, who was probably assisted by his nephew François-Noël, for the Ursuline nuns in Quebec City, is the most significant example. Between 1727 and 1736 the two altars of the chapel were adorned with a profusion of gilded sculptures in the baroque style. The pulpit was carved in 1726, surmounted with an angel playing a trumpet. The altarpiece survived the bombardment of the town by the British in the siege of Quebec in 1759, when some 80 percent of the buildings were demolished.

Other examples of quasi-miraculous survivals of baroque art in Canada are the polychromed low reliefs at the Oka Calvary (c. 1740–1817), near Montreal, which came very close to being razed by vandals. The sculptures made by Charles Chabouillez for the Récollet Fathers in Montreal were long believed to be lost, since the monastery for which they were created was destroyed. Scholars have since learned that before the Récollet church was torn down the retable was sold to a new parish, Saint-Grégoire de Nicolet, where it can still be seen, albeit with some additions and alterations. The Jesuit churches in both Montreal and Quebec were not so fortunate. They were completely destroyed; all that remains is Richard Short's 1761 engraving of the interior of the Jesuit chapel in Quebec, which gives us an inkling of its onetime splendor.

PAINTING

The circumstances that fostered the beginnings of a regional school of sculpture—the Canadian churches' demand for sculptures coupled with the constraints of importing—were experienced quite differently in the case of painting. The ease with which art on canvas could be carried along on the transatlantic voyage hindered the birth and development of painting in Canada. It appears that the paintings in all the important churches were imported, even when the subject matter was Canadian, as with the representation around 1664 of the Jesuit martyrs, at the Hôtel Dieu, Quebec, or even the ambitious post-1666 *La France apportant la foi aux Indiens de la Nouvelle-France*. This painting depicts the queen mother, Anne of Austria, instructing an Indian (on his knees) by showing him a painting of the Holy Trinity, Mary, Joseph, Anne, and Saint-Joachim. The Indian and the wigwam one sees in the background are based not on firsthand experience but on an engraving by Grégoire Huret, who never visited Canada.

On one occasion, a painter was brought to Canada in 1671 and commissioned to paint for the principal churches of the colony. Claude-François, who had taken the name Frère Luc as a Récollet friar, spent fifteen months in Canada, leaving here and there examples of his heavy and not too appealing style. Nevertheless, his stay in Canada fulfilled numerous commissions in short time. The Musée du Québec has his *Ange gardien* (1671) and the Hôpital Général his *L'assomption* (1671).

Some landscape paintings may have been done in Canada, but they seem not to have been a very popular genre. The Hôpital Général has some small imaginary landscapes that could have been done by a nun who painted during the period. There may have been more paintings, but they did not survive the conquest.

Portraits

The art of Canada that does survive consists mostly of ex-voto (votive) paintings and portraits. The great Iroquois chief Teganissorens had his portrait painted while on a diplomatic mission to Quebec; it was sent to Paris to be displayed. In 1700, while on another mission to the governor-general of Canada, a Récollet friar requested permission to paint his portrait. That portrait, too, has not survived. Most of the senior officials—governors-general, local governors, intendants—had their portraits done, probably in France, but some portraits of members of the Canadian noblesse have survived. The Ramsay Museum in Montreal displays a portrait of the intendant Jean Talon, attributed without solid proof to Frère Luc; the Séminaire de Québec has portraits of Bishop Laval (c. 1685) and of Bishop Jean-Baptiste de la Croix de Chevrières de Saint-Vallier (c. 1699). One can see at the McCord Museum in Montreal the striking portraits of the Hertel brothers, painted in the early 1700s; the older brother wears the cross of Saint Louis. Portraits of Pierre Le Moyne, sieur d'Iberville, and Jean-Baptiste Le Moyne, sieur de Bienville, survive in the Louisiana State Museum.

Especially in the religious communities, it was customary to have a painting done of a deceased person just before the burial. A painter was asked to come to a person's deathbed and to draw as faithfully as possible his or her resemblance. The saintly person could not protest on the basis of vanity, and it was the only means that the family or community had to preserve the memory of the deceased. One would not imagine that a great masterpiece could result from such a procedure, yet a more powerful, evocative, stunning, and truly beautiful portrait cannot be imagined than the deathbed likeness *Mère Marguerite Bourgeoys*, painted by Pierre Le Ber in 1700. In 1963 it was restored to its original splendor, showing the severe and emaciated face of a woman possessed of a powerful personality.

Ex-voto Painting

Ex-voto painting is an ancient genre. It flourished in Canada partly because of the fame of the shrine of Sainte-Anne de Beaupré, near Quebec, which may have been conceived on the model of Sainte-Anne d'Auvray in France, both famous places of pilgrimage. For example, when the captain of a ship feared losing his vessel in a sudden storm, he promised in desperation to give a painting, an ex-voto, meaning "by vow," to Sainte-Anne if he was saved by her heavenly intervention. The eventual painting customarily showed the peril from which he had been spared, with Sainte-Anne bestowing her blessing in one corner of the composition. When an ex-voto client was a person of status, it was customary to depict him in prayer but not to show the ill fortune that had beset him. A good example of this style is the *Ex-voto de Madame Riverin* (1703). Madame Riverin was abandoned by her husband and felt desperately in need of help for her little family. The painting was attributed to Michel Dessaillant de Richeterre, but without proof. When finished, the painting was hung in the church along with many others including the so-called *Ex-voto de Tracy*, governor-general of New France, 1665; it was in fact an *Education of the Virgin*, inspired by Rubens. It was large enough to be used as a main altar painting.

Most ex-voto paintings were modest, like the *Ex-voto des cinq naufragés de Lévis* (1754), which depicts the fate of five young people whose rowboats had capsized in the Saint Lawrence off the Île d'Orléans. They were able to glimpse the spire of Sainte-Anne de Beaupré. One of them must have been inspired to promise the painting to the saint. The votive was only partially successful; two of the youths drowned.

ART AND NATURE IN
A NEW WORLD

The efflorescence of the visual arts in New France is striking in its emphasis on religious subjects. Did not the vast expanse of the New World, its overpowering scenery, its exotic fauna and flora, its Native peoples, inspire painters or sculptors in New France? Perhaps they were moved and responded, but their works have not survived. An engraving depicting Niagara Falls appeared in *Nouvelle découverte d'un très grand pays,* published in 1697 by Father Louis Hennepin. A view of the Quebec basin, painted from the Lévis side of the river, showing the convoy of ships just arrived from France in May 1759, was displayed briefly at the McCord Museum before becoming part of a private collection.

One does, however, find many depictions of Canada in the cartouches of maps, illustrations in books, and on manuscripts. Some of the early explorers could make competent sketches, which were engraved in Paris. For example, Samuel de Champlain's journals and the accompanying maps are illustrated by his drawings, and in his *Brief discours* (1599–1601), the manuscript is illuminated by his hand; a copy is held at the John Carter Brown Library in Providence, Rhode Island.

The most remarkable example of this form of art is undoubtedly the so-called *Codex Canadensis,* which is at the Thomas Gilcrease Institute at Tulsa, Oklahoma. Originally this sketchbook was attached to the *Histoire naturelle des Indes occidentales* (1675), a manuscript written by Father Louis Nicolas, now held at the Bibliothèque Nationale, Paris. Nicolas depicts the flora and fauna of Canada, as well as the Indians, in an aesthetically pleasing fashion. Nicolas drew his inspiration from Konrad von Gesner's 1575 *Historia animalium* in sketching the animals, but he claimed more originality for his depiction of the flora.

The more one knows about this early period of the visual arts in Canada, the more one is persuaded of its originality. Canada compares well to New Spain for its religious paintings and to the English colonies for its taste in portraits. But both its religious paintings, more influenced by French classicism, and its portraits, more exuberant or naive than English counterparts, stand out as having a style of their own. The prescientific interest in fauna, flora, and Native peoples is for the northern part of the continent a source comparable to what is offered by Spanish authors such as Gonzalo Fernandez de

Oviedo y Valdés or José de Acosta. One only wishes that there was for Canada as good a publicist as the British colonies' Thomas Hariot and as talented an engraver as Théodore de Bry to give a better image of the cultures of its Native peoples.

BIBLIOGRAPHY

Berthiaume, Pierre, and Émile Lizé. *Foi et légendes: La peinture votive au Québec, 1666–1945.* Montreal, 1991.

Gagnon, François-Marc. *Premiers peintres de la Nouvelle-France.* 2 vols. Quebec, 1976.

Harper, John Russell. *Painting in Canada: A History.* 2nd edition. Toronto, Ontario, and Buffalo, N.Y., 1977.

Reid, Dennis. *A Concise History of Canadian Painting.* Toronto, Ontario, 1973.

Trudel, Jean, et al. *Le grande héritage: L'église catholique et les arts au Québec.* 2 vols. Quebec, 1984.

François-Marc Gagnon[*]

SEE ALSO **Home and Hearth.**

Louisiana

COLONIZATION OF FRENCH LOUISIANA began in the final year of the seventeenth century, yet early explorers and cartographers had already made watercolor renderings of geographic and special features of the new country. European artists commemorated early explorations in paintings and prints. John Law's Company of the West (later Company of the Indies) employed artists to produce propagandistic artworks to entice settlers to the area. One such painting, published in Paris about 1720 by François Gerard Jollain, was called *Le Commerce que les Indiens du Mexique Font avec les François au Port du Missisipi (The Mexican Indians Making Trade with the French at the Port of Mississippi).* It shows a mountainous paradise with docile gift-bearing Indians hospitably greeting European colonists and taking catechism lessons, while a lawbreaker is safely ensconced in jail. The scene imparts an overall view

[*] Special thanks are due to W. J. Eccles for his help with this essay.

of peace, prosperity, and law and order in a well-established environment.

In the 1720s and 1730s, architect-engineers Pierre le Blond de la Tour, Adrien de Pauger, and Ignace François Broutin drew city plans and architectural designs for the fledgling city. Alexandre de Batz, the first documented artist working in the colony, recorded indigenous flora, fauna, and sea life, as well as Native inhabitants and their architecture; several of his illustrations were published in Antoine Simon le Page du Pratz's *Histoire de la Louisiane* (1758), which chronicles sixteen years of observations in the fledgling colony. Jean Baptiste Michel le Bouteaux, Jean Pierre Lassus, B. Picart, V. Vanni, and Martinet also sketched Indian life and settlements in New Orleans, Mobile, Natchez, and Natchitoches. Reportedly, a Spanish artist, Lieutenant Miguel García, who sailed to the new colony with Jean-Baptiste le Moyne, sieur de Bienville, was referred to by the sailors as the "father of Louisiana artists." García's artistic output, if any, is unknown.

FROM CRAFTSMANSHIP TO PORTRAITURE

Much effort in early settlements went into creating home furnishings, and colonists imported furniture, artifacts, and portraits from Europe. Among the early immigrants were European-trained craftsmen, skilled slaves, and West Indies artisans, including goldsmiths, silversmiths, watchmakers, clockmakers, jewelers, potters, cabinetmakers, carpenters, and turners. Apprentices and residents, using imported articles as models, contentedly made their own furniture.

During the early years of colonization, it was economically unfeasible for artists to make a living in such an undomesticated locale, and there is no recorded activity in diaries and journals. Bienville himself had his portrait painted in Paris after he retired in 1743. As conditions became more prosperous, portrait painters arrived to take advantage of expanding opportunities.

José Francisco Xavier de Salazar y Mendoza, a native of Mérida in Yucatán, Mexico, is the earliest known artist to have succeeded at his profession. He arrived in Louisiana as an accomplished artist during the last quarter of the eighteenth century. His portraiture, which exhibits Spanish and Mexican eighteenth-century traditions, includes prominent planters and political, social, and religious personages of the city of New Orleans. Two disastrous fires at the end of the eighteenth century destroyed most of the city, both its architecture and its artifacts. Subsequently, Salazar's commissions included many replacement portraits. His daughter, Francisca de Salazar y Magaña, a portraitist who studied under her father, is the first known artist to have studied in the colony. Other artists, whose identities are yet unknown, imitated Salazar's painting style, creating a "school of Salazar."

Miniature painters, such as the Frenchman Ambrose Duval, found opportunities teaching and painting notable figures like William Charles Cole Claiborne, the first governor of Louisiana after it was sold to the United States in 1803. During this period, portraits were painted in the European tradition. Opportunities were also available to a few women who actively sought them, among them a miniaturist known only as Madame Prados; the first known native-born artist in New Orleans, she painted portraits during the first quarter of the nineteenth century.

John L. Boqueta de Woiseri, one of a number of itinerant artists who came to New Orleans, celebrated the occasion of the Louisiana Purchase in a painting and in November 1803 an aquatint engraving titled *A View of New Orleans Taken from the Plantation of Marigny*, an area just downriver of the Vieux Carré, or the Old Quarter, in New Orleans. Most conspicuous above the bird's-eye view is a depiction of an eagle, a reference to the American national bird, which holds in its beak a banner reading, "Under My Wings All Things Prosper." This depiction, which marks the end of the colonial period in French Louisiana, began a tradition of city views that continued throughout the years. Until this point, landscapes had been rare and had not existed as a painting genre. Likewise, no sculpture survives from the early period, nor is there any recorded activity of this endeavor.

With the Louisiana Purchase, opportunities opened up for artists and artisans. Their creative endeavors provided a rich cultural fabric representative of the cultural milieu of New Orleans, its customs, and its citizens.

BIBLIOGRAPHY

Mahé, John A., and Rosanne McCaffrey, eds. *Encyclopaedia of New Orleans Artists 1718–1918*. New Orleans, La., 1987. With bibliography. Offers biographical information on artists and artisans, both resident and visiting, who gravitated to New Orleans, which was already a cultural center when the greater Louisiana territory was still a frontier.

Poesch, Jessie. *The Art of the Old South: Painting, Sculpture, Architecture and the Products of Craftsmen, 1560–1860*. New York, 1983. Provides the best overall view of arts and architecture in colonial Louisiana. Includes extensive bibliography.

Judith Hopkins Bonner

SEE ALSO **Home and Hearth.**

THE SPANISH BORDERLANDS

PAINTING AND SCULPTURE in the Spanish Borderlands during the colonial period, initiated in 1540 by Francisco Vásquez de Coronado's entry into New Mexico and establishment of the first permanent Spanish settlement in 1598, is predominately religious in nature. Most of this religious art was intended for mission church decoration.

Roman Catholic missionaries accompanied military expeditions from the beginning of Spanish exploration in the Southwest, eventually remaining in the northern provinces of New Spain to convert and teach the Indian populations. Painting and sculpture played a significant role in this conversion. These were the tools of instruction, used to explain the religious ideas and symbols to the Native people and to inspire with their beauty. Fray Juan Ramírez, writing a letter from the Santo Domingo mission in 1659 in New Mexico, expressed the importance of church decorations and the difficulties typically encountered in importing ecclesiastical art to the northern provinces.

Inasmuch as it is not permissible to take out of this kingdom [New Mexico] any silver or goods other than cattle, and as such cattle would cheapen those which the governor sends out to El Parral, he closes the road with sinister purposes, and the kingdom is in want, we being forced to give a few sheep which are raised here for the purpose of bringing back ornaments, decorations for the chruches, and other necessities. Even when this entire *definitorio* (friar officials of the *Custodia*) went to the governor to ask license to do this, he replied that churches with decorations and costly ornaments were not necessary; that a few huts of straw and some cloth ornaments, with spoken (low) masses, were ample. The fact is, however, that these things are what we have the most care for, and procure at our expense and labor, for, if precept and virtue teach these natives, they are all influenced as well by the decency, ornamentation, and ritual of the churches. (C. W. Hackett. *Historical Document, Relating to New Mexico, Nueva Vizcaya, and Approaches Thereto, to 1773*. Vol. 3, pp. 188–189)

Of all the borderland regions, New Mexico has by far the longest history. Franciscan friars occupied the mission churches from the late sixteenth century until secularization in the nineteenth century. The painting and sculpture that filled the mission churches during two and a half centuries is the largest body of artistic work to be found in the borderlands region.

NEW MEXICO

Franciscan evangelization had achieved a lengthy, although erratic, history in New Mexico by 1700. Francisco Vásquez de Coronado's 1540 search for the reported seven golden cities and subsequent expeditions culminated in the 1593 colonizing efforts of Don Juan de Oñate and his group of settlers and friars. The Pueblo Rebellion of 1680 interrupted the efforts of the Franciscan order, causing the Spaniards to retreat south to El Paso for twelve years. When Captain-General Don Diego de Vargas reestablished Spanish control over the province in 1692–1693, the majority of the mission churches and their contents had been destroyed.

Out of necessity, a second building campaign was initiated. The adobe churches at Zia,

Isleta, Acoma, and Zuni were sufficiently preserved to be reoccupied. In Santa Fe the church of San Miguel was rebuilt in 1710 on the site of the pre-Revolt church, and the parish church of San Francisco was under construction from 1713 to 1717. A highly venerated statue of Our Lady of the Rosary, popularly known as "La Conquistadora," was placed in a lateral chapel of the parish church. The statue had arrived in New Mexico in 1625, and it participated in both the retreat and the re-entry of the settlers after the Pueblo Revolt.

The Franciscan missionaries subsequently erected numerous new mission churches in the outlying existing pueblos and villages. In some cases new pueblos were established, as at Laguna in 1699, and other pueblos were resettled, all of which required additional missions. The amount of energy and funds consumed by this renewed building campaign inhibited the decoration of church interiors with painting and sculpture, resulting in a delay, lagging far behind the decorating campaigns of Mexico. At the time of Bishop Pedro Tamarón y Romeral's ecclesiastical visitation to New Mexico in 1760, Mexico was well advanced into its most lavish decorating period, the *estípite* baroque, with altar screens that had reached the zenith of complexity. The word *estípite* refers to a kind of pilaster, a pilaster being a support that looks like a column but is not freestanding.

The Altar Screen

A combination of painting and sculpture, framed by architectural elements, the altar screen was often the major artistic work and the central decorative focus in the Roman Catholic church. The screen housed the titular saint, for whom the church was named. The finest available artists were involved in its production. Because of their prominence as artworks, their large size, and their central position, altar screens were often discussed in church documents and inventories, whereas individual paintings and sculpture might not be.

Spain. During the thirteenth century, changes in religious ritual within the Roman Catholic church of Europe contributed to the rise of this totally new art form. Until that time the priest had celebrated the Mass from behind the altar while facing the congregation. When the celebrant's position was moved to the front of the altar, a void was created that stimulated the development of the altarpiece, an ornamental screen rising behind the altar.

In Spain the altarpiece form, the *retablo,* had fully evolved by the mid fourteenth century and survived until well into the eighteenth century. In its generalized form, the Spanish altar screen consisted of a basic architectural structure housing paintings and/or sculptured images. The structure was generally composed of one or more stories, or horizontal tiers, resting on a decorated pedestal. Three or more bays rose vertically, topped by a crowning piece.

Mexico. With the Spanish conquest of Mexico in the sixteenth century, the format of the altar screen was transported to the New World, where it found a welcome home in the newly erected missions and cathedrals. Although New World church decoration initially consisted of frescoes, a simpler and more economical means of ornamentation, altar screens were erected as soon as was feasible in place of these murals. The sixteenth-century Mexican *retablo* faithfully adhered to the Spanish formula and was designed and built by European artists wherever possible. As in Spain, the altar screen, consisting of an intricate combination of artistic elements of architecture, sculpture, and painting, was never totally the work of a single artist. The altar screen was a composite of artistic pieces made by woodcarvers, wood joiners, sculptors, gilders, and painters. The resident priest or friar selected the screen's general iconographic theme. Production was closely dictated and supervised both by the guilds and by contractual agreement.

The type of column, specified in the contract, was the predominant artistic element in the *retablo.* Mexican altar screens are thus classified by their supports. When the altar screen form was transported from Spain to Mexico, the currently popular Renaissance style with its baluster or candelabrum column was transported also. The Renaissance style *retablo* was governed by a clearly defined architectonic structure, expressed through the use of such Renaissance elements as the classic orders, the entablature, and the pediment. Renaissance motifs consisting of cherubic heads, flowers, fruits, and garlands arrayed the architectural components, which were arranged in strict horizontality and verticality, thereby conveying a sense of balance and harmonious repetition.

This Renaissance style held reign in Mexico from the last half of the sixteenth century through the second quarter of the seventeenth, when the baroque style was introduced. Stylistic change initially showed little noticeable difference from the previous style other than the addition of the helicoidal (spiral) column—also known as salomonic, after King Solomon. As the salomonic baroque style developed, profuse foliage and ornamentation invaded every portion of the altar screen's surface.

The baroque affinity for ornamentation and magnificence found a special place in Mexico, where it reached phenomenal complexity and stimulated intense religious fervor. This stylistic movement climaxed with the *estípite* baroque phase, so named for its support, the *estípite* pilaster, a shaft composed of an inverted obelisk surmounted by an assortment of cubes, urns, medallions, and cherubic heads and topped by a capital, or column head, decorated with acanthus leaves in Corinthian style. The beginnings of the *estípite* baroque phase in New Spain can be traced to the Altar of the Kings, erected by Jerónimo Balbás between 1717 and 1737 in the Cathedral of Mexico. A Spanish sculptor, Balbás introduced the *estípite* type to Mexico in this altar screen based upon his previous work at Spain's Cathedral of Cádiz.

The *estípite* baroque struck a responsive chord with Mexican artists. Although derived from contemporary Spanish motifs, the Mexicans made it their own, extending and complicating the style far beyond even Spain's wildest imagination. The *estípite* baroque thus became a Mexican expression rather than merely another Spanish importation.

On the heels of the Altar of the Kings followed numerous *retablo* and church facade variations, based on the *estípite* style. The silver mining towns under the patronage of wealthy miners and the monastic establishments of the affluent Jesuit order proved particularly fertile ground for these expensive, dazzling, artistic extravaganzas. Gone was the sense of reason and calm, of architectural structure. At the ultimate of the Mexican baroque, no surface lay at rest, no area went undecorated. The pilasters flouted the laws of gravity through their amplification of parts and unstable appearance. Gone also was the visual prominence of the saints. Religious doctrine deferred to the single and sudden emotional impact upon the observer, submerging the saints into the ornamentation.

The final exuberance of the eighteenth century encouraged the dissolution of structure into a thoroughly plastic environment. *Estípites* were overwhelmed by the tall ornamental niche-pilasters located between them. Fabricated, appropriately enough, in a molded material rather than in carved wood or stone, this artistic development marked the last evolutionary stage of eighteenth-century Mexican *retablo* design.

With the founding of the Academy of San Carlos in Mexico City in 1781, a new era in colonial church design began. The delirium of the *estípite* baroque was rejected in favor of the revival of classical logic and reason. Gold and polychromy were replaced by white gypsum, marble, and jasper. In contrast to their baroque counterparts, neoclassic altar screens exhibited a certain sobriety. Many baroque altar screens were swept away in the purge, and Mexico again became the victim of an imposed, European style. With the Mexican War of Independence in 1821, the great era of the altar screen in Mexico came to a close.

New Mexico. During his visit, Bishop Tamarón only briefly reviewed the contents of New Mexico interiors, his interest lying with other matters, but he left the impression that the New Mexico missions, with the exception of the provincial capital, Santa Fe, were only sparsely adorned by 1760. At the parish church of Santa Cruz de la Cañada he observed, "The church is rather large but has little adornment," and at the Pueblo Indian mission of San José de la Laguna: "The church is small, and its adornment poor." His most extensive descriptions are of Santa Fe, where he mentioned that the parish church "is large, with a spacious nave and a transept adorned by altars and altar screens." Of the military chapel of La Castrense he expressed pleasure with the stone altar screen which was nearly complete during his visit.

Dedicated to Our Lady of Light, the altarpiece, completed in 1761, was a gift from the provincial governor. According to Bishop Tamarón's report, the stone for the *retablo* was quarried near the city, and upon completion, the entire altar screen was polychromed.

Carved, multistoried stone reliefs were more typically placed on church facades than in the interiors. In fact, stone *retablos* are rarely found throughout the Spanish Americas, and this altar screen exists as a solitary example in New Mexico.

Although incorporating the *estípite* pilaster, then popular in Mexico, the altar screen demonstrates a provinciality with its flat, shallow carving and simplification of motifs. It has been theorized that a provincial carver was imported from northern Mexico to execute the screen, probably with local assistance. Since no contract has been located, the question of authorship remains unanswered.

Not until Fray Francisco Atanasio Domínguez's was a full and detailed accounting of the New Mexico mission interior decoration recorded. Eight of the twenty-seven missions visited by Domínguez housed one or more altar screens as the focal point of decoration, providing evidence that, although meager, the Spanish tradition was maintained in colonial New Mexico. From these descriptions emerges a basic formula for the design and structure of the screens generally utilized throughout New Mexico. The altar screen composition, undoubtedly based on a simplified version of the Mexican altar screen, consisted of an architectural framework of painted wood with two levels, divided by architectural supports into three bays. The lower tier contained a central niche with the image of the mission's titular saint. Each of the other divisions formed by the supports housed either an oil painting on canvas (or hide) or a sculpted icon. To maintain this convention, New Mexican churches lacking adequate statuary and oil paintings to fill the sections sometimes painted directly onto the altar screen structure. Applying the image directly onto the screen, rather than attaching a painting or sculpture, was a New Mexican innovation that eventually gained a wide acceptance in the province.

During the forty-year period following Fray Domínguez's visitation of 1776, a great florescence of church ornamentation took place. Some sixty new altar screens were constructed in the mission churches of New Mexico. The number of *retablos* at the parish church of Santa Cruz de la Cañada, second in importance only to Santa Fe in the Rio Arriba area, increased from only one in 1776 to six by 1795.

Artists and Patrons

Franciscan missionaries were largely responsible for the interiors. Occasionally the friars themselves executed the altar screens. At Santa Cruz de la Cañada, Fray Andrés García was credited with making the main altar screen and some of the sculpted imagery. Two other friars who served at Santa Cruz made *retablos* for the nave and side chapels. Franciscans also traveled to other missions outside their jurisdiction to aid in their decoration.

Father García constructed the altar screen at San Gerónimo de Taos that was painted with earth iridescent with bits of mica, likely the same mineral paint used by the Taos Pueblo Indians for their pottery decoration. This method of achieving a gilt finish is only one of a variety of attempts by provincial artists to recreate the magnificence of Mexican art. San Francisco de Santa Fe's high altar was painted green with gilt veins to simulate the look of jasper. Attempts to achieve the illusion of perspective, although not always entirely successful according to ecclesiastical visitors, appeared in a number of altar screens. Interest in such effects demonstrate that Mexico exerted a marked influence on the decoration of her northern province.

Mexican artists evidently went north in search of work. No guilds were organized to train apprentices in painting and sculpture as in Mexican urban centers, but young assistants surely worked with masters to learn their skills in the tradition of the workshop.

In the seventeenth and eighteenth centuries many oil paintings and carved images of the saints, Mary, and Jesus were imported from Mexico in mission supply caravans. These decorations subsequently served as elements in locally made altar screens. On one occasion a wealthy donor, Bernardino Bustamante and his wife Feliciana Coca, imported two small altar screens from Mexico for the church of San Francisco in Santa Fe. These are the only known Mexican-manufactured altar screens in the northern province of New Mexico. The remaining *retablos* were apparently locally manufactured. Inventory statements, such as the description of the screen of the high altar at the Santa Fe parish church, suggest that the *retablos* were constructed of "the kind of wood common in this kingdom, which is fir, or pine."

Patrons, who tended to be civil officials and wealthy citizens, were often identified both in the ecclesiastical inventories and on the screens themselves. The identity of the artists, however, was only rarely recorded.

During the late eighteenth century, Antonio José Ortiz, a wealthy citizen of Santa Fe, funded the reconstruction and refurbishment of the Santa Fe parish church and four area chapels plus two private chapels at his home and ranch. The artist who executed the altar screen at the chapel of San Miguel of Santa Fe and likely the other chapels as well, remains anonymous but is called the Laguna Santero. Laguna Santero is the only eighteenth-century artist working in New Mexico for whom a large corpus of work remains extant. He has been identified, on the basis of style, as the maker of the surviving altar screens at San Miguel, Laguna, Acoma, Zia, and possibly Santa Ana.

Most of the patrons of these works were associated in one way or another with the Ortiz family. Only a man such as Ortiz had the economic means to bring an artist directly from Mexico. As indicated in the will of his wife, Rosa Bustamante, Ortiz had purchased artwork from Mexico. He was not only familiar with the artistic climate there, but would not likely have been satisfied with less than a Mexican artist to undertake the numerous commissions he donated to the churches. The Bustamantes, Ortiz's in-laws, had already imported the only known Mexican altar screens to New Mexico. However, planning to donate several altarpieces, perhaps Ortiz imported an artist, rather than an altar screen, into New Mexico. After completing the work for Ortiz, the artist moved on to other commissions from related patrons culminating as far west as Laguna and Acoma.

The altar screen at the chapel of San Miguel in Santa Fe is one of the oldest dated wooden altarpieces remaining in New Mexico. The dual cartouche inscriptions at its base identify the date, 1798, and the donor, Don Antonio José Ortiz.

Following the precedent set by both Mexico and eighteenth-century New Mexico, the altar screen was created solely as a backdrop for paintings and sculpture. Indeed, artists left spaces behind oil paintings unpainted. The oval oil paintings of saints and Jesus the Nazarene were probably imported from Mexico, as was the statue of the patron Saint Michael.

As one of the earliest extant wooden alterpieces of New Mexican manufacture, the San Miguel *retablo* occupies a unique position. Having only brief, written inventories of what preceded it chronologically in New Mexico, the influences shaping the formation of this piece can only be surmised. While following the same general format as other eighteenth-century New Mexican *retablos,* the altar screen exhibits signs of a synthesis of specific Spanish colonial elements combined in an unconventional manner.

The visibility of the architectural structure, with its clearly delineated sections and architectural members, is reminiscent of New Spain's sixteenth-century Renaissance style. The practice of filling all empty spaces with foliate motifs reflects prevailing Mexican taste throughout the sixteenth-century "plateresque" phase, an architectural style suggestive of the richly applied surface decoration of silver, which found its ultimate congestion in the eighteenth-century *estípite* baroque style. But notable differences exist. Whereas, in Mexico the forms were carved in relief, at San Miguel they are painted. The maker of the San Miguel screen substituted a painted profusion of foliage in the central niche for the elaborate carving seen in Mexico's early-eighteenth-century baroque altar screens. Painted vines are wrapped around the columns in lieu of the more convincing carved counterparts in Mexican churches. The pillars are the twisted salomonic columns so common in seventeenth- and early-eighteenth century Mexico. But by 1798, when this altar screen was completed, the salomonic column had long since ceased to be fashionable in New Spain and had been replaced by the more complicated *estípite* pilaster, which had already begun to lose favor to the neoclassic movement.

It has been suggested that the Castrense stone altarpiece served as the inspiration and prototype for the altar screen at San Miguel and other New Mexico *retablos.* Beside the most obvious discrepancy between San Miguel and La Castrense, the use of two different construction materials, the divergent use of column type, *estípite* at Castrense and salomonic at San Miguel, call into question the use of the Castrense as the prototype. It seems more logical to conclude that both were provincial interpretations of Mexican collaterals rather than one of the other. New Mexican colonists were not unaware of Mexican art as evidenced by the importation by Bustamante of the two gilded altar screens in the parish church of Santa Fe, as well as the exquisite Mexican painting of an altar screen signed by José de Alzíbar in 1783 and located in the chapel of Our Lady of Guadalupe in Santa Fe.

Inscribed in 1798, the same year as the altar screen of San Miguel, is the one at Nuestra Señora de la Asunción de Zia: "This altar was made through the devotion of Don Vitor Sandoval and of his wife Doña Maria Manuela Ortiz in the year of 1798." The mission church of Zia is one of a handful of New Mexican churches built prior to the Pueblo Revolt of 1680 that were in suitable condition to be reoccupied after the rebellion.

The Zia altar screen is the earliest surviving New Mexican example of a saint's image painted in tempera directly onto the architectural structure. Artists consciously attempted to replicate attached oil paintings by painting oval picture frames around the images of the saints in imitation of the San Miguel *retablo*. Perhaps this innovation on the part of the artist resulted from the poverty of the Pueblo Indian mission, which could not afford sufficient imported oil paintings to fill the screen.

The similarity of Zia's stylistic characteristics to those of the San Miguel altar screen provides the basis for attribution of the work to the Laguna artist. Both screens employ the same floral motifs and scalloped patterns. Salomonic columns, painted to accentuate their twisting curves, are incorporated into both. The underlying philosophy is the same: substitution of two-dimensional elements for three-dimensional components, whether artistic painted decoration for relief carving or painted architectural elements.

Painting and the Use of Prints

Scholars agree that San José at Laguna Pueblo contains the finest preserved wooden altarpiece in New Mexico. In the Laguna altar screen, architectural sculpture and painting merged fully. Freeing himself from the convention of provid-

ing a decorative backdrop for existing canvases, Laguna Santero painted the images directly onto wooden planks, filling the entire space with the image. The documented presence in the church of oil paintings from an earlier period suggests that he could have done otherwise. However, the artist chose to paint the titular saint, Saint Joseph, himself.

The full-length painted figure of Saint Joseph, occupies the central panel of the lower level, with Saint Barbara to the right and Saint John Nepomucene to the left. The choice of a Jesuit saint, John Nepomucene, although an unusual one for Franciscan New Mexico at the time of the construction of the Castrense altarpiece in 1761, was not peculiar by 1800. After the expulsion of the Jesuits from Mexico in 1767, ecclesiastical authorities reallocated the lavish and extravagant contents of their churches among the remaining orders. Jesuit saints consequently came to reside on altar screens alongside Franciscan, Augustinian, and Dominican saints in regular and secular churches.

Each of the saints depicted in the Laguna church is painstakingly correct iconographically, suggesting that the artist consulted a religious authority, probably a religious print, a practice quite common in Mexico and Spain. Devotional prints used as models for painted images of saints were readily available in Mexico, where they were sold at market stalls and shops near churches and at pilgrimage sites and shrines. Engraved illustrations in religious books also served as sources of artistic inspiration. Franciscans usually kept a variety of religious books to aid in instruction of the Indians.

Libraries, however, were exceedingly sparse in New Mexico. Only provincial governors, wealthy families, and clerics were likely to possess them. The library of the Custody was housed at the mission of Santo Domingo, which in 1776 had more than 250 volumes, including religious books, Spanish histories, Latin classics, dictionaries and grammars. Most of the citizenry were unable to read and fear of the Inquisition discouraged ownership of books other than religious volumes.

The artistic impact of the few available published engravings was thus disproportionally great. A woodcut on the frontispiece of the Santa Fe constitution of the Cofradía de la Congregación de Nuestra Señora de la Luz evidently served as a model for the stone panel of Our Lady of Light on the Costrense altar screen. The other relief panels exhibit a similar bookish flavor, and it is likely that they were copied from prints as well.

An 1807 Mexican copper engraving of the Holy Trinity by José Simón de Larrea displays a close stylistic affiliation with the painted Trinity panel crowning the altar screen at Laguna. Both illustrate the three-person Trinity seated amidst clouds and cherubic heads. Although Rome banned this image in 1745, Mexican and New Mexican artists consistently incorporated this icon into their works until the mid nineteenth century, and even later in the folk arts.

Wall Painting

The Laguna Santero also decorated the mission church's entire sanctuary. A hide altar frontal, a painted ceiling canopy, and a set of wall murals were applied to the projecting sanctuary walls flanking the altar screen. Damaged by roof leaks, they were completely covered with whitewash in the late 1960s.

Stretching from the ceiling to the level of the altar, they consisted of vertical registers of repeating bold foliate designs, bounded by horizontal registers. Their related motifs and patterns suggest that a single artist produced both the murals and the altar screen. As the following excerpt from the 1810 Laguna inventory suggests, the paintings' patterned registers imitated tapestry: "At its [the altar screen's] sides some curtains of perspective adorn painted of colors that embellish all the Presbytery." The surface tempera colors of black, gray, vermilion, and ochre were applied to a thin layer of whitewash covering the adobe plaster.

Wall paintings of gray and black, termed *grisaille,* combined with colored earth accents are found in Mexico in the monasteries of the sixteenth century. Examples include the convent of Huejotzingo, Puebla, and the cloisters of Acolman, Mexico; and the stairway and refectory paintings at the monastery of Actopan, Hidalgo. Book illustrations and printed marginalia that the artists enlarged evidently served as source materials for the frescoed borders, maintaining the gray and black coloration of the print with a few earth-colored accents. The wall paintings

at Laguna are highly reminiscent of the Mexican works and may also have used book illustrations as models.

Wall painting in colonial New Mexico was reported by inventories of several churches. Eighteenth-century New Mexico missions lacking altar screens resorted to sixteenth-century Mexican solutions. At Laguna itself, traces of early wall painting were found behind the altar screen. However, no wall painting with such a complex or sophisticated design as Laguna's has been recorded elsewhere in New Mexico. Friars trained in the monastic establishments of Mexico had undoubtedly seen such Mexican murals and had carried mental images of them to New Mexico. With funds and skill lacking for the construction of altarpieces, they initially substituted wall painting as the predominant decoration.

On the interior of the Santo Domingo church the presiding Franciscan had a small altar screen in perspective painted directly on the wall. In 1776 Fray Dominguez noted that the two-dimensionally painted saints were depicted as though they were sitting in three-dimensional niches. The wall paintings at San Ildefonso and San Francisco de Nambé, on the other hand, imitated tapestry designs.

Hide Painting

Ecclesiastical chroniclers observed large paintings on tanned animal hides, usually of saints, Mary, and Jesus, in the New Mexico missions. At least sixty-eight hide paintings are still extant, but documentary sources clearly suggest that hundreds were hanging on the church walls from the seventeenth century until around 1820, when representatives of the Bishop of Durango ordered their removal. Juan Bautista Guevara condemned the paintings as indecent and improper objects of devotion, as did succeeding visitors from the Diocese of Durango.

While there is some scholarly disagreement regarding the origins of the New Mexican hide paintings, seventeenth- and eighteenth-century documents from New Mexico clearly indicate that painted hides were shipped in numbers from New Mexico south to Mexico. Tanned hides were an important export commodity for the province. Painting on many of the hides may have been done in workshops where Indian painters were forced to labor.

Painted hides bearing devotional images hung on the mission walls had the added benefit of portability, allowing priests to carry paintings to the missions. In one instance, at the eighteenth-century church of Santo Tomás de Abiquíu, a Franciscan had arranged five hide paintings to create the appearance of an altar screen.

The painted hides served other uses as well. At the missions of Laguna and Acoma hides painted with floral designs constituted the altar frontals, while large hide canopies adorned with celestial images of the sun, moon, and stars hung above the altars. A hide altar canopy also existed at Santa Ana as early as 1712.

Hide paintings belonging to New Mexico residents also appear in the inventories of their estates and wills. Two extraordinary large hide paintings, known as the Segesser paintings, are named for Father Segesser who shipped them to his Swiss family in 1758. These are the oldest documented extant hide paintings believed to have been produced in New Mexico. One of them depicts the 1720 battle of the Villasur expedition from Santa Fe between the Spanish military and their Pueblo Indian allies against French and Pawnee forces in eastern Nebraska.

Sculpture

Fray Alonso Benavides took a small statue of Our Lady of the Rosary to New Mexico in 1625. Known popularly as "La Conquistadora," it is probably the earliest sculptural Christian image in New Mexico. Originally placed in the parish church of Santa Fe, Spaniards carried the Madonna south when the Spanish fled the region during the Pueblo Revolt of 1680. It accompanied the Vargas reconquest in 1692–1693. Today she is annually borne in a procession that commemorates this event.

The traditional Roman Catholic use of processional images in dramatic reenactments was transported to the New World, where it proved useful in the instruction and conversion of Native peoples. Even today, New Mexicans throughout the state carry processional images through community streets to bless and cleanse neighborhoods on the saint's feast day or at other important occasions in the Christian calendar. Images of revered Virgins, such as La Conquistadora, have lavish wardrobes of clothing and jewels.

Life-size figures of Jesus are often articulated at the shoulders, elbows, and knees, so that they may play differing roles in the dramatization of the Passion. During Good Friday processions, the Christ in the Sepulcher statue, carved by Fray Andrés Garcí before 1776, is carried from the church of Santa Cruz de la Cañada. Fray Domínguez credited Fray Andrés García with the production of sculptural images at other mission churches where he served, carving images for the niches of altar screens and processionals.

Domínguez also identified Captain Bernardo Miera y Pacheco, a Spanish-born military officer and mapmaker, as a New Mexican sculptor. Evidence also suggests that he was a painter as well, but no specific paintings can be directly linked to his hand. Miera y Pacheco carved a statue of Saint Phillip the Apostle for the altar-screen niche at the mission church of San Felipe Pueblo.

In the nineteenth century, native New Mexican artists began to satisfy the need for sculpture in churches and private chapels. José Rafael Aragón, whose career spanned more than forty years and included the production of numerous signed altar screens, panel paintings, and sculpted images for northern New Mexican communities, was among the most prolific of these artists. Aragón was undoubtedly influenced by the monuments of the eighteenth century in the capital city of Sante Fe, where he was born.

Though none of his sculptures are signed, documents identify him as a sculptor. In the 1867 inventory of Santa Cruz de la Cañada, Father Juan de Jesus Trujillo lists "two sculptured statues of Our Lady of Carmel, one of them made . . . by the sculptor Rafael Aragón who in turn would be paid for with his burial."

The amount of painting and sculpture produced in and for New Mexican missions and churches exceeded that of other borderland regions. The lengthy era of missionization and colonization necessitated the presence of substantial arts in service of the church.

TEXAS

Spanish exploration of Texas lasted for more than a century before settlements were finally established, but in the late seventeenth and early eighteenth centuries missions and *presidios* were established as buffers against French encroachment.

The Texas mission program differed from that of neighboring New Mexico, where mission churches were built at the sites of already existing Indian villages. In Texas, mission programs gathered tribal groups at three dozen mission compounds established at strategic points. Many missions were not very substantial and were plagued by attacks from raiding Apache and Comanche.

One group of missions that did prosper was that established beginning in 1718 along the San Antonio River near the river's modern municipal namesake. After building a series of temporary structures, the colonial regime initiated construction of permanent, grander mission churches. Three Texas missions, San Antonio de Valero (more popularly known as the Alamo), Nuestra Señora de la Purísma Concepción, and San José y San Miguel de Aguayo, all received elaborate facade and interior decoration. The less ornate mission churches of present-day San Juan Capistrano and San Francisco de la Espada were not intended as the final permanent buildings.

With the complete secularization of the missions in 1824, the Texas churches were abandoned and transformed into cattle enclosures and military establishments. The structures soon fell into ruin, experiencing collapsing roofs and walls, with the single exception of the Mission of Concepción. All of the missions subsequently required extensive rebuilding and repairs.

Architectural Sculpture

Three of the Texas missions have stone sculpture facades, an element not found on New Mexico mission churches. Carved ornamentation at Missions San Antonio de Valero and Concepción is shallow and delicate except for the projecting columns. Carved details and column styles were likely copied from Renaissance pattern books, and the facades have a sixteenth-century quality, far removed from their eighteenth-century date.

Statues of Saints Francis and Dominic have disappeared from their scalloped shell niches at Valero as has the Virgin of Immaculate Conception over the doorway of Mission Concepción. It is speculated that a master mason completed the Concepción facade in 1755 and then initiated reconstruction of Valero shortly thereafter. The master mason of Valero is known to be of Indian origin from central Mexico.

In contrast to the earlier sedate, shallow facades at Valero and Concepción, the carved stone facade at San José y Miguel de Aguayo is dynamic, deep, and organic. Fray Juan Agustín Morfí described the completed facade during his visit in 1777: "The facade is very costly because of the statues and ornaments with which it is heavily decorated, detracting somewhat from its natural beauty . . . no one could have imagined that there were such good artists in so desolate a place." A San José mission census lists Antonio Salazar, an Indian mason from Zacatecas. Salazar was probably the master carver at San José, founded by the Franciscan college in Zacatecas. Salazar likely worked at churches in Zacatecas, perhaps San Agustín, whose carving demonstrates some relationships to San José, before being sent north to build the new church.

The two-story stone facade is alive with scrolls, shells, swags, and foliate motifs. A good example of colonial baroque facades, it incorporates styles then prevalent in Mexico, unlike so many archaic borderland works. The iconographic program begins on the lower levels with Saints Joachim and Ann, parents of the Virgin, who appears as the Virgin of Guadalupe above the door. On the second level, the statues of Saints Dominic and Francis, founders of mendicant orders, flank the choir window. Above the window Saint Joseph stands holding the infant Jesus. An equally ornate sacristy window and interior doorways appear to be carved by the same artist.

Architectural Polychromy

The facades of San José and Concepción were further decorated with polychrome painting giving the appearance of colored ceramic tile and dressed stone surfaces common in central Mexico. At Concepción the two bell tower bases featured red and blue squares containing quatrefoil cross designs. Colorful painted bands and the architectural elements of the belfries, outlined in colorful reds and blues, framed the windows.

The portion of the San José facade not covered by stone also bore painted surface designs resembling the ceramic tiled facades of Puebla, Mexico. Red, blue, and yellow geometric designs covered the entire surface.

The San José and Concepción missions must have presented visitors a very different sight than they do today with only faint traces of the paint remaining. No evidence exists for polychromed exterior surfaces at the other San Antonio missions.

Figural Sculpture

In 1772 the Franciscan College of Querétero transferred jurisdiction over four San Antonio missions to the College of Zacatecas, which already administered San José mission. A detailed inventory, compiled for each of the former Franciscan missions, provides important information about the contents of the missions in the late eighteenth century. San Antonio de Valero housed fifteen pieces of figural sculpture according to the inventory. In addition to the images for the altar screen, the mission owned a life-sized Body of Christ used during Holy Week for the descent from the cross, with its cross, crown, and covering; also a statue of Jesus of Nazareth with its crown, garment, and silk cord for Holy Week reenactments. A statue of Our Lady of Sorrows, also associated with the events of the passion, had two taffeta cloak garments, one of trimmed cloth and another of velvet, with a silver dagger and crown. A cabinet stored an ivory statue of the Child Jesus to be used on Christmas Eve. All of these statues were used in the missions' program of Indian proselytization. The images, which appeared life-like with their glass eyes, inset teeth, human hair and eyelashes, were carried on the portable stands listed in the inventory, for feast day processions.

Two processional figures were constructed of corn pith, or *caña de maiz*, a process developed in pre-Hispanic Mexico and perpetuated in colonial Mexico. Missionaries were quick to note the merits of the lightweight construction. The freestanding statuary and oil paintings in the San Antonio missions were evidently imported from Mexico, probably during the eighteenth century.

Inventories and extant examples of figural sculpture demonstrate the narrow selection of iconography at the San Antonio missions. Figures of Jesus associated with the Nativity and events of the Passion; various advocations of Mary, particularly Our Lady of Sorrows, the Immaculate Conception, and the Rosary; Saint Joseph, Saint Francis, and Saint Anthony of Padua were the most common images.

CALIFORNIA

California's first settlement, the Franciscan mission at San Diego, was founded in 1769, 170 years after the colonization of New Mexico and some fifty years after the establishment of San Antonio. Along the coast from San Diego northward, a string of twenty-one missions reached to San Francisco Solano, the last one, founded in 1823. By this time Mexico was well advanced into the neoclassic stylistic era.

Like the other Spanish Borderland regions, most Spanish colonial artistic endeavors in California centered around the building and decorating campaigns of the missions. The Spanish Crown granted only about twenty-five *ranchos* between 1769 and 1821. Because most grantees remained impoverished, Spanish colonists lacked sufficient wealth to commission and purchase artwork. Even after the secularization of the missions in 1834, few families achieved the status of landed elite.

Oil Painting and the Use of Prints

Oil paintings and sculpted images for the California missions were, with few exceptions, imported from Mexico. While awaiting the arrival of this art work, Franciscans used engraved prints as a primary didactic device, probably distributing them among the Native converts.

Shipment requests and invoices list mission orders for large numbers of engravings from Mexico. The images most frequently requested identify the popular saints of the region in the late eighteenth and early nineteenth centuries.

The fourteen Stations of the Cross, which were hung in a series along the walls of the nave, were a particularly popular set of prints. These images were used temporarily until formal paintings arrived. Evidence documents the use of engravings as models for oil paintings. When Fray Junípero Serra ordered a painting of the patron saint for Mission San Juan Capistrano in 1775, he specified that they "should find a good engraving and have Paez paint it, or some other good artist."

A set of fourteen oils of the Stations of the Cross, painted in the early nineteenth century for San Fernando and now at Mission San Gabriel, were probably locally produced. The paintings, based upon Mexican engravings, suggest

329

that one or more Native Americans may have painted this series.

Wall Painting

Wall painting was the predominant form of church decoration produced locally in colonial California. Painted architectural ornaments, such as columns and entablatures, marbleized door and window panels and frames, along with floral, foliate, and geometric friezes abounded on the walls behind the altar, the nave, side chapels, and sometimes, even the ceiling. Several layers of paintings, with an intermediary layer of whitewash separating each have been found on the interiors of many of the missions, while exteriors also received painted decoration.

Santa Clara records boast the oldest documented wall painting, dating from 1784. At San Juan Bautista, the painting bore the date of 1800. An artist who produced images at both Santa Clara and San José worked there in the mid 1830s. Wall painting apparently spanned the history of the missions once permanent buildings were constructed.

Architectural treatises imported from Mexico as well as imported fabrics and wallpapers probably served as sources of artistic inspiration. The paintings generally had no iconographic content and were intended purely as ornamentation.

The painting on the ceiling of Mission Santa Clara, produced in 1835 or 1836, is a notable exception. The painter, Agustín Dávila, was from Mexico City where he likely saw the cathedral's painted dome. The ceiling, intended to depict the heavens, has the monogram of Jesus in the center with the four evangelists in adjacent corners, and the Immaculate Conception, the three-person Trinity, and Saint Joseph located above the altar.

Two-dimensional murals intended to emulate the sculptural quality of altar screens were painted in a number of mission sanctuaries. At Santa Inés the artist employed perspective in the painting to trick the eye into believing that a *retablo* stood behind the altar.

Both imported altar screens and locally constructed ones replaced wall paintings at several mission churches. In contrast to New Mexico, single sculptors did not produce multiple altar screens.

Because of the ravages of overpainting and natural disasters, only Mission San Miguel has preserved its original decoration. In 1821–1822, Esteban Munras, a Spaniard, covered the interior from floor to ceiling with decorative motifs; he also produced the altar screen.

Artists

With the multiple layers of wall paintings in the missions, often known only through fragments, as well as multiple painting styles within each layer, and the absence of reliable dating techniques, it is difficult to attach artists' names to individual works. Extant documentation indicates that a diverse groups of artists decorated the California missions.

At San Buenaventura, Indian artists produced all of the paintings, according to the Franciscan Mariano Payeras. The designs were probably based upon European pattern books. Although many other missions undoubtedly employed Native artists under missionaries' supervision, few other names were recorded. In 1771 the Franciscans at Mission San Gabriel ordered the book *How to Paint Without a Teacher*, suggesting that untrained artists were being used.

Little is known about missionaries working as artists. Fray Estevan Tapis was the decorator for the 1794 Santa Barbara Mission, the paintings of which are no longer extant. While at Mission San José, Franciscan José María de Jesús Gonzáles Rubio painted three large canvas curtains, also no longer extant, to decorate the church on special feast days: one for Christmas eve mass, another for Holy Thursday, and a funeral catafalque. Other such painted canvas curtains survive at Mission Dolores in San Francisco and at Santa Inés.

Artists from Mexico and Europe undoubtedly came to Alta California. Augustín Dávila, arriving in 1834 with the Híjar-Padres expedition from Mexico, decorated the missions of Santa Clara and San José where the original contract has been located. Esteban Munras, a Spaniard formerly of Peru, supervised the decoration program at San Miguel. And an American sailor, Thomas Doak, a ship's carpenter from New England, painted the main altar screen at San Juan Bautista Mission in 1817.

ARIZONA

Arizona was not a distinct Spanish colonial province. The missions at the Hopi pueblos in the north prior to the Pueblo Revolt were under New Mexican jurisdiction. No colonial settlements were established north of Tucson.

The two missions established in southern Arizona were within the province of Sonora, as were eight other Sonoran missions. These missions were among those founded by Jesuit Eusebio Kino in the region termed the Pimería Alta.

When the Jesuit order was expelled from New Spain in 1767, the Arizona missions were abandoned until Franciscan replacements arrived. The Franciscans began a new church at San Xavier del Bac, which was completed by the time of Fray Francisco Iturralde's 1797 report. Iturralde described the interior:

The church is very large. It has five altars, four in the crossing and the High Altar: the High Altar has a retable of burned brick and lime, and it is painted and gilded, and the other altars are only painted, and all are adorned with thirty-two statues of saints including the four that are in the four pillars in the body of the church, and all are very beautiful. Moreover, the walls of the church, the octagonal drum, the cupola, as also the choir are adorned with various images and mysteries in fine paintings which are applied on the wall, but in such a manner that they appear to be on canvas. (Bernard Fontana. "Biography of a Desert Church," p. 9)

San Xavier's interior is covered with adornment—wall paintings, five *retablos,* and some sixty figural sculptures. The artists are unknown. However, a 1795 census of San Xavier records the presence of twenty-nine Spaniards, whose presence would have been illegal unless they had been temporarily employed at the mission. A similar circumstance occurred at La Purísma Concepción de Tumacacorí, the second Arizona mission begun in 1801 and never completed. Tumacacorí later lost some twenty Spaniards in the 1805 census, while the Sonoran mission, La Purísma Concepción de Nuestra Señora de Caborca, gained thirty Spaniards.

All three churches share architectural similarities. The stone *retablo*-type facades at San Xavier del Bac and Caborca, which use the *estípite* column, are good borderland examples of the *estípite* baroque style, although this style was then some fifteen or more years out of fashion with Mexico.

The interior altar screens at Bac are also in the *estípite* baroque style. The main *retablo,* surprisingly constructed of brick and carved stucco rather than carved wood, while not overly ornate by Mexican standards, is extraordinary in comparison to other Spanish Borderland examples. A profusion of angels and cherubs, drapery swags, foliate, and other plaster embellishments, all richly coated in gilt, shimmer and undulate before the visitor's eye. The large number of sculptural images illustrate the proselytizing themes of the revelation of the Christian story and the salvation of mankind and were undoubtedly used by the missionaries in their conversion efforts. The main altar screen, whose iconography is a summary of the theme of redemption, represented by the Immaculate Conception, the events in the life of Jesus, and the founding of the Church, surmounted by an image of God the Father, is at the center of the thematic program. This work of art summarizes in a dramatic way the goal of the missionary effort in the Spanish Borderlands. The relationship between the Bac *retablo* and its Mexican counterparts indicates that the screen was produced by experienced, trained artists.

Artists likely produced most of the figural sculpture locally and in the vicinity of the mission, particularly those figures incorporating plaster. Laboratory analysis establishes that the wooden figures draped with solid plaster garments and other figures with plaster bodies are fashioned from the same materials as the plaster coatings of the mission walls. And the woods employed in the images grow locally.

BIBLIOGRAPHY

Adams, Eleanor B. "Bishop Tamarón's Visitation to New Mexico, 1760." *New Mexico Historical Review* 28 (April 1953):81–114; 28 (July 1953):192–221; 28 (October 1953):291–315; 29 (January 1954):41–47.

Adams, Eleanor B., and Fray Angélico Chavez. *The Missions of New Mexico, 1776: A Description by Fray Francisco Atanasio Domínguez.* Albuquerque, N. Mex., 1956; repr. 1975.

Ahlborn, Richard E. *Saints of San Xavier.* Tucson, Ariz., 1974.

Anderson, Barbara. "The Expulsion of the Jesuits and the Decline of Religious Iconography in Eighteenth Century Mexico." *New Mexico Studies in the Fine Arts* 1 (1976):37–39.

Archives of the Archdiocese of Santa Fe. Accounts, 1817. Book 62 (Box 5). Santa Fe. Acts of Guevara Visitation of New Mexico; Loose Document, 1795. No. 13. Abiquiú. General Census Chart and Report on Custody; Loose Document, 1810. No. 10. Laguna. Inventory of Church; Loose Document, 1867. No. 9. Santa Cruz. Inventory of Church.

Archives of Nuestra Señora de Guadalupe de Zacatecas. Inventories, 1772. Microfilm (Zacatecas 3 and 4). Archives of Old Spanish Missions Historical Research Library. Our Lady of the Lake University, San Antonio, Texas.

Bleser, Nicholas J. *Tumacácori, from Ranchería to National Monument.* Tucson, Ariz., 1989.

Boyd, E. *Popular Arts of Spanish New Mexico.* Santa Fe, N. Mex., 1974.

Bol, Marsha C. "The Anonymous Artist of Laguna and the New Mexican Colonial Altar Screen." M.A. thesis, University of New Mexico, 1980.

Chavez, Fray Angélico. *Our Lady of the Conquest.* Santa Fe, N. Mex., 1948.

Eckhart, George B., and James S. Griffith. *Temples in the Wilderness: Spanish Churches of Northern Sonora.* Arizona Historical Society Historical Monograph No. 3. Tucson, Ariz., 1975.

Fontana, Bernard. "Biography of a Desert Church: The Story of Mission San Xavier del Bac." *The Smoke Signal* 3 (Spring 1961); repr. 1971.

Goss, Robert C. *The San Xavier Altarpiece.* Tucson, Ariz., 1974.

Greenwood, Roberta S. "The California Ranchero: Fact or Fancy." In *Columbian Consequences: Archaeological and Historical Perspectives on the Spanish Borderlands West,* edited by David Hurst Thomas. Vol. 1. Washington D.C., 1989.

Grizzard, Mary. *Spanish Colonial Art and Architecture of Mexico and the U.S. Southwest.* Lanham, Md., 1986.

Hackett, C.W., ed. *Historical Documents Relating to New Mexico, Nueva Vizcaya and Approaches Thereto, to 1773.* Vol. 3. Washington, D.C., 1923–1937.

Iturralde, Francisco, O.F.M. *Visita de la Misiones de la Pimería por el P. Iturralde,* 1797. Franciscan Archive, Rome. Copy on file at Mission San Xavier, Tucson, Ariz.

Kelemen, Pál. "The Significance of the Stone Retable of Cristo Rey." *El Palacio* 61 (August 1954):243–272.

Montgomery, Ross Gordon, Watson Smith, and J. O. Brew. *Franciscan Awatovi.* Papers of the Peabody Museum of American Archaeology and Ethnology, vol. 36. Harvard University, 1949.

Morfí, Juan Agustín de. *History of Texas 1673–1779.* 2 vols. Translated by Carlos Eduardo Castañeda. New York, 1967.

Neuerburg, Norman. *The Decoration of the California Missions.* Santa Barbara, Calif., 1989.

———. "The Function of Prints in the California Missions." *Historical Account of Southern California* 67 (Fall 1985):263–280.

———. "Painting in the California Missions." *American Art Review* 4 (July 1977):72–88.

Ortiz Family Papers, New Mexico State Records Center, Will of Rosa Bustamante, 9 July 1814.

Lange, Yvonne. "The Impact of European Prints on The Devotional Tin Paintings of Mexico: A Transferral Hypothesis." In *The Art of Private Devotion: Retablo Painting of Mexico,* edited by Gloria Fraser Giffords. Fort Worth and Dallas, Tex., 1991.

Lee, Georgia, and Norman Neuerberg. "The Alta California Indians as Artists Before and After Contact." In *Columbian Consequences: Archaeological and Historical Perspectives on the Spanish Borderlands West,* edited by David Hurst Thomas. Vol. 1. Washington D.C., 1989.

McCarty, Kieran. "Bac." *Arizona Highways* 54 (January 1978):17–31.

Mather, Christine, ed. *Colonial Frontiers: Art and Life in Spanish New Mexico, The Fred Harvey Collection.* Santa Fe, N. Mex., 1983.

Pierce, Donna L. "The History of Hide Painting in New Mexico." In *The Segesser Hide Paintings: An Anthology* (tentative title), edited by Thomas E. Chavez. Santa Fe, N. Mex., forthcoming.

———. "Identification of the Warriors in the Frescos of Ixmiquilpan." *Research Center for the Arts Review* 4 (October 1981):1–8.

Quirarte, Jacinto. Decorative and Applied Arts at the Missions. Final Report, 10 August 1982. Research Center for the Arts, University of Texas San Antonio, Tex., 1982.

San Antonio Bicentennial Heritage Committee. "Church Art of Spanish Colonial San Antonio." *San Antonio in the 18th Century.* San Antonio, Tex., 1976.

Schuetz, Mardith. "Professional Artisans in the Hispanic Southwest." *The Americas* 40 (July 1983), no. 1. 1983.

Wroth, William. *Christian Images in Hispanic New Mexico.* Colorado Springs, Colo., 1982.

Marsha C. Bol

SEE ALSO **Architecture; Crafts; Home and Hearth; Mission Communities;** and **Native American Religions.**

CRAFTS

THE BRITISH COLONIES

To the modern reader, the term "crafts" often brings to mind those handmade objects produced through the skilled, regulated application of tools to such natural materials as wood, stone, earth, minerals, and plant fibers. A list of crafts made by producers in the British colonies of North America might include such functional categories as objects intended to focus social memory (gravestones, painted or engraved portraits, political cartoons), household furnishings (desks, chests, dishes, cutlery, domestic textiles), or mechanical implements (ploughs, clocks, guns, surveying tools). But in the seventeenth and eighteenth centuries, the term "crafts," itself a contraction of the period term "handicrafts," more often designated the particular trades responsible for the fabrication of such artifacts. Producers or artisans in early modern North America, therefore, conceived of themselves as "handicraftsmen" whose mastery of the "art and mystery" (*kräftig*) of a specific trade provided an economic livelihood and a sense of cultural identity.

For both immigrant and Creole colonists in Britain's North American possessions, the successful practice of one's craft usually culminated a protracted period of serving an apprenticeship,

working as a journeyman or day laborer, and garnering the resources needed to open and operate one's own shop. Thus a comprehensive historical approach to British crafts must concentrate on those trades and tradespeople whose skills and rules of acceptable work inform the design, workmanship, marketing, and symbolic meaning of artifacts produced according to recognized cultural standards.

Contemporary research on artisans also draws attention to the role that claims to "skill" and "strength" often played in colonial politics. Over the past two decades, historians have discovered that the colonial craftsman was a complicated, often contradictory figure. At times he could be the self-sufficient, proud, entrepreneurial hero of republican virtue that peoples the pages of Carl Bridenbaugh's pioneering study, *The Colonial Craftsman* (1950). Yet the same craftsmen who joined furniture, turned pots, blew glass, or printed newspapers by day met by night to mobilize patriotic sentiments into acts of rebellion. Against the myth of upward mobility and virtuous self-sufficiency, then, appeared the craftsman who felt the pain of poverty and discovered political consciousness in the darkened fractures of class difference. Indeed the *Oxford English Dictionary* (1989) offers as among the earliest definitions of "craft" the following: "Strength, power, might, force . . . Intellectual power; skill; art . . . ability in planning or performing." Without question the living memory of trade organization and civic political clout in late medieval guilds and the Masonic Order provided a ready model for American craftsmen searching for a social voice in such colonial centers as eighteenth-century Boston, New York, Philadelphia, and Charleston. And after the revolution, occupational slogans such as "By Hammer and Hand, All Arts Do Stand" drew attention to the assumption of political "strength, power, might, [and] force" by craft producers. Careful work on artisans, in summary, demonstrates that "skill" cut in two directions at once: it informed the virtuosity and control necessary to uphold standards of utility and aesthetic excellence; and it functioned as a source of reputation, political solidarity, and cultural capital. The 1681 footstone of Boston printer John Foster quoted an apt epigram from Ovid: "ARS ILLI SUA CENSUS ERAT—Skill Was His Cash."

MEANING IN EVERYDAY OBJECTS

Gravestone Imagery

As they crafted objects that both provided comfort and gave tangible contours to deeper cultural values, craftsmen played two important roles in colonial British society. They were at once the makers of symbols that spoke the collective voice of their community and links in the long chains of communication that connected England to North America, New England to the Chesapeake, and colonial urban centers to hinterland hamlets. Take, for example, the 1678 headstone of Joseph Tapping in Boston's King's Chapel burial ground. Cut in local slate by an anonymous craftsman known simply as the "Charlestown Stonecutter," the monument is divided conceptually into two sections. The upper half shows a grim, winged death's head staring out beneath the sculpted, double-scrolled pediment profile at the stone's topmost edge. Perched atop the glowering skull is a small hourglass. The lower section contains three panels. The left side reveals Tapping's age and date of death, while the right confronts viewers with the warnings *Vive Memor Loethi* (Live Mindful of Death) and *Fugit Hora* (Time Flies). These two panels flank a central engraved bas-relief that shows the figure of Time, equipped with requisite scythe and hourglass, staying the hand of Death

just as Death prepares to extinguish the candle flame of Tapping's mortal soul. Lifted from an illustration in Francis Quarles's *Hieroglyphiques of the Life of Man*, a popular emblem book published in London in 1638, the device dramatizes the eternal struggle between human vanity and the inevitability of death. The Tapping stone thus highlights the way in which one craftsman articulated the symbolic beliefs of British colonials through the narrative force of iconography.

Iconography has been the general method for "reading" the symbolic emblems that adorn many colonial gravestones in British North America. Burial grounds with emblematic stones like the Tapping monument punctuate the cultural landscape from Newfoundland through the Chesapeake down to South Carolina and Georgia. In New England, gravestone iconography attained its highest degree of complexity and local variation between 1670 and 1780. Scholars such as James Deetz and Peter Benes have broken colonial production into three phases: a period of "death's heads" (1670–ca.1730); an ensuing period of "winged cherubs" (ca. 1730–1760); and the beginning of a period of sentimental "urns and willows" design that continued into the middle of the nineteenth century (ca. 1760–1840). In Deetz's original and highly provocative argument, the break between the abstract "death's head" and the more realistic, personalized "winged cherub" phases correlates with the decline of "Puritan" fatalism and the Great Awakening's new emphasis on the joy of individual salvation. However, careful investigation suggests that the date ranges for these stylistic phases vary greatly as one moves from urban or coastal areas into the interior. As a result the neat alignment of gravestone iconography with religious transformation cannot be supported. For one thing, winged cherubs now appear to date from at least 1698—some thirty-five years before the awakening was a twinkling in Jonathan Edwards's eye—and death's heads continue until the 1780s. What is more, death's heads appear on the same stones as both winged cherubs *and*, more surprisingly, urns and willows.

Emphasis in the interpretation of gravestone iconography at present seems to fall on the side of how individuals are remembered rather than on how specific images might reference aspects of doctrinal change. Death's head designs urge that memory of the person be cast in terms of collective emblems of the soul, heavenly fruits, and a series of late medieval emblems of worldly vanity and fleshly transience: picks, shovels, hourglasses, winding-sheets, scythes, and imps of death. The winged cherub design may signify a desire to fix memory on the details of individual accomplishment and character, as a 1782 portrait stone of Reverend John d'Angier in the East Bridgewater, Massachusetts, burial ground suggests; the soul effigies on many stones in that design actually seem to take on the realism of period portraits. Finally, as romanticism began to wash ashore on the American strand in the 1760s, the earliest urn and willow stones argue the power of nature's beauty to mark the heroic passage of an individual to eternal life. In contrast to James Deetz's ambitious attempt to tie gravestone symbolism to specific religious beliefs, such scholars as Allan Ludwig and Peter Benes have demonstrated that American symbols are a direct extension of pan-European emblem tradition and that local stonecutters were able to combine a variety of motifs, depending on the desires of clients. Gravestone symbolism was thus a combination of the *ars memoria* tradition and the playfulness of skilled colonial cutters vying for competitive markets.

Clocks

The iconography of time's passage links the study of the stonecutter's craft to another group of symbolic objects produced in the British North American colonies: clocks. As elaborate mechanisms linked both to medieval models of the cosmos and to modern concepts of wage labor, efficient production, and industrial discipline, clocks fuse material culture and social history together as few crafted objects can. Clocks produced in the British colonies often had brightly decorated faces. A clock made by the German craftsman Jacob Graff in Lebanon County, Pennsylvania, in the late 1760s offers engraved tulips, classical funerary urns, and the proud maker's claim to its creation—*Jacob Graff Machet Dieses*—for the contemplation of viewers. Across its face as time passes, the moon, sun, and stars rotate with a kind of mechanical perfection that reminded its beholders that God was the original maker of this "clockwork universe." Often the corners of the clockface contained familiar icons of time's

vanity—winged cherubs very similar to those on colonial gravestones. Clockmakers were among the most specialized craftsmen working in the British colonies, and they often found that only in port cities could they locate necessary parts, specialized tools, a guaranteed market, and skilled workers able to supply the cases needed to house the timepiece.

Clocks and cases ranged widely in design from tall, foreboding clocks to portable shelf models, but all types commonly had a small side window permitting curious owners to view the miraculous mechanism itself. Between 1650 and 1750 the number of clocks owned in the British colonies increased dramatically. And although clocks were normally displayed in a house's parlor, a room traditionally marked for its ritual function, the passage of time became increasingly secularized. In part this process was linked to the ascendancy of a commercial capitalism that required crisp scheduling and prompt delivery of goods. Yet as Otto Mayr has persuasively argued, the popularity of clocks was also linked to their aptness as a metaphor for the secular, liberal vision of society and economy as self-regulating mechanisms—a vision that gained legitimacy in the American colonies in the decades preceding the revolution.

Property and Exchange

Finally, emblematic icons appear in the complex heraldic crests and coats of arms displayed on silver tankards and in attributes of colonials who sat for portraits. Such objects, like gravestones and clocks, were markers of specific moments in the passage of ritual time. Many events were structured in part by their material signs; in association with births, special beverages were consumed by pregnant women, midwives brought along special collapsible birthing chairs for use during delivery, and babies were given small red coral rattles symbolizing the purity of their quickened blood. Young women, in particular, marked the passage of their girlhood by concentrating on a range of needlework skills that culminated in exquisitely worked samplers. Young men found their lives consumed by the rigors of learning a trade as apprenticeship often took the years between their fourteenth and twenty-first birthdays. As marriage approached, the iconography of social passage became connected with the symbolic exchange of property. Indeed artifacts functioned as symbols not only through their iconic reference, but also as components of rites of passage and as objects of exchange or commemoration.

Many cultures in Western Europe mark the consolidation of kin relations with transferrals of goods. Without doubt, real estate, buildings, and livestock formed an important part of transactions in Britain's North American colonies. Usually these were the commodities offered to the marriage by the groom's side. The woman brought to the marriage a variety of craft objects that carried specific symbolic meanings. Chief among these were bed linens, clothing, cooking implements, and tools from her father's occupation. Textiles, in particular, argued the woman's pivotal role in control of the marriage bed and the care of children. To mark the ritual transfer of textiles, the bride's family often had elaborate storage chests made with the woman's initials and the date of her union. A cursory look at the members of the extended Smith family of Hadley, Massachusetts, for example, reveals that each of fourteen marriages was marked by the gift of a dower chest to the engaged daughters.

Symbolic exchanges of property also circumscribed ritual interactions of Anglo-Americans and Indians. Without question the role of trade goods in securing property rights was essential from the point of view of British colonists. Yet Indian peoples, whether Pennacook or Lenni Lenape or Cherokee, did not share the specific western concept of alienated individual property—although many Native groups recognized usufruct rights in tribal hunting grounds—and thus entered into asymmetrical exchanges unaware. They valued trade objects, however, for their own aesthetic and political reasons. A given trade object—a copper kettle, for example—if judged technically excellent and made of material whose polished, smooth surface reflected light, might be described as owning "manitto," or having power in its own right. Ample evidence demonstrates that members of Native societies valued trade goods because they believed their possession endowed them with additional authority in Indian circles; the aura of literacy and printed books as totems of spirit power extended in some cases to include clocks, guns, metalwork-

ing tools, and domestic objects as "ordinary" as furniture, pottery, and cooking utensils.

Indians, however, could integrate selected European trade goods into their everyday lives without disrupting the underlying structure of Native domestic traditions. In 1761 Ezra Stiles, minister at Newport, Rhode Island, visited Nihantic people living near present-day Stonington, Connecticut, and made seven sketches of two wigwams and their contents. The plan of the oval-shaped dwellings was traditional, with a central fire surrounded by raised sleeping platforms. Yet on the platforms rested English chests of drawers, boxes, and even a dresser for the display of trade ceramics!

Symbolic exchange between cultures inevitably raises problems in defining adequate compensation. Most English colonists seem not to have understood the function of gifts and gift giving in American Indian culture. The British knew well enough the concept of "return," or what anthropologists call "reciprocity." Thus when they presented a blanket or a plough to an Indian, they typically expected something in return from the same Indian who had received their gift. Yet in most Native American cultures, the idea of the gift does not automatically imply to the first party a reciprocal exchange. A gift might circulate to three, four, five, or more people before it "returns" very indirectly to the initial bearer. A "circular" exchange of this sort uses property to enclose and bind a wide set of social relations; by contrast the common European gift exchange was modeled closely on the asymmetrical, dyadic exchanges of the commercial marketplace. When English colonists gave gifts to Indians that were not instantly reciprocated, they concluded they were being cheated. Instead the Indians were making wider use of their exchange system before a gift or "payment" of corresponding value was returned to the colonial agent or merchant.

That British colonists should have overlooked (or ignored) this subtlety is surprising, since their own culture was fond of "indirect" exchanges in gift giving as well. The public presentation of silver or pewter objects to churches was a common way for colonial gentry to demonstrate their munificence to the community. Such a gift witnessed their public commitment to the common good. Yet it also implicated them in the rich symbolism of the communion sacrament, as every time the congregation participated in the Eucharist it was simultaneously renewing a holy covenant and receiving a sacralized version of the genteel hospitality that punctuated the members' secular lives. Thus while a "gift" of silver communion goblets brought no immediate reciprocal favor from the parish, it cultivated alliances and imaged obligations that could be indirectly "returned" at a future moment.

PATTERNS OF DIFFUSION

In these diverse ways, craftsmen were central to British colonial society because they were charged with actually *making and remaking* the symbolic world in a direct, material sense. Yet they also occupied a central place in how that symbolism was spread from place to place and how specific aesthetic styles and habits of design and workmanship changed over time. Studies of cultural transmission through crafts typically concentrate on what cultural geographers call "patterns of diffusion." Diffusion implies movement along two principal historical axes: geographic space and social space. Interest in the former has deep roots in the simultaneous development in the 1920s and 1930s of work by Hans Kurath on American English speech dialects and by Fred B. Kniffen on aerial reconnaissance of folk architecture. On the one hand, geographic diffusion studies suggested that the movement of culture across the landscape could be precisely mapped, and thus those studies provided a complement to the work of demographers and economic historians charting the migration of social groups. On the other hand, they gradually came to question the assumption of American exceptionalism that persisted through the 1950s. For if British craft traditions could be precisely mapped on the colonial American landscape, so, too, could antecedents to those traditions be discovered in England, Wales, Scotland, and the north of Ireland.

During the 1960s and 1970s, in particular, scholars such as Benno M. Forman, Henry H. Glassie, John T. Kirk, Robert F. Trent, and Robert Blair St. George were busy discovering, with the help of their British counterparts, that "American" craft traditions were more often continuous transferrals of Old World traditions than dramatically "American" innovations. As such, their publications provided an aesthetic corollary to arguments for transatlantic continuity made by such historians as David Grayson Allen and Timothy Breen. Fortunately many studies now exist that demonstrate the importance of British antecedents to American colonial furniture, textiles, ceramics, and metalwares including silver, pewter, brass, and iron.

One difficulty with the cultural geographic tradition in diffusion study was that it presumed the flow of cultural ideas without examining who, in particular, was involved as a bearer of a particular craft tradition. After all, it is one thing to assume the migration of British culture to the American colonies by finding, say, that a blanket chest made in Chester County, Pennsylvania, bears striking similarity to surviving church chests still used in southern Wales or in England's Lake District; it is quite another to identify specific joiners or cabinetmakers who migrated from Radnorshire in Wales to Radnor, Pennsylvania, in the 1720s. Diffusion study also lies at the core of another problem: how variations in the composition, structure, and decoration of an object correlate with the geographic location of its production (rural v. urban), the specific skill level of the craftsman (self-trained v. apprenticeship), and the wealth level of the client (poor v. highly mobile).

To redress these issues, some students of British craft traditions have tracked down and listed the specific local origins of joiners, carpenters, potters, blacksmiths, and thatchers (among others) who came to the New World between 1620 and the American Revolution. The impacts of these lists were several. First, they sensitized decorative arts scholars to the fact that Britain— and especially England—in the seventeenth and eighteenth centuries was never a cultural monolith, but rather consisted of a series of highly distinct and fragmented regional cultures, each of which sent its singular ways of speech, dress, and crafts to the North American scene. Based solely on the aesthetic texts woven from the strands of Britain's rich regional diversity, early America emerged more polyglot and multivalent than prior scholars had assumed. Add to this dynamic the complex exchanges of commodities and labor value between British colonists and both native American Indians and African slaves, and the place of crafts in early intercultural history becomes central.

PATTERNS OF PRODUCTION

Increased scholarly attention to craftsmen as known bearers of cultural tradition has shed incidental light on previously hidden aspects of domestic economy and on an early tendency in the colonies toward industrial production. Perhaps the myth of the colonial craftsman, if nothing else, raises a single useful question: exactly how "self-sufficient" were households where ready income depended on craft production? The answer to this inquiry is complex. In colonial port centers like Philadelphia, New York, Newport, and Boston, craftsmen maintained a degree of specialization in task organization. To be sure the boundary lines they patrolled between trades were not so sharp as those recognized by late medieval British guilds. In early Boston, for example, a carpenter confronted by lean economic times might be seen building houses, making coffins and furniture, or occasionally turning his tools to the fabrication of barrels. Yet in the countryside, rural artisans much more commonly diversified their skills. Whether in backwoods Pennsylvania or in the hinterlands of eastern Connecticut, farmers relied on part-time seasonal work in different trades to turn winter's slack hours to profit and also to fend off cycles of depression in the marketing of farm produce.

The impact of part-time work in skilled trades on farm families should not be underestimated. Many social historians have commented, for example, on the problems raised when a scarcity of land affected the inherited patrimony of New England families in the early eighteenth century. Certainly picking up one or two trades was a means by which younger sons could manage a household on a piece of land too small to support a profitable farm. In addition, as domestic crafts such as shoemaking, tailoring, or weaving complicated work schedules in a household, they invariably drew women, as well as

African and Native American slaves and servants, into the ranks of skilled producers. The production of domestic cloth makes this point especially clear. In British tradition weaving was always considered, like most other trades, a clearly male domain. And given the centrality of the cloth trades in England's national economy as well as the rising tide of bourgeois fashion that propelled rising consumer consciousness between 1680 and 1780, weaving to many promised profits with minimal capital investment. But it was also a trade that had always depended on household labor for the many tedious steps of fiber preparation—picking, cleaning, carding, and spinning—prior to weaving. Thus women clearly knew about and had participated directly in the totality of cloth production. Perhaps due to the political emphasis on colonial production on the eve of the revolution, women must have picked up weaving—as well as participated in public spinning contests—when demand for home production increased in the 1760s and 1770s.

Cloth production also draws attention to attempts to organize centralized, "industrial" enterprises in the British colonies. As historian Gary B. Nash has observed, Boston's town officers initiated in 1748 a scheme to employ that port's widows, children, and poor in an experimental textile factory. Under the aegis of the United Society for Manufactures and Importation, public leaders believed they could at once both "reform" the town's paupers and carry on a profitable linen weaving venture employing, for the most part, female labor. The factory was opened in 1751, but the venture collapsed in 1758 because its product was no cheaper than linen imports. Yet the point remains: the mid eighteenth century witnessed, in Boston as surely as in the Moravian community at Bethlehem, Pennsylvania, an attempt to commercialize craft production as a profit-making engine of expanding merchant capitalism. The earliest colonial attempts at industrialization came in the cloth trades and followed the lead of English experiments in Devon and Dorset in the 1720s. And while such colonial efforts were perhaps novel in their attempt to centralize labor at a single production site, they were built upon strategies of piecework and putting-out work to household producers that had characterized the urban economies of Boston and New York since the mid seventeenth century.

Three final aspects of the transmission of British craft traditions to the North American colonies warrant consideration: the circulation of "fashion" through printed books, the consumer revolution, and the problem of "regional culture." In many cases, ideas about proper designs in furniture, interior flooring patterns, drapery techniques, landscaping, and architecture moved from Britain to her North American colonies in the engraved illustrations printed in such pattern books as Batty Langley's *The City and Country Builder's and Workman's Treasury of Designs* (1745) and Thomas Chippendale's *The Gentleman and Cabinet-Maker's Director* (1754). These and many other published design books circulated in the American colonies; their presence may be discovered in newspaper advertisements and in the personal libraries of gentleman amateurs and practicing craftsmen alike. Elite clients may have imagined these design manuals as wellsprings of civilized imagery and classical reverie. Craftsmen, on the other hand, treated them as sources to be considered, weighed for their utility in local colonial contexts, and then selectively grafted onto their existing repertoires of creativity and workmanship.

Pattern books offered models for correct taste. By contrast, imported commodities provided immediate images that linked people to London's fashion world and, possibly, to other colonists who made similar purchases. Imported objects also, of course, provided working craftsmen with new ideas about design as well as access to new types of materials and technological processes; here, colonial enthusiasm for British creamware pottery, for Josiah Wedgwood's distinctive Etruria ware, and for the Staffordshire master's basalt tea services are cases in point. British craft products found a ready market as the colonial economy grew. As part of the eighteenth century "consumer revolution," new structures of desire and self emerged as increased advertising, colonial sensitivity to à la mode fashions flaunted by provincial officials, and, perhaps, a novelesque feeling that the simple possession of commodities—the latest in dinnerware, or avant-garde candlesticks—would somehow

magically change one's status lured people into the marketplace of images.

This consumer revolution affected different locations in the British colonies at different times and at different intensities. Between 1680 and 1780, however, most British colonials experienced both the liberating and the limiting qualities of the commercial world. Yet how did such changes affect different sections of colonial society? Here the common theory regarding the social diffusion of changes in craft production and distribution argues that changes in design and function began at the top of society's hierarchy—at the level of king and court. From there they percolated downward through the aristocracy and mercantile elite and finally reached the middle classes. The middle classes, the argument runs, waited with outstretched arms, eager to embrace the aura-exuding icons of royal and aristocratic taste. By the mid eighteenth century, receiving the healing power of the "king's touch" had largely passed from favor; now, however, owning china of a similar pattern or chairs with similar curved profiles as those of one's social superiors functioned to put one imaginatively "in touch" with them.

Yet any theory that argues that ideas flow from the aristocracy down to the popular classes runs amok when the power of vernacular design as a source of elite fashion emerges. In the sixteenth and seventeenth centuries, for example, "urban" architecture derived its basic forms from those rural forms that city inhabitants remembered from the villages of their birth; early structures in Boston are essentially vernacular farmhouses rearranged to fit on cramped town lots. In addition mid-eighteenth-century England witnessed a rediscovery of popular antiquities and folk culture by romantic critics. By the 1750s the upper classes had begun searching out vernacular objects as wellsprings of "uncorrupted" aesthetics. Horace, the son of minister Robert Walpole, eagerly displayed Welsh turned chairs in the front hall of his polite Twickenham villa. Country pottery, clothing, and architecture all served as sources of high-style taste in the eighteenth century. As a result the assumed dominance of high style over vernacular culture cannot be assured. Instead cultural transmission in colonial America described less a pattern of linear descent than one of circular movement, where low could influence high culture, and vice versa.

REGIONAL CULTURES

Craft objects, as ciphers from London drifting across the Atlantic divide in the 1720s or as ciphers from Philadelphia moving through the valley of Virginia in the 1770s, crossed cultural boundaries and thus challenge not only our understanding of cultural transmission but also the concept of regional culture that many students of British crafts and decorative arts have asserted was central to colonial life. For most scholars of early American crafts, regional culture derives its interpretive power from the work of cultural geographers from the late nineteenth century to the present. In France at the end of the last century, geographer Vidal de la Blache argued the utility of studying whole, living cultures in situated landscapes; the "way of life" of a people, he argued, is authentically written in their regional landscape—in the shape of their houses, the form of their chairs, and the decoration on their folk pottery.

Vidal's faith in the region as a useful, totalizing frame of analysis influenced such American geographers as Carl Sauer and Fred B. Kniffen. It was Kniffen, in "Folk Housing: Key to Diffusion" (1965), who attempted to outline three regional cultures (Northeast, Middle Atlantic, and South) in the eastern United States on the basis of artifact study. Kniffen's method and argument were then extended and refined by Henry Glassie in *Pattern in the Material Folk Culture of the Eastern United States* (1968), a work of diffusionist ethnology that quickly became a reference guide for other scholars interested in regional interpretation.

The concept of regional culture as signifying the common culture of a place and time emerges in many books and exhibition catalogs describing the furniture, pottery, textiles, and other craft forms made in British North America. Frequently these works explore the visual similarities of artifacts from a specific region—be it New England, the Eastern Shore of Maryland and Virginia, the Delaware Valley—and suggests that all artifacts from a given place and time indicate

a culture marked by consensual values. It is useful to point out examples of such surveys, some of which remain very helpful because of the details they provide about an object's provenance and function, if for no other reason than they seem to portray a cultural past at times at odds with the social past reconstructed by critical historians. The works of Margaret B. Schiffer, Benjamin A. Hewett, and James R. Melchior are typical examples from the wide-ranging literature available on colonial furniture. From work on early British colonial pottery crafts, one might point to Lura Woodside Watkins's 1968 monograph.

Often omitted from these studies, however, is the presence of objects from outside the region—precisely those objects which, as harbingers of expanding commercial desires, created tensions within the assumed seamless unity of colonial cultures. Similarly, many scholars omit analysis of labor itself, despite attending to such fine details as, in the case of furniture study, drawer construction, dovetail alignment, and the like. Some scholars, however, are careful to insist that any exploration of regional culture must include differences as well as assumed similarities. Arlene Palmer Schwind's 1984 essay on ceramic imports makes clear the amount and types of imported pottery sought after by residents of New York and its patroon hinterlands. Similarly, Harold B. Burnham and Dorothy K. Burnham's definitive study published in 1972, of early handwoven textiles in eastern Canada, argues the delicate interplay and persistence of ethnic traditions in regional textile forms.

Regional culture as an approach to British craft traditions that allows for the inclusion of the different themes we have discussed—symbolism, exchange, pattern books, and the consumption of fashionable commodities—continues to attract students. The Burnhams' emphasis on ethnic difference in eastern Canadian textiles as they explored patterns among English, French, German, and Scottish immigrants to the area represents an approach that has already shaped the interpretation of British crafts in early American. Developing lines of argument from cultural diffusion theory, some scholars have already demonstrated the extreme localism of craft traditions in the New World. The presence in early New England and the Chesapeake of joiners from East Anglia or the West Country is clearly evidenced by surviving objects. In the case of New England, for example, the complexity of various English subcultures is apparent when one confronts the impressive array of early joined furniture forms representing different English regional traditions. The domestic furniture made in seventeenth-century New England, for example, has known and traceable roots in London, Kent, Hampshire, Devon, Suffolk, and the Lake District. These strains of influence, in turn, established bases for regional patterns in succeeding generations. Extant objects from Maryland and Virginia suggest West Country influence, while those in southeastern Pennsylvania have firm Welsh antecedents.

In each case the ethnic diversity of first-generation crafts imprinted the complexity of regional culture in these respective areas. And in the eighteenth century, new migrations added still more diversity. In the midst of "English" New England, for example, a remarkably lively tradition of furniture developed in those southern New Hampshire communities, with names like Antrim and Londonderry, that were established by Ulster immigrants in the 1710s and 1720s. In this regard Charles Parson's 1970 study suggests Scottish antecedents, the forms and joinery techniques of which stand in stark contrast to the established canon of eighteenth-century furniture from regional centers like Boston, Newport, Philadelphia, Charleston, and Savannah.

At the same time, work done by archaeologists has steadily improved the recording and interpretation of below-ground survivals, of the way specific early crafts were actually practiced, and of the often difficult to trace interaction between British, African-American, and Native American peoples. The early eighteenth-century Virginia site of potter William Rogers described in Norman F. Barka, Edward Ayres, and Christine Sheriden's 1984 study is probably the most instructive craft site yet excavated. Not only does a key example of an early "craft to industry" transformation emerge, but the authors are also able to conclude that for some twenty-five years (1720–ca. 1745), Rogers and crew produced earthenware as well as brown salt-glazed stoneware as fine as any imported English materials.

Archaeological explorations have also yielded artifacts crucial to an understanding of how craft objects functioned in exchanges between British colonists and their American Indian neighbors. In early Rhode Island, for example, the availability of English tools allowed Narragansett Indians to carve steatite pipes of greater complexity and accuracy than Native stone tools did. Indian access to trade goods, then, allowed continuation and elaboration of Native aesthetics on occasion. Surely, however, trade more often implied Native dependency on colonial markets and culture brokers, and sites from Pentagoet in Maine to Fort Michilimackinac in western Pennsylvania suggest the asymmetry of power that developed between the dominant British and the subaltern Indians as the eighteenth century progressed. In sites from Massachusetts to Georgia, archaeologists are also uncovering the buried material lives of African slaves and freemen, and in almost every case the artifacts argue the poverty and immiserization of African-American peoples at the hands of British colonials. Yet at the same time some artifacts—along with written records—demonstrate that African Americans were often expert craftspeople whose skills with wood, stone, cotton, and iron helped to beautify the gracious houses, furniture, bed quilts, and gates of their Anglo-American owners. In eighteenth-century Virginia, for instance, slaves were sometimes skilled furniture producers. In 1770, when the Williamsburg estate of master craftsman Anthony Hay went at auction, one lot included "nineteen Negroes belonging to the said Estate, among them a very good Cabinet Maker." In 1733 Peter Scott, a Williamsburg shop joiner, sold "for Bills of Exchange or ready Money, Two Negroes, bred to the Business of a Cabinet-maker."

UNDERSTANDING NORTH AMERICAN DECORATIVE ARTS

In summary, the interpretation of crafts in the British North American colonies necessarily includes a wide variety of approaches and goals. Much of the literature in decorative arts is devoted to description, classification, and details of construction and nomenclature that will seem more directed to the connoisseur than to the critical historian. However, beneath discussions of such topics as furniture veneering techniques or sources for stoneware clay lie important interpretive issues that bind object description to historical analysis. As outlined, the principal interpretive frames linking artifact study to cultural history include those of symbolism and belief, transmission through space, time, and levels of social structure, and the emergence of regional cultures in the complex interplay of community and expanding eighteenth-century commerce.

A consideration of British crafts in the North American colonies allows the cultural historian to explore a wide variety of interdependent topics: the meaning of work and skill among craftsmen in colonial British society, the way crafted objects like gravestones and clocks link sacred and secular realities, the relationship between handicrafts and nascent industrialization, and the role of objects and advertising in constructing popular desire during a pivotal phase in the acceleration of consumerism. In each case crafts emerge as indices of technological shifts, as mediators of intercultural exchange, as emblems of aesthetic valuation, as icons of cultural power and public authority. Crafts in Britain's North American colonies may have been among what William Morris in 1883 called the "lesser arts," but they were always part of the way people communicated with one another.

BIBLIOGRAPHY

Allen, David Grayson. *In English Ways: The Movement of Societies and the Transferral of Local Law and Custom to Massachusetts Bay in the Seventeenth Century*. Chapel Hill, N.C., 1981.

Ames, Kenneth L., and Gerald W. R. Ward, eds. *Decorative Arts and Household Furnishings in America, 1650–1920: An Annotated Bibliography*. Winterthur, Del., 1989.

Barka, Norman F., Edward Ayres, and Christine Sheridan. *The "Poor Potter" of Yorktown: A Study of a Colonial Pottery Factory*. 3 vols. Denver, Colo., 1984.

Benes, Peter. *The Masks of Orthodoxy: Folk Gravestone Carving in Plymouth County, Massachusetts, 1689–1805*. Amherst, Mass., 1977.

Breen, Timothy H. "Persistent Localism: English Social Change and the Shaping of New England Institutions." In *Puritans and Adventurers: Change and Persistence in Early America*, edited by Timothy H. Breen. New York, 1982.

Bridenbaugh, Carl. *The Colonial Craftsman*. New York, 1950.

Burnham, Harold B., and Dorothy K. Burnham. *Keep Me Warm One Night: Early Handweaving in Eastern Canada*. Toronto, Ontario, 1972.

Campbell, Colin. *The Romantic Ethic and the Spirit of Modern Consumerism*. Oxford, 1987.

Chippendale, Thomas. *The Gentleman and Cabinet-Maker's Director*. London, 1754.

Conkey, Laura F., Ethel Boissevoin, and Ives Goddard. "Indians of Southern New England and Long Island: The Late Period." In *Handbook of the North American Indians: The Northeast*, Vol. 15, edited by Bruce Trigger. Washington, D.C., 1978.

Dethlefsen, Edwin, and James J. F. Deetz. "Death's Heads, Cherubs, and Willow Trees: Experimental Archaeology in Colonial Cemeteries." *American Antiquity* 31, no. 4 (1966):502–510.

Dow, George Francis, comp. *The Arts and Crafts in New England, 1704–1775: Gleanings from Boston Newspapers*. Topsfield, Mass., 1927.

Failey, Dean F. *Long Island Is My Nation: The Decorative Arts and Craftsmen, 1640–1830*. Setauket, N.Y., 1976.

Forman, Benno M. *American Seating Furniture, 1630–1730: An Interpretive Catalog*. New York, 1988.

Glassie, Henry H. *Pattern in the Material Folk Culture of the Eastern United States*. Philadelphia, 1968.

Gottesman, Rita Susswein, comp. *The Arts and Crafts in New York, 1726–1776: Advertisements and News Items from New York City Newspapers*. New York, 1938.

Hewett, Benjamin A., et al. *The Work of Many Hands: Card Tables in Federal America, 1790–1820*. New Haven, Conn., 1982.

Hyde, Lewis. *The Gift: Imagination and the Erotic Life of Property*. New York, 1984.

Kirk, John T. *American Furniture and the British Tradition to 1830*. New York, 1982.

Kniffen, Fred B. "Folk Housing: Key to Diffusion." *Annals of the Association of American Geographers* 55, no. 4 (1965):549–577.

Kurath, Hans. *A Word Geography of the Eastern United States*. Ann Arbor, Mich., 1949.

Langley, Batty. *The City and Country Builder's and Workman's Treasury of Designs*. London, 1745.

Ludwig, Allan I. *Graven Images: New England Stonecarving and Its Symbols, 1650–1815*. Middletown, Conn., 1966.

McKendrick, Neil, John Brewer, and J. H. Plumb. *The Birth of a Consumer Society: The Commercialization in Eighteenth-Century England*. London, 1982.

Mayr, Otto. *Authority, Liberty and Automatic Machinery in Early Modern Europe*. Baltimore, Md., 1986.

Melchior, James R., et al. *Eastern Shore, Virginia, Raised-Panel Furniture, 1730–1830*. Norfolk, Va., 1982.

Nash, Gary B. *The Urban Crucible: Social Change, Political Consciousness, and the Origins of the American Revolution.* Cambridge, Mass., 1977.

Parson, Charles. *The Dunlaps and Their Furniture.* Manchester, N.H., 1970.

Prime, Alfred Coxe, comp. *The Arts and Crafts in Philadelphia, Maryland, and South Carolina, 1721–1785: Gleanings from Newspapers.* 2 vols. Topsfield, Mass., 1929–1932.

Quimby, Ian M. G., ed. *The Craftsman in Early America.* New York, 1984.

St.George, Robert Blair. "Introduction." In *Material Life in America, 1600–1860,* edited by Robert Blair St.George. Boston, 1988.

———. *The Wrought Covenant: Source Materials for the Study of Craftsmen and Community in Southeastern New England, 1620–1700.* Brockton, Mass., 1979.

Schiffer, Margaret B. *Furniture and Its Makers of Chester County, Pennsylvania.* Philadelphia, 1966.

Schwind, Arlene Palmer. "The Ceramic Imports of Frederick Rhinelander, New York Loyalist Merchant." *Winterthur Portfolio* 19, no. 1 (1984):21–36.

Sturtevant, William. "Two 1761 Wigwams at Niantic, Connecticut." *American Antiquity* 40, no. 4 (1975):437–444.

Trent, Robert F. "New England Joinery and Turning Before 1700." In *New England Begins: The Seventeenth Century,* edited by Jonathan L. Fairbanks and Robert F. Trent. 3 vols. Boston, 1982.

Vlach, John Michael. *The Afro-American Tradition in Decorative Arts.* Cleveland, Ohio, 1977.

Watkins, Lura Woodside. *Early New England Potters and Their Wares.* Reprint. Hamden, Conn., 1968.

Robert Blair St.George

SEE ALSO **Architecture; Artisans; Home and Hearth; Patterns of Socialization; Rural Life;** and **Urban Life.**

THE DUTCH COLONY

IN 1728 DANIEL DEFOE commented that "the Dutch must be understood as they really are, the Middle Persons in trade, the Factors and Brokers of Europe." Defoe's observation distilled the essence of what New Netherland was to the Dutch: a colony for commerce founded on the exchange of worldly products for New World natural resources.

In the first decades of the seventeenth century, those products comprised mostly useful objects made in the Netherlands, which were exchanged with the Indians for furs. By mid century enough Europeans had arrived to satisfy their own need for many craft products, prompting New Amsterdam to regulate those who made them.

Beginning in the 1650s, men who had proper training for an occupation could register as *burghers,* giving them certain rights, including the freedom of the city to pursue their work. Apprenticeship was the accepted mode of training for a trade, and indentures between master and apprentice—for boys usually from age fourteen for seven years—were regulated by the city. Among the first burghers registered were men whose crafts were carpenter, chairmaker, cooper (barrel maker), locksmith, mason, painter (house and decorative), potter, blacksmith, and glazier (window glazing and glass decoration). Their products were used mostly to build and modestly furnish homes and shops in a town that was quickly expanding.

Yet the colonial Dutch were not so far removed from their golden age of culture at home. The painter-glazier Evert Duyckinck arrived sometime before 1640 and created the richly enameled church windows of the First Reformed Dutch Church of Albany (1656), which displayed the coats of arms of church members. They are evidence that elegance was valued at a very early date in the colony's history. Duyckinck and goldsmith-silversmith Jurian Blanck, Sr., who had begun practicing his trade by 1643, founded centurylong New York dynasties of glaziers and limners (portrait painters), goldsmiths, and silversmiths that included their sons and sons-in-law.

In the decorative arts and crafts of New Netherland, most craftsmen, like the population itself, were Dutch. But after the English conquest in 1664, specialization by nationality developed. For the next century, the more elite craftsmen—gold- and silversmiths, gunsmiths, painters and limners—remained mostly Dutch. The large craft of joiners, or furniture makers, was overwhelmingly English. Most pewterers, watchmakers, and clockmakers were English, too. After the revocation of the Edict of Nantes (1685), skilled Huguenots fled France, and many came to New York. They integrated (often by marriage) into their crafts, especially in the cases of gold- and silversmithing and joinery. Some crafts attracted a variety of nationalities, including glazing, pottery making, tinsmithing, turning (mostly chair making), and upholstering. Excepting upholstery and watch- and clockmaking, which began after 1700, all of these crafts had their beginnings in the New Netherland period. Freeman records, incomplete though they are, indicate that after 1700 English craftsmen introduced exotic new products through the trades of clothworker, wigmaker, carver, printer, bookbinder, linen draper, woolen draper, silk weaver, cabinetmaker, coachmaker, jeweler, and even ivory turner. By 1750 there were some twenty-five craft and art trades, less than one-sixth of all the trades represented in the cosmopolitan colonial city of New York.

While freeman and apprentice records are the most comprehensive sources for information on early arts and crafts, it must be remembered that much production was generated by less formally trained workers in shops and homes. Hired hands, indentured servants, and slaves assisted masters or produced for them goods not requiring skills at a professional level. In addition to doing housework, many wives and daughters produced textiles by spinning and weaving, then processed them by needlework into clothing and household "linens," sometimes embellishing them with sewn decoration.

In New Netherland society men also took a hand to domestic crafts. Among the decorative items produced were elaborately chip-carved objects of wood such as spoon racks (to hold spoons between meals), mangle boards (for pressing and rolling linens), and wooden shoes, all of which were traditionally made by a man for his wife. Evidence of this custom remains in the form of spoon racks from New York and New Jersey, often engraved with the wife or couple's initials and a date. All surviving examples that have been dated are from the eighteenth century, testifying by their lack of variation to how conservative some Dutch families were. Similarly the *kas*, or Dutch cupboard, was still being made as late as the early nineteenth century.

THE ANGLO-DUTCH ASSIMILATE ENGLISH TASTES

Most crafts, however, had long since dropped Dutch forms in favor of English ones. This was especially obvious in the cases of silver- and goldsmiths and portrait painters, who were following English prototypes as early as the 1690s. This seems ironic since both crafts were dominated by the Dutch well into the eighteenth century. What mattered, however, was what the patron wanted; and the wealthier New Yorkers, whether Dutch or English, had achieved prosperity and thus had their tasks formed under English rule.

We know their tastes especially well because they initialed and often dated their silver, which encompassed a wide variety of forms, functions, and styles. Richly molded and engraved brandy-wine bowls, salts, sugar and pepper casters, snuffboxes, porringers, tankards, teapots, and kettles, which are just some of the seventy known forms are indicative of lavish dinner and, sometimes, funeral parties. For the latter, silver mourning spoons or gold mourning rings, with last-minute engraved memorials, were given as gifts to pallbearers. Of the hundreds of surviving silver pieces engraved with names or initials or with family coats of arms, almost all were made locally by some seventy different silversmiths—not by Europeans—and were of a quality equal to that of imports.

These Anglo-Dutch were ordering English-style furniture, clothing, and other decorative objects well before the end of the seventeenth century, while their more conservative, and usually less prosperous, neighbors resented this forsaking of *Patria*. "Their language and customs begin pretty much to wear out," observed Dr. Alexander Hamilton in 1744, "and would very soon die were it not for a parcel of Dutch domines [clergymen] here, who . . . endeavour to preserve the Dutch customs as much as possible." Not surprisingly, then, communion beakers for Dutch churches continued to be made in the old Netherland style into the nineteenth century.

BIBLIOGRAPHY

Blackburn, Roderic H., and Ruth Piwonka. *Remembrance of Patria: Dutch Arts and Culture in Colonial America, 1609–1776.* N. p. 1988.

Gottesman, Rita S. *The Arts and Crafts in New York, 1726–1776.* New York, 1938.

Howard, Ronald W. "Apprenticeship and Economic Education in New Netherland and Seventeenth-Century New York." In *Education in New Netherland and the Middle Colonies.* Papers of the 7th Rensselaerswyck Seminar of the New Netherland Project. Albany, N.Y., 1985.

The New-York Historical Society. *Collections 1885. The Burghers of New Amsterdam and the Freemen of New York, 1675–1866.* Publication Fund Series, vol. 18. New York, 1886.

———. *Collections 1909. Indentures of Apprentices, October 21, 1718 to August 7, 1727.* Publication Fund Series, vol. 42. New York, 1910.

Rice, Norman S. *Albany Silver, 1652–1825.* Albany, N.Y. 1964.

Roderic H. Blackburn

SEE ALSO **Architecture; Artisans; Patterns of Socialization; Rural Life;** and **Urban Life.**

THE FRENCH COLONIES

THE CONTINENTAL COLONIES of New France could not compare in wealth with Spanish America or the West Indies, and thus could not support elaborate networks of artisans. Artisans in French North America produced few items for export, but did provide colonials with many of the manufactured products that they used in their daily lives.

WOODWORKING

Only the wealthiest immigrants to the French colonies brought their furniture with them to the New World. Most was manufactured in the colonies, making use of abundant supplies of wood and widespread skill at carpentry to produce serviceable items of solid, joined wood. In the seventeenth century even beds were a luxury for the habitants, but by the eighteenth century most households of New France were well supplied with furniture.

A good deal of this furniture was made by habitants at home—usually during the winter—for their own use. The remainder was produced by carpenters. Some of these professionals had their own shops and on occasion worked in the churches or homes where the furniture would be used. Other carpenters roamed the countryside in search of employment.

Canadian furniture tended to be simplified copies of French styles, the most important of which were Louis XIII, characterized by spiral turnings, beads, balusters, and geometric motifs, and Louis XV, distinguished by curved lines, spiral legs, crossbow shapes, carving, scrollwork, and rococo. These models were adopted in Canada after a lag of decades, and persisted after they went out of style in France. The most important items of household furnishings were the armoire and marriage bed. Other common items of furniture included chests, buffets, commodes, tables, and chairs.

Canadian craftsmen were particularly noted for their skill at wood carving. In the absence of sources of both stone suitable for carving and plaster, Canadians turned to wood to reproduce the effects obtained in Europe using these materials. The area that was to be decorated was covered with plain boards, to which were attached thin strips of carved wood. On an altar this ornamentation, known as appliqué, would be painted or gilded, and on a ceiling it would be whitewashed. In both cases, skilled craftsmanship produced works of great beauty.

METALWORKING

From the first years following the start of European settlement, local blacksmiths had always produced many of the metal items—from horseshoes to hinges—needed by the colonists of French North America. In the Saint Lawrence Valley, beginning in 1738, their efforts were supplemented by the Forges Saint-Maurice. A lack of qualified colonial ironworkers necessitated the import of skilled craftsmen from the metropole for this enterprise. Although small and incompetently managed, this ironworks, which was taken over by the state in 1743, produced anvils, pots, tops for brick stoves, shells, cannonballs, and a small number of cannon from local bog iron. Forged iron bars, a major product, were used in Canada, Louisbourg, and the French West Indies.

SILVER AND PEWTER

Domestic silver was used extensively by well-off colonials, whose spoons (the most common silver item), other flatware, hollowware, candlesticks, buttons, buckles, and snuffboxes of solid silver were a convenient place to store and also display their wealth. For the average French colonist, silver pieces were found in the church. Canon law demanded that the chalice and paten used in the celebration of the Mass be made of noble metals. Copper or pewter could be used for lesser vessels, but wherever possible, they too were made of silver.

In the seventeenth century, silverworking in New France was confined to the repair and maintenance of imported silver pieces by gunsmiths and armorers. In France guild regulations would have prevented them from working in silver, but in the colonies possession of the skills and equipment required for delicate metalworking were sufficient.

The armorer-silversmiths were only displaced in the eighteenth century, when increasing colonial populations and the concomitant increase in the number of churches created a steadily rising demand for ecclesiastic silver, which attracted immigrant professional silversmiths. Most of these professionals engaged in other economic activities, but in Canada between 1730 and 1750 the three most prominent silversmiths of New France, Roland Paradis, Paul Lambert, and Ignace-François Delezenne, all immigrants, were able to work full-time. At least one freed black slave, Dominique-François Mentor, worked as an apprentice and journeyman for Delezenne. In the last decade of French rule in Canada, a new outlet for the activities of silversmiths was found in the production of silver items for the fur trade, a trend that continued and expanded after the British conquest.

Since the French colonies lacked indigenous sources of precious metals, old silver pieces and specie were the only source of silver. Persons wanting a silver item—whether for domestic or ecclesiastic use—would generally have to provide sufficient metal for the piece and pay the smith. The silversmiths in New France had to cope with a shortage of metal, and the continual removal of silver coins from circulation for conversion into silver utensils was a serious problem for a colony that was chronically short of specie. This situation was somewhat alleviated by the arrival of thousands of French troops during the Seven Years' War, who were paid in coin.

Silversmiths of New France tended on the whole to produce competently executed but simplified copies of French provincial styles of Louis XIV. Decoration was produced by embossing, chasing, and engraving. Motifs included raised or engraved bands of stylized leaves, shells, or gadroons (oval shaped beadings, flutings, or reedings). Very often the coat of arms or monogram of the owners of domestic silver pieces was added.

In New France pewter was widely used as an inexpensive substitute for silver, for both ecclesiastic and domestic silver vessels, and many pewter pieces were based on silver models. Church vessels most commonly made of pewter were font basins, ewers for wine and oil, holy water basins, and censers. Imported pewter was common. Only one pewterer of the French regime is known by name, and large quantities of locally manufactured pewter did not appear until the nineteenth century.

GLASS AND POTTERY

The glass used in the French colonies was imported from France, and no evidence of colonial glassmaking exists. Much of the pottery used in the colonies was also imported. But local potters produced ceramic tureens, plates, pitchers, and pots, using designs based on metropolitan models, which met domestic demand and filled the gap when supply ships failed to arrive.

TEXTILE WORK

Although much of the better-quality cloth used in New France was imported, the decoration of textiles was an important craft there, and an important outlet for the artistic creativity of women in the French colonies. Much of this textile work was centered in the female religious orders. The Ursulines in particular, in their convents at Quebec, Montreal, and New Orleans, were renowned for their skill at knitting, crocheting, and embroidery.

For the nuns, the most important of these crafts was embroidery, which was of superior quality and whose sale provided an important source of income for religious communities. Using raw materials imported from France, the nuns embroidered clothing for lay customers and made religious textile products such as altar cloths and banners. They also made clothing, both for their own use and for sale to secular and religious clients. Lacemaking, although less important than embroidery, was practiced in these communities and used for religious ornaments. The nuns disseminated knowledge of these crafts throughout the French colonies by passing on their skills to young French and Amerindian women.

The nuns of New France were also known for their use of local products like birchbark, to produce boxes and containers of various sizes for secular and religious purposes. These items were decorated with porcupine quills and moose hair. This craft proved to be especially valuable after the British conquest, when bark boxes and model canoes found a market among soldiers of the occupying garrison who sought souvenirs and novelties.

GRAPHIC ARTS

In the mainland colonies of New France there was very little demand for printed matter, and the graphic arts—engraving, caricature, printing, and bookbinding—were neglected. Only in the French West Indies, where the demand for news and commercial forms was higher, was there a licensed printer and colonial newspaper, the *Gazette de Saint-Domingue*. In 1748 the governor general proposed that a press be established in Canada, but was told that this would only be possible if a private entrepreneur could be found who was willing to provide the necessary capital.

LOUISIANA

Louisiana's artistic heritage was impoverished when compared with that of Canada. Aside from the needlework of the Ursuline nuns, artistic creativity was channeled into furniture production for domestic consumption. Most early Louisiana furniture was fairly primitive, fashioned from the cypress. A viable furniture industry would not exist in Louisiana until the late eighteenth and early nineteenth centuries. Similarly, the ironworking industry for which the Crescent City became justifiably renowned was not spawned until the end of the Spanish era (1763–1803).

CONCLUSION

In the continental colonies of New France the struggle for survival in a harsh environment created societies in which few members had the leisure, skills, or inclination to write novels, paint pictures, or compose music. But French colonials did not neglect those opportunities that did exist for artistic expression. The men and women of New France could take pride in their handcrafted furniture or elaborate lacework. Professionals produced functional ceramics and elegant silver pieces. Their products might not be as elegant and refined as the work of the finest metropolitan artisans, but they were certainly comparable to the provincial products in France. Crafts in New France thus provided both many basic manufactured items needed by the colonials and an outlet for the creativity of the colonial artisans.

BIBLIOGRAPHY

Abrahamson, Una. *Crafts Canada: The Useful Arts.* Toronto, Ontario, 1974.
Adair, E. R. "French Canadian Art." *Canadian Historical Association, Report of the Annual Meeting,* (1929):91–102.
Barbeau, Marius. *Saintes artisanes: I. Les Brodeuses.* Vol. 1. Montreal, 1943.
Palardy, Jean. *The Early Furniture of French Canada.* Toronto, Ontario, 1963.
Traquair, Ramsay. *The Old Silver of Quebec.* Toronto, Ontario, 1940.
Trudel, Jean. *Silver in New France.* Ottawa, 1974.

D. Peter MacLeod

SEE ALSO **Architecture; Artisans; Patterns of Socialization; Rural Life;** and **Urban Life.**

THE SPANISH BORDERLANDS

WHEN THE SPANISH EXPLORERS and settlers reached the area known today as the Spanish Borderlands, they found indigenous societies in which there existed rich and complex cultural forms, including religious practices, language and literature, and visual and material arts. While the popular conception today is that the indigenous cultures were "primitive" and the incoming Europeans "civilized," in fact the difference between the two can better be understood as a question of values, of widely differing worldviews. The Indians were primitive in the true sense of this word: they held to a more primordial worldview in which there was not yet the decisive split between mind and body, between spirit and matter, between being and doing.

In such a view, utility and spirituality were not separated; useful tasks were not carried on in isolation from spiritual activities. Every facet of daily life had a spiritual significance, for there was not that solid wall between the mundane and the divine that has come to characterize European culture in the past five hundred years. Similarly, material objects made for these everyday tasks were not simply utilitarian. They were made and used within a spiritual context: all aspects of life, even the most mundane, were holy. Such a view prevailed among all the indigenous groups in the territories known today as the Spanish Borderlands. From Florida to California finely crafted items for fulfilling the full range of human needs were made in a wide variety of media, including stone, wood, bone, ceramics, textiles, and leather and encompassed basketry, painting, featherwork, and jewelry making.

For the incoming Spaniards the separation of sacred and secular had already begun. While they held some appreciation of the Indians' artisanal abilities, they could not directly utilize Indian products. The making and the use of these objects within the indigenous culture was too deeply imbued with spiritual considerations that were alien to the European worldview. For the Spaniards, more practical, that is, more purely utilitarian, forms and means of production were needed to satisfy the demands of urban and urbanizing market economies. As a result, the Spaniards attempted to transform the methods and products of the subjugated Indian artisans in the borderlands, utilizing their hand skills to produce items in conformity with European methods and uses. At the same time, European goods made in Spain or central Mexico were introduced to fill the needs of wealthier settlers in these frontier areas and served as models for indigenous artisans. These "superior" objects also served as symbols of Hispanic dominance and as vehicles of cultural change, often replacing indigenous forms.

THE BORDERLANDS AND THEIR CRAFTS

The various regions of the Spanish Borderlands extending from the Southeast to California have very different patterns of exploration, exploitation, and settlement. With the exception of New Mexico, until the late colonial period the Hispanic presence in the borderlands tended to be limited to soldiers, friars, civic officials, and a few traders and settlers. While the friars and a few others were actually of European ancestry (*españoles*), the majority of the "Hispanic" population was of mixed blood or were Hispanicized Indians. In the Southeast, in spite of the long period of Spanish occupation, particularly in Florida and extending as far north as Virginia and west into Alabama, the Spanish Crown was not successful in attracting Hispanic settlement. These territories remained little more than missions among the Indians and defensive outposts against the English and French. A similar situation prevailed in the large province of Louisiana, which was only for a brief period in the late eighteenth century under Spanish rule; many of the subjects of the Crown were actually French and English nationals.

In Texas the Hispanic population was somewhat larger but was much later in coming and by the late eighteenth century had not increased beyond two thousand to three thousand citizens located in four communities, the majority at San Antonio. Arizona remained essentially a mission and *presidio* outpost throughout the colonial period, with most of its small population living at

Tucson. Settlement in California did not begin until 1769 and was very limited in scope well into the nineteenth century, the population of non-Indian citizens totaling fewer than thirty-five hundred by 1821.

Throughout the borderlands, the friars, the soldiers, and the few settlers were dependent primarily upon imports and the subjugated Indian populations for their material needs. Since many of these areas were accessible by water, imported goods could be brought to the inhabitants in considerable quantities. There was, however, still a need for skilled Hispanic craftsmen, and in many remote areas the lack of them was a continual problem. Skilled craftsmen were also in demand in central Mexico, and it was difficult to entice them to move to a remote frontier where living conditions were severe. Often when craftsmen were convinced to emigrate to the borderlands, they did not stay long, returning as soon as possible to the comforts of a more civilized life in Mexico. The artisans who did come to the borderland outposts were those needed for basic maintenance of the clothing, tools, and equipment of the friars, soldiers, and settlers: blacksmiths to repair weapons and make horseshoes and simple farming implements; leather workers to make and repair shoes, outer clothing, and horse gear; weavers and tailors to make and mend clothing; carpenters with basic skills sufficient for making wooden carts and wheels, oxen yokes, and similar necessities; and masons knowledgeable in working with stone and adobe.

These artisans were sometimes employed by the friars to teach their trades to the Indians with the goal of establishing small-scale cottage industries in the missions, which could produce items in quantities sufficient both for local needs and for trade to other regions. In some cases, where outside craftsmen were lacking, the friars themselves had artisanal skills that they taught to the Indians. In California, for instance, in the late eighteenth century, artisanal activities were focused in the missions, where friars successfully developed small-scale cottage industries similar to what had prevailed in New Mexico in the seventeenth century. However, descriptions of Hispanic life in California in the 1790s still indicate an existence bare of local amenities even among the leading citizens.

With the exception of New Mexico and, to a much lesser extent, Texas and California, none of the Spanish Borderlands developed a viable and continuous Hispanic folk craft tradition. In New Mexico, although colonization began in a manner similar to that in the other areas, the situation was quite different. Small forces of soldiers accompanied by friars and a few settlers came to New Mexico in the late sixteenth century, establishing themselves among the Pueblo Indians. A stable rural and town-dwelling Hispanic population began to develop in the Rio Grande watershed, with significant communities in the well-watered areas near Taos Pueblo, Santa Cruz de la Cañada, Santa Fe, Albuquerque, and El Paso del Norte.

While the Pueblo Revolt of 1680 caused a temporary hiatus in Hispanic settlement in New Mexico, the reconquest, completed by 1696, brought a new influx of settlers from central and northern Mexico. By the mid eighteenth century the threat of nomadic Indian attack had been reduced, and the geographical isolation of the province continued to protect it from any serious incursions by the French and English. At this time the population began to increase rapidly. Arable lands were now available in more remote areas for those settlers who dared to venture beyond the relative security of the Indian pueblos and the larger Hispanic communities. The establishment of communities of detribalized and Hispanicized Indians known as *genizaros* also added to the population, and they served as buffers on the frontiers of the province to protect the Hispanic population centers from hostile Indian raids. By 1817 New Mexico had a sedentary population of over thirty-six thousand people, approximately ten times that of Texas or California.

Because of the remoteness of New Mexico, imported products could reach the colony only by a long and arduous overland route and thus were relatively scarce, affordable only by the wealthiest sectors of the population. As in other areas, the friars and settlers in the early colonial period had established cottage industries among the Indians, but the Pueblo Revolt gave the Indians a measure of independence after the reconquest, so that their products had to be purchased at market prices by the settlers. Since in the eighteenth century neither imports nor local Indian crafts were sufficient to meet the needs of the burgeoning Hispanic population, craft-making skills developed extensively in the Hispanic communities. The *vecino* artisans carried on Spanish-Mexican traditions, usually utilizing European technology (although simplified) and often perpetuating older European forms and motifs, ignoring the latest urban styles popular in central Mexico and Spain. In some cases they incorporated influences from the Native cultures with which they coexisted. Indian influence most often came from the incorporation of Indian women into Hispanic households, usually as wives of *mestizo* settlers or as servants. Hence the strongest Indian influences are to be found in women's domestic arts, such as preparation of foodstuffs and medical remedies and practices associated with childbirth. Traditional handcrafts carried on by women, such as pottery making and mud plastering, also show strong Indian influence. Other crafts, mostly male-dominated, show more subtle indigenous traits, usually limited to the introduction of some Native design motifs.

Crafts as practiced in the Southwest Borderlands during the colonial period are part of the larger pattern of provincial craft production found all over northern and central Mexico. Early recognition of these crafts by Anglo-American connoisseurs and scholars in the Southwest in the 1920s and 1930s placed unwarranted emphasis upon their peninsular Spanish origins and tended to overlook their Mexican antecedents. In the process of lauding the Spanish roots of New Mexican culture, its Mexican roots were downplayed or ignored. Crafts of Hispanic Southwestern origin were appreciated as products of a Spanish colonial past quite comparable in some eyes to the colonial traditions of the eastern United States.

In fact, there was little direct cultural communication between Spain and its American borderland settlements. Few settlers were of Spanish birth or of purely European ancestry; rather, the settlers were emigrants from Mexico, many generations removed from the mother country. These settlers brought to the borderlands Mexican cultural forms that were only indirectly Spanish in origin and that had been filtered through generations of usage in Mexico during which time Mexico's Indian cultures had had their impact. Thus the crafts in what is now the South-

west are a mixture of Spanish, Mexican Indian, and Southwest Indian forms and techniques, some, such as iron working, showing strong Spanish roots and others, such as weaving and adobe finishing, exhibiting much more indigenous influence.

WEAVING

The craft of weaving in the western borderlands was part of the larger picture of textile production in central and northern Mexico. Weaving had long been practiced by many indigenous groups prior to the Spanish Conquest both in central Mexico and in the borderlands, where the Pueblo Indians and their forebears in particular wove garments from locally grown cotton. Indian weaving in Mexico was part of household production, usually done by women on simple backstrap and frame looms, producing slowly, in conjunction with a myriad of other domestic activities, small quantities of clothing for family and ceremonial use.

With the conquest, the Spanish introduced domesticated sheep to North America, and they also introduced European industrial weaving methods, including the horizontal treadle loom. The treadle loom was, for the day, a highly efficient machine designed for high-volume commercial weaving. In terms of efficiency over Native methods its major advantages were three. At the beginning, an extremely long warp could be rolled on, so that long bolts of material, or many short pieces, could be woven without the need to attach a new warp. While weaving, the foot treadles allowed the operator to work quickly with both hands freed of the task of changing sheds, and the heavy beater efficiently packed all the newly woven weft thread with one movement. With this machine and other simple machines used in wool preparation, such as the spinning wheel, weaving was transformed from an intimate household art, usually the domain of women, to an industry on large or small scale in which bolts of yardage and blankets and serapes were turned out in large quantities by men in workshops (*obrajes*). Such a transformation had already taken place in most of Europe hundreds of years earlier. Thus, intimately handwoven garments, which among the Indians had important cultural and sacred connotations, were replaced by impersonal bolts of yardage made in an incipient factory ambience, later to be made into clothing by other artisans.

European weaving methods and large flocks of sheep came to the western borderlands with the early settlers. By the 1630s weaving workshops were in operation in Santa Fe and in other New Mexican locations. Treadle-loom weaving was also under way in the Indian missions of Baja California by the early 1700s and, by the 1770s, in the missions of Alta California. In New Mexico large quantities of coarse yardage (*sayal*), blankets, and other items were turned out on these looms, and much of the production was shipped south for trade in the populated areas of northern Mexico. At the same time, under supervision of the friars, the Pueblo Indians began weaving with wool on their vertical frame looms, producing considerable numbers of blankets as well as making other clothing items, such as wool stockings. Much of their production was collected as enforced tribute by the Spanish government. These local products were supplemented by the triennial mission supply train from Mexico and later by the efforts of private traders.

In the eighteenth century, with the reestablishment of the colony after the reconquest completed in 1696, the Pueblo Indians had more freedom to trade their woven products, which they continued to produce in quantities on their vertical frame looms. The Navajo Indians had also become active weavers, producing wool blankets of high quality. Among the growing Hispanic population, sheep raising was a major occupation, especially in the southern (Rio Abajo) area of New Mexico. Here large haciendas had their own textile workshops making yardage and blankets as part of their income-producing activities. By 1805, however, the quality of Hispanic weaving in New Mexico had become so poor that at the request of Governor Fernando Chacón, two master weavers, the brothers Ignacio Ricardo Bazán and Juan Bazán, were sent from Mexico City to Santa Fe. By introducing better techniques and new patterns to a large number of apprentices, the Bazán brothers inspired a revival of Hispanic weaving that continued to flourish through the nineteenth century.

Although in both Mexico and New Mexico Spanish methods and purposes seemed to dominate the craft of weaving, in at least one important area indigenous influence was still strong.

This was the creation of the serape. A poncho or blanket with a slit for the head, this ubiquitous article of male attire retained pre-Columbian elements in its design and use. The brightly colored serape designs, usually with central diamond motifs, have no direct antecedents in Spain, and in the colonial period and later they were an essential part of the costume of mestizo men, especially those of the rural *vaquero* and *ranchero* classes.

The serape was made all over the temperate regions of Mexico, but by the mid nineteenth century it was especially associated with the northeastern Mexican city of Saltillo. The Saltillo serape probably owes its origin to Tlaxcalan Indians, who were brought north by the Spaniards in the early colonial period to aid in subjugating the hostile tribes. A Tlaxcalan community was established as a barrio of Saltillo in the 1590s.

By the late colonial period, however, there is little evidence of commercial production of serapes in the Saltillo region or in Texas or elsewhere in the northeast frontier of New Spain. The 1812 report of Miguel Ramos Arizpe to the Spanish *Cortes* (parliament) states that weaving and other crafts were just beginning to develop at that time in Saltillo, the largest city in the northeast region of Mexico. Ramos Arizpe states that there were some sixty looms for weaving wool blankets and other items in Saltillo and in the neighboring barrio of Tlaxcala, as well as more than forty for weaving coarse cotton textiles. But he complains that an enlightened government should not allow the virtuous women of the region to continue working with such primitive equipment, although with their slow and laborious backstrap looms they are able to produce admirable weavings. As late as 1827 an American observer in Saltillo described the weaving of blankets and rebozos (shawls) by the Tlaxcalan Indian women by the use of backstrap looms. It appears that Indian methods were still commonly used on the northern frontier through the colonial period and that Saltillo serape production did not become fully mechanized until the 1830s or 1840s, soon becoming famous for creating the best and most beautiful Mexican serapes.

The people of the northeastern provinces including Texas, according to Ramos Arizpe, were being exploited by the greedy entrepreneurs of southern Mexico who bought their raw wool, cotton, and hides at low prices and sold them finished goods at high prices, not only draining the citizens of financial resources but also depriving them of the livelihood they would have gained if they had manufactured their own products. Saltillo is the only site he noted as having a nascent weaving industry; iron and woodworking were just beginning to develop also in Monterrey and Parras, although, disgracefully, all the iron farming tools were still imported from central Mexico. Clearly, crafts were not well founded in these northeastern cities by 1812, and further north on the Texas frontier they were even less so.

In New Mexico the surviving locally made blankets of Saltillo design all date from the mid nineteenth century, and it is not certain that these designs were introduced any earlier than the 1840s. In the eighteenth century there was considerable trading back and forth of design motifs among Hispanic, Pueblo, and Navajo weavers, and some local Indian techniques were still utilized in Hispanic weaving. While eighteenth-century Hispanic weaving in the Rio Abajo area was quite commercially oriented, in the north, where the mountainous land was less suited for large-scale sheep raising, there were many small landholders, and textile production was more often a family activity. Women were responsible for the wool preparation and often did the weaving. The treadle loom was used for weaving, but wool was still spun by women on the Indian drop spindle (*malacate*), the spinning wheel seldom being used until the late nineteenth century. In the north, the products of the loom were more likely to be made for family use or for local barter. Thus, isolated Hispanic communities maintained the craft of weaving through the colonial period and even into the twentieth century as an integral element of family and community life, producing beautiful weavings primarily for local use. In so doing, they drew upon both the early European and pre-Hispanic indigenous traditions in which beauty and utility had not yet suffered the separation caused by the dominance of rationalistic economic concerns.

WOODWORKING

Many of the pre-Columbian Indian groups in both the Southeast and the Southwest had strong woodworking traditions; wood was used to make carved and painted representations of animals and deities for ceremonial use, as well as utensils and components for building construction. The Spaniards had new needs for wood and brought new iron tools for working it. In many borderland areas, including Florida, Texas, New Mexico, Arizona, and California, the Indians were enlisted, whether willingly or not, in the construction of mission establishments, which required learning not only new masonry techniques but also new carpentry skills. The Indians were trained by friars or by artisans brought in from Mexico, and ecclesiastical reports usually indicate that they were quick in adapting to the new woodworking needs of the Europeans. More elaborate uses of wood characterized Hispanic building methods for both stone and adobe churches: large paneled and carved double doors at the entry, window frames, balconies, choir lofts with railings, decorated bond and ceiling beams, and supporting corbels.

In New Mexico, with the establishment of the missions in the 1620s, many Pueblo Indians were trained in carpentry, and they continued, along with some Hispanic carpenters, to fulfill woodworking needs of the colonists through the seventeenth and eighteenth centuries. This included not only the decoration of churches but also the making of farming tools, looms, and large wagons (*carretas*) used for transporting goods, as well as household and ecclesiastical furniture. In particular, the men of Pecos Pueblo had a reputation for excellent carpentry skills throughout the colonial period.

Seven Hispanic carpenters came with the first settlers to New Mexico in 1598, bringing with them their tools and presumably skills acquired through apprenticeship in the guild system then in place in Mexico. After the reconquest, a shortage of carpenters led to renewed demand for outside carpenters in the newly resettled region. This shortage continued through the first half of the eighteenth century. Governor Tomás Vélez Capuchín, writing in 1749 about two French carpenters who had just arrived in Santa Fe, stated that there were no carpenters resident in the city at the time, in spite of the great need for them. By 1790, however, there were at least forty carpenters in New Mexico, responding to the needs of a rapidly expanding Hispanic population. No formal guild system existed in New Mexico. Sons of master craftsmen tended to be their fathers' apprentices, so that the trade was passed down informally through families. Many generations of carpenters and blacksmiths in New Mexico are well documented in archival sources.

Furniture built out of local ponderosa pine wood by the Hispanic and Pueblo Indian carpenters included chests, chairs, stools, tables, clothes and dish cabinets, shelves, and other items. In style the pieces were devoid of the elaborate ornamentation of the deeply carved baroque and rococo furniture then popular in the urban centers of Mexico and Spain. Simple forms and low relief carving were characteristic of rural furniture made all over the northern frontier and hark back to sixteenth-century and earlier provincial Spanish work. Some of the designs are even more ancient, such as the rosette or spoked wheel and the opposed lion motifs on chest fronts, which are cosmic symbols deriving from the pre-Christian ancient Near East. These motifs were repeated by folk artists in both Europe and the Americas and survived in New Mexico through the eighteenth century. Some extant pieces of colonial and nineteenth-century furniture, including a few painted chests and painted and carved chairs, exhibit Pueblo Indian influence, but none of them are documented to known Pueblo carpenters. In spite of the difficulty of transportation, furniture was also imported into New Mexico; the most commonly owned items were the famous painted chests made by Tarascan Indians in Michoacán, where woodworking had been a major industry since the early colonial period.

Furniture-making may not have been the most important source of income for carpenters in the borderlands. Many travelers noted the lack of furniture in the homes even of the well-to-do, and colonial-period wills generally show that wealthy people with large homes owned little wooden furniture. Sparsely decorated homes were a cultural preference having roots both in Spain, probably a Moorish North African influence, and in the New World. In the adobe homes of the Southwest the few pieces of wooden furniture were often supplemented by mud-plaster benches, shelves, niches, cabinets, and fireplaces, all built into the walls. The craft of adobe finishing, including creating these built-in furnishings, was traditionally the work of women among the Pueblo Indians, a practice the Hispanic settlers adopted and carried on well into the twentieth century. In their furnishings, Hispanic homes combined the skills of both men and women, but the poorer people lived virtually without any wooden furniture, just as the Pueblo Indians did and just as the rural people did in Spain and North Africa.

BLACKSMITHING

Ironworking was not known among the Indians in the borderlands prior to the coming of the Spaniards. The working of iron in fact represents a criterion that separates the way of life of Renaissance Europe from that of the American Indians. Iron weapons, gunpowder, and horses were the three major factors that made the remarkable conquest of Mexico successful. After the initial conquest, iron weapons and tools made it possible to extend Spanish dominance over vast areas, including the northern frontier. Blacksmiths were essential to the establishing of outposts in the borderlands and to the continued maintenance of these often tenuous extensions of European culture: they kept the horses, mules, and donkeys properly shod; they maintained the firearms and other weapons in working order; and they made and repaired the immense variety of iron tools upon which the European way of life was so dependent.

Virtually every aspect of Hispanic life relied upon objects made of iron: weapons, armor, equestrian equipment, tools for farming and mining, tools for masons and other artisans, household utensils, door bolts, locks, crosses, ornamental iron for architectural use, and, of course, the blacksmith's own tools and equipment. Large quantities of these items were carried to the borderlands by the first settlers, and every successive supply train brought more. However, shortages of iron, which had to be imported from Spain, and lack of ironworkers were constant problems in borderland outposts, such as Texas, Arizona, and California, where the civilian population was small. All the borderland settlements, no matter how small the Hispanic population, needed blacksmiths to keep iron items in repair and to forge new ones when necessary. In the mission craft shops set up by the friars, ironworking was quickly taught to the

Indians, either by friars who had some proficiency in the craft or by outside blacksmiths brought in for the purpose.

At least two blacksmiths accompanied the Spanish explorer Juan de Oñate to New Mexico in 1598, and along with a substantial supply of iron items the Oñate expedition carried more than twelve anvils. Other blacksmiths came to the colony in the 1620s to aid in the building of the missions and the teaching of the craft to the Indians. That the Indians learned well was demonstrated in the Pueblo Revolt when, during the period of reconquest, the Spaniards found the Indians had set up blacksmith shops where they made weapons, such as iron-tipped lances. With the reconquest a number of newly arrived Hispanic blacksmiths established themselves in Santa Fe and later in other communities. Like woodworking, the ironworking trade was generally passed down in families. Successive generations of the Sena family of blacksmiths began with the arrival of Bernardino de Sena in 1693 and ended in the late 1920s when the last Sena closed his blacksmith shop in Santa Fe.

OTHER CRAFTS

Until the nineteenth century little silverwork was done in the borderland colonies due primarily to the lack of raw material. Most of the silverware in use was imported from Mexico by wealthy citizens; the northernmost silverworking center in the Southwest was the city of Chihuahua. New Mexican censuses of the 1780s and 1790s show a few silversmiths in the province, and a few also appear in late colonial censuses in Texas and California. Some blacksmiths may also have worked silver, making decorated horse gear such as bridle bits, silver buttons for the trousers of horsemen, and other items. By the 1830s New Mexican silver and gold workers had become renowned for their skill. The delicate craft of making gold and silver filigree jewelry was practiced in New Mexico by the 1830s and probably dates from the colonial period.

Fine leatherwork in the Hispano-Moorish tradition was done throughout Mexico in the colonial period. In the borderlands, leatherworking followed blacksmithing in importance as a craft necessary to the maintenance of Hispanic life. Leather was prepared and worked for a wide variety of uses and was especially important for the soldiers stationed at borderland *presidios*. Among the items made by leatherworkers were saddles and other horse gear, coats, jackets, boots (*botas*), shields (*adargas*), shoes, chests, boxes, and other containers.

Hispanic leatherworking traditions, introduced in some cases by the friars, had an impact on Native peoples of the borderlands. Indian men often wore leather garments in imitation of those of the Spanish soldiers and adopted Spanish-style saddles and other horse gear. Of great importance for Spanish military purposes were the heavy outer garments worn by soldiers, especially the jackets (*cueras de soldados*), and the sturdy leather shields to deflect arrows and lances. Heavy leather overcoats and chaps served to protect soldiers and horsemen riding through rough country full of cactus and brush. Leather chests, boxes, bags, and tobacco containers were made for household and personal use. The lightweight traveling chests known as *petacas* served to transport items from Mexico, then were used for household storage. A number of them have survived in New Mexico and probably were made in Chihuahua or further south. Many shoemakers (*zapateros*) appear in borderland colonial censuses. These individuals most likely were responsible for a wide range of leather goods, possibly including saddles and other horse gear. Some of the tailors (*sastres*) appearing in the censuses may also have been skilled in making leather garments.

Pottery making was carried on by many indigenous groups in the borderlands prior to the Spanish occupation. Hand-built, low-fired ceramics, often intricately painted or impressed with patterns, were made for household and ceremonial purposes. After the conquest, in the missions and military outposts from Florida to California, the Spaniards used both Indian ware and imported majolica for cooking and serving food, for storage, and for other domestic uses. Colonial sites all along the borderlands yield shards of both imported and Native pottery. Post-Conquest Indian ceramics often show influence from the colorful wheel-thrown majolica, most of which came from the city of Puebla in central Mexico, where there was a thriving pottery industry. In response to the needs of the settlers,

Indian potters copied and adapted popular European forms, such as soup bowls, bean pots, plates, and pitchers. For the churches they made ceramic chalices, censers, baptismal fonts, candlesticks, and other items. In some cases the decoration of Indian pottery was also influenced by Hispanic majolica ware.

The use of imported majolica items was generally limited to the wealthy Spaniards, while indigenous pottery was used by poorer Mestizos and the Indians. No majolica was made by artisans in the borderland settlements, and many settlers simply traded with the Indians for pottery. In New Mexico by the late eighteenth century, some Hispanic and Hispanicized women made simple utilitarian ware for household use, following Pueblo and Apache Indian techniques.

The end of the colonial period (1821) brought an influx of Anglo-American and northern European manufactured goods into the former Spanish territories, as well as the emigration of artisans from the United States and Europe and new tools and modes of distribution, producing many changes and adaptations in both the *vecino* and the Indian crafts. For example, in late-nineteenth-century New Mexico, the availability of milled lumber and more sophisticated woodworking tools, as well as access to Anglo-American designs, made possible the more elaborate and delicately decorated furniture and architectural decoration known as Territorial style. The ready availability of scrap tin from containers brought in by Anglo-American traders allowed the craft of tinwork to flourish after 1846. Today most surviving so-called Spanish colonial items in museums and private collections date from the post-1821 period, and many show Anglo-American influence.

BIBLIOGRAPHY

Adams, Eleanor, and Angelico Chavez, trans. and ed. *The Missions of New Mexico, 1776: A Description by Fray Francisco Atanasio Domínguez.* Albuquerque, N.Mex., 1956.

Ahlborn, Richard E. "Spanish Colonial Wood Carving in New Mexico, 1598–1848." M.A. thesis, University of Delaware, 1958.

Bannon, John F. *The Spanish Borderlands Frontier, 1513–1821.* New York, 1970.

Batkin, Jonathan. *Pottery of the Pueblos of New Mexico: 1700–1940.* Colorado Springs, Colo., 1987.

Boyd, E. *Popular Arts of Spanish New Mexico.* Santa Fe, N.Mex., 1974.

Boyd, Mark F. *Here They Once Stood: The Tragic End of the Apalachee Missions.* Gainesville, Fla., 1951.

Boylan, Leona Davis. *Spanish Colonial Silver.* Santa Fe, N.Mex., 1974.

Carrillo, Charles M. "New Mexican Hispanic Pottery as Evidence of Craft Specialization, 1790–1890." Ph.D. diss., University of New Mexico, in progress.

Fisher, Nora, ed. *Spanish Textile Tradition of New Mexico and Colorado.* Santa Fe, N.Mex., 1979.

Flint, Timothy, ed. *The Personal Narrative of James O. Pattie of Kentucky.* Cincinnati, Ohio, 1831; repr., Cleveland, Ohio, 1905.

Hann, John H. *Apalachee: The Land Between the Rivers.* Gainesville, Fla., 1988.

Jones, Oakah L., Jr. *Los Paisanos: Spanish Settlers on the Northern Frontier of New Spain.* Norman, Okla., 1979.

Larson, Lewis H., Jr. "Historic Guale Indians of the Georgia Coast and the Impact of the Spanish Mission Effort." In *Tacachale: Essays on the Indians of Florida and Southeastern Georgia During the Historic Period,* edited by Jerald Milanich and Samuel Proctor. Gainesville, Fla., 1978.

Myres, Sandra L. *The Ranch in Spanish Texas, 1691–1800.* El Paso, Tex., 1969.

Ramos Arizpe, Miguel. *Discursos, Memorias e Informes.* Mexico City, Mexico, 1942. (First published in Cadiz, Spain in 1812; English translation, Austin, Tex., 1950.)

Rolle, Andrew F. *California: A History.* New York, 1963.

Simmons, Marc, and Frank Turley. *Southwestern Colonial Ironwork: The Spanish Blacksmithing Tradition From Texas to California.* Santa Fe, N.Mex., 1980.

Taylor, Lonn, and Dessa Bokides. *New Mexican Furniture, 1600–1940.* Sante Fe, N.Mex., 1987.

Webb, Edith B. *Indian Life at the Old Missions.* Los Angeles, Calif., 1952; repr., Lincoln, Nebr., 1982.

Wroth, William. *Hispanic Crafts of the Southwest.* Colorado Springs, Colo., 1977.

William Wroth

SEE ALSO **Architecture; Artisans; Patterns of Socialization; Rural Life;** and **Urban Life.**

MUSIC AND DANCE

THE BRITISH COLONIES

Sacred Music

SACRED MUSIC in the British North American colonies included the activities of a variety of Protestant groups: Anglican, Congregational (Puritan), Baptist, and others. Between first colonization and political independence, these denominations developed divergent musical traditions. But the overarching story of British colonial sacred music is, as historian Richard Crawford has suggested, that of gradual transformation from ritual to art—much like the transition that occurred about a generation earlier in the small parish churches of Great Britain. English cathedral music, based on a long tradition of cultivated composition and requiring the presence of organs and trained choirs, touched the American colonies hardly at all.

Anglicans building a church at Jamestown, Virginia, in 1607, Pilgrims and Puritans arriving on New England's shores in the 1620s, and Scottish and Irish Presbyterians immigrating in the 1660s all followed John Calvin's injunction to sing versifications of the biblical psalms as a regular part of worship (referred to as "psalmody"). Their psalters were varied: Thomas Sternhold's and John Hopkins's *The Whole Booke of Psalmes* (1562 and many later editions) for adherents of the Church of England; Henry Ainsworth's *The Book of Psalmes: Englished both in Prose and Metre* (1612) for the separatist Pilgrims; *The Whole Booke of Psalmes faithfully Translated into English Metre* (1640 and many later editions), known as the "Bay Psalm Book," for the Massachusetts Bay Puritans; and the Scottish psalter, *The Psalms of David in Meeter* (1650), for the Presbyterians. Among Pilgrims and Puritans, instrumental accompaniment and professional singing leaders were eschewed; along with harmony and counterpoint, they were considered popish excesses. The Anglican southern colonies had no strictures against the use of instruments, but practical considerations long militated against their introduction.

By the revolution's end, many urban Anglican churches had replaced their unaccompanied clerk-led psalmody with the singing of both psalms and hymns to organ accompaniment. But the change in the Congregational churches of New England was more dramatic. In town after town, worshipers stood several times during the service to hear large groups of young men and women, seated together as choirs in the meeting-house galleries, perform four-voice tunes and anthems—some quite lengthy and florid, others containing rapid-fire imitative sections—occasionally with the accompaniment of bass viols or even of small "gallery orchestras." These youthful choristers (median age seventeen) were recent graduates of local singing schools, where they had learned the skills of musical sight-reading, vocal production, and ensemble performance. Many of the catchy new pieces they sang had been composed, perhaps even published, by local artisans and tradesmen of musical bent but little training.

In the colonial period, the changing musical traditions of New England Congregationalism clearly dominated not only music making in worship but music making as a whole. They touched nearly everyone in the New England region and many in the other colonies, actively involving thousands of people as singing masters and scholars, proponents and opponents of reform, and (toward the end of the period) composers, performers, and publishers of new sacred music. They gave rise to colonial America's first institutions for musical learning and performance as well as to its first musical imprints. Through all this, Congregationalist musicians produced materials and evolved practices adopted by worshipers of other denominations. (Very little survives to document the particular musical traditions of, for example, the Baptist church in America, associated with only one imprint containing music issued in the colonial period, or the Methodist church, associated with none.) Congregationalist music, musicians, and musical publications therefore take center stage in this essay.

EARLY CHANGE AND RESISTANCE

The progression of New England's sacred music from a subservient role in religious ritual to an assertive role as a creative artistic activity sparked two kinds of reactions. To some people, each new event in the process represented further declension from proper worship practice, an aesthetic mirror reflecting religious decline. For others, the changes brought opportunities for self-expression—a notion not consciously recognized in this tradition, but always a human need. In fact, the entire process was shaped by something universal and very old: the subversive, seductive power of music as a creative activity capable of distracting its practitioners from the controlling institution's "business at hand." In the Puritan-founded Congregational church, that business was the direct, uncluttered worship of God.

John Calvin's insistence that each and every worshiper sing God's praises, reinforced by tracts

such as Boston minister John Cotton's *Singing of Psalmes a Gospel-Ordinance* (London, 1647), firmly established a tradition of congregational singing on these shores. But the democracy inherent in Congregationalism added something else: an unspoken acknowledgment of each parishioner's right to praise God in song as he or she saw fit, unhampered by trained leadership. This philosophy, combined with an avoidance of instrumental accompaniment, a steady attrition of music books and of people who could decipher them (editions of the Bay Psalm Book with a supplement of only eleven or twelve monophonic tunes did little to shore up musical literacy), and the practice of "lining out," in which a deacon or clerk read each line of a psalm before it was sung, resulted, by the early 1700s, in a manner of congregational singing dramatically different from that of more musically literate worshipers in the cathedrals of the mother country.

In 1720 several Boston ministers began to protest in lectures and sermons (some of which were later published) the sound of the music in their churches. A passage from George Hood's pioneering *History of Music in New England* skillfully excerpts a polemic by the Reverend Thomas Walter, providing a vivid description of this sound:

Every melody was "tortured and twisted," (embellished?) "as every inskillful throat saw fit," until their psalms were uttered in a medley of confused and disorderly noises, rather than in a decorous song. The Rev. Mr. Walter says of their singing, that it sounded "like five hundred different tunes roared out at the same time;" and so little attention was paid to time, that they were often one or two words apart, producing noises "so hideous and disorderly, as is bad beyond expression." The manner of singing had also become so tedious and drawling, that the same author says, "I myself have twice in one note paused to take breath." (pp. 84–85)

In these phrases, clouded somewhat by the vitriol of a reformer's attack, are the main features of what became known as "the old way of singing": strongly independent individual lines, a lack of coordination between voices, perhaps considerable ornamentation, loud volume, extremely slow tempo, and scant regularity of rhythm.

Clearly, the "old way of singing" involved minimal reference to written materials. It was oral in practice and transmission; surviving accounts leave little doubt that by the early eighteenth century lining out had become essential to remind congregations of the text and tune to be sung, that only four or five tunes were used in most parishes, and that even with this limited repertory individuals frequently slipped from one tune into another before they had worked their way through a single stanza. (All these developments occurred somewhat earlier in English parish churches, as Nicholas Temperley has shown.) It is also clear that the "old way" was a practice dear to the hearts of many and that it was not given up without a struggle. Straddling ritual and art—remaining faithful to Puritan Congregationalist worship practice while offering a chance for self-expression—it could be effectively superseded only if its critics found something equally respectable and alluring to offer in its stead.

They did. The ministers themselves, in fact, had no inkling of how successful their replacement would become, nor of how far it would lead beyond their original intent. The idea was to encourage "regular singing" (singing by rule, or "by note"—that is, according to the way the music was notated) through the inculcation of musical literacy. This, in turn, the reformers reasoned, could not fail to improve congregational song. How to proceed? The Reverend Thomas Symmes of Bradford, Massachusetts, wrote in *The Reasonableness of, Regular Singing, or, Singing by Note* (Boston, 1720):

Would it not greatly tend to the promoting [of] Singing Psalms, if Singing Schools *were promoted?* . . . Where would be the *Difficulty*, or what the *Disadvantages*, if People that want *Skill* in *Singing*, would procure a *Skilfull Person* to *Instruct* them, and meet *Two* or *Three* Evenings in the Week, from *Five* or *six* a Clock, to *Eight*, and spend the Time in Learning to Sing? (p. 20)

This is just what happened. Although Anglican religious societies of young men had studied regular singing in Maryland as early as 1699, a singing master had taught in Virginia in 1710–1711, and psalmody instruction had been advertised in Boston in 1714, the singing school really came into its own in New England in the half century following the reform of the early 1720s.

Singing schools—taught in the Congregationalist parish of Windsor, Connecticut, in 1727, sponsored by New York's Anglican Trinity Church in 1753, or run by William Billings in a Boston schoolhouse in 1782—remained remarkably consistent in format and method throughout the colonial period. They tended to meet several evenings a week, as the Reverend Symmes had suggested, over a period of two or three months. Many used oblong tunebooks, printed or manuscript, as their texts, progressing from "the rudiments of vocal music" to actual tunes for practice. From the start singing schools were a youth activity, providing much-appreciated opportunities for social intercourse: most of the scholars were boys and girls between eight and twenty-one years of age, with the preponderance in their late teens. Before the revolution, most singing masters seem to have been hired by local parishes, as when Lewis Edson, Sr., of Bridgewater, Massachusetts, taught schools in next-door Halifax between 1769 and 1776—although the 1720s Connecticut River valley itinerancy of one George Beale provides a notable early exception to this rule. (By and large, the advent of the itinerant singing master was a late-eighteenth-century phenomenon, as was the self-sponsored singing school, where a singing master set himself up in business by advertising for scholars.)

FURTHER INNOVATIONS

"Regular singing" and the singing school, although introduced to enhance the ritual of Protestant worship, ironically brought an invasion of art into New England's meetinghouses. Striking innovations in themselves, they led to a series of additional changes, each of which took the churches' music one step further away from the Calvinist ideal espoused by the first settlers.

Eighteenth-century New England parishes were small democracies where church members voted on all questions brought before them. Many of these questions had to do with the music and texts for worship: Should regular singing be adopted? Who was to serve as chorister? Should the "New England version" (the Bay Psalm Book) be discarded in favor of Nicholas Brady's and Nahum Tate's *A New Version of the Psalms of David*, supplemented by some hymns by the nonconformist theologian Isaac Watts? Where in the meetinghouse should the choristers be seated? What tunes were to be sung in the worship service? Should a singing school be established? Who was to be hired as singing master, and what was his salary to be? Should the youngsters recently graduated from the singing school be allowed to sit together and help lead the singing? Might the choir be allowed to sing one psalm in each service on the Sabbath? Should a bass viol be admitted to accompany the singers? Was it time to discontinue lining out the psalms?

Discussions and decisions relating to these and similar issues are preserved in literally hundreds of New England town and church histories published in the late nineteenth and early twentieth centuries. These accounts, important sources for the historian of early American sacred music, are notable for two things: the consistency from town to town concerning what changed and when, and the degree of unhappiness and even strife that each innovation caused.

The first of these innovations—once it had been decided to sing "by rule"—seems to have been the most easily accepted: the appointment by the church of one or more men ("choristers") to sound the starting pitch of a tune with voice or pitch pipe and then to lead the singing. There are records of churches choosing choristers from the 1730s through the 1770s. (Parish clerks in smaller Anglican churches throughout the colonies were leading the singing during this same period.) The chorister's duties were performed in the context of lining out: a common sequence of events had the minister reading the entire psalm to be sung, a deacon repeating the first line or two of text, the chorister sounding a starting pitch and leading the singing of those lines, the deacon reading the next line or lines to be sung, the chorister leading the singing, and so on. (Even with an attempt to follow specified rhythmic values, reading and singing through a multiple-stanza psalm text could be a lengthy process.) Individual parishes are known to have resisted the appointment of singing leaders, and objections were voiced to the choristers' beating of time with their hands, to the use of instruments (pitch pipes) for setting the pitch, even to the setting of any specific pitch at all. But opposition to these early changes seems to have been neither particularly spirited nor sustained.

Toward mid century, in many parishes the number of singing leaders increased—to three, six, even eight men—and eventually these leaders were given leave to sit together. Presumably they would rise as a group to lead the congregation through a psalm at the appropriate point in the service.

In the meantime, however, singing-school graduates were proliferating in many New England communities. It was perhaps inevitable that these young people, having learned skills that set them apart from their elders, would not feel content to slip unobtrusively back into the congregation in order to bolster the general singing. They had tasted the pleasures of learning to sing new music at sight, of singing in parts, of regularly consociating with their peers. So they began agitating for the right to sit together in the meetinghouse and even occasionally to perform the tunes and anthems they had learned. Their requests met with opposition on various grounds, both social (seating in the meetinghouse directly reflected standing in the community) and religious (singing God's praises should be the duty of all, not the privilege of a few).

But perhaps it was felt that the young people's diligence in learning the vocal rudiments should not go unrewarded, for changes started to occur. In many towns the singers were allowed to sit as a body, first in the "hind seats below" and later up in the gallery (or balcony), formerly the preserve of the town's underprivileged, African American, and young male populations. And increasing numbers of churches instituted compromises such as allotting one psalm to the singers (to be sung in parts and not lined out) and one to the congregation. What these innovations added up to, of course, was the creation of the church choir. An unpublished list compiled by Richard Crawford and augmented by this writer shows that Boston's West and First churches were among the first to designate "singers' seats," in 1754 and 1758 respectively; towns following suit in the early 1760s included Salem and Newbury, Massachusetts (1761), Greenland, New Hampshire (1762), Ipswich and Medford, Massachusetts (1763), and Beverly and Hamlet, Massachusetts (1764). Twenty-three New England churches are known to have taken this step by the end of the 1760s and sixty-six by the end of the next decade.

Seating the singers as a body acknowledged their role as leaders of the musical part of the service. This development, perhaps abetted by increased affluence permitting more members of the congregation to purchase their own text collections, spelled the end of lining out. Indeed, in many churches the votes on seating the singers and on abolishing lining out were taken at the same time. In Worcester, Massachusetts, for example, on 5 August 1779 it was "voted, That the singers sit in the front seats in the front gallery. . . . Voted, That said singers be requested to . . . carry on singing in public worship. Voted, That the mode of singing in the congregation here, be without reading the psalms, line by line, to be sung." The same source describes the subsequent tearful exit from the meetinghouse of "the aged and venerable Deacon Chamberlain," whose job it had been to read the lines of the psalm. Deacon Chamberlain was not alone in his distress. In a survey of local histories for eighty-nine Massachusetts towns, individuals in seventeen—almost one-fifth of the total—were found to have left the meetinghouse, or refused to attend meeting, because of musical innovations.

A telling complaint about one choir was printed in the Portsmouth *New Hampshire Gazette* on 13 January 1764:

There are a set of Geniuses, who stick themselves up in a Gallery, and seem to think that they have a Priviledge of engrossing all the singing to themselves; and truely they take away a very effectual Method to secure this Priviledge, namely by singing such Tunes, as is impossible for the Congregation to join in. Whom they get to compose for them, or whether they compose for themselves, I will not pretend to determine; but, instead of those plain and easy Compositions which are essential to the Awful Solemnity of Church Music, away they get off, one after another, in a light, airy, jiggish Tune, better adapted to a Country Dance, than the awful Business of Chanting forth the Praises of the King of Kings. (Quoted in Louis Pichierri, *Music in New Hampshire, 1623–1800*, pp. 37–38)

This letter introduces two further innovations brought about by the singing school: the diversification of church music's repertory and style and the advent of the colonial American composer.

SACRED MUSIC IMPRINTS

By the revolution's official end in 1783, forty different titles containing sacred music had been issued in America. Ranging from the ninth edition of the Bay Psalm Book (1698) with its supplement of thirteen tunes to Boston composer William Billings's *Peace an Anthem* of 1783, these imprints provide another measure of the transition from ritual to art that is being traced here. They also document the dominance of Congregationalism and of the Puritan/Congregational model of musical worship in this period. Although several early tunebook compilers were not Congregationalists (Thomas Johnston, Francis Hopkinson, and Daniel Bayley were Anglicans; James Lyon became a Presbyterian minister), only eight of the forty colonial sacred-music publications were specifically aimed at non-Congregational worshipers (Reformed church, Anglican church, Baptist church), and the earliest of those eight was issued only in 1752.

Sacred music started its American career in print as an adjunct to sacred texts. With the single exception of Thomas Walter's *The Grounds and Rules of Musick Explained* (Boston, 1721; seven later editions through 1764), designed as a manual for instruction in "regular singing," every American imprint containing music issued before 1761 was either a collection of psalm or hymn texts with added tunes (interspersed throughout or gathered at the end) or a separately printed "tune supplement" designed to be bound or at least inserted into such a collection.

Even while playing an ancillary role to devotion, music made a strong showing in several of these early collections. Walter's tunebook, for example, offered among its twenty-four pieces eleven printed for the first time in the colonies. One of these, a simple four-phrase composition titled SOUTHWELL NEW TUNE, has not been traced to any earlier source and is thus a candidate for the first piece of music, both sacred and secular, composed in colonial America. A small tune supplement by John Tufts debuted in Boston in the same year (1721) that Walter's collection first appeared; no copies of early editions have been located, but the third edition of 1723, titled *An Introduction to the Art of Singing Psalm-Tunes* (eight later editions through 1744, under the title *An Introduction to the Singing of Psalm-Tunes*), offered thirty-four pieces, nine of which have not been found in previous American publications and one of which, 100 PSALM TUNE NEW, appears also to be American-composed. Little wonder that the church in Weston, Massachusetts—just outside Boston—at its meeting of 6 November 1724 voted a list of fourteen tunes to be used, requiring that "the Chorist[e]r do not Set any other publickly unless he has furth[e]r order fro[m] ye Church." Such anxiety about limiting the repertory for congregational song is typical of New England churches in this period.

THE RISE OF AMERICAN COMPOSERS OF SACRED MUSIC

The repertory did inevitably grow, however, and singing schools were the primary agent of its expansion. Singers with new skills wanted new music. It was only a matter of time before an enterprising singing master would try his own hand at composition. This is what James Lyon seems to have done for his tunebook *Urania* (Philadelphia, 1761; second edition 1767). *Urania* is a landmark in colonial American sacred music. It was the first collection that aspired to fill the needs both of beginners in psalmody and of experienced singers. As such, it represented a major step in the singing book's transformation from an accessory of ritual to a repository for art—a process that would result in collections such as William Billings's *The Psalm-Singer's Amusement* (1781), designed not so much for worship or instruction as for the enjoyment of trained choirs and experienced singing societies. *Urania* introduced sixty-nine pieces to the American tunebook repertory; at least ten of these, and possibly seventeen, were of American origin, including five probably by Lyon himself and three by William Tuckey, an immigrant Englishman active in the musical life of New York's Anglican Trinity Church. Further, *Urania* tapped a repertory hitherto unavailable in American musical imprints: the "fuging tunes" and anthems composed or compiled by a talented generation of English parish-church musicians, including Israel Holdroyd, Abraham Adams, John Arnold, Uriah Davenport, and Caleb Ashworth. From the collections of these men and a handful of others—William Knapp, William Tans'ur, Joseph Stephenson, Aaron Williams—almost all published between the 1730s and the 1760s, the first New England composers

of psalmody would draw their models and inspiration.

The fuging tunes in mid-century English collections had much to inspire young composers just out of singing school. Perhaps the most popular type set a four-line psalm stanza homophonically (chordally) to its midpoint, then at the third line of text brought in each voice separately, piling one on top of another for a closing section of rough and rousing four-part counterpoint. English anthems published at the same time display a similar liveliness. Fired by this material and following Lyon's example, several tunebook compilers in the mid and late 1760s introduced large chunks of the British repertory in their publications; the most extensive example is Daniel Bayley's almost literal reprinting of two tunebooks by William Tans'ur and Aaron Williams under the title *The American Harmony* (1769 and later editions). At the same time, colonial Americans began to compose in earnest.

None was composing more earnestly by the late 1760s than Boston tanner William Billings, who in 1770 at the age of twenty-four issued his first tunebook, *The New-England Psalm-Singer*. All 127 tunes, anthems, and canons in this collection were first printings; all 127, in fact, had been written by Billings, who moreover had "another Volume . . . consisting chiefly of Anthems, Fugues and Chorus's, of his own Composition" waiting in the wings. Further, several of the pieces are of high quality; the anthem "As the hart panteth after the water brooks," for example, is a work of considerable beauty and power. With its frontispiece by Paul Revere, its topical references, its settings of politically inspired texts, the lively prose of its ebullient author, and its torrent of homemade compositions that declare American musical independence and occasionally reveal an inspired creative talent. *The New-England Psalm-Singer* is a remarkable document in the history of American sacred music, of American music, of America itself.

Billings, not content with precocity, evolved rapidly as a musical artist after his audacious debut. His second collection, *The Singing Master's Assistant* (1778), is aesthetically light-years beyond his first. While *The New-England Psalm-Singer* included a large number of untexted psalm tunes, suggesting that it was partly intended for congregational singing, *The Singing*

Master's Assistant was almost exclusively a book for choirs—fully texted, containing eight anthems to the earlier book's four, and with pieces both topical (the anthem LAMENTATION OVER BOSTON, beginning "By the Rivers of Watertown we sat down and wept"; the patriotic hymn CHESTER, naming five British generals in its second stanza) and even prankish (the almost entirely dissonant JARGON). When one recalls the story of Worcester's aged Deacon Chamberlain tearfully exiting his meetinghouse because he could no longer line out the psalm, it is hard to credit that *The Singing Master's Assistant* had appeared in nearby Boston the previous year.

Billings's tunes and tunebooks seem to have given his New England contemporaries the courage to try writing their own music. The revolution limited tunebook publication, but large musical manuscripts dating from the mid 1770s by Daniel Read of Attleborough and Abraham Wood of Northboro, both in Massachusetts, make it plain that the composing of music was not affected. And in 1779 a new tunebook, *Select Harmony* by Andrew Law of Cheshire, Connecticut, introduced pieces by nine previously unpublished Americans—a sure sign that the creative urge was spreading.

There is one remaining innovation—one additional step away from ritual and toward art in the music of the Congregational worship service—to comment upon here: the introduction of instruments other than the human voice. Anglican churches had no prohibitions against instrumental accompaniment, purchasing organs to accompany their singing as soon as funds were available (Boston's King's Chapel in 1713 and the two other Anglican churches in that city by 1744; Saint Philip's Church, Charleston, South Carolina, and Christ Church, Philadelphia, in or around 1728; Trinity Church, Newport, Rhode Island, in 1733; New York's Trinity Church in 1737; five Virginia churches between 1737 and 1767; all three Anglican churches in Philadelphia by the mid 1760s). However, New England's Congregational churches, as we have seen, often had trouble accepting even the lowly pitch pipe. The next instrument to invade the Congregational sanctuary seems to have been the bass viol, introduced to support the singers by doubling the bass line. Once again, resistance was strong. Bass viols were referred to as "devil's

fiddles," and in Roxbury, Massachusetts, "one old church member stood at the church door and showed his contempt . . . by making a sort of caterwauling noise, which he called 'mocking the banjo.'" But in time the bass viol won a place in the meetinghouse gallery, as did (in some locations) the violin, flute, clarinet, bassoon, and other instruments eventually comprising the "gallery orchestra." (There was no organ in a Congregational church until 1770, in Providence, Rhode Island.)

In time, too, it appears that choirs took over the entire musical portion of the worship service in most Congregational churches. With this step, the transformation from ritual to art—for the worshiper, from participation in a religious act to appreciation of a performance—was complete. In its own way, music in the rural New England meetinghouse, like that of the urban Anglican church, had become as much an object for contemplation as a means of expressing sacred truths.

BIBLIOGRAPHY

Britton, Allen Perdue, Irving Lowens, and Richard Crawford. *American Sacred Music Imprints, 1698–1810: A Bibliography.* Worcester, Mass., 1990.
Buechner, Alan Clark. "Yankee Singing Schools and the Golden Age of Choral Music in New England, 1760–1800." Ed.D. diss., Harvard University, 1960.
Cooke, Nym. "American Psalmodists in Contact and Collaboration, 1770–1820." 2 vols. Ph.D. diss., University of Michigan, 1990.
Crawford, Richard. Preface to *Urania, or A Choice Collection of Psalm-Tunes, Anthems, and Hymns,* by James Lyon. Philadelphia, 1761; repr. New York, 1974.
———. "Psalmody." In *The New Grove Dictionary of American Music,* edited by H. Wiley Hitchcock and Stanley Sadie. London and New York, 1986.
———, ed. *The Core Repertory of Early American Psalmody.* Madison, Wis., 1984.
Crawford, Richard, and David Warren Steel. "Singing-school." In *The New Grove Dictionary of American Music,* edited by H. Wiley Hitchcock and Stanley Sadie. London and New York, 1986.
Ellinwood, Leonard. *The History of American Church Music.* New York, 1953.
Foote, Henry Wilder. *Three Centuries of American Hymnody.* Hamden, Conn., 1961.
Hood, George. *A History of Music in New England: with Biographical Sketches of Reformers and Psalmists.* Boston, 1846; repr. New York, 1970.

Kroeger, Karl, and Richard Crawford, eds. *The Complete Works of William Billings*. Vol. 1, *The New-England Psalm-Singer (1770)*. Boston, 1981.

Lowens, Irving. *Music and Musicians in Early America*. New York, 1964. See especially Chapter 2, "The Bay Psalm Book in 17th-Century New England," and Chapter 3, "John Tufts's *Introduction to the Singing of Psalm-Tunes (1721–1744)*: The First American Music Textbook."

McKay, David P., and Richard Crawford. *William Billings of Boston: Eighteenth-Century Composer*. Princeton, N.J., 1975.

Messiter, A. H. *A History of the Choir and Music of Trinity Church, New York from its Organization, to the Year 1897*. New York, 1906; repr. 1970.

Nathan, Hans, and Richard Crawford, eds. *The Complete Works of William Billings*. Vol. 2, *The Singing Master's Assistant (1778)*, *Music in Miniature (1779)*. Boston, 1977.

Osterhout, Paul R. "Note Reading and Regular Singing in Eighteenth-Century New England." *American Music* 4, no. 2 (Summer 1986):125–144.

Owen, Barbara. "Eighteenth-Century Organs and Organ Building in New England." In *Music in Colonial Massachusetts, 1630–1820, II: Music in Homes and in Churches*, edited by Barbara Lambert. Boston, 1985.

Pichierri, Louis. *Music in New Hampshire, 1623–1800*. New York, 1960.

Sonneck, O. G. *Francis Hopkinson, the First American Poet-Composer (1737–1791) and James Lyon, Patriot, Preacher, Psalmodist (1735–1794): Two Studies in Early American Music*. Washington, 1905; repr. New York, 1967.

Stevenson, Robert. *Protestant Church Music in America: A Short Survey of Men and Movements from 1564 to the Present*. New York, 1966.

Temperley, Nicholas. *The Music of the English Parish Church*. Vol. 1. Cambridge, England, 1979.

———. "Psalms, metrical." In *The New Grove Dictionary of American Music*, edited by H. Wiley Hitchcock and Stanley Sadie. London and New York, 1986.

Temperley, Nicholas, and Charles G. Manns. *Fuguing Tunes in the Eighteenth Century*. Detroit, Mich., 1983.

Wilson, Ruth Mack, and Kate Van Winkle Keller. *Connecticut's Music in the Revolutionary Era*. Hartford, Conn., 1979.

Nym Cooke

SEE ALSO various essays in RELIGION.

Secular Music and Dance

As EUROPEAN MIGRANTS established colonies on the North American continent, music and dancing continued to be part of their daily life. Most of the settlers carried familiar tunes, songs, and dances in their memories. Some brought instruments and written music as well. Once in America, they shared their music and dances with their friends and passed them on to their children. Throughout the colonial period, music and dance served to signal, soothe, animate, celebrate, intimidate, or immortalize, as colonists used them to satisfy personal or institutional needs.

Instrumental music and songs came from sources as varied as the colonists themselves. Dancing tunes and ballads passed aurally from generation to generation and were preserved in printed tunebooks, manuscript collections, and on broadsides. Old ballads about kings and knights, love and death, or accidents and supernatural happenings lasted for centuries. New ballads appeared criticizing contemporary personalities or describing local events. Sung to old tunes like "Chevy Chase" or "Children in the Wood," recently composed marches, opera arias, or stage dance tunes by composers like Henry Purcell, Jeremiah Clark, and George Frideric Handel, or even to familiar psalm tunes, they had broad appeal to all classes.

Working for his printer brother, Benjamin Franklin wrote ballads on up-to-the-minute events when he was a teenager. They were a great success but Franklin's father was not pleased and discouraged his efforts as inappropriate to his station in life. Throughout the colonial period the arts were haunted by class distinctions between those who practiced them professionally and sought patronage and the patrons who used them as recreation or display of status.

Economic and practical circumstances separated the music heard in governors' mansions from that heard in frontier cabins. Those with little to spend amused themselves with familiar songs and free-form community dances to the music of their own voices, perhaps enhanced by the hum of a Jew's harp held between the teeth or the lilt of a homemade flute or fiddle. Those with greater means purchased instruments and music, hired professional instructors, and enjoyed playing or listening to new compositions by British and European artists. They performed the latest dances learned from their teachers or from books ordered from London. In a society eager to show refinement, familiarity with the arts was a sign of gentility, affluence, and influence—evidence of sufficient means to obtain training and the leisure to practice skills.

DANCE FORMS IN COLONIAL TIMES

While there are references to social dancing before 1711, there is little specific information about dance forms used by British colonists before William Byrd's diary in which he speaks of dancing the minuet, French dances, and English country dances.

Because of the invention of a method of dance writing, the beginning of the eighteenth century was a watershed moment in social dance. Before that time, educated dancers in Britain and Europe performed galliards, courantos, branles, measures, English country dances, and other composed dances. English country dances described in words were preserved by John Playford in *The English Dancing Master* (London, 1651) and many later editions (*The Dancing Master,* 1652–1728), but the solo, duo, and other group dances existed only in sketchy descriptions.

Lower class people enjoyed free-form solo or duo jigs and hornpipes, reels for three and four dancers, and repetitive traditional round or line community dances. These forms are universal and timeless and were used throughout the colonial period.

At the beginning of the eighteenth century, French and English masters created a number of duo and solo dances and used a dramatically new dance technique, which had been developed in the court of Louis XIV over the last two decades of the previous century. A new notation system was used to record them. For the first time, composed dances were preserved in detail for future generations. The new dances used a vocabulary of basic steps and combinations set to the music of sarabandes, courantes, gavottes, passepieds, bourrées, allemandes, and minuets. Only the rhythm of the music changed the essential nature of the dance.

In 1711 a Virginian ordered a copy of Ebenezer Pemberton's *Essay for the Improvement of*

Dancing, written specifically for "masters that live remote from London." Henry Holt probably brought with him a recent English translation of Pierre Rameau's influential *Le Maître à Danser* (Paris, 1725) entitled *The Dancing-Master: or the Art of Dancing Explained . . . by John Essex* (London, 1728, second edition, 1731) prepared by his teacher—choreographer for London's Haymarket Theatre. This long narrative with fifty-seven illustrations showing style and technique may also have been in the library of Charles Stagg, a dancing master and theatrical producer in Williamsburg, Virginia. The inventory of Stagg's estate was made in 1735 and lists "a Book the art of Dancing by J. Weaver and D[itt]o by J. Essex." Weaver's work was probably *Orchesography or the Art of Dancing . . . by John Weaver* (London, 1706, second edition, 1722) translated from Raoul Feuillet's *Chorégraphie ou l'art de décrire la danse* (Paris, 1700), the first publication to describe the new dance writing system.

The Minuet
The minuet emerged as a dance of ceremony and ritual. For one couple dancing alone, it used a limited number of steps and a specific floor pattern and sequence of figures. Bows to the company and to partner opened and closed the dance. A symbol of precedence and power, the opening minuets were performed at formal dance events by the most prominent couples in attendance.

Jigs and Hornpipes
Among other notated dances in the new style were jigs or hornpipes (the names were used interchangeably). These free-form display dances for one or two dancers had music written in 3/2, 6/8, or 2/4 meter. At mid century as energetic new duple meter (two beats to a measure) hornpipe style emerged, later to be called the sailor's hornpipe, the older 3/2 tunes were dropped. Jigs continued to be written in 2/4 or 6/8 time. These dances were personal routines, created with step combinations and floor patterns particularly adapted to the skills of the soloist.

Reels
A group dance similar in nature to the jig was the reel. The reel was a dance for three or four

people in a line in which passages of solo dancing in place alternated with traveling in a figure-eight pattern around the other dancers. Because of their informal nature, reels were usually impromptu and were not notated.

The Country Dance

The best documented dance form was the English country dance, which involved many couples standing in a line, partner facing partner. Before 1690 the British colonists probably danced early forms of the English country dance using familiar Renaissance steps, the single (a step and close feet together) and the double (three steps and a close). Once the new French technique was introduced, the basic traveling step became a smooth pas de bourrée, with a half-coupé for setting and honors. The pas de bourrée is a compound step in which a demi-coupé (in first position, bend both knees and then step onto ball of one foot, straightening legs and bringing heel of free foot to other heel) is followed by two straight steps. Honors are the bows of respect made to partner and the company before and after dances, and setting is a movement in place, without traveling, within a dance.

Country dances were set to all kinds of popular music, from traditional ballad tunes to short marches taken from Handel's oratorios, from slow courante and minuet tunes in 3/2 and 3/4 to fast hornpipes in 6/8 or 2/4. The hornpipe was the ancestor of the traditional New England contra dance, which in turn was the ancestor of the traditional American square dance.

Cotillions

In the 1680s French masters developed a new form of country dance, terming it the *contredanse*. It was a nonprogressive dance, usually for a fixed number of dancers. In the 1760s English dancers adopted a form of French *contredanse*, the *cotillon*, anglicized as cotillion and usually but not always danced by four couples in a square. A group of figures formed the chorus of the dance; before each repetition, the dancers performed basic figures, termed changes. Cotillions employed steps similar to those used in country dances, but often in more complex combinations.

Cotillions were introduced into London ballrooms in the 1760s, adopted and promoted by dancing masters as a new dance which required far more schooling than the increasingly easier country dances. The earliest references to cotillions in the colonies are in the early 1770s when masters in several towns advertised that they could teach "these new French compositions." Like other new fashions, the cotillions were first taught by city masters who had quick access to the latest imports. They were soon carried to smaller towns by word of mouth and by itinerant masters.

MUSICAL TRADITIONS IN THE COLONIES

The Musical Puritans

Throughout all the colonies, but more often in Puritan-controlled New England, public furors between local magistrates and overly enthusiastic dancers and musicians broke out occasionally. However, such incidents were the exceptions rather than the rule, and the issue was more often the appropriateness of the time or place than the activity itself.

A few powerful clergymen in Boston perceived the pleasures of music and dance as threats to their congregations' spiritual lives, particularly when enjoyed on days set aside for lectures or worship. But the notion of total Puritan hostility to music and dance is a myth. Most early New Englanders welcomed music as a desirable recreation and dance as a useful physical and social skill.

The young people of Boston were as interested as their English cousins in songs describing the passion between the sexes. During his student days at Harvard in the 1640s, the Reverend Seaborn Cotton copied several of the most sentimental ballads imaginable. Apparently there was a ready market for such products. Puritan preacher Cotton Mather worried that "the minds and manners of many people" were being corrupted by the "foolish songs and ballads" that peddlers carried throughout the countryside.

One of Cotton Mather's colleagues in the church thoroughly enjoyed the latest songs and dances from both elite and vernacular sources. The Reverend Ebenezer Parkman's 1721 tune collection, whose contents ranged from psalm tunes to a tune from Handel's newly composed *Water Music,* reflected a growing interest in music within the church itself. Beginning in the 1720s, many New England churches established singing schools, paying music teachers to instruct young people in singing and in reading music. This in turn encouraged interest and participation in secular as well as sacred music; in 1729 the earliest known public concert was presented in Boston.

The Middle Colonies

An early reference to secular musical activities in New York concerns a private concert in 1710 attended by John Sharp, chaplain to the Governor. Balls were regularly held at the Fort and in other locations. In 1714 twenty-four shillings were paid to musicians for their work during the celebrations in honor of the coronation of George I, an event which featured a parade with hautboys and trumpets and a ball in the evening.

The following year a young lawyer, James Alexander, landed in New York with memories of social dances enjoyed with friends and fellow students in London. In 1730 he wrote out the figures for twenty-six English country dances to old tunes such as "Christ Church Bells," as well as for dances named for recent events such as "Marlborough's Victory."

Alexander was a Scot living in a formerly Dutch-controlled town. His tastes were guided by the leading citizens of his community, the English governor and his retinue. Alexander's Dutch-American wife may have sung lullabies from the Low Countries to her children and James might have danced a highland reel at home with his friends, but when the couple stepped together onto the ballroom floor in public, they chose the latest London fashion in dance. If Alexander wanted to make a political point in verse, he would have selected well-known English tunes for his songs.

Alexander has been credited with writing two highly critical political ballads in 1734 to the tunes of "All you fair ladies now onland" and "Now, now, you Tories all shall stoop," prompting the arrest of the publisher John Peter Zenger. The ensuing trial, in which Zenger was declared not guilty, set important precedents for freedom of the press in English-speaking America.

Rapid growth, general prosperity, and continuous immigration produced considerable cultural ferment, particularly in the middle colonies, but the power of fashion must not be underestimated. Although laborers from Ireland, craftsmen and merchants from Scotland, and musicians from Germany and Italy all brought their own musical traditions to the colonies, London continued to be the source of most of the public repertory.

Throughout the colonial period, trade controls favored Britain as the sole source for supplies. A steady stream of instruments, new music, and the latest dance books from London was unloaded onto colonial wharves. Passengers on incoming ships brought firsthand knowledge of the latest trends on the stage, in the public ballroom, and on the streets of the Old World. Some entrepreneurs traveled to England and the Continent to gather the latest repertory or to hire musicians and dancers for theatrical troupes. From Portsmouth to Savannah, they advertised that they used the most fashionable new material with the latest techniques, in the style of the greatest masters of London, Dublin, and Paris.

Some cultural minorities did maintain strong national traditions. Several Pennsylvania musicians formed manuscript collections containing both German and English compositions, perhaps reflecting the emotional tug-of-war between personal culture and current fashion. English and Scottish settlers who migrated to isolated parts of the Appalachians kept their ballads and tunes uncorrupted almost until the age of the phonograph. French fiddlers and dancers in northern New England have kept their traditions vigorous to this day.

The most concentrated musical culture in colonial America was that of Moravian communities in Pennsylvania and North Carolina. Settling in Bethlehem in 1741, members of this Protestant sect enjoyed an intense sacred and secular musical life. They accumulated substantial libraries of European music and maintained high levels of accomplishment in the performance and composition of instrumental and vocal music. In the midst of the revolutionary war, George Washington spent a night at Bethlehem and found pleasure and solace in a concert of chamber music by the Moravian brethren. However, these religious enclaves were quite insular and had little impact on the broad current of the arts in the colonial period.

Musical Tradition in the South

Music and dance in the southern colonies followed the same patterns as in the North, filling the social and personal needs of the people. Because Anglican and other Protestant sects as well as the Catholic church encouraged instrumental and vocal music in their liturgies, musical life in areas not under Puritan control was much less segregated. Colonists were free to enjoy the arts as they pleased, and music and dance thrived in the free market environment, unhindered by civic controls and spiritual threats. In fact, secular music seemed at times to edge out the sacred arts in the more hedonistic lives of the upper classes of the south. Distances were greater between towns and settlements smaller than in the North and plantations were spread out. But travel and correspondence brought southerners the latest fashions, usually within the time span of a voyage.

Throughout the colonies, theatrical troupes and other professionals traveled between population centers; the hardiest entrepreneurs traveled as itinerants between plantations in the South or between villages in the North. Sometimes they had contracts or sponsors in the next place, but more often they simply moved to a new location when the time seemed right and the new venue offered fresh audiences. For example in the south, large numbers of people came together for a few weeks or months for circuit court and legislative sessions. With leisure and money to spend, they attended concerts, plays, balls, and assemblies, and they took books of music, songs, and handwritten notes back home. Although a small town might not have been able to support music and dance professionals most of the year, there was plenty of demand for such entertainment during these "sessions."

Southern colonists enjoyed the same trade with London as their northern cousins. Henry Holt perceived Charleston, South Carolina, as fertile ground on which to make his fortune. In 1734 he opened a dancing school and began sponsoring public balls there.

The first Charleston theater season opened on 24 January 1735, and it is likely that Holt was involved in the featured ballet pantomimes, the earliest musical theater pieces of record to be performed in America. In 1737 Holt moved on to New York to continue his successful career teaching and performing.

AFRICAN-AMERICAN MUSIC AND DANCE

African-American music and dance were closely tied to occasion, part of life at work in the fields, at play with family and friends, alone mourning separation, or playing for parties of friends, owners, or employers. A number of blacks, both slave and free, attained considerable status as dance musicians throughout the colonies.

While African music appeared at first to have little impact on European models, it was ultimately to have far-reaching influence on the course of American music. Since most of the music played by black musicians for white audiences was outside of black musical traditions, it is likely that, as they played, blacks integrated their own musical ideas with the European music they were expected to play. The violin, also known familiarly as the fiddle, was the first instrument of European origin to be used by black Americans; it was played by them as early as the 1690s. As to how they obtained these instruments, Eileen Southern suggests that slaves made them if they had to, or were provided them by their owners. A letter written by a Philadelphian Quaker in 1719 supports these suppositions. The writer asked his friend in England to buy a strong well-made violin with two or three sets of spare strings to replace the instrument his slave had made for himself.

African music was passed on in aural tradition and without notation. Vocal music was often sung in a call-and-response pattern, occasionally in two or three parts. Drums of many varieties were the most common instruments and were often supplemented by hand clapping and rhythmic foot stamping. Instruments with plucked strings, similar to the lute and harp, and blown reed instruments were also used. Ostinato, which is basic to African music, is built on the reiteration of brief patterns in the bass rather than the use of contrasting tunes in the melody and bass lines.

Africans believed in the reality of the spirit world, and their rituals and ceremonies, centered on music and dance, brought all members of the community together, strengthening their social bonds and common values. None of this ceremonial music remains, but a unique dance form was observed by Nicholas Cresswell in Alexandria, Virginia, in 1775. Called a "Negro" or "Virginia Jig," it is an early example of the adoption of an African form by white Americans. Danced between the country dances, these "everlasting jigs" were danced by one couple at a time successively "to some Negro tune."

Several journalists recorded seeing these dances performed by blacks as well as whites in various colonies and most references associate the jigs with Virginia. Traveling in the middle colonies in 1759 and 1760, the Reverend Andrew Burnaby likened the dance to the *trescone* of the Tuscans in Italy. He was told that the dances he saw were borrowed "from the Negroes," and were "without any method or regularity." "A gentleman and lady stand up, and dance about the room, one of them retiring, the other pursuing . . . after some time another lady gets up, and then the first lady must sit down, she being, as they term it, cut out . . . The gentlemen perform in the same manner." Cresswell noted a difference between African-American and white dancing. Black dances were "most violent exercise . . . irregular and grotesque." He also saw an unusual instrument: "something in the imitation of a [English] guitar, with only four strings and played with the fingers in the same manner."

This instrument, called a banjer or banjar, was brought to the colonies by West African slaves as early as the seventeenth century. The modern banjo is a nineteenth-century commercial adaptation of this old instrument which the Reverend Jonathan Boucher described in 1775: "Its body was a large hollow gourd, with a long handle attached to it, strung with catgut."

MUSIC IN PUBLIC PLACES

Concerts

Selection of what music to play at concerts, both public and private, and what dances to dance depended entirely on the occasion and the participants. Outside, a military band might parade, playing spirited British marches and familiar song and dance tunes for all to hear. Indoor concerts, which were at first private and by invitation, featured concertos, songs from opera or oratorio, instrumental duets, and overtures. As populations grew and more citizens acquired appreciation of the cultivated arts, or wanted to give the impression that they had, concerts were organized as commercial ventures to which anyone might buy a ticket, a reflection of the rise of the middle class as a patron of music. Depending on the taste and level of sophistication of the expected audience, programs included fewer abstract pieces, more popular songs in English, and selections rather than whole works.

The earliest known public concert was held in Boston at Enstone's Dancing School Room on 18 February 1729. The following year, the Men's Musical Society of Boston sponsored a concert in honor of Saint Cecilia, the patron saint of music. As early as 1735, Charleston musicians gave public concerts in honor of Saint Cecilia. In 1762 the local gentry formed the Saint Cecilia Society in order to pool their resources for a series of concerts, but these were entirely private. Admission to the society was through a letter of application and a two-thirds vote of the members.

These musical clubs provided a means of entertainment for their members, who often formed the nucleus of the group of performers. They also fostered growth and cultivation of musicianship in their communities by attracting and supporting professional musicians.

Theater

Public musical events were sometimes held in conjunction with theatrical productions. These attractions were like variety shows: a serious play followed by a comedy, with overtures and entr'actes of unrelated instrumental and vocal music, dancing, and sometimes tumbling and acrobatics. Entrance to the theater was open to anyone who could afford a ticket; the price structure for the seats served to group the spectators by social class. Prices remained relatively stable throughout the 1700s. Eight, six, and four shillings were the usual fees for box, pit, and gallery respectively.

Music for these events might be chosen from English stage works like John Gay's popular *Beggar's Opera* (1728), Handel's operas and oratorios, and works of Henry Carey, Johann Friedrich

Lampe, and Charles Dibdin. Instrumental pieces were selected from the works of Johann Christian Bach, Johann Hasse, Arcangelo Corelli, John Reid, Johann Stamitz, and other British and European composers. Songs by such British composers as Richard Leveridge, James Oswald, William Boyce, George Alexander Stevens, and Thomas Arne were among the favorites just as they were in England at the time.

Some American compositions were performed occasionally as well, often by the composer himself. Giovanni Gualdo managed concerts in Philadelphia and included several of his own works on programs between 1769 and 1771.

In another way, most musicians were composers, arrangers, or orchestrators as well as performers of music. Indeed, sometimes the arranger received credit as composer on concert programs, later confusing scholars. Many pre-composed scores consisted of only a melody and a bass line; the music had to be transposed for the available instruments, harmonies realized, and inner parts developed before the music could be played. In a period when new compositions were routinely transmitted in manuscript or from memory, a definitive composer's score was a rarity.

Public Dances

To encourage theater attendance, promoters often permitted the audience to dance after performances in the theater or concert hall, taking advantage of the fact that the hall was open, lighted, and warm and the musicians were already hired. The broad stage or another large space within the building served as the ballroom. While technically anyone holding a ticket could join the dancing, the level of performance and the quality of clothing of the participants made it clear who was and who was not welcome.

Dances usually included minuets, country dances, perhaps a choreographed solo to a minuet, sarabande, or gavotte tune (usually referred to as French dances) by one of the stars of the preceding performance, and undoubtedly some informal reels. Minuet and saraband tunes were characteristically in two-measure phrases of triple time (three beats to a measure) while gavottes were in duple time usually with a half-measure anacrusis (upbeat). The details of tempo and dance technique was subject to local fashion

during the colonial period and changed often. Beginning in the 1770s, cotillions were also danced.

Military Music

The musicians who played in military bands were employed as independent contractors by the officers of regiments. They were expected to provide music for social events and for public ceremonies involving troops. A number of British bands served in America, and the officers of several American regiments maintained bands as well. The usual instrumentation comprised paired oboes, clarinets, French horns, and bassoons.

Music for the everyday management of the troops was played by enlisted soldiers. The fife, which had dropped out of military use in the seventeenth century, was reintroduced in the British army during the French and Indian War (1754–1763). By the Revolutionary War, two fifers and two drummers were usually required for each foot company and a bugler for mounted troops.

Most of the tunes played by military musicians were of British origin: signals, marches, airs, and dance tunes. One simple march melody became thoroughly associated with the American cause and was taken up by military and civilian musicians alike. Although its origins have yet to be determined, the tune of "Yankee Doodle" was played by British bands as they landed in Boston in 1768. The title the British gave it implied that they intended to insult the citizens by playing it. However, the melody was soon effectively used by the Americans as a counterirritant. Topical songs were written to it, and by 1775 it had become a signature tune for the patriots.

Taverns

Music was often heard in taverns as well as in concert halls and theaters. Some tavernkeepers employed musicians as regular staff, and many ran public balls at their establishments. Anthony Hay, manager of the Raleigh Tavern in Williamsburg, Virginia, ran a number of balls in 1763 in his Apollo Room, where Thomas Jefferson danced with Rebecca Burwell, his "fair Belinda."

More often, however, the patrons provided the music for themselves, particularly in times of political stress. In 1769 John Adams recorded that he and 350 other "sons of liberty" dined at a tavern in Dorchester, Massachusetts. After dinner someone sang John Dickinson's new "Liberty Song," and everyone joined in on the choruses. It was a call to unity: "Come join hand in hand, brave Americans all, and rouse your bold hearts at fair liberty's call . . . in freedom we're born, and in freedom we'll live." Set to a tune originally written by Englishman William Boyce, Dickinson's song was one the very few secular pieces to be published with its music in colonial America.

MUSIC IN PRIVATE SETTINGS

At Home

Philip Fithian, attending a large party at a Virginia plantation in 1774, watched an elegant company dance minuets, country dances, and reels to the music of a French horn and two violins in one room. In another, a noisy company of men sang liberty songs "in which six, eight, ten or more would put their heads near together and roar."

In smaller groups at home, wives and daughters were often asked to show off their polite skills by playing, singing, or dancing for guests. Sometimes more informal activities were preferred. Fithian reported with disgust that two of his students had slipped off several times to dance and play music with the black servants. Even among adults such activities continued. Thomas Jefferson's young brother "used to come out among the black people, play the fiddle and dance half the night," according to the "Memoirs of a Monticello Slave" cited by Helen Cripe.

Clubs

Mens' clubs and other exclusive organizations became popular in the early 1700s in England, where they provided business and social networks for their members. Similar clubs quickly sprang up in the colonies. Music and dance were often an important part of club activities, particularly in private gatherings.

The Tuesday Club of Annapolis met regularly between 1745 and 1756. Its motto was "Fiddlers, Fools, and Farces." In 1752 club members included five string players, two flutists, a keyboard performer, and possibly a bassoonist. Sev-

eral members composed songs and short oratorios for performance at their meetings, the earliest secular music known to be written in America. George Washington may have attended a concert with club members in March 1757, although he would not have participated in the music making. Washington enjoyed music enormously and danced well but did not play an instrument.

Washington also attended local lodge meetings of the Society of Freemasons throughout the colonies. The Masons supported music strongly and used it in their secret rituals as well as in public events. Several Americans wrote lyrics promoting masonic brotherhood and virtue and many lodges commissioned performances of existing pieces as well as compositions of new music.

Another type of club was the dancing assembly, which was composed of leading citizens who were invited to participate. Local assemblies sponsored series of dances, with admission controlled by the members, who also hired the musicians, arranged for the hall and other amenities, and selected a master of ceremonies or manager from among their number. Formed for their value as exclusive organizations through which members could express their power and wealth, these clubs existed at various times in most urban centers throughout the colonies, and in many small towns as well. One of the earliest clubs, and one that is still active, is the Philadelphia Assembly, founded in 1748.

MUSIC AND DANCE AS A BUSINESS

Although few entrepreneurs lived solely on the arts, music and dance provided significant business opportunities throughout the colonial period. Shops specializing in musical wares were located in larger towns, and teachers were in demand everywhere. Like the colonists, teachers came from Germany, France, and Italy, but most were British.

Music lessons were given in the home of the pupil or in schools where both private and group lessons could be held. Dancing schools met in any building where a large hall was available.

In rural areas and particularly the plantation areas of the South, enterprising teachers set up tours, moving from location to location to meet groups of youngsters for several days of instruction. In the North, such itinerants planned six- or eight-week sessions in successive towns, with classes meeting two or three times a week.

In addition to seeking lessons, early colonists wishing to study music used a popular English text: John Playford's *Introduction to the Skill of Musick*, first published in London in 1654 and reprinted for nearly a century. Later students used instructional works by Peter Prelleur and Francesco Geminiani.

Although tutors for all instruments were easily available in Boston, in 1769 book publisher John Boyles attempted to reap some of the profit by publishing *An Abstract of Geminiani's Art of Playing on the Violin, and of another book of instructions for playing in a true taste on the violin, German flute, violoncello, and the thorough bass on the harpsichord.* Perhaps seeing a similar market potential, the Philadelphia publishers David Hall and William Sellers published a tutor for the fife in 1776.

The English musician Edward Enstone supplemented his income with teaching and sales. He arrived in the colonies in 1715 from England and was hired as organist for King's Chapel in Boston. He soon opened a music school, presenting himself as "master of music and dancing," and sponsored public balls. Within two years, Enstone established a music store in which he sold musical wares including flageolets, flutes, oboes, bass viols, violins, bows, strings, reeds, instruction books, and books of ruled paper for composition or copying. He also repaired and tuned all instruments. He prospered in these enterprises for several years which indicates that there was a good local market for music, musical instruments, and other wares.

Music was a reasonably profitable business in large urban areas like Boston, Philadelphia, Charleston, and later in the colonial period, New York. Michael Hillegas managed a tavern and music store in Philadelphia in the 1750s and 1760s. In 1759 he advertised a harpsichord, a violoncello, English and Italian violins, German [transverse] flutes imported from Italy, and an enormous assortment of music. A few years later he published a list of more than fifty mostly contemporary composers whose music he carried, among them Domenico Alberti, Tommaso Albi-

noni, Boyce, Corelli, Handel, Johann Hasse, John Pepusch, Johann Quantz, Alessandro and Domenico Scarlatti, Stamitz, Giuseppe Tartini, and Antonio Vivaldi.

Advertisements in James Rivington's *New York Gazette* show that in the period of 1773–1783 the following instruments were available in New York: bagpipe, barrel organ, bassoon, bugle horn, clavichord clarinet, common flute, cornet, drum, tenor fiddle, French horn, German flute, guitar, harp, harpsichord, hautboy, hunting horn, organ, pastorale, forte piano, spinet, tabor and pipe, trumpet, viola, violin, violoncello, voice flute, and Welsh harp.

Imported forte pianos were sold in New York in the early 1770s, and John Behrent of Philadelphia advertised that he had built one in 1775. In 1773 a forte piano as well as a glass harmonica were in use at Robert Carter's Virginia plantation, Nomini Hall. The glass harmonica was probably the instrument developed by Benjamin Franklin in the early 1760s.

SUMMARY

The first colonists arrived from a world where the arts were divided. On one side were the cultivated arts of music and dance, enriched by centuries of patronage from the court, the nobility, and the church. Music and dance were consciously learned and practiced to occupy leisure time and to serve as tools for managing and enhancing social position.

On the other side was the music of the people. The laboring, farming, and servant classes had little access to cultivated music. They did not understand it, and they did not need it. Their long-lived ballads, airs, and dance tunes were seldom consciously learned but rather absorbed by frequent hearing and were an integral part of people's sense of community identification.

Class distinctions in the colonies, in contrast to the stratification of Great Britain, were blurred by new opportunities. Arriving in a place without established traditions, colonists set out to establish ways of life like those they had left behind. In America, landed gentry, wealthy merchants, and political leaders assumed the role of the Old World courts in setting fashion. They banded together to promote and enjoy abstract music and dance, trying to keep alive the distinctions in musical sophistication and social context of performance that excluded those with less privilege.

But a democratizing of the arts was occurring. This new openness depended on a critical mass of population with the means, the leisure, and the inclination to support such endeavors. As the middle classes rose in wealth and power, they demanded access to the cultivated arts as tokens of their new status. In turn, enterprising businessmen developed ways to make those arts available. The new system of dance writing and the publishing of instruction books in English gave the public access to dances formerly available only through private lessons. Publishers flooded the market with method books written for those who wished to learn to play instruments or to dance without incurring the expense of a master.

Changes in the repertory mirrored this effort to bring elite arts to a level understandable by the new consumers. In social dance, the minuet and the country dance enjoyed enormous popularity because they were flexible enough to be performed with either practiced or common skills. Dance on the theater stage abandoned abstract bourrées and gigues and became character dances. With story lines added, these were soon expanded into full pantomimes.

Music itself changed. Seventeenth-century musical compositions were linear; each voice was composed and each melodically important. Slowly the emphasis shifted to a melody-based music, for which a simple bass line provided the intended harmonic structure and certain conventions dictated the realization of the performance. This reduced the cost of printing scores, and early in the eighteenth century collections of songs, opera excerpts, and instrumental music became available in inexpensive editions and were exported to America.

Although the elite tried to retain a wall of privilege through adoption of ephemeral fad and fashion, the sheer size of the market serving the tastes of the emerging middle classes attracted many artists, musicians, publishers, and entrepreneurs. Performers and teachers organized public concerts, balls, and recitals at which their skills could be showcased, hoping that lucrative teaching sessions would follow. Tavernkeepers and dancing masters gave public parties at which their patrons and students could display their wealth and polite accomplishments.

Although these changes occurred throughout the Western world, they were magnified in the American colonies where power and control were less deeply entrenched in a ruling elite. A steady stream of emigrants from all corners of the Old World brought new kinds of music and dance traditions. Some of these were lost; some found fertile community support and flourished; and some, like African-American fiddling, grew into new arts and a new American music.

BIBLIOGRAPHY

Benson, Norman Arthur. "The Itinerant Dancing and Music Masters of Eighteenth Century America." Ph.D. diss., University of Minnesota, 1963.

Camus, Raoul F. *Military Music of the American Revolution.* Chapel Hill, N.C., 1976.

———. *National Tune Index: Early American Wind and Ceremonial Music, 1636–1836.* New York, 1989.

Farish, Hunter Dickinson, ed. *Journal and Letters of Philip Vickers Fithian, 1773–1774: A Plantation Tutor of the Old Dominion.* Williamsburg, Va., 1943.

Hamm, Charles. *Music in the New World.* New York, 1983.

Hitchcock, H. Wiley, and Stanley Sadie, eds. *The New Grove Dictionary of American Music.* London, 1986.

Keller, Kate Van Winkle. *"If the Company Can Do It!" Technique in Eighteenth-Century American Social Dance.* New York, 1990; 2nd ed. Sandy Hook, Conn., 1991.

———. *Popular Secular Music in America Through 1800: A Preliminary Checklist of Manuscripts in North American Collections.* Philadelphia, 1981.

Keller, Kate Van Winkle, and Carolyn Rabson. *National Tune Index: 18th-Century Secular Music.* New York, 1980.

Keller, Robert M. *Dance Figures Index: American Country Dances, 1730–1810.* Sandy Hook, Conn., 1989.

Lambert, Barbara, ed. *Music in Colonial Massachusetts, 1630–1820.* 2 vols. Boston, 1980, 1985.

Leppert, Richard D. *Music and Image: Domesticity, Ideology and Sociocultural Formation in Eighteenth-Century England.* Cambridge, England, 1988.

Lowens, Irving. *A Bibliography of Songsters Printed in America Before 1821.* Worcester, Mass., 1976.

Sonneck, Oscar G. *A Bibliography of Early Secular American Music (18th Century).* Revised and enlarged by William Treat Upton. New York, 1964.

———. *Early Concert-Life in America (1731–1800)*. 1907; repr. New York, 1978.

———. *Early Opera in America*. 1915; repr. New York, 1963.

Southern, Eileen. *The Music of Black Americans: A History*. New York, 1971; repr. 1983.

Talley, John Barry. *Secular Music in Colonial Annapolis: The Tuesday Club, 1745–1756*. Urbana, Ill., 1988.

Wells, Paul. "Fiddling: A Little-known Avenue of Black-White Musical Interchange." Paper presented at a conference of The Sonneck Society for American Music. Hampton, Va., April 1990.

Kate Van Winkle Keller

SEE ALSO **Drama; Festival Traditions; Native American Aesthetics; Recreations; Rural Life;** and **Urban Life.**

THE FRENCH COLONIES

THE HISTORY OF MUSIC and dance in New France, which follows that of the mother country, is based, depending on the period, on intermittent references to entertainments in the open air, at church, at the governor general's residence or in private homes, especially in Quebec and Montreal. Period sources for tracing this history are scarce; they include the *Histoire de la Nouvelle-France* (Paris, 1609) by Marc Lescarbot, the *Relations des jésuites* (1632–1673), *Le journal des jésuites* (1645–1668), contracts, travelers' accounts, and correspondence. Musical sources are even rarer. Apart from the manuscripts containing Indian-language adaptations of liturgical chants and sacred songs, including the well-known *Jesous Ahatonhia,* one should mention the prose sequence *Sacrae familiae,* attributed to Charles-Amador Martin, and roughly 120 motets. These motets are preserved in the Archives of the Monastery of the Augustinians of the Mercy of Jesus and the Monastery of the Ursulines, both in Quebec and founded in 1639.

THE BEGINNINGS

A summary of the principal facts in chronological order starts with the staging of Lescarbot's *Le Théâtre de Neptune en la Nouvelle-France* at Port Royal (later Annapolis Royal) sur l'Équille (Annapolis River) on 14 November 1606: trumpet calls, a short song, a chorus, and cannon fire make up the musical elements of the first dramatic work ever conceived and performed in French North America. Later, the development of seventeenth-century musical life was centered in Quebec. In November 1645 the small bell of the parish church was replaced by a larger one, and a wedding was celebrated to the sound of two violins. From then on, the occasional comment refers to song and instrumental music (on the violin, flute, or viol) during religious ceremonies. Five years after the arrival of François de Laval, the vicar apostolic and future bishop, the first Canadian-made bells swung in a Quebec belfry. It was apparently in the same year (1664) that an organ brought from Paris by Monseigneur de Laval was first used. This organ was later to be copied by a gifted cleric who made organs for several churches, solely in wood, which produced an agreeable sound.

Outside the church, the parishioners would sing and dance on special occasions. Witnesses report seeing dancing to the sound of a hurdy-gurdy in 1636 and the performance of "une espece de balet" (a sort of ballet), and that the governor general held the first ball in Canada in 1667. That this new entertainment was given a warm reception may be assumed from the order issued on 16 February 1691 by Jean-Baptiste de la Croix de Chevrières de Saint-Vallier, the second bishop of Quebec, in which the prelate denounced the holding of dance parties and other entertainments on feast days and Sundays, and even during divine service.

The fondness of the governors and intendants of New France for pleasures imitating those of the court of France explains the passion of the Canadian population for dances of which the minuet is the prototype. In the meantime, however, in Montreal, Louis-Armand de Lom d'Arce, baron of Lahontan, complained that it was always Lent there. The situation was to be changed radically by the growth of the city's population; the correspondence of Élisabeth Bégon (née Marie-Éliasbeth Rocbert de la Morandière) between 1748 and 1753 lists numerous balls and even specifies that everyone was learning to dance. The situation is confirmed by a certain J.-C. B., who wrote, in the account of his travels in Canada from 1751 to 1761, that his evenings were spent in the distraction of society balls.

LATER DEVELOPMENTS

The last years of the French regime contain few surprises. The intendant Jacques Raudot, in office 1705–1711, treated his guests to "un concert mêlé de voix et d'instruments, qui faisaient une charmante harmonie" (a concert of voices and instruments, which made a charming harmony). On several occasions he sent his musicians to sing in the Hôtel-Dieu's church. The same Raudot and Governor General Philippe de Rigaud de Vaudreuil entertained Major John Livingston most handsomely when he visited Quebec in 1710–1711. He noted that on 10 December, "I supped at ye Intendants, was very hansomly entertained, ye Governor, Gentlemen and Ladies of ye town were guests, and were diverted with musick and dancing," and, on 21 December, "Being their New Year's Day sup't this night at the Intendants, had a splendid entertainment with musick and dancing, and had ye drums and musick at my door." Livingston wrote that on 25 December, "The Govr. Genll. had a supper this night, where were at least 50 persons of distinction, and ye whole entertainment in great splendour," and on the following day, "The Governor Generall and myselfe were invited to sup at ye Intendant's, where was much company, great plenty, with dancing and musick to admiration."

Among other events we should mention the contract drawn up in 1721 between the Chapter of Quebec and Paul-Raymond Jourdain dit Labrosse, an organ builder in Montreal, for the construction of a seven-stop instrument. This was followed by the purchase in 1753 of a one-manual instrument with pedal pull-downs built by Robert Richard of Paris, rendered unusable by the bombardments of 1759.

The musical life of Quebec tended to become the norm in Montreal, particularly in the parish church. The first organ there was installed between 1698 and 1705; the church's most famous organist was doubtless Jean Girard, who, on coming to Canada in 1724, brought a large handwritten collection of anonymous pieces for the organ, which came to light in the early 1980s and has since become known as the *Livre d'orgue de Montréal*. In 1729 bells were installed in the church's new tower. Two years later, we learn about the state of teaching and practice of singing from the records of a jubilee that was held in the church: "Numerous Maidens of the City were taught Sacred Songs and Motets and sung them either at the Sermon or the Benediction."

The scarce, but reliable, sources allowing the musical life of New France to be partially reconstituted mention churches, the palace of the governor general or the intendant, and the open air as the sites of musical activities. Churches are associated with bells, organs, and, for a large part, singing. Dancing, ballet, and instrumental music were used for entertainment in certain private residences. Lastly, military music and music accompanying the theater were performed outdoors. As in France, the accomplishment of ritual and observance of protocol dictated for the most part the type of performance and the music to be played; the frequency of society entertainments may reveal a need to compensate for the severity of the existence of the young colony's inhabitants.

BIBLIOGRAPHY

Sources

B., J.-C. *Voyage au Canada dans le nord de l'Amérique septentrionale fait depuis l'an 1751 à 1761.* New ed. Paris, 1978.

Bégon, Élisabeth. *Lettres au cher fils: Correspondance d'Élisabeth Bégon avec son gendre (1748–1753).* Edited by Nicole Deschamps. Montreal, 1972.

Gallat-Morin, Élisabeth, and Antoine Bouchard, eds. *Témoins de la vie musicale en Nouvelle-France.* Quebec, 1981.

Headlam, Cecil, ed. *Calendar of State Papers, Colonial Series, America and West Indies, 1710–June 1711, Preserved in the Public Record Office.* London, 1924.

Laverdière, Charles Honoré, and Henri Raymond Casgrain, eds. *Le journal des jésuites.* Quebec, 1871; repr. Montreal, 1892, 1973.

Lescarbot, Marc. *Les muses de la Nouvelle France.* Paris, 1609.

Relations des jésuites. Paris, 1632–1673.

Translations

Lescarbot, Marc. *Neptune's Theatre: The First Existing Play Written and Produced in North America.* Translated by Edna B. Polman. New York, 1927.

————. *Nova Francia: Or the Description of That Part of New France, Which Is One Continent with Virginia.* London, 1609. New ed. *History of New France.* Edited and translated by W. L. Grant. 3 vols. Toronto, Ontario, 1907–1914; repr. New York, 1968.

Thwaites, Reuben Gold, ed. *The Jesuit Relations and Allied Documents: Travels and Exploration of the Jesuit Missionaries in New France, 1610–1791.* 73 vols. Cleveland, Ohio, 1896–1901; repr. in 36 vols. New York, 1959.

Music Anthologies

Livre d'orgue de Montréal. Edited by Élisabeth Gallat-Morin and Kenneth Gilbert. 3 vols. Saint-Hyacinthe, Quebec, 1985.

The Motet in New France. Transcribed and edited by Erich Schwandt. Victoria, British Columbia, 1981.

Sacred Choral Music I. Vol. 2, *The Canadian Musical Heritage.* Edited by Clifford Ford. Ottawa, 1984.

Studies

Amtmann, Willy. *Music in Canada, 1600–1800.* Montreal, 1975.

Desautels, Andrée. "Les trois âges de la musique au Canada." In *La Musique,* vol. 2, edited by Norbert Dufourcq. Paris, 1965.

Gallat-Morin, Élisabeth. *Le livre d'orgue de Montréal: Un Manuscrit de musique française classique: Étude critique et historique.* Paris and Montreal, 1988.

Kallmann, Helmut. *A History of Music in Canada, 1534–1914.* Toronto, 1960; rev. ed. 1987.

Kallmann, Helmut, Gilles Potvin, and Kenneth Winters, eds. *Encyclopedia of Music in Canada.* Toronto, Ontario, 1981.

Lemire, Maurice, ed. *Dictionnaire des oeuvres littéraires du Québec I.* Montreal, 1978.

McGee, Timothy J. *The Music of Canada.* New York, 1985.

Voyer, Simonne. *La danse traditionnelle dans l'est du Canada.* Quebec, 1986.

Lucien Poirier

SEE ALSO **Drama; Festival Traditions; Native American Aesthetics; Recreations; Rural Life;** and **Urban Life.**

THE SPANISH BORDERLANDS

FROM THE LATE SIXTEENTH century on, music and dance were an essential part of everyday life in the Spanish Borderlands. From the cradle to the grave, music leavens and sweetens both private and public rituals. When breath becomes song and inspiration finds words, people are transformed; the passions of the spirit are shared, and the passions of the flesh are extolled. Questions of destiny, history, love, death, and immortality become suddenly clear, and there is room for tears as well as laughter. Like life itself, music is both sacred and profane, always overflowing with vitality. The corporeal expression of the same exuberant energy is dance, which for centuries has been a major social and cultural activity of a far-flung frontier society. The allegorical line dances of the *matachines* re-enact the coming of Christianity to the Americas, the geometric symmetries of courtly dance styles form a visible metaphor of hierarchy and social order, and the popular gambols and reels of the region revel in a more earthly and anarchic joy of living.

The expressive culture the Spanish brought with them to the Americas served both as a solace in an unfamiliar environment and as a reminder and reaffirmation of who they were. The first music and dance forms that expressed their actual experience in New Spain and recorded the fateful encounter of cultures were ballads and allegorical dance drama. Spain enjoys a thousand-year-long ballad tradition rooted in the epic poetry of the eleventh century and the historic struggle between Christianity and Islam on the Iberian Peninsula. The invading conquistadores knew and sang these romance ballads as they undertook their own struggle, which they perceived as no less epic. As in medieval times, heroic ballads were written to commemorate victories and defeats.

In 1540 Francisco Vásquez de Coronado led an expedition to the Spanish Borderlands in a futile search for the fabulous Gran Quivira and its golden cities of Cíbola. His army wandered empty plains and valleys unopposed. Frustrated but undaunted, his pride was celebrated in the oral tradition through the centuries to come:

> Coronado se paseaba
> Por toda la tierra fuera
> Y no hubo quien le pisara
> El paso de su bandera.

(Coronado marched around / all the far-flung lands / and none dared step on / his flag as it passed.)

> Por aquí, por allí,
> Qué bueno va;
> Por aquí, por allí,
> Qué bueno va.

(Over here, over there, / how proudly it goes; / over here, over there, / how proudly it goes.)

This tantalizing fragment, transcribed in 1940, is all that has been recovered of a much longer ballad.

RELIGIOUS MUSIC AND DANCE

Dances of the *Matachines*

The spiritual conquest of Mexico is idealized and reenacted in dance dramas at Christmas, Holy Week, and the feasts of the Virgin of Guadalupe and other saints all across Mesoamerica. In the northlands these are known as *matachines,* a term of Arabic origin that refers to masked dancers. The dance is an allegory of the coming of Christianity, the legendary conversion of Moctezuma, the fight for the first converts, and the defeat of the forces of evil, bestiality, or animal worship as symbolized by the *toro* (bull), one of the masked characters. Although there is variation in form and meaning from community to community, the *matachines* have persisted from their origins in the 1520s to the present. Scholarly debates as to the origins of the *matachines* stress possible Moorish roots and strong Mexican-Indian influence.

Ten, twelve, or more dancers are clad from head to toe in colorful garb, including shawls and ribbons that hang from their fringed helmets, which looks like a bishop's miter but in design more closely resemble the *cupil* crown of the Aztec nobility. In one hand they carry a *guaje* (rattle), and in the other a brightly decorated trident called the *palma* and said to represent the Trinity.

The dance captain, known as *Monarca* (monarch) or Montezuma, is dressed similarly except for his crownlike *corona. La Malinche* (the same name as the interpreter and consort of Hernán Cortés) is represented by a young girl in a white First Communion dress. She interacts with *Monarca* and the *matachines* in a series of dances or acts (that can vary from town to town) with names like "la procesión" (the procession), "la Malinche," "el Monarca," "la corona" (the crown), "la brincada" (the jump), "la mudada" (the change), "el toro," "la cruz" (the cross), and "la despedida" (the farewell). Each movement has its own music, which in the northern Rio Grande valley is played on the guitar and violin. The unadorned melodies are chromatic and the style European, but the constant repetition recalls the chants of the Native American tradition. Farther down the river, the instruments are violin and drum, and in Chihuahua and Sonora only the drum is used. The dancers are arranged in a two-line formation reminiscent of certain Aztec dances. The dancers wave their *palmas* in graceful curves and shake their *guajes* in time to the music as they dance in place in a kind of *zapateado* (step dance) while executing turns, marching, kneeling, and being led back and forth by *la Malinche* and *Monarca.*

While the dancing proceeds, a burlesque pantomime unfolds involving several other characters, including *Toro,* a young boy dressed as a bull, and clownlike figures with beast masks and whips who are called *abuelos* (grandfathers). They stalk and charge each other, and at the end of the dance the *abuelos* kill and castrate *Toro.* The clowns appear to ridicule the religious nature of the dance, but they probably have their roots in the indigenous tradition of *koshares* (sacred clowns who incorporate blasphemy and irreverence into Native ceremonies).

The dance is performed in both Indian pueblos and Hispanic towns, and is both a synthesis and a rapprochement of the two traditions. Its cultural and religious meanings can be radically different for each community that stages it. For Hispanos the dance has a sacred character, and dancers often participate to fulfill personal promises to a saint. For Indians the dance can have both sacred and burlesque aspects. There is a legend from San Juan Pueblo in which Emperor Moctezuma travels to New Mexico before the arrival of the Spanish to teach the dance as a way of preparing the people to live with a new culture.

The Spanish and Mexican settlers of the Spanish Borderlands brought with them the sacred and secular music and formal and vernacular dance forms that were current in their day, from the sixteenth- and seventeenth-century colonization and recolonization of New Mexico to the eighteenth-century settlement of Arizona, California, and Texas. As each successive generation modified and added to the traditional repertory, distinct regional styles emerged. Surrounded by vigorous and sometimes threatening Indian cultures, the Hispanicity of the European and mestizo settlers of the borderlands was by nature militant, defying indigenous influences. Of the vernacular forms, only in the *matachines* dance drama and the *indita* dances and ballads of New Mexico can the inspiration of Native American music and sacred dance traditions be heard and seen.

Formal Music

Characteristically, the Spanish Borderland colonial culture, including music, has two aspects: the formal, which is part of the official program of church and government, and the informal, which includes the Native culture and the values of the people.

From the start of the Spanish conquest in 1521, music was officially recognized by the church as a key to the conversion and indoctrination of the Native Americans. Indians found musical activities to be highly attractive, and missionaries incorporated Native melodies into regional liturgies. Since musicians in pre-Hispanic Native cultures enjoyed great prestige, after the conquest many willing pupils presented themselves to the friars for instruction in European musical ways. Juan de Zumárraga, the first bishop of Mexico, encouraged his missionaries to use as much music as possible in their work. The first music school in the Americas was founded in 1523, immediately following the conquest of Mexico, by Pedro de Gante, a Franciscan who was a member of the private chapel of King Charles V. Indians were taught plainchant, musical notation, and the use and construction of European wind and string instruments, especially the Spanish bow and hand viols—*vihuela de arco* and *vihuela de mano*—predecessors of the

violin and the guitar. Within two decades of the conquest, Indians were composing in the European tradition, copying scores for the cathedral archives, and, with the exception of the organ, making the instruments they used.

The educational methodology that Gante developed was used extensively by his pupils, who included missionaries from his own order. The chronicles of the sixteenth and seventeenth centuries offer glowing commentaries on the musical talent and aptitude of the natives, from the Aztecs in the south to the Puebloan people of New Mexico in the north. There were so many enthusiastic Native American musicians that decrees were issued in the mid sixteenth century raising the qualifications of singers and musicians, lowering the numbers of members in choirs, and limiting the use of instruments in church.

During the sixteenth century, thirteen books of liturgical music and texts were published, beginning with the *Ordinarium* of 1556. They contain hymns, antiphons, psalms, and the music that accompanies the Ordinary and Proper of the Mass, as well as Passion music for Holy Week. Although the first sacred music to be played and sung in New Spain was in the style of the Gregorian chant, the polyphonic style of multiple-part harmony was employed very early on, first with psalms and motets, and later with settings of the Mass: the Magnificat, the Te Deum, and the Passion.

In an exchange involving the cathedral archives of Seville, Toledo, Mexico City, and Puebla, the latest compositions by the great Spanish composers Tomás Luis de Victoria, Cristóbal de Morales, and Francisco Guerrero were sent to New Spain and performed. Before long a considerable repertory of sacred music was written in New Spain by composers such as Hernando Franco and Juan de Lienas in the sixteenth century, and Juan Gutiérrez de Padilla and Francisco López Capillas in the seventeenth century. Their work is part of the polyphonic Spanish tradition and is virtually indistinguishable from contemporary sacred music from Spain. Colonists of the Spanish Borderlands most certainly heard this music in the churches of major cities as they made their way north. The farther they roamed from the great urban and cultural centers, the more they hastened a process that has been termed "folklorization." What they carried of their formal culture became less formal as it was incorporated into a regional folk tradition.

The Repertory of Folk Religious Music

Hispanic religious music in New Spain included an extensive informal repertory. Indian choirs all across the north and the south learned sacred music that was not part of the formal liturgy and which already was, or soon became, part of the folk tradition shared by the Indians' Spanish neighbors. These compositions include *villancicos* (Christmas carols) and *coplas* (couplets with a religious theme), as well as the music from the *pastorelas* (shepherds' plays about the Nativity) and from the *autos* (folk morality plays about the life and passion of Christ). Occasionally a composer would write formal settings for popular music, such as when Miguel Mateo Dallo y Lana arranged the *villancicos* that the famous poet Sor Juana Inés de la Cruz wrote in the Náhuatl language of the Aztecs in the 1670s and 1680s.

When Franciscan friars established their missions in New Mexico, California, and Texas, and the Jesuits theirs in Arizona, music was a central component in the project to Christianize the Native Americans. Their pedagogical use of music was encoded in the antiphonal call-and-response structure of the *alabado* ballad hymns still sung in northern New Mexico by the *penitente* brothers of the Hermandad Piadosa de Nuestro Padre Jesús Nazareno (Pious Brotherhood of Our Father Jesus the Nazarene). Historically many members of this brotherhood were *genízaros* (detribalized Indians) from tribes at war with the Spanish and Pueblo Indians. Membership in the brotherhood hastened the process of their Hispanicization. Although the friars introduced and composed many of these hymns, they quickly became part of the paraliturgies of the folk Catholicism of the borderlands. Many of the *alabados* were undoubtedly composed by the *penitente* brothers after the friars were long gone. In performance the *rezador* (prayer leader) sings successive stanzas of the hymn and the group responds to each with the principal stanza or chorus. As can be seen in the verses and chorus of "La Pasión" (the Passion), the *alabados* focus on themes of sacrifice and redemption as they narrate and contemplate the passion of Christ and the suffering of his mother. This anonymous piece, found in handwritten notebooks across New Mexico,

was one of the best known and most popular among the brothers.

> Mi Dios y mi Redentor,
> En quien espero y confío,
> Por tu pasión, Jesús mío,
> Abrázame en vuestro amor. Coro

(My God and my Redeemer / in whom I hope and trust / by thy passion, my Jesus / embrace me in thy love. Chorus)

> Escuchen con atención
> Lo que padeció Jesús:
> Desde el huerto hasta la cruz,
> En su sagrada pasión.

(Listen with attention / to what Jesus suffered / from the garden to the cross / in his sacred passion.)

Alabados are sung in unison and a cappella, with the occasional accompaniment of the *pito* (wooden flute). In its fipple structure and range, the *pito* resembles the soprano recorder. Its flourishes are said to represent the crying of the Virgin Mary and the souls in purgatory. Sung in a slow, mournful tempo, the melody lines are frequently modal in character, and the vocal style is melismatic (with stylized wavering around each note), reminiscent of Moorish and Sephardic singing.

According to specific textual references, *alabados* are sung during specific ritual activities, such as processions; the following example, "Con mansedumbre y ternura" (with mildness and tenderness), accompanies the sacrament of Communion or actual communal feasts. In the latter the brothers eat while the *rezador* sings each stanza, then pause and join in the singing of the chorus.

> Con mansedumbre y ternura
> En señas de un fino amor,
> Les previene a sus discípulos
> La última cena el Señor. Coro

(With mild tenderness / and signs of a love so fine, / he prepares for His disciples / the Lord's last supper. Chorus)

> Pues en este sacrificio
> Era sangre de animales,
> Y en el nuevo, el de Cristo,
> Por redimir los mortales.

(Well in this [prior] sacrifice / it was the blood of animals, / and in the new, that of Christ, / to redeem all mortals.)

Plays, Processions, and Paraliturgies

Already credited with the development of the Stations of the Cross service, the Franciscans were especially fond of using religious plays and processions that accompanied or built upon the seasonal feasts, dance dramas, and ceremonies of the Indians.

The lyrical folk music of the Christmas season is especially well known and loved. *Villancicos* in Spanish as well as in Native American languages were widely sung. One of the most popular of all tunes is "Vamos Todos a Belén" (Let us all go to Bethlehem.)

> Vamos todos a Belén
> Con amor y gozo,
> Adoremos al Señor,
> Nuestro Redentor.

(Let us all go to Bethlehem / with love and joy, / let us adore the Lord, / our Redeemer.)

> Derrama una estrella
> Divino dulzor,
> Hermosa doncella
> Nos da el Salvador.

(A star pours forth / divine sweetness, / a beautiful maiden / gives us the Savior.)

This *villancico* is sung for the Christmas processions called *las posadas* (the inns) as well as for the *pastorelas* (shepherds' plays).

Las posadas were originally performed on the nine nights prior to Christmas to enact the search of Joseph and Mary for a lodging place where Jesus can be born. After the procession stops at a designated house, the devil appears and prompts the owners not to let the Holy Family in. After knocking on the door, members of the procession sing:

> ¿Quién les da posada
> A estos peregrinos
> Que vienen cansados
> De andar los caminos?

(Who will give lodging / to these pilgrims / who are tired from / traveling the roads?)

After being turned away, as in the Scriptures, Joseph and Mary are finally invited into the inn with its stable and manger. The verse of invitation is:

> Entren, santos peregrinos,
> Reciban este rincón,
> No de esta pobre morada,
> Sino de mi corazón.

(Come in, holy pilgrims, / receive this corner, / not of this poor dwelling, / but rather of my heart.)

Los Pastores, the shepherds' Nativity play that takes place on or a few days before Christmas Eve, contains some of the most memorable melodies in the entire folk repertory. The plot is simple and the setting familiar to both settlers and Indians, many of whom were shepherds in their daily lives. Shepherds watching their flocks by night see the Christmas star and hear of the birth of Christ. Their journey to Bethlehem is interrupted by Lucifer, who is finally defeated in a duel by the Archangel Michael. Bartolo is a lazy shepherd whose antics delight the spectators and whose statements often provide a source of social humor. Different characters are known for their individual arias, including Lucifer's song, "Aprended, flores de mí" (Flowers, learn from me), whose lyrics are from poetry by Luis de Góngora, Spain's most famous baroque poet. Perhaps the most memorable aria is a lullaby for the infant Christ:

> Duérmete, niño lindo,
> En los brazos del amor,
> Mientras que duerme y descansa
> La pena de mi dolor.

(Sleep, beautiful child, / in the arms of love, / while the pain of my grief / sleeps and rests.)

> Chorus: A la ruu, a la mee,
> A la ruu, a la mee,
> A la ru, a la ru, a la me,
> A la ru, a la ru, a la me.

The cycle of miracle plays served their original purpose of teaching Christianity to the Indians, but the music of some is so appealing that the plays are still performed in the borderlands and throughout Mexico. With the secularization of the borderland missions and the disappearance of first the Jesuits and then the Franciscans, Hispanic religious music passed into the realm of the folk tradition.

SECULAR MUSIC AND DANCE

Rites of Passage

As a result of a perennial shortage of priests to minister to the remote inland provinces, a paraliturgy evolved through which the community was able to observe important rites of passage, such as marriage and death, in the lives of its members. Several of the *alabados* are moving funeral hymns called *despedimientos* (leave-takings), which use the first-person voice of the deceased to take leave of family and friends one by one, as in "Adiós acompañamiento" (Farewell, companionship):

> Adiós, mis amados hijos,
> Adiós, mi esposa querida,
> Adiós, mi acompañamiento,
> Que voy para la otra vida.

(Farewell, my beloved children, / farewell, my cherished wife, / farewell, my accompaniment, / I am going to the other life.)

> De la tierra fuí formado,
> La tierra me ha producido,
> La tierra me ha sustentado,
> A la tierra estoy rendido.

(From earth I was formed, / the earth has produced me, / the earth has sustained me, / to the earth I return.)

The voice of the person who has died narrates his own *velorio* (wake) and the departure for the cemetery, and at the side of the grave reminds us of our fate.

The most complex ceremonial music in the paraliturgical repertory is the *entriegas* (delivery songs), especially the *entriega de novios* (delivery of the newlyweds), in which the community unites to give its approval to a new couple. The song is performed at the wedding reception, which may precede the nuptial Mass by many months in the absence of a priest or follow the Mass if a priest is available. After invoking divine approval and that of the public in the first sung verses, several sections ensue. Since each performance is uniquely adapted to the particular couple, the order can vary:

Versos de la Santa Escritura (verses from the Holy Scriptures) give examples of the biblical models for marriages—the first couple, Adán y Eva (Adam and Eve), and the Sagrada Familia (Holy Family).

> Hizo Dios que Adán durmiera
> En un hermoso vergel,
> Dándole por compañera
> A una piadosa mujer.

(God made Adam sleep / in a beautiful garden, /giving him as companion / A compassionate woman.)

> Volvió Adán de su sueño
> Con una voz admirable,
> "Te recibo como esposa
> Por obedecer al Padre."

(Adam awoke from sleep / with an admirable voice, / "I receive you as my wife / to obey the Lord.")

Versos de la iglesia (verses from the church) describe the wedding, if it has already occurred, especially if it was held far from the village where the reception is being held. The guests who missed the ceremony can therefore receive a report of it.

> El padre les preguntó
> Si se quieren casar, di.
> Y la iglesia los oyó
> Que los dos dijeron "sí."

(The priest asked them / "Say if you want to marry," / and the church heard / that both said "yes.")

> Cuatro palomas volando,
> Salieron de la iglesia:
> El padrino y la madrina,
> El esposo y su princesa.

(Four doves in flight / came out of the church: / godfather and godmother, / husband and his princess.)

In *Consejos* (advice) verses the singer offers advice to the newlyweds and their families. The wedding changes all past relationships and is the beginning of new ones for everyone concerned. These verses are often humorous but always appropriate and full of traditional wisdom.

> El estado no es para un rato
> Ni para un día ni dos;
> Es por la eternidad
> Mientras vivan ambos dos.

(Marriage isn't for a moment / nor a day or two; / it is for eternity / as long as you both shall live.)

> Ahora me dirijo al novio
> Y también le haré saber,
> Ya no hay padre ni madre,
> Ahora lo que hay es mujer.

(Now I address the groom / and I'll let him know, / no more father and mother, / now what you have is a wife.)

Versos de la gente (verses for the people) are composed of anywhere from eighteen to twenty-six quatrains and take about half an hour to perform. The length of this last section depends on how many people are present at the reception and the size of the extended families in attendance. This segment takes as little as fifteen minutes and as long as an hour or more. Personal qualities are often mentioned; blessings are offered, and there is much humor in evidence. During this section people often pass by a rug in front of the singer where they leave their tips, known in Spanish as *la gala*.

> También a Facundo Martínez
> Un saludo y un cariñito,
> ¿Que viva su preciosa esposa
> Y toditos los de El Rito!

(Also to Facundo Martínez / greetings and a caress, / long live his lovely wife / and everyone from El Rito!)

> Los tíos de la novia,
> Tampoco los quiero olvidar.
> Son José y Aurora González.
> Dios se los ha de cuidar.

(The aunt and uncle of the bride, / I do not want to forget. / They're José and Aurora González. / God is sure to keep them!)

In this ceremonial song, a new set of social relationships is opened up: the bride and groom are "given" to each other, the parents are "given" a new son- or daughter-in-law as they relinquish a son or daughter, and two families are "given over" to each other as they enter into a new and promising relationship with many rewards and new resources for both. The agents for this exchange are the *padrinos* (sponsors or godparents), who are chosen especially for the wedding.

Community Dances

Weddings are also the occasion on which most of the traditional repertory of dances is performed. For centuries *bailes* (community dances) or *fandangos* (as they were known in California) were a lively focus of frontier life. The instrumental music of the *bailes* is a catalog of the popular dances and tunes accumulated over three centuries. The *marcha* (march) was a special wedding folk dance in which a line of men behind the groom and a line of women behind the bride promenaded in single file; they then joined as couples, circling and grouping until all had formed a single line. These actions represented the realignment of the social group to accommodate the new couple and join their families in a new relationship.

Courtly Dances and Their Diffusion

Political and ceremonial occasions of the viceregal court in Mexico City were celebrated with courtly dances such as the *pavana* and French gavotte, which were seldom performed outside larger cities. Their complex geometrical choreography was analogous to the order and hierarchy of royal society. In New Spain, as in Europe, some court dances made their way into other sectors of society and eventually into the far-flung villages of the frontier.

One popular example of this cultural diffusion is the *cuadrillas*, a set of dances descended from the French quadrilles (square dances). These include *cuadrillas*, in 2/4 time; *la mano derecha* (the right hand), in 6/8 time; and *cutilio* (cotillion), in 3/4 time. Movements were precise and symmetrical, and only those who knew the dance well participated in it; those who did not were spectators. This distinction, plus the social display of dress and position within the group, symbolized class and status within the society. One group dance with folk origins is the *cuna* (cradle), from New Mexico, in which groupings of two couples face each other, join hands, swing under the arms, and make a cradle out of four intertwined arms that rocks as the group dances and turns in place.

Dances for Two

Couples' dances represented an individualistic break with the more organized and patterned courtly dances. Descended from Austrian spring dances, the *valse* (waltz) had swept Europe by the late eighteenth century and was being enjoyed by nobles and commoners alike. More attuned to erotic expression than stateliness and form, the *valse* may well have reached the borderlands before the Spanish colonial period ended there. Other couples' dances with folk origins would be introduced to the court of Emperor Maximilian in the 1860s, making their way north and developing fascinating regional variations. Most of what is known as the "Spanish colonial" repertory of folk dances actually dates to this period, when the Spanish Borderlands had already been annexed to the United States.

Ballads

The secular repertory of music in the Spanish Borderlands includes the instrumental music of the allegorical, formal, and vernacular dances, as well as a unique constellation of ballads and songs. As the colonists first settled into the rhythms of their daily lives, the ancient *romances* they had sung in Mexico and Spain were still on their lips. Since the people were themselves making history, the epic romances of European wars were forgotten in favor of the novelesque themes of illicit loves and the burlesque ballads that have always entertained children. Popular in all of Spain and Latin America even today, "La Delgadina" (Slender lady) fascinated its listeners with a tale of incest and tragedy. In the ballad a rejected father imprisons his daughter, who dies of thirst and hunger.

> Cuando salieron de misa
> Su papá le platicaba,
> "Delgadina, hija mía,
> Te pretendo para dama."

(On returning from Mass / her father told her, / "Delgadina, my daughter, / I would have you as a woman.")

> "No permita Dios, Papá,
> Ni la Reina Soberana,
> Es ofensa para Dios
> Y traición para mi mama.

("God does not permit it, Father, / nor the Sovereign Queen, / it is an offense to God / and a betrayal of my mother.")

The ballad reinforced the settlers' belief that devotion to family was corruptible, and only devotion to divine law could preserve the human endeavor.

In the rigorous life of the frontier, humor had an important place. Children's ballads and games were often of great antiquity. In kitchens and bedrooms, parents sang traditional old ballads like "Don Gato" (Sir cat), whose animal characters poked fun at the conventions of courtly and bureaucratic life:

> Estaba el Señor Don Gato
> Sentado en su silla de oro
> Gastando medias de seda
> Y zapatos colorados.

(Sir Cat was sitting / on his golden chair / wearing out silk socks / and scarlet shoes.)

The pretentious Don Gato falls in love, pursues his Moorish lady across the rooftops, falls off, and dies a lover's death. The jubilant mice dress in red and celebrate:

> Los ratones de alegría
> Se visten de colorado
> Y los gatitos chiquitos
> Se quedan desconsolados.
> Miau, miau, miau. . . .

(The mice to show their joy / dressed all in scarlet / but the kittens / were inconsolable. / meow, meow, meow. . . .)

The Spanish Borderlands were traumatized over centuries of Indian warfare. The colonists customarily celebrated victories with the ancient military play *Moros y cristianos* (Moors and Christians). By the eighteenth century, this type of folk drama had become localized, as evidenced in the play *Los Comanches*, which celebrates the final defeat of these formidable foes. In this period can be found the origins of the *indita* (little Indian) ballads, so named by the people because the majority of the ballads are about relations between settlers and Indians in matters as diverse as warfare and love.

Some of the earliest and latest *inditas* are called *cautivas* (captives) because they sing of the travails of captivity faced by women on the frontier. Because of continual depredations throughout the eighteenth century, captives were often taken and slavery was widespread. In 1777 the town of Tomé, south of Albuquerque, suffered a particularly merciless attack in which every man, woman, and child was killed. Since men were usually killed in battle, captives were usually women and children. Their sad lament could be heard in ballads and songs such as "La cautiva Marcelina," about the pathetic woman whose fate it was to witness the murder of her family and wander the plains with her captors, having nothing to eat but mare's meat.

> La cautiva Marcelina
> Cuando llegó a los cerritos,
> Cuando llegó a los cerritos
> Volteó la cara llorando,
> "Mataron a mis hijitos,
> Mataron a mis hijitos."

(Marcelina the captive, / when she reached the hills, / when she reached the hills, / looked back, crying, / "They killed my children, / they killed my children.")

"Por eso ya no quiero
En el mundo más amar;
De mi querida patria
Me van a retirar." Coro

("That's why I no longer / want to love in this world, / from my beloved homeland / they are taking me away." Chorus)

Known all over New Mexico, this ballad was collected as far south as Mexico City as late as 1914, in a version called "La Infanta Margarita" (The princess Margarita), whose refrain includes the mention of mare's meat. In some areas it is sung with tragic overtones, while in others it has the same sarcastic or playful tone as a nursery rhyme; many versions are fragments of earlier ballads.

The "Indita de Cochití" is representative of a kind of raucous love song that is quite distinct from the *indita* ballads, which speak of tragedies or the experiences of captives. The common point is that both types of *inditas* relate interactions between Hispanics and Indians, although here the aggressive role is reversed:

Indita, indita, indita,
Indita de Cochití,
No le hace que seiga indita
Si al cabo no soy pa' ti.

(Little Indian, little Indian, / little Indian girl of Cochití, / it doesn't matter that you're Indian / if in the end I'm not for you.)

Indita, indita, indita,
Indita del otro día,
¿En dónde andabas anoche
Que traigas barriga fría?

(Little Indian, little Indian, / little Indian girl from the other day, / where were you last night, / that your belly is so cold?)

Here there is implied abuse of Native American women, with overtones of sarcasm rather than of tragedy. In most of its many versions, the Indian girl is pregnant and is abandoned not because she is Indian but because the singer "just isn't for her."

There are many popular verses that satirize Comanches in this vein. The following *verso* is sometimes used as a lullaby or to entertain children. The thought of the Comanche couple selling their children to satisfy their sweet tooth is both horrifying and humorous:

El Cumanchi y la Cumancha
Se fueron pa' Santa Fe,
Se fueron pa' Santa Fe,
A vender a sus hijitos,
A vender a sus hijitos,
Por azúcar y café,
Por azúcar y café.

(The Comanche and his woman / went to Santa Fe, / went to Santa Fe, / to sell their little children, / to sell their little children, / for sugar and coffee, / for sugar and coffee.)

Musically, *inditas* are interesting because the melodies often alternate with choruses that emulate the syllable singing and pentatonic scales of traditional Indian music. Ballads have gone through a continual evolution from the sixteen-syllable verse *romances* to the octosyllabic verse *inditas* of the region to the *décimas* (a ten-verse stanza form), and, in the late nineteenth and twentieth centuries, to the *romance corrido*. Despite these formal differences, ballads have shared a common theme in their fascination with the violent and inspiring events that shape people's lives and destinies.

The *Trovo*

One secular form that enjoyed great popularity during colonial times was the *trovo*, a dueling song in which poets matched wits, trying to outdo each other in improvising verses on love, philosophy, and theology. The names of famous *trovadores* (troubadours) of the past, such as El Viejo Vilmas, Gracia, and Chicoria, and their encounters with each other were memorialized in the *trovo*. This type of music was popular on the great yearly *conductas* (caravans) that took the trade goods produced in the north to market in Chihuahua and beyond. On the trail each night, the *trovadores* would provide entertainment and challenge the local poets of any towns the *conducta* passed through. The *trovo* below uses the fictional characters "Mr. Coffee" and "Ms. Corn Gruel" to argue the virtues of Native culture and products compared with what is imported from the south:

Café:
Yo soy el Café
Y de todos conocido,
En la América del Norte
De todos soy preferido.
En el mundo soy distinguido

Con satisfacción completa.
En tacitas todos me usan,
Bebiendo mi aguita prieta.

(Mr. Coffee: / I am Coffee / known to all, / in North America / everyone prefers me. / In the world I'm distinguished / by complete satisfaction / people use me in little cups, / drinking my dark water.)

Atole:
Yo también soy el Atole
Y aquí te hago la guerra.
¿Qué bien mantengo a mi gente
Con sólo labrar la tierra.
Y tú, Café orgulloso,
Que sepa el mundo entero,
Sacrificas a mi gente
De comprarte con dinero.

(Ms. Corn Gruel: / I am also Corn Gruel, / and here I give you battle. / How well I nourish my people / Just for their working the land. / And you, proud Coffee, / may the whole world know, / you sacrifice my people, / who buy you with money.)

In this contest Ms. Corn Gruel wins, since she nourishes her people rather than impoverishing them, as the exotic Mr. Coffee does.

The *Canción*

The last and in many ways the most popular and prevalent of the musical genres of the Spanish Borderlands was, and still is, the *canción* (song), the ubiquitous popular lyric whose multifaceted themes of love and its consequences pervade the imagination of the folk. The following *canción* is a *jota,* a typical folk rhythm and dance of northern Spain whose subject matter is definitely of the American hemisphere. In New Spain, as elsewhere in the Spanish Empire, a mestizo fusion of peoples and cultures emerged, known collectively as *la raza* (the people), celebrated here in the *jota serrana* (mountain jig).

Con una jota serrana
Venimos a saludar
Estas lindas mexicanas
De bello y dulce mirar.

(With a mountain jig / we come to salute / these Mexican beauties, / so comely and sweet.)

Que vivan las niñas
De tu bello suelo.
¿Qué tienen tus ojos,
Qué tienen tus ojos
Del color del cielo?

(Long live the maids / of your beautiful land. / What do your eyes have, / what do your eyes have / of the sky's blue?)

Con alegres españoleñas
Venimos a saludar
A estas hermosas trigueñas,
Bellas hijas de Anáhuac.

(With happy Spanish maids / we come to salute / these lovely dark ones, / pretty daughters of Anáhuac.)

The singer expresses his obsession with the dark-eyed women of New Spain (Anáhuac), whose eyes have very little to do with the color of the sky.

The *canción* is such a popular genre, expressing so many different thematic concerns, that it is in seemingly endless supply. Even so, an important source of *canciónes* that made their way north consisted of the popular songs of the theater in the cities of the south. Many plays had musical intermissions as sets were changed, and some *zarzuelas* (Spanish operettas) made their way to Mexico, to the delight of audiences, who gradually spread the most popular arias to the provinces. The origins of the famous *canción* "Don Simón de mi vida" (Don Simón of my life), may lie in the theaters of Mexico City, but Don Simón is well known in the Spanish Borderlands. His name is practically synonymous with the complaints of the older generation, permanently scandalized by the changing styles and progressively outrageous behavior of the young:

Don Simón, Don Simón de mi vida,
En los años que me dió el Señor,
Nunca he visto lo que ahora he mirado.
¿Ay, qué tiempos, Señor Don Simón!

(Don Simón, Don Simón, of my life, / in the years that the Lord gave me, / never have I seen what I am seeing now. / Oh, what times, Señor Don Simón!)

En mis tiempos las niñas usaban
Sus rosarios en la procesión,
Y sus ojos mostraban humildes.
¿Ay, qué tiempos, Señor Don Simón!

(In my day the young women used / their rosaries in the procession, / and they showed humility in their eyes. / Oh, what times, Señor Don Simón!)

Ahora, casí les salen los dientes
Cuando escriben cartitas de amor,

Y cuando sus padres les hablan, se ríen.
¿Ay, qué tiempos, Señor Don Simón!

(Now, they almost bare their teeth / when they write their little love letters, / and when parents talk to them, they laugh. / Oh, what times, Señor Don Simón!)

Judging from the archaic styles of clothing described in older versions of *Don Simón de mi vida*, the song has been popular since the early nineteenth century. With each generation new verses are added that register new complaints. Sequels about "Doña Chepita," Don Simón's wife, have also appeared over the years.

CONCLUSION

The rough-cut, unpolished, and elemental qualities of sacred and secular music and dance in the Spanish Borderlands were first commented on by nineteenth-century English and American observers and collectors like Charles F. Lummis, who traveled across the southwestern United States by foot in 1884. In the introduction to his songbook, he wrote: "In arid, lonely, gaunt New Mexico . . . music has taken the imprint of its surroundings." He wondered why the flawless singing styles and prodigious musicianship so easily found in Mexico and the south seemed to be absent in the north. Then, as today, the music of the region speaks not of embellished refinement but, rather, of a stark sense of necessity.

BIBLIOGRAPHY

Campa, Arthur L. *Spanish Folk Poetry in New Mexico.* Albuquerque, N. Mex., 1946.
———. *The Spanish Folksong in the Southwest.* University of New Mexico Bulletin, Modern Language Series 4, no. 1. Albuquerque, N. Mex., 1933.
———. *Spanish Religious Folktheatre in the Southwest, Second Cycle.* University of New Mexico Bulletin, Modern Language Series 5, no. 2. Albuquerque, N. Mex., 1934.

Champe, Flavia Waters. *The Matachines Dance of the Upper Rio Grande: History, Music, and Choreography.* Lincoln, Neb., 1983.
Espinosa, Aurelio M. "Romancero Nuevomejicano." *Revue Hispanique* 33 (1915):446–560.
Gonzales, Dolores, ed. *Canciones y juegos de Nuevo Mexico/Songs and Games of New Mexico.* New York, 1974.
Lamadrid, Enrique R. "*Las entriegas:* Ceremonial Music and Cultural Resistance on the Upper Rio Grande: Research Notes and Catalog of the Cipriano Vigil Collection 1985–87." *New Mexico Historical Review* 65, 1 (January 1990):1–19.
Lamadrid, Enrique R., and Jack Loeffler, recordist. "Tesoros del Espiritu/Treasures of the Spirit: A Portrait in Sound of Hispanic New Mexico." Audio exhibit and compact disc set produced by Museum of International Folk Art, Santa Fe, N. Mex., Hispanic Heritage Wing, 1989. Transcript publication forthcoming. Transcript includes all verse texts quoted in the present article except for those of *Las entriegas* (see entry above).
Lummis, Charles F. *The Land of Poco Tiempo.* New York, 1893; repr. Albuquerque, N. Mex., 1966.
Mendoza, Vicente T., and Virginia R. R. de Mendoza. *Estudio y clasificación de la música tradicional hispánica de Nuevo México.* Mexico City, 1986.
Paredes, Américo. *A Texas-Mexican Cancionero: Folksongs of the Lower Border.* Urbana, Ill., 1975.
Rael, Juan B. *The New Mexican Alabado.* Stanford, Calif., 1951; repr. New York, 1967.
Robb, John Donald. *Hispanic Folk Music of New Mexico and the Southwest: A Self-Portrait of a People.* Norman, Okla., 1980.
Sedillo, Mela. *Mexican and New Mexican Folkdances.* Albuquerque, N. Mex., 1937.
Stark, Richard B. *Juegos infantiles cantados en Nuevo México.* Santa Fe, N. Mex., 1973.
———. *Music of the "Bailes" in New Mexico.* Santa Fe, N. Mex., 1978.
———. *Music of the Spanish Folk Plays in New Mexico.* Santa Fe, N. Mex., 1969.

Enrique R. Lamadrid

SEE ALSO **Drama; Festival Traditions; Native American Aesthetics; Native American Religions; Recreations; Rural Life;** and **Urban Life.**

DRAMA

THE BRITISH AND DUTCH COLONIES

THE THEATER OF the British North American colonies was the theater of Great Britain, transplanted virtually intact on new soil. Architecturally and artistically, its structure and content were the same. The old and new popular plays from the London stage were performed in front of scenery that usually had been painted in London, by actors and actresses from London, Dublin, and Edinburgh, wearing the latest London fashions, before an audience of British colonists.

Occasionally colonists participated in professional theater as performers, playwrights, or scene painters, but they never dominated their own theaters, nor did they think of their theater as separate or different from that of England. Even in 1768, a Philadelphia critic seeing Lewis Hallam, Jr., as the slave Mungo in Isaac Bickerstaff's *The Padlock* described him, significantly, as the best Mungo on the *British* stage. Hallam had been in the colonies for more than fifteen years at the time.

The real differences between the British colonial theater world and its progenitor were more in the framework of social and geographical situations surrounding performances than in events inside the theaters themselves.

AMATEUR THEATER IN THE EARLY COLONIES

Professional actors did not begin immigrating to the colonies until the mid eighteenth century, but the first generations of British colonists, like Britons elsewhere, were enthusiastic amateurs. Military officers and their families, and other gentlemen and ladies of high rank, performed drama for the public; college students especially, in the colonies as in Great Britain, were active in the amateur theater that emerged by the end of the seventeenth century.

As early as 1690 Harvard students put on a play, *Gustavus Vasa*—of which local authorities disapproved. Boston, New York, Philadelphia, Providence, and other northern cities were home to a number of dissenting Protestant groups—Methodists, Quakers, Presbyterians, and Puritans—that objected to theater, and the activities of amateurs in Boston ultimately led to the passage of a law banning theater in 1750. (So strong was that city's opposition to plays that the only professional production ever presented in colonial Boston was not a play at all, but a popular stand-up comedy routine called *The Lecture on Heads*.) The Dutch colonists may have had some amateur activity prior to New Amsterdam's capture by the English in 1664, but there are no records of early productions in New York.

The same oppositional religious groups existed in England, but by the beginning of the eighteenth century they were not as geographically concentrated or as politically powerful as they were in the northern British colonies. The Puritans had outlawed the theater during their time in power in England, but dramatic performances regained legal sanction—and took on a new form—with the restoration of the monarchy in 1660.

THE FIRST COLONIAL THEATER BUILDING

In the one hundred years between Shakespeare's death and the building of the first theater in the British North American colonies in 1717, British theater greatly changed. Drama came to be performed almost exclusively indoors, with movable scenery, and with women onstage—all influences from Charles II's French exile. In the colonies, Anthony Aston, a semiprofessional actor from England, had briefly organized productions in a few cities in 1704, but he left no architectural legacy. Amateur players acted in colleges, taverns, and private homes until William Levingston, a Scottish merchant without any prior theatrical experience, built his theater in Williamsburg, Virginia, in 1717.

Levingston's performers were indentured to him before he left Great Britain; they were probably unemployed actors and dancers whom he indentured for the purposes of his theater and dancing school. The first recorded performance at Levingston's theater was in 1718. But Williamsburg was a new, small city unable to support a permanent theater, and by 1723 Levingston was out of business.

New owners continued to use Levingston's property as a theater. Lively, well-attended amateur performances by William and Mary students and even by such local personages as Governor William Gooch's son and sister continued into the 1730s. Other genteel amateur groups opened their own theater buildings—in 1733 in New York and in 1735 in Charleston. These well-organized groups performed a small repertory of a few favorite plays. By mid century, colonial capitals were more populous, prosperous, and playgoing than ever, yet without professional players. It is not surprising that someone in Great Britain should have noticed the possibilities.

FROM GREAT BRITAIN TO THE COLONIES

The Theatres Royal

In Great Britain, the theatrical world centered around the Theatres Royal, the licensed theaters that had a legal monopoly. In London, these were Drury Lane and Covent Garden; in Dublin, Smock Alley under joint management with Aungier Street equaled just one theater; and by mid century Edinburgh also had a Theatre Royal.

Great Britain's Licensing Act of 1737 had fixed strict controls on theater, chiefly to restrict political commentary and direct, personal satire. The result might be compared to closing down off-Broadway and off-off-Broadway playhouses and leaving only the biggest, most conservative mainstream theaters operating legally. This monopoly gave managers of the Theatres Royal considerable power and leverage. Audiences had few theaters among which to choose, and actors had little choice about where to work.

Unlicensed Theater

Inevitably, unlicensed theaters carried on. Popular among these was the London theater operated by William Hallam, the son of a substantial Covent Garden actress. Probably to avoid controversial new plays, and perhaps also out of personal taste, Hallam produced Shakespeare's plays as 25 percent of his repertory. Hallam also employed one of the best scene painters, John de Voto, and was noted for discovering and training new talents.

The regular audience at Hallam's theater at Goodman's Fields included many ships' captains, and when the management of Drury Lane had the law enforced against this successful competitor to the theater monopoly, his patrons may have encouraged him to export his trade. The Hallam family was talented and connected enough to form a company to take abroad: William's brother, Lewis Hallam, and Lewis's wife had been playing in the provincial circuits in Bath and Kent. They had begun their careers with minor roles at Covent Garden and played at least one season at Samuel Foote's unlicensed and often outrageous Haymarket Theatre. Performers from Lewis Hallam's recent Bath company and William Hallam's Goodman's Fields

Company, along with de Voto's excellent scenery, thus set sail for Virginia as the London Company of Comedians. The arrival of this group, neither big stars nor poor strollers, made the British North American colonies into the newest, best, and biggest provincial theater circuit.

Provincial Theater

London or Dublin actors went, respectively, to Bath or Cork to act in the summers; unsuccessful players in the capitals sought further training and polishing in the provinces before returning to try again. Joining this flow of personnel, the colonial theaters eventually had a circulation of performers to and from England, Ireland, and Scotland. Some used the colonies as a springboard for better British careers; others used their British experience and training to become stars in the colonies.

As early as 1745, a young Irish actor named John Moody had started a professional company in the British colony of Jamaica, with the financial backing of local patrons and performers recruited from Great Britain. Moody was often absent from his company, performing in British theaters (he eventually settled at London's Drury Lane), and in those theaters, consequently, word of Moody's colonial venture spread.

Moody's precedent may explain why Thomas Keane, an aged actor whose London career was long over, went to the colonies and then was joined in 1749 in Philadelphia by Walter Murray and a group of other relatively unknown actors. Although Murray was apparently a capable, experienced actor, the company's overall quality was uneven and its corporate survival was brief. Among other things, the somewhat wild young men tended to prolong bloody battle scenes in plays; the company managers neglected to prune the plays to suit the morality of audiences in Philadelphia and New York, and its unfavorable reception spurred the company to move on to Virginia in 1751.

A Williamsburg tavern-keeper, Alexander Finnie, built a new theater for Murray and Keane's anticipated arrival. Since Virginia and Maryland never had any antitheatrical laws, actors could count on a good reception there. Yet even their season in Williamsburg proved unprofitable for Murray and Keane's company (although Williamsburg supported a new professional group very well the next year, for a full eleven months). Murray and Keane's company then embarked on touring small towns in Virginia and Maryland that hosted annual horse races with potentially lucrative crowds, but still the company dissolved.

All in all, the company's history suggests that they simply were not very good. Their legacy, however, was in having bridged the gap between amateur and professional theater in the colonies. In New York, Robert Upton left Murray and Keane's company in an unsuccessful attempt to establish yet another semiprofessional theater group. Upton had ostensibly come to the colonies as the advance agent for the Hallams' theatrical company, which successfully followed Murray and Keane in Williamsburg. They tested the responses of various cities to the advent of professional theater, and, unfortunately, they lived in a manner that left a reputation which future, more circumspect, performers arriving from Great Britain would need to overcome.

Actors and Audiences

The constant influx of new people must have kept the colonial theater current in new trends. Criticism of the worst habits of faulty actors can paint a picture of eighteenth-century theater as stylized and exaggerated, but descriptions of the better actors and contemporary treatises on the actor's craft reveal an emphasis on feeling the character's feelings, understanding the character's motives, and using the tones and gestures of real life. (Eighteenth-century Britons in real life were self-conscious of deportment and grace; therefore so was the drama.) Thomas Sheridan, an actor and manager at Dublin's Smock Alley, claimed he totally became the character, forgetting himself and the audience; at least six, and perhaps more, of the actors and actresses who worked professionally in the colonies had spent time in Dublin under Sheridan's management. Others who came to the colonies had worked with the naturalistic actor Charles Macklin in London and in the provinces, or with Macklin's former student Samuel Foote.

Acting was a highly skilled trade, often handed down in families. It involved long working hours, with rehearsals at ten o'clock in the morning and performances at six o'clock at night, with a constantly rotating repertory of fifty to sixty different plays. Each of the three to five nights a week that a theater was open, a different play was presented—a five-act main piece and a short afterpiece. Acting was anything but a life of leisure, which perhaps explains why none of the colonial amateur groups turned professional.

In general, however, the professional performers who came to the colonies improved their incomes and their careers. Actors earned their livings solely from ticket sales—except for occasional summer tours of lectures and concerts, or giving music and dance instruction—and colonial ticket prices were fairly high, so the income could be quite lucrative; some colonial performers made one hundred to three hundred pounds in a year. But the life of a performer also involved expense and inconvenience. Scenery was a major investment, as were the high-fashion clothes worn for most of the plays. And since even in the largest colonial capitals, the audience for drama was a market that would be used up in a year, the acting trade required relocating often; actors always lived in rented lodgings.

Since amateurs in the colonies already had careers as doctors or military officers, or were college boys, or ladies of good family, they could act for pleasure and rehearse at leisure. To turn professional was to go into a trade, a step down that only a very few colonists took—perhaps another reason that professional theater was essentially imported to the colonies. Acting was not universally regarded as disreputable, but neither was it much regarded as an elevated calling. It was a business, a trade. Its most skilled and successful practitioners in both Great Britain and the colonies were respected and admired; they mingled socially with the upper classes, but did not share their social rank. Theater people had all the accomplishments of gentlemen and ladies, and the social standing of a tradesman or tavernkeeper.

The Audience
The typical colonial theatergoer was Anglican, city-dwelling, and had close ties with London or Edinburgh, either by travel or correspondence for business, fashion, education, or family. Professional theater came to such an audience not from afar, but from "home." Although an average colonist might be a small farmer, an average colonial theater patron was more likely to be a prosperous tailor, a few years from London himself, a purveyor of London fashions and a self-styled critic.

The theater was not frequented exclusively by the well-to-do, however. Everyone, from slaves to gentry, apprentices to college students, male and female, and occasionally children could and did attend, and all could be critics. There was no professional, written criticism of colonial theater beyond newspaper letters and editorials. The influential critics were the audiences, who were sometimes severe, but usually just.

In all British theater, opening-night audiences judged new plays. Sometimes their criticism had personal, factional motivation, but normally it was based on taste and judgment. Audiences had not yet taken to hissing at villains and cheering for heroes, nor had the curtain call (a novelty even in the early nineteenth century) been instituted. Actors and playwrights received both good reviews and bad reviews aloud and instantaneously during a performance. Speeches and moments deserving applause received it immediately; material that was poorly written, poorly acted, or otherwise offensive could be hissed and booed, or the actors even bombarded with orange peels and cries of "Off! Off!"

Audiences were usually attentive. They came, after all, for the play. Nonetheless, a certain noise level was typical: quiet conversation, eating, drinking, changing seats to visit friends, and tea and cards in the expensive boxes. It was unwise for actors, so dependent for their income on pleasing everyone and offending no one, to chastise unruly patrons. But if a party grew too loud, the rest of the audience might hiss the offenders into silence.

THEATER COMPANIES IN THE COLONIES

The London Company
With the arrival of the London Company, British colonists began to enjoy a real share of the British theatrical world. Williamsburg was wisely chosen for Lewis Hallam and the London Company's debut in 1752; despite the defection of their advance man, Robert Upton, to Murray and Keane a year earlier, the Hallams managed to

acquire Finnie's theater, improve it, and with the support of the populace convince a cautious Governor Robert Dinwiddie to grant permission for them to play. Williamsburg was fashionable and fun-loving. Virginians habitually traveled many miles for pleasure and society. Wealthy planters and their families, and people from other small settlements, came to this small capital for social life, business, shopping, government, and, now, theater. After a successful season in Williamsburg, the London Company toured New York, Philadelphia, Charleston, and Kingston, Jamaica, from 1753 to 1758.

The American Company

After Lewis Hallam died in Kingston in 1758, his company underwent a metamorphosis. Hallam's widow married David Douglass, the manager of John Moody's Jamaican theater, and they formed a reorganized theater group that was eventually called the American Company. Under Douglass, the American Company toured all the colonies that tolerated theater and persistently tested those that would not. Although Douglass succeeded in persuading, politicking, and advertising his way around the inevitable objections in New York and Philadelphia, he was eventually driven out of Rhode Island by antitheater legislation.

Theatrical seasons in the north in any case tended to be very short, even as brief as two months. New York theaters were small and impermanent. It was not until 1767 that northern opposition to theater faded sufficiently for the American Company to build larger, permanent theaters and play full, regular seasons repeatedly. Meanwhile, a fall-winter-spring season was standard in London, the Caribbean islands, and Williamsburg. In southern capitals with permanent theaters, such as those in Williamsburg or Charleston, a typical theater had three different seating areas for the audience—cheaper galleries, the middle-priced pit, and the exclusive boxes. These theaters also had backstage dressing rooms, a greenroom (where players could relax offstage), and storage areas. Onstage were fixtures for the support and movement of the wings and backdrops and for candles as lighting overhead and as footlights.

Not only the capitals in the south, but even some of the smaller towns that held weeks of horse races in the summer welcomed and proved profitable for actors. When the races or other opportunities called, a warehouse in Upper Marlboro or a tavern in Alexandria could suffice for several weeks as a theater. The American Company occasionally visited small towns, but Douglass had established a company of a size and ability, in its ever-changing membership, to produce masterfully any play the London stage could produce. Along with the old standards that comprised much of the repertory in all British theater, the American Company offered the best new London plays, which often opened at one of the permanent theaters in a colonial capital later that same year. In 1768, for instance, Hugh Kelly's *False Delicacy*—known as a comedy of wit, satire, sentiment, and morality—became a great success in London and then in the colonies, where Douglass opened this play in the north.

The Virginia Company

That same year, some of Douglass's new recruits left him to form another company in the south. At the helm of this new group was William Verling, who had married a Norfolk, Virginia, woman and chose Williamsburg for the first season of his Virginia Company of Comedians. He had in his favor the dancing talent of his cousin, James Verling Godwin, the versatile talents of beautiful Henrietta Osbourne, and a large repertory. He also had some considerably less talented minor players, a large investment in scenery, and bad weather in the spring. After a season in Annapolis, the Virginia company fell apart. Some of its members returned to the American Company, others retired from the stage, and some faced financial trouble and legal problems.

EMPLOYMENT IN THE THEATER

As professional theater became an established enterprise in the North American colonies, the extent of colonial participation in the theater increased. Most colonial residents who took part in the theater were behind the scenes: printers printing playbills and tickets, tavern-keepers selling tickets. Important behind-the-scenes personnel like the prompter—a job similar to a stage manager, who also prompted—were British, but it is probable that scene shifters, box keepers, and various house servants were hired locally as needed. Successful performers had personal servants, slave or free, and it is likely that these were in many cases native-born colonists. A woman slave from the King's Arms Tavern in Williamsburg apparently ran off with Verling's (renamed) New American Company, but as there were no roles for black women in the repertory—and those few for black men were played by whites in makeup—it can only be guessed that she may have served as a seamstress or a personal servant.

Although scenery was frequently imported from London, Jacob Snyder of Rhode Island temporarily was scene painter to the American Company in the mid 1760s. In 1759, two colonists with the improbably paired names of William Williams and Alexander Alexander worked for Douglass in Philadelphia. Williams built and painted scenery; Alexander constructed a new theater.

Local musicians, both amateur and professional, contributed to music in the theater. A few amateur actors, especially during Verling's Annapolis season, paid the manager for the privilege of playing a leading role onstage with the professional company for a night. This could attract the wealthy amateur's important friends, so managers endured the practice.

One colonist contributed a comedy that was almost produced, but Colonel Thomas Forrest's *The Discovery* contained such obvious characterizations of his acquaintances that it was withdrawn. Like many popular comedies, it was ribald and earthy and poked fun at society—in this case, the story involved Blackbeard's treasure.

Another colonist wrote a tragedy that actually was produced. Mercifully, Thomas Godfrey of Philadelphia was already dead when the American Company performed his overwrought verse tragedy, *The Prince of Parthia*. Unlike *The Discovery*, it had no local or American themes, but simply imitated, quite poorly, popular exotic, heroic tragedies like Aaron Hill's *Zara* (taken from Voltaire's *Zaïre*). *The Prince of Parthia* must have been hissed into oblivion. It was published, but never performed again.

Only five colonial residents are known to have become professional actors, although there may have been more; the origins of some actors yet are unknown. The first colonist to become a performer had been Nancy George, who disappointed her wealthy Philadelphia family by joining Murray and Keane. She, like most of that company, ended in theatrical obscurity. Another colonist who undertook professional theater was Thomas Charlton, a native of London who had joined his older brothers in Williamsburg but declined to take up their respective trades of tavern-keeping and wig-making. Charlton was one of the unfortunate minor actors of William Verling's Virginia Company. Wig-maker Edward Charlton was at the time a co-owner of the Williamsburg theater building; perhaps Verling was indebted to him for hairdressing and rent, and agreed to take a stagestruck younger brother off his hands. Charlton amounted to little as an actor, and his brothers had to go to court to take care of his debts.

More successful were Mary Richardson, Samuel Greville, and Richard Goodman. Like Nancy George—and unlike Thomas Charlton, who came from the ranks of skilled tradesmen—these three were from genteel families and after some amateur experience had turned professional. Richardson and Greville were reliable secondary players for a number of years. Goodman was a gifted comic who also had a knack for playing aged roles well even when he was still very young.

"BRITISH" THEATER THROUGH THE REVOLUTION

Colonial audiences never demanded an "American" theater. The works of Shakespeare, then as now, were sure to draw audiences. The passionate tragedies of British playwrights Thomas Otway and Nicholas Rowe, and Edward Moore's modern tragedy about the gambling craze, *The Gamester*, reliably drew tears and sold tickets. Frequently performed were the late-seventeenth- and early-eighteenth-century comedies of George Farquhar, John Vanbrugh, and Colley Cibber, where wit and rakishness held the stage for four acts and a convenient moral tied up the fifth. Equally popular were the new sentimental comedies such as those by Hugh Kelly and Richard Cumberland and farces such as those by David Garrick and Samuel Foote.

These were the plays that George Washington and Thomas Jefferson saw—and saw often. Following Verling's two years in Virginia and Maryland, Douglass brought his company south for the next three years. From 1768 through 1772, these two southern colonies had constant professional entertainment. Whether the actors were in Annapolis, Williamsburg, Petersburg, or Alexandria, George Washington was often in the audience. During an October court in Williamsburg, for example, he attended plays two or three nights a week for several weeks in a row, seeing two different plays each night.

On the eve of the revolution, the American Company was finally achieving real acceptance in the north. The quality of the actors, costumes, and scenes was continually improving; the colonial theater was able to attract new performers from the Theatre Royal in Edinburgh and London. The famed Thomas Wignell, of Garrick's Drury Lane, sailed for New York in 1774 to join David Douglass. The day after his arrival he received the news that the Continental Congress had banned theater as a frivolity that diverted money and effort from the war.

Amateurs carried on, and at Washington's request, Joseph Addison's 1713 tragedy, *Cato*—about liberty versus tyranny in ancient Rome—was performed by amateurs at Valley Forge. "It is not now a time to talk of aught but chains or conquest, liberty or death," says Cato, exhorting the African prince Juba to put off thoughts of love and marriage in the face of a war for freedom.

With a few exceptions, however (John Paul Jones was once an actor in Jamaica), professional actors and managers avoided the issue of the war with great energy and occasional obsequiousness. Controversy was fatal to their livelihoods. Social connections with an unpopular British government had proved disastrous for Dublin's Thomas Sheridan; in the American Company there were Irish veterans who could remember the resulting theater riots. Since no one knew who would win in North America, loyal colonies like Jamaica and Barbados, as well as the home theaters of Great Britain, were viewed as more secure places to sustain careers. Some actors permanently relocated.

John Henry was able to play Othello in London, yet came back to the new United States after the war. His wife, Maria, one of Dublin's four "child star" Storer sisters who came to the colonies as teenagers, resumed playing leading roles in North America as well. Mrs. Douglass, the original Mrs. Lewis Hallam of the 1752 London Company, died in Philadelphia in 1774. David Douglass remained in Jamaica.

Lewis Hallam, Jr., then joined with William Dunlap, a New Yorker and the first American and nonperformer to manage a theater company. The first plays by American playwrights, such as Royall Tyler's *The Contrast* and Dunlap's *Major Andre,* had largely British casts. These two plays, a comedy and a tragedy, concern events and consequences of the American Revolution, but most of the repertory still consisted of the new London plays such as Richard Brinsley Sheridan's work. The transition to a truly American theater had barely begun. The drama that played in the United States in the 1780s was under new management, but it was still the best and biggest British provincial circuit.

BIBLIOGRAPHY

Charke, Charlotte. *A Narrative of the Life of Mrs. Charlotte Charke (Youngest Daughter of Colley Cibbler [sic], Esq.).* Reprint. Gainesville, Fla., 1969. Autobiography of an English actress whose daughter, Catherine Harman, acted in the colonies, with some details of her daughter's life.

Daly, Charles P. *First Theater in America: When Was the Drama First Introduced in America? An Inquiry. Including a Consideration of the Objections That Have Been Made to the Stage.* Reprint. Port Washington, N.Y., 1968. Lacks information on Virginia and Maryland; good source on early amateur productions, especially in New York.

Fennell, James. *An Apology for the Life of James Fennell.* Reprint. New York, 1969. Autobiography of an actor of the eighteenth and early nineteenth centuries who worked in England, Scotland, and America.

MacMillan, Douglas, ed. *Plays of the Restoration and the Eighteenth Century: As They Were Acted at the Theatres-Royal by Their Majesties' Servants.* New York, 1931. Good collection of some of the favorites.

Rankin, Hugh F. *The Colonial Theatre: Its History and Operations.* Williamsburg, Va., 1955. Contains a thorough chronology of events in colonial theater, but is not entirely accurate on acting technique nor informed on actors' British background.

Rosenfeld, Sybil. *Strolling Players and Drama in the Provinces, 1660–1765.* Cambridge, England, 1960. Early careers of many colonial players.

———. *The Theatre of the London Fairs in the Eighteenth Century.* Cambridge, England, 1960. More on early careers of colonial players.

Seilhamer, George O. *History of the American Theatre, Before the Revolution.* Vol. 1. Reprint. New York, 1968. Excellent source for complete lists of roles played by each actor, plays performed in various cities, and citations of advertisements, criticism, and laws. Occasional inaccuracies in other areas.

Sheldon, Esther K. *Thomas Sheridan of Smock-Alley: Recording His Life As an Actor and Theater Manager Both in Dublin and London, and Including a Smock-Alley Calendar for the Years of His Management.* Princeton, N.J., 1967. A number of actors and actresses in the colonies came from Smock Alley Theatre, with Sheridan's style of acting and management. Important background for their lives; good list of performances from their Dublin careers.

Trebman, Simon. *Samuel Foote: Comedian, 1720–1777.* New York, 1971. Biography of one of the Hallams' early influences; good details on the world of unlicensed London theaters.

Patricia Kearney

See also **Architecture; Literature; Music and Dance; Painting and Sculpture;** and **Recreations.**

THE FRENCH COLONIES

NEW FRANCE IN THE SEVENTEENTH CENTURY

THEATER, IN ITS VARIOUS FORMS, was an important ingredient in the culture transplanted from France to North America in the first decade of the seventeenth century. It was more central to the intellectual elite, as represented by the classically educated Marc Lescarbot, author of the first dramatic text composed and performed in New France. It was a popular entertainment as well, familiar to the common folk who, in this as in every other colonial venture, soon represented the bulk of the population of New France.

Thus popular elements are visible in Lescarbot's good-humored *Le Théâtre de Neptune en la Nouvelle-France* (performed at Port Royal [later Annapolis Royal] on 14 November 1606). The text, however, like most dramatic texts published in Europe at the time, is predominantly elitist, replete with neoclassical references and other learned allusions typical of the late Renaissance in France. It clearly belongs also to the dramatic subgenre known as a *réception,* a semiritualized series of addresses, long popular in the Jesuits' colleges in France, such as the one Lescarbot had attended. This combination of familiar and exotic, of imported and indigenous elements, is one of the principal characteristics of the theater composed as well as performed in Canada for the rest of the colonial period. There is no reference to dramatic activity in Louisiana before the 1760s, and after Lescarbot's play there was no French drama in Acadia before the 1860s.

What is more surprising, given the sparse population of New France throughout its history, is the frequency of theatrical activity for most of the seventeenth century. From the early 1640s performances occurred quite regularly in Quebec, most of the plays being imported, with marked preference for the recent classical dramas of Pierre Corneille. But there are references also to dramatic texts composed in the colony, as Lescarbot's had been, to mark special occasions such as the arrival of a new governor or the visit of a church or lay dignitary. An intriguing example dates from 1640: local amateurs who had been preparing a tragicomedy for public performance were directed by the governor to include in their program elements of a *mystère* (medieval mystery or miracle play) for the edification of Amerindian spectators. As described by the author of the Jesuit *Relation* for that year, in the *mystère* the soul of an unbeliever was pursued by two demons speaking in Algonquian and was then cast, before the spectators' eyes, into a flaming hell. The natives in attendance, according to the Jesuit reporter, were duly impressed by these stage effects, visual and aural.

One of these "local" texts survives, and is an excellent example of the symbiosis between European inspiration and North American reality. Composed by teachers and performed by students at the Jesuits' school in Quebec in the summer of 1658, it is clearly another *réception.*

Here however, unlike Lescarbot's play, the references are all topical, couched in four Amerindian tongues with consecutive translation into French. The intention is blatantly political: the Jesuits who composed the text sought to persuade newly arrived Governor General Pierre de Voyer d'Argenson to launch an immediate military strike against the perceived common enemy, the Iroquois confederacy. It proved unfortunate for future development of the colony that d'Argenson heeded their advice on this occasion.

By mid century theater had become almost a routine aspect of life in Quebec, with performances of recent plays such as Corneille's *Héraclius* (1651) and *Le Cid* (1652) attracting only passing mention by Jesuit chroniclers. Drama had also become a tradition in the schools, both the boys' school established by the Jesuits in 1635 and the girls' school founded by the Ursuline nuns four years later. Most of the plays performed were of the type called *actions*, edifying tragicomedies often based upon the lives of saints or Christian heroes, composed by European members of the Jesuit order for performance in their standardized schools. But it is clear also that some texts continued to be composed locally, especially for the Ursulines' pupils, well into the eighteenth century.

The normal evolution of theater in New France was curtailed as a result of a memorable confrontation between religious and civil authority in 1693–1694. Governor General Louis de Buade de Frontenac had aroused the wrath of Bishop Jean-Baptiste de la Croix de Chevrières de Saint-Vallier with his announced intention of staging Molière's controversial *Tartuffe*, after successful performances of plays by Jean Racine and Corneille that same winter. It is worth noting that a very similar conflict was taking place in France at the same time, between proponents of the public stage and some members of the church hierarchy under the moral leadership of the great bishop Jacques-Bénigne Bossuet.

In the mother country, however, the multiplicity of dioceses and the divergence of episcopal views allowed for great diversity in local attitudes toward the stage. In New France, with its single diocese, no such nuances were possible. The bishop's immediate solution to the quarrel was to offer Frontenac a handsome bribe not to stage *Tartuffe*. But in typical fashion, Saint-Vallier used the incident as a pretext to prohibit all types of public theatrical activity in the colony. A few years later, in 1699, when a dispute arose between the bishop and the Jesuit order in Canada, he expressly forbade even the modest performances in the Jesuits' schools.

NEW FRANCE IN THE EIGHTEENTH CENTURY

References thereafter to public drama in New France virtually disappear: there are only four for the period 1699–1763, when the Treaty of Paris sealed the colony's fate. A musical comedy of some sort was staged at the intendant Jacques Raudot's residence in 1706. Play and intendant were swiftly condemned by the church hierarchy. Next came an anomalous performance of a self-serving *réception* composed at Saint-Vallier's request and performed for him and other dignitaries in 1727 by young female students from a charitable institution founded by the bishop himself. The text of this playlet has survived, the last of its kind from the French regime in Canada. Then there is an intriguing first reference to theater in Montreal, in a letter written by a local resident, Élisabeth Bégon, in 1749, alluding to a play apparently staged in conjunction with the *carnaval*, and at a safe distance from the bishop's palace in Quebec. The diary of the Marquis Louis-Joseph de Montcalm for 1759 mentions a play composed and staged by the troops stationed at Fort Niagara in that year, again safely removed geographically from possible clerical intervention. Scholars also know that an amateur production of a French comedy was staged in the early 1760s at the New Orleans home of Jean-Jacques Blaise d'Abbadie.

It is reasonable to speculate that there was in fact a good deal more theatrical activity than we shall ever be aware of during this period, since after Saint-Vallier's proclamation any such activity had, by definition, to escape official notice. But the bishop's interdiction would continue to have a negative effect on the development of public drama in French Canada for most of the next two centuries. There is evidence that the educational institutions, particularly the Séminaire de Québec (founded in 1663) and the Ursulines' convent, soon quietly revived the drama programs that were so central to their pedagogic traditions. But they did so with a great deal more circumspection than before, and their students' performances remained essentially private.

The church adapted its tactics to suit conditions. When denunciation from the pulpit of plans for a theatrical season in Montreal in 1789–1790 attracted far too much public attention, Bishop Jean-François Hubert instructed the pastor in question, François-Xavier Latour-Déséri, to continue his campaign against public theatricals, but exclusively through the confessional. This tactic appears to have been followed, with varying degrees of severity, by his successors until the very end of the nineteenth century.

Largely because of Saint-Vallier's intervention, the evolution of dramatic arts in all of the French colonies in North America would be delayed until well after the British conquest.

BIBLIOGRAPHY

Doucette, Leonard E. *Theatre in French Canada: Laying the Foundations, 1606–1867.* Toronto, Ontario, 1984.

Waldo, Lewis P. *The French Drama in America in the Eighteenth Century and Its Influence on the American Drama of That Period, 1701–1800.* Baltimore, Md., 1942.

Leonard E. Doucette

SEE ALSO **Recreations; Rural Life;** and **Urban Life.**

THE SPANISH BORDERLANDS

WHILE THE FOLK THEATER tradition was established throughout the Southwest, it was strongest initially in New Mexico and later developed in Texas and California. There is no strong evidence for the existence of a theater tradition in Florida; however, documents are constantly surfacing, and we may find the pattern described here applicable to the Spanish Southeast as well.

ON THE BANKS OF THE RIO GRANDE

The poet-soldier Captain Gaspar Pérez de Villagrá left in his *La historia de la Nueva México,* an epic poem first published in 1610, the oldest historical record of a theatrical presentation in what is today the American Southwest. Villagrá describes the performance of a play after the Spanish conquerors arrive at the banks of the Rio Grande:

> And then after the chores were done
> A grand comedy was performed,
> Composed by the noble Captain Farfán,
> And whose main plot was to demonstrate
> The great reception given to the Church. (*La historia.* Vol. 2, p. 76)

Captain Farfán was a member of the colonizing expedition undertaken by Captain Juan de Oñate, the acknowledged founder of New Mexico. The dramatic representation penned by Farfán was performed on 30 April 1598 in honor of the Lord's Ascension and to celebrate taking official possession of the recently discovered lands of New Mexico in the name of Spain's reigning monarch, Philip II. The impetus for colonization and exploration of the Americas, which had begun in 1492, continued unabated, spurred by hopes of finding and founding new empires such as those of Mexico and Peru. Tales of the Seven Cities of Cibola and of the treasures of the Great Quivira brought back by Francisco Vásquez de Coronado, Estebanico the Moor, and Fray Marcos de Niza, intrepid explorers of the Southwest during the first half of the sixteenth century, served to whet the appetites for gold and other precious metals of the ambitious and restless conquistadores.

Colonization was also motivated by the challenge posed by England to the newly discovered but yet uncolonized Spanish territories. Of particular importance was the incursion that the English pirate, Sir Francis Drake, made in the San Francisco Bay area. Spain was determined to retain its American lands, and so Philip II granted exploration rights in order to foment colonization in the outermost northern territories of New Spain. A royal decree of 19 April 1583, signed by the king and sent to the viceroy of Mexico City, granted the right to colonize the territories in the New Mexico area.

The successful colonization of New Mexico was undertaken by Don Juan de Oñate, a wealthy miner from Zacatecas. On 26 January 1598 his expedition began its journey toward the territory to be known as New Mexico. The route required crossing deserts, mountains, and other inhospitable terrain. The convoy experienced extreme weather conditions, and many times the settlers suffered severe thirst for several days. When they eventually reached the banks of the Rio Grande in April, the men and women comprising the expedition were exhausted but at the same time grateful they had survived the ordeal. Captain Oñate consequently ordered a period of rest and religious activities. The religious observances were designed to convey the settlers' gratitude to the Almighty, while the period of rest was to provide respite from the arduous journey. This was the context in which various festivities, including the theatrical representation cited by Villagrá, transpired.

According to Villagrá, the main plot of the Farfán play involved a great multitude of Indians from New Mexico who were receiving the holy teachings of the church and who humbly "requested on their knees their sins be washed with the baptismal waters." The drama resembled the *auto sacramentales* (liturgical dramas) that had been popular during the medieval period and Spain's "Siglo de Oro" or Golden Age (1492–1650) and appealed to the religious spirit of the colonizers.

Another reference by Villagrá in *La historia* to festivities and dramatic enactments describes the presentation of a *Los Moros y Cristianos* (The Moors and the Christians) play. The play was part of the festivities connected to the opening ceremonies of the first church built in San Juan de los Caballeros, New Mexico, and marked the founding of the town as well. The construction of the church was completed on 8 September 1598 with the help of hundreds of Indian laborers. That afternoon the men and women celebrated the event with secular plays, one being the battle between Moors and Christians. The play featured the Moors on horseback with lances and daggers and the Spaniards on foot with harquebuses. The clamourous noise made by the weapons and the boisterous, warlike behavior of the performers frightened the amazed audience, which was composed mainly of Native Americans from the surrounding areas.

Villagrá reports that there were also tilting matches, a bullfight, and, as part of the closing festivities, a *comedia,* or play, "cheerful and well-written—perhaps from the muse of Farfán the Sevillian." The above comments are the first historical references we have regarding the origins of European theater in the Spanish colonial period of today's American Southwest.

HISTORICAL PLAYS

Los Moros y Cristianos

The *Los Moros y Cristianos* play dates back to the twelfth century in Aragon, Spain. George M. Foster posits that it probably spread throughout Spain during the Muslim occupation, which lasted over seven hundred years (711–1492). By the fourteenth and fifteenth centuries, Foster asserts, the play was regularly enacted during the feast of Corpus Christi. The play is impregnated with ideological overtones designed to raise the superior moral forces of Christendom over the "heathen" religious beliefs of the Muslims. Two versions evolved in Spain during the Reconquest era: one was elaborate, stylized, and sophisticated, while the other has been described as involving "huge structures which served as castles to be assaulted and burned, and ships which were burned and sunk, sometimes in artificial lakes during simulated naval combats." Such spectacles were important symbolic representations of the power and might extant in the newly consolidated Spanish Empire. The drama signified the victory of Good (Spain) over Evil (the Moors); it conveyed the triumph of order over chaos.

Encoded within the drama's plot was the message of unity and might that the newly united monarchs of the Spanish Peninsula, Ferdinand and Isabella, wanted to spread. The repeated performances of the drama served to drive the message home and inculcate a fear and respect for the power of the state and church. Since the Reconquest of Spain was completed in 1492 and the colonizing enterprise in the New World began in precisely that year, the play was an important element in the continuation of the culture of conquest in the newly discovered lands. The aggressive, warring Spanish impetus that had triumphed over the Moorish element was displaced to the Americas, and the dark-skinned Native Americans replaced the Moors as the object of conquest, colonization, and evangelization.

The *Moros y Cristianos* plot is simple and straightforward. The Moorish leader, Sultán, a Turk, plans to steal the holy cross from the Christians with the help of his underlings and then demand a handsome ransom for its return. Moma, one of Sultán's soldiers, is charged with the task, and he plans to inebriate the Christian guard, Eduardo, and then steal the cross. The strategy works, and after obtaining the holy cross, Sultán demands a ransom; but Don Alfonso, the Christian leader, refuses and a battle ensues. The Christians are victorious and the Sultán, upon witnessing such power and valor, professes his conversion to Christianity.

Although John E. Englekirk, an expert in folk theater, avers that the folk plays found in the New Mexico area probably date back no further than the nineteenth century, circumstantial evidence suggests otherwise, especially for the *Los Moros y Cristianos* plays. These plays were widely diffused throughout the Iberian Peninsula, Mexico, and the American Southwest during the colonial period. In fact Fray Francisco Atanasio Domínguez mentions the play's being performed in one of the missions of New Mexico in the late eighteenth century. Fray Francisco, in his description of the rise of the cult of Our Lady of the Rosary, details how in each year beginning in 1771, a celebration was held in the Virgin's honor. He details the festivities for 1776, noting that "there are three days of festivity, with performances of Moors and Christians, tilts, a comedy, and bullfights." Other scholars, such as Arthur L. Campa, assert that there was an unbroken continuity of folk theater performances up to the present in New Mexico.

Los Comanches

Historical Background. The second major historical drama believed by many scholars to date to the colonial period is *Los Comanches*. The play is based on two major battles between the Spanish colonists and the Comanche in the years from 1774 to 1779.

When the Spaniards trekked the thousands of miles from the Mexican plateau to the northern frontier, they did not find an empty land devoid of population. In fact the area comprising Colorado, New Mexico, Texas, Oklahoma, Kansas, and the southern part of the Great Plains was inhabited by a fierce group of peoples known to the Indian Ute as the Komanchi. The Comanche, as they were later called by the Spaniards, referred to themselves as the Nermernuh, or the People, and were the southern branch of the great Shoshone family that eventually came to inhabit a large area of land from the Canadian border to the Sonoran desert in the American Southwest.

Most of the settlements instituted by Juan de Oñate when he colonized New Mexico were raided and harassed by the Apache in the seventeenth century. It was not until the beginning of the eighteenth century that the Comanche defeated the Apache and began to make incursions into New Mexican settlements. Continuous attacks and raids on New Mexican settlements took place between 1716 and 1760, and the Spaniards responded in kind. In 1771 Governor Fermín de Mendinueta, hoping to stop the violence against the Spanish colonists, signed a treaty with the Comanche. The raids, however, did not stop. A devastating massacre in Tomé in 1777, which left no one alive, instigated an expedition under the command of Don Carlos Fernández to track down the Comanche.

Hostilities nevertheless continued, and in a 1779 battle, Don Juan Bautista de Anza defeated the Comanche chief Cuerno Verde. The Spaniards attacked in the early morning and the battle, which reportedly took place near the source of the Colorado River, lasted all day. The Comanche suffered terrible casualties, and many were taken prisoner. According to historical records, the Comanche did not attack New Mexican settlements after De Anza's victory. This is the battle that was immortalized by an anonymous author in the lyrics of the historical play, *Los Comanches*.

The Play. There are two extant plays by the name *Los Comanches*: one a religious play and the other a historical play. The historical play, the much better known of the two, is considered here.

Both Aurelio Espinosa and Arthur L. Campa believe the play was written by a participant in the battle between the Comanche and the Spaniards. Campa comments that "*Los Comanches* was written by someone well informed on the history of Spanish military activities in the Southwest; someone who knew the Indian tribes and the men who commanded the garrison in Santa Fe. In addition, the author had an excellent command of heroic-sounding Spanish." The hand-copied manuscript of *Los Comanches* was passed down from generation to generation. Campa reports that by 1929 there were only three manuscripts left.

The play is a short one, consisting of only 515 lines in octosyllabic verse. Campa writes that the play was "staged in the open spaces, where a battle on horseback could be enacted, and the plains of Galisteo and the high mesas around Taos were favorite sites where both audiences and participants could enjoy the drama." Campa adds that "real Indians often took the parts of the Comanche braves, and as the battle that is the climax of the play opened, both sides became caught up in the action."

The plot is a simple one: the action begins as Cuerno Verde and other Comanche warriors challenge the Spaniards. The Spaniards respond in kind, and this preliminary verbal duel sets the stage for the battle. After the verbal dueling ceases, the physical battle commences. The drama closes with the routing of the Comanche. There are a total of twelve characters: six Comanche (Cuerno Verde, Oso Pardo, Cabeza Negra, Lobo Blanco, Zapato Cuenta, and Tabaco) and six Spaniards (Don Carlos, Don José de la Peña, El Teniente, Don Salvador Rivera, Don Rubio Ortiz, and the comical character Barriga Duce).

The play presents a classic example of discourse of subjugation in which the rhetorical style employed underscores the superiority of one people or nation over another. The author is obviously a Spaniard, and the characters are presented from the Hispanic point of view. The Comanche in the play are depicted as worthy adversaries of the Spaniards: they are brave; skilled in warfare; and ready to die for their cause. This, of course, suits the ideology of the conqueror. To present the Comanche as a coward would detract from what the play is trying to achieve, which is to demonstrate the power of the Spaniard as an object lesson to the remaining Comanche and other Indians. The enact-

ment is faithful to history in that the Comanche indeed had the reputation of being the most feared Plains Indians because of their bravery and skill in warfare. However, it is not true to history in having Cuerno Verde, the Comanche chief, express himself in eloquent Spanish. Cuerno Verde begins the verbal duel with a challenge to the Spaniards and highlights his prowess as a vanquisher of nations around the world. He proceeds to enumerate all the nations he has conquered, thus demonstrating his outstanding accomplishments in warfare. In this first speech, Cuerno Verde elaborates upon his adversaries in the most respectful terms. The Indian chief ends his monologue with the challenge to the Spanish leader to fight. Don Carlos answers with the epithet learned in the wars against the Moors: "Stop you wretched infidel!" Don Carlos parallels Cuerno Verde's speeches by describing the glorious achievements of Spain.

Each leader takes counsel from his followers and asks their consent to make war. All the Spaniards agree to fight the mighty tribe. Each Spanish soldier offers his consent with a speech in which he expounds on his own valor and throws invectives at the Comanche. The Spaniards invoke the help of the Virgin Mary and Santiago. However, on the Comanche side there is one chief, Tabaco, who does not wish to fight the Spaniards. Tabaco expresses his admiration for the Spaniards, describes his nation's peaceful relations with them, and asserts that he does not want to break this peace. The play ends with the speech of Barriga Duce and the routing of the Comanche.

The historical drama was ritualistically enacted each year to commemorate the Spanish victory over the feared Comanche. The play therefore served as a sign reminding the Comanche as well as other Indians of the power and might of the Spaniards and the futility of engaging in battle with such a formidable adversary. Performed in an open field, the play reproduced the events as fully as possible.

Los Matachines

Los Matachines is the third most important historical play dating from the colonial period, according to informants interviewed by Flavia Waters Champe. The first reference to a *matachines*-type dance is by Bernal Diaz del Castillo, who states,

399

"One part of the city was entirely occupied by Montezuma's dancers, of different kinds, some of whom bore a stick on their feet, others flew in the air, and some danced . . . Matachines."

The etymology of the word *matachines* raises various possibilities. One source suggests a possible derivation from the Italian *mattacinos,* "a kind of sword dancer in a fantastic costume." Another states that *matachines* are "men ridiculously disguised with a mask . . . giving each other blows with swords and bladders." Other theories point to a Nahuatl origin, from *matlachines* or *malacatonzin.* Still another points to the Spanish word *matar* (to kill) as the basis for *matachines.*

The *matachines* enacted in New Mexico is a dance-drama performed by Indians and Mexican Americans during the Christmas season or other important feast days in the Catholic calendar. The dance-drama is performed as a series of ritualized dance steps; there is no dramatic text, only a series of musical compositions played in accordance with the ritualized dance steps of the participating actors. Within the dance choreography, there is a mock bullfight that provides a touch of comic relief.

The cast of characters includes: El Monarca (the Monarch), the leading man, who may represent Moctezuma (Montezuma), the Aztec ruler; Los Capitanes (the Captains), four men dressed similarly to the Monarch with a miter-like crown headpiece; and Los Matachines, from twelve to sixteen men who dance together as a group. In addition to all the male dancers there is a female character, La Malinche. Her role is represented by a very young girl, from seven to twelve years old, dressed all in white. She presents a dramatic contrast to the tall, masked, colorfully clad, and crowned Monarca and Matachines. (The Malinche was the name of the Aztec woman who served Hernán Cortés, conqueror of Mexico, as adviser and as lover.) Other characters are the Abuelo (the grandfather), represented by a masked man who carries a whip, and the Toro, or bull. Aside from the main protagonists in the dance-drama, there are also some assistants who help the dance group with costumes or props. Of major importance to the production of the *matachines* dance are the musicians, who normally consist of violin, guitar, and drum players.

Scholars have proffered various interpretations as to the meaning of the *matachines* dance.

Ramón Gutiérrez suggests that *Los Matachines* recounts "the defeat of the Aztec Emperor Montezuma, his acceptance of Christianity, and obeisance before the mendicants. . . ." Mary Austin interprets the various *matachines* dances in a similar vein:

In the story *El Monarch* figures as Montezuma—head of the Aztec nation. *El Toro* is the figure of Pagan Deviltry; *El Aguelo* [sic] [*Abuelo,* the grandfather] is the lusts of the flesh, and the Bride [La Malinche] is the Soul which is to be won over to Christianity. Thus in the dance the story of Aztec conversion is revealed. ("Folkplays of the Southwest," p. 603)

RELIGIOUS DRAMA

The second major type of drama production in the colonial Southwest is that of liturgical drama, or religious folk plays including *autos sacramentales.* As with the other dramas discussed, their date of origin is a point of debate among scholars. John Englekirk asserts that the religious folk dramas extant in New Mexico today are derived from nineteenth-century printed texts. Most scholars, however, point to an uninterrupted tradition of performances of liturgical plays from the period of colonization to the present. The most popular religious plays, which have been collected and published by Arthur L. Campa, include *Comedia de Adán y Eva* and *Caín y Abel o el primer crimen.* These two plays depict scenes from the Old Testament and are classified by Campa as belonging to the First Cycle of religious folk theater in the Southwest. The Second Cycle of plays is derived from the New Testament and have also been published by Campa. They include *Coloquio de San José, Coloquio de pastores, Auto de los Reyes Magos,* and *El niño perdido.*

Comedia de Adán y Eva

The *autos sacramentales,* or mystery plays, date back to medieval Europe. In Spain the first such written drama of which a fragment still exists is the *Auto de los Reyes Magos* (Play of the Three Kings). This *auto* dates back to the twelfth century.

The Golden Age of Spanish theater began at the turn of the sixteenth century. Juan del Encina, court poet in the 1490s, was writing *eglo-*

gas (eclogues) to celebrate important dates in the liturgical calendar. His *eglogas* included the shepherds and other rustics that the *pastorelas* inherited. The shepherds included in Encina's *eglogas* are directly descended from the classical shepherds from Sannazaro's *Arcadia* (1504). Encina had traveled to Italy and after his return wrote three *eglogas* in which Arcadian shepherds such as Fileno, Zambardo, and Cardonio appear. Of particular interest is Fileno, since a character by that name appears in the *pastorela*, *La Aurora del Nuevo Día* and the *Coloquio de San José.*

The convention of introducing shepherds as protagonists in literary works dates back to the Latin author Theocritus, whose work *Idyls*, written in the third century B.C., incorporates the pastoral in its descriptions of the simple life of rustics and shepherds. Later, Virgil in his *Eclogues* further refined and popularized pastoral conventions.

In the late fifteenth century, when the colonization of the Americas was beginning, the missionary friars found the *autos sacramentales* particularly useful in the evangelization of the American Indian masses. The play *Adán y Eva* was a favorite, and its diffusion and popularity extended to the American Southwest. In the *Comedia de Adán y Eva,* published in 1934 by Arthur L. Campa from a manuscript dated 1893 and owned by Propéro Baca, a resident of Bernalillo, New Mexico, the Devil, Lucifer, Adán, and Eva appear as the main characters. Minor characters include Appetite and Sin and the positive forces, God and Mercy.

In this New Mexican play, Lucifer assumes a prominent role while Adán plays a secondary one with significantly fewer lines. Lucifer is portrayed as a Renaissance figure; he is articulate and knowledgeable, and reason and logic pervade his dialogues. As is true of other folk plays, humor is an important element in balancing the tension of the drama; the figures of Appetite and Sin provide comic relief.

At the inception of the play, we find Lucifer expounding his grievances to Appetite and Sin—mainly that he, a favorite of God, has been exiled from heaven and sent to hell and that two humans in the image of God (Adam and Eve) have been created. Lucifer, consumed with envy and anger, seeks revenge. He will, of course, succeed in tempting Eve to eat the apple and in having the couple expelled from paradise, just as he had been banished from heaven.

The second play in Campa's First Cycle, *Caín y Abel o el primer crimen,* depicts the biblical conflict between Abel and his brother Cain. Caín murders Abel, and the Lord holds Caín responsible for his deed. The play is very short and is done in a sentimental form, with Eve playing a particularly weepy character.

Los pastores

Of the four plays appearing in Campa's Second Cycle (the New Testament–based plays), the most popular one has been the many versions of *Los pastores*, also known as *pastorelas*. The play depicts the shepherds Lizardo, Bato, Gila, Abelicio, Bartolo, Menalpas, Dina, and Melideos tending their sheep when an Angel announces the news of the birth of Jesus and directs the shepherds to go to worship him at the grotto in Bethlehem. On their journey to the grotto, the *hermitaño,* or hermit, joins them. The Devil appears and tries to divert the shepherds from their journey by using the hermit to distract them.

Los pastores is the most widely diffused liturgical play in the Americas. There are hundreds of variants, which attest to its popularity. A common structural variation in the drama is found within the tricks the Devil plays on the shepherds when trying to intercept their pilgrimage to worship the infant Jesus. The Devil may use any of the Seven Deadly Sins in trying to tempt the shepherds to forget their journey, but those most commonly used are Lust, Gluttony, and Greed.

Las posadas

Las posadas is often associated with the shepherds' plays, although they do not necessarily have to be performed at the same time. *Las posadas* reenacts the pilgrimage that Joseph and Mary made to Bethlehem and their unsuccessful search for an inn. The ritual drama usually is performed on the nine nights preceding Christmas and culminates on Christmas Eve. It does not have a set text but involves a group of people singing the verses that reenact the Holy Family's quest. The singers go from house to house asking for a room, whereupon each house refuses to let them in. A designated home will finally admit them, and a festive party ensues. Part of the *Coloquio de San José* involves a *Las posadas* passage.

401

Coloquio de San José

The *Coloquio de San José*'s plot revolves around the marriage between San José and the Virgin Mary. It depicts the miraculous manner in which Joseph, the humble carpenter, was selected to wed Mary and how, after their betrothal, she receives the news of her impregnation by the Holy Ghost. The play also includes the pilgrimage of the Holy Family to Bethlehem and the refusal of the innkeepers (at Satan's instigation) to grant them lodging, as in *Las posadas*. At the conclusion of the play, the shepherds Arminda and Fileno join in the worship of the infant Jesus. Throughout the play the devils Luzbel and Satanás, as well as their cohort Astucias, try to cause as much mischief as they can for Joseph and Mary. However they are not successful, and Good eventually triumphs over Evil. Other characters prominent in the play include Isabel and Zacarías, Mary's close relatives, and the Angel Saint Michael.

Auto de los Reyes Magos

Prospero Baca, a folk poet from Bernalillo, New Mexico, had in his possession a manuscript of the religious play *Auto de los Reyes Magos*, which Campa was able to obtain and publish in his Second Cycle. This play details the journey of the three kings Baltazar, Gaspar, and Melchior in search of the infant Jesus. The play describes the meeting between the three kings and Herod, the ruler of the Roman province of Judaea. When Herod discovers the intent of the three kings to find and worship the New King, he tries to extract more information from them. Upon failing to find the New Born King's whereabouts, he orders every male child under the age of two to be murdered. Joseph and Mary flee from the region, hoping to escape the edict. The play ends with the successful escape of the Holy Family.

El Niño perdido

As with the manuscript for the *Los Reyes Magos* play, a New Mexican native preserved a version of the religious drama, *El Niño perdido*. Juan Tenorio from Taos, New Mexico, had in his possession a manuscript for *El Niño perdido*, which Campa published in his Second Cycle collection. The play's plot details the biblical passage concerning Jesus' earliest excursion away from his parents and his debate with the learned rabbis. While Joseph and Mary are frantically looking for Jesus, the young twelve-year-old is out by himself in the local town. The young child first encounters a miserly Rich Man who refuses to feed the hungry boy. It is a woman, Gosabel, who feeds him and who eventually will inform Mary of his whereabouts. After the incident with the Rich Man, Jesus joins the learned rabbis at the temple and discusses with them philosophical and religious issues. The rabbis declare him the most learned of them all. At the conclusion of the drama, Joseph and Mary find Jesus. Mary rebukes him for straying, whereupon Jesus informs her he is only doing his Father's business.

Las cuatro apariciones de nuestra Señora Guadalupe

A very important colonial drama related to the December cycle of festivities was *Las cuatro apariciones de nuestra Señora de Guadalupe*, which Aurora Lucero-White Lea has published. This folk drama depicts the miraculous apparition of the Virgin of Guadalupe to the young Indian Juan Diego at the Cerro del Tepeyac in present-day Mexico City. The Virgin appeared to Juan Diego and expressed her desire to have a temple built on the spot. Juan Diego repeatedly conveyed the message to the bishop of Mexico, but because of the former's low status as an Indian, the church authorities did not give credence to his message. Apparitions appeared four times, and the last time the image of the Virgin of Guadalupe was imprinted on Juan Diego's *tilma*, or robe. With the miraculous imprint before his eyes, the bishop had no choice but to believe Juan Diego.

A church in honor of the Virgin of Guadalupe was built on the Cerro del Tepeyac. The apparitions appeared in 1531, and the cult of the Virgin of Guadalupe grew rapidly throughout Mexico and the American Southwest. The play is performed during the feast of the Virgin of Guadalupe on 12 December.

All the liturgical dramas included in Campa's First and Second Cycle were enacted during the Christmas season until 6 January, when the play *Auto de los Reyes Magos* concluded the cycle of Nativity play performances.

DRAMA: SPANISH

CONCLUSION

Both the historical plays and the liturgical dramas had as their main ideological objective the indoctrination of the Native Americans either to fear the power and the might of the Spanish Empire or to accept the teachings of the Catholic church, which was at the time an important extension of the Spanish Empire. The plays served their function well, for the color and pageantry caught the eye of the curious Native American audiences. Once their attention was captured, the encoded messages were easy to drum in through the plots and narrative structures of these theatrical performances. Colonial theater in America was so successful that these historical and liturgical dramas are still performed today throughout the Southwest.

BIBLIOGRAPHY

Bibliographical Sources

Acuña, René. *El teatro popular en Hispanoamérica: Una bibliografía anotada.* Mexico, 1979.
Heisley, Michael. *An Annotated Bibliography of Chicano Folklore from the Southwestern United States.* Los Angeles, Calif., 1977.
Igo, John. *Los Pastores: An Annotated Bibliography with an Introduction.* San Antonio, Tex., 1967.

Critical Studies, Historical Works, and Plays

Austin, Mary. "Folk Plays of the Southwest." *Theatre Arts Monthly* 17, no. 8 (1933):599–610.
Brown, Lorin W., et al., eds. *Hispano Folklife of New Mexico.* Albuquerque, N.Mex., 1978.
Campa, Arthur L. *Hispanic Culture in the Southwest.* Norman, Okla., 1979.
———. "Los Comanches: A New Mexican Folk Drama." *University of New Mexico Bulletin* 7, no. 1 (1942):127–131.
———. "The New Mexican Spanish Folktheater." *Southern Folklore Quarterly* 5, no. 2 (1941):127–131.
———. "Spanish Religious Folktheatre in the Spanish Southwest." *University of New Mexico Bulletin* 5, no. 1 (1934):1–74; 5, no. 2 (1934):1–157. Comprises First Cycle and Second Cycle.
Carrasco Urgoiti, Soledad. "La fiesta de 'Moros y Cristianos' y la cuestión morisca en la España de los Austrias." In *Actas de las jornadas sobre teatro popular en España,* edited by Joaquin Alvarez Barrientos and Antonio Cea Gutiérrez. Madrid, 1987.
Carreter, Fernando Lázaro. *Teatro Medieval.* Madrid, 1965.
Castillo, Bernal Díaz del. *The True History of the Conquest of Mexico.* Translated by Maurice Keatinge. 2 vols. New York, 1927.
Champe, Flavia Waters. *The Matachines Dance of the Upper Rio Grande: History, Music, and Choreography.* Lincoln, Nebr., 1983.
———. "Origins of the Magical Matachines Dance." *El Palacio* 86, no. 4 (1980–1981):34–39.
Cole, M. R. *Los Pastores: A Mexican Play of the Nativity.* Boston and New York, 1907.
Comunidad de Madrid. *El auto religioso en España.* Madrid, 1991.
Díaz, Joaquín, and José Luis Alonso Ponga. *Autos de Navidad en León y Castilla.* León, Spain, 1983.
Domínguez, Fray Francisco Atanasio. *The Missions of New Mexico, 1776.* Albuquerque, N.Mex., 1975.
Donovan, Richard B. *The Liturgical Drama in Medieval Spain.* Toronto, Ontario, 1958.
Engelkirk, John E. "Notes on the Repertoire of the New Mexican Spanish Folktheatre." *Southern Folklore Quarterly* 4 (1940):227–237.
———. "The Source and Dating of New Mexican Spanish Folk Plays." *Western Folklore* 16, no. 4 (1957):232–255.
Espinosa, Aurelio M. "Los Comanches: A Spanish Heroic Play of the Year Seventeen Hundred and Eighty." *University of New Mexico Bulletin* 1, no. 1 (1907):1–45.
Espinosa, Gilberto. "Los Comanches." *New Mexico Quarterly* 1, no. 1 (1931):132–146.
Feder, Norman. "Matachines: A Photo Essay." *American Indian Tradition* 8, no. 2 (1962):79, 82.
Fernández de Lizardi, José Joaquín. "Pastorela en dos actos." *Obras. II Teatro.* Mexico City, 1965.
Foster, George M. *Culture and Conquest: America's Spanish Heritage.* New York, 1960.
García, Luis Navarro. *La conquista de Nuevo México.* Madrid, 1978.
Gillmor, Frances. "*Los Pastores* Number: Folk Plays of Hispanic America—Forward." *Western Folklore* 16, no. 4 (1957):229–231.
Grant, Blanche C. *Taos Today.* Taos, N.Mex., 1925.
Gutiérrez, Ramón A. *When Jesus Came, the Corn Mothers Went Away: Marriage, Sexuality, and Power in New Mexico.* Stanford, Calif., 1991.
Hammond, George P., and Agapito Rey. *Don Juan de Oñate, Colonizer of New Mexico, 1595–1628.* Albuquerque, N.Mex., 1953.
Kurath, Gertrude P. "The Origins of the Pueblo Indian Matachines." *El Palacio* 64, nos. 9 and 10 (1957):259–264.
Lea, Aurora Lucero-White. *Coloquio de los pastores.* Santa Fe, N.Mex., 1940.

———. *Literary Folklore of the Hispanic Southwest.* San Antonio, Tex., 1953.

———. "More about the Matachines." *New Mexican Folklore* 11 (1963–1964):7–9.

Lowther, María López de. *Los Pastores (The Shepherds): An Old California Christmas Play.* Hollywood, Calif., 1953.

McCrossan, Sister Joseph Marie. *The Role of the Church and the Folk in the Development of the Early Drama in New Mexico.* Philadelphia, 1948.

MacGregor-Villarreal, Mary. "Celebrating *Las Posadas* in Los Angeles." *Western Folklore* 39, no. 2 (1984):71–104.

María y Campos, Armando de. *Pastorelas Mexicanas.* Mexico City, 1985.

Menéndez Pidal, Ramón, ed. "Auto de los reyes magos." *Revista de Archivos, Bibliotecas y Museos* 4 (1948):453–462.

Muñoz Renedo, Carmen. *Representación de "Moros y Christianos" de Zujar.* Madrid, 1972.

Ortega, Pedro Ribera. *Christmas in Old Santa Fe.* Santa Fe, N.Mex., 1973.

Pearce, T. M. "The New Mexican 'Shepherds' Play.' " *Western Folklore* 15, no. 2 (1956):77–88.

Preminger, Alex, ed. *Princeton Encyclopedia of Poetry and Poetics.* Princeton, N.J., 1974.

Rael, Juan B. *The Sources and Diffusion of the Mexican Shepherds' Plays.* Guadalajara, Mexico, 1965.

Ricard, Robert. *The Spiritual Conquest of Mexico: An Essay on the Apostolic and the Evangelizing Methods of the Mendicant Orders in New Spain, 1523–1572.* Translated by Leslie Byrd Simpson. Berkeley, Calif., 1966.

Robb, J. D. "The Matachines Dance—a Ritual Folk Dance." *Western Folklore* 20, no. 2 (1961):87–101.

———. "The Music of *Los Pastores.*" *Western Folklore* 16, no. 4 (1957):263–280.

Robe, Stanley L. "The Relationship of *Los Pastores* to Other Spanish-American Folk Drama." *Western Folklore* 16, no. 4 (1957):281–289.

———, ed. *Coloquio de Pastores from Jalisco, México.* University of California Publications, folklore studies, 4. Los Angeles, 1954.

Roeder, Beatrice A. "*Los Comanches:* A Bicentennial Folk Play." *Bilingual Review/Revista Bilingüe* 3 (1976):213–220.

Romero Salinas, Joel. *La Pastorela Mexicana: orígen y evolución.* Mexico City, 1984.

San Martin, Beatriz. *Pastorelas y Coloquios.* Mexico City, 1987.

Stark, Richard B. *Music of the Spanish Folk Plays in New Mexico.* Santa Fe, N.Mex., 1969.

Sturdevant, Winifred. *The Misterio de los reyes magos: Its Position in the Development of the Medieval Legend of the Three Kings.* Johns Hopkins Studies in Romance Literature and Language, vol. 10. Baltimore, Md., 1927.

Valdez, Luis. *La Pastorela: The Shepherd's Play.* San Juan Bautista, Calif., 1989.

Villagrá, Gaspar Pérez de. *Historia de la Nueva México.* Alcalá de Henares, 1610; rev. ed., 2 vols., 1900.

Warman, Arturo. *La danza de Moros y Cristianos.* Mexico City, 1972.

Wilson, Margaret. *Spanish Drama of the Golden Age.* New York, 1969.

Maria Herrera-Sobek

SEE ALSO **Literature; Recreations; Rural Life; and Urban Life.**

NATIVE AMERICAN AESTHETICS

VISUAL ARTS

At the time of first contact with Europeans (as before and after), the indigenous peoples of North America were producing a wealth of visual forms in a great variety of techniques under many different social and economic conditions and for a multitude of purposes. They made use of the materials, opportunities, and challenges offered by a range of ecological zones, stretching from the treeless tundra to the subtropical forest. Much as the only significant meaning of the term "Indians," by which these populations came to be called, derives from the perceived contrast between them and the European "self," so the various Native American aesthetic traditions shared little besides their difference from the modern European concept of "art" that was then beginning to emerge fully.

The European distinction between "art" and "craft," which marks the emancipation of aesthetic form from functional form, was apparently unknown among Native North Americans, as was a term for "art" as a discrete domain. Nowhere were visual forms made or preserved exclusively for their artistic merit.

FACTORS SHAPING NATIVE AMERICAN ART

While lacking this ultimate specialization, Native American tribes differed in the extent to which the production of visual forms was restricted to certain groups and to which it was permeating and permeated by other aspects of their culture, including especially social prestige, religion, or nonvisual forms of expression.

The most basic mode of allocating related tasks to certain classes was the division of labor by gender. Although the principle itself is nearly universal, the specific assignment of types of production to the female or male domain is not. In Native North America, most textile techniques (including basketmaking and needlework) were woman's work, but weaving and embroidery were done by the men among the Pueblo peoples of the Southwest. Carving was generally a male concern, but woodcarving was assigned to females among some prairie tribes (such as the Pawnee or Omaha). Pottery was made and decorated by women; the fact that the makers often included male transvestites in the pueblo of Zuni illustrates the gender- rather than sex-related character of the practice. Painting and similar graphic modes of decorating two-dimensional surfaces were generally done by the same class of persons that had produced or prepared the respective surface. Thus painting on wood was commonly a male task, while painting on pottery was assigned to females. Tanned animal skins could be painted by either group.

The prevalent gender-specific production of visual arts led to the widespread presence of gender-specific styles. Plains Indian skin painting, done by both men and women, clearly illustrates the point. Male painting was representational, autobiographical, and mostly related to war honors; whereas female painting was abstract and symbolic. The representational versus abstract distinction between male and female styles is frequently encountered in other arts but is far from universal.

Occupational specialization whereby certain individuals plied certain crafts was probably present to some extent in most sedentary Native American societies. But nowhere did it fully replace the gender-based distinction. In some cases specialization was limited to the fact that ritual specialists monopolized the production of certain artifact types, the ritual knowledge being necessary for the item's production. Pictography was used to notate song texts in the western Great Lakes area or historical events on the Plains, in each case by specialists only. Among the peoples of the Upper Missouri River some crafts were considered sacred, and their practice was limited to members of special guilds. The specialized knowledge needed for their exercise was passed on by these societies, membership in which had to be obtained by purchase.

The presence of wealthy elites among the peoples of the Northwest Coast promoted professionalization (as it had in the Southeast before the arrival of De Soto and the subsequent collapse of the Native populations there). This process addressed the need for prestige goods while encouraging excellence in technical quality and stylistic sophistication. In some instances patron-craftsperson relationships developed.

Locally distinct styles or techniques formed the basis for the role that the visual arts played in expressing their makers' local or ethnic identity. Their uniqueness could stimulate the exchange of these distinctive products, especially in cases where crafts were related to the availability of certain resources. Certain Indian towns in New England, for example, were said to have supplied their neighbors with wooden bowls.

A significant group of technological features may also be found to distinguish Native American from European modes of artistic production. All of indigenous America lacked iron tools (except for a few traded from Siberia across the Bering Strait by the Eskimo), and even copper tools were fairly rare. Likewise, all uses of true rotary motion were unknown, including wheeled transportation, the potter's wheel, and the lathe. The absence of these implements was often compensated for by notable manual dexterity, as in the regular building up of pots by manipulating the clay or the exquisite carving of wood, stone, or ivory.

The lack of a separate domain of "art" is obvious from the fact that nowhere in Native North America were visual shapes produced just to satisfy aesthetic criteria. Usefulness and beauty were generally regarded as part of the same goal, rather than as standing in opposition to one another. Thus, works were always appreciated in a context of performance and in conjunction with nonvisual experience. The production and use of dry paintings of colored sands and pollen made for religious purposes in the Southwest were generally accompanied by songs or the recitation of myths; masks were viewed only when in movement, usually when worn by dancers following rhythmic patterns supplied by music.

The following brief survey must necessarily focus on the most prominent genres of the visual arts in Native North America. It is based on the media used, since these generally regulate the artistic division of labor and therefore also of styles.

THREE TECHNIQUES OF BASKETRY

Basketry was one of the most widespread arts in Native America, although it was relatively unimportant in the Arctic, sub-Arctic, and Plains regions. Of the three major techniques (plaiting, coiling, twining), coiling was more prominent in the West and plaiting in the East, where split river cane was traditionally cut into strips and woven into checkered or twilled patterns. Some of the resulting baskets were double woven (showing different patterns on the inside and outside). While most of the designs were abstract and rectilinear, the Chitimacha of Louisiana and their neighbors produced complex curvilinear patterns. Plaited wicker baskets (with rigid warps and flexible wefts) were found among the Pueblo people and were highly developed among the Hopi of Oraibi, who thereby created representational patterns.

The Hopi of the Second Mesa, on the other hand, produced coiled baskets made from yucca leaves. Coiling consists of sewing a spiraling foundation together with decorative stitches. Representational designs are somewhat easier to create with this technique, yet the vast majority of designs were geometric. Among the Salish of the Intermontane Plateau, a scaly, patterned surface is produced by imbrication, in which a decorative thread is caught under each weft stitch.

Twining, in which active wefts are twisted around passive wefts, allows a great profusion of structural and nonstructural decorative techniques. Although a few exquisitely twined baskets have survived from the Northeast, the most spectacular products of this tradition originate from the Northwest coast. There Europeans encountered basketry hats depicting whaling scenes during their first contact with the Nootka in the late eighteenth century. As a preserve of the indigenous upper class, whaling and, by extension, depictions of whaling were privileges of the elite. Aleut twining was strictly ornamental, but with up to thirteen hundred stitches per square inch, it displayed the greatest delicacy of any Native American basketwork.

WEAVING AND APPLIQUÉ ON PLIABLE FABRICS

Twining was also the most widespread technique in making pliable fabrics. Soft bags, belts, and burden straps with rectilinear designs (including some zoomorphic representations) were woven of nettle fibers, "Indian hemp" (apocynum), or grasses in the Northeast and the Northwest. Twined textiles reached an apex of development among the Tlingit of Alaska, who in the late eighteenth century began to introduce representational motifs into a purely abstract textile art. A nineteenth-century result of this development was the famous Chilkat blankets, which displayed crests of noble families. They were woven of cedar bark and the wool of mountain goats by women on the basis of pattern boards painted by men. Farther south in central California, twined blankets were covered on the outside with simple designs of feathers.

The loom (and thus true weaving) were limited to the Southwest, where cotton had been grown in the pueblos since pre-European times. The Navajo adopted weaving from the Pueblo people and sheepherding from the Spanish during colonial times, and they later became the master weavers of the whole region. Whereas many of the Pueblo textiles were dyed, painted, or embroidered, the Navajo went beyond simple striped patterns and employed tapestry weaves for complex geometric designs.

Although embroidery (and in a sense coiled basketry) were the most typical expressions of "needlework" of the Southwest, the Native women of eastern North America employed bone awls and sinew thread mostly for appliqué on tanned hides. East of the Rockies, dyed and flattened quills of the porcupine were the most commonly used decorative material thus sewn onto surfaces, but they were sometimes replaced by split bird quills, moose hair, or vegetal fibers. Less commonly, narrow bands were produced by threading quills through a loose grid of sinew threads, a technique generally referred to as "woven quillwork" and most highly developed in the sub-Arctic. In the Northeast, porcupine quills were also used to decorate baskets of birch bark in a simple kind of embroidery technique, which is probably post-European in origin. While woven quillwork invariably produces rectilinear patterns, quill appliqué was also employed in curvilinear styles, some of them with floral connotations and others in simple zoomorphic representations.

Shells, either naturally fitted with holes, like dentalium, or drilled to produce generally disk-shaped beads, were also used in appliqué work and were traded far from the coasts where most of them had originated. The tiresome process of making the beads and the usual limitation of the shells to one color (white, and only rarely, purple) laid the basis for the enthusiastic acceptance of European trade beads of glass since the time of first contact. Despite the possible availability of many different colors, white and blue glass beads were favored by Native American artisans well into the nineteenth century.

One of the best artifact types made of shell beads was the wampum belt, which became widely known to whites through their use in the protocol surrounding political deliberations, negotiations, and treaties. On the northeastern Atlantic coast, the belts were made of tubular white and purple shell beads, whose manufacture was extremely rare in pre-European times, and were strung on sinew of leather thongs before being woven into patterns; some of them acquired symbolic meanings, especially among the Iroquois. In the seventeenth and eighteenth centuries, other groups in the eastern woodlands used various items woven of wampum beads for personal decoration.

There is little evidence for textile appliqué prior to the arrival of Europeans, but afterward trade cloth (and subsequently silk ribbons) became widely used for this purpose. The introduction of steel needles undoubtedly helped to increase the popularity of decorative arts based on sewing.

PAINTING AND INSCRIPTION ON ROCK, POTTERY, AND OTHER MEDIA

Of all surfaces that can be painted or engraved, rock is distributed most widely in North America. Pecked, abraded, or incised petroglyphs and monochrome (mostly red or black) rock painting are thus all found in many areas and styles, many of which are still difficult to date and interpret. Polychrome rock paintings are found mainly in California and the Southwest. Some of the most complex of these are attributable to ritual specialists among the historic Chumash of southern California. In the rock art of the Southwest, a relationship can be seen with both pottery painting and murals.

Painted murals represent a local development of the three centuries just prior to Spanish contact (1300 to the end of the sixteenth century), but were continued in simpler form into later periods. Painted in fresco secco on adobe walls of ceremonial chambers for specific ceremonies, up to one hundred superimposed layers of painting have been found, indicating the less-than-permanent nature of this art form. It thus resembles the dry painting of the pueblo dwellers and their neighbors (most notably the Navajo), which were destroyed immediately after the end of the ceremony for which they had been made.

Pottery painting is very typical of the Southwest, where its roots go back to the first millennium A.D. As in rock art and in mural painting, polychromy had developed on the basis of simple red-on-buff and black-on-white styles. Rectilinear and curvilinear abstract as well as representational styles were traditionally used in the several different pueblos, a repertoire to which floral elements and more realistic animal figures were added under Spanish colonial influence.

By contrast, pottery in eastern North America was more typically decorated by other modes of surface treatment such as textile impressions, cord markings, or incisions. This focus on line rather than color is likewise found in the decoration of other surfaces in the region. Of special importance were incised or sgraffito-like scratched designs on the outer layer of birch bark among peoples all across the sub-Arctic, some of whom employed stencils to produce clearly delineated floral patterns. Engraved and chip-carved wooden boards and other artifacts were encountered in the temperate woodlands of eastern North America. Incised horn, bone, and shell had an even wider distribution. In the Arctic, on the other hand, the most favored material for incised decoration was walrus ivory. Its stylistic development since prehistoric times is well documented and includes generally earlier curvilinear and often abstract patterns as well as later pictographic representational styles.

Pictography is also the hallmark of the male skin-painting tradition of the Plains, which seems to be related to the pictographic engraving on bark and wood found farther east. Early examples of painted bison robes or buckskin shirts display highly stylized images of humans and animals with limbs shown in profile combined with frontal faces. It was not until the nineteenth century that, under white influence, more realistic representations were developed from this traditional style of painting. Another male skin-painting tradition of the Plains may be termed visionary, since the symbols of protective powers painted on shields were often inspired by dreams or visions. Some such designs, both on shields and the covers of tipis, also took on heraldic functions.

Perhaps the most highly sophisticated painting and engraving tradition of Native North America was the one developed by the professional artists-craftsmen of the Northwest coast. Wood is the primary medium on which it is expressed, but it is also found on leather, stone, horn, bone, and even copper. In its most conventionalized form it is found among the Tlingit of southeastern Alaska and their neighbors, including the Haida and Tsimshian of British Columbia. It served to display the heraldic crests of the noble families, which were rendered in a stylized, curvilinear manner. Many works of this tradition display a keen sense of the possibilities for exploiting the tension between lines, a limited number of shapes from which images are constructed, and pictorial space. Built around a compositional device that has become generally referred to as the form-line structure, which uses three colors (black, red, and green or blue) to define the hierarchy of lines, it employs a complex grammar of formal expression whose knowledge is essential for understanding the often ambiguous meaning of the designs.

This style has also influenced wood carving styles on the Northwest Coast, which otherwise embrace a wide range, from highly conventionalized and almost abstract renderings of faces to strikingly naturalistic portrait sculptures. Apart from masks used, for example, in the elaborate dramatic performances staged by secret societies during the winter season, the area's best-known type of wooden sculpture is the "totem pole." Like so many other art forms of the Northwest coast, it serves to display inherited privileges. Totem poles were either raised in front of the communal houses of a kin group, employed as memorials for deceased dignitaries, or used on ceremonial occasions when the validation of a group's rights were called for.

To the north the Alaska Eskimo, especially in the Bering Sea region, carved masks that range from modestly realistic to abstract and surrealistic. Inspired by the visions of shamans, they are a prime example of the semiprofessional art of ritual specialists and their helpers. Compared to the strictness of the rules for Northwest coast carving, Eskimo carving seems rather individualistic, although a core of shared features seems to exist.

Wooden masks were also carved in the northeastern woodlands, where the very expressive "False Faces" of the Iroquois, used in healing, are the only type to have survived the changes in religious practices brought about by white contact. A group of exquisitely carved items, including masks, which were recovered from an early historic context on Key Marco in Florida, clearly illustrates the professional quality of carving that must have existed. Other forms of carving, particularly including clubs and household utensils such as ladles or bowls, also attest to the former importance of wood carving in the East.

Stone sculpture in the East during the historic period was limited mostly to the production of pipe heads from soft stones. Like some of the other arts noted in this survey, pipes became an item in the growing "tourist art" market, which since early colonial times led many native artists/craftspeople to produce more-or-less compromised traditional items such as souvenirs for whites.

BIBLIOGRAPHY

Feest, Christian F. *Native Arts of North America*. London, 1980.

Harrison, Julia, et al. *The Spirit Sings: Artistic Traditions of Canada's First Peoples*. Toronto and Calgary, 1987.

Holm, Bill. *Northwest Coast Indian Art: An Analysis of Form*. Seattle, Wash., 1965.

Mathews, Zena Pearlstone, and Aldona Jonaitis, eds. *Native North American Art History: Selected Readings*. Palo Alto, Calif., 1982.

Maurer, Evan M. *The Native American Heritage: A Survey of North American Indian Art*. Chicago, 1977.

Wade, Edwin L., ed. *The Arts of the North American Indian: Native Traditions in Evolution*. New York, 1986.

Christian F. Feest

SEE ALSO **Mission Communities** and **Native American Religions.**

MUSIC AND DANCE

NATIVE AMERICANS BEHELD a relatively pristine universe before European contact, a universe filled with thousands of species of animals and plants, where great vistas were not yet diminished by air pollution and the night sky was not diluted by artificial light. American Indian artists used visible and invisible forms, such as dance and music, to reflect, exalt, preserve, and commemorate that universe—its wonders and realities.

Although some music and dance existed for entertainment, usually these art forms affected or were affected by religion, lifeways, and worldview. Many Indian ceremonies concentrated on renewing the world or keeping it in balance. Pueblo Indians, for example, maintained reciprocity with deities, the supernatural world, each other, and strangers through music, dance, and ceremony, as did most other Indian peoples.

HISTORICAL SOURCES

Archaeological evidence of Native music and dance prior to European contact exists through surviving instruments, ceremonial regalia, and depictions of music and dance in pottery, pictographs, and petroglyphs (symbols and pictures incised on rock surfaces). Following European contact, diaries and drawings by explorers offer accounts of indigenous music and dance that provide a sense of the sounds, colors, and movement of Native art, but the descriptions are sometimes sensationalized.

Music, dance, and other art forms are not as easy as some other social phenomena for a layman (such as a soldier or traveler) to describe, and recording technology has existed only since the late nineteenth century. Since ethnomusicology and dance ethnology lack the time depth of most historical documents, we can only try to reconstruct American Indian music and dance at the time of contact and through the colonial era from records such as those described above and from using what we know of the present and working backward.

The watercolor paintings of John White, an early colonist and governor, and the travel notes (published in 1588) of English scientist Thomas Harriot supply a few details about the characteristics of the Native music and dance they encountered during the early colonial period. White's surviving drawings of people, their architecture, and their social and economic activity came from his residence on Roanoke Island, and from them we learn to recognize Indian men, women, and children. Indian people are shown in both ordinary and ceremonial dress (sometimes adorned with body paint), listening to a shaman around the fire, and dancing during the Green Corn or First Fruits festival. Harriot describes a lively communal dance and solemn feast held in the evening that attracted villagers and visitors alike. He says that the participants kept time by striking gourds and branches against posts while wildly singing and dancing for the celebration of this solemn feast.

Harriot thought the dances were held for various reasons: socialization, amusement, exercise, commemoration of war, of peace, and of hunting, or to celebrate planting, harvest, capture of enemies, and religious festivals. He further believed that almost every occasion was celebrated by a dance (and, by extension, music and personal adornment).

One of White's drawings suggests both men and women singing and praying around a fire. Harriot implies that they are making merry after returning home from some dangerous activity, and they accompany themselves with gourd rattles.

English colonist William Strachey, author of a 1612 manuscript titled *The Historie of Travell into Virginia Britania,* asserted that song and dance were so akin in the mind of the aboriginal Virginian that the Indian word for song and dance there was the same. In observations recorded in 1609 he describes responsorial singing in Virginia, mentioning a short groan by "the rest of the priests" at pauses in the invocation of the chief priest. He talks about amorous songs and parodies ridiculing the Europeans. He also mentions a cane flute and gourd rattles of differing pitches.

We can still observe these instruments and the responses and groans that Strachey relates in the music and oratory of the Delaware, Cherokee, Shawnee, and many other formerly eastern tribes. Likewise we still find parodies and love lyrics. Strachey also describes a ceremonial that resembles greatly the Green Corn ceremony still observed by the Creek and other formerly southeastern tribes—a circular dance around a sacred fire with complicated choreography and men at the rear keeping order with switches.

Some early sources offer more details on the music itself. Some Indians, such as the Ojibwa or Chippewa, used written mnemonics to notate their songs on birch bark or other materials. The first European attempt at notating Native American music appears in the work of chronicler Marc Lescarbot in 1617. Using a seventeenth-century solfège method, Lescarbot describes tunes that use three- or four-tone scales, have the range of a fourth, and feature a soloist with a chorus response. The text appears to employ both words and vocables (standardized but nontranslatable syllables).

SONG AND DANCE FORMS

In all of North America, Indian music was primarily vocal, and vocal style is still one of the most important musical characteristics that helps us distinguish one area's music from another. Several types of song forms were used: strict unison; unison chorus, after the leader had sung the first line of the song to identify it; responsorial, with leader-chorus alternation; or strophic songs, with alternating chorus and verse parts. Strophic songs (in which the same music is used for each stanza) were common, particularly for animal dances and narratives. Yells, animal cries, and parlando formulas (suggestive of speech) occurred at important structural points in the songs. These markers not only expressed the exuberance of the dancers and singers, they were crucial to music making and choreography without notation or conductors. Songs tended to be short, but performances were long; songs had many repetitions, and some were arranged in cycles.

Musical contexts for nonprivate ceremonies and social occasions, many involving dance, are well documented. However, private songs used for practicing medicine and curing, praying, conducting initiation, hunting, storytelling, controlling nature, putting children to sleep, performing magic, playing games, and courting were equally important.

Sacred numbers, color sequence, and other symbols were important in playing out the songs and dances. For example, songs might have four or seven repetitions, or multiples thereof; colors and directions might be mentioned in a specific order denoting clockwise or counterclockwise motion; and so forth. Ritual speech was perceived by outsiders as having a songlike character.

Music and dance were adapted for large and small spaces, indoor and outdoor ceremonials, hard and soft surfaces, and loud and quiet observances. Dances used both exaggerated and subtle movements—as appropriate to the setting, the occasion, and the content of the observance—and had many elements particular to the traditions of various regions. Along the eastern seaboard and inland to the Great Lakes and Mississippi, for example, dances were most often performed in a counterclockwise manner. Larger motions and louder sounds occurred in the South and in all outdoor ceremonies, while the ceremonial longhouses of the North held more restrained celebrations.

MUSICAL INSTRUMENTS

Musical instruments were either worn on the body or held in the hand and were shaken, blown, or beaten upon. Hard rawhide drums were used in the Plains, the Southwest, the Northwest Coast, and among the Eskimo Indians (more properly known as the Inuit, Inupiat, and Yupik). The primary drum in the East and among the Navajo and the Apache was the water drum, a vessel partially filled with water, covered with a dampened, soft hide stretched tight, and beaten with a hard stick (unique to North America). Hand-held rattles of gourd, bark, horn, and turtle shells, along with strung rattles of deer hoof, turtle shell, and marine shell, were used by both dancers and singers.

Ceramic, wooden, and cane flutes were widespread in North America; they were double, single, and multiple, like panpipes. The courting flute, a male instrument, produced music that echoed and embellished well-known melodies, often drawn from love songs. Its influence was intended to draw a player's sweetheart to him.

The Apache fiddle (made from a mescal stalk) and musical bows are examples of early string instruments, although pre-Columbian evidence is difficult to find for these. Given the rapid adoption and adaptation of stringed instruments such as guitars, fiddles, and the like, especially in the Spanish Borderlands and French territory, either a few stringed instruments already existed before contact so that the European instruments were embraced as familiar, or the novelty was too appealing to resist.

REGIONAL FEATURES IN INDIAN MUSIC AND DANCE

The Arctic and Sub-Arctic
Among the Eskimo in Alaska and Canada the most important occasions for music and dance were midwinter gatherings in their large community houses. Several men would sing the same melody while each singer also played a large frame drum. These round drums were constructed from the bladders of large sea animals, stretched over driftwood hoops with attached handles. They were played from underneath with long slender wands. Mostly the male and female dancers acted out hunting, fishing, and other daily activities, often holding decorated dance fans woven from grass and animal hair.

The Northwest Coast
On the Northwest Coast of the United States and Canada, including Alaska, Indian music and dance are often part of compelling ritual dramas and ceremonies. These rituals—featuring elaborately painted screens, ceremonial dress, and multipart singing accompanied by rattles, drums, and whistles—rival grand opera in their conception and execution.

Many Northwest Coast Indians became members of the Russian Orthodox church beginning in the early nineteenth century and then translated hymns into their native languages. They also adopted some of the Russian harmonies and incorporated them into a few Native songs.

California
Indians of Northwest California had little prolonged contact with Europeans until the gold rush in the 1840s. Their ensemble music and dance, characterized by a sobbing, pulsating vocal quality, layers of ostinatos underlying the soloist, and paucity of instruments, is mainly ceremonial. Personal songs are used primarily to affect nature and one's daily affairs. Organized, ceremonial team gambling—generally a male activity—is a popular venue for music, and the instruments used are drums and rattles.

In central and southern California, the vocal style is somewhat relaxed, and the rattle serves as the primary instrument. Other than a few Spanish loanwords (in Diegueño bird songs from the Yuma tribal area near the Mexican border) the music in more southerly regions of California also reflects little influence from outsiders.

The Southwest
Kiva murals of the fourteenth to the sixteenth centuries, and Spanish accounts starting in 1540, show that masks, decorative textiles, and body painting were important arts to Pueblo Indian culture. The flutist Kokopeli adorns many petroglyphs and pieces of ancient pottery throughout the Southwest. Archaeologists have found prehistoric pottery depicting copper bells worn by dancers.

The large Pueblo rawhide and wooden drums, hand-held gourd rattles, and the turtle-shell, deer-hoof, and marine-shell strung rattles, worn by the dancers, are the most important instruments. The singers rehearse together to create a full-unison choral sound. Many of the dances involve men singing and dancing simultaneously in lines or moving in a procession. Women participate in the winter as featured dancers in front of the men; in the summer they join in couples' dances and in large group dances.

Among the Apache and Navajo, both personal and ceremonial songs were important. Curing rituals and girls' puberty ceremonies are the best-known contexts for music among the southern Athabascan. The water drum, the rattle, and voice are the primary instruments. The bullroarer, a thin, whirling wooden plaque suspended on a string—which survives in American popular culture as a child's toy—was still being used at the end of the twentieth century for ritual and ceremonial events, primarily in the Southwest. The Navajo use it in the Yeibichei and the Apache in the Mountain Spirit Dance.

The Plains

The "Indian music" best-known by the general public is that of the Plains. From Canada to Texas one can find singers and dancers performing ancient ceremonies. The smaller, more isolated bands of the colonial period did not have the large drums that became associated with twentieth-century Indians. For sacred ceremonies they used small hand-held frame drums, each beaten by a singer. If several men were singing together, each held a drum and played it in unison with the others. The pulsating vocal style (a variation in both pitch and loudness), often loud and somewhat individualistic, is a hallmark of the Plains singer. In addition to drums, rawhide rattles accompanied singing. Flutes were reserved primarily for love songs.

The East

Music of the Eastern Woodlands, the Northeast, and Southeast shared many traits. Many of the dances and songs were responsorial, incorporated shouts and animal cries, were performed by both genders, and circumscribed a counterclockwise dance area. Most featured hand-held rattles and water drums along with strung rattles worn on the dancers' bodies. Vocally, the singing tended to be nasal and somewhat high-pitched. Among the Iroquois of the Northeast, many of the ceremonies occurred in the longhouses, particularly in midwinter. In the Southeast most occurred outdoors with the summer First Fruits or Green Corn ceremony as the centerpiece.

THE CLASH OF COLONIALISM AND NATIVE AESTHETICS

Indian music for the most part was regarded by the early colonists as "the devil's work," and like folk, popular, and African musics, it had little influence on the musical life of colonial America. Indian religious practices, the nexus

for most dances, in fact were often banned by the churches and colonial governments. European clerics and settlers in the North American colonies converted many Indians to Christianity (often by coercion) and drove them from their aboriginal lands. Missionaries frequently performed the quasi-governmental role of overseeing the education and Christian life of Native Americans, which involved extermination of Native practices, religions, and languages. As a result, many singers, dancers, and traditional religious practitioners were no longer able to perform their arts and lifeways in their customary places at the accustomed times.

Recognizing that Indians loved music, missionaries began early to capitalize on that knowledge and use it to proselytize. Often Indians were lured to the missions to learn and sing new songs. Many Indians became Christians, and some began translating and composing their own hymns. While most sang melodies without harmony, the Cherokee and Tlingit were famous for their improvised harmonies based on the European models.

During the 1680–1696 Pueblo Indian revolt in New Mexico and Arizona, which forced the Spanish conquerors and missionaries south to El Paso, the Indians gained a few concessions concerning moderation of religious persecution from the Europeans. After the revolt, the Native religions and dances were practiced, to some extent, alongside Catholic rituals.

CONCLUSION

Music pervaded Indian life starting from creation stories and ending with death and memorial. Like other Americans, Eskimo and Indian peoples sang and danced to many varieties of music while reserving their own sacred and traditional music for special occasions. Indian musicians composed music to fit the times, sometimes mimicking their colonial counterparts, while keeping many of their old styles, forms, and contexts intact. Alternately, Indians embraced Western, popular and religious music, often integrating those styles with their own texts and tunes. American Indian music had little influence on colonial American society, but emphasized and continues to emphasize the traditions and values of Indian people. For many centuries Indians of North America danced; played and sang music, performed speeches and ceremonies; and carved and painted walls, ornaments, and everyday household items exhibiting group and individual artistry. These traditions survived alongside European-derived forms primarily because of their value to the individual Indian societies.

BIBLIOGRAPHY

Collaer, Paul. *Music of the Americas: An Illustrated Music Ethnology of the Eskimo and American Indian Peoples.* New York, 1973.

Davis, Ronald L. *A History of Music in American Life.* Vol. 1, *The Formative Years, 1620–1865.* Huntington, N.Y., 1982.

———. *Handbook of North American Indians.* Edited by William C. Sturtevant. Vols. 9 and 10, *Southwest,* edited by Alfonso Ortiz. Washington, D.C., 1979, 1983.

Hulton, Paul. *America 1585: The Complete Drawings of John White.* Chapel Hill, N.C., 1984.

Jones, Charles C., Jr. "Music and Musical Instruments." In his *Antiquities of the Southern Indians, Particularly of the Georgia Tribes.* New York, 1873.

Lescarbot, Marc. *The History of New France.* Edited by W. L. Grant and H. P. Biggar. Toronto, Ontario, 1907–1914. Originally published in 1617.

Quinn, David B., and Alison M. Quinn, eds. *The First Colonists: Documents on the Planting of the First English Settlements in North America, 1584–1590.* Raleigh, N.C., 1982; rev. ed. of *Virginia Voyages from Hakluyt.* London and New York, 1973.

Stevenson, Robert. "English Sources for Indian Music Before 1882." *Ethnomusicology* 17 (1973):399–442.

Strachey, William. *The Historie of Travell into Virginia Britania, 1612.* Edited by Louis B. Wright and Virginia Freund. London, 1953.

Charlotte Heth

SEE ALSO **Mission Communities** and **Native American Religions.**

XV

EDUCATION

THEORIES OF EDUCATION
PATTERNS OF SOCIALIZATION
SCHOOLS AND SCHOOLING
HIGHER EDUCATION

THEORIES OF EDUCATION

THE BRITISH, DUTCH, AND FRENCH COLONIES

THE POWER OF religious belief, always an incentive for the sea venturers who earlier had found a new world for Europeans, was paramount in establishing the tone, purpose, and method of seventeenth-century colonial schooling. In the earliest years of European settlement, simple lessons from the Bible, in a catechism, were often used to teach literacy. Teaching was done informally by anyone whose obligation or desire was to instruct the young. Missionaries and settlers with authoritative church connections took on the formal role of teacher along the eastern coast and the riverways of the northern reaches of colonization.

Beside the Saint Lawrence River in New France, Jesuit fathers taught a Roman Catholic catechism and Thomistic ethics, convinced that with this knowledge their charges, including those Native Americans whom they were able to convert from religions of nature, would escape hell and reach heaven. Similarly, Puritan parents, clergymen, and schoolmasters in New England, introduced their children to a determined Protestantism. Schoolmasters of New Amsterdam (later Manhattan), hired by the Dutch West India Company and licensed by the Classis of Amsterdam, taught disciplined behavior and a catechism from the Calvinist Dutch Reformed church. In the early years of colonization in Virginia, children were educated only by home instruction until some planters set up a few scattered schools where teaching generally comported with Church of England views. These views were reinforced gradually with the arrival of Anglican schoolmasters and tutors for the sons and daughters of rich planters. When William Penn's colony in 1700 was absorbing the educational ways of Quakers, as it later would absorb those of Lutheran Palatinate Germans and the Presbyterian Scotch-Irish, the remarkable variety of sectarian Protestant schooling was increasingly visible.

Despite intercolonial differences of theology and sponsorship, there was still an overall Christian educational consensus that worked locally for effective if not strong relationships among school, church, and civil authorities and that dictated the hiring, where possible, of schoolmasters who were screened for their piety and good character. In the absence of licensed teachers, all kinds of literate and devout people took up the task.

Christian indoctrination dominated primary educational theory for almost a century. In retrospect, it offered a rather well-worn chronicle for historians until the late twentieth century when Bernard Bailyn and Lawrence A. Cremin used a wider lens to view the American educational past as the transmission of cultures. Their newer historiography did not remove Christian belief as the centerpiece of educational theory, but their suggestions for social and comparative history, together with those of ethnohistorians, did underscore the singular and narrow legacy of early educational theory. White European settlers projected theories of learning that were incompatible with the cultural ways and beliefs of Native Americans and that were either withheld from or forced guardedly upon the other immigrant group, enslaved black people. Although a comparative study of colonial education thus becomes a wide inquiry into the history of differing and often conflicting cultures, the *theory* of primary education viewed as a system of formal ideas visited upon each "rising generation" of white colonists remains one of Christian premise. It moves but gradually with advanced instruction into the main channels of the Atlantic intellectual world carrying classical, Renaissance, and seventeenth-century scientific learning.

No clearer contemporary challenge to the exclusive character of liberal Western learning in the colonies can be summoned to mind than Samson Occom's chastising comment in 1770 to Eleazar Wheelock, renowned founder of Dartmouth College and earlier Occom's teacher. Occom, a Native American Mohegan, ordained minister, and extraordinary fundraiser in England for the college, wrote to Wheelock that it was the "general Sentiment of Indians" that Dartmouth would "never have much benefit" for them and that the College, founded in part to educate them, instead of becoming *Alma Mater* "will be too *Alba* [white] *Mater*."

A critical comparative view of colonial education must point, finally, to the scarcity of education for girls beyond primary Christian instruction and some reading. A small percentage attended general town schools or dame schools where they were taught household arts, "polite" social skills, music, possibly some arithmetic, or even some Latin. Talented, inquiring, and self-educated women were notable throughout the colonies, but the cause of women's education was not widely urged until after the revolution. Though colonial educational theory, initially pious and forceful, gradually became at advanced levels secular in tone and even elegantly stated in behalf of liberating intellect, it was meant chiefly for the instruction of young white males.

EDUCATING AND CONVERTING THE INDIANS

Church-sponsored education went hand-in-hand with seventeenth-century nationalism and the growth of overseas empires. The farthest ranging, the most dramatic, and, ultimately, the most tragic effort to spread simple Christian education was made from the late sixteenth century to about 1673 by missionaries to the Native Americans. Early in the annals of New France, Jesuit fathers, working within their well-organized and disciplined Society of Jesus, walked or paddled in birchbark canoes across vast distances to bring their gospel teachings to Native American tribes in the Great Lakes and the upper Mississippi Valley regions. Within the history of Catholicism and in the saga of European exploration and empire building, these teacher-priests and explorers are heroic and well-remembered for their individual perseverance and iron will to teach their faith to the unconverted in uncharted lands and to convert the Native Americans. Their exploits are set forth in their annual reports from 1632 to 1672, *Jesuit Relations,* and in the writings of the gifted and magisterial nineteenth-century American historian Francis Parkman. Six Jesuit missionaries to the Huron who met torture and death in the 1640s at the hands of Iroquois allies of the British were canonized in 1930. One of these missionaries, Isaac Jogues, by himself taught the faith to some two thousand Huron. By 1689 Father Claude Jean Allouez is reported to have baptized ten thousand Indians.

On a smaller scale, in seventeenth-century New England two Puritan ministers, "Apostle" John Eliot in Massachusetts Bay and Roger Williams in Narragansett Bay, met their Native American neighbors on equal terms, and converted them to Christianity. Like the Jesuits, the ministers learned their language and even composed an Indian-language catechism and dictionary. The first Bible published in America was John Eliot's, in the Indian language. Eliot's "praying Indians" by 1676 numbered at least one thousand in fourteen villages where there were ordained Indian ministers and missionaries. Along the Delaware River in New Sweden the Swedish Lutheran minister and missionary John Campanius earlier had translated Martin

Luther's catechism into the Delaware Indian language. Extensive Protestant missionary and teaching efforts among the Indians were made by the Moravians (Renewed Church of the United Brethren) under the leadership of Count Nicholaus Ludwig von Zinzendorf. From Bethlehem and Nazareth, both in Pennsylvania, Moravians sent about fifty missionaries from Maine to the Carolinas in mid-eighteenth-century British North America.

Despite memorable successes at teaching Christianity to a relatively small percentage of seventeenth-century North American Native people, the missionary experience with interracial tolerance had largely failed by 1763 when France surrendered Canada to Great Britain. Recolléts and Sulpicians took their place in New France, but the early-seventeenth-century zeal for establishing missions waned. One missionary father reported in 1750 that the small villages of New France held only a few converts and much irreligion. Following King Philip's War in Massachusetts Bay (1676) only four of John Eliot's villages of praying Indians survived. After two centuries of work, missionary educators turned out to be minor actors in a long and complex drama of clashing empires, border warfare, enduring enmities among Native American tribes, antagonism between Catholic and Protestant colonies, land hunger in white settlers, and inept colonial administration. In all of this, the Western grand educational theory of Christianizing the Indian became of secondary importance.

Lost within the imperial struggles was the recognition of flaws within the missionary theory itself. In reality, one culture imposes its ideas upon another only with difficulty; at times all attempts end in futility. Education is a fragile instrument of cultural and national expansion that can be too easily replaced with instruments of power. In the case of Indian-white relations a Christian theory of education was hardly adaptable to Indian belief and tradition. For the Native Americans, personal sinfulness was an alien concept, although wrongdoing was to be avoided. Punishment for wrongdoing by a supernatural being who has established a moral code not to be transgressed was beyond the Indians' ken. Generally Native Americans strove to avoid thoughts and actions that would disturb the harmony of nature and the universe. Evil for them

came from whatever upset this natural balance. The Native American moral code was, moreover, group-centered, not individual. Moral transgressions meant jeopardizing the safety of a village or even of a tribe. Missionaries preaching the existence of a supernatural being who would judge one's destiny for eternity, the idea of hell, or the Puritan idea of individual unceasing efforts to deserve salvation were not in tune with Indian religions of nature and temporal harmony. Native Americans were, however, receptive to the ideas of living together for the common good and of a caring, not a vindictive, Great Spirit. These concepts Indians could place alongside traditional beliefs and taboos.

EDUCATION IN NEW FRANCE AND NEW AMSTERDAM

In contrast to these great themes of cultural tension and to the enormous efforts of missionaries in New France, theories of formal schooling for settlers' children there are but a footnote. And by contrast with the English colonies, New France had a small population: in 1763 there were only about 75,000 people in the Saint Lawrence region, compared with more than 250,000 in the English colonies. The primary theory and objective of all early schooling was instruction in Roman Catholicism and preparation for church membership. The chief teaching tool was always a catechism, whether employed by the parish priest or members of the religious orders: Jesuits, and later Ursulines, Sisters of the Congregation of Notre Dame, Capuchins (in Louisiana), and Sulpicians, using the pedagogical theories of Saint John Baptist de LaSalle, a Christian Brother. Catechisms were generally similar in commanding Christian duty, obedience to church laws, piety, and social rectitude. Rigid classroom discipline characterized teaching in New France as throughout the other colonies. A tradition of dull and repetitive lessons was partly broken in the *petites écoles* of Sulpician schoolmasters and of the Sisters of the Congregation in Quebec; these groups attempted to improve teacher-student relations and to group students according to ability. Even so, absolute classroom silence and sober decorum were the rule. Only with the arrival of Christian Brother programs at the beginning of the eighteenth century, introduced by the Sulpicians, was primary instruction aimed at discovering talent and aptitude in each child, at nurturing a kind and paternal attitude toward the child, and at cultivating the senses as the basis of intellectual life. Concentration and reflection, so taught de LaSalle, were the focus of true education as opposed to mere training. The method in the rural schools involved senior students' instructing junior students. A student's passing to the next grade was dependent upon demonstrable mastery of the subjects.

Two developments in Quebec represented departures from seventeenth-century educational tradition. Girls were generally educated better than boys in convents and schools run by laywomen. Formal training for the legal and medical professions had to be pursued in France, and an apprenticeship system served in the training of artisans. An excellent school of hydrography was established in Quebec to train pilots and cartographers. At the college level Latin was pervasive, as at Harvard and Yale, but at the Collège de Quebec, the teaching of moral theology took on a different emphasis from that found at the British colleges. At the Collège de Québec the flavor of learning was Thomistic, tending to Aristotelian inquiry and, again in contrast to Calvinism, holding a mildly optimistic view of humanity's capacities to direct its own destiny.

Theories of education in the relatively short-lived Dutch colony of New Amsterdam generally accorded with those in Puritan New England. Yet here educational practice differed in that girls were educated on an equal footing with boys, leading to a high literacy rate among women. The intent of education, here as elsewhere, was conversion and sectarian loyalty but also, in keeping with Dutch mercantile policies, the preparation of the rising generation to strengthen national commerce.

NEW ENGLAND PURITANISM AS EDUCATION

Nowhere in the polyglot experiment of European cultures in an alien environment was the design of educational ideas more clearly drawn or more enduring in American history than in New England. Some of the most penetrating and most memorable writing by twentieth-century American historians has dealt with the life and ideas of seventeenth-century Massachusetts Bay Puritan communities. Throughout these closed, corporate, orthodox Congregational villages, daily existence and spiritual life were intertwined. Intense Calvinist conviction founded these communities and dictated methods for instructing the young. Indeed, there were no "theories" of education in the sense of programs unrelated to church doctrine. There was, however, a prevailing theory of the child, a mixed medieval and Calvinist picture of young human nature as corrupt and willful. Because "in Adam's fall, we sinned all"—that famous line from *The New-England Primer* (1690)—education was aimed at commencing Christian regeneration. Learning to overcome one's natural depravity was the first step for every child, whose entire life was expected to be a preparation for salvation.

The universal teaching device for the very young who could not yet read was a catechism, questions with set oral responses on church doctrine and biblical knowledge and on the child's earthly and spiritual duties. As moral injunction it became memorized social prescription. From some five hundred catechisms, most of them composed by Bay clergymen and graded for various age levels and capacities, a few were given to the child to master at home up to the age of seven or eight years. Much used in the first decades of the colony was *The Foundation of Christian Religion, Gathered Into Six Principles to Be Learned of Ignorant People That They May Be Fit to Heare Sermons With Profit, etc.* (1591), written by William Perkins, the revered Puritan divine of Christ College, Cambridge University. By mid seventeenth century the Westminster Assembly's *Shorter Catechism* (ca. 1647) became popular with family catechists, but even more popular was *Spiritual Milk for Boston Babes in Either England* (1656), written by the leading Boston minister and Puritan polemicist John Cotton.

The first reading lessons were couched in Christian belief. They customarily began with a hornbook, a single page protected by a transparent sheet of horn, on which were written the alphabet, some syllables to be sounded out, and the Lord's Prayer or the Apostles' Creed. The hornbook was used together with a simple catechism. After came a primer or a small reader on the elements of the Christian faith, always including the Lord's Prayer, the Apostles' Creed, and the Ten Commandments (Decalogue). In the first decades of the colony Edmund Coote's *The English Schoole-Maister* (1596) was the primer most used. By about 1690 *The New-England Primer* came into lasting fashion. This renowned little book was the only New England grammar-school textbook in use for the next fifty years and remained in use for another fifty. More than three million copies of *The New-England Primer* were sold, and it ranks with the Bible, Thomas Paine's *Common Sense* (1776), Noah Webster's blue-backed *Spelling Book* (1783), which replaced it, and Harriet Beecher Stowe's *Uncle Tom's Cabin* (1852) as an all-time best-seller in early American history.

All the Puritan instructional tools were loaded with injunctions to piety, upright character, obedience to parental and civil authority, industry, and frugality—aspects of Puritanism that twentieth-century critics such as H. L. Mencken and D. H. Lawrence lampooned in a stereotype of grim dutifulness and sobriety. Moderns, however, miss the essential purpose of these teaching weapons of orthodoxy if they forget their overarching context. The Puritan adult, as well as the child, lived in a world of belief, of mystery, of lingering medieval superstitions, and of agonizing spiritual self-concern. The God whom they feared, sought, and worshiped was ever-present, all-knowing, and all-powerful, and ultimately transcended human understanding. The aim of Puritan education was to authenticate this belief system and this world within the young and to bring them to a realization of their lowly condition before the Almighty.

Educating to strive for election to heaven—although salvation was never ensured for anyone—carried as many implicit social as explicit religious commands. It is hard to separate the social and the religious in Puritan dogma, as in other cultures of faith, considering the closely knit structure of Puritan villages. The immediate social agent of teaching was, of course, the family, a condition true of almost all North American colonial settlements. But the special alliance between New England clergy and families guaranteed the power of belief as social perspective. The clergy, most of whom in the first generation of settlement were graduates of Emmanuel College, Cambridge, a font of Puritanism, prized learning, an attitude proven by the establishment of the Boston Latin School in 1635 and enhanced by the presence of at least 114 university-trained people in the colony by 1640.

From a vast literature of sermons and discourses, the family emerges as the guarantor of a literate community. Within each "little commonwealthe"—or each "little cell of righteousness," Edmund S. Morgan's modern label—the father was master of all things. He was responsible for the education and the religious welfare of all under his roof, including servants and apprentices, who might have come from neighboring families. Obedience to the father by each member of the family mirrored a hierarchy of social authority and deference among believers in the community at large. The village minister speaking in support of paternal authority relied on another key Puritan doctrine, reiterated in turn by family catechists even to the very young: one's obligation in life was to be diligent in following one's proper calling. The idea that everyone has an appropriate station in life conformed generally to the ancient image of a Great Chain of Being in which humankind is stationed above the brutes but beneath the angels. It was well expressed in the Italian Renaissance by humanist writers like Giovanni Pico della Mirandola, refined as Protestant doctrine by John Calvin, and delivered as Puritan text by William Perkins in his *Treatise of the Vocations or Callings of Men* (1603). Puritan writers always cited 1 Cor. 7:20 as their first authority: "Let every man abide in the same calling wherein he was called." Commitment to a calling, so the young were instructed, was one's portion in fulfilling the covenant that the whole community had made with God. What a later age may see as acquiescence in social apathy or political domination, the Puritan taught as the promise of community harmony in a precarious existence facing a wilderness.

COTTON MATHER: PREPARING FOR SALVATION

Although his most effective years bridged the seventeenth and eighteenth centuries, Cotton Mather epitomizes the role of the clergyman-teacher in seventeenth-century New England.

Indefatigable pedant and celebrant of Congregational orthodoxy, though not the primitive Calvinist that Jonathan Edwards soon came to exemplify, Mather brilliantly made real the image of pastor as educator set forth by John Calvin in his *Ecclesiastical Ordinances* of 1541 and reaffirmed by the Synod of Dort in 1618–1619. Neither schoolmaster nor professor, Mather began assisting his father, Increase Mather, at Boston's Second Church in 1680. He made the pulpit his teaching podium and turned his writings—there were some 450 books from his quill pen—into texts for the faithful of all ages. His ministry taught as it preached and matched, if it did not in some ways exceed, the intellectual leadership of his two grandfathers, John Cotton and Richard Mather, and of his father.

Four sermons preached and published by Mather between 1696 and 1708 demonstrate the kind of community instruction under clerical admonition for which he and his predecessors were famous. His exhortations deal with what a later secular age would call the "social process" of education. Mather's first purpose was, of course, to fix everyone's mind upon the elusive goal of salvation. But along the way he told his people much about the daily utility and community aims of learning. In *A Good Master Well Served* (1696), he explained in fifty-five pages all the duties and responsibilities of masters and their servants or apprentices. With infinite care and biblical justifications he promulgated an educational code for training in a trade or vocation. In his *A Family Well-Ordered* (1699) he went to the root of education, proclaiming that families are the "*Nurseries of all Societies. . . . Well-ordered families* naturally produce a *Good Order* in other *Societies*. When *Families* are under an *Ill Discipline,* all other *Societies* being therefor *Ill Disciplined,* will feel that Error in the *First* Concoction." In his *Cares About the Nurseries* (1702) he underscored the parental duty to catechize children regularly, calling upon parents to teach children well "in a profitable calling" and to make children "beneficial to human society." He warned against the "mischief of ignorance," by which he meant not only impiety but also the social uselessness of the uneducated person. In *Corderius Americanus* (1708), his famous verse elegy to the venerated Boston schoolmaster Ezekiel Cheever, Mather praised one who had sent forth his charges to "all

Good Employments" as well as to "the Tabernacle."

Mather's pronouncements after 1700 reflected changes occurring, in worldly and sometimes subtle ways, in educational thought as Puritan authority declined in Boston. As is often the case in times of intellectual change, deep currents of tradition persisted. In Mather's case these carried some of the medieval vision of Saint Augustine, in which humanity has a questioning but submissive relationship to God, there is a hierarchy of being, order and symmetry exist in nature and in human affairs, and a community of souls in the love of the same good can create the city of God on earth. Mather of course colored these ideas with Calvinism: human efforts and horizons are contained within the concept of the total sovereignty and central place of God as revealed by the Bible, rather than by reason or nature.

Even so, a new view of the cosmos crept around these thoughts. Isaac Newton had startled the world of learned Christians in the century between William Perkins and Mather. In keeping with his lifelong amateur interest in scientific inquiry, Mather was subject to the age of reason and passed beyond the jeremiads of his younger days. He acquired a new sense of the God of cosmic order. Mather wrote in *The Christian Philosopher* (1721): "It is now plain from the most *evident Principles,* that the Great GOD not only has the Springs of this immense *Machine,* and all the several Parts of it, in his own Hand, and is the *first Mover;* but that without His *continual Influence* the whole Movement would soon fall to pieces."

Confronting the new science, the bustle of commerce, and the rise to power of worldly men in his commonwealth, Mather modified his role as teacher and enforcer of orthodoxy in only one respect. The community, he preached, must work to save itself in this life as well as in the next by doing good. This was the message of his *Bonifacius* (1710), a sermon that Benjamin Franklin later made famous. Mather attempted to model his own advice by setting up schools for slaves and the poor, establishing Indian missions, distributing tracts, and generally urging others to found voluntary societies for good works. But these all must be aimed, so he insisted, at glorifying the Creator, not at furthering enlightened self-interest. So the problem of salvation remained constant and paramount with him. Life was after all a long education for the world to come.

Although this essay is concerned with educational theory, not result, one cannot leave Mather without commenting on the educational legacy of his teachings. Granted, their impact was mixed and is still the subject of historical debate. Mather left an air of intellectual rigidity touched with wonder, a self-righteousness, and an arrogance of faith common to many Puritan leaders, whose legacy passed along pride in one's tribe that a later age has finally come to repudiate as ethnocentrism spilling over into racism. Mather projected that pride into his history of the New England people as they heroically overcame adversity, *Magnalia Christi Americana; or, The Ecclesiastical History of New-England* (1702). This first ambitious and compendious history written in the colonies suggested a white, Christian mission to save a continent. And as with other cultures of the era, Puritan instruction, under Old Testament literal authority, segregated women within their own social sphere, though not spiritually, and expected wives to submit to their husbands. Against these concepts one can weigh Mather's work and that of his forebears in fostering a literate people with schools and colleges to support them, in unyieldingly teaching the ideal of the good community, and in teaching adherence to a moral code (not forgetting that theirs became at times exclusive and vengeful) so that moral men do not become an immoral society or succumb to barbarism.

BENJAMIN WADSWORTH AND NATURAL THEOLOGY

A tract derived from some sermons preached in 1712 by Benjamin Wadsworth and distributed widely repeated a theme familiar to Puritans: *The Well-Ordered Family: or, Relative Duties. Being the Substance of Several Sermons, About Family Prayer, Duties of Husbands & Wives, Duties of Parents & Children, Duties of Masters and Servants.* Though repetitive and didactic, this educational essay illustrates well the turn of mind among colonial teachers and preachers after 1700. In New England the high Calvinist texture of teaching was becoming frayed, though not dissolved, by mundane concerns within the region's economic and political life. The writings of John Locke would not be read for yet another five years, and the age of American Enlightenment was well over a half-century away. But seventeenth-century scientific ideas, particularly the mechanical conception of nature, were becoming part of advanced Puritan thinking. In England, Robert Boyle's work of 1663, reinforced by John Ray's in 1691, set forth in Puritan terms the ancient image of nature as God's clockwork. A divine providence, they argued, had fashioned the clockwork of nature to operate with preordained regularity for all time. This premise became eighteenth-century natural theology. It was introduced first to Massachusetts by the correspondence between Boyle and Increase Mather and by the arrival in 1688 of Boyle's student, Charles Morton, to assume the ministry at Charlestown.

Though learned Puritans came to rejoice in "the light of nature" shed upon human affairs, there was ever the crucial matter of where and how one chose to apply the concept. All agreed that the light of nature was second to the divine light of revelation through the Scriptures. But in his argument for the well-ordered family, Wadsworth argued for family piety first on the ground that "the very light of nature" reveals God's ruling providence in governing human affairs. Preaching on the same subject thirteen years earlier, Cotton Mather had gone first to the sanction of Scriptural law. Wadsworth emphasized civic stability through family order here and now for its own sake, whereas Mather had accented civic stability for community salvation. Though he was as much dedicated as Mather to home education to prepare his people for conversion and ultimately for salvation, Wadsworth stressed family harmony and piety for the sake of "Practical Godliness." Indeed, practicality was the hallmark of Wadsworth's thirty-year ministerial career at Boston's First Church and his term as president of Harvard in his final twelve years. Liberal in his educational policies and ever aware of shifting intellectual currents, he taught churchgoers and students to see the old Puritan verities with fresh emphasis from the age of reason.

JOHN LOCKE AND HIS FOLLOWERS

The name of John Locke is written large across the eighteenth-century Anglo-American Enlightenment. In education no less than in philosophy, political thought, and early psychology, Locke was guide or inspiration for transition into new ways of thinking. His impact upon America is analogous to that of Charles Darwin and Sigmund Freud in the next two centuries: every educated person knew about him, but it is hard to determine how many people actually read him. That issue is one that puzzles historians, but it may be profitless. His ideas and writings became widely known through frequent and glowing references in the press and in public discourse, and his books were well represented in colonial libraries. The first testament to his influence, however, is the wide readership accorded popularizers of his educational views. These writers simplified and built upon Locke's *Essay Concerning Human Understanding* (1690), the first major treatise on the empirical theory of knowledge and the first work to establish a psychological context for educational theory. Popularizers also referred to Locke's *Some Thoughts Concerning Education* (1693), a short book of advice to teachers that dealt with the need for a sound and healthy body in their pupils, the inculcation of virtue, and the employment of a useful curriculum.

The Lockean revolution in educational theory meant (1) recognition of the plastic or malleable nature of the newborn child, whose mind Locke conceived of as a blank tablet possessing no innate ideas, (2) acceptance that experience, not authority, develops simple ideas in the mind and that these ideas, when mixed with other ideas, become increasingly complex and guide our actions, (3) knowledge that children are to be nurtured or cultivated in their development, not indoctrinated first with received authority, and that they are to be treated as individuals who have different paces of learning. Throughout his writings Locke's style and temperament were balanced, moderate, and practical—hardly revolutionary, though his ideas were. In Locke's schema, teachers and students alike came to experience education as a process rather than a rigid program. Locke did not repudiate programmed instruction: he argued for less classical and more modern studies, but he did reject rote learning and rigid memorization. And despite his contemporaries' suspicions about his religious views, it became clear that Locke was a Christian and an Anglican even though his theology was latitudinarian and benign, like his attitude toward children. When it came to teaching the concept of virtue, Locke meant teaching behavior in accord with Christ's lessons. Teach virtue by practice, he advised, not by rule.

John Clarke

A book by an English schoolmaster, John Clarke, titled *Education Upon the Education of Youth in Grammar Schools* (1720) clarified systematically the ideal curriculum of a Latin grammar school. It became widely used in England and America and had gone into a third printing by 1740. (Clarke signed himself John Clarke of Hull in order to distinguish himself from others of the same name.) Although John Locke's little book on education, *Some Thoughts Concerning Education,* had appeared almost three decades earlier, and even though Clarke, as an admirer, filled his own book with copious quotations from Locke, his essay proved to be more serviceable than Locke's to grammar school and academy teachers for two reasons.

Clarke advised instruction in small private schools, which was in keeping with the development of numerous colonial private academies and which represented a compromise with the private tutoring for gentlemen's sons that Locke supported. Private tutoring was simply unworkable in the colonies, except for some of the wealthier, isolated southern planters' families, principally because not enough qualified tutors were available. Moreover, schooling in eighteenth-century America increasingly meant a collective, not an individual, learning situation, especially in New England and in the Middle Atlantic colonies, where the schoolhouse was replacing the family home as the place of formal elementary instruction. A second and more important reason is that Clarke's *Essay* went beyond Locke's by offering a detailed plan of studies for a classical grammar school. Clarke elaborated a Lockean method of schooling, and his clear, vernacular style demonstrated that Locke's ideas about education could be made revolutionary within education.

Lockean precepts detailed by Clarke were to become staples of modern schooling. Clarke taught that young people have their own rates of intellectual development, that learning means a progression from the simple to the complex, that it is futile to learn rules without experience, and that indiscriminate corporal punishment kills initiative in the pupil as well as creativity in the teacher. He also believed that utility and an economy of time and effort are indispensable in teaching and that the "vulgar" method of teaching Latin by constant memorization had to be abandoned in favor of using ponies or trots and learning the rules of grammar from one's teacher rather than by the book. Above all, Clarke stressed clear writing in English as the vehicle of clear thinking, not merely the learning of Latin for its own sake. In the age of the *Spectator* and of freshened economic life that mandated more education for English people, clear reasoning counted most. The thrust of Clarke's substantive advice is well-stated toward the end of his essay and summarizes the purpose of liberal education since his day: "The Art of Reasoning well, is the greatest and noblest Endowment of a human Mind, next to Virtue itself; and the Man that is happy in the Enjoyment of that Talent, will ever distinguish himself in all the Business he engages in."

Isaac Watts

The English dissenting clergyman, lay philosopher, religious poet, and hymn writer Isaac Watts did more to retain the name of Locke in the American public mind than any other popularizer. Watts through his books was as much a teacher of adults as of children. There was a continuing increase in England at mid eighteenth century in adult male literacy among tradesmen, artisans, and yeomen; the commercial and mercantile classes were expanding; there was a proliferation of newspapers, journals, and books; and schools for children of the middling classes were multiplying. Parallel developments occurred in America, though at first on a smaller scale, and they were slower in transforming colonial society. It was in the heightened cultural tempo of port cities—Boston, New York, and Philadelphia—that initial demand arose for instructional and inspirational manuals on self-improvement. Watts's books met this need, and his name became synonymous with "useful learning."

His works were composed with remarkable orderliness and simplicity to satisfy popular middle-class culture. *The Improvement of the Mind, To Which Is Added, A Discourse on the Education of Children and Youth* (1751; first published in 1741 without the *Discourse*), known to generations of Americans as "Watts on the Mind," went out of fashion only after a century of use. It was essentially Lockean in philosophy. Maintaining that "all persons are under some obligation to improve their understanding," Watts repeated Locke's axiom about sensation and reflection as the basic experiences that furnish knowledge. But he added his five "eminent means" of improving knowledge: observing, reading, attending lectures, engaging in conversation, and pursuing study. In his section on teaching he underscored reason and understanding as the two primary faculties of the mind that he would have the teacher cultivate in students like "a skillful gardener"—an analogy that occurs in nineteenth-century child-study literature. His theme that teachers must understand youthful characteristics and tailor their methods to "the temper and inclination of the child" is Lockean, liberal, and modern. Two centuries later John Dewey would make a similar argument profoundly, though not so clearly.

In the *Discourse* Watts sustained Lockean sentiments by urging teachers to stimulate children's curiosity and to teach children to observe their surroundings. Memory must be trained; judgment and reasoning must be built upon the child's own experiences and reflections. At the level of academy instruction Watts argued for practical subjects—logic, mathematics, geometry, astronomy, natural philosophy (the nascent biological and physical sciences), and history—and he included poesy. He did not stress different subject matter for boys and girls, though he approved the custom of educating younger girls for "the affairs of the household" as ordained in Titus 2:5 and Tim. 5:14. And he advised parents of the "middle and lower ranks

425

of life who design their children for trades and manufactures" to avoid sending them to Latin and Greek schools.

He was not one to propose social revolution through education; a deferential and class-conscious society was his world. But for him the religious sanction of education served as a kind of egalitarianism. Just as the Puritans had preached that all people are equal as sinners in the sight of God, so too, for Watts, were his compatriots made "equal," so to speak, by piously educating themselves to a calling in life that could through their industry gain them economic and material equality with one another. Thus the Puritan ethic merged with the myths and the reality of expectant capitalism. Isaac Watts was reinforcing Benjamin Franklin's example.

John Witherspoon

The most significant book on child training written by an American between the time of Cotton Mather and the year of Horace Bushnell's *Views of Christian Nurture* (1847) was John Witherspoon's *Letters on Education*. They were written in 1765 in Scotland, where Witherspoon achieved prominence as a leader of the Evangelical Party of Presbyterianism; they were first published in the *Pennsylvania Magazine* in 1775, seven years after Witherspoon's arrival in New Jersey to head the College of New Jersey (now Princeton University). Here he became not only a memorable college president who guided an astonishing array of future leaders through their undergraduate years, but also a great civic leader in his own right, one who led in the movement toward American independence, signed the Declaration of Independence, and helped to ratify the Constitution.

The *Letters*, which were reprinted five times by 1822, illustrate an accommodation of religious belief to secular social conditions that characterizes American education from the prerevolutionary years through the mid nineteenth century. They are professedly concerned with the religious upbringing of children. But what really emerges from them is counsel to parents on how to raise their children to fit a culture that was increasingly secular, interdependent, urban, and upwardly mobile, though still deferential toward its leaders. The result is advice that mixes Calvinist doctrine with some Enlightenment concepts of child rearing. The Bible is no longer the primary authority; it is a support. A family must seek divine approval, but there is little talk of salvation or damnation, aside from asserting the reality of hell. The injunctions and rewards of a good life are essentially social, this-worldly, and humane. One must live, Witherspoon wrote, so as to make religion appear respectable. Children evince a religious spirit if they are taught to follow parental examples of social grace, kindliness, humility, generosity, and dignity. Piety and politeness merge. Witherspoon turns child training from a religious to a moral process. Parents are instructed to guide their children toward social harmony rather than to teach them first the way to salvation. Doubtless it was their concern with the present condition of the child and his or her future place in the world, written with the tone of old religious authority, that made the *Letters* so well received.

The *Letters* are partial to Lockean inductive logic: in reasoning it is safer "to trace facts upward than to reason downward." Their advice on parental discipline is also Lockean: solemnity is preferable to severity, though "the rod itself is an evidence of love." At this point, however, Witherspoon begins to leave Locke. Parental discipline dispensed without passion must be dictated by a sense of duty and by conscience. This innate conscience, or moral faculty, is the key instrument in Witherspoon's discussion here and throughout his writings. It demarcates Scottish common-sense academic philosophy, whose first spokesman in America was Witherspoon, from the Lockean picture of individuals born without innate ideas. The presence of an inborn moral sense in small children, Witherspoon contends, makes them susceptible to good example. Through discipline, when necessary, recalcitrant children have their consciences awakened. With this simple picture of young human nature, Witherspoon introduced Americans to a changing way of thought that modified Lockean teaching and helped to greet a nineteenth-century optimistic view of human potential.

BENJAMIN FRANKLIN: PRINTER

Benjamin Franklin defies easy characterization. There is some paradox in the educational influence he yielded upon a great number of his fellow Americans. On one side, professing no theory of education, he educated Americans in a way of life that sought fulfillment and success. So he in effect sponsored a theory of education with a broad social definition. Much impressed by Cotton Mather's *Bonifacius,* which he knew from his years as an apprentice printer in his native Boston, Franklin formed his Junto, or club for self-improvement and mutual assistance, with some friends four years after he arrived in Philadelphia in 1723. Mather's advice to form voluntary associations and adult education groups to promote religion and civic morality was turned by Franklin to the ends of secular practicality and specific vocational need. The discussions in his Junto of mundane and philosophical issues were, to Franklin's mind, no less moral than Mather's proposals. Likewise, as Poor Richard in his widely read *Almanack* (1732–1757), he instructed an aspiring people in the ways of getting ahead or of acquiring middle-class habits. He not only articulated Mather's and Isaac Watts's advice, but he also spoke for two American ways of thought, the Puritan and the pragmatic—one formed long before his time and the other promulgated long after him. These two channels of thought, so opposed to each other as formal "systems" of ideas, cut deeply into the American character and into American schooling.

On the other side, Franklin the astute civic leader knew precisely where a formal educational theory was most needed. He addressed this need with two proposals for secondary schooling. The first was his *Proposals Relating to the Education of Youth in Pennsylvania* (1749), which outlined the subjects to be taught in an academy. His theme was typically utilitarian, asserting that it would be well if students "could be taught *every Thing* that is ornamental: But Art is long, and their Time is short. It is therefore propos'd that they learn those Things that are likely to be *most useful* and *most ornamental,* Regard being had to the several Professions for which they are intended." The second specific proposal was his *Idea of the English School* (1751), in which he argued that a good command of written English, emphasizing thought and expression, is basic to a useful education. The term "English School" was in his day the name for a school that distinguished

its curriculum from the traditional Latin and Greek preparatory studies.

Franklin's *Idea* was largely adopted when the Philadelphia Academy opened in 1751 with Franklin as the first president of its interdenominational board of trustees. Its practical studies, its secular though intensely moral ethos, and its socially liberal style became the model for the Age of the Academy that marked American formal schooling after the revolution. Displacing Latin grammar schools as the chief means of secondary education for a growing school-aged population, academies offered broader curricula of English grammar, ethics (but not theology), practical mathematics, commercial subjects, and foreign languages. In these respects Franklin's design anticipated the modern public high school.

In all of this it must not be forgotten that Franklin, though an autodidact with little formal schooling, was an unusual man of high learning, indeed, almost a Renaissance, or broadly learned, man, and an enlightened or empirically guided scientist in one person. At the time of the American Enlightenment, he personified the theory of enlightened intellect.

HIGHER EDUCATION

The theory of education in the first three colleges established in the colonies was defined by common purpose. Founded in 1636, in 1650 Harvard College received its charter, which spoke to "the advancement of all good literature, arts and sciences" and "the education of the English & Indian youth of this Country in knowledge: and godliness." At the College of William and Mary in Virginia, which did not begin college-level instruction until about 1729 although it was chartered in 1693, the founding instrument intended that "the Church of Virginia may be furnished with a Seminary of Ministers of the Gospel and that the Youth may be piously educated in good Letters and Manners, and the Christian Faith may be propagated amongst the Western Indians." The third colonial college, Yale, was founded in 1701 by ministers so that "youth may be instructed in the arts & sciences, who through the blessing of Almighty God may be fitted for publick employment, both in church

& civil state." Confirming this purpose, the Yale Charter of 1745, still in force today, declared that the school would continue to train "many worthy persons for the service of God in the state as well as in church." These intentions were echoed in the founding of the six remaining colonial colleges.

All but one were religiously inspired; the exception was the College of Philadelphia (1740). But none of them required Protestant religious tests for admission, and, although they did prepare students to enter the ministry, they were not thought of as theological seminaries. The common aim was to provide the kind of education that John Milton in England called "complete and generous [when it] fits a man to perform justly, skilfully, and magnanimously all the offices, both private and public, of peace and war." If these small colleges did not attain this ideal in every respect, their lapses resulted from their wilderness or provincial locations, a dearth of interest among their potential clientele, and the intensity of their religious atmosphere as reflected in their curricula. By the eve of the American Revolution the colleges had turned out only about five thousand graduates, of whom some twenty-five hundred were then living. As testimony, however, to the partial fulfillment of Milton's ideal, these alumni were leaders in colonial and early national life in a larger proportion to the total population than their small number suggests.

The curriculum that carried the burden of realizing the liberal ideal was a mixture of medieval, Renaissance, and Reformation subject matter; it was grounded upon proficiency in Latin, Greek, and some Hebrew; and it was slow to change. One hundred years after President Henry Dunster in 1642 had set the course of studies at Harvard, Yale College was teaching the same program with only minor changes. Distributed over four years (though only three until about 1652), the Harvard program began with a review of Latin and Greek, which were admission requirements, then added, in the second year, logic, Hebrew, rhetoric, and introductory natural philosophy. The third year offered natural, mental, and moral philosophy and geography; in their final year students reviewed Latin, Greek, logic, and natural philosophy, and they began mathematics. Divinity in the form of catechism followed them through all four years.

The slowness of the curriculum to change was due in part to the universal reluctance in any faculty to adopt change and in part to the unwillingness of religious dogma to yield ground. But change did come, and often within courses that retained their titles. Some contend, as does Samuel Eliot Morison for Harvard, that gradual liberalization of the curriculum was always going on at an institution indebted as much to the Renaissance as to the Reformation. The means of change were many: the development abroad of critical literature and of early biblical criticism, the constant attempts to shore up Puritanism by sharpening replies to antinomians, the *libertas philosophandi,* or freedom of discussion, and pamphlet disputes among colonial clergy intimately connected with affairs of the colleges, and, most of all, the arrival of the new sciences. The battle against secularization of the curriculum was unending, and it was losing. Increase Mather's correspondence with the English Illuminati, Boyle and Ray, in the 1690s was an early demonstration of the keenness of Puritan interest in scientific inquiry.

By 1728 President Benjamin Wadsworth of Harvard installed Isaac Greenwood as the first Hollis Professor of Mathematics and Natural and Experimental Philosophy. Greenwood's teaching not only brought fresh thinking to the college course; it also helped Harvard to adjust to the increasing emphasis on practical subjects common among private academy masters, in contrast to the wholly classical training of the grammar schools. As Harvard succumbed to "worldliness," throughout New England devout people looked to Yale as the bastion of orthodoxy. But even there, where earlier young Jonathan Edwards had excitedly read Locke, students by mid century were familiar with Descartes, Newton, and Copernicus.

Though slow to change, the college curriculum was far from static. Not only did the Enlightenment in America expand the place of natural science and mathematics; it also introduced into the curriculum in the 1760s the concept of the "man of letters" and belles lettres in the form of English orations, history, poetry, and literature. Reason and observation came to supplant divine law in the study of ethics. The theory of education became the theory of the liberal arts as enlightened intellect.

The Independent Reflector

In 1753 three young Presbyterian lawyers in New York City led an attack on a plan for Anglican control of a proposed college, to be called King's College (now Columbia University). The Anglicans, who resented Harvard and Yale as "nurseries of sedition," had been planning a college for several decades, had raised funds for it by a lottery, had appointed a substantial majority of Episcopalians as trustees of these funds, and had selected the Anglican Samuel Johnson as first president. The legal trio—William Livingston, John Morin Scott, and William Smith, Jr.—feared that the plan to establish the new college would lead to an Anglican establishment in the province and decided to publish their Presbyterian Whiggish views in their weekly journal, *The Independent Reflector*, whose first issue had appeared 30 November 1752. (The Anglicans, in turn, believed that their critics meant only to weaken the proposed college so that the recently established, Presbyterian-dominated College of New Jersey would lack competition.) Despite the efforts of *The Independent Reflector*, King's College was chartered, albeit in an atmosphere of suspicion and religious rivalry. The new college pursued a liberal direction under Johnson, and its board of control, like that at the College of Philadelphia, was interdenominational. Yet it never flourished in the years before the revolution because of Presbyterian and legislative opposition.

This episode linked issues of educational theory and of academic control directly with that of religious and intellectual freedom. *The Independent Reflector* was generally Miltonian and Lockean in tone. It echoed the anticlericalism and the Protestant latitudinarianism of eighteenth-century English Whiggism, especially the writings of Thomas Gordon and John Trenchard, two pamphleteers whose Lockean essays widely influenced American political thought before the revolution.

While it is tempting to read an inevitable future into the controversy over King's College, *The Independent Reflector* did not announce the arrival of modern secular and scientific arguments for academic freedom. It did, however, clearly portray the changing premises of higher learning that were forged out of the struggle for sectarian equality and religious freedom. Its argument that the state should favor no particular church or sect came as much out of the circumstances of sectarian rivalry as it did out of Lockean theory about religious toleration. Yet its argument for government impartiality toward all sects anticipated the consensus that eventually created the first American state universities.

Even more significant in retrospect are the specific teaching credo and theory of the essays that appeared in *The Independent Reflector*. They advocated the toleration of various creeds and biblical interpretations within a Protestant context, which modified Calvinism and formed the "American" character of higher education in British North America. Their petition for a modification of religious sponsorship and academic practice was answered in most of the colleges by the 1790s. Impelled by an American Enlightenment, by a drive for national cultural identity, and by the social stirrings within the new republic, a revised theory of purpose claimed higher education. Morality over theology, prudence over absolute norms of behavior, a combination of humane, scientific, and practical subjects in addition to classical learning, preparation for public life as well as for the ministry—these became the new standard for educational theory.

BIBLIOGRAPHY

The following works are guides to late twentieth-century literature in a vast field that includes educational, intellectual, and religious history. The books by Bailyn and Cremin inaugurated a new era in writing the history of American education; they include extensive bibliographies. Only some of the most relevant works that have appeared since their publication are also cited here.

Ahlstrom, Sydney E. *A Religious History of the American People*. New Haven, Conn., 1972.

Axtell, James. *The European and the Indian: Essays in the Ethnohistory of Colonial North America*. New York, 1981.

——. *The School Upon a Hill: Education and Society in Colonial New England*. New Haven, Conn., 1974.

Bailyn, Bernard. *Education in the Forming of American Society: Needs and Opportunities for Study*. Chapel Hill, N.C., 1960.

Cremin, Lawrence A. *American Education: The Colonial Experience, 1607–1783*. New York, 1970. Cremin's exhaustive bibliography includes full citations of works by authors mentioned in this essay, Edmund

S. Morgan and Samuel Eliot Morison, and the modern reprinting of *The Independent Reflector,* edited by Milton M. Klein.

Fiering, Norman. *Moral Philosophy at Seventeenth-Century Harvard: A Discipline in Transition.* Chapel Hill, N.C., 1981.

Foster, Stephen. *Their Solitary Way: The Puritan Social Ethic in the First Century of Settlement in New England.* New Haven, Conn., 1971.

May, Henry F. *The Enlightenment in America.* New York, 1976.

Middlekauff, Robert. *The Mathers: Three Generations of Puritan Intellectuals, 1596–1728.* New York, 1971.

Rudolph, Frederick. *Curriculum: A History of the American Undergraduate Course of Study Since 1636.* San Francisco, 1977.

Silverman, Kenneth. *The Life and Times of Cotton Mather.* New York, 1985.

Smith, Wilson, ed. *Theories of Education in Early America, 1655–1819.* Indianapolis, Ind., 1973.

Wilson Smith

SEE ALSO **Artisans; Childhood and Adolescence; The Legal Profession;** and **Literacy.**

THE SPANISH BORDERLANDS

THIS ESSAY FOCUSES on the theories that guided educational practice in the Spanish Borderlands. Because the borderlands were a part of New Spain, a great deal of the discussion centers on educational theory in that context. Education being broadly defined as the transmission and reproduction of culture, the discussion goes beyond theories that support formal pedagogy to include its social purposes. Thus the relationship between social and economic policy and educational practice is placed within the context of the conquest and colonization of the Native peoples of the borderlands.

SPAIN IN 1492

The year 1492, besides being the beginning of a new era for Spain as an imperial power, also marked the end of the long struggle to establish Christian hegemony over the Iberian Peninsula. With the defeat of the Muslims in Granada, all that remained to be accomplished was the eradication of Muslim and Jewish culture. The policy that emerged consisted of offering the Muslims and Jews the choice of either leaving or converting to Christianity. Thus began the policy of incorporating the conquered into the Spanish sociocultural milieu, a policy that was to have a tremendous impact on the Native people of the Americas who were soon to become subjects of the Spanish Empire.

The role of education in the formation of the nation was well-established by the end of the fifteenth century in Spain. The Renaissance and the humanist movement had a tremendous impact. Among the changes brought by the Renaissance was an increased role for education. The title *caballero* had become synonymous with "literate." Nearly every transaction, from simple economic agreements to major treaties, were put into writing. By the end of the fifteenth century, over four thousand new primary schools and several universities had been established in Spain.

The impact of the humanist movement in this transformation was enormous. Among the more influential of the humanists were Juan Luis Vives, Cardinal Francisco Jiménez de Cisneros, and Elio Antonio de Nebrija. In 1509 Cisneros founded the University of Alcalá de Henares, which he dedicated to free inquiry. In 1514 he gathered several humanist scholars, and in 1517 they completed the first Polyglot Bible. Among his visions was a system of education for the poor into which the religious life would be integrated. It was at Alcalá that Vives espoused a new and modern concept of education which was based on the idea that schooling should be for all, including women, regardless of economic status. Nebrija prepared a Latin-Spanish dictionary and the first modern Spanish grammar, which officially made Castilian the language of the nation and solidified the use of language as an instrument of empire.

The year 1492 found Spain in the midst of rapid change. Mired as it was in a crisis of reform versus tradition, the New World offered an escape from the attraction of absolute antiquity and Christian tradition. For the humanists the newly acquired territories offered the laboratory into which to project dreams and utopias. It was in this milieu that the early missionaries who came to the Americas, students of the humanists, undertook the task of reconstructing the world of the American natives.

NATIVE INTELLECTUALS

The enormous territory, the magnitude of the Native population, and the minuscule number of missionaries presented a monumental problem for the religious. This could have easily been solved by the creation of a Native clergy, an issue that became highly controversial. The College of Santa Cruz de Tlaltelolco, established in 1536, was founded for the purpose of creating a Native intellectual elite and a Native clergy. Natives were taught reading, writing, music, Latin, rhetoric, logic, philosophy, and medicine. On a visit to the college one Spaniard commented that the students could speak Latin with the elegance of Cicero. The experiment, however, was under tremendous pressure from opponents, and a great debate ensued over the degree of education the natives should receive and the ordination of Native priests.

Critics argued that the education of the Indians increased their resistance to accepting their lot as subjects in the new order. Moreover, the college, it was feared, would become a hotbed of heresy because the Indians were not spiritually capable of interpreting Scripture. To place the Bible in their hands would be to open the gates to widespread misinterpretation.

Ultimately, pressure from the Spanish settlers as well as from a large portion of the clergy was too much for the optimism of the founders of the college. Even Bernardino de Sahagún, one of its strongest supporters, eventually admitted publicly that the experiment was a failure and that Indians were not ready for the priesthood. The synod of 1555, which forbade the ordination of mestizos, Indians, and blacks, and the Códice Franciscano, which in 1570 stated that Indians should not be ordained, sealed the fate of the college and the experiment.

The use of the Indian languages in instruction was also controversial. The early missionaries, faced with the realities of a widely spoken lingua franca, Nahuatl, learned the language and utilized it as the language of instruction. Sermons

and catechisms were translated into Nahuatl. In order for the natives to become integrated into the new society, opponents argued, the use of the Spanish language was necessary. In 1550 Emperor Charles V (King Charles I of Spain) urged the religious to promote the use of Castilian in instruction, arguing that the only way to gain the conversion of the Indians to Christianity and to secure the learning of European customs and way of life was through the use of Spanish. In practice the message was by and large ignored by the missionaries throughout the century. Thus, in 1634 King Philip IV was forced to decree that the Indians must learn Spanish.

The Spanish Borderlands presented a unique problem for the missionaries in that there was not a lingua franca such as Nahuatl in use. In New Mexico, the primary borderland missionary field in the sixteenth and seventeenth centuries, there were several languages spoken in the various pueblos. This circumstance made it necessary for the missionaries to depend on Native translators under their tutelage in order to communicate with the natives. These young *doctrineros* from the pueblos became the link between the missionaries and the natives. Besides the language problem there was the shortage of missionaries in the borderlands; thus the issue of the degree of education the Indians should receive had strong ramifications. As late as 1706, Fray Juan Alvarez, who visited all of the missions in New Mexico, argued that because the missions were so few and so far apart, it was necessary to entrust to the Indians themselves the care of the doctrine; the missionaries would visit periodically.

The practice of educating a few young boys from the pueblos and utilizing them as aides in the indoctrination of the rest of the villagers was customary in the Spanish Borderland missions. It was not without its pitfalls, however, for the Spaniards, as is evident in the case of Estevan Clemente, a native of the Tompiro nation in the middle of the seventeenth century. Educated by the friars and literate in Spanish and Latin, Clemente became the governor of all of the Salinas pueblos just east of present-day Albuquerque. Highly trusted by the Spaniards, he ministered to the Indians and wrote an essay urging against participation in Native dances and worship of Native deities. Unbeknownst to the Spaniards, he was plotting their expulsion, an offense for which he was hanged.

RELIGIOUS SYNCRETISM

A major theoretical debate was waged over the inclusion of indigenous practices in the educational process. A prime example was the conflict over the cult of the Virgin of Guadalupe, at Cerro de Tepeyac in the Valley of Mexico, among the religious in the sixteenth century. The site, which had been the destination of pilgrims long before the arrival of the Spaniards, was where the Mexican Indians paid reverence to the female deity Tonantzin. The archbishop of Mexico, Alonso de Montúfar (1553–1572), supported the cult, as had his predecessor Juan de Zumárraga, who organized the building of a chapel on the site in the 1530s. Most Franciscan missionaries, however, were vehemently opposed to the practice, viewing it as the perpetuation of idolatry.

Unable to obliterate the Native practices, the missionaries were compelled to incorporate them into their pedagogy. The Virgin of Guadalupe became the patron saint of the Native Americans. The religious Christianized a great deal of the Native song and dance. The contemporary Mexican song form *corrido*, for example, emerged from the pre-Columbian Mexican *tocotín*. In the borderlands this was a common practice. The Santuario de Chimayó in northern New Mexico is one example of a pre-Columbian place of worship converted into a Christian shrine that still attracts tens of thousands of pilgrims from throughout the Southwest. A great deal of Spanish colonial religious art from New Mexico also reflects this trend in religious syncretism, with Native motifs contained in Christian themes. Much of the folkloric song and dance still practiced by the Chicano people of New Mexico, such as the Comanche dances dedicated to the Holy Child of Attocha, had its origins in this period.

FEAR AND EDUCATION

While the humanist-influenced religious (particularly the Franciscans) promoted the use of reason in education to achieve a voluntary conversion of the Indians, in practice, much of the education was based more on the use of fear. It was common practice among some of the early missionaries in New Spain to burn animals alive to demonstrate the concept of hell. In the Spanish Borderlands the burning was extended to humans. In the Río Grande pueblo of Arenal in New Mexico, over four hundred males were burned alive in 1540 as an example to other natives who refused to submit to Christianity. While the use of education as a means of voluntary conversion, as espoused by the humanists, continued, in practice it was fear of the military power of the Spaniards that ultimately forced the Indians to submit.

THE ENLIGHTENMENT AND ITS IMPACT ON EDUCATION

The Bourbon reforms, initiated by Charles III in the middle of the eighteenth century, were part of a move to increase monarchical authority in the colonies and rejuvenate the imperial economy. The reforms were economic, administrative, political, and military. Among them were tax increases, the promotion of industry, increased communications in the outlying areas, fortification of defenses, and decreasing the power of the church. Administratively, the reforms had a direct impact on the Spanish Borderlands. The region was reorganized and placed in the jurisdiction of the Provincias Internas.

The theoretical shift in Spanish policy toward its largest colony had a tremendous impact on the role that education was to play. During the first two centuries after the conquest, the focus of education had been to construct a new society which the Spanish authorities now feared was out of their control. Among the changes were the secularization of the missions and the expulsion of the Jesuits from the colonies (1767). The military was no longer to focus solely on the defense of the borders; it was also to ensure internal security. The issue of social control in New Spain had become paramount.

After a significant portion of the population had been successfully detribalized and population centers in the borderlands had increased, there was a shift in focus from the reconstruction of Native culture to the maintenance of the new social order. The famine of 1785–1786 in New

Spain, one of the worst demographic catastrophes of the century, sparked a concern over the large numbers of hungry and potentially violent children who filled the streets. The social fabric that had been established was in danger of coming apart, and schools for the children of the poor were seen as the solution. Among the rationales for promoting the founding of primary schools was the perceived increase in the corruption of customs among the lower classes. This signified a shift in the responsibility for maintaining social order from the church and the family to the state. It was argued that it was a Christian duty for those with means to contribute to the education of the children of the poor. All over New Spain, schools that had been created for the children of the elite were now taking in children of the lower classes.

The issue of language use, which attracted much attention during the sixteenth and seventeenth centuries, was never fully resolved in the Spanish Borderlands. Although there are contradictory reports during the near century and a half of missionization, some missionaries in the mid eighteenth century were writing to their superiors that aside from the *doctrineros* the Pueblos were still not able to speak Spanish. The issue of language use among the natives was given great emphasis, and in 1782 Charles III ordered the establishment of primary schools for the Indians to learn Spanish. The authorities were urged to use noncoercive means to persuade the Indians to send their children to those schools.

The last two decades of the eighteenth century saw a tremendous growth in primary schools in all areas of New Spain. While this increase was especially important in the larger population centers, primary schools also began to emerge in the borderlands. One new trend that emerged in New Mexico was the growth of primary schools in the Indian pueblos. Previously, education in the pueblos was solely the charge of the missionaries. The primary schools that appeared during this period were most often administered by private teachers who contracted with the pueblos. In fact, one government official arguing for the establishment of primary schools among the Navajo cited the peaceful nature of the pueblo and the existence of schools in their communities as a rationale.

Militarily the reforms brought about a new policy that included making peace with the Comanche and the elimination of the Apache, a policy with educational implications. The militarily superior Comanche were able to make war on the Apache and sell captured children to the New Mexicans. The borderland settlers, working from the accepted theory that encouraged the purchasing of young Indian captives to save their souls, felt morally justified in acquiring them from the Comanche. Consequently many Apache children were incorporated into the settler populations through a process of informal education, which occurred mainly in the homes of their owners. The children of the Comanche leadership, on the other hand, received a different, more formal education in schools in Santa Fe. Thus education served the maintenance of social order by the elimination of the Apache as a threat through the incorporation of their children into a new social order, while the children of the more politically influential Comanche were educated on a voluntary basis.

Perhaps the greatest impact on demographics and the construction of a new social order was the commonly held theory that gave the populace moral justification for ransoming captives. Whether this was in fact the sole rationale among the settlers is difficult to ascertain. There were priests as late as the eighteenth century who argued that the captives were merely being introduced into a form of bondage. There is ample evidence that some of the captives were treated more as slaves than as neophytes being brought into the fold of Christianity. The ideological basis for this practice was embedded in the widely held belief that Indians who did not submit to Christianity willingly could be captured so that their souls might be saved. In 1752 the governor of New Mexico argued for the toleration of the practice to ensure Indians' instruction in the Catholic faith, and ultimately their salvation.

The theoretical frameworks that had emerged in Spain during the fourteenth and fifteenth centuries remained very influential throughout the sixteenth, seventeenth, and eighteenth centuries in the Spanish Borderlands. The idea that the conquered should be converted and integrated into the dominant Spanish sociocultural milieu, first utilized in response to the

Muslim and Jewish population in the Iberian Peninsula after 1492, also served as the rationale for the incorporation of the Native Americans. In essence the theory led to the widely utilized practice of colonizing the borderlands with the Native Americans themselves. Thus, while colonization by the English focused on importing settlers to move to the conquered territories and removing the natives, the Spanish utilized a form of mental colonization. That is, the objective was a conquest through education: the reconstruction of the Native mental frameworks and the consequent reordering of Native society. In general, theoretical debates among educators in New Spain centered on language use, the degree to which the Indians should be educated, and the incorporation of Native customs and practices into the new social order. Ultimately, resolution of these issues rested on more practical considerations, such as the shortage of priests and the resilience of the natives in maintaining their practices.

By the eighteenth century a new social order had become well established, and the role of education changed from reconstruction to maintenance of the new order. Within the new order the poor classes had become a threat to the social fabric, and education was perceived as the solution, prompting a tremendous growth of primary schools throughout the province, including the Spanish Borderlands.

BIBLIOGRAPHY

Barth, Pius J. *Franciscan Education and the Social Order in Spanish North America, 1502–1821.* Chicago, 1950.

Blackmar, Frank W. *Spanish Institutions of the Southwest.* Glorietta, N.Mex., 1976.

Cordova, Gilberto Benito. "Missionization and Hispanisization of Santo Tomás Apostal de Abiquiu, 1750–1770." Ph.D. diss., University of New Mexico, 1979.

Gallegos, Bernardo P. *Literacy, Education, and Society in New Mexico, 1693–1821.* Albuquerque, N.Mex., 1992.

Gonzalbo, Pilar. *El humanismo y la educación en la Nueva España.* Mexico City, 1985.

Gurza, Francisco Arce, Mílada Bazant, Anne Staples, Dorothy Tanck de Estrada, and Josefina Zoraida Vázquez. *Historia de las profesiones en México.* Mexico City, 1982.

Gutiérrez, Ramón A. *When Jesus Came, the Corn Mothers Went Away: Marriage, Sexuality, and Power in New Mexico, 1500–1846.* Stanford, Calif., 1991.

Heath, Shirley Brice. *Telling Tongues: Language Policy in Mexico, Colony to Nation.* New York, 1972.

Leonard, Irving A. *Baroque Times in Old Mexico.* Ann Arbor, Mich., 1959.

Ricard, Robert. *The Spiritual Conquest of Mexico.* Berkeley, Calif., 1966.

Tanck de Estrada, Dorothy. *La educación ilustrada, 1786–1836.* Mexico City, 1977.

———. *La ilustracion y la educación en la Nueva España.* Mexico City, 1985.

———. "Tensión en La Torre de Marfil: La educación en la segunda mitad del siglo XVIII mexicano." In *Ensayos sobre historia de la educación en Mexico,* edited by Josefina Zoraida Vázquez, Dorothy Tanck de Estrada, Anne Staples, and Francisco Arce Gurza. Mexico City, 1981.

Todorov, Tzvetan. *The Conquest of America: The Question of the Other.* Translated by Richard Howard. New York, 1984.

Vázquez, Josefina Zoraida, "El pensamiento renacenista español y los orígenes de la educación novohispana." In *Ensayos sobre historia de la educación en Mexico,* edited by Josefina Zoraida Vázquez, Dorothy Tanck de Estrada, Anne Staples, and Francisco Arce Gurza. Mexico City, 1981.

Bernardo P. Gallegos

SEE ALSO **Childhood and Adolescence; Literacy;** and **Mission Communities.**

PATTERNS OF SOCIALIZATION

THE BRITISH COLONIES

THROUGHOUT BRITISH NORTH AMERICA, socialization served the same function: to inculcate in the young certain behavior, values, and skills deemed appropriate and useful by their elders. This transmission of culture across the generations was infinitely complex, involving both formal and informal agencies, having unintended as well as deliberate consequences, with the family generally dominating the entire process. Along the frontier, where other communal institutions were rather weak, children were socialized almost exclusively by parents and siblings and perhaps a relative or two.

In older and more densely populated settlements, the family could usually draw upon the services of preachers, pedagogues, and an established network of kin and friends. Yet even there the family was still the primary educative agency, preparing the young for whatever else the church, the school, or apprenticeship training might impart.

The colonial family was typically nuclear in household, patriarchal in orientation, and extended in thought and conception. Its importance can hardly be exaggerated. The household was the basic unit both in society and in economic production, and the way mothers and fathers nurtured their young fundamentally shaped co-lonial culture, in both the seventeenth and eighteenth centuries.

Child rearing was everywhere much the same, typically falling into three stages of seven years each. If the parents remained alive and well, the child usually spent the first six or seven years in its own household, playing mostly but also beginning religious and literacy training. Over the next six or seven years, the youth would likely do some work about the house, shop, or farm and spend some time in formal schooling. The extent of schooling varied, but boys usually received significantly more schooling than girls. Then, during the next seven or so years, the young man or woman began serious occupational training, either through college, apprenticeship in a trade or profession, or some work experience that was less formal. If the three seven-year stages were more or less common throughout the colonies, however, there were still significant differences stemming from regional or cultural circumstances.

PURITAN NEW ENGLAND

Religion was a major component of socialization in all of colonial America. This was particularly true in early New England, where the Puritans of Massachusetts Bay maintained cultural hegemony throughout most of the region. Puritans were English Calvinists who came to America on a divine mission, to build a "city upon a hill."

Children played a pivotal role in this holy errand into the wilderness. "You came hither for your Children, Sons and Daughters," wrote the Reverend John Wilson in 1677, "and for your Grandchildren to be under the Ordinances of God." The family itself was called a "little commonwealth," the very foundation of both church and state. According to their elaborate covenant theology, Puritans were bound to one another and to the Lord through interlocking obligations that sanctified the household, the congregation, and the government. Children, for example, owed parents respect and obedience, and parents were likewise obliged to bring up children in the fear of the Lord and to some worthy calling.

Socialization for the Puritan infant began at the mother's breast, and most were apparently breast-fed. Two important early rituals were baptism, usually taking place within two weeks of birth, and the selection of a name. Baptism incorporated the child into the congregation, the extended family of faith; the name bestowed upon the infant often carried with it significant meaning. Firstborn sons and daughters commonly bore the forenames of their parents—yet another manifestation of the emphasis upon the conjugal family in Puritan life. Other children might be named after grandparents or biblical figures—like David, Sarah, Samuel, or Ruth—and were reminded of the faith and virtue of those whose name they bore. Regardless of what they called their children, Puritan parents followed child-rearing practices that clearly reinforced their particular religious convictions.

Calvinism taught that mankind was evil, redeemable only by God's unmerited and irresistible grace, and that salvation was limited to the predestined few, known as the elect. Therefore, infants were totally depraved, without any knowledge or capacity for goodness, and children were naturally inclined to do evil. The tantrums of small children were said to manifest man's corrupt and selfish nature. Godly parents were instructed to subdue the perverse will of the evil child; that was basic in Puritan child-rearing lore.

Breaking the child's will required the concerted efforts of both parents, with the father usually playing the larger role. The rigors of will-breaking varied with the disposition of parents, but the practice was common among Puritans in both England and America. Corporal punishment might be inflicted, but generally not upon a young child; the method of choice was apparently reward and deprivation of food, attention, and affection.

Breaking the child's will was just the beginning. According to Puritan writers, children needed discipline far more than affection, and parents were repeatedly warned that fondness for their offspring might well keep them from following proper child-rearing practices. Perhaps because they did not quite trust themselves, Puritan fathers and mothers routinely "sent out" their children to grow up in another household, where sons and daughters were expected to learn better manners and behavior than at home. Children might be sent out at any age, but they were usually apprenticed or bound out as servants between the ages of ten and fifteen, which meant they underwent the adjustments of puberty and adolescence outside their own family.

The pitiful protests of their crying children was almost more than Cotton Mather and Samuel Sewall could bear, but the two Puritan fathers still sent them out. "Children should not know, if it could be kept from them," wrote the Reverend John Robinson, "that they have a will of their own, but in their parents' keeping." Although Puritan parents loved their children and wanted love in return, will-breaking and sending out were just two important mechanisms in a system of child rearing that encouraged sons and daughters to view their parents with a mixture of fear and awe. In fact, many Puritan children treated their mothers and fathers with almost ritualistic deference.

Within the household itself, New England children began both religious and occupational training. Puritans recognized that basic literacy skills for boys and girls were crucial for understanding the Bible and growing in the faith. The father himself might teach reading to the children of his household, including his own and those bound to him, or send them all to a local schoolmaster. But even before children learned to read, Puritan parents began teaching them one of several acceptable catechisms. All of these were designed to convey in terms youngsters could understand the covenant theology peculiar to Puritanism as well as basic Calvinistic doctrines on human depravity, unconditional election, limited atonement, irresistible grace, and perseverance of the saints. Family prayer and Bible reading also inculcated Puritan tenets, and devout fathers, both lay and cleric, counseled their children to prepare themselves for God's saving grace.

Puritan parents also passed on to their children the tensions inherent in their faith. On the one hand, Puritans considered themselves God's chosen people, especially favored by his special covenant. On the other hand, they also believed in predestination and acknowledged that no one could be certain of salvation. Spiritual anxiety was the result, and children might absorb it early from their parents.

Children were made literally to confront death, by viewing and sometimes kissing the deceased relative or friend lying in the casket. Despite predestination, Puritans urged the young to prepare their hearts for salvation, thereby implying that preparation was somehow connected to divine election.

Along with religious instruction, Puritan mothers and fathers were especially concerned that their children learn a trade. In Calvinism, an occupation was a religious calling, and doing one's work well was regarded as an act of worship. As New Englanders well understood, there were two spheres of work, one male and the other female. Daughters had little choice, even those well versed in reading and writing; they were trained for housewifery, usually by their own mothers, but it was common for them to spend some time working in the household of another, frequently that of a relative or friend. Girls learned by doing, helping their mothers or mistresses with the cooking, cleaning, sewing, gardening, canning, and child care. The work of the conscientious housewife was never done, and even with the assistance of older children or servants, it could be drudgery. Puritan writers did exalt the good wife and mother, however, and young women understood the importance of their domestic calling for the good of the family and society.

Sons could follow a number of vocations, but most were born to farming, and that was the life they prepared for. As the population increased and trade expanded, greater economic specialization occurred, multiplying opportunities in commerce and crafts. Many sons learned farming or a craft from their fathers; others were sent out and learned a trade while living and working in the households of relatives, family friends, or acquaintances. A formal indenture was commonly written, especially in the seventeenth century, defining the terms of the apprenticeship, including what the boy would learn, how long he would serve, and how he would behave.

Such contracts also legalized the master's right to act in loco parentis and often obligated him to provide three months' schooling for his apprentice. An apprenticeship with a master craftsman, merchant, doctor, or lawyer was highly prized and usually required not only years of service from the youth but also a substantial fee. A select few boys went to grammar school, after which they usually entered college or began an apprenticeship in commerce, medicine, or law. Ministers were expected to go to college, and families rich and poor frequently dedicated one son to the church, which was an expensive enterprise.

Confirming the socialization efforts of the family was the local church, whose meetings formed the center of community life in New England. Ministers were the spiritual leaders, and their lengthy sermons on Sunday and lecture days were intended to instruct both young and old alike in their duty one to another and to God. Throughout the seventeenth century, ministers and lay leaders alike reiterated that catechizing was central to family devotional. To make sure that household catechizing was continuing apace, however, congregations began in the 1640s to require that children come to the church one evening a week to recite the catechism and be questioned about the previous Sunday's sermon.

Gradually but steadily, the congregation began to assume more control over catechizing, dividing the catechumen, both girls and boys, into groups according to ability, increasing the doctrinal content and mandating more detailed answers as the young person grew. The decline in conversion experiences among the children of the Puritan founders, which led to changing the rules to allow church membership through the Half-Way Covenant in 1657, encouraged congregational catechizing. Girls were catechized until age sixteen, and boys continued even beyond that. Adults of either sex who were new to the faith were also catechized. Although catechumen still practiced at home, they also rehearsed at the meetinghouse or at the parsonage, and the focus of catechizing became the public recitation led by the pastor every Sunday before the congregation. Catechizing played a crucial role in sustaining the forms of Puritanism among the rising generations long after the substance of the faith had begun to wear thin.

Provincial and local governments in Massachusetts and Connecticut made the family primarily responsible for nurturing and educating the young. In the case of orphans, local magistrates routinely bound them out to another family. Provincial law instructed children to obey their father and mother, and if children became "rude, stubborn, and unruly," local magistrates could take them away from their parents and bind them to a master for good discipline. A rebellious son or any child who should "smite or curse his parents" could be sentenced to death, though that penalty was never applied.

Obversely, abusive parents or masters and mistresses could be prosecuted and the ill-treated child removed from the household. Fear that the family was faltering in its educational duties inspired the famous Massachusetts ordinance of 1642 ordering parents and masters to teach their children and servants "to read and understand the principles of religion and capital laws of the country," and to keep them employed in some useful occupation. The law was enforced, and so was the "Old Deluder Satan" law of 1647 requiring English schools in towns of fifty families and Latin grammar schools in towns of one hundred families. Evidence indicates that because of the Puritan tradition of Bible reading, backed by positive laws calling for literacy training and schooling, almost all Massachusetts boys and about half the girls learned to read, giving New England the highest literacy rate in colonial America.

QUAKERS IN THE MIDDLE COLONIES

Quakerism, or the Society of Friends, emerged from the religious radicalism of the Puritan's Revolution in England. Like the Puritans, English Quakers, especially those associated with William Penn's enterprise in Pennsylvania, saw in America an opportunity for shaping society and government according to their fundamental beliefs. The Quakers were not Calvinists, however. In many ways more censorious than the Puritans, Friends rejected the legitimacy of the coercive state and embraced religious toleration, thereby relying upon the conjugal family and that larger family of faith, the Quaker meeting, as their primary engines of social reform.

Under Quakerism, the conjugal family was extraordinarily child-centered, and members of the meeting were especially devoted to the spiritual nurture of boys and girls. Unlike the Puritans and the English generally, the Quakers believed that fear had no legitimate place in familial relations. Rather, family members were bound together by love and compassion, and from the immediate kinship circle those virtues should flow outwardly into all dealings among the faithful and beyond into worldly society. Not surprisingly, Quakers rejected the concepts of predestination, human depravity, and limited atonement, three Calvinist doctrines that clashed with their social ethic of love.

Quakers taught that nothing was more important than raising children correctly. Indeed, it was the primary function of the family, and though the husband was definitely the head of the household, Quaker wives were regarded more as partners than as subordinates in the familial hierarchy. Like the Puritans, Quaker mothers generally breast-fed, unless health reasons necessitated wet-nursing. The Quaker baby was formally announced to the community of faith not by christening or baptism, both deemed too ceremonious by the Friends, but by a solemn ritual registering of the child's name with his local Quaker meeting.

In the Delaware Valley, Quakers commonly named their firstborn children after grandparents, giving the first son the name of the maternal grandfather and the first daughter the name of the paternal grandmother. Such bilateral naming represents a concern for onomastic equality between husband and wife. Along with equality, Quakers stressed the virtues of simplicity and plainness, and perhaps for that reason they were far less likely than Puritans to give their children biblical names, especially not the more elaborate ones.

Quakers and Puritans disagreed sharply over the basic nature of the child. George Fox, the founder of Quakerism, did occasionally talk of keeping the child in subjection and breaking his will. Richard Barclay and other Quaker apologists nonetheless denounced as ridiculous and barbaric the Calvinistic doctrine that children were born evil, doomed to hell should they die in infancy, as so many did. "There is no fear," wrote the American Quaker John Hepburn in 1714, ". . . that Christ will cast away such holy, harmless, righteous, and innocent Creatures, as little Children are."

Children were born saintly, but Quakers did acknowledge that they could grow depraved. Commentators agreed that parents should be on their guard for the tilt toward sin once the child possessed enough reason to know right from wrong. At that stage of development, the child could begin to cultivate the "inward light," whereby one gained knowledge and understanding of the Lord. The guidance of the family— particularly of the mother and father—during this spiritual odyssey was crucial; the very salvation of their children was at stake.

Quaker parents were urged to "bend the twig," rather than break the will, and to do it gently, in love and with godly conversation. Parents were told to be good examples, or role models, for their offspring. The Quaker family was designed to protect children from the world, whose corrupting influences threatened life eternal. Because "living in the light" meant living the Quaker virtues of plainness, simplicity, and equality, children were taught by example as well as by explanation. Therefore, both parents had to be constantly vigilant, and so did all the Friends, lest their failure in word or deed lead the young astray.

Quaker child-rearing practices were designed both to develop the "seed of goodness" that all children possessed and to prepare the young for sober and edifying occupations. Religious as well as occupational training took place mainly in the home, usually at the hands of loving parents. Indeed, Quaker parents may well have restricted and supervised the young even more closely than the Puritans did. Children were brought up in the plain style of speaking, dressing, and behaving. Family prayer, Bible reading, and discussions of spiritual matters made clear to youngsters the importance of their faith. Parents generally began taking their children to meeting at age four, despite the difficulties of trying to keep small children quiet during the long silences that usually characterized the two-hour services.

Many Quaker parents, if not most, certainly began teaching their children to read and write, though a local school would often finish the job. According to David Fischer, about 70 percent of Quaker men could sign their names, as opposed to about half that many Quaker women. Higher learning was not generally prized by the Quakers, who took pride in not having a specially educated "hireling ministry." But Bible reading was important, and so were literacy skills in terms of occupational training.

Just as Quaker children learned about religion from their parents, so also did most of them learn occupational skills. Boys followed their father's calling, which, as in the case of the Puritans, was most commonly farming. Girls learned housewifery alongside their mothers. Unlike the Puritans, the Quakers did not recommend sending out, believing that it was generally better for the child to grow up in his or her own family. There was apprenticeship, of course, especially in the crafts and commerce. Should apprenticeship training be desired, it was usually arranged through the meeting, with the youth being assigned to another Friend. Moreover, in accepting apprentices or in hiring servants, Quakers were instructed to make sure they were of the faith. In terms of occupations, Quakers favored "God's trades" before man's. J. William Frost notes that according to one Quaker, the former included farming and shepherding, as opposed to less natural tasks like handicrafts or commerce. Above all else, children should consider "such honest lawful *Callings,* as the Lord inclines them to, or make them *Capable* of."

The Quaker family included not just the mother, father, siblings, and grandparents but all members of the faith, especially those of the local meeting. The meeting assisted the family with its child-rearing chores, affirming the familiar tenets of plainness, simplicity, and equality in the faith.

Should parents falter in their duty toward children, or should children become unusually truculent, a committee from the meeting would likely intervene, perhaps arranging apprenticeship contracts or finding work for older children in good Quaker homes. A Quaker master accused of mistreating his apprentice might be brought before the meeting to answer charges against him. The meeting also took the lead in arranging schooling, sometimes subsidizing the schoolmaster or dame and providing a building for the school. Ideally, the local meeting wanted the child taught by and apprenticed to Quakers, though its efforts varied from one Quaker community to another.

Given the persecution they had received at the hands of government, Quakers were reluctant to enlist the aid of the state in dealing with domestic matters. In fact, their views on strictly separating church and state prevented them from doing so. In Pennsylvania, only two laws were passed supporting parents against unruly offspring. The Great Law of 1682 called for anyone who assaulted or threatened his parent to be jailed and put to hard labor "during the pleasure of the said parent." This statute was modified in 1700 to provide a punishment of six months in prison and a public whipping of "thirty-one lashes, well laid on."

Before 1700 some Pennsylvania Quakers talked about provincial government support of schooling, but the growing religious diversity of Pennsylvania convinced the Friends that any state involvement with religion might threaten the educational efforts of the local meetings. In short, Quakers opted for sectarian schooling or none at all. Of course, in Pennsylvania and elsewhere in colonial America, town or county government took charge of the education of destitute or orphaned children, if their parents or other relatives made no provision for them.

PLANTERS IN THE SOUTHERN COLONIES

The pattern of socialization that developed in the tidewater South was much different from that of either the Puritans in New England or the Quakers in the middle colonies. The Chesapeake colonies of Virginia and Maryland led the way. Before 1700 thousands of white indentured servants and hundreds of planters died trying to wrestle wealth from the disease-infested lands of the region. Gradually, with the growth of a native white population and the shift to black slavery, Chesapeake society in the early eigh-

teenth century stabilized and emerged as perhaps the most secular, materialistic, and hierarchical in colonial America.

A planter aristocracy arose, and its views of family and child rearing shaped the standards of the entire region. The Chesapeake household was typically nuclear in structure, patriarchal in organization, and thoroughly extended in orientation and association. A Virginia planter and his wife would likely have fewer living children than either a Puritan couple or a Quaker couple, but their household would usually still be much larger, including white and black servants, a white apprentice or two, and perhaps children of a deceased relative.

The Carolinas and Georgia went through a somewhat different founding and early development, though the mortality rate from seasoning was much like that of the Chesapeake. Moreover, North Carolina always had fewer slaves and a higher proportion of small planters than either South Carolina or the Chesapeake colonies, just as Georgia outside of Savannah remained pretty much an emerging frontier until after the American Revolution. However, plantation agriculture came to dominate the economic development of the colonial South, and planter elites developed throughout the region, much alike in both their familial structure and aspirations but different in detail from the Chesapeake aristocracy.

In terms of aping the English upper class, the wealthy South Carolina planters even outdid their Maryland and Virginia counterparts, but their attitudes toward family and child rearing, like those of planters in North Carolina and Georgia, were very similar to those of Chesapeake planters, whose domestic practices have received considerably more scholarly attention than planters in the rest of the South.

Family relations in the Chesapeake were characterized by what has been called domestic patriarchy. Indeed, throughout the colonial South, the father was firmly at the head of the family, and the economic roles of male and female were usually sharply separated. Although subordinate to her husband, the wife ruled over everyone else in the planter household. Children were highly prized, in part because roughly 40 percent of them died before adulthood. A couple whose marriage joined together two landed families would likely name the children after their grandparents, perhaps even bestowing the maternal family name upon the first or second son. Relatives celebrated the birth of a child, and grandparents, uncles, and aunts typically served as godparents when the babe was baptized. In most cases, children grew up in the same neighborhood and played with cousins in their numerous extended family.

Tidewater mothers generally breast-fed their young, though some wealthy families with numerous children also used wet nurses, both white and black. Unlike the Puritans, Chesapeake parents, most of whom subscribed to a comfortable Anglicanism, did not regard their children as naturally evil. They tended to indulge the infant, whether it wanted to nurse, play, or fret. Much the same could be said for children of wealthy planters throughout the planter South. In 1728 Virginian Thomas Jones happily reported that his infant nephew "struts around the house and is as noisy as a bully." Another relative complained that Jones's own two year-old son either did what he wanted or else "he is ready to tear the house down." Visitors observed that children seemed to have the run of the plantation, black and white children playing freely, with little adult supervision.

This permissive child-rearing regime continued into adolescence, and its freedoms startled strangers. Daniel Blake Smith noted that in 1783 the German traveler Johann Schoepf was surprised to find that a "Virginia youth of fifteen years is already such a man as he will be at twice that age." There was method behind the apparent madness. Young men—and young women, too—allowed and even encouraged to grow up quickly, acquired the habit of command and decision-making even in youth. During the seventeenth century, perhaps no more than one-fourth of the children who lived to eighteen still had both parents living. In the Carolinas and Georgia, demographic conditions were much like those in the Chesapeake. For their own good, and for the good of the family fortunes, young people needed to be ready to assume adult roles early in the Southern colonies.

Child rearing among Southern planters was, however, much more deliberate than many observers thought. Until five or six years old, children of both sexes typically wore long robes and played about the house near their mothers. Thereafter, boys were dressed in breeches and shirts, and their fathers began to draw them away from the domestic world of their mothers and sisters and into the manly world of business, politics, and sport. Chesapeake parents wanted their children to have a strong and secure sexual identity, one that generally developed from years of sex-segregated learning. Each sex had its proper sphere and knew it. Although the evidence is less abundant, planters in the Carolinas and Georgia apparently felt much the same way.

Young girls learned from their mothers, or perhaps in the home of a female relative, that they were destined to be helpmates and domestic managers. Mimicking came first. "It is curious to see the Girls imitating what they see in the great House," wrote tutor Philip Fithian from Virginia in 1774. Robert Carter's two young daughters, Fithian reported, were constantly playing at household chores, "sometimes tying a string to a chair & then run buzzing back to imitate the Girls spinning; then getting Rags & washing them without water." Although only six and ten years old respectively, the Carter girls also took delight in stuffing rags under their clothing and pretending they were pregnant women.

As they grew older, girls would begin to do domestic chores or else assist their mothers in managing the household. "They are every Day up to their Elbows in Housewifery," boasted William Byrd of his growing daughters in 1725, "which will qualify them effectually for useful Wives and if they live long enough, for Notable Women." Young women often developed very close bonds with their mothers and sisters and belonged to a network of female relatives and friends that provided comfort and support throughout their lives. They also learned from both experience and observation that wives and mothers were extremely important in Chesapeake society, though always subordinate in the scheme of things to husbands and fathers.

Fathers were almost always deeply involved in the education of their sons. In large families, younger sons might be informally farmed out or even legally apprenticed to an uncle or friend, but the father almost always made all the arrangements and kept a watchful eye on things. Like their sisters, sons learned by watching and by doing; they might carry their fathers' instructions among several plantations, assist in supervising the planting or harvesting, or look over western lands for investment purposes. Sons frequently accompanied their fathers into the fields, to the county court, to church, or to the horse races. They learned how to command, to manage the estate, and to be gentlemen by copying what they saw their fathers and older males do. Sons of humbler planters usually learned working shoulder to shoulder with their fathers, brothers, and family slaves. They too learned their place in this hierarchical social structure.

The plantation society of the colonial South valued literacy and even learning for its upper classes, but for the rest of the population, even literacy was neglected. "Good Education of Children is almost impossible," lamented William Fitzhugh of the scarcity of teachers and preachers in Virginia in 1687. Fitzhugh thought it "better to be never born than to be ill bred," that is, unschooled and lacking in refinement. This concern led many Chesapeake planters, Fitzhugh included, to send one or more of their children to England for schooling, a practice that continued well into the eighteenth century despite the increasing number of preachers and teachers serving the Chesapeake.

An Anglican preacher would now and again run a school in his home, but generally his educational impact was limited to Sunday sermons; the church was usually too distant for the pastor to do much catechizing. In fact, young children did not commonly make the trek to church, receiving whatever religious instruction they secured from their parents in family discussions and devotional or from tutors and schoolteachers.

Wealthy and aspiring planters wanted their children to be literate, girls as well as boys. Any learning beyond literacy for girls was generally deemed unnecessary, though it had status value as a mark of distinction and class refinement. Martha Laurens and Eliza Lucas, both of South Carolina, were among the few very well-educated exceptions who proved the rule. On the other hand, sons of the elite were expected to know at least some Latin and Greek, with more specialized learning for those preparing for careers in the law or medicine. Private tutors taught in the households of many wealthy families, instructing

boys and girls in subjects ranging from basic reading and writing, the catechism, and arithmetic to Latin and Greek. The Chesapeake upper class also hired dancing masters, who conducted schools for their sons and daughters, moving from one plantation house to another. Dancing was ritualistic recreation; it not only brought young men and women as well as adults together for socializing but also reinforced the attitude that living life properly, like performing the dance properly, meant abiding by the agreed-upon rules. In the hierarchical society of the Chesapeake, nothing so much distinguished the gentleman and gentlewoman as the ability to dance well.

Throughout the seventeenth century, provincial law in Virginia, Maryland, and the Carolinas enjoined county magistrates to look after the education of poor children and orphans. The apprenticeship indentures made for such children often demonstrated concern for the rudiments of literacy, though occupational training was of primary importance. Wills of parents possessing even a little property almost always called for their children to have some schooling, especially in the eighteenth century.

Like so much else in the Chesapeake, literacy was not only hierarchical but gender biased. According to Philip Bruce, between 1641 and 1700 in Virginia less than half of the white males could write and only one-fourth of the women. The discrepancy between male and female literacy improved some in the eighteenth century, but evidence is very sketchy for females. Kenneth Lockridge has estimated that between 1705 and 1762 the male literacy rate was 66 percent, with the figure being 100 percent for upper- and upper-middle-class males. While the gap in literacy between the rich and the poor narrowed elsewhere in colonial America, it actually became significantly larger in Virginia, and no doubt Maryland, too.

THE BACKCOUNTRY

Yet another pattern of socialization emerged in the colonial backcountry stretching from western Pennsylvania southward into the valley of Virginia and western Maryland and the uplands of the Carolinas and Georgia. Although some

Germans, Huguenots, and English Quakers could be found there, the backcountry was largely settled by people from the borderlands of northern Britain, especially the Scotch-Irish from Ulster in northern Ireland.

Family bonds were especially strong in the backcountry. They had to be; husband, wife, and children depended upon one another in ways unique to the hardships and hazards of their surroundings. Backcountry men and women married young, usually had numerous children, and more commonly than settlers in other parts of America might share their household with parents or with siblings and their spouses. "There is not a Cabbin but has 10 or 12 Young Children in it," the Anglican missionary Charles Woodmason wrote of the South Carolina backcountry in 1768. "When the Boys are 18 and Girls 14 they marry—so that in many Cabbin You will see 10 or 15 children. Children and Grand Children of one Size—and the Mother looking as Young as the Daughter," observed the peripatetic parson. Woodmason was not far from the mark, though the best evidence is that men were usually about twenty-one and women nineteen when they wed, which was still quite young for marriages relative to others in colonial America.

Backcountry settlers from the British borderlands thought of family not just in terms of their immediate kin but also in terms of the derbfine, defined as all the kin within four generations. Beyond the derbfine were kinsmen known as the clan. Loyalty to the family, the derbfine, and the clan was fundamental to the ethical system that the British borderlanders transferred to the uplands of the colonial South.

Following the traditions of the British borderlands, gender roles dictated that men were primarily warriors and hunters and that women not only did domestic chores but also shared in the hardest work. Of the backcountry settlers in Virginia and Carolina, William Byrd II described the men as "Slothfull in everything but getting Children," while the women did all the work. Other travelers agreed. "The ordinary Women," wrote one commentator, "take care of Cows, Hogs, and other small Cattle, make Butter and Cheese, spin Cotton and Flax, help sow and reap Corn, wind Silk from the Worms, gather Fruit, and look after the Home." And of course, much more. The men were seldom as shiftless as they seemed, and most labored long and hard to make a crop and protect their families. Yet the backcountry was the most male-dominated society in colonial America, and the women of the southern frontier were much more likely to do what elsewhere in the colonies would be termed men's work.

Regarding the many children in the backcountry, Governor James Glen of South Carolina complained in 1753 that their parents failed to "bestow the least Education on them, they take so much Care in raising a Litter of Piggs, their Children are equally naked and full as Nasty. . . ." Governor Glen failed to recognize or appreciate that the parental style of the settlers was from the British borderlands.

The influence was also reflected in the child-naming customs of the backcountry. The most common forenames included biblical names like John, Sarah, and Rachel; Teutonic names like Robert and Richard; and the names of borderland saints like Andrew, Patrick, and David.

Child care was of considerable concern to backcountry parents and their kin, but it was different from elsewhere in Anglo-America. Preparation for childbirth began with pregnant women consulting one or several of the old grannies whose knowledge of superstitious lore, magic, and herbal remedies might protect the child's health and reveal something of its future. Wet nursing was rare, and travelers reported that backcountry parents were indulgent and permissive toward their children. "They are very fond of their little ones," reported François-Jean, marquis de Chastelleux, from the Virginia back settlements in 1782, "and care much less for their children." Infants were pampered, not only by parents but by older siblings. Children were probably no less loved, but early on were given considerable freedom and encouraged toward their respective gender roles.

Males and females were raised quite differently. According to David Hackett Fischer, boys were nurtured in ways that fostered "fierce pride, stubborn independence and a warrior's courage." Early on they began following their fathers around, working with them in the fields and hunting with them. They were given knives, hatchets, and guns as soon as they could barely use them. They sat at the table with fathers and brothers and were served by their mothers and sisters. Boys learned quickly that men enjoyed privileged status in their society.

Other than at crucial times for planting or harvesting, boys did much as they pleased, running about the hills and valleys playing with their peers, hunting, and fishing. All this was not so much play as a struggle for dominance among their cohorts. Mastering the game or competition by the rules was less important than winning. The results of such socialization could be seen in young men who were courageous and cunning but also hot-tempered, undisciplined, and generally hostile toward any restraint. Young men matured early to the extent that they had learned how to survive and provide for themselves and others; it was expected of them. They could be and often were loving husbands and fathers, but they were given to strong drink and prone to fighting, and they could and sometimes did respond with violence when angered by wife or offspring.

If boys were taught to be self-asserting, girls learned to be self-denying. Watching and helping their mothers with work both inside and out of the house, they learned quickly the rules of the backcountry maleocracy. Young women, sometimes still children themselves, frequently took charge of the younger children; they had to because many mothers simply could not do it all. They learned to cook, to keep house, to tend the garden and crops and livestock, and to raise children. After they married, they had to contend usually with about twenty years of almost perpetual pregnancy while being responsible for doing all those things their mothers had done. Indeed, young women were taught in word and in deed by their mothers and other female kin that their role was one of sacrifice, first for their husbands and then their children, especially their sons.

Marriage was the only option available to young women, who, like their brothers, matured early; spinsterhood was regarded as an unfortunate state and only barely tolerated. Premarital pregnancy was higher on the frontier than elsewhere and seemed to be fairly well accepted. Woodmason estimated that in ninety-four out of every one hundred couples he married, the bride was already pregnant, more than a few of them "very big" with child. This was partly

due to the scarcity of preachers and magistrates to perform marriages, but it also indicated an openness about sexuality that characterized the backcountry. Much the same attitude prevailed in the British borderlands.

The same was true of the female network of support into which young women were gradually incorporated. However privileged sons might be in the family, mothers and daughter were usually close, sharing an intimacy that fathers and sons seldom achieved. Neither did most husbands and wives, despite the interdependence of the conjugal couple in day-to-day existence. Backcountry women—mothers and daughters, nieces and aunts—helped one another cope with the hardships that made many of them "sullen, grave, and of a retiring disposition." Aging grandmothers were likely to be self-assertive, but young women knew they had years of self-sacrifice to endure before they reached that status.

Girls were much less likely than boys to have any schooling, but the backcountry generally had a reputation for being ignorant and proud of it. Critics have apparently distorted the extent of illiteracy, however. One backcountry settlement, Williamsburg, South Carolina, founded by Scotch-Irish settlers, had extraordinarily high male literacy rates (98 percent) at the time of the revolution. Huguenot and German settlers averaged highest (more than 90 percent), and the Scotch-Irish overall male literacy rate has been estimated between 70 and 80 percent. At the same time, the female literacy rate was almost surely the lowest in the colonies for white women, and the rising generation that so much concerned Woodmason and other critics may well have been less literate than their parents, given the disruptions first of the Seven Years' War and then of the American Revolution.

Schooling was scarce throughout the backcountry, especially in South Carolina and Georgia. Itinerant teachers served the region, and because they depended largely on the subscription of parents from year to year, they frequently found it necessary to move from place to place or to stop teaching altogether. Nevertheless, teachers would become available now and again. The few Anglican preachers who ministered in the backcountry almost always tutored a few young men; Woodmason had twenty at one time.

Some of the Presbyterian preachers certainly held school, and a few Scotch-Irish settlements tried to keep a teacher, though usually with little lasting success.

The influence of provincial government upon education in the backcountry was slight. County government impacted much more, usually requiring the rudiments of literacy for orphans and children bound to apprenticeship, but schooling and formal learning were less important in the upland regions than elsewhere in Anglo-America. Book learning was certainly not scorned, especially among preachers who were expected to have it, and a few substantial libraries could be found among the backcountry elite. Nevertheless, backcountry settlers were oriented toward the spoken word rather than the written language. Traditions were handed down from father to son, and those who rose to leadership spoke the language idiomatically like the people and knew how to appeal to the values, experiences, and customs of the region.

EIGHTEENTH-CENTURY DEVELOPMENTS

There were of course other patterns of socialization in early America. Dutch New Yorkers, for example, were Calvinists, but they were definitely not Puritans. Many Pennsylvania Germans were sectarians, but they were not Quakers. Consider too the Moravians, German Lutherans, and the German Reformed, not to mention Amerindians or African Americans, slave and free, or even that medley of English Dissenters who inhabited Rhode Island, denounced far and wide by the more orthodox as the "latrine of New England." Their respective child-rearing methods were similar yet different in detail because the culture-shaping experiences of the various ethno-religious groups were never exactly alike and in many instances had been quite distinctive.

Philip Greven has masterfully attempted to conceptualize socialization in terms meaningful enough to provide insight into the child-rearing habits of all Americans. Although there are shortcomings in any such generalized paradigm, Greven has identified three primary parenting styles among Anglo-Americans in both the seventeenth and eighteenth centuries. Shaped by religious ideology, each style represented a particular perspective of the Protestant temperament toward the self.

Insecure and driven by fear and love for its offspring, the evangelical temperament deprecated the self; felt compelled to break the will of the naturally depraved child; and sought to impose its repressive vision of harmony, unity, and selflessness upon all society. Authoritative rather than authoritarian, the moderate temperament wanted to control rather than annihilate the self; the child was innocent, but tending toward sin, so its will must be bent by appeals to love and duty, not fear. Thoroughly self-assured, the genteel temperament was indulgent and affectionate toward children, whose self-assertions were encouraged, though kept within proper bounds by love and reverence.

Comparatively speaking, Greven's evangelical, moderate, and genteel temperaments essentially correspond to the central tendency of the Puritan, Quaker, and Chesapeake styles of child rearing discussed at the beginning of this essay; the "will-enhancing" backcountry does not quite fit his model. Greven nevertheless rightly insists that the three Protestant temperaments cut across virtually all Anglo-American religious groups and social classes. Yet Greven found an expanding moderate majority in the years after 1700, with increasing numbers of genteel temperament, drawn largely from the more prosperous classes.

This emphasis on the moderate temperament was everywhere reflected in the child-rearing literature that proliferated after 1725. The writings of John Locke, especially *Some Thoughts Concerning Education* (1693), that deal with teaching and nurturing provided the intellectual and religious underpinnings for the moderate style of child rearing.

In eighteenth-century America, a well-stocked colonial library usually contained Locke's writings on education, and they were widely advertised by booksellers in the newspapers. By the 1750s, well-read mothers were deliberately applying Locke in their child nurture. Even more widely read were the writings of those who expanded and popularized Locke's enlightened views, especially James Burgh, Philip Doddridge, and Isaac Watts, all of whom, unlike the Anglican Locke, were Dissenters.

The rise to dominance of the moderate and genteel styles suggests certain fundamental changes in familial relations. Increasing commercialization, greater urbanization, and rising levels of literacy are all factors social scientists have associated with modernization. Another is the development of more affective relations within the family itself, between husbands and wives and children and parents. Colonial marriages in the eighteenth century seem to have been increasingly more companionate and less patriarchal. Letters between husbands and wives, children and parents, were usually warm and affectionate. Children loomed larger at the center of domestic life; one measure of this change is the explosion of literature about and for children.

In New England, routinely sending children out of the parental household drifted out of fashion in the eighteenth century. According to Barry Levy, the Quakers of the middle colonies led other colonial Americans in developing affective domestic relations. The Dutch settlements of New Jersey and New York in the seventeenth century nonetheless also demonstrated warm familial bonds not driven by a dominating religious ideology. Regardless of who was first and why, clearly the trend by 1750 was toward the modern companionate, child-centered family.

Modes of schooling vastly expanded, catering to the changing social and economic needs of colonial society. Massachusetts alone had a system of provincially mandated and locally controlled town and village schools worthy of the name, but elsewhere in New England and throughout the middle colonies, towns, congregations, and neighborhoods were taking the initiative and sponsoring this schoolmaster or that. Even in the less densely populated southern colonies, the availability and variety of schooling increased significantly.

Non-British Americans—Dutch New Yorkers and German settlers generally—sometimes maintained a teacher to propagate their respective languages among the young and perhaps teach Latin, too. Even before but especially after the Great Awakening, religious competition between various sects and denominations also led to the founding of schools, both to maintain the faith among their own young but also to proselytize among children whose parents followed another creed.

Private schoolmasters were everywhere, especially in the colonial cities of Boston, New York, Philadelphia, and Charleston, and in secondary centers like Williamsburg, Annapolis, Albany, and Lancaster. They taught not only English and Latin, but also an ever-expanding curriculum. In 1723 John Walton, a recent Yale graduate, advertised his school in New York City where he taught "Reading, Writing, Arethmatick, whole Numbers and Fractions, Vulgar and Decimal, the Mariners Art, Plain and Mercators Way; Also Geometry, Survey, the Latin Tongue, the Greek and Hebrew Grammers, Ethicks, Rhetorick, Logick, Natural Philosophy and Metaphysicks, all or any of them for a Reasonable Price." Such eclectic schooling reflected the cultural and economic trends of the day, propagating both a goodly amount of Enlightenment thought and occupational skills.

Evening schools, which had begun to emerge before 1700 to serve apprentices who worked all day, multiplied and enlarged their subjects, attracting not only apprentices but young tradesmen and workers.

In fact, apprenticeship apparently declined in importance, and regulations imposed by the municipal governments were left unenforced. The shortage of laborers had made it difficult from the beginning of settlement to maintain the English law and custom of seven years of service before graduating to journeyman status. For many craftsmen, it was easier to hire a conscientious young man to help, without being legally obligated to teach him a trade and at the same time be responsible for such things as literacy training and public behavior.

All along, of course, most young men, like most young women, received their occupational training from their family. Fathers taught their sons the art and mystery of their craft, just as mothers initiated daughters into housewifery. But if apprenticeship became even less important than it had been before, schooling in collateral fields of learning became all the more important. A young clerk, for example, might find it to his advantage to study bookkeeping; in fact, his employer might require it.

Apprenticeship, however, still prevailed in the elite professions of law, medicine, and commerce. Indeed, this very specialized training often cost the parents of an aspiring young man a considerable sum, sometimes several hundred pounds. The apprentice, or rather his father, was paying not only for what he was learning but also for the opportunity gained through acquaintanceship with the people he was meeting as he studied with his master. As the eighteenth century progressed, college training was generally expected before one began an apprenticeship in law or medicine. Such professional training usually took the youth further away from his particular ethnic and religious traditions and into an expanding cosmopolitan world of the provincial upper class. Commerce, politics, and learning all propagated English culture among old and young alike, but those most influenced were the young, whose socialization mixed customs and traditions of the past with the changing imperatives of early American society.

BIBLIOGRAPHY

General and Theoretical Works

Bailyn, Bernard. *Education in the Forming of American Society.* Chapel Hill, N.C., 1960.

Beales, Ross W., Jr. "The Child in Seventeenth-Century America." In *American Childhood: A Research Guide and Historical Handbook,* edited by Joseph M. Hawes and N. Ray Hiner. Westport, Conn., 1985.

Bremner, Robert H., ed. *Children and Youth in America: A Documentary History.* 3 vols. Cambridge, Mass., 1970–1974.

Bridenbaugh, Carl. *The Colonial Craftsman.* New York, 1950.

Calvert, Karin Lee. "Children in American Family Portraiture, 1670–1810." *William and Mary Quarterly,* 3rd ser., 39, no. 1 (1982):87–113.

Cremin, Lawrence A. *American Education: The Colonial Experience, 1607–1783.* New York, 1970.

DeMause, Lloyd, ed. *The History of Childhood: The Untold Story of Child Abuse.* New York, 1988.

Demos, John, and Virginia Demos. "Adolescence in Historical Perspective." *Journal of Marriage and the Family* 31 (1969):632–638.

Fischer, David Hackett. *Albion's Seed: Four British Folkways in America.* New York and Oxford, 1989.

Greven, Philip. *The Protestant Temperament: Patterns of Child-Rearing, Religious Experience, and the Self in Early America.* New York, 1977.

Hawke, David Freeman. *Everyday Life in Early America.* New York, 1988.

Hiner, N. Ray. "Adolescence in Eighteenth-Century America." *History of Childhood Quarterly* 3 (1975):253–280.

———. "The Child in American Historiography: Accomplishments and Prospect." *Psychohistory Review* 7 (1978–1979):13–23.

Jernegan, Marcus Wilson. *Laboring and Dependent Classes in Colonial America, 1607–1783: Studies of the Economic, Educational, and Social Significance of Slaves, Servants, Apprentices, and Poor Folk.* Chicago, 1931.

Laslett, Peter, and Richard Wall, eds. *Household and Family in Past Time: Comparative Studies in the Size and Structure of the Domestic Group over the Last Three Centuries in England, France, Serbia, Japan, and Colonial North America, with Further Materials from Western Europe.* Cambridge, England, 1972.

Morris, Richard B. *Government and Labor in Early America.* New York, 1946; repr. 1965.

Quimby, M. G., ed. *The Craftsman in Early America.* New York, 1984.

Sommerville, C. John. *The Discovery of Childhood in Puritan England.* Athens, Ga., 1992.

New England

Axtell, James. *The School Upon a Hill.* New Haven, Conn., 1974.

Demos, John. *A Little Commonwealth: Family Life in Plymouth Colony.* New York, 1970.

Fleming, Sandford. *Children and Puritanism: The Place of Children in the Life and Thought of the New England Churches, 1620–1847.* New Haven, Conn., 1933; repr. New York, 1969.

Greven, Philip. "Youth, Maturity, and Religious Conversion: A Note on the Ages of Converts in Andover, Massachusetts, 1711–1749." *Essex Institute Historical Collections* 108 (1972):119–134.

Hiner, N. Ray. "Cotton Mather and His Children: The Evolution of a Parent Education." In *Regulated Children/Liberated Children: Education in Psychohistorical Perspective,* edited by Barbara Finkelstein. New York, 1979.

Lockridge, Kenneth A. *Literacy in Colonial New England: An Enquiry into the Social Context of Literacy in the Early Modern West.* New York, 1974.

Mather, Cotton. *Diary of Cotton Mather.* 2 vols. New York, 1957.

Sewall, Samuel. *Diary of Samuel Sewall.* Edited by Harvey Wish. New York, 1967.

Stannard, David E. *The Puritan Way of Death: A Study in Religion, Culture, and Social Change.* New York, 1977.

The Middle Colonies

Frost, J. William. *The Quaker Family in Colonial America: A Portrait of the Society of Friends.* New York, 1973.

Howard, Ronald. "Apprenticeship and Economic Education in New Netherland." In *A Beautiful and*

Fruitful Place: Selected Rensselaerswijck Seminar Papers, edited by Nancy Anne McClure Zeller. Albany, N.Y., 1991.

Levy, Barry. *Quakers and the American Family: British Settlement in the Delaware Valley.* New York and Oxford, 1988.

Nash, Gary. "Poverty and Poor Relief in Pre-Revolutionary Philadelphia." *William and Mary Quarterly,* 3rd ser., 33, no. 1 (1976):3–30.

Tully, Alan. "Levels and Educational Development in Rural Pennsylvania, 1729–1775." *Pennsylvania Magazine of History and Biography* 39 (1972):301–312.

Wells, Robert V. "Family Size and Fertility Control in Eighteenth-Century America: A Study of Quaker Families." *Population Studies* 25 (1971):73–82.

The Colonial South

Fithian, Philip Vickers. *Journal and Letters of Philip Vickers Fithian, 1773–1774: A Plantation Tutor of the Old Dominion.* Edited by Hunter Dickinson Farish. Williamsburg, Va., 1943; repr. Charlottesville, Va., 1968.

Griffin, Lucille, ed. "English Education for Virginia Youths: Some Eighteenth-Century Ambler Family Letters." *Virginia Magazine of History and Biography* 69, no. 1 (1961):14–16.

Kiple, Kenneth F., and Virginia H. Kiple. "Slave Child Mortality: Some Nutritional Answers to a Perennial Puzzle." *Journal of Social History* 10 (1977):284–309.

Kulikoff, Allan. *Tobacco and Slaves: The Development of Southern Cultures in the Chesapeake, 1680–1900.* Chapel Hill, N.C., 1986.

Morgan, Edmund S. *Virginians at Home.* New York, 1952.

Rutman, Darrett B., and Anita H. Rutman. " 'Non-Wives and Sons-in-Law': Parental Death in a Seventeenth-Century Virginia County." In *The Chesapeake in the Seventeenth Century: Essays on Anglo-American Society,* edited by Thad W. Tate and David L. Ammerman. Chapel Hill, N.C., 1979.

————. *A Place in Time: Explicatus.* New York, 1984.

————. *A Place in Time: Middlesex County, Virginia, 1650–1750.* New York, 1984.

Smith, Daniel Blake. *Inside the Great House: Planter Family Life in Eighteenth-Century Chesapeake Society.* Ithaca, N.Y., 1980.

Sobel, Mechal. *The World They Made Together: Black and White Values in Eighteenth-Century Virginia.* Princeton, N.J., 1987.

Spruill, Julia Cherry. *Women's Life and Work in the Southern Colonies.* Chapel Hill, N.C., 1938; repr. New York, 1972.

The Colonial Backcountry

Bridenbaugh, Carl. *Myths and Realities: Societies of the Colonial South.* Baton Rouge, La., 1952.

Brown, Richard M. *The South Carolina Regulators.* Cambridge, Mass., 1963.

Campbell, John C. *The Southern Highlander and His Homeland.* 1921; repr. Lexington, Ky., 1969.

Chastellux, François-Jean, marquis de. *Travels in North America in the Years 1780, 1781, and 1782.* 2 vols. New York, 1968.

Dickson, R. J. *Ulster Emigration to Colonial America, 1718–1775.* London, 1966.

Dunaway, Wayland F. *The Scotch-Irish of Colonial Pennsylvania.* Chapel Hill, N.C., 1966.

Hanna, Charles A. *The Scotch-Irish; or, The Scot in North Britain, North Ireland, and North America.* 2 vols. New York, 1902.

Leyburn, James G. *The Scotch-Irish: A Social History.* Chapel Hill, N.C., 1962.

Miles, Emma Bell. *The Spirit of the Mountains.* New York, 1905; repr. Knoxville, Tenn., 1975.

Woodmason, Charles. *The Carolina Backcountry on the Eve of the Revolution: The Journal and Other Writings of Charles Woodmason, Anglican Itinerant.* Edited by Richard J. Hooker. Chapel Hill, N.C., 1953.

Ronald William Howard

SEE ALSO **African-American Culture; Artisans; European Languages; Patterns of Community;** and **Schools and Schooling;** and various essays in FAMILIES AND THE LIFE COURSE.

THE DUTCH COLONY

TO BECOME FUNCTIONING members of their communities, the boys and girls of New Netherland required training in practical skills as well as grounding in the fundamental values of their elders. In both areas the family assumed primary responsibility, with church and schools offering supplementary instruction. Parents introduced their offspring to the work roles they would fill as adults, instilled in them an appreciation for the religious and moral truths that imparted meaning to existence, and in many instances, taught them to read.

SEPARATE EDUCATIONAL PATHS

The division of labor between males and females in New Netherland society mandated separate educational tracks for boys and girls. On the colony's farms, children were valued as a source of labor, and the sooner they could contribute to the family economy, the better. Fathers saw to it that their sons mastered the techniques of cultivating crops and managing livestock while mothers taught their daughters how to perform the myriad tasks involved in running a farm household. Parents taught by example, and children learned by experience.

The range of occupations open to boys in the urban areas of New Netherland was much broader than in farming communities. Parents therefore were required to select a fitting occupation for each son, one that would be consonant with the family's social rank as well as take into account the child's aptitude. In the majority of instances, New Netherland boys were instructed in the mysteries of their craft by their own fathers or close kinsmen. Such associations were informal but nonetheless efficient.

Under certain circumstances formal apprenticeships were warranted. Legal documents were drawn up and signed by parents so that their son could be trained under the supervision of a master artisan, a merchant, or the practitioner of a profession. When it was deemed appropriate for a boy to enter a trade not represented in the family circle, he would be apprenticed to a community member skilled in that trade. Boys (and girls) who had lost one parent or both or were otherwise left in a vulnerable position were customarily apprenticed to members of the community by officials called orphanmasters, who were charged with ensuring the child's welfare should avaricious relatives attempt to plunder the parents' estate. Apprenticeship contracts followed Dutch precedent by including provisions for instruction in reading and writing.

Though the system of apprenticeship was well established in the seventeenth-century Netherlands, apprenticeship contracts were un-common in New Netherland prior to the last decade of settlement. Frontier conditions, the dearth of colonists, and the limited range of occupations practiced made such formal arrangements unnecessary in most cases.

Boys in New Netherland had some choice regarding their adult occupations. Girls, however, were destined to become housewives. Consequently, their immersion in household skills began early in life and proceeded by stages as they matured. Taught by mothers and older sisters, they learned to prepare traditional Dutch meals, to make clothing according to Dutch designs, and to adhere to the high standard of cleanliness typical of Dutch households in the Netherlands.

While the ability to fashion a chair, shoe a horse, or cook a favorite Dutch dish signified readiness for adult status in New Netherland, children's education was considered incomplete without exposure to the spiritual and moral values of their family. Parents strove to familiarize youngsters with the contents of the Bible as well as to inculcate the key elements of the Reformed faith. Reading aloud from the *Statenvertaling*—the 1637 translation of the Bible into the Dutch vernacular authorized by the States-General of the Netherlands—was the centerpiece of Dutch family religious education. Fathers and mothers also sought to impress spiritual truths on their offspring by including them in family prayers and allowing them to observe the adults in private devotions. Children were initiated into the life of the religious community by accompanying their parents to worship services where the minister's sermons introduced them to Reformed theology and they first heard the congregation singing the psalms.

ROLE OF THE DUTCH REFORMED CHURCH

Complementing and reinforcing family religious education were common schools sponsored by the Dutch Reformed church. By the end of the era of Dutch rule, such schools had been established in nine of New Netherland's towns. Here, the precepts of Reformed doctrine were taught, using the Heidelberg Catechism and the Bible as texts.

BIBLIOGRAPHY

De Jong, Gerald F. *The Dutch Reformed Church in the American Colonies.* Grand Rapids, Mich., 1978.

Howard, Ronald W. "Apprenticeship and Economic Education in New Netherland and Seventeenth-Century New York." In *A Beautiful and Fruitful Place: Selected Rensselaerswijck Seminar Papers,* edited by Nancy Anne McClure Zeller. Albany, N.Y., 1991.

Kilpatrick, William Heard. *The Dutch Schools of New Netherland and Colonial New York.* Washington, D.C., 1912.

Joyce D. Goodfriend

SEE ALSO **African-American Culture; Artisans; European Languages; Patterns of Community;** and **Schools and Schooling;** and various essays in FAMILIES AND THE LIFE COURSE.

THE FRENCH COLONIES

IN NEW FRANCE, the greater part of the socialization of children took place within the family. Formal and religious education was provided by the church or was under its supervision. Trades and professions were learned through apprenticeship.

FAMILY

The education of children began within the family. Once past infancy, children became involved in productive activities that made an important contribution to the family economy. They performed simple agricultural and household tasks like gardening, caring for smaller children, herding livestock, sweeping floors, fetching water, and gathering firewood. As they learned to be productive, children also ascertained what kinds of behavior were expected of members of their society by watching older members of the family work and interact socially. Children determined much of what was right and wrong and which thoughts and actions were permissible or forbidden as they watched their parents acting out social roles as men and women, consumers and producers, farmers and craftsmen, and French subjects and members of the Catholic church.

FORMAL EDUCATION

The Catholic church held the responsibility for formal education. All children received instruction in catechism, which prepared them for their First Communion by teaching them Catholic doctrine, ethics, and morality, together with subordination and respect for authority. First Communion—an important step toward becoming an adult member of society—took place soon after puberty. On the whole, the church was fairly successful in guiding the moral development of its charges. Safe from the baneful influence of competing ideologies, the church was able to prescribe community standards of behavior, which were generally accepted if not always observed.

For most children, formal education began and ended with catechism. Among the habitants, young women were more likely to be literate and numerate than young men. Female religious orders, in particular the Congrégation de Notre Dame, were devoted to the education of young women, and they established small schools in both the towns and rural areas. Speaking of these sisters, a traveler in the mid eighteenth century noted that "in many places in the country, there are two or more of them, [and] their business is to instruct young girls in the Christian religion, to teach them reading, writing, needlework and other feminine accomplishments."

For the upper classes, the schools of the Ursuline nuns at Quebec, Trois-Rivières, and New Orleans and that run by the nuns of the Hôpital Général of Quebec instructed students in social graces, genteel accomplishments, and Christian virtues. The Ursuline schools were for young girls of good family. In New Orleans, some Indian girls were taken in as well; no comparable institutions existed for boys in Louisiana.

Schools were more common in the towns than in the countryside, but even there, illiteracy remained the norm. Priests did most of the teaching. Some went so far as to found *petites écoles* (primary schools), where reading, writing, and arithmetic were taught concurrently with catechetical instruction that seldom lasted for more than one year. The Sulpicians introduced the pedagogy and methodology of Jean-Baptiste de la Salle and the Christian Brothers in their *petite écoles* in 1701 at Montreal. This included the streaming of students according to ability, quiet study habits, group work, and good teacher-pupil rapport. Lay teachers were licensed by the ecclesiastical authorities and confirmed by the intendant.

Educated *fils de famille* (young men of good family) who had been exiled from France were an important source of lay schoolmasters, as were notaries who taught to obtain a second source of income. Many lay women who had been educated by nuns passed on their knowledge to their own children and the children of their neighbors. Except in some rural parishes, students receiving primary education were segregated by gender.

Secondary education was restricted to males, who could receive instruction in Latin, rhetoric, philosophy, and theology at seminaries in urban centers. Louisiana youth had to travel to France for a comparable secondary education. Potential priests and young men seeking further education could obtain a classical education at the Collège des Jésuites at Quebec.

MILITARY

For males over age sixteen, education in the harsher side of life was available through mandatory service in the militia. Through intermittent militia musters young men received rudimentary instruction in military skills and discipline.

APPRENTICESHIP

Young men or women seeking to enter a craft or profession were generally apprenticed to an established practitioner, who was most often either the father or a relative of the apprentice. Young women apprenticed exclusively as seamstresses. The most popular crafts for young men were those whose products were in steady demand: blacksmithing, shoemaking, cooperage, and joinery. The professions of New France—notary, surgeon, and merchant—were also learned by apprenticeship, usually to a relative.

Apprenticeship normally lasted for three years, between the ages of thirteen and nineteen. Instruction was customarily provided without cost, except for the labor of the apprentice. High-status craftsmen like silversmiths, gunsmiths, and armorers, as well as merchants, however, could expect payment for instructions. Apprentice seamstresses generally paid for their education, so that their education could be completed as quickly as possible, and they could return home and begin to work.

An apprentice was obliged to obey his or her master but was often exempted from menial tasks not related to the master's craft. When the obligation to perform these tasks was included in contracts, the tasks generally included gathering firewood, carrying water, and performing farm labor.

The master was expected to pass on the skills of his or her craft to the apprentice. In most trades, the master further agreed to provide food, clothing, shelter, and in some cases cash payments to the apprentice. These payments increased as the apprentice gained skill. Moreover, masters were obliged to look to the moral and religious development of their apprentices. Contracts for apprentices under sixteen obliged the master to release the apprentice to attend catechism classes until the apprentice's First Communion.

STANDARDS OF BEHAVIOR

Metropolitan officials tended to deprecate the socialization of children of New France. They displayed a marked tendency to characterize the children of New France as unruly, disobedient, vain, and lazy. Indeed, colonial behavior may not always have approached the ideals of the more rigorous clerics or officials.

Yet, by about the age of twenty, residents of New France had been instructed in formal ethics and religion by the church, in their profession through family instruction or apprenticeship, and in the mores of their society by watching and participating in the life of their family and community. Although they would not reach the legal age of majority until age twenty-five, these women and men were ready to leave childhood behind and take their places as full members of adult society.

BIBLIOGRAPHY

Hardy, Jean-Pierre, and David-Thiery Ruddel. *Les apprentis artisans à Québec, 1660–1815.* Montreal, 1977.

Jaenen, Cornelius J. *The Role of the Church in New France.* Toronto, Ontario, 1976.

Moogk, Peter N. "*Les petits sauvages:* The Children of Eighteenth-Century New France." In *Childhood and Family in Canadian History,* edited by Joy Parr. Toronto, Ontario, 1982.

D. Peter MacLeod

SEE ALSO **African-American Culture; Artisans; European Languages; Patterns of Community;** and **Schools and Schooling;** and various essays in FAMILIES AND THE LIFE COURSES.

THE SPANISH BORDERLANDS

THIS ESSAY TOUCHES the surface of the socialization enterprise in the Spanish Borderlands, primarily what is now the southwestern United States. It examines the role of the missions as evangelizer to the indigenous populations and spiritual leader of settlers, the importance of the family as a socializing agent, and the parts played by trade craftsmen and other workers as they trained others.

The imposition of Spanish civilization presented a major challenge to Iberian institutions, but devotion to their Christian beliefs and the overwhelming desire to find gold and other treasures motivated the Spanish Crown and church to mount a vigorous combined effort. The Crown

first entered the northern reaches with soldiers and followed up with missionaries and, on their heels, all types of fortune-seekers looking for mineral wealth or, at least, land and Indian labor. Colonizing the Southwest meant that the Spanish language and Spanish religious, political, and economic systems had to be taught to the "uncivilized" indigenous peoples of the region. It also meant that Spanish officers, settlers, miners, soldiers, farmers, cattle ranchers, governors, and priests had to uphold Spanish ways of life at all times if "civilization" and colonization were to flourish in the New World.

ALLIES IN CONQUEST— CROWN AND CHURCH

By the end of the sixteenth century, it was obvious to the Spanish Crown that violence was not the best way to subdue the indigenous population. The success of the colonizing enterprise required order, peace, and stability so that Spanish settlers could take advantage of the natural resources that abounded in the colonized area. In the Spanish Borderlands, as in New Spain, labor was needed in the mining enterprises, as well as in production of food and supplies for the *presidios,* colonial settlements, and mining camps, requiring the use of Indian workers. Since 1543 Francisco de Vitoria and Francisco Alonso de Castro had recommended to the Crown that "the people of the Indies [should] receive instruction regarding the liberal arts and the Holy Scriptures. Because, who are we to show discrimination that Christ never showed." Both the Crown and the church knew that the nomadic and semisettled way of life that prevailed among the Indians had to be changed if their labor was to be utilized in the service of the colonies. The church, with its evangelical bent, provided an excellent solution in self-sufficient utopian communities where Indians were brought together to receive the message of Christianity while learning the ways of Spanish civilization; that is, the Spanish missions. In 1599 the Spanish viceroy Gaspar de Zúñiga y Azevedo, count of Monterrey (located in the state of Nuevo Leon in northern Mexico) wrote to King Philip II of Spain that "the expense [for the missions in Chihuahua and elsewhere] has proven worthy because the state of the borders has improved from not being able

452

to go from one group of mines to another, now one can travel with great security." Franciscan missionaries assigned to the Kingdom of New Mexico and, later, Jesuit missionaries sent into Chihuahua, Texas, Sinaloa, Sonora (southern Arizona), and Alta and Baja California brought their fervor and devotion to God and king. Even members of the Dominicans participated in the mission work. Saving souls thus improved order and control to the benefit of the king.

For over two hundred years, the church through its various orders participated in the process of colonization, teaching Spanish Christian beliefs as well as practical European techniques of agriculture, artisanship, and artistry to the indigenous population. Although the missions were founded to serve the indigenous peoples, often the friars tended to the spiritual and ritual needs of and provided moral guidance to soldiers and settlers, as well.

The Spanish state relied on the Roman Catholic church to uphold the principles of a good society. The complex intertwining of church and state that was characteristic of the entire medieval period in Europe was imported to the Spanish Borderlands: as the Crown sought riches, the church sought souls. Each played its part and kept in sight the importance of its role in Europe's project of conquest.

Missionaries, the spiritual arm of conquest, continued their traditional role as teachers and guides to settlers sent from Central Mexico and Spain, as well as making efforts to "civilize" the Indians and acculturate them. This dual role was maintained throughout the colonial period.

The mission as a mechanism for the "civilizing" of Indian peoples represented the principal socializing institution for indigenous groups. Meanwhile, the maintenance of Catholic practices among the settlers—seeking guidance, learning catechism, listening to sermons, and receiving the Sacraments, especially confession and matrimony—enabled the church to instill patterns of culture and to perpetuate systems of power and social structure that originated in faraway Spain. Through the teachings of the church and the legal and social structure mandated by the state, colonial society learned that ethnicity, gender, and class were not only appropriate but almost a part of nature.

Ethnicity (Spanish, Indian, mestizo, mulatto, or black), gender, and class determined how people participated in economic production and how they were trained. Only those considered Spanish were allowed to study for and join the Catholic priesthood or the professions. By the first half of the sixteenth century several religious orders had organized schools to educate those young men called to serve Christ. But it wasn't until 1551, when Prince Philip (later King Philip II of Spain) signed the founding charter of the Royal and Pontifical University of Mexico, that it was possible for colonial young men to study for a profession. Within a few years theology, canon law, civil law, medicine, and arts (philosophy) were taught, and the university awarded bachelors degrees and doctorates in these disciplines to worthy students. It was possible for the sons of well-to-do families of the faraway borderland settlements to attend the university. How many actually did is not clear, but it is known that some graduates of the university did settle in the northern provinces, some for extended periods.

ECONOMIC PATTERNS

As necessary as it was to have lawyers and doctors in frontier communities, the settlements had even more need of artisans. Although Spanish society considered anyone who worked with his hands to be inferior to one who lived off his lands and the fruits of war, artisans gained status on the frontier because their skills were so necessary. Outside Mexico City, where the sixty guilds that existed in the mother country ruled with an iron fist, deciding all points regarding guild membership, training, prices, and standards, the need for skilled workers was so great that guild policies were not enforced. There was always a need for blacksmiths to make and maintain tools, plows, door hinges, ironwork for yokes and harnesses, axes, hammerheads, chisels, and axles for carts—in fact, dozens of items. Although smithing was ostensibly restricted to those of Spanish background, records indicate that mestizos and mulattos often practiced this trade outside of Mexico City. In one case, a mulatto arranged an apprenticeship with the best blacksmith in Mexico City with the understanding that he would learn everything necessary to become a journeyman within a year and a half and then would go to the provinces to work.

Guild restrictions made it clear he would never reach the title of master, but the apprenticeship allowed him to learn the trade and to practice successfully in the provinces. It is likely that some of the artisans who settled frontier communities had similar backgrounds.

Juan de Oñate headed an expedition into what became the Kingdom of New Mexico in 1598. The roster for that journey listed, among the soldiers and settlers, one man described as a carpenter, Francisco Hernandez Cordero of Guadalajara. Six other settlers carried tools that identified them as carpenters as well. The need for skilled carpenters was so great that friars in central Mexico convinced guild members to allow Indians to serve as apprentices and to learn the trade.

In the social scale of trades, silversmiths and blacksmiths were close to the top, while carpenters were close to the bottom. Nonetheless, their products and skills were highly prized. The carpenter's guild classified skills into numerous specialties. An apprentice could choose to train for *carpintero en negro*, that is, a carpenter mechanic skilled in producing "wheels and screws for horse-powered mills, the presses for an oil mill; the spindle for a winepress; a pump; a waterwheel; and various kinds of machinery." Necessary too were *carpinteros en blanco*, those who designed moldings and complex adornments. These categories boasted several subspecialties. The best known was the *maestro de obras* (master builder), who designed doors, windows, and moldings. Today this title is given to those sufficiently knowledgeable that they can take the place of an architect or even an engineer.

The specialty of the *ensemblador*, or joiner, described a cabinetmaker. It was the *entallador*, or wood carver, who created impressive and often majestic altars and altar screens for the churches. A highly respected specialist of the carpenter guild, the *violero*, or instrument-maker, was responsible for the making of clavichords, lutes, harps, and various types of guitars. In addition to carpenters and blacksmiths, documents record the existence of armorers (to maintain guns), weavers, silversmiths, tailors, saddlemakers, and barbers.

Life on the Spanish frontier, even after more than one hundred years of settlement, remained difficult. The artifacts made by tradesmen promoted a sense of "civilization" among the settlers as they enjoyed the warmth of a well-built room with close-fitting doors and windows, a steady table, and even a chair or two. Attending Mass on holy days in a church filled with beautifully carved and dressed statues of saints and listening to the imported organ or the clavichord made by a passing *violero* enabled men and women to face the isolation and loneliness of their frontier lives. In turn, artisans fared well. Documents mention several carpenter families who, through hard work and astute investments, acquired lands and businesses beyond the trade.

The world market for precious metals and minerals as well as the local needs of the colonial settlements promoted other profitable occupations—farmers to grow grains, vegetables, and fruits, *vaqueros* (cowboys) to tend cattle for hides and meat, shepherds to raise sheep for wool for their blankets and cloth. And then there were those often unsung heroes of the *Camino Real*—the muleteers. These occupations were usually left to the mestizo population and sometimes to the Indians. Each of these occupations could be carried out under very different economic and social conditions. It was possible that a free Spaniard, having received a merced of land, would not have the resources to hire Indians or landless mestizos to till his land or to herd his sheep; but other Spaniards, wealthy thanks to grants from the Crown, *encomiendas*, and, later, *repartimientos*, simply ordered Indians to do the work.

The *encomienda* was a grant given by the Crown to a person entitling him or her the right to the labor of a certain group of Indians. In exchange for free labor, the *encomendero* (beneficiary of the grant) was responsible for the religious education of said Indians. Later, due to numerous abuses suffered by Indians at the hands of the *encomenderos*, the Crown devised *repartimientos*, which also responded to the need for labor but were based on personal services. Under *repartimiento* all Indians had to provide a certain amount of labor rather than just the groups of Indians included in *encomiendas*. This was considered to be more equitable and persisted until the end of the colonial period. The Indians in question might live in a pueblo or a village or they might be slaves. Mestizos, too, might be free or slaves.

THE ROLE OF THE FAMILY

Socializing children and preparing them to take productive roles in society is a major function of families in all cultures. So it was in colonial New Spain. Laws and policies regulating marriage and the family indicate the importance accorded the family by the Crown. Together with the church, where the regulation of sexual behavior and the teaching of children were of primary concern, colonial authorities did everything possible to place the patriarchal family at the center of a good moral order for colonial settlements in the Spanish Borderlands. Orders for expeditions to colonize New Mexico and, later, Texas and California specifically sought families and marriageable women. Organizers considered married artisans to be the most desirable settlers. Unfortunately conditions in the borderlands were considered primitive, harsh, and dangerous by most. As a result, not all artisans who signed on with their families became permanent settlers. Those who did remain tried to maintain the customs and ways long established in Spain and in central Mexico.

The Spanish patriarchal family defined roles for men and for women, giving each different responsibilities in the joint effort to form a moral, productive household. Parents were expected to ensure that their children and all members of the household learn the teachings of the church, obeyed royal authorities, and complied with the tenets of good upbringing. The father, as head of the family, was responsible for the behavior of all members of his family. As the ultimate authority, he was also the disciplinarian. The mother took responsibility for religious instruction, making certain her children learned how to pray and studied their catechism, whether taught by the mother, church officials, or an *amiga,* a woman, usually unmarried or widowed, who taught religion to small children and, occasionally, reading and writing, as well. The mother was particularly responsible for bringing up her daughters.

Spiritual guidance was considered so important that the church provided surrogate spiritual parents through the institution of *compadrazco.* When a child was baptized and, later, received the sacrament of confirmation, an adult was invited to assume responsibility for the child's spiritual and, if necessary, material well-being. At a time when many women died in childbirth and men often were absent for long periods or died young, the church considered that the family needed support in its responsibilities.

The socioeconomic status of the family determined the type of socialization that was available to children. For example, the legitimate daughter of one of the elites (a land-owning Spaniard or a high-ranking officer) would be educated for marriage to someone of at least her own class. Her mother, sometimes helped by a live-in nun or a governess, would be expected to imbue her with the importance of love of God, duty to the church, respect for her parents (especially her father), and obedience to authorities, while teaching her to handle the responsibilities of running a Christian household. Central to all was teaching the daughter to behave in such a way that the family honor was maintained. For unmarried women this meant remaining pure and chaste above all. To be a virgin was of utmost importance, and the mother was expected to teach her daughters the importance of proper sexual behavior and to supervise her charges constantly.

After marriage, the wife was expected to be faithful to her husband in order to protect his honor. Regardless of marital status, women were admonished never to violate any of the rules of chastity, modesty, respect, obedience, submissiveness, and kindness that governed the behavior of a well-brought-up woman of honor. In all their dealings women were to show prudence and patience, to avoid gossip, and to speak only as appropriate. Women were taught to stay home and take care not to be known as someone who went into the streets without protection. Modest women learned how to protect their *partes vergonzosas* (shameful parts) from any eyes and certainly from touch. Above all, honor had to be protected and maintained.

SOCIALIZATION OF WOMEN

Daughters of families of the Spanish elite on the frontier were educated to marry or to enter the church. In some cases they were taught reading and writing as well as traditional needlework, and they learned domestic work according to their station. An outstanding exception to this rule were the daughters of the Marquis de Aguyo, governor of Texas, who believed his daughters should be well educated. Ignacia Javiera de Echeverz, wife of José Azlor, inherited titles of nobility that allowed her husband to hold a place of honor in the court of the Spanish Empire. She came from a family in which daughters were educated, and, as she traveled to the northern lands of Nuevo Leon and Texas to settle frontiers for the king, she insisted that the excellent library in her husband's family be brought to her home, La Hacienda de los Patos, in present-day Nuevo Leon. She also sought the best tutors in Madrid to be brought to La Hacienda de los Patos. Her youngest daughter, Maria Xaviera Azlor, went on to become a member of the Company of Mary, a religious order devoted to the education of women, and in 1754 founded the first schools for women in New Spain to teach grammar and numbers as well as reading and writing. Dozens of young women from both the elites and the lower echelons of society became nuns and teachers as a result; each school had to have one section reserved for poor students who could not pay but who would nonetheless receive the same education as the wealthy.

Wealthy settlers often had libraries, so it is likely that numerous well-born young women learned how to read. Reading aloud to a group was a common form of entertainment throughout the colonial period. Even the settlers struggling to survive cherished the Spanish custom of gathering in late afternoon and seeking the cool shade after a hot desert day or the warmth of a sun-filled corner on a winter day to exchange news or to read and reread the novel that had arrived two months earlier. These customs survive even today in southwestern pueblos.

Daughters born outside the legitimacy of wedlock, often of mixed ethnicities and as a result of adulterous behavior, quickly entered the work force, serving as domestic helpers, doing the most menial labor, working in fields, or serving as helpers in the *obrajes* (sweatshops). From these sources came the domestic armies needed to maintain the "civilized" households of Spanish settlers. Census reports amply document the existence of households with servants, often a euphemism for men and women held in slavery.

Girls soon learned how to wash clothes, to iron in pleats, and to avoid scorching prized linen from Brussels, while others specialized in invisible mending, a skill greatly prized in a land where new clothes usually required a sizable investment as well as a long wait. Seamstresses were trained by women already well versed in turning a straight hem. Seamstresses always needed helpers to stitch the long hems for sheets, tablecloths, napkins, and swaddling for babies. Moving from helper to seamstress was a worthy promotion. Women taught girls necessary household skills—how to wash; how to sew; how to cook; how to care for babies; how to polish silver; how to set a table; and how to survive while under the control of master, mistress, children, and even priests or lovers.

Any midwife, regardless of her ethnicity, who brought children into the world and knew how to care for the mother as well was a welcome member of the community. Usually, during their tenure midwives would identify a young girl as an assistant. Oral tradition among *parteras* of the borderlands points to close apprenticeships where the midwife (*partera*) shared her knowledge with her assistant. Not only did she teach physical techniques of massaging and rubbing, but also demonstrated the use of herbal teas, prayers, and often the laying of the hands during childbirth. These age-old teachings, combining Iberian techniques and beliefs with indigenous learning, are still in use today in many parts of the Southwest.

MISSIONARIES AND THE INDIANS

The Crown repeatedly instituted policies supporting the teaching of Spanish to Indian peoples. However, priests, friars, and monks concluded that it was not possible to use Spanish to explain Christian beliefs adequately to people whose understanding of the language was so limited, and so, with varying degrees of success, they learned the languages of the Native Americans. Not only did this practice mean that Christian teachings could be explained more thoroughly; eliminating the need for the Indians to learn Spanish also separated the Indian groups from settlers and helped the missionaries control Indians more effectively.

Missions tried to create self-sufficient Indian communities where all participated in the work and all shared in its products. A substantial portion of the labor went to the maintenance and the glorification of Christian ritual and services. Some of the products of the communities were donated to other missions or sold to nearby *presidios* or settled communities. Some priests apparently were well-schooled in various trades and crafts, such as masonry and metal- and leatherwork, as well as in agricultural techniques, and undoubtedly the Indians, who were often skilled in their own crafts, could with little difficulty apply their dexterity to new techniques.

For example, Fray Alonso de Benavides, a Franciscan who served in New Mexico from 1625 to 1629, left a memorial, written in 1630, describing, among other facets of missionary life, the excellence of Indian craftsmen who taught their skills to the missionaries: "The Indians are instructed in all the arts and crafts and have their schools like the others." The trades described include tailoring, shoemaking, carpentry, and blacksmithing. However, records indicate that not all missions were built with Indian labor exclusively. For instance, San Xavier del Bac appears to have risen with the use of artisans from Spain and central Mexico.

The use of Indian labor in building and in trades did not follow identical patterns in all missions or all *presidios*. Following European traditions of patriarchy, young Indian men who appeared to be leaders, more capable, more "intelligent," were selected to learn how to read and write and often formed part of the choir and chorus at the mission. To these chosen students, the missionaries taught European agricultural technologies. The plow, for example, radically changed planting practices. Although some indigenous groups already used irrigation, missionaries taught them the ancient *asequia* system learned from the Saracens in Spain, which used a central canal with numerous branches at various levels for irrigation; the process transformed previously uncultivated land into productive wheat fields. Wheat grows more easily than corn in most desert areas, and for Indians in the Arizona-Sonora desert (the extensions of the Chihuahua desert), wheat became a basic product. Not coincidentally, the host used in the Catholic Mass could be made only from wheat

flour. In addition, fruit trees, varieties of cotton, olive trees, grapes, and even flowers were introduced.

As Indians learned to cultivate in new ways, they were taught the basic teachings of Christianity. As Native Americans came to value the food and clothing provided by the mission church as a lure to attract and keep them close by, they also absorbed the Christian values of absolute obedience to the priests, hard work, and marital monogamy.

THE SOCIAL FUNCTION OF THE CHURCH

If honor had begun as a privilege and prerogative of warriors during the Reconquest of Spain and of the conquistadores of New Spain, in the Spanish Borderlands it was part and parcel of the cultural baggage of all Spanish settlers and soldiers. Honor distinguished the conquering society from the conquered. Thus, even in households devoid of luxury, daughters were taught their "honorable" roles by their parents and by the church.

Behavior was monitored by family and by self-appointed community matrons who used gossip as a powerful control. Adding to these forces, church priests were expected as part of their duties to exercise vigilance over the behavior of Spanish settlers. Parents took their cue from the church; that is, missionaries in the northern frontiers represented the voice of the church and of God in arbitrating the norms and practices of Spanish society.

Missionaries possessed numerous resources with which to teach, inspire, and guide their flocks. First, there were the catechism classes for all those unschooled in the basic teachings of Christ and of the church. After receiving and learning the basics, settlers could make their first Holy Communion. From then on, confession with a priest was to take place at least once a year. Only by adhering to these rules could people later receive the sacrament of Holy Communion and other sacraments such as matrimony, holy orders, and extreme unction. To be excommunicated, that is, detached from the church and not allowed to partake in the sacraments, exiled the person from Christian contact and was the most extreme punishment a Christian could suffer, particularly in isolated frontier communities.

Second, the church could reach people by the pulpit reading from the Gospel offered at least weekly by a priest, who would also explain the meaning of the passage through parable or through example. Sermons were often taken from the compilation prepared, for use by their missionaries, by various religious orders. For example, Jesuits returned to their provincial houses at least once every two years for spiritual renewal. Their beliefs reinvigorated, they then returned with new materials to help them in the task of caring for settlers, soldiers, and Indians.

Missionaries, using techniques long used by European Christians, organized processions (such as the one held on the day of Corpus Christi, still popular today in some communities) and formal theatrical pieces. Christmas was celebrated with numerous enactments, some beginning on the sixteenth of December and culminating on the twenty-fourth, telling of the birth of Christ, from the Annunciation to the birth of the Holy Child. *Pastorelas* (dramatic pieces enacting the birth of Christ) were produced all over the Southwest. Even dances were utilized. Many Indian dances were adapted to teach Christian religion. *La Danza de los Moros y los Cristianos* (the dance of the Moors and the Christians) already had a long history in Spain, as Christians celebrated their victories over the heretical Moors. In the colonies it was taught by the missionaries to the Indians with the twist of casting the neophytes as Moors. Today numerous variations of this dance can still be seen in Mexico and in the Southwest.

Catholicism in medieval Europe had demonstrated the didactic impact images can make on an illiterate population. As soon as possible missionaries in the Spanish Borderlands erected churches in which, surrounded by high walls and with light shining down on the altar through openings in the ceiling, the illuminated crucified Christ took center stage. Painters and wood carvers became important members of colonial settlements, and any traveling artist was welcome at missions, for there was always some corner or wall that needed adornment. Private images of patron saints often traveled along with the settlers.

From the published sermons and the confessional guides used by missionaries in Spanish Borderland settlements, we know that priests reinforced strict rules of behavior for all members of society—men, women, and children. At the same time, sermons constantly reminded the faithful (settlers, soldiers, and Indians) that they should have utmost reverence for the church, as represented in its priests. All authorities were to be obeyed and respected. Frequent reminders to obey and respect one's parents alternated with exhortations to parents to bring up their children to respect authority and their betters. Often from the pulpit came words reminding everyone how grateful all must be to live under a kingdom that both brought peace in this life and made it possible to participate in eternal happiness.

Colonial documents are filled with examples proving that, in spite of great odds and geographic isolation, the basic tenets of proper behavior for men and women found firm adherents in the settlers of the Spanish Borderlands.

CONCLUSION

In spite of late-twentieth-century scholarship devoted to the understanding of the Spanish colonial past in the borderlands many questions remain. Sources such as census reports, notary archives in regional depositories, inventories of private and ecclesiastical libraries, private collections of letters and documents are yet to be mined adequately. Newer techniques using ethnographies and oral tradition to bring understanding to present-day rituals and performances promise clearer pictures of how popular cultural forms have been preserved and transmitted. Further study of prayers and religious practices as they evolved in the Southwest using linguistic, literary, and anthropological methods will undoubtedly reveal the existence of spiritual lives as yet unknown to us.

BIBLIOGRAPHY

Buss, Fran Leeper. *La Partera: Story of a Midwife.* Ann Arbor, Mich. 1980.
Castañeda, Antonia I. *Presidarias y Pobladoras: Spanish-American Women in Frontier Monterrey, Alta California, 1770–1821.* Ph.D. diss., Stanford University, 1990.

Foz y Foz, Pilar. *La revolucion pedagogica en Nueva Espana (1754–1820)*. Vol. 1. Madrid, 1981.

Gonzalbo Aizpuru, Pilar. *La Historia de la Educacion en la Epoca Colonial: El Mundo Indigena*. Mexico City, 1990.

———. *La Historia de la Educacion en la Epoca Colonial: La Educacion de los Criollos y la Vida Urbana*. Mexico City, 1990.

Gutiérrez, Ramón A. *When Jesus Came, the Corn Mothers Went Away: Marriage, Sexuality, and Power in New Mexico, 1500–1846*. Stanford, Calif., 1991.

Mather, Christine. *Colonial Frontiers: Art and Life in Spanish New Mexico*. Santa Fe, N.Mex., 1983.

Spicer, Edward H., ed. *Ethnic Medicine in the Southwest*. Tucson, Ariz., 1977.

Spicer, Edward H. *The Yaquis: A Cultural History*. Tucson, Ariz., 1980.

Taylor, Lonn, and Dessa Bokides. *New Mexican Furniture: The Origins, Survival, and Revival of Furniture Making in the Hispanic Southwest*. Santa Fe, N.Mex., 1989.

Raquel Rubio-Goldsmith

SEE ALSO **Artisans; European Languages; Mission Communities; Patterns of Community;** and **Schools and Schooling;** and various essays in FAMILIES AND THE LIFE COURSE.

SCHOOLS AND SCHOOLING

THE BRITISH COLONIES

PUBLIC SCHOOLS, FAMILIAR to citizens in the United States in the nineteenth century—free, universal, locally controlled, and eventually compulsory—did not exist before the War for Independence. Modern public schools were a product of an increasingly urbanized, more technologically complex, competitive economic organization that developed after the War of 1812; this structure competed with a parallel, although smaller, private system that arose for both secular and religious reasons. In the English colonies before the War for Independence, however, schools were essentially private, sparse, scattered, controlled by a large variety of denominational and secular groups and individuals, and designed for sundry purposes. They ranged from dame schools for the youngest children, to a variety of petty schools, to reading and writing schools and Latin grammar schools for older children, particularly boys. In addition, a plethora of private teachers offered a wide variety of academic and practical subjects to anyone, children as well as adults, interested and able to pay. In short, they were heterogeneous, serving a small, ever-changing segment of the population and catering to diverse needs and interests. Schools were not, then, a vital part of most children's lives in British North America, but they did appear in all of the colonies to some degree and were part of the rich tapestry of colonial social, educational, cultural, religious, political, racial, and economic life.

SCHOOLING IN ENGLAND

Schools in the British colonies were influenced, in part, by the colonists' cultural baggage and previous experiences. During the sixteenth century and into the seventeenth most children in England did not attend any sort of school, for reasons that were often economic. Younger children, girls as well as boys, who did experience the scattered private-venture, fee-charging petty schools learned spelling, reading, and religion. The masters, both male and female, suffered from menial work and low status. Often the parish clerk assumed teaching responsibilities. There were also short-term private writing schools in some towns, both for children over eight who could read and for adults.

The sons of middle- and upper-class families might attend grammar school, perhaps as a stepping-stone to Oxford or Cambridge. A master, pious and university trained, would teach Latin, Greek, and sometimes Hebrew, along with rhetoric, classical history, ancient geography, mythology, and religion to boys from eight to fourteen or fifteen years of age. Discipline was strict and the curriculum narrow. There were also private tutors for boys whose parents could afford tuition. After about 1600, it was not considered unusual for wealthy girls to have private teachers or even to attend boarding schools where they learned reading, writing, music, dancing, needlework, household skills, and perhaps French and Latin, essentially practical skills. All schools were somewhat disrupted during the 1640s and 1650s because of the English Civil War and its aftermath, but with the restoration of the king in 1660 the traditional patterns reemerged, albeit with some variations.

Religion and schooling were closely intertwined. Since the mid sixteenth century the Church of England had controlled or influenced most schools, although Dissenters, either Puritans or Catholics, had been active as well. Historians traditionally have argued that the Puritans were more committed than others to widespread literacy in English and taught in petty schools as well as at home in order to encourage the laity, particularly men, to read the Bible. While this may have been true, Puritan-controlled grammar schools closely resembled the Anglican schools before the Civil War. The former, too, focused on a classical curriculum that stressed Latin, with perhaps more emphasis on reformed logic and Bible study, and favored Puritan-authored texts. From the Act of Uniformity following the Restoration to the Toleration Act of 1689, nonconformists were forced to teach in relative secrecy, with their academies moving from place to place.

By the eighteenth century there were various schools in England, including endowed parish schools teaching rudimentary literacy to the poor, funded grammar schools, English schools and private academies, and a wide variety of private-venture as well as charity schools. The latter "free" schools often emphasized vocational training and moral education for the poor. While there seems to have been a general falling off of educational zeal in England by the mid eighteenth century, there was nonetheless somewhat greater institutional diversity there.

THE PUBLIC NATURE OF NEW ENGLAND SCHOOLS

School founders and promoters in the colonies drew upon this English legacy in their quest to establish an institutional base for their ideas and goals. Although those who settled in New England were the most zealous in connecting schooling with learning, piety, and stability, a plethora of schools eventually sprang up in every colony for both religious and secular reasons. While there was little uniformity, or even continuity, some similarities existed: schools were for children and youth; and they concentrated on teaching a limited range of academic and practical skills as well as piety. Formal schooling was more for boys than for girls, and more for whites than for nonwhites, but all were included to some degree.

Seventeenth-Century Roots

The development of the Massachusetts schools exhibited an interesting combination of public and private initiative underscored by the colony's religious fervor, although educational uniformity and persistence were always illusory. Individuals in various towns early on began teaching small groups of students in their homes, as did Philemon Pormort in Boston in 1635, succeeded in the following year by Daniel Maude, who taught until 1643. Although attendance was both free and voluntary—Pormort and Maude were subsidized by the town's leaders—few boys participated. Some towns, such as Boston, Charlestown, Ipswich, and Dorchester, established Latin grammar schools for more advanced scholars. Others—Newbury and Salem, for example—stressed only reading and writing. Qualified teachers were always difficult to attract and retain. These early schools were generally funded through the rental of public town lands, supplemented with support from private endowments or public rates.

The General Court's emphasis on community organization and development, which required educated leaders and a literate citizenry, led to calls for more coordinated actions. Only seven of twenty-four Massachusetts towns had early on encouraged formal schooling. The reluctance of the other towns prompted the government in 1642 to pass a law promoting literacy. While a few dame schools emerged, the law had little public effect, since only Roxbury and Dedham founded grammar schools in the next few years. In 1647, so "that learning may not be buried in the grave of our fathers in the church and commonwealth," the legislature directed all towns of at least fifty households to "appoint one [person] within their own town to teach all such children as shall resort to him to write and read." The eight towns that each consisted of at least one hundred families were instructed to "set up a grammar school" with a qualified Latin grammar master. Five had already complied, and the remaining three, under pressure, soon capitulated. Funding would be either public or private, depending on each town's circumstances.

School costs varied according to the teacher's salary and various other expenses. Boston not only paid the master's salary, but sometimes provided him with a dwelling as well as a separate schoolhouse. Revenues came from the rental of town lands, a general town rate (or tax), and a growing dependency in many towns on tuition payments. Charlestown and Dorchester's "free" grammar schools disappeared after mid century, for example, as more emphasis was put on parental contributions. And there were also ostensibly private grammar schools—for example Elijah Corlet's in Cambridge, which was still partially subsidized by the town in the 1660s. The larger towns were theoretically required to support both a reading and writing and a Latin teacher, but many combined the two in a general school. Parents and children often had scant interest in classical education.

If the larger towns generally complied with the grammar-school provision of the 1647 law, the fourteen smaller communities of at least fifty families had problems. By 1660, nine still had no petty schools, and those that did had difficulty retaining their teachers. As additional towns came within the law's purview, they were slow to hire teachers. Twenty years after the law's passage, only ten of the eligible twenty-six towns had responded positively by maintaining a master under community control, paid by a heavy dependence on the town rate and supplemented by tuition payments and land-rental fees. Instruction in reading and writing was all the law required, but some of the teachers also covered ciphering, which was elementary arithmetic, Latin, and other subjects, thereby blurring the line between petty and grammar schools. The county courts reluctantly threatened to fine the recalcitrant towns. Local conditions did prompt some communities to secure teachers and even to build schoolhouses by the early 1670s. These

facilities were generally simple, primitive, and uncomfortable, filled with long plank desks attached to the walls and often dominated by the master's table. Parents supplied wood for the large fireplace.

The General Court's preference for grammar over petty schools was demonstrated in 1671. A new law doubled the fine to £10 for eligible towns that did not support grammar schools. Braintree and Beverly were quickly reprimanded. Other growing towns were also now cited for refusing to support a reading and writing teacher. Colonial leaders naturally feared some educational backsliding. Another amendment to the 1647 law, in 1683, mandated towns of two hundred families to provide two grammar and two writing schools. The law was largely symbolic. Until the century's end—facing continued financial hardships, wars, and political dislocations—some towns offered only Latin instruction, others both reading and grammar schools, while most had a general school combining the two. A majority of the fifty-family towns supported some sort of reading and writing school, particularly after the inclusion of an education provision in the Province Laws of 1692 that underscored their legal obligation.

By the early eighteenth century the grammar schools—headed by college-trained, perhaps professional Latin masters who served boys at least seven years old—were quite similar in the twenty-six large towns. None could match Boston Latin, where the notable Ezekiel Cheever served as master for seventy years. The reading and writing schools, however, were hardly uniform in the seventeen smaller towns. Meeting three or four months during the winter, sometimes another two in the summer, they had a constant turnover of teachers, who were sometimes poorly trained. The curriculum in all schools emphasized a select few readers and Latin grammars.

While the Massachusetts Bay colony set the pace and style for public schooling in New England, its neighbors followed suit in various ways. They were also influenced by Puritan notions equating literacy with piety, by the need for learned leaders, and by their common English background. The founders of Newport, Rhode Island, established a town school in 1640 and built a schoolhouse four decades later. Connecticut enacted a school law in 1650. In New Haven, a 1651 ordinance instructed the new town school-master that "his worke should be to perfect male children in English, after they can read in their Testament or Bible, & to learne them to wright." Grammar schools were valued by local leaders but difficult to maintain, as New Haven discovered in the 1670s. Plymouth colony recommended petty schools to its towns in the 1650s and mandated grammar schools in 1677.

Existing side by side with the New England town-sponsored masters were a variety of private schools, teachers, and programs. They presented boys and girls with opportunities beyond parental instruction. The ubiquitous dame schools, for example, proliferated by the 1690s and offered rudimentary reading and perhaps writing to boys and girls as young as two or three years old, plus sewing and knitting to the girls. Usually taught by women in their homes, who charged a nominal fee to the parents or who were paid by the town, the dame schools lifted some educational burdens from thankful mothers and fathers. The diary of Boston's Samuel Sewall records that he sent some of his daughters to Dame Sarah Walker, his two-year-old son Joseph to "Capt. Townsend's Mother's," and another daughter to learn reading and knitting from "Mrs. Thair" (Deborah Thayer).

Private male masters who charged tuition also offered instruction at various levels starting in the 1630s. In the later part of the century, Joseph Dassett, Edward Mills, and Peter Burr presided over grammar schools in Boston. Charging £2 per pupil per year, Burr taught Latin and writing to both boys and girls. In 1722 Mills became master of the town's public writing school. Sponsored by the Society for the Propagation of the Gospel in Foreign Parts (S.P.G.), the missionary arm of the Church of England, Mills had earned £15 in 1721 for offering grammar, writing, arithmetic, and church catechism, remuneration that was considerably less than that of his public counterparts, who received a larger sum and perhaps even a rent-free house. Private writing masters usually taught spelling, reading, writing, arithmetic, and even Latin to young boys and girls, offering competition to the town-supported masters. Local leaders in Marblehead, Sudbury, Rowley, and Braintree believed the presence of private teachers fulfilled their legal obligation to support a writing school.

Similar to their public counterparts, many of the private teachers combined writing and Latin instruction in a rather general curriculum.

EIGHTEENTH-CENTURY DEVELOPMENTS

The basic school patterns established in the seventeenth century continued in the eighteenth throughout New England: a mix of private and public instruction; support from public sources, tuition payments, or both; separate levels of dame, writing, and grammar schools, although many seem to have been a combination of the latter two; school entry as young as two years old, with boys (and sometimes girls) entering the higher levels at seven or eight for another seven years; and a curriculum generally stressing both literacy and memorization. How many children attended school and for how long is unknown.

Teachers proliferated as the population increased, particularly in the larger towns, but few were publicly supported. Boston had only two grammar schools and three writing schools for most of the century, free only for the town's residents. Masters of these five public schools, sometimes assisted by an usher, served for various lengths of time, although twelve lasted for more than twenty-five years as teaching developed into a profession. While the grammar schools offered a classical curriculum, mandatory for college admittance, the writing schools stressed penmanship and prepared boys to become merchants or clerks. Enrollment in the five schools was substantial, and between 1760 and 1766 they annually trained more than nine hundred boys, generally sons of the wealthier families, and absorbed a full one-third of the town's budget.

For students able to pay, desirous of a broader curriculum, and wary of the "charity" tinge of the public schools, other opportunities beckoned. Many came to Boston from other colonies, including the West Indies, boarding with a teacher. In 1709, Owen Harris offered geometry, surveying, navigation, astronomy, writing, and arithmetic. In his boarding school James Ivers taught girls arithmetic, writing, embroidery, needlework, and painting on glass. The nearly unlimited range of subjects and practical skills available through private instruction also included shorthand, bookkeeping, modern languages such as French, drawing, dancing, and mechanics. Some teachers, like Thomas Grainger at the S.P.G. school, taught religion through the Anglican catechism.

Schooling opportunities were less available in the region outside Boston. Towns continued to ignore the mandatory grammar school laws. Between 1731 and 1765, eighteen towns in Worcester County and nine towns in Middlesex County, for example, failed to provide grammar schools. County courts were reluctant to impose fines, even though they punished eight guilty towns in rural Hampshire County before the revolution. By 1765, approximately 65 of the Bay colony's 144 larger towns supported Latin grammar schools.

In Connecticut only four towns after 1700 were required to support grammar schools— New Haven, New London, Hartford, and Fairfield. They generally complied. By mid century, however, at least fifty towns in the colony had more than one hundred families and were required to support schools; the number of towns with grammar schools nonetheless remained at four, though some smaller villages employed college graduates for their writing schools. In New Hampshire, about half of the towns supported writing or grammar schools. The situation was bleaker in Rhode Island. Newport sustained three public schools only with great difficulty, including a grammar school in a substantial building erected in 1739. There were also Quaker, Congregational, Baptist, Episcopal (supported by the S.P.G.), Moravian, and other private schools in the town, where religious pluralism flourished. In Providence, George Taylor conducted an S.P.G. school, which welcomed charity and tuition students from 1735 until the revolution. A few dozen white boys and girls and occasionally a black child attended daily. In addition to dame schools, there were also Quaker, Baptist, and independent masters in the community.

Population growth and dispersal combined with economic problems to prompt some towns to move their writing and grammar schools around the community. These were called "moving" schools. In Watertown, Massachusetts, for example, in 1701 the town meeting agreed to alternate the grammar school once each quarter between two sites. Worcester transformed its standing school to a moving school in 1731. About the same time the reading and writing master in Londonderry, New Hampshire, temporarily moved to seven different locations in one year. By mid century moving schools were a common response to educational demands from families in the outlying vicinities of the towns. There was constant tension between the newer and older areas of growing communities for schools and other services.

The public schools were essentially for boys, but girls also were present. Indeed, of the 132 children attending Ephraim Fellows's school in Stonington, Connecticut, between 1746 and 1762, half were girls. While an extreme case, it illustrates the flexibility of prevailing attitudes. If boys and girls were enrolled at the same private school, they were often instructed in separate rooms or scheduled for different hours. Generally, however, girls attended private single-sex schools taught by women, emphasizing reading, writing, arithmetic, and sewing, sometimes French, English grammar, geography, and history. Boarding schools existed in a few towns such as Boston and Newport. Female schooling was practical, directed toward instilling the morality, utility, and gentility considered suitable for future wives and mothers.

By the revolution there was a plethora of public and private schools in New England. The earlier community emphasis on public Latin schools was gradually replaced by an interest in vocational and English subjects, particularly in the private writing and specialized schools springing up in the cities and towns. Dame schools proliferated for the smaller children. Poor children had more limited opportunities compared to their wealthier neighbors.

DISPARATE ORIGINS IN THE MIDDLE COLONIES

Schooling was also widespread in the middle colonies, but the configurations were necessarily different. Lacking the strong religious and community bonds characteristic of New England, the middle colonies demonstrated less public interest in writing or grammar schools. Rather, various communities, religious organizations, and individuals established a multitude of schools, offering a mix of academic, practical, and religious subjects.

New York

When the English captured New Netherland in 1664, they inherited both an elementary and a grammar school in New Amsterdam, although only the elementary school survived. Originally under both secular and church control, the school continued in New York City under the sponsorship of the Dutch Reformed church, which had as a stated goal the promotion of literacy and piety through elementary schooling. Instruction remained exclusively in Dutch. The master's salary came mostly from tuition fees. Admitting both boys and girls who ranged in age from seven to fourteen, the school concentrated on religious instruction, reading, writing, and ciphering. Clinging to the Dutch language until the 1770s, the school became marginal and could not attract even thirty charity students in 1767. A second Dutch school existed from 1743 to 1757.

Other Dutch schools in the eighteenth century included one in New Harlem where the small community faithfully provided the Dutch teacher with financial support and a house. The central Flatbush school, under joint church and town control, survived into the 1770s; it introduced English only in the 1750s. The nearby New Lotts school was exclusively in English. Schools also existed in Albany, Bergen, Kingston, and other older Dutch communities. Stressing reading, writing, and religion, classes were held in the teacher's house, as in New England. Girls and boys normally sat apart.

The English in the New York colony were also concerned about schooling, but their lack of sustained interest in public support for teachers or school buildings meant New York's children for the most part depended on a variety of religious and secular private schools. Matthew Hiller operated a combined private writing and grammar school in the 1670s on Manhattan. A short-lived Jesuit Latin school also existed. A free Latin school was established in 1702, and a master, licensed by the bishop of London, was procured two years later. This public school

lasted until 1710. Until 1722, the S.P.G. briefly supported a free grammar school taught by the Reverend Robert Jenny. In addition, the Shearith Israel congregation provided Hebrew teachers for its children. In the 1730s the provincial assembly also supported a public grammar school, where Alexander Malcolm taught twenty boys Latin, Greek, and mathematics.

The Anglican Trinity Church partially supported New York schoolmaster William Huddleston starting in 1702; by 1709 the S.P.G. funded this free school. Paid only ten pounds and a shipment of books per year, Huddleston taught fifty-one pauper children by 1719. Joseph Hildreth was later schoolmaster of this charity school and taught reading, writing, ciphering, and the catechism for three decades before the revolution. In 1720, Huddleston received a slight public subsidy to teach reading to a few poor children. During the next decade a small charity school served Greenwich Village.

The religious schools had stiff competition from a variety of individual teachers. At least sixteen separate private schools existed in the city between 1690 and 1720, and for the next twenty years twenty-four masters offered some sort of instruction. Private teachers had itinerate lives, and they probably never exceeded thirty in number before the revolution. Joshua Ring advertised in 1737 to teach reading and writing for twelve and a half shillings a quarter. A few teachers accepted both boys and girls, as did George Brownell in 1731, promising the elementary subjects, languages, bookkeeping, dancing, and needlework. The same year Martha Gazely, a new arrival from London, published an announcement offering to teach girls needlework as well as how to make artificial fruits and flowers, while others taught French and Spanish. There were also a few dame schools. Many masters taught intermittently while practicing other trades.

Young children attended classes during the day, but their older siblings, particularly apprentices, enjoyed a variety of evening schools, open generally for two quarters during the winter. Some teachers offered both day and evening classes. Since many indenture contracts called for instruction in reading, writing, and ciphering, there was a ready market for private evening instruction beginning in the late seventeenth century. In 1723 John Walton advertised instruction in reading, writing, arithmetic, fractions, and the "Mariner's Art" to apprentices. These schools generally combined academic as well as practical matters. Bookkeeping was offered, as was astronomy and surveying, along with ancient and modern languages, geography, ethics, rhetoric, logic, and other subjects. Some masters rented schoolhouses or rooms from private owners, a common practice also for regular day schools, which shared the same quarters. While many of the schools addressed the needs of apprentices, others catered to both young men and women, together or separate, seeking an education. Evening schools were popular in New York City, Boston, Philadelphia, Newport, and Charlestown, towns with a sizable number of young people.

New Jersey

The schooling patterns in New York, both the city and colony, were essentially mirrored in neighboring New Jersey. In Bergen the Reformed church established a Dutch school in 1661 that was also supported by the community, a practice continued until after the revolution. There were other Dutch schools, as well as a few Swedish schools, along the Delaware River. These schools sometimes survived into the eighteenth century but faced a shortage of pastor-teachers, financial difficulties, and waning interest in parochial education.

Quaker schools, on the other hand, rudimentary during the seventeenth century, grew somewhat through the 1750s, appearing in at least sixteen communities. Rare were teachers such as John Woolman of the Quaker school at Mount Holly, who devoted himself to the ideals of literacy and a more humane spirit. Greater interest in schooling, particularly for the poor, emerged in the 1760s as the Quakers withdrew from prerevolutionary politics, but real improvement did not come until the revolutionary years. The Quaker influence helped nurture the colony's 1758 and 1774 poor laws, which provided for elementary instruction for bound children.

The S.P.G. was also active in New Jersey, with mixed results. Before 1763 at least seven of its schoolmasters were in the colony, teaching reading, writing, arithmetic, catechism, and Christian morality. Despite many difficulties, including competition with the neighboring Quaker school and the problem of uncooperative parents, the teacher of the school in Burlington, started in 1712, remained for twenty-five years. Shrewsbury's master lasted about seventeen years. S.P.G. charity schools welcomed both white and black children. The few Lutheran schools, such as the one in Cohansey, concentrated on reading pious literature and on preparation for confirmation.

Presbyterian schools appeared in the 1760s, including grammar schools and academies whose classical curriculum prepared boys for college. They were often semipublic, dependent on private subscription but occasionally erected on public land, as in Newark. Presbyterian schools in a few towns reflected the Puritan emphasis on public education, particularly in the areas that New Englanders settled in East Jersey. In 1676 the Newark town meeting set aside land for a schoolhouse, finally built in 1700. Woodbridge had a schoolmaster as early as 1680, who was apparently supported by tuition fees until late in the century when the town paid his salary. The East Jersey assembly in 1693 encouraged towns to appoint three men to supervise a town rate to pay the teacher's salary, underscoring their commitment to free schools. Such centralized action disappeared after 1702 with the advent of royal government and waning Puritan influence. These town schools lingered along with the various religious and other private schools that focused on reading, writing, ciphering, and catechism. For more rudimentary skills, particularly learning the alphabet and sewing, boys and girls studied in the numerous dame schools.

Pennsylvania

Neighboring Pennsylvania, equally marked by religious diversity and cultural decentralization, had a rich array of schools, particularly in Philadelphia. The Quakers held a strong presence in education because of their concern for literacy and piety, but they lacked a monopoly of educational institutions. Soon after its founding, in 1683, the Provincial Council appointed Enoch Flower to teach reading, writing, and ciphering in Philadelphia; six years later the Friends monthly meeting named Thomas Makin master of another petty school in the burgeoning town.

George Keith became master of a public grammar school the same year, which grew so fast he was quickly assisted by Makin, who divided teaching responsibilities between classical and practical subjects. With a new charge and charter in 1701 to offer instruction in "good literature" as well as in "languages, arts & Sciences" to boys and girls, the Friends School became the keystone of the city's educational edifice.

The Friends (William Penn Charter) School experienced a turnover of masters and mistresses until the forty-year tenure of Anthony Benezet began in 1742. As the Quaker elite increased, they became more interested in the Latin curriculum. Other Quaker teachers were also controlled by the Philadelphia monthly meeting, such as Ann Brientnall, who taught reading and sewing in the 1760s. In 1779, at least ten teachers worked in Friends schools, offering instruction free, for the poor, that ranged from the classical subjects to English and arithmetic to rudimentary instruction for boys and girls. Generally supported by voluntary subscriptions, the schools also depended on various legacies and an occasional bond issue; schoolhouses were built on donated land.

The Friends' educational zeal was almost matched by other denominations and individuals in Philadelphia. Several schools appeared by the late 1690s, including one in an Anglican parish and another sponsored by the Swedish church. Within a few years girls could learn sewing from Mrs. Andros or serving from Mrs. Monckton. By mid century, after attending one of the numerous dame schools, boys could study Latin, Greek, mathematics, and other subjects from Master William Robbins, or accounting and surveying from Andrew Lamb or Theophilus Grew. Evening schools served those who worked during the day. Noel Ledru offered classes for young women in writing, arithmetic, and pattern drawing. Girls learned French from Mrs. Rhodes and boarded with the itinerate teacher George Brownell, who offered reading, writing, ciphering, dancing, and needlework.

Along with the private teachers, two German schools—Reformed and Lutheran—a Moravian elementary school, and in the 1750s a Baptist grammar school added to the mix. Most important, in 1751 Benjamin Franklin published *The Idea of the English School* and founded, with others, the nonsectarian Academy and Charitable School, which soon added a college curriculum (the College of Philadelphia). The academy was highly respected, featuring both a Latin and an English department, although within a few years the latter was given little support by the trustees and lost enrollment. The charity school soon served about one hundred boys and half as many girls. Students came from other colonies to attend Philadelphia's wide range of boarding and day schools. Despite the fame of the Penn Charter School and the academy in preparing boys for college, as in Boston there was a growing demand for a more practical, business-oriented curriculum.

The Quakers' interest in formal education at the elementary level carried throughout the colony. Teachers appeared in Byberry and Germantown, as well as in Bucks, Montgomery, Chester, and Delaware county communities. Usually under the supervision of the local monthly meetings, with strong prodding from the Philadelphia Yearly Meeting, the schools served both pay and free scholars, who studied reading, English, writing, arithmetic, sewing, spelling, needlework, and religion. Classes were held five and a half days a week, seven to eight hours a day. Most teachers were men, but the Quaker emphasis on gender equality meant that women were hired to teach girls as well as boys.

The variety of schools throughout the colony reflected local conditions. The Germantown schools illustrated the typical complexities of such a situation. The general court of Germantown appointed Francis Daniel Pastorious, with three years of experience in the Philadelphia Friends School, teacher of the local school in 1701; he taught both day and evening classes. Anthony Benezet had his own Quaker-oriented school from 1739 to 1742, and a school apparently opened in the Mennonite church building in 1708. The Moravian School, operated by John Bechtel in the 1740s, soon moved to Bethlehem. Overall, however, the established churches scarcely supported schools. Only Saint Michael's Lutheran Church made much of an effort; teachers were hired in the 1740s, and a schoolhouse was erected in 1771.

The real impetus for formal instruction came from nineteen men who formed the Union School (later Germantown Academy) in 1759.

Within a year they had constructed an imposing two-story stone building. The school offered separate English and German sections, a general curriculum, and even night classes for the mostly male students. Two smaller schools also enjoyed secular support: the Harmony School in 1745 and the Concord School in 1775. None of the Germantown schools was particularly sectarian, preferring to stress literacy and other practical skills. Private masters also offered a variety of subjects, including one who taught Latin and Greek in 1761 for "the Poor as well as the Rich, without any Distinction as to Sect or Persuasion." Children seem to have attended the nearest school.

Germantown was unusual in its lack of sectarian schooling. Still, it reflected the colony's educational and religious heterogeneity. The S.P.G. had six schoolmasters in Pennsylvania from 1714 to 1763, mirroring the small Anglican population. Private teachers struggled along throughout the colony—such as Rowland Jones in Chester and Radnor, who applied in vain to the S.P.G. for support. On the frontier Scotch-Irish Presbyterians established petty and grammar schools in an attempt to educate the scattered population. Moravians operated a secondary boarding school for girls in Bethlehem as well as various day and boarding schools for other students, although after 1754 they concentrated on educating their own children. Christopher Dock taught Mennonite children in both Skippack and Salford by 1738, alternating three days a week at each. The large German immigration meant both an influx of teachers from Germany, twelve alone in the fall of 1749, and the need to offer instruction in two languages in schools with a religious and ethnic mix of students. In many communities Lutheran and Reformed ministers often doubled as schoolmasters.

In light of the difficulty of maintaining schools, the poverty of many German families, and concern about their loyalty, in 1754 a London-based philanthropic organization called the Society for Propagating the Knowledge of God Among the Germans in Pennsylvania set about to establish its oversight in the colony. Under the supervision of the Reverend William Smith, also provost of the Academy and College of Philadelphia, and funded by donors in England and Scotland, the society by 1759 supported English-language schools in New Providence, Upper Dublin, Northampton, Lancaster, York, New Hanover, Reading, and Chesnut Level. While the emphasis was on teaching English and basic skills, there was also instruction in Latin and Greek. By 1763, however, the charity-school movement dissipated. Strong opposition came from the Quakers and the quietist sects. Many Germans feared losing their language, and funds from England became scarce. Thus, a charity-school system designed to promote language (and even religious) conformity was short-lived in heterogeneous Pennsylvania.

SPORADIC SCHOOLING IN THE SOUTHERN COLONIES

Schools were established in Pennsylvania and its neighbors by a variety of organizations and individuals, unlike the more public nature of New England's schools. In contrast Virginia and the other southern colonies had little organization on any level. Schooling was sporadic and essentially a private matter. This was not intended, but factors including the resistance or inertia of the colonists themselves continually succeeded in frustrating larger organizational schemes. Indeed, in 1622 the Virginia Company donated a thousand acres to maintain a public free school at Charles City. The project was still-born.

More successful was Benjamin Syms's bequest in 1635 of two hundred acres (80 hectares) and eight cows for a free school in Elizabeth City. Four years later Thomas Eaton donated five hundred acres (200 hectares), two slaves, twelve cows, two bulls, and twenty hogs to support another school in the same community. In 1675 Henry Peasley of Gloucester County bequeathed sufficient funds for a local charity school, which survived for many years despite its low attendance. A total of six schools operated in Virginia in 1689. In comparison, there was one school in Maryland at the time.

Virginia

During the eighteenth century three types of schools appeared in Virginia for white children:

endowed free schools, private community schools, and individual-venture schools. They concentrated on reading, writing, and arithmetic, although some of the private teachers occasionally taught the classics. Few children attended, however, and the planter elite depended on private tutors for their children. There were at least twelve attempts to establish endowed schools, with mixed results. Mary Whaley donated land for a free school in Williamsburg in 1706, with additional funds coming from her estate after her death in 1743. The income from Samuel Sandford's 3,420 acres (1,368 hectares) supported a successful school in Accomac County after 1710, and two schools succeeded in Nansemond County because of John Yeates's bequest in 1731. Primarily intended for poor children in need of basic instruction in reading, writing, and arithmetic, the free schools, considering the lack of competition, also accepted those who could pay. The College of William and Mary, founded in 1693, contained a grammar school as well as an Indian school, and the latter also accepted local white youth interested in reading and writing.

Scattered, private tuition-supported community schools existed where neighbors might have pooled their resources, built a schoolhouse or offered part of another facility, and advertised for a teacher. Sometimes individuals would initiate the effort. Devereux Jarratt, basically self-taught in reading and arithmetic, was invited by Jacob Moon to run a school in Albemarle County, although few pupils appeared. Perhaps two dozen Anglican and dissenting ministers conducted schools or served as tutors in the eighteenth century. Thomas Jefferson and James Madison attended such schools, which commonly offered a grammar-school curriculum. Jonathan Boucher's school in Caroline County was most successful in the 1760s, with thirty boys within a short time boarding on the property.

In the colony's three towns—Williamsburg, Norfolk, and Fredericksburg—there were a few private teachers. John Walker advertised to teach reading, writing, arithmetic, and even the classics to Williamsburg's boys in 1752. Bartholomew Le Petit had a short-lived school in Norfolk, then moved to the capital in 1773. Three years later Mrs. Neill proposed a boarding school for girls, a decade after Mrs. Arniston opened one in Norfolk to teach reading, writing, needlework, and other female skills. There were also more specialized dancing and music schools.

Maryland

In Virginia, with its scattered population and lack of community orientation, schools were scarce and generally focused on basic skills for the poor and classical subjects for the more privileged. In the rest of the South the situation was similar. The Maryland legislature finally passed an act in 1724 promoting county-supervised charity schools, but few were established. There was apparently only one endowed free school—King William's School at Annapolis—several Catholic and Presbyterian schools, and a few others initiated by German religious groups, offering both elementary and grammar curricula. Private teachers were active in Baltimore. Most inclusive was Somerset Academy in the city, which in 1769 offered a range of courses: English, spelling, writing, Latin and Greek, geography, navigation, and surveying.

THE CAROLINAS

North Carolina provided even fewer schooling choices to its children. Its colonial government struggled to support a school, and finally in 1766 did approve using tax funds for a schoolhouse in Newbern. There were Presbyterian schools along the western frontier, a Moravian school in Wachovia, some Quaker teachers, and probably an assortment of private masters from time to time. The Reverend David Caldwell opened a classical school near Newmarket, North Carolina. In South Carolina, on the other hand, a flourishing city and a wealthier economy meant a somewhat larger realm of educational opportunities. The assembly first encouraged schools in 1694. In 1712 it allowed parish vestries to build schoolhouses and pay teachers, though actual progress was slow. The endowed Winyaw Indigo Society School at Georgetown was opened in 1756, and three S.P.G. teachers operated in the colony in the eighteenth century, including Benjamin Dennis in Goose Creek and Thomas Morritt in Charleston.

Charleston offered a variety of schools and teachers by the mid eighteenth century, a recent situation reflecting its status as a growing metropolis. There was a short-lived Congregational school in the 1690s. James Douglas started an Anglican free school, funded by the colony, early in the new century, with a classical as well as a practical curriculum featuring mathematics, surveying, navigation, and merchants' accounts. At the time there was also the Reverend William Guy's classical school, supported by the S.P.G. and tuition payments. A few years later, in the 1720s, the S.P.G.'s Thomas Morritt had fifty-four students, most studying Latin. By the 1730s there were various private-venture day and night schools, presenting subjects including dancing, arithmetic, astronomy, bookkeeping, drawing, needlework, and much else to young men and women. The elite were being served, along with some poor scholars in the free school and charity schools sponsored by the South Carolina Society, the Fellowship Society, and the German Friendly Society. Just before the revolution various boarding schools opened, including the coeducational academies of Osborn Straton and William Walton.

Georgia

As the last colony founded, Georgia had less school development, although white children there still had some opportunities. Charitable contributions in England were early designed to promote schooling, but what in fact developed were essentially private initiatives, with one major exception. The Bethesda Orphan Asylum in Savannah, organized by George Whitefield in 1739, included a school that was also free to the town's children. Grants from Parliament funded the orphanage school, as well as teachers' salaries at Vernonburgh, Acton (later Savannah), and Augusta, which lasted through the revolution. There was a strong religious cast to the schools. Private-venture teachers, licensed by the bishop of London or the royal governor, offered Latin, French, and mathematics, as well as more mundane subjects such as dancing, fencing, and music. Educational support also came, in the early years, from the S.P.G., which funded two teachers, and the Society in Scotland for Propagating Christian Knowledge. By the revolution

Georgia offered a variety of educational possibilities, including boarding schools for boys and girls, particularly in Savannah.

SCHOOLING FOR NATIVE AND AFRICAN AMERICANS

All of the British colonies ultimately offered a wide range of schools and schooling experiences to their white children. There were also schools for Indian and black children (and sometimes adults), although they were sparse, scattered, and based on a desire to Christianize and "civilize"— one of the main spurs of colonization. Indian schools were a product of colonial governments or missionary societies, established by strong-willed individuals. They needed Native cooperation to succeed. Authorities in Virginia early proposed Henrico College and the East India School for Native children, but the Indian uprising in 1622 and the subsequent royal takeover of the colony frustrated the plan. There was no Native school for seventy years, when the founding of the College of William and Mary included a provision for Indian instruction in reading and writing. Statistics for the years prior to the revolution show varying attendance, ranging from twenty-four in one year to one or two at other times. A school was also established at Fort Christanna in 1714, with a large enrollment, although it lasted only three years.

A few Puritan ministers and others in New England were also interested in establishing schools in order to acculturate and Christianize the natives. Funds came from the English-based New England Company. Thomas Mayhew encouraged Peter Folger to open an Indian school on Martha's Vineyard in 1656, which limped along through the eighteenth century. Native students studied in Elijah Corlet's grammar school in Cambridge, the Roxbury Grammar School, and schools in some of the "praying villages" with Native teachers through the middle decades of the seventeenth century. Praying villages included natives who had ostensibly converted to Christianity and who lived in proximity to English communities in New England. By the 1750s there were various missionary-schoolmasters as well as Indian teachers throughout New England, stimulated by the Great Awakening. The boarding school at Stockbridge had sixty students at one point, but it suffered during the 1750s. Most unusual was Eleazar Wheelock Moor's Indian Charity School, first in Lebanon, Connecticut, then in Hanover, New Hampshire, which boarded both Native and white, male and female, charity students starting in 1754.

In the middle and southern colonies, various denominations attempted to establish Indian schools. The Presbyterian minister David Brainerd organized one in 1746 at Crosswicks, then moved to Cranbury, renamed Bethel, in New Jersey. Upon his death his brother John took over the work, and the school soon had fifty students in writing, Bible reading, and catechism; he later had a similar school and mission at Edgepillock. In Pennsylvania the Moravians established a number of missions and schools. The S.P.G. was somewhat active in New York, operating a school for seven years among the Mohawks beginning in 1712 and another one in 1769. A few S.P.G. schoolmasters serving white children in the early eighteenth century also accepted a small number of Native American students, as did Benjamin Dennis at Goose Creek Parish in South Carolina. A joint Methodist-Moravian school for the Yamacraw children in Georgia was directed by Benjamin Ingham and Peter and Catherine Rose, but outside factors caused its demise after it had been open for only a few months in 1737.

The Europeans' desire to acculturate the Indians through missionary work and schooling had little overall effect, partly because of Native resistance. The missionaries and their supporters also suffered from a lack of sustained will and from continual disruptions and distractions. Schooling for blacks, on the other hand, took on a different cast because of their more servile status and degraded image. The white goal was essentially to control, through the mechanism of slavery, although there were scattered humanitarian attempts to teach literacy and piety.

In New England the free and slave black population was quite small, about 3 percent of the population; schooling remained rudimentary, but black children might attend classes with their white neighbors. The Puritan divines John Eliot and Cotton Mather supported schools, and the latter had a short-lived evening charity school for African and Native American students in 1717. The S.P.G. was also somewhat active in New England, but to a greater extent in New York where it supported Elias Neau's Negro Catechetical School. Evening classes in Christianity for adult slaves there started in 1705. While attendance was high for a few years, it declined because of the 1712 slave uprising. Others, including William Huddleston, continued the school after Neau's death in 1722. John Beasley held classes for blacks in his home in Albany, teaching reading, writing, and catechism. And the S.P.G. opened another school in New York City in 1760, offering reading, writing, arithmetic for all, along with sewing for girls.

Both Anglicans and Quakers in Pennsylvania promoted some schooling for slaves and free blacks. The Reverend George Whitefield planned two schools, neither of which ever opened. Christ Church in Philadelphia launched a school strictly for black children in 1758, and it soon enrolled thirty-six pupils. Competition emerged three years later from the splinter Saint Paul's congregation. The city's Quakers organized a school for black (and white) children in 1770, upon the prodding of Anthony Benezet, who soon served as the schoolmaster. Indeed, he had already tutored blacks in the evening for twenty years in his home. In smaller communities African-American children occasionally attended Quaker schools with whites. Despite the Quakers' growing antipathy to slavery in mid century, the group was nevertheless slow to establish schools for the children of slaves or freedmen.

With its large slave and free black population, Virginia had a greater challenge to educate black children but lacked the will to provide much schooling. Some support came from Thomas Bray's Associates in England, a charity promoting religious instruction for blacks and Indians in the colonies. One school was established in Williamsburg, with Anne Wager teaching thirty pupils at a time until the school's demise with her death in 1774. A similar school was opened in Fredericksburg in 1765; it closed five years later. The S.P.G. was also active, particularly in Charleston, South Carolina, where Alexander Garden founded a school in 1743. For the twenty years of its existence it had an average attendance of sixty pupils. And in 1740, Mr.

Boulson, converted by the Reverend Whitefield, had transformed his dancing school into a reading school for blacks. Although he was charged with violating the slave code by teaching reading, he was allowed to continue.

LITERACY AND SCHOOLING

In modern society it is common to link literacy rates to school attendance. This was not the case, however, in the British colonies, where literacy was widespread but schooling haphazard for most. Male literacy, however measured, was quite high in the seventeenth century, higher than in northern Europe, and it increased in the eighteenth century. In all of the colonies the ability to read, and even to write, was commonplace before the revolution, with rates ranging from 90 percent in New England to greater than 70 percent in the southern colonies. Literacy was greater in urban than rural areas, although the gap was closing. Female literacy was somewhat less, perhaps more than 60 percent in New England by the 1770s, and lower in the middle and southern colonies. Girls did attend a variety of schools, particularly in New England, studying both academic and practical subjects, but how much this influenced their ability to read and write is difficult to discern. These high rates have been substantiated by numerous studies of signature literacy in various communities, as well as by studies of the sale and ownership of reading materials. Considering the fitful nature of school attendance for boys and girls, it would appear that literacy was essentially learned at home in every colony, often stimulated by religious orientation, political ferment, and commercial development.

CONCLUSION

Schooling was widespread in the British colonies, ranging from community-sponsored schools in New England, to denominational schools in the middle and southern colonies, to a plethora of private-venture teachers in many communities. Both boys and often girls attended these diverse establishments, learning reading, writing, arith-

metic, piety, and a whole range of other activities and skills. At the lowest level dame schools took in children as young as two or three years old. Most children attended only a primary school, if anything, for a few years, although attendance rates are unknown. The Latin grammar schools were designed for boys contemplating college. Indians and blacks also had some limited schooling possibilities. Thus, schools were available in all of the colonies in their many configurations, and surely touched the lives of numerous children (and adults). But they were not particularly significant, except perhaps in New England and a few coastal cities. Parents remained the central educational influence in most children's lives throughout the colonial period.

BIBLIOGRAPHY

Axtell, James. *The School upon a Hill: Education and Society in Colonial New England*. New Haven, Conn., 1974.

Bridenbaugh, Carl. *Cities in Revolt: Urban Life in America, 1743–1776*. New York, 1955.

———. *Cities in the Wilderness: The First Century of Urban Life in America, 1625–1742*. New York, 1955.

Bullock, Thomas K. "Schools and Schooling in Eighteenth-Century Virginia." Ph.D. diss., Duke University, 1961.

Burr, Nelson R. *Education in New Jersey, 1630–1871*. Princeton, N.J., 1942.

Calam, John. *Parsons and Pedagogues: The S.P.G. Adventure in American Education*. New York, 1971.

Cohen, Sheldon S. *A History of Colonial Education, 1607–1776*. New York, 1974.

Cremin, Lawrence A. *American Education: The Colonial Experience, 1607–1783*. New York, 1970.

Grubb, F. W. "Growth of Literacy in Colonial America: Longitudinal Patterns, Economic Models, and the Direction of Future Research." *Social Science History* 14 (1990):451–482.

Kaestle, Carl F. *The Evolution of an Urban School System: New York City, 1750–1850*. Cambridge, Mass., 1973.

Kilpatrick, William Heard. *The Dutch Schools of New Netherland and Colonial New York*. Washington, D.C., 1912.

Lawson, John, and Harold Silver. *A Social History of Education in England*. London, 1973.

Middlekauff, Robert. *Ancients and Axioms: Secondary Education in Eighteenth-Century New England*. New Haven, Conn., 1963.

473

Morgan, John. *Godly Learning: Puritan Attitudes Towards Reason, Learning, and Education, 1560–1640.* Cambridge, England, 1986.

Murphy, Geraldine J. "Massachusetts Bay Colony: The Role of Government in Education." Ph.D. diss., Radcliffe College, 1960.

Seybolt, Robert F. *The Evening School in Colonial America.* Urbana, Ill., 1925.

———. *The Private Schools of Colonial Boston.* Cambridge, Mass., 1935.

———. *The Public Schools of Colonial Boston, 1635–1775.* Cambridge, Mass., 1935.

Sommerville, C. John. *The Discovery of Childhood in Puritan England.* Athens, Ga., 1992.

Szasz, Margaret Connell. *Indian Education in the American Colonies, 1607–1783.* Albuquerque, N.Mex., 1988.

Teaford, John. "The Transformation of Massachusetts Education, 1670–1780." *History of Education Quarterly* 10 (1970):287–307.

Updegraff, Harlan. *The Origin of the Moving School in Massachusetts.* New York, 1908.

Ronald D. Cohen

SEE ALSO **Childhood and Adolescence** and **Mission Communities.**

THE DUTCH COLONY

EDUCATION HAD LONG BEEN a matter of concern in the Netherlands, and therefore it is not surprising that it also received attention in New Netherland. Although there is no evidence of a schoolmaster residing in the colony before the 1630s, it is likely that children were receiving some formal training before that time. Religious leaders in New Netherland, who were sent out jointly by the Dutch Reformed church and the directors of the Dutch West India Company, were specifically instructed to keep in mind the educational needs of the colony's youth. The charter of 1629 establishing the patroon system stipulated that patroonships be provided with ministers and schoolmasters "as quickly as possible."

INSTRUCTION UNDER DUTCH RULE

The mandates regarding religious leaders and education applied not only to ordained ministers but also to lay pastors. The first lay preacher in New Netherland was Bastiaen Krol, who at age twenty-eight was sent as a *Ziekentrooster* (literally, comforter of the sick) to Fort Orange in 1624. In 1626 Jan Huygens was sent in a similar capacity to New Amsterdam, and in 1628 New Amsterdam received its first ordained minister, the Reverend Jonas Michaëlius. Unlike the *Ziekentroosters*, who frequently had very limited training, Michaëlius, a graduate of Leiden University, was a learned man. In addition to speaking Dutch and French and being acquainted with classical Greek, he wrote praiseworthy Latin poetry and showed a great interest in the practice of mathematics.

The first person designated to serve specifically as a schoolmaster was Adam Roelantsen. The exact year he arrived at New Amsterdam is uncertain, but it likely occurred in the early 1630s. His school became the forerunner of what is today the Collegiate School. Although Roelantsen's school enjoys great prestige in the late twentieth century, its beginnings were anything but auspicious. For many years it had no permanent home; classes were held in rented rooms or the teacher's house. Its first quarters were at the Battery on the southern tip of Manhattan Island. As New York City expanded northward, the school was relocated more than a dozen times until it reached its present site on Manhattan's Upper West Side in 1892. Roelantsen himself had a checkered career, being a party to numerous lawsuits, most of which were not to his credit. Salaries were low and not always fully paid. As a result it was not uncommon for the early teachers to supplement their income by working as barbers, launderers, carpenters, or gardeners. Furnishings in the school were meager, consisting of little more than a desk and chair for the teacher and backless benches and writing tables for the pupils.

EDUCATION UNDER BRITISH RULE

Education was improving by 1664, when New Netherland fell to the English. By that time all but two of the eleven chartered towns in the colony had schools, and better teachers were appearing on the scene. Evert Pietersen is an example of the superior kind. He arrived at the Dutch settlement of New Amstel on the Delaware River (at the present site of New Castle, Delaware) in 1657 to serve as *Ziekentrooster* and schoolmaster and immediately opened a school that had twenty-five children. In 1661 Pietersen accepted the position of *Ziekentrooster* and schoolmaster at New Amsterdam, which offices he held until his retirement in about 1687.

School curricula, as described in the contracts of that day, generally called for instruction in "reading, writing, and ciphering" and the teaching of "good morals." The latter included instructing the pupils twice a week in the common prayers and the Heidelberg Catechism. Basic elementary readers were liberally sprinkled with excerpts from the Bible, especially the Psalms and Proverbs.

The office of schoolmaster continued to be of a semi-ecclesiastical nature in Dutch communities long after 1664. For example, when Gerrit Van Wagenen was appointed *Ziekentrooster* to the Dutch Reformed congregation of the Garden Street Church in New York City in 1733, his instructions included teaching school in the "Low Dutch Language." Similarly, when Anthony Welp was appointed schoolmaster of the Dutch Reformed settlement at Flatbush, Long Island, in 1773, he was expected to devote one afternoon each week to catechizing the children. He was required also to assist the minister during Sunday worship services, to read from an approved book of sermons on those Sundays when the pastor was absent, and to assist at funerals. It was also a customary practice for local ministers and church consistories to join the secular authorities in approving teachers and school curricula. At Bergen, New Jersey, for example, the consistory of the local Dutch Reformed congregation continued to appoint schoolmasters until 1790.

The shift to British rule eventually brought about demands for the instruction of English among the Dutch schools. The transition was slow, however. The authorities of the Dutch school at Flatbush, on Long Island, for example, did not advertise for someone to teach English until 1751, and the Dutch school at Bergen, New Jersey, did not do so until 1773. In explaining the survival of Dutch in the schools, it should be noted that at the time of the American Revolution almost all of the nearly one hundred Dutch Reformed churches in the colonies were still using the Dutch language exclusively in their worship services.

OTHER FORMS OF SCHOOLING

Education for girls in New Netherland received less attention than that for boys. Girls had to content themselves largely with domestic training at home and some rudimentary work in reading and writing.

Parents who wanted their children to receive more education than was available in the schools could resort to some form of tutoring or send them to school elsewhere. For example, the Reverend Johannes Magapolensis, who served at Rensselaerswyck from 1642 to 1649 and then at New Amsterdam until his death in 1670, instructed his son Samuel in Greek and Latin for several years, after which he sent him to Boston in 1653 to continue his studies for three years and then to the University of Utrecht in the Netherlands for another three years. A few prominent merchant families sent their sons to the Netherlands for special business training. Young men who went into medicine or law usually secured their training by hiring out as apprentices to a practicing physician or attorney.

BIBLIOGRAPHY

Corwin, Edward T., ed. *Ecclesiastical Records, State of New York.* Vol. 1. Albany, N.Y., 1901.

DeJong, Gerald Francis. "The *Ziekentroosters* or Comforters of the Sick in New Netherland." *New-York Historical Society Quarterly* 54, no. 4 (1970):338–359.

Dunshee, Henry W. *History of the School of the Collegiate Reformed Dutch Church in the City of New York from 1633 to 1883.* New York, 1883.

Kilpatrick, William Heard. *The Dutch Schools of New Netherland and Colonial New York.* Washington, D.C., 1912.

Zeller, Nancy Anne McClure, ed. *A Beautiful and Fruitful Place: Selected Rensselaerswyck Seminar Papers.* Edited by Nancy Zeller. Albany, N.Y., 1991. See especially the following papers from Rensselaerswyck Seminar VII on "Education in New Netherland and the Middle Colonies": William Lee Frost, "356 Years of Formal Education in New York City"; Massimo Maglione, "Evidence for the Establishment of Collegiate School in 1628"; Gerald F. De-

Jong, "The Education and Training of Dutch Ministers"; Ronald W. Howard, "Apprenticeship and Economic Education in New Netherland"; Howard G. Hageman, "The Dutch Battle for Higher Education in the Middle Colonies"; and Leo Hershkowitz, "Abigail Franks and Jewish Education in Early New York."

Gerald F. De Jong

SEE ALSO **Childhood and Adolescence.**

THE FRENCH COLONIES

THE FRENCH WORD *éducation* means far more than its English cognate. It means not merely learned but well-bred. Thus a person could be *bien instruit* (learned) but *sans éducation* (ill-bred, lacking good manners, uncivilized). It was this concept that dominated in the schools of New France, but always within a framework that required the schools to inculcate the tenets of the Roman Catholic church, loyalty to the Crown, and strict obedience of the king's commands.

In that day and age everyone believed in the existence of heaven and hell. It was everyone's desire to avoid going to hell after death and to enter heaven, as belatedly as possible. To achieve this end, for members of the Roman church, the mediation of the clergy was essential; they alone could administer the required sacraments, save for baptism in the prolonged absence of a priest. The French settlers in America had no need to read the Bible to achieve salvation, and they certainly were not to place their own interpretations on its contents. Thus they did not have the same urge to learn to read and write as the Protestants did in the English colonies.

In that era schooling usually began at the age of ten, since prior to that age most children lacked the manual dexterity to write with the only instrument available, the quill pen, let alone sharpen and split the nib with a pen knife. Blood-splattered paper was not conducive to good penmanship. The boys of farm families were needed to work on the farm as soon as they were big enough, and so only the girls could be spared such chores for a few years. Thus it was that more women than men in New France were literate.

The curriculum and high standards of the schools were also likely factors in discouraging literacy. The children were taught the catechism, reading, writing, Latin, arithmetic, contracts, and civility. They were not moved into a higher grade until they had mastered the work of the class they were in; they were not to begin learning French grammar before they were well versed in Latin. Such a philosophy and curriculum would not seem to have had much appeal or utility for the vast majority of the male population that spent its meager time on this earth felling trees; tilling the soil; paddling a canoe to the far west to trade with the Indians; voyaging to hunt seals in the Gulf or to trade at Louisbourg, the Antilles, or France; or in acquiring a skill in a manual trade.

The ability to sign one's name is a dubious test of literacy; in New France some people could do that and no more. Others could only sign their names with the aid of a wooden stencil. Yet the notarized contracts of voyageurs with the merchants who hired them to paddle canoeloads of trade goods to the western posts do give an indication of the literacy rate of the humbler class of Canadians. A random sampling of the contracts for six years between 1688 and 1751 reveals that 1,112 declared themselves to be unable to read and write, and 102 signed their contracts. Some 11 of the signatures are so shaky that one suspects they could merely scrawl some semblance of their names instead of the more customary X (or perhaps they had staggered over to the notary's office straight from a tavern). A much larger sampling of those contracts would most certainly produce similar results.

CANADA

There was no desire on the part of either the church or the Crown, as has been alleged, to keep the people in submissive ignorance. It was the aim of both the Crown officials and the clergy to have a school in every parish. By the second quarter of the eighteenth century, Canada was well on the way to achieving that goal.

The clerical and secular authorities were faced with two major problems: a shortage of parish priests and schoolmasters. To solve the first of these problems, Bishop François Laval de Montigny, after his arrival at Quebec in 1659, established a seminary. Its main aim was to provide a native Canadian clergy, but boys who lacked the vocation were not excluded. It cannot be claimed that the institution enjoyed over-whelming success.

The regimen perhaps explains why. The boys were admitted at the age of ten. They arose at four in the morning during the summer months, slept in until four-thirty in winter. They attended classes and devotions until eight at night, then retired to bed. They wore a distinctive uniform, a blue parka coat with a sash, and a wide brimmed hat. Their hair was cut short; their meals were Spartan, providing the bare minimum to sustain good health; and they were permitted to bathe no oftener than was absolutely necessary, for the sight of their own naked bodies might inculcate licentious thoughts. Plays and all other forms of amusement had to be shunned, and the boys were required to keep their parents and siblings at arm's length, to avoid forming an attachment to the secular world. Of the first 200 students admitted, 135 dropped out, most of them after two years' incarceration. Over a ninety-year period the seminary took in 843 students and 188 were eventually ordained.

In 1727 although a schoolmaster was paid only 375 livres a year, less than a skilled artisan earned, it was deemed necessary to establish standards. Legislation was enacted requiring would-be teachers to submit to an examination, to obtain the sanction of the intendant and the bishop, and once appointed to be under the surveillance of their parish priest. Male teachers, unless married, could not teach girls without special permission; the same applied to spinster teachers where boys were concerned. Teachers were required to set a good example by staying well clear of taverns, games of chance, persons of the opposite sex, and the company of any known to live too freely.

In Canada the seigneurs, senior officials, and well-to-do merchants were able to obtain as good an education for their children in the colony as they could in France. The boys could attend the Sulpicians' Latin school at Montreal or the Jesuits' college at Quebec, founded in 1635, where the same curriculum and standards were maintained as at the order's colleges in Europe. The Jesuits also had a school of hydrography at Quebec to train pilots, navigators, and cartographers. Boys of the lower stratum of society could obtain a degree of schooling through the apprenticeship system. Skilled labor was in such short supply that boys apprenticed to a master craftsman paid little if anything for their training, and some parents stipulated in the apprenticeship contract that the master would teach their son to read and write.

By 1707 the Sisters of the Congregation of Notre Dame had ten schools for girls in the rural parishes, and by the end of the French regime about half the parishes had schools, the others likely being sparsely populated. Lieutenant Colonel Louis Franquet of the elite French engineering corps, whilst on a tour of inspection of the Canadian fortifications on the eve of the Seven Years' War, wrote that the Canadian girls of the humbler class were far too well educated, hence they entertained ambitions to rise above their appointed station in life: they declined to marry men of their own social milieu but sought to marry into the bourgeoisie, even the noblesse, to live in town, and to wear silk every day. A few of them succeeded.

The daughters of the Canadian gentry were educated at the Ursulines' schools in Quebec, Trois-Rivières, or Montreal. They were taught reading, writing with a good hand, mathematics, chemistry, biology, and botany and were given a thorough grounding in Latin before French grammar, syntax, and literature were studied. In addition the young ladies were trained to be civil, to use the social graces, and how to converse, to charm, and to deal with the advances of young men; in short all the arts and skills requisite for persons of their future station in life.

Peter Kalm, professor of the natural sciences and member of the Swedish Academy of Science, noted during his tour of New France in 1749 that the Ursulines were eminently successful in their appointed task. He found the Canadian ladies to be very charming and coquettish. He noted, among other things, that they wrote with a better hand than he did himself. He ascribed this partly to the fact that every girl was eager to write billets-doux to her lover without having to seek anyone else's assistance.

LOUISBOURG

On Île Royale (Cape Breton) the fortress of Louisbourg was constructed immediately after the 1713 Peace of Utrecht. It was intended as a base for the navy, the French fishing fleet, and privateers in wartime. It soon became the major entrepôt for the commerce of the northwest Atlantic. The minister of marine responsible for the construction of the fortress, Jérôme Phélypeaux, comte de Pontchartrain, did not concern himself about schools; he left that to the Bishop of Quebec. In 1720 the *commissaire-ordonnateur* proposed to use royal funds to build a school, but Pontchartrain spurned the suggestion. By the mid 1720s there were over three hundred children of school age at the fortress and adjoining town. Parents thus had two options if they wanted their sons to receive a decent education: hire a private tutor or send them to the Collège des Jesuits at Quebec.

In 1727 Bishop Jean-Baptiste de la Croix de Saint-Vallier sent Marguerite Roy, soeur de la Conception (Sister of the Conception), a member of the Congrégation de Notre Dame, to Louisbourg to establish a school for girls. Despite a chronic lack of financial support the school managed to survive, giving the girls the rudiments of an education. By the 1740s there were probably six sisters and a hundred students, who paid thirteen livres a month, which by 1755 had increased to twenty-one livres a month, for their tuition and lodging—a fee that put the school out of reach for all but the more affluent.

LOUISIANA

The state of education in Louisiana more closely resembled that of Louisbourg than that of Canada. Education was neglected by both secular and ecclesiastical authorities; only the Ursuline nuns were effectual in establishing and operating a successful school. The first school in the colony was likely begun by a Capuchin monk, Father Cecil, in 1725. It lasted six years and failed as a result of the indifference of the colonists and lack of financial support. The church failed to establish a seminary on the lower Mississippi Valley. Most children of the elite received only a rudimentary education from their European parents. Parents who desired their sons to have a classical education had to send them to France.

Girls fared better. In 1727 seven Ursuline sisters arrived at New Orleans to establish a hospital and a school. Within a year there were twenty boarders whose parents paid one hundred livres, but orphans and children of the poor paid nothing. In 1734 the sisters moved to the handsome building, still standing today, on Chartres Street. There the young Creole ladies received the same education as did the girls with the Ursulines in Canada and France.

ÎLE ROYALE

At Louisbourg, French schooling came to an end in 1758 when the British captured the fortress. In Canada, during the siege of Quebec in the summer of 1759, the students of the Collège were mustered into a militia unit, aptly named the Royal Syntax Company, and were involved in the savage skirmishing that preceded the fateful battle of Quebec on 13 September.

With the war over, Canada ceded to Britain, and the Canadians abandoned as had been the Acadians before them to the none-too-tender mercies of their conquerors, the Canadians managed to preserve their schools, but not the Jesuit college. Their *collèges classiques* proliferated after the French Revolution, and the Ursulines continued to educate the girls; indeed many of the British officers and officials sent their daughters to the sisters for their education. Thus the language, religion, culture, the old regime values of the Canadians (soon to be referred to as French Canadians) were preserved in essence down to the present day.

BIBLIOGRAPHY

Franquet, Louis. *Voyages et mémoires sur le Canada par Franquet.* Montreal, 1974. Shrewd remarks on Canada and the Canadians.

Frégault, Guy. *La Civilisation de la Nouvelle-France (1714–1744)*. Montreal, 1944. Essays by a leading scholar. See especially pp. 252–266.

Gosselin, Amédée. *L'Instruction au Canada sous le régime français (1635–1760)*. Quebec, 1911. Written from a cleric's point of view; thorough but dated.

Groulx, Lionel. *L'Enseignement français au Canada*. 2 vols. Montreal, 1933–1934. Exhaustive; by a cleric and arch French-Canadian nationalist who regarded New France as a golden age.

Johnston, A. J. B. *Religion in Life at Louisbourg, 1713–1758*. Kingston and Montreal, 1984. Sound work.

Kalm, Peter. *Peter Kalm's Travels in North America: The English Version of 1770*, edited by Adolph B. Benson. 2 vols. New York, 1937. Astute comments on the Canadians' way of life, contrasted with that of the English colonials.

Landres, Yves. *Orphelines en France pionnières au Canada. Les Filles du roi au XVIIe siècle*. Montreal, 1992.

Noble, Stuart G., and Arthur G. Nuhrah. "Education in Colonial Louisiana." *The Louisiana Quarterly* 32, no. 4 (1949):759–776. Superficial.

O'Neill, Charles Edwards, ed. *Viel: Louisiana's Firstborn Author with Evandre, the First Literary Creation of a Native of the Mississippi Valley*. Lafayette, La., 1991.

Trudel, Marcel. *Initiation à la Nouvelle-France*. Montreal and Toronto, 1968. Essential reference work on New France. Published in English translation as *Introduction to New France*.

W. J. Eccles

SEE ALSO **Childhood and Adolescence** and **Mission Communities.**

THE SPANISH BORDERLANDS

THIS ARTICLE CONTAINS an examination of education in the Spanish Borderlands. Because of its large and stable population throughout the period and the availability of data, a great deal of the discussion will focus on New Mexico. The patterns in the other borderland areas, however, were very similar to those discussed here.

Education in the Spanish Borderlands existed in many complex and interrelated forms. Among Native populations there were a variety of indigenous forms of pedagogy that secured the intergenerational reproduction of culture. Beginning around 1540, however, European soldiers, missionaries, and explorers began to penetrate their world. It was within this context, the meeting of two very different worlds, that the history of schools and schooling in the Spanish Borderlands began. The first European educators, the Spanish missionaries, accompanied by their Mexican assistants, began to conduct educational activities and establish schools among the natives with the intent of restructuring their worldviews, culture, and mental life. Military conquest alone could not transform the collective consciousness of the Native Americans, a task that was educative in nature. What emerged to accomplish the task in the borderlands were educational institutions called missions, organized by men of the various religious orders, in particular the Franciscans and to a lesser degree the Jesuits. These institutions were sites of cultural struggle characterized by resistance, contention, and consent on the part of the natives, and of much negotiation and concession on the part of the missionaries. Ultimately, what resulted was a variety of forms of cultural syncretism common throughout the Spanish and Portuguese colonies in the Americas. The educational process thus was instrumental in the reconstruction of the culture of the indigenous population and the emergence of a new culture among large groups of Native Americans that reflected components that were both European and American in origin. Their descendents are the people who today identify themselves as Mexicans and Chicanos.

NATIVE EDUCATION

Prior to the arrival of the Europeans, forms of education in the Native communities varied greatly, as did the cultures themselves. In the Pueblo communities along the northern Rio Grande Valley, boys were educated in institutions called *kivas*, where various aspects of culture were transmitted. The *kiva* was the place where young boys were introduced to the symbolic world of their societies. It was in these educational institutions that boys were trained to become spiritual and cultural leaders. It was here that the collective knowledge of the villages was transmitted intergenerationally. Education took the form of song, dance, and other ritual ceremonies occurring throughout the year and designating important times in the symbolic world of the Pueblo.

Native communities in other areas of the borderlands differed greatly from those of the Pueblo in New Mexico, who lived in large villages, practiced advanced horticulture, and carried on commerce with surrounding peoples. In fact Native cultures of the borderlands varied greatly in terms of territory, economy, and living arrangements. Because of this the missionaries were forced to adapt their pedagogy to local conditions. Thus among the New Mexican Pueblo, missions were introduced into already established villages, while in areas such as present-day California and Texas, entire village complexes had to be constructed and natives forced to move in.

THE FORM OF
MISSION EDUCATION

The type of education provided in the missions of the Americas was influenced greatly by the Native societies, especially in the Mexican Empire. The pre-Columbian Mexican educational structure consisted of two formal schools, the Calmecac and the Tepochcalli, in addition to several forms of ritual for education of the masses. While the Tepochcolli focused on military training for the masses, the Calmecac was the institution for the formation of Mexican intellectuals; there young boys of the elite classes resided from around the age of four or five to adulthood. These students had a rigorous educational experience that included reading, writing, oratory, science, mathematics, and history. It was these intellectuals, brought together after the conquest by the Spanish religious orders, who began to bridge the intellectual worlds of Europe and the Americas. Working with the missionaries Bernardino de Sahagún, Pedro De Gánte, and others, they wrote a description of Mexican life, society, and history and translated aspects of Catholic doctrine into the Nahuatl language.

The European educators utilized the basic form of the Calmecac, selecting the children of the elite, bringing them to live in the missions, and subjecting them to a rigorous educational experience. This structure became the standard

for missions in all of New Spain. The youth who were schooled in the missions were called *doctrineros,* and they became a very important bridge between the mental life of Native Americans and that of the missionaries. The role that they played cannot be overstated. In addition to translating sermons and catechisms, both orally and in writing, they accompanied the missionaries as aides to all parts of New Spain.

The education of the villagers in the borderland missions consisted of weekly sermons to the married couples and daily lectures to the unmarried. As previously discussed, the absence of well-organized permanent villages outside of New Mexico forced the missionaries to organize entire villages as well as teach agriculture and establish other forms of industry; many of the latter, such as basketmaking in the California missions, were influenced by the Native cultures, which already practiced the craft of basketmaking. The missions were in operation up to the end of the Spanish period in 1821; however they declined in number, especially in New Mexico, in the second half of the eighteenth century as the Bourbon reforms generated a policy shift toward the secularization of missions.

RITUAL AS PEDAGOGY

Pre-Columbian Mexican life was filled with much ritual in the form of music, art, dance, and oratory, all of which served the function of transmitting culture from one generation to the next. Spanish educators used to their advantage what was already in existence, replacing the symbolic messages that were transmitted but retaining much of the Native form. An example of this is the Matachine dances that are still performed in villages in New Mexico. While the dance and musical form are Mexican, the symbolic essence is the Native acceptance of Christianity, with the dance culminating in Moctezuma's paying obeisance to the Christian God. Several other forms of educational drama incorporating music and dance emerged throughout New Spain. In New Mexico *Los Comanches,* utilizing plains-style music, dance, and dress, is another example, with the participants giving adoration to the Christian deity Santo Nino de Atocha. This type of pageantry was practiced in the communities of the settlers as well as those of the mixed bloods and *genizaros* (detribalized Plains Indians living in Spanish villages).

INFORMAL EDUCATION

The education of the settlers who came to the borderlands from other parts of New Spain, as well as that of the *genizaro* Indian and mixed-race populations who resided in the Spanish villages outside of the pueblos or the missions, took several forms and served a variety of functions, beginning with the intergenerational transmission of the Christian worldview. Among the primary custodial obligations of adults was to provide a moral education for the minors in their households, be it their own or their captive Indian children. All legal guardians of children were obliged to provide education in the basic principles of the Catholic faith. This expectation was taken seriously by the authorities, and there were several instances of children being removed from households because of the failure of the adults to provide the necessary religious training.

Outside of the missions, formal schools were scarce until the last two decades of the eighteenth century. Until then most of the children learned how to read and write through private instruction. Parents who could hired tutors to instruct their children in the arts of reading and writing. Several wills and settlements of estates make references to money owed to tutors for the literacy instruction of children. This form of literacy education was quite accessible. Since data regarding literacy rates comes from an analysis of military establishment papers that specified whether an enlistee could read and write, male literacy rates can be determined. Such documents do not exist for women. The average literacy rate for males throughout the eighteenth century was around 34 percent. Many of the tutors were also scribes and public readers, as was the case with Estevan Rodriguez the African in Santa Fe in the early part of the eighteenth century, who, besides being the official public reader in Santa Fe, also provided literacy instruction to children.

PRIMARY SCHOOLS

There is little evidence of formal schools other than the missions before the last three decades of the eighteenth century. In Santa Fe around the turn of the seventeenth century there was a school in operation under the direction of a Fray Alvarez in which reading and writing were taught. It was not until the latter decades of the eighteenth century, however, that formal primary schools began to emerge. In the New Mexican mission communities, the responsibility for primary education shifted from the missionaries to private instructors operating schools where reading, writing, and arithmetic were taught. The teachers were often under contract with the respective pueblos to provide instruction to the children and were usually paid in agricultural products. These schools often served both the children of the pueblos as well as those of the surrounding *vecinos* or all persons not residing in Indian pueblos, including mestizos, mulattoes, Africans, Europeans, and *genizaros*.

In the beginning of the nineteenth century, schools for the children of soldiers, retired soldiers, and surrounding settlers were in operation around the *presidios*. In Santa Fe the schools began operation in 1806 and continued to function until the end of the Spanish period in 1821. Children who attended them received instruction in reading, writing, mathematics, and religion. In the sequence of instruction, reading was taught first, followed by mathematics, religion, and, finally, writing.

VOCATIONAL EDUCATION

Practicing a trade such as blacksmithing, weaving, or tailoring required entering into an apprenticeship arrangement with a master craftsman. Boys entered into apprenticeship arrangements only after having learned how to read and write. The apprentice lived with the master, who provided him with food and shelter as well as the necessities of the trade, such as clothing and tools. In the beginning of the nineteenth century, the authorities brought two master weavers to New Mexico to teach the craft. The contract of the two masters stipulated that they were to create masters of the craft and that they would be provided with all of the materials necessary to accomplish their task. Many of the other industries revolving around sheep raising were taught in the home.

HIGHER EDUCATION

The Spanish Borderlands had no institutions of higher education. Therefore those students who sought an education beyond the primary level were forced to attend schools in other parts of New Spain. Durango was one of the places to which several of the youth of New Mexico went for higher education. Several of the Native priests of New Mexico were educated at the Tridenite Seminary in Durango. Another city with a college was Querétaro. Youth who attended these institutions were generally children of the landed elite of the upper-ranking military officers. Around the turn of the nineteenth century, several citizens of Santa Fe sought funds to establish an institute of higher learning there, but the college never materialized.

CONCLUSION

Education in the borderlands took many forms and served a variety of social purposes. The missions were the formal educational institutions that existed in the greatest number over the entire period. In fact throughout most of the seventeenth and eighteenth century they were the only formal educational institutions. Thus, probably the most literate individuals in the borderlands besides the missionaries and some of the government officials were the *doctrineros*, who were educated in the missions. In fact the majority of public readers in both the Spanish and Indian villages in New Mexico were identified as "Indios Ladinos" of such and such a tribe or nation. Ladino in this context referred to Indians who were acculturated into colonial society and could read and write.

Until the last two decades of the eighteenth century, education for the *vecinos* consisted mainly of private tutoring for those who could afford it. Around the turn of the century however, formal schools in the settlements of *vecinos* began to emerge, at first around the military *presidios*. It was also at this time that schoolteacher begins to appear on the census records as an official occupation.

In the broader sense, it was informal education within the family structure that played a most important role in the construction and maintenance of colonial culture. It was also in this context that captive Plains Indian children were incorporated into *vecino* culture, making the informal educational process integral to the reproduction of colonial culture as well as the transformation of Native culture in the borderlands.

BIBLIOGRAPHY

Adams, Eleanor B. "Two Colonial New Mexico Libraries: 1704, 1706." *New Mexico Historical Review* 19, no. 2 (1944):135–167.

Adams, Eleanor B., and Angelico Chavez, eds. and trans. *The Missions of New Mexico, 1776: A Description by Francisco Atanasio Domínguez, with Other Contemporary Documents.* Albuquerque, N.Mex., 1956.

Adams, Eleanor B., and France V. Scholes. "Books in New Mexico, 1598–1680." *New Mexico Historical Review* 17, no. 3 (1942):226–270.

Ayer, Emma Augusta, ed. and trans. *The Memorial of Fray Alonzo de Benavidez, 1630.* Albuquerque, N.Mex., 1965.

Bannon, John Francis. "The Mission as a Frontier Institution: Sixty Years of Interest and Research." *Western Historical Quarterly* 10, no. 3 (1979):303–322.

———. *The Spanish Borderlands Frontier, 1513–1821.* New York, 1970; Albuquerque, N.Mex., 1974.

Blackmar, Frank W. *Spanish Institutions of the Southwest.* Glorietta, N.Mex., 1976.

Bolton, Eugene Herbert. "The Mission as a Frontier Institution in the Spanish American Colonies." In *New Spain's Far Northern Frontier: Essays on Spain in the American West, 1540–1821,* edited by David J. Weber. Albuquerque, N.Mex., 1979.

Cordova, Gilberto Benito. "Missionization and Hispanization of Santo Thomas Apostol de Abiquiu, 1750–1770." Ph.D. diss., University of New Mexico, 1979.

Costo, Jeannette, and Henry Costo. *The Missions of California: A Legacy of Genocide.* Oakland, Calif., 1987.

De Aragon, Ray John. *Padre Martinez and Bishop Lamy.* Las Vegas, N.Mex., 1978.

De Nevi, Don, and Noel F. Moholy. *Juniper Serra.* Berkeley, Calif., 1985.

Gallegos, Bernardo P. *Literacy, Education, and Society in New Mexico: 1692–1821.* Albuquerque, N.Mex., 1992.

Gonzalbo, Pilar. *El humanismo y la educacion en la Nueva Espana.* Mexico City, 1985.

Greenleaf, Richard E. "The Inquisition in Eighteenth-Century New Mexico." *New Mexico Historical Review* 60, no. 1 (1985):29–60.

Guest, Francis F. "An Examination of the Thesis of S. F. Cook on the Forced Conversion of Indians in the California Missions." *Southern California Quarterly* 61, no. 1 (1979):1–78.

Gutiérrez, Ramón A. *When Jesus Came, the Corn Mothers Went Away: Marriage, Sexuality, and Power in New Mexico, 1500–1846.* Berkeley, Calif., 1991.

Hackett, Charles Wilson, ed. *Revolt of the Pueblo Indians of New Mexico and Otermin's Attempted Reconquest, 1680–1682.* Vols. 8 and 9. Albuquerque, N.Mex., 1970.

Jenkins, Mary Ellen. "Early Education in New Mexico." *National Education Association-New Mexico School Review* 53, no. 1 (1977):2–14.

Kelly, Henry K. "Franciscan Missions of New Mexico, 1740–1760." *New Mexico Historical Review* 15, no. 4 (1940):345–368.

Kessell, John L. *Friars, Soldiers, and Reformers.* Tucson, Ariz., 1976.

———. "The Making of a Martyr: The Young Francisco Garcés." *New Mexico Historical Review* 45, no. 3 (1970):181–196.

Matson, Daniel S., and Bernard L. Fontana, eds. and trans. *Friar Bringas Reports to the King: Methods of Indoctrination on the Frontier of New Spain, 1796–1797.* Tucson, Ariz., 1977.

Moyers, Robert A. "A History of Education in New Mexico." Ph.D. diss., George Peabody College for Teachers, 1942.

Read, Benjamin M. *A History of Education in New Mexico.* Santa Fe, N.Mex., 1911.

Ricard, Robert. *The Spiritual Conquest of Mexico.* Berkeley, Calif., 1966.

Richman, Irving B. *California Under Spain and Mexico: 1535–1847.* Boston, 1911.

Scholes, France V. "Civil Government and Society in New Mexico in the Seventeenth Century." *New Mexico Historical Review* 10, no. 2 (1935):71–111.

Ortiz, Alfonso. *The Tewa World: Space, Time, Being, and Becoming in a Pueblo Society.* Chicago, 1969.

Walter, Paul A. F. "Address Before the History and Social Science Section of the New Mexico Educational Association at Santa Fe, November 5, 1926." *New Mexico Historical Review* 2, no. 1 (1927):67–82.

Bernardo P. Gallegos

SEE ALSO **Childhood and Adolescence** and **Mission Communities.**

HIGHER EDUCATION

CIVILIZATION VERSUS BARBARISM

Europeans seeking to preserve their values and ideas in the North American wilderness were afraid of being overwhelmed by the untamed world and its primitive inhabitants. Whether they bent their efforts toward Christianizing and acculturating the Native population—as in the Spanish Borderlands and New France—or toward establishing enclaves of European civilization—as in the Dutch and English colonies—their objective was the same. They hoped to keep at bay the barbaric influences of the natural environment by preserving the heritage of western civilization. The task of transmitting this heritage to future generations of settlers was assigned to higher education.

There were essentially five ways to ensure that higher learning would continue among European settlers. The first was to depend upon the continued emigration of highly educated individuals from Europe. The second was to send native-born youths back to the metropolis to complete their education. The third was to rely on private tutors. Fourth, young people could be instructed in academies that were really the households of educated adults. The fifth way to provide for higher education was by chartering colleges in the colonies.

When European exploration and conquest in North America gave way to settlement and the exploitation of natural resources, colonists tried at least one of these approaches to higher education. The French largely depended on the religious orders to supply highly educated missionaries from home and to teach the indigenous population. The Jesuits established a college in Quebec and subsequently a school of hydrography to train pilots, navigators, and cartographers. There were no universities in the Spanish Borderlands, so children of the elite were dispatched to Europe or to universities in Latin America. Several of these had been founded in the New World early in the colonial period, primarily to train priests, canons, lawyers, and a few physicians. Spanish colonists in Florida sent their children to universities in Santo Domingo or Mexico City, while those residing in what would become the southwestern part of the United States used Mexico City for higher education. Colonists in New Netherland relied on educated immigrants and sent their youth back to Holland for training in the ministry and secular professions, most often to the University of Leiden. This practice continued until the mid eighteenth century, long after the British capture of New Amsterdam (New York). The English made use of all five strategies, which culminated in nine chartered colonial colleges before 1770. They also articulated most fully the role of higher education in the conflict of civilization versus barbarism. Thus, the ideas and efforts of Anglo-

Americans provide a reference point for the history of higher education in the North American colonies.

SEVENTEENTH-CENTURY HIGHER EDUCATION

The main goal of higher education in the seventeenth century was to preserve learning in the wilderness. This meant instructing in the classical languages and literature in order to prepare leaders for public and professional positions. Institutions such as the family, the church, the army, or the apprenticeship system could also prepare leaders. But it had come to be expected that those who occupied public office would be men of some learning. This generally meant knowledge—however rudimentary—of Latin and Greek, and a familiarity—however remote—with the writings of classical authors. Professional preparation built on the same foundation, for occupational specialization was still in the future. Educated men, particularly in the colonies, were likely to teach themselves professional skills in several areas after their college years: clergymen might practice medicine; farmers might be teachers; lawyers might also be magistrates.

Traditional sex roles excluded women from leadership, so there was no reason to educate them beyond basic literacy. They were taught to read and write in order to study the Bible and instruct their children. They were not expected to exercise intellectual curiosity, although exceptions might be found among girls educated by the Catholic religious orders. For women in the English colonies who delved into theology, the banishment of Anne Hutchinson from Massachusetts Bay in the 1630s was a sobering reminder to keep their knowledge to themselves. Elsewhere in Anglo-America, even basic literacy might be neglected. In the eighteenth century, otherwise articulate women apologized for their inability to write or to spell. Colleges were closed to them, and, without benefit of the classical curriculum, females were at a disadvantage in the company of intellectuals. Perhaps one can imagine the chagrin with which Jane Colden, an accomplished botanist, depended on her father,

Cadwallader Colden, to translate Linnaeus from the Latin for her.

Colonial colleges had the special mission of transmitting the classical heritage, together with an appropriate body of divinity. Boys who attended and received a degree were initiated into the ranks of educated men at a public commencement ceremony. No matter what their calling, they were expected to return the benefits of their learning to the community by preserving civilization in the wilderness. Careful provisions for higher education among French and English colonists in the seventeenth century illustrate these ideas.

Quebec College

The total French population in Quebec numbered only about five hundred in 1635 when the Jesuits opened a college. The college had its beginning when an aspiring Jesuit's parents, the marquis de Gamaches and his wife, Francoise Mangot, gave 48,000 livres to the society with the suggestion that the funds be used to found a college in New France. True to the mission of the teaching order, the college was to educate the upper classes and further the conversion of the heathen.

At first, according to Professor W. J. Eccles, the students were young and the teaching rudimentary. Ten boys, aged six to fifteen, met in the Jesuit residence at Quebec in 1635. The curriculum was that of a petite école (lower school), consisting of reading, writing, mathematics, and Latin grammar. College level instruction began in the 1660s in response to a growing population and as an incentive for emigration. Some of the settlers declared that they would never have considered coming to Quebec if their sons had not been able to obtain a good education there. Between fifty and sixty students were attending in 1670. By 1712 the Superior of Quebec, Joseph-Louis Germain, reported to his provincial that everything was being done at the Quebec college as in the Jesuit colleges in Europe, and perhaps with more regularity, exactitude, and better results than in some French colleges.

The curriculum in Jesuit colleges was quite standard. Derived from the pedagogical concepts of Descartes, Bossuet, Fénelon, the Oratoriens and the Messieurs de Port-Royal, and the Jesuits themselves, the system was based on three major works: *Les Constitutions, Le Ratio Studiorum,* and *De ratione descendi et docendi. Le Ratio Studiorum* was the course of instruction universally accepted in Europe after 1603, and it consisted of a résumé of the methods, procedures, and usages of the Collèges of the Society of Jesus. After Henri IV's university reforms in 1596, Latin was the basis of education as well as being the language of instruction, and all educated persons were expected to be able to use it. Four years had to be devoted to mastering its grammar, rules, and principles.

At Quebec, according to Professor Eccles, there were five Latin classes: one of rhetoric, one of humanity, and three of grammar which included Greek. Geography and history were covered in classes in grammar and rhetoric; science was taught as part of philosophy, although the works of Galileo, Descartes, Pascal, and Newton were used in mathematics and physics. The complete course of study *"de lettres"* at Quebec College took at least five years. The first three were devoted to grammar, and a year of humanity studies prepared the students for rhetoric. The science courses lasted three years. Students were also exposed to drama and performed Corneille's *Heraclitus* in 1651, *Le Cid* the following year, and Nicomède and Racine's *Mithridate* in 1694.

The professors at Quebec were of three ranks: ordained priests, prefects who were waiting to begin their course in theology and ordination, and *freres coadjuteurs adonnés* who performed manual tasks. Although Jesuit colleges were generally recognized as the best in Europe, they did not grant degrees. Quebec College followed the practice of the Society of Jesus in this regard, but it did hold public disputations. In 1666 Louis Jolliet defended his thesis in Latin before the leading political figures of the colony and was closely questioned by them. He would later become the well-known explorer of the Mississippi.

Harvard

At the same time that the French imported a Jesuit collegiate model and its curriculum, the English in the Massachusetts Bay colony set about meeting their need for higher learning on their own. They chose not to depend on the continued immigration of educated people. Nor did those Puritans who had left in disillusion display much interest in sending their sons back to England. Rather, the earliest settlers acted immediately to establish a college.

The sense of urgency is shown in a proposal of 1633, within three years of the first colonization, to establish a college in Massachusetts. John Eliot, teacher of the church at Roxbury and in later life a missionary to the Indians, followed up an expression of interest from Simonds D'Ewes in England. Eliot suggested that D'Ewes perpetuate his name and honor by donating money for a college. Eliot described the need for a library, college buildings, university rituals, and instruction in arts and sciences, law, and divinity. As it happened, it was not D'Ewes but John Harvard, a recent immigrant who had settled in Charleston, who lent his name and fortune to the college in Massachusetts, but Eliot's letter shows the importance attached to higher education and its necessary components.

Plans for Harvard came to fruition in 1636 when the Massachusetts Bay colony legislature voted four hundred pounds for the project. Unlike the self-governing universities of Oxford and Cambridge, Harvard was placed under community control. A board of overseers, consisting of six prominent magistrates and six leading churchmen, governed the college until the charter of 1650 set up a corporation of the president and fellows; thereafter, the overseers and the corporation shared power over Harvard. This departure from the governance of the English universities can perhaps be traced to the European Reformation. Protestant reformers had founded gymnasia under the control of their local communities, which provided ready models for the American Puritans. It is also possible that these models were followed by default rather than by desire because learned faculties who could be immediately entrusted with self-government were lacking in the colonies.

Instruction began 1638 in the small community of Newtown, which was promptly renamed Cambridge. Choice of the name was not coincidental. In his study of Harvard's origins, Samuel Eliot Morison identified a hundred men with connections to Cambridge University in England, thirty-two to Oxford, three to Dublin, and two each to Leiden and Franeker in the Netherlands. Thirty-five Cambridge men had direct links with Emmanuel College, a relatively new foundation in England with strong Puritan leanings and a special interest in ministerial training. The colonists wished to supply properly educated ministers for their churches. But their view of higher education encompassed more than a theological seminary and drew from the classical tradition. The Harvard charter of 1650 referred to "the advancement of all good literature, arts, and sciences." Good literature was a direct translation of the Ciceronian phrase *bonae litterae*, which had come to mean a body of polite literature, knowledge of which conveyed a veneer of gentility. Similarly, the reference to arts and sciences simply meant the traditional university curriculum.

Educated persons on both sides of the Atlantic conceived of higher education in the seventeenth century in qualitative more than quantitative terms. The experience of university life together with exposure to the classical corpus were what mattered. By the time Harvard was established, the English universities had gained respectability and popularity after more than a century of turmoil. Attendance at the universities and at the Inns of Court for legal education increased in the early seventeenth century and permeated to lower ranks of society. Scholars destined for the professions that required formal learning were being joined by other men whose studies were desirable but not necessary. Concurrently, the emergence of colleges as centers of instruction as well as residential living, added to the informal, extracurricular aspects of university life. As Lawrence Cremin has noted, seventeenth-century Harvard was not dissimilar to the individual colleges within the great universities of Oxford and Cambridge. Each consisted of twenty to fifty residential scholars, a president, two or three tutors, and a small staff of servants.

For the nine or ten students who gathered in Cambridge, Massachusetts, in mid 1638 the most exciting event of that summer was probably the earthquake that shook Boston on the first day of June. It is certain that students discussed college discipline and the food served by the president's wife, Mistress Eaton, in whose home they boarded. Nathaniel Eaton, president of Harvard between 1638 and 1639, was removed from his post within a year for physical cruelty towards the students: during the hearing, his wife's housekeeping also came under attack.

After this dismal start, Henry Dunster served as president from 1640 until 1654. A graduate of Magdalene College in Cambridge, Dunster introduced a curriculum covering a three-year program. He provided for freshman classes at 8 A.M. and 2 P.M. daily, second-year classes at 9 A.M. and 3 P.M., and senior classes at 10 A.M. and 4 P.M. Instruction early in the week focused on developing skills in logic, ethics, and mathematics. Wednesdays were devoted to Greek and Thursdays to other biblical languages. Fridays featured rhetoric. Saturday morning classes were on religion and natural history. An additional year of study at the freshman level was added by Dunster's successor, Charles Chauncy, who served from 1654 to 1672, whereupon the median age of entry dropped to between fifteen and sixteen years of age where it remained.

Another of President Dunster's contributions was to acquire a charter for Harvard from the Massachusetts colony legislature in 1650. The college had awarded degrees since 1642 but without being authorized to do so by any executive, legislative, or academic body. Apparently, Dunster sensed the weakness of the college's position and sought legitimacy from the colonial government. The charter of 1650 set up a corporation consisting of the president, treasurer, and five fellows. The corporation was empowered to hold property, make rules and bylaws, conduct meetings, appoint college officers and servants, and—with the cooperation of the overseers—perpetuate the corporation by filling vacancies in its membership. This kind of legal body, whether created by the imperial or the colonial government, would be the prototype for the governance of higher education in the Anglo-American colonies.

The charter contained one objective that would not have been found in any European prototype; namely, the education of Indian youth along with the English. Seven years earlier, a pamphlet promoting Harvard in England, called *New England's First Fruits,* was prefaced by an anecdotal account of the beneficial effects of white settlement upon the Indians. It brought to mind the contrast between civilization and barbarism, and the contribution anticipated from higher education. Money raised in England for missionary efforts among the Indians was used to support John Eliot's work among the natives of New England. But after 1650 President Henry Dunster acquired some of the money to support Indian education at Harvard. In 1656 a building known as the Indian College was erected: almost at once it was appropriated for the education of white students. Only four Indians are known to have attended Harvard in the seventeenth century, and Caleb Cheeshahteaumuck alone completed a bachelor's degree. One may view these efforts as well-intentioned but doomed to failure because of the cultural misconceptions on which they were based. Alternatively, they may be seen as deceptions used to divert charitable donations for the Indians to the education of whites. A better case for this latter interpretation can be made in Virginia.

William and Mary

The well-publicized visit to London by the Princess Pocahontas, a convert to Christianity and seemingly to western civilization, may have generated interest in educating the Indians in Virginia. In 1617 King James I authorized a collection in England to establish churches and schools for Indian children in Virginia, after which the Virginia Company added the words college and university to describe the scheme. The appeal was so successful that more than two thousand pounds was raised. By 1622 a large tract of land in Virginia had been set aside for Henrico College and indentured servants sent to cultivate it. A rector had been appointed, and there were the beginnings of a library. But the rest of the money raised in England had been diverted by the Virginia Company into other projects. The Indian uprising in 1622 took away the impetus if not the ability of the colony to set up the college. Dissolution of the Virginia Company three years later terminated the effort.

A century would pass before college-level education was available in Virginia. In the meantime, the colonists looked to England for advanced learning, with those who could afford it sending their sons home for training. Educated immigrants were also hired. Churches in Virginia were usually staffed by expatriate clergymen from England or Scotland. Educational initiatives by the Virginia legislature in the early 1660s came to nothing. Finally, in 1693 the ruling oligarchy secured a charter from the Crown authorizing the creation and administration of a colonial college. Even then, the College of William and Mary was not able to offer higher learning until the 1720s, when qualified faculty were hired. In the Chesapeake area a stable social structure and a population sustained by natural increase did not come about until late in the seventeenth century, and both were necessary for the colony to begin to assert intellectual autonomy.

A grammar school and schools of philosophy and divinity were proposed to a clerical convention in Virginia in 1690. The legislature voted support and named the Reverend James Blair to go to England to seek royal approval. Blair, who held an M.A. from the University of Edinburgh, was a recent immigrant and an influential Anglican. Blair's trip was a singular success. He returned in 1693 with a royal charter, including revenues, Anglican patronage at the highest level, and a share of the estate of Robert Boyle to support an Indian school at the College of William and Mary.

Blair's original instructions from the Virginia assembly said nothing about Indian education. The petition to the king and queen argued for ministerial training and the general benefits of a liberal and virtuous education for "our youth." But a petition drafted in 1690 to London merchants mentioned that a Virginia college might assist in converting the heathens. This and Blair's later bid for the Boyle bequest do seem to be rather disingenuous. The charter of College of William and Mary subsequently specified three aims: the supply of ministerial candidates, the pious education of youth, and the conversion of the Indians. Although Indian enrollment at the college fluctuated quite widely, the Boyle legacy was drawn upon to add an impressive building known as the Brafferton in 1723 and to buy books for the college library in 1732.

The charter of 1693 set up a self-perpetuating board of eighteen visitors from the colonial elite empowered to make rules and statutes for the college. Blair was appointed president for life and a visitor, serving from 1693 until 1743. Six other professors or masters were to instruct up to a hundred scholars in divinity, philosophy, languages, and arts and sciences. Following the practice in English universities, William and

Mary was afforded the patronage of a chancellor, the Bishop of London, and was assigned a representative in the Virginia legislature. However, the college was also subject to Scottish influences from Blair's hand.

In a public ceremony in 1699, five students at the College of William and Mary made formal speeches to an audience that included Virginia's leading citizens. The speeches presented the reasons typically given to the colonial community to justify local colleges. First there was a general oration in praise of learning directed at the minority who already possessed formal education. Then it was argued that higher education in Virginia was preferable to going abroad because it was cheaper, and avoided the risks of travel, sickness, and corruption by the metropolis. Parents could keep better control over their offspring nearer home. Also, the college would benefit the province by preventing the export of wealth; in fact it would probably bring money into the colony if students attended from elsewhere. It would certainly stimulate the local economy by providing markets and employment. Furthermore, the reputation of Virginia would be enhanced if it supplied its own ministers, physicians, lawyers, and statesmen. It was commonly thought that men qualified to hold positions of local authority were lacking. This was especially true in Virginia because the hard labor required to survive had left no time for study. As the educated immigrants had died, learning had disappeared and the native-born Virginians were scarcely able to read and write. Ignorance and barbarism in seventeenth-century Virginia were not just evocative threats, they were real.

After the auspicious start in 1693, the college project became bogged down in imperial and provincial politics. There was a struggle over the salary that Blair demanded, and then the college building, erected from Sir Christopher Wren's plans, burned. Instruction was irregular before 1720, and new financial support had to be sought in 1726. The value of attending William and Mary during the eighteenth century may have been the political and social contacts it provided in the capital city of Williamsburg more than the formal education. Many students did not obtain a degree, attending the college before or after private tutoring or a trip to England.

Yale

By the time that sons of the elite in Virginia could acquire higher education and elements of gentility at the College of William and Mary, three generations of fortunate young men in New England had been offered a Harvard education. They had filled various roles in church and state, but by the second third of the seventeenth century, few were choosing the ministry. To some observers this signaled a loss of piety at Cambridge, and the possibility that orthodox preachers to fill New England's pulpits would be lacking. A group of clergymen resolved to found another college, more convenient to their homes in Connecticut, where pious youths could be properly educated for service in church and state.

Yale College was the work of Harvard alumni. Of the ten trustees who met in November 1701, all but one were born in the colonies. Nine had attended Harvard, seven were ministers, and three had been ordained in the same year, 1685. The desire for a college in southern New England had been expressed before. Now was the time. In their first meeting, the trustees claimed to be fulfilling the "grand errand" of bringing Christianity and learning to the wilderness.

Grand errand notwithstanding, Yale actually began in a very modest way. Although a charter was obtained from the Connecticut legislature, for five years instruction took place in the home of the first rector, Abraham Pierson. From 1707 until 1720 the college location was in dispute and small groups of students followed their tutors from place to place. Higher education must have seemed like private instruction, except that the college bestowed degrees with all the solemnity and ritual of a medieval university. Brooks Mather Kelley's modern history of Yale pieces together an account of the 1717 commencement, held for the first time in New Haven. It was an all-day event, open to the public but probably attended only by the educated few and their parents. All the dialogue was in Latin. It started with a prayer and a salutatory oration. Then candidates for bachelors' degrees showed their learning by engaging in syllogistic disputations. After lunch, candidates for masters degrees delivered prepared speeches or responded to public questioning on a written thesis submitted beforehand. The rector then presented the candidates for degrees to the trustees and asked if it pleased them, to which the trustees answered that it did. The rector spoke individually to each candidate, saying "I admit thee to the First [or Second] Degree in Arts . . . , together with the power to lecture publicly on any one of the Arts which thou hast studied." The ceremony concluded with a valediction by one of the new masters of arts and a closing prayer.

The college's fortunes had begun to change by 1720. Elihu Yale made an important donation and had his name attached to the institution. A college building was erected in New Haven. And nearly eight hundred books sent by Jeremiah Dummer had arrived. In the long run, the books were the most important. Dummer had gathered recent publications from the greatest minds of the age—Locke, Newton, Descartes, Boyle, Milton, and the most notable clerics. They represented the first winds of rationalism to blow through academic halls in America.

In reality, the origins of formal higher education in North America were modest at best. Claims made for its importance were not. Listen to Harvard tutor Jonathan Mitchell in 1663: "Wee in this Country, being farre removed from the more cultivated parts of the world, had need to use utmost care & diligence to keep up Learning & all Helps of Education among us, lest degeneracy, Barbarism, Ignorance and irreligion doe by degrees breake in upon us." The survival of civilization, as Mitchell knew it, depended on preserving learning in the wilderness. Instead of these fears diminishing in the eighteenth century as the settlements matured, they were regenerated by new circumstances.

EIGHTEENTH-CENTURY HIGHER EDUCATION

The population of mainland British North America grew in the eighteenth century at an unprecedented rate. Most of this increase was due to high fertility and low infant mortality. The rest came about through immigration. The influx brought men, women, and children from many parts of Europe and from distant corners of the British Isles. The result was diversity in language, folklore, manners, values, and belief

that shattered the homogeneity of the seventeenth-century settlements. Uneven economic development left some regions prosperous and others poor. Religious conflicts and signs of materialism in the 1730s and 1740s were noted with lamentation. Imperial warfare in the 1750s and 1760s, plus growing estrangement between England and the colonies, compounded the sense of crisis. Once again, the question posed was how to transmit values and a cultural heritage from one generation to another.

The phenomenon of religious revival reached its zenith in 1740 with the Great Awakening. Among its initial effects was a heightened concern for religion that made many colonists seek church membership. Coupled with evangelical and missionary efforts among the unchurched and recent immigrants, there was a dramatic increase in the size of most denominations. New denominations like the Baptists appeared. Many established churches fell into rival factions, with New Side or New Light preachers supporting evangelical methods while the Old Side opposed them. Historians today can see demographic, social, economic, and political reasons for the religious confusion, but contemporaries saw only the hand of God or of the Devil.

The impact of the Great Awakening on higher education was most visible in the 1740s when George Whitefield, the best known itinerant preacher of the time, publicly attacked Harvard and Yale, in part because of the books being read by Harvard students. In a public response in 1744, the faculty bridled at Whitefield's brash arrogance. He replied that he had commented merely on the omission of evangelical writers. In fact, Whitefield was attacking the rational religion, comfortably ensconced at Harvard since the 1720s, in which ministerial candidates were being trained. Whitefield and the other New Light itinerants claimed that ministers must demonstrate that they had been converted before they presumed to show others the way.

Yale, under Thomas Clap, rector and president from 1740 to 1766, was not about to stay out of the controversy. Dissension and disorder had come to New Haven with the Great Awakening. Clap had denied degrees to two master's candidates in 1741 because they supported the revival. The case of David Brainerd was more notorious. He was expelled in 1741 for "saying that Tutor Whittelsey had no more grace than a chair." To Clap, this attitude proved that the Awakening was not God's work. He felt fully justified in expelling John and Ebenezer Cleaveland in 1744 because they had attended a religious meeting not to Clap's liking. By the mid 1740s, Clap publicly espoused a conservative, orthodox role for Yale. He was out of step with his times and had to contend with a resentful and often unruly student body. But he did see quite correctly that the issue raised by revivalism was the control of ministerial education.

Among eighteenth-century immigrants, the Scotch-Irish left a considerable mark on higher education. Their expectations about a learned ministry were particularly strong, for their clerical leaders had enjoyed the finest education in the Scottish universities. Douglas Sloan identified twenty-six of the original Presbytery of Philadelphia and found that twelve had attended the University of Glasgow and four, Edinburgh University. Following a practice used in Ulster for preparing ministerial candidates, the Scotch-Irish clergymen sometimes opened their homes as academies where the classics and religious studies could be passed to the younger generation. At their best, as in William Tennent's Log College, Samuel Blair's Faggs Manor, Samuel Finley's Nottingham Academy, or Francis Alison's Newark Academy, they were equivalent to the chartered, degree-granting colleges that succeeded them. They not only preserved traditional learning but also transmitted new ideas from the Scottish universities and from academies founded by English religious dissenters.

Douglas Sloan has demonstrated the widespread influence of Scottish education in the eighteenth century. The Scottish universities were centers for the Enlightenment, distinguished by some of the greatest philosophers and teachers of the age. They had seen reforms in curriculum and pedagogy, including the use of English instead of Latin as the language of classroom instruction. Professors were specializing in a discipline rather than teaching all subjects. Science was studied with modern methods and practical demonstrations. As for medical education, Scotland probably offered the best in the western world. These ideas were emulated on both sides of the Atlantic. Students in the academies were led into science and the *belles lettres* as far as the abilities of their mentor would permit. Emphasis was on a broad yet practical curriculum, although the classical languages were also stressed.

Colonial academies became focal points for a struggle over ministerial training and ordination. The paternal style of education in the academies enabled the Evangelicals to imbue young ministerial recruits with their ideas. However, their efforts were foiled in denominations where the Old Side controlled ordination and required that candidates for the ministry hold a college degree. Academies were not chartered, nor did they grant degrees. But the Evangelicals tended to eschew the three chartered colleges because of their rationalist leanings. The answer lay in new American colleges, duly authorized to award degrees to Evangelicals who would possess the formal credentials for ordination.

While denominational faction stimulated educational activity, the influence of European rationalists, especially John Locke, raised expectations. Locke provided insights into the workings of the mind which suggested that education could change individuals as well as societies. Teachers could mold impressionable young people by controlling their environment and developing their capacity to reason. Societal diversity, provincial and sectarian competition, Scottish innovation, and Lockean psychology combined to produce a strong catalyst for the founding of colleges in Anglo-America in the mid eighteenth century.

From the Urban Environment: Philadelphia College and King's College

Benjamin Franklin suggested an academy for Philadelphia in *A Proposal Relating to the Education of Youth in Pensilvania* (1749), which he distributed free to the principal inhabitants. At least fifty citizens pledged money to a subscription, whereupon the twenty-four largest donors were chosen as trustees. Although Franklin was among the trustees, the project passed into the hands of the urban elite.

Franklin's *Proposals* showed the pragmatic approach to higher education typical of the mercantile community. Since his own formal education had ended when he was ten years old, Franklin was not inclined to believe that classical studies were a mark of intellect. He advocated a thoroughly practical curriculum that would prepare one for a useful, comfortable life in this world rather than the next. In place of classical languages, Franklin preferred a thorough schooling in English. "As to their STUDIES," he wrote, "it would be well if they could be taught *every Thing* that is useful, and *every Thing* that is ornamental." But because "Art is long, and their Time is short," Franklin recommended "those Things that are likely to be *most useful* and *most ornamental*, Regard being had to the several Professions for which they are intended."

This was too radical for most trustees. Franklin gave in to "persons of wealth and learning," whose money and support were needed. The Constitutions of the academy, adopted by the trustees in 1749, provided for both Latin and English schools. In 1753 the proprietor incorporated the trustees by charter and in 1755 a second charter grafted a three year college onto the academy giving it degree-granting powers. By the early 1760s the institution, known as the College and Academy of Philadelphia, had about three hundred students.

The institution was to be secular, independent, and supported through private donations. However, Anglican influence was gradually asserted. The Presbyterian Francis Alison, an eminent classicist who joined the faculty in 1752 and served until 1779, was soon overshadowed by the Anglican William Smith. Both Alison and Smith had been educated in Scottish universities. But Smith, at the age of twenty-eight, was named provost as much because of his enthusiastic Anglicanism as for his innovative ideas on higher education. He dominated the institution from 1755 until 1779.

The curriculum at Philadelphia College did depart from tradition. William Smith had published a pamphlet entitled *A General Idea of the College of Mirania* (1753) expressing some ideas similar to Franklin's, including different training for practical occupations and for the professions. Classical languages were only needed for the latter. As provost, Smith's curriculum for Philadelphia College was probably based on his own education and recent reforms in Aberdeen, Scotland. The result was a three-year program in which the classics were taught from a modern perspective. Logic and metaphysics in the first year were superseded by moral philosophy later. Mathematics, natural history, astronomy, and physics were studied throughout. The significance of these innovations should not be overesti-

mated. Smith continued to believe that the classics enshrined the wisdom of the ages, and that the purpose of higher education was to transmit the cultural heritage, including the precepts of Christianity.

New Yorkers had been jealous for a long time about the careful provision for higher education in New England. When chartered colleges appeared in New Jersey and Pennsylvania, envy flared into ambition and then into controversy.

Two groups were in contention in New York. One, consisting of recent Yale graduates and lawyers, was led by William Livingston. They sought to raise the intellectual and cultural level of New Yorkers. Several had connections with Princeton, founded in 1746. Livingston himself was a Presbyterian and concerned that Princeton and Yale stood to lose from a rival college. Local pride prevailed, however, and Livingston's party advocated a New York college in a series of essays published as *The Independent Reflector* in 1753. In the tradition of English Dissenters, they presented the anti-clerical, Whig perspective.

On the other side was the Anglican party, composed of clerics, rural squires, and city merchants, and supported by the imperial Anglican establishment. With Harvard, Yale, and Princeton seemingly in the hands of Dissenters and the Philadelphia academy founded as a secular institution, New York's Anglicans were by 1750 in an aggressive mood. They supported the movement for King's College (Columbia University) on the assumption that they would be able to control it.

A bitter controversy over control was waged in the press and the legislature. Through a compromise in 1756, the college received a charter but only half the promised lottery funds as the price for Anglican control. The King's College charter was modeled after those of Yale and Princeton. It incorporated a board of trustees dominated by Anglicans and closely tied to the royal administration. The inclusion of Dutch, French, Lutherans, and Presbyterians was a recognition of New York's diversity. College admission was nondenominational but Anglican prayers were used.

The charter, dated 31 October 1754, named the leading colonial Anglican, Samuel Johnson, as president. Johnson had already begun teaching the previous July in the vestry room of Trinity Church, instructing eight students who had responded to the announced opening of the college. The curriculum was modeled on that of Yale. Having a special interest in philosophy, Johnson's teaching emphasized ethics, and he viewed education as a way to discover the Divine Purpose. Johnson hoped to nurture a generation of rational, ethical young men who would preserve English cultural values in a fragmented community. He served as president of King's College until 1763.

From Evangelical Origins: Princeton, Rutgers, Brown, and Dartmouth

Twenty years after the conflict began, a split in the Presbyterian Synod of Philadelphia over ministerial ordination led to the creation of the College of New Jersey (Princeton). A group headed by Jonathan Dickinson and Aaron Burr withdrew in 1745 to form the Synod of New York. Five men were alumni of Yale and one had been educated at Harvard. They wished to found a college where New Light Evangelical ministers could be trained for the growing number of congregations in the middle colonies and Virginia. But Princeton was also to transmit the cultural heritage.

The group obtained a college charter from the New Jersey government in 1746. Revisions to this charter generally expanded membership of the trustees, first to supporters of the late William Tennents's academy known as Log College, then to the colonial government, and then to the lay element which added other denominations. Trustees came from New York and Pennsylvania as well as New Jersey. The revised charter of 1748 stipulated that Princeton was open to all students regardless of their church affiliation. The college itself remained under Presbyterian control and had to seek funds from outside New Jersey.

Jonathan Dickinson was chosen as the first president, and the college officially opened at his home in Elizabeth, New Jersey, in May of 1747. Dickinson died in September of that year, so Aaron Burr took over the handful of students and the single tutor who comprised the college. When Burr died ten years later, there were about seventy students and three tutors housed in an impressive building known as Nassau Hall in Princeton. The next three presidents died prematurely. The choice fell next on the eminent

Scottish churchman, Dr. John Witherspoon, who arrived in 1768.

President Aaron Burr fashioned a curriculum at Princeton that drew initially from Yale. Letters from young William Shippen described his studies at Princeton between 1751 and 1754. As a freshman, Shippen read Latin and Greek authors and Hebrew grammar. He also studied logic, geography, astronomy, and rhetoric and had difficulty finding time for French, algebra, and English literature. Classical studies continued in the second year, with rhetoric and natural philosophy. Ethics and moral philosophy were added in the third year. The senior year seems to have been used for review. Samuel Finley, who had run his own academy at Nottingham before becoming president of Princeton in 1761, introduced chronology, and more study of English authors during his five-year tenure. With the arrival of Dr. Witherspoon, Scottish influence was more marked. Witherspoon improved teaching methods and tightened academic standards; he added to the library and in 1771 purchased the famous orrery constructed by David Rittenhouse that mechanically depicted the solar system. In public relations literature, Witherspoon stressed the similarities between Princeton and the English and Scottish universities.

The founding of Queens College (Rutgers University) followed the pattern of Princeton. Like the Presbyterians, the Dutch Reformed in America were seriously divided over the question of revival. In the 1740s the evangelical wing, led by Theodore J. Frelinghuysen, attempted to train ministerial candidates in their homes. But the Classis of Amsterdam, which supervised the colonial church, retained control over ordination. Not only did the Classis insist that candidates travel to Holland for ordination, it also remained fundamentally opposed to revivalism. The liberals wanted their own college to train ministers in America, together with the authority to ordain them. Conservatives thought this would destroy their link with the Church of Holland guaranteed in 1664, and would threaten their Dutch culture and identity.

The struggle lasted for two decades after 1740. The conservatives tried to blunt the movement for a Dutch college by negotiating with Princeton and then with King's College to allow ministerial candidates to be trained there. The Evangelicals tried to convince the Amsterdam Classis of their case. The response from the Amsterdam Classis in 1756 was typical: "Yes, a UNIVERSITY! What queer notions! With no consideration of the treasures necessary for its support; or the place where it should be located; or the plan for its government; or the protection necessary for its welfare; or where Professors . . . could be found."

Leadership of the college movement after 1761 was assumed by Jacob Rutsen Hardenberg, who had married into the Frelinghuysen family and remained prominent in college affairs until his death in 1790. Hardenberg informed the Amsterdam Classis that the college would go ahead with or without its blessing. The New Jersey government was petitioned for a charter in 1766. The charter granted in 1770 mandated a large board of trustees with a majority from the Dutch Reformed Church and stated that the students would be taught English.

The provision for English instruction came out of a long-standing dispute about cultural identity. One hundred years after the English conquest of New Netherland, the Dutch population was still largely unassimilated. Educated leaders had been supplied from the Netherlands or had been sent there to train. In 1769 the Amsterdam Classis was informed that ministers who were called from Holland would probably have to start to preach in English because the younger generation in New York was becoming unfamiliar with the Dutch language. Yet the older generation still had difficulty writing in English. A petition from the Rutgers trustees, presumably some of the best educated men in the Dutch community, was written in labored language that was probably learned phonetically. The trustees thanked the administration for the first charter:

by which favours your Esqs & Honors disCovert a most tender and im pasioN re grardt for the good of all man kined in ginarle & for Removing those Devickletis the Duch in thise parts laybert onder of sending thar youth to halland to be adecaytet for the Cosspel ministry in pertikoler. ("The Petition of the Trustees," Archives of Rutgers University)

Rutgers was intended by its founders to accelerate the adoption of the English language among the Dutch. They argued that the country was English anyhow and it did not matter much what the language was so long as their religion was preserved. The first commencement in 1774 demonstrated this process. Presiding over the affair was Jacob Rutsen Hardenberg whose family had been in America for over a hundred years. Hardenberg still regarded Dutch as his mother tongue and made a public apology for his faulty English. The lone graduate, however, "delivered Orations in Latin, Dutch and English with high applause."

By the 1760s the Baptists were almost the only major denomination without a college. The sect had not been split in the Great Awakening, for the Baptists had generally favored evangelicalism. They had not required their preachers to be formally educated but attitudes were changing. In 1756 the Philadelphia Association pledged support for a Latin grammar school. Hopewell Academy lasted for eleven years. James Manning and David Howell, who would be leaders in the Baptist college, were educated at Hopewell before graduating from Princeton. They participated in the movement for Rhode Island College (Brown University) in much the same way that graduates of the Presbyterian academies helped to found the College of New Jersey.

A college was probably recommended to the Association by Morgan Edwards who was reputed to be a classical scholar. The idea was taken up in 1762 by the young James Manning. He selected Rhode Island because of Baptist influence in the colony's government and the fact that it was without a college. Manning visited Newport in 1763 to consult with the city's leading Baptists and other interested parties. A series of bitter conflicts followed. A bid to secure support from the Congregationalists went awry. Indecision over the location of Rhode Island College was settled in favor of Providence but angered people in Newport who started to plan a rival college. Brown actually opened in James Manning's parsonage at Warren with a single student in 1765. David Howell was appointed tutor in 1767 but the college remained small, with most students coming from outside the colony. The charter disavowed religious discrimination of any sort yet the college was viewed as sectarian. The Baptists controlled it, but they paid the price in reduced community support and public funds.

Dartmouth College, chartered in 1769, was the outcome of Eleazar Wheelock's evangelicalism. After receiving a Yale education, Wheelock entered the Congregational ministry and became a leading supporter in Connecticut of the Great Awakening. When the revivalistic fervor died down, he sought another outlet for his compulsive energies. He settled on the conversion and education of Indians.

The Great Awakening had motivated some white missionaries to work in Native settlements. However, Wheelock preferred to bring Indian youths into white communities where they could acquire what he regarded as true religion and civilization. Returning to their tribes, they would encourage a new mode of life based on sedentary agriculture, Protestantism, and loyalty to the English Crown. While the Indians were among the English, white missionaries could learn their languages. The presence of Indians among the English might also discourage hostile Indian attacks on the whites.

Wheelock's ideas were based on the success of Samson Occum, a Mohegan Indian who was his pupil in the 1740s and had become an ordained minister. In the 1750s and early 1760s, Wheelock devoted himself to the education of Indian boys and girls who were sent to his parish in Lebanon, Connecticut. When Colonel Joshua Moore donated two acres (about 1 hectare) of land to support the work, Wheelock embarked on a campaign to obtain a charter and funds for the charity school. This brought him into contact with the metropolitan and colonial governments, the New England Congregationalists, the Society for the Propagation of the Gospel, and the Society in Scotland for the Promotion of Christian Knowledge. Such a complex web of support would eventually become strained by rivalries and suspicions. Wheelock was always a hard man to work with, especially when a sum of twelve thousand pounds, a very large amount, was raised in Britain for the Indian Charity School.

Meanwhile, Wheelock was re-evaluating his program. His *Narrative* published in 1771 showed his educational expectations as well as his disappointments:

I have turned out 40 Indians who were good readers, writers and were instructed in the principles of the Christian religion, sufficiently advanced in English grammar, arithmetic and a number considerably advanced in Latin & Greek, one of them through college, others carried through a course of learning as expensive as a college course. Well behaved while with me and left school with unblemished character. Many of them went at once into a business they were qualified for, mostly as school masters and interpreters; but by contact with the vices of their tribes (mostly drunkenness) not more than half preserved their characters unstained. The rest are sunk into as low, savage and brutish a way of living as they were before and many of the most promising have fallen lowest. And six of those who did preserve a good character are now dead. Most of them run their schools well for the first year but when they are broken up by hunting parties etc. have not enough energy to reassemble them. (Leon B. Richardson. *The History of Dartmouth College.* Vol. 1, p. 78)

This overall record, coupled with the increasing number of white youths in his school, caused Wheelock to shift his attention. From Anglicizing the Indians, Wheelock changed to training white missionaries, and then to founding a college where the English could be educated as ministers and leaders. In 1768 he chose to move his school to New Hampshire. The white population there was short of trained men and it was the only colony north of Maryland without a college. Wheelock's efforts to persuade his British backers of the continuity between the original plan, for which money had been raised, and the projected college were labored and unconvincing. A solution was found in dual boards to administer funds: one based in London would control the Indian charity school; another in America would supervise a larger institution known as Dartmouth College. In the college's charter the American board had twelve trustees, eight of them New Hampshire residents, seven of them laymen, with no denominational requirements.

In 1770 Wheelock moved with about thirty students, including three Indians, to Hanover in New Hampshire and Dartmouth College opened. The record of the college did little to mitigate the impression that Wheelock had altered his original purpose. Only two Indians passed through the charity school to graduate from Dartmouth during Wheelock's presidency. The college itself contributed few white missionaries to work with the Indians. At the first commencement in 1771, only two of the four graduates planned to be missionaries.

"College Enthusiasm!" Ezra Stiles wrote sarcastically in a diary entry for 6 April 1770 as he recorded the conversion of Wheelock's Indian school into Dartmouth. He noted three other college projects that would turn out to be stillborn. In 1770 George Whitefield was trying to obtain a royal charter to elevate his orphanage in Georgia to a college. A group was petitioning the South Carolina legislature for authority to open a college in Charleston. Nearer to home for Stiles, citizens of Newport were still scheming for a second college in Rhode Island to rival the Baptist college in Providence. Not all attempts to provide for colonial higher education through formally chartered colleges were successful; some would not see the light of day until after the republic provided new expectations for higher education.

OBJECTIVES OF HIGHER EDUCATION IN ANGLO-AMERICA

The underlying goal of eighteenth-century colleges was to prepare leaders. The educational objectives were to transmit learning, to prepare for adult occupations, to develop good citizenship, and to nourish virtue. Each of these contributed to leadership.

Transmission of learning remained at the heart of the enterprise and continued to be defined conservatively. Modernization of the curriculum in the eighteenth century did not mean that classical learning was abandoned. While some practical subjects were introduced to meet the needs of colonial communities, both the colleges and the academies prescribed the classics for higher education. Probably the most vivid example was the schooling designed by Eleazar Wheelock: the clergyman and his Indian and white students were literally out in the wilderness conjugating Latin verbs! Wheelock believed that classical learning was necessary for leadership, no matter what the vocation.

The classical heritage also included essential Christian doctrine. No matter how heated the debate about the control of an institution, the nature of the curriculum, or the paternalism of the president, there was implicit agreement that youth should seek philosophical and moral truth and that it would be Christian. True philosophy and sound doctrine were thought to go hand in hand. Educators encouraged students to browse in the college library, but they expected that this would serve to confirm belief not weaken it. William Livingston, arch critic of denominational control over education (at least by the Anglicans), nonetheless required undergraduates to attend church and daily prayers in the college. Religious freedom must not, in his words, become a "Cloak for Licenciousness."

Occupational preparation continued to build on the foundation of classical learning but it was becoming more specialized as colleges responded to societal needs. Population growth in the eighteenth century placed new demands on colleges to increase the number of educated men for leadership in church and state. The shortage of trained ministers was particularly acute. Educated men were in demand as local magistrates. Schoolteachers were being hired. The supply of physicians and lawyers was inadequate. All candidates needed higher education and, in the case of doctors, lawyers, and ministers, formal postgraduate training was coming to be expected as well. Aspiring colonial physicians who found the apprenticeship system inadequate journeyed to Europe for medical education. In the 1760s, however, both the College of Philadelphia and King's College provided for the study of medicine at home. An objective of the Livingston group in New York was to raise the standards of legal education. This was accomplished at William and Mary by the appointment of George Wythe as professor of law. Creation of the Hollis professorship of divinity at Harvard formalized theological study.

The redefinition of professional education was paralleled by some vocational specialization at the undergraduate level but not much. In keeping with Franklin's pragmatic recommendations, Philadelphia College offered a practical alternative to those not destined for the learned professions. Yet Provost Smith continued to stress gentlemanly accomplishments as a desirable outcome of education at the college. Eleazar Wheelock taught vocational skills in the Indian charity school although the program was dropped at Dartmouth. Typically, the undergraduate education offered at the denominational colleges did not differentiate between young men destined for the ministry and those who were not. Potential leaders in state as well as church needed to be exposed to learning and virtue as undergraduates. Post-baccalaureate ministerial study would take care of the clergy.

Developing good citizenship was a traditional objective for higher education. In the Anglo-French struggle in the first half of the eighteenth century, this meant securing the loyalty of the Indians and frontier settlers for the English—hence Wheelock's program. The problem in the middle colonies was the high ratio of non-English-speaking immigrants whose commitment to the English Crown was problematic. Princeton and Philadelphia College proposed to help by educating students from among the German immigrants. Assimilation would be achieved because these young men would adopt the values of the Anglo-American intellectual elite. With their understanding enhanced by college education, they would reject petty differences and seek to create harmonious, integrated communities. Samuel Johnson promised as much for King's College, which he saw as a nursery for British loyalty. Rutgers was in fact accomplishing this assimilation for the Dutch. The possibility that higher education offered a way to ameliorate differences in society put a new gloss on the importance of citizenship training in the early eighteenth century.

The conception of good citizenship was actually being reformulated by Anglo-American intellectuals. A debate in England had been waged between 1660 and 1700 on the proper education for a gentleman. The Renaissance definition of virtue as it was associated with gentility yielded to a more typically Christian version that stressed piety and godliness. John Locke then combined civility and piety into virtue as a requirement for the gentry. His ideas were popularized in the colonies by Isaac Watts, Philip Doddridge, and James Burgh. They shifted the focus to virtue as a sense of one's public responsibilities—in other words, citizenship. The role of exemplary citizen was therefore attainable by those who had been made virtuous by an enlightened education.

The objective of developing virtue in youth through higher education acquired fresh credibility through Locke's psychology. Rationalists like Franklin, Provost Smith, and Richard Peters in Philadelphia, and Samuel Johnson and William Livingston in New York assumed that reason generated virtue; thus, the more educated people were, the more ethical their behavior. Despite their Calvinist belief in predestination, the evangelical educators also used higher education to inculcate virtue by creating the circumstances for students to experience conversion. Locke had argued for the importance of youth as a formative period: the attraction of young people to evangelical religion in the Great Awakening acted as confirmation. Driven by millennial fervor after the Great Awakening, many New Light intellectual leaders expected higher education to reform society by bringing forth virtuous men.

CONTRIBUTIONS OF HIGHER EDUCATION IN ANGLO-AMERICA

If higher education was to foster virtue in youth coming of age at mid century, conflicts between students and faculty were not a promising start. But disorderly behavior occurred at many colonial colleges, with some episodes serious enough to be called riots. President Thomas Clap's harsh regime at Yale was plagued by student protests, and Harvard, despite the mild administration of President Edward Holyoke, saw the authority of the tutors challenged several times. Published biographical studies of the graduates of Harvard, Yale, and Princeton offer these glimpses of student life in the eighteenth century, together with important demographic data. Taken with unpublished dissertations that study institutional history, they suggest some contributions of higher education in Anglo-America.

One question is whether attendance at a colonial college changed career opportunities or provided upward social mobility. In the first three decades at Philadelphia College and Kings College, approximately two-thirds of the students came from upper-class families. These students entered the most lucrative professions or followed their fathers into business. Higher education probably added little to the social and economic advantages their families already possessed. The remaining one-third of Philadelphia and King's College students belonged to nonelite but still well-to-do families. These students tended to become ministers or schoolteachers, less profitable careers but with many job opportunities. Where these occupations surpassed those of their fathers in prestige, a college education may have provided upward mobility. Perhaps the evangelical colleges that recruited for these occupations gave ambitious young men from rather humble origins a foot on the professional ladder.

College education anywhere in the eighteenth century was expensive. James Axtell estimated that about three thousand men graduated from American colleges between 1746 and 1776. This was more than twice the number graduated in the preceding century. Even so, it involved perhaps one person among two hundred potentially eligible by age and gender. The barriers were wealth, educational preparation, and family status and aspiration.

Family status was the key that opened doors in the eighteenth century. Though higher education was an asset, it probably continued to function as it had for Harvard graduates in the seventeenth century, "to complete and confirm their qualification, right, and obligation to govern that already existed," in Axtell's words. If the revolutionary generation produced leaders who were also learned men, it was the rule rather than the exception. The unusual circumstance was that the political crisis gave them a chance to put into practice ideas they had studied in college.

David W. Robson has described the political awakening of faculties and students in the 1760s and 1770s. College presidents and faculty were politicized by the Seven Years' War and British imperial policies. Students followed their precepts and copied their behavior. The older generation was applying lessons drawn from the classical political texts that they taught. Robson shows that many of the assigned authors belonged to a canon now known as Commonwealth Whig ideology, which interpreted history as a struggle of liberty and virtue against tyranny and corruption. In the British imperial context, liberty depended on regenerating virtue—in England if this were possible; if not, then abroad among the American colonists. Differences on this point made educated men into Loyalists or Patriots.

BIBLIOGRAPHY

Audet, Louis-Philippe. "Programme et professeurs du Collège de Québec (1635–1763)." In *Les Cahiers des Dix, No. 34.* Montreal, 1969. Recommended by W. J. Eccles.

Axtell, James L. *The School upon a Hill: Education and Society in Colonial New England.* New Haven, Conn., 1974.

Bronson, Walter C. *The History of Brown University, 1764–1914.* Providence, R.I., 1914.

Campeau, Lucien. *La première mission des Jesuites en Nouvelle-France (1611–1613) et les commencements du Collège du Québec (1626–1670).* Cahiers d'Histoire des Jesuites, no. 1. Montreal, 1969. Recommended by W. J. Eccles.

Cremin, Lawrence A. *American Education: The Colonial Experience, 1607–1783.* New York, 1970.

Demarest, William. *A History of Rutgers College, 1766–1924.* New Brunswick, N.J., 1924.

Dexter, Franklin B., ed. *Biographical Sketches of the Graduates of Yale College.* 6 vols. New York, 1885–1912.

Ellis, Joseph J. *The New England Mind in Transition: Samuel Johnson of Connecticut, 1696–1772.* New Haven, Conn., 1973.

Erenberg, Phyllis Vine. "Change and Continuity: Values in American Higher Education, 1750–1800." Ph.D. diss., University of Michigan, 1974.

Franklin, Benjamin. *The Educational Views of Benjamin Franklin.* Edited by Thomas Woody. New York, 1931.

———. *The Papers of Benjamin Franklin*, edited by Leonard Wood Labaree et al. 25 vols. New Haven, Conn., 1959–

Gegenheimer, Albert F. *William Smith, Educator and Churchman, 1727–1803.* Philadelphia, 1943.

Gongora, Mario. *Studies in the Colonial History of Spanish America.* Cambridge, England, 1975.

Gordon, Ann D. "The College of Philadelphia, 1749–1779: Impact of an Institution." Ph.D. diss., University of Wisconsin, 1975.

Gosselin, Amédée. *L'Instruction au Canada sous le regime francais (1635–1760).* Quebec, 1911.

Harrison, Richard A. *Princetonians, 1769–1775: A Biographical Dictionary.* Princeton, N.J., 1980.

Herbst, Jurgen. "The First Three American Colleges: Schools of the Reformation." *Perspectives in American History* 8 (1974):7–52.

———. *From Crisis to Crisis: American College Government, 1636–1819.* Cambridge, Mass., 1982.

Hofstadter, Richard, and Wilson Smith, eds. *American Higher Education: A Documentary History.* 2 vols. Chicago, 1961.

Humphrey, David C. *From King's College to Columbia, 1746–1800.* New York, 1976.

Kelley, Brooks M. *Yale: A History.* New Haven, Conn., 1974.

Livingston, William. *The Independent Reflector; or, Weekly Essays on Sundry Important Subjects, More Particularly Adapted to the Province of New York.* Edited by Milton M. Klein. Cambridge, Mass., 1963.

McAnear, Beverly. "College Founding in the American Colonies, 1745–1775." *Mississippi Valley Historical Review* 42 (1955):24–44.

McClellan, B. Edward, and William J. Reese, eds. *The Social History of American Education.* Urbana, Ill., 1988.

McLachlan, James. *Princetonians, 1748–1768: A Biographical Dictionary.* Princeton, N.J., 1976.

Miller, Howard. *The Revolutionary College: American Presbyterian Higher Education: 1707–1837.* New York, 1976.

Montgomery, Thomas H. *A History of the University of Pennsylvania From Its Foundation to A.D. 1770, Including Biographical Sketches of the Trustees, Faculty, the First Alumni and Others.* Philadelphia, 1900.

Morison, Samuel E. *The Founding of Harvard College.* Cambridge, Mass., 1935.

Morpurgo, Jack E. *Their Majesties' Royall Colledge: William and Mary in the Seventeenth and Eighteenth Centuries.* Williamsburg, Va., 1976.

Richardson, Leon B. *The History of Dartmouth College.* 2 vols. Hanover, N.H., 1932.

Robson, David W. *Educating Republicans: The College in the Era of the American Revolution, 1750–1800.* Westport, Conn., 1985.

Sibley, John L. et al., eds. *Biographical Sketches of Those Who Attended Harvard College.* 17 vols. Boston, 1873–1975.

Sloan, Douglas. *The Scottish Enlightenment and the American College Ideal.* New York, 1971.

Solomon, Barbara M. *In the Company of Educated Women: A History of Women and Higher Education in America.* New Haven, Conn., 1985.

Szasz, Margaret C. *Indian Education in the American Colonies, 1607–1783.* Albuquerque, N.Mex., 1988.

Warch, Richard. *School of the Prophets: Yale College, 1701–1740.* New Haven, Conn., 1973.

Wheelock, Eleazar. *The Microfilm Edition of the Papers of Eleazar Wheelock.* Hanover, N.H., 1971.

Wertenbaker, Thomas J. *Princeton, 1746–1896.* Princeton, N.J., 1946.

Wright, Bobby. " 'For the Children of the Infidels'?: American Indian Education in the Colonial Colleges." *American Indian Culture and Research Journal* 12, no. 3 (1988):1–14.

Margaret W. Masson

SEE ALSO **Church and State; Literature;** and **Scientific Inquiry;** and various essays in THE LIFE OF THE MIND.

XVI

RELIGION

CHURCH AND STATE

THE BRITISH COLONIES

WHEN THE FIRST AMENDMENT to the U.S. Constitution went into effect in 1791, contemporary observers realized that its provisions for the separation of church and state applied only to the national government. The amendment's stipulation that "Congress shall make no law respecting an establishment of religion, or prohibiting the free exercise thereof" did guarantee that the federal government would not be entangled with the institutions of religion. At the local level, however, it was a different story. Five of the nation's fourteen states (Vermont had joined the union earlier that year) provided tax support for ministers, and those five plus seven others continued religious tests for public office. Only Virginia and Rhode Island practiced the kind of separation of church and state that has since become an American commonplace; that is, where government provides no money for churches and imposes no religious conditions for participation in public life. With less than a handful of exceptions, even the defenders of religious liberty in Rhode Island and Virginia did not object when Congress or the president proclaimed national days of prayer, when branches of the federal government began their meetings with prayer, or when military chaplains were appointed and funded by law.

From the standpoint of the late twentieth century, the coexistence of the amendment's sweeping endorsement of religious liberty on the national level with governmental backing for churches and religion-inspired legislation in the states may appear to be an anomaly. But from the standpoint of British colonial history, it was not surprising at all. Rather the situation reflected the colonists' allegiance to varied meanings of liberty, which they defined both "negatively" (as the absence of external political coercion) and "positively" (as the opportunity to govern their lives as they desired). Even more, it reflected the complicated tangle of negotiated local compromises that had been worked out with nearly infinite variation since the first days of British colonization.

TIGHTENING BONDS BETWEEN CHURCH AND STATE

Despite the persistent mythology that features "religious liberty" as a critical stimulant for British migration to North America, the first colonies actually instituted tighter government control of religion than existed in the Old World. New England's "Puritan way" was premised on an ingenious plan that, while it liberated the settlers from Britain's establishment, constructed new connections between religion and politics. In Virginia the Church of England gained a complete legal preeminence, as it eventually did in Maryland (but only after a singular effort in that colony to establish religious freedom). In both New England and the Chesapeake, the kind of freedom that mattered most turned out to be a "positive liberty" that enabled colonists as a group to structure their lives as they had been prevented from doing in Great Britain, not a "negative liberty" where individuals were free to do as they pleased.

New England

The five Puritan colonies of New England—Plymouth, Massachusetts Bay, Connecticut, New Haven, and New Hampshire—unanimously and resolutely rejected the English pattern of religious establishment in which bishops of the Church of England exercised hierarchical lordship in both church and state. At the same time, however, these colonies were guided by leaders who held that a well-ordered commonwealth needed a distinctly Christian character. In Plymouth and New Hampshire, the church-state ties were weakest. A history of persecution and wandering had left the Plymouth "pilgrims" with little stomach for doing unto others as had been done unto themselves. In addition Plymouth leaders like Governor William Bradford held that the church should be separated from the world, and this conviction led to a relatively passive role for the state in promoting religion.

In New Hampshire, founded as a royal province in 1679 and troubled by war and boundary disputes throughout its early history, the colonial assembly ordered each town to establish a church and support its minister. But its failure to provide means for implementing these guidelines, combined with the early presence of Quakers, Baptists, Presbyterians, and Anglicans meant that New Hampshire enjoyed a broad toleration within its formal Congregational establishment.

At the opposite extreme New Haven, founded in 1638 under the Reverend John Davenport and Governor Theophilus Eaton, witnessed the most complete Puritan effort to link the purposes of church and state. Because they believed that God had provided clear guidelines in Scripture for organizing every area of life, and because they now enjoyed the liberty to establish church and state as they saw fit, Davenport, Eaton, and their associates adopted and enforced laws (patterned on the civil government of the Old Testament) that established purified churches and vigorously promoted public morality.

Arrangements for religion and politics were not identical in Connecticut (to which New Haven was annexed in 1662) and Massachusetts Bay (which absorbed Plymouth in 1691). But the pattern established in Connecticut aimed at the same goals and exploited the same means as in Massachusetts' larger and more visible settlement. In the free air of the New World, Governor John Winthrop, the Reverend John Cotton, and other early leaders of the colony devised a plan that seemed to accomplish the goals for which Puritans had long striven in England. The plan had two essential innovations. First, it would call for individual confessions of personal faith as a condition for church membership (thus tying together holiness of self and of the church). Second, it would allow only male church members to vote for the colony's magistrates (thus linking purity of churches and purity of public life).

The result was a more democratic polity than had existed in England, since proportionately more males were members of New England churches than had been able to meet property requirements for the franchise in Britain. As spelled out in the Massachusetts Body of Liberties from 1641, the churches also enjoyed a broad gift of freedom: "Every Church hath full libertie to exercise all the ordinances of god, according to the rules of scripture." But the same Body of Liberties also made clear that civil life would be regulated by the Puritans' understanding of Scripture. For instance it provided capital punishment for twelve offenses, eleven of them (including idolatry, blasphemy, bestiality, homosexual practice, and adultery) drawn from the regulations of the Pentateuch. The Body of Liberties also contained provisions such as the following, which ensured that the colony's government would maintain a certain standard of religious life: "Civill Authoritie hath power and libertie to see the peace, ordinances and Rules of Christ observed in every church according to his word, so it be done in a Civill and not in an Ecclesiastical way."

The New England "way" of linking church and state did not escape opposition, but it did prevail. The most momentous early challenge came from the sweet-tempered but intellectually cantankerous Roger Williams, a Puritan minister who arrived in Massachusetts shortly after the colony's founding in 1630. Williams was not a modern thinker and so did not promote the separation of church and state as a defense for private rights. He did, however, feel that any governmental legislation touching the inward exercise of faith or its outward expression could only damage true religion and lead the state toward the grossest hypocrisies. These views—especially when combined with Williams's charge that the Massachusetts authorities had illegally appropriated their land from Native Americans—were not appreciated by the colony's leaders. For maintaining them with a vigorous Puritan obstinacy, Williams was banished from the colony in 1635. The next year he founded the city of Providence in what would become Rhode Island.

That colony was the New World's vanguard of religious liberty, taken in its modern sense. It established no church, legislated no tithes for supporting any church, and ordained a nearly absolute freedom of worship. These policies led to the settlement in Rhode Island of Quakers, Baptists, a wide range of those who practiced no religion, eventually a very small but significant number of Jews, and others who faced persecution or civil disabilities in Europe for their religious beliefs and practices. When he was in England in 1644 to secure a regular charter for Rhode Island, Williams published a notable tract, *The Bloudy* [i.e., Bloody] *Tenent of Persecution, for Cause of Conscience in a Conference Between Truth and Peace*, defending Rhode Island's radical support of religious liberty. John Cotton responded on behalf of the Bay colony with *The Bloudy Tenent. Washed and Made White in the Bloud of the Lambe* (1647) to defend the need for Massachusetts to ensure its social well-being by securing the proper forms of religion. Williams shot back with *The Bloudy Tenent yet More Bloudy* (1652), in which he reiterated his arguments about the damage done to religion when government coerced its observation.

Williams's prose was gnarled, but his intent was plain. It was not a message, however, that made much of an impression in the colonial period. Williams's exhortations lay fallow, and none of his pamphlets were reprinted until the time of the American Revolution. Only then did dissenting publicists like the Baptist leader, Isaac Backus, draw on Williams to defend the proposition that governmental establishment of religion inevitably harmed both church and state.

During the Commonwealth period in England, when oversight of the colonies was a low priority, Massachusetts took even stiffer actions against dissenters from its "way." The first Quakers, followers of the radical dissenter George Fox, had arrived in Boston in 1656. When they persisted on returning to disturb Massachusetts Bay with their promotion of the Inner Light of Christ and criticism of formal, external religion, they were fined and then whipped. Before England could regain a measure of direct control of the colonies after the Restoration of Charles II in 1660, Massachusetts, its patience exhausted by Quaker persistence, hanged four of Fox's followers for sedition, blasphemy, and persistent disturbance of the peace.

Virginia

It was the Church of England rather than Puritan Congregationalism that received the support of the state in Virginia, but the result was the same: the gradual loosening of governmental control over religion that took place in England over the course of the seventeenth and eighteenth centuries did not occur in Virginia until considerably later. The early legal codes of Virginia established the Church of England; they also provided for mandatory attendance at Sunday services and harsh laws against adultery, extravagant dress, and violation of the Sabbath. Because the mother church did not provide a bishop for its colonies, it was left for lay leaders—the governor, his council, and local vestries—to shape the religious character of the colony. Many of the activities normally carried out by English bishops—like assigning ministers to parishes or issuing marriage licenses—were taken over by the governors, several of whom were ardent supporters of the Anglican establishment.

In Virginia the establishment represented traditional Anglicanism adapted to the needs and wants of a colonial gentry. The result was an established church that frequently frustrated church officials. But it was also an establishment that just as successfully prevented the growth of rival churches as did the Congregationalists in Puritan New England. Only with great difficulty after the mid eighteenth century, and sometimes in the face of concentrated violence from the planter-vestrymen did non-Anglican Protestants painfully win the right to practice religion as they saw fit.

Maryland

The route to a secure Anglican establishment in Maryland was quite different than in Virginia, but the result was nearly the same. Maryland was founded in 1632 by a grant from Charles I to Cecil Calvert, second baron of Baltimore. Calvert and his family were Roman Catholics who hoped to make Maryland (named after Charles's Catholic queen) a profitable feudal barony as well as a haven for their co-religionists. The motives of the Calverts in promoting an unusual degree of religious toleration in their colony have been the subject of intense historical debate. Was it merely pragmatic prudence or commitment to principle that lay behind this provision of religious liberty?

Whether arising from principle or pragmatism, the Calverts' intention to foster general toleration in Maryland as a way of providing specific protection for Catholics faced an uphill struggle. Richard Ingle, an English Puritan, led a short-lived rebellion in 1645 during which several Catholic families were exiled. In 1648, as an effort to placate Protestant resentment, Cecil Calvert appointed a Protestant as the executive officer on site. The next year he arranged for an Act of Toleration to be issued as a further effort to calm religious tensions that were then rising to a fever pitch because of England's civil war between Puritan roundheads and Anglican cavaliers.

The provisions of this act have been justly hailed as a remarkable innovation in a century otherwise thoroughly committed to principles of religious coercion. It prohibited blasphemy, the denial of the Trinity, and the rejection of the divinity of Christ (punishable by death and confiscation of property) as well as "any reproachfull words or Speeches concerning the blessed Virgin Mary . . . or the holy Apostles or Evangelists" (crimes previously punishable by fines, whipping, and imprisonment). But it forbade Maryland's residents from slandering each other with religious epithets. And after these provisions, it also guaranteed "the free exercise" of religion and perfect protection from disturbance or disability in the practice of any Christian religious faith.

Remarkable as these stipulations were for their day, it is questionable whether they had much of an impact at the time. Nor does it appear that they were even remembered as landmark sentiments until nineteenth-century Americans began to celebrate the virtues of separating church and state.

The Calverts continued to promote a policy of toleration until the Glorious Revolution of 1688 (and an answering local Protestant rebellion in Maryland) brought the colony's experiment in religious liberty to an end. Maryland's new charter of 1691 banned Roman Catholics from holding office and taxed all inhabitants to support the Church of England. After this transition Maryland's vestrymen exercised the same mix of civil and religious functions that were being performed by their Virginia counterparts. Although Maryland remained the center of Catholic settlement in the thirteen colonies, and although non-Anglican Protestants were also present, the Anglican establishment dominated the religious life of the colony until the revolution. Only then did an alliance of Catholic gentry, non-Anglican Protestants, and Anglican Loyalists secure a broader toleration and advance the first steps toward separating church and state.

The strength and stability of the Anglican establishments in Virginia and Maryland were matched in one other colony, South Carolina. After a policy of broad toleration dating back to the early days of settlement in the 1660s, a series of laws was passed from 1698 to 1710 that established the Church of England. The colony's ten parishes became the administrative units of colonial government, and its ministers were supported by payments from the public treasury. As in Virginia and Maryland, local vestries wielded considerable power over Anglican churches and their ministers, but that provision simply meant that the lay gentry (rather than nonexistent bishops) dictated the terms of the church-state marriage. South Carolina did grant a generous toleration to non-Anglican Protestants, who were also allowed to serve as elected officials if they would swear an oath of allegiance. Not until 1778, however, did South Carolina adopt a more tolerant system in which a general Protestant establishment replaced the Anglican state church.

The Strength of Colonial Establishments

In summary, before the mid eighteenth century church and state were bound together more closely in New England (with the exception of Rhode Island) and the Chesapeake colonies of Virginia and Maryland (along with South Carolina) than they were in England at the same time. As part of the settlement of William and Mary as monarchs in 1689, the British Parliament passed "An Act for exempting their Majesties Protestant subjects, dissenting from the Church of England, from the penalties of certain laws." This guaranteed freedom of worship to Trinitarian dissenters even as it continued past restrictions on dissenters' attendance at the universities, membership in Parliament, and service as officers in the army or navy. (Roman Catholics and Unitarian Protestants continued to suffer harsher disabilities.) The New England and Chesapeake colonies in which religious establishments prevailed formally acknowledged this Act of Toleration, but their practice regularly restrained New England's non-Puritans and the Chesapeake's non-Anglicans more closely than non-Anglicans were restrained in England.

For these colonies, therefore, the judgment of historian John Murrin is apt:

More than a century after the first settlements, most of the people in British America lived within a narrower band of religious choices than fellow subjects enjoyed in England. A mere half-century before the drafting of the Bill of Rights, a well-informed observer could not easily have detected in most of the American colonies much of a popular base for the active separation of church and state as proclaimed in the First Amendment. ("Religion and Politics in America," p. 21)

ANOTHER WAY: RELIGION IN THE COLONIES AFTER 1660

If the history of New England and the Chesapeake colonies explains much of the intermingling of church and state that remained in the American states of 1791, where, then, did the advanced notions about the separation of church and state, as embodied in the First Amendment, come from? Part of the answer to this question is contained in the history of these vigorous establishments. Lonely voices like Roger Williams's and momentary outbursts of toleration like the Maryland Act of 1649 did point, however feebly at the time, to a more complete separation of church and state. Moreover the fact that various denominations were established in different colonies meant that the growing sense of a unitary "America" forced supporters of these contrasting establishments to rethink the national future of their particular churches.

The colonies founded after the restoration of Charles II in 1660 are the places to look for nontraditional, more liberal relations between church and state. The path to religious toleration, looser connections between church and state, and religious freedom (in the negative sense of the term) began most clearly in New York, New Jersey, Pennsylvania, and Delaware.

In North Carolina and Georgia, colonies founded late in the period of British rule, the Church of England would be established by law. But the paucity of Anglican ministers, neglect from colonial officials, and the presence of numerous dissenting churches meant that church-state relations in these two nominally Anglican colonies resembled those in the mid Atlantic provinces more than those in Virginia, Maryland, or South Carolina.

New York

In New Netherland (New York) under its original Dutch settlement, regulations providing for the church were as firm as in Massachusetts and Virginia. Although a certain degree of toleration was extended to New England Puritan churches on Long Island, leaders of the colony, especially Governor Peter Stuyvesant, aggressively suppressed religious organizations sponsored by Quakers, Lutherans, and Jews. Nonetheless the presence under Dutch rule of groups embracing these faiths (along with Roman Catholics, Mennonites, and French Huguenots) ensured that the formal establishment of the Dutch Reformed church was always contested.

When in 1664 the brother of Charles II, James, duke of York, mounted a successful expedition against New Netherland and gained the colony for England, formal recognition of religious toleration matched the reality on the ground. Earlier in 1642 a Jesuit missionary had recorded eighteen different languages among the still tiny population of the province. Under James a freedom of worship to accommodate this diversity of tongues became the norm. Although James's own Catholic proclivities moved him to grant religious liberty to all Christians, New York's position as an English colony meant that religious toleration would be regularly challenged by the Anglican tradition of establishment.

Efforts to promote an Anglican regimen intensified over the first three decades of New York's English existence. In 1675 Governor Edmund Andros tried to impose an Anglican clergyman on the Dutch Reformed congregation in Albany, even though that action violated provisions of the 1664 agreement by which the Dutch had yielded the colony. After the Glorious Revolution and the reorganization of English colonial rule, an even more spirited effort was made to bring New York's church life into line with the Anglican establishments in Virginia and Maryland. In 1693 Governor Benjamin Fletcher secured from the New York assembly a Ministry Act to make the Church of England the established church in New York City and the three neighboring counties. This Ministry Act, however, was beset with problems from the start. For one thing its language was vague enough so that several non-Anglican denominations felt they also qualified for public money to support their churches. For another New York's religious and ethnic diversity was already so great that it proved impossible for the colonial government to secure a monolithic establishment.

It was not, however, for lack of effort. A steady stream of missionaries from the Society for the Propagation of the Gospel in Foreign Parts (SPG) worked to extend the sway of Anglicanism in New York City and upstate. Even more, a series of governors labored might and main to make the establishment a reality. Most aggressive in that effort was Edward Hyde, or Lord Cornbury, governor from 1702 through 1708 (and also of New Jersey during the same years). Cornbury, whose lengthy list of eccentricities included dressing publicly as a woman,

sought every means possible to impede religious competition and promote the Anglican cause.

Cornbury's most memorable effort at restraining other religious bodies came in a clash with the nascent Presbyterian movement. In 1707 Francis Makemie, the father of Presbyterianism in the colonies, stopped in New York on his way to Boston and sought permission to preach. Cornbury refused, but Makemie nonetheless delivered a sermon in a private home. In response Cornbury had Makemie arrested for preaching without a license. In the trial that followed, Makemie claimed both that England's 1689 Act of Toleration secured his right to preach and also that England's laws about religion did not extend to the colonies. (Hence there was no need to appeal for toleration.) The jury returned a mixed verdict, acquitting Makemie but ordering him to pay court costs. Makemie's victory in promoting an ideal of religious liberty was more complete.

Cornbury and the governors who followed were relatively successful in the gradual process of wooing dissenters, dissatisfied for some reason with their own churches, into the Anglican fold. When the Anglican SPG provided French Huguenots with schools and clergymen, it was a natural consequence for Huguenots simply to become Anglicans, as many of them did. A similar path was followed by some prominent members of the Dutch Reformed church who, when revivalistic, populist, or democratic elements grew too insistent in their church, removed to the safe haven of the Church of England.

In the end, however, the anglicization of New York's churches could go only so far. Major controversies at mid century and after indicated that opposition to an Anglican establishment (and also to the principle of establishment itself) was pervasive. When a group of Anglicans proposed to establish King's College (later Columbia University) as the first institution of higher learning in New York, the response from a "Presbyterian" party was swift, decisive, and unabashed. Led by William Livingston, opponents of the college used their journal, *The Independent Reflector,* to protest an Anglican educational monopoly. In the process arguments for toleration were transformed into arguments for a much more complete break between the institutions of church and state. According to Livingston, who was borrowing language and conceptions of liberty from England's "real whigs," the creation of an Anglican-dominated college made him think that he "already beheld *Slavery* triumphant, and *Bigotry* swaying her enormous, her despotic Sceptre" in America. In any event Anglicans did succeed in establishing the college under their control, but Livingston's party had measurably advanced its position with the public at large.

With defenders of colonial liberties elsewhere in the colonies, some New Yorkers were also vociferous opponents of Anglican efforts to secure an American bishop. In 1767 Thomas Bradbury Chandler, an Anglican minister from Elizabethtown, New Jersey, published *An Appeal to the Public in Behalf of the Church of England in America.* This *Appeal* called for the presence of a bishop in America as a means of promoting the spiritual life of Anglicans, and it reassured other colonists that a bishop would not do anything inconsistent with their rights and safety. William Livingston and those who felt as he did saw it much differently. As he put it, if the American colonies received a bishop, it would "lead directly and necessarily to the full and complete establishment of episcopacy." And that would, in turn, "load Americans with burdens which neither they nor their forefathers could bear." On the question of a bishop, defenders of negative liberty like Livingston won not only the battle (there would be no episcopal bishops in America until after independence) but also the war. (There would be increasing concern over government promotion of religion by any means.)

New York, in summary, witnessed a pattern that led directly to the principles of the First Amendment. Diversity of churches was simply too great to allow one denomination to be favored by law. Principles of liberty were expanding too rapidly to allow defenders of ecclesiastical establishments a chance to recover.

New Jersey, Pennsylvania, and Delaware

The story, for different reasons and with diverse local issues predominating, had the same conclusion in New Jersey, Pennsylvania, and Delaware. New Jersey, which became a single royal colony in 1702 after having been divided into East Jersey and West Jersey, had such a range of denominations that no one group was able to secure a legal preference. Quakers, as the dominant early

body in West Jersey, retained considerable political influence in the unitary colony, but never enough to control public life. After the assumption of English control, Governor Cornbury and other earnest Anglicans tried to pass laws favoring the Church of England, but without avail. Quarrels among the Anglicans, the need for Anglican proprietors to encourage settlement, and the small number of Anglicans in the colony effectively squelched establishment aspirations. By mid century Presbyterians had become a major force in the eastern part of the colony. They succeeded in founding and controlling the College of New Jersey (later Princeton University). But apart from occasional concessions from the colonial legislature (for example, permission to hold a lottery as a means of raising money), the Presbyterians were no more successful than Quakers or Anglicans in securing legal preference for their faith. As in New York there were simply too many religious bodies and, increasingly after mid century, too many objections in principle to the kind of establishments that New Jersey's residents had experienced in Anglican England or Presbyterian Scotland.

In Pennsylvania and Delaware, the impact of William Penn's liberal attitudes was strong from the first. Penn did envisage Quaker control of the colony, but he also favored a wide measure of toleration for other Protestant bodies. Quakers dominated the Pennsylvania assembly from the colony's founding in 1681 until 1756, when warfare with France and its Indian allies made it impossible for Quaker pacifists to continue to govern. From the start, however, Penn's policy of religious toleration had led many widely diverse groups to migrate from Britain and the Continent (including substantial numbers of pacifist Mennonites, Church of the Brethren, and, a little bit later, Moravians). The "Pennsylvania Charter of Liberty" that Penn had written in 1682 did provide that all officials of the colony "shall be such as possess faith in Jesus Christ" and that "every first day of the week, called the Lord's day, people shall abstain from their common daily labour." But it also stated without equivocation,

That all persons living in this province, who confess and acknowledge the one Almighty and eternal God, to be the Creator, Upholder and Ruler of the world;

and that hold themselves obliged in conscience to live peaceably and justly in civil society, shall, in no ways, be molested or prejudiced for their religious persuasion, or practice, in matters of faith and worship, nor shall they be compelled, at any time, to frequent or maintain any religious worship, place or ministry whatever. (Framcos Newton Thorpe. *Constitutions.* Vol. 5, pp. 3062–3063)

Unlike the similar declaration in Maryland of 1649, the Pennsylvania proclamation of toleration stuck.

In Delaware, which came under the control of Penn's proprietorship in 1682, the same general pattern prevailed. Its charter of 1701 began with the statement that "no People can be truly happy, though under the greatest Enjoyment of Civil Liberties, if abridged of the Freedom of their Consciences, as to their Religious Profession and Worship." Like Pennsylvania, Delaware guaranteed complete religious freedom to all "who shall confess and acknowledge *One almighty God*, the Creator." Also as in Pennsylvania, office holding was restricted to those "who also profess to believe in *Jesus Christ*, the Saviour of the World."

In his provisions for religion, William Penn was literally more than a century ahead of his time. By requiring citizens to be theists and by promoting religious observances common to Christian denominations, while at the same time guaranteeing a wide religious toleration within those bounds, he anticipated the kind of church-state arrangements that prevailed in most of the states after national independence. In the context of the eighteenth century, it was a testimony to the liberality of Penn's vision that Pennsylvania was the only one of the thirteen colonies in which Roman Catholics were allowed to gather publicly for worship.

The Great Awakening and the Enlightenment

If the religious pluralism of the middle colonies and the encouragement of principles like those promoted by William Penn paved the way for the First Amendment to the Constitution, so also did larger cultural circumstances of the eighteenth century. From opposite ends of the ideological spectrum—the upsurge of Calvinist piety known as the Great Awakening and the increasing American attachment to the ideals of the European Enlightenment—came growing support for principles of toleration and religious freedom.

The Great Awakening had two major consequences for questions of church and state. First, by fragmenting the traditional Congregationalist churches in New England, it created some of the same religious diversity that was propelling the separation of church and state in the middle colonies. Second, by effectively spreading the message of personal piety in the Chesapeake, it created forceful new opponents to Anglican establishments in that region.

In New England between 1740 and 1744, the awakening left in its train a wide assemblage of local congregations dissatisfied with the faith and polity of established Puritan Congregationalism. Some of these were "separate" churches that retained Congregational theology but rejected the indiscriminate mingling of the born again and the community at large. Others became Baptists who rejected the baptism of infants as well as the traditional New England polity.

Both "separates" and Baptists, along with other sectarian bodies, objected strenuously to efforts by the state churches to quash dissent. George Whitefield's dramatic revivalistic tour of New England occurred in the fall of 1740. In 1742 Connecticut passed a law requiring itinerant preachers (who were following Whitefield's example) to obtain permission from a parish's clergyman and a majority of his congregation before being allowed to preach. Failure to comply, the Connecticut assembly stipulated, would result in fines and banishment from the colony. The most widespread response of the revivalists was to flaunt the law. But there were also published replies, most notably a lengthy pamphlet by Elisha Williams entitled *The Essential Rights and Liberties of Protestants* (1744). Its argument combined principles from the Protestant Reformation (on the sole ultimate authority of Scripture) and from Locke (on the retention of natural rights under government) in a way that would become very common during the revolutionary era.

The New England establishments did not give way easily. Not until well after the revolution and the addition of its potent political arguments to the religious impulses of the awakening was Congregationalism completely disestablished in

Connecticut and Massachusetts. Yet the arguments developed in the 1740s continued to be heard, and with increasing force, as the leaders of the New England establishments themselves began to complain about the unjust repression of the British Parliament.

Isaac Backus led a Baptist delegation in 1774 to the first Continental Congress in Philadelphia, where he sought an interview with the Massachusetts representatives, including the staunch Congregationalists John and Sam Adams. In a spirited exchange that lasted over four hours, Backus tried to convince the Adamses that Baptist complaints against Congregationalist oppression (Baptists' tax money could be used without their consent to erect Congregationalist churches) were just as legitimate as complaints by the colonial patriots against the British Parliament. John Adams conceded that there was an establishment in Massachusetts but contended that, because it was possible for Baptists and other dissenters to petition for exemption from its provisions, the establishment was "a very slender one, hardly to be called an establishment." When Backus pushed further to complain about the need for such exemptions, Adams retorted that "we might as well expect a change in the solar systim as to expect they would give up their establishment." In the short run, Adams was right; in the long run, Backus.

The effects of the Great Awakening on church-state issues in the South, where it ran its course from about 1750 to 1770, were almost as direct. The arrival of Baptists and Presbyterians in the backcountry of Virginia and the Carolinas set up an immediate challenge to Anglican hegemony. Church of England officials took steps at once to stop the itinerations of ministers who had to travel to meet with the scattered groups of these dissenters. But a reply came quickly. In 1752 Samuel Davies, a powerful Presbyterian preacher, dispatched a petition to the Bishop of London, nominal supervisor of Virginia's Anglicans, asking if indeed it was illegal to itinerate. To Davies it was clear that the liberties granted by England's Act of Toleration should extend to the colonies. Anglicans took these sectarian admonitions with even less grace than did Massachusetts's defenders of its establishment. Through and beyond the time of the revolution, Baptist and other dissenting conventicles were

occasionally, sometimes brutally, disrupted by Anglican ministers and their gentry allies.

Not all of Virginia's elite approved, however, and that disapproval illustrated the growing power of Enlightenment sentiments in opposing traditional patterns of ecclesiastical establishment. Led by Thomas Jefferson and James Madison, a number of Virginians joined other advanced thinkers throughout the colonies in the conviction that coercion on behalf of a religious establishment was as misguided for humane reasons as the sectarians felt it was for religious reasons. Madison, for example, wrote a college classmate in January 1774 that of all the problems besetting Virginia, religious intolerance was the worst, "That diabolical Hell conceived principle of persecution rages among some and to their eternal Infamy the Clergy can furnish their Quota of Imps for such business." Similar feelings about the evil of religious establishments lay behind the efforts of Jefferson to promote complete freedom of religion in Virginia, a goal that would be reached with the Virginia Act for Establishing Religious Freedom of 1785.

In contrast to the dominant patterns in the first century of English colonization, the cultural trends represented by the Great Awakening and the Enlightenment worked against the tight regulation of religion by the state. In further contrast to the well-entrenched traditions of establishment in New England and the Chesapeake, church-state connections were always much looser in New York, New Jersey, Pennsylvania, and Delaware. As the eighteenth century wound on, the social resources and the ideological certainties that had meant most in the creation of strong colonial establishments began to lose their cogency. Or at least they did so in the thirteen British colonies that would break from Britain in 1776. In Britain's other New World provinces, it was a different story.

Canadian Counterpoint

By shortly after the mid eighteenth century, Britain's possessions in the New World also included two settlements in what is now Canada. In 1710 the British, as part of ongoing struggles with France, had taken control of Acadia (modern Nova Scotia) on the Atlantic coast north of Maine. The Treaty of Utrecht of 1713 that ceded Acadia to the British contained the critical church-state provision for the Acadians that allowed these French speakers the right "to enjoy the free exercise of their religion according to the usage of the Church of Rome so far as the laws of Great Britain do allow." An era of general toleration ensued in the region until further French-British conflict intervened.

When Britain erected a fortified colony at Halifax in Nova Scotia as a result of imperial struggles in the mid 1740s (known as the War of the Austrian Succession [1740–1748] in Europe and King George's War [1744–1748] in North America), the colony soon attracted several thousand settlers to what had been previously a thinly populated province. They came from Scotland, Ireland, England, and the Continent as well as New England. Earlier the Anglican SPG had supplied school teachers to the region. And later (in 1758) the first meeting of the Nova Scotia assembly gave Anglicans preference in law. But in deference to the religiously and ethnically diverse population, toleration was extended to all (including the small number of Jews and Catholics).

Religious toleration in the maritime provinces survived even the British evacuation of the Acadians, which took place in 1755 as part of the Seven Years' War. Despite the anti-Catholicism that, in part, inspired this British action, surprisingly good relations continued between Protestants and Catholics. So pleased were British rulers with the loyalty of the Catholic subjects who remained that the Nova Scotia assembly even instituted an annual grant to Abbé Mailard, spiritual leader of the largely Catholic Micmac Indians and the remnant of Acadians who survived removal. Colonial developments in the maritimes hinted at the kind of church-state relationships that would later prevail widely in Canada, where full toleration was combined with selective governmental subsidies to churches and religious organizations.

Colonial policy in Quebec, which had become a British colony through the Treaty of Paris in 1763, showed yet another—and, given British religious sentiments in the eighteenth century, surprising—form of church-state relations. Britain's official policy immediately following its assumption of control in Quebec was to anglicize the French Canadians, including their religion. (In 1763 almost all of the province's sixty thousand residents were Roman Catholics; they were served by nearly two hundred priests. These totals were several times higher than the figures for Catholics in the thirteen colonies that later made up the United States.) But practice did not follow principle. Successive British governors allowed the Catholic church to go its own way. Delicate negotiations involving Quebec's senior clergy, the British governor, and the Vatican led to the appointment of a Catholic bishop under British oversight. (At this time the Catholic hierarchy was still outlawed in Britain.)

Britain's accommodating spirit toward Quebec became a matter of heated controversy in the colonies to the south when Parliament passed the Quebec Act in 1774. This legislation gave up the pretense of anglicization and ratified a number of traditional Quebec customs that had remained in limbo after the British takeover. Under this Act the Catholic church secured clear title to its hereditary lands; it was granted the right to tithe its members; and French civil law was recognized (along with the institution of English criminal law). Most remarkably, Catholic citizens received full civil rights fifty years before their fellow-religionists in Britain obtained a similar dispensation and at a time when most of the thirteen colonies still enforced civil disabilities on Roman Catholics. In these colonies, where anti-Catholicism was as deeply entrenched as in England and Scotland, the Quebec Act indicated to many patriots that Parliament had sold out to the pope, the embodiment (as they saw it) of civil and ecclesiastical tyranny. In Quebec, by contrast, the generosity of the Act played a considerable part in securing the loyalty of the Quebecois during the crisis of American independence that followed shortly thereafter.

NATIONAL DISESTABLISHMENT, INFORMAL LOCAL ESTABLISHMENT

In the thirteen British colonies that declared their independence in 1776, public expressions of formal religion were almost completely monopolized by forms of Protestantism. The fact that the forms were different contributed to the acceptance of religious toleration. The fact that they were almost exclusively Protestant made colonial affirmations of religious freedom parochial rather than global. In addition most colonists in 1776 held to the Old World conviction that religion of some sort was a necessary foundation for civil health. Yet Old World beliefs about the necessity of an establishment—where a single denomination was recognized as the church of a realm, the resources of government were devoted to maintaining that church, and the state church devoted part of its energies to sanctifying the government—had come under severe strain well before Lexington and Concord. If the thirteen former colonies had not succeeded in establishing a national government, anti-establishment convictions might not have matured so rapidly. But the basic ingredients of what would become the First Amendment to the Constitution were present before hostilities with Britain began.

The sequence may have been important. The growing sense that it was necessary to be liberated from ecclesiastical establishments imported from Britain was probably one of the predisposing conditions for feeling that it was necessary to be liberated from Britain.

On the other hand, there were British colonies (Nova Scotia and Quebec) where the conviction persisted that ecclesiastical establishments could coexist with, and perhaps even augment, the well-being of a society. These colonies would not find it necessary to pursue liberation from the mother country. And again there may have been a connection.

Along with the powerful events of the revolution, the circumstances of the colonial period go far to explain those of the early United States, where a national separation of church and state enshrined in the Constitution coexisted with functioning establishments (of Protestantism or a particular form of Protestantism) at the local level.

Those minority groups that had not exercised, or been allowed to exercise, a significant public role in the development of the British colonies continued in an ambiguous situation during the first decades of the new United States. In the colonial period, Roman Catholics enjoyed full civil rights only in Pennsylvania, Rhode Island, and (for a relatively few decades) Maryland. The link between France and Catholicism exacerbated the situation of Catholic civil rights during and after the Seven Years' War. Even William

Livingston, in the act of upbraiding New York's Anglicans for their establishmentarian pretensions, felt that, "for political reasons," it was necessary to "exclude *Papists* from the common and equal Benefits of Society." Sam Adams, otherwise a stalwart for liberty, in 1772 proclaimed that Catholics should not be tolerated because they teach "Doctrines subversive of the Civil Government under which they live." Popular attitudes that underlay the resistance to Catholic civil rights spurted to the surface with a vengeance when the first Continental Congress in 1774 addressed the British people on the Quebec Act: "Nor can we suppress our astonishment, that a British Parliament should ever consent to establish in that country a religion that has deluged your island in blood, and dispersed impiety, bigotry, persecution, murder and rebellion through every part of the world." Even Isaac Backus, who during the revolutionary period revived Roger Williams's arguments to defend the rights of non-Congregationalist Protestants in Massachusetts, did not feel that Roman Catholics should be allowed to serve in public office.

For reasons having more to do with prejudicial ignorance than active opposition, Jews were in roughly the same civil situation as Catholics throughout the colonial period. Protestant attention to Jews was minimal in the British colonies, mostly because they were so few. In New York, Jews found a relative toleration in practice, and in 1710 a rabbi was even emboldened to petition the governor for the same kind of civil exemptions enjoyed by Protestant clergymen. (The response does not survive.) Yet even in Rhode Island, where Jews had been present since the mid-seventeenth century, where they had worshiped without restraint, and where they had built a synagogue, they still could not vote or hold colonial office.

African Americans existed even further below the horizon of consciousness on these matters than Jews. Several colonies had passed laws by the first decade of the eighteenth century to confirm the fact that Christian baptism did not convey civil or religious liberties to black slaves. No black church was allowed to be formally organized until the 1770s, and then only because of revolutionary turmoil and the sufferance of British authorities.

Atheists were furthest beyond the pale. In 1689 John Locke's famous *Letter Concerning Toleration* had excluded atheists from the freedom he proposed for almost everyone else. Echoing Locke as well as expressing a nearly universal colonial opinion, a Connecticut minister, Moses Dickinson, on the very eve of independence opined that it was "absurd to speak of allowing atheists Liberty of Conscience."

The best student of colonial church-state relations, Thomas J. Curry, draws upon the Puritan antagonists in Massachusetts's first decade to explain the complex attitudes that prevailed in the late colonial period. Regarding those attitudes, he writes:

Americans could not achieve unity on any one religious belief, but they agreed that the government could have no authority in defining or imposing a belief on the populace, and that each person was entitled to the free exercise of his or her religion of choice. They disagreed on whether government should provide support for ministers and decided that in this religious matter, government had no power. In these decisions they followed Roger Williams. Where they did not disagree, however, is in the belief that government should promote the religious symbols and customs they shared in common. In this they followed John Cotton. (*First Freedoms*, p. 272)

By the end of the colonial period, "no establishment" meant not having the church-state relationship that Anglicans and New England Congregationalists had once enjoyed in at least half of the colonies. "Religious liberty" meant both the negative freedom of worshiping as one pleased and the positive freedom of being allowed to restrict non-Protestant or non-Christian religions. In this as in many other areas of colonial life, principles like those concerning the freedom of religion could guide, but never escape, the circumstances in which they were announced.

BIBLIOGRAPHY

Balmer, Randall H. *A Perfect Babel of Confusion: Dutch Religion and English Culture in the Middle Colonies.* New York, 1989. Especially valuable for New York.

Berlin, Isaiah. "Two Concepts of Liberty." In *Four Essays on Liberty.* New York, 1969. Offers shrewd definitions of "negative" and "positive" forms of liberty.

Bradford, William. *History of Plymouth Plantation, 1620–1647.* New York, 1981. Reveals Bradford as a Puritan but one who was accommodating on some issues of religious freedom.

Bridenbaugh, Carl. *Mitre and Sceptre: Transatlantic Faiths, Ideas, Personalities, and Politics, 1689–1775.* New York, 1962. Features the civil and religious strife over an Anglican bishop for the colonies.

Curry, Thomas J. "Church and State in Seventeenth and Eighteenth Century America." *Journal of Law and Religion* 7 (1989):261–280.

———. *The First Freedoms: Church and State in America to the Passage of the First Amendment.* New York, 1986. Offers the best general treatment of the subject.

Gaustad, Edwin S. *Liberty of Conscience: Roger Williams in America.* Grand Rapids, Mich., 1991. A solid recent biography emphasizing the religious motives behind Williams's views on church and state.

Isaac, Rhys. "Evangelical Revolt: The Nature of the Baptists' Challenge to the Traditional Order in Virginia, 1765–1775." *William and Mary Quarterly*, 3rd ser., 31 (1974):345–368. Perceptive account of both Baptists and the Virginia gentry who deeply resented the rise of sectarian Protestantism.

Kurland, Philip B., and Ralph Lerner, eds. *The Founders' Constitution.* Vol. 5, *Amendments I–XII.* Chicago, 1987. Sixty-nine well-selected documents from 1536 to 1833 pertinent to the religion clause of the First Amendment.

Livingston, William. *The Independent Reflector. . . .* Edited by Milton M. Klein. Cambridge, Mass., 1963. Strongly argued statements from colonial New York in favor of greater separation of church and state.

McLoughlin, William G., ed. *Isaac Backus on Church, State, and Calvinism: Pamphlets, 1754–1789.* Cambridge, Mass., 1968.

———. *New England Dissent, 1630–1833: The Baptists and Separation of Church and State.* 2 vols. Cambridge, Mass., 1971. With McLoughlin's very useful material on Isaac Backus, the most complete account of the Pietist challenge to New England's Congregationalist establishments.

Miller, Perry G. *Orthodoxy in Massachusetts, 1630–1650.* Boston, 1933. Pioneering modern work on the genius of the New England "way."

Moir, John S. *The Church in the British Era: From the British Conquest to Confederation.* Toronto, Ontario, 1972. Reliable survey on the accommodation of church and state that developed in the colonies that remained loyal to Britain.

Morgan, Edmund S., ed. *Puritan Political Ideas.* Indianapolis, Ind., 1965. Outstanding collection of documents.

Murrin, John M. "Religion and Politics in America from the First Settlements to the Civil War." In *Religion and American Politics from the Colonial Period to the 1980s,* edited by Mark A. Noll. New York, 1990. Argues persuasively that in New England and the Chesapeake there was less freedom of religion than in Britain until the mid eighteenth century.

Polishook, Irwin H., ed. *Roger Williams, John Cotton, and Religious Freedom.* Englewood Cliffs, N.J., 1967. Well-chosen documents from the major proponents of "negative" and "positive" freedom in early New England.

Raboteau, Albert J. *Slave Religion: The "Invisible Institution" in the Antebellum South.* New York, 1978. Full treatment of civil disabilities for African Americans.

Rawlyk, George A. *Revolution Rejected, 1775–1776.* Scarborough, Ontario, 1968. Well-selected documents, including church-state-related reasons why Nova Scotia and Quebec remained loyal during the revolution.

Stokes, Anson Phelps. *Church and State in the United States.* Vol. I. New York, 1950. An older standard work.

Thorpe, Framcos Newton. *The Federal and State Constitutions, Colonial Charters, and Other Organic Laws of the States, Territories, and Colonies Now or Heretofore Forming the United States of America.* Washington, D.C., 1909. The fullest collection of colonial charters and basic laws.

Walsh, H. H. *The Christian Church in Canada.* Toronto, Ontario, 1956.

Wilson, John F., ed. *Church and State in America: A Bibliographical Guide—The Colonial and Early National Periods.* New York, 1986. Excellent bibliographies, which are also informative essays, by Randall H. Balmer, "Church-State Issues in the Middle Colonies from Colonization to the Mid-Eighteenth Century"; Mark Valeri, "Puritanism and the Civil Order in New England from the First Settlements to the Great Awakening" and "Church and State in America from the Great Awakening to the American Revolution"; and Leigh Eric Schmidt, "Church-State Relations in the Colonial South."

Wilson, John F., and Donald L. Drakeman, eds. *Church and State in American History.* 2nd ed. Boston, 1987. The best one-volume collection of documents, with extensive materials on the colonial period.

Mark A. Noll

SEE ALSO **Taxation** and various essays in EDUCATION.

THE DUTCH COLONY

WHEN JONAS MICHAËLIUS arrived in New Amsterdam as the first Dutch Reformed minister in the colony, he advocated a careful and calculated distance between church and state in the newly organized colony. Writing to a friend back in the Netherlands in 1628, Michaëlius remarked that although "political and ecclesiastical persons can greatly assist each other, nevertheless the matters and offices belonging together must not be mixed but kept separate, in order to prevent all confusion and disorder." Michaëlius's prescription for the relation of church and state ultimately prevailed in New York, and this formula of maintaining an official distance between religion and politics (though often violated in practice) emerged as a forceful precursor for religious disestablishment in the United States Constitution.

Michaëlius, who had come from Holland to New Netherland by way of Brazil, doubtless inherited his ideas about church and state from the "two kingdoms" configuration of religion and politics that had emerged with the triumph of Calvinism in the Dutch Reformed church. Reformed churchmen, who had chafed under the political and religious oppressions of Spanish Catholicism, believed that the church should function without political interference. For the most part, the Dutch West India Company (WIC), which governed New Netherland, respected that arrangement in its New World entrepôt out of deference either to precedent or, more likely, to profits.

Although the WIC insisted formally that the Dutch Reformed church was the only religion tolerated in New Netherland, the colony's burgeoning pluralism demanded some concessions. As early as 1638, the company allowed that in matters of conscience "every man shall be free to live up to his own in peace and decorum." In 1657 Quakers on Long Island drafted the Flushing Remonstrance, expressing their desire to be entirely free of obligations to the Dutch Reformed church. Peter Stuyvesant, director-general of the colony for the WIC, initially resisted any attempts to undermine the favored status of Dutch Calvinism, but by 1663 he had received word from the company to back down. The merchants in Amsterdam advised Stuyvesant to "shut your eyes, at least not force people's consciences, but allow every one to have his own belief, as long as he behaves quietly and legally, gives no offense to his neighbors and does not oppose the government."

DUTCH RELIGION UNDER THE ENGLISH

The English Conquest of 1664 altered forever the colony's landscape and brought changes to its religious configuration. The duke of York, who became the colony's new proprietor, appeared initially to evince a broad and general liberality on religious matters, especially toward Catholics, among whom he numbered himself. The Articles of Capitulation, signed when the Dutch surrendered to the English, ensured that the Dutch "here shall enjoy the liberty of their consciences in Divine Worship and church discipline." That guarantee, however, soon proved illusory. The duke, along with Governor Edmund Andros and most Englishmen, held to an Erastian theory of church and state; that is, following the precepts of Thomas Erastus, a sixteenth-century political theorist. They believed that the church should be subject to the powers of the state and, indeed, should advance the prerogatives of the state. In Restoration England, Erastian theory was well established, but in colonial New York the Church of England was nonexistent in 1664, and the English were badly outnumbered by other ethnic groups.

The new rulers, then, sought to subvert religious toleration through indirect, devious means. In 1675 Nicholas Van Rensselaer, a renegade Dutchman with Anglican orders and a checkered past, arrived in New York with instructions from the duke of York to Governor Andros to place him in a Dutch church. Andros assigned him to the Dutch Reformed church in Albany, even though that church already had a minister. Although the Dutch clergy initially protested the appointment, it eventually backed down in deference to English rule. The clergy learned, however, that the English were hardly benign when it came to church-state relations.

The best course seemed to lay in accommodation. The Dutch clergy, by and large, cooperated with the English government, much to the consternation of its less affluent communicants, many of whom joined Leisler's Rebellion in 1689. After the rebellion had been quashed two years later, the English magistrates sought to establish the Church of England in New York. Governor Benjamin Fletcher, acting on instructions from London, eventually cajoled the Assembly into passing the Ministry Act of 1693, which legally (if not effectively) established Anglicanism in the four lower counties of the colony. The success of the Church of England in the middle colonies, however, had less to do with the Ministry Act, which religious dissenters managed to frustrate, than with the beneficence of several governors and the arrival of missionaries from the Society for the Propagation of the Gospel.

The dissenters, and the Dutch in particular, suffered under the administration of Edward Hyde, Viscount Cornbury, who served concurrently as governor of New York and New Jersey. Though often dismissed as a buffoon, Cornbury was quite effective in promoting the Church of England, recognizing that religious assimilation in the colony would bring political quiescence. Cornbury tried to install Anglican missionaries in Dutch and Huguenot churches, and he encouraged the formation of English schools, which proved to be the most effective long-term strategy for ensuring the triumph of English language, culture, and institutions in colonial New York.

RELIGIOUS PLURALISM

Despite the Ministry Act and the success of Anglican schools, however, the Church of England never attained the religious hegemony that its leaders coveted. The middle colonies were the most religiously and ethnically diverse region in the North Atlantic, thereby anticipating the pluralistic culture that would engulf the new nation in the nineteenth century. Non-English denizens of New York, including many of the Dutch, stoutly resisted the use of public funds for the founding of an Anglican school, King's College (Columbia University), in 1754, and the prospect that the Church of England might dispatch a bishop to America unleashed torrents of protest in the colony in the 1760s.

New York's state constitution of 1777 institutionalized the colony's long tradition of religious diversity, even though it limited somewhat the religious freedom of Roman Catholics by imposing an anti-Catholic naturalization oath. By the American Revolution, political leaders in New York had found religious establishment unworkable for the very same reason that the Dutch had found it untenable a century earlier—the existence of religious pluralism.

BIBLIOGRAPHY

Balmer, Randall. *A Perfect Babel of Confusion: Dutch Religion and English Culture in the Middle Colonies.* New York, 1989.

Pointer, Richard W. *Protestant Pluralism and the New York Experience: A Study of Eighteenth-Century Religious Diversity.* Bloomington, Ind., 1988.

Rink, Oliver A. *Holland on the Hudson: An Economic and Social History of Dutch New York.* Ithaca, N.Y., 1986.

Smith, George L. *Religion and Trade in New Netherland: Dutch Origins and American Development.* Ithaca, N.Y., 1973.

Randall Balmer

SEE ALSO **Taxation** and various essays in EDUCATION.

THE FRENCH COLONIES

INFLUENCED BY THE WRITINGS of American Francis Parkman (1823–1893), historians have long described the relationship between church and state in New France as a struggle between an overpowering and suffocating Roman Catholic theocracy and a society that began to liberate itself only after the British conquest of Canada in 1760. Revisionists have since challenged this interpretation showing the coincidence of interests and substantial agreement of church and state and emphasizing the beneficial role of the church in the welfare of Canadian society at large.

THE UNPLANNED EVANGELIZATION

In the early days of French expansion, and at least until the early 1650s, the Roman Catholic church regarded its involvement in the New World as directed mainly at the Indians. All French colonizing expeditions made their conversion to Christianity a proclaimed objective, which was clearly stated in all the royal charters granted to commercial companies. There is no evidence, however, that any colonizing expedition included clergy. As for the spiritual care of the Europeans, most probably an unknown number of priests accompanied the fishing fleet to the North Atlantic banks. A number of exploring expeditions also had priests among their members. The Crown favored their presence, and in 1604 King Henry IV asked the Jesuits to send two priests with the fishing fleet. Since these ships were regarded as extensions of the crew's home territory, no missionary work among the Indians was envisioned.

The little evangelical action that was taken was uncoordinated and unplanned. It also took a long time finally to solve the Catholic and Protestant (Huguenot) rivalry in the New World. The Edict of Nantes (1598, revoked 1685) had not specifically extended religious toleration to Canada, but it had not forbidden it either. Furthermore, the regional provenance of the ships' captains and crew members had made Huguenot presence in the New World colonies a reality. Huguenots were involved in abortive colonization schemes in Canada (1541), Brazil (1555), and Florida (1562). Each side deeply resented the other's presence. In 1621 the Franciscan Récollets and the colony's governor, Samuel de Champlain, petitioned King Louis XIII to exclude Huguenots from New France. In 1625 the Crown banned in Canada the exercise of all religions except Roman Catholicism, specifically extending the prohibition to Acadia (Nova Scotia) in 1659. The religious unity of the European colony was thus assured, although Huguenot merchants remained active in the colony in the eighteenth century.

Not until 1610, when French secular priest Jessé Flesché (Fléché) visited Port Royal (now Annapolis Royal, Nova Scotia), did a priest cross the North Atlantic to attempt the conversion of the Indians. He was followed by the Jesuits in 1611 and the Récollets in 1615. The great missionary drive in New France, intellectually nurtured and financed by the devout circles of the Catholic Reformation, coincided with the political rise of Armand Jean du Plessis, Cardinal Richelieu (1585–1642), architect of the expansion of the French colonial empire who simultaneously launched an attack against the Huguenots at home. In New France, the English conquest of Acadia (1628) and of Quebec (1629) temporarily disrupted these plans.

THE CHURCH AND THE AMERINDIANS

When New France was returned to France (1632), the Capuchins replaced the Récollets (who returned to Canada in 1670) in Acadia, and the Jesuits became the only missionaries in Quebec and Huronia. (The Congregation of the Holy Ghost, the Hospitaller Order of Saint John of God, and the secular clergy, including the Sulpicians, arrived later.) Both orders had a long experience of missionary work around the world. Until then all missionaries had derived their spiritual powers from the pope. The Jesuits tried to maintain a sort of operative independence from Rome, whereas the Capuchins (who left Acadia in 1655) regarded themselves as dependent on the Congregation for the Propagation of the Faith (founded 1622).

When the Crown decided to develop its North American colonies, neither the fur trade business community nor the state bureaucracy had the means or the desire to carry on any significant scheme of colonization. Only the church was willing and prepared to fulfill this role, as it had been doing for almost half a century in India, China, and Japan. Regular orders were not only highly motivated but also largely self-financing through substantial donations and

gifts. Their independence, however, was limited. The members of their French branches were mostly French-born and could not conceive of acting against or even outside the Crown's will. Furthermore, the pope encouraged them to cooperate with the French Crown, since licenses to travel, permission to establish missions, protection from outside enemies, and (after the 1650s) a large proportion of their revenues emanated from the Crown.

From 1633 to the 1650s the clergy, and the Jesuits in particular, were indispensable to Canada. Not only did they provide the colony with moral leadership but they also were instrumental in maintaining the Franco-Huron trade alliance, and their substantial investments in the colony gave it hard cash, permitted land clearing, and lured to Canada laborers and many of the few settlers it received. (Between 1626 and 1655 the clergy's expenditures composed about 20 percent of the colony's budget.) Furthermore, they created and staffed the institutions that would transform Canada into a real settlement (as opposed to a simple commercial outpost like Acadia). In 1635 a college was founded in Quebec (a year before Harvard), and in 1640 the colony, with a population of 356 individuals (of whom 29 were Jesuits), also had schools and a hospital. In this, the Jesuits were assisted by a number of female religious orders (the Ursulines and the Augustines Hospitalières de la Miséricorde de Jésus arrived in 1639), and by groups of devout French laymen, like the secret Compagnie du Saint-Sacrement, under whose auspices Montreal was founded in 1642.

Ironically, the overall influence of the church on the colony increased as its failure to evangelize the Indians quickly became evident. The Iroquois destroyed Huronia, the showcase of Jesuit missionary methods (1649); the institutions meant for the Indians (schools, hospitals) failed to attract them; and voluntary support from the devout in France faded. Furthermore, the 1650s brought the colony economic development and an overall increase in population. (In 1650, for the first time, the French in the Saint Lawrence valley outnumbered the Indians.) This necessitated a reassessment of the European population's spiritual needs, and the church was ready to meet them. Its considerable financial and human investments had earned it a major role in colonial society. The church, the largest Canadian landholder, controlled all educational and welfare institutions, and wielded considerable prestige and political influence.

To date, the church's influence in the colony had not led to any major conflict with the state. The church was expected to perform various basic functions that the state could not perform by itself. Its primary responsibility was to minister to the spiritual needs of the people by praying, preaching, administering the sacraments, setting a personal example of piety and temperance, and elevating the standards of public morality. It also was entrusted with instructing the young and policing public morality. Furthermore, the church was expected to keep accurate, vital statistics and to care for persons requiring public assistance (the sick, the poor, the aged, and abandoned children). Through these functions, the church served to bind the society firmly together and to maintain social order. The role of the church did not differ substantially in France and New France, although in the latter the priests also maintained the Franco-Indian alliance. Furthermore, the colony profited greatly from the French climate of religious revival, and attracted to Canada the best-trained members of the regular orders.

THE ESTABLISHMENT OF A BISHOPRIC

As the growth of the colony made itself felt at the ecclesiastical level, clerics sought the establishment of a bishopric. The transfer of spiritual authority from Europe to the colony generated questions of ecclesiatical accountability: Would the new bishop answer directly to Rome or would the Gallican tradition apply? The Gallican church (a sort of French national church) recognized the pope's spiritual authority but, by also recognizing the king's divine mandate, considered itself entitled to special rights and privileges. In Canada, the appointed bishop, François de Laval, was first made vicar apostolic (1658), a title that ensured the new bishop's jurisdictional dependence on Rome while capitalizing upon the French Crown's assistance through subsidies,

staffing, and protection. Laval became full bishop of Quebec in 1674. The long delay was caused more by foreign policy difficulties between Rome and Paris and by bureaucratic slowness than by any scheme to curb or enlarge ecclesiastical power in the colony.

Laval, very much his own man, started as a missionary leader in a savage country. His austere background would have favored papal leadership over the king's, yet he soon changed his attitude, if not his opinion. By and large, his administration signaled the decline of the church's political influence in the colony. Under King Louis XIV and his principal minister, Jean-Baptiste Colbert, the bishop was deprived of his right, which he exercised jointly with the governor, to appoint and dismiss members of the Sovereign Council, and his presence there became virtually honorary. The church's economic role also declined. Whereas in 1663 the church held 11 percent of the conceded land, only four *seigneuries* were granted to religious institutions between 1663 and 1743, when this practice was forbidden by royal decree. (Yet by the end of the French regime, the church still held 25 percent of conceded lands, and about 34 percent of the French-Canadian population lived on them.)

THE STATE TAKES OVER

Colbert's instructions (1665) to Intendant Jean Talon made it clear that it was "absolutely necessary to hold in just balance the temporal authority . . . and the spiritual authority"—the king's representatives in the colony and the bishop—so that "the latter be inferior to the former." Nevertheless, royal subsidies to the church were raised as its role as dispenser of spiritual assistance, instruction, welfare, and Indian diplomacy continued to be sought and valued. More hospices (Montreal 1688, Quebec 1692), hospitals (Quebec 1639, Montreal 1642, Trois-Rivières 1702), and houses for the poor (1688) were built. In the eighteenth century Crown subsidies amounted to somewhere between 30 and 40 percent of all church revenues. (The balance was provided by the tithe, gifts, seigneurial profits, and ecclesiastical benefices.) In Louisiana, the church was entirely financed by the state. Financial dependence curbed any attempt by the clergy to adopt an independent political role. Laval spent increasingly long periods in France lobbying for his church, whereas he never visited Rome. His successors were even more France-oriented, and some hardly set foot in New France. The oath of office (1741) of Bishop Henri-Marie Dubreil de Pontbriand is revealing: "I promise His Majesty that . . . I will be his faithful subject and servant, that I will strive . . . to serve and to further the well being of his state." State officials valued the church's loyalty, and complained that the lack of priests in the colony left many without proper spiritual assistance.

Disputes between bishops and royal officials were numerous, just as in France, but these were mere squabbles arising from personality conflicts and never challenged the complementary roles of church and state. The only significant issue on which the two parties clashed was the sale of alcoholic beverages to the Indians, which was opposed by the church (for humanitarian reasons) and upheld by the state (as a passport to trade). The latter view eventually prevailed. Most quarrels took place within the church itself, particularly in Louisiana. By and large, the de facto severance of the Canadian church's relations with Rome (which, after Laval, limited its role to the approval of the bishop's coadjutors and future successors) well shows the clergy's complete submission to the French Crown.

AFTER THE BRITISH CONQUEST

The church in Canada sought after 1760 the same relationship with the new state, which was not only linguistically different but also Protestant. Survival through accommodation became the official policy of the church leaders, who immediately found themselves in a subordinate position. As early as 1762, Vicar General Étienne Montgolfier, the church's interim leader, ordered that a *Te Deum* be sung throughout the colony on the occasion of the coronation and marriage of the new king of Great Britain, George III. Complete loyalty to Great Britain was preached by all successive bishops of Quebec, whose case was made even stronger by the Amer-

ican and French revolutions. As for the new state, Great Britain (just like France) valued the roles of the church in spiritual assistance, education, welfare, Indian diplomacy, and social order. It soon officially recognized the church's hierarchy, paid salaries to the Indian missionaries and eventually to the bishops, and enlisted the church in keeping social order among Irish immigrants widely perceived by authorities as unruly.

BIBLIOGRAPHY

Dickinson, John A., and Brian Young. *Diverse Pasts. A History of Quebec and Canada.* Toronto, Ontario, 1986.

Eccles, W. J. "The Role of the Church in New France," In Eccles's *Essays on New France.* Toronto, Ontario, 1987.

Jaenen, Cornelius John. *The Role of the Church in New France.* Toronto, Ontario, 1976.

Moir, John Sargent, ed. *Church and State in Canada, 1627–1867. Basic Documents.* Toronto, Ontario, 1967. In line with the Parkman tradition.

Trudel, Marcel. *L'Église canadienne sous le régime militaire, 1759–1764.* 2 vols. Quebec, 1956–1957.

Luca Codignola

SEE ALSO **Roman Catholicism** and **Taxation;** and various essays in RELIGION.

THE SPANISH BORDERLANDS

ROMAN CATHOLICISM WAS THE OFFICIAL state religion in Spain and in its entire colonial empire for its duration from the fifteenth century to the beginning of the nineteenth century. The particularly close relationship that developed between the Church of Rome and the Spanish state was forged during the long centuries of the Reconquest, between A.D. 711 and 1492, when the monarchs of Spain's kingdoms slowly curtailed the spread of Islam on the Iberian Peninsula and pushed the Moors back onto the African continent. For defending Catholicism, for proclaiming it as the one and only true religion in the realm, and for promising to convert the infidel in newly conquered territories, the popes of Rome reciprocated, granting Spain's kings extensive rights over ecclesiastical matters, rights that ultimately curtailed papal power.

The concessions of royal patronage that the kings of Spain enjoyed were known collectively as the Real Patronato. They were codified in a series of papal bulls, the most notable being Pope Innocent VIII's *Orthodoxe fidei propagationem* (1486), and Pope Julius II's *Illius fulciti presidio* (1504) and *Universalis ecclesiae* (1508). In these bulls Spain's monarchs gained the right to establish all ecclesiastical institutions in the realm, to present to the Holy See nominations for all ecclesiastical appointments and benefices, to establish diocesan boundaries, to collect and reapportion church revenues, and to review (and even veto) all communications between the pope or the generals of the religious orders and clerics.

With the conquest of America, the Real Patronato was extended to the Indies, adding the administration of ecclesiastical affairs to the king's jurisdiction over military, judicial, legislative, and commercial matters. The favorite sixteenth-century metaphor for the dual functions the monarch performed as king of the realm and vicar of the church in the Indies was that of a warrior wielding two swords, one temporal and one spiritual.

THE THREE COLONIAL BUREAUCRACIES

The Spanish Crown exercised its civil and ecclesiastical functions in its colonies through three bureaucracies. The first of these was the office of the viceroy, who administered all civil and military matters through a number of provincial governors, district constables, and local subordinates. Viceroys had the power to legislate on a whole series of routine matters. But on more substantive issues, they were bound by the *Recopilación de Leyes de los Reynos de las Indias* (1681), a compilation of Spain's extensive legal codes, and actions.

The second bureaucracy of import in the empire was the *audiencia*, the district court of appeal. It administered justice through a coterie of judicial officers and advised the viceroy and governors on legislative issues. Theoretically the *audiencia* was totally independent, answering only to the king. But in reality it was subordinate to the viceroy. When clashes between the two arose, the jurisdictional balance of power often was determined by the personalities involved and by the extent to which the Crown wished to intervene.

The colony's third bureaucracy, the church, was administered by bishops. They were charged with all ecclesiastical matters but had to cooperate with royal agents on issues of ecclesiastical taxation and clerical appointments because the viceroy was also legally the vice-patron of the church. On such administrative matters bishops answered directly to the king through the Council of the Indies. On issues of faith, morals, and clerical discipline, bishops answered directly to the pope. But given the centrality of religious language in the discourse of colonial politics, it was often quite impossible to view conflicts involving the church and its clerics as simply administrative or doctrinal matters with a clear jurisdictional locus.

Indeed, fuzzy and overlapping boundaries precipitated most of the disputes that developed between church and state in the Spanish Borderlands. The regular clergy routinely clashed with the viceroy and his governors about the place of the Indian in the colonial scheme, the friars arguing that all matters bearing on the Indians related to the regulation of the faith and thus fell under their domain. They were also at odds over the *fueros,* or special immunities, that the regular clergy enjoyed in disciplinary matters, and about the prerogatives of the viceroy and his governors as vice-patrons of the church.

The structure of institutional arrangements was established by the Crown so that the viceroy, the *audiencia,* and the church were relatively autonomous but nonetheless fundamentally interdependent. The Crown organized matters in this way because it distrusted its overseas officers. Ill-defined and overlapping jurisdictional boundaries provoked endless litigation among the viceroys, *audiencias,* and bishops, effectively checking the power of each group and keeping the Crown well informed of its affairs in the remotest corners of the empire.

THEOCRATIC CLAIMS TO AUTHORITY

To understand the political conflicts that developed in the Spanish Borderlands between the church and state during the colonial period, one must examine the broad sweep of that era. From 1539 to Mexican independence in 1821, two diametrically opposed theories of government and power animated the principal political actors in the borderlands. Spain's empire in America began with a theocratic theory of government and ended with a secular one. How the church and state negotiated their prerogatives and boundaries during these three centuries, as the secular theory of government gained ascendancy over the religious, will occupy our attention below.

The initial conquest of the Spanish Borderlands of North America was governed by a theocratic theory of government and power inspired by the Scriptures and formulated by clerics and canon lawyers. This theory described power as emanating in God and descending from Him to the king, and from the monarch down through the whole hierarchy of beings. "There is no authority except from God," stated Rom. 13:1, the oft-quoted scriptural basis for this theory, "and those that exist have been instituted by God." A second theory, best characterized as secular, was rooted in pagan sources, in Aristotle, and in medieval law and custom. Here power and authority were described as ascendant, rising from the populace to the sovereign. This secular theory gained currency with the ascendancy of the Bourbon monarchs to Spain's throne in 1700 and increasingly came to dominate how the state viewed itself and its relationship with the Roman Catholic church.

The ecclesiastical theory of government that dominated the political discourse of the church and state during the seventeenth and most of the eighteenth century was Franciscan in inspiration, the Franciscan order being the most numerous in New Spain, and was based largely (though not exclusively) on Fray Juan Focher's *Itinerario*

del Misionero en América (1574), and Fray Gerónimo de Mendieta's *Historia Eclesiástica Indiana* (1596). Focher and Mendieta envisioned a theocracy in New Spain in which ecclesiastical authority reigned supreme, and they generally interpreted the specifics of the Real Patronato in such terms. Their positions were based on an interpretation of the pastoral functions assigned to the papacy in Saint John's Gospel. When Christ said to Peter, "Feed my sheep" (John 21:15–17), Peter became vicar of all sheep, whether they had heard Christ's voice and entered into the fold (John 10:1–20) or not. The pope as Peter's successor enjoyed the "same authority held by the Blessed Peter as Vicar of Christ on earth," wrote Focher. His exclusively was the right to appoint the shepherds who would lead faithful and infidel alike. But given the enormous scope of the task, the pope had delegated some of his authority over the flock in America to the Crown in the Real Patronato. Nevertheless, those priests sent directly by the pope to the New World, as the Franciscans in New Spain had been, exercised sacerdotal powers as vicars of Christ. The powers the king enjoyed over the church in America were his as a vicar of the pope, and *not* as a vicar of Christ.

Focher and Mendieta maintained that when the first twelve Franciscan "apostles" departed for New Spain in 1523 to begin the conversion of the Indians, they were being dispatched by Fray Francisco de Los Angeles Quiñones, the minister general of their order, as "vicars of Christ." Indeed, these friars had been granted quasi-episcopal powers by Pope Leo X (reiterated by Pope Adrian VI in the 1522 bull *Omnimoda*) in those areas where there was no episcopal see or where it was two days distant. This included the right to administer all the sacraments except those requiring episcopal ordination; to act as ecclesiastical judges; to bless chalices, altars, and churches; and to impose and absolve excommunications.

From this Franciscan theory of ecclesiopolitical authority flowed several religiously inspired representations of the polity. According to this perspective, the most perfect model for the terrestrial order was the Trinity. The relationships of deference and authority among Father, Son, and Holy Ghost, each with his own role but subordinate to the Father, was what the friars wanted humanity to aspire to. One has to read no further than the "Act of Possession and Submission," read to the Indian lords of New Mexico in 1598, to imagine such a political order:

In the name of the most holy trinity and the indivisible eternal unity, deity, and majesty, Father, Son, and Holy Spirit, three persons in one, the one and only true God, who, with His eternal love, omnipotent power, and infinite wisdom, rules, governs, and orders . . . in whose hands rest the eternal pontificate and royal priesthood, the empires, kingdoms, principalities, governments and states, large and small, families and individuals . . . Jesus Christ, son of the living God, universal head of the church . . . because of His sorrowful and painful death and triumphant and glorious resurrection [was] . . . granted omnipotent power, authority, and jurisdiction, in civil and criminal cases, over high and low, and power of life and death, both in the kingdoms of heaven and on earth. . . . He left as His earthly vicar and substitute, Saint Peter, the prince of the apostles, and his legitimately elected successors. To them He entrusted the Kingdom, power, and empire, and the keys of heaven, in the same manner as Christ God himself had received them from His eternal Father as the head and master of the universe. (Ramón A. Gutiérrez. *When Jesus Came*, p. 97)

Echoing this trinitarian model of hierarchy and emanating directly from the role ascribed to the church therein was an anthropomorphic image of Christian society as a *corpus mysticum*, or mystical body with Christ as its head. For Franciscans on the borderlands, be it in Florida, New Mexico, or California, this body was of triune parts—head, arms, and feet—reflecting the structure of the Trinity. The head governed the body and singularly regulated its various parts. In Christian society the pope was the social head. Since authority over the church flowed from Christ to Peter to the popes, and from them to the Franciscans, the order's prelates continuously asserted that as vicars of Christ, they were the head of the body politic and therefore reigned supreme over all provincial religious matters.

Imagining the body politic in this way led Fray Antonio de Artega, one of New Mexico's first Franciscan prelates, to assert that the role of the provincial governor and the soldier-settlers was to serve as the church's "arms and hands that defended and protected it from heretics and other enemies." The Indians were "the feet which sustain and carry the weight of the entire body." They were forced to pay the Spanish *encomenderos* tribute in return for protection and indoctrination in Christian culture.

From the early 1600s clear into the 1800s the Franciscans, as the main order of priests and lay brothers who administered religious affairs in the Spanish Borderlands (the only exception being a brief period of Jesuit activity over the missions of southern Arizona), asserted their claim to headship over the body politic as vicars of Christ. They tried as well to impose their will through three ecclesiopolitical institutions: the prelacy, the Holy Office of the Inquisition, and the Office of the Holy Crusade. The Franciscan superior in every province, known as a *custos*, or custodian, exercised quasi-episcopal powers as prelate and ecclesiastical judge ordinary, settling everything from domestic discord to imposing or lifting ecclesiastical censures. The "final and surest authority," said some, was the Holy Office of the Inquisition. First established in the Spanish Borderlands in New Mexico in 1626, it was responsible for deracinating heresy and imposing religious orthodoxy. Widely feared was the Inquisition's warrant to impound the property of its accused, to demand public penitence, and to relegate to oblivion in its secret prisons those deemed incorrigible.

Least feared of the ecclesiastical tribunals was the Office of the Holy Crusade (*Santa Cruzada*). Conceived initially as the purchase of a papal indulgence to benefit the participants of the crusades to Jerusalem, the *Cruzada* evolved in Spain into a tax earmarked for the propagation of Catholicism. The *Cruzada* first reached the borderlands in New Mexico in 1633, where despite repeated complaints from the settlers that they too were waging a crusade against the infidels and should be exempt from the purchase of indulgences, the officers of the Holy Crusade continually levied the tax and seized intestate property.

In most areas of Spanish America, these three institutions were administered by different segments of the clergy, secular and regular, who were often at odds with each other over ends and means. But in the Spanish Borderlands where there were few priests, all three ecclesiastical bodies were controlled by the Franciscans. Under the terms of the Real Patronato both they and their assistants were theoretically immune from civil jurisdiction and impingement by vice-regal functionaries on doctrinal matters and issues of clerical discipline. The concentration of these ecclesiastical roles in the hands of a small group of friars gave them enormous power to fashion the religious commonwealth according to their own vision—a vision that was vigorously contested by the provincial governors as the king's representatives and by many of the colonists.

ROYAL CLAIMS TO AUTHORITY

Baroque as the theoretical justifications of Franciscan authority in New Spain were, the legal reality was that Spain's sovereign was both king and high priest over the Indies. Inspired by medieval theories of divine kingship, Spain's monarchs since the Iberian Reconquest had insisted on episcopal consecration and anointment to authenticate their authority as deriving from God. When a bishop as a Christ anointed the body of a king with holy chrism, that body was imbued with divinity, conjoining the human and divine, and thus reflecting on earth that kingdom which the *pater noster* said existed in heaven.

Fundamental to the exercise of divine kingship were the legal rights over the church that the papacy had conceded to Spain's monarchs in the Real Patronato. Royal jurists maintained that by virtue of the bulls of royal patronage, the king was the vicar of Christ. As vicar he administered the church and guaranteed Indian instruction. As king he governed and upheld justice. One has to look no further than the already cited 1598 "Act of Possession and Submission," read by Don Juan de Oñate to the Pueblo Indians, to see how the document could also be read as a writ for royal authority. In it, Christ is depicted as "eternal holy pontiff and king . . . son of the living god, universal head of the church . . . omnipotent power, authority and jurisdiction, in civil and criminal cases . . . not only king and judge, but also universal shepherd of believers and unbelievers." Understandably such formulations of royal authority angered the Franciscans, who advanced their own vicarial claims on the basis of this document and asserted that the king was simply a papal legate. Indeed, learned disquisitions on divine kingship were nothing but apologias for the extension of royal absolutism at the expense of the church's universalist claims, asserted the Franciscans.

The instrument through which kingship was exercised at the local level was the office of the governor. Theoretically governors were the visible instantiations of the king's secular authority as ruler, warrior, and judge; they stood in structural opposition to the clerics, who administered the monarch's sacerdotal functions through the prelacy, Inquisition, and Holy Crusade. The governor's power and prestige were rooted in the prerogatives of office: the right to assign Indian tributary grants (*encomiendas*), to grant land to settlers, to exploit an area's resources (often for personal profit), to administer justice to the entire population in civil and criminal cases, to legislate as needed, and to organize the province's defenses. Governors technically answered to the viceroy, at whose favor and command they served. But most of the settlements of the Spanish Borderlands were at least two thousand miles (3,200 kilometers) from Mexico City, a distance that took the fastest horseman several weeks to traverse. Therefore, communication was always slow, effectively placing local affairs beyond close supervision. Many a governor imposed his will as law, silencing opposition by prohibiting travel and censoring mail.

THE COLONISTS' ROLE IN CHURCH-STATE CONFLICT

Had representatives of the church and state been the only participants in disputes between these two institutions, the exact lineages of power might be disentangled easily. But the realities of power at the local and regional level were such that conflicts were often born not only of ambiguous and conflicting jurisdictional boundaries, but also from the contingent and independent role the colonists could play in politics. The loyalties of the colonists were never predictable, and could go either way—depending on the situation. The colonists owed allegiance to the king and his duly appointed officers. Whatever status and material rewards they enjoyed had been granted to them by the king. They shared a common culture with the governors but not with the Franciscans, who saw their lives as reproaches to the vainglories of the world and the spoils of human domination.

The colonists, then, stood as a pivotal group in determining whose claims to dominance over provincial affairs, those of the Franciscans or those of the governors, would prevail. If a settler had a highly developed eschatological sense and entrenched interests in the status quo, he might side with the friars against the comparatively transient governors. If, on the other hand, one were godless, anticlerical, or disgruntled with the state of affairs, one might ally with a recently arrived governor, hoping thus to obtain satisfaction or redress for past oppressions and slights. The delicate balance of power in the local resolution of church-state conflict was often in the hands of the colonists. Without them neither the governors nor the friars could effectively have their way or impose their will in local politics.

CONFLICT OVER INDIAN LABOR AND ECCLESIASTICAL PRIVILEGES

The vast and complicated relations that developed in the Spanish Borderlands between the church and state are best summarized thematically rather than by region. Although particular issues and personalities changed from place to place, the theoretical issues that precipitated conflict remained rather constant over time. The two issues that dominated church-state relations on the Spanish Borderlands from 1539 to Mexican independence in 1821 were first, the place of the Indian in the colonial scheme, and second, the rights and prerogatives of the church (and its clerics) as a privileged institution.

Throughout the colonial period, from Florida all the way west across the continent to Alta California, the Franciscans imagined themselves as the principal protectors of the Indians. They expected to control fully the minds and bodies of the Indians, forcing them to build churches and convents, till the fields the church owned, manufacture livestock by-products, and perform various liturgical roles as choir members, sacristans, catechists, and church wardens. They ra-

tionalized such uses of Indian labor by arguing that these activities were sure to lead the Indians to God.

Since much of the Spanish Borderlands was devoid of mineral wealth, the only way a governor, his constables, and the colonists of a particular area could profit from the conquest was to exploit the same resource the friars guarded so jealously: Indian labor. If animal pelts were going to be tanned for resale, if corn and wheat were going to be milled and sold as flour, if cotton and wool were going to be spun and made into cloth, it had to be through Indian labor.

The competition for Indian labor was often, if not always, litigated under the guise of much loftier issues. For example, it was not uncommon for the governor of a particular region to urge Indians not to attend Mass, not to offer their services to the friars without compensation, not to obey the rules of Christian morality concerning sexual behavior, and not to curtail the performance of their ancestral or, as the friars called them, "pagan" rituals. The clear intention of secular officials, when they encouraged such comportment, was the weakening of clerical authority over Indian communities.

When such events occurred, the friars would usually launch an investigation by the Inquisition and make formal complaints with the viceroy, claiming that the governor was fomenting liberty of conscience among the Indians and uttering heretical words about the power and authority of the church. If these charges were to stick, as they indeed did stick against several governors in Florida and New Mexico during the 1600s, the legal argument had to be couched so as to claim a doctrinal assault, over which, theoretically, the friars had jurisdictional recourse. Governors often countered such clerical complaints in the idiom of their own legal prerogatives, namely that the friars were demanding excessive labor from the Indians, and that clerical flocks were trampling civilian crops. They also asserted that the mission's sexual regime was excessively harsh, and that the friars were failing in their vow of obedience—in this case failing to obey and respect the governor as the king's representative in the Indies.

The Crown usually responded to such squabbles by relieving the litigants of their duties, transferring or promoting them to other posts, or urging civil and ecclesiastical officials to obey the laws of the kingdom and to live in peace and harmony with each other. Peace might reign for a short period, but as soon as a new governor and/or a new prelate arrived in a particular locale, the same old tensions that were at the root of the colonial enterprise—profits for the governor and colonists, converts and souls for the friars—would again precipitate open breaches and conflicts.

The second major irritant in church-state relations was the extensive privileges the church and its clerics enjoyed in America. As members of a corporate and privileged religious institution, the clergy was immune from civil jurisdiction, no matter if the issue at hand was financial improprieties and fraud, sexual misconduct, or insubordination before civil officials. Churches were legally safe havens that could not be violated by state officials. Such immunity was often a bitter source of controversy, particularly when asylum was offered to rebellious Indians, notorious criminals, or individuals intent on challenging civil authority.

Of course one must bear in mind that conflicts over ecclesiastical prerogatives were profoundly implicated in challenges involving the place of the Indian in the colonial scheme. This was indeed why conflicts between the friars and local governors were so bitter and often quite impossible to disentangle or to resolve easily to anyone's satisfaction.

BOURBON REFORMS

With the ascension of the Bourbon monarchs to Spain's throne in 1701, the relationship that had existed since the conquest of America between the church and state was radically renegotiated. Gradually the church's power was curtailed so that the institution lost its primacy and its privileged place in society. The Bourbon monarchs were intent on extending royal absolutism and toward this end reversed centuries of Hapsburg policy, slowly secularizing the missions and thereby removing Indians from direct church control, curtailing ecclesiastical immunities, and eventually subjecting the clergy to royal courts in civil and criminal affairs. Where the Hapsburg kings had intentionally left the legal boundaries of church and state ambiguously defined, thus forcing overlaps into the courts where they would ultimately decide all matters, now the Bourbons clearly delineated state power.

The Bourbon reform movement, generally known as the "Bourbon reforms," was most active during the reign of King Charles III (1759–1788). During his rule Spain was beset by deep economic stagnation, a stagnation that only worsened with Spain's defeat in the Seven Years' War (1756–1763). To rejuvenate the colonial economy, King Charles III undertook a massive reorganization of the empire's resources in the form of a social, political, and economic reform movement described by historian John Lynch as the "second colonization" of Spanish America. If the first colonization had subjugated the Indians, the second was organized to exploit the colonists and the natural resources of the empire.

The economic woes of Spain and its American empire were complex and multifaceted. Yet in the minds of the Caroline reformers, one of the central obstacles to development and prosperity was the enormous power and wealth that the Catholic church had been allowed to accumulate over the years. Much of the indigenous population of the Americas was under clerical tutelage of one form or another. Enormous tracts of land were under ecclesiastical production and supervision. The church controlled education almost exclusively. It was a major source of finance capital. Its clerics held an enormous amount of power over the daily lives of royal subjects, subjects who all too easily forgot the primacy of royal rule, particularly in their interactions with clerics who felt that they were totally above civil law. If Spain's imperial economy was to be rejuvenated, the power of the church had to be curtailed.

King Charles III proceeded in this task by rationalizing and centralizing control over the vast bureaucratic apparatus of the Spanish Empire. The royal administrative bureaucracy was streamlined and filled with peninsular Spaniards who were militantly loyal to the king. Corporate bodies, particularly those with entrenched privileges that were deemed antithetical to economic progress—the church, the nobility, the guilds, the Inquisition—were gradually subordinated and their privileges slowly dissolved.

In his relationship with the church, Charles III clearly wanted to subordinate it to the rational imperatives of the absolutist state. Toward this end the state asserted itself aggressively in education, until then a largely ecclesiastical domain. In 1767 he expelled the Jesuit order from the empire, arguing that the educational institutions they ran and the curricula they taught had to be put in the service of the state. The Jesuits were loyal not to the king but to the pope, and the extremely productive farms and Indian communities they controlled were not creating prosperity but backwardness due to their insularity.

Since the Jesuits answered directly to the Pope and, as his troops, fought the Reformation, they became the most visible scapegoats for the Caroline reformers. It was the church's judicial power vested in ecclesiastical courts that became the target of the most far-reaching changes. Historically, ecclesiastical courts had regulated all private and public personal behavior that fell into the spiritual domain broadly defined, including sexual sins, marriage and divorce, most probate matters, and litigation involving clerics and their property. As part of his larger assault on privileged institutions, Charles sharply curtailed the power of ecclesiastical courts, leaving in their jurisdiction only matters that were strictly spiritual while moving most property matters to secular courts. Clerics were theoretically immune from prosecution in secular courts, and this privilege, maintained Charles, encouraged resistance to royal imperative and state rule. He sharply limited the immunities churchmen could claim.

In the Spanish Borderlands, the Bourbon assault on the church's power and on the authority of its priests represented a new resolution of the conflicts that had marked church-state relations in previous centuries. Formerly, conflicts had been resolved in such a way as to preserve the harmonious marriage between church and state. Now that partnership was being severed in favor of ecclesiastical subordination. As a result the conflicts on the borderlands took on a much more anticlerical tone.

Provincial governors, who wanted the missions secularized so that they could have full reign over Indian land and labor, constantly brought charges against the friars which claimed that they were being remiss in their duties, both to their Indian neophytes and to the Spanish communities they served. They claimed that the Franciscans said Mass infrequently and were lax in administering the sacraments. The friars were accused of failing to teach the Indians Spanish, seizing Indian crops and livestock for themselves, and selling the excess for personal profit. The Franciscans hotly contested all of these charges as malicious lies. Certainly there were a few weak and dissolute priests, they acknowledged, but the majority were said to be models of virtue. They asserted that the false testimony the governors raised against the friars was but a ploy to rob the Indians of their true protectors, the Franciscans, and to expose them to unbridled exploitation.

But despite clerical opposition, the imperatives of the state reigned supreme. The secularization of the missions progressed, as did rulings to deprive the friars of Indian service, to strip them of ecclesiastical wealth, to curtail their clerical immunities before the civil courts, and to abrogate many of the legal functions they controlled through the ecclesiastical courts. By the beginning of the nineteenth century, then, the church had been relegated to a largely ritual and ceremonial role with control only of spiritual matters. The king had emerged as an absolute secular ruler.

BIBLIOGRAPHY

Bannon, John F. *The Spanish Borderlands Frontier, 1513–1821*. New York, 1970; repr. Albuquerque, N.Mex., 1974.

Bayle, Constantino. *El Culto del Santísimo en Indias*. Madrid, 1951.

Borges, Pedro. *Métodos Misionales en la Cristianización de América, Siglo XVI*. Madrid, 1960.

Boxer, Charles R. *The Church Militant and Iberian Expansion, 1440–1770*. Baltimore, Md., 1978.

Canedo, Lino Gómez. *Evangelización y Conquista: Experiencia Franciscana en Hispanoamérica*. Mexico City, 1977.

Egaña, Antonio de. *La Teoría de Regio Vicariato Español en Indias*. Rome, 1958.

Farriss, Nancy M. *Crown and Clergy in Colonial Mexico, 1759–1821: The Crisis of Ecclesiastical Privilege*. London, 1968.

Focher, Juan. *Itinerario del Misionero en América*. Madrid, 1960.

Giménez Fernández, Manuel. *El Concilio IV Mejicano*. Seville, Spain, 1939.

Góngora, Mario. *Studies in the Colonial History of Spanish America.* Cambridge, England, 1975.

Gutiérrez, Ramón A. *When Jesus Came, the Corn Mothers Went Away: Marriage, Sexuality, and Power in New Mexico, 1500–1846.* Stanford, Calif., 1991.

Hernáez, Francisco J., ed. *Colección de bulas, breves y otros documentos relativos a la iglesia de América y Filipinas.* Brussels, 1879.

Kessell, John L. *Kiva, Cross and Crown: The Pecos Indians and New Mexico, 1540–1840.* Washington, D.C., 1979; Albuquerque, N.Mex., 1987.

Lynch, John. *The Spanish American Revolutions, 1808–1826.* New York, 1973.

Mendieta, Gerónimo de. *Historia Eclesiastica Indiana.* Mexico City, 1945.

Phelan, John Leddy. "Authority and Flexibility in the Spanish Imperial Bureaucracy." *Administrative Science Quarterly* 5, no. 1 (1960):47–65.

———. *The Millennial Kingdom of the Franciscans in the New World.* Berkeley, Calif., 1970.

Scholes, France V. "Church and State in New Mexico, 1610–1650." *New Mexico Historical Review* 11, nos. 1–4 (1936): no. 1, 9–76; no. 2, 145–178; no. 3, 283–294; no. 4, 297–349; and 12, no. 1 (1937): 78–106.

———. "The First Decade of the Inquisition in New Mexico." *New Mexico Historical Review* 10, no. 3 (1935):195–241.

———. *Troublous Times in New Mexico, 1659–1670.* Albuquerque, N.Mex., 1942.

Sylvest, Edwin Edward. *Motifs of Franciscan Mission Theory in Sixteenth Century New Spain: Province of the Holy Gospel.* Washington, D.C., 1975.

Ramón A. Gutiérrez

SEE ALSO **Mission Communities; Roman Catholicism; and Taxation;** and various essays in EDUCATION.

ROMAN CATHOLICISM

THE SPANISH BORDERLANDS

EXPLAINING THE PRESENCE of Roman Catholicism in the "Spanish Borderlands" requires a careful, historical analysis since it was so unlike the quest for religious freedom that characterized the coming of European religions along the eastern seaboard of North America and their incorporation into the mainstream of American life. The conversion of Native peoples to Christianity and their integration into the Spanish Empire were primary goals in Spain's conquest of the Americas. Roman Catholicism frequently replaced or combined with Native American religions through an elaborate process of evangelization because the acceptance of Christianity by Indian nations offered greater political and economic security for both colonist and native. By contrast, the faith practiced among Spanish colonials was characterized by a high degree of tradition and intense loyalty to the institutional church.

"SPANISH BORDERLANDS"

Before analyzing the process of evangelization, a brief discussion of the concept of the "Spanish Borderlands" is in order. For almost a century it has been the vogue in academic circles to address Hispanic and Native American issues under the label "borderlands." This descriptive sobriquet was popularized by the historian Herbert Eugene Bolton in the early twentieth century in an attempt to accommodate his concept to the frontier hypothesis of Frederick Jackson Turner. Turner's theory tried to explain American history in terms of a westward-expanding, Anglo-American frontier; the "borderland" concept countered with a northward-expanding, Spanish frontier that converged geographically in the regions of the present border. In the latter part of the twentieth century the concept has been restricted to the areas of contemporary United States–Mexican political borders.

Thus, the original "borderlands" thesis has unwittingly truncated the reality of the cultural dynamic essential to understanding the spread of the Spanish Empire and the acculturation of its peoples. Still, for the purposes of this discussion, the Spanish Borderlands are simply those regions of the United States once occupied by Spain. The presence of Roman Catholicism there is not due exclusively to evangelization by Spaniards; it is a complex phenomenon that can be explained only by the convergence of different historical and religious dynamics.

DYNAMICS OF THE CONVERSION PROCESS

The first element in these dynamics is historically remote. It begins with a Spanish conquest of the Americas that was as much religious as secular. Its origins go back to Christopher Columbus and beyond—to Spain's perception of its role in world history. The *Reconquista* under Ferdinand and Isabella, as understood by the Spaniards, was a valiant attempt to rid the Iberian Peninsula of "infidel" religions and adherents. Not only were the Moors soundly defeated and driven from the land in 1492, but those Jews who were unwilling to accept Christianity were expelled the same year. Spain was manifesting a pious intolerance toward peoples who rejected an invitation to conversion.

Curiously, Columbus's search for a western route to Asia that same year failed admirably when he discovered an unsullied New World that was ripe for evangelization. No missionary accompanied Columbus on the first voyage because his purposes were wholly secular; the second voyage, however, carried missionaries to convert the heathen New World to Christendom as well as to claim land and peoples for Spain. From 1493 onward it is difficult to separate Spanish secular intentions from religious motivations.

The second dynamic, which will be dealt with below, concerns the waning of Spanish missionary support in the late eighteenth century and its total collapse after Mexico's war of independence. The near vacuum of religious ministry, the paucity of priests, and the inability of non-Hispanic churchmen to deal with apostolic needs in territories newly acquired from Spain and Mexico set the stage for the rise of "folk Catholicism" throughout the borderlands.

EVANGELIZATION AND SPANISH EXPANSION IN THE AMERICAS

The discovery of the Americas came as a shock to a Europe that was unconsciously poised on the edge of a new age. Generalizations abound to explain the demise of the medieval world and the emergence of the Renaissance. Whatever reasons truly explain social phenomena in the fif-teenth and sixteenth centuries lie beyond the scope of this essay; the fact is that Europe underwent profound changes, and Spain was very much in the vanguard. After centuries of invasions by outsiders from the north and east, new self-images fortified the notions of regaining lost lands, redefining regions, and asserting new authority. Conquest was in the air.

Furthermore, the dominant role of the papacy in sanctioning secular rule was widely accepted, and there was a pervading fear of Muslim expansion into Europe. The counterattack against infidels marched under the banner of the Crusades, and the notion of conquest was usually understood as liberation of lands for the practice of the Christian faith. In this sense, Spain's conquest of Granada in 1492 occasioned the establishment of a system of royal patronage. The Crusades, indeed, laid the foundation for the rise of the *Real Patronato*, through which Spain conducted its most intimate imperial expansion.

From the earliest moments when lands were retaken from the infidels in Spain, the Catholic kings were obligated to build and support churches and clergy. Although the roots of the patronage system trace well back into Roman times and into earlier Spanish history, the bull of Pope Innocent VIII, *Orthodoxe fidei propagationem,* or the "Bull of Granada," of 13 December 1486, granted to Ferdinand and Isabella powerful privileges and obligations regarding the expansion and maintenance of the Catholic faith. These privileges and obligations are summarily known as the Real Patronato. Although the Real Patronato was initially conceded for application in the known kingdoms of Europe, it was soon extended to the Americas as a part of the Spanish Empire. Ultimately, the Real Patronato set the distinct character of Roman Catholicism in the borderlands.

THE REAL PATRONATO

The Real Patronato can be nominally defined as "royal patronage," by which is understood the monarch's privilege to name the clergy who are to serve particular churches in return for donations of land, building and maintaining the churches, and providing of endowments. While this privilege may seem disproportionate when weighed against its obligation, it was the Crown's surest way of keeping close control over perhaps the most sensitive element in the sociopolitical structure—the people as a community.

The Bull of Granada anticipated the functioning of the Real Patronato in the Americas when Innocent wrote:

This we gladly confer, and as a reward of their crusade make them [the Catholic kings] rulers, guardians, and keepers of the lands they conquer and the people there resident. They have a right to be assisted in a manner helpful to them and generally beneficial, so that they may possess and control the churches, monasteries, and other ecclesiastical benefices and occupied territories regained by them in the enterprise to which they consecrated themselves by vow.

Although America was still to be discovered, the character of Spanish conquest was confirmed, and the Real Patronato was at its heart. Columbus had hardly returned to Europe with news of his discoveries than Pope Alexander VI stressed the obligations of the Catholic kings to convert the newly known peoples to Christianity. Ferdinand and Isabella responded with undeniable clarity in their instructions before Columbus's second voyage in May 1493, when they exercised the privilege of the Patronato by appointing Padre Fray Bernal Buil and reaffirmed their royal duties for the conversion of the Native peoples. Likewise the instructions to Governor Fray Nicolás de Ovando in 1501 read more like a church document than a recitation of civic duties.

The history of the Real Patronato is firmly established with the promulgation of the bull of Julius II *Illius fulciti presidio* of 15 November 1504. The pope conferred on the Catholic monarchs the full rights and duties of the Patronato:

Let them determine the size and style of the metropolitan and cathedral churches . . . and see to their building. And let them erect and institute the respective ecclesiastical dignities in their cities and dioceses, the canonries, prebends, and other ecclesiastical benefices with or without charge of souls. And let them conserve and plant other spiritualities, as they think expedient, for the increase of the divine worship and salvation of souls.

As stated above, the place of the Real Patronato in establishing Roman Catholicism in the Spanish Borderlands appears historically remote, but in reality it explained the nature of the presence of the Roman Catholic faith throughout the region. Countless criticisms have been lodged against the church in the frontier, but most of the criticisms stem from a faulty understanding of the position of the church and the operation of the Real Patronato. Churchmen are sometimes accused of bilking unwary natives of their limited wealth in order to enrich the church, when in reality the source of monies for the churches and mission communities was the royal treasury; the Native communities were actually the beneficiaries of mission building. Native peoples in mission territory, which comprised nearly all of the Spanish Borderlands, were not taxed—although they may have been obligated to very limited, communal work for the church, which benefited the mission community and not the clergy or the Crown. On the other hand, colonial properties were subject to *diezmos* (tithes) that were paid to the Crown but generally returned to the hierarchy for distribution under the system of ecclesiastical benefices. Benefices fueled the building and operation of the secular church, whereas the mission system was exclusively operated by members of religious orders and not by secular clergy. Thus the missions were precluded from benefices and direct hierarchical support.

It would be helpful to recall the distinction between secular and regular clergy in the Americas, because the regulars were the primary ministers of the Native enclaves. The hierarchical structure of the Roman Catholic church under the papacy divides into "secular" and "regular" clergy. The seculars answer to the local ordinary (bishop); the regulars follow approved *regulae* (rules or institutes) and answer to a religious superior other than a bishop. The missionaries were routinely instructed to sign official documents as "Padre 'Juan Fulano,' *ministro de su Magestad*," to assert their independence from episcopal authority. Financial holdings of the regulars, through their orders or approved institutes, were also independent of the hierarchy and the bishops. This procedure ensured that the task of the regulars would be the conversion and acculturation of Native peoples and not the aggrandizement of the church. The secular clergy, on the other hand, ministered to the Spanish colonials and communities that were already long-since converted. While the distinction between regular and secular must not be overdrawn, it does help to explain the character of the mestizo church, which was spawned by the intermarriage of Indian converts and Spanish settlers in many borderland areas. This distinction also aids in understanding the role of the mestizo and Indian communities in the nineteenth-century movements for political independence.

The royal government accepted and exercised its privileges and duties under the Patronato throughout the Americas, including the northern frontiers of New Spain. This exercise meant that the church was not enriching itself under the protection of the Crown, but rather that the Crown was using the church as the primary instrument of social integration. Not only did the church pursue its religious goals, it also accepted responsibility for schools, hospitals, and every form of social service. Because of the provisions of the Patronato, local churches and church activities were endowed with land and other investments that met the financial burden of the church's varied activities. Many critics have incorrectly attributed the church's extensive holdings to the greed of the clergy rather than to the mandates of law. Another, almost singularly important point is that the organization of the Roman Catholic churches under the Real Patronato does not correspond with the Anglo-American model, which postulates the separation of church and state. Nor, in the case of the Anglican church, where coalescence of power was recognized, was the identification of church and state equivalent to the Spanish model—perhaps the strongest difference residing in the Spanish monarchs' total reluctance to interfere in doctrinal matters.

These characteristic differences created the social context for the kind of Roman Catholic Christianity that evolved throughout the borderlands. The incipient churches in Native communities exercised strong independence from episcopal control (and support). Later steps toward secularization, such as the process of incorporating the mission church into the jurisdiction of a local bishop, involved new obligations and taxes to which the Native peoples were unaccustomed. A knowledge of how Catholic communities formed and evolved throughout the borderlands is essential to understanding the church that eventually emerged. Despite the pious desires of some bishops and clergy, the Roman Catholic faith in the borderlands was never tight and univocal—yet it was in every way a genuine conversion from older beliefs and practices.

THE MISSION SYSTEM

As much as the mission system has been studied in the history of the borderlands, its role in the evolution of Roman Catholicism in these regions has been significantly underestimated, particularly since the Patronato mission system was abolished in 1821. Continuity in the evolution of the Catholic communities was interrupted. The secularization of the missions in the nineteenth century was simply incapable of coping with the immense array of social and economic responsibilities that the missions had dealt with and for which the Crown had paid. Furthermore, the goals and expectations of secular jurisdiction were nearly incompatible with the needs of the Indian and mestizo churches that came under the immediate care of the various dioceses through secularization.

Succinctly stated, the mission system was Spain's program for the conversion of Native peoples under the Real Patronato. The system came directly under the control of the Council of the Indies and was operated in the different viceroyalties of the empire through agreements with several religious orders. In the case of northern New Spain, the Order of Friars Minor (Franciscans) and the Society of Jesus (Jesuits) were the chief orders involved. They accepted responsibility for recruiting missionaries from among their ranks to send to the districts under their control. Generally speaking, the districts were geographically separate and usually ethnically homogeneous; that is, the two orders rarely worked among the same linguistic or cultural communities. This is why it is important not to insist on a monolithic explanation of the mission system.

The Franciscans set the precedents for the evangelization of the borderlands with their early entry into New Mexico and the central plains. Their men, who attempted gallant and isolated ministries, were soon martyred for their efforts to change the beliefs and practices of the Indian nations. Not until substantial attempts had been made by Spaniards to settle in the Indian country were the missionary ventures successful. Franciscan missions stressed community living in preference to prolonged one-man missionary involvement.

The Jesuits also entered partially settled territory along the Pacific slopes, but their ministerial techniques tended toward sustained isolation from the colonial settlements. They followed a much less monastic tradition, and their missionaries frequently lived alone among the Indian communities. This condition encouraged syncretism in the practice of the Christian faith. The effects of this methodology will be discussed below in the section on the administration of the sacraments.

Historiographically, the English-reader is usually introduced to the mission system according to the late-eighteenth-century model of the Alta California missions. This is unfortunate, because these missions, as well as those of Texas, were established and operated under drastically changed rules and regulations after the military and economic reforms of the 1770s and 1780s of Charles III of Spain wrenched control away from the religious orders in the missions and subjected the mission communities to stringent political controls.

Prior to the Bourbon reforms of the mid eighteenth century, the typical borderland mission was characterized mostly by its environmental setting and the Native community. Missions were established in or very near existing Indian villages. Their primary tasks were conversion and the betterment of community life, not the unfettered control of land and labor for secular purposes. Hostility between missions and colonials was not uncommon in northern New Spain because the missions relied on cattle and crops for growth and survival but the Spanish settlers saw the production of these items there as an encroachment on growth and profits. The missions were able to outdo their colonial competitors in prices and productivity. Missionary control of the Indian labor pool caused untold jealousy. But with the advent of the Bourbon reforms, the altruistic aspects of the missions took a decidedly secondary place.

Before the reforms the missionary was effectively a Crown agent responsible for the protection, care, and growth of the community. He could, and often did, call on the local military post for assistance, but he was not subject to their jurisdiction as in Bourbon times. Once the control of temporalities (material welfare) was wrested from the missionaries and placed in the hands of local military commanders, the missions were transformed into supply bases supported with Indian labor. Native American labor was no longer protected from harsh conditions and unfair compensation. These later decades are the ones that Indian nations recall with such bitterness in the twentieth century. The earlier and more stable decades, when the missions were centers of "friendly persuasion," were the ones that truly shaped the future of the mestizo church in the borderlands.

With all this in mind, it is possible to distinguish the religious experience and formation of the Indians of New Mexico and Arizona from those of California and Texas. The long years of contact between Franciscans and Pueblos explain both the origins of the Pueblo Revolt of 1680, and the peaceful resurgence of Catholicism after the reconquest of 1692. In Arizona the Pima and Papago (Tohono O'odam) have remained strongly Catholic to this day, despite some incidents of rebellion. These Native American communities have also maintained a presence and identity into this century. By contrast, the Christian Indian communities of California and Texas, which were formed largely under the Bourbon system, have all but vanished. They are, at best, poorly integrated into contemporary society because Spanish and Anglo immigration swamped their lands and peoples, and there was no effective old-style mission system to protect them.

Another problem in understanding the effects of the missions on the shaping of the Christian community has been the overly mechanical description of the mission system—rising to the bells, morning liturgy, catechism, communal work in the fields. This has produced a monolithic concept of missions that distorts the diversity of the conversion phenomena. What the neophyte understood about the sacraments, the nature of God, and the teachings of the *doctrina* (catechism) were fundamental to his formation as a Catholic. Because the native convert came from a totally different cultural background than a European, the religious traditions that he developed were radically different from those of the Spanish Catholic. A superficial review of conversion records will not reveal these staunch differences because religious priests were anxious to indicate the success of conversion through the trappings of conformity. It is always easier to point to social conformity as a sign of interior conversion than to measure actual ideological changes. Although missionaries themselves were quick to point out the acceptance of external practices as a sign of conversion, they often confessed doubts about the thoroughness of changes of faith in their unofficial correspondence.

Under the older Spanish system Indians invited missionaries to reside in their villages. Churches and residences were constructed at Crown expense, and communal fields were designated for the support of mission communities. Indian neophytes were assigned rotating work schedules in the fields and with livestock. Their work earned them food and clothing that accrued with the amount of time they contributed to the common effort, and they received a minimum wage. Each neophyte was required to attend mass, catechism, and special education sessions. The children were all educated at the mission school, which had primary responsibility for language, math, and music training. Depending on his language skills, the resident missionary taught the doctrine, but when he lacked such competence, he resorted to interpreters or Native *temastians* (catechists).

Throughout the mission period, disputes arose over the primacy of language—whether the native tongue should be incorporated or everything should be taught exclusively in Spanish. Obviously fluency in Spanish drew a Native community closer to the Spaniards, while Native languages provided the Indians with a relatively safe and secretive haven for their traditional preferences.

MISSIONS, ORTHODOXY, AND THE COUNCIL OF TRENT

Missions have seldom been analyzed in their ecclesiastical context. Robert Ricard's landmark study, *The Spiritual Conquest of Mexico,* is superb for the early missionary activities of the mendicant religious orders, but it ends with the arrival of the Jesuits, who were indisputable pacesetters for borderland missions. Ricard rightly criticizes the view that eighteenth-century Alta California missions typify the Spanish mission system, but he errs in giving the impression that Mexico was "conquered" spiritually in the first half-century of contact. The nearly two centuries of mission expansion in the north, which fall outside both Ricard's mendicant phase and the later Alta California phase, were those which formed the borderland church. Furthermore, the decrees of the Council of Trent (1545) and Mexico's own Third Council (1585) lie outside the scope of his study.

Throughout the sixteenth century the discovery of America and the Reformation vied for Europe's attention. In studies of the post-Reformation period, few writers have ever alluded to the fact that no prelate from the New World was involved in the deliberations of the Council of Trent. In effect, America presented no issues of orthodoxy that were not theoretically addressed in the issues of preserving an unsullied faith in Europe. Thus, the immensely complex problems of acculturation, inculturation, and syncretism were left unresolved, with the consequence that the clergy of America were sensitized about issues that were hardly comparable. Yet the non-Christian beliefs and practices of the Native Americans did fall under the council's concerns about orthodoxy; clerical reports on catechism, baptism, penance, and communion had to follow strict guidelines. Differences of belief were simplistically categorized as superstition and diabolic intervention; Native religious ministry was seen as witchcraft or pure shamanism.

Therefore, whenever Roman Catholicism in the borderlands comes under discussion, certain presumptions about conciliar theology and pastoral necessity come into play; for example, the process of conversion itself, as conducted by the missionaries, had to accommodate not only Native sensitivities but also the concerns of the Council of Trent regarding orthodoxy. This process is illustrated by the compilation of "approved" catechisms, catechetical instructions, and the administration of baptism that adhered to the strictures of the council. But once the Native American had accepted baptism, conversion was still not considered complete by the missionaries; the process continued, less as a test of orthodoxy than as a shaping or refinement of newly acquired religious and cultural practices.

CONVERSION AND ACCULTURATION UNDER THE MISSION SYSTEM

Although the stated evangelical goals of the various orders may have been conversion to the "one true faith," the manner of conversion was not uniform, nor were the criteria by which conversion was evaluated exactly the same. Granted that dogmatic orthodoxy was subject to the same evaluative norms (a creed, the Commandments, and prayers), allowances for syncretic understandings and practices were rather broad. For example, belief in the dogmas of the creed were left open to some degree of nativistic interpretation, as long as the neophyte accepted belief in a Trinitarian Godhead and the incarnation of Jesus Christ. But, for example, the acceptance of a Trinity did not necessarily require the rejection of the sacredness of the four cardinal points of the compass that played such an important part in Native agricultural rituals. Gentle forms of syncretic faith can be seen in the belief in God the Father, God the Son, and God the Holy Spirit, together with the symbolism of the four-armed cross as a universal Christian sign of life and death. Probably more than anything else, missionaries feared that the Indians would continue in idolatry, even to the point of imputing idolatrous meanings to the crucifix and images of the saints.

By the time extensive missionary efforts were being made in the borderlands, some standardization was being imposed by the church. Baptism without catechesis was not allowed except in the case of the dying or of very young infants. This practice had changed rather significantly since the early days of the conquest, when the sacrament had been administered soon after the neophyte had given signs of accepting the most rudimentary aspects of the faith. Learning could take place later. However, in the light of both experience and the changed climate of the Council of Trent, it was considered both prudent and practical to delay baptizing adults until there was certain knowledge of their intellectual conversion as well as their abandonment of "sinful" pagan practices. Infants were baptized immediately on request by the parents, but missionaries did not baptize every infant merely on sight. Children were baptized soon after successful demonstration of their grasp and acceptance of the *doctrina*. Thus, over time, the nucleus of a trained Christian community emerged, and it was essentially a church of the young.

The sixteenth century brought important changes to the formation of religious communities. If nothing else, the widespread use of the printed word made the catechism a popular device in the quest for doctrinal orthodoxy. Throughout previous centuries Christian belief had depended heavily on familial instruction, the spoken word, and pictorial declamation. The Reformation, however, moved immediately to employ the printed word in declaring its doctrinal fundamentals; the leader of each sect from Martin Luther onward proclaimed his teachings in a "catechism." The Roman Catholic church responded with its own series of catechisms, which were stringently controlled by the decrees of the Council of Trent. Although the council had promulgated its own *Catechism*, the church's pastoral theologians wrote adaptations that were usually briefer and more manageable for training less sophisticated neophytes.

In New Spain, the Franciscans had anticipated the doctrinal concerns of Trent in the matter of catechisms; Fray Alonso de Molina composed a Nahuatl text that became widespread and popular. The Jesuits, on the other hand, came on the scene after Trent and employed variations on catechisms written by members of the order who had participated in the council. The Mexican version of the Tridentine catechism that was approved by the Third Mexican Council was written by Jesuit father Juan de la Plaza, but it was too ponderous for field use. The versions that became more popular and widespread were those of Fathers Gerónimo de Ripalda and Bartolomé de Castaño; only a few of them have survived in Native-language translations.

These catechisms concentrated on explanations of the common prayers: the Our Father (*Padre nuestro*), the Hail Mary (*Ave*), the Creed (*Credo*), and the Hail Holy Queen (*Salve Regina*). Group recitation of the prayers of the catechism served linguistic as well as religious purposes. These prayers were often chanted or set to melodies that appealed to the Indians' sense of music and rhythm. The catechism went on to discuss the Commandments and the rules of Christian living, which included the sacraments, works of mercy, theological and cardinal virtues, gifts of the Holy Spirit, the Beatitudes, and the last things. In actuality, the missionaries were quite sensible in their demands about how Indians grasped the catechism; they knew the process could be completed only over time.

THE ROLE OF THE SACRAMENTS

Enough has already been said about baptism as the rite of initiation into the Christian community. Since the goal of conversion was to save souls from eternal damnation, and the goal of initiation into the Christian community was to protect the individual from evil, baptism was considered extremely important. Not infrequently in missionary experience, a deathly ill child or elderly person returned to health in a matter of days after baptism, and the occurrence was used by the missionary to explain that since the sacrament was intended to give the recipient eternal life, the cure was a sure sign of its power. Whether one thinks of this as miracle or chicanery, baptism took on powerful significance in the mission communities because it opened the door to a whole new world of temporal and spiritual support. The pouring of baptismal waters has always been a clear and simple human ritual to express the idea of cleansing and nurturing, but the full impact of the sacrament went beyond the ritual purification.

Remembering that baptism was the sacrament of initiation into the Christian community, its reception brought a whole new set of personal relationships with established members of the community. Among the most significant was the *compadrazgo* or the spiritual relation of the godparents. The idea of having "spiritual parents" in the faith created a guarantee that the new Christian would have a proper upbringing in the faith. Because the missions were established in pagan territory, these relationships were particularly important. And over the years *compadrazgo* evolved into an especially strong social institution; families were knit together through these networks of spiritual relations. In the earlier stages of conversion these godparent relationships helped to reinforce the barriers against intermarriage among close relatives.

Confirmation as the sacrament of ratification in the faith has had a very confusing history. In the post-Reformation climate, churchmen were anxious to administer the sacrament as a bulwark against backsliders. The requirements generally were a more thorough preparation in Christian doctrine and a long probation that established the habitual practice of the religion. Hence, children were schooled more intensely in the doctrine prior to the conferral of the sacrament. The conferral, however, presented a serious problem, since by tradition it was done by the local ordinary (bishop). In continental Europe it was easily done because hundreds of bishops were available. In America the number of bishops was minuscule by comparison. Along the vast northern frontier of New Spain, only two bishops held jurisdiction and they were required to ride thousands of miles to administer the sacrament. Missionaries successfully appealed for the powers to confirm, but it was never a clear issue since it seemed to detract from the privileges of the hierarchy. A compromise was reached in the seventeenth century, when the power to confirm was granted to the person who held the office of *visitador;* theoretically this person visited each mission once a year and could administer the sacrament at that time. Practical difficulties of travel, health, and weather led to the uncertain administration of the sacrament and contributed to the theological dispute over whether confirmation should be administered together with baptism. More and more, the administration of confirmation was restricted to the bishops, and their infrequent visitations of their vast dioceses led to a sense of isolation and an awe of ecclesiastical power. The social effect of the sacrament was minimal, but its ecclesiastical implications were evident.

The sacrament of matrimony had profound effects on the Native communities. Baptism brought with it the acceptance of all other Christian practices, and the church insisted vehemently on the sanctity of monogamous marriage. Each Indian tribe adhered to slightly different norms of sexual conduct, and monogamy was not a universally preferred practice. Nevertheless, the missionaries held rigidly to the laws of the church, and a Native couple married in the church were closely monitored regarding faithfulness and the care of their children. Indians were not permitted to move freely between missions and towns for fear that a man might neglect his wife and children. In the event of a marriage, the couple's background was checked against mission records to establish freedom to marry, and the Indian communities were somewhat grateful for the imposition of an authority that promised some degree of marital stability.

Controversy seems always to rage over the place of holy orders in the New World. The prospect of a Native clergy seemed to terrify the church hierarchy, and in a relatively short time it decided against the ordination of Indians. *Cédulas* or decrees of the Catholic kings of Spain also prohibited the ordination of Native clergy. This proscription endured throughout the colonial period, enforced through the requirement of *limpieza de sangre*, literally "purity of blood," which was a carry over from Inquisition precepts against Jews and Moors on the Iberian Peninsula. Unfortunately, this prohibition worked to alienate the Christian community from the clergy, who had always to be replaced by a cultural outsider. This was not unacceptable to the Native Americans, though, because the practice placed the priest in a class apart from the people—just as they often did with their own *hechiceros* (shamans or medicine men).

Although baptism, confirmation, and matrimony were sacraments that helped to shape the Christian community and to create new networks of moral obligations, no sacrament touched the Indians' daily lives as strongly as the celebration of the Eucharist. In mission communities the neophytes were obligated to attend Mass to listen to the word of God being preached by the missionary—often in an unintelligible language. Since Christianity has always insisted on the primacy of the Eucharist as the central sign of Christian union and life, the Indians were drawn closely into the celebration of the liturgy. No other circumstance involved cultural adaptation as much as the liturgy and related practices.

During the conduct of the Mass, the priest read and preached on the Scriptures according to his individual competence, so that these essential lessons were conveyed either in Spanish or in a Native dialect. Obviously, there was a wide range of success and failure. When the priest enjoyed the services of a trained *fiscal*, an official representative who held the "cane of office" and was usually a level above the temastian or teacher, these readings or lessons were conducted by him, and the priest confined himself to the celebration of the sacred mysteries. Once again, the regulations and rituals of the church were at odds with the Native cultural preferences. Mass was said under a an open-air shelter or ramada and later within a church because the Roman Catholic ritual and the Judeo-Christian tradition insisted that holy places are contained and covered, as evidenced in the "holy of holies." Following that tradition, the Eucharist was always celebrated, like the Passover supper, in a designated room. But this religious preference ran counter to the Native understanding that the outdoors is sacred. Religious services were conducted on raised platforms; only priestly, secretive, preparatory rites were performed in *kivas* (Pueblo ceremonial structures) or caves. This inversion was never really recognized by the Catholic clergy although in the sixteenth century they readily conducted outdoor services where thousands of Indians gathered in the atrium of the monastery churches to hear Mass. For the Indians this was sacred; for the clergy this was merely keeping the unbaptized from entering into the sacred temple for believers.

Native American sensitivity for the sacredness of the open air partially explains the great success of morality plays and processions that always took place outside the church buildings. The dramatic processions of the *Posadas* prior to Christmas and the dramatizations of the Passion during Holy Week are among the more elaborate examples. Perhaps the best example of the conflict between the holiness of the outdoors and the sacredness of the sanctuary occurs with the culmination of *Semana Santa* (Holy Week) events on Holy Saturday.

In many pueblos of northern Mexico elaborate paraliturgical ceremonies are held from Palm Sunday through Easter, depicting the struggle between good and evil, between virtue (life) and sin (death), and between Christ and the devil. Customarily, a *hermandad* (religious brotherhood) was established among the people to assume the role of the Jews and the Pharisees, who were seen as those responsible for the death of Christ. The "Judios" and "Fariseos" were granted a tacit license for mischievous conduct in the community, which reached its height during the Holy Week pageantry. Wearing outlandish masks, reminiscent of Indian dance costumes, they spoke in falsetto, disrupting processions and tormenting the faithful. They represented the force of evil in the world; their day of exaltation came on Good Friday, when Christ was crucified—often dramatized by strapping a young man to a cross in the village. On Holy Saturday the ritual leader of the town burned an effigy of Judas at dawn as a sign that punishment was about to fall on the evildoers. Throughout the town the Judios and Fariseos prepared themselves for the coming flagellation, which occurred immediately prior to the *Misa de la Gloria*. The faithful crowded into the church proper, and then the forces of evil attacked the building. Waves of Judios and Fariseos were repulsed by whip-wielding *soldados de la Virgen*. The whole event, which took place shortly before noon, was choreographed as a clumsy ballet that reached a peak when the evil ones penetrated the church. The townsfolk lashed the invaders with willow branches until blood broke across their backs. With bleeding bodies the Judios and Fariseos fell on their knees and crept through the main aisle, while righteous Christians continued to lash them with branches. Now duly chastised for their mischief, the penitent men approached the altar to make a special offering for reinstatement as God-fearing Christians. Until this sacred moment, all of the paraliturgical ceremonies had taken place outside; the final entry into the church was genuinely symbolic because at that moment the church bells rang out in joyous victory. Lent ended with the recitation of the Gloria and ringing of bells.

Another very popular paraliturgical ceremony, which occurred at Christmastide, depicted Joseph and Mary's search for a resting place. The *Posada* has been a staunch favorite of Spanish devotion for centuries, but they held a particular affinity for the Indians because of their processional and outdoor character. To the Spaniard it was poignant because it was the Holy Family's search for interior shelter; to the Indian it was the trek of the sacred through the open world. And the Posadas, like the other outdoor processions, provided excellent opportunities for "wild" dancing that was far more religiously expressive for them than passive kneeling.

Probably no other religious ceremony was more sacred or mysterious to the Indian community than the Eucharist itself. Clearly, this was the central act of worship among the Catholics. While controversy raged in Europe during the Reformation over the real presence of Christ in the Eucharist, the problem in the New World was to educate the Indian that this ceremony was not idolatrous. Aztecs were quick to understand the Eucharistic symbolism of bread and wine, because they themselves held a reverential respect for tortillas and pulque. They understood that these symbols expressed the radical need for man to be nurtured by the goods of the earth—and these more than any other. The challenge for the missionaries was to make a theological shift, so that Native peoples saw in the Eucharist a need to be nurtured by the living presence of the Son of God. Manifestly, this is sublime theology confronting basic human perceptions. No one has satisfactorily explained exactly how the Indians grasped this profound Christian mystery, but they did perceive its importance.

First of all, according to the practice of the times, they were permitted to receive the Eucharist only once a year. It was a moment made so sacred that only the priest was permitted to consume the Sacred Species daily—and even then only after fasting and abstinence. The Spanish liturgical traditions enhanced the mystery because no one was allowed even to touch the empty chalice except with special cloths. Even the water to be mixed with the wine had to be administered with a spoon. Throughout the year the communities were invited to adore the Eucharist on special feasts when Benediction was conducted. Only the finest vessels were permitted to touch or display the Sacred Host. It was high, transcendent drama for a convert struggling to understand Christianity.

The Eucharist was linked to another staunch Christian sacrament, that of penance. Church law prescribed that baptized Christians receive the Eucharist once a year and that this occur during Eastertide. Ascetic scrupulosity twisted this law so that everyone understood that he or she was not to receive the Eucharist *except* once a year. A minimalist precept thereby became a maximalist practice. Furthermore, the reception of communion was to happen only when the individual was in "the state of grace," a moral condition of the soul that was certain only following confession. So the reception of communion became closely linked to the reception of the sacrament of penance. The Spanish church had long emphasized the feast of Corpus Christi, which extolled the mystery of the Real Presence; every good Christian therefore wished to receive communion on or near that feast. The clergy literally worked overtime in preparing the faithful for the reception of the Eucharist by hearing endless hours of confessions. The faithful, on the other hand, tended to postpone going to confession until the social pressure of Corpus Christi drew them into the church. This practice remained in effect until the late nineteenth century, when frequent communion was advocated by Rome, thus making this religious practice seem rather odd to twentieth-century Catholics. The effect was clear; it made contact with the central act of Christian worship awesome, fearsome, and transcendent—almost a reversal of the theology of incarnation.

The sacrament of penance was not exclusively linked to the reception of communion; it was administered with much greater frequency. The reception of the Eucharist, however, followed the Latin ascetic tradition whereby one never presented himself at the altar without previously confessing. The Council of Trent had stressed the practice of a complete and thorough confession; the missionaries were very careful to implement this directive because it was useful in shaping the Christian community. Catechism classes were used to train the faithful in the proper manner of confession, making it possible to discuss personal sins in an impersonal context. Some doctrinal manuals show an ingenious mixture of language practice, societal vocabulary, and moralizing: "I talked back to my grandmother." Or, "she made her uncle angry," and "he stole food from his godfather."

Because Trent had also demanded that penitents confess all their sins according to number and kind, priests had to train neophytes in whole new categories of morality. The Indians responded well but frequently surprised priests by producing a small knotted cord or notched stick to help in a careful recitation of their sins and faults. This was a typical application of the "history" stick or cord known among many nations in northern New Spain. As Indian traditions lapsed, these mnemonic devices disappeared, but it is fascinating to contemplate the effect on American Indians worked by a decree of a church council.

Naturally, no Native Americans were subjected to public chastisement or penance for anything mentioned in confession. Public punishment was restricted to publicly known offenses, as determined by law. The church was always careful to guard the sanctity of the private forum of confession. Private penances, from what we are able to determine, were usually confined to devotional prayers; only in the event of theft or damage were penitents obliged to some kind of restitution.

The church long ago raised anointing the sick to the status of a sacrament. For many years it was known as extreme unction because it was administered only to the dying, *in extremis*. When possible, the dying person was also given the Eucharist, and this was called *viaticum*, because it suggested that the Lord accompany the person on his journey to death. On the frontier death was a constant companion. Christian and Native views of death differed radically; many accommodations took place and persist to this day.

It is commonplace to read in the record that priests rode through the night to visit a dying person who had requested baptism or extreme unction, depending on his status in the church. It was not unusual for a priest to baptize the person and soon after to anoint him. These actions underscored the importance that the church placed on salvation and life after death; no one was left to die alone and unattended—a circumstance that Christians found repugnant. Distance and isolation made the administration of these sacraments difficult and precarious, but this situation never seems to have generated stronger lay participation. Christians attending a dying believer might join in prayers, but there was always that haunting and empty feeling that lingered after death if the priest had not arrived in time to anoint the person or give viaticum.

THE SACRAMENTALS

Clearly, the sacraments had the direct social effect of incorporating the believer in the life of the church. Baptism was initiation; confirmation, a reaffirmation; the Eucharist, a nurturing; penance, a reconciliation; matrimony, an interweaving in sacred procreation; holy orders, special service in the church; and extreme unction, a sacred departure to eternal life. However described, these were all aspects of the life of the church. But the priest also made extensive use of his power to bless a wide variety of things. While some of these benedictions served church purposes, such as the blessing of sacred vessels and vestments, more frequently they were entrées for the church to express its concern for the daily well-being of the faithful.

The eighteenth-century practice of writing clerical manuals gives certain evidence of the sacraments known in the borderlands. Priests had all sorts of special blessings: for new houses and farm implements; for seeds to be planted; for protecting fields from worms, beetles, and birds; for crops to be harvested and farm animals; for weather, drought, and polluted waters; for pilgrims; for eggs, bread, and fruits. In short, there was a blessing for everything—a reflection of the pervasiveness of Christian practices. In many instances these blessings paralleled daily concerns that had been attended by Native shamans, but, more accurately, they demonstrated the clergy's efforts to reach out into the community to sacralize all people, things, and events.

For every social and human condition there was a measured response—a procession, a festival, a litany, a blessing, or a prayer. Everything came within the compass of the church's concern—life, death, drought, flood, plague, public disturbance, and particular thanksgivings. The only limitation on the church's policy was the scarcity of priests to express it—a problem that the faithful resolved by developing intense commitments to private devotions, which became the foundations of "folk Catholicism."

THE INQUISITION IN THE BORDERLANDS

No discussion of Spanish Catholicism is complete without mention of the Holy Office of the Inquisition. This ecclesiastical investigatory and judicial unit of the royal government, established by Ferdinand and Isabella to ferret out Jews and Muslims after the *Reconquista* in Spain, was transferred to the Americas in the late sixteenth century. More often than not, it dealt with oddities of colonial behavior rather than the substance of religious practice. Tribunals were set up in Mexico City, Lima, and Cartagena, so its influence over northern New Spain was diluted by distance and the paucity of colonial residents. From the beginning, the Holy Office was precluded from dealing with Indians, concentrating on suspicious activity among the nonindigenous population. As in peninsular Spain this power was employed by the clergy to redress instances of injustice, especially when churchmen felt that their rights were being violated. In a relatively short time, the Inquisition was embroiled in power struggles between clergy and secular society.

In the case of the borderlands, the Holy Office in the mid 1620s appointed Alonso de Benavides, superior of the Franciscan community, as its first *comisario* in New Mexico. There had been serious altercations between the Franciscan missionaries and Governor Juan de Eulate, and Fray Esteban de Perea had appealed to the Inquisition in Mexico City for help. The historical details are less important than the fundamental relationship between clergy and secular authority. The presence of an agent of the Inquisition in New Mexico brought with it the customary fear and suspicion that always attended this powerful juridical arm of the Crown and the church. In the case of New Mexico, nearly two thousand miles north of the court of the Inquisition, it is no wonder that secular officials trembled when the friars were discontent, because a mere accusation could be enough to send them in shackles for trial in Mexico City.

Another serious problem in addressing the activities of the Inquisition in the borderlands is the unfortunate fact that the ordinary records of church affairs in New Mexico were totally destroyed; but the records of the Inquisition, which were sent to Mexico, have been preserved in some detail. This has led to rather distorted characterizations about the church, based on the impious exaggerations of frustrated clergymen and culturally insensitive theocrats. Sound comparative studies about the church in the borderlands are difficult, given the imbalance in the extant archival record. Slowly, the authority of the Inquisition was eroded during the Bourbon reign of the eighteenth century, and it was abolished in 1813.

Probably one of the most penetrating effects of the Inquisition throughout the frontier was the restriction of Enlightenment ideas because of the Index of Forbidden Books. This was not felt directly because it blocked the importation of "unsuitable" books, which typically came overseas on ships that were routinely inspected for intellectual contraband. Only rarely did books of this nature make their way northward. In the late eighteenth century forbidden books did come more easily into northern New Spain by way of contact with English and French frontiersmen, but the strength of the Holy Office was so depleted that violations against possessing forbidden books were overlooked.

As mentioned above, the Inquisition held no jurisdiction over indigenous peoples. Idolatry, witchcraft, and immorality practiced by Indians were to be punished by missionaries, not by the secular church. This is precisely why such trouble arose in New Mexico, where members of the regular clergy (in this case the Franciscans) were both missionary and Inquisitor: the fine line of jurisdiction had to be drawn by one and the same person. Hence, laypersons were accused of heresy, bigamy, and witchcraft, but at the behest or under the influence of neighboring Indians. Very little can be learned from these instances about the nature of belief among Roman Catholics, but a great deal can be learned about the bizarre thinking of the times.

THE SECULAR CHURCH IN THE BORDERLANDS

Since the vast population of northern New Spain was indigenous, and later mestizo, the presence of the secular clergy was minimal. In the earliest days of colonization, when Spanish mining towns grew up in the silver-rich mountains of the central plateau, the secular clergy soon appeared on the scene to attend to the spiritual needs of the settlers. Again, their number was so limited that the regular clergy, assigned to missions and Indian towns, were prevailed upon for religious services. There was nothing uniform or consistent about such assistance, except for the fact that religious superiors guarded against the practice at all possible times.

Two dioceses were erected for the northern territories, one at Guadalajara and the other at Durango. The bishopric at Guadalajara tended to oversee expansion to the northwest, and at Durango, to the north; the history of the two dioceses is filled with jurisdictional struggles. By the middle of the eighteenth century Durango had established precedence as far as New Mexico. It is noteworthy that no other diocese was erected in the north until 1780, when Antonio de los Reyes, a former Franciscan missionary, was appointed the bishop of Sonora. Arriving at his see in Arizpe, the capital of the Interior Provinces, in 1783, Reyes stayed only briefly before moving his residence to Alamos, the richest silver district in the northwest. His plan for the diocese of Sonora was to erect four new Franciscan *custodias* to oversee both lay and Indian Catholics.

Prior to the erection of Sonora, the bishops of Durango had made tortuous visitations throughout their jurisdiction. It is informative to review the detailed visit of Don Pedro Tamerón y Romeral, who spent three years traveling nearly fourteen thousand miles (22,400 kilometers) visiting his diocese. There were only a handful of colonial towns in his jurisdiction and several hundred Indian pueblos still overseen by missionaries. This once again emphasizes the character of the colonial church throughout the borderlands: it was chiefly indigenous, later heavily mestizo, and thoroughly impregnated by syncretic practices.

As the role of the missions declined in the last decades of the eighteenth century, the burden of religious care often fell on the shoulders of military chaplains. These men were primarily concerned with the spiritual welfare of *presidio* garrisons and their families; their spirituality tended always to be traditional and perfunctory, in contrast to the missionaries' concern for the Indian community and wider evangelization. Hence, the final years of the Spanish Empire in the borderlands witnessed a sharp decline in the rate of conversions and a concern to maintain a status quo among practicing Catholics. Emphasis on Marian devotions and patronage remained strong, as well as growing devotions to Jesus as popularized in those of the Sacred Heart, the Sacred Head, and the Sacred Blood. Looking back on these decades, it seems that a lugubrious sensitivity had infected religious practice, which resonated well with Spanish mysticism and the Native cult of the dead. These sentiments so deeply affected the devotional aspects of Catholicism that they were not effectively countered until well into the twentieth century.

Several popular conceptions of the Catholic church in the borderlands really are not characteristic of the colonial church. One widely known group among the Catholics was the *penitentes,* or brotherhoods, especially in New Mexico, that practiced extreme forms of penance, outlawed even by the local bishops. This form of devotional behavior had its roots in the kinds of paraliturgical events described above in regard to Holy Week; but the growth of these particular sects generally came after the close of the Spanish colonial period, when religious and secular ministry was nearly extinguished. Left to their own insights and instincts, the penitential groups embraced the cultist fads of bloody flagellation, bodily pain, and corporeal exertion. The ascetic aspect centered on the sufferings of Christ and their own sense of rejection and frustration in the aftermath of Spain's collapse as an empire and Mexico's inability to concern itself with a distant frontier.

New Mexico's *penitentes* were also known as *moradas,* or lodges that served as meeting halls and storage rooms for paraliturgical paraphernalia—masks, crosses, *pasos* (processional floats), and vestments. There was a curious admixture of peninsular Spanish and Native American traditions. The members of the brotherhoods were expected to live a strict moral life, including personal conduct and marital faithfulness. Very rigorous examinations preceded entry into the confraternity, and year-round vigilance over members was maintained. Strict adherence to the tenets of the Catholic faith was expected, as was unstinting charity to the brotherhood and the local community. There was every reason for the *penitentes* to express pride in their loyalty to the church through its long years of neglect and isolation. The ascetic aspects of their devotional behavior cannot be taken as a measure of the ascetic practice of the church. In colonial times, monastic discipline was still held in high esteem by both religious and lay persons. Self-flagellation, horsehair scapulars, and body chains were considered salutary instruments to overcome temptation and human weakness in man's struggle with the devil. And without the presence of religious authority and guidance, many of the *penitentes'* practices reached masochistic dimensions. Again, caution is essential here because the goals of the *moradas* were not sadistic liturgies but self-discipline and sacrifice for the good of the community.

The eighteenth century experienced some of the worst exaggerations in ascetic practices known in the history of the church. The extreme division between spirituality and temporality, particularly as evidenced in the influence of Jansenism, permeated the church; and on the frontier some very distorted devotional practices flourished because of the absence of episcopal guidance. To use the *penitentes* to characterize the whole of frontier Roman Catholicism would be an egregious generalization; however, the number and extent of these brotherhoods did emphasize community concern for traditional orthodoxy and intense commitment.

CONCLUSIONS

Roman Catholicism was widely and well established throughout the borderlands before it suffered from the westward movements of Anglo-

American expansion. The myth of a virgin land was true only in the minds of the northern European pioneers who occupied Spanish and Native American lands by conquest. Religious acculturation had already happened among thousands of Native peoples, and the regions were essentially Christian, but of a kind of Christianity that was unacceptable to those Protestant sects which continued to seek special freedoms in the West. The colonial church that they encountered was a weak catechetical church sustained by independent devotion and fierce loyalties. It was a church abandoned, isolated, and bent on survival. It was a dormant church that awaited—and awaits—revitalization. But on awakening, it will find the world changed and many of its still-active traditions anachronistic.

BIBLIOGRAPHY

Ahlborn, Richard E. *The Penitente Moradas of Abiquiú.* Washington, D.C., 1968.

Aspurz, Lazaro de. *Aportación estranjera a las misiones españolas del patronato regio.* Madrid, 1946.

Bayle, Constantino. *Expansión misional de España.* Barcelona, Spain, 1936.

Borges Morán, Pedro. *Misión y civilización en América.* Madrid, 1987.

Bossy, John. *Christianity in the West, 1400–1700.* Oxford and New York, 1985.

Castañeda, Carlos E. *Our Catholic Heritage in Texas, 1519–1936.* 7 vols. Austin, Tex., 1936–1958.

Egaña, Antonio de. *La Teoría del regio vicariato español en Indias.* Rome, 1958.

Espinola, Nicolás de. *Diario quadragésimal y desagravios de Christo para el santo tiempo de la quaresma.* Mexico, 1728.

Farriss, Nancy M. *Crown and Clergy in Colonial Mexico, 1759–1821: The Crisis of Ecclesiastical Privilege.* London, 1968.

Greenleaf, Richard E. "The Mexican Inquisition and the Enlightenment, 1763–1805." *New Mexico Historical Review* 41 (1966):181–196.

Gutiérrez, Ramón A. *When Jesus Came, the Corn Mothers Went Away: Marriage, Sexuality, and Power in New Mexico, 1500–1846.* Stanford, Calif., 1991.

Kessell, John L. *Kiva, Cross, and Crown: The Pecos Indians and New Mexico, 1540–1840.* Washington, D.C., 1979.

Lejarza, Fidel de. *Conquista espiritual del Nuevo Santander.* Madrid, 1947.

Payne, Stanley G. *Spanish Catholicism: An Historical Overview.* Madison, Wis., 1984.

Pérez de Ríbas, Andrés. *Historia de los triunfos de nuestra santa fe entre gentes las mas bárbaras y fieras del Nuevo Orbe conseguidos por los soldados de la milicia de la Compañía de Jesús en las misiones de la Provincia de Nueva España.* Madrid, 1645; repr. 1944.

Polzer, Charles W. *Rules and Precepts of the Jesuit Missions of Northwestern New Spain.* Tucson, Ariz., 1976.

Recopilación de leyes de los reinos de las Indias. 1681. Reprint. 4 vols. Madrid, 1973.

Ricard, Robert. *The Spiritual Conquest of Mexico: An Essay on the Aposolate and Evangelizing Methods of the Mendicant Orders in New Spain, 1523–1572.* Translated by Lesley Byrd Simpson. Berkeley and Los Angeles, 1966.

Ripalda, Gerónimo de. *Catecismo mexicano.* Mexico, 1758.

Shiels, W. Eugene. *King and Church: The Rise and Fall of the Patronato Real.* Chicago, 1961.

Silva Antonio da. *Trent's Impact on the Portuguese Patronage Missions.* Translated by Joaquim da Silva Godinho. Lisbon, 1969.

Simmons, Marc. *Witchcraft in the Southwest: Spanish and Indian Supernaturalism on the Rio Grande.* Flagstaff, Ariz., 1974.

Tamarón y Romeral, Pedro. *Viajes pastorales y descripción de la diócesis de Nueva Vizcaya.* Annotated by Mario Hernández y Sánchez-Barba. In *Viajes por Norteamérica.* Madrid, 1958.

Venegas, Miguel. *Manual de Párrocos.* Mexico City, 1857.

Weigle, Marta. *Brothers of Light, Brothers of Blood: The Penitentes of the Southwest.* Albuquerque, N.M., 1976.

Wroth, William. *Images of Penance, Images of Mercy: Southwestern Santos in the Late Nineteenth Century.* Norman, Okla., 1991.

Charles W. Polzer

SEE ALSO **Church and State; Higher Education; Mission Communties;** and **Schools and Schooling.**

THE FRENCH COLONIES

ALL RESIDENTS OF New France of European origin publicly professed to be Christians. Given the regional provenance of the ships' captains and crew members, French Protestants (Huguenots) were quite active in sixteenth-century and early-seventeenth-century French colonial enterprises. A desire to find a religious haven partially motivated their involvement in abortive colonization schemes in Canada (1534), Brazil (1555), and Florida (1562). Later, they took an active role in the fishing and fur-trading expeditions in Acadia (present-day Nova Scotia and New Brunswick) and along the Saint Lawrence. These were not times of religious tolerance. Just as the exercise of Roman Catholicism was banned in all British continental colonies—except for a short time in Maryland during the mid seventeenth century—all religions except that of Rome were excluded from New France. The charter granted to the Compagnie des Cent-Associés (Company of One Hundred Associates, 1627) forbade its members "to carry over [to North America] any foreigner . . . other than natural-born French subjects, professing the Catholic religion." After that date, a Huguenot presence in the colony was not tolerated except for some settlers who were part of the great immigration waves of the 1650s and 1660s, and again in the eighteenth century, when the authorities in New France relaxed their opposition in special cases. Thus, New France was a Catholic colony throughout the seventeenth and eighteenth centuries until the end of the French regime in 1763.

In New France, the European community consisted of a single body of lay Catholic men and women who were held together, under God's guidance, by the sacraments administered by the clergy. The latter comprised one bishop, a number of secular priests, and the male and female members of the regular orders. The male members of the regular orders were ordained priests who had also pledged themselves to some special vows. In principle, the same description applied in France. In fact, the relationship between church and state, the role of the church within the state, and the state's obligations toward its Catholic population was the same on both sides of the Atlantic Ocean.

THE INDIANS AS PART OF THE CATHOLIC COMMUNITY

In the early days of French expansion there was, however, one major difference between France and New France. The small Catholic community of New France lived side by side with the Indian nations. Although the Indians vastly outnumbered the French, it was believed that the Indians could become part of the overall Catholic community. A few in fact did. At least until the 1650s, the Catholic church regarded its role in the New World as proselytizing to the Indians. The first clergyman who attempted to convert the Indians was the secular priest Jessé Fléché, who visited Port Royal, Nova Scotia, in 1610. Fléché was an exception, as were the few secular priests who followed him (nineteen between 1634 and 1663), because until the 1650s missionary work in Canada and in Acadia was left in the hands of male and female regular orders. At times they were assisted by devout members of the laity.

The Jesuits were in Acadia from 1611 to 1613 and in Canada from 1625 to 1629 and from 1633 to 1800. In Quebec, they had been preceded by the Recollets (1615–1629, 1670–1849). The latter were also active in Acadia (1619–1624, 1630–1634). In 1632 the Capuchins joined the Recollets in Acadia. They left the colony in 1655 and returned in the late eighteenth century (1785–1827). Both the Franciscans—of which the Recollets and Capuchins were a branch—and the Jesuits had had a long experience of missionary work around the world, including Spanish and Portuguese America. New France was regarded as fertile ground for Christianizing. The clergy would also minister to the spiritual needs of the Europeans whenever required, but they considered their main duty to be the conversion of the Indian "multitudes," not the welfare of the French settlers who still numbered fewer than twenty-five hundred.

We know very little about the experience of the Capuchins with the Indians of Acadia. They were active among the Micmac and in 1644 were instrumental in bringing Madame de Brice to Port Royal, where she organized a school for Indian boys and girls. The Capuchin presence was seriously hampered by rivalries within the order both in Acadia and in France, and by the order's role in the civil war. Although the Capuchins had residences in Port Royal, Saint-Jean, Pentagoüet, La Hève, Miscou, and Canseau, and two confrères were for a time with the Indians of present-day Maine, their overall success with the Indians was apparently very limited.

As for the Recollets, early experience among the Huron and the Montagnais had convinced them that the Indians had first to be "civilized," made to adopt a European way of life, and then converted. The Indians were encouraged to abandon their nomadic habits, to live close to European villages, and to send their children to French schools. The Recollets enjoyed even less success than the Capuchins. In the twelve years between 1615 and 1627 they baptized only fifty-four Indians, of whom thirty-nine were moribund and two recanted.

Contrary to efforts by the Capuchins and the Recollets, the Jesuit attempt at converting the Indians met with relative success. The Jesuits, who entered Huronia in 1634, were tolerated by the Huron, their presence linked by the natives to the politics of the fur trade and to a military alliance. The Jesuits learned Indian languages and customs and won the respect of the Indians while managing to survive in a hostile physical and human environment. At the same time, they taught the Indians not only the theoretical tenets of the Catholic faith, but also how to adapt their daily lives to Christian commandments. As was the case with other missionary orders, the Jesuits generally tried to exercise patience and compromise whenever possible, realizing that a rigid approach to local customs would lead nowhere. Yet they remained adamant in administering sacraments to Indians only on point of death, for fear of abjuration, or after the Indians had led an almost saintly life over a period of months and even years.

Between 1634 and 1650 some ten thousand Huron were baptized and became part of the North American Catholic community. Because many died soon after baptism, it is difficult to evaluate the number of converts at any given time. The number of baptisms and conversions grew rapidly after 1647. By then Huron society was disintegrating from within, due to the profound division between the converted and unconverted, and from without, owing to ongoing Iroquois assaults. By 1650 the Huron were destroyed as a nation by the Iroquois, and the converted who had survived left Huronia to live close to the French settlements. Although these Native converts were now outcasts from Native society and marginal to the French one, they still had become part of a larger Catholic community.

The involvement of both the laity and the female regular orders in missionary work was a typical feature of the early phase of New France's Catholicism. Many laymen and laywomen in France regarded it as their duty to assist financially the missionary endeavors in Canada and Acadia. In fact, the survival of the colony in the 1630s and 1640s owes much to their donations. Some of them, such as Madame de Brice, Marie-Madeleine de Chauvigny de La Peltrie, and Paul de Chomedey de Maisonneuve, traveled to New France. Maisonneuve was the first governor of Ville-Marie (present-day Montreal), whose establishment in 1642 was conceived for purely missionary motives by French laymen belonging to the Compagnie du Saint-Sacrement and the Société de Notre Dame de Montréal. Voluntary lay assistants, known as *donnés*, performed useful, mundane tasks for the Jesuits (ranging from hunting to teaching). Their female counterparts, the *données*, worked in hospitals and hospices.

As for the female regular orders—the Ursulines, the Augustines Hospitalières de la Miséricorde de Jésus (from 1639), and the Religieuses Hospitalières de Saint-Joseph (from 1659)—were allowed to establish de facto uncloistered communities in New France on account of the crucial social and educational tasks they performed. Like their male counterparts, the Ursulines went to Canada to assist in the conversion of the Indians. When it became evident that their efforts were not meeting with success they debated whether to return to France, but in the end they decided to stay on and devote themselves to the French community. As in France, members of the female regular orders took care of the education of young boys and girls and gave assistance to the sick, the poor, and the derelict. The Soeurs de la Congrégation (Filles Séculières de la Congrégation de Notre-Dame, established 1658), the Frères Hospitalières de la Croix et de Saint-Joseph (a male community, 1688–1747), and the Soeurs Grises (established 1737), were secular communities performing similar tasks. In 1727 the Ursulines established a separate community in New Orleans to teach and care for the sick.

The 1650s were a major turning point in the history of the Catholic community of New France. Huronia had ceased to exist, institutions meant for the Indians, such as schools and hospitals, had failed to attract them, and voluntary metropolitan support from devout circles was beginning to fade. Furthermore, in 1650 for the first time the French in the Saint Lawrence Valley were more numerous than the Indians. Indian missions continued to exist and, in a few cases, to thrive, as some missionaries continued to carry on their apostolic duties among the Indians well into the twentieth century. But most of the human and financial resources of the Catholic church were used for the non-native community. To this day, in fact, the aboriginal Catholic community and the community of European origin remain distinct.

The practice of intermarriage followed a trend that reflected the development of the overall relations between the two ethnic groups. In the early days, miscegenation was encouraged, as such unions were deemed to favor Indian cultural and religious adaptation to European ways and to be a way to increase the colony's population. Because marriages were permitted only between Catholics, Indians were brought into the faith. In practice, not many such marriages took place. According to Canadian historian Cornelius J. Jaenen, only seventeen intermarriages took place, although many Indian women simply chose to cohabit with the Europeans, between 1644 and 1700. Early expectations on the part of the French authorities later gave way to disillusionment and prejudice against such unions, since the offspring, in the eyes of the Crown officials, manifested the worst features of both races. It is more likely that these children, the founders of the Métis nation, demonstrated an independent spirit not to the liking of French officialdom.

Mixed unions were never a major factor in Canada. Conversely, the frontier conditions of the Illinois and the lower Louisiana settlements, where French women were scarce and relations with the Indians an everyday occurrence, made intermarriage very common. For example, according to the historian Charles Edwards O'Neill, the available records for Kaskaskia and Fort de Chartres for the years 1695–1730 show an average of one French-Indian legal marriage for every unmixed union. In the eighteenth century, French authorities tried to stop these unions many times, because they feared that such inhabitants would leave settlements like Mobile to live in the Indian villages of the interior. The clergy, however, recognized that such unions did exist and that to refuse the marriage sacrament would simply favor concubinage and profligacy. In Louisiana, marriages between the Indians and the French were soon outnumbered by liaisons between the French and the black slaves, manumitted or not. In Canada after the French regime, the ecclesiastical authorities were faced with the great practical and doctrinal problems created by marriages between Catholics and Protestants. In both cases, the ecclesiastical authorities sought to adapt to the new environment.

CHURCH ORGANIZATION

Catholic countries were divided into a number of dioceses, which were in turn subdivided into parishes. Spiritual jurisdiction emanated from the bishop (the head of the diocese) downward to the curé (parish priest), who was in direct contact with the laity. Theoretically, the appointment of a bishop was the pope's decision. In practice, the French king had gained over the years the power to select candidates to the bishoprics, who the pope then had to appoint, according to the so-called Gallican liberties. During the reign of Louis XIV (r. 1643–1715), these powers over the church were equal to those that Henry VIII (r. 1509–1547), king of England, sought and obtained only at the price of schism with Rome. Still, both the bishop and the parish priest would have in their own territory members of regular orders whom they could control only partially as, theoretically, the latter were exempted from any territorial jurisdiction and answered directly to the pope.

Prior to 1658 the above system did not apply in New France. Missionaries were being sent to the colonies to convert the Indians, not to export the French church to the New World. Furthermore, the Capuchins, the Recollets, and the Jesuits fell under the newly founded Sacred Congregation "de Propaganda Fide" (1622), the Holy See's agency responsible for missionary activity. The Capuchins and the Recollets did not oppose the Propaganda's overall jurisdiction and entertained good relations with the Roman cardinals. Conversely, the Jesuits struggled and successfully maintained a sort of operative independence from the Propaganda.

Spiritual jurisdiction over the population at large was, in fact, very unclear. For example, the churches in Quebec, Trois-Rivières, and Montreal were regarded by the people as parish churches, and there the sacraments of baptism, Communion, and matrimony were administered by whomever was available, mostly by the Jesuits. (In 1657 the Jesuits of Montreal were replaced by the Priests of the Society of Saint Sulpice, who were detached from their Paris seminary and established their own seminary in Montreal.) But parish churches they were not, as there was no bishop in the colony who could define their respective boundaries and appoint or recall their parish priest. Furthermore, for almost two decades François de Harlay de Champvallon, the archbishop of Rouen, one of the riverine towns of France having close links with French America, tried to impose his own jurisdiction over New France as if Canada were a simple extension of metropolitan France. In the end, Champvallon's attempt was stalled by the Jesuits, who feared for their independence; by the Holy See, which did not want an extension overseas of the Gallican church; and by the first bishop of Quebec, François de Laval (1623–1708).

Laval's appointment became a complicated matter. Owing to bureaucratic slowness and overall difficulties in Rome's foreign policy, Laval was first made vicar apostolic in Canada (1658) with episcopal powers as bishop of Petraea *in partibus infidelium* (a formula recently devised for Portuguese Asia, whereby the candidate was granted full spiritual powers as bishop but no territorial jurisdiction). Only much later, in 1674, was Laval appointed bishop of Quebec. The need for a bishop had long been felt in New France, as there were certain sacraments a simple priest could not administer. For example, only a bishop could confirm the faithful and ordain new priests. This meant that, unless a bishop were appointed, French colonists would have to travel to France to be confirmed and ordained. Furthermore, a proper parish system had to be put in place and education for prospective priests be provided in the colony.

Laval arrived in Canada in 1659 and canonically established the first parish church (Notre-Dame-de-Québec, 1664). By 1724 thirty-nine more parishes were erected, adding up to about one hundred in Canada by the end of the French regime. In 1663 Laval established the Séminaire de Quebec, to which the Petit Séminaire was attached in 1668. During the French regime, it accepted 843 students, of whom 118 were eventually ordained. Conversely, Louisiana produced only one priest, Étienne Viel, who was ordained in France.

Laval made the Quebec seminary into an original institution from which parish priests were drawn and to which they could be recalled upon the bishop's orders. The seminary centralized and administered the church's revenues, including the tithe paid by the residents of Canada toward the cost of maintaining their parish priest. Consequently, the seminary took charge of all material needs of Canadian priests, such as subsistence, lodging, and travel expenses. The seminary was the keystone of Laval's church. The underlying concept was that the priests' primary allegiance was to the seminary rather than to their own parishes; thus they would regard themselves not as individual priests, but as members of a real community. This system differed greatly from the Gallican tradition, and toward the end of the seventeenth century the system in New France was modified by Jean-Baptiste de La Croix de Chevrières de Saint-Vallier, who succeeded Laval as bishop in 1688. However, most original features were retained. For example, in spite of the Crown's efforts to the contrary, the bishop kept his right to recall all parish priests at his will. By and large, the ecclesiastical structure that Laval put in place during his mandate was not substantially altered by the bishops who followed him during the French regime. From Saint-Vallier's mandate (1688–1727) onward it would have been difficult to distinguish the diocese of Quebec from a diocese in France.

Contrary to what was commonly believed in Protestant circles, New France was not overpopulated by priests, although the ratio of priests to the overall population was higher in the seventeenth century than in the eighteenth century and was therefore more influential. In 1640 there were 64 families in New France served by 29 Jesuits whose primary duty was to the Indians. Toward the end of the French regime in 1759 there was one priest for every 350 faithful. Comparisons are difficult to make, but one may note that in Rome, until 1740, there was one priest for nearly every fifteen persons; in lower Canada in 1790 the ratio had dropped to one to 1,400; while in Ireland in 1800 each parish priest was responsible for an average of 2,676 parishioners. Numbers, however, tell only part of the story. The point is that in European Catholic countries complaints were often heard about the disproportionate number and power of the clergy within society. Conversely, in New France both the civil authorities and the population at large always considered the number of available priests insufficient for the many tasks—spiritual, educational, and social—that they needed to perform. It must also be noted that, especially in the second half of the seventeenth century, a few of the secular priests could not cope with the special problems posed by New France, such as the climate and the distances they needed to travel, and they asked to be recalled to France. This, in turn, made the task of the remaining priests ever more difficult, as some had to serve several parishes. That most of them did remain is a measure of their dedication.

In moving west along the Great Lakes and south along the Ohio and Mississippi rivers toward the vast region of Louisiana, the Catholic church exported itself to the new lands made available by French expansion into the interior of the continent. Biloxi, Mobile, and New Orleans were established respectively in 1699, 1702, and 1718. The bishop of Quebec retained spiritual control over French Catholics wherever they might be, including the Indians converted by the French. Distance and difficulties in communication, besides the growing population in certain areas, made it necessary for the bishop to appoint priests as his vicars general in Quebec, Montreal, Trois-Rivières, Michilimackinac, Acadia, New Orleans, and Paris. They acted as his local representatives. As simple priests, however, the vicars general enjoyed limited spiritual powers. They could not, for example, confirm the faithful or ordain new priests.

Members of the regular orders, including some Montreal Sulpicians and some priests of the Quebec seminary, continued to perform their missionary duties with the Indians, who were numerous, especially in the midwestern region of the continent. In spite of distances, the bishop retained final control. In Louisiana, Jesu-its, Capuchins (who arrived in 1721), and Quebec seminary priests were constantly at odds. Their only recourse was to refer complaints to their bishop and await his decision, which at best was received a year later. Louisiana was the only region under their jurisdiction that Quebec bishops never visited. In eighteenth-century Acadia members of the Congregation of the Holy Ghost (Spiritans) and of the Brothers Hospitallers of Saint John of God were also active, the former as missionaries to the Micmac and the Abenaki (1735–1762), the latter as chaplains at Louisbourg (1716–1758). In 1713 peninsular Acadia (present-day Nova Scotia) was acquired by the British Crown. With the grudging compliance of the British government, Acadians were allowed to continue the exercise of their religion. In practice, local priests were left under the jurisdiction of the bishop of Quebec.

Nearly all members of the male regular orders were French-born, but in contrast by 1760 seventeen of the twenty-four Recollets were Canadian-born. The secular clergy, except for the Sulpicians, soon became largely Canadian. By 1760, four-fifths of the seventy-three parish priests were born in Canada. The bishops, however, were all born in the Old World. Likewise, after their initial establishment, most of the members of the female regular orders were drawn from among Canadian families.

STANDARDS OF THE CLERGY

The educational, moral, and economic standards of the clergy of New France were much higher than those of their counterparts in France. Jesuits and Sulpicians were exceptionally well-educated and highly motivated, and the members of the secular clergy were specially selected by the directors of the Séminaire des Missions-Étrangères in Paris, an institution with formal links to the Séminaire de Quebec. The standards imposed by the Quebec seminary upon its students were also quite demanding, although they were somewhat relaxed after the overly rigorous early years, when 135 out of the first 200 students dropped out.

As for moral standards, there is little or no evidence of misbehavior on the part of the clergy, and certainly the bishops led exemplary lives.

Yet it has to be said that the bishop Louis-François Duplessis de Mornay never went to Quebec, Laval and Saint-Vallier respectively spent twelve and seventeen years in Europe during their mandate at Quebec, and Pierre-Herman Dosquet spent only one year out of six in Canada. Comparisons can only be made with the contemporary clergy of European Catholic countries and with the attitude of the same clergy during the subsequent British regime. European clerical standards were known to be very low, and instances of moral shortcomings were common knowledge in France as well as, for example, in Ireland. Still, higher standards were required in the whole of North America, not only in New France. For example, in 1788 the bishop of Baltimore, John Carroll, remarked that in his diocese "[s]obriety in drink is expected from clergymen to a great degree," and that what "in many parts of Europe would be esteemed no more than a cheerful and allowable enjoyment" would be regarded in that colony "as an unbecoming excess." Under the British regime in Canada, instances of immoderate drinking and sexual impropriety, together with an excessive preoccupation with money, abounded. Yet they must be ascribed to the new English- and Gaelic-speaking clergy of Irish origin who were active in the Maritimes, not to the old Francophone clergy of Quebec, who did not have instances of various abuses. Among the latter (responsible for a much larger population), in the years 1760–1830 only twenty drunkards, thirty "libertins," five illicit births, and thirty interventions of the bishop on the issue of relations between the priests and their female servants came to light.

The financial standing of the church in New France was much in line with the general trend in society. The church was neither rich nor poor—the immense wealth of some bishops and cardinals in France and the extreme poverty of some rural parish priests was not the rule in New France. Canadian bishops enjoyed an income of some ten thousand livres a year but used most of it in performing their functions. Furthermore, Laval and Saint-Vallier used a great deal of their own personal patrimony to provide for the needs of the colonial church. The income of parish priests varied, as their revenues came in part from their own parishioners, in part from the bishop himself. This meant that a parish priest in an urban area or in a very productive seigneury would earn more than his counterpart who lived in a poor or underpopulated region. The latter, however, would be compensated by a larger share of the Crown's special funds distributed through the bishop. By and large, in the eighteenth century parish priests would not be expected to live on less than one thousand livres a year. In the same period, in France, annual incomes varied from seven hundred to three thousand livres, the former being considered a very low figure.

In France the total income of most parish priests derived from the revenues of tithes and beneficed lands, fees collected through the performing of their sacred functions (weddings, funerals, masses, the selling of pews, donations and gifts) and civil functions (the keeping and issuing of official records), augmented by special privileges such as free lodging. Regular and secular communities enjoyed extra revenues as they were able to own and manage large properties collectively. In Canada a similar situation applied, as the bishop, the Sulpicians, and the Jesuits had been granted large and profitable stretches of land under the seigneurial system. The Sulpicians and the Jesuits also received large sums from their own mother houses in France. As for benefices, the bishop enjoyed the revenues of some French abbeys, although the actual figures have never been properly calculated and may not have amounted to much. In Louisiana, tithes were not collected, and the clergy was almost entirely financed by the Crown.

The French Crown had recognized the church's role in society by endowing it with land and substantial sums of money variously allocated. The French system was exported to New France. By the end of the French regime, the church in Canada held slightly over 25 percent of the conceded land, and about 34 percent of the population lived on it. In early New France the Jesuits had been responsible for keeping the colony alive, and by doing so their political power had been recognized even by civil authorities. Although after 1663 the Crown fully regained its control over the church, the amount of money it continued to grant the Quebec church showed that the church performed its task to the Crown's satisfaction. Toward the end of the seventeenth century, about eight thousand livres a year went toward the stipends of parish priests, but special projects, such as the building of a church or of the episcopal palace, were often financed by the Crown. In the eighteenth century, Crown subsidies amounted to somewhere between 30 or 40 percent of the entire church revenue.

RELIGIOUS PRACTICE

The Catholics of New France believed they could be saved from an eternity in Hell and be given access to Heaven. They were expected to pray at various times during the day; to visit their church periodically; to abstain from eating meat at appropriate times during the year; never to be avaricious, to drink to excess, to blaspheme, or to lead an irregular sexual life; to behave properly toward their neighbors and their relatives; and to forgive their enemies. Still, it was expected that most people, although well aware of what God demanded of them, would regularly fall into sin and then be pardoned through confession, penance, and Communion.

Catholics believed that a saintly life could be led only by a handful of men and women—not necessarily only members of the clergy—and that worldly success would neither prove nor guarantee salvation. Indeed, they acknowledged that the poor and the lowly were more likely to be welcomed in Heaven than the wealthy and the powerful. Similarly, they acknowledged that a personal dialogue with God, mainly through prayer and a variety of rituals, such as making the sign of the cross, would help them achieve salvation. But at the same time they admitted that salvation was not possible without the personal intervention of the ordained clergy. The clergy could assist laymen and laywomen throughout their lives, allow them to become members of the church through baptism and soldiers of Christ through confirmation, to be absolved from their sins through confession and penance, to receive God through Communion, to procreate in matrimony, and to be prepared to meet their Maker with the last rites.

To what extent were these general expectations reflected in New France's society? The general framework outlined above applied not only to Catholics in New France, but also to all Catholics throughout the world. Within this framework, however, there was ample room for variations based on the historical period, the social standing and age of the individual, and the location of the community. In the case of France and New France, some variations did occur.

In France the determined efforts of the Catholic Counter-Reformation had converted thousands of Huguenots to Catholicism. This conversion brought with it the problem of instruction in the tenets of Catholicism. By the same token, the Catholic church also recognized the low level of religious instruction and practice among the French peasantry; like the "savages" of North America, they needed education in religion. By and large, in New France these problems did not exist because the settlers were aware of their duties as Catholics. Nevertheless, New France's society went through a number of different stages that are easy to discern.

Until the mid 1630s, Canadian society consisted of a small community whose members were praised by the Jesuits for their religious piety and observance. Around 1634, however, some problems became evident. The Jesuits had envisaged a system of reservations that would protect the Indians from various influences of the French community that were not in keeping with Catholic teaching. The Jesuits especially feared the examples offered by fur traders, who were keen to adopt the liberal sexual customs of the Indians. Despite these moral improprieties, the fur traders remained practicing Catholics. In the eighteenth century, before setting off on western expeditions in which few opportunities would exist for meeting a priest, the fur traders would stop at Saint-Anne-de-Bellevue, the most westerly church in the colony, where they would be absolved from their sins through confession and Communion and made ready for a trip from which some might not return.

The surviving sources, which provide a picture of the moral standard of Canadian colonial society before 1663, show a society where blasphemy, drunkenness, illicit sex, and poor religious observance did not exist to a large degree. Canadian historian Marcel Trudel lists sixty recorded instances of criminal behavior in the years 1636–1663, most of which concerned illicit sex, drunkenness, and blasphemy. After 1663 when the royal government began, the increase in the number of immigrants (many of whom were indentured servants and soldiers) and the lessened role of the church (the ratio between clergy and faithful having markedly decreased) brought a general increase in criminal behavior.

The eighteenth century witnessed an even further decline in moral standards, mirroring a trend well known in European society at the same time. No real anticlericalism was evident in Canada, yet both religious and civil authorities complained about the growing lack of respect for the church and the clergy. The absence of important urban centers, which given the large number of people are more conducive to crime, and the total absence of French immigration limited this negative tendency in Acadia. Conversely, Louisiana, where the number of residents never exceeded five thousand during the French regime, was notorious for the deep immorality and disorderly behavior of its population. At times in Canada edicts were posted outside churches suggesting that women dress modestly and ordering men not to speak loudly, squabble among themselves, or walk out at the beginning of the sermon. Bishops petitioned Rome so that the number of feast days, some forty until 1744, be reduced or celebrated on Sundays, as such days created opportunities for brawls, intoxication, and excesses of all sorts, as did participation in ceremonies such as baptisms and weddings. Even so, one must note the central importance of religion and of the Catholic church in the life of all residents of New France.

THE INFLUENCE OF RELIGIOUS OBSERVANCE

All year long, and throughout any given day, the residents of New France were reminded of their duties toward God. The sound of the church bells, the ornate carved woodwork of the church interiors, the smell of incense, the gold and silver accoutrements of the altar, the processions, the clerical garb, the priest's sermon from the pulpit, the Roman liturgy, the Latin language used in most rituals, the Gregorian singing of the choir, the music of the organ, the stations of the cross that visualized Christ's agony—all this was a constant appeal to the faithful's senses

and a physical reminder of the afterlife. Naturally enough, the inhabitants of distant rural areas enjoyed fewer opportunities to partake in the life of the church and to be reminded of God's presence on Earth. In fact, in the seventeenth century Governor General Louis de Buade de Frontenac complained that a number of Canadians were only able to hear mass, confess, and take Communion a few times during the year.

The relationship between the clergy and the laity was not limited to church attendance. The influence of the Catholic church was much more pervasive and not limited just to the spiritual domain. Baptismal, marriage, and death certificates, for example, were issued by the clergy on behalf of the Crown and had to be used and shown on a variety of occasions during one's lifetime. Those aspiring to high office under the Crown, such as a judge, had to provide a certificate from the clergy declaring their good moral character. Attendance at mass and communion was compulsory at least once a year, usually around Easter Sunday, and both were certified by the parish priest. Priests acted as royal notaries in remote rural parishes. Civil authorities used mass and other religious gatherings to make announcements and read decrees. Banns announcing a forthcoming marriage were published and read aloud to the faithful on three successive Sundays in order to ensure that there were no known impediments, such as a former marriage in France. Dispensations from other impediments (usually related to young age or kinship) were granted by the Holy See via the bishop and the parish priest. Instruction was invariably given by the clergy and members of the various orders. In entering hospitals and almshouses, the unfortunate individual expected to be assisted, for the sake of his or her body and soul, by members of the church. Furthermore, through inner knowledge gained through confession, and because of their generally superior education, priests played a major role in society, being called upon to find spouses for parishioners, reconcile broken marriages, sedate personal quarrels, quench social rebellions, or simply poll the community's attitudes.

Church ceremonies served to remind colonists that just as they were expected to keep and act according to their social status in civil society, they were also expected to adhere to the hierarchical framework of the church. The faithful could not simply march in a procession in any row they liked or sit anywhere they pleased during mass. For example, major squabbles at Notre-Dame-de-Québec between church wardens (*marguilliers*) and the nobility over which group should come first obliged Laval to suspend all processions, illustrating the importance attributed to the honor of marching nearest to the officiating priest. Similarly, the pews closer to the altar were reserved for prominent members of the community and their families. These pews were purchased and the contract was inherited. The seigneur and his family received Communion and incense first, their names were mentioned in the officiating priest's prayers, and they were entitled to inhumation in the church itself, under their own pews—vertically in subsequent generations. Seigneurs were among the few who were granted such honors, which emphasized their high social standing and enabled them to look down on the rest of the faithful as people of lesser importance. By accepting this system, the habitants recognized their lower status in society.

On matters of sin and salvation, French colonists were dependent on the clergy and had to comply with their commands. Yet ordinary parishioners recognized that certain matters fell outside of the spiritual domain, such as the payment of the tithe and the selling of alcohol to Indians, and for these facets of life Canadians showed surprising independence. When Laval arrived in Canada in 1659, he sought to finance the church through the payment of dues by the habitants, according to the custom of northern France; that is, one-thirteenth of the yearly fruits of human labor and general production. Yet Canadians complained that the spiritual services they enjoyed were not worth that amount, and they simply refused to pay it. Moreover, Frontenac supported them. After a few years of painful negotiations, the amount collected by the parish church was fixed at one-twenty-sixth per year, and even that amount was limited to wheat, oats, and peas, all of which could be stored. The issue was hardly solved. In 1717 Saint-Vallier threatened to refuse absolution to those who denied the church what it claimed as its due, but some parishioners continued to refuse payment of their tithes, or they gave the church the worst portion of their crops.

The nefarious effect of alcohol on the Indian population was common knowledge among Canadians. In fact, the second criminal offense to be punished in the colony was for intoxicating Indians (1636). Laval and his successors fought hard to prohibit the sale of alcohol, but to no avail. Although it was eventually forbidden to carry alcohol to Indian villages, alcohol could be sold freely in colonial villages or to Indians whose dwellings fell outside those lands claimed by France. From Laval's time onward, bishops tried to cope with the problem of alcohol by excommunicating or denying absolution to those who contributed to the drunkenness of Indians. Pierre Aigron, a seaman who furnished liquor to the Indians and was known as Lamothe, was twice excommunicated by Laval (1660, 1661), but he was also absolved on both occasions after submitting to public penitence. The denial of absolution was a matter of grave concern, for it meant that the sinner would be destined to eternal damnation. As with the case of a refusal to pay tithes, however, no such threats could discourage some Canadians from pursuing immoral and illegal activity. Indeed, some royal officials connived in it. In fact, Frontenac maintained in a dispatch to Louis XIV that insobriety was no more prevalent among the Indians than it was among the English and Dutch.

Canadians also showed some degree of independence from the clergy through a church institution known as the *fabrique*, a body elected by parish members and one that also existed in France. The *fabrique* consisted of a small group of laymen, known as *marguilliers*, who were chosen to manage the ecclesiastical goods of a church—the church itself, the presbytery, and the cemetery. They were also responsible for overseeing the church's financial affairs, with the exception of the tithe, which was collected directly by the parish priest.

Because the members of the *fabrique* were usually chosen through elections from which no male parishioners were excluded, this unique French colonial representative body has often been compared to the American trusteeship system. Still, the democratic nature of this institution should not be overemphasized. *Marguilliers* were invariably elected from among the prominent habitants, who served without pay and considered such service an honor, and they limited themselves to ecclesiastical matters and had no official say in the selection of their parish priest. In sum, such an institution never undermined the hierarchical structure of civil society. However, at times parish priests themselves successfully enlisted the *fabrique's* support to voice their opposition to their bishop. In comparing North American trustees with French colonial *marguilliers* differences, rather than similarities, should be stressed. In Nova Scotia, New Brunswick, and the United States the legal incorporation of churches required that they be managed by a body of trustees. In the United States, the trustees could appoint their parish priest, stop his salary at any time, and dismiss him at will, irrespective of the bishop's intervention. The annual choice of trustees became a regular occasion for an electoral campaign, fought in the same vein, and often with the same violence, as political campaigns. Nothing of that sort ever occurred in New France.

CONCLUSION

Prior to the mid 1650s, the emphasis on missionary work among the Indians in New France often paralleled the church's activities in France, where Catholic missionaries worked among Huguenots or a peasantry that was reputed to be virtually pagan. After the mid 1650s, the organization of the French colonial church, its doctrine, and the religious observance and practice of the faithful continued to follow the model of France. However, variations did occur, and this explains some of the unique elements found in the Canadian church. (Acadia and Louisiana, for various reasons, proved to be different from Canada proper.) Laval's Quebec seminary, the center of a secular community of priests, was distinctly Canadian, and the bishop's power to recall parish priests also shows the tightened structure of the Canadian church. Comparatively speaking, the economic standards of the Canadian church were more equitable. As for the levels to which the commandments of the Catholic religion really influenced and shaped the everyday lives of the clergy and of the faithful, the educational and moral standards of the Canadian church were far superior to those of the French church. The economic standards of the Canadian church were also relatively more equitable.

BIBLIOGRAPHY

Brasseaux, Carl. "The Moral Climate of French Louisiana." *Louisiana History* 27, no. 1 (1986):27–41.

Campeau, Lucien, S. J., ed. *Monumenta Novae Franciae.* 5 vols. Rome, Quebec, and Montreal, 1967.

Eccles, W. J. "The Role of the Church in New France." In his *Essays on New France.* Toronto, Ontario, 1987.

Jaenen, Cornelius J. *The Role of the Church in New France.* Toronto, Ontario, 1976.

Lemieux, Lucien. *Les XVIIIe et XIXe siècles: Les années difficiles (1760–1839).* Vol. 2 of *Histoire du catholicisme québécois,* edited by Nive Voisine. Montreal, 1989.

O'Neill, Charles Edwards. *Church and State in French Colonial Louisiana: Policy and Politics to 1732.* New Haven and London, 1966.

Thériault, Michel. *The Institutes of Consecrated Life in Canada from the Beginning of New France up to the Present: Historical Notes and References.* Ottawa, 1980.

Trudel, Marcel. *Histoire de la Nouvelle France.* 3 vols. Montreal, 1963–1983. See especially vol. 2, *Le comptoir, 1604–1627,* and vol. 3, *La seigneurie des Cent-Associés, 1627–1663.*

———. *Initiation à la Nouvelle-France: Histoire et institutions.* Montreal and Toronto, 1968.

Luca Codignola

See also **Church and State; the French Settlements; Higher Education; Indian-Colonist Contact; Mission Communities; and Theories of Education.**

THE BRITISH AND DUTCH COLONIES

MARYLAND

THE FIRST SUBSTANTIAL PRESENCE of Roman Catholics in English America began with the arrival on 25 March 1634 in the Potomac River of the tiny ships *Ark* and *Dove,* carrying the founders of Lord Baltimore's colony of Maryland.

The Maryland colony was the dream of George Calvert, Lord Baltimore, onetime secretary of state to King James I. Calvert converted to Roman Catholicism sometime around 1624 and was for that reason excluded from further government service. In 1621 Calvert had sent out a colony to the Avalon peninsula of Newfoundland. No oath affirming the king's supremacy over the church was demanded, and the Avalon charter provided only that "no interpretation be admitted thereof whereby God's holy and true Christian religion, or the allegiance due to us, our heirs and successors may in any thing suffer any prejudice or diminution"

John Courtney Murray, the twentieth-century Roman Catholic church-state theorist, complained of "the somewhat impenetrable thinking" of Baltimore and his son and successor, Cecilius. Neither their practice nor their thinking was impenetrable. The Baltimores held for equal civil treatment and equal religious toleration for all faiths within their domain. During the last years in Newfoundland, an Anglican parson and a Catholic priest shared the proprietor's home for their services, to the evident distress of church authorities both in Rome and in London.

Giving up on Newfoundland, Baltimore sought a grant north of Virginia. The grant was made on 20 June 1632, but George Calvert had died two months earlier, and the award was to his son, Cecilius, the second baron. The charter, like that of Avalon, established a government modeled on the county palatinate of the bishop of Durham at the fourteen-century apex of its independence. Baltimore had powers second only to the king himself. The colony was to be largely autonomous, its laws to be "consonant to reason and be not repugnant or contrary, but (so far as conveniently may be) agreeable to the Laws, Statutes, Customs and Rights of Our Kingdom of England."

Maryland (named for Charles I's French queen, Henrietta Maria) was founded from "a laudable and pious Zeal for extending the Christian Religion and also the Territories of Our Empire." Roman Catholics were prohibited in Stuart England, liable to various penal laws. Although Baltimore's colony was not a "Catholic" colony, either in numbers or in purpose, it did have Catholic beginnings. The colonists sailed aboard the 360-ton (324-metric ton) *Ark* and 60-ton (54-metric ton) pinnace *Dove* on 13 November 1633 from London. On board were about two hundred servants and laborers, most of them Protestants, seventeen "gentlemen adventurers," most of them Catholics, and two Jesuit priests and a lay brother.

Catholics constituted the social, economic, and political elite of the party. As gentlemen adventurers, they took up most of the land in the proprietor's gift. For every £100 paid for transportation of five men, each of the gentry received four hundred acres (160 hectares) and a share in colonial trade. They formed the first colonial assembly and were the nucleus of "the Proprietor's party" in colonial debates. But Catholics were always a numerical minority. Their power waned as Protestant servants worked out indentures and as immigrants, Puritans and others, made their way to Maryland.

Leonard Calvert, younger brother of Cecilius Calvert, Lord Baltimore, was lieutenant-governor of the colony. He was a Catholic, as were John Lewger, a former Anglican who became colonial secretary, and Captain Thomas Cornwaleys, the military commander. The colony's priests were Andrew White and John Altham, also known as Gravener; they were accompanied by Brother Thomas Gervase, S.J. The Jesuits paid for thirty servants; fourteen were assigned to their credit by other gentry. Among Andrew White's servants was "Mathias Sousa, molato," who appears later as a free man in the assembly of 1641 to 1642.

Five documents bear on the colony's foundations: the charter of 1632; two promotional pamphlets published in 1633, *An Account of the Colony,* and *Objections Answered*; Lord Baltimore's *Instructions,* also in 1633; and Andrew White's *Relatio itineris,* translated as *Narrative of a Voyage to Maryland,* a report sent to the Jesuit superior-general at Rome in April 1634. The documents came of an English Catholicism that in the crucible of Elizabethan England had come to understand "that Priests of whatever order ought not by force of arms to plant or water the Catholic faith," and that in religious matters, men and women have the right to be free from physical coercion. They clearly distinguished between political and religious loyalty: sovereigns and laws were for them incompetent in matters of conscience, and religious affiliation could not be used to command political commitment.

The charter of 1632 was a royal document, not in itself the product of contemporary English Catholic thinking; but Baltimore chose to interpret it according to his own lights, and the Church of England was not established in Maryland. Neither the laws of mortmain (dealing with the ownership of land by religious bodies) nor the anti-Catholic penal laws were in force. The Catholic church was not established or given government subsidy. The Jesuits were supported by the land they took up as gentlemen adventurers. The system worked well for Catholics, but not for others. Lack of government financial support inhibited the growth of Anglican church structure and left three-quarters of the people basically unchurched.

The promotional pamphlet *An Account of the Colony* listed spiritual and temporal advantages of the venture. The author laid stress on converting the indigenous peoples to Christianity. The Eurocentric cultural perspective prevented the Baltimores from extending their views on religious toleration to Native Americans or to African religions. The pervasive "Christian" character of the enterprise and its accompanying literature also would have discouraged Jews from coming. In any event, they had been excluded from England since their expulsion in 1290, and there were none in any colony when the *Ark* and the *Dove* set sail. The second pamphlet, *Objections Answered,* took up three economic questions and the problem of toleration of popery in the Maryland colony, arguing that English Catholics were exchanging their "pleasant, plentiful . . . and native country" for "a wilderness among savages and wild beasts." If the Crown tolerated the Native Americans, "undoubted idolators," why should it not allow papists to exist in America?

Baltimore's *Instructions* revealed an irenic and pragmatic approach to religious topics. Unity and peace were foremost. To achieve them, Catholic practice on board the *Ark* and

the *Dove* and afterwards in Maryland was to be unobtrusive. No offense was to be given to Protestants. Religious debate was to be avoided. Officials were to treat Protestants "with as much mildness and favor as Justice will permit." Once the colonists were settled, only Anglican emissaries were to be sent to the governor of Virginia and to Captain William Claiborne, who controlled Kent Island in the Chesapeake. Baltimore ordered a chapel built as part of the settlement; its denomination was not specified.

Andrew White's *Narrative of a Voyage to Maryland* records the story of the transatlantic voyage and the first day on Saint Clement's Island in the Potomac, the river the colonists named after Saint Gregory:

On the day of the *Annunciation of the Most Holy Virgin Mary* in the year 1634, we celebrated the mass for the first time, on this island. This had never been done before in this part of the world. After we had completed the sacrifice, we took upon our shoulders a great cross, which we had hewn out of a tree, and advancing in order to the appointed place, with the assistance of the Governor and his associates and the other Catholics, we erected a trophy to Christ the Savior, humbly reciting, on our bended knees, the Litanies of the Sacred Cross, with great emotion. (John Tracy Ellis. *Documents of American Catholic History,* p. 104)

Catholic religious practice was not as unobtrusive as Baltimore anticipated. For English Catholics, finally free to worship publicly, the enthusiasm on Saint Clement's Island was understandable. It was also the harbinger of troubles to come.

The colonists laid out a town they called Saint Mary's. The Jesuits had their own cabin and in it Maryland's first chapel. Their land claims under the conditions of plantation amounted to 28,500 acres (11,400 hectares). They took immediate possession of 3,400 acres (1,360 hectares) in and about Saint Mary's, including Saint Inigoe's manor and Saint George Island. In 1638 the recently arrived head of the Jesuit enterprise, Thomas Copley, reported to Jesuit headquarters in Rome on the religious state of the colony: reception of the sacraments was equal to that in Europe, the young were taught catechism, feast-day sermons were regular. Mass was offered daily and attended by Catholics and Protestants. Priests assisted the sick and dying. The *Spiritual Exercises,* the program of meditation and prayer outlined by the Jesuits' founder, Ignatius Loyola, had been introduced with good results.

Copley pointed out incidents touching on religious toleration. In two cases where Catholics had taken issue with Protestants, authorities sided with the latter and fined the Catholics, providing in one case that the fine be held in escrow until the arrival of the first Protestant minister, when it would be applied to his support. An act of the assembly excused the Jesuits from attendance, to which, as property owners, they were otherwise obliged, and when Governor Calvert deputized a priest to serve a warrant on a cattle rustler, the assembly ruled that such confusion of church and state not be allowed. The early colonists made genuine efforts to preserve freedom of religious practice. They also freely invited those of faiths other than their own to immigrate into the colony, as we know from the diary of the Puritan governor of Massachusetts Bay colony, John Winthrop:

The Lord Bartemore being owner of much land near Virginia, being himself a papist, and his brother, Mr. Calvert, the governor there being a papist also, but the colony consisted both of Protestants and papists, he wrote a letter to Captain Gibbons of Boston, and sent him a commission, wherein he made tender of land in Maryland to any of ours that would transport thither, with free liberty of religion, and all other privileges which the place afforded, paying such annual rent as should be agreed upon, but our Captain had no mind to further his desire herein, nor had any of our people temptation that way. (James Hosmer, ed. *Winthrop's Journal.* Vol. 2, p. 150)

There was conflict between Lord Baltimore and the Maryland assembly over the code of laws by which the province was to be governed, as well as between the proprietor and the Jesuits. The latter fight was two-pronged. One issue was the right of the Jesuits, already claimants to thousands of acres, to receive additional land as a gift from Native American chiefs. The second disagreement had to do with the recognition or non-recognition of rights claimed from time immemorial by clergy in Catholic states. The Jesuit protagonist was Thomas Copley, born in Spain of English descent, who came to Maryland in 1637. Although he was aware of the Catholic

situation in an English Protestant empire, Copley held that "while the government is Catholique," as it was in Maryland, priests should enjoy traditional immunities. His great and ultimately successful adversary was John Lewger, the colonial secretary.

Working with Lord Baltimore, Lewger devised a system that prescinded from canon law, either Roman or Anglican, and made no special provision for clergy or church. Some quiet concessions were made to avoid entanglement of church and state, as in the case of the clerical process server employed by Governor Calvert, and priests were excused from judging capital crimes, but otherwise they were treated as if canon law did not exist. Lewger's position was that despite appearances, Catholicism was not publicly allowed in Maryland and had no claims on the state. Copley replied with a catalog of grievances and thinly disguised threats of excommunication. His complaints were many: contact with the natives was legally restricted; priests were taxed and their servants liable to arrest; militia duties were imposed on the servants; the clergy were liable to levies for the defense of the colony; restrictions on manorial holdings were proposed; and unmarried women had to forfeit landholdings after seven years. This last militated against the church-approved state of virginity.

Matters moved further when a new set of conditions for plantations placed limitations on the church's power of acquiring property. Copley put all Jesuit property in the hands of a lay trustee. A further complication developed when the Jesuits accepted property at Mattapany on the Patuxent River from a Native chief. The proprietor claimed that land in the province was in his gift, not that of the Natives, and confiscated the estate. A many-sided battle resulted, involving Lord Baltimore, the Jesuit provincial superior in England, and the general superior in Rome. In the colony, pro-Jesuit and proproprietor parties sprang up. The matter was finally laid to rest by Jesuit Father General Muzio Vitelleschi, who wrote to his men in Maryland, "I should be sorry indeed to see the first fruits, which are so beautifully developing in the Lord, nipped in their growth by the frost of cupidity." The more serious threat posed by an increasing Puritan presence soon ended the intramural

Catholic quarrel, but, as Thomas Spalding has commented:

While Baltimore's refusal to recognize Jesuit claims precluded the development of a special status under the law in English-speaking America that future churchmen might cite as precedent, the Jesuits' stand forestalled the growth of a tradition of unquestioning subservience to the state on the part of the church itself. The principles of separation and of free exercise were alike strengthened by the controversy. (Thomas W. Spalding. *The Premier See*, pp. 3–4)

Throughout the colonial period, the Jesuit mission was supported from the more than twenty thousand acres (8,000 hectares) that Jesuits owned. The income from these properties was supplemented by property inherited by individual Jesuits and by substantial gifts from lay benefactors. Legally, the property was held by lay trustees or passed by will from one Jesuit to another. There is no evidence that collections for church support were even taken at religious services.

The colonists and Lord Baltimore tangled over the question of initiating legislation in the colony. The fight over the Jesuits' privileges was part of the struggle. Finally, in 1639, the assembly passed a set of statutes, among them one that declared: "Holy Churches [*sic*] within this province shall have all her rights and liberties." The original text added the word "immunities," but this was dropped in the final version. Whether the use of "her" is, as Spalding suggests, "a grammatical absurdity," or, as seems more likely, simply an obsolete usage for "their," we know from an appeal to the text in a later prosecution of the Jesuit Francis Fitzherbert that "all churches" were meant. Baltimore had wished the adjective "Christian" inserted into the text. The assembly adopted the broader version.

England's Civil War came to Maryland in 1645. Maryland Protestants, with help from Virginia Puritans, assumed control. White and Copley were sent in chains to England and tried there for violating the penal law that forbade English priests ordained abroad to enter the kingdom. They were let off because their return was involuntary, but they were sent into exile. The Jesuit mission was in shambles. Of fourteen missionaries since 1634, four stayed only briefly, eight were dead, and two were exiles. The Cal-

verts reasserted themselves, but Leonard Calvert died in 1647 and his temporary Catholic successor, Thomas Greene, was replaced by a Protestant, William Stone. The oath of office Stone took suggested the changing temper of the times in a clause that promised not to hinder the Catholics' free exercise of religion. Leonard Calvert's personal affairs were cared for by Margaret Brent, whose handling of mutinous soldiers won from the assembly the accolade, "It were better for the collony's safety at that time in her hands than in any mans else in the whole Province." But her demands for a voice and two votes in the assembly, one as attorney for the Calvert estate and one as landowner in her own right, were denied. With her brothers she left Maryland for the Virginia shore of the Potomac in 1651.

Catholics probably still had a slight majority in the Maryland assembly of 1649, which adopted an act concerning religion that marked a giant step back from earlier policy. Toleration was restricted to Trinitarian Christians, and severe penalties, including death, were inflicted for a whole range of religious offenses. None of this was in the draft submitted to the assembly by Baltimore, nor was it consistent with earlier acts of the assembly itself. The act's harsh phrases reflected a compromise. They sounded like pronouncements in the Presbyterian-controlled English parliament in the spring of 1648.

The situation worsened. The assembly repealed the act of 1649 and "in the Name of his highness the Lord Protector" [Oliver Cromwell] prohibited exercise of the Catholic religion. Peace did not return until 1657.

With restoration of proprietary rule in 1660, conditions improved. Charles, third Lord Baltimore, lived in the province from 1661 to 1684. The Catholic community was a declining minority, but one with social and in many cases economic importance. Families like the Carrolls, Brents, Darnalls, Diggeses, Brookes, Sewalls, and Neales were untitled colonial aristocrats, often closely related to the Calvert family. Other families ranked only marginally lower on the social ladder and regularly intermarried with the magnates. Both sons and daughters were generally well educated. Regular convoys took youngsters to France and Flanders, where they entered the exiled English Jesuits' college of Saint Omer (later in Bruges) or one of a host of English-run convent schools. Some went on to law or medical studies; others returned home after secondary school to take over family plantations. During the colonial period, forty-nine Americans entered seminaries; nearly half of these returned to work as Jesuits in Maryland, while others worked in England or in continental Jesuit schools. Thirty-three colonial women became nuns in cloistered convents of Benedictines, Poor Clares, Sepulchrines, Dominicans, and Carmelites. Only two ever returned home, when, in 1790, the first Carmelite convent, and the first religious house of women, in the thirteen colonies opened at Port Tobacco, Maryland.

Thomas Spalding has termed the period between the restoration of proprietary rule and the revolutionary year of 1689 "the golden age of Catholic aristocracy in Maryland, the Glorious Revolution." Catholic gentry prospered, Catholic farmers were well off, and the Jesuit clergy, augmented by two or three English Franciscans between 1672 and 1720, went about their itinerant spiritual ministry, traveling by boat, or sulky, or on horseback to distant missions from their plantations, which were worked by upward of a hundred African-American slaves. Ralph Crouch ran a school at Newton Manor in the 1650s, admitting both Protestants and Catholics. Edward Cotton was its first benefactor, endowing it with "a horse and mare, the stock and all its increase forever." A visiting missionary from the Iroquois country of northern New York wrote during the 1670s that he had met in Maryland "two of our English fathers and a brother; the fathers dressed like gentlemen, the brother like a farmer, having charge of a farm which serves to support the two missionaries."

With the lord proprietor back in power, the act of 1649 was once more in force, but political and economic considerations prevented a complete return to the pre-Puritan era. Business interests challenged the feudal structure of Maryland's economy, and growing political consciousness reacted against limited suffrage and nepotism in government. The colony's demography changed. By 1677 the third Lord Baltimore counted Quakers as the largest single denomination, followed by Presbyterians, Independents, Anabaptists, and Anglicans. Catholics came last.

The end of the Baltimores' feudal domain came after the Glorious Revolution in England. In 1691 Maryland became a royal province. A year later the Church of England was established by law, and in 1694 the capital was transferred from Catholic Saint Mary's to Protestant Annapolis. Penal laws were imposed on Catholics. Included were compulsory attendance at Anglican services, a Test Act, which effectively barred Catholics from public service and the legal profession, and denial of the right to vote. A heavy tax, similar to that on African slaves, was imposed on importation of Irish servants, although there was no tax on white Protestants. Ministers lamented "the great number of Irish Papists continually brought into this Province." The census of 1790 showed a larger percentage of Catholic southern Irish in Maryland (7 percent of the total population) than in any other original state.

Although Catholics smarted under the constraints occasioned by their religion, the penal laws were not rigorously applied. A leading Catholic, Charles Carroll of Annapolis, fumed that he would move to French Louisiana, but he was still the wealthiest person in Maryland after the death of fellow Catholic Richard Bennett III in 1749. Family connections, especially in the provincial council, and the social standing of their wealthier members shielded Maryland Catholics from the worst consequences of outlaw status.

The third Lord Baltimore, although deprived of political authority, remained a presence in colonial life. He gave regular alms to support the missionaries, but that ended with his death in 1715. His son and successor, Benedict Calvert, conformed to the Anglican Church in 1713. He died seven weeks after his father, leaving a Protestant heir, Charles, to whom the proprietorship was restored in 1715, some months after Benedict Calvert's death. Until the American Revolution, Maryland Catholics remained disfranchised. In 1705 Queen Anne permitted private Catholic worship, and many manor houses had private chapels. A separate church building was built at Newtown in 1766, apparently without protest from the civil authorities. But the Newtown church is the sole such example of a freestanding Catholic church from the colonial period.

The wealthy Brent family had plantations on the Virginia shore of the Potomac, where its members lived peaceably, took an active part in political life, and hosted regular Catholic church services. In addition, the Maryland Jesuits pushed west to Frederick in the 1740s and expanded their activity to the head of the Chesapeake and to Maryland's Eastern Shore. A classical and commercial preparatory school was opened in 1741 at Saint Xaverius mission, popularly called "Bohemia Manor," a Jesuit farm in Cecil County. Plans were made by the 1760s for a center in Baltimore, where a ministry to Acadian refugees from Nova Scotia was developing.

The immediate pre-revolutionary years saw a change of political alignment on the part of Maryland's Catholic magnates. They and their coreligionists had every reason to fear popular movements. Nevertheless, in the person of their leading representative, Charles Carroll of Carrollton, they moved from Tory to Whig allegiance. Educated abroad, Carroll was a man of the Enlightenment. The Jesuits introduced him to the thought of Locke and Montesquieu; he regarded his teachers as "men of Republican principles, who will not fail to inspire the youths with a love of liberty."

Charles Carroll was a partisan of civil and religious liberty, opposed to state interference in religious matters and to religion's ties with the state. "Unlimited toleration" and free conversation among people of all sects seemed to him the way to eliminate religious tensions. Historian David Skaggs considers Carroll's political shift to the popular party "one of the most significant developments on the road to minority rights, not only in Maryland, but in America generally." A somewhat awed John Adams wrote of his vigorous participation in the revolution: "He continues to hazard his all, his immense fortune, the largest in America, and his Life." Charles Carroll's views were shared by his cousin, John Carroll, who in 1789 was ordained the first Roman Catholic bishop in the United States. Writing to the Philadelphia magazine *The Columbian* in the summer of 1787, he summed it up: "Freedom and independence acquired by the united efforts, and cemented with the mingled blood of Protestants and Catholic fellow-citizens, should be equally enjoyed by all." This thinking was consistent with that of the Calverts and the early Maryland assembly. It founded what has come to be called the Maryland tradition of religious liberty.

THE SOUTHERN AND THE MIDDLE COLONIES

There were few Catholics elsewhere in the thirteen colonies. Jesuits from Florida tried from 1570 to 1572 to establish a mission on the Virginia coast, but the effort failed and all but one of the band were killed. Irish convicts were deported in considerable numbers to Virginia, but there was no organized church activity among them. Only in the Brent plantations on the Northern Neck were there colonial centers of Catholic practice. The Carolinas and Georgia had no Catholics in colonial times, except for occasional Spanish explorers and, in Georgia, Franciscans like the five friars who were killed there in 1597.

In William Penn's colonies of Delaware and Pennsylvania, Catholics, although debarred from holding public office and from the legal and teaching professions, enjoyed *de facto* toleration. From 1730 on, plantations and towns in Delaware were visited by itinerant missionaries from Bohemia Manor, the Jesuit center in northeastern Maryland. Land for a church, the first in Delaware, was purchased in 1772 at Coffee Run. In 1708 mass was said in Philadelphia and in 1729 the Jesuit Joseph Greaton became the first resident priest. Within a few years, Saint Joseph's Church was opened, the first Catholic "town church" in the colonies. The more elegant Saint Mary's followed in 1763 and became a parish of upwardly mobile merchants and professional people. In addition to the town churches, congregations formed in the southeastern counties. In 1717 John Digges from Maryland took up land in the Conewago valley. He was followed by German Catholics among the "Pennsylvania Dutch" recruited in the Rhineland by William Penn's agents. They were cared for by German Jesuits, one of whom was stationed in Philadelphia to assist in the multilingual churches of that cosmopolitan seaport.

A few Catholics appear in New Jersey's early history. They came from Ireland and France to work in the salt mines and claypits. In 1668 a Catholic, William Douglass, was elected from

Bergen County to the assembly, but he was disqualified because of his religion. Jesuits from the short-lived New York mission said mass and baptized Catholics at Woodbridge and Elizabethtown in the 1680s. Throughout the eighteenth century, there were Catholics in small numbers working in the iron mines and foundries and in glassworks. John Tatham, a pottery maker, was named governor of West Jersey in 1690, but his Catholicism prevented him from taking office. Circuit-riding priests from Philadelphia ministered to the scattered Catholics during the colonial period.

A Dutch West India Company regulation in 1624 stipulated that in the colony of New Netherland (later New York), "they shall . . . hold no other services than those of true Reformed religion." During the years of Dutch rule (1626–1664), public Roman Catholic worship was forbidden, but there was practical toleration of Catholics. They were occasionally reported at New Amsterdam (New York City) and there were regular contacts between company officials and French Jesuits working among the Five Nations upstate. The Dutch rescued from Mohawk captivity the Jesuits Isaac Jogues and François Bressani, and Simon LeMoyne visited and carried on a correspondence with Dominie Johannes Megapolensis. Their exchange was amiable, but not "ecumenical" in the modern sense of the word, as each held vigorously to sharply opposed theological opinions.

NEW YORK AND NEW ENGLAND

Under the rule of the younger brother of King Charles II, James, Duke of York, who became a Catholic in 1672, Catholics held public office in New York and an Irish Catholic, Thomas Dongan, became governor. In 1682 he brought English Jesuits with him; they later had a chapel in Fort James at the tip of Manhattan and a school on the "King's Farm." Dongan planned for them to move north and replace French Jesuits among the Iroquois. This scheme, as well as the 1683 Charter of Liberties and Privileges granting complete religious toleration, was scrapped in the aftermath of the Glorious Revolution and a rebellion in New York led by the German Jacob Leisler. Penal laws against Catholics were instituted, some of which remained in effect until 1806.

Connecticut and Massachusetts had a common Puritan heritage that discouraged Catholic settlement. No colonial Catholics were reported in Connecticut, although the French Jesuit Gabriel Druilettes paid a visit in 1651 as a trade commissioner for New France. Massachusetts passed laws excluding Catholic priests in 1647 and again in 1700, but, apart from those who came from Canada as trade commissioners, none visited the colony until the revolution. Irish exiles from Barbados made their way to Massachusetts in the seventeenth century, but there was no organized Catholic community. One such refugee, Ann Glover, was hanged as a witch in 1688. She was pursued relentlessly by Cotton Mather, and her prosecution had strong anti-Catholic overtones.

Rhode Island's founder, Roger Williams, was no admirer of papists, but he did advocate toleration. The colonial charter after 1689 excepted Roman Catholics from the general toleration it accorded, but this exception was not in earlier versions of the document. In any case, there were no Catholics in colonial days. The same was true of New Hampshire, where early laws denied any who might come the rights of free men and excluded them from public office. Jesuit missionaries were active among the Saint Francis tribe in northern Vermont, where Swanton claims the first Catholic church (1700). When the mission era ended, there were no Catholics until the nineteenth century.

Maine's story differed from that of the other colonies and is properly considered within the context of French colonial history.

CONCLUSION

The story of Roman Catholicism in the colonies ended with a flurry of activity over the Quebec Act, passed in 1774 by the British Parliament, which allowed French Canadians freedom to practice their religion and collect tithes as they had under French rule. Americans found the act offensive to Protestant sensibilities, and it seemed to foreclose any westward territorial expansion. The act was one of the five "Intolerable Acts" that prompted calling of the first Continental Congress. That body in September and October 1774 made its own "Suffolk Resolves," which condemned the Quebec Act as "Dangerous in an extreme degree to the Protestant religion and to the civil and religious rights of all Americans." But the Spanish and French alliances helped. Congress in a body went four times to services at Saint Mary's Church in Philadelphia. Religious hostility by no means ended, but change was in the air. As American Roman Catholics turned their attention to structuring their church in the new republic, the church itself began to change, with new and diverse immigrants arriving on every ship. A new constitutional solution to the problem of church-state relationships was in the making. The colonial era had ended.

BIBLIOGRAPHY

Guides

Ellis, John Tracy, and Robert Trisco. *A Guide to American Catholic History.* 2nd ed. Santa Barbara, Calif., 1982.
Hennesey, James. *American Catholic Bibliography 1970–1982.* Notre Dame, Ind., 1982.
———. *Supplement to American Catholic Bibliography 1970–1982.* Notre Dame, Ind., 1983.
Vollmar, Edward. *The Catholic Church in America: An Historical Bibliography.* 2nd ed., New York, 1963.

Books and Articles

Axtell, James L. *The Invasion Within: The Contest of Cultures in Colonial North America.* New York, 1985.
Berlin, George. "History of the Jews in Maryland: Struggle for Liberty." In *The History of Religious Toleration in Maryland,* edited by James F. Brewer. Baltimore, Md., 1985.
Burnett, Edmund C., ed. *Letters of Members of the Continental Congress.* 6 vols. Washington, D.C., 1921–1931.
Carr, Lois Green. "Toleration in Maryland: Why It Ended." In *The History of Religious Toleration,* edited by James F. Brewer. Baltimore, Md., 1985.
Commager, Henry Steele, ed. *Documents of American History.* 7th ed. New York, 1963.
DeJong, Gerald Francis. "Dominie Johannes Megapolensis: Minister to New Netherland." *The New-York Historical Society Quarterly* 52 (1968):7–47.
Ellis, John Tracy. *Catholics in Colonial America.* Baltimore, Md. 1965.
———. ed. *Documents of American Catholic History.* Rev. ed. Wilmington, Del., 1967.
Hanley, Thomas O'B. *Charles Carroll of Carrollton: The Making of a Revolutionary Gentleman.* Washington, D.C., 1970.
Hennesey, James. *American Catholics: The History of the Roman Catholic Community in the United States.* New York, 1981.
———. "Catholicism in the English Colonies." In *Encyclopedia of the American Religious Experience,* edited by Charles H. Lippy and Peter W. Williams. New York, 1988.
———. "Roman Catholicism: The Maryland Tradition." *Thought* 51 (1970):282–295.
———. "Several Youths Sent from Here: Native-born Priests and Religious of Colonial America, 1634–1776." In *Studies in Church History in Honor of John Tracy Ellis,* edited by Nelson H. Minnich, Robert B. Eno and Robert F. Trisco. Wilmington, Del., 1985.
Hosmer, James, ed. *Winthrop's Journal.* 2 vols. New York, 1966.
Hughes, Thomas. *History of the Society of Jesus in North America, Colonial and Federal.* 4 vols. New York, 1907–1917.
Lahey, Raymond J. "The Role of Religion in Lord Baltimore's Colonial Enterprise." *Maryland Historical Magazine* 72 (1979):492–511.
Lapomarda, Vincent A. "A Catholic in Puritan Society." *American Benedictine Review* 41 (1990):192–208.
———. "The Jesuit Missions of Colonial New England," *Essex Institute Historical Collections* 126 (1990):91–109.
Megapolensis, Johannes. *Reply of Rev. Johannes Megapolensis, Pastor of the Church of New Amsterdam, to a Letter of Father Simon LeMoyne, a Jesuit Missionary of Canada, 1658.* New York, 1907.
Melville, Annabelle. *John Carroll of Baltimore: Founder of the American Catholic Hierarchy.* New York, 1955.
Miller, Kerby A. *Emigrants and Exiles: Ireland and the Irish Exodus to North America.* New York, 1985.
Murray, John Courtney. *We Hold These Truths: Catholic Reflections on the American Proposition.* New York, 1960.
Skaggs, David Curtis, *Roots of Maryland Democracy, 1753–1776.* Westport, Conn., 1973.
Spalding, Thomas W. *The Premier See: A History of the Archdiocese of Baltimore 1789–1989.* Baltimore, Md., 1989.
Stokes, Anselm Phelps. *Church and State in the United States.* 3 vols. New York, 1950.

James Hennesey

SEE ALSO **British Settlements, The Chesapeake; British Settlements, The Middle Colonies;** and **Church and State.**

ANGLICANISM

After forty religiously troubled years, England's national church emerged in 1559 through the Elizabethan Settlement. The Church of England was a magisterial Protestant body (one endorsed, supported, and controlled by princely government). As such it took its place in Europe's religious spectrum alongside similar churches: Lutheran, Zwinglian, and Calvinist. Like them it stood between the Roman Catholic church and the papacy on the one hand and the free conventicles, or assemblies, of the Anabaptists and the Spiritualists on the other. Later this church would be seen as a *via media,* a middle way between Roman Catholicism and Genevan Calvinism.

It was the Elizabethan church that came to America. What was its character? Basic to its faith were the three classical creeds of Christendom: the Apostles, the Nicene, and the Athanasian. Providing further definition were, first of all, the Thirty-nine Articles of Religion (1563) and the first and second *Book of Homilies* (1547, 1571). The latter were often read aloud in parishes in America and England. Their presence in all churches, together with Desiderius Erasmus's *Paraphrases* (of the Gospels) (1547), was commanded for the people's theological and moral guidance. The church had a single order of worship drawn from many liturgical sources, crafted largely by Thomas Cranmer and contained in the famous *Book of Common Prayer* (1559). Central to the church's worship was the Bishops' Bible (1568). Until the King James version in 1611, it was the official English translation appointed to be read in churches. Finally, Anglicanism was given a formal defense in John Jewel's *Apology of the Church of England* (1564).

Of equal importance were two highly popular works. The first of these was the celebrated Geneva Bible (1560), which was found in nearly every English household and ran to seventy full editions during the eighty years after its initial publication. (The Bishops' Bible had nineteen editions.) Second was John Foxe's *Acts and Monuments* (1563), or as it was called, Foxe's Book of Martyrs, a clearly Protestant, if controversial, volume that sought to remember the heroes and heroines of the English Reformation.

Since it retained bishops the church was episcopal in polity, and since the queen was its "supreme governor," it was royal. In judicial process it remained medieval and professional rather than evangelical and pastoral. In other words, the church in part relied more upon external and traditional legal structures than upon inner persuasion as the result of a more immediate engagement with Christian faith. The church's economy was chaotic; there were pluralities of benefices, and the distribution of endowments bore little relation to pastoral needs.

Without doubt the church was comprehensive. That is to say, the elements that made up her life were drawn from many sources: from the early church fathers (particularly Augustine);

from the biblical and theological scholars of the sixteenth century—Erasmus, Martin Luther, Huldrych Zwingli (the Swiss Protestant reformer), Martin Bucer (the Alsatian who sought Protestant unity and furthered reform in the cities of Germany and in England), and John Calvin; and from the treasure of universal liturgies.

If modern historians agree that these are the elements of Elizabethan Anglicanism, they disagree on their significance. Some would call Elizabeth's church classical Anglicanism; others argue that the later, more "catholic" church of William Laud deserves that title. Likewise there are those who see a distinctly Anglican ethos in the early days of the Settlement, one that already distinguished the church from continental Protestantism. Others point to Jewel's alignment of the church with Luther and Zwingli. It is agreed that the Calvinist influence on the ordinary Elizabethan clergy and laity was profound. Certainly at the time all acknowledged the three pillars of Protestantism: the sufficiency of Scripture, justification by grace through faith, and the priesthood of all believers. Elizabeth herself was educated by young reformed scholars.

The queen's role was crucial. Since Elizabeth believed in the divine right of kings to rule, she refused to be outmaneuvered by anyone. Much of the intelligentsia wanted the restitution of "primitive Christianity" and a "purer," less formal, more independent church. When, as early as 1559, these reform-minded "Puritans" took religious matters into their own hands—and overplayed them—the queen asserted her authority. Later she had to counter papal threats against her throne and her life. She needed tradition to uphold her rule; she wanted moderation to keep it peaceful. She sought national unity and tried to avoid persecution. Elizabeth paid a price for her Settlement. Her restrictions on reform of the church's structure and on the *Book of Common Prayer* and her desire for ancient vestments drove moderates into the arms of the more extreme reformers.

EVOLUTION OF THE CHESAPEAKE BAY CHURCH

What Massachusetts Bay was to Puritanism in New England, the Chesapeake Bay was to colonial Anglicanism. Since Jamestown gave evidence of a Puritan religious character, how can one account for the difference between the two colonies? While both shared a common Protestantism, their different dates of settlement are important. Jamestown reflected the English church in 1607, not in 1630. By the later date, Puritans despaired of reform and were leaving the mother country as dissenters in all but name. In addition the settlers of Massachusetts had gone beyond basic statements of Protestant theology and had become more concerned with piety and the cure of souls. Meanwhile in Virginia, after the colony's disastrous beginning (between 1607 and 1624, 5,400 out of 6,400 immigrants died), the church went its own way.

What was that way? First, account should be taken of the leaders' Puritanism. In the early years, dire straits prompted strong measures. Religious observance was compelled in Sir Thomas Gates's stern *Articles, Lawes, and Orders, Divine, Politique and Martiall* (1610–1611), misnamed Dale's Laws. These and the long prayer appended to them reflect predestinarian, covenantal theology and—since the settlers were not yet motivated by a common religious purpose—a demand for disciplined behavior by people from every social class.

The influence of Puritanism can be seen in the choice of books for the colonists' small, highly prized libraries. In particular the tone was set by the first four volumes sent to the proposed but unrealized college at Henrico for Christianizing and civilizing Indians. Three of them were the works of William Perkins of Christ's College, Cambridge, and the fourth was Augustine's *The City of God*. The works of Calvin himself, Richard Sibbes, William Ames, John Owen, Francis Turretin, and other theologians also indicate Puritan Calvinism. Only later did the great work of the anti-Puritan traditionalist, Richard Hooker, author of the *Laws of Ecclesiastical Polity* (published between 1594 and 1662), appear in Virginia. Thereafter, along with Charles I's *Eikon Basilike* (1649), the writings of Caroline Anglicans such as Richard Allestree and Jeremy Taylor graced Virginia libraries.

The predisposition of the clergy also attests to the early reformed character of the church. On the basis of matriculation at either Anglican or Puritan colleges in Oxford and Cambridge, the sixty-seven clergy who came from England between 1607 and 1660 can be categorized as follows: eleven Puritan Independents, twenty-two conforming Puritans, another twenty-two whom we cannot identify by a category, four conforming clergy not episcopally ordained, and eight royalists.

As the risks to life by Indian attack and disease diminished, and as the colony expanded, stability was achieved. From 1625 to 1635, the General Assembly passed a series of acts that made religion uniform. As a result social mutuality replaced "Lawes Martiall." Personal conduct was regulated by the reporting of moral offenses to churchwardens. It has been noted that when couples had children too soon after marriage, they were required as punishment to appear in church in white robes carrying white wands. (White was the symbol of chastity; wands such as the one with which Moses parted the waters of the Red Sea [Exod. 14:16ff.] were symbols of power, intensity, and direction; hence a white wand implied reformed sexual behavior.) Cohabitation before marriage and other forms of sexual promiscuity were serious threats to conjugal, family, and social stability.

There were other punishments. Any person habitually drunk had to stand at the church door with a pot around his neck. Skipping church on Sunday was an offense punishable by fine or by participation in road or bridge building so others could get to church more conveniently. In the early Stuart period, when people felt a hollowness at the center of life, such disciplinary measures, especially in a strange land, were reassuring. Moreover, as has been recognized, the closeness to the local grain of the ministers and vestries of Virginia helped produce civility and a sense of community.

Emergence of Low Church Anglicanism

The evolution of the Virginia church is seen not only in the developing consociational character of its conforming Puritanism but in its differences from the church in England. Throughout the colonial period, first by circumstance, then by inclination, Virginians failed to transplant the hierarchy. Gone were those medieval ranks of clerical functionaries that had bothered the Puritans: archbishops, diocesan and suffragan bishops, deans, clerical prebendaries, and canons. Cathedrals and collegiate chapels did not exist in colonial America; even the simplest of traditional vestments—surplices—were at first in short supply (and not required in any case). While the verbal order of the prayer book was maintained, the trappings of worship were minimal by English standards. Clergy always preached and often conducted entire services in academic black gown and bands. Church ornaments were limited to a Bible for reading the lessons, two large prayer books (for clerk and minister), an alms basin, vessels for the service of Holy Communion, "fair white linen" for the holy table, a pulpit cloth and cushion, and a font for baptisms, often of wood or silver rather than the canonical stone. Moreover ecclesiastical courts, that crucial means of maintaining hierarchical rule, were wholly absent. As a result Virginia was low church.

In 1720 Robert Carter, a leading Anglican layman, sent a letter to his agent in London regarding the education of his sons that summed up what had become traditional in America:

I resolve the principles of our holy religion shall be instilled into mine betimes; as I am of the Church of England way, so I desire they should be. But the high flown, up-top notions and great stress that is laid upon ceremonies, any further than decency and conformity, are what I cannot come into reason of. Practical godliness is the substance; these are but the shell.

In his lack of enthusiasm for those elements that had become, for the Caroline churchmen, the glories of English catholicity—episcopacy and ceremonies—Carter reflected the attitude of Virginia's founders.

To this church's moderate Puritanism (her Calvinism, her lack of medieval orders and vestments, and her church discipline), to her localism, and to her simplicity should be added her shortage of clergy. In the early days, ministers died along with everyone else. In 1615 there were 15 clergy in a colony of 350 people (a ratio of one to twenty-three); in 1660 there were eleven for twenty-five thousand laity (or, 1 to 2,273). So high was the death rate in the early decades that the median tenure of a clergyman prior to 1660 was only from four to five years. From 1660 to 1720, when the number of ministers doubled, the median tenure was ten years. Thus it is not surprising that Huguenots (French Calvinists) and others should minister to Anglican congregations.

By the end of the century, the church in Virginia was the only Anglican establishment in North America. Of the seventy-five parishes in the colonies in 1690, all but one were in the South, and of those fifty were in Virginia. These churches prospered. First, they were tax supported; that is, clerical salaries were taken from the uniform, flat tax of two shillings per one hundred acres (40 hectares) levied on all males sixteen years and older, white and black. (Slave owners paid the tax on their slaves.) Ministers' wages were legislatively mandated by the General Assembly, not negotiated between pastor and congregation as in Massachusetts. Moreover, though legislators complained, remuneration was generous, varying from £80 to £100 per annum in the seventeenth century and up to £167 by 1760. Payment was actually made in the staple crop, tobacco, which was then sold on the London market. Second, parishes were controlled by local justices of the peace who were also the vestrymen. Parish administration was then a quasi-governmental function of the county in which the laity collected money for the minister's salary as well as the alms for the poor. Third, Episcopal churches were well attended by young and old alike. Congregations were active and growing. What is more they remained without rivals until the advent of the Presbyterians, Baptists, and Methodists after 1745. With the exception of a Quaker minority which was by 1700 in decline, Virginia was for 135 years uniformly Anglican.

The Lay Character of Virginia's Anglicanism

The local laity was the most significant group in the church. They held the rights of advowson. This meant that the prerogative of choosing the minister, that is, ecclesiastical patronage, belonged to the group alone and did not reside in the Crown, the university college, the municipality, or the bishop. Often vestries, without consulting anyone, did not institute, that is, formally and permanently install ministers as rectors but kept them on a year-to-year basis. This state of affairs came about during England's Civil War. At that time the royalist governor, Sir William Berkeley, sailing before the political winds, also, prudently shifted responsibility for uniformity from himself to the vestries. As a result the laity

could not only fire their ministers at will but, if they chose to do so, could retain those of ecclesiastical pedigree. Sometimes they did this against the wills of the subsequent governors. Such was the case of the vestry of St. Mary's White Chapel when it successfully defended its unorthodox Presbyterian rector, Andrew Jackson, who served from 1686 to 1710. There were similar cases involving nonepiscopally ordained clergy.

At first vestries were chosen in parishwide elections. In 1662, however, they were permitted to fill their own vacancies. Thus vestries became self-perpetuating bodies. This privilege corresponded with the emergence of the powerful gentry, who were increasingly moving toward the use of black slaves. Stratification in society was thereafter sharpened. Much time was spent by the aristocracy establishing its social supremacy over poorer whites as well as over blacks. They did so by horse racing, gambling, and demanding special forms of address from inferiors. Yet all belonged to Anglican parishes. As many historians have shown, when the lower class was swept up by the Baptists in the Great Awakening, the fragile alliance of the Anglican gentry with the yeomanry came apart.

In the meantime wealthy planters increasingly set the tone in the parishes. Their competitiveness, individualism, and materialism caused yet another change in the church's character. Since there was no one powerful enough to call the gentry to account, religion for Anglicans in the Chesapeake became a private rather than a communal matter. As there had been a change from martial authority to communal discipline, so now there was one to private faith.

Virginia's "Believing Wives"

By the end of the seventeenth century, a potentially dangerous gap appeared between public worship on the one hand and solitary devotion on the other. Into the ethical, moral, and educational void that resulted stepped women, Virginia's "believing wives."

A woman's role in seventeenth-century England and America has been variously described as that of Eve, the temptress to sin, or the lascivious witch. Did such views give way to the ideal of true womanhood in the eighteenth century, or did differing views exist earlier, side by side? Authoritative for women in Virginia was Anglican Richard Allestree's *The Ladies' Calling* (1673). On the basis of Pauline doctrine (1 Cor. 11:3ff., 14:34ff.; Eph. 5:22ff.; 1 Tim. 2:8ff.; compare with Jesus in Luke 10:38–42), women were barred from the ordained ministry and from serving on vestries. Nonetheless, Allestree asserted, women had souls "of as Divine an Original" and as "endless a Duration" as men. They had a "native propensity toward virtue" that "closelier fenced them in from temptation." And according to Allestree, women showed modesty as opposed to wantonness. Though they "need instruction," women evidenced a "peculiar aptness" toward piety, especially in the home.

It was there, says Joan Gundersen, that women developed their own domain, entering into religious and theological discussions freely (which, along with passing judgment on sermons, Allestree frowned upon). In the home popular piety and moral behavior were shaped by women's design. There they prayed aloud, taught, catechized, and converted. Since baptisms, marriages, and funerals were conducted in homes, the ceremonial of those occasions was also under the direction of the wives.

Women's role was significant. They passed on the faith to future generations. They also enjoyed more control over their property than their English counterparts. At times they also expanded their normal participation in church affairs. In 1685 Mary Taney, wife of the sheriff of Calvert County, Maryland, boldly wrote the archbishop of Canterbury, calling his attention to the "sad condition" of his "stray flock." Taney wanted a settled Anglican ministry in Calvert County that would "prove a nursery of religion and loyalty through the whole Province." As much as the vestries, wives and mothers exemplified the lay character of Virginia's Anglicanism.

The Church Adopts the Planters' Perspective

In the Old Dominion, the alliance between aristocracy and church—to the partial exclusion of governor and Crown—was greatly aided by James Blair, one of the most powerful clerics in all of colonial America. Arriving in 1685 Blair became the representative, or commissary, of the bishop of London, who had assumed a measure of control over American churches. Blair was commissary for fifty-three years. For fifty

years he was a member of the King's Council in Virginia, and for forty-nine years he was president of the College of William and Mary, which he had founded in 1693. This "very vile old Ffellow," as Governor William Gooch called him, was contentious, high-handed, and farsighted. In theology he was moralistic and in politics manipulative. By introducing a quasi-Presbyterian system of church government imported from his native Scotland, Blair gave the clergy for the first time a corporate identity that led to its successful if ill-conceived demand for power and higher wages in the Parsons' Cause (1755–1763). Blair cemented the alliance of the ministers with the aristocracy, into which he himself had married. Though he could not ordain ministers, Blair could plan for the future. Whereas his college provided only three clergy in 1744, by 1776 William and Mary graduates in the ministry numbered twenty-six, outstripping Oxford (five) and Cambridge (seven).

Virginia's clergy reflected planter attitudes toward black slaves. It has been suggested that the Anglican ministers took the lead in cruel racial and spiritual repression of blacks. Others see the clergy following social attitudes and practices already in place. A few, such as the Rev. Morgan Godwyn in *The Negro's and Indian's Advocate Suing for Their Admission into the Church* (1680), took a strong stand and came into conflict with his parishioners. A few, like Francis Le Jau of South Carolina, persevered. Le Jau remained an outspoken critic of his parishioners. Others sought advice from England. Short of defying the planters, most ministers tried to catechize and admit slaves where and when they could. For their part neither blacks, Indians, nor white indentured servants took part in white religious services. They remained unchurched. Baptisms of slaves, it was correctly understood by whites, implied an equality before God which, in turn, might mean that one Christian should not keep another in bondage.

THE DRIVE FOR THE ANGLICIZATION OF THE COLONIES

After 1700 a remarkable change took place in the attitude of the Anglican church in America. A new era of aggressiveness was inaugurated.

Leaders of ability emerged, both lay and clerical. Many of them were Tories (those who put Crown over Parliament); mostly they were conservative Whigs (supporters of the rights of Parliament). All were imperial minded and sought to establish Anglicanism by law in all of the colonies; to place her local parishes at the center of life; to make the parishes the normal agents of education, welfare, and public worship; and to create a common spiritual center in America. England's church was henceforth to be the spiritual arm of the first British Empire. "Fur, flag, and faith," as John K. Nelson remarks, expresses the purpose of colonial Anglicanism. In the politics of the Atlantic world this church would offer, it was hoped, a powerful counterweight to the empires of Catholic France and Spain. Other colonists saw matters differently with respect to Anglicanism, as well as to Roman Catholicism.

In Massachusetts and Connecticut, Puritans feared Anglicization would mean the reimposition of that absolute royal authority which had caused them to flee England in the first place. In most of the colonies, religious pluralism was so firmly entrenched from the start as to constitute what became an American pattern.

In New York the church was established in the four lower counties of the province, but Anglicans, though growing in number, were still in the minority. In Rhode Island, New Jersey, and Pennsylvania (with Delaware), there had never been any kind of enforced religious allegiance. The Quakers, like Roger Williams, believed none were permitted to have "power or authority over men's consciences in religious matters." In once-Catholic Maryland, with its tradition of toleration, Anglicanism became the establishment (1702) but pluralism continued.

South of Virginia the Church of England was everywhere outnumbered by other religious groups. In North Carolina, where establishment came in fits and starts (1701, 1705, 1711, 1715, 1720, and, finally, 1765), religion was chronically diverse and, from an Anglican perspective, unstable. In South Carolina the church (established in 1706) was outnumbered three to one by dissenters. As the century wore on, moreover, its clergy and laity, as S. Charles Bolton reminds us, were the most ardent anti-imperialists of all Anglicans in the colonies. Georgia (where establishment came in 1758) was far and away the most religiously diverse colony in America. Perhaps more than any other place in its century, it fulfilled the universal need for refuge for all persecuted groups.

One of the chief inspirers of the founding of Georgia was the unwitting father of imperial Anglicanism, the Reverend Thomas Bray. In early 1700 Bray arrived in Maryland as commissary. He was a keen, determined farmer's son who had taken his Master of Arts degree at Oxford as a *puer pauper,* a poor boy. Bray emerged in England as a major reformer. The colony to which he came was torn by religious strife among Quakers, Presbyterians, Roman Catholics, and recently augmented Anglicans. Bray met with the seventeen clergy of Maryland's Church of England parishes. Recognizing American needs, he saw that he could be of more use in England as an advocate for the colonies.

Bray had already observed the success in fulfilling their several objectives of voluntary groups of German pietists, the Society of Friends (Quakers), and even the Society of Jesus (Jesuits). As a result, in 1698 he founded the Anglican Society for the Promotion of Christian Knowledge (SPCK). Its purpose was to provide theological libraries for rural England and America. He also saw the need for a centralized missionary body to send clergy to the New World. The result was the Society for the Propagation of the Gospel in Foreign Parts (SPG), founded in 1701. Both organizations were supported by voluntary contributions from many sources including the Crown. Ever the self-deprecating improviser, Bray constantly sought fresh ways to fulfill the promise of the gospel. In doing so he brought a new authority to the American church.

In what ways did Anglicanism succeed? Why did it fail ultimately to provide the spiritual tie that bound the empire together?

Successes in the Spread of Anglicanism
On the one hand, the accomplishments of the two societies were noteworthy. The SPCK disseminated nearly one hundred libraries of more than one hundred volumes each and some of over one thousand. The works of Anglican theologians abounded, including Bray's own popular *Catechetical Lectures* (1696). The SPCK contributed heavily to what was perhaps the most momentous shipment of books in all colonial his-

tory, that of Jeremiah Dummer to Yale. This famous collection was placed on the shelves in 1718, just in time for student Jonathan Edwards to read the works of Isaac Newton and John Locke and for tutor Samuel Johnson and Yale's president, Timothy Cutler, to read Anglican apologetics.

The results were astounding, and the month in which they occurred—September 1722— proved to be one which changed the course of colonial history. In New Haven, as a result of their reading and conversing, Johnson, Cutler, and other faculty shook the foundations of Congregationalism by announcing their decisions to seek ordination in the Church of England. Johnson, the Hebraist and philosophical theologian, had become impressed with Anglican claims to apostolic succession. Meanwhile, in his first pastorate along the banks of the Hudson River, Jonathan Edwards, scientist and biblical theologian, was impressed by God's immediacy and by "an inward, sweet sense" of the beauty of Christ. The result was the renewal of covenant theology in Lockean terms. Many Americans trace their spiritual ancestry to one event or the other.

Thomas Bray's SPG was no less influential. In the course of the century, it sent 329 missionaries to North America. The charter stipulated that these missionaries were to preach "the great Fundamental Principles of Christianity, and the Duties of a sober, righteous, and godly life," to live simply, and to make themselves masters of the church's doctrine "as contain'd in the Articles and Homilies . . . Liturgy and Canons." Daily prayer and Bible reading were required. They were to instruct people in the nature and use of the sacraments as a means of grace. A "Spirit of Meekness and Gentleness" toward Dissenters was to be matched by a concern for the conversion of Quakers, "Heathens and Infidels," Indians, and blacks. It was by and large a clear and attractive call to service, and men of ability and character answered it.

Many, like Elias Neau and John Bartow in New York and Charles Woodmason in the backcountry of South Carolina, championed the poor. Woodmason, the American Jonathan Swift, brought reforming energy to his work and left a priceless diary. There were many others who served with great distinction. But it often proved more politically rewarding, if not more challenging, to convert Puritans than Indians.

By 1730 there were twelve SPG missionaries in South Carolina, five in Georgia, two in North Carolina, nine in Pennsylvania, five in Delaware, seven in New Jersey, seven in New York, four in Connecticut, three in Rhode Island, and four in Massachusetts. In 1748 there were thirty-six in New England alone. But the greatest growth was to come in the period 1761–1775, especially in Connecticut, as historian Bruce Steiner has shown. There significant converts were made among physicians, attorneys, and merchants as well as among poor farmers.

Largely as a result of the work of the SPG, by 1775 there were 144 churches stretching from what is now Maine to the Delaware Valley with approximately ninety-three ministers. In Virginia and Maryland (where the majority of ministers were not SPG missionaries), there were 143 churches and 136 clergy. In the Carolinas and Georgia, there were forty-seven churches and thirty-five ministers. There were 270,000 Anglicans in America in 1775 out of a population of 2.5 million. While the church had dropped from second place in 1700 to fourth place (behind Congregationalists, Presbyterians, and Baptists) by 1775, its growth rate for the 1760s of 22.5 percent was behind the Baptists with 31.4 percent but equal to or ahead of all others.

In addition to books, missionaries, and churches, Anglicans added two educational institutions. In one they had considerable influence; in the other they exercised complete control. The College of Philadelphia (1749), now the University of Pennsylvania, had as its first provost the Reverend William Smith; and King's College (1754), now Columbia University, had as its first president Samuel Johnson. King's was designed to offset Harvard, Yale, and Princeton. There were also numerous catechists, private tutors, school teachers, and propagandists on behalf of the Anglican cause in America. Among the latter were Bray himself, who inaugurated a genre of unofficial reports to England with his *A Memorial Representing the Present State of Religion on the Continent of North America* (1700). Others followed suit: ex-Quaker and collaborator with Bray, George Keith, *A Journey of Travels* (1706); Hugh Jones, *The Present State of Virginia* (1724); James MacSparran, *America Dissected*

(1752); William Smith, *A Brief State of the Province of Pennsylvania* (1755); and Samuel Johnson, *Raphael, or the Genius of the English America* (ca. 1763). A number of colonial newspapers were favorable to the Anglican cause. In addition the SPG printed Bibles, prayer books, and other publications in the German, Dutch, French, Welsh, Swedish, and Iroquoian languages.

New York became the hub of advancing Anglicanism. There the important Ministry Act (1693) did not legally establish the church, but an aggressive royal governor made sure that its provision for a "Protestant ministry" meant Anglican. The church was outnumbered seventeen to one by Dissenters, was bitterly opposed by Presbyterians, and was suffering internal divisions between Whigs and Tories. Nevertheless, New York Anglicans received significant aid from the SPG. That is because the Hudson River from New York to Albany proved to be the most important line of defense in all America against the expansion of the French. Had it fallen under enemy control, British America would have been divided, with New England separated from the colonies to its south.

From New York City and its environs, Anglican missionaries moved in three directions. North to Albany and the Five Nations of the Iroquois went John Ogilvie, who in addition to speaking Dutch translated the prayer book into the Mohawk tongue. South to Burlington in West Jersey went the high churchman John Talbot to found St. Mary's Church (a deliberate slap at Quakers, who believed that God was incarnate in everyone equally). East into Connecticut went Judge Caleb Heathcote and the Reverend George Muirson. Their efforts were matched by George Pigot and James MacSparran, who moved west into Connecticut from Narragansett Bay.

Anglican development thereafter remained an affair of missionary activity from other strategic towns. From Burlington new congregations were founded in New Jersey, the Delaware Valley, and Pennsylvania. In Connecticut, Stratford and New London became the bases for further growth along the coast and inland. From Boston, with the first King's Chapel (1689) and Christ Church (1723), clergy of high caliber founded some twenty churches along the shores of Massachusetts Bay and into New Hampshire and what is now Maine. Unlike the Connecticut ministers, however, they failed to penetrate the interior. Aside from some bankers and merchants in Boston, the majority of Anglicans in Massachusetts were from the lower-class people in seafaring and related trades. There and in Connecticut such persons were not welcomed into the elite Congregational churches.

In South Carolina, Charles Town produced aristocratic parishes along the coastal tidewater, but Anglican clergy were unwilling for the most part to work in the backcountry. Prior to 1750 the church in North Carolina and Georgia was a failure. In the meanwhile, as growth was proceeding in the northern and middle colonies, Virginia's and Maryland's churches stood still.

Limits to the Church's Growth

Why did Anglicanism, with its new energy, fail to unite Americans? First, the Old World ideal of *cuius regio, eius religio* (in a [prince's] country, his religion must be followed) might work in stable Virginia and Massachusetts. Elsewhere it was impossible to realize. Immigrants to eighteenth-century America (who contributed to a 34.5 percent increase of the population per decade) were too diverse. Since the paupers of one decade became the "princes" of the next, their churches flourished accordingly. Few saw any need to change allegiance.

Second, Whitehall's missionary expectations were one thing, American realities another. For example, the hope of converting the warlike Yamasee Indians of South Carolina as a defense against Spain proved so farfetched that missionary Samuel Thomas ended by ministering to whites along the Cooper River. In addition, communication between the SPG and clergymen in America was difficult; missives were often delayed or lost. The requirement of long reports to the mother country proved onerous, the pay was miserable, and the requests for additional clergy were impossible to meet. There was confusion over instructions and arguments over duties.

Most colonial church traditions, whether magisterial or radical, were organized, administered, and supported locally. Outside of Virginia and Maryland, though, Anglican activity was not. For all American-born clergy of the Church of England, ordination and licensing involved a three-thousand-mile (4,800-kilometer) trip to

England, not a two-hour service at the local church. Storm and death from smallpox in London took their toll. Once in the New World, Englishmen found no settled parishes at all but large tracts of land and scattered inhabitants who saw little need to help ministers already supported by London. Well might English planners insist on liturgical niceties in worship; such things had little to do with local hardships and were ignored. Not surprisingly some men moved to Maryland and Virginia, where the pay was higher. Others stayed on, augmenting their salaries as teachers (they were the best educated in the colonies) and serving with great fidelity.

Third, the idea of uniting Americans in the national church was shattered when the religious lid blew off in the awakenings of the 1740s. That the leader and unifier of these revivals should have been an Anglican priest is one of the ironies of colonial history. In his seven trips to America, George Whitefield reinvoked the theology of the English reformation. He took seriously the three pillars of sixteenth-century Anglicanism. First was the sufficiency of Scripture. So vivid were the stories in the Bible to Whitefield that he discovered his identity in them and then drew others into the biblical web. Second was justification by grace through faith. Whitefield unabashedly declared that none who came to Christ's feet were ever turned away, however dark their sin. The priesthood of all believers was the third pillar. He simply swept aside, insolently and unabashedly, all hierarchy, rank, denomination, and social class. For Whitefield, Americans—Anglican and otherwise—did not have to be completed by Crown or mitre but by that "new sense of the heart" that Edwards had experienced in 1722. For other than spiritual reasons, Benjamin Franklin agreed and asked Whitefield himself to be chaplain of a great army of settlers to people the Ohio Valley.

Whitefield became the first American folk hero, someone either loved or hated, then as now. Either he was God-intoxicated or self-intoxicated. It has never been quite clear which. Most of the Anglican clergy hated him, but most of their parishioners flocked to hear him and some were converted. Old James Blair invited the twenty-five-year-old to preach at Bruton Parish. What has been overlooked by historians, but not by those who heard him, was the invocation

of the Thirty-nine Articles of Religion against moralism on the one hand and rationalism on the other. In making this invocation Whitefield appealed to tradition and thereby caused a spiritual revolution not unlike that which had produced the Articles of Religion in the first place.

For those who disliked impulsiveness, exaggeration, and accusations against sober men of policy, Whitefield's presence was not without its rewards. Anglican Arthur Browne of Portsmouth, New Hampshire, noted that the loss of a few members to evangelical enthusiasm was more than compensated for by "ye addition of thirty-six to our Communion notwithstanding the indefatigable Industry of some crackbrained zealotts to disturb our Peace and promote division."

Whitefield's spiritual ecumenism was carried on in the 1760s by English Methodist laity who constituted the revival wing of Anglicanism in America. Still part of the church, they formed cell groups in parishes, sometimes encouraged by local clergy like Devereux Jarratt of Virginia. These awakened Anglicans harked back to earlier attitudes in their stress on intimacy, mutual respect, and communal discipline.

The fourth reason for the church's failure to become the tie that bound the empire was the agitation for the episcopate, which resulted in a colossal political uproar. Known as the Bishop's Controversy, it raged from 1763 to 1770, but its antecedents went back to the 1710s.

Historians disagree about whether there was a concerted effort on the part of colonial Anglicans to obtain the episcopate. There are three groups: first, denominational historians who saw the struggle for the episcopate as largely an in-house issue; second, those taking a transatlantic and Dissenter perspective, who saw the controversy as a factor in the coming of revolution; and third, Frederick V. Mills, who first noted transcolonial resistance to the episcopate, not just by Dissenters but by a majority of Anglicans as well. Agitators in favor of an American episcopate, Mills claims, were a small, vocal coterie of northern high churchmen.

Colonials conjectured about whether the ample homes of clerics such as East Apthorp of Cambridge, James MacSparran, or John Talbot might not have been intended for episcopal palaces. There were rumors in the press that

Whitefield himself might be made a bishop. Historians have busied themselves with the possibility of secret consecrations. Documentary evidence, however, is lacking.

What is certain is that churchmen blundered both in America and in England by attacking Dissenters' religion. Puritans, declared the bishop of Llandaff in 1767, were "without remembrance or knowledge of God." The pamphlet warfare that ensued involved Anglicans Apthorp, Thomas Bradbury Chandler, and Archbishop Thomas Secker on the one hand and Jonathan Mayhew, Charles Chauncy, William Livingston, and Francis Allison on the other. Defensive coalitions formed on both sides. New York and Connecticut Anglicans gained important experience in learning to cooperate by holding conventions. From their ranks came Loyalist pamphleteers such as Samuel Seabury and Charles Inglis. Their politics damaged the church in the eyes of many. Yet of the 286 Anglican clergy in 1776, 144 were Patriots; there were as well about 160,000 Patriot laity and 110,000 Loyalists.

HOW ANGLICANS WORSHIPED IN AMERICA

What of Anglican worship? Some historians claim that it was devotional rather than instructive, liturgical rather than homiletical. Others note that pews more often faced the pulpit than the holy table and that interiors were designed for preaching, not to attract the eye. People saw themselves and their world under divine governance. God was not passively mysterious and obscure, waiting to be sought out and apprehended by His worshipers but actively mysterious in deliverances, epidemics, dreams, weather, and the like. Though he was hidden, one felt his hand and submitted to his will. Life's goal was not to behold him in beatitude but to try to do the right thing. Acceptance of death—for instance that of a child—was a virtue colonial Anglicans cultivated. William Byrd II's seeming callousness toward the death of one of his children was a protective attitude adopted in a time of high infant mortality both for theological and psychological reasons. If Byrd occasionally slept in church, he was just as likely to shed "tears of repentance," though too loud grief was frowned upon as ungentlemanly. In the later eighteenth century, it was felt that Christianity did not contradict the "Principles of Natural Reason." As a result emphasis on the free grace of God in Jesus Christ was replaced by "sound morality or deep studied Metaphysics."

In the Chesapeake the rhythm of business practices, marriages, and holidays was governed as much by the church calendar as by the crop cycle, Christmas being the most popular holiday. The order of service for an average Sunday morning was Morning Prayer, Litany, Ante-Communion, and sermon. For three centuries this was the normal Sunday for Anglicans, extended at special times in the year by the completion of the eucharist. There were no processions, only a few hymns, but psalms sung in meter. Anglican chorister Thomas Ravenscroft's *Whole Booke of Psalms, with the Hymnes Evangellical and Songs Spirituall* (1621) contained about 150 psalm tunes with treble, alto, and bass parts; before that settlers at Jamestown in 1607 sang the Old Version of Sternhold 'and Hopkins using Thomas Est's musical settings. Ravenscroft's tune book was used in both Massachusetts and in Virginia; each sang the same hymns from the same metrical psalms. The first book to be published in British America was the immensely popular (on both sides of the Atlantic) Bay Psalm Book (1640), used by Anglicans and Puritans alike. In colonial Anglican churches, the parish clerk would announce one of a mere dozen hymn tunes and then, since there were never enough tune books, he would line out the psalm that the congregation would dutifully—if it could remember the line—sing back until the end.

In the eighteenth century, two hymn books increased musical possibilities for congregations, Anglican and otherwise: George Whitefield's *A Collection of Hymns for Social Worship* (1765) and Francis Hopkinson's *A Collection of Psalm Tunes, with a few Anthems and Hymns* (1763), written for Christ Church and St. Peter's in Philadelphia. The first organ was a four-stop chamber instrument placed in King's Chapel, Boston, in 1713. In 1739 Trinity Church, New York, installed a three-manual organ. Thereafter in the 1750s David Tannenberg built some forty organs, many for Episcopal churches, as did Thomas Johnston of Boston. Church bells were common; instrumental music, other than the organ and the venerable bass viol, were not.

Families sat together, usually in box pews that were sold as private property (often including the ground under them); they could be passed down through generations. The location of one's pew indicated rank in the community. The most desirable were nearest the front of the church. Seats generally ran along three sides of the rectangle or square, with a door on the fourth side opening onto one of the aisles. Pews were decorated according to taste, some of which was questionable. There were no liturgical colors or eucharistic vestments, but the combined services provided a hefty serving of Scripture. The Holy Communion was administered four times a year in Virginia (at Christmas, Easter, Whitsunday, and Michaelmas), six times a year in Maryland, and monthly in larger churches in coastal towns. Clergy preached twice on Sunday and on weekdays during Lent. Sermons were short by New England standards, rarely over twenty minutes. Ministers catechized children in Lent. Otherwise there was little teaching in parishes. There were no Sunday schools.

The buildings in which Anglicans worshiped were generally derived from English models. On the basis of St. Luke's, Smithfield (1632–1638), and the records and ruins of others, Virginians built English Gothic churches in the seventeenth century. Amid the travail of pioneering, it was comforting to step back into a familiar medieval building where grace descended from above.

In the eighteenth century colonial Anglicans copied the Georgian baroque churches of Christopher Wren and, later, of James Gibbs. Some, such as simple St. Paul's, Wickford, Rhode Island (1707), and clean, erudite Christ Church, Philadelphia (1744), took on provincial coloration. Others were triumphantly imperial, such as King's Chapel, Boston (1749), and St. Paul's Chapel, New York City (1766). A few, like solid, confident Christ Church, Lancaster County, Virginia (1732), were markedly original.

Anglicans may have been held to the fixed forms of the prayer book, but when it came to the liturgical setting of worship, they felt free to experiment. There were different arrangements of pulpit, holy table, font, and the like. On panels where all could read them were the Lord's Prayer, the Apostles' Creed, and the Decalogue. (The latter was required by canon to be displayed.) Closeness to the people was, it seems, the rule for pulpit and reading desk.

FAILURE TO PRODUCE A POWERFUL IDEOLOGY

We must return once again to our main question: Why did not Anglicanism become the pervasive force in American life that Puritanism became? As the established church in Virginia, America's largest colony, it was poised to do so. To put it differently: Why was this church and its religious tradition unable, amid the rhythms of daily life, to supply the beat and toll the bells for communicants and noncommunicants alike? Put specifically: Why did the Church of England, with its *Book of Common Prayer* and its Protestant, even Calvinist, articles and homilies, its powerful laity, and its missionary societies, fail to communicate its spiritual feel and sensibility to the emerging nation? If New England Puritanism has been metamorphosed into American Puritanism, like it or not, why did not tidewater Anglicanism become American Anglicanism?

Behind this failure is a cumulation of circumstances. First was geography. The magnificent bay of the Chesapeake was rich beyond measure, but it was, for seventeenth-century settlers, also disease ridden. At the outset life was simply a matter of individual survival. There was no ideologically united community of faith and intellect to strengthen any will to endure. Promising Puritan-minded but conforming clergy, like Richard Buck and Alexander Whitaker, did not live long enough to put their imprint on the colony. As a result, for the first two decades unification eluded them.

Second, the development of dispersed tidewater plantations discouraged the growth of towns, where lively theological debate and education were most likely to occur. It took only six years after their arrival in 1630 for the Puritans of Massachusetts to found Harvard College; it took seventy-five years for the dream of the college at Henrico to be realized as the College of William and Mary in 1693. Plantation life, moreover, meant that the space occupied by Virginians was three or four times greater than that of eastern Massachusetts. As a result parishes were often over 100 square miles (260 square kilometers), ten times larger than comparable parishes in Massachusetts, even when the settled regions of the two colonies are included. Virginia parishes of this size included over two thousand whites, double and triple the size of Massachusetts' churches. Church attendance was difficult, even when there were outlying chapels. Those who did not have horses and carriages had to walk from eight to ten miles (about 13 to 16 kilometers) to church. It was these people who in the eighteenth century became dissatisfied with the balance between the benefits received and the taxes paid. Loyalty to the church was thus weakened.

Third, instead of modifying class differences, as did the Massachusetts Bay Puritans, Virginians and Marylanders sharpened social distinctions over the course of the seventeenth century with the introduction of indentured white servants and black slaves. Both societies would agree with John Winthrop that all people are "thus [by divine providence] rancked into two sortes, riche and poore." However, Chesapeake planters would be unlikely to agree when, in "A Modell of Christian Charity," Winthrop declared that "in [our] duty of love wee must love brotherly without dissimulation . . . wee must beare one anothers burthens, wee must not looke only on our owne things, but allsoe on the things of our brethren." In the slave-owning areas of the colonial South, one might love God but be selective about neighbors. Few there objected to this reading of the Great Commandment (Mt. 22:37–40ff.; Luke 6:31ff.). Thus the Anglican church failed to commend itself to a large segment of the population.

Fourth, religious pluralism in the middle colonies and in the deep South became so much a part of cultural life that no church could dominate. In New York, New Jersey, and Pennsylvania, denominations other than the Church of England declared their prerogatives loudly and convincingly, while in South Carolina nonreligious interests shaped society. Since Georgia was a refuge for the religiously persecuted and others, assimilation into the Church of England was never an option.

Fifth, the theological climate changed. By the time Williamsburg became the provincial capital of the Old Dominion and the college was founded, there was no compelling covenant theology either to be modified or reclaimed, as occurred in New England in 1660 and 1734 respectively. Throughout the colonies a more comprehensive—and moralistic—Anglicanism, reflecting English sources, appeared in books by high churchmen, latitudinarians, and eventually, deists. The combination of high-church claims to historic Anglican authenticity (the unbroken succession of bishops from the apostles, or apostolic succession) and Enlightenment rationalism altered the scene.

In the northern colonies, the Church of England became a haven for Puritans who, in the light of the new European scientific learning, found themselves disillusioned by their own provincialism. In the 1720s and 1730s they asked, What is the good society and by what rubric is it to be governed? Ex-Puritans like Samuel Johnson found comfort in a communal legitimacy guaranteed by historic episcopal succession and, thus, valid priestly ordination. To Johnson it seemed that God planned in advance and then worked in the world, through the authentic church and her clergy, to achieve His plan. For Johnson, Samuel Seabury, and others, as a result, Anglicanism became a clearly illuminated path between the darkness of Roman superstition on the one hand and the caterwauling of the followers of Whitefield on the other.

For Jonathan Edwards and the awakened preachers, communal harmony, authenticated by a new aesthetic and moral "sense of the heart," was itself the most convincing evidence that the good society was being created afresh every day. To them the true church was in the hearts and in the minds of those whom God had touched with His spirit regardless of their religious tradition. They thus reflected those ideals of unity in the faith of such sixteenth-century reformers as Martin Bucer. Moreover for Edwards there was no division between God's planning and his working; for God to conceive as actual was for Him to make to be actual. Apostolic succession, in this view, could be nothing less than an affirmation of God's continuous—and continuing—act of creation. To believe anything less (such as mere tactical succession) was idolatry.

With such a division in America, Anglicanism could hardly hope to dominate. But what is important to recognize is that by the second quarter of the eighteenth century, the American church was evidencing a variety that would itself make definition—and influence—increasingly difficult to achieve. To be the uniting spiritual arm of the first British empire, the church had to be more than a refuge for Anglophiles and more than the local southern gentry at prayer. It was not enough to subscribe to Hugh Jones's little dictum,

> God bless the church and George its defender;
> Convert the fanaticks and baulk the Pretender.

It was not enough for high churchmen in the northern colonies to rely on a concept of fixed authority in Crown, Parliament, and bishop beyond which there was no appeal. Increasingly Americans looked to fundamental law by which all of whatever rank must abide. While desire for a constitution embodying that law grew, the northern Anglicans' desire to adhere to a fixed imperial and ecclesiastical authority dwindled alarmingly after 1760 and finally came unstuck in 1776.

To Harriet Beecher Stowe, who from her maternal grandparents came to understand colonial Anglicanism and who eventually joined the Episcopal church (the name given after the revolution to the Church of England in America), belongs the last and most perceptive word: theologically the Anglican church provided a gentle rain but no thunder. She wrote,

> It remains a mystery to my mind how a church which retains such a stimulating and inspiring liturgy *could* have such drowsy preaching,—how men could go through with the "Te Deum" and the "Gloria in Excelsis," without one thrill of inspiration, or one lift above the dust of earth, and after uttering words which one would think might warm the frozen heart of the very dead, settle sleepily down into the quietest commonplace.

Human nature, she judged, "is, above all things, lazy, and needs to be thorned and goaded up those heights where it ought to fly."

BIBLIOGRAPHY

Bolton, S. Charles. *Southern Anglicanism: The Church of England in Colonial South Carolina.* Westport, Conn., 1982.

Ellis, Joseph J. *The New England Mind in Transition: Samuel Johnson of Connecticut, 1696–1772.* New Haven, Conn., 1973. Intellectual biography of Anglicanism's leading colonial educator.

Fithian, Philip Vickers. *Journal and Letters of Philip Vickers Fithian.* Edited by Hunter Dickinson Farrish. Williamsburg, Va., 1965. Provides a northerner's view of religion and planter life in eighteenth-century Virginia.

Gundersen, Joan. "The Anglican Ministry in Virginia, 1723–1776." Ph.D. diss., University of Notre Dame, 1972. A major revisionist work on Virginia clergy.

Jones, Hugh. *The Present State of Virginia, from Whence Is Inferred a Short View of Maryland and North Carolina.* Edited by Richard L. Morton. Chapel Hill, N.C., 1956. An indispensable account of the Church of England in Virginia written in 1724.

Mills, Frederick V., Sr. *Bishops by Ballot: An Eighteenth-Century Ecclesiastical Revolution.* New York, 1978. An essential study of Anglicanism in revolutionary America.

Nelson, John K. "Anglican Missions in America, 1701–1725: A Study of the Society for the Propagation of the Gospel in Foreign Parts." Ph.D. diss., Northwestern University, 1962. Groundbreaking analysis of the early SPG.

Steiner, Bruce E. "New England Anglicanism: A Genteel Faith?" *William and Mary Quarterly,* 3rd ser., 27 (1970):122–135.

Woodmason, Charles. *The Carolina Backcountry on the Eve of the Revolution: The Journal and Other Writings of Charles Woodmason, Anglican Itinerant.* Edited by Richard J. Hooker. Chapel Hill, N.C., 1953.

Woolverton, John F. *Colonial Anglicanism in North America.* Detroit, Mich., 1984. Contains a seventeen-page bibliography.

John Frederick Woolverton

SEE ALSO **Higher Education; Music and Dance, The British Colonies, Sacred Music; Philosophy; The Structure of Society;** and **Taxation.**

PURITANISM

PURITANISM HAS GENERATED more scholarship than nearly any other subject in American history, yet misconceptions and controversies abound. Popular attitudes still reflect a vestigial Menckenism that regards Puritans as self-righteous busybodies who soured American culture for everyone else. Although scholars discarded this stereotype long ago, they continue to dispute the Saints' (believers') influence. Impressed with its high piety and social activism, some historians rate Puritanism the most signal factor developing colonial New England, at times virtually equating place and faith. Others, rightly pointing out the region's entrepreneurialism, social homogeneity, demographic growth, and inherited English folkways, downplay its impact and seem occasionally to disregard it altogether. Resulting from different sources and research strategies, these contradictory assessments also betray an underlying terminological vagueness. Pressed to identify a consistent "Puritanism" critical of, yet aligned with, the post-Reformation church, English historians have contested the term's precise meaning, but their American cousins fix primarily on colonial developments, where recognizing a Puritan mainstream is easy, and presume the definition implicitly. Reviewing English historiography underlines the subject's transatlantic sweep and warns against regarding it as solely the New World's spawn. Understanding Puritanism in America requires engaging both the Tudor-Stuart background and the definitional stew.

DEFINITION

The name "Puritan" first surfaced in England in the 1560s as an epithet denouncing Protestants perceived as excessively earnest in their efforts to purify the English church of Catholic "corruption." Those so tagged initially dismissed the name, claiming it falsely implied their affinity with sects such as the thirteenth-century Cathars, who asserted human perfectibility on earth. Abhorring the notion, Puritans preferred to call themselves "the godly," but, like others slandered throughout the ages, ultimately accepted the slur. Until the 1640s, prelates and laity disputed with the "precisians" (a synonym for "Puritan," connoting people overly "precise," or scrupulous, about conforming strictly to Scripture) in their midst; a few modern historians, however, dispute the existence of a distinct movement, arguing that "Puritanism" disguises the church's essential unity by exaggerating secondary differences of opinion. Charles H. and Katherine George interpret Reformed Protestantism as primarily a medium for legitimizing the capitalist market system. Thus they can identify the "Puritan ethic" advocating industry and frugality in one's calling to gain the riches of heaven (and earth) as a common Protestant value. More concerned with church affairs, Patrick Collinson has at times subsumed Puritanism within a broader English Protestant consensus concerned, at least until the 1620s, with Reformed dogmatics, effective preaching, and moral reforms. The first view, as Collinson himself explains, dismissed religious ideas too readily; the second, as scholars like J. Sears McGee argue, minimizes partisanship within the church. Both neglect the historical reality that contemporaries, spying Puritans in pulpits and pews, sought either to join or to denounce them. Too much evidence of conflict between the self-professed godly and their detractors survives to support dismissing Puritanism as a historical entity. Describing it, however, takes more care.

Colonial historians have taken little interest in defining Puritanism because the problem appears either irrelevant or solved. From a purely American perspective, the fervor of seventeenth-century New Englanders for building a holy commonwealth so distinguishes them from other settlers that detailing the nuances of their beliefs becomes moot; Puritanism means Calvinist doctrine and moral police. Perry Miller had apparently decided the issue in his majestic corpus, most notably *The New England Mind.* Although cognizant of the Saints' "Augustinian strain of piety," Miller defined Puritanism as essentially an intellectual program, anchored in the dialectical dichotomies of Peter Ramus and in the Reformed covenant theology, which conceived the relationship between individuals and God, Miller thought, as a bilateral contract consummated by voluntary partners. Knighting Puritanism with the sword of rational respectability changed its interpretation forever. No longer could scholars dismiss it as unthinking fanaticism or derogate its significance for New England's past; Puritanism had provided the educated elite with a system to fathom the spiritual universe and dominate noetic life. Asserting its importance in molding colonial New England and dramatizing preachers' toils to preserve their scheme against Enlightenment humanism and backsliding congregants, Miller limned how the original synthesis unraveled despite piecemeal attempts to stitch it together. Declension, the paradigm of Puritanism's rise and fall, explained New England's transformation from religious hothouse to secular society.

Historians of English Puritanism have occasionally duplicated Miller's ideational slant— Marshall Knappen called Tudor Puritanism a "chapter in the history of idealism"—but they confront a phenomenon less easily categorized as primarily an intellectual one. With good reason they have characterized Puritanism equally as a drive to spiritualize worship, overthrow the prelates, hedge in (and ultimately behead) the king, or dictate one's neighbors' habits. People might advance one or more of these agendas, and some (e.g., bishops committed to the hierarchy inherent in episcopacy but enthusiastic about improved preaching) discountenanced one Puritan reform while espousing another. Defining English Puritanism as primarily an intellectual movement fails to explain either its political vitality or its programmatic diversity, and its existence in tension with but not absolutely separate from the established church makes identifying its proponents problematic. When did nonconformity lapse into schism? English historiography subordinates Puritanism's words to its world—the networks of gentry who sheltered dissident preachers, the local struggles between the godly and their fellow parishioners to control behavior in church, townhouse, and street—and, noting how Reformed Protestant theology prevailed among the church's creeds and clerics, distinguishes the Saints as paragons of holy zeal. Puritans, to quote Patrick Collinson, were a "hotter sort" of Protestant, outstanding for their passion to labor in God's name.

Puritanism, then, comprised a special religious sensibility, an intensity to celebrate the Lord by performing his commands. The psychological roots of this ardor grew in conversion, the "new birth" of John 3:3 elaborated by Puritan preachers into an emotional confrontation with grace borne by the Holy Spirit in the Word. Its manifest content channeled by the doctrines of Reformed Protestantism, conversion involved believers in a protracted experience prompting them to join self-selected groups of devout ministers, magistrates, and laity dedicated to purifying church and society. Grace flourished in a particular sociopolitical milieu: Saints sought, exhibited, and sustained their individual faith within a community populated, ministered, and, as much as possible, governed by their spiritual peers. Defining Puritanism as foremost a religious temperament demands locating its historical environment, binding it to a specific time, place, and theology. To detach the sensibility from these moorings reduces it to a synonym for a certain kind of self-righteous moralism and blunts its analytic utility.

The "declension" model that has so tightly framed perceptions of colonial New England posits an essential Puritanism, complete at its American debut, disintegrating (declining) over time. Assuming that one moment defines the entire movement, this model comprehends change as departure from an ideal type. Such a static theory was rhetorically useful to preachers urging their congregants to repent, but it biases historical interpretation by prejudging any alteration in Puritan practice or belief as necessarily devolutionary. Identifying Puritanism as a religious mentality allows a more dynamic approach by admitting that ideas, practices, and institutions evolve. In this light, Puritanism did not depreciate, but adapted as preachers refined their doctrine, ministers and laity contested for power, and the godly gained the chance to erect their biblical commonwealth unhindered by ancient structures of church and state. The history of Puritanism features accommodation to historical circumstance, and its narrative properly begins with faith.

DOCTRINE AND SENSIBILITY

Doctrinally, Puritanism belongs to the theological genus usually named Calvinism after the preeminent Genevan churchman but more appropriately denominated Reformed Protestantism to recognize that contributors in some fifty cities hammered out its tenets. Reformed Protestantism appropriated Martin Luther's central insight that salvation comes through faith alone, and further incorporated a theory that God dispenses grace by means of a covenant. In England, continental thought built upon foundations poured by early Protestants like William Tyndale and John Bradford, and by the later sixteenth century the resulting edifice housed the English church.

Reformed dogmatics presupposes a sovereign, omniscient God who created the world to manifest his glory and who demands obedience from all creatures. Totally immersed in the world's operation, God decrees what shall transpire and then effects it through his will (Providence). Scripture discloses the essentials of his plan, and human beings can discern its progress by using book and faith to decipher portents in a falling sparrow or a rising tax, but they can never plumb his mind through reason and can comprehend his grace only through faith. God displays his mercy by granting eternal life to all who perform his commandments, and his justice by damning everyone who disobeys. The first man, Adam, had the ability to fulfill God's law but chose to sin instead, so deranging his sensate powers (faculties) that subsequently he could only dimly think, will, or feel the good. Adam's progeny inherit both his constitutional debility (the Puritan notion of original sin) and his guilt; they cannot perform good works—precluded by the innate corruption of body and soul—and deserve death, waiting under a sentence waived only through the intervention of Jesus Christ. God incarnate, Christ performed God's law but took on and atoned for humanity's sin, sacrificing himself on the cross to make his perfect righteousness available to degenerate humanity. Christ offers redemption freely, and to accept him is all a sinner needs to attain heaven; he saves only those who embrace him as their personal savior.

Reformed Protestants explained how God works redemption as a series of logical steps commencing with his determination to save some and damn the rest. Both election and reprobation evince his glory, but why he predestines particular souls for heaven or hell lies beyond human ken. Few doctrines in the history of theology have received more polemical and scholarly attention than predestination, variously described as the hub of Reformed dogmatics, a denial of free will that turns humans into puppets on the hand of a capricious god, and a savage teaching that dooms people for not doing what they cannot possibly do. In fact, predestination figured little in Reformed preaching (although it emerged as a polemical flash point in fights with other creeds), did not abrogate human choice in the conduct of one's daily affairs (asserting only that one cannot will one's own salvation), and, understood within its doctrinal context, intended to console, not condemn. Predestination explains the observation, otherwise inexplicable, that some people live godly lives while others do evil and, by pronouncing that God saves the elect infallibly, guarantees that he will never fail them, supreme comfort against fears that one might fall away.

Puritans believed that God offered Christ by means of a covenant. In the most sophisticated rendering of this idea, preachers argued that originally God had established a "covenant of works" with Adam, promising salvation if he satisfied divine law flawlessly, but that, in Eden's wake, God enacted a "covenant of grace" pledging eternal life on the sole condition that one take Christ as one's savior. Covenant theology neither demeaned God's sovereignty nor held him to a deal; it held that God compacts solely with those he has elected to save, who gain faith only because he grants it, not because they earn it. The covenant concept is better understood as an attempt to incorporate a recurrent biblical motif into Reformed theology than as an effort at dictating salvation's terms to an awesome lord. Nevertheless, the bilaterality of the covenanting process proved useful for Puritans to understand other agreements that both sides did enter voluntarily: those between God and the people in his chosen nation, rulers and the ruled within a state, and members of a church with each other.

From William Perkins in the late sixteenth century to Samuel Willard in the late seventeenth, Puritan systematizers added few novelties to Reformed doctrine. The ministers' greatest contributions came as "physicians of the soul," master psychologists of a religious sensibility established through conversion. People strive vainly to win salvation on their own, they warned, for original sin vitiates the exercise; with every action corrupted by inherent disability, unregenerates cannot merit grace. In time, however, God calls the predestined elect to Christ, who imputes his righteousness to them and adopts them into God's family. The Holy Spirit reorders believers' faculties and partially restores their pristine capacity to obey God's law, although enough corruption remains to ensure that they will never cease to sin on earth. Complete purification and deliverance from the law's curse come only after death, but meanwhile regenerate believers can gain assurance that they are saved, confidence that grows as their spirituality matures.

The genius of Puritan preachers lay with imaging grace in the flesh, transforming abstract doctrines into tears and smiles. Conversion's passage evokes a characteristic emotional pattern. As the Holy Spirit awakens unregenerates to their transgressions, conscience stabs them and they dread its pricks. Frantic efforts to reform prove futile because their deeds lack saving efficacy, and realizing that they cannot save themselves induces holy desperation. Convinced of their doom, they give themselves up for lost and implore Christ's aid. Fear and terror mark a period of preparation for grace, after which Christ calls, the soul answers, and regeneration begins. No specific emotion identifies the moment of grace, but in time sensations of joy and peace dispel anxiety. Suffused with divine love (agape), Saints beam their affection to God and their fellows. By "love" Puritans meant a passion imbued with duty and manifested in work. Agape rouses desires to serve the Lord in all things, and whereas unregenerates drudge from fear of punishment, believers labor with infatuated obligation made possible by a sense of power that is conversion's corollary.

In the Puritan rendering, original sin destroys one's ability to come to God, but pride naturally deludes unregenerates into thinking that they can, and they respond to conscience's first pangs by trusting in their own powers to merit grace. Preparation climaxes in humiliation, the horrific insight that no amount of toil can overcome inner depravity. Taking Christ revitalizes the faculties and endows them with new power to do good. For a Saint, grace correlates with a cycle of emotions and a sense of power that, once learned, can be reiterated. When corruption raises doubts about salvation, inspiring fear and impeding holy labor, Saints can work through the now-familiar affective cycle and recover their strength. Theologically, conversion translates Saints into grace; experientially, it empowers them.

Neither the Bible nor Reformed dogmatics dresses conversion in any emotional style. Why Puritans alone should have so emphasized the new birth's feelings and potency is unclear, but the most intriguing hypothesis points to faith's political contexts. French Huguenots, squeezed by the Catholic majority into fortified enclaves, expressed an extroverted piety in picaresque tales of redemption from sin and persecution. Aggrieved with their church but not alienated from it, alternately suppressed and tolerated, Puritans did not have to defend themselves against such outward aggressions and instead ruminated on their own failings, glimpsing sin in a looking glass rather than the prosecutor's face. Whatever the reason, Puritan religiosity exhibited typical concerns. To better obey God's will and to compile evidence of their own salvation, Saints scanned the world for clues to his decree. An ugly wound or a sudden storm was not a random tic of history and nature but a providential sign illustrating an ultimate design. To interpret the meanings, clergy and laity turned to Scripture.

Equating the Bible with God's word, Puritans took it as the mandatory blueprint for godly living and strove to follow it exactly, although fidelity to the text did not entail mindless literalism. Scripture does not err, they held, but neither does it prescribe every duty; reason must play over its pages, filling gaps and explaining why some rules, like the Old Testament's ceremonial laws, no longer apply. God does command a crusade against sin, however, and personal convictions to purge evil from oneself should energize campaigns to purify church and society. When successfully completed, this moral program would erect not some "progressive" utopia but the truly godly community realized in ancient times though long degenerated by Catholic corruptions. The Bible's precepts lead back to the church's primitive perfection, an ideal Puritans reached for by marching ahead to the past.

Whether millennialism—the belief in Christ's imminent return and the attendant radical restructuring of the world—comprised an essential element of Puritan piety is controversial. The religious excitements of Tudor-Stuart England and America encouraged speculation about the Lord's impending advent, encouraging some Puritans to anticipate the Last Days. They seem, however, to have adopted millennialism only at certain times or in response to events deemed especially apocalyptic. John Cotton pored through the Book of Revelation as the English Civil War erupted, and Increase Mather took cues from a tableau of wars, plagues, and messianism among eastern European Jews that he thought foretold their incoming to Christ. John Eliot's fervor waxed and waned according to the progress of his Amerindian mission and the exigencies of Anglo-American politics. Perhaps the most judicious view would acknowledge millennialism as a frequent but not essential Puritan trait. The Puritans' sensibility centered on providentialism, moral activism, bibliolatry, primitivism, and an exclusivist attitude toward the nonelect, all of these qualities suffused with God's hallmark: conversion-induced intensity.

GENESIS AND EXODUS

Puritanism emerged to contest what dissatisfied Protestants considered England's ruling ills: the church's arrested Reformation and a disintegrating social structure epitomized by increased mobility and decreased communality. The Acts of Supremacy and Uniformity (1559) had fixed the church with the monarch as supreme governor and a Protestant liturgy but had not eradicated ritual practices like using the sign of the cross in baptism or improved the clergy's competence. Nor had it instituted correct discipline, which in fully Reformed churches meant instructing the congregation in morality, surveilling their behavior, protecting the sanctity of the Lord's Supper by prohibiting the impure from celebrating it, and excommunicating the scandalous. Outraged reformers, many of whom had spent the 1550s in exile on the Continent absorbing the latest Protestant ideas, began to agitate for an end to "popish superstition" and the installation of Reformed procedures regarding discipline.

Matters first came to a head in 1566 when, with Elizabeth's blessing, Archbishop Matthew Parker insisted that ministers conducting public rites must wear the proper ceremonial vestments, whatever their scruples that the ornate garb stank of Rome, and suspended thirty-seven London clergymen who refused. Nonconformists next tried to legislate reformation through Parliament, but the bishops beat down their bills. Stymied by the religious and political establishment, radical Puritans plotted to replace the episcopal hierarchy with a presbyterian scheme that would have placed discipline in the hands of church officers chosen by each congregation—the consistory—and organized ecclesiastical government around a graduated series of self-governing groups: local consistories would form classes, which would send representatives to regional synods, the whole topped by a national council.

Unequivocally patriotic, the radicals nevertheless challenged the English state's religious buttressing and drew the queen's ire for sedition. Presbyterianism allocated discipline to the consistory instead of the existing church courts and denied the magistrate's right to dictate church policy, a program that, if instituted, would have eliminated the episcopate and dashed the royal supremacy. Elizabeth wanted none of it. Archbishop John Whitgift jailed nine leading presbyterians in 1590, and the movement collapsed.

The crackdown deterred Puritans from overt political action for a generation, but a handful, despairing that the church would ever reform, had already broken away. Separatists refused to take Communion with regular parishioners, who shared the sacrament with "ungodly folk," and gathered congregations on their own, spooking the government because withdrawing from the parishes fractured the ideal of a national English church and transgressed the monarch's authority as its head. The resulting persecution drove Separatists underground or overseas, where they berated nonseparating Puritans for embracing an untrue church. Separatists willingly removed themselves from the Puritan mainstream, and they provided concrete examples of how believers could raise a church outside the established hierarchy by voluntarily covenanting together.

The Puritan majority rejected separatism for impugning Saints still within the English church and roiling the authorities against them all. With prospects for institutional reform dim, they directed their energies into spreading the gospel. Puritanism was always a religion of the sermon, and the godly gadded about the English countryside to hear a favorite preacher. Yeomen, goodwives, traders, artisans, and lawyers filled the audiences, so associating nonconformity with the middling orders makes some sense, but interpreting the movement primarily in class terms or imputing its appeal to its supposedly procapitalist message misconstrues it. Members of the gentry endowed lectureships for preachers outside episcopal control and, as local civic leaders, promoted moral reform. Some of the poor were likewise born again, particularly if they worked in godly households. The much-discussed "Puritan ethic" did not extol acquisitive enterprise. Saints were expected to be frugal, industrious, diligent, and honest, and to perform their particular (occupational) calling in respect of their general vocation as Christians; one prospered little by gaining the world but losing one's soul.

Puritanism may have helped small entrepreneurs survive in England's urban economies of scarce resources and plentiful competition—fair dealing satisfied customers and careful management kept businesses functioning despite endemically small profit margins—but earning a modest competence, especially when one sells goods at a "just price" determined by an item's social value and affordability, does not evince unchecked acquisitive enterprise. Some justification exists for linking Puritanism with commercial activity, especially in market towns and their hinterlands. Towns provided the fiscal density to fund such extramural godly activities as independent lectureships, and the population density to support covenanted associations. Puritanism did not extol the road to riches, but it flourished in environments with income levels high enough to support the social apparatus of godliness.

As the "spiritual brotherhood" spread the gospel of new birth, lay converts formed bands to study, to pray, and to edify each other. Collecting around "powerful" (inspiring) preachers, they covenanted among themselves to walk rightly before God, in the process generating small cells of born-again Christians within the larger, more spiritually torpid body of the church. Concentrated in southern and eastern England, they probably did not comprise more than 5 percent of the population overall, but their energy, directed at instilling godly discipline in both parish and town, magnified their influence. The notion of a holy commonwealth where regenerated Saints ran the church and regulated their neighbors' behavior first played out in those localities where covenanted assemblies grew large enough to contest their neighbors' ways. Forcing refractory ministers to strip off their vestments, hounding youths to quit maypole dancing, and, where they counted magistrates among them, prohibiting recreation on the Sabbath, Puritans combined reforming the church with improving society. Sometimes, as at Banbury, they succeeded, but frequently they angered neighbors resentful of self-righteous "hypocrites" who disturbed frolics and who, the propaganda went, secretly committed all the sins they so piously denounced. Local fights between the godly and their antagonists, waged with pamphlets, sneers, ordinances, and fists, went on for decades before the 1640s, when both sides mounted cannons.

Government activity against dissenters swelled and ebbed. King James I (r. 1603–1625) once threatened to "harry" Puritans from the land, and his bishops intermittently suspended nonconformist preachers, but his government had neither the means nor the inclination to contrive a concerted effort, and Puritans even received official church support in some of the "dark corners of the land," where their proselytizing zeal made them ideal shock troops to infiltrate zones of irreligion and Catholic recusancy. Nevertheless, by the end of his reign James I had correlated religious dissent with political subversion and had set the throne firmly against the Puritans, a policy his son Charles I (r. 1625–1649) amplified. Charles preferred Arminians—who propounded a more liberal theology of human cooperation in conversion and a more exalted view of ritual ceremony than did Reformed orthodoxy—in high positions in the church, based his foreign policy on *raison d'état* rather than Protestant alliances (even marrying a French Catholic princess), dismissed Parliament in 1629 (thereby choking off Puritan agitation for moral legislation in the House of Commons), and allowed increased harassment of nonconformists.

Diminished hopes for reform and augmented fears of persecution inspired thoughts of flight. The Netherlands, a haven for dissenters from across Europe, presented an obvious destination, but even there matters did not always turn out as refugees expected. John Robinson's Separatist congregation settled in Leiden only to face economic hardship, a softening of their religious discipline and ethnic identity, and the threat of Spanish invasion. The classes of the Dutch Reformed church monitored the theology of ministers like Thomas Hooker and silenced them when they spoke too independently. The colonization of Virginia and Bermuda suggested an alternative refuge: America. The Leiden Separatists contracted with an association of English investors eager to start a private plantation in Virginia, although they eventually settled in Plymouth. Contractual troubles with their sponsors plagued the Pilgrims for years, but they could not have outfitted the voyage alone. In contrast, Puritans controlled the companies that launched their two major transatlantic colonizing efforts.

The first aimed toward New England, its offshore waters known since the late fifteenth century as fertile fishing grounds, and in 1624 the Dorchester Adventurers entered the business. Dorchester had an active Puritan movement, and one-sixth of the company's associates were ministers; the Adventurers planned to establish a permanent base to supply the yearly fishing fleets with logistical and spiritual support. The endeavor failed, and in 1628 investors from London and East Anglia took over the enterprise, intending to found a Puritan sanctuary. The next year they received a royal charter establishing the Massachusetts Bay Company that, for reasons unknown, did not specify where the company had to locate its headquarters. As Charles I sent Parliament packing and nonconforming ministers lost their livings, a portion of the company mobilized to take advantage of the loophole. Agreeing to emigrate, they bought out those members who demurred and took the company's government with them, the better to secure their colony against unfriendly interference.

Geopolitics joined religion and commerce in directing the second enterprise. In 1630, twenty wealthy Puritans organized the Providence Company to settle the islands of Providence and San Andreas off the coast of Nicaragua. By that date English enterprisers had already organized three colonies in the eastern Caribbean, upwind from hostile galleons, but the Providence Company nestled its venture squarely in the Spanish maw because, along with marketing agricultural products and building a holy society, they wanted a forward base against the foe. At a time when Stuart diplomacy appeased Catholic powers too readily for Puritan tastes, the company believed that attacking Spanish operations in the Caribbean would weaken England's foremost Catholic adversary and advance true Protestantism. Providing a godly asylum mattered much to organizers of both the Massachusetts Bay Company and the Providence Company, but the latter's religious nationalism, a reversion to Elizabethan foreign policy and a harbinger of Oliver Cromwell's, envisioned a far more aggressive program than did the former's.

The "Puritan hegira" occurred within a larger folk wandering; between Plymouth (1620) and the battle of Edgehill (1642) that opened the Civil War, eighty thousand people followed their hopes out of England, primarily to the North American mainland and the Caribbean.

Puritans fanned out beyond New England and Providence, settling in Virginia, Maryland, Bermuda, and, later in the century, Cape Fear (North Carolina) and the West Indian islands of Eleuthera, Jamaica, and New Providence. Evidence of characteristically Puritan interest in a Reformed church and moral order exists for all of these places, but in none did that influence predominate or survive long enough to ground society and culture. Governor William Berkeley enforced the use of the Anglican liturgy in Virginia after 1643 and pressured nonconformists to leave; some three hundred moved to Maryland, where they agitated for changes in the colony's Act of Toleration (1649) that excluded non-Trinitarians, and during the 1650s led a coup against Lord Baltimore's government. In the end, although dissenting Protestantism figured heavily in Maryland's politics, no Puritan church order developed, and the colony established Anglicanism in 1702. Bermuda and Jamaica also had nonconforming populations without holy commonwealths, the efforts on Cape Fear and Eleuthera quickly petered out, and the Spanish military destroyed Old Providence and New Providence.

The bulk of the Puritans went to Massachusetts Bay during the Great Migration of the 1630s and from there "hived out" into Connecticut, New Haven, New Hampshire, Maine, and Rhode Island, the "sinkhole" for all heterodoxies the mainstream banned. By 1650 New England counted some twenty thousand inhabitants. No single explanation accounts for the migration; some came for adventure, others because family or friends beckoned. East Anglia's depressed textile industry provided an economic incentive to leave England for the New World, as did the prospect of landownership. Not every voyager was a Saint, nor did religion alone animate those who were, but Puritanism endowed the elite and probably a majority of the passengers with its distinctive zeal and outlook. Providentialism read God's controversy with England in stilled looms, bickering among neighbors, episcopal high-handedness, and absolutist politics, intimating a more godly life overseas. The demography of the exodus implies its religious coloration; against the makeup of contemporary movements to other colonies—typically young, single men on the make—the nature of the Great Migration

stands out for its more balanced sex ratios, the number of mature adults, the prevalence of families, the presence of groups originating in the same town or congregation, and an unusually high percentage of university graduates—the building blocks of covenanting communities expressed as sociological categories. They moved not so much for "religious freedom"—certainly not for tolerating other faiths—as for setting up a holier, more disciplined community in the diaspora than England would allow.

THE HOLY COMMONWEALTH

The trinity of church, state, and family expressed institutionally Puritanism's sociopolitical triumvirate of ministers, magistrates, and laity. Each organization retained its own especial sphere but joined the others to instill and maintain moral order. By "church," Puritans understood only the body of regenerate believers covenanted together to enforce godly demeanor, not the inclusive group of Saints and sinners who composed the congregation. According to this definition, migrants did not quit the Church of England, because they claimed to keep communion with Saints who remained behind (although in time this geographic separation became a denominational one). A church should consist only of Visible Saints, people whose character and carriage palpably demonstrated their election, and the higher the percentage of Visible Saints who also belonged to the Invisible Church (the body of regenerates God has elected in all times and places), the purer that particular group of worshipers.

Even to approach the ideal was impossible in England, where "church" referred to the parish's edifice and inhabitants, who, whether pious or profane, took the sacramental bread and wine. Free at last to prosecute any reform they wished, Puritans promoted congregational autonomy in the service of purity and discipline, a form of church government, argued by seventeenth-century theologians John Cotton, Richard Mather, and Thomas Hooker among others, that presumed to re-create the church structure of the primitive Christians; in fact, it elaborated on both the writings of theorists like Thomas

Cartwright and William Ames, and practices like the Separatists' church gatherings. Distrusting the episcopal structure that gave the central administration control over individual parishes, and ecclesiastical courts that dispensed discipline clumsily at best, they devised the New England Way, a congregational system that made each church its own supreme governor, although ministers could (and did) convene informal associations to keep abreast of events and to advise each other. The laity founded churches—seven or so known righteous men examining their godliness before each other and then covenanting to worship the Lord and follow his laws—and played an important role in running them: calling the minister, choosing the officers, certifying membership, and ratifying excommunication. The most striking innovation established examination of a candidate's conversion as a condition of membership; restricting the church to God's elect as much as possible had led to evaluating an individual's personal experience, an entirely subjective procedure since no human could authenticate another's grace with absolute certainty.

English Puritanism had evolved as a movement with dual evangelical goals: to preach the gospel to nominal Christians, heretics, and non-Christians (what might be called the "external mission") and to increase the piety of Christians within the church (the "internal mission"). Preachers always proselytized the former groups, especially before Reformed Protestantism had swept the parishes, but the greater effort lay in heightening the piety of ordinary professors through the new birth. In first-generation New England, meetinghouses filled with substantial numbers of Visible Saints, so that the major task lay more in sorting migrants into convenable congregations and in formalizing the church order than in pressing for immediate conversions; most settlers were either regenerate or could reasonably be expected to become so soon. The outward mission, however, confronted people far more alien than any the Puritans had encountered in England: the mostly Algonquian-speaking Amerindians of the eastern woodlands. The common ethnocentric assumption that Europeans had to civilize the Amerindians before Christianizing them gained added currency among Puritans because of the high piety and

discipline they demanded; to be born again and take the Lord's Supper, natives had to learn the subtleties of Reformed theology, necessarily accomplished only by first apprehending the artifacts and demeanor that embodied it.

Along with the disdain Puritans accorded peoples they considered culturally inferior, the real necessity for organizing their own system, and Amerindian bands' disinterest in receiving the whites' religion while they maintained their own intact, the gulf between deerskins and doublets helps explain the colonists' delay in proselytizing the natives. Activity began in the 1640s, prodded by criticism from foes in England who reproved Massachusetts for ignoring the directive, emblemized on the Bay Company's seal, to evangelize the heathen. The major efforts were undertaken by John Eliot among the Massachusetts, and Thomas Mayhew, who began his family's generations-long mission to the Martha's Vineyard Wampanoag. At the height of Eliot's success, in 1674, eleven hundred "Praying Indians" inhabited fourteen towns built on colonial models; the Mayhews, more liberal about letting the natives retain their material culture, also attracted hundreds.

Perhaps three hundred to five hundred Amerindians experienced the new birth during the seventeenth and early eighteenth centuries, and several thousand more were acculturated enough to adopt some Christian practices—not an overwhelming number, given the precontact population of the area, but the most successful effort of any English mission during the colonial period. Contact with the Amerindians did not affect Puritanism. The conquerors' revealed truth did not absorb discrepant beliefs, and its categories conveniently described the Amerindians' estate as a prime example of human depravity and their ritual as witchcraft. Amerindians who accepted Puritanism made a transcultural leap, although in conceiving Christ as a shaman while failing to cognize conversion's affective cycle, they beheld grace through Native eyes.

Saints relied on the magistrates to uphold morality and support the religious order, a charge magnified by the New England Way's abolition of church courts and the absence of any ecclesiastical authority superior to the individual congregation. Church and state occupied separate spheres—magistrates could not make doctrine, nor could ministers hold office—but they cooperated closely to make the commonwealth holy. Puritans organized colonial governments more according to this functional imperative than by any theoretical one. The voluntarism of covenanting as the mode of founding churches imparted a tendency toward some popular participation in politics—at least for men.

Godly men called (male) magistrates to office just as they called (male) ministers to the church, and the laity's participation in the church's disciplinary proceedings passed over institutionally into town meetings, a distinctively New England form of local governance. Whatever "inclusivist" political proclivities (the word "democratic" would be anachronistic) Puritans entertained, however, were balanced by their desire to keep disciplinary mechanisms in godly hands and by the general English acceptance of social inequality's just inevitability. The theology of particular vocation supported this belief: industry in one's task glorified God; hence every occupation was honorable in serving him, whether performed in castle or cot. Superintending both voluntarism and hierarchy was the commitment to government as protector of the moral order. Constitutional arrangements mattered less than successful prosecution of God's Law; whether an executive was hereditary or elected meant little compared with that agency's success in upholding good behavior.

The specific structure of the Massachusetts Bay Colony's government, which became normative for New England, derived from the company's charter elaborated by political exigency: a general court consisting of governor, deputy governor, and assistants, to which the settlers added deputies elected for individual towns (who eventually sat as a separate legislative house). Within this central structure, power belonged to the Puritan gentry and wealthy freeholders, counseled by (but not subservient to) the ministry; New England governments enforced morality through legislation—the Connecticut General Court guarded the Sabbath in 1676 by forbidding sports on Sunday night—and by trying offenders in county courts; they upheld the New England Way by convening synods for ministers to address pressing religious issues and by quashing dissent.

Within Massachusetts' first decade, civil authority twice removed major threats to the mechanism of church-state cooperation. The recurring appearance of Separatists and sectarians should dispel any lingering notions that Puritans thought as a single mind, or that a passive laity silently acquiesced to every minister's positions. Animated by religious fervor and the bedrock Protestant belief in the priesthood of all believers, and accustomed to covenanted study groups that annotated life by Scripture, lay Puritans kept up constant religious dialogues that sometimes spun them out of orthodoxy's orbit. New England's migrants harbored heterogeneous beliefs, and their rulers could tolerate, within certain narrow limits, variations in the Way: James Noyes and Thomas Parker, for example, organized the Newbury consistory along presbyterian lines.

When critics espoused heretical doctrines and contravened the cooperative moral activism of church and state, however, magistrates moved against them. In 1635 the Massachusetts General Court banished the minister Roger Williams for, among other offenses, denying civil authority's right to punish religious infractions and urging his congregation to renounce the colony's other churches for having allowed this infringement on their autonomy. Anne Hutchinson posed an even greater threat, at the height of her influence winning over virtually the entire Boston church (save Governor John Winthrop and pastor John Wilson). Hutchinson advanced a species of antinomianism—belief that the law of God was irrelevant to regenerates, who were guided solely by the Spirit—that is usually considered an outcropping of Reformed thought, although research in the latter half of the twentieth century locates it substantially closer to the orthodox range. The court expelled her in 1637; excommunication from the church followed the next year.

In calling the family a "little commonwealth," Puritans compared an efficient state to a well-run household and implied the latter's importance for the former. Abhorring individuals in solitary—unrestrained by not having to share godly obligations with other people—they expected everyone to live under family government. According to ministers' prescriptions, a godly husband protects his wife from harm, provides for her physical well-being, befriends her, shares her bed, and chastises her when necessary, although never by force. A godly wife cares for her mate, runs the household economy, takes primary responsibility for raising the children, and submits to her husband's authority—as long as he obeys God. When he errs, he deserves her rebuke.

Husband and wife (she as his deputy) govern children and servants, raising, providing for, and educating them in both particular and general callings. Fathers teach sons a trade, mothers instruct daughters in housewifery, and either may help a child read. The state intervened when it perceived families failing to educate; in 1642 the Massachusetts General Court ordered town selectmen to determine if parents and masters were instructing their charges in reading, religion, colony laws, and a skill, and in 1648 specified that parents must catechize children and apprentices in orthodox doctrine. The other Puritan colonies followed suit. Family exercises— Bible reading, prayer, discussion, and meditation—instilled Reformed religion. Parental training could not guarantee salvation—no human work could—but, for whatever reasons, the children of godly parents, preachers knew, manifested grace more often than did others. Christian instruction was an obligation to both God and the state that prepared youths to behave properly in society.

The reality of Puritan family life was of course more complex than writers prescribed. Assuming that a wide range of personalities and behaviors exist in any society, whatever its values, and allowing too that some Saints did beat their spouses, dangle hell before disobedient children, or exploit their servants, the caricatures of straitlaced adults unable to enjoy each other and intent on crushing their children's wills are overdrawn; the history of Puritans' intransigence toward rulers, ministers, and each other should suggest their child rearing did not inhibit willfulness. Puritans may have understood love as a rational passion, freighting it with notions of duty, but they did know how to love, and expressed an affection that still warms the letters and journals that survive. Parents treated children with kindness and care but, on the other hand, did not romanticize their young. Every infant was innately depraved, they believed, and taming its corrupted faculties a necessity. Puritans encouraged obedience, not initiative; an ordered society needs people who follow God's law. God having revealed the knowledge essential for salvation, innovation was at best a mixed blessing too often the avenue for heresy and vice. Households had a duty to monitor themselves and their community. "Watchful loving kindness" extended family government to the neighbors, its moral oversight an informal mechanism by which each little commonwealth might contribute to the moral order of the public one.

THE SECOND PURITAN REFORMATION

Puritanism suffused seventeenth-century New England, but it neither shaped institutions similarly nor inspired uniform devotion. Husbandry, fishing, and secular architecture, for example, developed independently of overt religious influence (although Saints engaged in them, of course), and no population anywhere ever accepts even core values uniformly. At the culture's core were regenerated Saints, surrounded (in descending order of Puritan religiosity) by would-be Saints, professing churchgoers, and nominal Christians. Nonbelievers (if any) flitted around the periphery, with sectarians mimicking but not identifying with the core. Only a minority (how small one cannot say) attempted the godly life the creed demanded, yet Puritanism's effects were profound, the result of its status as a privileged ideology the majority accepted. The difficulties of Reformed theology notwithstanding, Puritanism was not the intellectual plaything of a cloistered ministry but a discourse on God shared by preachers and people; faith mixed with magic to breed a common credulity, albeit with variations between elite and folk. Providentialism urged people to seek portents, the rage for reporting remarkable events as footnotes to God's decree edging into necromantic speculation about his plans that ministers berated but could not entirely disown because in some degree they fostered it themselves.

Witchcraft affords perhaps the best example of how elite and folk versions of the collective mentality interacted. Everyone in colonial New England believed in the existence of people, usually women, who by acquiring infernal powers through compacting with Satan inflicted the assorted nastinesses neither grace nor technology could deflect: rancid butter, lamed cattle, horrific storms, incurable illness. Everyone wanted them purged. Villagers, however, feared most for their persons and property, sought evidence of diabolism in physical effects and gossip, and did not scruple to fight black magic with white. Ministers and magistrates worried more about the witch's worship, preferred eliciting a confession, and opposed fighting wizardry with wizardry. The two perspectives clashed at trials, with villagers pressing for a verdict that would rid them of the malefactor and judges, though agreed on witchcraft's noxiousness, increasingly reluctant to convict individuals on the basis of the signs and talk the plaintiffs adduced as proof. The witch panic at Salem in 1692 temporarily reversed the process when the special Court of Oyer and Terminer disregarded ministers' warnings to use spectral evidence very carefully; in the wake of twenty dead, however, magistrates hardened their legal skepticism and, although still believing in witches, declined to prosecute more complaints.

Puritanism had fastened on New England in a particular context: its strength among the political and clerical elites who organized the society, their consensus on establishing a holy commonwealth, the high percentage of migrants who had undergone or would undergo conversion, the relatively compact settlement patterns of early towns (which facilitated discipline), and little foreign interference. Those conditions altered as the seventeenth century grew old. Commerce, first vigorously pursued during the economically depressed 1640s, generated a mercantile class whose transatlantic interests and capitalist ethic stood against the majority's New England–centered moralism and ambivalence about the free market. Imported luxuries subjected merchants (and their customers) to criticism from the more abstemious, and their political affiliations, evident as early as their support for Anne Hutchinson, set them against the Puritan gentry, who hoarded their own power as long as they could. Rapid population growth, issuing after 1640 from marriages rather than incoming vessels, crowded town lands, prompting movement to the outskirts, the formation of new communities, and bitter contentions about covenants broken and fellowship denied.

A new generation arose that knew not England nor its persecutions, and whose members did not convert frequently enough. Expansion abraded Amerindian tribes, and in 1675–1676 the sachem Metacom (King Philip) and his Wampanoag organized a pantribal alliance that, before its defeat, inflicted the most casualties per capita on an "American" population in history, arresting territorial growth for decades. The English government took stock of colonial trade and its haphazard administration, moving to engross the former by strengthening the latter. Royal officials began to poke their noses into the holds of New England's ships, sift through the colonies' legal claims to political autonomy, and demand greater tolerance for other denominations.

Puritans tried to maintain their faith and its institutional expression in holy commonwealths as well as they could, their reactions comprising what might be called the Second Puritan Reformation. The first had aimed to establish a moral order and culminated (in America) in the system codified by the Cambridge Platform of 1648. The second hoped to preserve New England's holy commonwealths intact.

Responding politically did not require many modifications. General Courts continued to call occasional days of fasting or thanksgiving, convene synods, and harass dissenters—Massachusetts even executed four Quakers between 1659 and 1661. County courts took on more cases as townsfolk, disputing neighbors they did not meet in church fellowship, increasingly litigated their conflicts rather than mediating them in church. In general, however, New England societies remained relatively moral and politically stable; unlike the Chesapeake that endured several major rebellions against constituted authorities in the seventeenth century, New England experienced only one such revolt, against Governor Edmund Andros in 1689, who was expelled because his government superseded the old order. Defending holy commonwealths against English intervention took greater political action than policing them, especially in Massachusetts, which claimed allegiance to the Crown but denied its jurisdiction, an opinion neither Charles II (r. 1660–1685) nor James II (r. 1685–1688) could tolerate. A moderate faction within the General Court advocated compromising in order to mini-

PURITANISM

mize English regulation, but the extremists prevailed and refused to comply with imperial demands. The Crown vacated the Massachusetts
Bay charter in 1684 and incorporated New England into a single dominion. The Bay Colony
received a new charter in 1691 that included
old Plymouth but destroyed the state's capability
to enforce church discipline. Connecticut regained its charter, leaving the church-state synthesis intact.

Greater accommodations occurred in the
churches, although not in formal doctrine, which
changed little. Preachers encouraged a renewed
appreciation for baptism and the Lord's Supper
as vehicles for heightening pious sensibilities,
but the basic theology of redemption did not
change. The clergy did, however, refigure the
basis of their authority. Ministering to Puritans
always necessitated a certain charisma, despite
the doctrinal sureties that grace operated independently of a cleric's personality; the social origins of Puritanism had lain in the laity's flocking
to sermons and voluntarily covenanting around
powerful pastors. New England's founding ministers arrived, often with settled congregations
in tow, reputed for their homiletic skills and their
loyalty to the cause of godliness. Their successors—cheated of minting renown from sacrifice
by growing up in a godly place, and seeking
the call within an operating church system that
transformed heroic commitment into a job
search—could not as a class elicit the same awe
as Hooker and Cotton. Never-absent tensions
between ministers and laity flared. Congregations complained that preachers floundered in
the pulpit or demanded too much money; ministers reacted by exalting the sacerdotal origins
of their office in Christ's commission to them
rather than in a congregation's call, and by pressing for consocation that would give their semi-
formal associations powers to ordain and to administer discipline to individual churches.
Connecticut sanctioned consociations in the Say-
brook Platform of 1708; Massachusetts had narrowly failed to adopt a similar arrangement three
years earlier.

Ministers also elevated the exhortation of
regeneration through repentance to first place
in their ceremonial rhetoric. The jeremiad, as
this voice became known, raised veneration for
ancestors into a cultural myth—extolling the first

generation's achievements and using them to box
their children about the ears. It reminded audiences that God had contrived a national covenant
with his New English people to bless them if
they took him as Lord, but that he would punish
them for continued sins by abrogating the pact.
Periwigs, unregenerate children, and congregational bickering (not to mention penury) had
brought frontier war and customs agents,
warned the Synod of 1679, and worse would
follow unless New England reformed. The jeremiad's politics of national redemption chided
the magistracy (to their faces in the General
Court) for failing to maintain moral order. Nevertheless, the sermon always ended with the
promise that God would forgive his chosen if
they repented (as they surely would). Interpreted
against the backdrop of ministers' discontent
with the magistrates' casualness in stemming a
perceived rise in bad behavior and the younger
laity's abandonment of the quest for grace, the
jeremiad became a political stick with which one-
third of the Puritan triumvirate hoped to prod
the other two-thirds.

Finally, the clergy reworked their rituals and
recruitment mechanisms to fit new conditions
of evangelism. In England, Puritan preachers
had trolled for converts in the seas of the Church
of England or had attracted schools of individuals to themselves; urged by circumstance
(preachers never controlled the official liturgy)
and the Reformed persuasion, their congregational preaching served satisfactorily as the major
recruiting tool. The first American ministers
spoke to a self-selected godly band requiring
Christian maintenance more than conversion.
By the late seventeenth century, however, the
children's failure to convert in requisite numbers
forced ministers to augment the machinery of
appeal. Reliance on weekly sermonizing, adequate to collect the godly piecemeal, did not suffice when one wanted to regenerate a whole society instantly. Gadding about, the laity's device
for finding powerful preachers among a mass
of homily readers, was irrelevant when sermons
rang from every pulpit, and impracticable given
churches' power to make listeners attend their
local service. A return to the "primitive" English
situation—gathering the godly into new
churches of the pure—was unwise as long as
the government could suppress such activities

as dissent, and inconceivable as long as ministers and godly presumed (as they still did) that New England as a national entity (not just a haven for the Elect) lay under covenant with God. The solution lay in pouring old doctrine into new containers, vivifying rituals of public communion, and expanding the means of recruitment.

Although constituting more a form of official address than a proselytizing tool, the jeremiad rehearsed traditional themes in a novel setting. The rhetoric of trespass and repentance re-created in political terms conversion's rhythms of doubt and relief. Manuals of popular devotion had sustained piety in England, and now the expanding transatlantic book trade, a silver lining in commercialism's dark cloud, made such manuals more available in the colonies. Ministers encouraged their use, and they became handbooks for resurgent lay fellowship. Congregations reaffirmed their vows in public rehearsals of their original bond. The Boston church had renewed its covenant as early as 1636, but in the second half of the century the ceremony became more frequent, with Saints spending a day fasting and praying together to remind themselves of their duties to God and each other.

Jeremiads, devotional manuals, and covenant renewals underlined traditional piety; sacramentalism and revivalism reached out to potential new members. Puritans believed that baptism sealed a child's covenant with the church, and although not necessarily auguring conversion, it did bring one under the church's care. Regenerated Saints could baptize their young, but when those children grew up without experiencing conversion, as congregants (but not members) of the church they could not bring their own children into the fold. Rather than risk losing such people, synods in 1657 and 1662 fashioned a device, dubbed the Halfway Covenant, to allow the nonregenerate baptized to bring their children to the font, thereby preserving them in covenant. Solomon Stoddard recast the Lord's Supper as an evangelical tool. Puritan discipline had restricted it to Visible Saints; now Stoddard invited everyone to the table, hoping to awe them into conversion.

The Halfway Covenant and Stoddardeanism did not go unopposed. A decade passed before the baptismal reformers could convince their colleagues and a powerful minority of the laity that the Halfway Covenant did not traduce the church. Increase and Cotton Mather, the two most prominent ministers in Massachusetts, excoriated Stoddard for demeaning discipline. But Stoddard pressed ahead, and by such means he revitalized the Northampton church in a series of "refreshings," seasons of intensified religiosity that brought new converts into the church more quickly than occurred under normal events, and that presaged the most dramatic recruiting tool of all—the revival. The Saints may have recovered the relative numerical strength they had enjoyed at New England's founding, but, even if not, the rising number of conversions and the continued official publicity of Puritan values as the seventeenth century closed suggest that the second Reformation did not fail completely.

AWAKENING AND EVALUATION

The date by which "Puritanism" ended depends upon defining the term. Considered as a sociopolitical reform movement implemented through the cooperative agency of church, state, and family, Puritanism in America may be said to have culminated (in Massachusetts at least) in 1684, with the vacating of the Bay Company charter, or in 1691, when King William III granted a second charter that knocked the magistrate's leg off the institutional tripod undergirding the holy commonwealth. Suffrage, the king held, belonged to propertyholders, whether godly or not, and the state had to tolerate other faiths; congregational churches retained their hold on public taxes but no longer enjoyed the "special relationship" by which government upheld their interests.

Doctrinally and experientially, however, the changes were not so dramatic. Eighteenth-century ministers invoked the deities of Enlightenment learning and gave their sermons a superficially more rational cant, but the dogmas and message remained the same: humans were depraved creatures unable to save themselves and doomed to perdition unless God elected them for regeneration by the Holy Spirit. Yet if Puritanism as faith and experience had not essentially changed, the context of its practice had. The rate of church formation kept more or less abreast of the rising population, but the number of conversions did not. In some sense, early Georgian New England's ecclesiastical situation had come to resemble Elizabethan England's: an established church, theologically (and more so liturgically) reformed, incorporating the majority of the population, most of whom fell short of the high piety demanded by the elect. The wheel had turned almost full circle.

At that point Jonathan Edwards, George Whitefield, and other charismatic preachers touched off the Great Awakening, understood most precisely as the revival that shook New England from 1740 to 1745. Once again bands of spiritually excited laypeople moved about the countryside to hear powerful sermons, charging their own ministers with insufficiency or, more damningly, unregeneracy if they could not fire their words with Spirit. The Awakeners had prototypes of revival at hand in the Northampton refreshings, and corresponded with British brethren likewise immersed in revivals, but the medium of large crowds as apt vehicles for advertising grace testifies more to the preachers' rhetorical abilities than to their organizational agency; Edwards attributed the mass audiences to a providentially miraculous outpouring of grace and left it at that. But if not self-consciously planned, the Great Awakening demonstrated the utility of gathering people from different churches together and preaching for their souls, a recruitment vehicle more efficient (in terms of numbers reached) and concentrated (in terms of time elapsed) than the tradition of weekly sermonizing.

Revivalism stirred up religious fervor, and the rate of conversion soared. In this respect, the Great Awakening climaxes Puritan religious sensibility, an explosion of fervor ignited by the Reformed theology of grace, but at the same time, it represents the last hurrah. Orthodox church order and doctrine shattered in disputes over the extent to which grace manifests itself in extreme physical demonstrations, the practice of judging fellow congregants as unregenerate, and the necessity for ministers to be born again. Adjudging their churches no longer true, New Lights (revival's advocates) launched a new separatism, founding their own denomination and defecting to the Baptists. Surveying the smashup of the standing order in the Awakening's emotional chaos, Charles Chauncy mused about sin-

ners in the hands of a reasonable God—a rational deity would not dangle a soul over hellfire without allowing it a chance to will its escape—and started down the path to universalism. By the late eighteenth century, some Reformed divines were taking the theological low road to Arminianism, the notion that the human will coactively works with God to obtain faith. Its churches and theology fragmenting, Puritanism ended with a bang, not a whimper.

Defining Puritanism as a religious sensibility amalgamating ministers, magistrates, and laity helps assess how it did (and did not) configure New England. Settlers owed their plows, their courts, and (usually) their names to English ways; whatever their devotion to the Bible, Saints worshiped in a meetinghouse in Boston in Massachusetts (an Algonquian word), not in the temple of Jerusalem in New Judah. Enlisting Puritanism to explain New Englanders' entrepreneurialism accounts neither for the merchants' antagonism to Saintly government nor the enterprising energies of Virginia planters and Philadelphia traders. But limiting the movement's horizons does not mean obliterating them. Puritanism fixed New England with a dominant denomination and religious rhetoric. Godliness and communal discipline provided the ideological framework for the region's social integration and political stability, both unusual in the seventeenth-century colonies. Buoyed by a high regard for education, manifested in the Massachusetts compulsory-school law of 1647 and the founding of Harvard College in 1636, New England's literacy rates surpassed those of other colonies; dampened by communal morality, its illegitimacy rates stayed below them. Accustomed to judging any person in the light of his or her sanctity, Puritans held no brief for divine right and distrusted arbitrary power, clerical and magisterial, an attitude that helps account for the region's notorious political feistiness.

Puritanism was not antiauthoritarian per se—it proposed, after all, to discipline society—but it exalted no particular form of (political) authority and set itself against corruption. The language of revolution in New England incorporated a Puritan lexicon. In the 1760s and 1770s beleaguered British ministers would routinely describe dissenting Protestants as Cromwellian republicans in pious garb, an exaggeration that misconstrued why New Englanders opposed imperial reorganization but correctly linked resistance with their religious mentality.

In its historical form, Puritanism no longer exists. The collaboration of church and state to enforce right doctrine contravenes the Constitution, although moral reform movements from antebellum Sabbatarianism to prohibitionism to antipornography campaigns have enlisted the magistracy against sin. Some churches retain predestinarian theories of redemption, but modern revivalism has long spoken Arminianism. Calls for the new birth abound, but their sensibility arms unregenerates with far more agency than a Puritan could abide. As a myth, however, Puritanism remains one of America's most powerful cultural icons. Whether celebrating it as the vehicle of faith's golden age or, more usually, exorcising it as the demon of repressive hypocrisy, Americans from Nathaniel Hawthorne to Arthur Miller have measured themselves against its decree.

BIBLIOGRAPHY

Definition

Foster, Stephen. *The Long Argument: English Puritanism and the Shaping of New England Culture, 1550–1700.* Chapel Hill, N.C., 1991.

Doctrine and Sensibility

Bozeman, Theodore Dwight. *To Live Ancient Lives: The Primitivist Dimension in Puritanism.* Chapel Hill, N.C., 1988.
Cohen, Charles L. *God's Caress: The Psychology of Puritan Religious Experience.* New York, 1986.
Miller, Perry. *The New England Mind.* New York, 1939; 2 vols. Cambridge, Mass., 1953–1954.
Stoever, William K. B. *'A Faire and Easie Way to Heaven': Covenant Theology and Antinomianism in Early Massachusetts.* Middletown, Conn., 1978.
Wallace, Dewey. *Puritans and Predestination: Grace in English Protestant Theology, 1525–1695.* Chapel Hill, N.C., 1982.

Genesis and Exodus

Collinson, Patrick. *The Elizabethan Puritan Movement.* Berkeley, Calif., 1967.
———. *Godly People: Studies on English Protestantism and Puritanism.* London, 1983.

———. *The Religion of Protestants: The Church in English Society, 1559–1625.* Oxford, 1982.
Cressy, David. *Coming Over: Migration and Communication Between England and New England in the Seventeenth Century.* New York, 1987.
George, Charles H., and Katherine George. *The Protestant Mind of the English Reformation, 1570–1640.* Princeton, N.J., 1961.
Knappen, Marshall M. *Tudor Puritanism: A Chapter in the History of Idealism.* Chicago, 1939.
McGee, J. Sears. *The Godly Man in Stuart England.* New Haven, Conn., 1976.
Seaver, Paul. *Wallington's World: A Puritan Artisan in Seventeenth-Century London.* Stanford, Calif., 1985.

The Holy Commonwealth

Axtell, James. *The Invasion Within: The Contest of Cultures in Colonial North America.* New York, 1985.
Breen, Timothy H. *The Character of The Good Ruler: Puritan Political Ideas in New England, 1630–1730.* Chapel Hill, N.C., 1970.
Gura, Philip F. *A Glimpse of Sion's Glory: Puritan Radicalism in New England, 1620–1660.* Middletown, Conn., 1984.
Hall, David D. *The Faithful Shepherd: A History of the New England Ministry in the Seventeenth Century.* Chapel Hill, N.C., 1972.
Kupperman, Karen Ordahl. "Errand to the Indies: Puritan Colonization from Providence Island through the Western Design." *William and Mary Quarterly,* 3rd ser., 45, no. 1 (1988) 70–99.
Morgan, Edmund S. *The Puritan Family: Religion and Domestic Relations in Seventeenth-Century New England.* Rev. ed. New York, 1966.

The Second Puritan Reformation

Bercovitch, Sacvan. *The American Jeremiad.* Madison, Wis., 1978.
Hall, David D. *Worlds of Wonder, Days of Judgment: Popular Religious Belief in Early New England.* New York, 1989.
Hambrick-Stowe, Charles E. *The Practice of Piety: Puritan Devotional Disciplines in Seventeenth-Century New England.* Chapel Hill, N.C., 1982.
Holifield, E. Brooks. *The Covenant Sealed: The Development of Puritan Sacramental Theology in Old and New England, 1570–1720.* New Haven, Conn., 1974.
Middlekauff, Robert. *The Mathers: Three Generations of Puritan Intellectuals 1596–1728.* New York, 1971.
Stout, Harry S. *The New England Soul: Preaching and Religious Culture in Colonial New England.* New York, 1986.

Awakening and Evaluation

Bushman, Richard L. *From Puritan to Yankee: Character and the Social Order in Connecticut, 1690–1765.* Cambridge, Mass., 1967.

Gaustad, Edwin Scott. *The Great Awakening in New England.* Gloucester, Mass., 1965.

Heyrman, Christine Leigh. *Commerce and Culture: The Maritime Communities of Colonial Massachusetts, 1690–1750.* New York, 1984.

Charles L. Cohen[1]

See also **British Settlements, New England; Church and State; Dutch and French Calvinism; Literacy; Philosophy; Music and Dance, The British Colonies, Sacred Music;** and **The Structure of Society.**

[1] The author wishes to thank David D. Hall, Michael McGiffert, and Robert Middlekauf for their helpful commentaries on this chapter.

QUAKERISM

QUAKERISM IS A RELIGIOUS MOVEMENT, born in seventeenth-century England as the vision of George Fox, an intense, semiliterate young man whose quest for meaning within the Church of England drew only ridicule from its curates. Forced back on his own resources, Fox discovered God. In the late 1640s and early 1650s, he wandered through the countryside preaching about an Inner Light whereby the holy spirit was revealed to and acted through man. Gathering to himself followers who shared the zeal born of spiritual discovery, Fox at first imposed no discipline upon them. After all, if the Inner Light transformed individuals into vessels of God's will, then rules, ministers, and even the church as an institution might be done away with.

QUAKERISM IN ENGLAND

But Fox and his followers did not stop at the rejection of church tradition. The Puritans had gone that far, and there can be little doubt that Quakers inherited such Puritan attitudes as the attachment of primary importance to personal experience, especially the conversion to a godly life; the concept of man as a pilgrim, a stranger to the world, yet a voyager determined to remake the world for the Lord; and consequently a seemingly limitless capacity for moral protest against the world's wicked ways. Thus Puritans outraged Anglicans by denying man-made church tradi-

tion, citing the Bible as their only guide. In turn Quakers infuriated Puritans by claiming that the Scriptures alone were not guidance enough. Robert Barclay, the first man to attempt a systemization of Quaker thought, declared that the Bible was "a declaration of the *fountain*, but not the *fountain* itself." The written word was not to be a restraint on the Inner Light. Where Puritans were literal, Quakers were mystical.

The contrast was more than theological. George Fox was the son of a weaver whom neighbors contemptuously referred to as a "Righteous Christer." His mother, too, was deeply religious. Fox's preaching attracted men and women like himself, spiritually thirsty and, if not always of humble origins, at least disdainful of the polite conventions which acknowledged a social hierarchy that was generally accepted as inevitable. Puritans could count among their number members of the gentry, and they supported both the principle and the practice of social stratification. Indeed their belief in predestination and election, the restriction of salvation to a chosen few, reflected an elitist attitude. Conversely Quakers believed that any and every person could discover the Inner Light. Quaker zeal was fired with a belief in the possibility of achieving earthly perfection.

A zealous perfectionism demanded the elimination of human obstacles on the road to spiritual attainment. No time, no place, no conditions were inappropriate for the preaching of the

Word, even if church services must be disrupted or bizarre behavior was necessary to attract attention. Perfectionism also dictated a disregard for meaningless social distinctions symbolized in dress, custom, and manner of speaking. William Penn, one of the most aristocratic of the early converts, stated flatly, "We are not to respect persons." Yet it was these very excesses of the first Quakers that led increasing numbers of them to call for self-restraint.

To the monarchical government that came to power with the Restoration of 1660, the behavior and aims of the Quakers seemed quite extreme. In 1661 over four thousand Quakers were jailed, and for a decade after that time their number in prison almost always exceeded a thousand. It was in this period of persecution that they were joined by William Penn. Being in the spirit of its first members, he was bent on converting a reluctant world to righteousness, stopping at nothing to preach the Truth. He was imprisoned four times for publicly stating his beliefs in word and print. Penn's willingness to withstand the harshness of these confinements when he might have used the position of his father, Admiral Sir William Penn, to obtain release, as well as his missionary efforts on the Continent, convinced other Quakers of his commitment and paved the way to his position of leadership at a time when Quakerism was in process of change.

"A Faith that overcomes the World" began accommodating to the necessities of social survival. Quakers were being imprisoned almost at the caprice of public officials. Persecution did not deter the Quakers, but this alone did not ensure the perpetuation of the group. The alternative was to combat persecution through organization. It was during the Restoration that the individualistic Quakers coalesced into the Society of Friends.

This conscious transformation did not occur without a struggle over strategy. Some of the most vital men in the movement were the persons most resistant to corporate discipline. Complicating matters even more was the problem of leadership. The death or confinement in the 1660s of the most prominent of the early Quakers, coupled with the fact that future leaders such as Penn were only then joining the ranks, made discipline more imperative but also more difficult

to achieve. Again it was the boundless energy of George Fox that turned the tide.

Emerging from a long imprisonment in 1666, Fox began a four-year canvass of England and Ireland in the cause of group discipline. He set up Men's Monthly Meetings, separate from the weekly worship meetings held on First Day (Sunday), to handle such business as defining membership, preserving good conduct (by means of Quakers keeping watch on one another), and giving mutual aid through funds collected in the name of charity. A parallel system of Women's Meetings was also instituted, as well as a Meeting for Sufferings that was initiated to collect and publish accounts of state persecution and was later utilized to defend Friends against such official acts. Spontaneity and self-expression were becoming less characteristic of Quakers than regularity and group discipline. Submission to persecution and martyrdom was being replaced by legal challenge and political lobbying. The expectation of converting the world to righteousness ebbed, superseded by the hope of obtaining toleration of religious dissent by state and society.

William Penn's Leadership

The same move from zeal to moderation was evident in William Penn's life. Penn never modified his devotion to liberty of conscience, the basic principle of his political thought and action, and he always favored practical steps to alleviate persecution. The alteration came in his tactics. In his tract, *England's Great Interest in the Choice of This New Parliament* (1679), he made clear his determination to engage in politics to eliminate persecution. In the interim the English political picture had changed as party platforms were enunciated on the two great issues of the seventeenth century: the constitutional conflict between king and Parliament and the religious struggle between the Church of England and Dissenters.

The Tories, advocates of the throne and the national church, were not without appeal for Penn, since he numbered among his friends Charles II, the king's brother James, Duke of York, and several influential courtiers, all of whom he had approached on the Quakers' behalf. But with political principles deriving from his study of classical republicanism and a vital interest in dissent, Penn naturally gravitated to the opposition group, the Whigs. He had already encouraged fellow Quakers to compile a record of persecutions, institutionalized in the Meeting for Sufferings that he took the lead in organizing in 1675, and to lay petitions before Parliament. *England's Great Interest* was issued as one of the first clear statements of Whig policy.

THE BEGINNINGS OF THE "HOLY EXPERIMENT"

Within the Society of Friends, however, there was resentment against the worldly involvements that Penn's tactics entailed, and older Quakers stymied his strategy. Nor did Penn's foray into politics serve him well, since the Whigs faded before a Tory resurgence. Frustrated in England, Penn turned toward America as a locale for applying his political and religious principles.

For a quarter of a century, Friends had been traveling to the New World, not to escape but to sow the Word. "In 1655 many went beyond the sea," wrote Fox, "where truth also sprang up; and in 1656 it broke forth in America." But in Massachusetts Quaker truth was considered a falsehood, and the early arrivals there were jailed, deported, whipped, and finally executed. Quakers fared better in New York, Virginia, and Maryland and best in Carolina and Rhode Island, where they held positions in government. As early as 1660 the Quaker Josiah Coale, a friend of Penn's, spoke to the Susquehanna Indians about purchasing land. By 1674 two Quakers were in possession of West New Jersey.

The complications of organizing a colony as encumbered by personal and legal conflicts as West New Jersey showed Penn, not the most patient of Quakers, the virtues of clear and single proprietorship as a prerequisite to planting a settlement. Proceeding alone he could obtain a royal charter through his connections while concealing his plans for Pennsylvania as a "holy experiment," a whiggish combination of republicanism and religious toleration. In addition he took personal satisfaction from his role as sole proprietary lord, despite his proclaimed republicanism and Quaker egalitarianism.

Thus the gradual Quaker movement into the New World was capped by the founding of Pennsylvania. It strengthened the Friends' position in America, yet it was tied to England in spirit and by direct correspondence. It was of more than symbolic significance that in 1681 the London Yearly Meeting issued its first letter abroad, and that William Penn was a member of the Epistle Committee. Quakers in Pennsylvania would never be unaware of their counterparts across the sea.

Old World experience, stimulated by New World opportunity, would turn the holy experiment into a thriving enterprise. Some eight thousand people, almost all English, Welsh, and Irish Quakers had migrated to Pennsylvania by 1685. As the zeal and religious individualism characteristic of the first Quakers was being subjected to group discipline, the emphasis among them in England changed from the reform of society to toleration by it. In contrast Pennsylvania, offering the alternative of a fresh start, appeared not as a violation or modification of Quaker ideals but as the very way to put them into practice. Thus where Friends had once gone to America as missionaries into alien communities, braving threats and almost expecting martyrdom, they now were going in a body to establish a separate place for themselves. Penn asked the prospective settlers to contribute nothing but themselves to the holy experiment. In Pennsylvania, the wilderness laboratory, they would have the opportunity to work out the experiment with fuller control over their own destinies.

Quakers, of course, were not known for their submissiveness, and it is likely that those least sympathetic to group discipline in England were the ones who immigrated to America. Their Old World experience with government, as with organized religion, had been as adversaries. Where they were not indifferent they were hostile to form, structure, and institutions, the very stabilizing forces of society. Unsurprisingly the Quaker colony did not develop in accord with the proprietor's original vision. When he mustered the support of Quaker merchants to help underwrite the founding of Pennsylvania, rewarding with political office those who immigrated, Penn thought he could establish an elite faithful to his interest. But challenges from outside the proprietary circle and defections within produced a coterie of Quaker politicians, merchants, and landowners who by 1688 controlled the colony's government for their own purposes.

RETURNING TO THE PEACE TESTIMONY

It was not, however, the accumulation of wealth and power by a few Friends that put Quakerism to the test. Rather, it was the demands of public service juxtaposed with the Quaker opposition to war. In 1740 England declared war against Spain and demanded support from her colonies in King George's War. Most of the American provinces responded promptly and obediently to this summons. But in Pennsylvania the assembly replied that the religious principles of a majority of its members did not allow them to "preserve good Consciences and come into the Levying of Money and appropriating it to the uses recommended."

The assembly's responses to similar requests in the past had not foreshadowed this adamant refusal. In 1693 the assembly voted on a "bill for the support of Government," an action consistent with the Quaker belief that governments, installed by God, were owed obedience by their subjects. If the money contained in the bill was to be used for military purposes, that was not the assembly's responsibility, though Quakers did not deny a nation's right to defend itself. When a subsequent royal demand for aid in Queen Anne's War was laid before the legislature in 1709, the assembly refused to contribute to the military expedition but did offer an amount smaller than requested as "a Present" to the queen. Faced by another requisition for the military two years later, the assembly responded with a sum "for the Queen's use," fully aware that a portion of it would be diverted directly to military operations. In justification it was said that these martial activities would be conducted outside of Pennsylvania, where the provincial government had no jurisdiction. From a constitutional point of view, Quaker politicians took shelter under their subordinate position in the empire. They had not abandoned the peace testimony but only found ways to reconcile it with their commitment to the government.

Between the end of Queen Anne's War in 1713 and the beginning of King George's War in 1740, Quakerism underwent significant change, symbolized by the fact that by 1725 the first-generation founders of Pennsylvania were dead. And what had been a Quaker colony was now a heterogeneous society, with Friends clearly in a minority. As their preponderance diminished and their original leaders died, the Friends lost sight of their sectarian characteristics. Pennsylvania Quakers now reflected rather than reformed their environment. Wealth and class consciousness increased, mirrored in the Society of Friends through the elegance of the rich Quakers' life-style and in the fact that this economic elite provided religious leadership as well.

In 1737 the practice of birthright membership in the Society was accepted by the London Yearly Meeting. This was an attempt to keep younger Quakers within the fold. By the third decade of the century, it was recognized that delinquency in the Society was sharply rising; far and away the major offense was "marrying out" to non-Quakers. It was the general practice at this time to attempt to bring the wayward back to righteous behavior, an emphasis on correct conduct suggesting that, for a substantial number of Quakers, once-vital beliefs bearing upon states of inwardness were being relegated to the status of dogma.

Yet worldly and spiritual Friends alike continued to regard at least one of the original Quaker principles as vital. In September 1739 the Philadelphia Yearly Meeting circulated a letter calling for strict adherence to the peace testimony, a position adopted by Quakers elected to the assembly in October and relayed to the governor in the summer of 1740 in response to his request for military funds. But when England declared war against France in 1740, the Quaker-dominated assembly finally responded to the demand for a defense contribution. The money (£4,000) was voted "for the King's Use" and designated specifically for the purchase of "Bread, Beef, Pork, Flour, Wheat or other Grain . . . within this province." Benjamin Franklin's witty recollection that the governor understood "other Grain" to mean gunpowder was probably apocryphal but, as usual, the philosopher grasped the larger meaning of the gesture. His characterization of the Quaker politicians struck at their dilemma: "They were unwilling to offend government, on the one hand, by a direct refusal [to grant aid for military purposes]; and their friends, the body of the Quakers, on the other, by a compliance contrary to their principles; hence a variety of evasions to avoid complying, and modes of disguising the compliance when it became unavoidable."

Legislators were again put to the test when, fifteen years later, news came that bands of Ohio Indians had massacred settlers in the Tulpehocken and Forks of Delaware regions. Angry frontiersmen appeared in Philadelphia. The proprietor quickly granted £5,000 for defense while the assembly voted £55,000 but excluded the proprietary lands from taxation. Franklin's bill creating a voluntary militia was accepted by the assembly, with four Quakers dissenting, and by the governor, though with hesitation. This was the first legislated armed force in the province.

As the war continued and Indian allies of the French attacked Pennsylvanians, the assembly voted more funds for defense. When the governor and his council prepared a declaration of war and offered a bounty on scalps, a Quaker petition opposing these bellicose measures, signed by Philadelphia's weightiest Friends, was ignored. The assembly was not consulted until after the declaration was issued on 14 April 1756. The province was officially in violation of pacifist principles for the first time in its history.

On 4 June 1756, despite the governor's suspension of hostilities a day earlier, six Quakers resigned their assembly seats, unable to serve when "the present Situation of Public Affairs call upon us for Service in a military Way." In July, Friends who believed that the Society should intercede in making peace with the Indians rather than letting the government carry on negotiations alone gathered subscriptions (largely from Quakers but also from Mennonites and Schwenkfelders) and formed The Friendly Association for Regaining and Preserving Peace with the Indians by Pacific Measures.

Conscientious Friends now pointed to the spiritual decline implicit in the compromises Quakers had been drawn into during their years of political, economic, and social dominance in Pennsylvania. These spiritual Quakers intended to return the Society to its original ideals, the violation of which was thrown into relief by the declaration of war. And their message was heard. When Friends refused to pay the property tax in 1757, it was clear that Quaker consciousness had been raised to a level at which no war levies would be paid.

QUAKER BENEVOLENCE

Another index to the Society's altered perspective could be seen in its new attitude toward delinquents. Previously pardoned, they were now punished. One-fifth of those who had been Friends in 1760 were disowned by the time of the revolution.

But despite the mentality of retreat and the urge to purify, conscientious Quakers could not forsake the world. They put their principles into practice through the organization of alternatives to the status quo. Within the Society the Yearly Meeting's correspondence committee in 1756 became a Meeting for Sufferings, which was given funds to lobby and provide legal defense for Quakers. Outside the Society the Friendly Association was organized to implement pacifism by dealing fairly, but extralegally (since foreign affairs were in the government's domain), with the natives.

And there was another way to avoid tangling with the government while influencing public affairs, a method utilized so effectively by Benjamin Franklin: the private voluntary society. Friends who found officeholding repugnant, thus rejecting the union of temporal and spiritual matters that was fundamental to William Penn's holy experiment, discovered an alternative in voluntary association that could put into practice the principles of reformist Quakers without drawing them into complicity with the government or conflict with their more compromising brethren. This second holy experiment, characterized not by the buoyant optimism of its predecessor but by an admonishing moralism born from a feeling of crisis, demonstrated a new approach to working in the world that disdained politics and, in addition, expanded the areas of charity to people previously on the periphery of Quaker consciousness.

Friends who had disregarded the religious needs of fellow Europeans in the early eighteenth century now came to the aid of Acadians deported from Nova Scotia in 1755. At the same time aid was extended to refugees, both the white settlers and the Native Americans, who suffered from Indian attacks. Forsaking their focus on in-group charity, a large number of Friends turned their attention to the Pennsylvania Hospital and the Overseers of the Poor.

Condemning Slavery

These activities put Quakers in the forefront of benevolent activities. But their work with African Americans actually set them apart from their fellow Americans. Friends were forced by the egalitarian implications of their theology and the pronouncements of such leaders as George Fox, who had advocated preaching to blacks and some form of manumission, to confront the realities of slaveholding and living with African Americans. Of the dozen or so condemnations of slavery appearing in the American colonies before 1750, most were written by Quakers. By 1760 Quakers could see no alternative to the compulsory manumission of slaves, though abolition had as yet not been endorsed by the Yearly Meeting and few slaves held by Friends were freed before 1755. On the eve of the American Revolution, Friends stood apart from other Americans on the issue of slavery.

THE AMERICAN REVOLUTION: QUAKERS UNDER ATTACK

Because they were pacifists, the Quakers found the revolution to be a difficult period. They consistently opposed the war and refused to support the revolutionary government. In the midst of their own reformation, they viewed as imperative a testimony against war. They disowned those Friends who could not honor pacifism and declared their intention to resist "with Christian firmness" any efforts to conscript them into the fighting or to impose "tests not warranted by the precepts of Christ or the laws of the happy constitution under which we and others long enjoyed tranquillity and peace," a resolution referring to the affirmation of support for Pennsylvania's new constitution. As General William Howe approached Philadelphia in 1777, Congress advised the Pennsylvania government of Quaker disaffection, which led to the arrest, im-

prisonment, and deportation to Virginia of some Quakers. When the patriots returned to Philadelphia after the British and the Loyalists had exited, two Friends were hanged, most were subject to public ridicule, and the property of all of them was vulnerable to seizure.

The reformation in the Society that led to the adamant opposition to war as an expression of Quaker purity also raised the question of the Friends' relationship to the surrounding civil community. Previous to and even during the revolution, the British government generally accepted the Quaker desire to stand apart. But idealistic revolutionaries, in other states as well as in Pennsylvania, were suspicious of passivity and virtually forced Friends to take a role in society at large. In response Quakers made a contribution of their virtue. They conducted a large-scale program of war relief in the form of money, clothing, and provisions for noncombatants. And they publicly proclaimed their morality, most notably their views on slavery. The captive in the clutches of a tyrannical master was a metaphor used liberally by American propagandists after 1763, but to Friends it was more than imagery. It fit a judgment they had already made on the institution of black slavery. As other Americans drew back from the implications of total equality, Friends moved forward.

And a final irony could be found in the Society's new social role. As the revolution began, Quakers looked to their origins, when they were similarly at odds with the state. Thus they conceived of their role as apocalyptic, quoting in 1777 Penn's *To the Children of Light* (1678): "We are the people, above all others, that must stand in the gap, and pray for the putting away of wrath, so that this Land may be not made an utter desolation." Yet as Quakers pressed their principles on the larger society, Penn's idea of a final purifying upheaval sent from on high was less relevant to their lives than active reforming carried on below, though abolitionism would later create an earthly cataclysm. It was the Quakers, more than any other religious group, who would serve as the conscience of the nation.

BIBLIOGRAPHY

Barbour, Hugh. *The Quakers in Puritan England.* New Haven, Conn., 1964.

Besse, Joseph. *A Collection of the Sufferings of the People Called Quakers.* 2 vols. London, 1753.

Dunn, Mary Maples. *William Penn: Politics and Conscience.* Princeton, N.J., 1967.

Dunn, Mary Maples, and Richard S. Dunn, eds. *The Papers of William Penn.* 5 vols. Philadelphia, 1981–1987.

Endy, Melvin B., Jr. *William Penn and Early Quakerism.* Princeton, N.J., 1973.

Fox, George. *The Journal of George Fox.* Edited by John L. Nickalls. Rev. ed. Cambridge, England, 1952.

Illick, Joseph E. *Colonial Pennsylvania: A History.* New York, 1976.

James, Sydney V. *A People Among Peoples: Quaker Benevolence in Eighteenth-Century America.* Cambridge, Mass., 1963.

Janney, Samuel M. *History of the Religious Society of Friends from Its Rise to the Year 1828.* 4 vols. Philadelphia, 1859–1867.

Jones, Rufus M. *The Quakers in the American Colonies.* London, 1911.

Levy, Barry. *Quakers and the American Family: British Settlement in the Delaware Valley.* New York, 1988.

Marietta, Jack D. *The Reformation of American Quakerism, 1748–1783.* Philadelphia, 1984.

Nash, Gary B. *Quakers and Politics: Pennsylvania, 1681–1726.* Princeton, N.J., 1968.

Tolles, Frederick B. *Meeting House and Counting House: The Quaker Merchants of Colonial Philadelphia, 1682–1763.* Chapel Hill, N.C., 1948.

———. *Quakers and the Atlantic Culture.* New York, 1960.

Joseph E. Illick

SEE ALSO **British Settlements, The Middle Colonies; Marriage;** and **Schools and Schooling.**

DUTCH AND FRENCH CALVINISM

THE REFORMED TRADITION traces its theology to the sixteenth-century reformer John Calvin, who, following the lead of Martin Luther, dissented from Roman Catholicism, especially on the doctrines of papal infallibility, the sale of indulgences, and the transubstantiation of Holy Communion. While Luther directly challenged Rome and asserted the primacy of Scriptures in matters of faith and doctrine, Calvin provided the Protestant Reformation with a systematic theology, *The Institutes of the Christian Religion*, which went through several editions and took its final form in 1559. There, Calvin elaborated on Luther's notions about salvation by grace alone; we are all abject sinners, Calvin declared, and we can do nothing to earn forgiveness. God, however, in his infinite mercy, has chosen to save some, the elect, from damnation.

Reformed theology animated the Puritans in England, especially after the Marian Exile of 1553–1558 had exposed many of England's Protestant leaders to Calvin's ideas. The Church of England, however, never fully embraced Calvinism. Charles I's appointment of William Laud as archbishop of Canterbury—Laud was openly hostile to Calvinism and to the Puritans—prompted the migration of Puritans to Massachusetts in 1630. But Calvinism had other apologists outside of New England: the Presbyterians in the middle colonies and, to a lesser degree, the Baptists of Rhode Island and Virginia. The most prominent representatives of the Calvinist tradition in the middle colonies of New York and New Jersey were the Dutch and the French.

After 1685, when the civil and religious liberties of French Protestants (Huguenots) were revoked by Louis XIV, many made their way to the coastal cities of Anglo North America by way of England or the French West Indies. With the exception of a few Huguenot agents of metropolitan companies at Quebec in the 1750s, the practice of French Calvinism was excluded from New France.

A Huguenot colony on the Atlantic coast had been established in the 1560s, but it was very soon destroyed by Spanish forces sent from newly founded Saint Augustine. There were a few Huguenots living in Louisiana during the eighteenth century, despite the official ban against their presence.

The Dutch Reformed church established a foothold in North America when Jonas Michaëlius arrived in New Amsterdam (present-day New York) from Brazil in 1628 to organize a congregation and serve as its minister. From the outset Michaëlius recognized that, due to the unique and diverse character of his congregants, he faced a formidable challenge. "At the first administration of the Lord's Supper which was observed, not without great joy and comfort to many, we had fully fifty communicants—Walloons and Dutch," Michaëlius noted in a letter to Amsterdam in 1628, adding that "one cannot observe strictly all the usual formalities in making a beginning under such circumstances."

603

Michaëlius proceeded to carve out a small congregation in New Amsterdam. Soon, with contributions exacted during a besotted wedding feast, Dutch Calvinists constructed a chapel in the new trading entrepôt of the Dutch West India Company. Even though religion was not the highest priority for either the merchants in Amsterdam or the settlers in New Netherland, the Dutch Reformed church managed to organize thirteen congregations by 1664, from Fort Orange (Albany) and Schenectady along the Mohawk and Hudson rivers in the north to New Amstel (New Castle) along the Delaware.

THE ENGLISH CONQUEST

The English Conquest of 1664, however, radically altered the fortunes of Dutch Calvinism in the middle colonies. Although the Articles of Capitulation stipulated that the Dutch "here shall enjoy the liberty of their consciences in Divine Worship and church discipline," English rulers, both in the colonies and at Whitehall, soon reneged on that promise. In 1675 the duke of York gave Governor Edmund Andros instructions to place Nicholas Van Rensselaer, a Dutchman with Anglican orders and a checkered past, in one of the colony's Dutch Reformed churches. Andros assigned Van Rensselaer to Albany, where his presence triggered a major controversy. The Dutch clergy initially resisted the move but soon recognized that the path of least resistance lay in accommodation to English rule. Other members of the Dutch church, notably Jacob Leisler and Jacob Milborne (later Leisler's son-in-law), fought the appointment through the courts and all the way to the governor's council where, with the apparent complicity of the Dutch clergy, they were rebuffed and forced to pay court costs.

The Van Rensselaer case sowed the seeds of later discontent. Following the English conquest, a deep fissure opened within the Dutch Reformed church over the issue of accommodation to the English. Most of the Dutch merchants, realizing that control of the colony lay securely in the hands of the English, saw that their interests were better served by assimilation. They readily accommodated to English rule, customs, and institutions. Some even Anglicized their names. The lower classes among the Dutch, however, had migrated to the New World seeking economic opportunity, and the English takeover placed them one remove farther from the prospect of such advancement.

LEISLER'S REBELLION

The festering discontent within the Dutch community erupted into rebellion when news of England's Glorious Revolution reached New York. On 31 May 1689 the militia took control of the fort amid wild (and unfounded) speculations about an invasion of the colony by Roman Catholics. Jacob Leisler, a militia captain who was bitterly opposed to Roman Catholicism, James II, and English magistrates in general, was chosen leader of the insurrection and assumed the rank of lieutenant-general. Leisler and Jacob Milborne, however, insisted that they were merely securing the colony on an interim basis for the new English monarchs, William and Mary. For Leisler and many of his lower-class Dutch followers, the specter of Catholic oppression was very real indeed. They explicitly linked Catholicism with both religious heresy and political tyranny, and they equated William of Orange's triumph over James II with William the Silent's victory over Philip II of Spain a century earlier.

While Leisler and Milborne enjoyed the support of the lower classes, they met with determined opposition from Dutch traders and, significantly, from the Dutch clergy. Leisler, who viewed himself as a champion of Dutch liberties against the yoke of English oppression, regarded the clergy's resistance to his provisional government as nothing short of treachery. He sought and failed to exact some gesture of obeisance from them. When English rule was restored in 1691 the clergy, especially Henricus Selyns of New York, argued that Leisler and Milborne should be hanged as speedily as possible so as to stanch any further restiveness in the colony.

The Dutch clergy, however, seriously underestimated the level of discontent among their less affluent congregants. After Leisler and Milborne were executed on 16 May 1691, the Dutch Reformed ministers faced large-scale attrition in their churches: 80 percent on Long Island and as high as 90 percent in New York City, where Selyns had led the opposition to Leisler. The clergy's salaries, notoriously difficult to collect in the best of times, fell deeply into arrears. In the New York church Leislerians remained aloof, although they sought each year to win seats on the consistory; by 1699 they had captured a majority, and the next year, much to the chagrin of Selyns, every seat was filled with a supporter of the rebellion. Amid a changing political climate, the Leislerians won another victory over their erstwhile opponents in general, and Selyns in particular. After reviewing the trial and executions, the English Parliament in 1695 ordered the return of Leisler's and Milborne's property to their families, passed a bill legalizing their rule, and removed the attainder of treason. Leislerians then obtained permission from the magistrates to exhume the bodies and, after a parade in 1698 and amid great fanfare, the corpses were reinterred in the Dutch Reformed church in New York City, a powerful statement about the deep and persistent divisions within Dutch Calvinism.

THE JUGGERNAUT OF ENGLISH CULTURE

But if the clergy faced dissent within its churches, the external pressures were even greater and, in the end, overwhelming. This held true for both Dutch and French Calvinism in the middle colonies. French Protestants, better known as Huguenots, began arriving in the New World in 1685, fleeing persecution after the revocation of the Edict of Nantes. Initially the Huguenots found the pluralism of colonial New York congenial, but they soon faced the dilemma of either maintaining their ethnic particularity or bowing to the considerable pressures to assimilate. Because of the relatively small size of the French community and, most likely, the absence of fond associations with France itself, the Huguenots surrendered more quickly than the Dutch to the juggernaut of English culture. In some cases Dutch and French Calvinists closed ranks, with the French congregations generally folding into Dutch churches, but the pressures they faced from English rulers were similar.

When Governor Benjamin Fletcher finally cajoled the General Assembly into passing the Ministry Act of 1693, the Church of England became the legally established religion in the four lower counties of New York. Although the Dutch and other dissenters sought, with some success, to frustrate several of the bill's provisions, they faced more effective assaults from the Society for the Propagation of the Gospel. Missionaries from the society flooded the North Atlantic colonies after 1701, and they enjoyed considerable success in New York and New Jersey because of the cooperation of successive governors. Edward Hyde, Lord Cornbury, was especially ruthless in his attempts to disrupt the religious affairs of Dutch and French Calvinists. He sought to install Anglican ministers in Dutch Reformed and Huguenot churches. In 1703 he supported the intrusion of Bernardus Freeman, a schismatic, into the Dutch Reformed churches on Long Island. Freeman's presence there provoked a bitter schism that lasted the better part of a decade and had the effect of enervating Dutch Calvinism throughout the colony.

More important to the long-term success of Anglicanism at the expense of Dutch and French Calvinism was the formation of Anglican schools. Justifying his appointment of an Anglican to the Dutch Reformed church in Kingston, Cornbury wrote: "Now I am of Opinion that if as ye Dutch Ministers dye, those Churches were supply'd with English ministers that would with schools be a means to make this Colony an English Colony, which I am afraid will not easily be done without it." On 27 November 1702, shortly after Cornbury's arrival, the Assembly passed "An Act for Encouragement of a Grammar Free School in the City of New-York," which provided "for the Education and Instruction of Youth and Male Children of Such Parents as are of French and Dutch Extraction, as well as of the English." One of the society's missionaries even proposed outlawing Dutch schools in order to accelerate the process of Anglicization.

Such measures were not necessary. Dutch Calvinism remained deeply divided after Leisler's Rebellion, largely along socioeconomic lines. According to contemporary accounts, a large number of erstwhile Leislerians migrated across the Hudson River to New Jersey at the turn of the eighteenth century, seeking both rich farmland and political respite. Back in New York, the Dutch Reformed church lost many of its more prosperous congregants to the Church of

England in the early decades of the eighteenth century. The wives of these congregants, however, perhaps recognizing that their rights had been constricted under English rule, remained within the Dutch Reformed church, sometimes in direct defiance of their assimilated husbands.

TWO CULTURES, TWO CHURCHES

Early in the eighteenth century, then, Dutch Calvinism split into two distinct churches. Although the traditionalist Dutch clergy, centered in New York and Long Island, continued to curry favor with the English rulers, just as it had beginning in 1664, there was a subtle shift in their posture. Somewhat paradoxically they began to emphasize their loyalty to the Classis of Amsterdam, which retained ecclesiastical oversight over the colonial churches, the importance of liturgical formality, and their fealty to Dutch culture in general, including Dutch-language preaching.

The Dutch Reformed churches in New Jersey and in the upper Hudson Valley, on the other hand, evinced a rather different character. These congregations, consisting in part of erstwhile Leislerians, preferred the pietism articulated by preachers like Freeman, Guiliam Bertholf, John Henry Goetschius, and, most notably, Theodorus Jacobus Frelinghuysen, who arrived in the New World in 1720. Like their confreres across the Atlantic, the pietists attacked the cold formalism of Dutch Reformed orthodoxy and advocated instead a warmhearted piety and high standards of probity. The new evangelical piety eventually prevailed, especially in the Raritan Valley of New Jersey, but not, once again, without a struggle. Frelinghuysen's withholding of the sacraments, ostensibly an attempt to enforce higher standards of godliness, very often degenerated into a tool wielded against his critics. He roundly denounced the traditionalist Dutch clergy for its lack of piety, even though Frelinghuysen apparently fell short of the mark himself, at least by the standards of eighteenth-century Calvinism; Frelinghuysen faced repeated (and apparently unrefuted) charges that he and his schoolmaster, Jacobus Schuurman, were homosexuals.

The Dutch Calvinism that emerged from the Raritan Valley and from the upper Hudson Valley was decidedly evangelical, long before the stirrings of what historians generally refer to as the Great Awakening in New England. Frelinghuysen, in fact, was responsible for tutoring Gilbert Tennent, the Presbyterian revivalist, in the rudiments of continental pietism while both men served churches in New Brunswick. The two often traded pulpits, which underscores another trait of Dutch Calvinistic pietism in the middle colonies—its ecumenical character. While the traditionalist clergy in New York clung to Dutch language, customs, and traditions as a kind of safe harbor in a sea of change, Frelinghuysen and other pietists blended into the evangelical culture that was emerging in the American colonies. They cooperated with New Light Presbyterians and with such luminaries as George Whitefield. Jonathan Edwards in Northampton, Massachusetts, was well aware of Frelinghuysen and the Dutch pietists in the middle colonies.

COETUS AND CONFERENTIE

While Dutch Calvinists in New Jersey embraced the revival, traditionalists in New York vilified it, thereby forcing a final showdown between the two camps. In the 1740s, amid the enthusiasm of the Great Awakening, the pietists began agitating for a *coetus* (pronounced SEE-tus), which would allow the colonial clergy to rule on ecclesiastical matters while retaining its formal subordination to the Classis of Amsterdam. The traditionalists saw this as an opportunity for the revivalists to perpetuate their mischief. They vigorously opposed the move, but the Classis of Amsterdam, wearied of the incessant bickering on the western shore of the Atlantic, allowed the movement to proceed. When the American Coetus was gaveled to order on 8 September 1747, the traditionalist clergy refused to attend and later organized themselves into the rival Conferentie party, which insisted upon maintaining strong ties to Amsterdam.

Within a few years the Coetus, dominated by pietists, or Evangelicals, sought to establish itself as an American classis, thereby severing all remaining formal ties to the Netherlands. In addition the Pietists proposed an indigenous academy or seminary for the training of evangelical ministers. This, they reasoned, would have several advantages. First, it would circumvent the requirement, irregularly enforced, that Dutch Reformed ministers be graduates of a Dutch university and secure their ordinations from the Classis of Amsterdam. The former stipulation especially rankled the Pietists because most ministerial candidates for the New World had come out of the University of Leiden and were, in the Pietists' judgment, deficient in personal piety, too urbane in demeanor, and unnecessarily scholastic in theology. An indigenous academy would allow the Pietists to shape the spiritual lives of ministerial candidates, and it would also ensure that they spoke acceptable English, a requirement that became more and more important as the eighteenth century wore on.

Dutch Reformed traditionalists in New York also faced the language issue. By the middle of the eighteenth century Dutch children in New York, in the absence of Dutch schools, could no longer understand the sermons of Netherlands-trained preachers. As the younger generation drifted off either to the Presbyterians or the Church of England, the New York congregation finally faced the inevitable in 1763 when it hired a Scottish-trained minister, Archibald Laidlie, to preach in English. As for an American academy, the Dutch of New York, while opposing Coetus plans for an indigenous seminary, cooperated with the Anglicans in the founding of King's College (Columbia University) in 1754. The Coetus proceeded with its plans for an academy sympathetic to Dutch Pietism; Queen's College (Rutgers University) was chartered in 1766.

As the revolution approached, divisions within Dutch Calvinism hardened. The Conferentie party, historically solicitous toward English rule, largely remained loyal to the British, or at least tried to remain neutral. The Coetus ministers and their congregations, on the other hand, overwhelmingly supported the Patriot cause, recognizing—sometimes explicitly—the connection between ecclesiastical independence from the Netherlands and political independence from Britain.

Indeed, with the securing of political independence from the British, the Dutch churches quickly effected their ecclesiastical independence from the Netherlands. In October 1784 they assumed the name of "The Synod of the Reformed Dutch Churches of New York and New Jersey." Later in the decade, the synod authorized a translation of the psalm book and the *Articles of the Synod of Dort,* "since the English language is our national tongue, and is making progress, and has already been adopted wholly or in part in worship in most of our congregations, and the rising generation seem to be little acquainted with the Dutch tongue."

Dutch and French Calvinism in the middle colonies were linked inextricably with ethnicity. For both groups religious life became the focus of ethnic identity. The Huguenots, lacking a strong and cohesive community, assimilated into other ethnic groups, either the Dutch or the English. The Dutch, once the rulers of the colony, sought at various times to resist the forces of Anglicization, but they too succumbed to the juggernaut of English culture.

BIBLIOGRAPHY

Balmer, Randall. *A Perfect Babel of Confusion: Dutch Religion and English Culture in the Middle Colonies.* New York, 1989.

Butler, Jon. *The Huguenots in America: A Refugee People in New World Society.* Cambridge, Mass., 1983.

Hackett, David G. *The Rude Hand of Innovation: Religion and Social Order in Albany, New York, 1652–1836.* New York, 1991.

Rink, Oliver A. *Holland on the Hudson: An Economic and Social History of Dutch New York.* Ithaca, N.Y., 1986.

Tanis, James. *Dutch Calvinistic Pietism in the Middle Colonies: A Study in the Life and Theology of Theodorus Jacobus Frelinghuysen.* The Hague, The Netherlands, 1967.

Randall Balmer

SEE ALSO **Church and State; Puritanism; Revivalism and the Great Awakening;** and **Roman Catholicism.**

PROTESTANT PLURALISM

Here bee not many of the Church of England; few Roman Catholicks; abundance of Quakers preachers men and Women especially; Singing Quakers, Ranting Quakers; Sabbatarians; Antisabbatarians; Some Anabaptists; some Independents; some Jews; in short, of all sorts of opinions there are some, and the most part [are] of none at all.
Governor Thomas Dongan, New York, 1687

THE ORIGINS OF AMERICAN religious pluralism, and of pluralism among Protestants especially, are correctly thought to lie in the colonial period. Between 1607 and 1776, America emerged from a relatively narrow if nonetheless plural Protestant religious spectrum to a Protestant cornucopia so overflowing that many men and women of the time found it disturbing rather than reassuring. This pluralism appeared in two main forms: diverse views on theology and ecclesiastical policy within single denominations or movements, and an increasing number of denominations or movements themselves. Pluralism in the British colonies never equaled or even approximated the religious pluralism of American society after 1800 and especially after 1880, but on the eve of the revolution religious pluralism was indelibly shaping that society. Most important, it turned America toward the issues of religious diversity that have continually characterized the development of modern United States society.

Religious pluralism and Protestant diversity were European inventions, although Americans are sometimes inclined to think of them as unique to their own society. An extraordinary variety of religious belief characterized Europe long before—and long after—the Christianization of the Roman Empire, much to the chagrin of church authorities. For centuries before the Protestant Reformation, the Roman Catholic church tolerated substantial differences in theology and liturgy by way of accommodating both intellectual diversity and regional and national differences. The great crises of the church reflected the deep differences not always well contained within the church. During the period of the so-called Avignon Captivity (1305–1378), three different men claimed the papacy, each representing important forces within the church. The contest ended only when one died and secular powers forced a compromise between the two remaining contenders.

The Protestant Reformation enlarged religious diversity in early modern Europe. Between 1517, when Martin Luther posted his Ninety-five Theses on the door of the cathedral at Wittenberg, and 1589, when Henry of Navarre abjured even the new Protestantism to become Henry IV of France—two years after the English had attempted the ill-fated colony at Roanoke Island off what is now North Carolina—Protestants divided among themselves, often bitterly, even as they also contested with Catholics for local as well as Continental spiritual supremacy. By 1600 Protantism was divisible into three

609

principal groups: Lutherans, Calvinists (followers of the Genevan theologian, Jean Calvin), and a host of other groups whose small numbers frequently were dwarfed by the tenacity of their beliefs. These "sectarians" included Zwinglians (followers of the Zurich reformer, Huldrych Zwingli), advocates of the so-called "radical reformation" such as the mystical Kaspar Schwenkfeld of Swabia, Jacob Hutter and the Hutterites, and the Swiss Brethren led by Conrad Grebel and Balthasar Hubmaier. The group also included England's adamant "Puritans," who came close to remodeling the Church of England before Elizabeth I drove them underground in the 1580s, just as England was beginning serious efforts at New World colonization.

Popular religious apathy sometimes intertwined with this multiplicity of Protestant beliefs to make early modern Europe a scene of both religious ferment and spiritual instability, at least in the minds of critics who saw both as the work of the devil. Despite stunning political success in Germany, Switzerland, Scotland, England, the Netherlands, and even France, Protestants commanded lay obedience and voluntary worship no better than Catholics. All authorities, both Catholic and Protestant, reported lax church attendance. Lay Catholics attended Easter services much more frequently than did Protestants (roughly 80 percent in France, for example, as opposed to 30 or 40 percent in England), but both reported extremely low weekly attendance (15 to 40 percent in face-to-face rural communities with priests or ministers, fewer than 10 percent in urban places).

The law, however, seldom sanctioned religious diversity, even in Protestant countries. Throughout the early modern period, European law gave primacy to the state church. In most countries, the law recognized only a single religion and proscribed severe penalties, including death, for those who practiced any other. Sometimes the law recognized social reality only in perverse ways. In 1685 Louis XIV used a real decline of Protestant strength in France to declare that it no longer existed and that he therefore was no longer bound by the protections granted to Protestants in 1598 by the Edict of Nantes; the result was a massive and successful anti-Protestant pogrom that effectively destroyed Protestantism as a major force in French politics and culture.

Everywhere, authorities used the law to protect state-sanctioned religion. Whether in Catholic France or Anglican England, the law gave privileges to adherents of the state church and denied them to anyone who rejected it. They typically included voting and office holding, but sometimes involved a wide range of "privileges" from oath taking to burial. Although the law never exterminated popular anticlericalism and criticism of state-church corruption, it achieved greater successes in preventing the expansion of competing religious groups than historians have sometimes admitted. Swedes may have made lethargic and even cynical Lutherans, and Spaniards may have held the church in open contempt, but this did not mean that they necessarily exercised other religious options. Few Swedes became Baptists or Unitarians and few Spaniards became Protestants of any kind, due in large part to the legal pressure that government placed on religious dissent and dissenters.

Thus Europe offered complicated models for colonial leaders rethinking the problem of religious diversity. No European nation tolerated all religions or religious views. Most approved of only one religion and applied a wide range of penalties to citizens unwise enough to reject it. Only a few legally tolerated even a narrow variety of groups—among them, England after adopting the Act of Toleration in 1689—and this toleration was new, continually controversial, and limited. Not surprisingly then, multiple Protestant groups emerged only slowly and not always smoothly in colonial America. On the eve of the American Revolution, Protestant pluralism (and to a much lesser extent, a larger and more general religious pluralism) was a reality in colonial America, but it did not yet constitute a new American religious ideal.

PROTESTANT PLURALISM IN THE EARLY COLONIES, 1607–1680

Arriving from an already religiously complex society, British settlers brought to America only some, not all, of the religious opinion they knew at home. Nor was that variety of opinion expressed in all the colonies with equal force. Still, although relatively narrow in range, the pluralism found very early among Protestants in both New England and the Chesapeake demonstrated that orthodoxy would be no easier to maintain in North America than in Europe. It provided a foundation for the far more vigorous pluralism that emerged in colonial Protestantism after 1680.

New England Before 1680

The emergence of pluralism among New England's seemingly orthodox Puritans graphically demonstrated the complexity of both Puritanism and English Protestantism, as well as of the congregational form of church government that New Englanders adopted. At the same time, with the notable exception of Quakerism, this pluralism remained almost wholly Calvinist, exhibiting little influence from non-Calvinist Continental sources or even from the spiritual radicalism that flourished during the English Civil War and Commonwealth of the 1640s and 1650s.

New Englanders resisted pluralism, sometimes bitterly, although they were the products of English religious pluralism. Historians of these New Englanders have not made the task of understanding that paradox any easier. On the one hand, the circumstances of early Puritan migration to New England masked quite natural divisions and unresolved tensions even among settlers committed to Puritanism. Attacked by both James I and William Laud (the archbishop of Canterbury from 1633 to 1645), Puritans tended to overestimate their own doctrinal unity and to underestimate their capacity for dividing over extremely precise theological points ("Precisionist" was as common an epithet used against them as "Puritan"). Moreover, like their enemies, historians have tended to exaggerate Puritan orthodoxy while undervaluing the flux of Puritan opinion between the 1620s, when colonists first began arriving in New England, and the 1670s, when the distinctly religious migration to New England had all but ended.

Ironically, perhaps, both ecclesiastical principles and a fear of centralized religious authority encouraged New England church authorities to establish a system of church government that made it difficult, at best, to establish a firm orthodoxy while at the same time actually fostering theological pluralism. This system was New England Congregationalism. Each congregation recognized no ecclesiastical authority higher than itself; a minister was ordained only to serve a specific congregation; and although ministerial and church councils could debate doctrinal, disciplinary, and ecclesiastical issues, they possessed no power to enforce any collective views they might adopt.

Ecclesiastical decentralization ended up stimulating an extraordinary plurality of views that authorities met with coercion, their Congregational principles notwithstanding. In 1635 the authorities exiled Roger Williams to Rhode Island after he rejected the union of church and state and criticized the government's refusal to negotiate with Indians for land that the immigrants were occupying, thus threatening both religious and social order. In 1637 they tried Boston's Anne Hutchinson for sedition after she began explicating sermons delivered by Boston ministers in their pulpits and criticized ministers whose theology she rejected, all in sessions held with friends and neighbors in her home. Worse, she savored so-called antinomian principles that placed her above the law because, she said, she was saved and, therefore, sinless; she did not need laws passed to regulate the sinful. And in 1654 they forced Henry Dunster's resignation as Harvard's first president after Dunster's biblical study led him to adopt Baptist principles that restricted the rite of baptism to consenting adults, although like many others who adopted Baptist principles, Dunster remained a Calvinist who believed both in predestination and in the uselessness of good works to achieve salvation.

Throughout the 1650s, 1660s, and 1670s, doctrinal diversity among New England's Congregationalist churches produced further collective action, although many congregations failed to heed it. The 1648 Cambridge Platform, drawn up to provide a common doctrinal foundation for the rising number of New England town churches, skirted important issues like church membership standards and sanctification (the presence or lack of sinfulness among the saved) because of the variety of opinion and the inability of the region's leaders to enforce the Platform. The 1662 Halfway Covenant met similar results. Theoretically, it changed church membership standards by providing full membership for adults who "owned" a congregational covenant but a new "halfway" membership for adults who had not yet owned the covenant but had been baptized as children. Yet as many as half of New England's congregations ignored the Covenant, in part because they rejected it doctrinally and in part because they rejected the authority of the ministerial council that wrote it. Ironically, then, Calvinism seemingly guaranteed doctrinal plurality as much as it solidified order or orthodoxy.

Baptist congregations and Quaker meetings constituted New England's first formal dissenting religious groups. Baptists first organized in Rhode Island and immediately made pluralism and institutional separation characteristics of what was still a narrowly Calvinist society. In 1639 Roger Williams, fresh from his expulsion from Massachusetts, helped form a church in Providence, Rhode Island, that upheld adult baptism, although it lacked any formal relationship to England's Baptist congregations and denominational institutions. But Williams, constantly seeking religious truth, withdrew from the congregation after only a few months, and the remaining worshipers soon began to dispute about predestination, a doctrine that Calvinist Baptists upheld but that Arminian Baptists rejected. By 1652 the division had split the congregation into two churches, while a similar dispute divided the Baptist congregation at Newport in 1656. A further division shattered Arminian Baptists in 1671, when a Seventh-Day Baptist congregation worshiping on Saturday also emerged in Newport, and several other Seventh-Day Baptist congregations organized in western Rhode Island.

Massachusetts's Baptists experienced less internal doctrinal turmoil, perhaps because their dissent from the colony's legally established, tax-supported Congregational churches bore significant personal risks. Between 1649 and 1660 efforts by several Congregational church members to withdraw to form Baptist congregations met stiff legal sanction; in Rehoboth, for example, town officials forced the dissidents into exile in Rhode Island. Nonetheless, Baptists successfully formed congregations in Boston in 1665 and in Woburn in 1677, and a Welsh Baptist congregation was formed in Swansea in Plymouth Colony in 1663. With the exception of the Swansea congregation, which was the town church and as much ethnically Welsh as Baptist, Massachusetts's Baptists constituted a direct challenge to the colony's Congregationalist establishment because they drew members from settlers who ought to have supported the legally sanctioned churches. Embittered town authorities forced continued payment of taxes to support their old churches, as much a penalty for ruining town cohesion as for the doctrinal differences the Baptists had exposed and now furthered.

Quakers paid the highest price for bringing Protestant pluralism to New England. Emerging out of the Commonwealth Puritan milieu, yet rejecting many distinctive Puritan tenets—Calvinism, the sacraments, and traditional worship—Quakers emphasized universal salvation through an "inner light," silent weekly worship, and, ultimately, pacifism. Quakers also sent missionaries—"Public Friends"—to New England as early as 1656. After imprisoning and ejecting the first missionaries and passing laws to ban their proselytizing, Massachusetts authorities had hanged four Public Friends by 1661, then harassed successive missionaries through the 1680s.

Quakerism found adherents nonetheless in both Massachusetts and Rhode Island before 1680. In Massachusetts, Quaker meetings emerged in both Salem and Boston, where Baptist congregations also existed, although both meetings remained small. Quakerism found more numerous followers in Rhode Island, Nantucket, and eastern Long Island, which developed closer relations with New England than with New York in the seventeenth century. As a result, and before the colonization of Pennsylvania, these early Quaker gatherings, strung out along the New England coastline from Providence to Portsmouth, led to the first distinctive Quaker Yearly Meeting in the New World held in Newport, Rhode Island, in 1661.

Through the 1680s, then, Protestant pluralism in New England emerged unevenly. Connecticut remained almost untouched by the institutional expression of Protestant diversity except for the variety of opinions still contained inside its Congregationalist churches; as a result, through 1680 the colony lacked a single dissenting Baptist congregation or Quaker meeting (unless one counts the Quaker meetings on eastern Long Island, an area Connecticut claimed through the colonial period). Elsewhere, Protestant diversity remained largely a seaport phenomenon (especially notable in Salem, Boston, Providence, and Newport), with the occasional exception of a small ethnic enclave like the Welsh Baptists of Swansea, Massachusetts. Nor was this pluralism necessarily valued. It thrived in Rhode Island both because Roger Williams and the Rhode Island authorities refused to adopt the traditional English church-state relationship and because Massachusetts, which did use coercion shamelessly, sent so many of its own spiritual dissidents there. And in Massachusetts, dissidence persisted although it produced substantial court action, including fines, property confiscation, and exile, as well as execution. Massachusetts was the only province in the entire colonial period that used capital punishment to suppress religious diversity among Protestants.

The Middle and Southern Colonies Before 1680

Protestant pluralism in the middle and southern colonies before 1680 can be construed as both narrower and broader than that found in New England. On the one hand, it proved more limited and less vital both because organized religious activities of any kind, including tax-supported worship, proved more limited and less vital than in New England and because, the Chesapeake aside, this area experienced relatively limited European colonization before 1680. On the other hand, a considerable diversity within officially sanctioned churches paralleled that found among New England's Congregationalists, while ethnic diversity, with its potentially important religious implications, almost single-handedly transformed colonial Protestantism between 1680 and the 1770s. As a result, even in the half century before 1680, the sometimes phlegmatic Protestant pluralism of the middle and southern colonies more clearly anticipated the emerging Protestantism of pre-revolutionary America than did the more vibrant but narrower pluralism of early New England.

Like many other European colonies in America, New Netherland reflected no special religious origins, although also like others, its founders proclaimed desires to proselytize among American Indians. Ironically, however, its commonplace commercialism brought to it a remarkable religious diversity, even in its earliest years. This was because the colony, like the Netherlands itself, attracted an eclectic, cosmopolitan population drawn from virtually all the European nations actively pursuing international trade. Very early, and certainly by the eve of the first British conquest in 1664, New Netherland already contained Dutch Protestants (who, as in England, were subtly divided into several religious "parties" inside the Dutch Reformed Church), Walloons (Protestants from the area that now is modern Belgium), French Protestants (or "Huguenots"), and German-speaking Protestants (some Lutherans and some "German Reformed" Calvinists), as well as Catholics and Jews.

Nevertheless, even well after the final English conquest of 1664, the only formal and sustained collective religious worship in the colony remained the Dutch Reformed church, which was supported by the local Dutch government (again, the exception being eastern Long Island, whose ownership was disputed with Connecticut). Recognizing this diversity, the Dutch Reformed ministers in New York City held at least occasional Walloon and French services and later supported formation of a French-speaking congregation at New Paltz in 1683, although a Dutch Reformed congregation already existed in nearby Kingston.

The Delaware and Raritan valleys experienced an initial colonization that, however politically unsuccessful, prefigured the spiritual eclecticism that ultimately prospered in New Jersey, Pennsylvania, and Delaware between 1680 and the 1770s. Although the Dutch conquered the colony of New Sweden (settled on the Delaware River) in 1638, and the English assumed jurisdiction over the area after their own conquest of the Dutch in 1664, descendants of the Swedish settlers continued to support one or two Swedish Lutheran congregations throughout the American colonial period, usually hiring ministers directly from authorities in Stockholm who, in turn, tended to associate with Church of England clergymen, especially after 1700. New England immigrants from Connecticut settled Newark and Woodbridge, New Jersey, in the 1680s and brought with them their Congregational church. Dutch settlers from New York slowly filtered into New Jersey, especially into the Raritan Valley, where they established Dutch Reformed congregations. And Scottish immigrants, leaving home when Scotland's religious climate was still eclectic and not nearly so Presbyterian as it became in the eighteenth century, represented several religious views—Presbyterianism, of course, but also the Church of Scotland (essentially Anglican) and Quakerism, which had made considerable inroads in southern Scotland between 1665 and 1680. As in New York, however, the multiple religious inclinations of many residents in the Delaware and Raritan valleys had to be fulfilled individually rather than collectively, since organized congregations—whether Presbyterian, Dutch Reformed, or Quaker—remained relatively scarce until the population expanded after 1680.

The early southern colonies replicated the patterns found in the middle colonies, sometimes in exaggerated form. In Maryland, the contrast between the variety of individual religious beliefs and the failure or inability to develop a significant collective religious life scarcely could have been greater. Maryland's origins as a colony founded by the Baltimores naturally attracted Catholic settlers and, before 1660, a number of Catholic priests. But non-Catholic Englishmen soon predominated in the population, and anti-Catholic prejudice was evident during Maryland's several governmental upheavals between 1640 and 1690, a period of vandalization of the colony's Catholic chapels and a time when Catholic worship was largely driven into private homes.

Maryland's famous "Act Concerning Religion," passed in 1649, might be thought to signal the prosperity of diverse Protestant groups in early Maryland and to have signaled the inevitability of England's Act of Toleration of 1689. It prohibited a wide variety of epithets that Marylanders might use to slur "unorthodox" neighbors: "heretic, Scismatic, Idolator, puritan, Independent, Presbiterian, popish priest, Jesuite, Jesuited papist, Lutheran, Calvinist, Anabaptist, Brownist, Antinomian, Barrowist, Roundhead, [and] Separatist." The 1649 act was almost a plea for any sort of organized religious worship, especially among Protestants, because up until the 1680s non-Catholic public worship fared poorly in the colony. No church was established by law, Anglicans managed the organization of only two or three working parishes at best, and no dissenting Baptist or Presbyterian groups are known to have enjoyed a long-term existence in Maryland before 1680. Between 1660 and 1680 only Quakers managed to sustain even the semblance of steady organized worship there,

and these in only two or three gatherings perhaps involving 150 worshipers at most.

Virginia represented a similar situation despite formal Church of England establishment in the colony. Early Puritan sentiment evident among Virginia Company shareholders and some early Puritan-inclined clergymen gave way to a half century of spiritual drift following the collapse of the Virginia Company of London in 1624. Although the colony formally established the Church of England and gave directions for laying out parish boundaries, initiative for sustaining parish life remained in local hands. Many parishes existed in name only, others employed ministers only briefly and erratically, and a certain eclecticism characterized the few that sustained worship across several decades. In Nansemond County, Puritanism prospered from the early 1640s into the 1650s, until Governor William Berkeley exiled two ministers sent from New England to serve the parish churches and finally forced Nansemond's Puritan partisans into exile across the Chesapeake in Maryland, where their congregation soon disbanded. Other parishes exhibited similar diversity or even eccentricity. The library of the Reverend Thomas Teackle, who served Eastern-Shore parishes in Accomack and Northampton counties between 1652 and 1695, contained far more books on Puritanism, Catholicism, and even occultism than on Anglicanism, although how Teackle or his parishioners synthesized the divergent strands represented in the books remains unknown.

As in Maryland, however, this diversity of interests and instincts among Virginia's laity and clergy produced few of the dissenting groups that characterized Virginia by 1750. Through the 1680s, not a single Baptist or Presbyterian congregation had been organized there, and as in Massachusetts, none of the radical and infamous English sectarian groups thrown up by the Civil War and the Commonwealth prospered in Virginia either. Quakerism, however, won followers in Virginia's southern-shore counties, including Nansemond, where Puritan-inclined residents remained, and several Quaker meetings were established there in the 1670s. But even in these areas, Quakerism remained more important as a symbol of individual religious diversity than as a powerful religious force, since it appealed to no more than 1 or 2 percent of the population, even in a colony often poorly served by both the established Church of England and the several other dissenting denominations active in England and dominant in New England.

In some regards, the area south of Virginia that now is North and South Carolina exemplified the combination of Protestant diversity and institutional lethargy common to the middle and southern colonies. Settled haphazardly by Englishmen who had often straggled in from other colonies, the area lacked even the Catholic presence hated by so many Englishmen but present in Maryland; nor was there much sign of the Church of England or any Baptist, Congregational, or Presbyterian activity. As in both Maryland and Virginia, Quakerism filled the bill for a few. When the Quaker founder, George Fox, traveled through the area in the 1670s, he met a ready response, although he was surprised by the settlers' ignorance of even the most elemental Christian doctrine and form. Nonetheless, the Quaker stress on the "inner light" and especially its use of silent worship, along with its lack of resident ministers who needed a salary, glebe, and house, fitted well the sometimes grim economic realities of early- and mid-seventeenth-century settlement south of Virginia.

THE TRANSFORMATION OF COLONIAL PROTESTANTISM, 1680–1770

The nine decades between the 1680s and the 1770s thoroughly transformed colonial American religion, including early American Protestantism, in ways that would have astonished early-seventeenth-century colonists, even in places like New York or Maryland, much less New England. By the time of the American Revolution, a once somewhat lethargic American Protestantism had become so institutionally robust that it was viewed as a model for European Protestants. Even among English settlers, post-1680 colonial Protestantism was far more theologically diverse than was its earlier-seventeenth-century predecessor. Moreover, new ethnic and racial dimensions extended this theological and liturgical diversity even farther. Not surprisingly, as early as the 1750s and certainly by the 1770s,

both foreign and domestic observers had begun to detect distinctively American themes in colonial Protestantism. In the main, these themes remained only embryonic. The increasingly diverse pre-revolutionary colonial Protestants were still largely dependent upon European sources and they were, therefore, overwhelmingly "colonial." Yet they also were shaping a religious configuration hitherto unknown in Europe, one that the success of the revolution further transformed in ways that ultimately became indelibly American.

Statistics dramatically express the expansion of diversity within colonial American Protestantism between 1680 and the 1770s. More than three-quarters of all congregations organized in the American colonies had their origins in the years between 1680 and 1770 rather than in the earlier decades of settlement. Indeed, the thirty years immediately preceding the revolution brought the greatest rush of congregation-building to the colonies, since some 60 percent of all colonial American congregations were formed between 1740 and 1770 alone.

The transformation of colonial Protestantism between 1680 and 1770 reshaped relations among the colonial denominations. Before 1680 two denominations—Congregationalism and the Church of England—accounted for 90 percent of all colonial American congregations and Congregationalism comprised the vast majority of these because it embraced virtually all of New England's congregations, which greatly outnumbered the working Anglican parishes in early Virginia. By the 1770s, however, Congregationalism, although still strong, amounted to only about 20 percent of colonial congregations, and the Church of England to approximately 15 percent. In contrast, English and Scottish Presbyterians now accounted for about 18 percent of the colonial congregations and English and Welsh Baptists for about 15 percent, while Quakers constituted about 10 percent of the colonial congregations. Finally, where non-English congregations made up only a small proportion of all Christian congregations in the colonies (including New Netherland) before 1680, by 1770 they comprised between 20 and 25 percent of all colonial congregations.

The expansion of colonial settlement into vast new territories between 1680 and 1760 further exaggerated the importance of this new, vigorously diverse colonial American Protestantism. Only New England remained relatively homogeneous. Indeed, the sheer number of Congregationalist churches there, more than six hundred in the 1770s, accounted for virtually all of that denomination's churches in all the colonies and for its ranking as the largest denomination in the British colonies. But in the politically and culturally important middle and southern colonies, diversity, even seeming chaos, reigned. Anglicanism accounted for no more than a third of the region's churches; another third were Baptist, and nearly a quarter were Presbyterian.

Diversity was even more pronounced in the middle colonies. German congregations made up a full third of the region's congregations and by the time of the revolution they were divided between two main groups—Lutherans and Calvinist German Reformed churches—and four smaller groups—Amish, Mennonite, Moravian, and German Baptist. English-speaking congregations were divided among Presbyterian, Baptist, Quaker, and Anglican churches. Finally, testifying to the region's spiritual pluralism, even Catholicism was rising there, with some dozen Catholic churches being established in the middle colonies in the late 1760s and the 1770s alone.

Origins of Modern Pluralism, 1680–1740

What historians frequently call the "second colonization" of colonial America—the final English conquest of New Netherland in 1664 and the establishment of the new colonies of East and West Jersey, Pennsylvania, Delaware, and North and South Carolina after 1680—thoroughly erased the old Calvinist-Anglican domination of the English religious order. It transformed Presbyterian and Baptist congregations from occasional curiosities into powerful denominations, it ultimately reinvigorated the Church of England, and it brought Continental Protestantism to America in a way that signaled the increasing importance of ethnicity to Protestant identity and success in the nineteenth- and twentieth-century United States.

Quakerism was the earliest beneficiary of England's second colonization in America. Before 1680 Quakerism grew in limited ways through the labor of Quaker proselytizers, Public

Friends, who worked among English colonists in America. Between 1680 and 1710 Englishmen who had long since converted to Quakerism at home, including many second-generation Friends, immigrated to America in unparalleled numbers. First coming to the East and West Jerseys in the 1670s, then settling in Pennsylvania in greater numbers after William Penn established the colony in 1681, these new settlers shaped the colony and the denomination that Americans would for all time think of as the model home of American Quakerism. Between 1675 and 1700 the number of Quaker meetings grew from perhaps eight or ten scattered throughout New England and the southern colonies, to well over fifty concentrated primarily in New Jersey, New York, Delaware, and, of course, Pennsylvania. Moreover, in the Jerseys and Pennsylvania, Quakers quickly came to dominate both government and society, transforming themselves from a frequently derided minority at home into a powerful, triumphant majority in several American colonies.

Baptists and Presbyterians likewise made their first major appearance in the colonies during the second colonization. Welsh and English Baptists immigrated to the Jerseys and Pennsylvania in substantial numbers between 1680 and 1740 and thoroughly outstripped the older Baptist congregations confined to the New England coast. By 1710 more than twenty Baptist congregations had emerged in this area, and by 1740 their number had grown to more than sixty, the vast majority of them located in the area between New York and Annapolis.

Presbyterians arrived in even greater numbers. Whereas in 1680 no more than a handful of Presbyterian congregations existed anywhere in the American colonies, by 1710 nearly 30 had been formed, and by 1740 the number had reached more than 130. Some of the congregations were formed among English settlers in places like Boston, New York City, and Charleston. A few, like the original Congregationalists at Newark and Woodbridge, New Jersey, finally abandoned their Congregationalist principles to become Presbyterians.

But many of the new Presbyterian congregations stemmed from a combination of immigration and proselytizing among immigrants. "Scots-Irish" immigrants—Scotsmen who had first been settled in Ireland to aid in the subjugation of the Irish but who subsequently immigrated to America—comprised one group of these immigrants, some settling in the Jerseys and Pennsylvania, others settling after 1730 in the North and South Carolina backcountry. Immigrants coming directly from Scotland offered another, though more complicated, source of Presbyterian adherence. Especially before 1710 these immigrants reflected Scotland's exceptional eclecticism in religion, some being Presbyterian, some being Anglicans (Church of Scotland), and some being Quakers. But as in Scotland, Presbyterianism in New Jersey and Pennsylvania soon overwhelmed the earlier religious commitments; by the 1740s to be Scottish was, in the main, to be Presbyterian. On both sides of the Atlantic, then, the term "Scotch [sic] Presbyterian" was an eighteenth-century creation, not a tradition deriving straight from the Reformation.

New splinter groups and sects, most small and short-lived, demonstrated that the English capacity for derision, dissent, and division, with its subsequent result in religious diversity, extended far beyond seventeenth-century New England. In New England itself, a group first formed in 1677 by the Rhode Island dissident John Rogers, and called the Rogerenes, split off from already-dissident Baptists, worshiped on Saturdays (as did the Seventh-Day Baptists), and stressed the use of prayer in healing (a tenet accepted by all Christian groups but not to the exclusion of medicine, something at which the Rogerenes at least hinted). Although the group outlived its founder, Rogerene congregations never extended beyond Rhode Island and eastern Connecticut, and these declined after 1740.

A near-disastrous schism in the 1690s among Pennsylvania and New Jersey Quakers tested the limits of toleration in Pennsylvania and at least briefly produced a new religious group. After fashioning a biting critique of Pennsylvania's prestigious Public Friends that criticized their pretentious, overweening authority, disciplinary lethargy, and doctrinal sloth, the Scottish Quaker George Keith stimulated a schism so serious that Philadelphia Quaker authorities finally used the court system to prevent Keith's printer, William Bradford, from publishing, on grounds of libel. Lacking support among Quakers in England as well, Keith took his several hundred followers on a dizzying theological ride. Between 1694 and 1697 they called themselves Christian Quakers; then they adopted the rite of baptism and from 1697 to about 1710 called themselves Keithian Baptists. In the meantime, Keith became an Anglican and launched a proselytizing tour in the American colonies to convert his old enemies, the Quakers. But he met no better fortunes among them than he did among supporters of his schism, who worshiped separately for several years until finally merging with more orthodox English Baptists in the 1710s.

The ability, willingness, and success of English settlers to create powerful denominational institutions kept much of colonial Protestantism from exploding into chaos and accounted for the increase of dissenting Protestant congregations in the colonies, especially south of New England. Between 1680 and 1710 Philadelphia easily displaced Boston as the capital of colonial Protestantism and the model of colonial denominational organization. By 1685 Quakers in the region of the Delaware Valley had established their distinctive meeting system of monthly and quarterly meetings capped by a Yearly Meeting initially held in Burlington, New Jersey, but quickly moved to Philadelphia. The Yearly Meeting contained the region's most important Friends, gained direct jurisdiction over Quaker meetings between New York and Maryland, and became a model for the smaller Yearly Meeting held in Rhode Island for New England Friends and for the Yearly Meeting formed in the 1740s in Virginia to manage affairs for Quakers in the southern colonies.

Baptists and Presbyterians likewise established their modern denominational headquarters in Philadelphia. Baptist congregations had gathered informally in Pennsylvania and New Jersey between 1693 and 1706, but in 1707 they established a more powerful association later simply called the Philadelphia Baptist Association. Organization of the first presbytery in the American colonies also occurred in Philadelphia. Claiming fewer congregations than the Baptists, but spurred by a suggestion for a presbytery from several local ministers, the Presbytery of Philadelphia held its first meeting in September

1706. By 1716 the Philadelphia presbytery was sufficiently large to warrant formation of the first synod in the colonies—the Synod of Philadelphia—and to divide its members into regional presbyteries, which numbered no less than six by the 1740s.

The new denominational institutions proved to be authoritative, although not necessarily authoritarian. Power in each flowed down from the top rather than up from the bottom; in the main, they were dominated by a small number of adherents who exercised ministerial functions—Public Friends among the Quakers, preachers and elders among the Baptists, and ordained ministers among the Presbyterians. Their gatherings settled disputes within and among meetings and congregations, established standards for entrance into the ministry, and assigned ministers to congregations (among Baptists and Presbyterians). Their most important and successful function involved their stimulation of denominational enlargement. Even Quakers, who all but abandoned proselytizing among non-Quakers after 1700, encouraged formation of new meetings to serve Quaker settlements in Pennsylvania's expanding backcountry, while Baptists and Presbyterians vigorously promoted new congregations in the recent settlements as well. These colonial denominational institutions proved far more vigorous than their counterparts in England, probably because they were proselytizing in new settlements rather than in old ones. The expansion of denominational growth among Baptists, in particular, contrasted sharply with stasis and even decline among late-Stuart and early-Hanoverian Baptists in England.

The state-church tradition revived during this period as well, and a major campaign by Church of England authorities thoroughly reinvigorated Anglicanism in the North American colonies. Anglicanism suffered in the colonies because many settlers were indifferent or hostile to the church and because parliamentary politics both before and after the English Civil War precluded naming a new bishop or bishops to manage Anglican affairs in the overseas colonies. The changes that occurred especially between 1680 and 1710 compensated for these earlier difficulties in ways that transformed much of colonial American religious life.

The Anglican transformation took two principal courses, both evident in Virginia between 1680 and the 1730s. First, the church strengthened legal prerogatives implicit in its establishment as Virginia's state church in the 1620s but compromised by a half century of institutional lethargy. The Virginia burgesses renewed the parish structure, more vigorously pressed for creation of parishes as settlement expanded, and strengthened the powers of parish vestries. In addition, London authorities secured the appointment of a commissary, or agent of the Bishop of London, to strengthen Anglican ecclesiastical authority in the colony, an appointment made all the more important by the man first named to the position: the dynamic if often controversial James Blair, who after 1690 vigorously pressed Anglican parish development in Virginia for more than a half century until his death in 1743. As a result, the number of Anglican parishes in Virginia more than doubled in the years from 1685 to 1710, more than thirty parishes churches were constructed, and the church achieved a significant part of the glory and power that its legal position implied.

Anglican authorities pursued similar ends in other colonies with similar, if not identical, means. Between 1680 and 1710 they won legal establishment in South Carolina, North Carolina, Maryland, and New York (the latter a partial establishment in New York City and five surrounding counties) that allowed them to found parishes and support ministers using the legal and fiscal power of the colonial government. The effect in Maryland was particularly dramatic. Where the colony had only four or five regularly gathered Protestant churches or meetings in 1685 (two or three Anglican churches, one Presbyterian church, and several Quaker meetings, all of them small), Maryland had some thirty working Anglican parishes by 1710, virtually all of them with new church buildings and two-thirds of them staffed with resident Anglican clergymen.

In colonies where legal establishment proved impossible or where it proved lax (as in North and South Carolina), the church used two new institutions to bolster its American position. In 1699 Anglican authorities created the Society for Promoting Christian Knowledge (SPCK) to commission and publish books useful in Anglican evangelizing, and in 1701 they established the Society for the Propagation of the Gospel in Foreign Parts (SPG) to provide ministers for English settlers in the American colonies. Explicitly modeled on what Anglican reformers (especially Thomas Bray, who had briefly served as Anglican commissary in Maryland) took to be ideal denominational institutions among Dissenters, Anglican authorities raised enormous sums of money in England that were disbursed throughout the American colonies to build Anglican churches, pay ministerial salaries, and distribute books in places where legal establishment proved impossible and to bolster Anglican enterprises in colonies where it had succeeded.

As Anglicanism challenged older dissenting congregations for preeminence, dramatic visual changes sometimes occurred in the colonial cities. Between 1680 and 1720 Anglicans erected the largest church buildings yet constructed in the American colonies. They deliberately named and designed Boston's King's Chapel to irritate descendants of the city's Puritan founders, constructing an ornate building that symbolized both Anglican liturgicalism and its headship by the king. Trinity Church in New York City, Christ Church in Philadelphia, and Saint Phillips' Church in Charleston performed similar functions. Nor were they empty symbols. They represented the vigor with which Anglicans diversified early-eighteenth-century colonial Protestantism. Between 1680 and 1710 Anglicans constructed no less than eighty-five church buildings in the colonies, most of them in rural parishes, and between 1710 and 1740 they constructed nearly one hundred more, again, usually in rural areas where the colonial population was expanding most rapidly. As a result, the church headed by the English monarch became for the first time vigorously present in the colonial American religious configuration.

Non-English immigrants from the European continent made colonial Protestantism even more diverse. Huguenots fleeing Louis XIV's persecution in France in the 1680s were the first of these immigrants, and between 1680 and 1700 they established congregations in the cities of Boston, New York, and Charleston as well as in rural New York and South Carolina. Yet Huguenots assimilated so well in early-eighteenth-century colonial society that they also disap-

peared as a significant ethnic and religious group. Several rural settlements in New England collapsed quickly. In the cities, the refugees began to intermarry with English (and in New York, with Dutch) residents and left the Huguenot churches. Rural congregations in New York and South Carolina affiliated with the Church of England, which aggressively recruited them as part of its drive to regain influence in the colonies, and Huguenots never established a denominational institution to unite their congregations and to provide the institutional leadership increasingly characteristic of other Protestant denominations.

By the 1750s only two independent Huguenot congregations still existed in the colonies, in New York City and in Charleston. Both were using English in their worship, as now was true in the rural congregations that had become Anglican parishes, and their membership was extremely small. Some "members" belonged to Anglican and Presbyterian congregations where they and their children married and baptized infants. Their formal attachment to the surviving Huguenot congregations was primarily a matter of sentimental attachment rather than active or exclusive support, and it well symbolized the reduction of French Protestantism to little more than a curiosity in colonial society.

German immigrants brought a far more significant variety to colonial American Protestantism. The first German immigrants to Pennsylvania, who arrived in 1683 from the Rhine town of Krefeld, represented the theological volatility of seventeenth-century Protestantism. Formerly Lutherans, they had themselves only recently converted to the Mennonite faith. When this group settled in the area north of Philadelphia, soon called Germantown, they encountered other similarly disposed, theologically volatile settlers. Some professed Quaker principles, some Lutheran, some pietistic, some mystical, some millennial, and some a mixture of all. Out of this mélange, a mystically inclined immigrant, Johann Kelpius, formed one of the earliest communitarian settlements in the colonies. Kelpius and his followers lived in caves along Wissahickon Creek awaiting the "Woman of the Wilderness"—the onset of the millennium as described in Revelations 12:1. Some members of the community, which disappeared by 1710, subsequently joined the more important communitarian settlement at Ephrata, a German Seventh-Day Baptist community near Lancaster that became a mecca for colonists pursuing mystical, perfectionistic goals; in fact, the settlement did not disband until the 1940s, and it lives on in Thomas Mann's novel *The Magic Mountain* (1927), where a principal character is based on the figure of Conrad Beissel, Ephrata's most important mid-eighteenth-century leader.

German-speaking immigrants accounted for other sectarian groups as well. A Maryland Labadist settlement formed in the 1680s by an ex-Jesuit, Jean de Labadie, contained many German residents, some coming from Kelpius's communitarian group outside Philadelphia, others being disaffected members of the Ephrata settlement who arrived in the 1730s and 1740s. Members of the Church of the Brethren—a group formed among Pietists in the German Palatinate around 1700 by Alexander Mack and derided as Dunkers because they baptized adults using total immersion—arrived in Germantown about 1719, but rather quickly moved to the relative isolation of rural Pennsylvania west of Philadelphia. In 1728 the first Schwenkfeldians, followers of a tradition founded by the German reformer Kaspar Schwenkfeld (1489–1561), arrived in Georgia, and more Schwenkfeldians settled in Pennsylvania after 1734. These were, in turn, followed by the first Moravians—members of the Church of the United Brethren (or Unitas Fratrum), disaffected and pietistically inclined former Lutherans led by the aristocratic Count Nicolaus Zinzendorf. The Moravians first settled in Georgia in 1735, then spilled out into North Carolina and, finally, Pennsylvania, especially Nazareth and Bethlehem in Lancaster County, the town names suggesting how intently Moravians sought to recreate a new Israel in the American wilderness.

German Lutherans and German Calvinists (the latter called the German Reformed church) proved more numerically and culturally important in reshaping colonial American Protestantism after 1680. Their emigration from the Continent in the eighteenth century was far more important than the earlier wave of the seventeenth century. The new arrivals laid the foundations of what would become their respective denominations in eighteenth- and nineteenth-century America.

The dramatic rise of emigration from the German principalities after 1680, and especially after 1710, made Lutheranism a major religious presence in the middle colonies and even in some southern colonies. Before 1680 only four Lutheran congregations had yet been formed in the colonies, all of them in the area of the old Swedish colony on the Delaware River. Between 1680 and 1710, however, more than fifteen Lutheran congregations were formed in the same region; then, between 1710 and 1740 more than seventy Lutheran congregations emerged in this area, well over half of them in Pennsylvania alone, the remainder scattered from New York to Georgia. Only New England lacked a Lutheran presence by 1740.

Nonetheless, before 1730 poor organization and meager financial support hobbled many of the new Lutheran congregations. Lutheran ministers immigrated to the colonies on their own rather than at the instigation of denominational authorities. Once arrived, they found themselves at the mercy of miserly congregations that worked their will with hapless clergymen and that lacked the traditional supervision provided by bishops at home. In Germantown, settlers seldom attended churches and gave them little financial support. Worse, contemporaries and historians alike have noted that Lutheran authorities in Germany did nothing to improve the situation until the German sects—especially the Moravians—began arriving in the colonies in significant numbers. In short, competition from dreaded sectarians rather than sensitivity to long-standing complaints about misbehavior and disorder in German Lutheran congregational life brought discipline to New World Lutheranism. Lutherans—laity and clergy alike—meanwhile had experienced the taste of freedom or chaos all too readily.

German Reformed congregations experienced similar anomalous conditions between 1680 and 1740. Where there were only three or four German Reformed congregations established in the colonies by 1710, nearly fifty were established in the thirty years between 1710 and 1740. Even more than with Lutherans, most of these congregations were located in Pennsylvania in the expanding agricultural settlements west of Philadelphia. The nature of the German emigration may have reinforced the disorder of early German Reformed congregational life in

Pennsylvania. Most of the Germans who might have gravitated to the German Reformed churches were indentured servants—redemptioners—and their lack of family and kinship groups, not their class, mitigated against active church involvement in America as much as it did at home. With that circumstance added to congregational problems like those that plagued Lutherans and to sometimes vigorous personal disputes among German Reformed ministers, the 1730s proved to be as tumultuous for German Reformed congregations as they were for Lutheran ones. Still, the leadership of individual clergymen like John Philip Boehm and George Michael Weiss, the sheer numbers of potentially and partially committed adherents, and an important, sometimes almost idyllic, physical isolation in the rural countryside—which confined religious competition to other German groups—made the German Reformed tradition (like Lutheranism) viable, if not yet vital, in this New World environment—quite unlike the environment for French Protestants, whose distinctive religious tradition already was dying.

The Maturation of Protestant Pluralism, 1740–1770

The last thirty years of the colonial period proved more tumultuous, more creative, and more stabilizing than any other period in colonial American Protestant religious history. Previously quiet Protestant denominations broke out into enormous controversies over the increasing resort to revivalism. Virtually all denominations accelerated their proselytizing to bring the unusually large number of unchurched colonists under their influence. New, more powerful, denominational institutions made proselytizing more viable, and ultimately they largely contained the often divergent groups found among both ministers and the laity. And more new groups emerged, demonstrating that the colonies had scarcely exhausted their attraction as a place of spiritual refuge and their capacity to absorb and perhaps even encourage religious creativity. The result, on the eve of the American Revolution, was spiritual ecstasy as well as confusion, a combination that perhaps explains why and how pluralism prospered so among colonial Protestants.

Between 1740 and 1770 Protestant diversity accelerated even more rapidly than it did be-

tween 1680 and 1740. The depth and range of this acceleration are dramatically measured in statistics. Between 1740 and 1770 more than twelve hundred congregations, virtually all of them Protestant, were organized in the American colonies—more congregations than were organized in the entire period since 1607. The pattern of congregational formation proved equally interesting. The power of state-church connections to shape the American religious landscape remained astonishingly impressive. The principal beneficiaries of this power, which was manifested in advantages such as the power to tax and other legal privileges, were Congregationalists in New England and the Church of England in New York, Maryland, Virginia, and North and South Carolina. These two denominations accounted for nearly a third of the total of newly organized congregations—about 150 congregations formed by the Church of England and about 257 congregations formed by New England Congregationalists.

At the same time, denominations that expanded without governmental aid accounted for no less than two-thirds of the church expansion in pre-revolutionary society. The classic English dissenting denominations accounted for the largest segment of this growth: Baptists for about 200 new congregations and Presbyterians for more than 275 new congregations. The principal German denominations expanded dramatically in this period as well, with German Lutherans and the German Reformed denominations each adding about 125 congregations. Even the Dutch Reformed church added some forty congregations between 1740 and 1770, mostly in New York and New Jersey; their members came almost entirely from descendants of old immigrants rather than from new immigration. The result solidified the pluralist tradition in American religion and colonial Protestantism never slipped back into the older, relatively homogeneous patterns of the early and mid seventeenth century.

The massive denominational expansion of the 1740s, 1750s, and 1760s paralleled an evangelical revivalism that both stimulated and undermined denominational stability. Distinguished by emotional outpourings and a "born-again" religious experience, evangelical revivalism was controversial in the mid-eighteenth-century; not surprisingly, it also has produced sharp disagreement among historians. Some have equated it with American anti-intellectualism and bigotry; others have found it not only distinctively American but intellectually creative; still others have seen it as a major source of American democracy. Yet, however evangelical revivalism is assessed, there is no doubt that it further complicated an increasingly tangled colonial Protestantism. After 1740 evangelical revivalism recast colonial theology and brought division and schisms to many of the nascent colonial denominations even as continental European immigration continued to enrich, enlarge, and sometimes perturb colonial Protestantism.

Like immigration and even traditional English religious pluralism, revivalism reshaped colonial Protestantism by its suddenly expanded range and influence, not by its uniqueness. In many ways, Protestant revivalism had been born with the Reformation in groups that stressed personal religious experience, emotionalism, and individual commitment to Christ—all of which were to be manifested not only in personal introspection and commitment but in a renewed church membership. This kind of revivalism made appearances in the American colonies long before the 1740s, most notably among the so-called Singing Quakers on Long Island in the 1680s; among Dutch Reformed congregations in New Jersey in the 1720s; in Northampton, Massachusetts, in the 1690s, where the great Solomon Stoddard used it to revive flagging membership in the town congregation; then in Northampton again in the 1730s, when Stoddard's grandson, the even more renowned Jonathan Edwards, promoted a revivalism that combined intense emotionalism with substantial disciplinary demands that tested the congregation as severely as it expanded it.

The arrival of the Anglican evangelist George Whitefield in 1739 raised evangelical revivalism to unparalleled heights. Extraordinarily handsome, afflicted with an eye tic that induced mystery as well as compassion, possessed of an actor's voice and skills, and bearing an extraordinary sense of public relations, Whitefield was perhaps the archetype of the modern revivalist. From his first American revival tour in 1740 to his last in 1773, Whitefield specialized in spiritual spectacle. He attracted enormous crowds in the colonial cities—reputedly ten thousand people

flocked to see him in Philadelphia in 1741, for example. He induced even the cynical to empty their pockets for a contribution, including Benjamin Franklin, already notorious for his critical attitude toward institutional Christianity. And he shaped the language of subsequent American evangelicalism by the simple question he made famous—"What must I do to be saved?"—the question, more than the answer, remaining the theme of his sermons for more than thirty years. Most important, Whitefield became a model for evangelistic revivalism among Baptists, Congregationalists, and Presbyterians, and he strengthened revivalistic tendencies among some German groups as well.

Colonial revivalism, Whitefield's as well as that spawned in the colonial denominations, exhibited transatlantic and provincial characteristics simultaneously. On the one hand, both leaders and participants saw their own revivalism as part of a larger revivalistic movement throughout Western society, from well-known and well-publicized revivals in both Scotland and Wales to pietistic and sectarian movements in the German principalities. The Atlantic became a conduit of revival fervor, as revivalists laced the shipping lanes with reams of letters describing their successes (and some failures) in letters eagerly shared with their listeners, publicly as well as privately. Whitefield openly used his transatlantic reputation to enhance his prestige on both sides of the ocean, and journals such as *The Christian History,* published in both Boston and Edinburgh, swept readers up in an evangelical drama of international dimensions.

Yet the revivals also proved to be surprisingly conservative, seldom more than momentarily floating out beyond their colonial moorings. New England revivals plumbed tensions introduced by increasing materialism, widening disparities of wealth, and increasing social stratification, with revivalists in the main offering themselves as critics of the new, less-mobile society. Revivalism in the middle colonies became more closely tied to growing ethnic consciousness among first- and second-generation immigrants, both among the Scots and among the Germans. And in the southern colonies it sometimes bore distinctly political marks—as in Virginia, where revivalism's backers deliberately affronted the colony's political and religious elite and, in the main, recruited converts among poor settlers long uninvolved in the politics or religion of the now 150-year-old colony.

The colonial revivals also proved to be episodic and surprisingly narrow in their social implications, at least by modern standards. This perhaps befitted colonies still more efficiently connected to London than to each other. Their dependence on ripe local conditions together with occasional open resistance on the part of both listeners and ministers meant that they rose and died in one place even before they popped up in another. Their greatest, most consistent appearances occurred in New England in the early 1740s, where they had all but expired by the early 1750s. In the middle colonies the revivals were almost exclusively confined to Presbyterian ranks among English colonists; Baptists there remained surprisingly unaffected by them, although Baptists were deeply involved in New England revivals. And in the southern colonies, significant widespread revivals did not even begin until the 1760s, where they were largely dominated by Baptists, and even continued into the period of the revolution, although such was not the case elsewhere.

Ultimately, most colonial revivalism tended toward enduring forms of cultural conservatism. Early revivalists like Gilbert Tennent called ministerial opponents "Pharisee-shepherds" whose parishioners should abandon them in favor of truly converted ministers, including unordained preachers and ministers from other denominations. Itinerants like James Davenport scandalized opponents with claims of revelatory experiences, book burnings, and contemptuous ridicule of existing denominations. But revivalists like Jonathan Edwards or Whitefield never adopted such views, and Tennent and other supporters quickly modified them. Men dominated revival leadership and allotted no substantial roles to women. The revivals also never turned to miracle working, although the revivalists' critics regularly compared them to London's notorious French Prophets of the 1710s, who claimed to perform such acts. The revivalists' stress on both conversion and personal rectitude fostered an active, often severe paternalism whose watchfulness sometimes verged on sheer nosiness. Ultimately, Jonathan Edwards's Northampton congregation found his severity and unrelenting stress on personal discipline authoritarian, distasteful, and certainly not democratic or popular; in 1750 his congregation simply fired him.

The bitterness induced by Edwards's revivals in Northampton well symbolized the divisions that revivals frequently produced wherever they occurred. Connecticut, remarkably homogeneous in its religious complexion through the seventeenth century and the scene of only modest Baptist activity in the early eighteenth century, became almost notorious as an evangelical battleground. New London was the home of James Davenport's "Shepherd's Tent," where Davenport held seemingly wild evangelistic revivals and conducted his book burnings. More significant, Congregationalists as well as Baptists divided over the revivals. Congregationalists and Baptists split into New Light and Old Light groups; the fury of these divisions split congregations, towns, and finally the colony itself. For better or worse, then, the revivals made Connecticut as spiritually modern as other American colonies.

In dividing denominations, revivalism also created new ones, and these groups frequently stressed institutional prowess even more vigorously than had their predecessors. In the middle colonies, the Presbyterians' Synod of Philadelphia fought about revivalism through the early 1740s; the pro-revivalists and anti-revivalists formally split in 1745. But rather than giving more authority to local congregations and less to the synod or presbyteries, pro-revivalists formed the Synod of New York and pursued opposite policies. The revivalists demanded classical learning as well as a conversion experience in their ordained clergymen; they vigorously disciplined wayward ministers, especially when the offenses involved adultery and sexual misconduct; and they demanded that congregations support and obey clergymen whose training, reputation, and even holiness the synod guaranteed.

This commitment to institutional prowess outlasted the bitterness and divisiveness produced by the flush of revivalism in the 1740s and accounted for the continuing expansion of the vast variety of Protestant congregations that characterized the immediate pre-revolutionary period. Saddened, and to a degree even embarrassed, by their schism, the pro-revivalist Synod of New York and the anti-revivalist Synod of

Philadelphia reunited in 1758. Most important, the united synod and its regional presbyteries worked steadily to both create and fill demands for new congregations and ministers. They sent ministers on preaching tours of the middle and southern colonies, and as a result the number of congregations and ministers nearly doubled in the twenty years before the revolution.

Baptists, Lutherans, and the German Reformed denominations acted similarly, irrespective of their positions on evangelical revivalism. In the 1760s the Philadelphia Baptist Association began keeping membership statistics—the first denomination to do so in the colonies—that revealed its expansion from twenty-five to forty congregations between 1740 and 1770 and a growth in congregational size from fifty to seventy adults. As part of an effort to grapple with colonial population mobility, the association even tracked the number of persons who had been "dismissed by letter" to a Baptist congregation elsewhere. The result was only partially encouraging: half of the Baptists who moved joined a Baptist congregation in their new communities, but half became lost to the Baptists, some presumably joining other congregations, others rejoining the majority of colonists who still lacked affiliation with any denomination.

Lutherans and German Reformed authorities also turned to institution-building to foster an order that previously had eluded them. Arriving in Philadelphia in 1742, Henry Melchior Muhlenberg subtly employed institutional devices to reinforce his personal labor and, ultimately, his personal prestige. If he organized congregations almost single-handedly and traveled alone through much of western Pennsylvania to solidify his creation, he also established the Lutheran Ministerium of Pennsylvania in 1748 and used its authority to advance Lutheran stability in the colony. German Reformed ministers acted similarly. Plagued by disorder despite sometimes herculean efforts by individual laity and ministers alike, Pennsylvania's German Reformed ministers formed the region's first *coetus*, or yearly convention, in 1747, which they used principally as a vehicle for furnishing ministers to an expanding number of congregations.

New religious groups also appeared in the colonies with substantial force after 1740, as well as new theologies that exercised enormous influence without any institutional presence. French-speaking Protestants three generations removed from the Huguenot exodus from France in the 1680s emigrated from Switzerland to New Bordeaux, North Carolina, in 1765. This new Huguenot group succeeded no better than did the first Huguenots who came in the 1680s or two other small groups of settlers who settled in Manakin, Virginia, in 1701 and Purrysburg, South Carolina, in 1732. By 1771 the New Bordeaux settlers already had petitioned the Society for the Propagation of the Gospel in Foreign Parts for an Anglican-ordained minister because they could not support one on their own and because no Huguenot denomination existed in the colonies to help them.

Three new sectarian groups proved more enduring—Sandemanians, Swedenborgians, and the Amish. Sandemanians descended from the work of a Scot and former Presbyterian, Robert Sandeman, who immigrated to Connecticut in 1764. He and his followers formed four congregations there while proselytizing in England and Scotland as well, stressing a highly enthusiastic, emotional ministry, adult baptism by immersion, weekly communion, and vegetarianism. The Sandemanians persisted in New England into the antebellum period, where they constituted something of a model for antebellum religious seekers and claimed further attention by the lifelong membership of the great British scientist Michael Faraday (1791–1867).

The spread of doctrines of the Swedish mystic Emanuel Swedenborg demonstrated the power of print to shape religious conviction and attract followers in a theologically eclectic, volatile society. Swedenborg's explication of visionary experiences, the use of trances to gain religious knowledge, and his enthusiastic promulgation of intensely millennial themes all circulated through the colonies through English translations of his works published in London in the 1750s and 1760s. Swedenborg's views were widely known to theologically informed colonists before the revolution and appear to have had some attraction both to scientifically inclined colonists, who also knew of Swedenborg's work in metallurgy (also connected to occult alchemy), and to some Evangelicals initially intrigued by Swedenborg's enthusiasm. No Swedenborgian congregations were formed in America, however, until after the revolution. Like the Sandemanians, the Swedenborgians subsequently attracted attention because of the interest taken in the movement by a great figure—in the Swedenborgian case, the American intellectual Ralph Waldo Emerson, whose reading in Swedenborg was central to the shaping of American transcendentalism.

The Amish also first appeared in significant numbers in Pennsylvania in the 1760s. Part of the Mennonite movement but more conservative in matters of dress, discipline, and technology, the Amish had been founded in the 1690s in Germany by Jacob Amman. Amish immigrants first arrived in Pennsylvania with the larger German immigration of the 1720s, but the principal Amish immigration occurred in the 1760s. Like other German immigrants, including those of the principal Mennonite movement, they settled in Lancaster County. Even in the eighteenth century their "old-fashioned" ways made them distinctive and often disliked, and they were not the only sectarian group to find the rural American wilderness inviting more because of its isolation than its beauty.

The Protestant group that subsequently shaped nineteenth- and twentieth-century American religion most dramatically—Methodism—had only weakly appeared on the eve of the American Revolution, and the group very nearly disappeared because of its support for the Crown rather than for American independence. Methodism was a peculiar anomaly before 1770. Not unlike early Puritanism, Methodism was a spiritual reform group within the Church of England. It was formed in the 1730s by John Wesley, who with his brother Charles, the famous hymn writer, promoted an anti-Calvinist, Arminian theology that stressed the ability of individuals to achieve salvation through personal piety exemplified in an experience of personal spiritual regeneration. Methodist views first gained credence in America through the revivals of the 1740s and 1750s, since the evangelist George Whitefield was associated with the Wesleys for many years, although they later split over Whitefield's adamant Calvinism. But like Swedenborgianism, Methodism attracted attention through the distribution of Wesley's innumerable books and tracts, which circulated through the American colonies in large numbers long before any Methodist missionaries appeared there.

Through the mid 1760s, Methodism remained an informal movement, and the first sep-

arate Methodist congregation in the colonies was not established until 1766, in New York City. By 1776 only eight Methodist congregations had been established anywhere in the colonies, most of them in the Chesapeake in Maryland and Virginia, where they seemed to benefit from the dissent laid against a still-dominant Anglicanism by Baptists. Moreover, Wesley's behavior during the revolution itself came close to dooming the movement. Deeply conservative in politics and stressing obedience more than freedom, Wesley not only vigorously supported George III but angrily withdrew all of his colonial missionaries, forcing all of them home to England except Francis Asbury, whose presence and backing for independence almost single-handedly salvaged Methodism's reputation after 1776, if not all its early converts. Despite Asbury's work, however, the revolution brought Methodism's advance to an abrupt conclusion, and its subsequent phenomenal success in nineteenth-century America was due entirely to its rebirth after the revolution, not to its origins in the colonial era.

The pre-revolutionary record of expansion among religious groups contained one major exception that ironically became a foundation for yet additional pluralism within American Protestantism—the death of traditional African religious systems in Britain's American colonies. Despite a growing slave population, continuing importations from Africa, and the development of family life and kinship systems within native-born slave populations, not a single traditional African religious system—Ashanti, Ibo, Yoruba, among others—survived, much less prospered, in the mainland colonies. While some discrete rituals and customs survived, such as burial rites and "conjuring" to cure diseases, the larger religious systems that originally created and sustained those beliefs and practices failed to emerge as a new African-American society emerged. As a result, enslaved Africans began turning to Protestantism, thereby laying the foundations for the distinctive African-American Christianity that challenged white Protestantism—and American society—in the nineteenth century.

Both the Protestant conversions of slaves and the ways in which slaveholders allowed their slaves to worship shaped the subsequent development of African-American religion in the United States. Slave conversion to Christianity in the British colonial period should not be exaggerated. It was rare in the seventeenth century, when slavery itself was uncommon, and it was still uncommon in the eighteenth century, when slavery was emerging full force throughout the colonies. Nonetheless, Christian conversion occurred and was important when it did. In New England, it frequently depended on the isolation of slaves in an overwhelmingly English society, while in the southern colonies, it was resisted by planters and slaves alike, if for quite different reasons (planters because they worried that conversion would make slaves feel "uppity," slaves because it was both foreign and the religion of their captors).

The Christian conversion that did occur, however, made the Protestantism of even early African Americans different from the Protestantism of European settlers in America. Beginning in the 1740s and 1750s, first among Anglicans, then among evangelical Presbyterians and Baptists, slaves were converting to Christianity in sufficient numbers to make congregations undertake special provisions for their worship. But Christianized slaves remained a distinct minority, as much among slaves as among whites. They also remained separate. Whether in prestigious parishes or poor ones, converted slaves never were treated as equals. At best, they sat with their owners; at worst, they sat in back pews or in balconies. They did not preach. They did not read the Scriptures. They did not exercise discipline. And they always worshiped in the company of Europeans rather than independently, at least so far as Europeans knew or could discover. Quite unlike English and continental European immigrants, then, the religious experience of the slowly growing numbers of Christianized Africans in pre-revolutionary America became an experience of discrimination and segregation—a pattern that shaped American religion and American society profoundly, not only in the pre-revolutionary period, but in the next two centuries as well.

The decades between 1740 and 1770 also witnessed the earliest emergence of the syncretic creativity that especially shaped African-American Protestantism in antebellum and postbellum society. Within a tightly controlled worship, signs of rites and rituals important in later African-American Christianity were emerging. In New England—oddly, perhaps, since so few slaves lived there—Christianized African Americans already were merging secular holidays created for and by slaves with religious expression, especially music and dance. In the southern colonies, emotionalism that seems to have been indelibly part of African religious ceremonialism merged with the emotionalism also characteristic of English evangelicalism to shape a spiritual fervor increasingly characteristic of southern evangelicalism. And in both northern and southern colonies, "conjuring" of a distinctively African character began to merge with Christian miracle working and prayer to form a spiritual regimen that was later fully developed in nineteenth-century African-American Christianity and in twentieth-century American Pentecostalism.

Deism—an intellectual construct that approached institutional form only in the Freemasonry movement, which was perhaps more fraternal than religious—nonetheless shaped colonial society, politics, and especially the American Revolution far more profoundly than colonial American religious groups. Deism was a seventeenth-century creation, its principles perhaps most influentially expressed in John Locke's *The Reasonableness of Christianity* (1695). It had its greatest influence in the eighteenth century, however, and like Swedenborgianism and early Methodism it gained ground through books and pamphlets rather than through missionaries, again demonstrating how thoroughly intellectual and spiritual matters intertwined in the eighteenth century.

Deism's principles, often maligned by both contemporaries and historians, stressed reason and ethics. Deists did not deny the existence or even the power of God—the word "deism" literally meaning belief in God—but recognized one Creator alone without any belief in Christ's divinity or in God's willingness (if not inability) to become involved in the world. Rather, Deists believed that men and women bore obligations to use the reason with which God had imbued them, along with the learning that distinguished Western culture and Christianity, to shape a better, more moral world. In short, Deism stressed the principles, not the personages, of Christianity. What mattered were virtue, ethics, and learning: virtue that made it possible to discern truth, ethics that shaped individual and collective behavior, and learning that provided the intellectual foundation of moral action.

Ultimately, like other groups Deism thrived on its constituency, and its constituency scarcely could have been more distinguished, or at least more important. Deism did, in fact, find adherents in nearly all the major colonial Protestant groups—Anglican and Congregational especially, but also Presbyterian—except those that were most vigorously evangelical. But it was Deism's appeal to the colonial elite, especially to its public figures—legislators, magistrates, members of the colonial council, and governors—that made Deism important and powerful. It was no accident that virtually every one of the so-called Founding Fathers was a Deist. From Benjamin Franklin and George Washington to Thomas Jefferson and Alexander Hamilton, these men evidenced interest in religion's instrumental capacities. None were evangelical; few accepted Christ's divinity, and few accepted Christianity as the only true religion. Yet all saw in Christianity the expression of extraordinarily "useful" moral and ethical principles to guide public life, both before and particularly after the revolution. Some, especially Jefferson and Franklin, expressed interest in the historical Christ. Jefferson even cataloged Christ's ethical principles in a compilation he drew from his own reading of the New Testament. In some regards, the Deism of the Founding Fathers, often criticized, may have guaranteed the survival of religion altogether in the revolutionary and post-revolutionary period. In Europe many intellectuals and political leaders turned against religions generally and Christianity specifically in the mid and late eighteenth century. But in the North American colonies, intellectuals and political leaders became more moderate Deists. Their immediate choice scarcely pleased Evangelicals, but their very moderation, both in what they believed and how they believed it, also ultimately guaranteed Protestant Christianity an influential place in both pre- and post-revolutionary societies seeking principles to shape-independence and protect a new, untried order.

THE CHARACTER AND LEGACY OF PLURAL PROTESTANTISM

In the main, the pluralism so strongly present in early American Protestantism, especially after 1680, was a pluralism of fact rather than a pluralism of principle. Even before 1680 colonists in New England and the Chesapeake understood all too well that whatever the fate and character of their dominant religious traditions—if indeed any tradition was dominant—no orthodoxy held sway at the expense of other opinions or likely ever would. Even the Boston authorities who hanged Quaker missionaries in the 1660s were criticized by contemporaries and neighbors for introducing new and ugly elements of coercion into colonial religious patterns. The only other time that colonial authorities sought to corral opinion about things supernatural and spiritual by threatening—and obtaining—executions, it was against witches—an exercise that also succeeded only in New England. These executions ceased after 1692.

Yet it is difficult to find in the colonial era a celebration of pluralism itself. Quite correctly, colonists saw the reality of pluralism related directly to the failure of the state-church tradition, a tradition that also was decaying in Europe, even if more slowly. The advance of communications and technology that made the rise of the modern nation-state possible—the kind that transformed the weak authority of Henry VII into the strikingly powerful monarchies of Henry VIII and Elizabeth I and that also brought England to bloody civil war in the 1640s—proved unable to contain the spread of highly variegated religious opinion and doctrine. Indeed, printing, new channels of communication, improved roads, and expanded ocean technology all hastened the spread of new religious doctrines, even if they did not shape their substance or guarantee their audience.

In this sense, France's successful use of violence to suppress French Protestantism proved less a model for subsequent activity than England's inability to reestablish Church of England hegemony after the restoration of the Crown in 1660. English authorities successfully crippled the Independents (Congregationalists) and Baptists and probably stopped the continuing expansion of Quakerism. But they also failed to exterminate these groups, try as they might—as Louis XIV all but did to the Protestants in France. The result was the 1689 Act of Toleration. Although the act was passed grudgingly, was limited, was frequently slighted, and certainly did not praise the value or legitimacy of a plurality of religious views (even a plurality limited to Protestant views), it did nonetheless prevent the state from the worst kind of violence against dissenting Protestants, and it furnished a model for a colonial society ultimately more plural than that of England itself.

Even by 1776 few colonists advocated pluralism, whether among Protestants, among Christians, or in religion generally. New Englanders did not so much accept Baptists, Quakers, or Anglicans by the 1680s as they abandoned older, failed notions about religious orthodoxy that they had been unable to enforce since the 1640s. William Penn promoted pluralism less than he decried religious violence and touted settlement in a colony that was as commercial as it was idealistic. Anglicans tried to circumscribe Presbyterian preaching in New York in 1707 and in Virginia as late as 1750 by demanding enforcement of laws requiring preaching licenses, although in each case the authorities knew that the efforts would likely backfire, as they did.

These limitations and failures suggest that colonial America backed into pluralism, even within Protestantism, much as did Britain. In both places, pluralism was something that existed, not something that was desired. In both places as well, it existed because the traditional state church simply could not control or manage public religious expression within even very modestly drawn boundaries. Although historians often point up the failures of the Church of England to dominate religious expression in the colonies where it was established—the Carolinas, Virginia, Maryland, and part of New York—the more spectacular failure of the state-church tradition really occurred in New England. The nature of early New England immigration, the commitment to Puritanism, and the region's geographical compactness offered conditions close to ideal for shaping and sustaining a religiously homogeneous society. But even in New England, several kinds of Puritanisms had emerged by 1650, to say nothing of 1680 or 1750. In this context, the failure of the Church of England to prevent the expansion of competing Protestant groups hardly seems pathological.

Colonial authorities also proved unable to prevent the arrival of new religious views in America, much as was true at home. New England authorities never advertised for colonists of differing religious views, but colonists of several persuasions came anyway, and the society nurtured others after they immigrated. And elsewhere, as in Pennsylvania, New York, and the Carolinas, colonial authorities openly welcomed settlers of divergent religious backgrounds—preferably Protestant, of course—and sometimes even advertised for them.

Not surprisingly, the plurality of Protestant views in colonial America more frequently proved derivative than creative. Substantial intellectual and theological interchange among colonial Protestants remained uncommon and largely undesired, in contrast to the antebellum society of the 1830s and 1840s. Cooperation among Protestants occurred briefly in colonies like Pennsylvania, but usually over quite pragmatic issues such as the temporary loss of worship space due to church fires or the desire to commemorate battle victories (in New York City in 1763 the ceremonies even included the hazan from Congregation Shearith Israel). But the interchange produced no groups or movements of consequence. The Rogerenes, Christian Quakers, and Keithian Quakers died out and could not in any case match the significance of antebellum groups like the Mormons or Disciples of Christ, which persisted to become major American denominations, the latter distinctly Protestant, the Mormons sometimes claiming to be a new religion altogether.

Thus, although religious variety was a part of everyday life and was welcomed by the individual groups that found refuge through it, for the culture as a whole the pluralism within colonial Protestantism was always vaguely distressing and uncomfortable. Colonial commentators often sighed as they contemplated the luxuriant flotsam of America's increasingly unstructured spiritual variety. The French traveler Hector St. John de Crèvecoeur spoke of its national implications in his *Letters from an American Farmer*, published in 1782. Crèvecoeur associated pluralism with religious indifference. Noting correctly that most colonists did not attend church, in part because the churches failed them and in part because they simply were not interested, Crèvecoeur linked this indifference to the combination of a seemingly limitless landscape sprawling with an almost incomprehensible variety of Protestant groups and sects: "Zeal in Europe is confined; [but] here it evaporates in the great distance it has to travel; there it is a grain of powder inclosed; here it burns away in the open air and consumes without effect."

Nevertheless, before independence colonists thought in narrower, more precise terms about the implications that pluralism held for individuals, many of whom remained confused by the bewildering choices available to them. Charles Woodmason, an Anglican who itinerated through the southern backcountry in the late 1760s, caught some of this variety and much of the exasperation that accompanied this pluralism throughout the colonial period. In this still-colonial society, perceptions of order and orthodoxy that were unrealistic even in the Old World powerfully shaped the ways men and women thought about Protestant diversity in the New. Not until after 1776, and then often not without considerable reluctance and controversy, would diversity of Protestant opinion (much less a positive regard for religious pluralism generally) come to be something not only valued but protected and encouraged as something uniquely American.

Next Day, I returned and preached the 27th [of January] in my Way back at Lynch's Creek [in Virginia] to a great Multitude of People assembled together, being the 1st Episcopal Minister they had seen since their being in the province—They complain'd of being eaten up by Itinerant Teachers, Preachers, and Imposers from New England and Pennsylvania—Baptists, New Lights, Presbyterians, Independants, and an hundred other Sects—So that one day You might hear this System of Doctrine—the next day another—next day another, retrograde to both—Thus by the Variety of Taylors who would pretend to know the best fashion in which Christs Coat is to be worn[,] none will put it on. (*Journal*, p. 13)

BIBLIOGRAPHY

Original Sources

Aland, Kurt, ed. *Die Korrespondenz Heinrich Melchior Muhlenbergs: Aus der Anfangszeit des deutschen Luthertums in Nordamerika.* 3 vols. to date. Berlin, 1986– .

Backus, Isaac. *The Diary of Isaac Backus.* Edited by William G. McLoughlin. Providence, R.I., 1979.

Edwards, Morgan. *Materials Toward a History of the Baptists.* 2 vols. Edited by Eve B. Weeks and Mary B. Warren. Danielsville, Ga., 1984.

Gillette, A. D., ed. *Minutes of the Philadelphia Baptist Association from A.D. 1707 to A.D. 1807.* Philadelphia, 1851.

Hinke, William J. *Life and Letters of the Rev. John Philip Boehm, Founder of the Reformed Church in Pennsylvania, 1683–1749.* Philadelphia, 1916.

Kelpius, Johannes. "The Diarium of Magister Johannes Kelpius." Translated and edited by Julius Friedrich Sachse. *Pennsylvania German Society Proceedings and Addresses* 25, pt. 1 (1914–1915).

Klett, Guy S., ed. *Minutes of the Presbyterian Church in America, 1706–1788.* Philadelphia, 1976.

Michener, Ezra. *A Retrospect of Early Quakerism; Being Extracts from the Records of Philadelphia Yearly Meeting and the Meetings Composing It.* Philadelphia, 1860.

Minutes and Letters of the Coetus of the German Reformed Congregations in Pennsylvania, 1747–1792. Philadelphia, 1903.

Muhlenberg, Henry Melchior. *The Journals of Henry Melchior Muhlenberg.* 3 vols. Translated and edited by Theodore G. Tappert and John W. Doberstein. Philadelphia, 1942–1958.

Perry, William Stevens, ed. *Historical Collections Relating to the American Colonial Church [of England].* 5 vols. Hartford, Conn., 1870–1878.

Whitefield, George. *George Whitefield's Journal.* London, 1960.

Woodmason, Charles. *The Carolina Backcountry on the Eve of the Revolution: The Journal and Other Writings of Charles Woodmason, Anglican Itinerant.* Edited by Richard J. Hooker. Chapel Hill, N.C., 1953.

Modern Histories

Ahlstrom, Sydney E. *A Religious History of the American People.* New Haven, Conn., 1972.

Alderfer, E. G. *The Ephrata Commune: An Early American Counterculture.* Pittsburgh, Pa., 1985.

Balmer, Randall H. *A Perfect Babel of Confusion: Dutch Religion and English Culture in the Middle Colonies.* New York, 1989.

Benz, Ernst. "Ecumenical Relations Between Boston Puritanism and German Pietism: Cotton Mather and August Hermann Francke." *Harvard Theological Review* 54 (1961):159–191.

Boller, Paul F., Jr. *George Washington and Religion.* Dallas, Tex., 1963.

Bolles, John Rogers, and Anna B. Williams. *The Rogerenes: Some Hitherto Unpublished Annals Belonging to the Colonial History of Connecticut.* Boston, 1904.

Bonomi, Patricia U. *Under the Cope of Heaven: Religion, Society, and Politics in Colonial America.* New York, 1986.

Butler, Jon. *Awash in a Sea of Faith: Christianizing the American People.* Cambridge, Mass., 1990.

Cantor, Geoffrey N. *Michael Faraday: Sandemanian and Scientist: A Study of Science and Religion in the Nineteenth Century.* London, 1991.

Carroll, Kenneth. *Quakerism on the Eastern Shore.* Baltimore, Md., 1970.

Chu, Jonathan M. *Neighbors, Friends, or Madmen: The Puritan Adjustment to Quakerism in Seventeenth-Century Massachusetts Bay.* Westport, Conn., 1985.

Coalter, Milton J., Jr. *Gilbert Tennent, Son of Thunder: A Case Study of Continental Pietism's Impact on the First Great Awakening in the Middle Colonies.* New York, 1986.

Commager, Henry Steele. *The Empire of Reason: How Europe Imagined and America Realized the Enlightenment.* Garden City, N.Y., 1977.

Creel, Margaret Washington. *"A Peculiar People": Slave Religion and Community-Culture Among the Gullahs.* New York, 1988.

Curry, Thomas J. *The First Freedoms: Church and State in America to the Passage of the First Amendment.* New York, 1986.

De Jong, Gerald F. *The Dutch Reformed Church in the American Colonies.* Grand Rapids, Mich., 1978.

Dunaway, Wayland F. *The Scotch-Irish of Colonial Pennsylvania.* Baltimore, Md., 1985.

Durnbaugh, Donald F., ed. *The Brethren in Colonial America: A Source Book on the Transplantation and Development of the Church of the Brethren in the Eighteenth Century.* Elgin, Ill., 1967.

Frantz, John B. "The Awakening of Religion Among the German Settlers in the Middle Colonies." *William and Mary Quarterly* 3rd ser., 33 (1976):266–288.

Frost, J. William. *A Perfect Freedom: Religious Liberty in Pennsylvania.* New York, 1990.

Gladfelter, Charles H. *Pastors and People: German Lutheran and Reformed Churches in the Pennsylvania Field, 1717–1793.* Breinigsville, Pa., 1980.

Gollin, Gillian Lindt. *Moravians in Two Worlds: A Study of Changing Communities.* New York, 1967.

Gura, Philip F. *A Glimpse of Sion's Glory: Puritan Radicalism in New England, 1620–1660.* Middletown, Conn., 1984.

Hall, David D. *Worlds of Wonder, Days of Judgment: Popular Religious Belief in Early New England.* New York, 1989.

Hudson, Winthrop S. "The American Context As an Area for Research in Black Church Studies." *Church History* 52 (1983):157–171.

Ireland, Owen S. "The Ethnic-Religious Dimension of Pennsylvania Politics, 1778–1779." *William and Mary Quarterly* 3rd ser., 30 (1973):423–448.

James, Sydney V. *A People Among Peoples: Quaker Benevolence in Eighteenth-Century America.* Cambridge, Mass., 1963.

Jones, George Fenwick. *The Salzburger Saga: Religious Exiles and Other Germans Along the Savannah.* Athens, Ga., 1984.

Klett, Guy Souillard. *Presbyterians in Colonial Pennsylvania.* Philadelphia, 1937.

Kreider, Harry J. *Lutheranism in Colonial New York.* New York, 1942.

Landsman, Ned C. *Scotland and Its First American Colony, 1683–1765.* Princeton, N.J., 1985.

Lewis, R. Barry. "The Failure of the Anglican-Prussian Ecumenical Effort of 1710–1714." *Church History* 47 (1978):381–399.

Lovejoy, David S. *Religious Enthusiasm in the New World: Heresy to Revolution.* Cambridge, Mass., 1985.

McLoughlin, William G. *New England Dissent, 1630–1833: The Baptists and the Separation of Church and State.* 2 vols. Cambridge, Mass., 1971.

MacMaster, Richard K. *Land, Piety, Peoplehood: The Establishment of Mennonite Communities in America, 1683–1790.* Scottdale, Pa., 1985.

MacMaster, Richard K., Samuel L. Horst, and Robert F. Ulle. *Conscience in Crisis: Mennonites and Other Peace Churches in America, 1739–1789: Interpretation and Documents.* Scottdale, Pa., 1979.

Marietta, Jack D. *The Reformation of American Quakerism, 1748–1783.* Philadelphia, 1984.

May, Henry F. *The Enlightenment in America.* New York, 1976.

Mead, Sidney E. *The Lively Experiment: The Shaping of Christianity in America.* New York, 1963.

Morgan, Edmund S. *Visible Saints: The History of a Puritan Idea.* New York, 1963.

Pestana, Carla Gardina. *Quakers and Baptists in Colonial Massachusetts.* New York, 1991.

Pointer, Richard W. *Protestant Pluralism and the New York Experience: A Study of Eighteenth-Century Religious Diversity.* Bloomington, Ind., 1988.

Raboteau, Albert J. *Slave Religion: The "Invisible Institution" in the Antebellum South.* New York, 1978.

Rothermund, Dietmar. *The Layman's Progress: Religious and Political Experience in Colonial Pennsylvania, 1740–1770.* Philadelphia, 1962.

Sachse, Julius Friedrich. *The German Pietists of Provincial Pennsylvania, 1694–1708.* Philadelphia, 1895.

Sanford, Charles B. *The Religious Life of Thomas Jefferson.* Charlottesville, Va., 1984.

Schelbert, Leo. *Swiss Migration to America: The Swiss Mennonites.* New York, 1980.

Schwartz, Sally. *A Mixed Multitude: The Struggle for Toleration in Colonial Pennsylvania.* New York, 1987.

Smith, George L. *Religion and Trade in New Netherland: Dutch Origins and American Development.* Ithaca, N.Y., 1973.

Smylie, James H. *American Presbyterians: A Pictorial History.* Philadelphia, 1985.

Sobel, Mechal. *Trabelin' On: The Slave Journey to an Afro-Baptist Faith*. Westport, Conn., 1979.

———. *The World They Made Together: Black and White Values in Eighteenth-Century Virginia*. Princeton, N.J., 1987.

Stoeffler, F. Ernest, ed. *Continental Pietism and Early American Christianity*. Grand Rapids, Mich., 1976.

Stout, Harry S. *The Divine Dramatist: George Whitefield and the Rise of Modern Evangelicalism*. Grand Rapids, Mich., 1991.

Tanis, James. *Dutch Calvinistic Pietism in the Middle Colonies: A Study in the Life and Theology of Theodorus Jacobus Frelinghuysen*. The Hague, 1967.

Thorp, Daniel B. *The Moravian Community in Colonial North Carolina: Pluralism on the Southern Frontier*. Knoxville, Tenn., 1988.

Tolles, Frederick B. *Quakers and the Atlantic Culture*. New York, 1960.

Trinterud, Leonard J. *The Forming of an American Tradition: A Re-examination of Colonial Presbyterianism*. Philadelphia, 1949.

Van Horne, John C. "Impediments to the Christianization and Education of Blacks in Colonial America: The Case of the Associates of Dr. Bray." *Historical Magazine of the Protestant Episcopal Church* 50 (1981):243–269.

Walker, Williston. "The Sandemanians of New England." In *Annual Report of the American Historical Association for the Year 1901*. Washington, D.C., 1902.

Westerkamp, Marilyn J. *Triumph of the Laity: Scots-Irish Piety and the Great Awakening, 1625–1760*. New York, 1988.

Wolf, Stephanie Grauman. *Urban Village: Population, Community, and Family Structure in Germantown, Pennsylvania, 1683–1800*. Princeton, N.J., 1976.

Woolverton, John Frederick. *Colonial Anglicanism in North America*. Detroit, Mich., 1984.

Worrall, Arthur J. *Quakers in the Colonial Northeast*. Hanover, N.H., 1980.

Jon Butler

JUDAISM

THOUGH THERE WERE no Jewish delegates to the Constitutional Convention of 1787, there was an Old Testament presence, an interweaving of Judaism and American colonial experience. Benjamin Franklin, one of the first contributors to the rebuilding of Mikvah Israel synagogue in Philadelphia, had suggested during the revolution a design for the Great Seal of the United States depicting Moses (George Washington) standing on the shore of the Red Sea, hand extended, with George III as pharaoh about to be destroyed. The motto for the new country, taken from Leviticus, would be "Rebellion to Tyrants Is Obedience to God." Thomas Jefferson and John Adams had suggested a few modifications but concurred with this concept. Jefferson, like Franklin, considered Americans as political descendants of ancient Hebrews. He probably would have also accepted the notion of Ezra Stiles, president of Yale, that the Constitution, being a sacred document, should be written in a sacred language, Hebrew. Though not adopted, the suggestions mirrored the hopes of a people striving to found and perpetuate a society that would be governed in accordance with divine scripture. Some, like Franklin, held that this new country was to be an asylum for refugees from Europe, the promised land for all who would leave the wilderness of the Old World.

For colonial Americans it did not take much imagination to see parallels with biblical events as a chosen people emerging from slavery and chaos to build a "city on a hill." Reverend Samuel Langdon of New Hampshire viewed the Constitution as a new Ten Commandments and Washington as a contemporary Moses. While such felt connections with the Old Testament did not necessarily carry over into more practical, day-to-day relationships between Jews and non-Jews, ancient traditions did touch American society.

There was another, more immediate, Jewish involvement with the Constitution relating to questions of religious liberty, a concern shared by other minorities. There were not many Jews in the United States at the end of the revolution, probably no more than from twenty-five hundred to three thousand in a population of three million, with most of them to be found in New York, Pennsylvania, Rhode Island, South Carolina, and Georgia. Yet, they had an influence and an importance beyond their number.

Jews had accomplished much for themselves and their country since their first arrival in New Amsterdam in 1654, although perhaps some at the Convention needed to be reminded even of recent achievements. On 7 September 1787 a leading Philadelphia-New York merchant, Jonas Phillips, sent a letter to the delegates noting that "Jews . . . have been foremost in aiding and assisting the States with their lives and fortunes, they have supported the cause, have bravely fought and bled for liberty" which they would not enjoy if religious tests were to be part of the new government. Phillips's letter was a tribute to the significant legacy of Jewish patriotism and sacrifice during the revolution and a summary of the Jewish colonial presence.

Abraham Solomon fought at Bunker Hill. Philip Moses Russell, a surgeon's mate, endured at Valley Forge and earned the gratitude of Washington. Francis Salvador died in 1776 as a result of combat against the British in South Carolina. During the fighting around Beaufort, South Carolina, in 1777, Joseph Solomon was among those killed and Ephraim Abrams was wounded. They were members of Captain Richard Lushington's militia company of sixty, which included about twenty-five Jews and was known, perhaps sarcastically, as the "Jew Company." David Salisbury Franks and Solomon Bush became lieutenant colonels, the highest rank held by Jews in the Continental Army during the war. Bush was badly wounded at Philadelphia in September 1777. Franks fought through the Saratoga campaign of 1777. Haym Salomon, a Polish immigrant, raised some £200,000 for the government as chief broker to the superintendent of finance. He freely lent money to Baron Friedrich von Steuben, General Thaddeus Kościuszko, James Wilson, and James Madison. The latter would fight long and hard for passage of the First Amendment and remember Salomon and the "kindness of our little friend, in Front Street."

PERSECUTION IN NEW SPAIN

It is difficult to date the arrival of the first Jews in the colonies. A widely held view, especially among Puritans, was that Native Americans were the lost tribe of Israel. But historically, Jewish contact with the New World went back to 1492, when Spain expelled its Jews. (Portugal followed suit in 1497.) Those who wished to remain had to convert, becoming what were called New Christians or *conversos* as well as Marranos (literally pigs or accursed). Thus ended a long Jewish "Golden Age" and the beginning of a diaspora as Jews migrated around the Mediterranean area and then to northern and eastern Europe.

New Christians were with Columbus on his voyages of exploration. At least six of those on his first voyage were New Christians, including the interpreter Luis de Torres. Significant numbers were in New Spain, especially after the initial period of blood and rapine associated with Cortés and Pizarro. Of Mexico's population of twenty thousand whites in the seventeenth century, two thousand may have been New Christians. Throughout the region they played a major role in business and trade. Some in government, such as Luis de Carvajal, were of Jewish-Portuguese background. In 1579 he was made governor of Nuevo León, a region that stretches from Tampico to what is now San Antonio, Texas.

Many New Christians continued to observe (albeit secretly) traditional Jewish rituals and holidays, even though they may not have always understood the significance of them. Such observances were extremely risky, since Spain and its colonies were hardly models of religious toleration. Church and state were ever on the lookout for signs of heresy, and many *conversos* were tortured or burned to death on the slightest suspicion. Mexico's first verified auto-da-fé (a ceremony held in conjunction with a judgment of the Inquisition) occurred in 1528, and the last of some seventeen hundred individual trials was conducted as late as 1815. Forty-nine *conversos* were burned to death. Most of the others were imprisoned or sent to galleys.

SAFE HAVENS IN DUTCH BRAZIL AND THE CARIBBEAN

The Dutch, French, and British colonies of the New World offered Jews a far more inviting prospect than did Spain's dominions. Much more than Spain, northern Europe emerged from medieval patterns of thought and behavior during the sixteenth and seventeenth centuries. The Reformation decimated the power of the Roman Catholic church there, while the growth of strong nation-states gave greater sway to secular goals such as the pursuit of commerce. The development of a spirit of free scientific inquiry, unhindered by clerical authority, further weakened the hold of religious dogma over society. Labor and industry determined national greatness. Natural laws of supply, demand, and free competition replaced restrictive edicts. Slowly ghetto walls would tumble. Therefore while anti-Semitism remained rife, Jews were no longer judged exclusively as Jews. Their potential worldly contributions to society also figured in the formulation of colonial policy.

The Netherlands and its colonies were the first to welcome Jewish refugees from the Iberian peninsula—not because they were Jews, but because they were productive individuals and useful allies against hated Catholic Spain, with whom Dutch Calvinists had been frequently at war since the mid-sixteenth century. Cities like Amsterdam and The Hague sheltered remnants of Portuguese-Spanish (Sephardic) Jews. Active in the Netherlands were Manasseh ben Israel, rabbi and political propagandist, the philosopher Baruch Spinoza, and the physician Don Balthazar de Castro.

In 1629 the Dutch, on their way to creating a vast worldwide empire, seized Portuguese-held Recife in Brazil. They controlled that territory until 1654. Dutch-held Brazil had a Jewish population of from six hundred to one thousand. It was perhaps one-third of the entire population and was concentrated mostly in Recife. Recife's recapture by the Portuguese in January 1654 led to the first significant Jewish contact with North America.

Most of the Jews went to the Netherlands, but others scattered around the Caribbean. Some of the refugees went to the French West Indies, and particularly to the islands of Martinique and Guadeloupe. Although their presence stirred opposition and harassment from local Jesuits, it suited the mercantilist policies of French statesman Jean-Baptiste Colbert, who was seeking to strengthen France economically. In 1671 he legalized the presence of Jewish merchants in the French West Indies; however, a 1685 order expelled them from the islands. Many refugees went to Curaçao and other Dutch islands of the Antilles, where they were admitted as settlers, promoters of trade, and allies in its eternal wars with Catholic Spain. By the mid eighteenth century some fourteen hundred Jews were on Curaçao where the capital, Willemstad, had a Joodenstraat and Joode Kerkstraat (Jewish Synagogue Street). Families like the DeCasseres, Fidanque, and deFonseca, some with descendants still on the island, helped establish a permanent, very important and flourishing society that contributed a great deal to the prosperity, history, and culture of the region. Mikve Israel (Hope of Israel), the oldest existing Jewish sanctuary in the New World, is located there. Dedicated in 1732, an earlier house of worship was built in 1703, replacing those used in 1651 and 1692.

Some refugees went to Barbados and other islands in the British West Indies. British authorities, like Colbert, saw Jews as industrious and therefore useful. The Brazilian refugees helped develop British Caribbean trade and commerce. Eventually, they were found in every British possession in the area. Families like the Touro's of Jamaica and Valverde's of Barbados were particularly active in sugar traffic, and such merchants made up a substantial portion of trade with British North America. Religious life was actively maintained, and a synagogue was established at Bridgetown, Barbados, in the early 1650's, later called Nidhe Israel (the Scattered of Israel), one of the oldest in the English-speaking world. Numerous other synagogues and schools were situated throughout the West Indies, all reflecting an involvement in the Caribbean.

Nevertheless, local legislatures imposed various disabilities upon Jews. They could not vote or hold office and paid special taxes, among other burdens.

ESTABLISHING A PRESENCE IN NEW AMSTERDAM

The impact of Recife's fall reached New Amsterdam in early September 1654, when a group of twenty-three Jews arrived. In this small frontier city of perhaps fifteen hundred people, the history of Jews in North America began. Most had been in Recife and had left in January 1654. Their destination is uncertain—possibly they intended to return to Holland. At any rate they were caught up in a series of misadventures and eventually deposited in New Amsterdam. Here they found at least two other Jews, Jacob Barsimon and Solomon Pieterson, who had arrived in the summer of 1654.

Though most of the twenty-three were Sephardic, some were not, and neither were Barsimon nor Pieterson, who were both eastern European (Ashkenazim). This was also true of Asser Levy, the most noted of the early community. He was the only one who could properly be called a permanent settler. He died in New York in 1682.

Although New Amsterdam was known as a polyglot community where, according to Father Isaac Jogues, eighteen different languages were spoken, Director General Peter Stuyvesant regarded Jews as usurers and did not want them to stay. But the newcomers found support among the directors of the Dutch West India Company, which controlled most of the Netherlands' possessions in the New World. Investors in the company, some of whom were Jews, favored the Dutch colonies. On 15 February 1655 the directors of the company—in a historic step—granted Jews the right to settle and trade in the colony. Still, Stuyvesant and members of the Calvinist community tried to bar them from holding real estate, engaging in retail trade, obtaining membership in the militia, having a burial ground of their own, or building a synagogue. These restrictions were, between 1655 and 1657, essentially lifted through the efforts of individuals such as Levy, Barsimon, David Ferara, Joseph d'Acosta, and Salvador D'Andrada along with the "Lords Directors" in the Netherlands. In April 1657 full burgher or citizenship rights had been reluctantly granted by Stuyvesant, the only reservation being a prohibition on public worship. The small transient group did not make an issue of this, since most did not plan to stay long enough to feel a need for a synagogue.

For most the wilderness outpost had little to offer. But through Asser Levy, a Jewish presence was maintained—though barely. At the time of the surrender of the colony to the British in 1664, only two Jews seem to have resided in New Amsterdam, one being Levy. There was a degree of religious practice in the earliest years of settlement, although there may not have been a formal congregation. Services may have been held on a regular basis. A Torah owned by Levy was available, but little else beside prayer books and shawls existed. The Sabbath seems to have been observed, and in 1660 two Jews— Levy again being one—were licensed as butchers serving the religious requirements of the small community. A burial ground was purchased in 1656, but there is no record of any interment. Some Jews did well economically, especially Levy. He had a varied trade in flour, wheat, tobacco, and furs throughout New Netherland as well as with the Netherlands, the Caribbean, and British colonies in America. Levy seems to have been readily accepted by the community at large. He moved easily among non-Jews. His partner in a slaughterhouse opened in 1680 was not Jewish.

PROSPERITY AND TOLERANCE IN NEW YORK

Jews had been expelled from England in the thirteenth century. Barely a decade before the British conquest of New Amsterdam in 1664, Oliver Cromwell—lord protector of the Commonwealth—decided to readmit Jews. At war with the Dutch, primarily over commercial rivalries and control of the high seas, Cromwell could use any support available. By mid century Jews were entering England. In subsequent decades they gained, if not full citizenship, then the right to trade and protection of the law.

The British seizure of New Netherland brought major changes to the province. English common law, representative government, and a clearer definition of citizenship were introduced. Until 1685 New York was a proprietary colony owned by James, duke of York, later James II; then it became a royal colony. A permanent assembly was granted after 1691. In 1686 New York City and Albany obtained the right of corporate government through a mayor appointed by the governor and an elected common council. Perhaps more important, as a British colony New York benefited from enlarged markets through trade access to the mother country and its possessions, and it had enhanced military protection as well. The Trade and Navigation acts, passed between 1651 and 1696, helped develop a growing and increasingly prosperous colony by encouraging shipbuilding, stabilizing trade, and promoting settlement.

English law helped to assure a stable and lasting Jewish presence. The Rabba Couty case of 1671, involving the seizure by Jamaican authorities of the ship of a New York Jewish merchant, resulted in establishing the right under English law of resident Jews to conduct business in Britain and her colonies. Naturalization acts of 1715 and 1740 further encouraged immigration, while law and custom extended civil rights, including the right to vote, hold office, and conduct public worship.

At the beginning of the eighteenth century, a new influx of merchant immigrants augmented the small handful of Jews previously found in the city. Among this new group were Jacob Franks, his father-in-law, Moses Levy, related by marriage to Asser Levy, Nathan Simson, Rodrigo Pacheco, and several members of the influential Gomez clan, including Mordecai and patriarch Luis. Most came from the West Indies, England, and Germany. By 1695 a synagogue had been established in rented quarters. As with the earlier Jewish immigrants, wholesale trade was the economic underpinning of the small group. Only a very few, like "Israel the Jew, soapmaker," conducted retail trade and crafts. These merchants were closely identified with the chocolate, cocoa, and spermaceti candle trade, but they also participated in all manner of commerce including slaves, cloth, and sealing wax. The mix was typical of colonial merchants.

In traffic to England, the Caribbean, and the Atlantic Coast, New York Jewish merchants accounted for anywhere from 2 percent of all trade to as much as 40 percent of commerce with Jamaica after 1730. The percentages were lower after the early decades of the eighteenth century, but Jews remained an important factor in trade. Significantly, Sampson Simson was a prominent member of the New York Chamber of Commerce beginning in 1768.

Population data for the colonial era is not precise, but it appears that while in 1664 there were, as noted, only two known Jews, by 1722 there were thirty-one Jewish families in the city. They constituted about 2.3 percent of the total population of the city of eight thousand and paid about 2 percent of the taxes. This appears to have been near a population peak in terms of percentage, because for most of the century the Jewish population was about 1 percent of the total. (This presumably explains why the percentage of trade in Jewish hands declined, as previously observed.) Most lived by choice in the South and Dock wards alongside the East River; however members of the Simson family lived in Oyster Bay, Long Island. David Elias resided in Southampton, also on Long Island, in the

1720s. Daniel Gomez and members of the Hays family lived in Westchester and Orange counties.

Putting Down Roots

Two developments indicate the permanence of the early-eighteenth-century Jewish community. By 1730 Congregation Shearith Israel (Remnant of Israel) had been formed. It followed Sephardic rites, although many members, including its first president, Jacob Franks, were Askhenazic. In April 1730 the first services were conducted in a small, just completed synagogue on Mill Street (present South William Street). It was the first such structure in British North America. It could easily be argued that with this event, the community, before then perhaps something of an experiment, came of age, and that with the dedication of the synagogue a permanent Jewish society was established.

It was also in 1730 when, it could be said, the community's political maturation became evident. In that year the assembly passed a law specifically giving Christians and Jews protection from attacks by slaves. While information about debates regarding the act is minimal, it would seem that along with economic success came a degree of political power.

There was no law specifically giving Jews the right to vote, nor was there a law depriving them of the franchise. (A heated, often anti-Semitic debate on the matter occurred in 1737, when the assembly resolved to deprive Jews of the right to vote, but apparently this did not have the force of law.) Jews did vote, although how many is unclear. Jacob Franks, Samuel Levy, and Moses Levy were elected as constables and assessors; these, however, were generally not sought-after positions. Some served in the militia. Rodrigo Pacheco, along with several others, was named temporary colonial agent for New York to represent the colony as a lobbyist during the Sugar Act debates. It was surely the highest position held by a Jew in colonial America. Daniel and Mordecai Gomez served as Spanish interpreters, the first in Supreme Court, the latter in Admiralty Court.

Events indicative of a type of problem inherent in a basically open society were the marriage in 1742 of Phila, daughter of Jacob and Abigail Franks, to a notable member of the Anglican aristocracy, Oliver DeLancey, and the marriage of her brother David in 1743 to Margaret Evans, daughter of a prominent Philadelphia family. Explanations can be found in the tolerant attitudes prevailing in New York, the economic achievements of the Franks family, and perhaps the secular attitude of the mother, Abigail, a daughter of the Enlightenment. Fluent in Spanish and French, Abigail had her son, Naphtali, regularly send her the works of Montesquieu, Pope, Addison, and Steele from London. An avid reader of history and literature, she moved freely in the lay world, much more so than in that of the synagogue. Abigail regarded religion as little more than superstition, and her dislike of members of the Sephardic community and others of the congregation limited the choice of marriage partners for her children. Her closest friends were Christian. By the end of the century, the Franks in New York and England had lost their identity as a Jewish family. Most Jews remained within the community, though its continuity depended on incoming immigrants, who reinforced stability and structure.

As an indicator both of a permanent Jewish commitment to New York and of the opportunities open there, Jews could increasingly be found in the crafts and professions and less exclusively in wholesale trade. Elias Woolin, among others, was a physician, and Michael Solomon Hays, a watchmaker. The well-known Myer Myers, a silversmith and goldsmith, was native to the city and served the needs of more affluent New Yorkers. He also made beautiful silver ornamental pomegranates (*rimonim*) to adorn the scrolls of law at Shearith Israel. He did the same for Philadelphia's Congregation Mikve Israel (Hope of Israel). In 1774 Isaac Abrahams became the first Jewish graduate of King's College and went on to become a physician.

New York was the focal point of the emerging Jewish-American experience. The success of the New York community persuaded others to build new settlements in British America. Anti-Semitism of a private kind existed everywhere, but not usually in the law. Overtly hostile incidents were rare and generally not violent or organized. These included a 1752 performance of *The Merchant of Venice* in Williamsburg, Virginia, featuring a stereotypical Shylock, and an attack on "Jew landlords" in a German newspaper in Pennsylvania in 1764.

SETTLEMENTS IN NEW ENGLAND

A few years after the initial New York contact, Jewish tradesmen had settled by 1654 in the other British colonies. By 1659 individual merchant-peddlers had appeared in Connecticut. By the turn of the century Isaac de Medina, originally from New York, was in Hartford, and by 1721 some Jews were located in Stamford, Branford, and Norwalk. Michael Judah was in Norwalk by the 1740s and remained there until he died about forty years later. After 1755 Jews were found in New Haven and Derby. It is difficult to be sure of how well they were received or treated by local Congregationalists. Perhaps the best indication is that during the revolution, many of the Jewish community in British-occupied New York moved, even if temporarily, to a number of Connecticut towns, including Wilton and Stamford. But no synagogue was built, and Connecticut was at most a distant outpost, with Massachusetts being even more distant.

In the Bay Colony Judah Monis, whose 1735 Hebrew grammar was the first published in the colonies, converted to Congregationalism in 1722, probably in order to teach at Harvard. This was regarded as a distinct triumph for the Congregationalists. But there were reservations about Monis's sincerity, and Ezra Stiles felt "Jews will never become incorporated with the people of America." At any rate, there were not many other such victories, although attempts at proselytizing were common, especially in Puritan Massachusetts.

Jewish Merchants in Newport

The major center of Jewish settlement in New England was Rhode Island, a colony founded, at least in part, by independent Baptists. Roger Williams, an ardent advocate of separation of church and state, supported the right of Jews to practice their religion without government interference. Perhaps as early as 1656, some Jews may have migrated from New York across Long Island Sound to Newport. In 1678 a burial ground for Jews was purchased in Newport by Mordecai Campanall and Moses Pacheco of Barbados. Many of the early Jewish settlers in Newport were from that Caribbean island, but for an unknown reason the Barbadians left in 1685. They were soon replaced by others, most notably by a group of some ninety Jews who apparently arrived from Curaçao in 1693. By 1712 there was a "Jew's Street" in Newport. The town prospered during the eighteenth century, and given the growing trade between New York and Rhode Island a number of leading Jewish families in New York, including the Polocks, Isaakses, Lopezes, and Harts, left the Hudson River city for Rhode Island. Some fifteen Jewish families were in Rhode Island in 1755.

As testimony to the success and permanence of the settlement, by 1756 a formal congregation had been organized. First known as Nephuse Israel (the Scattered of Israel), by 1769 it had become Yeshuat Israel (the Salvation of Israel). With the help of the New York community, construction had begun by 1759 on the oldest extant synagogue in the country, the famous and elegant Touro Synagogue, designed by the noted American architect, Peter Harrison. Named after Isaac Touro of Amsterdam, the building, finished in 1763, was and is one of the glories of colonial architecture.

The Jewish community in Rhode Island was the second most important and secure one in British America. Here merchants like Jacob Rodriquez Rivera and Aaron and Moses Lopez developed a flourishing trade in spermaceti candles, fish, rum, marine supplies, and many other products. Prosperity brought recognition. In August 1773 the Rhode Island General Assembly appointed Aaron Lopez to a committee of three to petition the British government for recognition of the colony's right to fish in Canadian waters, including cod fishing in the Gulf of Saint Lawrence. Ezra Stiles remembered Lopez as a merchant "of the first eminence . . . probably surpassed by no merch[an]t in America . . . the most universally beloved . . . of any man I ever knew." Like New York, Newport—with possibly some two hundred Jews in a population of nine thousand in 1774—was an example of Jewish accomplishment. Still in 1776 Moses Michael Hays, though an active supporter of the revolution, complained of not being allowed to vote. Much was done, more remained.

THE MIDDLE AND SOUTHERN COLONIES

The success of Jewish Americans was also evident in Pennsylvania, where in the 1730s—after a period of sporadic individual contact—small numbers of Jewish merchants settled. Most came from New York, including Nathan Levy, son of Moses Levy, David Franks, and Isaac Mendes Seixes. The great majority of them settled in Philadelphia. By 1747 rented quarters on Sterling Alley served as a synagogue to meet the needs of the community of perhaps three hundred, about 1 percent of the overall population of the city. In 1771 Congregation Mikve Israel was in place at its own building in Cherry Alley. In 1754 Barnard Gratz, an immigrant from Upper Silesia, arrived in Philadelphia and quickly established members of that family as leading mercantile factors. In 1765 eight Jews signed the Philadelphia nonimportation agreement, 2 percent of the approximately four hundred signers. Two of the eight were Gratz brothers. There were also settlements in interior Pennsylvania, notably at Lancaster and Easton. Mordecai Moses Mordecai, formerly of Easton, had a farm close to Fort Pitt (Pittsburgh). Merchants with close ties to major fur traders, like Joseph Simon of Lancaster, were of considerable importance in opening the West.

While there was no Jewish community in either New Jersey or Delaware, a number of individual Jews lived and worked there. The same was true for Maryland, Virginia, and North Carolina.

Georgia and South Carolina had Jewish settlements. There may have been Jews in the latter colony as early as the 1680s, but there was only a handful through the first decade of the eighteenth century. In the 1740s Charleston was the fourth largest colonial city, with seven thousand inhabitants, and was also an increasingly important center of trade. Members of the New York Franks family and other Jews moved there. Samuel Levy and Moses Solomon carried on their trade in Charleston, as did Isaac DaCosta, among others. By 1749 a synagogue had been established in rented quarters, serving the needs of some twelve families. It used Sephardic liturgy, though half the Congregation Beth Sholom (House of Peace) was Ashkenazic. By 1776 about fifty Jewish families, or approximately two hundred people, lived among some ten thousand Charlestonians. Jews also went to the back country and to other port settlements such as Beaufort, just across the Georgia border.

Georgia began as a model colony where the deserving poor could reestablish their lives and at the same time help protect South Carolina from Spanish attack. The Georgia trustees, proprietors of the colony, were aided by wealthy members of Congregation Bevis Marks in London, who wanted to support their less fortunate co-religionists and at the same time reduce the financial burdens associated with alms giving. There was considerable opposition to Jewish settlement on the part of some trustees. But on 11 July 1733, six months after the colony's founding, over forty Jewish settlers came to Savannah as a single group, one of the largest instances of the mass migration of Jews in the colonial period. About thirty more Jews landed at Savannah in November 1733. Governor James Oglethorpe generally welcomed Jewish newcomers. His attitude was likely influenced by the work of Dr. Samuel Nunez, a Jewish physician who quelled a serious outbreak of illness in the infant colony. Jews quickly purchased home lots and by 1735 Congregation Mikve Israel was established in the usual rented quarters. However the original settlement did not last through a war with Spain that commenced in 1739.

Fear of Spanish attack from Florida as well as certain prohibitory policies of the trustees, such as barring the use of slave labor, caused many inhabitants, Jews and non-Jews, to leave the province for New York, Charleston, Lancaster, and the Caribbean. After the end of the last colonial war in 1763, Georgia—since 1752 a royal colony—resumed its development. As population and trade grew, the number of Jews increased so that by 1770 there may have been one hundred in the colony. In 1774 Mordecai Sheftall organized a service in his home. Some left the colony with the coming of the revolution, but others served in the war. Jews could be found in other scattered areas of the colony, but only in very small numbers.

TRACES IN LOUISIANA AND CANADA

Elsewhere in North America Jewish merchants, including Isaac Rodrigues Monsanto, were in places such as New Orleans by 1760, though most of them left several years later when Spain took over the formerly French province of Louisiana. A law first instituted by Cardinal Richelieu in the seventeenth century, and strictly enforced after, prevented a Jewish presence until after the British conquest in 1763. There were possibly some Jews in French Canada, but only as isolated individuals. One of the most notable to establish themselves after that date was Aaron Hart, reportedly the wealthiest Jew north of Lake Champlain. There were a few families in Quebec, Trois-Rivières, and Montreal as well. In the latter, it has been suggested, regular religious services were being conducted by 1768. In 1775 Lazarus David bought land on Saint Janvier Street for use as a cemetery, while in 1777 a synagogue was erected on Saint James Street, the third one in North America. It has been estimated that there were fifty Jewish families in Canada by 1776, with somewhere from one hundred to one hundred and fifty people. Canada did not attract many Jews, perhaps because of a lack of economic opportunity as well as a marked degree of religious intolerance.

CHARACTERISTICS OF THE JEWISH SETTLEMENTS

Jewish colonization in North America began tentatively and slowly and was often marked by a transient quality. Immigration came in waves and many of the arrivals left before long. Therefore it took time for permanent, stable Jewish communities to form. Two developments marked such communities: the existence of a significant number of Jewish craftsmen and the construction of synagogues. Both indicated the possession of nonportable assets: land, buildings, inventories, and a degree of political power. Even where Jews were not welcomed, the general community was at least tolerant. This brought its own problems, especially in regard to maintaining group identity.

Most Jews seemed to have little knowledge of Hebrew, as witness the need for Monis's grammar and the publication in 1760 in New York of an English translation of Joseph Jesurun Pinto's Hebrew prayer of thanks for the conquest of Canada. Rosh Hashanah, Yom Kippur, and Shabbat services were translated in 1761 and 1766. The practice of religion was also impeded by difficulties in obtaining services of *shohets* (kosher butchers), *mohels* (circumcisers), and those who knew how to conduct services. There were no ordained rabbis in the colonies. Questions relating to law were usually answered by London rabbis. Trial and error usually served as a convenient guide in matters of observance. Religious education was provided by most congregations, but it was difficult to obtain teachers and the funding to hire them. All this made it hard to maintain discipline and orthodoxy. The intermarriages of the Franks family, referred to above, are perhaps illustrations of a general communal laxity and a tendency to assimilate.

Certainly the old saying, "the law of the land is the law," was followed by the community in achieving economic and social well-being. Peter Kalm, a Swedish naturalist, visited New York in 1748 and commented on the status of many Jews in the city who besides "great privileges . . . have a synagogue and houses, and great country seats of their own property. . . . They have likewise several ships, which they freight, and send out with their own goods. In fine, they enjoy all the privileges common to the other inhabitants of this town and province."

CONCLUSION

The Jewish colonial experience in the British and Dutch territories was generally a happy one, not only because Jews prospered, but also because they contributed so substantially to the well-being of society in general. Surely members of the Constitutional Convention would concur. The vision of a "New Zion," a country without ghetto walls, "Jew codes," and official anti-Semitism, had been largely secured. Jews had found a home and by the revolution were active, if not fully equal, participants in the affairs of an emerging nation.

BIBLIOGRAPHY

Chyet, Stanley F. *Lopez of Newport: Colonial American Merchant Prince.* Detroit, Mich., 1970.

Grinstein, Hyman B. *The Rise of the Jewish Community of New York, 1654–1860.* Philadelphia, 1945.

Gutstein, Morris A. *The Story of the Jews of Newport: Two and a Half Centuries of Judaism, 1658–1908.* New York, 1936.

Hershkowitz, Leo, and Isidore S. Meyer. *Letters of the Franks Family, 1723–1748.* Waltham, Mass., 1968.

Liebman, Seymour B. *The Inquisitors and the Jews in the New World: Summaries of Procesos, 1500–1810, and Bibliographic Guide.* Coral Gables, Fla., 1974.

Marcus, Jacob R. *The Colonial American Jew, 1492–1776.* 3 vols. Detroit, Mich., 1970.

Oppenheim, Samuel. "The Early History of the Jews in New York, 1654–1664." *Publications of the American Jewish Historical Society* 18 (1909):1–91.

Resnikoff, Charles, and Uriah Z. Englesman. *The Jews of Charleston.* Philadelphia, 1950.

Schappes, Morris U., ed. *A Documentary History of the Jews in the United States, 1654–1875.* 3rd ed. New York, 1971.

Wolf II, Edwin, and Maxwell Whiteman. *The History of the Jews of Philadelphia: From Colonial Times to the Age of Jackson.* Philadelphia, 1975.

Leo Hershkowitz

SEE ALSO **Church and State; Protestant Pluralism;** and **Puritanism.**

NATIVE AMERICAN RELIGIONS

In 1528, ALMOST A CENTURY before the founding of Jamestown, the Spanish explorer Álvar Núñez Cabeza de Vaca survived a shipwreck near American shores. After wandering through northern Mexico and Texas, he was rescued in 1536 and recounted stories about seven golden cities. When the news reached Spain, Spanish explorer Fray Marcos de Niza, guided by Esteban, Núñez's slave, was sent to find these cities, in an expedition that led to the Zuni villages of the American Southwest. There were indeed seven villages, but rather than being constructed of gold, they were pueblos whose adobe probably appeared golden in the sunlight. Throughout the colonial period in these borderlands, the image of the Indian was inseparable from newcomers' perceptions of them, and so it is even today.

The "Indian" was an image invented as a foil for addressing colonial identities. It was centuries before any attempt was made to see these peoples as they see themselves. Indeed, the term "cultures" as a plural was not used until the late nineteenth century, when that concept finally opened the way to comprehending the integrity and distinctiveness of the many Indian nations. Furthermore, the term "religion," which denoted Christianity from the colonial period through the nineteenth century, was almost unthinkable as a designation of anything "Indian." It was "true" religion—that is, Christianity—that was being provided to help these "heathen" peoples.

To refer to Native American religions prior to and during the colonial period is thus a re-creation refined by twentieth-century ideas about both Native Americans and "religion," which is now seen merely as a dimension of all cultures. It requires the difficult task, using not-altogether-reliable methods, of trying to see the actual peoples reflected in the images invented of them.

RELIGIONS ON THE EVE OF COLONIALISM

Diversity, Complexity, and Theological Opacity

The fundamental fact is that there never was a "Native American religion"—that is, a single, consistent religious practice, set of beliefs, institution, and history that existed throughout the Americas or even North America. There was no "Indian language," "Indian culture," or "Indian way"; diversity, variety, and complexity characterized Native American religions. This does not, however, preclude common themes, patterns, or types. A brief outline of their cultural and linguistic variation will help not only to establish this point but also to provide necessary context.

How long the Americas have had human inhabitants is a subject of continuing controversy, yet incontestably it has been many thousands of years. During that period peoples spread throughout the Western Hemisphere and developed a variety of cultures; various methods have been used to analyze and present their complex array. The most common is the designation of culture and language phyla. Culture-area designations are delimited geographically, based on the consistency of cultural patterns. Signal among the distinguishing factors is the mode of subsistence; this, in turn, is reflected throughout the cultural patterns, particularly through the shaping of material culture (houses, tools, artworks). Of the nine language phyla in North America, hundreds of distinct languages have been identified. Language classification provides one line of evidence, complementing the archaeological, for discerning the history of tribal cultures. As yet there is no system for classifying native religions, other than designating the culture area and subsistence mode.

The diversity of Native American religions can be appreciated in a variety of frames. For example, while it is commonly held that subsistence patterns—simplified as hunting and agriculture—correlate with modes of religion, cultures with similar subsistence patterns show considerable variety. Bear ceremonialism, for example, has been understood as a core feature of hunting cultures with religious practices throughout the sub-Arctic regions and from the Labrador Peninsula to western Canada and Alaska, maintaining a continuity with religious practices from antiquity. Throughout this region there is evidence of the belief in a master or mistress of the animals, a magicoreligious character to the practice of hunting, and special treatment of the bones or other parts of the killed game. Yet, despite these common features, diversity is found across the enormous bear-hunting area. In some tribes, hunting was linked with individual and shamanistic activities; in others it was a community activity involving elaborate ceremonies, including dance and drama.

Almost all North American tribes gained some subsistence from hunting. Even the Pueblo tribes of the American Southwest, so strongly identified with agriculture and a sedentary way of life, depended on seasonal hunting. The Pueblo hunted in a ritually prescribed manner,

and hunting and animals were prominent subjects in their oral traditions. Religious and cultural diversity also occurred among cultivators in latitudes from southern Canada to South America.

Most research on the spiritual and theological conceptions of these tribal peoples has been directed toward the search for evidence to establish theories about the evolution of religion. Some scholars have looked for a high god in North America to demonstrate that the earliest form of religion was monotheism. Others, holding that the high god is a product of religious evolution culminating in Christianity, have attempted to show that such figures were unknown in North America. As a product of European (predominantly Protestant) thought, such theorizing has drawn a veil over Native American conceptions of the spiritual world.

Even fundamental questions about Native American categories of the spiritual, supernatural, and theological have not been adequately raised—much less, extensively dealt with. Obviously, no single set of theological terms is adequate or explicit, and the common terminology derived from Western religious traditions (including such concepts as god, deity, spirit, and supernatural) will not suffice to convey the diversity, complexity, and theological opacity of Native American religions.

Belief in a Spiritual World

An important factor common to Native American religions was a deep belief in a spiritual world, which was described in myth, encountered in ritual, and inhabited by various figures, forces, and powers. Some cultures named and otherwise identified at least one major spiritual figure, either male or female. A cosmic creator did not always exist, and a highly developed story tradition associated with creator figures was unusual. After the Creation some figures were so removed from the human world that they were never addressed in prayer or through ritual; others were close at hand and approachable. For some tribes a pervasive spiritual power—*orenda* for the Iroquois, *manitou* for the Algonquin, and *wakan* for the Lakota (or Sioux)—not only pervaded all existence but also could be conceived of in a personified form, such as Gitchi Manitou and Wakan Tanka.

644

Apart from spiritual presences of extraordinary power and prominence, beings of almost untold variety pervaded the oral and ritual traditions. Mythological figures reflected theological conceptions and commonly were animated aspects of the natural world: waters, winds, celestial phenomena, animals, insects, and plants. Other mythological figures had no human or natural counterparts.

Native Americans did not regard or encounter the world in merely physical terms: every plant, animal, object, and point of orientation be it a geographical landmark, star formation, or point of the compass was the subject of a story in which personal, moral, and spiritual dimensions shaped everyday human life. Theological conceptions were also expressed through ritual personification in masked and dramatic performances, acts of prayer, vision and guardian-spirit quests, shamanistic performances, and hunting and planting rites. A variety of entities were foundational to belief.

Modes of Expression

Native North American languages did not have an alphabetic counterpart to the spoken word and therefore could not be written. The freedoms and limitations of this exclusive orality was a shaping force in Native American political and social structures, technological development, patterns of thinking, and most certainly religion. With no written histories, recorded scriptures, formal statements of doctrine, or second-order traditions of critical and interpretive thought presented in writing, Native Americans instead gave concrete expression to religion through their characterization of the landscape, in the shapes of their houses and other architectural forms, in costumes, dances, masks, and medicine bundles, and in such oral forms as song, prayer, and story. Any tradition not kept vital and not passed on to the next generation through use and performance was lost forever.

At transitions in the annual cycle, passages in the life cycle, the onset of an illness, or moments of community needs, religious actions were performed, not to celebrate these occasions but to effect change. Thus, new-year rites brought about the change of the year, rites of passage transformed a child into an adult, and funerary practices conducted the deceased person to the land of the dead.

Religious events were inseparable from the evocative and emotive effects inspired by their performance. These occurred on many levels, from the transmission of culture from one generation to another, to the reaffirmation of positions and relationships in the social structure, to the highest level of re-creating or reaffirming the natural order. Native American religions were powerful and essential because of what they did even more than because of what they meant.

Native Americans effectively utilized the reversal of norms to increase the vitality of religious actions. Performances by clowns were widespread, and through them—almost always in a ritual setting—a community shared the experience of foolish actions, forbidden, and even unspeakable actions, proceeding from human needs gone out of control. There were widely told stories of figures such as the coyote, raven, mink, and raccoon, who acted out and explored the reversals and extremes of the ordered human world. The creatures slept with their daughters, ate their children, were slow to learn, and satirized many they encountered. Often they acted foolish themselves and were the butt of many a joke. These animals were not considered deities and had no supernatural powers. They were utopian in their rejection of the rules of order and their accompanying restrictions. By demonstrating the suffering brought upon these characters through their persistent defiance and reversal of the expected order, these stories effectively reaffirmed order. Thus, these comic-story figures and ritual clowns participated in the ongoing religious process by reaffirming the order of the created world.

The dominant patterns and themes that characterized each Native American religion were repeatedly expressed in landscape, architecture, material culture, and the oral traditions. For example, a predominant arrangement among tribes on the Plains was the circumscribed cross whose arms correspond to the cardinal or semicardinal directions. The pattern took such forms as medicine wheels, tipi orientations, and shield decorations. The cross represented unity and wholeness, balance amid differentiation.

Among the Tewa, a Pueblo people of the Southwest, such a dominant pattern expressed a complexly mediated duality that was replicated in physical and mythological geographies (designated by a mountain and lake in each of the four cardinal directions), in calendrical and seasonal distinctions (corresponding to the four annual seasons), in economic and sustenance activities (agriculture and hunting), and in village and house structures.

In many cultures this dominant symbolic complex centered on a single object with manifold uses and interpretations. Such objects included corn (and cornmeal and corn pollen), tobacco (and also the pipe and the smoke), and other plants such as squash, beans, and cacti. Many animals also served as dominant symbols, such as the eagle, bear, and wolf.

The broken or open circle, which characterized the Navajo religious worldview, was replicated in cosmology, ritual patterns and procedures, craft and material objects, house structures, and cultural practices. It expressed the idea that openness and motion are essential to life, that relationships are more important than entities, and that incompleteness and gaps are keys to creativity.

Native American art also was a form of religious expression. Though the wooden false-face masks now so strongly identified with the Iroquois apparently did not develop until the early nineteenth century, other types of masks were used prior to colonization. Among the Iroquois, they were associated with ritual healing. Masks were never carved as works of art intended to be hung as decorative objects. Rather, they were ritual objects that bridged the material world of human experience and the spiritual and mythological world. The figures presented in masks were revealed to the mask makers and mask wearers through dreams and mythological traditions. Masks were used among the Alaskan Eskimos south through the Pacific Northwest coast, throughout the Southwest, from the Northeast south, and occasionally in other areas.

Sand paintings, kiva murals, effigy pipes, clothing and pottery designs, weavings, and the many other items likely to be identified as works of art were primary bearers of religious values and worldviews and were often religiously powerful. Effigy pipes, used throughout the East, were carved in the image of the spirit guardian and were often aligned to face the smoker. As strong tobacco was smoked for extended periods

in one of these effigy pipes, the smoker not only looked eye to eye with his guardian, he also exchanged breath with it.

For Native Americans, it was the creation and use of these objects for religious purposes that was valued, rather than their possession and display as art objects. They were forms of religious expression and, more important, they were used in religious actions.

Religion and the Landscape

For Native Americans the landscape was the site upon which was projected and through which was concretized a gradient of values, a set of important categories and distinctions that constituted their religious worldviews. The landscape gave form to religious ideas in many ways. Fundamentally, the landscape was seen as bound spaces—that is, as territories—and this conception was expressed in both temporal and spatial dimensions. Its limits were defined by the physical extent of a culture's domain, and the home territory or land was coextensive with the world of order and meaning. Many tribes delimited them by distinctive features of the land. Mountains, rivers, lakes, and forests marked the center (or perimeter) and defined the principles of human orientation.

The landscape gave expression to intent and value by serving as the setting for the journey along the road of life. For the Hopi in the Southwest the orientation of life, goodness, health, and happiness was toward the east; for the Oglala of the Plains it was toward the south. Many cultures designated cardinal or semicardinal directions (sometimes in combination with the zenith, nadir, and center) and endowed them with values and attributes. Prayers were offered and houses oriented with regard to direction, and most architectural forms had cosmological significance. Ritual processes were conducted constantly with an eye to orientation. Pilgrimages, of both body and mind, had directional orientations, usually expressed as journeys through a landscape.

The extent of a culture's territory was pragmatically defined by the movements and places of occupancy of its people, and the religious character of the land was often reflected in practical activities. Hunting, for example, involved a religious relationship between people and animals that took form in spatial terms. Hunters lived in human homes in the human world; while the game lived in dwellings, usually inaccessible to human beings, under the guidance of a protector of animals. The preparation for the hunt was one of spiritual communion with the game or with the game's master or mistress. The hunt was a journey by both hunters and animals into a mediating landscape—the hunting grounds—where the hunter played host to game that, upon being killed, played host to the hunter seeking nourishment.

The landscape also gave language to religion in the form of story traditions of the world's creation and history. Native Americans generally did not have Creation stories in which the physical world was made from nothing. Their stories commonly told of the primordial or ancestral designation, transformation, and orientation that resulted in the present landscape: how the world was found, how its shape gained significance, and how human beings should orient themselves within this landscape. These stories told how life not only became livable but also meaningful.

Although there were major creator figures who brought order to the world, such as the Winnebago Earthmaker and the Laguna Thought Woman, other figures contributed to its origin and primordial ordering. For example, in the widespread earth-diver story, many animals and birds attempted to obtain, from the bottom of the primordial sea, a bit of soil for creating the world. In western North America creation stories often involved the theft of something essential to life, such as fire or light, that had been secreted away by a mythological figure. In other regions, the character of the world and of human life was attributed to mythological siblings who fought and counteracted each other's efforts to establish the world. In some oral traditions there was an abundance of magical flights to spiritual worlds, of long migrations in search of a livable place, and of major catastrophes that transformed the world. In all these stories the result was the world, the land imprinted with a gradient of values observable by those living within it.

The landscape was also the arena of history; and natural features served as mnemonics—from points on the migration routes of mythic ancestors to points on historical journeys. There were physical reminders of wars, of great individual achievements, of former residences, and of revelations and visions. For Native Americans history was told in stories read from the landscape's features.

American colonial history seemed to require the progressive displacement of Native Americans from territories that had been their sources of meaning. Of necessity, these displacements resulted in radical transformations and innovations. Displaced peoples had to redefine themselves and re-create their worlds, often in unfamiliar lands and in cities where there was no land for a tribal culture. The importance of land in the cultural and religious identity and continuity of Native Americans was paramount.

Religion and Health

Health and healing were common religious concerns, and physical and psychological health often reflected the social, cultural, and spiritual aspects of the world in which one lived. In this view, the individual is integral in a complex web of relationships and dependencies, the disturbance of which—even if remote from the individual—may have an impact signaled by symptoms and feelings of illness.

Curing techniques thus often focused not directly on the symptoms but on what were determined to be the causal factors. The restorative, rectifying, and re-creative actions were commonly identified primarily as healing processes and might be successfully performed without any accompanying improvement in the symptoms. Thus the treatment's success was defined in terms derived from specific tribal conceptions. Although Native American curing practices undoubtedly produced significant physical and psychological effects, they were probably secondary to the intent: to give an illness meaning, to rectify and repair relationships at a human or spiritual level, to restore an individual and a community to a context in which life and death might have meaning.

Shamanism, by which certain forms of healing practices are now commonly identified, has a Siberian origin. While the term has come to refer to worldwide phenomena, the Siberian examples stand as prototypes. Consequently, shamanism is most commonly seen as a magicoreligious process of curing and divination, whereby techniques of entrancement are used to achieve an extraordinary psychic and spiritual status. In North America entrancement techniques were not widely used beyond the region from the sub-Arctic through the Pacific Northwest into California and, here and there, across Canada.

The extraordinary spiritual power of shamans was intended to influence the world through spiritual forces. Shamans gained power through spiritual alliances with animals and natural forms, with ghosts, and with mythological beings. Individuals acquired spiritual power by quest, inheritance, election, or purchase; hallucinogenic drugs were rarely used in North America. Initiatory experiences were customary, although they did not often involve—as is common outside of North America—strong imagery of skeletonization (being stripped of flesh), spirit flights, or death. These themes are found in Eskimo shamanism, which was related to Siberian shamanism.

The shaman's most widespread function was healing, and two disease theories and conjoined curing techniques were most common. First, illness was attributed to either the loss or the theft of life's vitality, or soul. The associated cure was to determine the cause of the loss and the location of the departed life form, and to rescue and restore it to the suffering person. The techniques included magical flight and ritually dramatized rescue missions. Second, illness was alternatively attributed to some object of malevolence that had penetrated the sufferer's body. The intruder might be thought of as the source of the felt pain, and the curing technique was to remove it by such means as sucking, blowing, singing, or using formulas. Other common shamanistic functions were associated with divination, serving hunting and agricultural needs, and war activities.

Death

Native Americans rarely regarded death as natural or accidental. Often only a nonviolent death in old age after a full and meaningful life is easily accepted; otherwise death requires an explanation. Inquiry and reflection help the family and acquaintances of the deceased to understand the improper actions or relationships that could explain the death, which is an occasion for reinforcing the community's social and religious principles.

Funerary practices reflect a variety of views. Whereas the Navajo regard the dead as powerful pollutants to be avoided, the Pueblo peoples believe that the dead (at least those who lived a proper life) become cloud spirits and katcinas (spirit messengers) who serve the living by bringing rain and an abundance of food. Some Native Americans, perhaps showing Christian inspiration, envisioned the afterlife as consisting of two roads—one leading to rewards for a good life, the other to punishments. The Milky Way is a common depiction among North American tribes of the actual road taken by the deceased. Caution is needed to avoid the primitivist notion of Native Americans as preeminently hunters who believe in a "happy hunting ground" afterlife.

The Individual and Society

One might suspect that the customs, procedures, and structures of a small tribal society would put constraining pressures on the individual, inhibiting personal freedom and creativity. Although Native American cultures strongly influenced individual actions, views, and characters, it does not necessarily follow that the individual suffered a loss of identity and freedom.

A culture shapes individuals and demands conformity through many institutions and structures. Kinship is a major basis for aligning relationships and activities, from marital to occupational, ceremonial, and religious. Ancestry, clan, and family roles are often defined and given religious significance by oral traditions, which establish the origins of these societal orders and their responsibilities and characters. In many cultures gender distinctions determined and limited activities ranging from work to religion; yet there was usually a balance in the division of activities, and some assumed exclusions do not exist. Women, for example, were sometimes leaders, respected elders, owners of property, and religious practitioners.

Age often determined societal roles and responsibilities, and most cultures had some form of initiation of the young, which often corresponded to the instilling of religious awareness and the acceptance of religious responsibilities. This transition was commonly effected through a formal religious rite of passage. Age sets—that is, groups of people closely related in age—were occasionally a formal base for societal distinctions. The advancement of wisdom, knowledge, and respectability was a widespread correlate of the advancement of age.

In many cultures individuals were initiated into formal religious societies, which corresponded to the culture's structure of political and religious authority. Members took on enormous responsibilities for the community. There were war societies, medicine-bundle societies, ritual and religious orders, priesthoods, and curing and medicine societies in which individuals had to conform to highly—and often very narrowly—defined roles; there were no alternatives. A Native American could not reject his or her culture and survive—much less live a meaningful life. Life virtually depended on maintaining a good standing in society.

Despite pressures for conformity, many Native Americans developed distinctive personalities and acquired considerable individuality. Status and accomplishment were measured by an individual's performance in socially defined roles. For example, warriors in many societies recounted their abilities and accomplishments in public pronouncements. Likewise, hunters publicly recalled and proclaimed their feats, and agriculturists told of their plentiful and fine crops. Food preparers were known for the delight imparted by their food; potters and weavers were distinguished by the fineness, beauty, and usefulness of their works. Shamans and medicine people often publicly displayed their spiritual powers by eating live coals, plunging their arms into boiling water, and cutting their flesh only to heal it instantly. They also told of their successes in curing, finding lost objects, and performing other tasks. While roles, occupations, and certain limitations were culturally set, these structures were also the means for developing individual personalities and enjoying freedom.

The balance between social conformity and freedom of individual development is perhaps most evident in the rites of passage. In most Native American cultures, a child had to undergo a rite of passage to become recognized as an adult and consequently to take on the privileges and responsibilities of adulthood. Although closely monitored by the elders, the ritual process often focused on the individual undergoing the initiatory experience and to that extent was shaped by that person. In the widely practiced rite of passage that involved vision questing, for both male and female initiates, the content and form of the experience were owned by the individual, and the vision therefore became a vehicle to individuality and personal distinctiveness.

In general, creativity, freedom, and individuality were found more in the exercise and perpetuation of long-established societal forms than in transforming and transcending them. Freedom was won through tradition; personhood and individuality were achieved as a dimension of societal structures.

Religion and Authority

Because of the exclusive orality of Native Americans, the character of religious authority was different from that in written religious traditions. In cultures without writing, tradition and continuity are always on the brink of extinction, since all history, experience, knowledge, and wisdom must be borne in the minds of the living. With good reason, Native Americans recognized a close connection between religious responsibility, knowledge, experience, and authority. Age was honored and was often the basis for authority because of awareness that knowledge, experience, and the accompanying wisdom are acquired only over time. Authority, especially religious authority, therefore was commonly vested in elders.

Authority was exercised in several forms, including through the structures of religious and ritual societies and through religious offices and occupations. Notable among these were the storytellers and the story elements by which the various levels of authority were proclaimed. Stories set in the primordium—in the beginning, in mythological times, when human beings and animals spoke the same language—asserted their claim to authority in their very setting and form. These temporal settings are not to be confused with an effort to establish a historical precedent or line of historical development. By proclaiming that there is no precedent to the events and knowledge revealed in the stories, the setting is a statement of authority, equivalent in some ways to the canon in literate traditions. Furthermore, especially when compared with other forms of tales and legends, stories with a mythological or primordial setting were more commonly accompanied by a strict prohibition against change or alteration when told or transmitted from one generation to the next. These creation stories probably remained remarkably stable over long periods.

Forms of authority related to specific oral traditions varied widely among Native American cultures. One example is that of Zuni oral traditions, in which an individual was designated to be Kĩaklo, the mythical figure responsible for knowing and formally telling the extensive creation-story cycle. Once every four or eight years Kĩaklo came to Zuni to tell the story. Few Zuni likely ever heard it all on one occasion; yet many storytellers retold parts of it, adding their own interpretations and applications where relevant. These second renderings held the storytelling of Kĩaklo as "canon," and they amounted to an exegetical exercise.

Religion and History

Presented here as they likely were on the eve of colonization, Native American religions are referred to in the past tense, although much of what is described still remains vital and active, and is far from bygone. It would be mistaken to assume that the only authentic Native American religions are those that preexisted European colonization—that any Native American religion that has changed is no longer authentically Native American. Such a view is tantamount to saying that Native Americans are nonhistorical, that they live in a golden era without change. While Eastern and Western religions are described in terms of history, Native American religions are often compressed not only into a common "Indian religion" but also into a timeless past.

Native Americans frequently are compared to Americans of European ancestry in a simple binary contrast centering on the category of time. They are characterized as experiencing time in cycles, as ahistoric or uninterested in making history, and as relying more on intuition and feeling than on logic and reason. Americans, on the other hand, are generally considered to experience time as linear—as a progression or decline—and seen as much interested in making history, in development, in progress. According to this logic, Americans are rational, more than intuitive or spiritual, beings. This superficial view is born as much of false imagery as of a sound characterization of the peoples in question. One might argue that there is nothing inherently geo-metric about the experience of time, and that such metaphors do more harm than good, reducing diversity and complexity to simplistic characterizations.

In a strict sense, Native Americans were not interested in history because they did not produce a written record of the past. But in nearly every other sense they were historical beings as much as any others. Their traditions and religious institutions were the instruments of development, change, and encounter with outsiders. They served as effective defenses against pressure to change, to acculturate, and to undergo radical transformation.

Despite a lack of written records, Native American religions did have histories, and a simple example demonstrates this point. While sun worship is as stereotypical of "the Indian religion" as the northern Plains warrior is of "the Indian," the sun dance, practiced across the northern Plains, has a complex history spanning the last several centuries. The Lakota, most widely associated with the sun dance, were not Plains tribes until the early eighteenth century, when they were displaced from the woodland and lake regions surrounding the Great Lakes by other tribes responding to the westward expansion of European Americans set off by colonialism along the East Coast. Arriving on the Plains and taking advantage of their new access to horses, introduced by Spanish colonists in the borderlands, the Lakota became hunters and warriors. Their strength lay in their capacity to change and adapt their historical situation to their advantage. Influenced by sedentary agriculturists along the Missouri and Mississippi rivers and their tributaries, as well as by nomadic hunters living in small bands along the eastern side of the Rocky Mountains, the Lakota newcomers developed new religious forms, and the sun dance was soon to be practiced by many tribes across the Plains. Outlawed by the Bureau of Indian Affairs in the late nineteenth century, the sun dance was revived in the mid twentieth century.

Native Americans have a strong interest in history, and stories of important events in an individual's lifetime—or, frequently, well before it—were common. Much oral tradition was based on maintaining and using history without the convenience of writing. In winter-count records, kept by some tribes, a graphic image served as a reminder of the past year's significant events. Major natural events, such as floods, earthquakes, and eclipses, served as markers by which to orient historical events.

Finally, while Christian and European influence is usually thought to coincide with the initial contact, this influence may have had an effect long before. In some areas there is evidence that years before their first actual contact with Christians, tribes had heard about and adopted certain patterns of Christianity. For example, Native Americans from the northeastern United States traveled to the northwestern United States at least a decade prior to European Americans. They told the tribes in the area about the coming "white men" and "Long Coats"—that is, Christian missionaries. Mythology and ritual incorporated even the anticipated arrival of these newcomers.

ENCOUNTERS WITH CHRISTIANITY

For many tribes, the first contact with Europeans was with their missionaries, though in the earliest period of contact it was debated whether "Indians" were sufficiently "human" to be Christianized, and often they were killed even before missionaries had their chance. Among surviving Native Americans, missionaries maintained a constant presence and often learned Native American languages. For many tribal languages missionaries were the principal linguists, writing the only grammars and dictionaries that existed.

Missionaries established the first schools among Native American communities to teach reading and writing so that the Scriptures might be read and also to provide the civilizing element thought necessary in Christianizing "the Indians." Native practices that competed with Christianity, regarded as barbaric, savage, and heathen, were often suppressed and discouraged.

The equation of religion with Christianity is strongly evidenced in the field of American religious history, which has included Native Americans only insofar as they have entered American mission history—that is, only insofar as they have become Christians. The encounter with Christianity seems to have been rather one-sided, with Native American religions not only ignored but also suppressed; Christianity has been the measure and the only acceptable religious presence. This encounter is often cited to demonstrate the evils of Christianity and the glories of the "Indian religion," and both Native Americans and European Americans have participated in the polemic. Such a position is far too superficial, leading to a misunderstanding of both missionary history and Native religious traditions.

Two areas illustrate something of the richer character of this encounter. First, many missionaries were profoundly interested in tribal customs, and much of what is known of Native American religions in the colonial period derives from their records. The French Jesuits wrote extensively of the cultures in which they lived, and their writings were collected as "Relations" sent to Paris annually from 1632 to 1674. They were published with English translation and notes in seventy-three volumes by Reuben G. Thwaites between 1896 to 1901 as *The Jesuit Relations and Allied Documents*. This remarkable material demonstrates that the Jesuits were interested in the cultures that they missionized, primarily the Iroquois, far beyond what was essential to do their job. Similar records were kept by the Franciscans in the Southwest Borderlands, but few of them have been published, and warehouses filled with these documents remain untouched in Spain.

Second, many Native Americans became Christians as a result of the missions—a victory from one point of view; a failure, from another. Unfortunately, from either point of view conversion has usually marked the end of the story, when in a sense it should serve as the beginning. The important influence of Christianity on Native American cultures and religions has been underappreciated and the acceptance of Christianity regarded as synonymous with the loss of Native American traditions.

A few examples, dating from the postcolonial period but resulting from a process initiated during the colonial period, will suggest the importance of reconsidering Native American Christianity. An Apache community sings Christian hymns during their worship service—but in the Apache language, accompanied by music sounding more Apache than European American. In 1834 a Christian hymnal was translated into Seneca; it is still used today. But the Seneca terms for God and for related Christian theological concepts reflect traditional Seneca ideas more than Christian ones. The Yaqui of Arizona perform a dramatization of the events of Easter that involves a sizable portion of the community for most of Holy Week; many are involved throughout Lent. The Yaqui encounter with Christianity dates from the early seventeenth century. Christian churches are the dominant architectural feature in most Pueblo villages. These churches are attended not only for Mass but also for dances and other tribal religious performances. At Zuni, life-size depictions of tribal religious figures were painted on the walls of the Catholic mission church in the nineteenth century. A Comanche eagle doctor in Oklahoma uses Bible verses to describe her doctoring practice. Jesus is commonly prayed to in peyote meetings.

Such examples reflect the adaptability and creativity of Native Americans in their encounters with Christianity and demonstrate how elements of Christianity were absorbed in a way that developed and enriched Native American religious traditions.

BIBLIOGRAPHY

Beck, Peggy V., and A. L. Walters. *The Sacred: Ways of Knowledge, Sources of Life.* Rev. ed. Tsaile, Ariz., 1990.

Brown, Joseph Epes. *The Spiritual Legacy of the American Indian.* New York, 1982.

Gill, Sam D. *Native American Religions: An Introduction.* Belmont, Calif., 1981.

————. *Native American Religious Action.* Columbia, S.C., 1987.

————. *Native American Traditions: Sources and Interpretations.* Belmont, Calif., 1983.

Hallowell, A. Irving. "Ojibwa Ontology, Behavior, and World View." In *Culture in History: Essays in Honor of Paul Radin,* edited by Stanley Diamond. New York, 1960.

Hertzberg, Hazel W. *The Search for an American Indian Identity: Modern Pan-Indian Movements.* Syracuse, N.Y., 1971.

Hultkrantz, Åke. *The Study of American Indian Religions.* New York, 1983.

Hymes, Dell. *"In Vain I Tried to Tell You": Essays in Native American Ethnopoetics.* Philadelphia, 1981.

Kroeber, Karl, ed. *Traditional Literatures of the American Indian: Texts and Interpretations.* Lincoln, Neb., 1981.

Michaelsen, Robert S. "The Significance of the American Indian Religious Freedom Act of 1978." *Journal of the American Academy of Religion* 52 (1984): 93–115.

Murdock, George P., and Timothy J. O'Leary. *Ethnographic Bibliography of North America.* 4th ed. New Haven, Conn., 1975.

Ortiz, Alfonso. *The Tewa World: Space, Time, Being, and Becoming in a Pueblo Society.* Chicago, 1969.

Sturtevant, William C., ed. *Handbook of North American Indians.* Washington, D.C., 1978–.

Thompson, Stith. *Tales of the North American Indians.* Cambridge, Mass., 1929.

Thwaites, Reuben G., ed. *The Jesuit Relations and Allied Documents.* 73 vols. Cleveland, Ohio, 1896–1901.

Sam D. Gill

SEE ALSO **The First Americans; Indian-Colonist Conflicts and Alliances; Literature; Medical Practice; Native American Aesthetics;** and **Repeopling the Land;** and various essays in the sections THE ARTS and RACIAL INTERACTION.

MAGIC AND WITCHCRAFT

THE BELIEFS AND PRACTICES of magic, witchcraft, and witch-hunting were widely present in seventeenth-century America. The colonists of New France and New Spain brought them from Europe, as did the English who settled in the Chesapeake, New England, the middle colonies, and the lower South. Native Americans and the Africans who were forcibly transported to the New World had traditions of their own concerning prophecy, spirits, and magic.

Only in New England did witch-hunting play a significant role in the social system. A scattering of accusations and prosecutions occurred in the middle and southern colonies; in two, Virginia and Bermuda, there were multiple executions. Everywhere the process of witch-hunting came to an end by the close of the seventeenth century. Popular lore survived much longer, as did a social role for persons who practiced healing, located lost objects, and told fortunes.

No single definition of magic can encompass the range of meanings that it had for the several cultures that existed side by side in early America. From a western European perspective, magic designates ideas about the supernatural that seem contradictory to religious orthodoxy; in anthropologies that rest on schemes of evolution through stages, it means a way of thinking about nature and the supernatural that is regarded as more primitive than religion. Increasingly, however, the boundary between magic and religion is being understood by historians and anthropologists as permeable and fluid. The apparent antagonism between magic and science has given way to the recognition that in early modern Europe magic had close connections with experimental and theoretical science. So too in the case of witch-hunting and witchcraft, historians have shown that accusations of witchcraft arose out of the tensions and conflicts of everyday life; witch-hunting was a recurring aspect of social relationships.

THE EUROPEAN BACKGROUND

The Origins of Magic

A useful definition of magic, offered by Valerie Flint, is "the exercise of a preternatural control over nature by human beings, with the assistance of forces more powerful than they." Belief in such a phenomenon emerged very early in world history and became prominent in antiquity among the Greeks and Romans. The cultures of the Near and Middle East were rich sources of magic and left their mark on the Old Testament, which refers to sorcery, divination, wizards, shape-shifting, and enchantments. I Sam. 28:8–25 tells of King Saul consulting the witch of Endor, who conjured up the spirit of the dead Samuel to give him advice. Other forms of magic included astrology and alchemy. Astrology, which rested on the principle that extraterrestrial

653

bodies exerted power over nature, involved the prediction of natural events and human fate (judicial astrology). Alchemy, a form of chemistry, concerned the transmutation of baser metals into gold and the search for the alkahest, or universal solvent. Alchemy and astrology may be considered branches of occult science. The word *occult* in its root sense means hidden; by connotation it refers to knowledge that is mysterious and esoteric. According to tradition, the occult originated in Egypt.

Even in the ancient world, some of these beliefs were troubling; the writers of the Old Testament described God as condemning divination and sorcery, and Exod. 22:18 states, "Thou shalt not suffer a witch to live." The rise of Christianity added greatly to the tensions between magic and acceptable beliefs. The New Testament describes a trial of magic between Peter and Simon Magus (Acts 8:9–24); in this and other contests, persons described as "magi" always lose. From cults of the period, Christianity absorbed the concept of demons who possess supernatural power and use it to make humans suffer. Some early Christian writers blended the concept of evil demons with that of magic. Always the church condemned demons and their *maleficia* (evil acts) while rejecting astrology as contrary to the providence of God. Yet the early church also acknowledged the reality of acts that seem very close to being magic, like shape-changing and prophetic dreams. It renamed such events "*miracula*" and "wonders."

This mixture of *miracula* and *maleficia* was inherited by the Middle Ages. As that epoch gave way to the Renaissance and Reformation, there was a startling revival of magic initiated by persons who proposed using the occult to achieve immortal perfection and who attempted a synthesis of esoteric lore drawn from astrology, mathematics, the cabala, hermetic philosophy, alchemy, and Neoplatonism. Forerunners of this movement in the early sixteenth century included Cornelius Agrippa, the mythical Hermes Trismegistus, and the physician-philosopher Paracelsus, whose theory of medicine involved Neoplatonist principles. Important figures in the resynthesizing of hermetic traditions included the Italians Marsilio Ficino and Pico della Mirandola and the English mathematician John Dee, who may have helped to found the Rosicrucians.

Dee was a controversial figure who spent time in prison. Much less controversial was the low version of astrology that was popularized through continental and English almanacs. Almanacs, issued annually to serve as calendars, were among the best-selling publications in seventeenth-century England. Many of them contained predictions based on astrology; some included the image of the man of signs, which linked parts of the body to the signs of the zodiac. Other forms of magic also became broadly popular.

The Protestant reformers were uneasy with both high and popular magic. John Calvin denounced judicial astrology; the English minister William Perkins called for a purified almanac. Protestants accused Catholics of perpetuating magic and superstition, citing, for example, the rite of exorcism (which Protestants rejected) and the belief that saints' relics could work miracles. Protestantism discarded many of the accommodations that Catholicism had forged between magic and religion.

Yet Protestants held onto magical ideas because of the premise, still credible, that the natural world was subject to preternatural forces. Stories were told of Protestant martyrs who foretold the future. Stories also circulated of "strange" and "wondrous" events, as of apparitions in the sky, "monstrous" births, and shape-changing devils. This lore was gathered up in books like Thomas Beard's *The Theatre of Gods Judgments* (1597). New England minister Increase Mather compiled a similar collection, *An Essay for the Recording of Illustrious Providences* (1684).

Witchcraft and the Devil's Pact

Protestants and Catholics agreed, moreover, on the existence of witches and witchcraft. In the centuries just before the Reformation, the concept of "witch" underwent a crucial change. An older lore, still plausible to many in the Renaissance, linked witchcraft to image magic (the infliction of harm upon someone by manipulating a puppet), to the sexual lusts of demons known as incubi and succubi (known in England as a witch's "familiars"), and to night gatherings attended by demons and the witches they transported through the air. To these older beliefs was joined in the fourteenth and fifteenth centuries the assertion that witches were apostates and heretics who signed a compact with the devil (see Isa. 28:15) to establish a new society in which every form of order was inverted, as in sexual license and the witches' Sabbath. It was commonly assumed that the devil sealed this compact by imprinting a special mark on the witch's body.

In the Christian theology of these times, the devil was regarded as the supreme opponent of God. Behind this single word lies a complex series of references in the Old and New Testament to dragons, fallen angels, Beelzebub, and archfiends. By the end of the Middle Ages, these figures had been largely replaced by the Prince of Evil who, although ultimately under the control of God, was ever conspiring to destroy the community of believing Christians.

Demonologists who claimed to be skilled in witch-finding spun out elaborate descriptions of the devil and his minions. Two German Dominicans, Heinrich Kramer and Jacob Sprenger, both experienced inquisitors, wrote one such codification, the *Malleus Maleficarum,* or "Devil's Hammer" (ca. 1486), a text that is notable for the bias it displays against women, whose sexuality is depicted as especially threatening. The *Malleus* and its successors also advised on the procedures to follow in a judicial trial. A handful of writers criticized the demonologists; the most vigorous critic was the Englishman Reginald Scot, author of *The Discovery of Witchcraft* (1584).

The figure of the witch as agent of the devil threatened Christian orthodoxy. In the fourteenth and fifteenth centuries, the Catholic Inquisition (a general name for procedures aimed at uncovering and eliminating heresy) became active in detecting witches. But the heyday of the great witch-hunts was the sixteenth and seventeenth centuries, when secular courts—backed by the civil state—took on the task of eradicating witches and suppressing heresy. Not all of Europe was equally affected by these witch-hunts. Nor can it be said that Catholics were more zealous than Protestants, or vice versa. In the older literature, the toll of those who died in the witch-hunts was vastly exaggerated. It is likely that the total approached one hundred thousand, not the millions that are sometimes suggested. The regions where the most intensive witch-hunts occurred were France (especially in the southeast and southwest), Germany, Switzerland, and Poland. Trials occurred in the Scandinavian countries, eastern Europe, and Russia. The parts of Europe that came under Spanish rule and that constitute present-day Italy experienced relatively little witch-hunting; here, church courts had jurisdiction. In some episodes the victims numbered in the hundreds, and the situation approached mass panic. But much of the activity was localized and small-scale. Prosecution was intermittent, not continuous; a graph of the trials over time would display sharp peaks and valleys.

The statistics for England and Scotland deserve particular attention. Relative to the population, the number of executions in Scotland was far higher than in England, where the incidence was quite low compared to most of Europe. The first great wave of witch-hunting in Scotland occurred in 1591; the period of the most sustained activity fell between 1640 and 1662, after which prosecution steadily declined, to vanish altogether in the early eighteenth century. In England witch-hunting commenced slightly later and began to subside as early as the 1620s, though the mid 1640s brought a burst of executions. The last execution in England occurred in 1685, and the last recorded witch trial was held in 1717; in 1736 the law was changed so that witchcraft (or pretensions to perform the same) became an instance of fraud.

In England, as elsewhere, the great witch-hunts arose when magistrates and clergy transformed the suspicions and conflicts of rural society into evidence of a devil's conspiracy. A key step was the 1604 "Act against Conjuration, Witchcraft, and Dealing with Evil and Wicked Spirits." Previously, Keith Thomas observes, witchcraft had been understood as "an activity—doing harm to others by supernatural means—not a belief or heresy." It had been made a felony in 1542, but, Thomas notes, on the grounds of "hostility to the community, rather than . . . relations with the devil as such." The new law made it a felony to "consult, covenant with, entertain, employ, feed, or reward any evil and wicked spirit." Even under the new statute, however, most accusations of witchcraft continued to involve image magic, curses, and similar acts that were alleged to harm persons and their goods. Only in extraordinary witch-hunts such as those conducted in 1645 and 1646 by the professional witch-finder Matthew Hopkins did the devil's compact play a major role. Otherwise, witchcraft and witch-hunting in Tudor-Stuart England involved the traditional lore of *maleficium*.

The distinction between witchcraft as heresy and witchcraft as acts of harm to others is crucial to understanding the social and intellectual history of witch-hunting. The lore of witches as persons who did harmful things antedated the concept of the devil's pact. This lore was an aspect of popular culture and oral tradition; it flourished in rural societies along with a closely related lore connected with healing, fortune-telling, and discovering lost objects. These abilities were credible to peasants and villagers who welcomed any services that lessened the perils and inexplicable suffering that were part of everyday life. The persons who performed these services (*devins* in France, "cunning persons" in England) were accepted and even welcomed for their services. Yet toleration was tinged with suspicion, for the power to heal implied its opposite, the power to harm. It should not surprise us that "cunning people" were frequently accused of *maleficium*.

But the majority of accusations sprang from tensions between neighbors in rural communities. Villagers used the name "witch" for persons with whom they had quarreled or who seemed to threaten them in some respect. This name-calling, though it sometimes led to lynchings, did not produce witch-hunts. The latter occurred when secular and ecclesiastical courts moved in and imposed the concept of the devil's pact on local conflicts. The key testimony became confessions that were sometimes elicited by torture. The essential difference between the traditional lore and the beliefs acted on by the civil courts had to do with heresy and the devil: ordinary people talked about harmful acts, but the clergy and the courts focused on affiliation with the devil.

Why should heresy in the form of witchcraft suddenly have become so threatening? Some historians argue that the sixteenth and seventeenth centuries were a period of rapid social change, even of crisis, and that witch-hunting represents a response to social strain. According to one version of this argument, traditional village culture, with its norm of charity to neighbors, was in transition to an ethos of possessive individualism. Others have suggested that witch-hunting was linked to the newly emerging modern state, with its apparatus of legal rationality. It has also been argued that certain groups were using the hunts to extend their power over those who were marginal, disaffected, or of the lower classes; for example, some assert that orthodox Christians were attempting to erase elements of pagan folklore that lingered among a half-Christianized peasantry. Still other scholars have employed the sociology of deviance and regard witch-hunting as a means by which societies exclude outsiders. The weakness of these last two interpretations is that they ignore the long history of village conflicts out of which prosecutions arose (a history lasting, in some regions of Europe, well into the modern period), impose too much rationality on a process that was very intermittent, and overlook the disagreement among the upper classes about how to deal with local accusations. The strength of all these interpretations is that they have to do with order and disorder; in early modern Europe, the figure of the witch embodied wide-ranging fears of disorder, be it sexual, religious, political, or economic. Witchcraft was seen as a phenomenon that turned things upside down.

MAGIC, WITCHCRAFT, AND WITCH-HUNTING IN THE NEW WORLD

Magic, High and Low

Most of these interpretations are relevant to the history of witch-hunting in the New World. The major difference is that paganism, and the extreme opposition between magic and religion, were not reproduced on this side of the Atlantic. Magic made its way to the New World along with witchcraft and witch-hunting. By 1680 American almanacs included the man of signs and snippets of astrological lore. Many eighteenth-century almanacs continued to print such lore. Prognostications (predictions of the future) were another feature of the almanac. The lore of healing and fortune-telling also reappeared in America. Here as in Europe, "cunning people" were summoned to help women in childbirth and to advise on missing persons and future husbands. There is no way of knowing how many people played this role in the colonies. What is certain is that those who did were viewed ambiguously as both good and bad; of one such woman in New England, who faced accusations of having harmed her neighbors by witchcraft, a witness "did wonder that she should be both a healing and a destroying witch." A similar ambiguity surrounded perceptions of prophesying. It was widely believed in the seventeenth century that the Holy Spirit could enable someone to witness to God's purposes. Yet the Puritans rejected prophecy when it was performed by radicals like the Quakers and Anne Hutchinson. Associating religious heresy with illicit sexuality, and both of these with witchcraft, a Massachusetts court in 1656 ordered two Quaker women searched for witch marks.

The lore of high magic, or the occult, was discussed among a few persons in seventeenth-century New England. John Winthrop, Jr. (son of the famous governor of Massachusetts and himself a governor of Connecticut), began to acquire books on alchemy as early as the 1630s and eventually assembled an extraordinary collection. In the early 1640s, he became active in an iron-mining venture in Massachusetts that may also have involved a search for more esoteric metals. Friends who shared his speculations in alchemy and Paracelsean medicine included Robert Child and George Stirk (or Starkey), both of whom passed briefly through New England. A largely unrelated vein of esoteric lore entered Pennsylvania in the late seventeenth and eighteenth centuries via the migration of Johann Kelpius and other Germans who, in a tradition that dates back to Paracelsus, were attracted to the mystical and perfectionist aspects of hermeticism. Similarly the Pietist movement within German Protestantism helped to convey aspects of hermetic and alchemical lore to the colonies. In the second half of the eighteenth century yet another kind of magic, a lore of treasure hunting, began to inspire a rash of diggings in New England and the middle states. Some treasure seekers used enchanted stones, or seerstones, to find buried gold, none of which was ever recovered.

When we add to these expressions of magic those of countermagic, as in nailing horseshoes over doors, it becomes plain that magical beliefs and practices were widely diffused. In the case of someone like John Winthrop, Jr., an interest in esoteric magic coexisted with orthodox Protestantism. As in Europe, so in the New World,

religion and magic were often intertwined. Yet some clergy felt threatened by the "cunning people." The Boston minister Increase Mather condemned countermagic in writings of the 1680s; his son and fellow minister Cotton denounced astrology.

Witchcraft in New Spain and New France

At the close of the sixteenth century, the Spanish in Mexico began to establish permanent settlements in the province of New Mexico. Franciscans rapidly took up the task of converting the Pueblo Indians to Christianity. These missionaries saw witchcraft and sorcery at work in the conflict between the two cultures and attempted to eradicate such practices. That process resulted in violence, as in 1675 when four Indians were hanged, several dozen whipped and enslaved, and others jailed for practicing sorcery and killing seven missionaries. The Indians retaliated in the Pueblo Revolt of 1680, a defeat for the Spanish that was interpreted as the work of the devil.

Before and after the revolt, cases of witchcraft were investigated by missionaries and officials of the Catholic church. An early seventeenth-century case involved a wagon-train driver, Luís de Rivera, who confessed to entering into a compact with the devil. Taken to Mexico City for trial, he was released with only the obligation of modest penance. Several other cases that came before the mission church had to do with the complex relationship between Native peoples and the colonists. As late as 1800, illness or death among the missionaries was occasionally attributed to enchantments performed by the Pueblos. Other accusations of witchcraft grew out of social tensions within the colonial settlements. In general the church and the civil government dismissed these accusations as unfounded. Far more consequential was the witchcraft that was institutionalized among the Indians, who sometimes executed suspected witches among their ranks. It is possible that executions occurred as recently as 1900.

The Catholic religious orders that participated in the colonization of New France were well aware of the possibility of sorcery and witchcraft; as in New Spain and the British colonies, the French colonizers encountered Native American cultures in which sorcery, divination, and other forms of magic (both for good and for evil) were widely practiced. The missionaries labored to eradicate such practices and the beliefs behind them. Within their own settlements, the French occasionally had to deal with the phenomena of specters and demons. Individuals were occasionally accused of sorcery; two persons were ordered banished from their parishes as a result of such accusations, and on occasion the Conseil Supérieur (Superior Council), the appeals court, ordered that a suspect be kept under surveillance for a year. The low incidence of cases may be related to the shortage of women in seventeenth-century New France; more certainly, it is connected to the workings of the legal system, where no one was charged with a crime before a judge had made an investigation. The response of the church tended to be an intensified routine of prayer and other spiritual exercises. In France itself witch-hunting effectively ended during the 1680s.

Witchcraft in Virginia, Bermuda, and New York

Outside New England the most active naming of suspected witches occurred in Virginia and Bermuda. The surviving court records from Virginia indicate that between 1627 and 1705, nine cases came before the courts of persons accused of being witches; in another ten cases persons sued for defamation, with the majority of such suits coming after 1668. Only a single person—William Harding of Northumberland County in 1655—seems to have been convicted; his punishment consisted of whipping and banishment. The swimming test (an innocent person was supposed to sink in water) was applied in the last of the Virginia cases in 1705. Unique to the Virginia records are three reports of shipboard executions of women who reputedly were witches.

Witch-hunting in the island colony of Bermuda claimed its first victim, Jean Gardiner, executed in 1651. She was subjected to the usual search for witch marks and the swimming test, which she failed. John Middleton, executed in 1653, made a confession not to being in covenant with the devil but to committing other "sins," including disobedience to his parents and stealing turkeys. Two more women were executed in the 1650s. In all, by 1696 some twenty-three persons had been accused or had complained of defamation, with most of the court cases ending in dismissal.

During the period of Dutch rule in what became New York, the town of Easthampton, which was colonized by English settlers moving south from New England, indicted a woman for witchcraft; she was tried in Connecticut and acquitted. In 1665, the year after the English Conquest, a court heard the case of Ralph and Mary Hall; they were eventually acquitted. In 1670 Katherine Harrison, who had previously been accused of witchcraft while living in Connecticut, was investigated anew but not charged. A Swedish woman was tried and eventually acquitted in Pennsylvania in 1683. Occasional references to accusations may be found in the records of other colonies.

New England

Alice (or Alse) Young of Windsor, Connecticut, was the first person in New England to be executed for allegedly being a witch. A year later, in 1648, Mary Johnson of Wethersfield, Connecticut, confessed to "familiarity with the devil" and was executed. So was Margaret Jones of Charlestown, a healer and fortune-teller. By 1656 another nine persons had been tried, found guilty, and executed; others had been brought to trial but not convicted; and in still other cases, people had filed suit for defamation on the grounds of being falsely accused by their neighbors. Between 1656 and 1663, three more persons were executed. Thereafter, although juries pronounced several persons guilty, no court carried out the death penalty until 1688, when Goody Glover, an Irishwoman, was executed in Boston. Altogether perhaps as many as one hundred persons were accused of being witches (a figure that includes cases of defamation) in Massachusetts, Connecticut, and the then-independent colonies of Plymouth (which was merged into Massachusetts in 1691) and New Haven (which became part of Connecticut in 1665).

Only in Hartford, Connecticut, did someone's confession unleash multiple accusations and convictions. A young woman named Ann Cole blamed her fits of "possession" on an older woman who lived next door, Rebecca Greensmith. When she was questioned, Mrs. Greensmith described meeting with the devil and implicated her husband and several others in witch gatherings. Ann Cole also cried out against Elizabeth Seager. Suspicion eventually extended to at least nine more adults. The Greensmiths and one other person were executed, but the governor of Connecticut refused to carry out the jury's guilty verdict in the case of Elizabeth Seager.

Certain women lived for years under a cloud of suspicion. Mary Parsons of Northampton was twice accused of witchcraft, first in 1656 (she then sued for defamation) and a second time in 1674, when members of the same family that denounced Mary Parsons in 1656 blamed her for the death of a daughter. The impoverished Eunice Cole of Salisbury and Hampton, New Hampshire, was in and out of jail, or before the courts, for a period of twenty-five years. Katherine Harrison of Wethersfield, Connecticut, had a reputation as a fortune-teller and a healer; indicted and tried in 1669, she was ordered to leave the colony. Moving to New York, she was again complained against for witchcraft.

The testimony that was offered in the courts involved conflicts and misfortune. Witnesses also reiterated some of the traditional lore of witchcraft and witch-hunting. Witches came at night to trouble people in their sleep. It was alleged that some of the accused were attended by "familiars" in the form of small animals or birds. Cats, dogs, birds, and snakes appeared and disappeared mysteriously, and it was commonly reported that the suspected witch felt the blow if someone hit one of these shape-changing creatures. Women suspects were often searched for witch marks and witch teats (supposedly sucked by the "familiar"), though what constituted a mark was a matter of debate and confusion. The most frequent themes were sickness and death. Farm animals seemed highly vulnerable. So were very young children. A traditional connection between witches and infanticide runs through these cases. Rarely did a witness refer directly to the devil. In general the people who testified lived in the same community as the accused.

Another side of witchcraft in New England was the experience that contemporaries named diabolical possession. It consisted of "strange fits" manifested in bizarre contortions of the body. Physicians tried to cure these fits using natural remedies; when these failed to work, the alternative was to assume that the devil was attempting to control the person, a diagnosis supported by unusual forms of speech coming from the possessed. (Speaking in a deep voice, sixteen-year-old Elizabeth Knapp called her minister a "great rogue.") Those who fell into this condition were, with rare exceptions, young women and children. They were asked to identify the witches who participated in afflicting them. As in the Hartford witch-hunt, the response to these questions could touch off a series of accusations.

The Salem Witch-Hunt. During the winter of 1691 to 1692, certain children and young women in Salem Village (now Danvers), Massachusetts, began to experience the symptoms of diabolical possession. About this time there may have been some experimenting with magic and countermagic; one such experiment, the baking of a witch-cake (made from the urine of a suspected witch), led to the questioning of Tituba, a Carib Indian slave living in the household of the village's minister. She confessed to being in league with the devil and named two confederates. Under the leadership of the minister, Samuel Parris, the community initially employed the spiritual remedies of penitential prayer and fasting. But as the symptoms of the possessed intensified, arrests began in late February. The local magistrates examined some of the accused in March and early April. A former minister, George Burroughs, was brought back from Maine and examined in May. On 2 June a special Court of Oyer and Terminer convened in Salem Town and condemned Bridget Bishop to be executed by hanging; she died on 10 June. Five others were convicted by the end of June and were executed on 19 July.

Village feuds, reputations as "cunning people," and histories of difficulties with the law loom in the background of the accused in the early phases of the witch-hunt. Meanwhile the witch-hunt had spread to adjacent towns, especially Andover, where two of the "afflicted" girls came in early July to play the role of witch-finder at the request of a man whose wife was sick. The result was a veritable explosion of accusations and confessions. Further executions occurred on 29 July, 19 August, and 22 September for a cumulative total of nineteen (five men and fourteen women); Martha Corey's husband, Giles, died as a consequence of a procedure known as *peine forte et dure* (a slow crushing with weights), intended to make him participate in a trial. Several others died while in prison.

Even before the court heard its first case, the legal process—that is, the standards of evidence—was beginning to trouble certain ministers and laymen. During the trials themselves, dozens of ordinary people came forward to defend their neighbors. In October the governor of Massachusetts, Sir William Phips, ordered the court dissolved. Though the regular court convened in January 1693 and sentenced three more persons to death, no further executions occurred; those still in prison or under sentence (they numbered more than one hundred) were released under a general pardon. In all some 250 persons were named as possible witches. The great majority lived in towns in Essex County other than Salem and Salem Village.

The same year accusations of witchcraft spread through the Connecticut town of Fairfield. Mercy Disborough was convicted; five others were acquitted or, though accused, not brought to trial. A group of ministers questioned some of the evidence against Disborough, as did three of the magistrates. The government eventually reprieved her.

The Salem witch-hunt was unique in size. Yet in all but two respects, it grew out of and resembled the usual process of witch-hunting. Several of the victims had previously been accused of witchcraft. Two or three had reputations as healers and fortune-tellers. Witnesses recited the traditional lore of apparitions, shape-changing animals, and witches' meetings in the woods; they also dredged up old quarrels. What was special to the Salem witch-hunt was the contagious voicing of confessions and the assumption, argued by Samuel Parris, Cotton Mather, and others in their sermons that the devil had organized a conspiracy against the kingdom of Christ.

The feeling that the victims of the hunt were innocent became prevalent as soon as the trials had ended. Robert Calef, a resident of Boston, denounced witch-hunting in general and Cotton Mather in particular in *More Wonders of the Invisible World* (1700), a book that included certain documents exposing the procedures of the court. Occurring at the very end of the cycle of witch-hunting in Europe, the Salem witch-hunt was immediately publicized in ways that ensured its notoriety.

For all intents and purposes, organized witch-hunting came to an end in New England in 1693. A woman was indicted in Connecticut in 1697, and local fears and name-calling related to witchcraft occasionally reached the courts for another twenty years. But the authorities, both civil and clerical, were no longer confident that they could detect the work of the devil. By the early decades of the eighteenth century, the more educated were discarding the concept of witchcraft. The traditional lore lingered on, though without the same power to affect everyday life.

Underlying Patterns

Religious Underpinnings. Witchcraft and witch-hunting were related to broader patterns of values and social structure. Organized religion supported the witch-hunts. The ministers did not originate accusations of witchcraft—these welled up from conflicts and tensions among neighbors—but they lent the sanction of theology to the concept of the devil's pact. Charles Upham is among the historians who have laid the blame for witch-hunting in New England at the feet of Puritanism, citing its supposed literalism regarding the Bible and its aggravated concern with purity and evil. Yet witch-hunting occurred with as great or greater intensity in societies that were Catholic. It may be indicative that no trials occurred in Rhode Island, the one New England colony with religious pluralism and few clergy. What can be said for certain of the clergy is that it criticized popular lore and urged the courts to ignore such folk practices as the swimming test. The ministers also told their congregations that witchcraft and possession represented a struggle between good and evil, Christ and Satan, and urged them to overcome the devil by engaging in the spiritual exercises of prayer, fasting, and self-examination. Thus the minister who tended to sixteen-year-old Elizabeth Knapp in New England urged her to repent of secret sins. That so many people confessed to being tempted by the devil was related to the guilt and frustration that developed as a consequence of the ministers' expectations.

660

Despite the claims of nineteenth-century writers who often accused Cotton Mather of instigating the witch-hunt, Mather did not participate in any of the trials. In 1688 he claimed to have healed the most severely possessed of the Goodwin children of Boston by using the remedies of fasting and prayer. In 1692 he applied these same remedies to a young woman in Boston, and in the following year to yet another; he had also suggested taking the "aflicted" girls of Salem Village into his care. On each of these occasions, he refused to make public the names of those the possessed accused of afflicting them. This restraint, his marked preference for spiritual healings, and the warnings he and his father issued against judicial excesses deserve to be acknowledged. Yet he and his father defended the executions as justified by the evidence presented to the court, and a few contemporaries went far beyond him in criticizing the process of witch-hunting.

Religion contributed to a mentality of "wonder." When people saw apparitions and shape-changing black dogs, or said that the devil spoke to them, such testimony was credible. For the colonists, the natural forces at work in the world were overlain by and interwoven with moral, spiritual, and supernatural forces. It was always possible for everyday life to be interrupted by preternatural events, or wonders. A wonder was any unexpected event that reminded people of the radical contingency of their existence—of how insecure they were, and how vulnerable to divine judgment. At a deeper level still, the mentality of wonder drew on pre-Christian notions of nature as animate, or charged with spirits. What seem to us to be delusions were credible to people who thought of the relationship between the physical and the spiritual as plastic and open-ended.

Social Causes. Witch-hunting arose when social relationships were affected by misfortune. In case after case, village people accused neighbors of doing them harm—making them or their children sick, causing cattle and chickens to die, inducing the symptoms of possession. A general rule for understanding such accusations is that the suspected witch and her accuser had quarreled, or that the accuser had refused to per-

form a service for the witch. When angry words were followed by misfortune (an accident or sudden illness), it seemed plausible to attribute the event to vengeful anger. As a man who observed the Salem witch-hunt concluded, "If after anger between neighbors mischief followed, this oft bred suspicion of witchcraft in the matter."

In Salem Village a long history of quarrels over land, the organization of a church, ecclesiastical policy, and obligations to the minister reached their climax in the witch-hunt. According to an older interpretation, now no longer credible, the village minister, Samuel Parris, manipulated the accusations to strike back at his opponents. Paul Boyer and Stephen Nissenbaum have suggested that some of the families in Salem Village were falling behind economically as rural society began the transition to capitalism, and that the unease of these families was fuel to the fire of accusations. Hostility to religious outsiders may have been another factor.

The classic stereotype of the witch as a quarrelsome old hag contains further clues to patterns in the social history of witchcraft. The most important concerns gender. The cry of "witch" was raised against women far more often than against men. The raw numbers work out to a ratio of better than four to one, essentially the same ratio as in the European witch-hunts. When historians have compared the penalties imposed on women and men, further differences emerge; the men were less likely to be tried and convicted, and their sentences were less severe. Moreover, many of the men were husbands or sons of women suspects.

The vulnerability of women stemmed in part from traditional attitudes about women's sexuality and their role as mothers. In the New England cases, the references to a sexual relationship between women witches and the devil are relatively scant in comparison with those in some of the European witch-hunts. Yet the image of women as especially licentious played a role, as did tensions in the mother-child relationship. According to tradition witches were seen as especially threatening to infants and young children. Most of the women accused of being witches were over the age of forty, a pattern that may indicate other psychosocial tensions.

A normative rule in western culture during these centuries was that women were subordinate to men. Witch-hunting was a means of reaffirming this rule at a time when Protestantism was assigning to women a new importance within the household and when the system of inheritance was making some women economically independent. In New England these persons of independent means were vulnerable to accusations of witchcraft. So, in general, were widows who lacked male defenders, those who practiced healing, and anyone who challenged male authority. Carol Karlsen has argued that young women became possessed because of the strains they experienced in trying to reconcile the expected role for women with the possibilities for independence.

According to the traditional stereotype, the female witch was an impoverished troublemaker. These characteristics fit some victims of witch-hunting in New England. Within the most carefully studied group, the persons accused of witchcraft in Essex County, Massachusetts, some had frequently challenged the established authorities and become defendants in the civil courts. When witnesses described someone as "railing and scolding," they may have been accurate. Yet such testimony also flowed from a general uneasiness about anger in a society where the official ethics emphasized fellowship and charity. Several victims of the witch-hunts were impoverished, and in general (though with significant exceptions) the suspects were persons of lower economic status. All in all, however, the most reliable predictors of who would be accused of witchcraft are gender, age, and economic independence.

Were there any "real" witches in New England, persons who practiced the black arts? According to an interpretation that many historians regard as fanciful, an underground cult organized around covens and practicing devil worship (or perhaps pagan fertility rites focused on a goat-devil) had existed for centuries in Europe. Those who propose the existence of this cult regard the witches' Sabbath as having actually occurred. Most historians insist that tales of the witches' Sabbath were pure fantasy. This would surely seem the case for New England. When authorities searched the home of Goody Glover, an old woman accused in 1688 of tormenting four children in the Goodwin family of Boston,

they apparently found "several small images, or puppets, or babies, made of ragg"; she then confessed "that the way to torment the objects of her malice, was by wetting of her finger with her spittle, and stroking of these little images." Witnesses reported finding similar images among the possessions of Bridget Bishop of Salem Village. Whether these statements are credible remains in doubt. On the other hand, it is certain that ordinary people used curses, charms, and countermagic; Dorcas Hoar, a fortune-teller who was executed in 1692, consulted a book of palmistry. And since ordinary people regarded these forms of magic as efficacious, it is possible that threats and curses voiced by a suspected witch could affect another person's state of health. In this special sense, witchcraft was real.

THE LEGAL PROCESS

In early America, as in early modern Europe, civil courts conducted witch-hunts. The exceptions to this rule were Spain and Italy, where ecclesiastical courts investigated accusations of witchcraft. The transition from ecclesiastical to secular jurisdiction, which in most parts of Europe was occurring in the fifteenth and sixteenth centuries, set the stage for massive prosecutions to unfold, for the secular authorities were far more aggressive in securing convictions and in enlarging the scope of witch-hunts.

At the same time, the legal process usually resulted in failure to charge a suspect or in acquittal. The ratio varied over time and in different places, but the single conviction out of nine trials in seventeenth-century Virginia is characteristic. Prior to 1692 the rate of conviction in New England was about 17 percent; in the Salem witch-hunt, some one out of ten persons named as witches were convicted, and in Fairfield that same year, the one conviction (out of eleven accusations) was never carried out. The ratio was considerably higher in most parts of Europe, but there as in early America the point still holds that the judicial system distanced itself from the anger, ill-will, and folklore of the village community. In general the higher or more centralized the court, the less the likelihood of conviction.

Witchcraft was a capital crime. The statute enacted by Massachusetts in 1641 and reiterated in the law codes of the other New England colonies was succinct: "If any man or woman be a witch (that is hath or consulteth with a familiar spirit) they shall be put to death." No doubt with the severity of the sentence in mind and a due regard to procedures and rules, judges distinguished between presumptive and convictive evidence. Presumptive evidence encompassed the lore of witchcraft and much of what was attributed to the stereotypical witch—apparitions, extraordinary feats of strength, a malicious temperament, cursing, and the like. Convictive evidence had to do with the relationship between the devil and the witch, a relationship that, by definition, was hidden or invisible. Rarely if ever was a person observed performing acts of witchcraft; instead, the evidence consisted of sightings of apparitions and familiars, discoveries of the witch's teat, the tormented gestures of the possessed, and the fantasies of persons who confessed. Confession was the most important evidence of the devil's pact, though there could be problems in evaluating statements of this kind.

What counted as evidence, and especially evidence sufficient to impose the penalty of death, was disputed throughout the seventeenth century in England and America. A further complication was the rule in capital cases in New England that any action leading to conviction had to be observed by two witnesses. Early in the century two distinguished English ministers, William Perkins and Richard Bernard, both affiliated with the Puritan movement, advised against accepting certain aspects of the traditional lore and emphasized the importance of confession. Ministers and magistrates in New England drew on this criticism in 1662 during the Hartford witch-hunt, in 1692 during the Fairfield episode, and yet again in response to the waves of accusations taking place in Salem. Of special significance at Salem was testimony describing the appearance of someone in the form of an apparition, or specter. In June, and again in October, various ministers warned against relying on such evidence on the ground that the devil could impersonate someone who was innocent; the basis of guilt, they argued, "ought certainly to be more considerable, than barely the accused persons being represented by a specter unto the afflicted." Certain ministers, among them Increase Mather, also recommended against using as evidence the dramatic responses of the afflicted to the touch and gaze of suspected witches. Always at hand was the possibility of a medical diagnosis of possession as a form of mental illness or as consisting of fantasies stemming from disordered thinking.

At the moment that accusations began to circulate in Salem Village, political and legal institutions were in limbo as Massachusetts Bay awaited the new charter granted by William III and the man the king had appointed as governor, Sir William Phips. Arriving in May with the charter, Phips responded to the crisis by appointing nine persons, headed by the Deputy Governor William Stoughton, to a special Court of Oyer and Terminer. The deliberations of the judges do not survive, but the records include depositions by scores of witnesses (who produced the same kinds of evidence that had characterized witch-hunting in previous cases) and examples of questioning from the bench. The persons who confessed were not executed, perhaps because the court hoped to gain more information from them. In many of the European trials, torture was often the means of eliciting confessions. English common law, which also prevailed in New England, did not sanction torture, put the burden of judgment on a jury, and defined witchcraft as a civil crime. This last circumstance explains why convicted witches in New England were hanged, not burned. Whether torture was used in New England is partly a matter of definition, but without question the court sanctioned abusive treatment of a few male suspects in 1692.

MAGIC AND WITCHCRAFT IN THE AFRICAN-AMERICAN COMMUNITY

Traditional African religion encompassed spiritual methods of healing that were exercised by diviners and healers. The power to heal was closely related to the power of doing harm, or performing acts of witchcraft. The Africans who came as slaves to the New World brought with them, therefore, "a rich tradition of folk belief and practice, including conjure, herbalism, ghost lore, witchcraft, and fortune-telling." This lore survived within the slave community even after some African Americans began to accept Christianity. Because the slaves were excluded from political and judicial institutions, this lore, and any sorcery or magic that proceeded from it, never resulted in a witch-hunt.

DECLINE OF WITCH-HUNTING

The precipitous decline of witch-hunting happened at about the same time in western Europe, the American colonies, New France, and New Spain. A simple explanation for its cessation is that civil magistrates, often with the clergy as their allies, ceased to find credible the traditional lore. The withdrawal of the courts had much to do with a shift in attitude about the relationship between nature and the supernatural, for the educated classes were increasingly persuaded that hitherto mysterious "wonders" and the experience of possession all had natural causes. Though Cotton Mather worried that these new attitudes encouraged "Atheism," and though he and his father continued to assert the possibility of wonders, clergy such as John Hale and Samuel Willard realized that the debacle of the Salem witch-hunt necessitated a fundamental change of thinking.

Witch-hunting was a complex, multilayered phenomenon. In general, studies made in 1990 found that the distinctions between high and low magic, religion and magic, and the clergy and the people are inadequate to encompass these complexities. Nor does any single factor explain what happened in early America and early modern Europe.

BIBLIOGRAPHY

Boyer, Paul, and Stephen Nissenbaum. *Salem Possessed: The Social Origins of Witchcraft.* Cambridge, Mass., 1974. A social history that argues that tensions over capitalism divided the village where accusations first began.

Brooke, John L. *The Refiner's Fire: The Hermetic Tradition and the Origins of Mormon Cosmology.* Forthcoming.

Demos, John P. *Entertaining Satan: Witchcraft and the Culture of Early New England.* New York, 1982. A careful social history of local episodes prior to 1692, combined with psychoanalytical analysis. Includes a list of all accusations prior to Salem.

Flint, Valerie I. J. *The Rise of Magic in Early Medieval Europe.* Princeton, N.J., 1991.

Hale, John. *A Modest Enquiry into the Nature of Witchcraft.* Boston, 1702. The troubled reflections of a contemporary Massachusetts minister on the theology and procedures of witch-hunting.

Hall, David D., ed. *Witch-Hunting in Seventeenth-Century New England: A Documentary History, 1638–1692.* Boston, 1991. The documentary evidence for the major cases prior to Salem; includes a bibliography of scholarship relating to witch-hunting in Europe and American colonies.

Karlsen, Carol F. *The Devil in the Shape of a Woman: Witchcraft in Colonial New England.* New York, 1987. Explores the reasons for the preponderance of women among the accused.

Larner, Christina. *Enemies of God: The Witch-Hunt in Scotland.* Baltimore, Md., 1981. Reviews previous theories of witchcraft and witch-hunting; excellent discussion of religion and gender.

Levack, Brian P. *The Witch-Hunt in Early Modern Europe.* London, 1987. A sophisticated synthesis, useful for comparison.

Mandrou, Robert. *Magistrats et Sorciers en France au xviie siècle.* Paris, 1968.

Murchembled, Robert. *Culture populaire et culture des élites dans la France moderne.* Paris, 1978.

Raboteau, Albert J. *Slave Religion: The "Invisible Institution" in the Antebellum South.* New York, 1978.

Robbins, Rossell Hope. *The Encyclopedia of Witchcraft and Demonology.* New York, 1959.

Simmons, Marc. *Witchcraft in the Southwest: Spanish and Indian Supernaturalism on the Rio Grande.* Flagstaff, Ariz., 1974.

Thomas, Keith. *Religion and the Decline of Magic.* London, 1971. Argues for witch-hunting as endemic in village culture; differentiates popular from learned understandings of witchcraft, describes astrology, prophecy, and the "cunning people."

David D. Hall

SEE ALSO **African-American Culture; British Settlements, New England;** and **Crime and Law Enforcement.**

REVIVALISM AND
THE GREAT AWAKENING

A REVIVAL OF RELIGION has two basic meanings in the context of twentieth-century Christianity. First, the term refers to a series of special religious services intended to reinvigorate the religious life of a congregation. By holding a revival, a church seeks to intensify the piety of its members and to bring nonmembers to commit themselves to Christ. Second, the term refers to a period during which the piety of members intensifies and new members join the church in more than ordinary numbers. A church holds a revival hoping for a genuine revival of religion, an increase in holiness both in personal depth and in numerical breadth.

In British colonial America, however, churches did not "hold" revivals. To announce in advance a special season in which God's grace would be available in unusual abundance would have looked like a usurpation of divine sovereignty. Pious colonists believed that revival would come when God willed it and not because of human actions. Colonial congregations, nonetheless, often prayed and fasted for the outpouring of the Holy Spirit that would transform them into a sanctified people, and—with the Great Awakening—revivalism, the deliberate use of means to bring about a revival of religion, became an integral part of Protestant church life in British North America.

Numerous and dramatic conversions were the dominant element of the eighteenth-century revivals. Reformed Protestant theology taught that all individuals are born sinners and require the infusion of God's grace, called conversion or the New Birth, in order to be transformed into true Christians whose souls would enter heaven when they died. By the early seventeenth century, Reformed theologians had developed a standard pattern, or morphology, of the steps through which one passed from sin to grace. The process began with "awakening," the realization that one is a sinner, worthy and in danger of eternal damnation; it proceeded to "humiliation," the recognition that one could do nothing oneself to merit salvation, that one's good deeds would not bring salvation, and that one must rely totally on the mercy of Jesus Christ; and it culminated in conversion proper, an acceptance of Christ as one's own savior and in a total surrender to God. Conversion resulted in love of God and of neighbor and the desire to obey God's will. During the Great Awakening, revivalists preached principally for conversions, which came to be much more public, theatrical, emotionally intense, and condensed in duration than previously.

Proponents of the Great Awakening understood revivals to be more than simply the confluence of numerous individual conversions. Rather, they considered revivals to be the sanctification of their communities by the outpouring of the Holy Spirit for which their churches had so long prayed. With the Great Awakening, these communal experiences came to be looked on as discrete entities; they received close analysis, and accounts of them assumed a standard pattern. Just as Reformed theologians had described a morphology of conversion in the individual soul, theorists of the Great Awakening delineated a morphology of religious revival in the community. Paralleling the conversion narrative, the revival narrative emerged as a religious genre.

The Great Awakening is a term introduced in the mid nineteenth century to refer to those religious revivals of the years from 1739 to 1745 which were associated principally with tours of the British American colonies by George Whitefield, an itinerant Methodist evangelist. Subsequently historians have used it in relation to the movement of evangelical Pietism and the related revivals and controversies, principally in the middle colonies and New England, from about 1720 to about 1750. Sometimes the term refers to the general evangelical movement throughout British North America, including the South, over the course of the entire eighteenth century. The evangelical movement in eighteenth-century British North America was a regional manifestation of the broader, pietistic evangelical revival that had begun in Germany in the mid seventeenth century. No matter what one calls it, it possessed enough unity as a cultural and religious phenomenon to be treated as a single entity. The current essay takes the broadest view of the Great Awakening in order to assess its origins, progress, and consequences.

REFORMATION AND REVIVALISM, 1689–1720

Most accounts of the Great Awakening begin around 1720. To measure the significance of the Awakening, however, one needs to understand the important religious changes that took place during the preceding three decades. In that period New England replicated an English pattern in which the decline of the practical influence of the churches had led to experimentation with voluntarism. Disappointing results in turn led to disillusionment with human schemes for reformation and to reliance on the outpouring of divine grace to effect a revival of religion.

Voluntarism

To speak of an eighteenth-century "revival" of religion in America misleadingly implies that a piety vital in the seventeenth century had decayed by the eighteenth. Evidence suggests that familial traditions of lay piety remained strong into the new century and that much preaching in America's Reformed churches remained solidly evangelical. The Great Awakening was not so much a rebirth of evangelical piety as it was a matter of expressing that piety in new forms. In both Great Britain and British America, the secularization of the state that came with the enactment of religious toleration, the relative indifference of civil authorities to the regulation of morality, and the loss of the clergy's influence over social policy and popular mores induced religious leaders to experiment with voluntary organizations for spiritual and moral reform. As those efforts proved inadequate and as church membership came increasingly to depend on voluntary commitment, religious reformers adopted aggressive evangelism and revivalistic techniques as tools of persuasion.

The Act of Toleration of 1689 diminished the legal authority of the established church in England, crippling the power of its courts. In response a number of Anglican bishops took the lead in organizing voluntary efforts at spiritual and moral reform. They founded religious societies for prayer and pious discussion, promoted religious education through the Society for the Propagation of Christian Knowledge, and supported societies for reformation of manners. The Dissenters cooperated with the last, which prosecuted immorality in secular courts. After 1710 the Anglican religious societies and the nondenominational societies for the reformation of manners lost their prominence. By the 1720s annual lectures offered to the Dissenters in the reformation societies explained the inefficacy of the movement with the observation that reformation would not be lasting until God poured out his Spirit. Moral reform, they concluded, depended not so much on the execution of good laws as on the appearing of God's freely given grace among the people.

Voluntarism emerged gradually in seventeenth-century New England as a vehicle for maintaining the churches' influence. Within a decade of settlement, the New England Way of the Congregational churches had been implemented. The principal components of the New England Way were the autonomy of the individual church and the limitation of church membership to visible saints who covenanted with each other in the sight of God. Visible saints were those who not only lived an outwardly upright life but also could give a convincing narration of their conversion experience. Proponents of the New England Way confronted a crisis in the middle of the seventeenth century when few of the second generation were either willing or able to give witness to a conversion experience. When persons baptized in infancy on the basis of their parents' membership attained adulthood without undergoing the conversion experience, they were denied admission to the Lord's Supper and the right to present their own children for baptism. Facing the prospect that church members would become an ever-diminishing proportion of the population, in 1662 a synod recommended, and local churches began adopting, the Half-Way Covenant: baptized but unconverted members who "owned the covenant," submitting themselves to church discipline, were allowed to have their children baptized, but were still excluded from the Holy Eucharist and from voting privileges in the church.

Revocation of the Bay Colony charter in 1684 augmented the Half-Way Covenant's significance; because the civil magistrate could no longer be counted on to uphold the religious commitments of the community, the need of the churches to spread their influence throughout the community increased. Before the end of the seventeenth century, the Half-Way Covenant had become an evangelical tool for bringing in the unchurched. The renewal by particular churches of their covenants to walk together as Christians in the sight of God was another innovation used to stir up religious interest. Introduced during King Philip's War (1675–1676), covenants of reformation had become an ordinary part of church life by the end of the century. Covenant renewal was often used as an occasion for encouraging baptized adults and even the unchurched to own the covenant and, hence,

to accept halfway membership. In this way covenant renewal became an evangelical device.

The Glorious Revolution (1688) brought about the fall of the Dominion of New England and restored home rule to the New England colonies, but this did not mean a return to religious monopoly by Puritan Congregationalists. Toleration of most varieties of Protestantism became the law. New England's law courts became less concerned with punishing moral transgressions. At the same time, because of the increasing heterogeneity of the populace, churches became less important than civil law courts as tribunals for the resolution of local conflicts. Having lost their coercive authority, New England church leaders imported from England forms of voluntary association for the promotion of reformation and revival.

In New England during the two decades on either side of 1700, proclamations, sermons, and religious and reformation societies reflected the influence of the English movement for the reformation of manners. Boston minister Cotton Mather (1663–1728) led those who imitated these activities in New England. He founded societies of men to help the authorities in Boston suppress disorders and, for their guidance, published a manual and an abstract of Massachusetts's laws against vice, and he actively fostered the meeting of private groups for religious exercises. Sometime after 1710, however, Mather recognized that the voluntary societies had failed to reform New England or to revive piety, but in Mather's view they nevertheless continued to serve an essential function. Efforts to do good served as a basis of unity for true Christians. The union of Christians on principles of piety would prepare the way for the Second Coming, which would bring about the ultimate reformation. Mather came to rely on the faithful remnant awaiting the millennium, Christ's thousand-year reign on earth promised by Scripture. All that was left for Christians to do was to prepare and pray for the pouring out of God's Spirit promised to the church in the latter days.

During the first two decades of the eighteenth century Solomon Stoddard (1643–1729), minister at Northampton, Massachusetts, in the Connecticut River valley, underwent a similar change of attitude toward methods to effect a reformation of morals and revival of religion.

During the latter part of the seventeenth century, Stoddard had promoted his particular program for the reformation of New England as vigorously as had Cotton Mather. By the 1710s he had, like Mather, reevaluated his methods and had come to look for a shower of grace as the sole workable solution.

Addressing the problem of how to bring potential saints into the church, Stoddard before 1710 renounced the New England Way as a major obstacle: the power of religion had declined in the land not because the churches had been defiled by unregenerate members, but because too many people had been excluded from the means of grace. He redefined the relationship between conversion and the sacraments, dropping the requirement of evidence of conversion for full church membership and contending that the sacraments were means of conversion. Because salvation came through the church, it was important to bring as many people into it as possible.

By the second decade of the eighteenth century, Stoddard recognized that he had failed to convince his colleagues that the sacraments were converting ordinances. He began instead to assert that the gospel was the sole means of conversion and to advocate a new program for promoting vital religion. His new program hinged on the minister as preacher and pastoral guide to awakened sinners seeking Christ. For Stoddard religion would revive when God channeled abundant measures of grace through a conversionist, evangelical, gospel ministry.

The development of an evangelical preaching style in the Connecticut River valley was part of the general movement throughout European evangelical circles during the first quarter of the eighteenth century.

Preaching

A new, affective homiletic style was a major factor in the coming of the Great Awakening. The new style was influenced by Continental Pietism and by a new psychology of sense perception. It also arose from a reaction against moralistic, rationalist preaching and the spread of rationalist heterodoxies. The evangelically oriented clergy pressed their campaign for an evangelical style of preaching and pastoral ministry all the more urgently because of the rival clerical style of Enlighten-

ment rationalism, which they asserted stood in the way of a revival of religion.

Rationalist preachers focused on the reasonableness of Christianity, as opposed to the great mysteries of the faith, and described the chief end of religion as the happiness of mankind rather than the glory of God. They did so as defenders of Christianity against the attacks of deists and skeptics. Their sermons were polite discourses on philosophy, the conventional message of which was that a moral life leads to earthly benefits. This kind of pulpit eloquence emerged in the latter part of the seventeenth century in the established church in England, for which the sermonic style of Archbishop John Tillotson became the standard. By the turn of the century some Dissenters, particularly among Presbyterians and Congregationalists, had adopted the rationalist manner. Under these influences divisions within Dissent widened between rationalists, high Calvinists, and evangelical Calvinists. Rationalists emphasized man's ability to reason and choose the right for himself. High Calvinists believed that fallen man could do nothing to promote his own salvation. The Evangelicals, in contrast to the high Calvinists, urged the use of the means of salvation while awaiting God's grace to make them effectual; in contrast to the rationalists, they embraced the affections as central to the life of the soul.

The examples of Philip Doddridge and Isaac Watts illustrate the character of the evangelical Dissenters. Doddridge, minister of an Independent congregation at Northampton, England, rejected an emphasis on natural religion and moral virtue in favor of plain evangelical sermons that "awaken, revive, and enlarge the soul." His popular *Rise and Progress of Religion in the Soul* (1745) explicated the evangelical morphology of conversion. Watts was a respected Independent minister in London, the author of textbooks in numerous fields, a poet, and a hymnist, who concluded that the affections are at the center of true religion and that it is the preacher's duty to move them. In the numerous hymns for which he is famous, his chief aim was to awaken holy passions. The English Dissenters would not lead revivals until late in the eighteenth century. The influence of rationalism, legal bars to field preaching, and the small proportion of the population (about 6 percent) that constituted their audience inhibited revivalism among dissenting ministers. Although they would hold themselves aloof from English Methodists, leaders among the evangelical Dissenters would endorse the American and Scottish revivals.

In place of the traditional theory that the affections must be kept subordinate to the understanding so that the latter, not the former, would govern the will, leading evangelical theorists followed John Locke in adopting a unified conception of the psyche in which the affections, the understanding, and the will could not be separated from each other. Locke's theory that knowledge comes through sense perceptions shaped the Evangelicals' appeal to the passions. These theorists came to believe that one comes to love the good and the true through a perception of its beauty. Considering the sense of beauty to be a function of the affections, they appealed directly to the "heart" through a use of lively imagery.

Continental pietistic ideas and practices legitimized the Evangelicals' rhetorical appeal to the heart. Pietism on the Continent emerged in the latter seventeenth century as a reaction against the prevalence of a nonevangelical piety that taught a scholastic dogmatism, emphasized baptismal regeneration, accepted a complacent morality, and frowned on the public display of emotion. The Pietists sought instead greater emphasis on Scripture, assumption by laity of more responsibility for the work of the church, nurturing the piety of those training for the ministry, preaching that focused on conversion, and practical works of charity as the pious fruits of the new life in the soul.

By the mid seventeenth century English Puritan thought, through publications and the work of religious exiles, had helped shape a Dutch brand of Pietism which, in turn, influenced German Lutheranism. Philipp Jakob Spener energized the renewal movement in German Lutheranism by organizing lay groups, called *collegia pietatis*, in which members shared devotions and discussed their spiritual experiences. His *Pia Desideria*, or *Earnest Desires for Reform of the True Evangelical Church* (1675), widely propagated Pietism's goals. August Hermann Francke, professor of theology at the University of Halle, succeeded to the leadership of German Pietism. He advocated fervent evangelical conversionism

and the use of vivid imagery in preaching. German Pietist influence extended broadly through Great Britain and British America by the 1720s, and Francke's writings influenced all the early evangelical leaders. Pietism's direct appeal to the heart attracted ministers frustrated by their inability to halt the secularization of their societies or to effect any lasting improvement in prevailing moral standards. Its simple faith in Christ's person and its unquestioning commitment to puritanical moral standards proved comforting in the face of the theological and moral skepticism of the age.

In New England in the first quarter of the eighteenth century, two lines of development were under way that were conducive to successful evangelical revivalism. One group of preachers, centered in Boston and headed by Cotton Mather, gradually moved away from the traditional Puritan emphasis on formal reason and logic and urged the kind of vital piety described in Francke's writings. Mather's preaching came to focus on the person of Christ, paralleling a campaign for "preaching Christ" undertaken by evangelical Dissenters in England. In 1722 the defection of Timothy Cutler and several others at Yale College to the Church of England under the influence of rationalist literature proved to Mather that the decay of evangelical truth in England endangered "preaching Christ" in America.

Another group of preachers, centered in the Connecticut River valley and under the mentorship of Solomon Stoddard, was reaping evangelical fruits by means of a pastoral emphasis on conversion. Stoddard promoted a charismatic evangelism. Converted preachers, full of the Holy Spirit, appealing to anxious men and women to flee to Christ for safety, would revive religion while restoring the influence and status of the clergy. Stoddard urged ministers to move their auditors by portraying in vivid imagery the horrors of damnation and the ever-present danger of dying unconverted. He taught that ministers ought to instruct people in the examination of their hearts for signs of grace and that ministers could not reach men's hearts unless the ministers themselves were converted.

In Stoddard's preparationist theology, conversion involved two separate kinds of operations by the Spirit. First, there is preparatory work, in which the Spirit first frightens the individual into attempting moral reformation by making him sensible of his danger of damnation and then brings the individual to humiliation by showing him he has no power in himself truly to reform. Up to this point, no saving grace has been involved; the soul has done nothing good— rather, it has been passive. When the soul has been thus prepared, it is ready for conversion work. By illuminating the understanding with a vision of the glory and excellence of God, the Spirit produces love of God in the heart. The soul is now capable of faith, the accepting of the offer of salvation in the gospel, the first gracious act of the soul. Since this first closing with Christ is "the greatest change that men undergo in this world," men usually know the time of their conversion. Thus, from first awakening to final assurance, affections—fear, humiliation, love, and joy—are at the center of the conversion process. It is the preacher's job to engage those emotions.

By the first quarter of the eighteenth century, evangelical Protestants of different regions were promoting similar campaigns in support of "experimental," or what today is called "experiential," religion. The evangelical parties among the Continental Lutherans and Reformed, English Dissenters, Scottish and Scotch-Irish Presbyterians, and American Congregationalists and Presbyterians shared the same basic outlook. All focused on the necessity of the New Birth for eternal salvation. They insisted that pastors instruct the people on the distinction between the converted and the unconverted and on how to examine their own spiritual condition. Pastors were urged to preach differently to each category of hearer: sinners asleep in their sins, those awakened to a sense of guilt and those who were repentant and humbled, as well as newly converted but weak Christians and Christians strong in faith. The Evangelicals emphasized the centrality of the affections in religious experience and the proper place of emotion in self-examination, private devotions, and public worship. They encouraged the singing of psalms and hymns to engage pious feelings and placed particular value in Christian fellowship, making use of private groups variously called conventicles, religious societies, or assemblies of the pious. Each branch of Evangelicals sought the purity of the church by restricting access to the sacraments

and by other forms of ecclesiastical discipline. They treasured spontaneity and sincerity in worship and denigrated formalism and prescribed ritual.

REVIVALISM TO 1739

New England

From their early days, New England congregations had known seasons in which more than unusual numbers experienced conversions and applied for church membership. With the development of aggressively conversionist pastoral and preaching styles after about 1710, however, New England towns began experiencing more frequent and more intensive periods of religious revival. This was especially noticeable in the Connecticut River valley where, following Stoddard's lead, by the 1720s a group of preachers had developed a successful revivalist approach. By application of preparationist theology to their sermons, several clergymen in the valley enjoyed at least one period of religious revival in their congregations between 1712 and 1733. The growing frequency of sporadic local revivals seemed to confirm the efficacy of the renewed emphasis on evangelical preaching. Now the Connecticut River valley revivalists began to look for a general religious awakening.

The Connecticut River valley revival tradition came to full fruition with revivals in Northampton and some thirty other valley towns in 1734–1735. The leader and interpreter of that awakening was a grandson and successor of Solomon Stoddard, Jonathan Edwards. The progress of the revival in Edwards's Northampton fit the pattern set by the previous Connecticut River valley revivals. It began with the reform of the young people, who were gradually weaned from their late-night frolics and brought to a serious interest in religion. Forcefully reminded of their vulnerability by the deaths of two youths in 1734, the young people began meeting in small groups for prayer and pious discussion; their elders soon followed their example. In the fall, Edwards began a series of sermons on justification by faith alone. Religious concern spread quickly through the town, and many people gave public witness to conversion experiences. Private religious meetings became frequent and crowded. People resorted to the pastor's chamber instead of the tavern and stayed at home except for business or religion. A long-standing political feud lay dormant. The revival's ardor began to cool in June 1735 when the suicide of Edwards's uncle, Joseph Hawley, made people wary of religious introspection. The effects of the revival lingered, nevertheless, and the private religious meetings were kept up.

Solomon Stoddard and Jonathan Edwards perceived most clearly the implications and the potential of communal religious awakenings. In his account of the Connecticut River valley awakening, *A Faithful Narrative* (1737), Edwards formulated a previously imperfectly formed theory of revivals as the transformation by grace of a community. Following Stoddard's lead, Edwards fit the ideas and the phenomena together into a coherent whole. With *A Faithful Narrative* he not only perfected a new genre of religious literature, the revival narrative, but he also classified the revival as a unique phenomenon whose characteristics were unmistakable. By establishing expectations, his narrative became a blueprint for future revivals. *A Faithful Narrative*, first published in London, brought international attention to the American revivals and marked Edwards as their leading proponent and interpreter.

In 1739 Jonathan Edwards delivered a series of lectures at Northampton (published posthumously as *A History of the Work of Redemption* [1774]). In them he identified the local revivals that his congregation had witnessed with the outpourings of the Spirit throughout biblical and Christian history and posited that those local occurrences were forerunners of revivals that would usher in the millennial kingdom. Edwards magnified the Connecticut River valley revivals by portraying them as events central to the entire past and future of the relationship of God and man. He made the phenomenon of the revival the key element in the drama of redemption.

The Middle Colonies

The sizable immigration from the European continent to the middle colonies that began in the 1680s had by the 1730s brought to America not only Continental Lutheran and Reformed churches but also numerous Pietist sects, including Dunkers, Seventh-Day German Baptists, Amish, Mennonites, Moravians, and an assortment of mystics. The several varieties of Pietism were not all revivalistic; many reflected Lutheran quietist reliance on salvation by faith alone rather than Reformed striving for evidence of grace. While Pietism supplied a populace open to emotional conversion, revivalism came not from the sects but from the Pietist wings of the churches, in particular the Dutch Reformed and the Presbyterian. The revival in the middle colonies among the Dutch Reformed and the British Presbyterians reflected the activism of Pietists in the Netherlands and of Evangelicals in Scotland and Ulster.

The Dutch Reformed church in the Netherlands was divided into theological parties. The Pietist party sought to promote experiential religion: conversion and practical inner spirituality. To that end it organized private meetings for prayer and Bible reading and encouraged use of extemporaneous prayer in public worship. Members of the conservative party believed that those practices led to enthusiasm (mistaken claims of divine inspiration), mysticism, and heresy. They trusted in formal dogma and adherence to the established liturgy.

Theodorus Jacobus Frelinghuysen (1691–ca. 1748), German born but educated in Dutch Reformed Pietism, carried the dispute over pastoral style to America and in the process became the patriarch of revivalism in the middle colonies. Frelinghuysen arrived in America in 1720 to minister to Dutch Reformed congregations in New Jersey's Raritan Valley, where he introduced revivalistic methods and theology. Valuing zeal over formality, he allowed deviations from the prescribed liturgy, permitted the use of hymns as well as psalms in public worship, and preached searchingly on the necessity of the New Birth. His ministry resulted in numerous conversion experiences. By practicing emotional conversionism, denouncing nonevangelical preachers, and insisting on the right to examine the spiritual state of individuals before admitting them to the sacraments, he created divisions among his own congregations and aroused strong opposition from the traditionalist clergy. The conservatives were troubled as well that Frelinghuysen blurred denominational distinctions by cooperating with evangelical clergy of other churches.

Presbyterians in the middle colonies organized themselves as the Synod of Philadelphia in 1716. Within a decade divisions arose among them: between those educated in New England and those educated in Scotland or Ulster, and between conservatives and Evangelicals. The Scots and Scotch-Irish supported subscription to the Westminster Confession of Faith, conservatives as a way of assuring denominational unity and Evangelicals as a shield against heterodoxy. The New Englanders opposed subscription as an infringement on private conscience that placed a man-made text before God's word contained in Scripture. On itinerancy and clerical qualifications, issues that related more directly to revivalism, conservatives and Evangelicals divided. By controlling the right of ministers to preach in vacant congregations, the conservatives sought to maintain church discipline; by giving the synod the authority to examine the proficiency of candidates for the ministry who had been educated privately rather than in European colleges, they sought to preserve right doctrine and sound teaching. Evangelicals viewed giving either of those powers to church councils as hobbles on a zealous revivalism. They believed that congregations should be free to hear any clergyman who might do their souls good and that the piety of candidates for the clergy was as important as their education.

Members of the Tennent family championed the evangelical style among the middle colony Presbyterians. William Tennent, Sr. (1673–1746), an ordained minister in the episcopal Church of Ireland, concluding that there was no scriptural basis for many of that church's principles, left Ireland and was received into the Presbyterian Church in Philadelphia in 1718. In 1726 he set up his "Log College" at Neshaminy, Pennsylvania, where he trained many of the early evangelical leaders of Presbyterianism, including his four sons. Tennent, Sr., taught his students to value heartfelt practical piety over formal orthodoxy and liturgical decorum. One son, Gilbert Tennent (1703–1764), Presbyterian minister at New Brunswick, New Jersey, and later at Philadelphia, learned additionally from Frelinghuysen a searching style of preaching that brought auditors to discover their own spiritual condition. For the middle colony revivalists, the mark of the evangelical preacher was his differentiating among the various spiritual states of his hearers. Advocating passionate address to the affections, they preached the terrors of damnation. They

joined their voices to the English Evangelicals' call to preach Christ rather than natural religion and condemned nonevangelical preaching. Graduates of the Log College found that their preaching led, in their words, to "the conviction and conversion of a considerable number of persons."

As New England Congregationalists had their covenant renewals and public fasts, so the Scottish Presbyterians had a traditional ritual at which the revivalists had much of their success. This was the Communion season, a practice that had its origins in Scotland around the start of the seventeenth century. Congregations would hold solemn Communion services at which several ministers from a vicinity preached over a period of from three to five days, and which hundreds of persons from the surrounding parishes attended. Neighboring parishes would schedule their Communion celebrations over the course of a summer in such a way that local residents might have the opportunity of attending several such events. Participants at sacramental gatherings among the more radical Scottish Presbyterians during the rule of Oliver Cromwell and among Presbyterian conventicles during the Restoration period experienced many of them as occasions of special outpourings of divine grace. During the two decades following the Glorious Revolution and the reestablishment of Presbyterianism, the sacramental season became a regular feature of Scottish religious culture. As in Scotland, Presbyterians in the middle colonies customarily employed a period of several days to celebrate the sacrament, preceding the Sabbath day with days for preparation and following it with days for thanksgiving. During the Great Awakening religious feelings reached heights of intensity, and conversions were begun or consummated in large numbers at these meetings.

THE GREAT AWAKENING'S CONSTITUENCY

Many among the crowds who listened to the revivalists portray hell's torments were powerfully frightened, some reacting with groans, cries, fainting, and fits. Since the danger of death from various causes was no greater during the periods of revival than before—attempts to demonstrate geographical relationships between the destructiveness of epidemics and the effectiveness of revivals, for instance, have generally failed—one must look elsewhere to explain the heightened sensitivity to the preaching of terror. It is to feelings of guilt for sin that we turn for explanation, for it was not just death but punishment thereafter that filled people with fear. The Great Awakening has been characterized as a psychological earthquake, but it did not strike down its subjects indiscriminately. By identifying those groups most susceptible to revivalism, historians have tried to discover the roots of the anxiety that fueled the revivals.

The converts of the Great Awakening were disproportionately young people from their mid teens to mid twenties. This attribute suggests that problems of resolving sexual tensions underlay the anxiety manifested in the revivals. Premarital conceptions increased among Americans in the second quarter of the eighteenth century. This phenomenon may have resulted from the decline of the churches' disciplinary power and the relative lack of interest of the civil authorities in punishing transgressions of sexual morals. In New England it may have also resulted from the decrease of available land and the consequent diminished ability of parents, by withholding gifts of real property, to control their children. Adolescence had become a more difficult stage in life by the early eighteenth century, and religious conversion appeared as a way of resolving some of the resulting tensions.

The Great Awakening, however, was more than the manifestation of one generation's transition to adulthood. It was part of a broader psychological adjustment to significant social and economic changes. With commercialization—growth of markets, settlement of more distant frontiers, and greater opportunities in waterborne trade—eighteenth-century economic relations became more impersonal; as the elite consolidated its wealth and permanent classes of landless farm workers and urban wage laborers appeared, social groups grew farther apart. These developments led to increased clashes of economic interests, litigation, and political factionalism. Because these behavioral patterns contrasted with the ideal of Christian harmony, they produced feelings of guilt. Evangelicalism substi-

tuted alternative sources of authority, enabling converts to overcome the guilt they internalized for opposing the powers that be, to trust their own consciences, and as "new men" to survive in the newly competitive society.

Scholars disagree over whether to describe the Great Awakening as a movement of the middling sort or of the poor. In rural New England, converts of the revivals came principally from families of church members, established in their communities. In the prosperous commercial port of New London, Connecticut, however, the supporters of the radical revival, although not the dregs of society, consisted of those not integrated into the power structure. And the followers of the radical evangelists in cities such as Boston have been identified as the dispossessed, including slaves, servants, and the impoverished. While the Great Awakening's origins seem to have lain in the middling sort, it drew a following as well from those who were strangers to economic, social, and political power. Those alienated from mainstream culture, such as the Baptists of Virginia, were attracted by the movement's critique of those in authority and by its condemnation of contemporary morality and materialism.

In addition to age, locality, and economic status, a pious upbringing and religious education appear to have been crucial determinants of who was susceptible to revivalism. The core constituency of the Great Awakening consisted of members of families in which Reformed piety had been maintained. Societies for religious fellowship that met apart from regular church worship services nurtured the piety that was the essential foundation of a religious awakening. These groups of pious neighbors who met regularly to converse about their religious experiences, to pray, to sing psalms, and to read the Bible together often served as the nuclei of local revivals.

THE COURSE OF THE GREAT AWAKENING, 1739–1745

The Methodists and George Whitefield
Periods of intense revivalistic activity with extraordinary popular participation began in England and Wales in 1738, in the middle colonies the following year, in New England in 1740,

and in Scotland two years later. After 1742 the revivals subsided, but their consequences continued on. The immediate catalysts of the revivals in both Great Britain and America were leaders of an evangelical movement within the Church of England known as Methodism. Those leaders had mastered the preaching of conversionist doctrine with vivid imagery and dramatic flair.

In the mid 1730s the "Holy Club" at Oxford University, a society organized in the tradition of the Anglican religious societies, served as the spiritual nursery of some of Methodism's chief founders, including Charles Wesley, John Wesley, and George Whitefield. The Methodists rejected the rationalism and dry moralism of much Anglican preaching, asserted the necessity of conversion, and nurtured the religious passions. Their emphasis on sin, hell, the atonement, and salvation by faith alone distinguished them from most other Anglican ministers. They built their movement through itinerancy, small groups for prayer and religious instruction, and affective preaching.

The most influential of these preachers in America was George Whitefield (1714–1770). Born in Gloucester, England, the son of innkeepers, he studied for the ministry at Oxford, where he joined the Holy Club and embraced a life of passionate asceticism. His religious reading convinced him of the necessity of the New Birth, which he experienced in 1735. Ordained a deacon in 1736, he began preaching with an emphasis on the New Birth. After a missionary journey to Georgia, he returned to England in 1739 to be ordained a priest and to raise money for an orphanage in the young colony. By then the publication of nine of his sermons and his *Journals* of his voyage to America had made him vulnerable to criticism for spiritual pride, reliance on impulses, and enthusiasm. His writings had also offended many ministers of the Church of England with denunciations of their preaching. Finding himself excluded from most Anglican pulpits, Whitefield preached in the open air. With his actor's ability to make the drama of redemption come alive and a voice that could be heard and understood by audiences into the tens of thousands, he attracted and moved enormous gatherings. In addition to the New Birth, he began emphasizing the theme of salvation by faith alone and became a confirmed predestinarian. On the latter issue he broke with the

Wesleys, who believed in the ability of individuals to accept or reject the offer of grace.

In October 1739, preceded by a reputation as a zealous evangelist, Whitefield arrived at Lewes, Delaware, and undertook an evangelizing circuit through the middle colonies. He preached for ten days in Philadelphia, where he met William Tennent, Sr. He then set out for New York. Along the way he linked up with Gilbert Tennent, who accompanied him to New York City. There, denied use of a pulpit by the Anglican commissary, Whitefield preached in the Presbyterian meetinghouse as well as in the open air, along with Tennent. In December, Whitefield began a journey through the southern colonies from Maryland to Georgia. He spent the winter in the South, supervising the building of his orphanage near Savannah. During the winter he visited Charleston, South Carolina, where, denied use of an Anglican pulpit, he preached in the Presbyterian and Baptist meetinghouses. In the spring he left Savannah for Philadelphia and made a second tour of Pennsylvania, New Jersey, and New York. Guided by Gilbert Tennent to congregations receptive to evangelical preaching, Whitefield succeeded in stimulating religious interest wherever he went.

Reports of Whitefield's successes raised New Englanders' expectations of a revival of religion. Hoping to stimulate a similar phenomenon in their congregations, several Boston clergymen invited Whitefield to come and preach. They prepared their people for his visit by publishing works on evangelical preaching and reports from dissenting ministers in Charleston, South Carolina, that lauded Whitefield. When Whitefield arrived in September, a delegation of gentlemen met him and led him into Boston. Until the end of October he preached in New England towns. At each stop large crowds gathered to hear the Word and to feel the Spirit move in them. After a brief return to Georgia, Whitefield sailed for England in January 1741; he would not return to America until 1744. The interest in religion that Whitefield had aroused, Gilbert Tennent fostered by making an evangelizing journey through New England during the winter of 1740–1741. Beginning with Whitefield's visit, for a year and a half New England experienced numerous local revivals.

Whitefield built his success on several factors. First, through his oratorical art and theatrical skill he held the attention of his auditors and made each one sense that he was addressing him or her individually. By acting out the biblical drama of creation, fall from grace, and redemption, he provided a form of theater. He illustrated his message with familiar examples from daily life and addressed sinners directly, even to the point of speaking their own innermost thoughts. Second, his being an ordained priest in the Church of England who had adopted the evangelical message and condemned the dry morality of his church made him particularly attractive to the nonconformist denominations. To American Evangelicals he appeared to have been raised up out of the seat of formalism to preach a living faith and revive orthodox Reformed doctrine. Third, Whitefield adapted to evangelism commercial marketing techniques, including self-promotion, advance men, and newspaper advertising. Through them, he enlarged the market for religion far beyond local bounds and sought out clients among all ranks of people.

New Lights and Old

Several features of the revival movement quickly became controversial: extremes of terror and joy—often manifested by crying out, violent physical motion, and fainting—prominence of lay leaders, criticism of unconverted clergy, unwillingness to commune with the unregenerate, rejection of formalized prayers and liturgies, extemporaneous preaching, fervent singing of psalms and hymns, private meetings for prayer and religious fellowship, itinerancy, and interdenominational cooperation. New Englanders' attitudes toward these features ranged along a continuum from Old Lights, who used them as evidence against the divine origin of the revival, to New Lights, who defended them as by-products of an outpouring of grace. Old Lights were composed of rationalists, who sought to subject the passions to reason, and conservative Calvinists, who objected to revivalist innovations. New Lights ranged from radicals, who aspired to open themselves to divine impressions, to moderates, who labored to discriminate between the work of grace and human error.

In its initial stages in New England, the Great Awakening seemed to be producing the desirable effects expected from an outpouring of the Holy Spirit. Revivals were measured by the number of new converts. Quarreling neighbors patched up their differences. Youths gave up their frolics and merry meetings in favor of gatherings for prayer and pious reading. The pastor's chamber replaced the tavern as a place of common resort. The ministers were suddenly subject to demands for frequent public and private lectures and for private and group conferences. Benefiting directly from them, most settled ministers at first supported the revivals.

Soon things began to go wrong. The renewed respect for the minister was based not on his office but on his ability as a revivalist. Only those ministers who appeared to have the power to alarm their listeners with a sense of sin and to guide the awakened to conversion won the people's affection. Ministers who did not practice the more vigorous styles of revivalist preaching, failed to evoke an emotional response, or frowned on commotion in the meetinghouse might even find themselves denounced as carnal legalists. Congregations divided over loyalty to their pastors. People left their own preachers in order to hear men from whom they expected to get more good. Itinerant evangelists invaded the parishes of suspected carnal ministers. Laymen took on themselves the minister's function of expounding the Word, claiming extraordinary gifts. If charisma was the necessary quality of a good preacher, then of what use was human learning?

The career of James Davenport illustrates some of the extremes to which the radical revival went. In July 1741 Davenport, Presbyterian minister of Southold, Long Island, undertook a preaching tour through Connecticut and Rhode Island. During the tour he encouraged congregations to parade through the streets singing hymns, allowed lay speaking and praying in public worship, and welcomed emotional outbursts during his sermons. He assumed the right to examine local ministers on the state of their souls, and those whom he found unworthy or uncooperative he attacked by name from the pulpit. Brought into court for disturbing the peace in Stratford, Connecticut, he was judged "disturbed in the rational faculties of his mind" and was deported to Southold. When he appeared next in Boston, the pro-revivalist clergy repudiated him because his conduct discredited the Awakening. Preaching in several Massachusetts towns, Davenport exhorted his hearers to turn their unregenerate ministers out of their places. Again he was tried for disturbing the peace, found insane, and sent back to Southold. In March 1743 he led followers in New London, Connecticut, in burning many of their luxurious possessions and theological books. A year later Davenport published a recantation and apology for his aberrant behavior.

The yearning for a converted ministry and pure Christian fellowship, fanned into flame by the revivals and reflected by Davenport's following, led to the creation of the Strict Separate denomination. In more than 125 instances, comprising almost a third of New England's Congregational parishes, groups of New Lights withdrew from the standing church because they found the pastor's preaching unprofitable to their souls or because they objected to membership practices that allowed the unregenerate to share in the Lord's Supper. Spurning both open Communion, in which the requirement of a conversion narrative was waved, and the Half-Way Covenant, in which partial membership privileges were afforded the unconverted, they covenanted together in churches that sought pure regenerate membership.

Davenport's antics and the Separate movement were forceful weapons in the Old Lights' arsenal of arguments against the revivals. Many New Englanders concluded that such disorders could not be God's doing. Charles Chauncy, minister to Boston's First Church, emerged as the most effective critic of the revivals. In such works as *Enthusiasm Described and Cautioned Against* (1742) and *Seasonable Thoughts on the State of Religion in New England* (1743) he warned that the revivals were delusions produced by enthusiasts appealing to the animal passions of the people, the "conversions" mainly hysteria, and the reports of moral reformation exaggerated. Publication of Whitefield's journals covering the period of his New England visit, in which he stated that the majority of New England's clergy were unregenerate and that the light of truth had gone out at Harvard and Yale colleges, turned many New England clergymen against the revival. When Whitefield returned to New England in 1744, he found himself excluded from most pulpits. Critics of the revivals judged that the extreme distress of awakened sinners merely manifested unreasoned terror aroused by the evangelists' graphic depictions of the torments

of hell. They objected to the usurpation of pastoral functions by lay persons who counseled the spiritually awakened or who exhorted publicly. They found the converts to be self-righteous and censorious. They found that itinerating and intruding preachers, as well as laity who left their settled pastors, undermined the authority intrinsic to the clerical office.

Jonathan Edwards, an effective revivalist, emerged as the revivals' principal defender. On 8 July 1741, preaching on invitation at Enfield, Connecticut, he delivered what is perhaps the most famous sermon in American literature, "Sinners in the Hands of an Angry God" (published later that year). The sermon, the thesis of which is that the sinner has no security but the will of God, created such a commotion that Edwards had to pause in its midst until order had been restored. Edwards's effectiveness derived not from any flamboyance of delivery—he spoke in monotones, staring into space—but from the relentlessness of his argument and from the artistry of his imagery. Scholars have concluded that the Enfield sermon, employing imagery from none of the senses except the tactile, produced vertigo, conveying a sense of suspension without support. In such sermons Edwards brought sinners to experience with their senses their helplessness and need of reconciliation with God. In polemical works he defended the authenticity of the conversions wrought by such preaching. *The Distinguishing Marks of a Work of the Spirit of God* (1741), a sermon delivered in New Haven at the end of the summer of Davenport's first revivalist tour through Connecticut, argues that the revivals should be judged not by such epiphenomena as shouting, laughing, and fainting, nor by the censoriousness of some of the awakened, but solely by the evidence of the transformation of souls by grace. *Some Thoughts Concerning the Present Revival of Religion* (1742 [released March 1743]) a book-length treatise, develops this theme in depth. The two works became the standard defenses of the revivals in both America and Great Britain.

Among the chief tools that proponents used to promote the Awakening were revival narratives, twenty-five of which were written and printed in America between 1741 and 1745. Just as the conversion narrative traced the rise and progress of grace in the soul, so the revival narrative traced the rise and progress of grace turning a town from sin to holiness. The majority of the narratives followed the model of Edwards's *Faithful Narrative.* The Evangelicals viewed the local revival as a process, with a beginning, climax, and finite duration. In describing the individual local revivals, the narrators produced a blueprint by which participants in subsequent revivals could know how they should respond to the outpouring of grace.

Most of the American revival narratives appeared in *The Christian History,* published weekly in Boston from March 1743 to February 1745. The editor, Thomas Prince, Jr., patterned the magazine on British revival magazines that printed current news of evangelical religion and accounts of revivals in former times. By printing the British materials, as well as accounts of Continental Pietism and Christian missions in the East Indies, *The Christian History* placed America's Great Awakening into the context of the outpouring of God's Spirit for the revival and propagation of true religion throughout the world.

The revivals of 1739–1742 stimulated millennial speculation among Evangelicals. In *Thoughts on the Revival of Religion,* Edwards affirmed that the revivals presaged the millennium, which he asserted would probably begin in America, thus claiming for the New World the destiny of reforming the Old. To further that end, he proposed a day of fasting and prayer to be observed throughout the American colonies. After 1743, however, Edwards grew pessimistic about the prospects of a renewal of the Awakening and disillusioned by the decay of holiness in America. In the process, the focus of his millennialism became cosmopolitan. In 1744 a group of Scottish Evangelicals, among whom millennial hopes had been raised to great heights, proposed a seven-year observance of quarterly days of prayer for the renewal of the outpouring of the Holy Spirit and the spread of Christ's spiritual reign across the globe. Edwards immediately approved of this Concert of Prayer and became its chief American promoter. The Concert, renewed several times, spread to numerous evangelical congregations in America and was still being observed by some into the 1760s.

Denominational Developments

The Great Awakening affected the organization of many of the religious denominations in America, but not all uniformly. In the wake of the revivals, several of the Reformed denominations divided between Evangelicals and conservatives, only to reunite later in the century with the evangelical parties in ascendance. The Church of England grew in the northern colonies as those alienated from the evangelical churches joined it. Some of those who led the opposition to the Awakening planted the roots of a new liberal denomination, Unitarianism.

The major issues dividing middle colony Presbyterianism—revivalism, the training of ministers, and the right to itinerate—came to converge around the last named. The matter of itinerancy had been agitating the Synod of Philadelphia since the early 1730s, when a number of the Log College graduates had gone about preaching in vacant pulpits. In 1738 the Synod adopted an itinerancy act that enabled a single pastor in a presbytery to stop a roving minister from serving a vacant church. Gilbert Tennent brought the controversy to a climax on 8 March 1740, when he preached a sermon published that year as *The Danger of an Unconverted Ministry.* In this strongly worded condemnation of nonrevivalist preaching, he pronounced it right and beneficial to leave one's settled but unconverted pastor to hear a more spiritually profitable one. In response, at the meeting of the Synod of Philadelphia in the spring of 1741, the conservative, or Old Side, party expelled the Tennent faction. The Tennent, or New Side, faction then established its own Synod of New Brunswick.

Moderate revivalists of the New York Presbytery tended to oppose itinerancy, the intrusion of preachers on others' parishes, and congregations' leaving their settled pastors to hear more evangelical preachers. The radical revivalists' emphasis on believers' assurance of salvation also troubled them. In 1745, however, the intransigence of the conservatives in the Philadelphia Synod through several attempts to reunite synods propelled the moderate revivalists into an alliance with the New Side party. The New York Presbytery, led by ministers who were of the New England tradition, joined with the New Brunswick Synod, led by those trained in the Frelinghuysen-Tennent tradition, to form the Synod of New York. Not until 1758, when the clergy of the pro-revival New York Synod outnumbered those of the antirevival Philadelphia Synod by seventy-three to twenty-two, did the

Presbyterians reunite in the merged Synod of New York and Philadelphia.

Competing factions in the Dutch Reformed church in the middle colonies separated over much the same issues as did the Presbyterians. In 1747 the Pietist party organized the Coetus of New York, a clerical organization for mutual consultation, to promote unity and resolve disagreements among the Dutch Reformed clergy in America. Conservatives suspected the Coetus of seeking authority to ordain ministers and autonomy from the Classis of Amsterdam. Indeed, in 1754 the Coetus did adopt a plan for an American Classis and circulate it among the churches for consideration. At that time the New York provincial government was proposing to establish a new college (King's). Because it would create an Episcopalian sectarian institution, the plan angered most of the Dutch. A group of conservative Dutch clergymen, however, led by Domine John Ritzema, who hoped to be appointed to a professorship of divinity at the new college, favored the government's proposal while opposing an American Classis. Censured by the Coetus for their support of the college, Ritzema and his fellow dissidents withdrew from the Coetus and formed a rival conference, called the Conferentie. Although competition for political power was the ostensible basis of the schism, underlying the division was a fundamental disagreement over the nature of piety and the desirability of revivals. The Coetus and the Conferentie contended for recognition as the true Dutch Reformed church in America until the latter's demise in 1771.

The Unitas Fratrum, or Moravians, a group of followers of John Hus that survived the Thirty Years' War in Bohemia and Moravia, migrated to the estate of the Count Nicolaus von Zinzendorf in Bethelsdorf, Germany, in 1722 and adopted Zinzendorf as their bishop. Under the leadership of the count, who had imbibed Lutheran Pietism as a youth at Halle, the group came to be characterized by a devotion to the passion of Christ and an interest in evangelizing.

The first contingent of Moravian settlers in America went to Georgia in 1736 and in a few years moved to Pennsylvania. Late in 1741 Zinzendorf arrived in America to set up Indian missions and supervise the establishment of a Moravian settlement at Bethlehem, Pennsylvania.

Gilbert Tennent met Zinzendorf when the latter passed through New Brunswick. Finding that Moravians taught universal salvation, perfectionism (the possibility of becoming free from all inclination toward sin), and "stillness," in opposition to Reformed striving for evidence of grace, Tennent became their fervent opponent. The Moravians sought to unite the various German Protestant groups in the middle colonies under a single nondenominational umbrella, which they called the Congregation of God in the Spirit. Representatives of a number of those groups met several times during the 1740s, but by the end of the decade it had become clear that the Moravians would remain as only one among many denominations.

In New England several of the Separate churches, pushing the notion of regenerate membership to its logical conclusion, embraced believer's baptism, thus rejecting the practice of baptizing the children of members. Isaac Backus and Shubal Stearns led this group into the Baptist communion in the early 1750s. In 1767 the Separate Baptists formally united with the Particular (Calvinist) Baptists in the Warren, Rhode Island, Baptist Association. The Separates infused American Baptist churches with the ethos of revivalistic, evangelical conversionism. The Separate Congregationalists struggled in vain to retain their ecclesiastical identity, their members eventually becoming Baptists or rejoining the established churches, encouraged to do the latter as the standing churches gradually abandoned the Half-Way Covenant.

Anglicans responded to the revivalists in contrary ways. Many lay members of the Church of England attended Whitefield's preaching out of curiosity; some were moved by his eloquence to accept the revivals as genuine. Anglicans who embraced Whitefield's brand of evangelicalism could be found throughout the colonies. One such individual was Devereux Jarratt, an unlettered Virginia youth who, awakened by his reading of evangelical writers, including Whitefield, went on to become one of the South's leading evangelical preachers. As a rule, the Anglican clergy opposed both Whitefield and the Awakening. The Anglican churches in New England benefited from the Awakening, as some of the people who found themselves excluded by the Congregational churches' reinvigorated requirement of a conversion narrative discovered congenial homes in the Anglican communion. Others who were repelled by the emotional excess or theology of the evangelical movement also joined the Church of England. The new accessions came not only from the genteel classes but also from the poor, who achieved in the Church of England social standing and affirmation of their self-worth.

Although the first Unitarian church in America, King's Chapel in Boston, Massachusetts, did not avow itself so until 1787, and Unitarianism did not emerge as a recognizable denomination until the first quarter of the nineteenth century, the origins of American Unitarianism are traceable directly to New England ministers, including Charles Chauncy, who led the opposition to the Great Awakening. In place of revivalism's emphasis on an emotional transformation of the heart, these protagonists for liberal religion substituted reasonable belief in the truths of religion and conviction of the benefits of moral duties. They rejected the necessity of a conversion experience for church membership or for eternal happiness. Rather, they held that man was a free agent, capable of recognizing the truth and dedicating himself to the good. God did not predestine anyone to damnation but benevolently provided the grace to assist each as a rational creature to work out his own salvation.

THE REVIVAL IN THE SOUTH

The evangelical movement had little impact on religion in the southern colonies until the middle of the 1740s, when the New Side Presbyterian churches of the middle colonies began dispatching missionaries to preach the Gospel there, especially to the new settlements of Scotch-Irish in the back country. From then until the end of the colonial era, three successive surges of evangelicalism—Presbyterian, Baptist, and Methodist—moved through parts of the South.

During the 1740s, independent of both Whitefield's visits to Virginia and of the Presbyterian missionaries, an evangelical Pietist movement emerged in Hanover County, Virginia, where a layman named Samuel Morris organized neighbors for the reading of devotional and sermonic literature. When this group sought protection from prosecution under the Act of Toleration, they called themselves Lutherans because of the influence on them of Luther's *Commentary on Galatians*. William Robinson, one of the earliest of the New Side missionaries, brought the movement into the Presbyterian fold; and his successor, Samuel Davies, confirmed that identification.

The Baptist evangelical revival in the South had two phases. During the first, from 1752 to 1756, missionaries from Particular Baptist (Calvinist) associations in Philadelphia and Charleston turned the overwhelmingly General Baptist churches (Arminian) into Particular Baptist churches, in which conversion was a criterion of membership. The reorganized churches called themselves "Regular" Baptists. The second phase involved the rapid organization, under the leadership of passionately revivalist missionaries from New England, of Separate Baptist churches among the unchurched of the Virginia and Carolina backcountry. Sandy Creek, North Carolina, where a group of New England Separates under Shubal Stearns settled in 1755, became the center of a notable revival. The Separate Baptists' demonstrative emotionalism troubled the Regular Baptists, while the Regulars' rigid dogmatism made the Separates uneasy. Common practices and beliefs eventually overcame mutual suspicions, and union was accomplished in 1787.

During the colonial period, Methodism was still a movement of societies of pious Evangelicals within the Anglican communion. The first Methodist Society in America was formed in New York in 1766, and the first Methodist circuit in Virginia was established in 1774. By the time of the Declaration of Independence, there were some three thousand members of Methodist societies in America, mostly in parts of Maryland and Virginia. An independent Methodist Episcopal church was organized in 1784.

POLITICAL CONSEQUENCES

The Great Awakening changed American politics in two important ways, one easily documented and the other subtler but just as real. The movement brought church-state relations dramatically to the fore, and it transformed the character and tone of political discourse, rendering it at once more democratic and more confrontational.

In 1742 conservatives in the Connecticut General Assembly sought to limit the excesses of the Awakening by denying tax support to Connecticut ministers who preached in others' parishes; providing for the deportation of anyone not of the colony who taught, preached, or publicly exhorted without the permission of the settled minister and the majority of the church members; and instituting fines and jail terms for lay persons who publicly exhorted. Separates, in particular, suffered persecution under these laws. In most cases Separates argued for voluntary support of the gospel ministry. For refusing to pay taxes to support their former pastors, many were prosecuted, fined, and imprisoned in both Connecticut and Massachusetts. Separates espoused freedom of conscience, disestablishment, and the noninterference of the state in matters of religion; and they carried these tenets into the Separate Baptist communion, where they converged with traditional Baptist contempt for state-supported churches. In Virginia, where Separate Baptists refused as a matter of conscience to register as Dissenters under the law, legal prosecution of the Baptists began in 1768. In these conflicts lay the seeds of the defeat of church legal establishments.

The Great Awakening undermined patterns of deference to traditional authority. By emphasizing the rights of individual conscience and freedom of personal choice in religion, and by promoting greater lay participation in church affairs, the evangelical movement challenged the established churches. The fervent factionalism of the resulting political conflicts over toleration and taxation, sanctioned by each party's conviction that it was pursuing God's will, brought a higher level of contentiousness to the public arena while enlarging the number of those who took part in organized resistance to authority.

Evangelicals aroused intense hostility, especially from the Anglican establishment in the South. The movement attracted people who were dissatisfied with the culture of the gentry, as well as immigrants into the backcountry who had no ties to the leading families or to the customary ways of the tidewater. The Evangelicals' lack of deference and their rival system of values made them subversive in the gentry's eyes. The Baptists' somber, austere ways and their refusal to take part in gambling, horse racing, and dancing stood as affronts to the prevailing life-style. In place of conviviality and proud personal display, Baptists substituted close communal bonds of fellowship; in place of competitive confrontation, they substituted the intimacy of love feasts and feet washing.

Many scholars have attempted to draw links between the Great Awakening and the American Revolution. Some have concluded that it was the Calvinist New Lights, with their vision of a new society radically transformed by divine grace, rather than the rationalist religious liberals, who most fervently embraced the revolution. Others find the connection in the orality of evangelical culture. The revivalist's extemporaneous address in vernacular language to voluntary popular assemblies transmitted an implicit democratic message, undercutting habits of deference to the printed word and to the masters of polite style. The populace was mobilized in support of resistance to British authority in similar mass meetings, where the same democratic message was again implicit. Enthusiasm for liberty became as infectious as religious enthusiasm. Still others argue that the transformation of the tone and style of politics during contentions over the issues raised by the revivals paved the way for the Patriot movement.

It is unlikely that the Great Awakening was an indispensable factor in the making of the rebellion against British authority; there were sufficient causes apart from the evangelical movement for resistance to take shape. Evangelicals did overwhelmingly support the Patriot cause and notably contributed to its eventual success, but they contributed no substantial portion of its leadership, which was composed overwhelmingly of liberals who rationalized their movement using ideas of the Enlightenment and the ideology of British opposition Whigs. Evangelicals, however, were pivotal in fashioning the domestic revolution, the movement to make American society more egalitarian. Most Evangelicals espoused the revolution as a stage in God's design to bring about the millennium; God's kingdom on earth would be a radically reordered society. They did not, however, consider the struggle for liberty itself as a product of the outpouring of God's grace. Rather, they believed that freedom from the menace of political and religious tyranny would provide a context in which American society could increase in holiness.

RELIGIOUS CONSEQUENCES

As important as the Great Awakening was for American politics, evangelicalism was a religious movement first and foremost, and its influence on American religion was its most natural legacy. That legacy was theological, ecclesiastical, and cultural.

Jonathan Edwards and the New Divinity

In 1750 Jonathan Edwards lost his eminent position as pastor of the Congregational church at Northampton when the church, refusing to accept his renunciation of open Communion and reinstitution of a conversion relation as a requirement of membership, dismissed him. Edwards moved to the frontier town of Stockbridge, Massachusetts, where his congregation included Housatonic Indians. In 1758 he accepted appointment as president of the College of New Jersey but died soon after as a result of a smallpox vaccination. Despite Edwards's exile to the frontier and his premature death, he became one of the most influential of American theologians, establishing through his writings and his students an original theological school. Edwards employed modern psychology in support of evangelical Calvinism and of emotional religious experience, building an understanding of the nature of true virtue, a vision of the society of the saintly that would prevail when Christ established his millennial rule, and a powerful motive for voluntary benevolent activity.

Edwards taught that before his fall from grace man possessed an affection, or sentiment, for both self-interest and benevolence. God punished man for sin by removing the affection for benevolence. Man in his depraved condition was then capable of acting only out of self-love. Conversion, accordingly, is the arbitrary act of God's restoring the affection for benevolence to his elect. A regenerate heart is one that has perceived the excellency of God. The aesthetic sense of the excellency of God results in true virtue, benevolence, the consent to serve in the total divine scheme of things.

The gradual work of redemption is the spread of this perception and consent to more and more souls, resulting in the good ordering of society and eventually to the millennium. The ends of redemption pertain not solely or even primarily to saving particular men but principally to saving the human community.

Edwards taught that although the gift of grace is an arbitrary act of God, it occurs through natural means. Because conversion is the perception of the divine excellency, it takes place within the natural order of perception. The role of the minister is to help man perceive the divine excellency by giving him a true idea of it. Because God makes use of his church to channel his grace to his elect, it is possible and necessary for God's people to promote the work of redemption.

To Edwards's body of thought, his followers added ideas from the Scottish moral philosophers to promote moderate revivalism; to sustain the evangelical attack against liberal interpretations of free will, sin, and regeneration, and to defend evangelicalism against the charge that its predestinarian doctrines encouraged indifference to morality.

By locating true religion in benevolence, the Edwardseans, or New Divinity men, formulated a moral imperative for socially responsible engagement with the world. To the New Divinity men, the kingdom of God was within men to whom benevolence had been restored, and they encouraged moral activism as a means to hasten the millennium. In their attempts to present evangelical Calvinism in rational and humane terms, they emphasized God's benevolence rather than his justice and fashioned a man-centered rather than God-centered theology. The New Divinity thus foreshadowed both the attenuated Calvinism and the moral reform movements of the nineteenth century.

The Clergy

The Great Awakening altered the gospel ministry in America, an alteration illustrated by the

681

case of the New England Congregationalists. Radical Evangelicals challenged the standing Congregationalist churches with a revolutionary version of clerical legitimacy. In responding to that challenge moderate New Lights, conservative Old Lights, and liberals closed ranks to protect their common profession. In the process they subtly changed their own clerical emphases.

Experiences of preachers' being empowered to speak movingly for hours, extemporaneously and without preparation, of lay persons' exhorting with marked results, and of itinerant preachers'—ordained and not—producing revivals confirmed the radicals in the conviction that God called individuals directly to the ministry. Inspiration by the Holy Spirit, they maintained, not a college education or long hours of sermon preparation or membership in a clerical association, was what gave the ministry its legitimacy. This conviction stood in stark contrast to the traditional Congregationalist view that God manifested his calling of an individual to the ministry in the natural course of things, through such signs as an indication of piety, an inclination to theological study, a successful pastoral apprenticeship, and a call from a particular church.

Responding to the challenge, the established clergy united in asserting that a proper education was an essential qualification of a minister. They agreed with their critics that a minister should be converted, but they denied that the people could judge the souls of their preachers. A ministerial candidate's knowledge of divinity and of biblical languages, on the other hand, could be objectively tested. Furthermore, the established clergy reiterated that by virtue of his office, not his ability to arouse the passions of his auditors, the minister deserved respect. The experience of the Great Awakening, however, demonstrated that ministers retained their people's loyalty not because of the eminence of their office but through the personal affection they won through the pastoral relationship with their flocks. In place of lectures on the deference due them, the Congregationalist clergy began to emphasize a pastoral ethic of humility and service.

The Great Awakening produced no democratic restructuring of authority in the American churches. The radicals' version of ministerial legitimacy, however, was an alternative model that would resonate with the egalitarian rhetoric of popular religious movements of the early republic.

Evangelicalism and American Culture

The Great Awakening ensured that evangelicalism, not Enlightenment rationalism, would predominate in postrevolutionary America. It reinforced the denominational structure of American Christianity while providing a common evangelical culture that crossed denominational lines. It laid the foundation for the early republic's Second Great Awakening, during which evangelicalism confirmed its hold on the American religious landscape. And it established the religious revival as a phenomenon that would be a distinguishing feature of nineteenth-century American Protestant church life.

The preaching of the revivalists accelerated the Christianization of African Americans, which previously had been minimal; and the evangelical commitment to benevolence prompted pious men to undertake missionary work among Native Americans. Evangelical churches sought to assure the continuance of an evangelically trained ministry by founding the College of New Jersey (Princeton, 1746), the College of Rhode Island (Brown, 1764), Queens College (Rutgers, 1766), and Dartmouth College (1769). The evangelical movement created familial and communal traditions of enthusiastic, emotional religion on which radical new sects of the early national era drew.

Perhaps the most important result of the Great Awakening was the transformation it effected in the lives of countless ordinary people. Conversion gave individuals a sense of the divine, a foretaste of heavenly peace, and the assurance of self-worth. The evangelical movement, moreover, did not stop with the experience of conversion but led the individual into a new communal relationship. It brought converts together into close-knit voluntary communities of people who shared like experiences. Those communities helped their members to live up to new norms of behavior, norms that served as alternatives to those of an increasingly competitive, secular, and self-aggrandizing society.

BIBLIOGRAPHY

Balmer, Randall. *A Perfect Babel of Confusion: Dutch Religion and English Culture in the Middle Colonies.* New York, 1989.

Bonomi, Patricia U. *Under the Cope of Heaven: Religion, Society, and Politics in Colonial America.* New York, 1986.

Bonomi, Patricia U., and Peter R. Eisenstadt. "Church Adherence in the Eighteenth-Century British American Colonies." *William and Mary Quarterly,* 3rd ser., 39, no. 2 (1982):245–286.

Bumsted, J. M., and John E. Van de Wetering. *What Must I Do To Be Saved? The Great Awakening in Colonial America.* Hinsdale, Ill., 1976.

Bushman, Richard L. *From Puritan to Yankee: Character and the Social Order in Connecticut, 1690–1765.* Cambridge, Mass., 1967.

———, comp. *The Great Awakening: Documents on the Revival of Religion, 1740–1745.* New York, 1970.

Butler, Jon. "Enthusiasm Described and Decried: The Great Awakening As Interpretive Fiction." *Journal of American History* 69, no. 2 (1982):305–325.

Coalter, Milton J., Jr. *Gilbert Tennent, Son of Thunder: A Case Study of Continental Pietism's Impact on the First Great Awakening in the Middle Colonies.* Westport, Conn., 1986.

Cowing, Cedric B. *The Great Awakening and the American Revolution: Colonial Thought in the 18th Century.* Chicago, 1971.

Crawford, Michael J. *Seasons of Grace: Colonial New England's Revival Tradition in Its British Context.* New York, 1991.

———. "The Spiritual Travels of Nathan Cole." *William and Mary Quarterly,* 3rd ser., 33, no. 1 (1976):89–126.

Dallimore, Arnold A. *George Whitefield: The Life and Times of the Great Evangelist of the Eighteenth-Century Revival.* 2 vols. London, 1970–1980.

De Jong, Gerald F. *The Dutch Reformed Church in the American Colonies.* Grand Rapids, Mich., 1978.

Edwards, Jonathan. *The Works of Jonathan Edwards.* Edited by C. C. Goen. Vol. 4, *The Great Awakening.* New Haven, Conn., 1972.

Fiering, Norman S. *Jonathan Edwards's Moral Thought and Its British Context.* Chapel Hill, N.C., 1981.

Gaustad, Edwin Scott. *The Great Awakening in New England.* New York, 1957.

Gewehr, Wesley M. *The Great Awakening in Virginia, 1740–1790.* Durham, N.C., 1930; repr. Gloucester, Mass., 1965.

Gillies, John, comp. *Historical Collections of Accounts of Revival.* 2 vols. Glasgow, 1754; rev. ed. 1845; repr. of rev. ed. Fairfield, Pa., 1981. The 1754 edition was published in two volumes as *Historical Collections Relating to Remarkable Periods of the Success of the Gospel, and Eminent Instruments Employed in Promoting It.*

Goen, C. C. *Revivalism and Separatism in New England, 1740–1800: Strict Congregationalists and Separate Baptists in the Great Awakening.* New Haven, Conn., 1962.

Heimert, Alan. *Religion and the American Mind: From the Great Awakening to the Revolution.* Cambridge, Mass., 1966.

Heimert, Alan, and Perry Miller, eds. *The Great Awakening: Documents Illustrating the Crisis and Its Consequences.* Indianapolis, Ind., 1967.

Isaac, Rhys. *The Transformation of Virginia, 1740–1790.* Chapel Hill, N.C., 1982.

Lodge, Martin E. "The Crisis of the Churches in the Middle Colonies, 1720–1750." *Pennsylvania Magazine of History and Biography* 95, no. 2 (1971):195–220.

Lucas, Paul R. "'An Appeal to the Learned': The Mind of Solomon Stoddard." *William and Mary Quarterly,* 3rd ser., 30, no. 2 (1973):257–292.

McLoughlin, William G. *Isaac Backus and the American Pietistic Tradition.* Boston, 1967.

Mathews, Donald G. *Religion in the Old South.* Chicago, 1977.

Maxson, Charles Hartshorn. *The Great Awakening in the Middle Colonies.* Chicago, 1920; repr. Gloucester, Mass., 1958.

Miller, Perry. *Jonathan Edwards.* New York, 1949.

Nash, Gary B. *The Urban Crucible: Social Change, Political Consciousness, and the Origins of the American Revolution.* Cambridge, Mass., 1979.

Schafer, Thomas A. "Solomon Stoddard and the Theology of the Revival." In *A Miscellany of American Christianity: Essays in Honor of H. Shelton Smith,* edited by Stuart C. Henry. Durham, N.C., 1963.

Schmidt, Leigh Eric. *Holy Fairs: Scottish Communions and American Revivals in the Early Modern Period.* Princeton, N.J., 1989.

Stoeffler, F. Ernest, ed. *Continental Pietism and Early American Christianity.* Grand Rapids, Mich., 1976.

Stout, Harry S. *The New England Soul: Preaching and Religious Culture in Colonial New England.* New York, 1986.

———. "Religion, Communications, and the Ideological Origins of the American Revolution." *William and Mary Quarterly,* 3rd ser., 34, no. 4 (1977):519–541.

Tanis, James. *Dutch Calvinistic Pietism in the Middle Colonies: A Study in the Life and Theology of Theodorus*

Jacobus Frelinghuysen. The Hague, The Netherlands, 1967.

Tracy, Joseph. *The Great Awakening: A History of the Revival of Religion in the Time of Edwards and Whitefield.* Boston–New York, 1842; repr. Carlisle, Pa., 1989.

Tracy, Patricia J. *Jonathan Edwards, Pastor: Religion and Society in Eighteenth-Century Northampton.* New York, 1980.

Trinterud, Leonard J. *The Forming of an American Tradition: A Re-examination of Colonial Presbyterianism.* Philadelphia, 1949.

Westerkamp, Marilyn J. *Triumph of the Laity: Scots-Irish Piety and the Great Awakening, 1625–1760.* New York, 1988.

Whitefield, George. *George Whitefield's Journals.* London, 1960.

Winslow, Ola Elizabeth. *Jonathan Edwards, 1703–1758: A Biography.* New York, 1940.

Youngs, J. William T., Jr. *God's Messengers: Religious Leadership in Colonial New England, 1700–1750.* Baltimore, Md., 1976.

Michael J. Crawford

XVII

TOWARD INDEPENDENCE

The Reorganization of Empires
Crises of Empire
Ideologies of Revolution
Independence

THE REORGANIZATION OF EMPIRES

THE BRITISH COLONIES

WHO DECIDED POLICY IN Georgian Britain was a puzzle to European statesmen, and a source of confusion to many American colonists. The British "mixed form" of monarchical government was unique and, indeed, still in the process of evolution. But by the time of George III's accession in 1760 the main features of the political system had been established, and it is a long since exploded myth that he sought to turn back the constitutional clock to the time of royal power. The twenty-two-year-old new king fully accepted the curtailment of the royal prerogative that had developed since the Glorious Revolution of 1688. What he did insist upon was the sovereign's right to choose his ministers; having done so, he was content to let them govern. Policy decisions were made by the cabinet of six to twelve leading officeholders, and George III often had no positive opinions even on such important matters as the American crisis: not until virtually the outbreak of war did he strive to insist on a firm stance. Earlier he loyally backed the various policy shifts of his successive ministers. His appointments and dismissals of them derived from personal prejudices and not policy considerations, and the frequent ministerial changes of the 1760s were due to his desire to find a prime minister (the contemporary term was "the premier" or simply "the minister") whom he found congenial and who could command the support of Parliament.

George III, at first not realizing this last restraint, appointed his favorite, John Stuart, Lord Bute, in 1762. Within a year he had to turn to a politician with a parliamentary base, George Grenville. Grenville was dismissed in 1765 because he had personally antagonized the king; his successor, Charles Watson-Wentworth, marquess of Rockingham, was replaced a year later because George III deemed his ministry incompetent and had high hopes of William Pitt the elder, now made earl of Chatham. These hopes proved quite unfounded, and after he resigned in 1768 the ministry Chatham had chosen staggered on under the duke of Grafton, who resigned in January 1770 when confronted with an opposition led by Grenville, Rockingham, and Chatham. George III was saved from the humiliation of surrendering to this challenge by the advent to office of the respected and competent Lord North, an able parliamentarian who soon won the friendship as well as the gratitude of the king, and who survived for twelve years, until brought down by defeat in the American War. Little of this political turmoil had anything to do with America, and underneath the shifting policies of different ministers there was always the determination to maintain British control over the colonies.

Like their king, the ministers also had to take account of Parliament. While the king could appoint and dismiss a prime minister and his colleagues, approval of the House of Commons was necessary for both the successful enactment of the prime minister's policies and his tenure of office. The latter was rarely a matter of concern, although in 1782, as a result of the failure of the American War, Lord North was forced to resign, against the wishes of George III. More relevant to the day-to-day political scene was the need of parliamentary majority support for ministerial policies, and the nature of the contemporary British political system made that anything but a formality.

In 1929 Sir Lewis Namier first described what he called "the structure of politics" in mid-eighteenth-century Britain. He demonstrated that the House of Commons comprised not two contending parties, Whigs and Tories, but an assembly of more than five hundred members—from squires to merchants to sprigs of the aristocracy—who owed their seats to varying combinations of family influence, personal exertions, and financial expenditure. In contrast, barely 20 to 30 of the 558 members owed their election to ministerial assistance. All ministers were confronted with this body of "self-returning" members, and persuasion rather than bribery was the mode of influence employed to secure a majority among them.

For convenience of analysis, the House of Commons can be broadly divided into three types of allegiances demonstrated by members after their arrival at Westminster. There was "the court party" of some 150 alleged "placemen," ranging from army colonels to holders of sinecures, providing a makeweight, but no more than that, in favor of government. There were about one hundred "politicians," men attached to one of the several small factions in Parliament or perhaps acting on their own. These were the members who, with associated peers, were ambitious for the power and perquisites of high political office, and at any point in time some would be in government and some in opposition. Also sitting on both sides of the House of Commons were the three hundred "independents," some of whom might as regularly support the government as others would oppose it, but among whom there were many whose individual opin-

ions on ministerial measures would determine their attitudes toward them. They needed convincing, and that was why any successful prime minister had to be a good House of Commons man; only George Grenville and Lord North filled the bill in the era of the American Revolution. Success in this respect, however, was more than a matter of political skills.

Policies had to be tailored to suit the opinions and prejudices of the House of Commons. That ministerial measures on America invariably enjoyed large parliamentary majorities did not mean that Westminster approval was rubber-stamped. Soundings were taken and opinions canvased before policies were initiated, and the weight of prejudice in Parliament over America was increasingly against concessions to and conciliation of the colonies. In the mid 1770s this hard-line attitude proved to be a constraint on ministerial policy making.

From 1763 Britain ruled the entire continent of North America east of the Mississippi River. She had already held the Hudson Bay territories to the north, Newfoundland and Nova Scotia on the northeast seaboard, and the thirteen old settlement colonies along the Atlantic coast from New Hampshire to Georgia. By the Treaty of Paris, France ceded her Quebec colony and all claims to land north and south of the Great Lakes up to the Mississippi, while Spain gave up Florida and the coastal strip west to the Mississippi. These vast areas contained about one hundred thousand French, five thousand Spaniards, and some two hundred fifty thousand Native Americans. Many politicians and officials in Britain were worried about the difficulties of organizing these new territories, but the immediate problems arising from them were solved by the end of 1763. Although British ministers continued thereafter to study the Indian question and the seemingly intractable problem of the substantial French population in Quebec, Britain's American policy was concerned primarily with her older colonies.

Prior to 1763, in what has been called a century of "salutary neglect," the British settlement colonies on the Atlantic coast of North America enjoyed rapid economic and political development with little regulation from Britain. Colonial merchants had often paid only lip service to the trade laws. The small elected assemblies had acquired powers of legislation and taxation, and these mini-Parliaments were deemed by Americans to be equivalent in status to the mother Parliament at Westminster. But that was not the interpretation of the imperial constitution held in Britain. That the king's government now chose to act increasingly through Parliament, rather than through the royal privy council, was the root cause of the American quarrel with Britain, but there was also widespread resentment at the specific policies being implemented. For what happened from 1763 was that the British government, despite frequent changes of ministry, took advantage of a period of European peace to overhaul the empire, seeking both tighter control and financial contributions. Attention was given to the old problem of Ireland and the new one of India, but it was North America that became the main focus of interest.

THE BRITISH ARMY IN AMERICA

Already the exigencies of war had seen Crown encroachments on powers hitherto exercised by the colonies. In 1754, with the Seven Years' War imminent, the post of army commander in chief was created, with powers superseding those of governors and with direction of Indian affairs, hitherto a preserve of individual colonies. The latter function was delegated in 1755 to two Indian superintendents, northern and southern. In 1763 these wartime expedients became permanent peacetime practice. There was now an army commander in chief, normally residing at New York, with powers and responsibilities extending over the whole of British North America. It was one complaint in the Declaration of Independence that George III had "affected to render the Military independent of and superior to the Civil power." General Thomas Gage, who was army commander from 1763 to 1775, in fact contrived to give the minimum offense to the colonists. But it was inevitable that complaints would arise over the presence of an army, because of practical difficulties over its accommodation and transport, and especially because the British government intended to make the American colonists pay toward its cost. For when on 4 March 1763 the Bute ministry (1762–1763)

announced to Parliament a decision to keep in America a larger army than had hitherto been customary, members were assured that after the first year the cost would fall on the colonists.

The reason for the military decision was publicly stated to be France's retention of a twenty-thousand-man army in the West Indies. This potential threat from Britain's traditional enemy, and the need to overawe both the Indian tribes and the new French subjects of Canada, meant that the army would be garrisoned for the most part outside the old British colonies: in Canada, in Florida, along the southern coast, and in the wilderness of the Mississippi and Ohio valleys. But if the chief motive was defense, an important subsidiary aim in this deployment of the army was to avoid trouble with the Indian tribes by protecting them against unscrupulous exploitation by both cheating traders and settlers seeking to trick them out of their land. Parliament, however, could not be openly told this.

It was never a British intention to establish military control over the settlement colonies; no soldiers were stationed in recalcitrant Massachusetts until the behavior of Boston made a permanent military occupation there necessary from 1768. Nor was the American army to be the ten thousand men customarily stated. That was to be the establishment only for the transitional year of 1764. Thereafter it was to consist of seventy-five hundred men; successive cuts from 1770 reduced it to only sixty-two hundred men by 1773. Britain evidently was neither intending military rule nor expecting violent discontent. Failure to shift the financial burden of the army onto colonial shoulders was undoubtedly the cause of this reduction. No ministry was able to fulfill the promise made to Parliament in 1763, when the annual cost was anticipated at £225,000. In fact, despite the military economies, the actual cost averaged £384,000 in the years between 1763 and 1775.

THE QUARTERING ACT OF 1765

The total cost of roughly £384,000 per year did not include that of billeting soldiers who were stationed in, or in transit through, the older settlement colonies. Although they formed only a small part of the army, how these troops were to be accommodated soon became a bone of contention.

The American Mutiny Act of 1765, better known as the Quartering Act, was a response to Gage's complaints about colonial obstruction. The Grenville ministry (1763–1765) took great care to avoid a form of wording that would permit the billeting of soldiers in private houses. The solution was a clause authorizing billeting by local magistrates in uninhabited buildings if no barracks or inns were available. In such cases, so another clause stipulated, the colony should provide the soldiers, free of charge, with firewood, candles, bedding, and cooking utensils, as well as rum, cider, or vinegar.

Gage soon found that this solution was unsatisfactory. Billeting in private houses, previously not an uncommon practice, was now implicitly illegal. Worse still, the operation of the provisions clause depended on the mood of an assembly. Colonists perceived a double grievance: the clause was regarded as a tax and as an unfair tax, since its incidence was uneven and accidental. Some colonies, such as Virginia, escaped a military presence altogether; in contrast, New York, containing the main port for the arrival and departure of soldiers, had the heaviest burden. During 1765 and 1766 that colony's assembly refused several requests from Gage for supplies and, although a few other colonies were occasionally defiant or obstructive on the point, the Chatham ministry (1766–1768) decided to make an example. The New York Restraining Act of 1767 proposed to prevent the assembly there from meeting until it complied with the Quartering Act. But it so happened that the assembly gave way at the very time this legislation was being passed, and it never came into effect.

The Quartering Act remained an intermittent colonial grievance, and it was accordingly revised in 1769. One alteration sensibly permitted army officers and civil magistrates discretion to make mutually satisfactory arrangements. Another, never acted upon, allowed colonies to opt out of the Quartering Act if they passed their own legislation for the same purpose. In 1771 Secretary of State for the Colonies Wills Hill, earl of Hillsborough, devised a pragmatic solution when New Jersey refused to pay. Rather than coerce the colony, he withdrew the regiment sent there, so as to prompt appreciation of the financial and military benefits of an army presence. A regiment would spend its pay and maintenance costs locally, and might be useful in maintaining order.

The tactic caused other colonies to vote their contributions without delay, and the problem of the Quartering Act was virtually resolved, apart from the special case of Massachusetts. It was only because of the new difficulty of accommodating a large force in Boston in 1774 that another Quartering Act was passed. Contrary to persistent legend, this did not authorize billeting in private houses but merely transferred the authority under the 1765 act from the magistrates to the governor, so that there would be no obstruction to the placing of soldiers in taverns, halls, and barns.

WESTERN POLICY

In 1763, before measures to finance and billet the army were introduced, the major policy decisions concerning arrangements for the new territories were speedily taken. Charles Wyndham, Lord Egremont, as southern secretary the minister responsible for the colonies during the ministries of Lord Bute and George Grenville (until his death in August 1763), soon produced the broad outlines of a plan. The details were filled in by the Board of Trade and Plantations, at this time a government department exclusively concerned with colonies and commerce. Egremont proposed a western boundary beyond which settlement should not be allowed, for fear of alienating the Indians, and in July 1763 the Grenville ministry agreed that this should be the mountain watershed between the coastal plain and the Mississippi Valley. The two Indian superintendents were entrusted with the task of establishing this on the ground.

North and south of what would be an enormous Indian reservation three new colonies were devised for the areas where white settlers already lived. Quebec was limited to the Saint Lawrence River valley for the French inhabitants of that conquered colony. East and West Florida were created for the sparse Spanish population of that peninsula and the southern coast, respectively. Until they contained more British settlers, these new colonies, unlike the older ones, were not to have elected assemblies; and even in 1774 the Quebec Act, which guaranteed French civil law and the Catholic religion to the inhabitants of that colony, did not make such a concession.

The Proclamation of 1763, which established these territorial arrangements, was followed between 1764 and 1766 by plans for the management of the Indian tribes as the two superintendents developed an organization of commissaries, interpreters, and gunsmiths. The cost of what has sometimes been called an Indian Department, and much more so the unexpectedly great expense of maintaining a military presence throughout the forest wilderness, soon led to proposals by Gage for economy through withdrawal of most of the army garrisons. But William Petty, Lord Shelburne, southern secretary in the Chatham ministry, had plans to the contrary; in 1767 he proposed the creation of three new colonies south of the Great Lakes. Although this idea was quashed by Lord Hillsborough when he became the first secretary of state for America (1768–1772), British government policy was not firmly against westward settlement. When Northern Indian Superintendent Sir William Johnson in 1768 concluded Indian treaties for a settlement line well to the west of what had been intended in 1763, the indignant American secretary discovered that all his cabinet colleagues favored the idea of such expansion; he was driven to resign in 1772 when his opposition to a subsequently abortive scheme for a new colony of Vandalia in the Ohio Valley was overruled. Yet Hillsborough, on grounds of economy, had allowed Gage to evacuate such western forts as he thought fit, and twenty-four had been abandoned by 1773.

Britain's final solution to the western problem was embodied in the Quebec Act of 1774, which incorporated most of the wilderness into an expanded version of that colony by extending its boundary to the Ohio River. It thereby threatened to block the further potential westward expansion of such colonies as New York and Pennsylvania, and revived the settlement issue as a matter of colonial complaint, even though the 1763 Proclamation Line had been tacitly abandoned.

THE CURRENCY ACT OF 1764

Problems arising from the older colonies engrossed much more British attention than those of the new territories. The colonial assemblies issued their own paper money, which was used to repay debts to British merchants that often had been incurred in sterling. Among various grievances about American behavior, the depreciated state of certain colonial currencies had long concerned the Board of Trade and Plantations. Virginia, the worst offender, had already been warned by the Bute ministry to mend its ways, and on its refusal to do so the Board of Trade, on 9 February 1764, published a report condemning all colonial legal-tender paper money as fraudulent and suggesting a ban on new issues. Ministerial enactment of this ban was postponed because of the press of other business, but on 4 April an independent member of Parliament involved in American trade, Anthony Bacon, moved for a bill to ban all existing as well as future colonial currency. The ministry thereupon modified this to the Board of Trade and Plantations proposal. The Currency Act of 1764 did not, therefore, cancel existing paper money, and had little immediate effect. But all such money was dated to expire at specified times, and from the mid 1760s complaints about the growing scarcity of paper money began to reach London.

Lord Hillsborough refused to alter the Currency Act when he was American secretary, but in 1773 the North ministry (1770–1782) passed amending legislation that provided a viable compromise between the conflicting interests of American colonists and British merchants: the value of the paper currency was guaranteed for use in the payment of taxes and other public debts, but individual private creditors could still insist on being paid in sterling.

THE SUGAR ACT OF 1764

If the currency question was but a minor colonial grievance, that was partly because Americans had much else to complain about in other British policy measures. In 1763 Prime Minister George Grenville ordered a detailed investigation into colonial evasion of the trade laws; the investigation revealed a state of affairs intolerable to a man obsessed with legality and financial solvency. Evidence compiled by the Board of Trade and Plantations and the customs commissioners revealed a host of defects: the inefficiency, coercion, and corruption of many customs officials; difficulty in securing convictions in jury trials; and the immense task of patrolling such a long coastline. Administrative action preceded legislation. The navy was brought in to make war on the smugglers and stationed more than forty-four ships in American waters. Absentee customs officials were ordered to their posts and made to do their duty, on pain of dismissal, an almost unprecedented threat in that age of patronage.

The key measure was the complicated American Duties Act of 1764, which comprised an extensive overhaul of the trade laws and the methods of enforcing them. Among the more controversial changes was the creation of a new Vice-Admiralty Court at Halifax in remote Nova Scotia. In such courts decisions were made by judges, without juries. Eleven already existed in the colonies, to deal with maritime cases, but they had proved susceptible to local pressure. Hence the location of the new court, which would have both concurrent and appellate jurisdiction over all America, and to which customs officials would be encouraged to refer difficult cases.

These provisions in the Duties Act to alter and enforce the trade laws were overshadowed by the most important provision of the measure, which has often given it the name Sugar Act. This was the first deliberate attempt to tax the colonies. The act called for the conversion of an existing duty on molasses, a by-product of sugar refining used to make rum, into a source of revenue as well as a trade regulation. The Molasses Act of 1733 had imposed what was intended to be a prohibitive duty of six pence a gallon on molasses imported from foreign West Indian islands into British North America, the purpose being to preserve that market for the British islands. The act had been virtually a dead letter. Such a high duty encouraged smuggling, and in any case the British West Indies could supply only a small proportion of American needs. Grenville, apprised of these circumstances, decided to halve the duty and enforce it, aiming to produce a revenue estimated by the treasury at seventy-eight thousand pounds but forecast to Parliament as much less.

When Grenville announced this plan as part of his budget on 9 March 1764, he stated that the money would be put toward the cost of the army in America: there was never any substance in the myth that Britain sought by her taxation of the colonies to make them contribute toward the cost of the national debt incurred in the Seven Years' War. Since it would be quite inadequate for an army expense now estimated, Grenville said, at £360,000 a year, he informed members of Parliament of his intention simultaneously to introduce a stamp act for the colonies.

THE STAMP ACT OF 1765

This measure had been in preparation since the autumn of 1763. It would extend to the colonies stamp duties imposed in Britain itself since the later seventeenth century. They applied to a wide range of legal documents; to cargo lists for ships and other papers used in trade; to newspapers, to advertisements in them, and to many other items produced by printers, such as calendars; and to a miscellany of other items like licenses to sell alcohol, university degree certificates, playing cards, and dice. Such a measure would directly affect lawyers, merchants, and printers in the regular conduct of their business, and most other colonists at some time or another. It was even more of an innovation than the adaptation of the molasses duty to raise revenue, for the stamp duties would be taxes levied within the colonies and not merely on goods imported. When in the 1764 budget debate a few members of Parliament suggested that the colonists should first be informed and consulted, Grenville readily agreed to postpone this measure for a year and went ahead with the molasses duty only. His concession was intended, however, merely to allow Americans to suggest alternative Parliamentary taxation and not, as has sometimes been stated, to permit them to produce schemes for taxing themselves through their assemblies.

The American response was one of indignation. No colony made any suggestion about alternative parliamentary taxation. Instead at least eight of the thirteen old colonies protested the proposed Stamp Act as "taxation without representation"; only two seem to have complained about the Sugar Act as a tax, though others did so on economic grounds. This colonial challenge to Parliament's right of taxation over America merely stiffened the determination of the ministry to proceed with the measure. By the time

Grenville introduced the stamp bill into the House of Commons on 6 February 1765, the chief motive was assertion of parliamentary sovereignty rather than the raising of revenue. A few members did oppose the tax on grounds of folly and inexpediency, but the ministry won the day by 245 votes to 49, and there was no further test of parliamentary opinion.

The Grenville ministry thought the Stamp Act would be accepted under protest, and took care to avoid all reasonable objections to it. The wide range of duties had been devised to provide an equitable distribution of the burden. They averaged only about two-thirds of their equivalent in Britain, and the total tax revenue anticipated was small: estimates varied between fifty thousand and one hundred thousand pounds, and that sum, even with the molasses-duty revenue, would not pay half the cost of the army in America. The money raised would be handed over to the army in the colonies. (It was a contemporary fallacy that there would be any drain of specie from America.) Nor would there be a new group of officials sent out from Britain: the administration of the measure would be in the hands of colonists.

None of these concessions prevented the storm of protest that in 1765 nullified the operation of the Stamp Act by compelling these officials to resign. The Rockingham ministry (1765–1766), caught in the vise of the violent resistance in America and the consequent public indignation in Britain, accompanied repeal of the Stamp Act in 1766 with the Declaratory Act, asserting the right of Parliament to legislate for the colonies "in all cases whatsoever": taxation was included, though not specifically mentioned. It was not a mere face-saving phrase but an affirmation of a political faith almost universally cherished in Britain. Moreover, contrary to legend, the Rockingham ministry had not abandoned the idea of a colonial revenue and, indeed, devised the sole really productive tax to be levied on America in the revolutionary period: an adaptation of Grenville's Sugar Act of 1764.

The reduction in 1764 of the duty on foreign molasses had failed to deter smuggling, for the duty of three pence yielded only fifty-two hundred pounds in that year and forty-one hundred pounds in 1765. The duty was reduced in 1766 to a penny a gallon, and levied on all molasses entering America, British as well as foreign, thereby eliminating fraudulent declarations. The change was a financial success, for smuggling of molasses was now too unprofitable to be widely risked. Between 1766 and the War of Independence the molasses duty brought in a revenue that swelled to thirty or forty thousand pounds a year, approximately 10 percent of the American army costs. The Rockingham ministry had other taxation plans for the colonies involving import duties on wine, fruit, and other commodities; but Rockingham was dismissed from office before these ideas could be implemented.

THE TOWNSHEND DUTIES OF 1767

One of the first initiatives of the Chatham ministry (1766–1768) was a search for methods of taxing America, and various alternatives were considered before Chancellor of the Exchequer Charles Townshend returned to the idea of customs duties. This met what was generally, if erroneously, believed in Britain to be colonial acceptance of "external taxation," as distinct from such "internal taxation" as the stamp duties. Townshend discarded the Rockinghamite targets in his final list of taxable goods, introduced on 1 June 1767 into the House of Commons. He proposed small duties on paper, glass, china, and paint, to produce twenty thousand pounds, and a duty of three pence on two pounds of tea for another twenty thousand pounds. In reply to a Grenville taunt that these were "trifles," he stated that they were only a beginning. Townshend's death on 4 September put an end to any further plans.

The purpose of this revenue plan was to be quite different from that of the earlier taxation measures. When on 26 January 1767 Townshend announced to the House of Commons his intention to tax America, he had said that he would use the money to meet the costs of the American army. But within a few months he had changed his mind, and decided instead to use the duties to pay the costs of civil government in the colonies, an idea he had conceived as early as 1753. An idea obvious to British politicians steeped in historical knowledge of Parliament's use of its taxation power against the Crown, it was irrelevant to the American scene.

Few governors were entirely dependent on salaries voted by assemblies, and none had been coerced by this weapon. When Townshend's tactic was adopted in Massachusetts in the early 1770s, it proved not merely irrelevant but also counterproductive in its provocative effect.

Townshend did not anticipate the resistance to his new taxes that was to lead to the repeal in 1770 of all but the lucrative duty on tea, but he was well aware of the difficulties of enforcing the trade laws in America. His duties were therefore accompanied by three measures to remedy that situation.

One was the American Customs Board Act. The obvious motives were to ensure closer supervision of and greater support for the colonial customs service, but the act also aimed at affording merchants protection from local abuses of authority. By 29 July 1767 the British Customs Board had produced a plan for an American board of five members, with ten subordinate officials, at a net extra salary cost of two thousand pounds. It was established in November and based at Boston, rather than Philadelphia or New York, possibly because Boston was deemed the center of resistance. The location was a mistake. Devoid of military protection, the board had to flee the town in June 1768 and did not return until soldiers arrived in September. The board fled again for nine months when the soldiers left after the Boston Massacre of 5 March 1770, but it then returned and remained at Boston until the War of Independence.

Townshend's Revenue Act contained a clause that sought to extend the use of writs of assistance to all colonies. These writs authorized customs officials to search premises for smuggled goods. They had first been issued in Massachusetts some dozen years before, and after their legality had been vainly challenged there in a celebrated court case in 1761, political agitation over their use had virtually ceased. In 1768 the new American Customs Board instructed customs officials in the various colonies to obtain writs from their local law courts. There ensued an ongoing controversy that contributed to the alienation of the colonies from Britain. For the next few years, until South Carolina yielded in 1773, the local colonial courts unanimously refused to permit such general power to the customs service, although they were willing to issue writs for the search of specified buildings if good cause could be shown. The whole procedure came to be depicted as an attack on individual liberty.

In addition to the Customs Board and the writs of assistance, Townshend intended to use a third method of enforcing the trade laws. The experiment of the new Vice-Admiralty Court established at Halifax had been a failure. The distance deterred customs officials from taking cases there. In 1765 a clause in the Stamp Act therefore substituted courts at Boston, Philadelphia, and Charleston; but before they had been created, the complete repeal of that measure had the effect of nullifying this attempt to meet a colonial grievance. Townshend died before the relevant legislation was put before Parliament, but in 1768 four regional Vice-Admiralty Courts were established at Halifax, Boston, Philadelphia, and Charleston: each was to have original jurisdiction within its own area, and also appellate jurisdiction over the provincial courts. There was no outcry about this new system, for it met earlier complaints of both merchants and customs officials about the unreasonable distance to Halifax. The new judges, moreover, were to be paid by the Crown, to prevent both bribery against and financial bias toward convictions. But these courts soon became another cause of colonial discontent, as merchants such as Henry Laurens of Charleston encountered interference with their accustomed trading practices through frequent enforcement of the letter of the law.

THE AMERICAN SECRETARYSHIP

Set against this background of five years of close attention to the colonies, the creation of a secretaryship of state for the colonies has often been seen as the final step in the reform of Britain's American empire. The idea was not a new one. During the 1750s George Dunk, Lord Halifax, when president of the Board of Trade and Plantations, had sought on several occasions to have his office upgraded to an American secretaryship, with a seat in the cabinet. The change had been considered by the Bute ministry in 1762, the Rockingham ministry in 1766, and the Chatham ministry in 1766 and 1767. When the change took place on 20 January 1768, the presidency of the Board of Trade and Plantations remained separate until 10 June; it was then merged into the new and senior appointment. The motive was not merely recognition of the need to control the colonies; there was also the desire to reduce the enormous work load of the southern secretary, who was responsible for home affairs in both Britain and Ireland and for foreign policy with France, Spain, and southern Europe, as well as for colonial matters.

The British overhaul of imperial government from 1763 has sometimes been depicted as a coherent policy. That is too rational a concept. What occurred was a series of initiatives by men who could see there was much to be done, and by no means all of the measures attributed to the two most prominent ministers involved, George Grenville and Charles Townshend, can be credited to them personally. The idea of a "Grenville program" for America dissolves under detailed scrutiny. The measures of his ministry had diverse antecedents. The Proclamation of 1763 was in substance based on earlier wartime decisions. The policy of maintaining an army in America, and the consequent commitment to a colonial tax, were legacies of the Bute ministry. So was the Currency Act in principle, and its actual introduction was by an independent member of Parliament. The Mutiny Act was never thought of until complaints came from General Gage. What the conscientious and industrious Grenville did supply was a determination to do whatever seemed to be necessary. Charles Townshend, a man of volatile temperament, brought enthusiasm and knowledge to the problem of America, but Sir Lewis Namier exaggerated when declaring his aim to be "a remodelling of colonial government." The original purpose of his taxation was the same as before, to meet army costs; the payment of colonial officials was an afterthought, albeit an old idea of his. The other measures associated with him—the American Customs Board, writs of assistance, and Vice-Admiralty Courts—were merely ways of enforcing trade laws and not a policy in themselves.

The British policies of the 1760s were less a systematic plan than an imperial attitude, but they did represent a perspective that went beyond the traditional mercantilist view that economic benefits formed the prime motive of co-

lonization. Tighter control would be imposed on Britain's overseas possessions, and they should be made to pay their own costs. All this was a traumatic shock to Americans, who had virtually been left to go their own way for decades. Suddenly they were confronted with a settlement line, a curb on their supply of currency, interference with their commercial and maritime habits, and the presence of an army. These were grievances enough; but the central point of controversy was Parliament's claim to sovereignty over America, especially as assumed in the taxation measures and openly stated in the Declaratory Act. The significance of the British moves lay not in the various irritants but in this issue of constitutional principle.

Yet to many observers in Britain at the end of 1770, it seemed as if the American crisis was over. The colonial trade boycott imposed in retaliation for the Townshend duties had collapsed after the ministry of Lord North repealed all those duties except that on tea. This apparent governmental climb-down had been little more than a token gesture, for only the tea duty had produced any significant revenue. At a cabinet meeting on 1 May 1769 the then–prime minister, the duke of Grafton, had been outvoted, five to four, over his wish to repeal the tea duty as well. That decision can be seen, in retrospect, as the point of no return in the sequence of events leading to the American Revolution.

During the early 1770s the tea duty was paid on a sufficient amount of imports, over half a million pounds in 1771, to enable Lord North to fulfill in part Townshend's aim of paying colonial salaries out of the revenue. This period of comparative political calm, however, was deceptive, for the British attempts in the 1760s to impose American taxes had initiated a colonial debate about the constitutional structure of the British Empire. Americans were coming to dispute the power of Parliament to legislate for them even before the final crisis was precipitated by the Boston Tea Party.

That event, ironically, arose from a situation unrelated to British colonial policy. Britain's biggest commercial organization, the East India Company, was by 1773 suffering from a financial crisis caused by its inability to sell tea, which normally provided 90 percent of its revenue. Part of the rescue package devised by the North ministry was the Tea Act, which included tax and trade concessions enabling the East India Company to sell tea in America at a price that, including the Townshend duty, would be lower than that of the smuggled Dutch tea which captured most of the colonial market. Fearing the loss of their illicit trade, the merchants of New York and Philadelphia launched an immediate protest campaign, depicting the project as a ministerial plot to trick Americans into acceptance of taxed tea. By the end of November 1773 it was evident that the sale of East India Company tea would be prevented at both ports. But in Boston the legal tea merchants, given military protection, refused to surrender to popular pressure. This impasse led to the destruction of the company tea there on 16 December.

THE INTOLERABLE ACTS OF 1774

No revisionist interpretation of the American Revolution has attempted to dismiss the significance of the Boston Tea Party. It was an open challenge to Britain's authority that shocked public opinion there, opposition politicians like Lord Chatham and the marquess of Rockingham being as appalled as supporters of the ministry. The North cabinet at first simply intended direct executive action: legal punishment of the persons responsible and the closure of Boston harbor. This line of policy soon proved to be impractical, for there was no evidence to convict individuals. The ministry therefore decided to deploy the full weight of parliamentary legislation, thereby raising the stakes in any confrontation: continued colonial opposition would constitute a challenge to the authority of Westminster.

By the end of February 1774 the North cabinet adopted a policy not only of closing the port of Boston until the town paid compensation for the tea but also of altering the charter of Massachusetts, more democratic than those of the other royal colonies, because it was deemed to make that colony ungovernable. The Boston Port Act passed Parliament on 31 March 1774 without a vote against it, and the Massachusetts Government Act by the large majority of 239 to 64 on the third reading. The so-called Intolerable Acts were completed by the temporary Impartial Administration of Justice Act, to secure fair trials

for soldiers and officials concerned in the support of government. North disappointed some expectations by failing to offer any concessions whatsoever, and an opposition move to repeal the tea duty was crushed by 182 votes to 49 on 19 April. Popular opinion was strongly behind official policy, one opposition member of Parliament lamenting that "it is not an error of the ministry: it is an error of the nation."

Soon associated with these measures by the Americans was the Quebec Act, passed in June 1774, for there was much in it to arouse alarm and indignation in the thirteen older colonies. It had been long in the making, and what to posterity have seemed the most enlightened features of the legislation—the legality of Catholic worship and the use of French civil law—represented a consensus view in Britain. They were ideas inherited from the Grenville and Rockingham ministries of the 1760s and now belatedly enacted. The input of the North ministry was twofold. As early as 7 June 1771 the cabinet rejected the idea of an elected assembly as the colony's legislature in favor of a council nominated by the Crown: an assembly based on the small minority of no more than two thousand British settlers would be unfair to the French Catholic population of some one hundred thousand, while a papist-dominated one was unthinkable. The other North ministry decision was momentous: the incorporation within Quebec of the entire area north and south of the Great Lakes down to the Ohio River. This solution to the western problem infuriated expansionists in the older British colonies, and the establishment of French law and the Roman Catholic church fueled American fears and bigotry. The Quebec Act became another grievance, and its repeal a colonial demand.

The ministerial tactic in the Intolerable Acts had been to isolate Massachusetts, for many Americans had been shocked by the violence in Boston. It never looked likely to succeed, and news from the colonies during the summer and autumn of 1774 was ominous, the widespread decision to formulate a collective response in a congress. The colonial defiance, moreover, had now become a complete challenge to the legislative power of Parliament. The Continental Congress, representatives of twelve colonies meeting at Philadelphia, demanded repeal of the offending legislation and instituted a structured trade boycott, the Continental Association. The Congress was as uncompromising as Parliament had been, making no conciliatory gesture. Americans assumed that, as in 1766 and 1770, Britain would yield enough ground to avoid a confrontation.

Neither side yet envisaged a civil war. Congress had refused the military option favored by radical hotheads, and the North ministry did not consider armed repression as a policy. It is necessary to state this clearly, for some accounts of British policy making have confused the two distinct problems facing the North ministry at the end of 1774: the general colonial crisis and the particular need to recover control of Massachusetts, where militia virtually besieged the British army in Boston. Such remarks as George III's comment to Lord North on 18 November 1774 that "blows must decide" referred only to the Massachusetts situation. Early in 1775 the cabinet decided to send three thousand soldiers to reinforce the four thousand already in Boston. The ministry was hoping, by such prompt action, to prevent the escalation of the military standoff in Massachusetts into civil war. This tactic failed when the British army commander at Boston, General Thomas Gage, on 19 April dispatched a force to seize a colonial arsenal at Concord, thereby precipitating the armed clash at Lexington that launched the revolutionary war.

NORTH'S CONCILIATORY PROPOSAL OF 1775

The Battle of Lexington ruined any chance of success for the main policy initiative of the North ministry in 1775. Although the cabinet decided to answer the Continental Association by a ban on colonial trade and fishing, and the appropriate legislation was enacted in the spring of 1775, the cardinal feature of the ministry's American policy for that year was a conciliatory proposal devised by Lord North. This plan was that Parliament would refrain from taxing any individual colony that offered to pay its own civil government costs and its share of defense expenditure. This was North's concept of a permanent policy solution to the American crisis, and it became his ministry's war aim when the colonies refused to accept the proposal voluntarily. Delegation

of the power of taxation was to be the answer to the problem of imperial government.

When Lord North put forward this idea in Parliament on 20 February 1775, he had to fend off an attack by his own supporters over what many thought to be a disgraceful surrender to colonial resistance. This episode is a reminder of how much parliamentary opinion limited the ministry's freedom to make policy decisions. Any more generous proposal would have foundered at Westminster, where at first it seemed that even North's modest plan would be defeated. News of North's offer reached America after Lexington, and it never received serious consideration by the Continental Congress, which formally rejected it in July. This failure was more than a matter of unlucky timing. North's plan was based on the misconception that the imperial quarrel was still only about taxation, whereas in colonial eyes it had moved to the wider ground of parliamentary sovereignty. This misunderstanding also flawed the proposals of opposition spokesmen Lord Chatham and Edmund Burke. No British politician in 1775 could envisage any policy that would have satisfied colonial demands nor, in any case, would parliamentary approval have been forthcoming.

After news of Lexington reached London, the North ministry accepted the reality of a civil war, and much time during the next year was spent in military preparations for a major campaign in 1776. But North did not abandon his hopes of a negotiated settlement even when the famous Olive Branch Petition of the Continental Congress (1775) proved to contain no constructive proposals, to the chagrin of the few American sympathizers in Britain. The Proclamation of Rebellion, issued by George III on 23 August, did not signify the end of conciliation, for behind it lay a variety of tactical motives. They included the need to cut communications between America and Britain and the aim of rallying support for government policy. There resulted a national demonstration of patriotic feeling; resolutions voted on by public bodies produced 126 Addresses of support for the policy, against 26 Petitions of protest.

The policy North now envisaged was a peace commission to negotiate on his Conciliatory Plan of 20 February with individual colonies after each had been brought back under British control.

That was the thinking behind his so-called Prohibitory Act of late 1775, the most misunderstood part of North's American policy. It repealed the Boston Port Act and the 1775 legislation banning American trade, replacing them with a prohibition of all colonial commerce. But—and this was the crucial point—North's proposed peace commission would be empowered to remove this ban on any individual colony that came to terms. North's purpose was to give the peace commission the bargaining counter of this discretionary power. Contemporary criticism erroneously focused on the trade ban, and so has subsequent historical comment. Once again North's good intentions came to naught. Wrangling within his own ministry over both the personnel of the peace commission—eventually Lord Howe and General Howe—and the terms it could offer delayed its formal appointment until May 1776. Lord Howe did not arrive at New York until after the Declaration of Independence. American resistance leaders had taken care to ensure that the commission, known to be on its way, would have no chance of success.

CONCLUSION

The story of the British side of the American Revolution has been confused by a variety of misunderstandings, both contemporary and historical. Many colonists refused to accept that the official policies enjoyed popular support in Britain, ascribing them to a tyrannical ministry and a corrupt Parliament; but majority public opinion in Britain, however defined, did favor coercion of America. Then there is the hoary old myth that British policy was instigated by a king whose wicked constitutional plotting allegedly threatened liberty in both America and Britain.

George III in fact bore little direct responsibility for policy making, as the colonial leadership knew full well; not until 1776 did they blame him as a pretext for seeking independence. During the final crisis years the king did voice his support of firm measures, but these were to enforce the parliamentary supremacy of which by 1782 he was almost the last champion. Earlier he had passively supported whatever policies his various ministers chose to adopt as they initiated the imperial reorganization that provoked colonial resentment.

The basic quarrel between Britain and America did not concern the role of the monarchy; it was simply over whether Parliament should be the legislature for the British Empire. Before 1763 parliamentary supremacy over British colonies had been tacitly assumed rather than frequently asserted. The initial colonial challenge in the Stamp Act crisis led to the Declaratory Act of 1766, the first formal claim of full parliamentary power over the colonies; and that Britain then regarded America as being ruled by Parliament rather than the king was signified by the Massachusetts Government Act, which altered a charter granted by the Crown. Although Lord North proved willing to allow the colonies to tax themselves, neither his ministry nor British public opinion would accept the implicit demand for internal home rule that underlay the colonial challenge to Parliament. The gap between Britain's maximum concession, the power of taxation, and America's minimum demand, the right of legislation, could not be bridged.

BIBLIOGRAPHY

Barrow, Thomas C. *Trade and Empire: The British Customs Service in Colonial America, 1660–1775.* Cambridge, Mass., 1967.

Bradley, James E. *Popular Politics and the American Revolution in England: Petitions, the Crown, and Public Opinion.* Macon, Ga., 1986.

Bullion, John L. *A Great and Necessary Measure: George Grenville and the Genesis of the Stamp Act, 1763–1765.* Columbia, Mo., 1982.

Clark, Dora M. *The Rise of the British Treasury: Colonial Administration in the Eighteenth Century.* New Haven, Conn., 1960; repr. Hamden, Conn., 1969.

Dickerson, Oliver M. *The Navigation Acts and the American Revolution.* Philadelphia, 1951.

Donoughue, Bernard. *British Politics and the American Revolution: The Path to War, 1773–75.* London and New York, 1964.

Morris, Richard B., ed. *The Era of the American Revolution: Studies Inscribed to Evarts Boutell Greene.* New York, 1939; repr. 1965. Includes studies of writs of assistance and the office of army commander in chief.

Namier, Sir Lewis, and John Brooke. *Charles Townshend.* London, 1964.

Shy, John W. *Toward Lexington: The Role of the British Army in the Coming of the American Revolution.* Princeton, N.J., 1965.

Sosin, Jack M. *Whitehall and the Wilderness: The Middle West in British Colonial Policy, 1760–1775*. Lincoln, Neb., 1961.

Thomas, Peter D. G. *British Politics and the Stamp Act Crisis: The First Phase of the American Revolution, 1763–1767*. Oxford and New York, 1975. Offers a general account of British policy making as do the two other works by Thomas cited below.

———. *Tea Party to Independence: The Third Phase of the American Revolution, 1773–1776*. Oxford and New York, 1991.

———. *The Townshend Duties Crisis: The Second Phase of the American Revolution, 1767–1773*. Oxford and New York, 1987.

Peter D. G. Thomas

SEE ALSO **The European Contest for North America; Indian-Colonist Conflicts and Alliances;** and **The West Indies and North America.**

SPANISH

AT THE BEGINNING OF THE eighteenth century, Spain undertook a massive reorganization of its empire. The diverse sources motivating the complex process of reorganization, the delicately balanced, frequently unstable compromises achieved, and the progressive implementation of changes together constituted the broad set of policies known as the Bourbon reforms. These reforms radically altered social, political, and cultural processes in Spain and its empire, including the remote northern provinces of New Spain, some of which eventually became part of the United States.

The reforms themselves were part of a much larger process of change; intended in part to stop a growing crisis of empire, they in fact intensified it. In the long run (over decades) the reforms backfired, even though in the short run (over years) they were generally successful.

A fortuitous consequence of the Bourbon reforms for historians was the generation of numerous reports on frontier conditions. These reports not only described contemporary conditions but also attempted to reconstruct recent history. While the reports are certainly biased in the sense that they were written to develop and implement new administrative policies, they represent reasonable attempts at objectivity. Without them we would know far less about conditions throughout the Spanish Empire in the late eighteenth century.

BACKGROUND

One major source of the Bourbon reforms lay in European geopolitics and the changes sweeping the Continent in the eighteenth century. The reforms originated in the replacement of the house of Hapsburg by the house of Bourbon as the ruling family of Spain. The War of Spanish Succession (1702–1713) and the ensuing Peace of Utrecht confirmed the right of Philip V (reigned 1700–1746), the first Bourbon king of Spain, to the throne. Philip introduced a series of administrative reforms early in the eighteenth century. Included in the reforms was the establishment of a French-inspired system of intendants, which consisted of uniform administrative units to replace the former hodgepodge of jurisdictions. These reforms were meant to build a strong, centralized state and to facilitate communication with and control of local governmental units.

Later in the century, King Charles III (reigned 1759–1788) extended this reform program by devising a plan to remedy colonial problems. He sought to recolonize the Americas through economic, administrative, political, and military reforms. The new policies were intended to increase and regularize taxes, industrialize the colonies, colonize peripheral areas, improve defenses, and curb the growing independence of Spanish settlers.

In addition to his concern with administrative and fiscal reform, King Charles III was reacting to important changes in global political and economic rivalries. The Seven Years' War (1756–1763), which in North America motivated the French and Indian War, was, among other things, an unsuccessful attempt to abrogate British trade rights. The Peace of Paris (1763), while not solving the trade problem, did bring massive changes to North America. The British gained Canada and Florida; the Spanish gained Louisiana.

The subsequent Family Compact, a French and Spanish alliance, anticipated further conflict with Britain, since British and Spanish territories now bordered each other without an intervening French buffer. British merchants attempted to enter New Spain across this border. In Alta California, Russian fur traders threatened from the northwest.

In 1783 the Treaty of Paris ending the revolution returned Florida to Spain. For a while Spain claimed the Ohio River as the northern boundary, but with the Treaty of San Lorenzo (or Pinckney's Treaty) in 1795, Spain accepted the thirty-first parallel as the northern boundary of Florida. In 1800 Spain returned Louisiana to Napoleon in hopes of reestablishing a French buffer zone between the northern provinces and U.S. territory. This plan backfired when Napoleon sold Louisiana to the United States in 1803.

Meanwhile the independence of the British colonies led to new threats from westward moving American settlers and merchants. Thus Americans replaced the English as the major non-Indian threat to the entire borderland region from eastern Florida to New Mexico.

THE SCOPE OF COLONIAL REFORMS

These changes in international relations shaped the initial implementation and subsequent modifications of the Bourbon reforms. They began in 1765, were extended in 1778, and included Venezuela in 1789. The reforms in frontier administration focused primarily on New Spain, with only minor attention paid to Louisiana or Florida.

The main goals were strengthening of centralized state power over regional and local interests, economic growth, and abatement of British trade with the colonies. The institution of *comercio libre* (literally "free trade," but without the connotations that this term carries today) attempted to combat British trade with Spanish America by opening more ports to trade between Spain and her colonies in both Spain and America.

The commercial reforms changed trade patterns significantly. The proportion of colonial imports consisting of Spanish-produced goods increased from 15 percent in the late seventeenth century to about 50 percent in the late eighteenth century. This change in trade had the unintended effect of undermining colonial industries and favoring new commercial centers that competed with the older viceregal capitals of Lima and Mexico City.

Administrative reforms paralleled commercial reforms. Two *visitadores* (official inspectors) were dispatched by the king to the Americas to investigate conditions—José de Gálvez to New Spain in 1765–1771 and José Antonio de Areche to Peru and La Plata in 1777–1782. Both found bureaucracies dominated by local criollos (Spaniards born in, and permanently resident in, the colonies) who pursued their own interests at the expense of the Crown. Gálvez was appointed Minister of the Indies in 1776 and began instituting reforms intended to restore control of revenue to the Crown and to replace unreliable criollos with more trustworthy *peninsulares* (Spaniards born in Spain who viewed Spain, not the colonies, as their true home). Restriction of criollos to less than a third of all administrative posts in the Americas helped enhance royal authority.

In 1786 an intendancy system superseded the system of *corregimientos* (variable administrative units), thus replacing a patrimonial system that viewed offices as personal property with a bureaucratic system dedicated to efficient service of royal interests and staffed by competent administrators. The appointment of intendants was more tightly controlled than had been the case for *corregidores* (heads of the *corregimientos*). The viceregal and *audiencia* structures, however, were left in place. This led to bureaucratic conflict between the new superintendent, who was to have independent control of the treasury in New Spain, and the viceroy, who had supervised the treasury before the reforms. The viceroy won—the office of superintendent was abolished. The viceroy gained control of the exchequer and became the intendant of the viceregal district. However, feuding with intendants of the outlying districts continued. Such feuding was particularly troublesome for the northern provinces because of the time required to communicate with them.

The fiscal component of the Bourbon reforms met with considerable success. Tax farming (contracting with private individuals to collect taxes on a commission basis) was eliminated, and the royal monopolies on tobacco, silver, mercury, and gunpowder were tightened. Revenues from the sales tax (*alcabala*) doubled from 1.5 million to 3 million pesos between 1775 and the 1780s. Revenue from the tax on *pulque* (a locally made liquor) increased from about 470,000 pesos in 1775 to 810,000 pesos by 1779. Between 1765 and 1809 the tobacco monopoly generated some 177 million pesos for the Crown. Total silver production rose from 12 to 18 million pesos in the 1770s. Crown revenue from silver was 5 million pesos in 1789 despite tax reductions to miners. From the 1760s to 1779, Indian tribute increased from about 600,000 to 960,000 pesos. Between 1765 and 1782 revenues from silver produced in New Spain increased from 6 to 19 million pesos.

An increased military presence in the colonies served the triple purpose of defending against European rivals, providing improved control over a restless population, and controlling incessant Indian raids on the frontiers. Between 1758 and 1800 the military in New Spain increased from three thousand to over twenty-nine thousand. Criollo advancement was blocked systematically in the military as in administration. The insistence on augmenting special benefits for the military, called *fueros* (literally "rights," but generally referring to a special judicial jurisdiction or court), furthered rivalry between church and state because of overlapping and competing *fueros*.

Relations between church and state had always been difficult in the Spanish Empire. On the one hand, the church, in the form of missionaries, was a major instrument for the spread of Spanish authority and culture. On the other hand, there was an inherent conflict between saving Indian souls and employing Indian labor—free or coerced—to create wealth. A secondary conflict focused on whether Indian lands brought into production with Indian laborers under church supervision should be kept by the church, given to the king, or turned over to local colonists. Church-state relations tilted toward increasing antagonism as the Crown sought to extend its direct control over Indians and undermine the relative autonomy of the church by secularizing the missions. Jesuit autonomy and resistance to these changes, among other things, led to their expulsion from the New World in 1767 and a tighter control of church activities throughout the colonies.

The Bourbon reforms intensified conflicts between criollos and *peninsulares* throughout the colonial empire. Peninsular Spaniards were interested in career advancement, whereas settlers were interested in economic development and local social advancement. From the Crown's view, the reforms were an attempt to restore order and integrity to colonial government. In the criollo view, the reforms were a *peninsular* attempt to usurp their privileges and wealth. This antagonism contributed to the growing alienation of Spanish colonists and fueled the crisis that led to the independence movements in Spanish America.

REFORMS AND INDIAN RELATIONS

Defense was a vital concern to Spain on the far northern frontier of New Spain, in the region known as the *Provincias Internas,* or "Internal Provinces," for three reasons. First, the sedentary Pueblo Indians, who lived in over twenty villages, comprised several culturally and socially distinct societies, and spoke several mutually unintelligible languages, had succeeded in uniting in 1680 and forcing the Spaniards out of New Mexico. This was the first and only defeat of European colonists by Indians in North America. Second, Spain sought to protect its lucrative silver mines further south by establishing a northern buffer zone between the mining districts and potential European rivals and hostile nomadic Indians. These pressures led to colonization efforts in Texas and the *Pimería Alta* (now southern Arizona) in the early eighteenth century. Third, the church was interested in the salvation of Indians who had been converted to Christianity in the course of early explorations and colonization.

In 1692 and 1693 Diego de Vargas reconquered New Mexico. Soon after the reconquest Pueblo groups were forced into an uneasy alliance with Spanish settlers, with the resumption of a pattern of endemic warfare with nomadic Indians, the so-called *indios bárbaros* (literally, barbaric Indians, meaning nomadic or non-sedentary groups). The causes of this continual warfare are quite complex, but may be summarized briefly.

For the nomadic Indians, raiding was either an alternative to trading with Spaniards or the Pueblos, or a means to improving the terms of trade, especially for horses and guns. The Spaniards had their own motivation for raiding. Low pay for the military pushed Spanish leaders to supplement pay with booty obtained on raids—primarily captured women and children used as slaves. The taking of captives was a major irritant to nomadic Indians and provoked retaliatory raids. Both legitimate mistakes in identifying raiders (Indian or Spanish) and intentionally disguised identities fanned the flames of conflict into a state of endemic warfare. Despite continual raiding, Spanish villages on the extreme frontiers maintained trading relationships with specific Indian bands. This trade played an important role in the frontier economy.

In response to the concern with endemic warfare, Visitador General Gálvez made two recommendations in 1768 for the political and military reorganization of the northern frontier of New Spain. First, he recommended a system of intendants be established in the colonies. This was delayed until 1786. He also recommended the establishment of a *comandancia general* (general command), which was implemented in 1776.

In order to deal specifically with the frontier situation, King Charles III dispatched the Cayetano María Pignatelli Rubí, known as the Marqués de Rubí, to northern New Spain in 1765 to review and reorganize the defenses of the region. Rubí made his report in 1768, which resulted in the issuance of the *Reglamento* of 1772 on frontier defense and the appointment of Hugo O'Conor as commandant inspector of *presidios*.

Rubí reported that *presidios* (military garrisons) were scattered haphazardly across the frontier. The twenty-four outposts that existed lacked coordination. Corrupt practices of *presidio* commanders and unclear enlistment regulations led to low morale among the troops. He recommended consolidation to fifteen *presidios* strung along the thirtieth parallel, with an exception for New Mexico. He urged moving the El Paso garrison south to Carrizal and establishing a new garrison at Robledo, north of El Paso. He also recommended a more skeptical attitude toward Indian peace overtures and stronger guarantees of peace in negotiations with Indian leaders.

By 1776 the new line of *presidios* was built, but problems remained. As presidial commanders took their troops farther afield against hostile Indian groups, other Indian groups would raid, depleting the presidial horse herds. In New Mexico in 1775, the viceroy appropriated funds to replace 1,500 stolen horses. In Nueva Vizcaya, approximately the modern Mexican state of Chihuahua (including parts of what are now Texas and southern Arizona), Indians killed 1,674 people, captured 154 more, stole 68,256 head of livestock, and forced the abandonment of 116 ranches between 1771 and 1776. Even allowing for considerable exaggeration in contemporary reports, Indian raiding was a severe problem.

Teodoro de Croix was appointed commandant general of the *Provincias Internas* in 1776. His duties included annual inspection of all presidios, determination and coordination of military campaigns, and initiation of peace negotiations, subject to viceregal approval. He was to assure kindly treatment of prisoners and curtail the use of captives as booty. These reforms were intended to pacify the region, allow economic development, and enable the *Provincias Internas* to pay a portion of the expenses for their administration.

The commandant general was the highest official in the *Provincias Internas*, responsible to the king through the Minister of the Indies. Nevertheless he was to keep the viceroy informed of his actions. Since the commandant general had a status comparable to that of the viceroy and exercised jurisdiction over territory formerly controlled by the viceroy, feuding between the two was all but guaranteed.

The Nomadic Indians

The single most important goal and consequence of the Bourbon reforms in the *Provincias Internas* was the development and implementation of a policy of peace with nomadic Indians. This goal was largely achieved, despite many reversals, exceptions, and local failures. On the northern frontier, a twin strategy for dealing with nomadic groups emerged. On the one hand, Spanish officials sought peace with northern and eastern nomadic groups that lived in what is now western Texas, eastern New Mexico, and contiguous areas, especially the Comanche bands. On the other hand, they pursued a divide-and-conquer strategy against the numerous Apache bands who lived throughout what we know today as New Mexico and Arizona.

The processes by which these goals were achieved defy easy summary. Part of the problem was that few frontier administrators—and until recent decades few historians—understood the variety in the political organizations of aboriginal groups, especially nomadic groups that survived by hunting, gathering, and occasionally, gardening. These groups had fluid memberships and permeable boundaries, both ethnically and territorially.

This lack of understanding led to various errors, such as referring to one group by many different names, and to different groups by the same name. Thus, accurate identification of nomadic groups in the documentary sources is problematic. Furthermore, it is historically hazardous to read current "tribal" affiliations too far into the past. Centuries of warfare, and eventually the peace process engendered by the Bourbon reforms, actually created the tribal groups we know today. Thus, terms like "the Comanche *tribe*" and "the Apache *tribe*" give a false sense of cultural, social, and political unity that came into existence only in the late nineteenth and early twentieth centuries.

Peace was achieved with the Comanche bands in the 1780s under the leadership of two New Mexican governors, Fernando de la Concha and Juan Bautista de Anza. Both of these men had considerable frontier experience and were exceptional in their understanding of Indian political organization. Through several battles and the judicious use of gifts, they succeeded in compelling the Comanche bands to unite and to elect one central chief, Ecueracapa (Leather Jacket), in 1786. This led to an enduring peace between New Mexican Spaniards and the Comanche that lasted well into the era of American control (the late nineteenth century). It was, however, a specific peace with New Mexican Spaniards and did not include Spaniards in Texas or more southerly provinces. Comanches became stout allies in wars with other Indians, especially the Apache. They also served as a border police, patrolling the northern and eastern boundaries of New Spain in an arc running from south-central Colorado through western Kansas, Oklahoma, and Texas and reporting on the movements of non-Spanish Europeans.

The divide-and-conquer strategy that Spain applied to various Apache bands had a very different impact, forcing many of them to fragment and scatter. Comanche pressure gradually forced them southwest from the Plains into what is now southern Arizona and southern New Mexico. Because the Apache menaced interior communications and trade, there was no effort to unite them. Indeed, bands that sought peace were required to serve as allies in pursuing other Apache bands. There were for a while several *establecimientos de paz* (peace establishments, institutions roughly analogous to American Indian reservations), but attempts to make the Apache completely sedentary met with little success.

In general, though, the strategies of peace with the Comanche and divide-and-conquer with other nomadic groups worked. Indian raiding was attenuated considerably. In northern New Mexico, this facilitated movement further onto the Plains and expansion of sheep production. In southern New Mexico, it eased communications and trade. In Texas, Arizona, and California these strategies were less successful, and warfare with nomadic Indians remained a problem. Conflicts also continued in Louisiana and Florida.

The peace began to unravel in the early nineteenth century as the conflicts that accompanied the movement toward independence from Spain drained resources from the frontier. Here again there was a great deal of local and regional variation in the waxing and waning of Indian raids. At those times when the *Provincias Internas* were split into separate districts, coordination of policies toward nomadic Indians was nearly impossible, since Indian territories typically straddled these artificial, and from an Indian point of view, arbitrary geographic divisions. The constant reshuffling of provincial borders and administrative organization proved unsuccessful in dealing with this reality.

ADMINISTRATIVE, FISCAL, AND OTHER REFORMS

The *Provincias Internas* went through several organizational shifts. In 1786 Viceroy Bernardo de Gálvez divided the region into three commands. Just one year later, in 1787, his successor, Viceroy Manuel Antonio Flores, reorganized the *Provincias Internas* into two divisions: *Provincias*

Internas del Poniente included the Californias, Sonora, Nueva Vizcaya (approximately modern Chihuahua), and New Mexico; *Provincias Internas del Oriente* included Texas, Coahuila, Nuevo León, and Nuevo Santander (modern Tamaulipas). In 1793 a royal order reunited the provinces under a single command. The new *Provincias Internas* were composed of Sonora, Nueva Vizcaya, New Mexico, Texas, and Coahuila. The Californias, Nuevo León, and Nuevo Santander were restored to viceregal administration. In 1804 the divisions of 1787 were restored, but implementation was delayed until 1812 by the Napoleonic Wars. Sinaloa was added to the western division of the *Provincias Internas*.

As the threat of other Europeans to the Californias decreased and Indian problems grew, Chihuahua replaced Durango as the capital of the *Provincias Internas*. Chihuahua also became the commandant general's headquarters in 1814 for several reasons. Chihuahua was the legal capital and was centrally located. It was nearer than Durango to the frontiers, facilitating closer supervision of the Indian campaigns. It was closer to New Mexico, which required special attention because of increasing interest on the part of the United States. The move inconvenienced the commandant general, but pleased Chihuahua merchants.

Other reforms attempted to improve the extraction of resources from the frontier. The Spanish Royal Engineers received a commission to map the frontier, noting especially likely locations for mines. In their report they recommended opening new routes of communication running east-west across the northernmost provinces in addition to the existing north-south connections. These reports led to several exploratory expeditions. Commandant General Croix also had a mint built at Arispe, Sonora, to relieve the specie shortage that was retarding commerce. Royal monopolies on gunpowder, tobacco, salt, mercury, playing cards, and stamped paper generated revenues, but Indian tribute was virtually nonexistent in the *Provincias Internas*. The *media anata*, a tax of one-half of the first year's salary of appointed officials (the commandant general was exempt) was implemented. Still, because of military expenses associated with the Indian wars, the provinces were not able to become financially independent of the viceroyalty. Thus, these reforms met with minimal success.

In the late eighteenth century, attempts were made to concentrate settlers for improved defense. Fray Juan Morfi, who had traveled extensively in New Mexico and Texas and who had served as secretary to Commandant General Croix, wrote an extensive report on frontier conditions, including security and trade. In it, he suggested that dispersed settlements were an attempt by colonists to escape state scrutiny. Dispersion did facilitate contraband trade with nomadic bands, including participation in illicit trade in *punche,* a tobacco substitute of considerable importance in the local economy. Dispersed settlements also protected villagers from misdirected vengeance raids, since nomadic Indians had refined their skill in choosing targets and were careful not to attack trading partners.

While the Bourbon reforms achieved significant successes, they also engendered or exacerbated many frontier problems. The repeated reshuffling of the administration of the *Provincias Internas* promoted bureaucratic turmoil. Local governors often found themselves ensnared in the turmoil, or sought to manipulate it to their own advantage. Gubernatorial corruption remained a problem. In the 1790s it resulted in a royal order withholding one-fifth of a governor's salary as an advance on fines that were expected to be imposed for infractions committed while in office. Despite all the reforms and adjustments, the *Provincias Internas* remained unable to pay their own administrative and military costs and so continued to drain the royal treasury.

FRONTIER PROSPERITY

The reorganization of the northern provinces of New Spain, undertaken as part of the Bourbon reforms, helped establish relative peace on the frontier and so facilitated population growth, prosperity, and trade. (These effects were also part of the success of the Bourbon reforms throughout the empire.) One evidence of the increased prosperity could be found in population growth.

As problematic as census and population data are for the northern frontier regions of New Spain, the general patterns are quite clear: after the reconquest, population grew steadily, increasing rapidly after the initiation of the Bourbon reforms, even though the late eighteenth century was a period of relatively low immigration. The population of Albuquerque exceeded the population of Santa Fe for the first time by 1790. By 1817 the population of either city surpassed the total population of Texas, Baja or Alta California, or northern Sonora. As part of the reforms, efforts were made to increase the population of Texas (initially colonized in the 1710s), a remote frontier province with a sparse Spanish population. In 1769 Alta California was officially colonized in an attempt to make good on vague territorial claims and to preempt Russian and British rivals. Thus, until after Mexican Independence (1821), it was New Mexico, not Texas or California, that had the largest population of Europeans in the region.

With the Bourbon reforms and relative peace on the frontier, local production and trade with nomadic groups and with Chihuahua accelerated. New Mexico became increasingly dependent on Chihuahua for iron goods, fabrics, leather goods, and delicacies. Sheep, wool, animal hides, pine nuts, some Pueblo-made blankets, and a few captives were given in exchange. The articles traded south were generally of low value, whereas the imported items were expensive.

Pedro Bautista Pino, a resident of New Mexico, claimed in 1812 that the annual trade with Chihuahua involved purchases of 112,000 pesos and sales of 60,000 pesos. Pino reported that this trade regularly drained the province of specie—despite an annual government payroll of 38,000 pesos. Chihuahua traders used the specie shortage to promote several fictitious accounting schemes that worked to their advantage. Pino probably exaggerated the shortage of currency to gain sympathy, but the shortage of specie was real, and the new mint at Arispe did not entirely relieve the problem.

Growing trade and increasing trade deficits caused a steady pressure for further production of export goods, which in turn led to intensified local production and increased trade with nomadic groups. As noted above, relative frontier peace facilitated this economic growth.

Sheep production also flourished in New Mexico. Some estimates run as high as 250,000 sheep exported annually. In 1800 merchants sent 18,784 sheep south in a single caravan. In 1807, 15,000 sheep were also shipped south. Zebulon Pike estimated in 1806 that 30,000

sheep a year were shipped from New Mexico to Chihuahua. The exact extent of the sheep trade is unknowable, but it was both extensive and important to the local and regional economies.

Trade, and especially contraband trade, played an important role even in communities located on the farthest frontier. Jacobo Ugarte (1769–1791), commandant general of the *Provincias Internas,* attempted to incorporate trade in his pacification policies by instituting fairs where they could be regulated. Unregulated trade was dangerous. Injured parties, both Spanish and Indian, would frequently raid to remedy bad deals, initiating counter-raids. By regulating trade, Ugarte sought to break the cycle of raiding and counter-raiding. He met with only partial success for the reasons mentioned in Fray Morfi's report, namely that villagers depended on this trade in horses, hides, and captives for much of their livelihood.

LONG-TERM CONSEQUENCES OF THE BOURBON REFORMS

The Bourbon reforms fundamentally shaped the ebb and flow of economic growth, population growth, warfare, settlement, and class and ethnic relations. Trade affected economic development in multifarious ways. The major indirect effect of trade was the continued growth and prosperity of the local elite, which used trade profits to acquire land and build large sheep and cattle herds through the *partido* system (a shares system for raising livestock). The resumption of nomadic raids and population growth combined to make land more valuable. Increasing land value and increasing population spurred new settlements; increasing raids slowed such expansion. Colonization of new lands and requests for land grants, in turn, intensified conflict between Indians and Spaniards.

In many places these economic changes altered the local social and economic stratification. An apparent rise in debt servitude was shaped by changes in intensity of nomadic raiding and the availability and desirability of new land. When conditions were peaceful, attempts were made to coerce settlers into continuing to work for wealthier settlers. When conditions were more warlike, the temptation to found new settlements was low, and low wages were sufficient to keep the labor supply at hand. Similarly, when times were prosperous ethnic stratification tended to loosen: individuals and families crossed ethnic lines and changed identities. When times were difficult, ethnic stratification became more rigid. Within the Hispanic population, the elite class was gradually transformed from a legal nobility with little economic power to one with moderate local power due to its role in trade. Its wealth and power were tied to variations in peace, prosperity, and trade.

The key lesson here is the extreme volatility of frontier social conditions within a general pattern of increased prosperity. The prosperity was due to sporadically increasing capitalist trade, which in turn was a product of the Bourbon reforms. Within the general pattern, social relations varied locally, sometimes from one community to the next. Temporal changes were similarly volatile, with social relations and trends reversing in the course of a decade or so. Thus, the more closely one observes social conditions, the more chaotic they appear. It is only from a distant view that the general pattern within this fascinating volatility becomes visible.

The period between the middle of the eighteenth century and the middle of the nineteenth century was a time of transformation—the denouement of the Spanish era and the ascendancy of the American era. Ties to the Spanish Empire were loosening. The Bourbon reforms played a major role in precipitating the independence movements in Mexico. The events in the reform era shaped the American Indian groups we know today. In short, the Bourbon reforms left a legacy that continued to shape social processes for over a century.

BIBLIOGRAPHY

Bannon, John Francis. *The Spanish Borderlands Frontier, 1513–1821.* Albuquerque, N.Mex., 1974. This remains one of the best overviews of the borderlands.

Brading, D. A. *Miners and Merchants in Bourbon Mexico, 1763–1810.* Cambridge, England, 1971. A close history of the Bourbon reform era, focusing on the mining regions immediately south of the *Provincias Internas.*

Braudel, Fernand. *Civilization and Capitalism, 15th–18th Century.* Vol. 3, *The Perspective of the World.* Translated by Fiân Reynolds. New York, 1984. This famous history of capitalism provides valuable background on the reorganization of the New World colonial empires.

Griffen, William B. *Apaches at War and Peace: The Janos Presidio, 1750–1858.* Albuquerque, N.Mex., 1988.

———. *Utmost Good Faith: Patterns of Apache-Mexican Hostilities in Northern Chihuahua Border Warfare, 1821–1848.* Albuquerque, N.Mex., 1988. A pair of detailed historical narratives that focus on Apache relations with the Spanish and Mexican governments. Griffen gives a fine feel for the variability in these relations.

Gutiérrez, Ramón A. *When Jesus Came, the Corn Mothers Went Away: Marriage, Sexuality, and Power in New Mexico, 1500–1846.* Stanford, Calif., 1991. A pathbreaking analysis that uses marriage data to explore traditional questions about class, ethnicity, and gender, helping to correct the severe neglect of the latter topic. Chapter 10 is especially good on the Bourbon reforms.

Hall, Thomas D. *Social Change in the Southwest, 1350–1880.* Lawrence, Kans., 1989. A sociological analysis of ethnic and social change in the region, focusing on Indian-European relations. Like most sociological works, it argues an explicit theoretical position. Chapter 2 reviews the debates on these theories.

John, Elizabeth A. H. *Storms Brewed in Other Men's Worlds: The Confrontation of Indians, Spanish, and French in the Southwest, 1540–1795.* College Station, Tex., 1975. The finest detailed narrative history of the eastern Southwest (Texas and New Mexico) in print. An excellent counterpoint to Hall, Spicer, and Lang.

Jones, Oakah L., Jr. *Los Paisanos: Spanish Settlers on the Northern Frontier of New Spain.* Norman, Okla., 1979. A compendium on settlement of the *Provincias Internas.* A valuable resource on the region.

Lang, James. *Conquest and Commerce: Spain and England in the Americas.* New York, 1975. A sociological comparison of Spanish and British colonial practices. An excellent overview.

———. *Portuguese Brazil: The King's Plantation.* New York, 1979. A sociological comparison of Spanish, Portuguese, and British colonial practices. An excellent overview of the reorganization of colonial empires.

Reff, Daniel T. *Disease, Depopulation, and Culture Change in Northwestern New Spain, 1518–1764.* Salt Lake City, Utah, 1991. A detailed study of the effects of disease on Native cultures and Spanish administrative practices.

Rock, David. *Argentina, 1516–1982: From Spanish*

Colonization to the Falklands War. Berkeley, Calif., 1985. This history of Argentina offers much information on imperial changes in southern South America.

Spicer, Edward E. *Cycles of Conquest: The Impact of Spain, Mexico and the United States on the Indians of the Southwest, 1533–1960.* Tucson, Ariz., 1962. The classic history of Indian-European relations in the Southwest. The focus is primarily on the western Southwest (especially Arizona, Sonora, and Sinaloa).

Stein, Stanley J., and Barbara H. Stein. *The Colonial Heritage of Latin America: Essays on Economic Dependence in Perspective.* London and New York, 1970. An outstanding survey of the Spanish colonies.

Thomas, David Hurst, ed. *Columbian Consequences.* Vol. 1, *Archaeological and Historical Perspectives on the Spanish Borderlands West;* vol. 2, *Archaeological and Historical Perspectives on the Spanish Borderlands East;* vol. 3, *The Spanish Borderlands in Pan-American Perspective.* Washington, D.C., 1989–1991. An outstanding collection of current research on the borderlands. Many essays in these volumes shed light on the interplay between the actions of indigenous populations and Spanish colonial reorganization.

Wallerstein, Immanuel. *The Modern World-System: Capitalist Agriculture and the Origins of European World-Economy in the Sixteenth Century.* New York, 1974.

——. *The Modern World-System II: Mercantilism and the Consolidation of the European World-Economy, 1600–1750.* New York, 1980.

——. *The Modern World-System III: The Second Era of Great Expansion of the Capitalist World-Economy, 1730–1840.* New York, 1989. This account of the birth and growth of Europe's domination of world trade has many penetrating, if controversial, insights into changes in the organization and administration of New World colonies.

Weber, David J. *Myth and History of the Hispanic Southwest: Essays by David J. Weber.* Albuquerque, N.Mex., 1988. Essays 3 and 4 on Boltonians and John Bannon are especially valuable summaries and analyses of literature on the Southwest.

Thomas D. Hall

SEE ALSO **The European Contest for North America; Indian-Colonist Conflicts and Alliances; and The West Indies and North America.**

CRISES OF EMPIRE

BRITISH

NEVER WERE THE COLONISTS of British North America more proud of their British identity than in 1763, at the conclusion of the Seven Years' War (also known as the French and Indian War). Not only had colonial soldiers fought along with British regular troops in securing Britain's stunning victory, but that conquest promised to transform the future of North America. By the Treaty of Paris, Canada, all other French territory east of the Mississippi except for New Orleans, and Spanish Florida became British territory. As a result, colonists could suddenly look forward to freedom from those recurrent wars with Britain's "popish" enemies that had, over the previous seventy-five years, killed or injured an extraordinary proportion of American combatants, increased the colonial tax burden, and in general constituted a persistent detraction from the pastoral pleasures of provincial life. For the colonists, as for others touched by Enlightenment thought, British rule and liberty were synonymous; and freedom, they understood, had material as well as moral benefits. Colonial celebrators of British victory therefore predicted an unparalleled growth both in population and in wealth as virtually all of North America east of the Mississippi became British. In short, by all appearances a great watershed in American history had occurred with the British military victories at Quebec (1759) and Montreal (1760) and the fruits they brought in the peace settlement. That history would remember a greater breaking point in 1776 was unanticipated and undesired.

THE SUGAR ACT

The events that spurred American independence began with Britain's efforts to draw on colonial resources to relieve the strain on its treasury created by expenditures during and immediately after the Seven Years' War. The first of those efforts, the Revenue Act of 1764, better known as the Sugar Act, seemed at first to be only another in a chain of trade laws that colonists had accepted for over a century. American critics of the Sugar Act, among whom northern merchants and their legislative spokesmen were prominent, found much to oppose in the provisions for enforcing the act and in the duty of three pence per gallon on molasses from the non-British West Indies. But, particularly in the opening phase of opposition, they criticized the Sugar Act as unwise more than as a violation of rights. Some persons noticed, however, that the Sugar Act's preamble said it was meant to raise "a revenue . . . in America for defraying the expenses of defending, protecting, and securing the same." In other words, the Sugar Act was designed not to regulate trade through the imposition of economic incentives and deterrents, as Parliament had done in the past, but to raise money for the British treasury. It was therefore, as the North Carolina Assembly noted in October 1764, a tax "laid on us without our Privity and Consent, and against what we esteem our Inherent right, and Exclusive privilege of Imposing our own Taxes."

THE STAMP ACT CRISIS

By the time the North Carolinians acted, Americans' awareness of Parliament's decision to levy taxes on them had been raised by news of an impending Stamp Act, which Parliament finally approved in March 1765. That law, which laid an excise tax on items including colonial almanacs, pamphlets, broadsides, newspapers, newspaper advertisements, a wide range of legal documents, dice, and playing cards, was novel: Parliament had not previously imposed direct taxes on the colonists. Moreover, the law affected everyone, not just those involved in trade, and particularly hurt printers and lawyers, who had a strong influence on American opinion. By arrogating to itself the authority to tax colonists, Parliament threatened the power of colonial assemblies, which claimed an exclusive right to tax within their jurisdictions. In most colonies, the elected legislative assemblies were the only government institutions at the provincial level that spoke for the governed: the councils and governors with whom they shared the responsibilities of governing were (except in the charter colonies) appointed by the Crown or by a proprietor with the consent of the Crown. Colonists also took exception to the provision for trying persons accused of violating the Stamp Act in courts of Vice-Admiralty, which had no juries.

The Constitutional Argument
Under the British constitution, Americans insisted, taxes were "free gifts of the people," and could be granted only by the people or by their representatives. Since the colonists had no representatives at Westminster, Parliament could not tax them.

To the principle of "no taxation without representation" most British defenders of parliamentary right gave a ready consent. They insisted, however, that Americans were "virtually" represented in Parliament, whose members acted not only on behalf of those who voted for them but for everyone under the British flag. That included colonists as well as the substantial number of Englishmen who lacked the right to vote for members of Parliament.

Daniel Dulany of Maryland answered that argument in his *Considerations on the Propriety of Imposing Taxes in the British Colonies for the Purpose of Raising a Revenue by Act of Parliament*, a pamphlet first published anonymously at Annapolis in October 1765. In short, Dulany conceded that "virtual representation" might work in England, where all Englishmen—voters and nonvoters, those who sat in Parliament and those who did not—were together subject to taxes levied by Parliament and so had a common interest. It could not, however, extend to America, because no similar community of interest bound colonists and Englishmen. Indeed, their interests were opposed, since Parliament could ease the tax burden on its members and on those who elected them by increasing the taxes levied on colonists. If the Americans were not "virtually" represented in Parliament, Dulany concluded, they were not represented there at all; they were represented only in their provincial elected assemblies, which therefore alone could lay taxes upon them. Dulany's pamphlet was the first of a series to be extensively reprinted and circulated throughout the colonies, and he himself became a hero celebrated as, a few years earlier, were British officers who led the conquest of Canada such as generals Jeffrey Amherst or James Wolfe.

Before long, however, even Dulany's argument seemed too moderate. By 1766 the Virginia pamphleteer Richard Bland was ready to reject the legitimacy of virtual representation even for England; in *An Inquiry into the Rights of the British Colonies*, he prnounced the alleged "Fact" that "nine Tenths of the People of Britain" could not vote "a great Defect" in the British constitution.

Pettitions and Resolves
From the start, then, Americans reacted to British imperial reform with a torrent of arguments published in both pamphlets and provincial

newspapers. The bases of their opposition were also stated in formal petitions against the Sugar and Stamp acts passed by provincial assemblies and later by a Stamp Act Congress that convened at New York City in October 1765. Twenty-seven delegates from nine colonies (all except New Hampshire, Virginia, North Carolina, and Georgia) attended the congress, which, besides petitioning the King, House of Lords, and House of Commons, adopted a set of Declaration of Rights. It said that free men could be taxed only with their consent, that colonists were not—and, "from their local circumstances," could not—be represented in the British House of Commons, and that therefore no taxes could be "constitutionally imposed on them" except by their provincial legislatures. The congress also declared that trial by jury was "the inherent and invaluable Right of every *British* Subject in these Colonies."

Parliament refused to consider the colonial petitions, since they pertained to revenue laws and also questioned parliamentary right. Several colonial assemblies responded by passing resolutions that asserted or reasserted their exclusive right to tax. The Virginia resolves of May 1765 were particularly influential, in part because a series of radical resolves rejected by the legislature were published in other colonial newspapers as if they had been accepted by the House of Burgesses. One such resolution asserted that Virginians were "not bound to yield Obedience to any Law or Ordinance whatsoever, designed to impose any Taxation upon them, other than the Laws or Ordinances of the General Assembly." Another said that persons who wrote or spoke in defense of taxes imposed other than by Virginia's General Assembly were to be deemed enemies of the colony.

Popular Uprisings

Colonial opposition to the Stamp Act soon escalated from arguments, petitions, and resolutions to direct popular action. By the 1760s popular uprisings were a relatively familiar phenomenon in colonial life and had a certain acceptance and legitimacy because they frequently acted on behalf of a community where the laws or the powers of local magistrates were inadequate. In fact, the established agencies of contemporary law enforcement—the hue and cry, posse comitatus, and militia—depended upon the mobilization of private citizens, and the line between them and illegal mobs was sometimes open to interpretation. Participants frequently came from all segments of the population, including persons of wealth and standing and even local officials as well as the boys, servants, seamen, and "Negroes" often cited as the rank and file of colonial mobs.

Where issues of right were involved, moreover, American proponents of direct action could draw on a tradition in English thought that justified popular opposition to "tyrannic" authority and that went back at least to the seventeenth century. Ideas central to that Whig tradition were shared by those whom modern historians sometimes classify within several distinct schools of thought, but who shared a conception of government fundamentally at odds with the divine right of kings. Their essential argument began logically with an assertion of the contractual origins of government: all public officials exercised defined powers as agents of the people. If they exceeded the bounds of their lawful power, they acted without legitimacy and were justly opposed by the people, who had both a right and a duty to protect the lawful order and the liberty it sustained by holding their rulers in check. The people could resist isolated acts of tyranny or, where the abuse of power permeated the entire system of government, they could revolt, overturn the regime, and establish another.

The exercise of that right and duty to oppose wrongful authority was, however, subject to restrictions. The provocation could not consist of casual errors or private immoralities but had to pose a threat to the lawful order so serious and general that the danger was recognized by the "body of the people." Resistance and revolution could therefore not be the work of a minority. Moreover, all peaceful means of redress had to be exhausted before the "body of the people" resorted to force, and the force employed had to be proportional to the threat that provoked it. If there was no chance of success, forceful opposition was not to be attempted, since its failure would probably lead to even more severe repression. Although these "rules" often appeared in English and Scottish writings as descriptions of how the people had acted and would continue to act, in American writings of the 1760s they often assumed a prescriptive character. Resistance to Britain developed in conformance with those mandates, which helped guide the revolutionary movement away from anarchy and toward the establishment of a new legal order.

The first Stamp Act "riot" occurred at Boston on 14 August 1765. Early that morning an effigy of Andrew Oliver, the Massachusetts stamp distributor, appeared hanging from what would later be called the city's Liberty Tree. That evening a crowd took down the effigy, paraded it through the town, and burned it after destroying a building that was said to be Oliver's future "stamp office." Meanwhile, a segment of the crowd attacked Oliver's home. The next day, fearing further violence, Oliver announced that he was asking to be excused from his new position.

These events in Boston provided an efficient model for nullifying the Stamp Act. If stamp men everywhere could be persuaded—with force, if necessary—to resign, the stamps would not be distributed and the act could not be put into effect, as scheduled, on 1 November 1765. Before August was over, stamp distributors in Rhode Island, New Jersey, and New York had resigned due to actual or threatened violence, and those in all the other colonies except Georgia eventually followed suit, effectively blocking execution of the Stamp Act. Where no stamp men were present to provoke uprisings, colonists demonstrated a new militancy by staging demonstrations, such as mock trials for stamps and stamp men or "funerals" for liberty.

Violence, however, soon showed a tendency to spread. In Boston, participants in a second uprising on 26 August attacked the homes of royal officials associated with the Vice-Admiralty court or the customs service, then destroyed the elegant home of Lieutenant Governor Thomas Hutchinson. A group of Stamp Act opponents known as the Loyal Nine organized the first uprising, but merchants who feared they had been named in recent depositions on smuggling were apparently responsible for the second. An orderly demonstration at Newport on 27 August led to four days of virtually uncontrolled rioting, in which opposition to the Stamp Act was again intertwined with other local resentments.

Containing Violence

Such cascading violence, considered by many observers unjustifiable in itself, alienated supporters of the American cause in both the colonies and England. In its wake, therefore, leaders of American resistance made elaborate efforts to constrain their followers, sometimes by careful organization. The crowd that forced the Connecticut stamp distributor Jared Ingersoll to resign on 18 September 1765 resembled a militia company, and at Philadelphia in early October leaders took care to avoid an explosive direct confrontation between the stamp men and the crowds. Forms of coercion were also refined, as threats of violence against supporters of the Stamp Act gave way to threats of commercial boycott or social ostracism. In October 1765, for example, the freemen of Essex County, New Jersey, voted to have "no Communication" with Stamp Act supporters "unless it be to inform them of their Vileness." These efforts to avoid violence were not immediately effective everywhere. In early November 1765 New York City crowds, fearful that Britain planned to enforce the Stamp Act by force of arms, attacked a coach and sleigh owned by Lieutenant Governor Cadwallader Colden and destroyed a house rented by Major Thomas James of the Royal Artillery. Several days of "terror" followed, as rumors of a mass attack on Fort George circulated through the city. Peace returned after the stamps were removed from the fort and entrusted to local officials.

In late 1765 and 1766, peace and order were maintained in part by formal organizations of the Sons of Liberty, which apparently were first formed in New York City in late October or early November and quickly began to establish contact with similar groups elsewhere. Beginning in late December 1765 and continuing through the early spring of 1766, a formal intercolonial alliance of the Sons of Liberty was organized in New England, then extended to communities in New York outside Manhattan and to colonies further south. In general, local chapters were founded several months after the initial Stamp Act uprisings in response to outside initiatives or to some local event. For example, rumors that a local deputy stamp distributor might be appointed precipitated the formation of the Albany, New York, Sons of Liberty. The Sons of Liberty built upon earlier groups of Stamp Act opponents such as Boston's Loyal Nine and the Charleston, South Carolina, Fire Company. Known members, for the most part, belonged to the colonial middle and upper middle classes and included artisans, lawyers, merchants, and even local officials. Once organized, however, the Sons of Liberty made a conscious effort to broaden the movement's social base so it could speak for the "body of the people."

The Sons of Liberty were determined to prevent implementation of the Stamp Act—by an intercolonial military force if necessary. They also sought the resumption of legal and commercial business that had ceased on 1 November 1765 because the stamps or stamped documents required for their operation were unavailable. The Stamp Act constituted an assumption of power without right by Parliament, they argued, and was therefore null and void; to cease business because stamps were unavailable was, in effect, to concede that the act was legally binding. The Sons of Liberty were, however, equally dedicated to ensuring that civil government continued unimpeded where it was unaffected by the Stamp Act and that, as the New York Sons of Liberty put it in January 1766, no odium be cast on any persons or groups except insofar as they promoted or abetted the act. Their opposition, in short, was determined but limited, and by no means revolutionary in character. Resolutions passed by the Sons of Liberty characteristically professed a profound loyalty to George III and Great Britain; and when news of the Stamp Act's repeal arrived in March 1766, the local Sons of Liberty often organized the celebrations.

THE DECLARATORY ACT

The Declaratory Act of 1766, which asserted Parliament's power to bind the colonists "in all cases whatsoever," did not in general dissipate the celebratory mood. Most often it was interpreted as a face-saving device upon which Parliament did not intend to act. However, a handful of colonists were more pessimistic. Among them were Silas Downer in Providence, Rhode Island, Samuel Adams in Boston, Christopher Gadsden of Charleston, South Carolina, and, in New York, William Goddard. Adams suggested to Gadsden in December 1766 that Parliament might try to raise a revenue under the pretext of regulating trade, and that a tax so disguised (as it had been with the Sugar Act) would be as objectionable as the Stamp Act. Within a year the Townshend Acts of 1767, which attempted to raise revenue

for the support of royal officials in the colonies through duties on imported tea, lead, paper, glass, and painters' colors, made Adams's hypothesis prophetic.

THE TOWNSHEND CRISIS

Colonial opposition to Britain in the Townshend crisis of 1767–1770 was raised in good part by a series of essays by John Dickinson of Pennsylvania that began to appear in Philadelphia newspapers during December 1767 and were rapidly reprinted elsewhere. Dickinson's essays soon appeared in pamphlet form as *Letters from a Farmer in Pennsylvania to the Inhabitants of the British Colonies* (1768), of which seven editions were printed in America and others in London, Dublin, and Amsterdam. Dickinson began by calling attention to the New York Restraining Act approved by Parliament in June 1767, which suspended the legislature of New York until it agreed to comply fully with the Quartering Act of 1765. In June 1766 the New York legislature had voted to provision British soldiers stationed within the colony in accord with most but not all of the articles required by the Quartering Act. The legislators regarded the Quartering Act as a tax law because it demanded that colonists supply goods without their prior consent, and so refused to acknowledge its validity.

Dickinson endorsed that argument and the legitimacy of New York's refusal to comply with the act. He also condemned the Restraining Act as an infringement of colonial rights with dangerous implications that went well beyond New York and demanded the united opposition of Americans everywhere. Similarly, the Townshend duties, which were explicitly levied "to raise a revenue" from the colonists, were "as much *taxes* upon us, as those imposed by the Stamp Act." The duties, too, should be opposed, but not by "inflammatory measures." Instead Dickinson called for "a firm, modest exertion of a free spirit," which could take the form of "withholding from Great Britain all the advantages she has been used to receive from us" if American petitions for redress should again be rejected.

Nonimportation and Nonconsumption

Like Daniel Dulany in the Stamp Act crisis, Dickinson became an American hero as colonists everywhere praised and toasted "the Pennsylvania Farmer." Moreover, in keeping with his advice, they opposed the new duties by boycotting British imports. During the Stamp Act crisis, a rudimentary nonimportation movement had proscribed the purchase of selected nonessential British goods, including mourning clothes. It was sufficiently successful that pressure from British merchants hurt by the boycott helped persuade Parliament to repeal the Stamp Act. The nonimportation associations of 1768–1770 built upon that precedent but involved more people in a more organized movement. Compacts were first negotiated in New England and New York during 1768. The movement spread in 1769 as it became clear that petitions against the Townshend Acts had not won redress. In the North subscribers to the nonimportation associations were mostly merchants. Other supporters signed nonconsumption agreements by which they promised not to purchase proscribed goods or to patronize merchants who imported such articles. In the plantation colonies nonimportation associations were adopted from the start by broad-based public bodies, such as extralegal meetings of the provincial assemblies. The agreements prohibited somewhat different lists of goods from colony to colony and differed in other details. Where the Sons of Liberty reappeared in 1769 and 1770, they did so as fervent supporters of nonimportation and American manufacturing to supply needs usually met by imports.

The movement to restrict British imports had appeal for economic as well as political reasons. It made a virtue of an austerity that in the constricted colonial economy of the late 1760s was necessary for many, including debt-plagued southern planters; and it allowed merchants to sell off their stock of less desirable goods. In time, however, nonimportation caused suffering even among many artisanal manufacturers, who had much of the colonial market to themselves, but often needed imported materials to practice their trades.

The advantage of nonimportation as a peaceful means of gaining redress also proved somewhat illusory. Again, as in the Stamp Act crisis, social and economic boycotts were employed against those who ignored or violated the agreements. But fear of violence also encour-

aged cooperation and was itself sometimes sustained by explicit threats, such as the scaffold erected near a Liberty Tree that brought the submission of one New Yorker in September 1769. In Boston late that October ten to twelve persons "of some considerable rank," joined later by a far greater mob of less respectable persons, attacked the publisher of the *Boston Chronicle*, John Mein, whose charges of cheating leveled against members of the local nonimportation association had severely strained the entire movement.

As the associations expanded their base of support, they increasingly functioned like regularly constituted government agencies whose power came, in effect, from social compacts: they examined merchants' records, tried those suspected of violating the agreements, and imposed sanctions on the guilty. This assumption of authority by extralegal institutions threatened that of British officials, who called for royal troops to reestablish the power of the Crown. But the presence of redcoats itself provoked disorder. In New York repeated incidents between civilians and soldiers led in January 1770 to a clash remembered as the Battle of Golden Hill. In Boston, to which troops were dispatched in 1768 to reinforce royal authority, a long series of similar confrontations culminated on 5 March 1770, when royal troops shot into an angry crowd, killing five men in an event recalled by polemicists as the Boston Massacre. Thereafter, on the insistence of the town, the troops were withdrawn to Castle William in Boston Harbor.

The nonimportation agreements substantially reduced British exports to the colonies. However, they failed to cause significant distress in Britain, in part because manufacturers found alternative markets in northern Europe. Nonetheless, on 5 March 1770, the day of the Boston Massacre, the ministry of Lord North asked Parliament to rescind all the Townshend duties except that on tea. By then former Chancellor of the Exchequer Charles Townshend had been dead for over two years, and the duties adopted on his recommendation seemed injurious to British interests because they taxed British manufactures. The tax on tea was retained as a continued assertion of parliamentary right.

When news arrived of the impending partial repeal, the South Carolina General Committee wrote a circular letter to the other colonies calling for a continuation of nonimportation until the tea duty and other grievances were removed. But merchants elsewhere were eager to resume trading. After several months of division, and over the opposition of Sons of Liberty Isaac Sears and Alexander McDougall, New York's merchants decided in July 1770 to resume importation, and the agreements collapsed everywhere.

THE "QUIET PERIOD"

The years from 1770 to 1773 are sometimes described as the "quiet period" of the budding rebellion since agitation had apparently ceased. Samuel Adams wrote instead of a "sullen silence." The confidence in British justice that characterized the Sons of Liberty during the Stamp Act crisis and was reaffirmed by Dickinson in his "Farmer's Letters" had declined significantly in the intervening years. Colonists at first attributed their grievances to misleading reports from British officials in America, such as Governor Francis Bernard of Massachusetts who advised his superiors in England that only strong measures could secure the colonists' submission. But by 1770 agitation in England over Crown persecution of the radical John Wilkes, British policy in Ireland, and other developments had convinced many colonists that the source of their problems lay in England—in Parliament or the king's ministers. After King George III personally rejected petitions for redress, he, too, became the subject of criticism and suspicion. Even the prospect of independence was occasionally raised in newspaper essays of the early 1770s.

Meanwhile, a developing sense of common danger allowed local resistance cadres to overcome previous divisions founded on provincial politics. In Pennsylvania opponents of the Stamp Act were generally members of the Proprietary party and opposed by the Anti-Proprietary party, which wanted to make that province a royal colony. But by 1770 supporters of the Anti-Proprietary party such as Charles Thomson and Philadelphia's mechanics had joined the resistance movement. There were also signs that a division between two factions of the New York Sons of Liberty—one supportive of the DeLan-

cey party, the other of the Livingstons—had begun to heal. Correspondence networks between partisans of resistance in different colonies were also gradually established, and in November 1772 Boston founded a committee of correspondence that began systematically mobilizing other Massachusetts towns in what it understood as the defense of American freedom. That model was imitated elsewhere. Moreover, in March 1773 the Virginia House of Burgesses established a committee of correspondence and called on other colonies to do the same. It was moved to action after the Crown appointed a commission to investigate the destruction in June 1772 of the *Gaspée*, a royal warship used by the customs service, by a crowd of Rhode Islanders exasperated by its wanton use and unlawful plundering of local farmers. Participants identified by the commission were to be tried in England. By 1774 every colony except Pennsylvania and North Carolina had established committees of correspondence.

RESISTANCE TO THE TEA ACT

Because suspicions of Britain and intercolonial communications were so well developed, events moved quickly once news of the Tea Act of 1773 had arrived. By providing for the rebate of local English taxes on tea reexported to the colonies and permitting the East India Company to sell tea through its own agents, the act allowed the company to undersell smuggled Dutch tea. In that way Parliament hoped the company could dispose of its vast stock of tea and repair its perilous financial state. The Tea Act imposed no new tax on the colonists, but tea sold in America would remain subject to the remaining Townshend duty, which Parliament again refused to repeal. Colonists regarded payment of that levy as a tacit acceptance of Parliament's right to tax, which would inevitably lead to a long list of further taxes. The Tea Act also threatened the interests of American tea merchants, including smugglers, by giving the East India Company a monopoly of the American market.

The East India Company planned to send substantial shipments of tea to New York, Philadelphia, Boston, and Charleston. Opposition first appeared in New York, where protracted threats in newspapers and broadsides against local consignees—those appointed by the company as its agents in selling tea—led them to announce in late November that they were resigning their commissions. In Philadelphia, again, there was a barrage of threats. A mass meeting at the State House called on consignees to resign and declared persons who assisted in landing taxed tea "enemies to their country." The consignees resigned on 1 December 1773. In Boston, however, the consignees included two sons of Thomas Hutchinson, a victim of mob violence during the Stamp Act crisis whom the Crown had since appointed governor of Massachusetts, and Richard Clarke, the father-in-law of Thomas Hutchinson, Jr., and a leading importer of tea. Supported by the highest officer in Massachusetts, with royal troops stationed nearby and royal warships in the harbor, they refused to resign even after mobs had attacked Clarke's store on 3 November and the Clarke home two weeks later.

Against such unyielding opponents, resistance took highly organized forms. The Boston town meeting in early November had unsuccessfully demanded the consignees' resignation. The town's committee of correspondence and those of four neighboring communities later agreed to cooperate in preventing the landing and sale of taxed East India Company tea and solicited the support of other communities. The first tea ship to arrive in the colonies, the *Dartmouth*, sailed into Boston Harbor on 28 November 1773. The next day, an extralegal town meeting of some five thousand people, including the inhabitants of nearby towns and Bostonians unqualified to participate in regular town meetings, met at Faneuil Hall, then moved to more spacious quarters at the Old South Church. That meeting of the "body" of the people demanded that the imported tea be returned to England without payment of the Townshend tax and posted a watch to ensure that none of the tea was landed secretly.

In early December two other tea ships, the *Eleanor* and the *Beaver*, arrived, but attention remained riveted on the *Dartmouth*. As the first to arrive, it would be the first to reach the end of a legal twenty-day waiting period in the harbor. If the tax on its cargo was not paid in that time, the tea would be seized by customs men and, the Bostonians feared, secretly released to the Hutchinsons and their fellow consignees. Francis Rotch, the son of Joseph Rotch who owned the *Dartmouth*, finally agreed to send that ship back to England with its cargo unladen if it could get the clearances necessary to leave the harbor. But first the customs collector, Richard Harrison, and then Governor Hutchinson refused to grant them. Late on 16 December 1773, the day before the tea became subject to seizure and immediately after the failure of Rotch's last-minute plea to Hutchinson, the "body" meeting dissolved and a crowd of some sixty men—obscure laborers and mechanics side by side with local businessmen and prominent political figures—boarded the tea ships. In three hours they emptied some 340 chests of tea into the harbor. Careful efforts were made to prevent plunder and the damaging of private property other than tea. Although the event apparently began with noisy shouts as the crowd left the meeting, the destruction of the tea itself was carried out with remarkable discipline and quiet.

News of the Boston Tea Party helped prevent further violence elsewhere. In Philadelphia a mass meeting of some eight thousand people at the State House on 27 December 1773 convinced the captain of the *Polly* to depart, tea and all, for England the next day. Similarly, in mid-April 1774 a large crowd in New York City convinced the captain of the *Nancy* to leave without bringing his ship into the customs district or unloading its cargo of tea. Events proceeded somewhat differently at Charleston. After the *London* arrived in early December 1773, a mass meeting succeeded in getting the consignees to resign. The ship then remained in the harbor for twenty days. Since no one appeared to pay the duties, its tea was seized and stored in the customhouse, where it remained for over a year until local officials sold it to help pay the costs of the Revolutionary War.

Boston was not the only community to have a "tea party." In late April 1774 New Yorkers destroyed tea brought into the harbor on the *London*, whose captain had denied having tea on board. Annapolis patriots went further. They forced the owners of the *Peggy Stewart*, who in October 1774 actually paid the duties on tea, to make a public apology and destroy the tea as well as the vessel that had imported it.

THE COERCIVE ACTS

In the spring and summer of 1774 Parliament passed four Coercive Acts intended to strengthen royal authority in Massachusetts. The Boston Port Act closed that port until the town agreed to compensate the East India Company for the destroyed tea. Only food and firewood could be brought to Boston on coastal vessels, which required special passes and were subject to careful surveillance by officials from Salem, where the customhouse was relocated. The Massachusetts Government Act ended the election of the governor's council by the colony's lower house and made its members Crown appointees. In other ways, too, it cut back the democratic components of Massachusetts government. In the future, juries would be elected or summoned not by local constables but by sheriffs, who were Crown appointees; and no town meeting except the annual election meeting could be held without special permission from the royal governor. A third measure, the Administration of Justice Act, allowed the governor of Massachusetts to order that trials of customs officers or other public officers indicted for murder as a result of their efforts to suppress uprisings or enforce Parliament's revenue laws be held in another colony or in Britain. Finally, a new Quartering Act allowed the commander of British military forces in the colonies to quarter troops wherever they were needed.

Americans labeled these the "Intolerable Acts." Even those who regretted the destruction of tea at Boston argued that the town ought not to have been punished without an opportunity to defend itself. The elimination or weakening of popular institutions under the Massachusetts Government Act seemed of a piece with another parliamentary act of 1774 that colonists sometimes included among the "Intolerable Acts," the Quebec Act, which finally established a regular government for Canada. Parliament not only extended Quebec's boundaries to include lands in the Ohio Valley and Illinois country already claimed by other colonies, but also failed to include provision for an elected legisla-

ture. Laws would instead be made by an appointed council. Moreover, by waiving the Test Act in Canada and recognizing the legality there of the Roman Catholic church—even allowing it to collect tithes—the Quebec Act opened king and Parliament to the charge of establishing "popery," which for the British colonies' militantly Protestant population was the religion of despots.

Bostonians called the Administration of Justice Act the "Murder Act." It effectively gave royal officials a license to kill, they said, since no British official tried in England for killing colonists would ever be convicted. This act particularly aroused suspicion since the criticism of the Massachusetts legal system that had provided its pretext seemed so manifestly unfounded. Massachusetts had gone out of its way to give the soldiers indicted after the Boston Massacre a fair trial. Two attorneys prominent in the resistance movement, John Adams and Josiah Quincy, Jr., defended them on the urging of their political colleagues. In the end, Captain Thomas Preston and six of the eight soldiers tried were acquitted. The other two were convicted of manslaughter, not murder, allowed to plead benefit of clergy, branded on the hand, and released.

The "Intolerable Acts" seemed, in short, to prove that Britain was determined to rule the colonists arbitrarily, even, as the Quartering Act suggested, by military force. Any doubts were dispelled in April 1774 when news arrived that General Thomas Gage, commander of the British army in America, had been appointed royal governor of Massachusetts.

Parliament approved the Coercive Acts on the assumption that Bostonians would readily submit or, if they did not, could easily be forced into submission. Instead the cause of Boston became "the cause of America," as communities as far south as the Carolinas sent food and other supplies for the relief of Bostonians deprived of their livelihoods by the Port Act. The Boston committee of correspondence called for an immediate boycott of British imports, but other colonies insisted that a congress should first meet to coordinate resistance and avoid the inconsistencies that weakened the nonimportation movement of 1768–1770.

THE FIRST CONTINENTAL CONGRESS

Delegates from every colony except Georgia met at Philadelphia to form the First Continental Congress from 5 September to 26 October 1774. Although the congress included a substantial number of moderates, it took a decidedly radical stand when it endorsed a set of resolutions adopted on 9 September by Suffolk County, Massachusetts, and carried to Philadelphia by Paul Revere. The Suffolk Resolves not only called for disobedience to the "Intolerable Acts" and an immediate cessation of all trade with Britain, Ireland, and the West Indies, but also asked the people to elect militia officers and to learn the art of war—which, however, was to be used only defensively. In a Declaration of Rights and Resolves adopted in October, the congress rejected Parliament's right to tax the colonists and reaffirmed their rights of assembly, petition, and trial by jury, as well as their right to live unconstrained by a standing army. It also adopted a series of petitions and addresses—to the people of Great Britain and colonists in Canada, the West Indies, and Florida, as well as to the king—and established the Continental Association, a nonimportation and nonexportation agreement that was to be enforced by local committees elected by those qualified to vote for assembly representatives. Finally, the congress decided that unless the colonists' grievances were redressed, it would convene again in May 1775. By then the outbreak of war at Lexington and Concord on 19 April 1775 had obliged the Second Continental Congress to assume far greater responsibilities than its predecessor, including the raising, organization, and support of an army.

LOYALISM

In the wake of the First Continental Congress, many onetime moderates began to emerge as Loyalists, that is, persons who opposed American independence. As a group the Loyalists were extremely diverse: some opposed independence from conviction; others out of expediency—for example, siding with the Crown in 1776 because they thought the colonies would lose the war; still others from ignorance of recent political his-

tory, or simply because longtime local enemies had taken the other side. Like the revolutionaries, they were drawn from all parts of the colonial population—farmers and artisans as well as merchants and planters—and sometimes from the same families that produced ardent advocates of the American cause.

One group represented among Loyalists out of all proportion to its place in the American population consisted, not surprisingly, of British officeholders. Unassimilated ethnic or religious minorities, such as members of the Church of England in Congregationalist Connecticut, also tended to become Loyalists, perhaps from fear that their liberty would be less secure under majority rule than under the Crown. With rare exceptions, Loyalists were not "Tories"—that is, defenders of the divine right of kings—but "Whigs" who used old Whig arguments against the revolutionaries. They insisted, for example, that American opposition to Britain was the work of a minority, not the "body of the people," and condemned the colonists' resort to force because the peaceful means of securing redress had not been exhausted. Modern estimates suggest that American Loyalists, including wives and children, constituted about 20 percent of the total population.

TOWARD REVOLUTION

As of late 1774, however, not even the most radical colonists advocated independence. In his spirited *Summary View of the Rights of British America* (1774), Thomas Jefferson spoke of American independence only from Parliament, not Britain. If the empire consisted, as Jefferson suggested, of self-governing states bound together under the Crown, then redress could come only from the king. But hope in the king waned after George III failed to respond to petitions from the Continental Congresses and then, in 1775, declared the Americans traitors involved in a rebellion carried on to establish an independent empire.

Attention then turned toward the British people. Although in the Parliamentary election of 1774 British voters had strongly supported the king and ministry, many colonists continued to hope through 1775 that, provoked by the Continental Association and inspired by the colonists' armed resistance, uprisings in England would help bring down the "tyrannic" regime of George III just as they had ended that of James II in 1688. After prospects for such uprisings faded, leading radicals still failed to endorse independence because they were emotionally unprepared for it, or for political reasons: until the "body of the people" was ready for that step, independence would create only division and failure. In July 1776 when independence was finally declared, the Continental Congress attributed American grievances to the king not out of any new conviction of his guilt but to signal the advent of revolution. To blame the king—not his ministers—for infringements of rights was to announce the dissolution of legitimate government.

The revolutionary character of the American Revolution lay not in independence alone, as Thomas Paine later noted, but in the establishment of a "republican" government whose authority came entirely from the people. In 1763 republicanism had been as distant from American thought as independence; but by early 1776, when Paine's *Common Sense* called for a rejection of the British form of government as well as of British rule and the establishment of republican institutions, over a decade of American experience could support his proposals. First in the organized extralegal associations of the Sons of Liberty, then in the nonimportation associations and the Continental Association, and finally in the congresses and conventions of the mid 1770s, governmental authority had gradually passed to organizations whose power rested on the people. In that way a movement that sought to enlist the "body of the people" in opposing the extension of British power became an experiment in republicanism whose success allowed a crisis within the British Empire—a small thing in itself—to emerge as one of the world's great revolutions.

BIBLIOGRAPHY

Ammerman, David. *In the Common Cause: American Response to the Coercive Acts of 1774.* New York, 1974.

Bailyn, Bernard. *The Ideological Origins of the American Revolution.* Cambridge, Mass., 1967. Traces the long-term impact of arguments first raised during the independence movement.

———. *The Ordeal of Thomas Hutchinson.* Cambridge, Mass., 1974. An appendix summarizes the development of scholarship on Loyalists.

Brown, Richard D. *Revolutionary Politics in Massachusetts: The Boston Committee of Correspondence and the Towns, 1772–1774.* Cambridge, Mass., 1970.

Calhoon, Robert McCluer. *The Loyalists in Revolutionary America, 1760–1781.* New York, 1973.

Champagne, Roger J. *Alexander McDougall and the American Revolution in New York.* Schenectady, N.Y., 1975.

Christie, Ian R., and Benjamin W. Labaree. *Empire or Independence, 1760–1776: A British-American Dialogue on the Coming of the American Revolution.* New York, 1976.

Conser, Walter H., Jr., et al., eds. *The American Revolution.* New York, 1985.

———. *Resistance, Politics, and the American Struggle for Independence, 1765–1775.* Boulder, Colo., 1986.

Countryman, Edward. *A People in Revolution: The American Revolution and Political Society in New York, 1760–1790,* Baltimore, Md., 1981.

Gipson, Lawrence Henry. *The Coming of the Revolution, 1763–1775.* New York, 1954.

Jensen, Merrill. *The Founding of a Nation: A History of the American Revolution, 1763–1776.* New York, 1968. Provides a particularly useful, detailed narrative of events leading to independence.

———, comp. *Tracts of the American Revolution, 1763–1776.* Indianapolis, Ind., 1967.

Labaree, Benjamin Woods. *The Boston Tea Party.* New York, 1964. Provides an account of the tea crisis that goes well beyond Boston.

Maier, Pauline. *From Resistance to Revolution: Colonial Radicals and the Development of American Opposition to Britain, 1765–1776.* New York, 1972. Gives an overall account of how both American assessments of Britain and the forms of colonial opposition changed between 1765 and 1776.

———. *The Old Revolutionaries: Political Lives in the Age of Samuel Adams.* New York, 1980.

Morgan, Edmund S. "Colonial Ideas of Parliamentary Power 1764–1766." *William and Mary Quarterly,* 3rd ser., 5 (1948):311–341 and 6 (1949):162–177.

Morgan, Edmund S., and Helen M. Morgan. *The Stamp Act Crisis: Prologue to Revolution.* 1953; rev. ed. New York, 1963.

Nelson, William H. *The American Tory.* Oxford, 1961.

Norton, Mary Beth. *The British-Americans: The Loyalist Exiles in England, 1774–1789.* Boston, 1972.

———. "The Loyalist Critique of the Revolution." In Library of Congress Symposia on the American Revolution, *The Development of a Revolutionary Mentality*. Washington, D.C., 1972.

Ryerson, Richard Alan. *"The Revolution Is Now Begun": The Radical Committees of Philadelphia, 1765–1776*. Philadelphia, 1978.

Schlesinger, Arthur M. *The Colonial Merchants and the American Revolution, 1763–1776*. New York, 1918.

Shy, John W. *Toward Lexington: The Role of the British Army in the Coming of the American Revolution*. Princeton, N.J., 1965.

Tyler, John W. *Smugglers and Patriots: Boston Merchants and the Advent of the American Revolution*. Boston, 1986.

Walsh, Richard. *Charleston's Sons of Liberty: A Study of the Artisans, 1763–1789*. Columbia, S.C., 1959.

Young, Alfred F., ed. *The American Revolution*. DeKalb, Ill., 1976.

Zobel, Hiller B. *The Boston Massacre*. New York, 1970.

Pauline Maier

SEE ALSO **Ideologies of Revolution; Mercantilism; and Reorganization of Empires.**

SPANISH

MULTIPLE CRISES SHAPED the independence movements that swept through Spanish America in the early nineteenth century. As is generally the case with profound social changes, these movements had deep roots, some of which were tied to unintended consequences of the Bourbon reforms. The independence movements in the Spanish colonies had much in common. All were rebellions against Crown control of the economy, and all confronted complicated regional conflicts that had developed during the long colonial era. Conflicts centered on the competition between the old colonial capitals and their officials who sought to control trade, and regional and local elites who pursued local autonomy. There was competition between local and national merchants and between agricultural exporters and nascent manufacturers. These conflicts often persisted and recurred because competing groups had approximately equal strength. The details of each independence movement varied considerably, even while the underlying commonalities remained.

A full account of these multifaceted crises in the borderlands requires a three-tiered explanation. The general processes and international context of the independence movements that swept Spanish America make up the broadest level. At this level it was the jockeying for geopolitical advantage between Spain and the newly independent United States, and Britain and France, that led to the cession of the Floridas to the United States. The uneven movement toward independence of New Spain (approximately Mexico) provides the general context for the crises in the western borderlands. Patterns in New Spain differed from patterns found elsewhere in the Spanish Empire. Finally, the crises in the borderlands of northern New Spain differed in important ways from those in central New Spain.

OVERVIEW

To search for the one cause of revolution is a fool's errand. Momentous changes have complex causes. Rebellions and revolutions frequently take on a life of their own once begun. They may begin with one set of goals, one set of tactics, and one set of actors, but these factors tend to change quickly in the course of events, often in ways participants did not intend. Several sets of processes shaped the timing of Spanish American rebellions against overly autocratic Spanish rule and turned them into revolutions against Spanish control. These factors cut across the three levels discussed above (international, national, and local), sometimes working differently in different contexts.

Initially various groups rebelled against what they saw as excesses of reform-minded Bourbon administrators from Spain. In particular, they objected to new taxes, new Crown monopolies, and trade regulations. The objections to these changes varied with the vigor with which they were enforced. Objections increased when efforts to implement reforms intensified in response to Spain's need for increased revenues because of its involvement in European wars.

Several types of crises were brewing. There were conflicts between indigenous populations and Spanish settlers. There were conflicts between *peninsulares*, Spaniards born in Spain who were spending part of their careers in the Indies, and *criollos*, Spaniards born in the colonies and permanently resident there. *Peninsulares* were interested in career advancement, using time in the Americas as a stepping-stone to higher offices, whereas *criollos* were interested in local development and local social advancement.

Although the Bourbon reforms were intended to avoid crises, in the long run they increased them. There were also conflicts among merchants and customers and the state, as well as conflicts between frontier settlers and people in the more urbanized and developed central areas. The Bourbon reforms alienated every important colonial group: merchants, bureaucrats, clergy, and landlords, most of whom were *criollos*, whose taxes paid *peninsulares*'s salaries. The conflicts between these groups, especially between *criollos* and *peninsulares*, were mitigated by the tendency of the elites to intermarry but exacerbated by the steady flow of immigrant Spaniards to the Americas. Nearly all *peninsulares* were male. Those who stayed long in the Americas typically married into the *criollo* elite. Resentment over differential treatment was strongest among first-generation *criollos*, who experienced this difference most acutely.

Restriction of higher offices to *peninsulares*, with only lower offices open to *criollos*, exacerbated conflict between these two groups. The intention was to limit local corruption and provide more professional and objective administration attuned to the overall needs of empire. *Criollos*, however, perceived them as malicious attempts to undercut their privileges and power. In some situations the practice did lead to less efficient administration, for administrative effectiveness often depended on intimate knowledge of local conditions, which took years to gain. This situation was more common in frontier areas than in central, urbanized areas.

Some historians argue that the cleavage between *criollos* and *peninsulares* began early and lasted for the entire colonial phase. Other historians argue that it arose in the seventeenth century

with the growth of large landholdings. Still others argue that the rift developed in the last quarter of the seventeenth century and became acute just before independence. The *criollo-peninsulare* distinction is often tied to the Hispanic preoccupation with blood purity, demonstrated in the elaborate *casta* system (a system of distinguishing among, and ranking, many different types of racial mixtures). In any case, all agree that the split did become acute and played an important role in most Latin American independence movements.

The spread of Enlightenment literature and ideas throughout the Spanish Empire had some influence on colonial leaders. In Europe, in addition to the obvious objections to colonial independence, there was an underlying fear that a successful attempt at political autonomy might inspire European workers and peasants to seek similar changes. In discussions of these processes there is always controversy over how much ideas led people to action versus how much new ideas were used as rationalizations for actions undertaken for other motives. Generally, it is believed that both processes were at work. Debates among historians and social scientists usually revolve around the relative weights of these two processes.

The American and French revolutions constituted a third set of factors shaping the crises of empire. Typically, the American Revolution was held up as a model of action and the French Revolution as a model to be avoided. The very success of the United States in becoming independent from Britain established that it was possible for colonies to set a course for independence. The United States was admired, but it was also feared. It was large, it was expanding, and it was Protestant. The French Revolution (1789) similarly established that a radical reorganization of society was possible, but at the expense of considerable social disruption. By the early 1800s it was also clear that this kind of reorganization could have dire consequences for the international community.

Local considerations were the fourth major factor in each independence movement. When rebellions originating among the poorer segments of society—Indians, peasants, and so on— threatened not only *peninsulares* but also *criollos*, the two elites sometimes formed an alliance against the rebels. Indian rebellions were not rare in Spanish colonial history, but they were not a common source of independence movements. The ensuing *criollo-peninsulare* alliances spurred the formation of local identities. Regionalisms, as opposed to a pan-Hispanic Americanism, were developing. These regional movements were based on concerns with local economies, values, interests of local elites, and geographic particulars, which varied considerably from one part of Spanish America to another. They frequently gave rise to nationalist movements.

Finally, specific events often proved crucial. Which local leader joined with which other members of the elite often shaped alliances. For instance, when Francisco de Miranda stopped in Saint Domingue (now Haiti) in 1806 to regroup his small force headed for Gran Colombia (now Venezuela), his *criollo* supporters perceived his action as an attempt to form an alliance with rebellious slaves. This overstepped what they had in mind, so they turned against him. In fact Miranda did not seek such an alliance, but the widespread perception that he had done so undermined his support.

An important point, which applies to all levels of these crises, bears reemphasis. Different processes, social forces, and political goals were at times so evenly balanced that seemingly minor events could tilt the balance. This led to a great deal of diversity among the rebellions, or even between different rebellions in the same region, though overarching similarities remained. This is especially evident in the international context.

INTERNATIONAL CONTEXT

Major changes in Europe during the late eighteenth and early nineteenth centuries had profound effects on the relations between colonies and home countries. Throughout the Atlantic economy trade was increasing rapidly, beginning a long-term shift from mercantilism toward free trade. The industrial revolution was beginning in Britain. Britain and France were engaged in a series of wars. And France easily dominated a weak Spanish monarchy.

Under mercantilism, each country sought to monopolize trade with its colonies, limiting trade to national carriers operating from a restricted number of ports, manipulating that trade to the home country's advantage and typically to the colonies' disadvantage. The advance of free trade meant that anyone could trade with anyone else and that governments should minimize interference in trade through tariffs and other taxes. These changes were relatively gradual and occurred with many variations.

The importance of colonial exports for European development is still hotly debated among scholars. Debates revolve around the contribution of colonial exports to European economies: whether they merely assisted, or fueled, or were vital to economic development, the onset of the industrial revolution, and the rapid spread of industrial capitalism. There is general agreement that the colonies had some impact on European economies, and that many European leaders thought that the colonies were vital to European prosperity. The latter concern had been a major driving force behind the Bourbon reforms in Spanish America.

Colonial relations varied from country to country. Britain sought dominance primarily through trade. As British shipping, and later manufacturing, began to surpass that of all other countries, British leaders tended to support more open and freer trade. Britain imported mainly raw materials and exported mainly manufactured goods. Spain, which retained an essentially agrarian economy, sought domination and prosperity by monopolizing colonial trade, and by taxing imports and exports that passed through Spain going to or coming from its colonies. France pursued a strategy somewhat in between. Its colonial holdings were generally less profitable—with the major exception of Saint Domingue, which was the single most profitable colony in the Americas.

The difference between Spanish and British colonial policy is illustrated by the taxes taken from and trade with their respective colonies. British trade with its colonies was significantly larger than that of Spain with its colonies. Taxes, however, were very different. In the early 1800s Spain was taking approximately thirty-five times more tax from New Spain than Britain was taking from its North American colonies. These differences were clear to contemporary leaders. The much greater economic success of Britain relative to Spain was noted by *criollos,* causing some to question the benefit of continued domination by Spain.

France pursued an advantage in continental trade by using its geographic advantage of a land connection with the rest of Europe. Britain attempted to maximize overseas trade by pursuing its geographic advantages of a maritime location and the relative protection from invasion afforded by the English Channel. Spain's lack of development of industry, as compared with that of Britain and France, quickly left it out of the picture—except for its enormous colonial holdings and their massive exports of silver. Consequently, the major rivalry was between Britain and France. Each sought to gain control of the other's colonies, to block the other's trade while extending its own. Hence one motive behind French support for the North American rebellion was the harm it posed for British trade. Similarly, the French Revolution helped Britain in that it disrupted the French economy.

France and Britain were continually at war between 1793 and 1814, except for a brief interlude in 1802–1803. Spain joined with France against Britain between 1779 and 1783, between 1796 and 1802, and again between 1805 and 1808. The spread of *comercio libre* (free trade, but without its modern connotations) throughout the empire after 1778 opened more and more ports to British trade. Thus, the Spanish colonies were lucrative markets for British goods and helped replace European markets lost or limited by war with France.

When Napoleon deposed Ferdinand VII in 1808, Spanish royalists pursued alliance with Britain against France. This newfound alliance tempered British interests in the direct acquisition of Spanish colonies. In the colonies Napoleon's usurpation of power justified rebellion in the name of royalist support.

After independence the United States remained dependent on British trade, yet pursued its geographic advantage to gain a share of the trade with Spanish colonies. Whereas Britain was concerned with maintaining the Spanish alliance against France while trading with Spain's colonies, the United States sought to avoid retaliation by either Britain or Spain while increasing its trade with Spain's colonies. These conditions led both Britain and the United States to pursue nearly neutral policies with respect to independence movements in Spanish colonies. Much of the trade with foreigners was technically illegal, although there were many temporary, official exceptions.

British neutrality toward Spanish colonial independence was based on two sets of nearly balanced, yet opposing forces. The first set, already mentioned, consisted of the opposing interests in an alliance with Spain in Europe and access to Spanish colonial trade. Independence offered the opportunity for increased colonial trade but threatened the loss of Spanish support against France. The second set of forces dealt with opposing views on representative government. Having established a parliamentary democracy, Britain had ideological and political leanings favoring that form of government. As an owner of empire it sought to maintain imperial control of its colonies. Britain's experience of rebellion in its North American colonies demonstrated the danger and cost of such rebellions. However, subsequent experience showed that independence need not impede trade. It also suggested that seizure of Spanish colonies was not an attractive goal, whereas open trade with them was. British foreign officers became very adept at maintaining an acceptable neutrality with respect to the independence of Spanish colonies.

Similarly, the United States had two sets of opposing goals with respect to the Spanish colonies, but they were somewhat different from those influencing British policy. First, its rivalries were with Britain and not with France. Second, the territory of the United States bordered Spanish territory. After the United States had acquired Louisiana from France in 1803, when Bonaparte reneged on his agreement with Spain to keep it out of British or United States hands, the border with Spain was both larger and less clearly mapped. Hence acquisition of Spanish territories made sense to leaders in the United States. Still, Americans did not want to upset negotiations with Spain for peaceful transfer of territory by overtly supporting colonial rebellions. These negotiations led to the Adams-Onís Treaty (1819), which ceded the Floridas to the United States.

Finally, the slave rebellions in Saint Domingue in the 1790s tempered *criollo* ardor for rebellion. Saint-Domingue, the most productive colony in the New World, produced sugar through massive use of African slave labor. During the dissension among white overlords that followed the French Revolution, slaves rose in revolt on the island. The history of this revolt is complicated and not directly germane to the crises of the Spanish Empire, except in one dimension. It underscored the danger of an Indian revolt inspired by disunity or rebellion among Spaniards—*criollo* or *peninsulare*. Indians, and peoples of mixed racial ancestry, made up nearly two-thirds of the population of the Spanish colonies, and in some areas as much as 80 percent of the population. Thus, the threat of Indian rebellion promoted caution among Spaniards in the Americas.

European rivalries heightened the perception by Spanish officials of the need to protect the rich silver-producing areas of New Spain by maintaining expensive frontier provinces as buffers between them and their rivals. It should be noted that many of the factors that contributed to the drive for Mexican independence also contributed to Mexico's subsequent loss of territory to the United States, even though those events are beyond the scope of this article. For all these reasons it is important to examine more closely the crises that led to Mexican independence.

THE CRISES IN NEW SPAIN

The economy of colonial New Spain was typical of the Spanish colonies in many ways: it had a large indigenous population marked by many cultural distinctions and an infrastructure oriented toward export. Indians constituted 60 percent of its population. They supplied most of the labor on the haciendas (large landed estates) and in the mines, yet maintained semiautonomous villages and communally owned lands. The transportation system focused on Mexico City and Veracruz. There was little integration and development of internal trade in comparison with that in the United States or Britain. The economy was organized around primary exports, mostly silver. Acapulco was a secondary port that traded silver for Filipino and other Asian goods. The inadequate internal transportation system slowed economic development and hampered

administrative communication. Hence, the colonial administration had weak control over outlying areas.

New Spain was distinctive in several ways. First, it was a major source of revenue for Spain through taxes and especially silver. New Spain sent roughly 5 percent of its total production to Spain in the forms of taxes and remittances to the church, the largest percentage of any of the colonies. A nearly equal amount of taxes paid for the administration of New Spain and underwrote the costs of government and the defense of other Spanish colonies. As noted above, this tax burden far exceeded that imposed by Britain on its colonies.

Second, New Spain was large and well populated. It held approximately one-third of the entire population of the Spanish colonies, slightly over six million people in the early nineteenth century. This was only one million less than the population of the United States. Mexico City was the largest city in the Americas. In Spain only Madrid was larger.

Third, New Spain had prospered in the era of the Bourbon reforms. It was the most productive of all the Spanish or Portuguese colonies, but reached only about half the production per capita of the United States. There was a significant manufacturing sector, and a large internal and external trade. Thus, while relatively undeveloped compared with the United States or Britain, New Spain was better developed than most of the Spanish colonies.

Finally, the first rebellions against Spain in New Spain were strongly supported by the lower classes, although the *criollo* elite ultimately subverted them. While not unique, this was uncommon.

The class and ethnic structure in New Spain was in many ways typical of Spain's colonies. Indians made up 60 percent of the population. *Castas* (people of mixed racial ancestry) made up another 22 percent. The remaining 18 percent were Europeans, of whom nearly all were *criollos*. Only 0.2 percent, about fifteen thousand, were *peninsulares*, sometimes called *gachupines* (spurs, referring to the trappings of nobility).

The *peninsulares* were an imperial elite nearly monopolizing all the high offices in the colonial administration, military, and church. The *criollos* constituted both a local elite and a small but growing bourgeoisie. They held nearly two-thirds of colonial administrative offices, and filled the lower ranks of the military and clergy. *Criollos* also owned mines and haciendas and constituted the merchant class. The urban poor lived on the edge of starvation. They regularly faced food shortages and plagues in the last years of the colony, particularly in urban areas. In times or places where labor was abundant, concerns with ethnic purity surfaced and *castas* experienced discrimination. In areas or times where labor was short—typically in mining areas—such discrimination was significantly attenuated.

While economic growth had been significant in late-eighteenth-century New Spain, it remained slow compared with growth in the United States. A prime factor slowing economic development was a strong system of servile labor. The facile equation of landowning with feudalism, and hence political conservatism, has caused confusion about which classes initiated and which classes contained the rebellions. It is important to note that many of the estates in New Spain were not feudal but capitalist-oriented agricultural enterprises, despite an element of coercion involved in mobilizing that labor. The owners of these estates typically opposed tariffs on their products and on their imports. They resented Crown control of the economy and interference with their administration of local economies. Hence they were receptive to attempts to curtail or eliminate Bourbon centralized control.

Criollos felt threatened on several fronts. The reservation of high offices for *peninsulares* thwarted *criollo* ambitions. The Decree of Consolidation, issued in 1804 and repealed in 1808, required that mortgages held by the church be repaid speedily and that those repayments be remitted to Spain to help pay for war with Britain (Spain was now under French domination). This eroded *criollo* wealth and undermined economic growth by removing capital from New Spain. The elite ran the risk of diluting their wealth by marriage of their daughters to *peninsulares* through losses in the form of large dowries and eventual subdivision of their holdings. Economic stagnation, rising taxes, and bad investments—especially investments in haciendas and declining mines—also threatened their wealth.

When Napoleon deposed the Spanish king in 1808 and Spanish royalist opposition groups formed in Spain, the status of New Spain was called into question. Some factions, which included many *criollos*, argued that New Spain, like the components of Spain itself, was a kingdom with considerable local autonomy. Others, especially *peninsulares*, argued that it was a colony proper, with no local autonomy. Both sides argued over where proper loyalties lay. The educated *criollos* were familiar with the intellectual currents sweeping through Europe and the Americas, and generally took a liberal stance favoring local autonomy.

In 1809 a number of *criollos* conspired to break away from Spanish control. In 1810 they recruited a priest from the Bajío (central Mexico, the region around Guanajuato), Miguel Hidalgo y Castilla, in order to enlist his large Indian following. The Bajío was a region marked by stark class divisions and severe deprivations for workers during the grain shortages. Discovery of the conspiracy in September 1810 pushed Hidalgo into leading the rebellion. In October, Hidalgo abolished Indian tribute. This act further increased Indian and *casta* support. The support, however, soon got out of hand. The sacking of *peninsulare* haciendas to finance the revolution quickly spread to generalized looting of haciendas. As the revolt began to take on more of the character of a peasant-Indian revolt threatening all estate owners, the major landowners and the *criollo* elite joined with the royalists to quash the rebellion. By 1815 the revolution was defeated and order restored.

When a liberal revolution took place in Spain in 1820, the *criollo* elite seized power in the name of the king under a former royalist officer, Agustín de Iturbide, and declared independence in 1821. Despite royalist intentions, the need for revenue required enforced loans from local landowners and continued sale of Jesuit properties that had been seized under Bourbon rule. The royalist government failed because of the combined opposition of the merchant classes who had a vested interest in free trade and of similarly minded *hacendados* (estate owners) who supported the liberals. The landowners were interested not in restoring Bourbon centralism but in gaining autonomy to control policies in their own regions. The small capitalist class also opposed state practices that thwarted business development, although they were favorable to protection of their industries from foreign competition. Thus, Mexico became independent with a legacy of nearly balanced opposing factions that kept the government in chaos for the next fifty years.

THE NORTHERN FRONTIER

The northern frontier provinces of New Spain, known as the *Provincias Internas* (internal provinces), were different from the rest of New Spain. The region contained few haciendas or large ranches and held few servile Indians living on communal lands. Cattle and sheep were the major staple commodities. The region was sparsely populated, containing less than one-tenth of the Europeans in New Spain in an area accounting for nearly half its territory. A significant portion of it remained unmapped and unsettled, Spanish territory in theory only.

Spanish law was laxly enforced. Ethnic and class relations were more fluid than in central New Spain. There were numerous hostile, nomadic Indian groups who raided or traded with northern villages. The local elites were poorer than their counterparts in central New Spain. The northern provinces, especially New Mexico, absorbed more funds than they generated. New Mexico also had a trade deficit with the rest of New Spain. The primary purposes for holding on to these provinces were to provide a buffer between the outside world and the lucrative mining provinces farther south and to validate territorial claims against other European powers.

On the frontier there was a twofold dependence on trade. On the one hand settlers depended on supply caravans from Veracruz via Chihuahua City for European goods, news, and political and administrative regulation. Cattle, sheep, some wines, and products obtained from trade with Indians went south in return. On the other hand, there were lively localized trading relationships with nomadic Indians for various products including hides, piñon nuts, and captives—and occasionally guns that came from French traders via Indian intermediaries. Grains, metal, and especially horses were given in return.

The increases in trade that accompanied the Bourbon reforms in the late eighteenth century stimulated further agricultural development, especially in livestock. Trade in a local tobacco substitute, *punche*, created friction with respect to the Crown's tobacco monopoly. The economic prosperity generated by the Bourbon reforms contributed to relative peace with nomadic Indians and local population growth.

The combination of remoteness and lack of wealth generated in these provinces led to their relative neglect. When Spain became embroiled in European wars, the north suffered doubly. Taxes were increased, and administrative funds, troops, and supplies were cut. There was a constant barrage of letters to the viceroy requesting more troops and more money for gifts to peaceful Indians and for the support of local government. The net result was that in the last decade of the eighteenth century and the first decades of the nineteenth century, conditions on the frontier became more chaotic and warfare with nomadic Indians intensified.

Despite the isolation of the far frontier, geopolitics exerted important, yet differing, effects there as well. The establishment of Fort Ross, north of San Francisco, in 1812 increased fear of Russian encroachment. There was considerable concern about expansionist tendencies of the United States. In the short run, however, the indirect effects of United States–British expansion were more important.

As British colonists, and later citizens of the United States, moved west seeking trade and new land, more and more Indian groups were pushed west of the Mississippi. The intrusion of new groups—Indian and American—onto the Great Plains disrupted social relations and exacerbated conflict among Plains groups. This pressure pushed Comanche groups farther south, forcing a greater reliance on raiding, and led to even stronger pressures on Apache groups. The latter were now denied access to the Great Plains, and were increasingly forced to raid for subsistence. The trade in captives served to fuel the raiding. These pressures coincided with diminishing viceregal funds for frontier administration, further exacerbating the conflicts.

The effects of the independence rebellions were considerably attenuated on the far frontier. In Texas, Juan Bautista de las Casas staged a coup against the royalist government. This coup was short-lived. An agent of Miguel Hidalgo de Castilla, Bernardo Gutiérrez de Lara, with support from United States officials, raised a small army to invade Texas in 1812. His army was defeated the next year with considerable loss and disruption of the Texas economy.

There was some violence in California a few years later, but it was brief. Most of the effects of the independence struggle were indirect. The neglect that had begun in the previous decade accelerated sharply. The various peace arrangements with nomadic Indians disintegrated and the entire north returned to a state of endemic warfare.

The effects of the independence movement were mixed. Here and there in the north new town councils sprang up and frontiersmen began to enjoy increased local autonomy. This new trend persisted well into the Mexican era. However, the experiences of Texas and California led all northern governors to exercise caution in accepting independence in 1821 until they were sure which side had in fact won.

We owe much of our knowledge of frontier conditions in the early nineteenth century to a memorial to the Spanish Cortes (legislative council advisory to the king) written by Pedro Bautista Pino in 1812 in his capacity as official representative to the Cortes from New Mexico. This and other documents make it clear that the local elite, and even many citizens, favored increased local autonomy.

Overall, the crises of the Spanish Empire had significant effects on the borderlands. Their immediate effects on the interior provinces, especially those that later became part of the United States, were to increase warfare with nomadic Indians and to slow somewhat the economic growth engendered by the Bourbon reforms. European conflicts led directly to the cession of the Floridas to the United States, and indirectly to the Louisiana Purchase and, with several decades' delay, the independence of Texas and the losses associated with the Mexican-American War (1846–1848). The latter, of course, are beyond the time frame discussed here. But colonial conditions shaped both the social structure of those provinces and their subsequent loss by Mexico. Similarly, colonial conditions set Mexico and the United States on very different developmental paths. These differences continue to shape relations between the two countries today.

BIBLIOGRAPHY

Bazant, Jan. *A Concise History of Mexico: From Hidalgo to Cárdenas, 1805–1940.* Cambridge, England, 1977. An excellent summary of Mexican history.

Brading, David A. "Government and Elite in Late Colonial Mexico." *Hispanic American Historical Review* 53, no. 3 (August 1973):389–414. An insightful analysis of the elite in New Spain on the eve of revolution.

Bethell, Leslie, ed. *The Cambridge History of Latin America.* 7 vols. Cambridge and New York, 1984. An excellent compendium. David Brading, "Bourbon Spain and Its American Empire," vol. 1, pp. 389–439; John Lynch, "The Origins of Spanish American Independence," vol. 3, pp. 3–50; Timothy Anna, "The Independence of Mexico and Central America," vol. 3, pp. 51–94; and D. A. G. Waddell, "International Politics and Latin American Independence," vol. 3, pp. 197–228, are especially useful.

Coatsworth, John H. *Growth Against Development: The Economic Impact of Railroads on Porfirian Mexico.* DeKalb, Ill., 1981.

———. "Obstacles to Economic Growth in Nineteenth-Century Mexico." *American Historical Review* 83, no. 1 (February 1978):80–100.

Humboldt, Alexander von. *Political Essay on the Kingdom of New Spain.* Abridged translation by John Black, edited by Mary Maples Dunn. Norman, Okla., 1972. An edited text edition of a thoughtful observer's firsthand account of life in New Spain on the eve of the rebellion.

Lynch, John. *The Spanish American Revolutions, 1808–1826.* New York, 1973; 2nd ed. 1986. An important, thorough study of the revolutions in Latin America.

Moorhead, Max. *New Mexico's Royal Road: Trade and Travel on the Chihuahua Trail.* Norman, Okla., 1958. The best study of trade through New Mexico and the Provincias Internas.

O'Brien, Patrick. "European Economic Development: The Contribution of the Periphery." *Economic History Review* 2nd ser., 35, no. 1 (February 1982): 1–18. An excellent overview of the debates and evidence about how much colonies contributed to European development. The debate continues, but this is a good introduction to it.

Stein, Stanley J., and Barbara H. Stein. *The Colonial Heritage of Latin America: Essays on Economic Dependence in Perspective.* London and New York, 1970. An outstanding survey of the Spanish colonies.

Thomas D. Hall

SEE ALSO **Ideologies of Revolution; Mercantilism;** and **Reorganization of Empires.**

IDEOLOGIES OF REVOLUTION

BRITISH

IDEOLOGIES CONSTITUTE A HIDDEN but shared matrix of attitudes and beliefs that help shape social behavior. They operate as cognitive and expressive symbol systems that provide a pattern or a guide for organizing social and psychological processes. As such, ideologies comprise the unconscious propensity underlying political, religious, or social thought at any given moment to make facts congruent with ideas, and ideas with facts, in order to create a worldview that will support both the individual and the collective sense of identity. Ideologies are particularly important in periods of social turbulence; at such times they give clear meaning to the lives of otherwise bewildered individuals and groups. Such meaning provides a sense of rightness that allows—even impels—individuals and groups to act upon their beliefs.

The need for such clarity became imperative for a great many individuals living in the British mainland colonies of North America at the end of the Seven Years' War (1763). Following the successful conclusion of that conflict, Great Britain attempted to reorganize its empire in order to rationalize its structure and to increase British authority within the colonies. As a consequence, Parliament imposed a series of measures upon the American colonists that initiated a period of turmoil culminating in revolution.

Such actions by the British authorities elicited economic boycotts, street riots, and legislative protests from a wide variety of Americans. The articulation of colonial attitudes, however, fell to the provincial gentry. In their pamphlets, broadsides, and newspaper essays, these literate gentlemen struggled to create a rational discourse convincing enough to bring about alterations in British administrative policy. Instead their efforts resulted in something quite different: a rationale for revolution and regeneration. Responding to the intense political pressure of events occurring from 1763 to 1776, their disparate thoughts gradually became integrated into a comprehensive and forceful image of politics and society that penetrated widely and deeply throughout colonial culture.

SOURCES OF AMERICAN THOUGHT

As they struggled to create a compelling argument against the actions of Parliament, members of the gentry drew upon a varied array of intellectual sources. A familiarity with classical antiquity, the hallmark of a gentleman, pervaded their efforts. They focused their attention primarily on Cicero, Sallust, and Tacitus, all of whom wrote in the midst of periods of turmoil within the Roman republic or in a time of decline characterized by the decay of moral and political virtues. Their work drew a sharp contrast between the venality, cynicism, and corruption of their own time and the virtuous simplicity, patriotic character, and love of liberty exuded by all citizens during the earlier, glorious days of the republic.

American gentlemen found compelling similarities to their own situation in this classical literature. For them simple, honest, virtuous provinces faced a terrible threat from the corruption and tyranny overtaking a once-honorable mother country and its venerable constitution. Classical analogies thus provided a vivid language of outrage for the colonial authors; at the same time, though, they served more an illustrative than a determinative role in American thought.

The English common law, represented primarily in the writings of Sir Edward Coke and, later, in Sir William Blackstone's *Commentaries*, also contributed to colonial thought. Again, like classical allusions, common-law references embodying principles of justice, equity, and rights served to illustrate a particular interpretation of history that shed light and meaning upon present events. Most particularly such citations indicated that the British constitution representing the bright hope of liberty in the Western world had been corrupted by the machinations of greedy ministers and sycophantic placemen.

References to eighteenth-century European intellectuals also suffused the essays of provincial authors. Indeed Enlightenment rationalism assumed a prominent place in their thought. Pamphlets, essays, and legislative orations repeatedly cited John Locke regarding natural rights and the social contract between a people and its government. Nearly as often American authors drew upon Montesquieu in their efforts to construe British liberty and to construct the institutional arrangements necessary for its preservation. In addition they looked to Voltaire for insight into oppression by the church, to Cesare Beccaria for aid in reforming the criminal law, and to Jean Jacques Burlamaqui, Hugo Grotius, Samuel Pufendorf, and Emmerich de Vattel for help in understanding the proper principles of civil government as well as the laws of nature and of nations.

Nevertheless here, too, the gentry's use of such luminaries reflected an ofttimes superficial or confused understanding of their work.

Conservatives and radicals alike indiscriminately cited Jean Jacques Rousseau, Locke, or Montesquieu to substantiate their claims. Further they lumped such men as Henry St. John Viscount Bolingbroke and David Hume together with radical reformers or even treated such peripheral figures as Burlamaqui on a par with Locke if it suited their purposes. Even though Enlightenment thought pervaded colonial literature, like classical and common-law ideas it assumed a more ornamental than determinative place within colonial thought.

The Importance of John Locke

One Enlightenment writer, however, did exert a powerful shaping influence within colonial society. John Locke's thought pervaded the various colonies by the 1760s. His concept of the social contract, articulated in *Two Treatises of Government* (1690), stood out above all others. In Locke's mind, men living in a state of nature contracted to form governments in order to protect their natural rights of life, liberty, and property. If government broke that contract, if it threatened the natural rights whose protection was its sole purpose, for example, by taking a man's property without his consent, then the people had every right to reassess their action in creating that government. This could, as a desperate last measure, lead to rebellion. For his part Locke never denied that rebellion could be a dangerous thing; at the same time, though, he just as forcefully warned that its counterpart, slavery, was far worse.

Locke's conviction that the people retained the right to rebel against unlawful or oppressive authorities became firmly entrenched in the colonial consciousness. Writers in the *New York Journal*, for example, drew nearly verbatim upon Locke when they declared: "Good Laws and good Rulers will always be obey'd and respected." "Mobs and Tumults never happen but thru' Oppression and a scandalous Abuse of Power" (18 August 1768). Most petitions of colonial assemblies also assumed a Lockean cast. Although continuing to articulate their desires in terms of the traditional protection-allegiance covenant, legislators applied basic Lockean principles so as to reformulate this ancient covenant to fit their needs. Consequently in their agitation colonists shaped Locke's contractual ideas to emphasize the king's obligation to respect popular rights rather than the people's responsibility to obey constituted authority.

The Commonwealthmen

If Locke's ideas regarding the essential relationship between rulers and the ruled undergirded colonial governmental assumptions, other authors, who themselves assimilated Locke's fundamental ideas into their writings, furnished the colonial gentry with a theory of politics that simultaneously explained why the British behaved as they did in the post-1763 era and provided the ideological basis for an American response. These writers—eighteenth-century transmitters of the radical social and political thought of the English Civil War and Commonwealth era—offered Americans a cohesive set of concepts that fused classical thought, common-law theories, and Enlightenment ideas into a meaningful and coherent whole. The writings of these "Commonwealthmen" thereby helped the colonists clarify their opposition to Parliament while simultaneously investing that opposition with a clear sense of purpose.

The extreme libertarians John Trenchard and Thomas Gordon became the most influential of these writers in America. Their *Cato's Letters* (1720), a bitter attack upon early eighteenth-century English society and politics, literally pervaded colonial culture. In addition the writings of such men as Bolingbroke, Benjamin Hoadly, Robert Viscount Molesworth, Frances Hutcheson, Joseph Priestley, Richard Price, and James Burgh found a receptive audience in America.

Trenchard, Gordon, and the other "country" theorists wrote from a deep and bitter enmity toward the social, economic, and political forces altering English society throughout the decades after the Glorious Revolution of 1688. In these years a massive commercial and financial revolution worked unsettling and fundamental changes upon English life. The emergence of the Bank of England, huge mercantile firms, and stock markets combined with the spreading commercialization of agriculture, the increasing power of new moneyed men, and the appalling proportions of a steadily increasing public debt all seemed to threaten traditional values. In the minds of the Commonwealthmen, these changes meant that England was becoming degenerate and terribly diseased—falling prey to vice, luxury, and materialistic commercial values. Behind this perspective lay a political critique: excessive governmental power spawned the decadence and decay eating away at the very foundations of English society.

Opposition writers did not necessarily provide novel theoretical insights to the American colonists. Their primary concepts of natural rights, the contractual basis of government and society, and the unique, liberty-preserving nature of England's "mixed" constitution were virtually identical with mainstream political beliefs advanced since the late seventeenth century. While opposition writers employed commonly held modes of thought, they placed an entirely different emphasis upon these ideas and used them in unique ways.

In their minds, the stability praised by orthodox political theorists rested upon a methodical subversion of Parliament by the executive. For them the degeneration of social and political life they saw all about them resulted from one central cause: the self-seeking drive for power by corrupt ministers under the executive. Thus venal ministries, epitomized by Robert Walpole, consciously fostered such dangerous tendencies as luxury and extravagance, certain forerunners of indigence, dependence, and servility. After achieving power these officials fattened on the very corruption they had produced. Their actions were entirely predictable and included the passage of onerous taxes, the generation of burdensome public debts, and finally the creation of a standing army whose ostensible purpose was to protect the people but whose true function was to dominate them.

Such ideas elicited little support within English society and yet became immensely powerful in the American colonies. There the imposition of such measures as the Stamp Act (1765) and the Townshend Duties (1767) raised disturbing questions for which English radical and opposition writers provided uniquely relevant answers. As a result a comprehensive theory of politics emerged within the colonies that made sense of the bewildering changes facing a quite diverse range of eighteenth-century Americans.

The role of power, understood as the control or dominance of some men over others, became central to this emergent theory of politics. For many Americans power loomed behind every political action; it constituted the ultimate explanation for whatever political behavior affected their lives. Power was ubiquitous; worse, it inexorably sought to expand beyond its proper limits. The aggressive nature of power disturbed provincial writers deeply; in their minds justice, equity, and liberty always fell victim to its inordinate demands. Consequently they perceived the public world split into two innately opposed spheres: power and liberty. Power, ceaselessly and brutally assertive, must be resisted at all costs; liberty, envisioned as delicate, innocent, and passive, required the unrelenting protection of an ever alert citizenry. Thus the moral strength and vigilance of the people became central to the defense of liberty.

For generations none of this seemed relevant; Americans had long felt secure in their liberties. They were, after all, members of a sturdy, vigilant race of Britishers protected by the English constitution. Such confidence faltered, however, when, following the end of the Seven Years' War, evidence mounted in their minds that an independent Parliament, the primary safeguard for the maintenance of constitutional liberty, was being undermined by the corrupting machinations of the Crown. Such suspicions gained increasing credibility as the influence of opposition writers spread throughout the colonies. These authors lashed out with unrelenting intensity at both the degeneracy of the era and the viciousness of official corruption that fattened upon this decadence.

Given the influence of these authors, many colonists resolutely believed Britain to be yielding to the propensity, common throughout the history of nations, to degenerate with age and succumb to the corruptions of power. Considered from this perspective, the actions taken by Parliament following the Seven Years' War seemed to represent not only mistaken or even ill-advised behavior but also a deliberately planned attack upon the British constitution and with it all protection for individual liberties. Given such beliefs the Declaration of Independence of 4 July 1776 seemed not only eminently reasonable but critical to the survival of liberty in America.

THE COMMITMENT TO REPUBLICANISM

The deep conviction that they were confronting a ministerial conspiracy against liberty transmuted the meaning of colonial resistance in the minds of many colonists. No longer simply a constitutional quarrel over the power of Parliament to govern them, their cause now symbolized a world regenerative creed embodied in the political philosophy of republicanism. As a consequence American republicanism represented far more than merely the substitution of an elective system for a monarchy; it imbued the political break with England with a moral passion and an idealistic depth organically linked to the very character of American society.

While the commitment to republicanism inspired the American cause with extraordinary moral fervor, it also created anxiety and uneasiness among a great many Americans. Their familiarity with the classics and with historical precedent continually reminded these people of the delicate nature of republics, of how easily they could degenerate into tyrannies. Such tyranny generally resulted from moral decay rather than the force of arms; the character and spirit of the people, not military strength and material wealth, determined whether a republic prospered or failed. The solid qualities of the yeoman—courage, integrity, frugality, temperance, industry—embodied the true strength and character of a republican society. "Luxury," with its train of social distinctions, elegance, and effeminacy, enervated republics; it existed simultaneously as cause and symptom of social decay.

In order to survive, republics required the total absence of selfishness and luxury; indeed republics rested upon virtue; that is, the willingness of citizens to place the common good above their own private needs and desires. Thus for a great many Americans the sacrifice of personal concerns for the good of the larger community comprised both the vital core of republican beliefs as well as the utopian aim of the revolution.

When the revolution broke out, then, most Americans espoused a distinctive set of political and social beliefs that not only united them against the British but imbued their struggle with a true sense of purpose. Certain that history disclosed an incessant tension between the spheres of liberty and power, American revolutionaries swiftly shaped a consensus intended to shield liberty from the unremitting aggressions of power. This republican unanimity demanded public and private virtue, internal unity, social solidarity, and eternal vigilance against the perversions of power.

While republican ideas unified Americans in their struggle against the British, these ideas did not convey the same meaning for everyone involved. Indeed it soon became clear why republicanism was universally accepted so quickly: it rested on elusively abstract ideas. Americans agreed that republicanism meant an absence of an aristocracy and a monarchy, but beyond this all accord disappeared. The explicit form a republican government should assume and, more important, what composed a republican society remained ill defined. As time passed it became increasingly evident that republicanism and revolution conveyed different meanings in various regions of the country and even different meanings for distinct groups within the same locale. These varied perceptions of republicanism resulted from socioeconomic forces at work within eighteenth-century America that created a number of diffuse but very real needs among dissimilar groups of Americans.

The Perspective from Outside the Marketplace

Most Americans lived in remote rural areas where they drew meaning in their lives from traditional corporate communities. Residing in neighborhoods composed of subsistence farmers and mistrustful of higher authorities and commercial behavior, these people wished for little else beyond continued isolation, independence, and homogeneity. Any other environment would expose them to external interference, internal discord, and the social dislocations occasioned by inequitable allocations of power and wealth.

Constant changes generated by the demands of an encroaching market economy imperiled the desires of these Americans. While such changes affected their economic interests, the greatest threat was to the integral worldview in which these rural people found meaning and identity in their lives. As these threats accelerated, they intensified the urge for local independence, homogeneity, and isolation. Troubled by the painful realization that the simple, austere, and natural world that they knew and cherished was rapidly eroding in the face of an entrepreneurial, individualistic market society, many rural Americans sought moral regeneration. They

became ripe for a singular form of political mobilization.

Revolutionary republicanism accomplished this mobilization. Indeed the gentry's calls for political action cast in libertarian terms appeared to speak directly to the anxieties felt by so many rural folk. With its attacks upon aristocratic corruption and the tyranny resulting from the incursions of power into the realm of liberty, the dark, conspiratorial suspicions of country rhetoric resonated with the localist's fear of change and distrust of power. Consequently rural Americans took seriously the gentry's exhortations to seize control of their own lives, to defend themselves against the tyranny of oppressive and corrupt outside forces, and to return their country to its traditional virtuous course. Anxious for a reactionary, cleansing crusade and urged to take part in what they could only assume to be just such a cause, rural traditionalists fashioned revolutionary republicanism according to their most profound needs.

Views from Within the Market Economy

Conflicting perceptions of republicanism arose in those areas most affected by the presence of a market economy. The rapid and uneven accumulation of wealth and its consolidation among certain segments of society to the exclusion of others spawned anxieties that a few individuals were becoming wealthy at the expense of the majority. Those concerned by these seeming inequities, while puzzled by and perhaps drawn to market values, demanded economic justice as well as the preservation of social opportunity for themselves and their children. A growing urban underclass remained wedded to a moral economy of equity rather than a competitive market society. Like their more isolated rural compatriots, such folk understood republicanism to be a crusade to reclaim the corporate values of their past that seemed to them endangered in an increasingly threatening present.

The Middle Class. Simultaneously with the emergence of this reactionary ethos, a quite dissimilar outlook emerged in urban areas and in rural regions experiencing rapid growth and economic change. In these locales there emerged an aggressive, individualistic, acquisitive ethos characteristic of such men as the Green Mountain Boys on the New Hampshire Grants, fledgling merchants disputing the established junto for economic profit in Boston, and upstart planters challenging the Virginia squirearchy at the polls. Combined with thousands of fellow Americans whose economic enterprises detached them from the traditional corporate world of their forefathers, these individuals created a unique view of republicanism. Their republicanism blended John Locke's ideas with those of English country party radicals. Their comprehension of Locke emerged from their understanding of men such as James Burgh and Richard Price, who fused a bitter middle-class hostility toward the closed, aristocratic nature of the British constitution with the country party's deeply ingrained distrust of corruption and the misuses of power.

In his *Political Disquisitions* (1774), Burgh fashioned a profound amalgam of middle-class radicalism and country party ideas with Lockean principles of contract, the state of nature, and government as a trust of all the people. He instilled traditional opposition attitudes with a strident individualism drawn from an insurgent middle class. Thus when he castigated placemen, for example, his indignation sprang not simply from the threat such men posed to an independent House of Commons but also from his belief that they epitomized an idle profligacy that had for too long blocked the access of talented middle-class individuals to public office. No longer should lucrative and prestigious positions within the British government be allotted solely to unworthy nobles and members of the gentry. Merit, not hereditary privilege, should determine who earned governmental positions.

Richard Price, too, deftly integrated Lockean ideas, Commonwealth principles, and middle-class radicalism. In his *Observations on the Nature of Civil Liberty* (1776), Price infused an increasingly modern middle-class ethos into the country party's traditional hostility to capitalism. In his mind individuals who profited through unnatural means such as banks and paper money composed an idle and barren element within English society. Such an amoral class of nonproducers, like the idle poor, stood in marked contrast to the talented and industrious middle class.

The traditional language of classical republicanism underwent a transmutation in the writings of men like Burgh and Price: "corruption,"

for example, took on a new meaning. It now symbolized idleness, dissoluteness, an absence of productivity, and the total lack of talent and merit. A corrupt society denied public careers to men of talent and industry while rewarding unproductive and talentless drones. The true nation lay outside such a decadent government. It consisted of hardworking, diligent, and frugal individuals who desired both a meritocracy and a social order characterized by civic virtue. Such people steadfastly opposed an aristocracy resting on dependency or deference. In its stead they called for equal opportunity for merit and talent. In this way they shaped Locke's ideas on natural equality to mean a natural right to equal opportunity.

This perspective prompted a fresh conceptualization of virtue that blended a belief in the greater public good with industry and economic productiveness. Such a perception did not occasion a retreat from public activity to a privatized, selfish drive for material gain; instead it transformed the manner in which individuals considered the fundamental character of public conduct. Civic behavior alone no longer defined virtue and morality; economic enterprise now assumed importance as well. The common good remained the goal toward which all citizens must strive, but economic activity oriented toward private well-being became the most desirable mode of accomplishing this end. Thus, self-centered economic activity defined the man of virtue; a community of such men resulted in a society based on natural ability, not artificial privilege.

Although the rising entrepreneurial individuals in America, like their fellow countrymen, drew upon Locke, Price, and Burgh, their republicanism took on a special character. It was typified by aggressive individualism, interest-group politics, and an emphasis upon a competitive market economy. The entrepreneurs anticipated a society of opportunity for all deserving citizens as well as a government open to any man of talent and ability. Such men abhorred deference. In their minds it was characteristic of an aristocracy of privilege rather than a republican society led by men who earned their position as a result of their natural abilities.

The Gentry. As for the American gentry, its perception of republicanism could not have been more dissimilar. Like so many of their countrymen, members of the gentry also relied on Lockean principles; however, for them Locke stood as the protector of social hierarchy, not the advocate of personal autonomy and popular sovereignty. In this they resembled their English counterparts for whom Locke's ideas had seemed sufficiently conservative to adopt without a second thought as a suitable rationale for the rigidly structured English society of the eighteenth century. The English gentry presumed that Locke's *Two Treatises of Government* simply sanctioned the established legal order of English society. His principal ideas proved of inestimable value to the English ruling class in its effort to regain the right of political initiative. Locke lent credence to the idea that a just opposition to the king could legitimately coexist with a hierarchy of social authority.

Consequently the Glorious Revolution did not in the least weaken the firm psychological dependence of the populace upon the ruling class of clergy, gentry, and aristocracy. Rather, it established that while any individual enjoyed the theoretical right to challenge the legal order of society in the face of tyrannical oppression, the vital requisites of the social structure (peace, order, harmony, and social discipline) dictated that very few men could exercise this right responsibly. Further since the very legitimacy of the right of resistance rested logically on the responsibility with which it was employed, by definition only gentlemen of the ruling class were competent to assume such an awesome moral obligation. The great English lords readily embraced such doctrines in 1690; indeed these concepts served the ruling aristocracy well throughout the succeeding decades of the eighteenth century. Their hierarchical order rested squarely upon this foundation.

These same principles underlay the American gentry's perception of republicanism. For these gentlemen the social disciplines essential to a hierarchy had been unalterably severed from the legitimate order of English society by the American Revolution. In the minds of members of the American gentry, society's hierarchical authority and the affective force itself that made it credible had not disintegrated but had taken on a new and continued life within their own society. Habitually accustomed to considering themselves the embodiment of the "people" in the traditional sense of king and people bound to one another by the ancient covenant of reciprocal protection and allegiance, constituents of the gentry naturally took for granted that the august responsibility for leading the revolution fell to them. From their perspective the revolution entailed a rebellion against corrupt British officials, not a challenge to the principle of hierarchical authority itself. Indeed only such authority could hold society together.

Republicanism and Liberalism

In 1776, then, supporters of the revolution, regardless of their rank or station, professed a devotion to republicanism. Republicanism, though, did not mean the same thing to all Americans. Some ardently approved of the new world of market relations while others remained deeply anticapitalistic. Many favored a communal society resting on a social hierarchy. Others, with no regard for rank or status, insisted upon an open, competitive society. Still others desired a simple, homogeneous society of relative equality bound together by powerful corporate bonds. Such distinct predispositions comprised discrete fragments of the two cultural forces of republicanism and liberalism that affected the lives of Americans in the late eighteenth century. Often these forces appeared to run parallel to each other. At other times they seemed in direct confrontation, while at still others they merged into a nearly indistinguishable whole.

By and large republicanism, a familiar perspective accepted by persons in all walks of life, molded Americans' thoughts; it furnished meaning and identity in their lives. Liberalism, which was more an unarticulated behavioral pattern than a clearly delineated intellectual attitude, unselfconsciously shaped their day-to-day actions. A great many Americans clung tenaciously to a harmonious, corporate perception of themselves and their society even while acting in materialistic, competitive, and utilitarian ways in their daily activities. Thus even while actively moving their society in an open, competitive, modern direction, Americans doggedly insisted upon idealizing social harmony and a virtuous communal order.

Such behavior gained sustenance from the conflict with the British in the 1760s and the

1770s. Indeed by stigmatizing the values, attitudes, and institutions of a mother country poised on the verge of the industrial revolution, that confrontation injected fresh vitality into traditional republican values. Thus the revolution consecrated virtue (defined as the subordination of self to the greater good of the community), communal harmony, and corporate unity at the very moment in time when those ideals were rapidly becoming anachronistic. By this time Americans had domesticated classical republicanism to fit their contemporary needs; they quite unselfconsciously amalgamated traditional assumptions with their liberal behavior patterns.

This synthesis of republican ideas with liberal behavior patterns did not, however, ease the social tensions present throughout American society. While these strains had not necessarily caused the revolution, they did help shape the meaning and expectations that various groups invested in the revolutionary cause. Thus even though the gentry had mobilized a great variety of Americans of disparate desires and expectations by means of political exhortations ringing with libertarian rhetoric and promises of national regeneration, what these gentlemen meant by this agitation may well have been something quite distinct from the spirit in which many Americans—rural and urban, rising or declining—took them.

The vast majority of Americans shaped revolutionary rhetoric in terms of their innermost needs. What might happen if those needs were not met by the successful completion of the revolution remained obscured by the war itself. The problem would, however, reappear with increased intensity with the war's conclusion. At that time Americans could not avoid confronting the knotty question of what form of government and what type of society was to emerge within their new nation.

REPUBLICAN GOVERNMENTS

Even before that time, though, an intense excitement over the prospects for new republican governments that would drastically reorder the world Americans had known developed within the new states. Freedom from the corruption and restraints of Great Britain offered the opportunity for a new kind of politics, a new kind of government, that would alter the lives not only of Americans but of all people. Consequently, impelled by the ideological beliefs that brought them to revolution, Americans turned with a particular intensity to their state governments in an effort to translate these beliefs into institutional safeguards of republicanism.

Such intensity emanated from a belief common to many Americans that the very success of the revolution itself depended upon their attempts to forge new governments resting on enlightened and enduring principles. Striving to break free from oppressive centralized authority, Americans could not conceive of the formation of a powerful national state. Therefore the founding of republican governments in the states assumed tremendous importance; indeed for many Americans the proper establishment of these governments became the central objective of the revolution itself. Within their separate states, Americans assiduously discussed the great problems of sovereignty, representation, equality, the separation of powers, liberty, property, and the common good. There also Americans began their search for the best means to enshrine republican values so as to protect liberty from the ceaseless aggressions of power.

Framing the First State Constitutions

As Americans initiated this process, they attempted to translate into constitutional language the experiential foundation formed by their colonial past and viewed through a republican prism. Here the necessary first step involved stripping their governors of all prerogative powers. While no other state went so far as Pennsylvania, which eliminated the position entirely in favor of a council, every state severely restricted the governor's prerogatives. These executives now faced annual elections and sharply reduced terms of service. None could share in the lawmaking authority, nor did any enjoy the exclusive power of appointing judicial and executive positions. Consequently Americans eventually came to the conclusion that their governors should be restricted to the executive functions of government.

In their efforts to ward off oppression at the hands of governors, those who drafted state constitutions employed the concept of separation of powers. Although paying heed to Montesquieu's idea of separating the executive, judicial, and legislative functions, these individuals meant primarily to shield the legislative and judicial branches from encroachments at the hands of the executive. Actually, considering the legislature to be the true embodiment of the people in the government, the framers located nearly all power in that branch. Thus for all intents and purposes, the legislatures absorbed executive, legislative, and judicial powers. The power to make the law as well as the power to enforce it now rested entirely with the people.

Once state legislatures had been invested with such power, the framers proceeded with great caution; they wanted to make certain that these newly created bodies remained as free of corruption as was humanly possible. As a result they instituted short and regular legislative sessions as safeguards against abuses of the past. In addition, increasing representation and broadening the suffrage helped make the legislatures more responsive to the people.

Nevertheless, like the even more doctrinaire English libertarians, most framers remained suspicious of the poor. Such people might be manipulated by others; consequently those drafting the new constitutions favored restricting the suffrage to those with a stake in society. While not all Americans adhered to such a perception by 1776, all state constitutions did demand the payment of taxes and fulfillment of a residence requirement as minimal prerequisites for voting. Equal representation, however, stood as the surest safeguard of the integrity of the legislatures. Thus assemblies that were exact replicas of society and that were based on the fullest and freest suffrage of freeholders possible became the bastions of liberty in America.

A belief in the idea of such equitable representation, though, was not itself free of ambiguities. This resulted from the fact that a great many Americans adhered simultaneously to the concepts of virtual and actual representation. That is, their belief in the unity and homogeneity of the people led them to espouse the idea that each representative served a single organic society (virtual representation); yet their desire for the legislature to be an exact replica of society necessitated an explicit consent from the people divided into equal electoral districts with intimate ties to their own representatives (actual representation). Over time, as a growing number of Americans came to view their legislatures as made up of competing interests, they began to demand the authority to instruct their representatives on how to vote as well as calling for residential requirements both for voters and their assemblymen. Nonetheless abandonment of the idea of virtual representation meant the erosion of one of the vital intellectual foundations of republicanism, its dependence upon the organic unity of the people. Consequently most Americans demanded that their representatives respond to the individual needs and local interests of their constituents; at the same time, however, these same individuals clung to a perception of republicanism predicated on the existence of a harmonious, organic community.

The vast majority of Americans, throughout all their efforts to create new forms of government based upon republican principles, remained firmly convinced that only a correctly balanced governmental structure could protect them from oppression. As a consequence those responsible for writing the state constitutions assumed that a natural elite of talent and ability existed within their societies and should assume its legitimate place in the upper houses of their legislatures.

The senates, then, would be composed of the wisest and best men in society; they would be selfless individuals of superior talent, ability, and education who would place the public interest above all else. Such a presumption was natural enough given the proclivities of those who wrote the constitutions, but how to identify and set apart those capable of assuming a place in the senate raised troubling questions. To create an aristocracy, albeit a natural one, threatened republican principles; not to divide the legislatures, however, went against all received political knowledge and ran the risk of allowing the legislatures to gain overweening and thus potentially oppressive power.

With the passage of time, Americans' commitment to the idea of balanced government, combined with their fear of aristocracy, induced many individuals to alter their perception of the nature and function of the senate. Slowly and by degrees, an increasing number of Americans began to view the senate as simply one more means of checking the otherwise unrestrained power of the legislature. Most important this check did not create a special social or intellectual order in society; rather it stood for the people themselves. Thus by establishing a two-house legislature representing identical interests, Americans assured themselves of an institutional check upon the encroachment of power within their governments without creating a special interest that violated republican principles.

Few individuals had more than the slightest awareness of the meanings implicit in the resultant concept of double representation. Nonetheless this idea gradually became a vital element in a fundamental transformation taking place within American political thought. The nature of constitutional limitations on political power, the character of the relation between the people and their legislatures, and most important, the meaning of the sovereignty of the people formed the central components in this political transformation. Sporadic deliberations over these issues—conducted without comprehensive design or intent—propelled Americans quite unselfconsciously toward an entirely new political culture.

Redefining the Significance of Constitutions

The most fundamental change underlying this political transformation involved American attitudes toward a constitution. The struggle against parliamentary legislation in the 1760s convinced many Americans that the only means a people had at their disposal to protect their most basic rights was to remove those rights from the arbitrary power of any particular government. The fact that Parliament had claimed the right to interpret the English constitution and thus to legislate in any manner that it saw fit regarding the colonies, further convinced Americans that their fundamental rights could only be protected by creating a written constitution. Even more important such a constitution must exist both separate from and superior to government itself. It had to be superior even to the people's own representatives in the legislatures.

Such beliefs remained vague and inchoate throughout the revolution. Then, in a pamphlet entitled *Conciliatory Hints, Attempting by a Fair State of Matters, to Remove Party Prejudice* (1784), Thomas Tudor Tucker declared: "The authority of the people at large being the true sovereign authority, and superior to the legislative, a constitution framed by their express orders, and not made of force without first having the sanction of their approbation, would be superior to the legislative power, and therefore not alterable by it." With this statement Tucker succinctly articulated the new political perceptions that were emerging in a piecemeal, perhaps unintentional, manner throughout America. Such ideas thoroughly transformed the old relationship between the people and their rulers. Constitutions no longer represented covenants between separate competing groups; rather they now comprised the fundamental substructure of society itself and existed over and above government. Indeed constitutions brought governments into being and proscribed and limited their powers. In addition authority in every part of those governments stemmed entirely and completely from the people.

The belief that constitutions were superior to government carried with it a number of important implications. Perhaps the most crucial involved the manner in which the constitutions themselves were drafted. One fact stood out above all others: constitutions, to be entirely resistant to legislative interference, must be created by a power superior to the legislatures themselves. As a consequence Americans, quite without design, but nonetheless quite rapidly, came to consider conventions of the people as extraordinary constitution-making institutions distinct from and transcendent to their regularly elected legislatures. Such conventions offered the people a legitimate, peaceful means by which to retrieve the reins of government into their own hands; further, these bodies allowed the people to make whatever alterations they deemed necessary in order to guarantee their liberties and to defend their interests from the legislatures established over them. Thus the power of constitutional conventions revolutionized the old contract between the people and their rulers. Now the people themselves established their governments, which could only rule at their pleasure and under their careful scrutiny.

The Relocation of Sovereignty

This fresh perception of the relationship between the people and their governments inexorably raised questions about the meaning of sovereignty that became an integral part of the understanding of government and society emerging in post-revolutionary America. Discussions of sovereignty grounded in the belief that absolute and indivisible sovereignty must reside somewhere in any society led Americans to inquire even further into the proper relationship between the people and their legislatures.

In 1776 most Americans assumed that sovereignty resided in their legislatures. Such a belief made the idea of a confederation government of real power difficult, if not impossible, to envision. A strong central government raised the disturbing possibility of a divided sovereignty with two legislatures exerting power within a single state. As a consequence, attempts to enlarge the influence of the central government contradicted conventional wisdom regarding sovereignty as well as the ideological thrust of the revolution that promised the people more power over their own lives. At the same time, however, efforts by individuals within the states to control their own separate legislatures benefited from this ideological impetus.

As a consequence of these efforts within the states, legislatures increasingly came to be perceived as separate from the people and as objects of suspicion, an interest that had to be carefully watched. If not they would become the instruments of self-interested individuals or factions. Gradually a tension developed between individuals considering legislators to be simply agents of the people subject to their binding instructions and others who believed their representatives, once elected, to be independent of the people and thus free to deliberate for themselves upon the public welfare. Both groups accepted the concept of indivisible sovereignty; they differed only over where to locate that sovereignty. Those according their legislators independent status upon election believed that sovereignty resided in the legislature; those desirous of instructing their elected representatives felt that sovereignty rested with the people themselves.

Over time the position of those who considered their elected officials simply as limited advocates of the local interests of those who elected them gradually emerged triumphant. Ever growing numbers of people came to perceive representatives, senators, and governors without distinction as their agents; as a consequence, the various branches of government grew increasingly alike. No longer were the people represented in only a single branch of the government; instead they scrutinized, supervised, and managed their agents in all parts of the government. They now enveloped the entire government.

After 1776, then, Americans, caught up in the ideological thrust of their revolution, moved resolutely toward an acceptance of the complete and actual sovereignty of the people. Only with such an acceptance could a fresh, new republican government and society emerge in the Western world. And only with such an acceptance could the ideological promise of the American Revolution be fulfilled.

BIBLIOGRAPHY

Appleby, Joyce. *Capitalism and a New Social Order: The Republican Vision of the 1790s.* New York, 1984. Provides excellent insight into the liberal nature of American thought.

Bailyn, Bernard. *The Ideological Origins of the American Revolution.* Cambridge, Mass., 1967. A brilliant treatment of Commonwealth ideas as well as the resultant system of political thought that emerged in America.

Bushman, Richard L. *King and People in Provincial Massachusetts.* Chapel Hill, N.C., 1985. Provides sophisticated look into the changing relationship between the Crown and the people in eighteenth-century America.

Erikson, Erik H. *Young Man Luther: A Study in Psychoanalysis and History.* New York, 1958. One of the most perceptive works dealing with the dynamics of ideology.

Geertz, Clifford. "Ideology As a Cultural System." In *Ideology and Discontent,* edited by David E. Apter. London, 1964. Furnishes background into the functions of ideology.

Greene, Jack P. *The Quest for Power: The Lower Houses of Assembly in the Southern Royal Colonies, 1689–1776.* Chapel Hill, N.C., 1963. Shows how the American people gained increasing control of their governments over the course of the eighteenth century.

Kloppenberg, James T. "The Virtues of Liberalism: Christianity, Republicanism, and Ethics in Early American Political Discourse." *Journal of American History* 74, no. 1 (1987):9–33. A brilliant essay revealing liberalism and republicanism to be integrally related rather than competing paradigms.

Kramnick, Isaac. *Republicanism and Bourgeois Radicalism: Political Ideology in Late Eighteenth-Century England and America.* Ithaca, N.Y., 1990. Emphasizes the liberal character of eighteenth-century English and American thought.

May, Henry F. *The Enlightenment in America*. New York, 1976. Offers an insightful analysis of the broad intellectual environment within which American revolutionary thought developed.

Meyer, Donald H. *The Democratic Enlightenment*. New York, 1976. This book also provides background into the intellectual context of revolutionary thought.

Nash, Gary B. *The Urban Crucible: Social Change, Political Consciousness, and the Origins of the American Revolution*. Cambridge, Mass., 1979. Perceptively examines how the various social classes in America employed republican ideas.

Pocock, J. G. A. *The Machiavellian Moment: Florentine Political Thought and the Atlantic Republican Tradition*. Princeton, N.J., 1975. This book is central to understanding republican thought in the Western world.

Robbins, Caroline. *The Eighteenth-Century Commonwealthman: Studies in the Transmission, Development, and Circumstances of English Liberal Thought from the Restoration of Charles II Until the War with the Thirteen Colonies*. Cambridge, Mass., 1959. An outstanding analysis of Commonwealth thought.

Shalhope, Robert E. "Republicanism and Early American Historiography." *William and Mary Quarterly*, 3rd ser., 39, no. 2 (1982):334–356. Analyzes the literature of republicanism.

———. *The Roots of Democracy: American Thought and Culture, 1760–1800*. Boston, 1990. A discussion of the ideas of liberalism and republicanism within a broad cultural context.

Wood, Gordon S. *The Creation of the American Republic, 1776–1787*. Chapel Hill, N.C., 1969. A magisterial study essential to the understanding of republican thought in America.

Robert E. Shalhope

SEE ALSO other essays in this section.

SPANISH

AT THE OUTBREAK OF THE Mexican struggle for independence, the viceroy of New Spain presided over what was, in fact, a loose collection of political jurisdictions which would later make up the Mexican Empire (from September 1821 to March 1823) and then the federal republic. It is important not to assume a sense of unity among the various parts of the colonial state, because it was regional identity and aspirations for regional self-government that lay at the heart of the achievement of independence from Spain. The viceroy, with his capital in Mexico City, directly controlled only the center of Mexico, while the peripheral regions—including the separate *audiencia* (high court) region of Nueva Galicia (with its capital in Guadalajara), the northern provinces (the northern states of modern Mexico as well as the regions from California to Texas that later became part of the United States), Yucatán, and the separate *audiencia* region of Central America (known then as the captaincy general of Guatemala)—were all political dependencies that in the late colonial era took their orders directly from Spain and had a strong sense of their own identities. This tendency was particularly strengthened after Napoleon's conquest of much of metropolitan Spain in 1808, which cut the American colonies off from their monarch, and after the wartime government in Spain proclaimed the Spanish Constitution of 1812, which abolished the old viceroyalties and created direct political links between each province and the mother country. In Mexico, even after independence in 1821, there was a constant tension between the forces of centralism and the forces of regionalism. It is perhaps the dominant theme in Mexican history.

CLASS, COLOR, LANGUAGE, AND ETHNIC IDENTITY

Amid the complexity of a colonial society divided by region, there were many other dividing elements. These included class, color, language, and ethnic identity. In Mexico's 1808 population of 6,122,000, there were 1.1 million whites (themselves divided between 1 million Creoles, or American-born whites, and a small but politically dominant group of European Spaniards), 3.6 million Indians, and 1.3 million people of mixed background (mestizos, mulattoes, blacks) called *castas*. These categories, moreover, referred mainly to cultural and social identity rather than to color. Some Creoles were poor. Mexico's richest citizens were the wealthiest of all Spanish Americans (late colonial Mexico had more millionaires than the United States in 1810), and it was Spain's wealthiest, most populous, and most important colony; but most Mexicans were either agriculturalists and urban workers, or landless people of truly marginal economic status.

What united this otherwise disparate population, either by positive belief or by the inertia of three centuries, was their common ethos of king, empire, and religion. This ethos eventually broke down in 1808, when the French armies of Napoleon launched an attempted conquest of Spain, but important cracks in the ideology of colonial loyalty to mother Spain had begun to appear fifty years earlier. These doubts—and for most people they were not much more than worrisome doubts—appeared in the realms of ideas, politics, and economics, and for some people they were simultaneous and inextricable. Social perceptions and economic fears are the basic explanations for independence.

At the top of the social scale in colonial Mexico was the royal administrative and commercial elite who came from Spain to govern and control the state, the economy, the church, and the foreign trade of the colony. But of greater consequence in the long term were the Mexican-born, or Creole, domestic plutocrats, who were in most regards closely allied to the peninsulars. They were the great property owners, *hacendados*, miners, and merchants. Their complaints against the Spanish system were chiefly economic. They objected to the administrative reforms which the Spanish kings had implemented and which eliminated their access to high political office in the colony. They objected to the new taxes imposed by an empire that was constantly involved in foreign wars in the late 1700s. Most of all, they objected to the Decree of Consolidation of 1804, a royal decree that would have required the paying of all outstanding mortgages owed to the church so the funds could be transferred to Spain to pay for its wars in Europe. The church was the only lending agency in a colony that still had no banks. In effect the decree would have siphoned off up to two-thirds of all the capital in New Spain. Most of the rich would have been

ruined, for nearly everything they owned was mortgaged. Thus the decree brought the wealthiest domestic elite into a temporary union with the less wealthy Creoles, who had other complaints. If Spain would not protect the rich, what good was the mother country to them? It provoked a desire for autonomy among the rich, so that they could protect themselves in the future against such ruinous legislation from Spain. Though the Decree of Consolidation was revoked in 1808, the political damage was done.

The Spanish, the Creoles, and *Mexicanidad*

Below the rich in status, but still part of a general elite, was the population of Creole bourgeoisie—well educated, aspiring to appointments, dependent on commerce and the professions, but barred from further social advancement by royal decrees restricting political and economic dominance to peninsulars appointed from Spain. They were the creators of a sense of identity, often called "Creolism," that made them the first to realize they were not simply Spaniards living in America but Americans, and in particular, Mexicans. This identity was not yet strong enough to be called nationalism; it is best thought of as protonationalism. It was founded on a host of Creole grievances against Spanish administration, chiefly their feeling that the Europeans who held most of the important offices in the colonial regime were outsiders.

Throughout the three centuries of Spain's colonial rule, Europeans had denigrated the abilities, talents, physical vigor, and mentality of the Americans, while the Americans, in self-defense, had created a series of countermyths about themselves. By the 1780s Creole identity had assumed a unique form in Mexico. This sense of Creole identity, of *mexicanidad* or Mexicanism, was based on the myth that they were the heirs of the ancient Aztecs, a cultured society with a recognizable political state which had been invaded and conquered by the Spaniards in 1521. This is often called neo-Aztecism. It is a myth, because the real heirs of the Aztecs were the Native people at the bottom of the social scale—and the Creoles romanticized the original Aztecs, who had dominated the country through brutal conquest. Another prominent idea that emerged among the Creoles was their belief that the unique blend of the Indian and European cultures in Mexico was the true Mexican identity. This is a myth at least as far as it concerned the white Creoles; the real heirs of the mixed culture were the mestizo masses who shared the bottom of the social scale with the Indians. By 1810 this emerging consciousness of self was represented in the devotion of the Mexican people, particularly the masses, to the Virgin of Guadalupe, an apparition of a dark-skinned Virgin Mary who many Mexicans believed appeared to an Indian shortly after the Spanish Conquest on the hill of Tepeyac, just north of the capital, where the Indians had worshiped the mother of the ancient gods. Representing religious syncretism and the mestizos, the Virgin of Guadalupe emerged as the preeminent symbol of national identity, of folk identity, in Mexico.

The most important early statement of this Creole sense of Mexicanism came among a group of Mexican-born Jesuits, members of that order throughout Spanish America expelled from the empire by order of King Charles III in 1767. Of the 678 Jesuits expelled from Mexico, 400 were Creoles, and in the generation of exile in Europe that followed, they put into words the nostalgia for a culturally unique Mexican homeland. The ultimate expression of Mexico's glorious heritage was a book entitled *Historia antigua de México,* written by the exiled Mexican Jesuit Francisco Clavijero. Soon other Mexican writers, most notably José Servando Teresa de Mier, the intellectual mentor of Mexican identity, and the activist-philosopher-politician Carlos María de Bustamante, further defined the Creoles' sense of self-identification, of consciousness of self, distinct from the peninsular Spaniards and with differing political objectives. The fact that Mexico was the product of a unique mixture of Indian and European, in degrees and proportions not quite the same as in any other American country, was the core of *lo mexicano,* that which is Mexican.

THE BOURBON REFORMS

Among the Creoles, at least, this emerging identity was greatly enhanced by the sense of grievance against the king of Spain and his empire that resulted from the Bourbon reforms. These were the administrative and economic reforms introduced in New Spain and throughout the

empire, chiefly in the 1740s by Philip V, and again in the 1780s by Charles III. The expulsion of the Jesuit order was one grievance in the minds of Mexican Creoles, because most of the Mexican Jesuits were Creoles. In addition, there was a sense that the entire Bourbon regime was attacking the privileges of the Roman Catholic church—which was ironic, since the Bourbon monarchs were generally pious kings who nonetheless attempted to reduce the size of the clergy, restrain the foundation of new monasteries and convents, and in general force greater productivity upon the church. The attempts to limit the power of the church eventually caused alienation, particularly among lower-level parish priests in Mexico, many of whom communicated their grievances to their congregations.

In Mexico, one of the most far-ranging consequences of pressure on the church was the renewed missionary efforts by which various Jesuits and Franciscans followed up the pioneering missionary work in the north originally undertaken in the late seventeenth century by Fathers Eusebio Francisco Kino, Juan Manuel de Salvatierra, and others, to spread Spanish religion and power among the Indians in Sonora, Arizona, Alta California, and Texas. The famous Franciscan friar Junípero Serra founded missions in California after 1769. These missionaries were followed by a few soldiers and settlers, although the northern lands remained very sparsely settled and vulnerable to encroachment by the Russians on the Pacific and the Anglo-Americans in Texas. This danger of foreign encroachment led Spain in 1776 to create separate military governments in the far north in what were called the Interior Provinces of the East (Coahuila, Texas, Nuevo León, and Tamaulipas), and of the West (Sonora, Sinaloa, Chihuahua, and Nuevo México), thereby facilitating the sense of provincial identity in those areas. The last several viceroys of Mexico were deeply concerned about possible Anglo-American encroachment in Texas, particularly after the United States acquired the Louisiana territory in 1803. The 1819 Adams-Onís Treaty between Spain and the United States, which transferred the Floridas to the United States and fixed a border between Mexico and the United States, was not fully ratified until 1821, the year Mexico became independent.

The most significant Bourbon reforms were those of Charles III from the 1760s to the 1780s. They included several acts aimed at improving the economy and strengthening direct government control from Spain which, paradoxically, greatly speeded the development of regionalism and local identity in Mexico. The Spanish Crown began to cut back severely on the number of Creoles appointed to important government positions, particularly in administrative and judicial bureaucracies. Charles III, believing that the colonists' participation in government should be restricted, appointed peninsular Spaniards instead. Among other important political reforms was the creation, for the first time, of a standing army in Mexico and of various militia groups. These would provide aspiring Creoles the option of a military career, particularly since doors were being closed to them in administrative careers.

Politically, the most significant reform was the introduction of direct government by royal intendants in each province, decreed in 1786. Designed to increase governmental efficiency and to strengthen centralized royal power, the intendancies also greatly enhanced regional identity by giving some provinces their "own" government for the first time, thereby weakening the traditional power of the viceroy. Meanwhile, the economy of New Spain was restructured by opening foreign trade for the first time to Spanish merchants other than those in the great monopoly mercantile organizations, or *consulados,* in Spain and Mexico. This is generally called "free trade," though it is a misnomer, since no foreigners from outside the Spanish Empire were legally permitted to trade with Mexico. The essence of mercantilism survived; the Bourbons simply made it more efficient. Increased commercial opportunities provoked a rush of peninsular settlers to the colony, increasing the resentment of some Creoles.

Rebellion and Unrest from Below

At the bottom of the social scale in Mexico were the mestizo, mulatto, black, and Indian masses, numbering fully 82 percent of the total population. The poor lived on the margin of survival, dependent on the maize crop to provide their staple food. In the last century of the colonial era, New Spain suffered ten major cycles of agricultural crisis, price increases, and economic disruption. The last occurred in 1808–1810 and was the match that ignited the insurrection of the Indians under Father Miguel Hidalgo. These agricultural crises caused wide unemployment, sent thousands of destitute people flocking to the cities, and provoked major outbreaks of unrest and epidemic diseases. Of the ten major epidemics in the last century before independence, seven occurred in conjunction with agricultural crises. In the 1736–1739 epidemic, Mexico City lost nearly 50 percent of its population, and later epidemics each killed between 10 and 25 percent of the urban population. The last great epidemic was in 1813, in the midst of the fighting for independence. Between the 1790s and the outbreak of the insurrection in 1810, maize prices had increased over 300 percent. In 1811 close to half the per capita income of the poor was spent on maize. The masses were increasingly restive at the same time that the elites were feeling increasingly aggrieved.

The political and economic concerns of the elite and the misery of the poor never met across the massive gulf of class and color distinctions that separated them, even after the rebellions began. What is chiefly important about the effect of the economic and political anger building up against Spain is that it left the viceregal government more vulnerable and facing challenge on many fronts simultaneously. When Napoléon invaded Spain in 1808 and took its king, Ferdinand VII, captive in France, the center of the empire collapsed and the many American colonies of Spain moved gradually, over the next two years, to rebellion. In Mexico, the first crisis came in a debate over whether provincial juntas should be created to assume power following the collapse of the mother country. This was really an attempt by Creole elites to gain control of the viceregal government, but in September 1808 the European conservatives in Mexico City seized control of the government, overthrew Viceroy José de Iturrigaray (whom they accused of siding with the Creoles), and held power until Spain could send a new viceroy.

From beginning to end, the Mexican struggle for independence (1810–1821) was characterized by several different movements separated by class. The "wars of independence" were actually a series of civil wars in which the objectives of the Indian masses who made up the Hidalgo rebellion (1810–1811) differed from those of the mestizos who made up the rebellion led by José María Morelos (1811–1815), and those two failed rebellions differed yet again from the relatively bloodless rebellion of the Creole elites led by Agustín de Iturbide (1820–1821), which succeeded. Independence came about as the result of a complex process of elimination of alternatives rather than as a result of the wars alone. Although Spain sent a few expeditionary troops, at all times both the royalist and the rebel forces consisted primarily of Mexicans.

The mass insurrections, chiefly led by Hidalgo and Morelos but including many other rebellions in various regions, caused an estimated two hundred thousand to six hundred thousand deaths; devastated the country's haciendas, mines, and transport; required more than a generation to recover from economically; and produced no victory. This is because the viceregal regime, under viceroys Francisco Javier Venegas (1810–1813) and Félix María Calleja (1813–1816), was remarkably skilled in its ability to mobilize other elements of the population to resist the lower-class uprisings. Hidalgo (who was a rural parish priest) is honored by Mexicans as the "father" of independence; Morelos (also a priest) is honored as the skilled leader of an attempted social revolution. Each was captured and executed by royal arms, and their armies faded away, leaving a series of uncoordinated regional rebellions in the field but posing less of a threat to royal power. The Iturbide phase, on the other hand, began with his proclamation of the Plan of Iguala on 24 February 1821, and concluded in September 1821 with independence, all with no more than 150 dead.

This apparent paradox can be explained by the fact that there were really two different agendas, representing different social groups, in the process of independence. The Hidalgo and Morelos phases were rebellions of lower-class and rural campesinos and laborers—Indians in the case of the Hidalgo revolt, mainly mestizos in the case of the Morelos revolt. The Hidalgo uprising swept out of the Bajío region of Mexico (the richest agricultural zone) in September 1810 with such ferocity—Hidalgo had a force of eighty thousand unarmed and untrained Indian followers—that it terrified other elements of the population; it was the closest thing to a race war that

New Spain experienced. The viceregal government launched a skilled military and propaganda resistance, organizing regional command structures of new militias, urban regiments, ranchers, and merchants, simultaneously abolishing the Indian tribute, and convincing unaffected elements that the uprising had only destruction as its object. By the time the Morelos movement began, militarily much more skilled and consisting of small units of well-armed and well-trained rebels, the viceregal government had won the propaganda war, and through the use of conscription and forced loans it had been able to mobilize effective military units in many parts of the colony. Iturbide himself was a prominent commander of one of these royalist forces. The last three viceroys of New Spain, who had to fight the rebellions, took for themselves powers that would not normally be permitted; Spain, embroiled in its own war of liberation at home, was in no position to object.

The Creole Dilemma

The Creole elite of the colony, meanwhile, had come to support autonomy for New Spain as the foremost item on its political agenda. It gave enthusiastic support to the government of the Cortes, or parliament, that rose in war-torn Spain in the wake of Napoléon's invasion and proclamation of his brother Joseph as king. The American colonies were invited to elect deputies to the Spanish Cortes, which met at Cádiz in the far south of the peninsula. The Mexican provinces elected and sent deputies, several of whom became notable leaders of the Cortes. The Cortes, which in 1812 produced a constitution for the Spanish monarchy, the first in Spain's history, stimulated hopes in Mexico for provincial autonomy and home rule in each area of the vast empire. The Constitution of 1812 was the most radical in Europe at the time. It made the Cortes (rather than the king) sovereign, created elected provincial deputations (or legislative assemblies) and city councils, and took away many of the powers, and even the title, of the viceroy. The Mexican viceroys resisted, refusing to implement some aspects of the constitution.

In short, the rising sentiment of *mexicanidad* among the educated elements in New Spain led chiefly to aspirations for home rule, and from 1810 to 1814 developments in the mother country held out the promise that some form of autonomy, within a liberal constitutional monarchy, would develop. It is not so much that Mexican elites opposed or supported independence; rather, they opposed radical social revolution at the hands of the lower class at home, and favored liberal parliamentary and constitutional government with the substantial promise of home rule for each province in the empire at large. In the midst of destructive revolt at home and imperial collapse in Spain, the Mexican elites faced a terrifying dilemma. They rallied round the viceregal standard as their best defense against total destruction.

The Mexican elites held on for dear life, and in 1814 the imperial crisis began to be resolved. Napoleon was facing defeat in Europe, and he withdrew from Spain. The Spanish king, Ferdinand VII, held captive in France since 1808, returned home to a country that had been saved by his political enemies, the liberals. Having learned nothing and forgotten nothing, as the famous saying about the Spanish Bourbon monarchs had it, Ferdinand VII immediately issued a decree in which he abolished the Constitution of 1812 and declared all the acts of the Cortes null and void. In Mexico, Peru, and all the other parts of the empire where royal government had not yet been destroyed, the king's order was implemented and parliamentary constitutionalism was replaced with an even more intense form of absolutism than the traditional one. The elite's hope for Mexican home rule was ended by imperial fiat, but amid the life-or-death struggle against the lower-class rebels, relief was the dominant sentiment, at least for the moment.

The overthrow of the elected Cortes was, in many ways, the real turning point. The viceregal government in Mexico had already shown that the Indian and mestizo rebellions could be controlled, though the threat was not completely eliminated at any time. Smaller rebel groups remained in the field after the execution of Morelos in 1815, mainly in the south (where Vicente Guerrero remained in rebellion) and other areas outside central Mexico. But the primary item of the elite's agenda, home rule or autonomy, had been put aside in the resistance to the rebellion and had to await the rise of a movement that would both guarantee the survival of vested interests in Mexico—whether they be landholders, church, army, merchants, or bureaucrats—and simultaneously bring about political separation, or independence, from Spain. Despite the fact that future generations of Mexicans would perceive Hidalgo and Morelos as the great heroes of independence, the fact is that independence would not have come about because of radical lower-class rebellion. A political solution was required.

THE PLAN OF IGUALA

There is a clear continuum, in terms of political thought and aspirations, between the early expressions of autonomist sentiment in 1808; the rising expectations provoked from 1810 to 1814 by the Mexican provinces participating in the Cortes and the massive changes decreed in the constitution; and the final achievement of independence. The refusal after 1814 of the absolutist regime of Ferdinand VII to consider reform for the colonies, whether in trade, government, or civil appointments, convinced politically active Mexicans that the mother country would remain deaf to their pleas for change. Once the threat of social revolution was virtually ended, the Mexican Creoles could return to the main agenda—political autonomy. The Mexicans generally supported the Spanish Constitution, and when it was restored following a revolt of the royal army in Spain in 1820, the Mexicans rejoiced. Yet, the new liberal imperial government, which held power from 1820 to 1823, still refused to accede to the minimal demands of the Mexicans, or of the other colonials.

Thus the Plan of Iguala, issued by the Creole Agustín de Iturbide in February 1821 and immediately endorsed by southern rebel leader Vicente Guerrero, offered a political compromise—independence (under a separate constitutional monarchy), guarantees of existing status groups, creation of a Mexican congress to write a new constitution, and an invitation to the Spanish king to assume the throne of the Mexican Empire. It was a minimal program that met the basic needs of all groups, and although the political alliance it created lasted only briefly, it was enough to bring about independence. The Plan of Iguala was even accepted by the newly arrived Spanish head of government, Juan O'Donojú, a liberal, who signed the Treaty of Córdoba with

Iturbide. Spain rejected the agreement but could do nothing about it. In 1822 Iturbide was elected emperor by the Constituent Congress.

The guarantees in the Plan of Iguala, particularly its support for regional identity within the framework of the Spanish Constitution of 1812 (which was adopted for use in Mexico until a Mexican constitution could be produced), attracted the support of peripheral regions—such as the far northern provinces—where the wars of independence had not raged. Even Central America, which until 1821 had been almost unaffected by the passions searing the Mexican central provinces, enlisted under the Plan of Iguala in Iturbide's Mexican Empire. So did the captaincy general of Yucatán. For a brief period—no more than eighteen months—all of the Mexican and Mesoamerican subcontinent was joined in a greater Mexico running from Costa Rica in the south to California in the north. Yet so great was the tendency to home rule, now achieved for greater Mexico, that it soon spread to most of the individual provinces.

In 1823 the empire collapsed following Iturbide's abdication. Central America separated from Mexico and in 1824 created a federal republic. Meanwhile, the Mexican provinces declared themselves self-governing states, and in 1824 established a federal republic. The original dream of autonomy, now upgraded to self-rule for each province, was achieved. The tendency to regional identity and regional government, always contesting with the tendency to centralism, continued through the nineteenth century as the main thread in Mexican national affairs.

BIBLIOGRAPHY

The topic of Mexican independence and the late colonial era has undergone such fundamental revision since the 1970s that, with a few exceptions, this bibliography lists only the most major works published since 1969.

Anna, Timothy E. *The Fall of the Royal Government in Mexico City.* Lincoln, Nebr., 1978.
———. "The Independence of Mexico and Central America." In *Cambridge History of Latin America.* Vol. 3, edited by Leslie Bethell. Cambridge, England, 1985.
———. *The Mexican Empire of Iturbide.* Lincoln, Nebr., 1990.
———. *Spain and the Loss of America.* Lincoln, Nebr., 1983.
Archer, Christon I. *The Army in Bourbon Mexico, 1760–1810.* Albuquerque, N.Mex., 1977.
Benson, Nettie Lee., ed. *Mexico and the Spanish Cortes, 1810–1822: Eight Essays.* Austin, Tex., 1966.
Brading, David A. *Miners and Merchants in Bourbon Mexico, 1763–1810.* Cambridge, England, 1971.
———. *The Origins of Mexican Nationalism.* Cambridge, England, 1990.
Costeloe, Michael P. *Church Wealth in Mexico, 1800–1856.* Cambridge, England, 1967.
Farriss, N. M. *Crown and Clergy in Colonial Mexico, 1759–1821: The Crisis of Ecclesiastical Privilege.* London, 1968.
Flores Caballero, Romeo. *Counterrevolution: The Role of the Spaniards in the Independence of Mexico, 1804–1838.* Translated by Jaime E. Rodriguez O. Lincoln, Nebr., 1974.
Florescano, Enrique. *Precios del maíz y crisis agrícolas en México (1708–1810).* Mexico City, 1969.
Hamill, Hugh M., Jr. *The Hidalgo Revolt: Prelude to Mexican Independence.* Gainesville, Fla., 1966.
Hamnett, Brian R. *La política española en la época revolucionaria.* Mexico City, 1985.
——— *Revolución y contrarrevolución en México y el Perú: Liberalismo, realeza y separatismo (1800–1824).* Translated by Roberto Gómez Ciria. Mexico City, 1978.
———. *Roots of Insurgency: Mexican Regions, 1750–1824.* Cambridge, England, 1986.
Ladd, Doris M. *The Mexican Nobility at Independence, 1780–1826.* Austin, Tex., 1976.
Rodríguez O., Jaime E. *The Emergence of Spanish America: Vicente Rocafuerte and Spanish Americanism, 1808–1832.* Berkeley, Calif., 1975.
———, ed. *The Independence of Mexico and the Creation of the New Nation.* Los Angeles, Calif., 1989.
Torre Villar, Ernesto de la, ed. *Los "Guadalupes" y la independencia.* 2nd ed. Mexico City, 1985.
Tutino, John. *From Insurrection to Revolution in Mexico: Social Bases of Agrarian Violence, 1750–1940.* Princeton, N.J., 1986.
Weber, David J. *The Mexican Frontier, 1821–1846: The American Southwest Under Mexico.* Albuquerque, N.Mex., 1982.
———, ed. *New Spain's Far Northern Frontier: Essays on Spain in the American West, 1540–1821.* Albuquerque, N.Mex., 1979.

Timothy E. Anna

SEE ALSO other essays in this section.

INDEPENDENCE

THE BRITISH COLONIES

SAM ADAMS, THE CONSUMMATE militant from Massachusetts, had been spoiling for a fight since 1774, and probably long before. By the time the Second Continental Congress met in May 1775, he certainly favored, if he did not openly advocate, American independence. Pennsylvania's John Dickinson, on the other hand, although clearly an advocate of colonial rights, continued to hope for peaceful reconciliation more than a year later. As late as July 1776, he still could not bring himself to sign the declaration that would finalize Anglo-American separation from Great Britain.

CONSERVATIVES, RADICALS, AND MODERATES

The opinions of most delegates to the Second Continental Congress, the body which would ultimately declare independence from England, fell somewhere between those of Adams and Dickinson. In the months between May 1775 and July 1776, events would force a majority of them to abandon all hope for reconciliation and join Adams in supporting independence. The story of precisely how this happened remains to be told, but its outlines are clear.

The distinction among radical, moderate, and conservative in the spring of 1775 had little to do with a commitment to American rights. The Coercive Acts (1774) had convinced even determined Loyalists that the king and Parliament had overstepped the bounds of their authority in the colonies. It was now a perception of conditions in England that distinguished the degree of support for independence.

Conservatives believed that the British government had simply erred, that the king and Parliament were legislating under a misconception. They insisted that reconciliation remained possible, even probable. Patience and understanding would restore the empire. They reluctantly admitted the necessity for defensive measures in the colonies but resisted offensive actions and insisted on petitions for peace.

Radicals rejected these arguments. They argued that the British government was engaged in a deliberate conspiracy to reduce the colonists to a state of absolute dependence. Patience and petitions would only delay the inevitable. The colonists must separate from the corruption of England if they hoped to maintain their freedom. Delay would only allow the British to strengthen their position and make the inevitable separation more difficult to achieve.

Moderates, the largest group in Congress, fell somewhere between these two groups, and for several months it was they who determined American policy. They hoped for reconciliation but were less sanguine about the possibilities than were the conservatives. They supported both military action and petition and were more willing to use military force offensively if it seemed likely to achieve the long-term objective of return to the empire.

Those were the issues that divided the delegates. Other considerations united them. All delegates firmly supported the necessity of defending American rights. They rejected Parliament's efforts to tax the colonies and insisted on repeal of all such legislation. They unanimously condemned the Coercive Acts and generally supported the refusal of Massachusetts Bay to abide by those acts, which, they agreed, must be repealed if harmony were to be restored to the empire. Moreover, the British attack at Lexington and Concord (19 April 1775) had removed all divisions over the importance of supporting military measures. Even John Dickinson occasionally waxed eloquent on the need for opposing the British army by every means possible. In brief, the delegates generally concurred on what they wanted and that military action was, for the time being, necessary to defend Anglo-America (henceforth to be referred to as America) against the war that Britain had initiated. They differed on the means by which their objectives might be obtained.

The story of the American move to independence can be told most simply in terms of dwindling hopes for reconciliation. If the radicals could persuade other members of Congress that there was no hope for compromise, that the British were determined to force the issue with America, then independence was inevitable. In retrospect we know that the radicals were correct, that the British government had determined that compromise would irreversibly weaken the empire. All that remained was for George III and Parliament to assist the radicals in proving the accuracy of their assessment. And this assistance they readily provided.

George III pulled no punches. He had written as early as 1774 that the colonists must either "submit or triumph," and this conclusion enjoyed the support of the prime ministry and a majority in Parliament. Nor was there any likelihood that this support might erode. New elections had returned substantial majorities for Lord Frederick North as prime minister and the opposition, weak in numbers, was divided and ineffective. The vast majority in Parliament expected the colonists to submit. They firmly believed that past attempts at compromise had only weakened the authority of the mother country. If Britain would govern, it must govern. As Thomas Gage, last royal governor of Massachusetts, had put it in a letter to George III, "they will be Lyons whilst we are Lambs." Retreat was impossible. The colonists must understand there would be no backing down. King and Parliament would ultimately persuade the Americans of their determination; they would prove the radicals correct; and they would lose an empire.

SIGNIFICANCE OF LEXINGTON AND CONCORD

As Congress assembled in Philadelphia, the members were greeted by news of armed conflict in Massachusetts. The importance of Lexington and Concord in explaining the move toward independence cannot be exaggerated. Thomas Paine, in his pamphlet *Common Sense* (1776), later contended that this engagement marked the point of no return in the conflict between England and America. How, he asked, is it possible to "love, honor, and faithfully serve the power that hath carried fire and sword into your land?" Not an insignificant point. But beyond that, both in England and America, the conflict outside Boston carried implications that have often been overlooked.

In America, the battle at Lexington and Concord not only marked the beginning of military conflict; it also directly involved the other colonies in a confrontation that had previously been confined to Massachusetts. In October 1774 the First Continental Congress had struck a deal with the Bay Colony. Fearing the overzealousness of the New Englanders, the delegates had asked that Massachusetts avoid any type of offensive action and had promised, in return, that all America would support the colony if it was attacked. When, on 19 April 1775, the British attacked, the other colonies were honor bound to join the fray. It was this action which caused Congress to create an American army and to appoint a commander in chief. The creation of an army and the appointment of officers was a major, perhaps irreversible, step in the direction of independence.

The effect in England was similarly electric. When, in early 1775, the North ministry had ordered Gage to take offensive action in Massachusetts, it had been assumed that the colonists would offer no effective resistance. William Legge, Lord Dartmouth, wrote to Gage in no uncertain terms. The government expected little resistance and disagreed with Gage's view that such an offensive movement would signal the beginning of war. Should that be the case, however, the government thought it better to initiate military conflict immediately rather than wait for the colonies to further their state of preparedness.

News of the engagement at Concord hit London like a thunderbolt and persuaded the government that it must begin to prepare seriously for war. Halfway measures would no longer suffice. Thus in both the colonies and Great Britain, the battles at Lexington and Concord helped to persuade the opposing sides to fortify their positions and prepare for a lengthy conflict.

CONGRESS BEGINS ITS WORK

Despite differences of opinion in Congress, the delegates who assembled in Philadelphia in May 1775 faced a number of problems that could not be ignored. The army around Boston consisted not just of men from Massachusetts but from Connecticut and New Hampshire as well. Its organization, command, and supply were not provincial but continental issues. Despite the protestations of loyalty to the king, Congress must commission an army to oppose his troops. Money was another pressing issue. Surely Congress would be called upon to purchase supplies, pay soldiers and officers, and meet myriad expenses related to the conduct of military opposition. It might insist that it did not aim for independence, but was not the issuance of paper money and initially bills of credit the act of a sovereign power? There was, in addition, a fear of anarchy in the several colonies. Massachusetts

and New Hampshire had already asked Congress to authorize the establishment of provincial governments based on the authority of the people rather than of the king. Most delegates disavowed any intention of creating governments under any authority but that of England, but they most certainly could not permit disorder and anarchy to reign instead.

There were other problems as well. How were they to define treason? Could they effectively organize military action without adopting a continental plan of government? So long as they insisted that separation from the mother country was not a goal of their military action, could they expect to solicit foreign aid, especially from France?

The problem was, in brief, that the delegates were faced with the apparent paradox of preparing for battle against a government to which they proclaimed allegiance. Robert Middlekauff, in *The Glorious Cause*, points out that Congress "prepared for war while it begged for peace; it proclaimed its determination to protect American liberties while it petitioned for reconciliation; it expressed respect for the king while it promised death to his armies."

Jack N. Rakove has accurately noted that during the early meetings of the Congress, the conservatives launched an effort to reconsider some of the decisions made by the First Continental Congress and offer concessions. Dickinson and John Jay of New York proposed reconsideration of Parliament's right to regulate trade, and may even have suggested that Congress offer to pay for the tea destroyed at Boston. Scattered notes suggest that these two, no doubt supported by other conservatives, wanted to reconsider the Statement of Rights adopted in 1774.

Such efforts were of no avail. Military action in Massachusetts had almost certainly moved some of the delegates to more radical positions than they had previously held, and the Battle of Bunker Hill (17 June 1775) did nothing to moderate that swing. A majority of the delegates were unwilling to grant any rights to Parliament, as was evidenced by their refusal to petition that legislative body in either 1774 or 1775. When, indeed, they did draw up a petition to the king, they suggested no specific plan for reconciliation and left it, in essence, up to Great Britain to offer some concessions. Congress was committed.

CREATING AN ARMY

There was never a question that Congress would be forced to create an army after Lexington and Concord, but other events expedited that move. Perhaps the most startling was the news that Ethan Allen, Benedict Arnold, and the Green Mountain Boys had captured Fort Ticonderoga on Lake Champlain and Crown Point in May 1775. Although somewhat embarrassed by this less than defensive activity on the part of "American" troops, most of the delegates must have rejoiced at the event, since those forts controlled access to and from Canada. Nevertheless, the Congress debated at some length the proper response to this rather obvious act of aggression. The result would have been disingenuous had the Congress not been serious. The delegates voted to take a strict inventory of all arms and supplies in order that they might be returned after peace was restored.

Conservatives, moderates, and radicals found common ground in organizing military resistance. Given the British occupation of Boston and Gage's attacks on Lexington and Concord, even the most conservative of the delegates had to admit that it would be foolhardy to pretend that a state of war did not exist or to refuse to prepare for military defense against royal troops. They also agreed, at least outwardly, that independence was not an immediate option. The most radical of the delegates understood that popular opinion would not support an immediate break with the mother country, and most concurred, however reluctantly, that one last attempt at reconciliation must be undertaken. John Adams encapsulated the position of the Congress most concisely when, on 10 June, he wrote that it was necessary to "prepare for a vigorous defensive War, but at the same time to keep open the Door of Reconciliation—to hold the Sword in one Hand and the Olive Branch in the other." Adams himself thought it too late for reconciliation, but he admitted that the people were not ready for independence and must be allowed to find their own way to measures he already believed necessary. On 17 June he reasserted that position to his wife.

Throughout the month of June, Congress pursued these divergent policies. It created a Continental Army and appointed a commander in chief, George Washington, as well as other officers. Riflemen were sent to Boston from the middle and southern colonies, thus extending the direct impact of the war on the population beyond New England. The delegates adopted other measures necessary to the conduct of the war and, not incidentally, normally associated with the actions of a sovereign power. In mid June Congress issued two million dollars in paper currency and authorized North Carolina, which had asked for advice, to deal with the crime of treason if necessary. The delegates who had initially rejected a proposal to invade Canada soon reversed themselves. News of the Battle of Bunker Hill arrived on 22 June, and five days later John Hancock, writing as president of the Congress, authorized General Philip Schuyler to take Montreal if it proved agreeable to the French Canadians.

RESISTANCE SHORT OF INDEPENDENCE

During the first week of July, Congress attempted to explain its position to its constituents and to the world in two documents. The first, adopted on 6 July, was the Declaration of the Causes and Necessity for Taking up Arms. Two days later the delegates signed a second petition to the king, known as the Olive Branch Petition. The vote on the Olive Branch Petition was not unanimous, and some of the radical delegates feared that it might offer the British an opportunity to divide the colonists. Such men both expected and hoped for its rejection. John Adams once again analyzed the mood of Congress, noting that the majority still expected the ministry to back down when it learned of the battle of Lexington and Concord, the unanimity of the colonies, and so on. "I think," wrote Adams, "they are much deceived." Adams hoped that the ministry would reject the petition, and added that should Britain agree, he believed that "if we insist on our Liberties negotiations will terminate in nothing."

In the Declaration of the Causes and Necessity for Taking up Arms, Congress explained the decision to adopt military measures. Americans were, they said, simply defending their liberties against the revolutionary encroachments of a wicked government. The innovations of the British had left them no choice but to protect their ancient liberties against an unlawful ministry. They had, in fact, been "compelled by our enemies" to take up arms. This document, which set forth a policy of resistance short of independence, is perhaps the best statement of the American position prior to July 1776 and deserves more careful consideration.

In listing its reasons for taking up arms, Congress cited specific actions of king and Parliament. Those included the neglect of petitions from the First Continental Congress, Parliament's characterization of New England as being in rebellion, acts of Parliament cutting off commercial intercourse with foreign countries and prohibiting the colonists from British fisheries, Gage's occupation of Boston, and, of course, the attack on Lexington and Concord. As a result the delegates considered themselves "reduced to the alternative of choosing an unconditional submission to the tyranny of irritated ministers or resistance by force. The latter is our choice."

Bernard Bailyn has accurately noted that much about the colonial response to British measures can be explained by the fear of a conspiracy to deprive the colonists of their freedoms, and the Declaration of the Causes and Necessity for Taking up Arms reflects that concern. "We cannot," the delegates wrote, "endure the infamy and guilt of resigning succeeding generations to that wretchedness which inevitably awaits them, if we basely entail hereditary bondage upon them." Given the extent of this suspicion, it is not surprising that the measures Great Britain was already taking would drive the colonists to independence.

In the Declaration the delegates specifically mentioned both the question of independence and the possibility of securing foreign aid. Congress denied any immediate intention of adopting such extreme measures but did not rule out the possibility. The delegates surely expected the government to read between the lines, and they clearly raised the threat. In denying their intention of separating from their "fellow subjects," they noted that "necessity has not yet driven us into that desperate measure, or induced us to excite any other nation to war against them."

Even as the Congress adopted the Declaration explaining why the colonists had been forced to fight, the members were putting the finishing touches on the petition to the king reasserting their desire for reconciliation. Although this Olive Branch Petition is a rather vague expression of loyalty, it is possible to glean from its pages a general outline of what the Americans were fighting for.

It is notable, first of all, that the Second Continental Congress, like the First, did not petition Parliament. The delegates were unwilling to take any step that might suggest a recognition of the authority of the British Parliament to exercise any power over the colonies. As mentioned above, the more conservative delegates still held out some hope that Congress would recognize the right of Parliament to regulate trade, but a majority rejected that possibility and the petition did not even mention the issue. Even in the Congress of 1774 the supporters of such a right had been able to muster only five votes in its favor.

According to the Olive Branch Petition, America was "attached to your Majesty's person, family, and Government, with all devotion that principle and affection can inspire." The delegates declined "the ungrateful task of describing the irksome variety of artifices practised by many of your Majesty's Ministers" who were to blame for "a new system of statutes and regulations adopted for the administration of the Colonies." Congress could only protect the colonies from "those artful and cruel enemies who abuse your royal confidence and authority for the purpose of effecting our destruction."

In short, the petition expressed the hope of the moderates that George III had been deluded by his ministers. Once persuaded of America's loyalty, the king would intervene on behalf of the colonists, and restore peace and prosperity to the empire. The petition also reflected the importance of blaming the ministry as an explanation for the willingness of the colonists to take up arms. If, indeed, the Americans were attached to the empire through the king, and if the troops had been sent by ministers essentially disloyal to the king, then it was possible for Congress to have its cake and eat it too. They had armed, in essence, against troops hired by a ministry engaged in deceiving the king, mistreating his subjects, and abusing his "royal confidence."

BRITISH POLICY STRENGTHENS THE RADICALS

Unfortunately for the hopes of the conciliationists, George III fully endorsed the policies of the government. Both he and the cabinet believed that the colonial leadership was aiming for independence, and that the mother country must take a firm stand in order to avoid further disaster. Indeed, from the British point of view, the determination of Congress to reject the authority of Parliament was a move toward independence, and the government was correct in assuming that the empire, as they understood it, could not be restored except by conquest. The radicals in Congress, and an increasing number of moderates, also understood that point.

During August and September the Congress continued to pursue measures necessary for the defense of America and to await further news of developing British policy. In October that news began to arrive. The king, in a royal proclamation on 23 August, had condemned them as rebels and had refused even to receive the Olive Branch Petition. Additional troops were on their way to the colonies. The conciliationists were in disarray. Having persuaded the Congress to formulate yet another "humble petition," they could but shake their heads over the king's refusal even to consider it. Faced with the failure of their plan for restoring the empire, they could only adopt a wait-and-see attitude. The news continued to be bad.

In November, John Murray, earl of Dunmore and the governor of Virginia, extinguished any flickering hope for reconciliation in that colony when, writing from the safety of a royal warship, he called for a slave rebellion in the Old Dominion. Promising freedom for those who would join the king against their former masters, Dunmore sent a shiver of terror throughout the colony. Edmund Pendleton reported a rumor that slaves had flocked to Dunmore, but "I hope it is magnified." The Virginia Convention condemned Dunmore but showed that it had been alarmed by the proclamation when it offered pardon to any slaves who would surrender. If there had been any question about the sentiments of Virginia, Dunmore's proclamation eliminated them. On 1 January 1776, when he ordered the shelling, and consequent burning, of Norfolk, he only pounded an additional nail in the coffin of reconciliation.

By November 1775 Congress could no longer ignore the requests of several colonies for authority to establish essentially autonomous governments for themselves. New Hampshire was authorized to erect a temporary government basing its authority on the will of the people. Similar instructions to South Carolina resulted in the adoption of a constitution for that "colony" in March 1776, independent of all royal authority. Dunmore's actions in Virginia led to a congressional authorization for Virginia to follow suit and set up a government independent of British authority.

Many in Congress viewed any action by Congress authorizing the establishment of governments in the several colonies as the equivalent of declaring independence. Some of the more conservative delegates began to fear that Congress might declare independence colony by colony.

SENTIMENT FOR INDEPENDENCE INCREASES

By December 1775, independence was a constant subject for discussion both in and out of Congress, as is illustrated by the correspondence of the delegates. Joseph Hewes of North Carolina hoped it "might not come too soon. I fear it will be the case if the British Ministry pursue their present diabolical Schemes." Sam Adams, who could restrain himself only with difficulty, noted that "we must be content to wait till the Fruit is ripe before we gather it."

That the movement for independence was growing is also illustrated by the efforts of more conservative elements to stop the drift at the end of 1775. Urged on by John Dickinson, the government of Pennsylvania had specifically instructed its delegation not to agree to any separation from Great Britain. By January 1776 Delaware, New Jersey, and Maryland had followed suit. The fact that several colonies had specifically instructed their delegates not to agree to separation from the empire was used to prevent formal consideration of the issue by Congress. It was, the conservatives insisted, inappropriate to discuss an issue they were instructed not to approve. Moreover, they argued, these instructions showed that the people opposed independence, and Congress should not advance an issue that did not enjoy popular support.

The task of the anti-independence group was, however, a thankless one. By January the activities of the British government had begun to flood the newspapers, and nothing done on the other side of the Atlantic offered support to the conciliationists. News of the king's speech accusing the colonists of seeking independence, an express from Virginia with news of Dunmore's shelling of Norfolk, and private letters from England insisting that there was no hope for conciliatory measures fueled the radical movement in Congress. Rumors that the British were engaged in negotiations to engage foreign troops for action in the colonies added to the fire. Richard Smith of New Jersey noted in his diary that several delegates had said, on the floor of Congress, that if a foreign force were sent to America, they were "willing to declare the Colonies in a State of Independent Sovereignty."

For most of the delegates any thought of independence raised at least three other issues which would, of necessity, accompany—if not precede—that decision. Congress would need to authorize each of the colonies to establish a government based on the authority of the people rather than on that of the king. Moreover, if the decision for independence were to be carried out, the delegates would need to establish a continental government adequate to the prosecution of the war and to prevent intercolonial squabbling. Finally, the idea of independence was considered by many to be critical to negotiations with foreign powers in order to establish trade connections and secure aid.

Initially it seems to have been assumed that there would be an ordered progress in which each of these considerations would come in its own time. In the event the decisions were made rather haphazardly. Congress considered, but temporarily rejected, the appointment of a committee to establish a confederation, and would not achieve this objective for several years. The appointment of an unofficial envoy to France, Silas Deane, and authorization of independent state governments would both precede a declaration of independence, although neither step could be taken until the prospect of separation loomed fairly certain.

Other, less sweeping, measures continued to push the delegates toward independence. Rumors of possible attacks by British troops forced the adoption of measures to put the middle and southern colonies in a state of preparedness. Debates continued on opening colonial ports to all the world on 1 March, and on 24 January a motion was offered to create a War Office. And along with these major questions Congress was daily faced with a multitude of minor decisions ranging from how to deal with persons who refused to accept Continental bills to paying for music at the funeral oration of General Richard Montgomery, who had died at the battle at Quebec.

It is probable that by the beginning of 1776, a majority in Congress favored independence but, as John Adams and others were painfully aware, a majority would not do. The decision must be unanimous. Moreover, it could not simply be made by the Congress. Public opinion throughout the colonies must be brought to favor separation from the empire, and widespread hope for reconciliation remained among the population. The time was ripe for a major propaganda effort, and the propagandist was waiting in the wings.

THOMAS PAINE'S
COMMON SENSE

Thomas Paine's *Common Sense* (1776), like Harriet Beecher Stowe's antislavery classic, *Uncle Tom's Cabin* (1852), was an essential ingredient in moving a nation to war. Within a few months following its publication in January more than one hundred thousand copies of the pamphlet had come from the printing presses of America and had almost certainly been read to thousands more. That it was widely read in Congress is evident from numerous references in the correspondence of the delegates.

Whereas Congress, at least in its official documents, had attempted to avoid implicating the king in the conspiracy against the colonies, Paine went for the jugular. It was time, he insisted, to place the blame where it really belonged: on George III himself and on the "ancient tyrannies" of monarchy and aristocracy. Pointing out that government itself was a necessary evil, like clothing the "badge of lost innocence," he argued that the entire structure of the British government was faulty. It enshrined, he contended, the "base remains" of two tyrannies: the House of Lords and the monarchy. The few good kings throughout history were simply an exception to the rule. Any thinking person could easily discern that one honest man was worth all the crowned ruffians who had ever existed.

Paine paid very little attention to the specifics of the quarrel with Great Britain. Recently arrived in the colonies, he probably knew little about the events of the past ten years and, in any case, was not interested in the details of the conflict between England and America. It was the British system of government itself that aroused Paine's ire, imbued as he was with the doctrines of the radical opposition in England. The only legitimate part of British government, the very basis of the republic, was the House of Commons—and that had been poisoned by influence and corruption. The fate of Charles I had made kings more subtle, "not more just." Through a system of payoffs and influence, George III had engrossed the power of the Commons and was thus not only an ally of the conspirators but also the driving force behind them.

Paine also appealed to the messianic chord that ran deep throughout the colonies. Freedom was endangered throughout the world. Now that England had declared liberty unwelcome, it was only in America that liberty could hope for asylum. Thus the war for independence took on worldwide significance. It was not simply a war for American autonomy but a war to make the world safe for freedom.

Surely no true American could seek reconciliation with the corruption and tyranny of the Old World. And for those who continued to oppose separation, the bloody onslaughts at Lexington, Concord, and Bunker Hill had made the need obvious. Common sense, the love of liberty, and the future of the world called for independence: "The blood of the slain, the weeping voice of nature cries, 'Tis Time to Part.'"

WANING HOPES FOR RECONCILIATION

Even as Paine prepared his pamphlet, the British government continued its efforts to amplify the voice of the radicals. On 22 December 1775 Parliament had adopted the Prohibitory Act, forbidding any and all trade with the colonies. This act was widely viewed in the colonies as the final straw, and John Adams wrote that it, along with the Royal Proclamation of Rebellion (23 August 1775), had "convinced the doubting and confirmed the timorous and wavering." In February 1776 the colonists learned that England was attempting to hire foreign mercenaries, a move of enormous importance in hardening American attitudes. The idea that the mother country would enlist foreign troops to make war against her "children" was almost inconceivable to many.

Sentiment in Congress, advanced by the apparent shift in popular opinion and the obvious refusal of Great Britain to alter its course, hardened throughout February. An important event took place in Massachusetts when the Provincial Congress replaced Thomas Cushing with Elbridge Gerry, a move which John Adams welcomed as ending dissension in that delegation. The Bay Colony now spoke with a united voice in strong support of radical measures. Another sign of growing radicalism came when Congress, by a vote of seven to five, ignored conservative pleas that signing a foreign alliance would amount to independence and began active pursuit of that objective. The delegates gave further evidence of their sentiments in dealing with the memorial service for General Richard Montgomery. At the request of Congress, Dr. William Smith, provost of the College of Philadelphia, offered a sermon eulogizing Montgomery. The delegates subsequently refused to publish the address because Smith "declared the Sentiments of the Congress to continue in a Dependency on Great Britain."

March witnessed an increase in congressional militancy. Repeated discussions of independence on the floor of Congress increased pressure on those colonies that had instructed their delegates not to endorse separation without consulting their constituents. In addition, the Secret Committee of Correspondence appointed Silas Deane as envoy to France and instructed him to seek "aid, arms, and ammunition" from France. He was authorized to hint at independence. News of American reverses in Canada evidenced the need for a more unified central government and intensified sentiment for a confederation that would be necessary to pursue collective action against the British. Indications of a planned British attack on New York increased the need for immediate action.

Conservatives, increasingly on the defensive, were heartened in mid March when rumors circulated that Lord William Howe and General Jeffrey Amherst were authorized to treat with Congress and to offer real concessions. They grasped at such rumors and made them their last-ditch effort to stave off independence. Even so, on 15 March, John Hancock, writing as president of the Congress, expressed the opinion that "Our enemies mean to prosecute this cruel and unjust War, with unrelenting Fury. . . ."

News of the Prohibitory Act, by which Parliament authorized the seizure of all American ships and the confiscation of their cargoes, was perhaps the death knell of reconciliation. Joseph Hewes thought that "nothing is left now but to fight it out," and others in Congress agreed. John Adams suggested that the Prohibitory Act should be called the Act of Independence, and thought the British government had joined in "sundering this country from that I think forever." It decreed America independence, Adams opined, "in spite of our supplications and entreaties."

A lengthy debate during the last weeks of March resulted in an act of Congress authorizing the commission of privateers to prey on British trade. The sticking point in this debate was Sam Adams's insistence that the king, not the ministry, be blamed for America's distress. In the end, Adams failed in his objective, but accusatory mention of the king was included in a preamble for the first time. Paine's pamphlet had worked its magic.

By April 1776 nearly everyone in the Congress knew that independence was close at hand. The colonists had established both an army and a navy. Congress had appointed general officers, issued paper money, and begun negotiations with foreign nations for assistance. Surely these were the powers of a sovereign nation. American forces had invaded Canada and, although turned back at Quebec, had certainly ventured a step beyond "defensive warfare." George Washington had defined treason and threatened to hang prisoners of war if the British did so. On 6 April the Congress opened the ports of America to all the world except England. And it became increasingly clear that the arrival of the long-awaited commissioners would not materialize. When the City of London petitioned the king in behalf of America, his response, cold and formal, made no mention of negotiation. Richard Henry Lee thought that endorsement of independence was not far off.

No ground remained on which the conciliations could stand. Benjamin Franklin wrote, on 15 April, that England had been daily engaged in removing all obstacles to separation. One day later John Adams suggested that the colonies had, in effect, been independent since the Battle of Lexington and Concord, and Oliver Wolcott of Connecticut predicted that final separation was unavoidable. Indeed, England had left the conservatives little hope on which to base their opposition to separation. It had declared the colonies in rebellion, accused them of seeking independence, interdicted their trade, shelled their cities, encouraged their slaves to rebel, and refused their petitions for peace. It was difficult for even the most optimistic conservative to hold out hopes for reconciliation. On 24 April Thomas Stone of Maryland thought that if "the Commissioners do not arrive shortly and conduct themselves with great Candor and Uprightness to effect a Reconciliation, a Separation will most undoubtedly take place."

A MAJORITY FOR INDEPENDENCE

By the end of April it was almost certainly too late. It is doubtful that anything England could have done by then would have made a peaceful reconciliation possible. John Adams, as would so often be the case, hit the nail on the head. Writing on 27 April, he noted that a return to Great Britain was out of the question. It would create, he thought, an impossible situation: "perpetual Animosity, Discord Civil war; Encroachment and Usurpation on one side, and Discontent, Mutiny, Sedition, Riot and Resistance, on the other." When, in mid May, Congress learned that foreign troops were being paid by the British, the last hope for reconciliation vanished.

In effect the delegates declared independence from Great Britain on 15 May when they authorized the establishment in all colonies of governments not only independent of Parliament but also of the king. The preamble broke new ground by laying the difficulties of the colonists directly at the feet of the king, who now acted "in conjunction with the lords and commons." George III had "excluded the United Colonies from the protection of his crown" and, by implication, broken the contract of government. It was "irreconcilable to reason and good Conscience, for the people of these colonies now to take the oaths and affirmations necessary for the support of any government under the crown of Great Britain, and it is necessary that the exercise of every kind of authority under the said crown should be totally suppressed, and all the powers of government exerted, under the authority of the people of the colonies." This document declared, in no uncertain terms, that the colonies were absolved of loyalty to the Crown and, in doing so, severed the final ties which had bound the Americans to Great Britain. Carter Braxton of Virginia, a foe of independence, reported that the decision had been viewed out of doors as a declaration of independence, and John Adams thought it a total separation not only from Parliament but also from the king. Caesar Rodney of Delaware reported that the resolution was generally thought to amount to "a declaration of Independence. It certainly savours of it."

Slowly but surely the several colonies that had previously denied their delegates the authority to vote for independence reversed themselves. In March, South Carolina had implicitly authorized a vote for independence by giving its delegation the authority to take whatever steps were deemed necessary to protect American liberties. On 5 April Georgia freed its delegation from all restrictions, and on 12 April North Carolina specified that its representatives might join in a vote for independence.

The efforts of Congress, not surprisingly, were directed at assisting the radicalization of the reluctant colonies. When, during the second week of May, the delegates recommended the formation of independent governments, they almost certainly intended that their decision would assist the forces of independence throughout America. No doubt the rejection of royal authority asserted in the preamble proved useful to radical elements in the several colonies. It was particularly influential in Pennsylvania, where a conservative government, encouraged by John Dickinson, had done its best to slow the drift toward independence. Since the act not only rejected the authority of the Crown but also encouraged the several colonies "to adopt such a government as shall, in the opinion of the representatives of the people, best conduce to the happiness and safety of their constituents in particular, and America in general," it well suited the needs of more radical elements. In Pennsylvania the act helped effect peaceful revolution in government and resulted in an authorization for that province's delegates to commit to independence.

Much of the remaining opposition to independence that remained in Congress hinged on fears that the severing of ties with England would result in an excessively democratic government in America. As late as 29 June, Edward Rutledge of South Carolina expressed his fear of New England and its overriding influence in the government: "I dread their low cunning, and those levelling Principles which Men without Character and without Fortune in general possess, which are so captivating to the lower class of Mankind and which will occasion such a fluctuation of Property as to introduce the greatest disorder." Interestingly, as soon as it became clear that independence was a sure thing, even John Adams began to worry about its effect on colonial government. Unlike Rutledge, Adams had no fear of the New England colonies, but he did express concern about the future under more democratic governments. Paine's open advocacy of thoroughly republican government had somewhat unnerved the conservative Adams, and the approach of what had previously been only envisioned led him to commit his fears of popular government to paper. "I fear that in every Assembly members will obtain an influence by noise, not sense; by meanness, not greatness; by ignorance, not learning; by contracted hearts, not large souls. I fear, too, that it will be impossible to convince and persuade people to establish wise regulations."

THE VOTE FOR SEPARATION

Virginia led the way. On 15 May 1776 the Provincial Convention instructed its delegates, in a roll-call vote, to propose independence in the Continental Congress. The instructions were read to the Congress on 27 May, but not until 7 June did Richard Henry Lee move such an article on the floor. Even then it appeared that Pennsylvania and Maryland were unprepared for a declaration, and so a decision was put off until early July. It is not unremarkable that during the interim, copies of British treaties with the German states to enlist mercenaries against America had appeared in the newspapers. Similarly significant, although more difficult to document because he was not in Congress, was the influence of the commander in chief, George Washington, who was in Philadelphia during the latter part of May. His role in the movement to independence would be difficult to overemphasize. (It has been detailed by Curtis Nettels in *George Washington and American Independence*.)

On 10 June a committee was appointed to prepare a Declaration of Independence and instructed to report on 1 July. Congress assumed that the interval would permit those delegates without specific instructions to correspond with their respective provincial conventions. New York, Maryland, and Pennsylvania were the most important holdouts, but a number of other delegations hoped specific instructions might arrive before the deadline. On 14 June Pennsylvania released its delegates; only Maryland stood alone. Three days later Congress unanimously agreed upon the need for a confederation and appointed a committee to draw up the articles of union.

On 28 June a draft of the Declaration, penned by Thomas Jefferson, was presented to Congress; an unofficial vote two days later showed only South Carolina and Pennsylvania in dissent. Francis Lightfoot Lee of Virginia noted that Maryland's Provincial Convention had unanimously instructed its delegates to support independence, and that South Carolina would reverse itself the following day. The delegates from New York had abstained in the absence of instructions, and Delaware was divided.

When on 2 July the official vote in the Congress was recorded, the Declaration of Independence was adopted without dissent. New York still abstained, and would not add its vote for over a week, but what had seemed impossible six months earlier had been achieved. John Adams's prediction that Americans would forever celebrate the second of July with fireworks and thanksgiving has proven slightly inaccurate. Because it took time to present Congress with a clean copy of the document it had approved, and perhaps to prove that specific dates are less important than events, we celebrate the birthday of independence two days after it actually took place.

THE DECLARATION OF INDEPENDENCE

Perhaps the most striking feature of the Declaration of Independence is the radical statement of government it encapsulates. Having declared "all men" equal, and possessed of basic inalienable rights, Congress went on to set forth a simple purpose for the establishment of governments: the protection of basic human rights. If a government fails to fulfill this basic purpose, it is not only the right but the "duty" of the people to rise up and overthrow it. In short, the Declaration of Independence is more than an explanation of American action in 1776; it is a call to revolution anywhere that tyranny exists. It is notable that the Declaration of Independence, written in the eighteenth century, has been used in the twentieth century not only by the civil rights movement in the United States but also by revolutionaries worldwide. The document provided a statement of human rights which, more than two hundred years later, is still a challenge to mankind.

In the decades since the 1960s the author of the Declaration, Thomas Jefferson, has been often criticized for his hypocrisy in owning slaves even as he defended human liberty. The Founding Fathers, it is pointed out, either deliberately lied about the equality of "all men" or they were not paying attention when they signed the Declaration. The criticism is valid, but the story has another side. Most delegates, even from the southern colonies, disliked slavery and hoped for its ultimate demise. Jefferson himself feared for the nation the punishment of a just God; and Washington would promise, in his Farewell Address, never again to own a slave by purchase. The latter freed all his slaves upon his death. It is certain that Jefferson, and others, were aware of the implications of their statement about human rights and probable that, at least in theory, they believed it. It is also probable that the vast majority of the Founding Fathers would be cheered to know that their statement of principle ultimately helped the American people achieve what the founders could not.

Having set forth so specific an explanation for the purpose of government and the justification for its overthrow, the major portion of the Declaration is a list of the "long train of abuses and usurpations" on the part of the king of England which reveal his design to establish an "absolute Tyranny over these States." This breach of contract by the British monarch is the justification for a rebellion which is, indeed, not a rebellion at all. The Americans have, rather, been reluctantly forced to take up arms to protect their traditional liberties. Far from being revolutionaries, they are a people attempting to defend the existing framework of government.

Two points are notable. First, Congress clearly invokes the contract theory of government in which ruler and ruled enter into an agreement which can be abrogated by either side if the contract is breached. Second, here, as elsewhere in the activities of Congress, the concept of a concerted effort on the part of the British government to deprive the Americans of their liberties and reduce them to slavery is cited as the primary motivation for declaring independence. The Declaration does not suggest that any specific act justified revolution. Instead, the delegates cite the existence of a plan, or plot, having as its "direct object, the establishment of an absolute Tyranny over these states." When read closely, the Declaration of Independence is a case study of the mind-set which apparently drove the colonies to revolution.

This ideological framework further explains why independence came at a particular point in time. Even the ultraroyalist Thomas Hutchinson of Massachusetts believed that specific acts of the British government were unnecessary and unjust. But governmental error does not justify revolution. A governmental plot to deprive individuals of their natural liberties does. Consequently the decision to separate from Great Britain, and to declare that George III had broken the contract of government, could come only at the point when an individual or a colony concluded that the acts of the British government were not simply ill advised or ill conceived.

For this reason the delegates, after more than a decade of conflict with Parliament, chose to issue an explanation of their decision to separate from the mother country in which that body is never named. Indeed, only one vague reference is made to Parliament in a brief section charging that the king "combined with others to subject us to a jurisdiction foreign to our constitution, and unacknowledged by our laws; giving his Assent to their Acts of pretended Legislation."

Thus, by 1776, the Continental Congress denied that the colonies had ever been subject to the jurisdiction of Parliament. Obviously they had no need to declare their independence from a body upon which they had never been dependent. And, consequently, the major portion of the Declaration is given over to a listing of the many acts by which the king had violated his contract to govern America and thereby forfeited that authority.

Those who had sought independence had been vindicated, and Thomas Paine had said it best. Though perhaps "strange and difficult," the pamphleteer had written, "until an independence is declared, the Continent will feel itself like a man who continues putting off some unpleasant business from day to day, yet knows it must be done, hates to set about it, wishes it over, and is continually haunted with the thoughts of its necessity."

BIBLIOGRAPHY

Bailyn, Bernard. *The Ideological Origins of the American Revolution.* Cambridge, Mass., 1967.

Christie, Ian R., and Benjamin W. Labaree. *Empire or Independence, 1760–1776: A British-American Dialogue on the Coming of the American Revolution.* New York, 1976.

Countryman, Edward. *The American Revolution.* New York, 1985.

Greene, Jack P., ed. *The American Revolution: Its Character and Limits.* New York, 1978.

Jensen, Merrill. *The Founding of a Nation: A History of the American Revolution, 1763–1776.* New York, 1968.

Maier, Pauline. *From Resistance to Revolution: Colonial Radicals and the Development of American Opposition to Britain, 1765–1776.* New York, 1972.

Middlekauff, Robert. *The Glorious Cause: The American Revolution, 1763–1789.* New York, 1982.

Nash, Gary B. *The Urban Crucible: Social Change, Political Consciousness, and the Origins of the American Revolution.* Cambridge, Mass., 1979.

Nettels, Curtis P. *George Washington and American Independence.* Boston, 1951.

Rakove, Jack N. *The Beginnings of National Politics: An Interpretive History of the Continental Congress.* New York, 1979.

Ryerson, Richard Alan. *The Revolution Is Now Begun: The Radical Committees of Philadelphia, 1765–1776.* Philadelphia, 1978.

Shy, John W. *Toward Lexington: The Role of the British Army in the Coming of the American Revolution.* Princeton, N.J., 1965.

Wood, Gordon. *Radicalism of the American Revolution.* New York, 1992.

Young, Alfred F., ed. *The American Revolution: Explorations in the History of American Radicalism.* DeKalb, Ill., 1976.

David Leon Ammerman

SEE ALSO **Crises of Empire; Ideologies of Revolution; Reorganization of Empires;** and the map accompanying this article.

THE SPANISH BORDERLANDS

BACKGROUND

AT THE TIME OF the American Revolution, the inhabitants of the Spanish Indies showed little inclination toward rebellion. The Bourbon reforms of Charles III gave many American-born *criollos* the opportunity to participate in commercial, military, and political affairs within the colonial structure. Despite their awareness of the democratic features of the British-American experience and of the French Revolution late in the eighteenth century, the *criollos* as well as the peninsular Spanish in the New World remained loyal to the Crown.

In the opening decade of the nineteenth century, however, two events in Iberia dramatically challenged the loyalty of Spanish Americans. The first was the naval encounter in 1805 off Cape Trafalgar in which a superior British fleet destroyed the combined armada of French and Spanish warships. The second cataclysmic event, a massive invasion of Napoleonic troops south of the Pyrenees, virtually paralyzed the government of Ferdinand VII. Shortly thereafter the coerced abdication of the monarch and the imposition of the usurper Joseph Bonaparte upon the Spanish throne jeopardized the connection between the mother country and the colonial possessions.

Left without direct control from Madrid, the Spanish-American colonies began to drift. Consequently, various factions competed for authority to govern colonial Mexico in the absence of a ruling monarch.

In September 1810 the outbreak of a serious insurrection fomented by Manuel Hidalgo y Costilla, a disgruntled parish priest in the village of Dolores north of Mexico City, shattered the tranquility of the viceroyalty and sent reverberations outward to the borderlands. Little did royalist officials anticipate that this small uprising in an obscure backwoods village would flare into a bloody civil war lasting for eleven years.

RAMIFICATIONS IN TEXAS OF THE HIDALGO REBELLION

In Texas, a strategic province of some seventy-five hundred inhabitants northeast of the Rio Grande, Governor Manuel María de Salcedo grappled with the vexing problem of how to keep revolutionary ideas from infiltrating his jurisdiction. On the southwestern frontier, he faced the menace of insurgent sympathizers fo-

MEXICAN INDEPENDENCE IN THE SPANISH BORDERLANDS

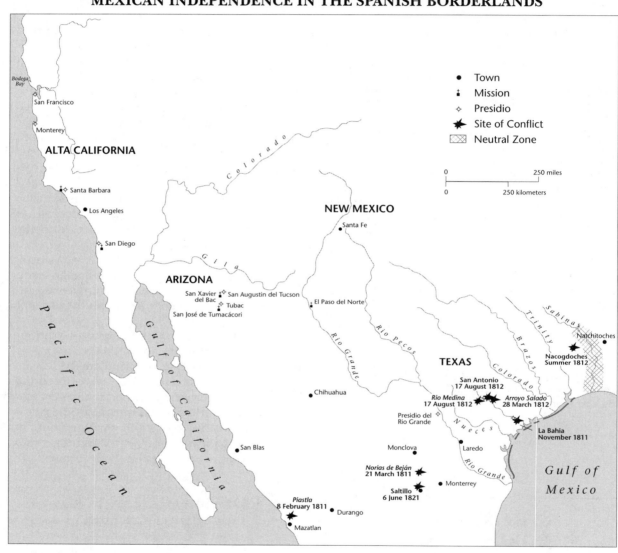

Legend:
- • Town
- ⚑ Mission
- ◇ Presidio
- ✹ Site of Conflict
- ▨ Neutral Zone

0 ————— 250 miles
0 ————— 250 kilometers

Bodega Bay

◇ San Francisco

◇ Monterey

ALTA CALIFORNIA

⚑◇ Santa Barbara

• Los Angeles

◇ San Diego ⚑

Colorado

NEW MEXICO

• Santa Fe

Gila

ARIZONA

San Xavier ⚑◇ San Augustin del Tucson
del Bac
◇ Tubac
San José de Tumacácori ⚑

• El Paso del Norte

Rio Pecos

Rio Grande

Sabinas

Trinity

• Natchitoches

**Nacogdoches
Summer 1812**

Pacific Ocean

Gulf of California

TEXAS

Brazos

Colorado

• Chihuahua

**San Antonio
17 August 1812**

Rio Medina
17 August 1812

Arroyo Salado
28 March 1812

Presidio del
Rio Grande ◇

Nueces

**La Bahia
November 1811**

• San Blas

• Monclova

• Laredo

Rio Grande

*Gulf of
Mexico*

Norias de Beján
21 March 1811

• Monterrey

**Saltillo
6 June 1821**

Piastla
8 February 1811

• Durango

• Mazatlan

menting chaos and disorder. On the thickly forested eastern border, Anglo-American filibusters, adventurers, and soldiers of fortune cast covetous glances at Texas. From both directions irregulars constantly menaced the stability of Governor Salcedo's administration of Texas.

The Overthrow of Royal Authority

In the opening weeks of 1811, an uneasy calm hovered above the rooftops of San Antonio de Béxar, the capital of the province. Although Governor Salcedo convened a special junta on 18 January to devise a united front to suppress incipient conspiracies, ideas of rebellion fomented by restless malcontents gripped the minds of a number of civilians and soldiers in the provincial capital. Juan Bautista de las Casas, a retired militia captain from Nuevo Santander below the Nueces River, assumed the leadership role by exploiting local discontent among the lower ranks of the military. On the night of 21 January he enlisted the support of four dissatisfied sergeants, who in turn brought their followers into the conspiracy. Before dawn the next morning, Las Casas and his confederates surrounded the Casas Reales, the local government house, and forced Salcedo and his staff officers to surrender.

After placing the royalists in detention, Las Casas plunged the province into utter confusion by his arbitrary actions. First he confiscated the royalists' property and that of their sympathizers. Next he proclaimed himself head of a provisional government in consort with the Hidalgo rebellion. Then he released the political prisoners of the Salcedo administration while arresting critics of his rule. Finally, after sending rebel agents to Nacogdoches, La Bahía, and other settlements and rural *ranchos,* he dispatched messengers to Coahuila to inform insurgent leaders of his successful coup d'etat in Texas. Anticipating that a vanguard of the Hidalgo rebellion would eventually reach Texas, Las Casas simply waited for high-ranking insurgents to recognize his contributions to the cause.

The longer Las Casas waited, the more tenuous his control became. Late in February, two emissaries of the Hidalgo revolt—Field Marshal Ignacio Aldama and Franciscan friar Juan Salazar, representing Mariano Jiménez, a superior officer in the northbound rebel Army of America—enroute to the United States, arrived in San Antonio de Béxar. Seeking maximum political advantage from the encounter, the usurper governor warmly welcomed the envoys. Viewing events from a discreet distance, old-line members of the town aristocracy compared the treatment Las Casas gave the insurgents with the harsh treatment he had given to some *vecinos,* landowning residents, and concluded that his ambitions did not coincide with the community's general welfare.

Counterrevolution

Meeting behind closed doors under the leadership of Juan Manuel Zambrano, subdeacon of the San Fernando church, the town elders resolved to oust Las Casas from power. Because no one suspected him of fomenting a counterrevolution, Zambrano was able to capitalize upon his clerical status to obtain from Fray Salazar a broad outline of the insurgent's plans to use Texas as a corridor to the United States.

Following a meeting on the night of 11 March outlining their commitment to the counterinsurgency, Zambrano's trusted associates proceeded to overpower the guards at the government house and boldly confront Las Casas. Surprised and without solid support anywhere, the prudent usurper surrendered. After placing Las Casas in a well-secured cell at the secularized Mission San Antonio de Valero (later renowned as the Alamo), the junta sent two loyal messengers (carrying forged credentials identifying them as emissaries from Las Casas) into rebel-held territory below the Rio Grande. Their assignment was to transmit oral messages conveying what had recently occurred in Texas to Nemesio Salcedo, commandant general of the Interior Provinces and uncle of Governor Salcedo, in Chihuahua.

South of the Rio Grande, the two couriers arrived at the town of San Fernando, where they learned from royalist sympathizers that the Texas prisoners were being detained at the Hacienda San Juan de Sabinas, the home of Colonel Elizondo. Informed of the countercoup in San Antonio and highly motivated by the news, Salcedo adroitly manipulated Colonel Elizondo's disappointment and frustration in not receiving either recognition and recompense for guarding the royalist prisoners or an assignment commensurate with his self-perceived military talent and experience. When Salcedo reminded Elizondo that Commandant General Nemesio Salcedo was his uncle and that a timely suggestion from the nephew might result in a coveted promotion—provided the rebel colonel redeemed himself—the captor denounced the Hidalgo rebellion.

Defeat of Insurgent Forces in Coahuila.

Elizondo and his followers joined Salcedo in planning a strategy to deal with the rebellion in Coahuila. In Monclova, on the night of 16 March, a small band of royalists overpowered Pedro de Aranda, recipient of revolutionary documents detailing vital information about the rebels, including reports from their recent defeats and the removal of Miguel Hidalgo from high command for demonstrated incompetence in combat. Five days later the counter-rebels overtook a band of insurgents on the road to Monclova and captured nine hundred men plus the entire high command of the curate of Dolores (Ignacio Allende, Juan Aldama, Mariano Jiménez, and Mariano Absalo).

Less than a week later, Governor Salcedo of Texas, assisted by a large complement of soldiers, escorted the principal leaders of the revolt on a long trek to Chihuahua, headquarters of Commandant General Nemesio Salcedo, where they arrived on 23 April. On 6 May 1811 Commandant General Salcedo appointed a military tribunal of seven members, with his nephew Manuel as presiding judge, to conduct proceedings against the conspirators. Owing to his status as an ordained priest, the tribunal scheduled Hidalgo's case as the last trial. On 14 June in full accord with the rules of canon law, the advocates of the church ordered the curate of Dolores to be publicly defrocked. Now reduced to the status of an ordinary layman, Hidalgo was shot by a squad of soldiers on 30 July.

Renewed Insurgency

Although he had participated in the capture of Hidalgo and other insurgents, the governor never doubted that the threat of insurrection would rise again. And, in fact, the following year insurgency surfaced again in Nuevo Santander south of the Rio Grande.

Bernardo Gutiérrez de Lara, a prosperous landowner from Revilla, intercepted the Army of America north of Saltillo and received from its leaders a commission of lieutenant colonel to lead a diplomatic mission to the United States for the purpose of obtaining foreign assistance. Arriving in Washington, D.C., late in 1811 Gutiérrez de Lara met unofficially with Secretary of State James Monroe. Given the American government's expansionist tendencies, the secretary expressed lively interest in a struggle for Mexican independence, but nothing constructive resulted from the meeting.

However, Gutiérrez remained in Washington for about two months building a network of contacts that included the Cuban-born adventurer José Álvarez de Toledo and John Graham of the State Department. Graham urged Gutiérrez to go to western Louisiana for the purpose of organizing an armed force to overturn the royalist government in Texas. On his way there, he met William Shaler, a special agent of the State Department with expertise in covert operations, who advised him on revolutionary strategies.

Encouraged in his mission, the Mexican colonel in March 1812 reached the Louisiana-Texas border region known as the Neutral Ground, which harbored a colorful assortment of American adventurers and fugitives. Conspicuous among the temporary residents was William Magee, a former army lieutenant and West Point graduate, whom Gutiérrez swiftly recruited to organize and train an expeditionary force. Commissioned a lieutenant colonel, Magee offered large parcels of land in Spanish Texas, forty dollars a month in salary, and spoils of war to prospective filibusters who enlisted in what he called the Republican Army of the North.

A vanguard of the motley Republican Army invaded east Texas in early August, causing Spanish defenses to collapse at Nacogdoches. With Nacogdoches as a forward base, the main unit of the Gutiérrez-Magee expedition pressed forward into Texas. Following several stalemates between the filibusters and the royalists and the death of Magee in February 1813, Samuel Kemper of Virginia assumed command. With their supplies almost exhausted and having sustained heavy filibuster firepower, the royalists on 19

February lifed the siege and withdrew to the capital, San Antonio de Béxar.

Reinforced by Indian auxiliaries and other mercenaries sent by Shaler, the filibusters reorganized their army before pursuing the royalists into the interior. On 28 March on the slopes of Salado Creek regular troops and militiamen, under the leadership of Colonel Simón Herrera, defended the road against the oncoming filibusters. Surprised by the sudden resistance, Kemper halted the march and sent mounted Indian auxiliaries to engage the enemy cavalry. The Indians quickly outflanked the royalists, who within about twenty minutes abandoned the battleground and scrambled for refuge in San Antonio.

Following Governor Salcedo's surrender on 2 April, Gutiérrez declared himself *generalísimo* and governor of Texas. He established a junta that promptly issued a death sentence for all royalists including Salcedo. This action sharply divided the filibusterer camp, causing many to return to the Neutral Ground. Complicating matters for Gutiérrez, the titular head of the filibustering army, José Álvarez de Toledo arrived in Béxar determined to supersede Gutiérrez. With flamboyant style, he slowly undermined the latter's authority over both Anglo-American and Mexican filibusterers before toppling him.

Royalist Reconquest

Learning of the coup and Salcedo's assassination, royalists below the Rio Grande resolved to recapture the province. In a normal succession of leadership, General Félix Calleja assumed duties as viceroy in Mexico City and, in turn, appointed Joaquín de Arredondo commandant general of the eastern Interior Provinces. At San Antonio de Béxar, Alvarez de Toledo, untested in combat, unwisely realigned the filibusters along linguistic lines. Warned by scouts that a royalist army bent on reconquest had crossed the Rio Grande at Laredo on 17 August 1813, the filibusters (renamed the Republican Army of North Mexico) moved toward the Medina River, southeast of San Antonio. The next day, tricked by a royalist ruse, Alvarez de Toledo foolishly led his entire force into a large V-shaped ravine, where Arredondo's forces virtually annihilated it.

Arredondo's victory at the Battle of Medina retarded the cause of Mexican independence in Texas for nearly eight years. Not only did he chase rebel fugitives into east Texas as far as the Sabine River boundary, but he chastised insurgent sympathizers everywhere. As punishment for permitting filibusters to enter the province, Arredondo disarmed the townspeople of San Antonio of every imaginable weapon, leaving them totally vulnerable to attack by belligerent Indians. As a result of this humiliation, the *ayuntamiento* (town council) became a highly conservative corporation suspicious of every irregular movement.

In the aftermath of Arredondo's harsh occupation of Texas, Colonel Antonio Martínez arrived in 1817 to take formal charge of the province. Like Salcedo and other predecessors, Martínez encountered a plethora of problems that taxed his initiative and resolution. At the top of his agenda was the threat of insurrection, which continually overshadowed his administration.

INDEPENDENCE ARRIVES

As in the borderlands frontier of Texas, so also in the central area of Mexico, the thundercloud of rebellion hovered above the landscape. Following the execution of Miguel Hidalgo in 1811, another warrior priest, José María Morelos, plunged the region south of Mexico into revolt. Although royalist defenders eventually defeated and attacked Morelos in 1815, other insurgent leaders, like Vicente Guerrero, picked up the fallen mantle of independence. But the level of insurrection fell lower than it had been in the time of Hidalgo and the years immediately after.

Events in Spain in 1820, however, reshaped political alliances in colonial Mexico and revived the independence movement. Restored to the throne after Napoleon's downfall in 1814, Ferdinand VII returned to Spain amid a wave of popular acclaim. A year later Ferdinand abrogated the liberal anticlerical constitution of 1812 and turned his wrath upon Spanish liberals everywhere. But in 1820 a royal army led by Colonel Rafael Riego disobeyed orders and marched directly to the royal palace in Madrid. Confronted by a rebellious army on the brink of toppling the monarchy, Ferdinand reluctantly restored the liberal constitution.

By midsummer, news of the constitutional restoration had reached government officials in Mexico City. Possibly more devoted to their portfolios than to their convictions, servants of the Crown accepted the constitutional changes without question or comment. But Colonel Agustín de Iturbide, a royalist officer removed from active command several years before, contemplated unhappily how the enforcement of the anticlerical provisions would affect Mexico's tradition-bound society. Coincidentally, a renewed insurgency of Vicente Guerrero south of the capital prompted the government to reinstate Iturbide to active command. Assigned to eradicate Guerrero's rebels late in 1820, the royalist colonel, harboring rebellious thoughts, departed Mexico City at the head of a large army.

Under a flag of truce, Iturbide and Guerrero met on 24 February 1821 in a verdant valley called Iguala, where the two leaders agreed to put aside past differences and to cooperate in a concerted drive to defend the country from the evils of the liberal, anticlerical ideas coming out of Spain. Accordingly the two commanders endorsed a Plan of Iguala; with its pledge of Three Guarantees—independence, religion, and unity—it was astutely designed to win broad-based support from various sectors of society. The two leaders further agreed to seek the allegiance of the provinces surrounding Mexico City (including the borderlands of Nuevo León, Coahuila, and Texas), reserving the viceregal center for the final capitulation.

Mexican Independence in Texas

News of Iturbide's revolution had spread into Nuevo León and Coahuila by the early spring of 1821. Commandant General Arredondo ordered Governor Martínez of Texas to implement forceful measures to deter the latest wave of insurrection. Left alone to confront the challenge, Martínez informed the extremely conservative *ayuntamiento* about Iturbide's independence movement. Alcalde José Angel Navarro boldly reassured the governor that the town council would defend the province with great vigor. Navarro's reply represented the general attitude of *cabildos* (municipal governments) in the bor-

derlands, which were the last bastions of royalism in Spanish North America.

In his four years of service in Texas, Governor Martínez never wavered in his loyalty to the Crown. Still, he recognized tell-tale signs everywhere that signaled a collapse of the royalist system he had sworn to uphold. Late in June the city of Saltillo fell into the hands of Iturbide's forces, leaving the road to Monterrey completely unguarded. In a matter of days Arredondo, unable to resist the enticing promises of independence, capitulated and signed the Plan of Iguala.

Within ten days a mail courier delivered to Governor Martínez the unbelievable news of Arredondo's surrender. In a terse message, the general advised the Texas governor to emulate his example. To Martínez's sense of propriety, capitulation was not an honorable option. While he still enjoyed flexibility of movement, the governor decided to pursue a proactive course allowing him and others to reconcile honor with reality by inaugurating Mexican independence in Texas before he was compelled to do so.

Aware that the key to an orderly transition resided with the *ayuntamiento*, Martínez on 16 July summoned Alcalde Navarro and associates to meet in his office the next day at 8:00 A.M. When Navarro objected that such meetings were contrary to local custom, Martínez diplomatically amended his directive to that of an urgent request that the *ayuntamiento* assemble in its municipal chambers on the afternoon of 18 July along with officers of the royal army and the San Antonio militia to discuss an issue of extraordinary significance.

Just prior to the afternoon meeting, a member of the governor's staff posted a bulletin in the plaza informing citizens that their presence was required the following morning at a public assembly for the purpose of taking a solemn oath. The same bulletin instructed militia and army personnel to stand in formation in the town plaza. After Martínez disclosed to the *ayuntamiento* and the officers that Commandant General Arredondo had endorsed Iturbide's Plan of Iguala, he outlined precise instructions concerning a private and public ceremony to be conducted the next day.

At 6:00 A.M. on 19 July, the municipal leaders reconvened on the east side of the town plaza.

Standing before Governor Martínez, they took an oath of allegiance to Mexico's independence and acknowledged Colonel Iturbide as *jefe superior*. Martínez led the delegation into the crowded plaza where the townspeople and troops waited in nervous silence. The governor confidently addressed the assembly, explaining the reasons for the convocation. Then he asked for their cooperation in an orderly transition. Alcalde Navarro also spoke to the audience, followed by the pastor of San Fernando church, Refugio de la Garza.

When the orations ended, Navarro briefed Father de la Garza on points of secular protocol. The priest then administered the oaths of allegiance. First, the military officers approached a table on which the priest had placed a Bible and a crucifix. In tandem they raised their swords and pledged to defend the Catholic church, to preserve Mexican independence, and to maintain public order for all inhabitants of Mexico. Next, members of the *ayuntamiento,* the clergy, and the civilian population took the same oath before an upraised crucifix. Finally military officers passed through the ranks of the soldiers to administer the oath, after which they dismissed the units. After the ceremony Martínez dispatched couriers to La Bahía and Nacogdoches to notify royalist leaders of the independence ceremony in Béxar, instructing them to replicate it.

With the ceremonies of 19 July in Béxar, *tejanos* celebrated Mexican independence two months before Iturbide led a triumphant march into Mexico City. The strict adherence to public order in Texas was a tribute to the vision and leadership of Governor Antonio Martínez and the *ayuntamiento* of San Antonio.

New Mexico

Situated directly north of the city of Chihuahua, headquarters of the commandancy general of the Interior Provinces, New Mexico was outside the mainstream of dependable communication. New Mexicans kept abreast of the trial and execution of Miguel Hidalgo in 1811 because the geographic proximity facilitated a flow of information. News of events that occurred south of Monterrey and Saltillo, on the other hand, usually took much longer to reach the provincial capital of Santa Fe.

Distance delayed the arrival there of reports about Agustín Iturbide's Plan of Iguala until three months after its promulgation in February 1821, and because of the barrier between the provinces, news about independence in Texas did not reach New Mexico until late in the summer. At that time Alejo García Conde, commandant general of the Western Interior Provinces, ordered Governor Facundo Melgares to swear allegiance to Mexican independence.

Not disposed to take any regional initiative, Governor Melgares in early September deferred to superior authority by requiring municipal officials in Santa Fe and *alcaldes* in other communities to affirm fidelity to the new political order. Extremely cautious about committing themselves beyond retrieval before the outcome was certain, however, New Mexico's leaders did not yet schedule any public events.

For the rest of the year, Melgares and his associates carefully examined reports from the south to the effect that Iturbide not only had triumphed and installed a Provisional Governing Junta of the Mexican Empire, but also that such fundamental changes had been endorsed by Bishop Antonio Joaquín Pérez Martínez and Captain General Juan O'Donojú, the last viceroy of New Spain. Finally convinced that colonial Mexico had truly discarded fealty to the mother country, Governor Melgares late in December scheduled a public ceremony.

Using a decree of the Provisional Governing Junta dated 6 October as a planning document, the governor and his confidants prepared a full program of activities for Sunday, 6 January 1822. To demonstrate broad support for Iturbide and the Three Guarantees, the ceremonies committee assigned oratorical duties to a trio of respected residents of Santa Fe, each symbolizing one of the guarantees. Alférez Santiago Abreu (Independence); Reverend Vicar and Ecclesiastical Judge Juan Tomás Terrazas (Religion); and Fray Francisco de Hozio, European chaplain of the royal troops (Union).

Although it was cold and overcast, the festive day began at dawn in the main plaza with the ringing of church bells, salvos of artillery, and an outburst of shrill music to accompany the unfurling of a white banner adorned with a tricolor heart on which were imprinted the words of the Three Guarantees. The crowd then slowly filed into the parish church for a solemn Mass to inaugurate independence day. When the liturgy ended about 10:00 A.M., the senior *alcalde* of Santa Fe, Pedro Armendaris, led a procession through the meandering, twisting streets of the town. Behind Armendaris walked Governor Melgares and members of the local *ayuntamiento,* followed in two lines by prominent citizens of the community.

The parade ended at the church plaza where it had formed earlier. Ignoring the cold weather, the crowd sang hymns of thanksgiving. At noon the townspeople moved toward the main plaza to watch a ceremonial dance performed by Indians from the pueblo of San Diego de Tesuque that lasted about an hour. Afterwards the spectators dispersed to observe, or to participate in, various games at the outer edge of the plaza.

In the evening, as the townspeople assembled in the plaza, four squads of soldiers took positions at each corner and fired salvos to complement the salute of the artillery. In sequence, after every volley, each squad shouted a litany of *vivas:* "Long live Religion!"; "Long live Union!"; "Long live Independence!"; and "Long live the Liberty of the Mexican Empire!" At the termination of the salvos of artillery and muskets, Alcalde Abreu, Father Terrazas, and Fray Hozio mounted the stage to recite long passages of a *loa,* a dramatic poem commemorating an historic event. After the *loa* invited guests, appropriately attired, entered the Palace of the Governors to attend a *baile* (dance) hosted by Governor Melgares. During intermissions in the dancing, the governor, the senior alcalde, and the Franciscan friar took turns entertaining the guests. At 4:30 A.M. the *baile* ended as merrily as it had begun. The independence celebration was over.

Southern Arizona

Spanish Arizona stood on the outer rim of the empire, seemingly cut off from its neighbors to the south. Early in the nineteenth century, Presidio of Tubac on the southern edge of Arizona protected Mission San José de Tumacácori and the village of Calabazas along the Santa Cruz River. At the northern fringe of Arizona, Presidio San Agustín del Tucson, forty miles (64 kilometers) north of Tubac, provided support to the nearby Mission San Xavier del Bac. To the east the land of the untamed Apaches formed a cultural barrier that restricted Spanish expansion, as did the Gulf of California on the southwest.

The authorized troop strength of Presidio of Tubac—eighty-four soldiers, two officers, and two sergeants—constituted the main population for the southern region, complemented by eight Spanish and twenty Indian families (the latter of whom with permission resided away from the missions). They all lived within an area of five square miles (8 kilometers). Near the northern confluence of the Santa Cruz River, Presidio San Agustín del Tucson's jurisdiction, covering only two square miles, incorporated a larger population of over one thousand soldiers, settlers, retired personnel, and Indian converts.

Miguel Ignacio de Arvizu, brevet captain, commanded the *presidio* of Tucson when partisans of Hidalgo raised the cry of insurrection in 1810. At the beginning of the following year, Captain Arvizu joined the royalist forces of Commandant General Alejo García Conde in a campaign against insurgents in the coastal corridor south of Tubac. On 8 February 1811, in the battle of Piaxla, fifty miles (80 kilometers) north of Mazatlán, the royalists confronted an insurgent army of seventy-five hundred men led by self-styled General José María González Hermosillo. Finding a royalist detachment commanded by Captain José Laredo wholly surrounded by an overwhelming force of six hundred rebels, Arvizu resolved to rescue his comrades in arms. Taking charge of a small squad of sixteen men, Captain Arvizu not only achieved his objective of rescuing a brother officer but captured an entire artillery battery from the insurgents. Turning the cannons upon González Hermosillo's numerically superior forces, Arvizu routed the enemy from the battlefield.

Colonel Arvizu was a formidable warrior. But as administrator of Tucson in peacetime from 1813 to 1819, he was found wanting. Arvizu effectively kept insurgents out of southern Arizona. But his harsh methods caused many civilian settlers to abandon Tucson.

The struggle over Mexican independence hardly touched the Arizona frontier. By the time that news of it finally penetrated this remote corner of the borderlands, the announcement had lost its celebratory fervor, and Colonel Arvizu simply acquiesced.

Alta California

As the last frontier of the Spanish Empire in North America, Alta California, was virtually isolated by time and distance from centers of authority in Mexico City, cost the government more to maintain than the nebulous security it provided in return. Founded in 1769 as a favorite project of Visitador General José de Gálvez to thwart Russian imperial designs in the Pacific Northwest, the colony initially received vital supplies and official dispatches through an overland route or by sea lanes from ports on the west coast of Mexico. Unfortunately, in 1781 an Indian uprising permanently sealed the Yuma Crossing at the Río Colorado, west of Tucson, leaving the maritime route, with its contrary winds and currents, as the only avenue of ingress and egress to California. Such geographic factors retarded communication with Upper California by an average of six months to a year.

By the decade of Mexican independence, Alta California was a fairly stable colony with a network of eighteen missions, four *presidios*, and three towns. The *presidio* of Monterey served as the provincial capital and political-military center. Colonel Pablo Vicente de Solá, a staunch royalist, administered the province from there, assisted by subordinate officers assigned to the other *presidios*. The Franciscan missionaries, practically all peninsular Spaniards ably led by Fray Mariano Payeras, enthusiastically supported the monarchy, which had promoted evangelization of the natives of California. Both Alta and Baja California, but especially the former, were bastions of Spanish royalism and resistance. The challenge to leaders in Mexico City was how to bring Alta California under the canopy of Mexican independence without bloodshed.

Since the Californias were at the edge of the Spanish Empire in North America, communication with them was slow. And so as late as January 1822, neither province had responded to dispatches from Iturbide's Provisional Governing Junta. Concerned about this silence and uneasy about rumors that Russian war ships had rendezvoused at Bodega Bay, north of San Francisco, Iturbide's government decided to send a commissioner plenipotentiary to the Californias to facilitate a declaration of allegiance, to inaugurate a new political system loyal to independent Mexico, and to implement changes in the administration of the Franciscan missions. Cognizant of the numerous missionaries laboring in California and wishing to provide tangible proof that it intended to protect Christianity from contamination by alien ideas, the new government appointed Reverend Agustín Fernández de San Vicente, canon of the cathedral of Durango, as special commissioner.

Empowered to remove uncooperative officials and to appoint replacements, Canónigo Fernández experienced various delays before finally arriving at Loreto in Baja California in June 1822. Meanwhile, in Alta California, Governor Solá carefully reviewed dispatches from Iturbide requiring allegiance to the new Mexican Empire and announcing an upcoming convocation of a congress of deputies to create a governmental structure.

Ever the royalist, Solá found ample reassurance in the communiqués that the new rulers in Mexico City, far from being firebrand liberals, were actually pragmatic conservatives. Thus satisfied, he summoned the commanders of the four *presidios*, Fray Payeras, Fray Vicente Francisco de Sarría (representing the rural vicar, Fray José Francisco de Paula Señán), and several other prominent residents of the province to help him formulate an appropriate response.

On 9 April 1822 Governor Solá assembled his guests as a formal junta to provide a foundation of legitimacy for the proceedings. After summarizing the contents of the dispatches he had received, he volunteered to be the first to swear allegiance to independent Mexico. Following his example, the four presidial commanders, Fray Payeras, and the captains of the military companies of San Blas and Mazatlán stationed in Alta California took the same oath.

Two days later, in a public ceremony, the junta members again subscribed to the same oath. In turn, they invited the civilian settlers, soldiers, and officers of the Monterey garrison and the Franciscan missionaries to swear allegiance to Iturbide's government. Within a few days, the governor scheduled similar ceremonies on a lesser scale at the *presidios* of Santa Barbara, San Diego, and San Francisco; at the three pueblos; and at the missions.

Seemingly oblivious to the imminent visit by the canon of Durango, Governor Solá waited more than a month before convoking an electoral meeting in Monterey to select a deputy to the Mexican Congress. The participants joining Solá on 21 May included Lieutenant José María Estudillo of the cavalry company at San Diego; Alférez José Mariano Estrada of the same unit; Lieutenant-Alférez Manuel Gómez of the artillery battery at Monterey; and five civilian electors from the *partidos* (jurisdictions) of San Francisco, Monterey, Santa Barbara, Los Angeles, and San Diego. Aside from their principal constituents, the electors also represented the Indian converts of the mission pueblos and other communities within their respective districts.

Governor Solá emerged from the meeting as the electors' first choice as Alta California's deputy to the Congress, with Captain Luis Antonio Argüello, of the *presidio* of San Francisco, as alternate. Thus by the time the Reverend Canon Fernández finally arrived in Monterey in late September, the province had not only already acknowledged the sovereignty of independent Mexico but also had begun to participate in the new system of government.

An Assessment of Mexican Independence

Mexico's independence movement fluctuated in scope and density in the borderlands. In the Coahuila–Texas corridor the battles of independence ravaged the countryside and deeply divided the loyalties of the inhabitants for almost the entire length of the insurgency. Texas royalists as best they could parried the thrusts of insurrection aimed at overturning colonial rule. Two times dedicated insurgents toppled the provincial government, and twice royalists regained control. After nearly a decade of turmoil, Agustín Iturbide proclaimed his Plan of Iguala with its captivating promises of religion, independence, and unity. Confronted by the reality of broadbased support for Iturbide's revolution, Governor Antonio Martínez persuaded royalist sympathizers in Texas to inaugurate Mexican independence there nearly two months before the insurgent army entered Mexico City in September 1821.

In New Mexico, Spanish Arizona, and Alta California, royalist officials waited until Mexican independence had actually triumphed before committing their support to it. The flamboyant celebrations organized by Facundo Melgares and Pablo Vicente Solá in Santa Fe and Monterey, respectively, were a matter of jumping on a winning bandwagon. But regardless of motives, the celebrations of Mexican independence in the borderlands formally closed three hundred years of Spanish colonial rule in North America.

MEXICAN INDEPENDENCE IN RETROSPECT

Like the American Revolution, Mexico's independence movement was essentially conservative. There was a dramatic shift in allegiance from a Spanish monarch to an abstract concept of nationhood and a shift in focus from Madrid to Mexico City, where a president governed the new nation with the support of a pliant congress. But except for some changes in political nomenclature, the governmental apparatus remained virtually intact.

States superseded colonial provinces, with the majority of them conserving their original names. An exception in the borderlands was Tamaulipas, which discarded its former Spanish identity (Nuevo Santander) in favor of an affirmation of an indigenous heritage. Likewise, Chihuahua replaced Nueva Vizcaya, but that change occurred in the final decades of Spanish colonial rule and not in the national period.

Law, language, religion, land-tenure patterns, place-name geography, livestock raising, business arrangements, family relationships, and weights and measures remained relatively intact. With the exception of some peninsular Spaniards who survived the trauma of independence and elected to leave Mexico, most *criollos* chose to remain as energetic participants in the fledgling years of the new nation. One noticeable difference was the active involvement of revolutionary generals in the swirl of national politics without changing from military uniform to civilian attire.

Mexican independence in the borderlands reflected the conservative nature of Mexican society. Governor Martínez of Texas, for example, stayed in office to become the first executive of an independent province under the rule of Agustín Iturbide. Spanish Franciscans remained in New Mexico and California to administer the old colonial missions until the government later mandated their final secularization.

Mexican independence was a political phenomena and hardly a social transformation. Unlike the United States of America, which after independence from England resolved to nurture social and economic ties with the former mother country, Mexico completely turned its back on Spain but retained many of the institutions that the Spaniards had transported to North America.

BIBLIOGRAPHY

Almaráz, Félix D., Jr. "Aspects of Mexican Texas: A Focal Point in Southwest History." *Red River Valley Historical Review* 2, no. 3 (1975):363–379.

———. *Governor Antonio Martínez and Mexican Independence in Texas: An Orderly Transition.* San Antonio, Tex., 1979.

———. *Tragic Cavalier: Governor Manuel Salcedo of Texas, 1808–1813.* College Station, Tex., 1991.

Bolton, Herbert E., ed. "The Iturbide Revolution in the Californias." *Hispanic American Historical Review* 2, no. 2 (1919):188–242.

Hamill, Hugh M., Jr. *The Hidalgo Revolt: Prelude to Mexican Independence.* Gainesville, Fla., 1966.

McCarty, Kieran, comp. *Desert Documentary: The Spanish Years, 1767–1821.* Tucson, Ariz., 1976.

Miller, Hubert J. *Padre Miguel Hidalgo: Father of Mexican Independence.* Edinburg, Tex., 1986.

Weber, David J., ed. "An Unforgettable Day: Facundo Melgares on Independence." *New Mexico Historical Review* 48, no. 1 (1973):27–44.

Felix D. Almaraz, Jr.

SEE ALSO **Crises of Empire; Ideologies of Revolution;** and **Reorganization of Empires;** and the map accompanying this article.

THE CANADIAN PERSPECTIVE

BRITAIN'S NORTH AMERICAN colonies detached the umbilical cord with their motherland in 1776. In 1783 their status as an independent nation was recognized by Great Britain. Some four decades later the Spanish colonies gained their independence from Spain. In startling contrast the French colonists in North America never displayed any desire for independence, for separation from France, save for a faint flicker just before the conquest of Canada by Great Britain in 1760. Instead they were cast away by their motherland: the colonists of Louisiana were abandoned first to Spain then to the burgeoning United States of America, whereupon the Louisianans were completely assimilated, their language and culture expunged. The French in Canada and its western hinterland found themselves in grave danger of sharing a similar fate, abandoned as they were to the none-too-tender mercies of their British conquerors.

THE CONQUEST OF 1760

The Canadian ruling class—the senior French officials, the Troupes de la Marine with its Canadian officer corps (most of them seigneurs and nobles), and some of the wealthier bourgeois merchants—left for France in 1760. The great majority of the Canadians, however—the habitant freehold farmers, the urban artisans, and the petty officials—had nothing to go to in France; hence they stayed in Canada, left leaderless save for the church. Of all the old institutions the Catholic church alone remained. But it too lacked a leader; it had no bishop, the incumbent having disobligingly died shortly before the capitulation of the French armies at Montreal. Thus no new priests could be ordained, and the British would not allow any to be sent from France.

Within a generation the Roman priesthood would be gone, and what then? Contemporaries wondered if the Canadians would become pagans or, worse still, be converted to Protestantism and face an eventual eternity in hell. The prospect for the Canadians was too horrible to contemplate. The remaining Canadian clergy therefore had to make every effort to persuade the British government to allow a bishop to be appointed for Canada. They had to cooperate with the British military government in every respect. Most Canadians did not take such a long-term view of things, until their own parish priest died and there was no one to take his place. For some Canadians the clergy came to be viewed as collaborators, *vendus,* who had sold out to the enemy, for the war between France and Britain was not yet over. It was hoped that Canada would be returned to France at the war's end, and then there would be the inevitable settling of accounts.

During the course of the war, the French government had paid for goods and services rendered by the Canadians with paper money. These *ordonnances* were nothing more than IOUs with a government stamp, to be redeemed in due course by the Ministry of the Marine. As the war pursued its course elsewhere in the world, payment of these vast accrued sums was held in abeyance. The French government was, of course, bankrupt. Canadian merchants who had trade goods in warehouses at La Rochelle and Bordeaux awaiting shipment could not get delivery and eventually had to sell them for a pittance.

Meanwhile the British merchants and settlers who had accompanied the armies of Major Generals James Wolfe and Jeffery Amherst as civilian supply corps could obtain ample goods for the fur trade and for domestic consumption from London suppliers on credit. This group—English, Scots, and Anglo-Americans—quickly took control of the Canadian economy and retained it for the ensuing two centuries. The old Canadian upper class—those of them who had stayed in the colony after the conquest for whatever reasons—were economically bereft. To fend off starvation they were forced to sell their marketable possessions—jewelry, silverware, china, furniture, fine clothing—to the British occupation forces, who alone had hard currency. So much land came on the market that farms and seigneuries had to be sold for a fraction of their worth. This was the short-term price of conquest.

During the siege of Quebec in the summer of 1759 the British, fearing that the town could not be taken, had systematically bombarded it, dismantling some 80 percent of the buildings and laying waste to all the farms along the Saint Lawrence. Thousands of homes, stables, and barns were pillaged then put to the torch, the cattle driven off or slaughtered, the crops burned. The British advance on Montreal the following year looked much the same. At Varennes some Canadian women were raped. It would take the Canadians at least two generations to restore what had been destroyed. Meanwhile, making do as best they could, the Canadians prayed for a quick end to the war, the restoration of French rule, and the redemption of the paper money owed them by the French government.

BRITAIN'S "NEW SUBJECTS"

In the summer of 1764, the first ships arrived at Quebec from Britain with heartbreaking news: by the terms of the Treaty of Paris, France had ceded Canada to Great Britain. Subsequently the Canadians learned that the French government refused to redeem, on a variety of pretexts, the paper money its officials had issued during the war. The economic capital of the colony was gone. Essential institutions, such as the Ursulines' convent school, the Hôtels Dieu that cared for the sick, the Hôpital, entrusted with the destitute, aged, and orphaned, were bereft. From this time on Canadians were referred to as His Britannic Majesty's "new subjects"; the British as "the old subjects." Most Canadians had no choice but to submit, put a crop in the ground, hunt and fish to put food on the table, accept whatever employment the British army and merchants offered, bow and scrape if necessary.

Defending newly claimed territory, however, proved a thorny problem for British authorities. The previous year, 1763, the Indian nations of the Great Lakes region and the Ohio Valley, outraged by the influx of Anglo-American settlers onto their lands in defiance of all treaty obligations, had suddenly struck back. Some thousands of British squatters were slaughtered. The majority fled back over the Allegheny Mountains, leaving the defense of the western frontier to the British army, which had been stripped to the bone for a campaign in the Caribbean. The meager British garrisons at the old French forts suffered heavy casualties before they succeeded in bringing the warring Indian nations to terms.

Two things vexed the British authorities on this occasion. First, the Canadian militia refused to serve when called up, declaring that the Indians of the region had always been their friends, never their enemies. Second, the Anglo-

American colonial assemblies, whose people had brought on the war, refused to provide men or money to restore peace in the west. The British government therefore concluded that a garrison force of some ten thousand men was needed in North America to defend the frontiers and keep the Canadians in subjection. Furthermore, it was decided that the Anglo-American colonists, the main beneficiaries of the recent war, should be required to pay their share of the massive national debt incurred during the conflict. The colonists rejected all such proposals out of hand, labeling them "Intolerable Acts."

With trouble brewing in the old thirteen colonies and France manifestly preparing for a war of revenge, Britain stripped its new province, Quebec, of most of its garrison troops and shipped them to Boston to preserve order there. In Quebec itself an awkward situation had developed, one that persuaded the British authorities that it would be politic to try to placate the Canadians and gain their support. The problem was partly economic, partly social in origin. The British officers and men had come into conflict with the Protestant merchant community over a number of issues. The officers were gentlemen, the merchants manifestly were not. The army became convinced that the merchants were cheating outrageously on every government contract; a group of them even had the audacity to offer Governor James Murray a percentage. Murray, his officers, and their men quickly came to despise the merchants. One of those considered most obnoxious, Thomas Walker, late of Boston, had his home invaded by a band of soldiers who cut off one of his ears. Despite a rigorous court of inquiry the perpetrators were never identified. In the eyes of aristocrats like Murray, his successor Guy Carleton, and their officers, men such as the merchants were not to be borne. Thus they invited the merchants' wives and daughters to their supper parties and balls but not their menfolk, who were obliged to use the tradesmen's entrance if they had occasion to call. For their part the merchants bitterly resented being ruled by a governor and his appointed council; they wanted an elected assembly, which they would dominate since only Protestants would be eligible for election.

Thus it was that the British officers discovered admirable but hitherto unrecognized quali-ties in their erstwhile foes, what remained of the old seigneurial class and the senior Roman clergy; the company of these two groups was much more to the officers' liking for they were, after all, gentlemen. At a lower social level many British soldiers, particularly those of the Scottish regiments, decided to take their discharge in Quebec; they married Canadian women, were quickly assimilated, and continued the way of life that they had known in the old country, which differed very little from that of the Canadian habitants.

A LEADER FOR THE ROMAN CATHOLIC CHURCH

Meanwhile the Roman church in Quebec was in a desperate situation. The number of priests was steadily declining. The British government would not allow any priests to be sent from France, and without a bishop none could be ordained in the colony. A Protestant king of England could not appoint a Roman bishop in his realm, nor could he allow the king of France and the pope to make such an appointment. It was a serious dilemma. Eventually a solution was found, typically British in its pragmatism. James Murray persuaded the government to allow a senior member of the clergy, Jean-Olivier Briand, the late bishop's vicar-general, a man of great tact and an adroit diplomat who had cooperated with Murray in every possible way, to be allowed to go to France and be quietly consecrated in 1766. The British could not, however, bring themselves to recognize him as bishop. They insisted that Briand's title be "superintendant of the Romish church," but he was, to all intents and purposes, a bishop of the church of Rome who could, and did, consecrate priests in the province. The religion, beliefs, and practices of the Canadians had been saved. For most of the ensuing two centuries the church remained the dominant institution in Quebec.

THE QUEBEC ACT

James Murray, during his term in office, came to hold the Canadians in high regard. Murray's successor, Guy Carleton, although initially sympathetic to the complaints made against Murray by the Protestant merchants, quickly came to share his predecessor's views. In 1774 at Carleton's behest the British Parliament enacted the Quebec Act. The new law granted the Canadians the freedom that they had enjoyed all along, the right to practice their religion; it also restored the old French civil law, allowed Canadians to hold office under the Crown, and extended the jurisdiction of the governor and council at Quebec to the Ohio territory. It did not allow, however, the establishment of a legislative assembly for the province. Given the great disparity in numbers between the British and Canadian peoples, an assembly was deemed impossible. Carleton would not allow the Canadians to be placed at the mercy of what he had come to regard as the rabid mercantile faction, nor could the British government of the day have countenanced allowing the Canadians to sit as members of an assembly, thereby rendering the British Protestant minority at their mercy.

Historians have long disputed the true intent of the Quebec Act. Was it the so-called Magna Carta for the Canadians, or was it really yet another attempt, albeit long-term, to assimilate the Canadians? Canadian historiography has viewed the Quebec Act as the recognition of two basic rights: religion and French laws, such as the right of Roman Catholics to hold office under the Crown and seigneurial tenure. In any event it succeeded in infuriating papist-hating New Englanders, who published vicious pamphlets attacking the recognition of the church of Rome. Another powerful faction, the land speculators of Virginia and Pennsylvania—including such notables as George Washington, Benjamin Franklin, and other future leaders of the American Revolution—were also outraged, because they had long coveted the rich lands of the Ohio territory for themselves.

THE ANGLO-AMERICAN INVASION AND FRENCH POLICY

In 1775 two motley Anglo-American armies invaded Quebec, occupied Montreal, and laid siege to the town of Quebec. Once again the Canadian militia was called out. Once again most of the men refused, despite being exhorted to serve under threat of excommunication by the bishop. They paid little attention, regarding the conflict as a purely British quarrel, until they were abused by the undisciplined Anglo-American troops, their religious ceremonies mocked, and their supplies of all sorts seized with barely the pretense of payment. In addition the New England pamphlets of the previous year, condemning the Quebec Act and referring to the Canadians in the most unflattering terms, had circulated throughout the province; as the American colonials now appealed to the Canadians to support their cause against the British and regain their freedom, the hypocrisy was too blatant to be endured. It soon became apparent that the Anglo-Americans could not take Quebec. When, in May, a British fleet with an army of regulars came up the Saint Lawrence to the capital, the Anglo-Americans fled back whence they had come.

If, when France in 1778 unmasked its guns and openly supported the Anglo-American cause, the Canadians hoped to see a French fleet and an army wearing the white uniforms of France appear at Quebec to liberate them from foreign rule and restore them to their motherland, they were disappointed. In the 1778 Treaty of Alliance with the Anglo-Americans the French foreign minister, Charles Gravier, comte de Vergennes, renounced all pretensions to regain France's former North American colonies. His Most Christian Majesty's erstwhile Canadian subjects remained expendable.

Vergennes was determined on two things. First, Britain's old American colonies had to gain their independence, thereby disrupting the British Empire, draining its economic base and hence its capacity for imperialistic adventures elsewhere in the world. Second, Canada must remain under the British Crown, since Britain would then have to expend its wealth and military strength to fend off the avaricious American republic that was determined to conquer the entire continent. Vergennes therefore issued strict verbal orders to the commander of the French expeditionary force, Lieutenant General Jean-Baptiste-Donatien de Vimeur, comte de Rochambeau, that under no circumstances were the troops under his command to be employed in an expedition against Canada nor any aid

NORTH AMERICA

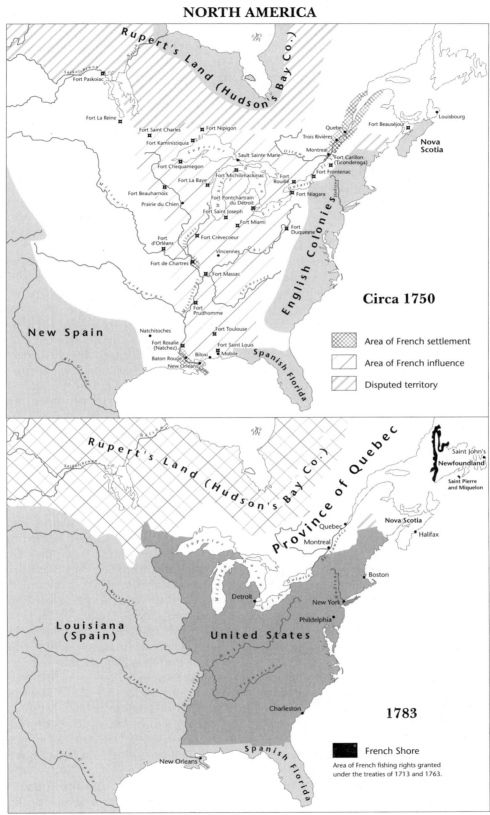

Circa 1750

Rupert's Land (Hudson's Bay Co.)

Fort Paskoiac
Fort La Reine
Fort Saint Charles · Fort Nipigon
Fort Kaministiquia
Fort Chequamegon
Sault Sainte Marie
Fort La Baye
Fort Michilimackinac · Fort Rouillé
Fort Beauharnois
Prairie du Chien
Fort Pontchartrain du Détroit · Fort Niagara
Fort Saint Joseph
Fort Miami
Fort d'Orléans
Fort Crèvecoeur · Fort Duquesne
Vincennes
Fort de Chartres
Fort Massac
Fort Prudhomme

Quebec · Fort Beauséjour · Louisbourg
Trois Rivières
Montreal · **Nova Scotia**
Fort Carillon (Ticonderoga)
Fort Frontenac

English Colonies

New Spain

Natchitoches
Fort Rosalie (Natchez)
Baton Rouge · Biloxi · Mobile
New Orleans
Fort Toulouse
Fort Saint Louis

Spanish Florida

	Area of French settlement
	Area of French influence
	Disputed territory

1783

Rupert's Land (Hudson's Bay Co.)

Province of Quebec

Saint John's
Newfoundland
Saint Pierre and Miquelon

Quebec
Montreal
Nova Scotia
Halifax

Boston

Detroit

New York

Phildelphia

United States

Louisiana (Spain)

Charleston

New Orleans

Spanish Florida

| | French Shore |

Area of French fishing rights granted under the treaties of 1713 and 1763.

These maps represent the fullest extent of French power in North America in 1750 and its abridgment by 1783 when the English colonists gained their independence and became recognized as the United States of America.

offered to the Americans should they make such an attempt.

Canada remained British. The Anglo-Americans could not conquer it on their own, and they could not countenance France regaining it; France did not want it back and was determined that the Anglo-Americans should not have it. The Canadians were mere pawns on this imperial chessboard.

In 1783, to the dismay and disgust of Vergennes, Great Britain ceded to the United States of America what it had no right to cede: its erstwhile territorial claim, which it had never succeeded in substantiating, to the lands between the Alleghenies and the Mississippi. The Indian nations whose lands these were thus were doomed to extinction. At the same time some forty-thousand Loyalists fled—actually these were but a small fraction of those who had supported the Loyalist cause; the majority remained in situ and became Federalists—or were driven out of their homes to seek sanctuary in Nova Scotia and Quebec. Those who arrived in Quebec found themselves in strange surroundings, among an alien people who had been their feared enemies a generation earlier. The civil law of the province was not the law they knew or could comprehend, the seigneurial land-tenure system was foreign to them, and there was no elected assembly where they could air their grievances and make their views known.

TWO CANADAS

To accommodate these people who had suffered much, lost everything, for their loyalty to the Crown, the British government, under the Constitutional Act of 1791, divided the province into Lower and Upper Canada—present-day Quebec and Ontario. Each was to have an elected legislative assembly, a governor, and executive and legislative councils, the members of both to be appointed. The assemblies could do little more than levy taxes, or refuse to do so. Such a division of powers was unworkable and inevitably led to political deadlock.

Yet at least the Loyalists and "Late Loyalists"—emigrants from the United States attracted by the offer of potentially rich free land—in Upper Canada were free of French influence and numerical domination, able to establish their own, familiar institutions and go their own way. On the other hand the old British subjects of the new province of Lower Canada were far from content. They found themselves a minority amid the mass of the French Canadians, and they saw any hope for the eventual assimilation of the French Canadians vanishing. Moreover, the French Canadians elected to the assembly rapidly mastered the techniques of parliamentary government and came to dominate the debates in the House, particularly after they gained the right to speak in their own language.

Thus, in Lower Canada politics became polarized; a French-speaking party, the Parti Canadien, controlled the assembly. In 1826 it became known as the Parti Patriote and adopted some of the concepts and slogans of the American revolution and of Jacksonian democracy. Essentially it was the party of the French Canadians whose leaders had been excluded from the commercial and industrial life of the colony, and who therefore had taken to the professions—law, medicine, journalism, politics. The British element wanted to raise revenues by taxing land for roads and canals, but the assembly refused to levy such taxes. Ironically, not all the members of Parti Patriote were French Canadians; some were British radicals, such as John Nielson and Dr. Edmund Bailey O'Callaghan.

In Montreal racial tension grew apace, and there were serious clashes in the streets. In 1837 the government issued warrants for the arrest of the Parti Patriote leaders, including the flamboyant speaker of the assembly, Louis-Joseph Papineau. Fighting flared as British paramilitary units roamed the streets, attacked the French, and sacked the homes of Patriote leaders. There were more serious clashes in the countryside as the French Canadians took up arms. Some of their villages were attacked, the churches desecrated, and the villagers' homes put to the torch—in midwinter. This so-called rebellion was quickly and harshly crushed. The leaders of the Parti Patriote fled to the United States. Twelve of their followers were hanged, and fifty-eight were deported to an Australian penal colony. The rebellion had been a fiasco, but it left bitter memories.

The aftermath was the union of the two Canadas in 1840. The English-speaking population in both provinces had grown immensely, as thousands of immigrants from the British Isles poured in. Thus there was no longer any fear of French domination, instead increasing hope, and determination, that the French Canadians would eventually be assimilated, their language and culture swept into discard. In 1867 came confederation of all the existing provinces in British North America. Thus there emerged a vexing double minority. The British in Quebec remained a minority, controlling the economy but ever fearful of the French majority that controlled the province's politics, and the French Canadians became more and more of a minority as new provinces, British-dominated, were admitted into the confederation. Yet, the French Canadians persisted tenaciously and retained their languages, their essential institutions, and their culture. At the close of the twentieth century the struggle to be *maîtres chez nous*—to be independent, perhaps form a sovereign state—had remained alive with many of them for two and a third centuries.

BIBLIOGRAPHY

Balthazar, Louis. *Bilan du nationalisme au Québec.* Montreal, 1986.

Dion, Léon. *Nationalisme et politique au Québec.* Montreal, 1975.

Eccles, William J. *France in America.* New York, 1972; rev. ed. Markham, Ontario, 1990.

Guindon, Hubert. *Quebec Society: Tradition, Modernity, and Nationhood.* Toronto, Ontario, 1988.

Hero, Alfred Olivier, Jr., and Louis Balthazar. *Contemporary Quebec and the United States, 1960–1985.* Cambridge, Mass., 1988.

Hughes, Everett C. *French Canada in Transition.* Chicago, 1943.

Levine, Marc V. *The Reconquest of Montreal: Language Policy and Social Change in a Bilingual City.* Philadelphia, 1990.

Linteau, Paul-André, René Durocher, and Jean-Claude Robert. *Quebec: A History, 1867–1929.* Toronto, Ontario, 1983.

Linteau, Paul-André, René Durocher, Jean-Claude Robert, and François Ricard. *Quebec Since 1930.* Toronto, Ontario, 1991.

Neatby, Hilda. *Quebec: The Revolutionary Age, 1760–1791.* Toronto, Ontario, 1966.

Robert, Jean-Claude. *Du Canada français au Québec libre.* Paris, 1975.

Séguin, Maurice. *L'idée d'indépendance au Québec: Genèse et historique.* Trois-Rivières, Quebec, 1971.

Trofimenkoff, Susan Mann. *The Dream of Nation: A Social and Intellectual History of Quebec.* Toronto, Ontario, 1982.

Wade, Mason. *The French Canadians, 1760–1967.* Vol. 1. Toronto, Ontario, 1968.

Jean-Claude Robert

SEE ALSO **Reorganization of Empires** and **Roman Catholicism.**

CONTRIBUTORS

Mathé Allain Member of the Department of French and Francophone Studies at the University of Southwest Louisiana. Author of *Not Worth a Straw: French Colonial Policy and The Founding of the Lousiana Colony, 1699–1769*. LITERATURE

Felix D. Almaraz, Jr. Professor of History at the University of Texas, San Antonio. Author of *Tragic Cavalier: Governor Manuel Salcedo of Texas, 1808–1813*, *The San Antonio Missions and Their Systems of Land Tenure*, and numerous books and articles. Member of the editorial board of *Colonial Latin American Historical Review*. Recipient of a Fulbright to Argentina. INDEPENDENCE

David Leon Ammerman Professor of History at the Florida State University. Author of *In the Common Cause: American Response to the Coercive Acts of 1774* and numerous articles on the coming of independence to the American colonies. Coeditor of *The Chesapeake in the Seventeenth Century*. INDEPENDENCE

Barry Jean Ancelet Distinguished Associate Professor of French and Francophone Studies and Director of the Center for Acadian and Creole Folklore at the University of Southwestern Louisiana. Author of *Cajun Country*, a forthcoming book on the Cajun and Creole Mardi Gras, and numerous studies on Louisiana French folklore and folklife. FESTIVAL TRADITIONS

Virginia DeJohn Anderson Associate Professor of History at the University of Colorado, Boulder. Author of *New England's Generation: The Great Migration and the Formation of Society and Culture in the Seventeenth Century*. BRITISH SETTLEMENTS

Timothy E. Anna Professor of History at the University of Manitoba. Author of *The Fall of the Royal Government in Mexico City*, *The Fall of the Royal Government in Peru*, *Spain and the Loss of America*, and *The Mexican Empire of Iturbide*. IDEOLOGIES OF REVOLUTION

G. Blaine Baker Associate Professor of Law at McGill University. Author of periodical literature on Canadian legal history published by the Osgoode Society, the *Law and History Review*, the Canadian Historical Association, and the *University of Toronto Law Journal*. THE LEGAL PROFESSION

Vaughan B. Baker Assistant Professor of History and Humanities and Associate of the Center for Louisiana Studies at the University of Southwestern Louisiana. Author of articles on women in colonial Louisiana during the French administrative period. Recipient of an NEH grant for her work on this subject and winner of the 1989 L. Kemper Williams Manuscript Prize in Louisiana History. INTERRACIAL SOCIETIES

Randall Balmer Associate Professor of Religion at Barnard College. Author of *A Perfect Babel of Confusion: Dutch Religion and English Culture in the Middle Colonies*, and *Mine Eyes Have Seen the Glory: A Journey into the Evangelical*

Subculture in America. CHURCH AND STATE and DUTCH AND FRENCH CALVINISM

Gunther Barth   Professor of History at University of California, Berkeley. Author of *All Quiet on the Yamhill*; *Bitter Strength*; *Instant Cities*; *City People*; and *Fleeting Moments: Nature and Culture in American History.* URBAN LIFE

John O. Baxter   Independent research consultant, Santa Fe, New Mexico. Author of *Las Carneradas: Sheep Trade in New Mexico, 1700–1860* and various articles concerning the history of the Southwest. FARMING, PLANTING, AND RANCHING

Ross W. Beales, Jr.   Associate Professor of History at the College of the Holy Cross. Author of articles on the history of the family, community life, and religion in early America. Currently researching eighteenth-century Westborough, Massachusetts, and its minister, Ebenezer Parkman (1703–1782). CHILDHOOD AND ADOLESCENCE

Jacqueline Beaudoin-Ross   Curator of Costume and Textiles at the McCord Museum of Canadian History, Montreal. Author of "Form and Fashion: Nineteenth Century Montreal Dress" and numerous articles on costume and textiles. DRESS

Ira Berlin   Professor of History at the University of Maryland, College Park. Author of *Slaves Without Masters: The Free Negro in the Antebellum South* and an editor of *Freedom: A Documentary History of Emancipation.* Director of the Freedmen and Southern Society Project, 1976–1991. FREE BLACKS

Roderick Hall Blackburn   Senior Research Fellow at the New York State Museum, Albany. Coauthor of *Remembrance of Patria: Dutch Art and Culture in Colonial America, 1609–1776,* and numerous articles on New York Dutch material culture. ARCHITECTURE, CRAFTS, HOME AND HEARTH, and PAINTING AND SCULPTURE

Wayne Bodle   Associate Director of the Philadelphia Center for Early American Studies at the University of Pennsylvania. Author of numerous articles on American colonial regional development, civil-military relations during the Revolutionary War, and the experience of women during the revolutionary era. BRITISH SETTLEMENTS

Marsha C. Bol   Associate Curator of Anthropology at the Carnegie Museum of Natural History. Former Curator of Latin American Folk Art at the Museum of International Folk Art, Museum of New Mexico. PAINTING AND SCULPTURE

Judith Hopkins Bonner   Associate Curator of Art at the Historic New Orleans Collection. Author of *Newcomb Centennial, 1886–1986: An Exhibition of Art by the Art Faculty* and numerous scholarly articles and critical reviews on southern art and artists. PAINTING AND SCULPTURE

J. F. Bosher   Professor at York University. Author of *The Single Duty Project*; *French Finances, 1770–1795*; *The Canada Merchants, 1713–1763*; *The French Revolution*; and *Men and Ships in the Canada Trade, 1660–1760.* Visiting fellow at All Souls College, Oxford, 1991–1992. THE COLONIAL MERCHANT and TAXATION

Henry Warner Bowden   Professor of Religion at Rutgers University. Author of *American Indians and Christian Missions: Studies in Cultural Conflict.* MISSION COMMUNITIES

Carl A. Brasseaux   Assistant Director of the Center for Louisiana Studies and Assistant Professor of History at the University of Southwestern Louisiana. Author of over twenty studies of the French experience in North America. LITERATURE

Chandos Michael Brown   Director, Commonwealth Center for the Study of American Culture; Associate Professor of History and American Studies at the College of William and Mary. Author of *Benjamin Silliman: A Life in the Young Republic* and "A Natural History of the Gloucester Sea Serpent: Knowledge, Power, and the Culture of Science in Antebellum America." SCIENTIFIC INQUIRY

Jennifer S. H. Brown   Professor of History at the University of Winnipeg. Author of *Strangers*

CONTRIBUTORS

in Blood: Fur Trade Company Families in Indian Country; author and editor of numerous other works on Native and fur trade history. General editor of the Rupert's Land Record Society at the University of Winnipeg. BRITISH SETTLEMENTS

Stuart Bruchey Allen Nevins Professor Emeritus at Columbia University and Libra Professor of History at the University of Maine. Author of *Enterprise: The Dynamic Economy of a Free People* and other books and articles. President of the Economic History Association, 1985–1986, and Co-President of the International Commission on the History of Social Structures and Social Movements, 1990– . THE COLONIAL MERCHANT

David M. Brugge Independent Anthropologist (retired from the National Park Service). Author of *Navajo Pottery and Ethnohistory*; *Navajos in the Catholic Church Records of New Mexico, 1694–1875*; *A History of the Chaco Navajos*; and *Tsegai: An Archaeological Ethnohistory of the Chaco Region*. SLAVERY

Bruce R. Buckley Professor Emeritus of American Folk Culture, Cooperstown Graduate Programs, SUNY-Oneonta. Author of *Living Tradition: Folk Arts of Schoharie County, N.Y.*; *Infinite Variations: Folk Art Quilts*; and *Horse High, Sheep Tight, and Hog Proof: The Stone Walls of Dutchess County, N.Y.* Honorary Vice President, New York Folklore Society. FESTIVAL TRADITIONS

Jon Butler William Robertson Coe Professor of American History at Yale University. Author of *Awash in a Sea of Faith: Christianizing the American People*; *The Huguenots in America: A Refugee People in New World Society*; and *Power, Authority, and the Origins of American Denominational Order*. PROTESTANT PLURALISM

Leon G. Campbell Visiting Professor of History at Stanford University. Author of *The Military and Society in Colonial Peru, 1750–1810* and numerous articles for *Hispanic American Historical Review* and *Latin American Research Review*. Contributing editor of *Research Guide to Andean History: Bolivia, Chile, Ecuador, and Peru*. MEN IN ARMS

Jack Campisi Associate Professor of Anthropology at Wellesley College. Author of *The Mashpee Indians: Tribe on Trial* and numerous articles. Coeditor of several books on North American Indians including *Extending the Rafters: Interdisciplinary Approaches to Iroquoian Studies* and *The Oneida Indian Experience: Two Perspectives*. INDIAN GOVERNANCE

Anthony J. Cárdenas Professor of Spanish at the University of New Mexico. Author of articles on medieval Spanish manuscripts and literature from philological, historical, and literary perspectives. Editor of *Noticiero Alfonsí*. EUROPEAN LANGUAGES

Craig M. Carver Senior Editor of the *Dictionary of American Regional English* at the University of Wisconsin, Madison. Author of *American Regional Dialects*, *A History of English in Its Own Words*, and many articles on English and its variants, including a bimonthly column, "Word Histories," in *The Atlantic*. EUROPEAN LANGUAGES

Jay Cassel Assistant Professor of History, York University. Author of *The Secret Plague: Venereal Disease in Canada, 1660–1760*, the forthcoming *The Military in Canada*, and various articles. INDIAN-COLONIST CONFLICTS AND ALLIANCES, MEDICAL PRACTICE, MEN IN ARMS, and OLD AGE AND DEATH

Antonia I. Casteñeda Assistant Professor of Women's Studies and Chicano Studies at the University of California, Santa Barbara. Author of various articles on women in colonial California, and coauthor of *Chicano Literature: Text and Context*. MARRIAGE

Wallace Chafe Professor Emeritus of Linguistics at the University of California, Santa Barbara. Author of various books and articles on the Caddoan, Siouan, and Iroquoian languages. INDIAN LANGUAGES

Charles E. Clark James H. Hayes and Claire Short Hayes Professor of the Humanities and Professor of History at the University of New Hampshire. Author of *The Eastern Frontier: The Settlement of Northern New England, 1610–1763*; *Maine: A History*; the forthcoming *The Public*

Prints: The Newspaper in Anglo-American Culture, 1665–1750; and several articles on early American printing and journalism. THE COLONIAL PRESS

Paul G. E. Clemens Professor of History at Rutgers University. Author of *The Atlantic Economy* and *Colonial Maryland's Eastern Shore: From Tobacco to Grain*. FARMING, PLANTING, AND RANCHING

William M. Clements Professor of English and Folklore at Arkansas State University. Author of numerous articles on Native American oral literatures. Editor of *Native American Folklore, 1879–1979: An Annotated Bibliography* and *Native American Folklore in Nineteenth-Century Periodicals*. LITERATURE

Luca Codignola Professor of History of Early European Expansion at the University of Genoa. Author of *Guerra e guerriglia nell'America coloniale*, *The Coldest Harbour of the Land*, and *Guide to Documents Relating to French and British North America in the Archives of the Sacred Congregation de Propaganda Fide*. CHURCH AND STATE and ROMAN CATHOLICISM

Charles L. Cohen Associate Professor of History at the University of Wisconsin, Madison. Author of *God's Caress: The Psychology of Puritan Religious Experience* and various articles on Puritan theology, colonial religious rhetoric, and the Amerindian reception of Christianity. PURITANISM

David Steven Cohen Senior Research Associate and Director of the Ethnic History Program at the New Jersey Historical Commission. Author of *The Dutch-American Farm*; *The Folklore and Folklife of New Jersey*; *The Ramapo Mountain People*; and numerous articles. Editor of *America, The Dream of My Life* and coeditor of *Pinelands Folklife*. Producer of television and radio documentaries and curator of museum exhibitions. FARMING, PLANTING, AND RANCHING; FESTIVAL TRADITIONS; INTERRACIAL SOCIETIES; SCIENTIFIC INQUIRY; and TECHNOLOGY

Ronald D. Cohen Professor of History at Indiana University Northwest. Author of

Children of the Mill: Schooling and Society in Gary, Indiana, 1906–1960 and other books and articles. Associate editor of *History of Education Quarterly*. SCHOOLS AND SCHOOLING

Richard C. Conn Chief Curator at the Denver Art Museum. Author of " 'Circles of the World': Native American Art in the Denver Art Museum," "A Persistent Vision: Art of the Reservation Days," and many articles on American Indian art. Recipient of McCloy Fellowship in Art, 1979. Member of the Board of the Native American Art Studies Association. TECHNOLOGY

Jacob Ernest Cooke Professor Emeritus of History at Lafayette College. Author of numerous books, including *Tench Coxe and the Early Republic* and *Alexander Hamilton: A Biography*. Coeditor of the thirteen-volume *A History of the American Colonies*. Formerly John Henry MacCracken Professor and Head of the Department of History at Lafayette College. *Editor in Chief*

Nym Cooke Lecturer in Music at College of the Holy Cross. Author of articles on American music published in *The New Grove Dictionary of American Music* and other publications. Editor of *The Music of Timothy Swan* for the series Music of the United States of America. NEH Fellow at the American Antiquarian Society, 1992–1993. MUSIC AND DANCE

Edward Countryman Professor of History at Southern Methodist University. Author of *A People in Revolution: The American Revolution and Political Society in New York, 1760–1790* and *The American Revolution*; coauthor of two other books and author of many articles. SOCIAL TENSIONS

Michael Craton Professor of History at the University of Waterloo. Author of general histories of the Bahamas, British slavery, and slave resistance; articles on slavery and the Caribbean; studies of a Jamaican state (Worthy Park) and its people; and coauthor of a two-volume history of the Bahamian people. THE WEST INDIES AND NORTH AMERICA

Michael J. Crawford Head of the Early American Branch, Naval Historical Center, U.S.

CONTRIBUTORS

Navy. Author of *Seasons of Grace: Colonial New England's Revival Tradition in Its British Context* and numerous scholarly articles. REVIVALISM AND THE GREAT AWAKENING

Charles R. Cutter   Assistant Professor of History at Purdue University. Author of *The Protector de Indios in Colonial New Mexico, 1659–1821*; *To Give to Each His Own: The Legal Culture of Northern New Spain;* and various articles on Spanish colonial legal history. CIVIL LAW, CRIME AND LAW ENFORCEMENT, THE LEGAL PROFESSION, and SOCIAL TENSIONS

Donald C. Cutter   Professor Emeritus of History at the University of New Mexico and O'Connor chair of Spanish Colonial History of Texas and the Southwest, St. Mary's University. Fulbright Scholar in Spain, 1961–1962, and Mexico, 1971–1972. Past President of the Western History Association. TECHNOLOGY

Bruce C. Daniels   Professor of History at the University of Winnipeg. Author of *The Connecticut Town: Growth and Development, 1635–1790*; *Dissent and Conformity on Narragansett Bay: The Colonial Rhode Island Town*; and *The Fragmentation of New England*. President of the Canadian Association for American Studies. LOCAL GOVERNMENT

George Dargo   Professor of Law at the New England School of Law. Author of *Jefferson's Louisiana, Roots of the Republic, Private Law and the Public Estate*, and a forthcoming history of the United States Court of Appeals for the First Circuit. THE FRAMEWORK OF GOVERNMENT

Kathleen A. Deagan   Curator of Historical Archaeology at the Florida Museum of Natural History and Joint Professor of Anthropology at the University of Florida. Author of *Spanish St. Augustine: The Archaeology of a Colonial Creole Community, Artifacts of the Spanish Colonies*, and numerous publications concerning archaeological perspectives on Spanish American colonial adaptations. SETTLEMENTS IN THE SPANISH BORDERLANDS

Gerald F. De Jong   Professor Emeritus of History at the University of South Dakota.

Author of *The Dutch in America, 1609–1974*; *The Dutch Reformed Church in the American Colonies*; and other books and numerous articles. SCHOOLS AND SCHOOLING

Jesus F. de la Teja   Assistant Professor of History at Southwest Texas State University. Author of a number of articles on eighteenth and nineteenth-century Texas. Compiler and editor of *A Revolution Remembered: The Memoirs and Selected Correspondence of Juan N. Seguín*. THE STRUCTURE OF SOCIETY and TRADE AND COMMERCE

Steven Deyle   Doctoral Candidate in American History at Columbia University. Author of several articles on race relations in colonial America and the early republic. INTERRACIAL SOCIETIES

John A. Dickinson   Professor and chair of the Department of History at the Université de Montréal. Author of *Justice et justiciables* and numerous books and articles; coauthor of *A Short History of Quebec* and *Les Européens découvrent l'Amérique*. CRIME AND LAW ENFORCEMENT, THE FRAMEWORK OF GOVERNMENT, and RELATIONS WITH THE PARENT COUNTRY

Robert J. Dinkin   Professor of History at California State University, Fresno. Author of *Voting in Provincial America, Voting in Revolutionary America*, and *Campaigning in America: A History of Election Practices*. THE SUFFRAGE

Leonard E. Doucette   Professor of French and Drama at the University of Toronto. Author of *Emery Bigot: Seventeenth-Century Humanist*; *Theatre in French Canada, 1606–1867*; and many articles on the history of theater in French Canada. DRAMA

W. J. Eccles   Professor Emeritus of History at the University of Toronto. Author of numerous books and articles on New France, including *Frontenac: The Courtier Governor*; *Canada Under Louis XIV*; *France in America*; *The Canadian Frontier, 1500–1673*; and *Essays on New France*. Honorary LL.D. degree from the University of Genoa. MANNERS, SCHOOLS AND SCHOOLING, and SEXUAL MORES AND BEHAVIOR

CONTRIBUTORS

J. Worth Estes Professor of Pharmacology at the Boston University School of Medicine. Author of *Hall Jackson and the Purple Foxglove: Medical Practice and Research in Revolutionary America, 1760–1820* and *Dictionary of Protopharmacology: Therapeutic Practices, 1700–1850.* Coeditor of *Medicine in Colonial Massachusetts, 1620–1820.* MEDICAL PRACTICE

Firth Haring Fabend Independent historian and editor. Author of *A Dutch Family in the Middle Colonies, 1660–1800* and various articles. Editor of *Tappan: 300 Years, 1686–1986.* LANDHOLDING and RURAL LIFE

Brian Fagan Professor of Anthropology at the University of California, Santa Barbara. Author of *The Rape of the Nile, Ancient North America, Kingdoms of Gold, Kingdoms of Jade,* and many other books about archaeology. Contributing editor to *Archaeology Magazine.* THE FIRST AMERICANS

Christian F. Feest Professor of Anthropology at the University of Frankfurt. Author of *Native Arts of North America* and *The Powhatan Tribes.* Editor of *Indians and Europe* and *European Review of Native American Studies.* NATIVE AMERICAN AESTHETICS

Norman Fiering Director and Librarian of the John Carter Brown Library at Brown University. Author of *Jonathan Edwards's Moral Thought and Its British Context* and *Moral Philosophy at Seventeenth-Century Harvard: A Discipline in Transition.* PHILOSOPHY

Janet R. Fireman Chief Curator of History at Natural History Museum of Los Angeles County. Author of *Spain's Royal Corps of Engineers in the Western Borderlands: Instrument of Bourbon Reform, 1764–1815* and various essays and reviews on exploration and discovery in Spanish North America. SCIENTIFIC INQUIRY

Ross H. Frank Landmarks Assistant Professor of History at American University. Author of *From Settler to Citizen: Economic Development and Cultural Change in Late Colonial New Mexico, 1750–1820.* Consultant at the National Museum of American History. CURRENCY AND FINANCE

Elisabeth Paling Funk Adjunct Assistant Professor at Manhattanville College. Author of forthcoming book on Washington Irving and the Dutch heritage and various articles on New Netherland literature and Dutch culture in American literature. LITERATURE

François-Marc Gagnon Professor of Art History at Université de Montréal. Author of *Paul-Émile Borduas: Biographie critique et analyse de l'oeuvre, La conversion par l'image, Ces hommes dits sauvaiges,* and *Hommes effarables et bestes sauvages.* Member of the editorial board of RACAR and the *Journal of Canadian Art History.* PAINTING AND SCULPTURE

Bernardo P. Gallegos Associate Professor of Social Foundations of Education at California State University, Los Angeles. Author of *Literacy, Education, and Society in New Mexico, 1693–1821.* SCHOOLS AND SCHOOLING and THEORIES OF EDUCATION

Charles T. Gehring Director, New Netherland Project. Translator and editor of the series *New Netherland Documents.* Fellow of the Holland Society of New York. DUTCH AND SWEDISH SETTLEMENTS and EUROPEAN LANGUAGES

Larry R. Gerlach Professor of History at the University of Utah. Author of numerous books and articles on sport and Anglo-American history. Member of editorial boards of several scholarly journals and the council of the North American Society for Sport History. RECREATIONS

James R. Gibson Professor of Geography at York University. Author and translator of numerous articles and several books on the historical geography of Russia, Russian eastward expansion, and imperial competition on the Northwest Coast, including *Otter Skins, Boston Ships,* and *China Goods.* Fellow of the Royal Society of Canada. THE RUSSIAN SETTLEMENTS

Sam D. Gill Professor of Religion at the University of Colorado, Boulder. Author of *Mother Earth: An American Story, Native American Religious Action,* and other books and articles; coauthor of *Dictionary of Native American Mythology.* NATIVE AMERICAN RELIGIONS

CONTRIBUTORS

Ives Goddard   Curator of the Department of Anthropology at the Smithsonian Institution. Author of articles on linguistic and ethnohistorical topics; coauthor of *Native Writings in Massachusetts*. Conducts research on endangered and extinct Native American languages. INDIAN LANGUAGES

Erlinda Gonzales-Berry   Chair of the Department of Spanish and Portuguese at the University of New Mexico. Author of a novel, *Paletitas de Guayaba*. Editor of *Paso por aqui: Critical Essays on the New Mexican Literary Tradition*. MANNERS

Deena González   Associate Professor of History and Chicano Studies at Pomona College. Author of forthcoming *Refusing the Favor: The Spanish-Mexican Women of Santa Fe, 1820–1880* and of numerous articles on Chicana frontier history. Editor of forthcoming *Dictionary of Latinas in the United States*. GENDER RELATIONS and OLD AGE AND DEATH

Joyce D. Goodfriend   Professor of History at the University of Denver. Author of *Before the Melting Pot: Society and Culture in Colonial New York City, 1664–1730* and numerous essays on early New York and the Dutch in colonial America. Winner of the Hendricks Manuscript Award in 1991. CRIME AND LAW ENFORCEMENT, PATTERNS OF COMMUNITY, PATTERNS OF SOCIALIZATION, SLAVERY, SOCIAL TENSIONS, THE STRUCTURE OF SOCIETY, and URBAN LIFE

Larry Dale Gragg   Professor of History, University of Missouri, Rolla. Author of *Migration in Early America: The Virginia Quaker Experience*; *A Quest for Security: The Life of Samuel Parris, 1653–1720*; *The Salem Witch Crisis*; and numerous articles and essays. TRANSPORTATION AND COMMUNICATION

Jack P. Greene   Andrew W. Mellon Professor in the Humanities at the Johns Hopkins University. Author of several books and articles in the field of early American history. COLONIAL POLITICAL CULTURE and COLONIAL POLITICAL THOUGHT

Robert S. Grumet   Anthropologist. INDIAN-COLONIST CONFLICTS AND ALLIANCES and INDIAN-COLONIST CONTACT

Ramón A. Gutiérrez   Founding Chair of the Ethnic Studies Department at the University of California, San Diego. Author of *When Jesus Came, the Corn Mothers Went Away: Marriage, Sexuality, and Power in New Mexico, 1500–1848* and a study of Hispanic literature. CHURCH AND STATE; DETRIBALIZED AND MANUMITTED INDIANS; FAMILY STRUCTURES; INTERRACIAL SOCIETIES; SETTLEMENTS IN THE SPANISH BORDERLANDS; and SEXUAL MORES AND BEHAVIOR

David D. Hall   Professor of American Religious History at Harvard Divinity School. Author of *Worlds of Wonder, Days of Judgment: Popular Religion in Early New England* and *The Faithful Shepherd: A History of the New England Ministry in Seventeenth Century New England*. MAGIC AND WITCHCRAFT

G. Emlen Hall   Professor of Law at the University of New Mexico Law School. Author of *Four Leagues of Pecos* and articles on the history of the southwestern natural resources. LANDHOLDING

Thomas D. Hall   Lester M. Jones Professor of Sociology at DePauw University. Author of *Social Change in the Southwest, 1350–1880* and numerous chapters on Native American and ethnic relations in the American Southwest. Coeditor of *Core/Periphery Relations in Precapitalist World*. BOUND LABOR, CRISES OF EMPIRE, and REORGANIZATION OF EMPIRES

Kimberly S. Hanger   Director of Research at the Louisiana State Museum and Adjunct Professor of History at the University of New Orleans. Author of articles on colonial Louisiana and the Caribbean and a forthcoming book on free people of African descent in Spanish New Orleans. DRESS

Kevin J. Hayes   Assistant Professor of English at the University of Central Oklahoma. Author of *Captain John Smith: A Reference Guide* and the forthcoming *William Byrd's Library*; coauthor of *Checklist of Melville Reviews*. LIBRARIES AND LEARNED SOCIETIES

James Hennesey   Professor of the History of Christianity at Canisius College and Christ the

King Seminary. Author of *American Catholics: A History of the Roman Catholic Community in the United States*, *The First Council of the Vatican: The American Experience*, and numerous books and articles. ROMAN CATHOLICISM

Bernard L. Herman Associate Director of the Center for Historic Architecture and Engineering, Associate Professor of Urban Affairs and Public Policy, and Associate Professor of History at the University of Delaware. Author and coauthor of numerous books and articles including *The Stolen House: A Land and Life Remembered* and *Architecture and Rural Life in Central Delaware*. HOME AND HEARTH

Maria Herrera-Sobek Professor of Spanish at the University of California, Irvine. Author of *The Bracero Experience*, *The Mexican Corrido*, and *Northward Bound: The Mexican Immigrant Experience in Ballad and Song*. Editor of *Beyond Stereotypes* and *Reconstructing a Chicano/a Literary Heritage*; coeditor of *Chicana Creativity and Criticism*. DRAMA

Leo Hershkowitz Professor of History at Queens College of the City University of New York. Author of *Tweed's New York: Another Look* and numerous other studies on Manhattan. Editor of *Wills of Early New York Jews* and *Letters of Abigail Franks, 1733–1748*. JUDAISM

Charlotte Heth Professor of Ethnomusicology and Systematic Musicology at the University of California, Los Angeles. Author and editor of numerous studies of American Indian music and dance including *Native American Dance* for the National Museum of the American Indian, Smithsonian Institution. Producer of six record albums and eight videotapes on American Indian music. NATIVE AMERICAN AESTHETICS

Jane H. Hill Professor of Anthropology and Linguistics at the University of Arizona. Author of *Mulu'wetam: The First People*, *Speaking Mexicano*, and many articles on the linguistics and sociolinguistics of Uto-Aztecan languages. INDIAN LANGUAGES

Peter Charles Hoffer Professor of History at the University of Georgia. Author of *Infanticide*

in England and New England, *Impeachment in America*, *The Law's Conscience*, and *Law and People in the American Colonies*, and other works. CIVIL LAW and CRIME AND LAW ENFORCEMENT

James Horn Principal Lecturer in the School of Historical and Critical Studies at the University of Brighton. Author of articles on early Chesapeake society and the forthcoming *Adapting to a New World: English Society in the Seventeenth-Century Chesapeake*. REPEOPLING THE LAND

Ronald William Howard Department Head and Professor of History at Mississippi College. Author of articles in *Dictionary of Literary Biography* and essays on New Netherland and early New York; coauthor of *The Twilight of British Rule in Revolutionary America: The New York Letterbook of General James Robertson, 1780–1783*. CHILDHOOD AND ADOLESCENCE; FAMILY STRUCTURES; MANNERS; MARRIAGE; OLD AGE AND DEATH; PATTERNS OF SOCIALIZATION; SEXUAL MORES AND BEHAVIOR; and THE STRUCTURE OF SOCIETY

Joseph E. Illick Professor of History at San Francisco State University. Author of *William Penn: The Politician* and *Colonial Pennsylvania: A History*. QUAKERISM

Robert H. Jackson Assistant Professor of History at Texas Southern University. Author of numerous articles on the social, economic, and demographic history of the Spanish Borderlands and of nineteenth- and twentieth-century Bolivia. RELATIONS WITH THE PARENT COUNTRY and REPEOPLING THE LAND

William H. Jacobsen, Jr. Professor of Linguistics in the Department of English at the University of Nevada, Reno. Author of numerous studies of western Indian languages, especially on the Washo, Makah, Hokan, and Wakashan groups. INDIAN LANGUAGES

Cornelius John Jaenen Professor Emeritus of History, University of Ottawa. Author of *Friend and Foe*, *The Role of the Church in New France*, *The French Relationship with the Native Peoples of New France*, and numerous collaborative works

CONTRIBUTORS

and scholarly articles. INTERRACIAL SOCIETIES, RURAL LIFE, SOCIAL TENSIONS, and THE STRUCTURE OF SOCIETY

Herbert A. Johnson Ernest F. Hollings Professor of Constitutional Law at the University of South Carolina School of Law. Author of *Essays in New York Colonial Legal History*, *John Jay: Colonial Lawyer*, and *History of Criminal Justice*. Editor of and contributor to *South Carolina Legal History*. THE LEGAL PROFESSION

Patricia Kearney Lead interpreter, theatrical interpretation, for the Colonial Williamsburg Foundation. DRAMA

Kate Van Winkle Keller Executive Director of the Sonneck Society for American Music. Author of bibliographies and studies of eighteenth-century popular music and social dance. Co-Director of the NEH-supported projects, *National Tune Index* and *American Performing Arts in the 18th Century: The Newspaper Sources*. MUSIC AND DANCE

Deborah Keller-Cohen Associate Professor of Linguistics, Associate Research Scientist, English Language Institute and Center for Human Growth and Development, University of Michigan. Author of articles on literacy in bureaucratic American institutions and on the history of colonial American literacy. Editor of the forthcoming *Literacy: Interdisciplinary Conversations*. LITERACY

Ralph Ketcham Professor of History and Political Science at the Maxwell School, Syracuse University. Author of *Framed for Posterity: The Enduring Philosophy of the Constitution*. THE ENLIGHTENMENT

Geoffrey D. Kimball Post-doctoral fellow in the Department of Anthropology at Tulane University. Author of *Koasati Grammar*, *Koasati Dictionary*, and numerous articles on southeastern and other American Indian languages. INDIAN LANGUAGES

Kenneth F. Kiple Professor of History at Bowling Green State University. Author of *The Caribbean Slave: A Biological History* and other

books. Editor of *The Cambridge World History of Human Disease* and the Cambridge History and Culture of Food and Nutrition Project. Recipient of Guggenheim fellowship, 1989–1990. MEDICAL PRACTICE

Milton M. Klein University Historian at the University of Tennessee. Coeditor of the thirteen-volume *A History of the American Colonies*. Associate Editor

Michael Edward Krauss Director of the Alaska Native Language Center and Professor of Linguistics at the University of Alaska, Fairbanks. Author of books and articles about Alaskan and related languages—Eskimo, Athabaskan, and Eyak. Editor of scientific and educational materials for these languages. Chair for the Committee on Language Endangerment of the Linguistic Society of America. INDIAN LANGUAGES

Shepard Krech III Director of the Haffenreffer Museum of Anthropology and Professor of Anthropology at Brown University. Author of *A Victorian Earl in the Arctic*, *Praise the Bridge that Carries You Over*, and numerous articles. Editor of *Indians, Animals, and the Fur Trade* and *The Subarctic's Fur Trade*. Editor of *Ethnohistory*, 1982–1992. Fellow of the Woodrow Wilson Center, 1992–1993. MEDICAL PRACTICE

Jon Kukla Director of the Historic New Orleans Collection. Author of *Political Institutions in Virginia, 1619–1660* and many articles. Editor of *The Bill of Rights; A Lively Heritage; The Capitol of Virginia: A Landmark of American Architecture; A Key to Survey Reports and Microfilm of the Virginia Colonial Records Project*; and several documentary editions. BRITISH SETTLEMENTS

Allan Kulikoff Associate Professor of History at Northern Illinois University, DeKalb. Author of *Tobacco and Slaves: The Development of Southern Culture in the Chesapeake, 1680–1800*. INTERNAL MIGRATION and RURAL LIFE

Alain LaBerge Assistant Professor of Canadian History at the Université Laval. Author of several articles on preindustrial, rural Quebec. Co-Director of *L'occupation des terres dans la vallée*

du Saint-Laurent: Les aveux et dénombrements, 1723–1745. LANDHOLDING

Enrique R. Lamadrid   Associate Professor of Southwest Literature and Folklore at the University of New Mexico. Author of *Tesoros del Espíritu: A Sound Portrait of Hispanic New Mexico* and numerous articles on popular culture, folk music, and literature of greater Mexico and Latin America. DRESS, FESTIVAL TRADITIONS, and MUSIC AND DANCE

Diane Lindstrom   Professor of History and Women's Studies at the University of Wisconsin, Madison. Author of *Economic Development in the Philadelphia Region, 1810 to 1850* and numerous essays on American industrialization and urbanization. MANUFACTURING AND EXTRACTIVE INDUSTRIES

Mason I. Lowance, Jr.   Professor of English at the University of Massachusetts, Amherst. Author of numerous books including *The Language of Canaan: Metaphor and Symbol in New England from the Puritans to the Transcendentalists* and a forthcoming book about *Uncle Tom's Cabin* and American culture. Editor of *Typological Writings of Jonathan Edwards* for the Yale edition of Edwards's works. Member of the editorial board of *Early American Literature*. Recipient of Guggenheim fellowship. LITERATURE

Robert McColley   Professor of History at the University of Illinois, Urbana-Champaign. Author of *Slavery and Jeffersonian Virginia* and many articles and reviews on American slavery, politics, and high culture. SLAVERY

John J. McCusker   Ewing Halsell Distinguished Professor of American History and Professor of Economics at Trinity University. Author of other books and articles on various aspects of the economy of the early modern Atlantic world; coauthor of *The Economy of British America, 1607–1789*. MERCANTILISM

Thomas Howatt McGovern   Professor of Anthropology at Hunter College, Graduate Center of the City University of New York. Author of numerous articles and monographs on environmental archaeology and the Scandinavian North Atlantic. Director of the Hunter Bioarchaeology Laboratory; coordinator of the North Atlantic Biocultural Organization (NABO). Conducted archaeological fieldwork in Greenland, Shetlands, and Iceland. THE NORSE SETTLEMENTS

D. Peter MacLeod   Assistant Professor of History at the University of Ottawa. Author of "The Anishinabeg Point of View: The History of the Great Lakes Region to 1800 in Nineteenth-Century Mississauga, Odawa, and Ojibwa Historiography," "Microbes and Muskets: Smallpox and the Participation of the Amerindian Allies of New France in the Seven Years' War," and other articles. CRAFTS and PATTERNS OF SOCIALIZATION

Russell Mario Magnaghi   Professor of American History at Northern Michigan University. Author of *Miners, Merchants, and Midwives* and of numerous articles on the Spanish Borderlands. Editor of Herbert E. Bolton's *The Hasinai*. PATTERNS OF COMMUNITY

Pauline Maier   William R. Kenan, Jr., Professor of American History at the Massachusetts Institute of Technology. Author of *From Resistance to Revolution: Colonial Radicals and the Development of American Opposition to Britain, 1765–1776* and *The Old Revolutionaries: Political Lives in the Age of Samuel Adams*. CRISES OF EMPIRE

Gloria Lund Main   Associate Professor of History at the University of Colorado, Boulder. Author of *Tobacco Colony: Life in Early Maryland, 1650–1720* and articles on colonial New England. FAMILY STRUCTURES

Jackson Turner Main   Adjunct Professor of History at the University of Colorado, Boulder (Ret.) Author of several books, including *The Social Structure of Revolutionary America* and *Society and Economy in Colonial Connecticut*. THE STRUCTURE OF SOCIETY and TAXATION

Peter C. Mancall   Associate Professor of History at the University of Kansas. Author of *Valley of Opportunity: Economic Culture Along the Upper Susquehanna, 1700–1800* and the forthcoming *Alcohol and Empire: The Origins of*

Indian Drinking in America. ECOLOGICAL CONSEQUENCES OF ECONOMIC DEVELOPMENT and LANDHOLDING

Margaret W. Masson Director of Graduate Admissions and Records at Towson State University. Author of articles on colonial American colleges and women's history. HIGHER EDUCATION

Jacques Mathieu Professor of History at the Université Laval. Author of *Les mémoires québécoises*, *La Nouvelle-France*, *L'occupation des terres dans la vallée du Saint-Laurent*, and *Les dynamismes de la recherche au Québec*. FRENCH SETTLEMENTS

Cathy Matson Associate Professor of History at the University of Delaware. Author of many articles on the economic thought of the early American republic and colonial New York and the political theory of Federalists and Antifederalists; coauthor of *A Union of Interests: Politics and Economy in Revolutionary America*. TAXATION

Russell R. Menard Professor of History at the University of Minnesota. Author of numerous articles in early American economic and social history; coauthor of *The Economy of British America, 1607–1789* and *Robert Cole's World: Agriculture and Society in Early Maryland*. GROWTH AND WELFARE

Joseph C. Miller Commonwealth Professor of History and Dean of the College of Arts and Sciences at the University of Virginia. Author of *Way of Death: Merchant Capitalism and the Angolan Slave Trade, 1730–1830*; *Slavery and Slaving in World History: A Bibliography, 1990–1991*; and scholarly works in African history. Editor of the *Journal of African History*. THE SLAVE TRADE

Lillian B. Miller Historian of American Culture at the National Portrait Gallery, Smithsonian Institution. Author of *Patrons and Patriotism* and other studies of American art and cultural history. Editor of *Collected Papers of Charles Willson Peale and His Family* and *Selected Papers*. PAINTING AND SCULPTURE

Dale Miquelon Professor of History at the University of Saskatchewan. Author of *New France, 1701–1744: "A Supplement to Europe"* and *Dugard of Rouen: French Trade to Canada and the West Indies, 1729–1770*. REPEOPLING THE LAND

Robert D. Mitchell Associate Professor of Geography at the University of Maryland, College Park. Author of *Commercialism and Frontier* and *Appalachian Frontiers: Settlement, Society, and Development in the Preindustrial Era*. Editor of *North America: The Historical Geography of a Changing Continent*. THE NATURAL ENVIRONMENT

Marianne Mithun Professor of Linguistics at the University of California, Santa Barbara. Author of *The Languages of Native North America*, *A Cayuga Grammar*, *Northern Iroquoian Texts*, *A Grammar of Tuscarora*, and numerous articles on grammar and discourse, historical linguistics, and the development of grammatical categories. INDIAN LANGUAGES

Peter N. Moogk Associate Professor of History at the University of British Columbia. Author of *Building a House in New France*, *Vancouver Defended*, and articles on the social history and numismatics of New France. ARCHITECTURE; BOUND LABOR; CHILDHOOD AND ADOLESCENCE; CURRENCY AND FINANCE; and URBAN LIFE

John H. Moore Professor of Anthropology at the University of Oklahoma. Author of over fifty books and articles on American Indians, including *The Cheyenne Nation: A Social and Demographic History*. Currently involved in the Human Genome Project and ethnohistorical research on the Mvskoke Creek Indians. NATIVE AMERICAN ECONOMIES

Philip D. Morgan Associate Professor of History at Florida State University. Author of *Slave Counterpoint*. Coeditor of *Colonial Chesapeake Society*, *Strangers Within the Realm*, and *The Slaves' Economy*. BOUND LABOR

David E. Narrett Associate Professor of History at the University of Texas, Arlington. Author of *Inheritance and Family Life in Colonial New York City*, a forthcoming book on frontier expansion and republicanism during the revolutionary and early national periods, and numerous articles including "Men's Wills and Women's Property Rights in Colonial New York." Coeditor of *Essays on Liberty and Federalism: The Shaping of the U.S. Constitution*. Winner of the 1992 Hendricks Manuscript Award. THE LEGAL PROFESSION

Gary B. Nash   Professor of History at the University of California, Los Angeles. Author of *Quakers and Politics*; *Red, White, and Black*; *The Urban Crucible*; *Forging Freedom: The Formation of Philadelphia's Black Community*; *Race and Revolution*; and *Race, Class, and Politics: Essays on American Colonial and Revolutionary Society*. URBAN LIFE

William J. Newbigging   Doctoral candidate in the Department of History at the University of Toronto. Author of several articles, reviews, and a forthcoming history of the French-Ottawa Alliance from 1613–1763. INTERNAL MIGRATION, MARRIAGE, and PATTERNS OF COMMUNITY

Jan Noel   Assistant Professor of History at the University of Toronto. Author of *Canada Dry: Temperance Crusades Before Confederation* and several articles on the history of women in French Canada. GENDER RELATIONS

Mark A. Noll   Professor of History at Wheaton College, Illinois. Author of *Princeton and the Republic, 1768–1822*; *A History of Christianity in the United States and Canada*; and other works in American religious history. Editor of *Religion and American Politics*. CHURCH AND STATE

Alison Gilbert Olson   Professor of History at the University of Maryland, College Park. Author of *Making the Empire Work*; *Anglo-American Politics, 1675–1775*; *The Radical Duke*; *Anglo-American Political Relations*; and numerous articles. RELATIONS WITH THE PARENT COUNTRY

Genaro M. Padilla   Associate Professor of English at the University of California, Berkeley. Author of numerous articles on the culture and literature of the Southwest. General editor of a University of New Mexico series dedicated to recovering the Hispanic literary heritage of New Mexico from 1610 to the present. LITERATURE

Edwin J. Perkins   Professor of History at the University of Southern California. Author of *Economy of Colonial America*; *Financing Anglo-American Trade: House of Brown, 1800–1880*; and *Prosperous People*. Editor of *Essays in Economic and Business History*. CURRENCY AND FINANCE

Carla Rahn Phillips   Professor of History at the University of Minnesota. Author of *Ciudad Real, 1500–1750: Growth, Crisis, and Readjustment in the Spanish Economy* and *Six Galleons for the King of Spain: Imperial Defense in the Early Seventeenth Century*; coauthor of *The Worlds of Christopher Columbus*. EMERGENCE OF EMPIRES

William D. Piersen   Professor of History at Fisk University. Author of *Black Yankees: The Development of an Afro-American Subculture in Eighteenth-Century New England* and the forthcoming *Black Legacy: America's Hidden Heritage*. AFRICAN-AMERICAN CULTURE

Ruth Piwonka   Freelance specialist in Hudson Valley social history and material culture. Guest curator, Livingston Manor tercentennial exhibition, Clermont State Historic Site and "Remembrance of Patria: Dutch Arts and Culture in Colonial America, 1609–1776," Albany Institute of History and Art. Author of several articles and other publications on Dutch cultural history. DRESS

Claude Poirier   Director of Trésor de la langue française au Québec and Professor of Languages and Linguistics at Laval Université. Editor of *Dictionnaire du français québécois* and *Dictionnaire du français plus*. EUROPEAN LANGUAGES

Lucien Poirier   Director and Professor of Music at Laval Université. Editor of three volumes of the *Canadian Musical Heritage* series, a collection of organ music, and the *Répertoire des données musicales de la presse québécoise*; contributor to *Dictionary of Canadian Biography* and *Encyclopedia of Music in Canada*. MUSIC AND DANCE

Charles W. Polzer, S. J.   Curator of Ethnohistory at the Arizona State Museum, University of Arizona. Author of *Rules and Precepts of Jesuit Missions*, *Presidio and Militia on the Northern Frontier of New Spain*, and *Pedro de*

Rivera and the Military Regulations of Northern New Spain. Director of the Documentary Relations of the Southwest. ROMAN CATHOLICISM

Bernard Alexander Pothier Senior historian, material culture at the Canadian War Museum. Author of *Course à l'Acadie* and numerous articles on the history of the Acadians. THE CONQUEST OF ACADIA

Jacob M. Price Professor Emeritus of History at the University of Michigan. Author of many books and articles, including *France and the Chesapeake* and *Capital and Credit in British Overseas Trade*. Past president of the Economic History Association and corresponding fellow of the British Academy. TRADE AND COMMERCE

James Pritchard Professor of History at Queen's University, Kingston, Ontario. Author of *Louis XV's Navy, 1748–1762: A Study of Organization and Administration* and numerous articles. SCIENTIFIC INQUIRY and TRADE AND COMMERCE

David B. Quinn Professor Emeritus of Modern History at the University of Liverpool. Author of many works on early America including *Roanoke Voyages* and *Explorers and Colonies: America, 1500–1625*. Member of Royal Irish Academy; Honorary Member of the British Academy, American Historical Association, Royal Historical Society. THE AGE OF RECONNAISSANCE and EMERGENCE OF EMPIRES

Jerome Reich Professor of History at Chicago State University. Author of *Leisler's Rebellion: A Study of Democracy in New York, 1664–1720* and numerous textbooks including *United States History, The Black American Experience, World History*, and *Colonial America*. TAXATION

Daniel K. Richter Associate Professor of History at Dickerson College. Author of *The Ordeal of the Longhouse: The Peoples of the Iroquois League in the Era of European Colonization*. Coeditor of *Beyond The Covenant Chain: The Iroquois and Their Neighbors in Indian North America, 1600–1800*. INDIAN-COLONIST CONFLICTS AND ALLIANCES

Oliver A. Rink Professor of History at California State University, Bakersfield. Author

of *Holland on the Hudson: An Economic and Social History of Dutch New York*. THE COLONIAL MERCHANT; CURRENCY AND FINANCE; EMERGENCE OF EMPIRES; THE FRAMEWORK OF GOVERNMENT; MEN IN ARMS; RELATIONS WITH THE PARENT COUNTRY; and TRADE AND COMMERCE

Robert Cowan Ritchie W. M. Keck Foundation Director of Research at the Huntington Library. Author of *Captain Kidd and the War Against the Pirates* and *The Duke's Province: A Study of New York's Politics and Society, 1664–1691*. MARITIME ENTERPRISES

Jean-Claude Robert Professor of History at the Université de Québec. Author of *Du Canada français au Québec libre* and numerous books and articles on nineteenth-century economic and social history; coauthor of *Quebec: A History, 1863–1929* and *Quebec Since 1930*. INDEPENDENCE

Raquel Rubio-Goldsmith Full-time instructor of history at Pima Community College. Author of various essays on the history of Mexican women in the United States. PATTERNS OF SOCIALIZATION

Robert Blair St. George Assistant Professor of Folklore and Folklife at the University of Pennsylvania. Author of *The Wrought Covenant: Source Material for the Study of Craft and Community in Southeastern New England, 1620–1700; Material Life in America,1600–1860*; and numerous essays and articles on material culture theory, vernacular architecture, and early New England culture. CRAFTS

Sharon V. Salinger Associate Professor of History at the University of California, Riverside. Author of *"To Serve Well and Faithfully": Labor and Indentured Servants in Pennsylvania, 1682–1800* and journal articles on labor and wealth structure in early America. TRAVEL AND LODGING

Marylynn Salmon Research Associate in History at Smith College. Author of *Women and the Law of Property in Early America*; coauthor of *Inheritance in America: From Colonial Times to the Present*. MARRIAGE

Mardith K. Schuetz-Miller Research Associate of Arizona State Museum, University of Arizona.

CONTRIBUTORS

Author of numerous articles, monographs, and books dealing with prehistoric and Spanish site archaeology, Spanish colonial history, and architecture. ARCHITECTURE

Ronald Schultz Associate Professor of History at the University of Wyoming. Author of *The Republic of Labor: Philadelphia Artisans and the Politics of Class* and numerous essays dealing with early American artisans. Coeditor of *Retracing the Past: Readings in the History of the American People*. ARTISANS

Robert E. Shalhope George Lynn Cross Professor of History at the University of Oklahoma. Author of *The Roots of Democracy: American Thought and Culture, 1760–1800* among other books and numerous scholarly articles. IDEOLOGIES OF REVOLUTION

Martha Dickinson Shattuck Historian and research assistant at the New Netherland Project, Albany. Author of "Women and the Economy in Beverwijck, New Netherland." CIVIL LAW

John Shy Professor of History at the University of Michigan. Author of *Toward Lexington: The Role of the British Army in the Coming of the American Revolution* and *A People Numerous and Armed: Reflections on the Military Struggle for American Independence*. MEN IN ARMS

Lucy Simler Associate Director, Center for Early Modern History, University of Minnesota. Author of numerous journal articles and conference papers on rural wage labor and on the process of transition from an agricultural to an industrial economy, particularly in southeastern Pennsylvania. Contributing scholar, Philadelphia Center for Early American Studies. HIRED LABOR

Marc Simmons Historian. Author of numerous books and articles, including *Spanish Government in New Mexico* and *The Last Conquistador*. THE FRAMEWORK OF GOVERNMENT

Billy G. Smith Professor of History at Montana State University. Author of *The "Lower Sort": Philadelphia's Laboring People, 1750–1800*. Coeditor of *Blacks Who Stole Themselves:*

Advertisements for Runaways in the Pennsylvania Gazette, 1728–1790 and *The Infortunate: The Voyage and Adventures of William Moraley, an Indentured Servant*. POVERTY

Wilson Smith Professor Emeritus of History at the University of California, Davis. Author of *Professors and Public Ethics: Studies of Northern Moral Philosophers Before the Civil War* and various essays. Editor of *Theories of Education in Early America*; *Essays in American Intellectual History*; coeditor of *American Higher Education, A Documentary History*. THEORIES OF EDUCATION

Jean R. Soderlund Associate Professor of History at the University of Maryland, Baltimore County. Author of *Quakers and Slavery: A Divided Spirit* and articles on women in the Middle Atlantic colonies; coauthor of *Freedom by Degrees: Emancipation in Pennsylvania and Its Aftermath*. GENDER RELATIONS

S. Dale Standen Professor of History at Trent University. Author of articles on politics, administration, and Amerindian relations in New France. Contributor to the *Dictionary of Canadian Biography*. FARMING, PLANTING, AND RANCHING and FAMILY STRUCTURES

Ian Kenneth Steele Commonwealth Scholar, Killam Fellow, and Professor of History at the University of Western Ontario. Author of *Betrayals: Fort William Henry and the "Massacre"*; *The English Atlantic, 1675–1740*; *Atlantic Merchant-Apothecary*; *Guerrillas and Grenadiers*; and *Politics of Colonial Policy*. THE EUROPEAN CONQUEST FOR NORTH AMERICA

Peter A. Stern Social Science Librarian and Latin American Specialist at Alexander Library, Rutgers University. Author of numerous articles on borderland history and the new information technology in the humanities and social sciences. INDIAN-COLONIST CONFLICTS AND ALLIANCES and INDIAN-COLONIST CONTACT

William C. Sturtevant Curator of North American Ethnology in the Department of Anthropology, National Museum of Natural History, Smithsonian Institution. Author of many publications on the cultures and history of the Indians of North America and the Antilles. General Editor of the *Handbook of North American Indians*. *Special Consultant*

Michael M. Swann Assistant Dean and Associate Professor of Architecture and Urban Design at the University of Kansas. Author of *Migrants in the Mexican North, Tierra Adentro,* and numerous articles and essays on migration, settlement, and town growth in the New World. INTERNAL MIGRATION

Barbara A. Tenenbaum Specialist in Mexican culture in the Hispanic Division of the Library of Congress. Author of *The Politics of Penury: Debts and Taxes in Mexico, 1821–1856* and *México en la época de los agiotistas, 1821–1857.* Editor in Chief of the forthcoming *Encyclopedia of Latin American History.* TAXATION

Peter D. G. Thomas Professor of History at the University of Wales, Aberystwyth. Author of *British Politics and the Stamp Act Crisis, The Townshend Duties Crisis, Tea Party to Independence, Lord North, The House of Commons in the Eighteenth Century,* and *Revolution in America.* REORGANIZATION OF EMPIRES

Roger Thompson Reader in American History at the University of East Anglia, Norwich. Author of *Women in Stuart England and America* and *Sex in Middlesex: Popular Mores in a Massachusetts County, 1649–99.* SEXUAL MORES AND BEHAVIOR

Frederick J. Thorpe Research Fellow at Canadian Museum of Civilization. Author of *Remparts lointains: La politique française des travaux publics à terre-neuve et à l'Île Royale, 1695–1758.* THE FUR TRADE, HOME AND HEARTH, and TECHNOLOGY

Elisabeth Tooker Professor Emerita of Anthropology at Temple University. Author of *An Ethnography of the Huron Indians, 1615–1649; The Iroquois Ceremonial of Midwinter;* and other books and articles. NATIVE AMERICAN FAMILIES AND LIFE CYCLES

Patricia A. Trautman Associate Professor of Family Material Culture at the University of

Connecticut. Author of articles on American dress as a reflection of its social setting. Past editor of *Dress: The Journal of The Costume Society of America.* Fellow of the Costume Society of America. DRESS

Marcel Trudel Professor Emeritus of History at the University of Ottawa. Author of over twenty-five monographs on the history of Canada including *Dictionnaire des esclaves et de leurs propriétaires au Canada français.* Member of the Académie des Lettres du Québec, chevalier de l'Ordre National du Québec; officer of l'Ordre du Canada. Recipient of numerous honorary degrees and awards. EMERGENCE OF EMPIRES

Dell Upton Professor of Architectural History at the University of California, Berkeley. Author of *Holy Things and Profane: Anglican Parish Churches in Colonial Virginia,* among other books and articles on American architecture, material culture, and cultural landscapes. ARCHITECTURE

Daniel H. Usner, Jr. Associate Professor of History at Cornell University. Author of *Indians, Settlers, and Slaves in a Frontier Exchange Economy: The Lower Mississippi Valley Before 1783.* SLAVERY

John R. Van Ness President, Museum of New Mexico Foundation. Author of *Hispanos in Northern New Mexico: The Development of Corporate Community and Multicommunity;* coauthor of *Cañones: Values, Crisis, and Survival in a Northern New Mexico Village.* Series editor for the University of New Mexico Press. RURAL LIFE

Alden Vaughan Professor of History at Columbia University. Author of *New England Frontier: Puritans and Indians, 1620–1675* and *American Genesis: Captain John Smith and the Founding of Virginia.* General Editor of the multivolume *Early American Indian Documents: Treaties and Laws, 1607–1789. Associate Editor*

Jack Warwick Professor of French at York University. Author of *The Long Journey: Literary Themes of French Canada* and many articles on Canadian and seventeenth-century French literature. LITERATURE

John J. Waters Professor of Early American History at the University of Rochester. Author of *The Otis Family in Provincial and Revolutionary Massachusetts* and numerous articles and reviews. Recipient of the Jamestown Award. Burgess Fellow at Columbia University, John Carter Brown Fellow at Brown University, and Charles Warren Fellow at Harvard University. PATTERNS OF COMMUNITY

Robert M. Weir Professor of History at the University of South Carolina. Author of *Colonial South Carolina: A History, "The Last of American Freemen": Studies in the Political Culture of the Colonial and Revolutionary South*, and various articles. BRITISH SETTLEMENTS

Peter H. Wood Professor of History at Duke University. Author of *Black Majority* and numerous articles; coauthor of *Natives and Newcomers* and *Winslow Homer's Images of Blacks*. Coeditor of *Powhatan's Mantle: Indians in the Colonial Southeast*. Member of the editorial boards of *Ethnohistory* and the *Journal of Southern History*. SLAVE RESISTANCE

John Frederick Woolverton Editor of the journal of *Anglican and Episcopal History*. Author of *Colonial Anglicanism in North America* and many articles in Episcopal church history; contributor to *American National Biography* and *Dictionary of Virginia Biography*. ANGLICANISM

William Wroth Former Curator of the Taylor Museum for Southwestern Studies, Colorado Springs Fine Arts Center. Author of *Christian Images in Hispanic New Mexico* and *Images of Penance, Images of Mercy*, among other books and articles on cultural history of the Southwest. Editor of *Hispanic Crafts of the Southwest*. CRAFTS

Neil L. York Associate Professor of History at Brigham Young University. Author of *Mechanical Metamorphosis: Technological Change in Revolutionary America* and *Neither Kingdom Nor Nation: The Irish Quest for Constitutional Rights, 1698–1800*. Editor of *Toward a More Perfect Union: Six Essays on the Constitution*. TECHNOLOGY

Michael Zuckerman Professor of History at the University of Pennsylvania. Author of *Peaceable Kingdoms: New England Towns in the Eighteenth Century* and *Almost Chosen People: Oblique Biographies in the American Grain*. Editor of *Friends and Neighbors: Group Life in America's First Plural Society*. MANNERS

INDEX

Boldface page numbers identify full articles; italic numbers signify tables.

Aataentsic (Indian deity), **2**:145b, **3**:220a
Abbadie, Jean-Jacques Blaise d,' **3**:395b
Abenaki Indians: balance-of-power diplomacy, **2**:231a; branches, **2**:240b–241a; British colonial wars, **2**:111b, 112a, 112b, 113b, 115a, 230a, 241a-b, 281a, 284a; French alliances, **2**:241a, 283a; French missions, **3**:35a, 35b, 548b; Iroquois war, **2**:245a, 246b; language, **3**:34b, 35a, 35b, 36a; resettlement, **2**:147a, 318b, 348b; tribal organization, **1**:451b–452a, 455a
Abiquiú (New Mexico), **2**:161a, 323a, 433a
Abó (New Mexico), **3**:295a
abolitionism: anti-Indian slavery movement, **1**:728a; in Britain, **2**:75a, 75b; colonial-era, **2**:70a, 71b, 77b–78a, 85b–86a; in French colonies, **2**:85b–86a; inefficiency argument, **2**:75a; Quaker, **2**:59b, 64a, 78a, 86a, **3**:600a, 600b; slave literature, **3**:97b–99b; urban, **2**:468b
abortion, **2**:698b
Abrahams, Isaac, **3**:638a
Abrams, Ephraim, **3**:634a
Abreu, Alférez Santiago, **3**:765b, 766a
Absalo, Mariano, **3**:762a
absolutism: British, **1**:253b, 257b, 258a; French, **1**:250b, 251a, 251b, 267a, 295a, 301a-b; Spanish, **1**:287a-b, 294b
Académie de Sciences (France), **3**:154a
Académie Royale des Sciences de Paris. *See* Paris Academy of Sciences
Academy of San Carlos (Mexico City), **3**:322b
Acadia and Acadians, **2**:289a–296b; British takeover (1710), **2**:278b, 281a, 282b, 285b, 507a; church-state relations, **3**:511b–512a, 518a, 548a; currency and finance, **1**:564a; deportation and diaspora, **2**:292a–295a, 348b, 435a, **3**:23b, 512a; dikes, **3**:242a; dress, **2**:616a; family patterns, **2**:668a–671b; farming, **1**:704a, 704b–705a; festival traditions, **2**:596a, 599a; French claims, **2**:279b; French community sense, **2**:426a-b, 538a; French landholding system, **1**:668a-b; French local government, **1**:344b, **2**:371a; French mapping, **2**:276b; French merchants, **1**:595a; French political culture, **1**:267a; French settlements, **1**:59b, 81a, 81b, 82a, 137a-b, **2**:33a, 240a, 317a, 319a; French settlers' origins, **3**:23a; French troops, **2**:500b, 502b; fur trade, **1**:83a, 641b; Huguenot ban, **3**:517b–518a; Huguenots, **3**:544a; Indian relations, **2**:109b, 240b–241a; language and dialects, **3**:23a, 24a, 34b; libraries, **3**:124a; in Louisiana, **1**:718b, **2**:294b, 295a-b, 296a, 320a, 427a, 435a, 616a; *métissage* in, **2**:172b; missionaries, **3**:518a, 544b, 548b; naval stores industry, **1**:615a, 617b, 737b; neutrality, **2**:290a, 290b, 291b–292a; Quaker aid, **3**:599b–600a; salt-marsh cultivation, **1**:705a; scientific inquiry, **3**:180b, 182a, 184b; sexual mores, **2**:700a; social homogeneity, **2**:426a-b; survival of, **2**:295b–296b; theater, **1**:81b, **3**:394a-b; water travel, **2**:638b, 639a. *See also* Cape Breton Island; Nova Scotia
Acapulco, **1**:544a, 565a, **3**:724a
accidents. *See* physical injury
Accomac County (Virginia), **3**:470a
accounting methods, **1**:582b–584b

acequia system. *See* water systems
Achumawi language, **3**:48a
Acoma Indians: enslavement, **2**:96a, 156a; pueblo destruction description, **3**:91b, 92a; sexual and marriage mores, **2**:732b; as Western Pueblo, **1**:454a
Acoma (New Mexico), **1**:117a, 118b, **3**:321a, 324a, 327a
Acosta, José de, **3**:318a
Act against Conjuration, Witchcraft, and Dealing with Evil and Wicked Spirits (1604), **3**:655b
Act Concerning Religion (1649), **3**:614a
Act of Possession and Submission (1598), **3**:523a, 524a
Act of Settlement (1701), **1**:310b
Act of Toleration (1649), **1**:196b, 197b, 307a-b, **3**:506a, 557b, 584a
Act of Toleration (1689), **3**:507a, 508b, 511a, 610b, 614a, 627b–628a, 666b, 679b
Acts of Duties (1660s), **1**:463a
Acts of Supremacy and Uniformity (1559), **3**:581b
Acts of Trade and Navigation. *See* Navigation Acts
Adai Indians, **1**:120a
Adams, Abigail, **2**:396a-b
Adams, Abraham, **3**:362a
Adams, John, **2**:197b; on Carroll (Charles), **3**:559a; and church-state relations, **3**:511a; concerns about republican government, **3**:756b–757a; and Enlightenment thought, **3**:156a, 160b, 161a; on gentleman's accomplishments, **2**:626b; on Independence Day, **3**:757b; and independence movement, **3**:143a, 370b–371a, 633a, 750a-b, 753b, 754b, 755a, 755b–756a; and learned societies, **3**:131b; legal defense of Boston Massacre, **1**:427a, **3**:717b; library, **1**:425b; on New York City vice, **2**:692b; on voting restrictions, **1**:364a, 365b; and women's rights, **2**:396a-b
Adams, Samuel: independence advocacy, **3**:159a, 713a, 713b, 715a, 747a, 752b; portraits of, **3**:306b, 309a; and religious toleration, **3**:511a, 513b
Adams, Thomas R., **3**:121a
Adams-Onís Treaty (1819), **2**:94a, 723b, 742b
adarga (shield), **2**:263a, **3**:248a
Addison, Joseph, **1**:260b, **3**:160b, 393a
Adena Indians, 39a-b
Administration of Justice Act (1774), **3**:717a, 717b. *See also* Intolerable Acts
admiralty law, **1**:422b, 424a
adobe, **1**:622a, **2**:142a, 465a, 585b–586a, **3**:249b–250a, 286b–287a, 287b, 288a, 289a, 290b, 291a, 295a, 297a, 298a, 299a, 320b–321a, 353a-b
Adrian VI, pope, **3**:522b
adultery: British colonial punishments, **2**:684b, 685a, 688b; British colonial rates, **2**:688a; British double standard, **2**:393a, 712a-b, 714b, 718b; as capital offense, **2**:393a, 411a, 685a, **3**:504b; as divorce grounds, **2**:438a-b, **3**:393a, 696b, 728a, 729a; in Dutch colony, **2**:696b; in French colonies, **1**:410a, **2**:698b; Indian view of, **2**:635b, 722a; Massachusetts definition, **2**:393a; Puritan legal prosecution, **1**:401a, 402a; in Spanish Borderlands, **2**:703b, 706a-b; Span-

ish double standard, **2**:410b, 706a-b; Spanish punishments, **1**:415a, **2**:410b–411a, 635a
advertising, **3**:117a
affaire du Canada (scandal), **1**:594a
Africa: Iberian exploration, **1**:52a, 75a. *See also* Canary Islands; slave trade
African-American culture, **2**:195a–206b; appearance and dress, **2**:201b–202b, 615a-b; colonial celebrities, **2**:85b; cooking, **2**:203a; crafts, **2**:202b–203a, **3**:341b; death and funerary customs, **2**:771b–772a, 776a; disease resistance, **1**:692a; ethnicity and nationalism, **2**:206a-b; farming practices, **1**:208a, 681a-b, 692a-b; festivals, **2**:205a-b, 592a, 594a-b, 595a; formation of, **2**:196b–197a, 531a; gambling in, **2**:561a-b; impact on Spanish language, **3**:27b; impact on white southern culture, **2**:80b–81a, 572b, 772a, **3**:18b–19a; Indian relations, **2**:182b, 204a; intragroup divisions, **2**:192a; language, **2**:197a–198a, **3**:18b–19a; literature, **2**:85b, **3**:61a, **96b–99b**; in Louisiana, **2**:90b, 174b–175b, 192a-b, 615a-b; magic and witchcraft, **3**:226a, 663b–664a; marriage and family structure, **2**:198a–199a, 342a-b, 666b, 715b–716a, 717a-b, 722a, 741b–742a; medical practice, **2**:204a-b, **3**:225b–227a; mercantile activity, **1**:601b, **2**:204a; music and dance, **2**:200b–201a, 561b–562a, 594a-b, 595a, **3**:368b–369a, 371a; naming practices, **2**:199a, 744a; in, New York, **1**:174b, 179b; racial stereotyping, **3**:97b; recreations, **2**:560b–562a; religion, **1**:209b, **2**:85b, 199a–200b, 342b–343a, 390b, **3**:97a, 99a-b, 513b, 625b–626b, 682b; rice cultivation, **1**:208a, 692a-b; slavery and development of, **1**:208a–209a, **2**:80a-b, 84b, 212b–213a; in South Carolina and Georgia, **2**:84a, 445a, 530b; work patterns, **2**:203b–204a. *See also* free blacks; interracial societies; slave resistance; slavery; slave trade
African Company, **2**:53b
African slave trade. *See* slave trade
afterlife, **2**:145b, 776b, **3**:648b
Age of Democratic Revolution, The (Palmer), **3**:161b
Age of Reason. *See* Enlightenment, The
Age of Reconnaissance. *See* exploration
agrarian areas. *See* farming, planting, and ranching; rural life
Agreda, María Jesús de, **3**:95a
agriculture. *See* farming, planting, and ranching
Aguayo, San Miguel, marqués de, **1**:713a, 714b
Aguilar, Antonio, **3**:292a
Aguilar, Isidro, **3**:297b
Aguilera, Teresa de, **3**:94b–95a
Aguyo, marquis de, **3**:456a
Ahasimus (New Netherland), **1**:146a
Aigron, Pierre (Lamothe), **3**:552b
Ai Indians, **1**:120a, **3**:39b
Ainsworth, Henry, **3**:357b
Aix-la-Chapelle, Treaty (Peace) of (1748), **1**:168a, **2**:284a
alabado ballad hymns, **3**:379a-b, 381a
Alabama: community patterns, **2**:432a; French settlement/trading posts, **1**:128a, 646a-b; Indian alliances and wars, **2**:252a-b; Mississippian cul-

Culloden, battle of (1746), **1**:209a
Culpeper, Nicholas, **3**:213b
Culpepper's Rebellion (1677), **1**:205b
Cumberland, Richard, **3**:392b
Cumberland, William Augustus, duke of, **1**:92b, **2**:285a, 286a
Cumberland Gap, **1**:190a
Cummings, Abbott Lowell, **3**:271b
cuna (dance), **3**:382b
Cupan language subgroup, **3**:44b
Cupeño Indians, **3**:44b, 45a, 45b
Curaçao: Dutch interests, **1**:225a, 532b, 533a, 533b, **2**:51b, 52b, 88a, 277b; French privateering, **2**:280a; horses, **1**:699b; Jewish settlers, **3**:635a, 639a
curés. *See* clergy
Curler, Arent van, **1**:146b, 149b
curling, **2**:552a, 556b
Currency Act (1751), **1**:554b, 557b–558a, 558b
Currency Act (1764), **1**:211a, 558a, **3**:691a-b, 695a
currency and finance, **1**:**551a–575a**; British colonial exchange rate, **1**:578b; British colonial inflation, **1**:376b; British colonial innovations, **1**:551a–552a; British colonial merchants' investments and accounting methods, **1**:582b–584b; British colonial retail trade, **1**:578a-b; British colonies, **1**:184a, 185a, 378a, **551a–559a**, **3**:691a-b; British prohibition on colonial paper money, **1**:211a; Continental Congress issuance, **3**:750b; Dutch colonial barter, **1**:560a–561a; Dutch colonial exchange rate, **1**:381b.*n.1*, 533b, 560a, 560b, 591a, 592b–593a; Dutch colony, **1**:**559b–561b**; Dutch trade credit and exchange, **1**:533b, 559b–561a, 590b–591a, 591b; fiat currency vs. bank notes, **1**:551a-b; French colonies, **1**:299a, **562a–564b**, **2**:373b–374a; French and Indian War and, **3**:346a, 770a-b; mercantilist view of, **1**:462a-b; Spanish Borderlands, **1**:552b, **564b–575a**; Spanish coins, **1**:552b, 560a, 562b, 578a; wampum inflation, **1**:560b. *See also* banking
Curry, Thomas J., **3**:514a
Curson, Henry, **1**:422a
Curtis, Edmund, **1**:197b
Cusabo Indians, **3**:39b
Cushing, Thomas, **3**:754b
Cushnoc trading post (Maine), **2**:111b
Custom of Paris (legal code), **1**:299b, 444a, 444b, **2**:375b, 376b, 427a, 453b, 456a; on marriage, **2**:669b–670b, 671b, 725b–726a
customs and duties, British colonies, **1**:272a, 332b, 337a, 377b, 379b, 585a, **3**:692a–694b, 695a, 695b–696a, 696b, 698b, 709b–710a, 711a, 713a–715a, 715b–716b, 725a; Dutch colonies, **1**:381b, 382b–383b; Florida, **1**:573b; French colonies, **1**:299a, 299b, 385a, 540a-b; in mercantilist theory, **1**:305a, 463a-b; Mexican treasury system, **1**:387b–388a; New Mexican, **1**:574b–575a; Texas, **1**:570a
Cutler, Timothy, **3**:569a, 669b
Cuyler, Cornelius, **1**:650a

Dablon, Claude, **2**:146b, 147b
DaCosta, Isaac, **3**:639b
D'Acosta, Joseph, **3**:636a
Dagyr, John Adam, **1**:623b
Daigre, Jacques, **1**:408a–409a
dairying, **1**:689b–690a, **2**:385a, 385b
Dakota Indians. *See* Sioux Indians
Dale, Sir Thomas, **1**:192b, 349a, 401a, **2**:227b
Dale's Laws (1611). *See Articles, Lawes, and Orders, Divine, Politique and Martiall* (Gates)
Dallas, Alexander J., **1**:426a
Dalles Rendezvous (Columbia River), **1**:727b
Dallo y Lana, Miguel Mateo, **3**:379a
Dalton, Michael, **1**:400b, 422a
dame schools, **3**:464a, 466b, 467b, 468a, 473a-b
dance. *See* music and dance; social dance forms
Danckaerts, Jasper, **1**:699a, **2**:182a-b, **3**:75a, 240a

D'Andrada, Salvador, **3**:636a
Dane, John, **2**:685b
Danforth, Samuel, **3**:71b
d'Angier, John, **3**:335a
Danvers (Massachusetts). *See* Salem
D'Anville, Jean-Baptiste-Louis-Frédéric de La Rochefoucauld de Roye, duc, **2**:284a
Darien (Georgia), **1**:209a
Darnall family, **3**:557b
Dartmouth, Lord (William Legge), **3**:749a
Dartmouth College: founding, **2**:151a, **3**:418a, 496a–497a, 498a; and Great Awakening, **3**:472a, 682b
Dassett, Joseph, **3**:464a
Dauphin Island, **2**:432a
Davaugour, Pierre Dubois, **2**:499b
Davenant, Charles, **1**:259b
Davenport, James, **3**:504a, 623a, 623b, 675b–676a
Davenport, John, **1**:163b, **2**:389b
Davenport, Uriah, **3**:362a
David, Lazarus, **3**:640b
Davies, Sir John, **1**:253a, 254b
Davies, Samuel, **3**:129a, 511a, 679b
Dávila, Augustín (Agustín), **3**:289a, 330a, 330b
Davis, David Brion, **2**:70a
Davis, Harold E., **1**:500b
Davis, Hugh, **2**:687a
Davis, John, **1**:58a, 87b
Davis, Samuel, **2**:200b
Davis Strait, **1**:58a, 60a
Dawkins, Henry, **3**:306a
Day (Daye), Matthew, **3**:112a, 113b
Day (Daye), Stephen, **3**:112a, 113b, 115b
Day of the Dead ritual, **2**:782a
Daza, Ignacio, **3**:294a
De. For names not found below, *see under* key word, e.g., Grasse, François Joseph Paul de
Deane, Silas, **3**:753b, 755a
death, **2**:**766a–773a**, **778a–782b**; African-American funeral practices, **2**:199b, 772a; Algonquian burial customs, **1**:37a; Anglican view of, **3**:572a; attitudes and practices, **2**:769a–772b; autopsies, **3**:209a; British colonies, **2**:**766a–773a**; burial mound builders, **1**:41a, 41b, 42a, 42b, 43a; Chesapeake planters' funeral practices, **2**:772b; in childhood, **2**:652a, 654b, 666a, 745a-b, 757a, 766a–767a, 768a–769a, 771a, 771b, 775a, 778a, 781b, **3**:196a, 200a-b, 209b; colonial causes of, **3**:209a–210a; Dutch colonial burial customs, **2**:770a-b, 775a; Dutch colony, **2**:**775a**; French Catholic funerary practices, **2**:779b; French colonies, **2**:**778b–780a**; gravestone carvings, **3**:304b–305a, 311a, 313b, 334a–335a; Indian afterlife beliefs, **2**:145b, 776b, **3**:648b; Indian view of, **3**:647a–648b; and Iroquois, **2**:776b, **3**:106b–107a; Mogollon burial customs, **1**:39a; and orphans, **2**:443a, 745b, 754a, 758b; preburial portraits, **3**:317a-b; Puritan funerary practices, **2**:769a, **3**:437a; Quaker funerary practices, **2**:770b–771a; Roman Catholic sacrament, **3**:539b–540a; Spanish Borderlands, **2**:680b, **781a–782b**, **3**:381a; tuberculosis as leading cause of, **3**:209a. *See also* disease; life expectancy; widows
debating societies, **1**:426a-b
debt peonage, **2**:13a, 35b, 36a, 38b, 40a, 41b–42a, 97b
De Bullion family, **2**:403a
DeCasseres family, **3**:635a
décima (verse form), **3**:93a
Decker, Johannes, **3**:281b
Declaration of Independence (1776): colonial leadership ambivalence, **1**:212b; Enlightenment influence, **3**:157a, 160b, 161a, 698a; events leading to, **3**:732a, 747a–757b; grievances, **1**:558b, **3**:689a, 719a; indictment of George III, **1**:311a; Lockean influence, **1**:259a; overview, **3**:757a–758b; signers, **3**:129b; and slavery, **3**:98b, 757b, 758a; Virginia and, **1**:200a
Declaration of Rights (1765), **3**:711a
Declaration of Rights (1776), **3**:157a

Declaration of Rights and Resolves (1774), **3**:718a
Declaration of the Causes and Necessity for Taking up Arms (1775), **3**:750b, 751a-b
Declaratory Act (1766), **1**:211b, 426b, **3**:159a, 693a, 695b, 698b, 713a-b
Decrees of Consolidation (1804), **3**:725a, 741a-b
Dedham (Massachusetts), **2**:525a, 525b, 528b, **3**:262b
Dee, John, **3**:125b, 165b, 654a-b
deer: Indian hunters, **1**:7a, 10a, 11b, 678b, 725b, **2**:554b; population variants, **1**:731b, 734b–735a; skin trade, **1**:478a, *515a–b*, 517b, 541b, 579b, 640a, 644b–645b, 646a, 646b, 728b, 734b–735a
Deerfield (Massachusetts), **2**:282a, **3**:63b, 64a–64b
Deetz, James, **2**:577a, **3**:334b, 335a
defendants' rights, **1**:400a-b, 401a, 403a, 405b–406a, 407b
defense. *See* forts; military; *presidios*
Defoe, Daniel, **1**:260b, **3**:343a-b
DeFonseca family, **3**:635a
de Fries, Johan, **2**:183a-b
De Gánte, Pedro, **3**:480a
deism, **3**:156a, 626b–627b
De Laet, Johan, **3**:176a
DeLancey, James, **1**:183b, **2**:534a
DeLancey, Oliver, **2**:534a, **3**:638a
De Lancey, Stephen, **1**:650a
DeLancey party, **3**:715a-b
deLange, Jacob, **3**:314a
Delanoy, Abraham, Jr., **3**:307a
Delaware: Anglican converts, **3**:569b, 570a; architecture, **3**:277b; creation of, **1**:145b; criminal justice, **1**:403b; Dutch control, **1**:152b, 698a; ethnic diversity, **2**:*315a–b*, 556a-b, 658a; export taxes, **1**:377b; housing, **2**:569a; and independence movement, **1**:185b–186a, **3**:752b–753a, 757b; Indian language, **3**:34b; interracial societies, **2**:183a; loan offices, **1**:378a; local government, **1**:349a, 357b–358a, 359b; political development, **1**:281b; religious pluralism, **3**:509a, 509b, 510a, 568a, 613b, 616b; Roman Catholicism, **3**:559b; slavery and slave trade, **2**:81b–82a, 88b; suffrage, **1**:365b, 366a, 369b; Swedish settlement, **1**:149a, 149b–150b, 225a, 357b, 358a; taverns, **2**:644b, 658a; taxation, **1**:373a, 373b. *See also* Delaware River and Valley; middle colonies
Delaware Bay, **2**:336a, 336b, 658a
Delaware County (Pennsylvania), **3**:468b
Delaware Indians, **2**:107a, 107b, 112b, 115a, 151b–152b, 231b, 236a-b; deerskin trade, **1**:645a; and escaped slaves, **2**:183a; French and Indian War, **2**:116b, 117a, 233b–234a, 234b, 284b; language, **3**:35a, 35b; marriage and sexual customs, **2**:667a, 695b, 697a, 722a; migrations, **2**:152a, 233a, 337b; Moravian missions, **2**:116b; music and oratory, **3**:106a, 410b–411a; and Pennsylvania colony, **2**:659a; prophet, **2**:234b, 253b, 287b; Protestant missions, **3**:419a; Susquehannock threat, **2**:237a; Walking Purchase, **1**:655a
Delaware River and Valley: British control, **1**:152a, 152b, 170a-b, 171a; Dutch conquest of New Sweden, **1**:147a-b, 149b–152b, 225a, 340a, **2**:497b–498a, 537a; Dutch dikes, **2**:240a; Dutch exploration, **1**:60a, 142a, 142b; Dutch forts, **2**:495b, 498b; Dutch migrations, **2**:336a, 369b, 370a; Dutch settlers, **1**:143a, 143b, 145b, 152b, 340a, **2**:237b, 424b; fur trade, **1**:148b–149a; housing, **2**:571a, 573b; Indian-colonist relations, **2**:115a, 231b, 236a-b, 238b; Indian conversions, **3**:418b–419a; Indian migrations, **2**:237a; landholding patterns, **1**:661b; old age in, **2**:763a; Protestantism, **3**:613b–614a, 620b; Quakerism, **2**:419a–420a, **3**:617b; road building, **1**:498a; schools, **3**:467a, 475a; social structure, **2**:360a; Swedish settlement, **2**:236b, 237b
De La Warr, Thomas West, Lord, **1**:192b
Delezenne, Ignace-François, **3**:346a
Delgado, Carlos, **2**:161a, 161b

Great Britain (*cont.*)
758b; cultural imports from, **3**:367b; currency, **1**:551a-b, 552a–553a; declarations of rights, **1**:401b; divorce in, **1**:438a, 438b; drama, **3**:387a, 387b–388a, 388b–389b, 390b, 393a; Dutch wars. *See* Anglo-Dutch wars; emigration (18th-century), **2**:310b, 311a–313a; emigration motives, **2**:304b–309a, 310b–313b, 335a; emigration (17th-century), **2**:303a, 341a; empire building, **2**:276a, 278b, 279a; English language, **3**:13a–14b, 15b–16b; Enlightenment in, **1**:254a, 261a–262b, **3**:152b–153a, 153b, 155b, 158b, 160a, 160b; evangelical dissenters, **3**:668b–669a, 670a, 673b, 674a; events leading to American Revolution, **3**:687a–698b, 709a–719a. *See also* American Revolution on eve of empire, **1**:84b–86a; exploration. *See* exploration; expulsion and return of Jews, **1**:69a, **3**:636b; family structure in, **2**:649a–653a; festival traditions in, **2**:591a, 592a; housing, **1**:469a-b; ideologies of revolution, **3**:158a, 158b; internal migration, **2**:740b–741a; Irish settlements, **1**:87a–88b; isolation from continent, **1**:83b–84a; landholding ideals and practices, **1**:653a–654a, 656a; legal profession in, **1**:422a-b; legal protection of property, **1**:403a; legal system in, **1**:398a–399b, 401a; literacy in, **3**:5b; medical training in, **3**:208b, 214b; mercantilism, **1**:460a-b, 463a, 487b, 616b–617a, 644b; monetary system, **1**:553a; music in, **3**:362a-b, 364b, 367b; nationalism, **1**:82a-b; old age in, **2**:652a-b; patent law, **3**:232b; piracy. *See under* privateering and piracy; political structure (mid-18th century), **3**:688a-b, 735a; political theory, **1**:252b–263a, 279b; Portugal as ally, **1**:524a; poverty and welfare in, **1**:373b, 484a-b; press censorship, **3**:116a, 119b; Protestantism in, **3**:610b, 627b–628a, 666b–667a; Puritanism in, **1**:197b, **2**:527b, **3**:138a, 139b–140a, 577b–579a, 581b–583a, 603a; Quaker emigration, **2**:658b; Quakerism in, **3**:595a–596b, 597b; recreations, **2**:553b–554a; reorganization of empire, **3**:687a–698a; Roman Catholicism in, **3**:554b–555a; Russian diplomatic relations, **1**:241a-b; schooling in, **3**:461a–462a; servitude in, **2**:19a-b; sexual behavior and marriage in, **2**:392a-b, 393a, 686b, 711a–714b; ship tonnage and types, **1**:495a-b, 628a; slavery in, **2**:19a–19b; slave trade, **1**:523a-b, **2**:60a, 62b–63a, 68b, 69a, 73a, 76b–77a, 81b, 84a-b, 86a-b; slave trade ban (1807), **2**:75a, 84b, 86a; social origin of indentured emigrants, **2**:28a; society (17th-century), **2**:357a–358a; and Spanish colonial independence moves, **3**:723a-b; Spanish rivalry with, **2**:276b, 513a-b. *See also* empire building; empires, European contest for; tobacco imports, **1**:519b; trade. *See under* trade and commerce; transatlantic ship travel times, **1**:496a-b; union of England and Scotland (1707), **2**:282a; warfare and diplomacy in, **2**:223b–224b. *See also* specific wars; wars with Netherlands. *See* Anglo-Dutch wars; witch-hunts, **3**:655b–656a. *See also* British settlements; French and Indian Wars; Ireland; Parliament; Scotland; Ulster
Great Corn (moon celebration), **2**:596b
Great Lakes, **1**:21a, 215a, 727a
Great Lakes region: first French community, **2**:346a-b; French migration to, **2**:345a, 345b, 345b–346b, 426a; French royal government, **1**:297b–298a; French settlements, **1**:137b–138a; fur trade, **1**:537b, 643a, 645b–646a, **2**:244a-b, 428a; Indian basketry, **3**:254a; Indian-colonist contact, **1**:727b, **2**:111b, 116a, 172b, 242b–243a, 249b, 346b; Indian-colonist marriage, **2**:725b; Indian inhabitants, **2**:244a-b, 249b–250a; Indian language, **1**:727b, **3**:34a–35a, 35b, 38a; Indian massacres, **3**:770b; Indian migrations, **2**:337b–338a; Indian tribe system, **1**:451b–452a; intertribal warfare, **2**:249b–250a; Jesuit missionaries, **3**:418b; Jesuit mission destruction, **1**:138a; local government, **2**:371b;

malaria, **3**:203a; Pontiac's War, **2**:234b, 253b, 287b; recreations, **2**:551b; smallpox outbreak, **3**:202a
Great Law (1683), **2**:688b
Great Migration (1629–1641), **1**:158b, 164a, 165a, 306a, **2**:418b
Great Northern War (1700–1721), **1**:518a, 691a
Greaton, Joseph, **3**:559b
Great Plains, **1**:4b, 6a, 7a, 12a, 726b; at end of colonial period, **1**:450a; farming conditions, **1**:724a-b; Indian language, **3**:42b; Indian tribe system, **1**:451b; Pawnee massacre of Spanish soldier, **2**:264b; Spanish explorers, **1**:55b. *See also* Plains Indians
Great Serpent Mound (Ohio), **1**:41b–42a
Great Sun (Natchez leader), **1**:453a
Great Wagon Road, **1**:199a, 498b, 499a, 501b, 502a, **2**:337a
Grebel, Conrad, **3**:610a
Greek contract workers, **2**:17a, 324a, 325b, 431b, **3**:290b
Green, Bartholomew, **3**:113a
Green, Samuel, **3**:112a–113a, 113b, 114a
Green, Samuel, Jr., **3**:114a, 114b
Green Bay (Wisconsin), **2**:147b, 148a, 244a, 250a, **3**:37b
Greenberg, Joseph, **3**:31a, 49b
Greenbrier Company, **1**:662b
Green Corn ceremony, **3**:411a, 413a
Greene, Thomas, **3**:557b
Greenland: Danish colony, **1**:225a; English survey, **1**:58a; fishing, **1**:630a; Inuit language, **3**:54a, 55a; Moravians in, **3**:55a; Norse settlements, **1**:49a-b, 106a, 106b, 107a, 107b, 108a–110b; Thule migration to, **1**:20a-b, 109b
Greenland (New Hampshire), **3**:360b
Greenlanders' Saga (Norse), **1**:107a
Green Mountain Boys, **2**:532b, **3**:750a
Greensmith, Rebecca, **3**:658b–659a
Greensted, William, **2**:190a
Greenwich Village (New York), **3**:466b
Greenwood, Isaac, **3**:428b
Greenwood, John, **3**:306b, 308b
Greer, Allan, **2**:723b
Gregorian chant, **3**:378b
Grenada, **1**:229a, **2**:287a
Grenville, George, **3**:687b, 688b, 690a, 690b, 691b, 692a-b, 695a, 696b
Grenville, Sir Richard, **1**:58a, 87b, 88b, 89a, 89b, 90b, 192a, 203a, 226b
Gresham's law, **1**:554a-b, 562a
Greven, Philip, **3**:445a-b
Greville, Samuel, **3**:392b
Grew, Theophilus, **3**:468a
Gridley, Jeremiah, **1**:426a, 508a, **3**:118b
Grignon, Antoine, **1**:595a
Grimm, Friedrich Melchior von, **3**:82a
Grindley, James, **1**:425b
grisaille (wall paintings), **3**:326a-b
Gronovius, Johann Friedrich, **3**:169b
Groseilliers, Médard Chouart, sieur des, **1**:214b, 215a, **2**:346a
gross national product (GNP), **1**:467b–468a, 471a, 471b, 472b
Gros Ventres. *See* Hidsata Indians
Grotius, Hugo, **1**:252a, 252b, 258a, 258b, 403b, 442b, **3**:176a, 730a
Groton (Massachusetts), **2**:395b
Groulx, Lionel, **2**:172b
Guachichil Indians, **2**:256b
Guadalajara, **1**:290b, 292a, 352a, **3**:541b, 545b, 740b
Guadalupe Hidalgo, Treaty of (1848), **1**:447a-b
Guadeloupe: and American Revolution naval battle, **1**:229a-b; British capture of, **2**:287a; French interests, **1**:224a, 229a, **2**:277a; Jewish settlers, **3**:635a; slave imports, **2**:63b; sugar industry, **2**:52a, 59b
Gua de Monts, Pierre. *See* Monts, Pierre du Gua de

Gualdo, Giovanni, **3**:370a
Guale Indians, **1**:125a; hostility to Spanish presence, **2**:134a; language, **3**:39b; population decline, **2**:321a; Spanish mission, **1**:126a, 128a, **2**:106a, 110a, 113a, 115a, 121a, 322b, 354a
Gualean Revolt (1597), **2**:120b–121a, 210b
Guamare Indians, **2**:256b
Guanabara Bay. *See* Rio de Janeiro, Bay of
Guanajuato, **1**:113b, 389a, 565a, 567b, 568a, **2**:256b, **3**:725b
Guanche Indians, **1**:52a, **2**:271b, 272a
Guatemala, **1**:113a, 290a, 290b, **3**:740b
Guázabas-Oputo (Arizona), **1**:120b
Gudeman, Stephen, **2**:677b–678a, 678b
Guebavi mission (Arizona), **2**:434a
Guerrero, Francisco, **2**:158b, **3**:378b, 745b
Guerrero, Vicente, **3**:763b, 764a
guerrilla warfare: French colonial tactics, **2**:246b, 253a, 502a-b, 506b–507a; French deerskin traders, **1**:646b; Huron-Iroquois tactics, **2**:243a; Indian tactics against British, **2**:247a-b; maroons, **2**:181a; Spanish Borderlands, **2**:255b, 258a
Guest, John, **1**:425b
Guettard, Jean-Étienne, **3**:184b, 185a
Guevara, Antonio de, **3**:123b
Guevara, Juan Bautista, **3**:326b
Guianas, **1**:224b, 225b, **2**:52b
Guicciardini, Francisco, **1**:252a
guilder, **1**:560a
Guilford (Connecticut), **2**:573b
Guinea Coast, **1**:52a, 224b, 225a, **2**:59a
Gulf Coast, **1**:55a, **3**:688b. *See also* Louisiana; Texas
Gullah (Creole language), **2**:197b
Gunston Hall (Virginia), **3**:271b
Gustavus II Adolphus, king of Sweden, **1**:147b
Gutiérrez, Rafael (*Quemaculos*), **1**:416a
Gutiérrez, Ramón, **2**:407b, 483a, 731a, 735a, 737a, **3**:400b
Gutiérrez de Lara, Bernardo, **3**:726b, 762b, 763a
Gutiérrez de Padilla, Juan, **3**:378b
Guy, William, **3**:471a
Guyana, **1**:92b, 542a
Guyart-Martin, Mme. *See* Marie de l'Incarnation
Guzmáan de Alfarache (Alemán), **3**:123a
Gyles, John, **3**:102a, 103b

habeas corpus, right of, **1**:253a
Hachard, Marie Madeleine, **2**:614b, **3**:82a
haciendas, **2**:23a, **3**:291a-b, 292b
Hackensack (New Jersey), **1**:698b
Hackensack Indians, **2**:237b, 238b–239a
Hackensack River and Valley, **1**:665a, **2**:183b
Hadley (Massachusetts), **3**:336a
Hadley Path, **2**:638a
Haerlem (New Netherland). *See* Harlem
Hague, John, **3**:235b
Haida Indians, **1**:23a, 240a, 242a, 453b–454a, **2**:402a, **3**:48b, 409a
hainault. *See* scythe, Dutch
hairstyles, **2**:202a, 606b, 611a, 614a-b, 624b
Haisla language, **3**:48b
Haiti (Saint Domingue): Acadian exiles in, **2**:294b; French control, **1**:224a, 229a, 297a, **2**:59b; independence, **1**:229b, 230a; Louisiana immigrants, **3**:23b; naming of, **1**:222a; slave plantation profitability, **1**:229a; slave revolt (1791), **1**:229b, **2**:63b, 75a, 218b, 219a, **3**:722a, 723b–724a; slave trade to, **2**:55b, 59b, 60a, 62a, 75a; sugar exports, **1**:539a. *See also* Hispaniola
Hakluyt, Richard, **1**:84b, 86b–87a, 89a, 90a, 93a, **3**:55a, 57a, 166b
Halchidhoma dialect, **3**:48a
Hale, Horatio, **3**:51b
Hale, John, **3**:664a
Hale, Sir Matthew, **1**:254a, 400b
"Half-freedom" system, **2**:189a-b
Halfpenny, William and John, **3**:272a